Exceptional Students

Preparing Teachers for the 21st Century

Ronald L. Taylor
Florida Atlantic University

Lydia R. Smiley
Florida Atlantic University

Stephen B. Richards
University of Dayton

 **McGraw-Hill Higher Education**

Boston   Burr Ridge, IL   Dubuque, IA   New York   San Francisco   St. Louis
Bangkok   Bogotá   Caracas   Kuala Lumpur   Lisbon   London   Madrid   Mexico City
Milan   Montreal   New Delhi   Santiago   Seoul   Singapore   Sydney   Taipei   Toronto

*Dedicated to the many students in
Introduction to Special Education courses
who motivated us to write this text.*

McGraw-Hill
Higher Education

Published by McGraw-Hill, an imprint of The McGraw-Hill Companies, Inc., 1221 Avenue of the Americas, New York, NY 10020. Copyright © 2009. All rights reserved. No part of this publication may be reproduced or distributed in any form or by any means, or stored in a database or retrieval system, without the prior written consent of The McGraw-Hill Companies, Inc., including, but not limited to, in any network or other electronic storage or transmission, or broadcast for distance learning.

This book is printed on acid-free paper.

1 2 3 4 5 6 7 8 9 0 QPD/QPD 0 9 8 7

ISBN: 978-0-07-286637-7
MHID: 0-07-286637-3

Editor in Chief: *Michael Ryan*
Publisher: *Beth Mejia*
Senior Sponsoring Editor: *Allison McNamara*
Marketing Manager: *James Headley*
Director of Development: *Dawn Groundwater*
Senior Developmental Editor: *Cara Labell*
Production Editor: *Catherine Morris*
Manuscript Editor: *Kay Mikel*
Art Director: *Jeanne Schreiber*
Design Manager: *Andrei Pasternak*
Text Designer: *Ellen Pettengell*
Cover Designer: *Scott Idleman*
Inside Cover Designer: *Linda Robertson*
Art Editor: *Emma Ghiselli*
Illustrators: *Dave Bohn, Rennie Evans, John Waller, Judy Waller*
Photo Research Coordinator: *Nora Agbayani*
Photo Researcher: *Judy Mason*
Supplements Producer: *Patrick McCarthy*
Production Supervisor: *Tandra Jorgensen*
Composition: *9.75/12 ITC Century Book, by Aptara*
Printing: *45# Pub Matte Plus, Quebecor World, Inc.*

Cover: Background © Japack Company/Corbis; Left © Bob Daemmrich/PhotoEdit Inc.; Middle © Bill Aron/PhotoEdit Inc.; Right © Gideon Mendel/Corbis.

Credits: The credits section for this book begins on page C-1 and is considered an extension of the copyright page.

Library of Congress Cataloging-in-Publication Data

Taylor, Ronald.
  Exceptional students: preparing teachers for the 21st century / Ronald Taylor, Lydia Smiley, Stephen Richards.
      p. cm.
  Includes bibliographical references and index.
  ISBN-13: 978-0-07-286637-7 (alk. paper)
  ISBN-10: 0-07-286637-3 (alk. paper)
  1. Special education teachers—In-service training.   I. Smiley, Lydia Ruffner   II. Richards, Steve III. Title.
  LC3969.45.T39 2008
  371.9—dc22

2007047022

The Internet addresses listed in the text were accurate at the time of publication. The inclusion of a Web site does not indicate an endorsement by the authors or McGraw-Hill, and McGraw-Hill does not guarantee the accuracy of the information presented at these sites.

www.mhhe.com

About the Authors

RONALD L. TAYLOR, ED.D. is currently professor of Exceptional Student Education at Florida Atlantic University. He received his bachelor's and master's degrees in Psychology at Austin College and Trinity University. He received his doctorate in Special Education from the University of Houston. Prior to coming to Florida Atlantic University, Dr. Taylor was a school psychologist and consulting teacher for a Title III grant that focused on working with culturally diverse students. He also served on the faculty in Special Education at Boston University. Dr. Taylor has published extensively, including 8 books (18 counting various editions) and over 20 chapters and 90 articles. He recently completed the eighth edition of his assessment text, *Assessment of Exceptional Students: Educational and Psychological Procedures.* He has received over 2 million dollars in grant funding. He is active in several professional organizations, having made over 60 presentations, and was editor of *Diagnostique*, the journal for the assessment division of the Council for Exceptional Children.

LYDIA R. SMILEY, PH.D. is a professor of Exceptional Student Education at Florida Atlantic University. She received her doctorate in Special Education from Georgia State University. Dr. Smiley co-authored *Language Delays and Disorders: From Research to Practice (1998)* and has also written several articles and chapters on a variety of topics. She teaches both undergraduate and graduate classes and has been the recipient of several teaching awards and the CLD Professional of the Year award. Her current interests are in methods of teaching students with mild/moderate disabilities and language disorders.

STEPHEN B. RICHARDS, ED.D. is an Associate Professor and Coordinator for Intervention Specialist Programs at the University of Dayton. He received his doctorate in Special Education from Florida Atlantic University. He teaches in both the undergraduate and graduate licensure programs. He has co-authored three textbooks, *Mental Retardation: Historical Perspectives, Current Practices, and Future Directions* (2005); *Single Subject Research and Design: Applications in Educational and Clinical Settings* (1999); and *Exceptional Children: Integrating Research and Teaching* (1995); in addition to journal articles on a variety of topics. His current interests are in assessing the preparation of pre-service teacher education candidates for their first year in teaching.

Brief Contents

Contents

PART ONE Special Education: Fundamentals and Processes

PART TWO IDEA 04 High-Prevalence Exceptionalities: Foundations and Instruction

PART THREE IDEA 04 Low-Incidence Exceptionalities: Foundations and Instruction

PART FOUR Other Exceptionalities: Foundations and Instruction

When we first started teaching the Introduction to Special Education course years ago, our classes were filled with students who were excited about becoming special education teachers. As the area of Special Education has grown and evolved over the years, we have found that our classes are no longer made up solely of future special education teachers. What began with a trickle of elementary, middle, and secondary school teachers taking the course has evolved into an introductory course with a significant number of both future special educators and future general educators. Clearly, no one teacher, no one person, can ever bear full responsibility for educating exceptional students, and we are glad to see that the Introduction to Special Education course reflects this reality.

We asked ourselves: how can we write a book that speaks to the range of students who take the course—including future special educators and future general educators?

The course continues to evolve, and we have struggled to find teaching materials that support the diversity of students we see in our classes. Many books focus on future special educators, but few reach out to both groups of future teachers—the special educator and the general educator. In response to this need, *Exceptional Students: Preparing All Teachers for the 21st Century* includes both foundational material that is at the core of understanding exceptionalities and practical information that is key to effective teaching. Using this format, we hope to provide future teachers with the knowledge and resources they need to be successful, no matter what role they play in the education of exceptional students.

An Emphasis on What Teachers *Need to Know* and *Be Able to Do*

Exceptional Students provides balanced coverage of the foundations of exceptionalities that future teachers *need to know* to understand their students and responsibilities, and the practical information they need to effectively teach their students. Although the general topics addressed are similar to those of other textbooks, coverage of these topics is enhanced within each chapter of *Exceptional Students*.

Coverage of practical information related to instructional content, instructional procedures, the instructional environment, and instructional technology has been expanded from its traditional treatment so that each chapter provides equal amounts of foundational and practical material. In addition, two topics crucial for future teachers to understand in order to best support their students—collaboration and students at risk—are stand-alone chapters.

CHAPTER OUTLINE

FOUNDATIONS	PRACTICE
What Are the Foundations of Learning Disabilities?	**What and How Do I Teach Students with Learning Disabilities?**
A Brief History of Learning Disabilities	Instructional Content
Definitions of Learning Disabilities	Types of Content Knowledge
Prevalence of Learning Disabilities	Areas of Instructional Content
	Transition Planning
What Are the Causes and Characteristics of Learning Disabilities?	Instructional Procedures
Causes of Learning Disabilities	**What Are Other Instructional Considerations for Teaching Students with Learning Disabilities?**
Characteristics of Students with Learning Disabilities	The Instructional Environment
How Are Students with Learning Disabilities Identified?	Instructional Technology
Response to Intervention	**What Are Some Considerations for the General Education Teacher?**
The Use of Standardized Testing	

Foundational Information for Understanding Exceptionalities

The first half of each exceptionality chapter is devoted to the foundational information about exceptionalities that future teachers need to know. This section discusses the history, definitions, prevalence, causes, characteristics, and identification procedures of the specific exceptionality. Devoting the first half of the chapter to foundational content provides future teachers with the groundwork they will need to make informed instructional decisions in the classroom.

Foundational coverage is also highlighted through the *An Important Event* feature, which presents a key event or the publication of seminal research that has helped shape special education today. Reflection questions, designed to help students consider their opinion or the importance of the event, accompany each discussion. Examples of important events include the founding of the Council for Exceptional Children, publication of Wang and Birch's proposal for the use of the Adaptive Learning Environment Model, and publication of the results of the Carolina Abecedarian Project. Even though *Exceptional Students* emphasizes practical applications, we believe it is vital for students to understand how special education has evolved and to consider their place in its continuing development.

Exceptional Students provides balanced coverage of the foundations of exceptionalities that future teachers need to know to understand their students and responsibilities, and the practical information they need to have to effectively teach their students.

Practical Information to Guide Classroom Planning and Instruction

The second half of each exceptionality chapter provides instructional and pedagogical information future teachers need to know to effectively teach students. This part of the chapter is organized around instructional content, instructional procedures, the instructional environment, and instructional technology, as well as specific considerations for the general education teacher. In addition, the general education section introduces topics that are important when planning and implementing instruction for students with special needs within the general education classroom. Practical strategies are also highlighted in the following features:

Chapter-opening Case Study and *Revisit* Opportunities

Each chapter begins with a scenario describing a student with special needs in the context of his or her educational experience. Throughout the chapter, readers are presented with related questions called *Revisits*, which ask students to apply key concepts they have just learned to an actual situation. These cases tie the chapter together, allow for contextual learning, and offer an instructor several additional topics for discussion. For example, in Chapter 8, the reader is introduced to Allison, a student with a hearing loss. Later in the chapter, the reader is asked whether Allison would be considered deaf or hard of hearing, what issues she might have with her identity, and how her teacher might plan for accommodations during literacy instruction.

INTRODUCING ALLISON

Allison is a 6-year-old girl who has just started the first grade. She has a hearing loss resulting from repeated and severe ear infections in infancy and throughout her early childhood. The infections resulted in a bilateral conductive hearing loss. Her loss is mild to moderate—she does not hear clearly until sounds reach a 40 decibel level. She experiences this hearing loss across all frequencies of sound detectable by the human ear. Prior to entering school, Allison received early intervention services at home from an audiologist and early childhood special educator. Because of her frequent illnesses, she only sporadically attended a center-based preschool program. With time, medical interventions greatly reduced the infections and their severity.

Allison uses hearing aids that make it possible for her to learn using her auditory channel. Her speech and language skills are delayed, likely the result of not hearing adequately in early childhood. Her parents are concerned about her literacy skills development as she begins school. Because she qualified for early intervention, the school and Allison's parents developed an IEP for her. She receives speech and language services regularly. An itinerant teacher for students who are deaf or hard of hearing provides consultation to her general education teacher. The team did not feel they should "pull out" Allison for resource room services if her literacy skills, which will be monitored and assessed frequently, can be developed in her general education class. Also, an audi-

ologist will provide consultation to Allison's parents, teachers, and speech and language pathologist to ensure her hearing aids are working properly, are being maintained, and are being used as effectively as possible. ■

Classroom Suggestions

While writing this text, we interviewed and surveyed hundreds of teachers, both in the classroom and in Colleges of Education. The universal cry for "more strategies!" rang through loud and clear. In response, each chapter includes several *Classroom Suggestions* with strategies and tips. These clear, concise strategies serve as mini-guides for future teachers, giving them confidence to enter their classrooms ready to handle myriad situations. Examples of *Classroom Suggestions* include Strategies to Promote Family Involvement, Guidelines for Implementing Cooperative Learning, Examples of Instructional Grouping Accommodations for Students with Intellectual Disabilities, and Accommodations for a Student Who Has Difficulty with Self-Control.

Classroom Example A Sample Team-Teaching Plan

The Plan

Learning Goal: Students will be able to use place values concepts to represent whole numbers and decimals using numerals, words, expanded notation, and physical models (Ohio Content Area Standards: Grade Three Mathematics: Numbers and Number Systems).

Lesson Objective: Students will be able to describe the multiplicative nature of the number system (e.g., 2520 can be represented as $2 \times 1000 + 5 \times 100 + 2 \times 10 + 0 \times 1$).

IEP Objectives (as appropriate): John will be able to apply principles of multiplication to solve computational and word problems with 90% accuracy.

Instructional Grouping: Students will be in one large group for initial instruction (one teach, one assist), followed by students being divided for smaller group instruction (parallel teaching), and finally divided into one smaller homogeneous group and one large homogeneous group (alternative teaching).

Classroom Examples

Exceptional Students does not just *talk* about what future teachers will find or use in class, but *shows* them by including classroom artifacts and sample handouts of real and relevant student and teacher work. For example, the text shares a sample Team-Teaching plan, a Contingency Contract, and a Social Story with picture cues to assist with waiting in line in the cafeteria.

Meet the Educator

As teachers, we know that students often forget concepts and definitions but remember stories. Each chapter devoted to a particular exceptionality includes a classroom case study presented in a teacher's voice that applies and personalizes the content. Teachers throughout the country provided us with their experiences to help future teachers experience real learning and teaching situations. The student's background, characteristics, learning challenges, and strengths are described alongside the teacher's implementation of instructional content and strategies, the instructional environment and technology, and collaboration. The feature is designed to show how the topics introduced in the practical half of the chapter are used in a real teaching situation. For example, in Chapter 4, educator Michael Woods shares his experiences teaching Kathy, an 11th grader who has a learning disability. Michael discusses how he has supported her study and self-advocacy skills to help her succeed in school.

In Practice Meet Educator Michael Woods and His Student Kathy

I teach learning strategies at an urban high school in one of the nation's largest school districts. I have taught for over 14 years, primarily at the high school level, though I have worked with students at all levels. My area of expertise is postsecondary transition and independent living skills. I was honored to receive the 2004 Teacher of the Year Award in my school district.

My student Kathy is an 11th grader who has been receiving services for learning disabilities since the 4th grade. She was in a pullout resource room setting through middle school. She was gradually included more and more in general education and now, with the exception of her learning strategies class, attends all classes in an inclusive general education setting. She is working on a standard diploma, and her IEP goals are directed at teaching her learning strategies to support her success in the inclusive environment.

Kathy has experienced success in her elective courses (art, physical education, cooking). However, she requires extensive support in her academic courses. These supports include teaching her cognitive and metacognitive learning strategies in reading comprehension, study skills, essay and short answer test taking skills, and report writing. Additionally, Kathy needs to develop self-advocacy skills. She shows some limitations when it comes to communicating her needs and/or questions to her general education teachers. She describes talking to her teachers as "difficult." When asked why, she replies, "I don't want to feel stupid ... there are only a few teachers I am good at talking with."

I had to help her feel more positive about her ability to meet these requirements. I pointed out that she could be successful if she tried hard and applied the strategies she learned in her strategies class.

Instructional Content and Procedures

Like many students with learning disabilities, Kathy and the students in my learning strategies course require ongoing instruction in organizational strategies, study skills, self-advocacy, and written expression. For that reason, whole group lessons have been created to provide both support and reinforcement of these activities. I have taught Kathy to use graphic organizers to better understand her reading assignments. She has learned to attend to the text organization patterns (for example, chronological, compare-contrast, or cause-effect) and to select a graphic organizer that she can apply to that particular chapter or text. She has also learned to attend to the visual cues in each of her texts, including bold print and marginal notes. As another example, I focus on note taking and

	Characteristics	Indicators You Might See	Teaching Implications	Methodologies and Strategies to Try	Considerations for the General Classroom and Collaboration
What IDEA 04 Says about Learning Disabilities: Learning Disabilities is an IDEA 04 category. IDEA defines learning disabilities as "a disorder in one or more of the basic psychological processes involved in understanding or in using language, spoken or written, which may manifest in an imperfect ability to listen, think, speak, read, spell, or do mathematical calculations." Disorders included are perceptual disabilities, brain injury, minimal brain dysfunction, dyslexia, and developmental aphasia. Disorders not included are learning problems that are primarily the result of visual, hearing, or motor disabilities; mental retardation; emotional disturbance; or environmental, cultural, or economic disadvantage. **Identification Tools:** The general classroom teacher often makes the initial identification based on classroom observation and performance, and state- or districtwide assessments. *Prereferral Assessment and RTI Approaches:* Possibly uses criterion-referenced testing, curriculum-based assessment, and criterion-referenced measurement. *Formal Identification:* Several sources are used for identification. They may include intelligence and achievement tests, tests measuring process skills, and language and academic tests. The response to intervention approach may also be used.	**Related to Reading**	May have problems with phonological awareness or processing; rapid automatic naming; word recognition (mispronunciation; skipping, adding, or substituting words; reversing letters or words; difficulty blending sounds together); and comprehension (due to lack of background knowledge, difficulty understanding text structure, and vocabulary deficits).	**Instructional Content** • Most students with learning disabilities will participate in the general education curriculum. They will most likely need intensive instruction in the process of learning and in the content of learning. • Consider need for the curriculum to include declarative knowledge, procedural knowledge, and conditional knowledge. • Consider the Direct Instruction program for reading. • Support content areas of reading (phonological awareness, decoding and comprehension), written language (teaching writing as a process), mathematics (computation and problem solving), and study skills (such as listening, note taking, time management, comprehending textbook usage and memory strategies). • Transition planning should include the development of goal setting and self-advocacy.	• Task Analysis (p. 113) • Direction Instruction (p. 113) • Cognitive Strategies (p. 115) • Metacognitive Strategies (p. 115) • Mnemonics (p. 117) • Attribution Retraining (p. 118)	Instruction generally occurs in the general education classroom. The general education teacher should: • Establish a positive climate that promotes valuing and accepting personal responsibility for learning. • Consider accommodations such as modified instructional methods or materials, assignments and tests, time demands and scheduling, and the learning environment. • Consider adapting the academic content. • Consider a parallel or overlapping curriculum.
	Related to Mathematics	Possible problems with basic number facts, calculation, application, language of math, problem solving, oral drills and worksheets, word problems, math anxiety, and retrieving information from long-term memory.	**Instructional Procedures** • Provide a structured instructional program with daily routines and expectations; clear rules; curriculum presented in an organized, sequential fashion; and a focus on learning tasks rather than extraneous stimuli. • In planning, consider what, how, and when to teach; provide activities for practice, feedback, and evaluation; organize and pace the curriculum; and provide smooth transitions. • Consider using task analysis and direct instruction. • Consider using cognitive and metacognitive strategies instruction. Consider whether using the Learning Strategies Curriculum would be of use in teaching academics and social interaction. Consider attribution retraining. • Effective instructional practices for ELLs include using visuals to reinforce concepts and vocabulary, utilizing cooperative learning and peer tutoring, making strategic use of the native language by allowing students to organize their thoughts in their native language, providing sufficient time and opportunity for students to use oral language and writing in formal and informal contexts, and focusing on rich vocabulary words during lessons to be used as vehicles for teaching literary concepts. Also consider providing simplified, appealing, multisensory lectures; adapting textbooks and assignments; and using supplementary materials.		**Collaboration** General and special educators should consult on: • Determining the curriculum • Developing accommodations • Choosing procedures and strategies • Planning the physical environment • Planning for assistive technology
	Writing and Written Expression Characteristics	Possible problems with handwriting, spelling, or written language/written expression (punctuation, vocabulary, and sentence structure).			
	Expressive and Receptive Language Characteristics	Possible problems with Producing and understanding language.			
	Cognitive-Related Characteristics	Possible problems with attention, memory, strategy use, and metacognition.	**Instructional Environment** • Reduce congestion in high-traffic areas, make sure you can see all students, make frequently used materials and supplies easily accessible, ensure that all students can see whole class presentations. • For preschool students, the environment should be structured and promote efficiency, accessibility, independence, and functionality. It should also promote language and literacy development. • For elementary and secondary students, the environment should be organized to prevent "dead time." Structure and routine are important. Space should be available for individual work, large and small group work, peer tutoring, and cooperative learning. Decrease possible distractions. • Effective grouping options include one-to-one instruction, small group, whole class, peer tutoring, and classwide peer tutoring.		
	Social and Emotional Characteristics	Possible social skills deficits, and problems with social cognition and relationships with others. May have fewer friends and less social status than peers. Possible behavioral problems include depression, anxiety disorders, and antisocial personality disorder. May also display learned helplessness.			

Practical Considerations for the Classroom

Concluding each chapter, *Practical Considerations for the Classroom: A Reference for Teachers* provides an at-a-glance practical summary the future teacher can take into the classroom. Sections of the feature include What IDEA Says about the Specific Exceptionality, Identification Tools, Characteristics, Indicators You Might See, Teaching Implications, Methodologies and Strategies to Try, Considerations for the General Classroom, and Collaboration.

Coverage of Collaboration

We strongly believe that helping our future teachers to be part of a collaborative team will result in a better educational experience for the exceptional student, the general education teacher, and the special education teacher. We dedicate a complete chapter (Chapter 3) to the foundations of collaboration. The chapter provides an introduction to collaboration including its history and key concepts and the roles of different team members. It also explores best practices in collaboration among schools and families, between school personnel, and between schools and communities. In addition, we've integrated issues of collaboration in individual chapters where relevant.

Coverage of Students at Risk

As part of our belief in including practical and relevant information for all future teachers, we have included a chapter dedicated to at-risk children (Chapter 13). Regardless of whether they receive services under Part C of IDEA 04, children at risk may be identified as needing services through Part B of IDEA 04. If identified early and addressed properly, the learning challenges of some of these students can be remediated without formal identification. This chapter enables future teachers to identify students who may be at risk and provide them with the appropriate supports.

Integration of Key Topics

Based on our experience teaching introduction to special education courses, we have chosen to integrate the coverage of several key topics throughout the chapters rather than isolate them in their own chapters. This approach better shows the topics' relevance to the exceptionality being discussed. Integrated topics include:

- *Inclusion:* The inclusive classroom is first introduced in Chapter 2 (The Special Education Process). To further emphasize the importance of this topic, and to discuss it in a relevant and practical manner, the final section of each chapter in Parts Two–Four focuses on the inclusive, general education classroom. As members of the collaborative special education team, both the special education teacher and the general education teacher benefit from fully understanding inclusion. It prepares the future general education teacher for a classroom with exceptional students and enables the future special education teacher to better understand general classroom needs, thereby fostering better collaboration.
- *Student Cultural Diversity:* Diversity is first introduced in Chapter 1 (An Overview of Special Education) and then discussed within each chapter. For example, effective instructional strategies for English language learners with learning disabilities are suggested in Chapter 4 (Students with Learning Disabilities); working with families from diverse backgrounds when implementing assistive technology for students with intellectual disabilities is discussed in Chapter 5 (Students with Mental Retardation/Intellectual Disabilities); and the underidentification of culturally diverse gifted students is explored in Chapter 15 (Students Who Are Gifted and Talented).
- *Technology:* Technology offers a range of support and learning opportunities for students. With the explosive growth of technology tools, an understanding of how and when to use these tools and their benefits should be discussed. Each chapter in Parts Two–Four presents a section on relevant technologies useful in the instruction and support of students with special needs.
- *Early Intervention and Transition:* Like technology, early intervention and transition issues vary by exceptionality. Coverage ranges from the importance of early intervention with children diagnosed with an autism spectrum disorder, to special transition support, such as for postsecondary education for students with learning disabilities.

Features That Support Student Learning

Students in our classrooms not only need to read textual information but also need to understand, analyze, and synthesize the large amount of material presented to them. *Exceptional Students* includes the following pedagogical aids as guides for future teachers, resulting in more application and a better understanding of special education.

- *Chapter Opening Outline:* Each chapter begins with a chapter outline designed as an advance organizer to prepare the reader for the content to come.
- *Check Your Understanding:* Concluding each major section are several questions presented to check understanding of key ideas. This allows students to learn and digest material in smaller chunks. By using this tool, students can work through the material at their own pace, checking that they fully understand one concept before moving to the next.

- *Marginal Definitions of Key Terms:* For easy reference, full definitions of key terms are presented in the margin next to where they appear in the chapter. These definitions are also available in the glossary at the end of the text.
- *Links to the Council for Exceptional Children (CEC) Standards:* Understanding CEC standards and how each concept and strategy supports those standards is of the utmost importance to future teachers. Marginal notations key relevant CEC standards to section content, thereby allowing students to see these standards in context. For instructors, these icons show where and how course materials are relevant to the relevant standards.
- *Chapter Summary:* Key concepts are highlighted to reinforce an understanding of the most important concepts and provide an effective tool for studying.
- *Reflection Questions:* Chapter-ending reflection questions encourage debate, collaborative projects, active learning, or, simply, reflection. They provide the instructor with easy ways to assign meaningful in- and out-of-class contextual learning opportunities.
- *Application Activities: For Learning and Your Portfolio:* These field-based activities provide students with an opportunity to apply what they are learning in real environments, to use real life materials and data, and to interact with people from the schools and community.

Supplemental Offerings

Exceptional Students is accompanied by a wealth of teaching and learning resources.

- **Instructor's Manual** by Tandra Tyler-Wood, University of North Texas. Each chapter includes an overview, objectives, outline, and key vocabulary list; teaching strategies; classroom activities; alternative assessment activities; possible responses to the Revisit questions asked in the text; and additional case studies and examples.
- **Test Bank** by Donna Kearns, University of Central Oklahoma. Each chapter is supported by multiple-choice and true/false questions categorized by type of question and level of difficulty, and essay questions.
- **EZTest Online Computerized Test Bank.** Test questions are available electronically through EZTest. EZTest is a flexible and easy-to-use program that enables instructors to create tests from book-specific items combined with their own items. Multiple versions of the test can be created, and any test can be exported for use with course management systems such as WebCT and Blackboard. In addition, EZ Test Online is accessible virtually anywhere via the Web, and eliminates the need to install testing software. Instructors also have the option of delivering tests through iQuiz™ via students' iPods™.
- **PowerPoint Slides** by Donna Kearns, University of Central Oklahoma. The PowerPoint slides cover the key points of each chapter and include charts and graphs from the text. The PowerPoint presentations serve as an organization and navigation tool, and can be modified to meet your needs.
- **Video Clips.** These clips offer a view inside actual special education and general education classroom settings, demonstrating the key concepts and a number of the instructional strategies covered in the text.
- **Classroom Performance System (CPS) Content** by Richael Barger-Anderson, Slippery Rock University. Each chapter includes objective and opinion questions to be used in a Classroom Performance System ("clickers") to gauge student understanding and spark discussion.
- **Course Management Cartridges.** Cartridges including material from the Online Learning Center and the test bank are available and can be customized to match your course. Our cartridges are free for adopting instructors.

- **Online Learning Center—Student Study Guide** with quizzes by Craig Rice, Middle Tennessee State University. The Online Learning Center houses a student study guide including a study checklist and practice quizzes, Web links for further exploration, and online appendices with additional classroom examples.
- *Annual Editions: Educating Children with Exceptionalities 07/08* by Karen Freiberg. This collection of reprinted contemporary articles from sources such as *Teaching Exceptional Children*, *Educational Leadership*, and *Intervention in School and Clinic* can be packaged with *Exceptional Students* for a reduced price.

Acknowledgments

We want to start by thanking our significant others— Yvette, Dave, and Joyce—for putting up with us for the many, many hours we ignored them as we were involved in this project.

Just as it takes a team to educate students with exceptionalities, so it does to write a textbook. We gratefully acknowledge the feedback, guidance, and contributions offered by our expert consultants who helped ensure current and comprehensive coverage in their areas of specialty; design consultants who commented on the cover and interior designs; peer reviewers who teach relevant college courses and were able to suggest how chapters or discussions could be improved to best meet the way they teach and their students learn the course content; and the practicing teachers who shared their experiences of teaching students with exceptionalities.

Finally, we would like to thank Tandra Tyler-Wood, Donna Kearns, Richael Barger-Anderson, and Craig Rice for their hard work on the supplements program.

Expert Consultants

Hank Bersani, *Western Oregon University*

Diane P. Bryant, *The University of Texas at Austin*

Barbara Clark, *California State University, Los Angeles*

Belva Collins, *University of Kentucky*

Maureen Conroy, *The University of Florida*

Thomas N. Kluwin, *Gallaudet University*

S. Jay Kuder, *Rowan University*

Janet Lerner, *Northeastern Illinois University*

Brenda Myles, *The University of Kansas*

J. David Smith, *University of North Carolina at Greensboro*

Joyce VanTassel-Baska, *The College of William and Mary*

Jo Webber, *Texas State University, San Marcos*

Sydney S. Zentall, *Purdue University*

Design Consultants

Patricia Campbell, *Valdosta State University*

Robert E. Faulk, *University of Memphis*

Holly Hoffman, *Central Michigan University*

Donna Kearns, *University of Central Oklahoma*

Craig Rice, *Middle Tennessee State University*

Susan Simmerman, *Utah Valley State College*

James Thompson, *Illinois State University*

Shirley E. Thompson, *Valdosta State University*

Peer Reviewers

Gary Allison, *University of Delaware*

Ellyn Lucas Arwood, *University of Portland*

Richael Barger-Anderson, *Slippery Rock University*

Dawn Behan, *Upper Iowa University*

Rebecca Newcom Belcher, *Northwest Missouri State University*

Dawn Berlin, *California State University, Dominguez Hills*

Carrie Ann Blackaller, *California State University, Dominguez Hills*

Sally Burton-Hoyle, *Eastern Michigan University*

Kathleen M. Chinn, *New Mexico State University*

Denise Clark, *University of Wisconsin-Oshkosh*

Martha Cocchiarella, *Arizona State University-Tempe*

Christina Curran, *Central Washington University*

Stephen Dempsey, *Emporia State University*

Douglas Eicher, *Missouri Western*

J'anne Ellsworth, *Worthman University*

Theresa Estrem, *University of Minnesota*

Richard Evans, *University of Texas, Permian Basin*

Bob Faulk, *University of Memphis*

Mary Fisher, *Purdue University*

Constance J. Fournier, *Texas A&M University*

Derrick Fries, *Eastern Michigan University*

Kenneth Coffey, *Mississippi State University*

Dan Glasgow, *Northeastern State University*

Blanche Jackson Glimps, *Tennessee State University*

Patrick Grant, *Slippery Rock University*

Barbara Green, *University of Central Oklahoma*

Holly Hoffman, *Central Michigan University*

Jack Hourcade, *Boise State University*

Susan Hupp, *University of Minnesota*

Nithya Narayanaswamy Iyer, *SUNY, Oneonta*

Donna Kearns, *University of Central Oklahoma*

Myung-sook Koh, *Eastern Michigan University*

Wilbert Corry Larson, *Eastern Kentucky University*

Marcel Lebrun, *Plymouth State College*

Barbara Lee, *Kean University*

Yeun joo Lee, *California State University, Bakersfield*

Joan D. Lewis, *University of Nebraska, Kearney*

Reid Linn, *James Madison University*

Carmelita Lomeo-Smrtic, *Mohawk Valley Community College*

Joy McGehee, *Northwestern State University*

Dianna McNair, *Central Washington University*

Joseph Merhaut, *Slippery Rock University*

Martha Meyer, *Butler University*

Dorothy D. Miles, *Saint Louis University*

N. Kagendo Mutua, *University of Alabama*

Joseph Nolan, *Indiana University of Pennsylvania*

Anne Papalia-Berardi, *Millersville University*

E. Michelle Pardew, *Western Oregon University*

Kathlyn Parker, *Eastern Michigan University*

Loreena Parks, *Eastern Michigan University*

Linda Parrish, *Texas A&M University*

Darcie Peterson, *Utah State University*

Barbara Rebhuhn, *University of Wisconsin–River Falls*

Craig Rice, *Middle Tennessee State University*

Patricia Rippe, *Peru State College*

Phyllis Robertson, *University of Texas, Austin*

Lynne A. Rocklage, *Eastern Michigan University*

Loline Saras, *Kutztown University*

Susan Simmerman, *Utah Valley State College*

Scott Sparks, *Ohio University*

Terry Spigner, *University of Central Oklahoma*

Georgine Steinmiller, *Henderson State University*

Linda Strunck, *Ball State University*

Linda Svobodny, *Minnesota State University Moorhead*

Kristine Swain, *University of Nebraska, Omaha*

James Thompson, *Illinois State University*

Shirley E. Thompson, *Valdosta State University*

Tandra Tyler-Wood, *University of North Texas*

Doreen Vieitez, *Joliet Junior College*

Phillip Waldrop, *Middle Tennessee State University*

Robin Wells, *Eastern New Mexico University*

Barbara Wert, *Bloomsberg University*

James Yanok, *Ohio University*

Dalun Zhang, *Clemson University*

Practicing Teachers

Joanne Bennett, *Horizon Elementary School*, FL

Juliana Berry, *Smith Elementary School*, TX

Kimberly DiLorenzo, *Forest Hills Elementary School*, FL

Carol Elder, *Graves County Central Elementary School*, KY

Barbara Gejer, *Arnold Elementary School*, CA

Christine Honsberger, *Early Steps*, FL

Toby Honsberger, *Renaissance Learning Center*, FL

Varie Hudson Hawkins, *Wesley Lakes Elementary School*, GA

Ingrid Huisman, *Williams High School*, TX

Amanda Norris, *Mason County Intermediate School*, KY

Carlotta Rody, *Cross Creek School*, FL

Jamie Mendelsohn, *P.S. 59 Beekman Hill Elementary School*, NY

Dian Trompler, *Remington Elementary School*, OK

Michael Woods, *Forest Hills High School*, FL

Jamie Worrell, *Howell L. Watkins Middle School*, FL

An Overview of Special Education

CHAPTER OUTLINE

This book is about teaching exceptional students—what both special education and general education teachers, and other professionals, can do to educate students with special needs to the maximum extent possible. It covers foundational information on the history, definitions, prevalence, causes, characteristics, and identification of exceptional students that teachers need to understand in order to make informed decisions for the classroom. Perhaps more importantly, in this book we discuss practical information regarding the instructional content, procedures, environment, and technology that teachers will use in their day-to-day activities. Teaching exceptional students is a challenging, rewarding, and sometimes both a frustrating and joyful endeavor. Through research and continued teaching, we are constantly discovering more and more about the characteristics, capabilities, and educational needs of exceptional students. Similarly, we have learned a great deal about the educational approaches to use with students with special needs. However, we have also learned that just as each student has individual characteristics, needs, and strengths and weaknesses, there is no single approach, theory, or philosophy that gives us all the answers or will be relevant for all exceptional students. Current federal law requires that students with disabilities be taught using scientifically based instruction. With this in mind, the approaches, models, and techniques discussed in this text are supported by research. We share this research-based information for you to use as you begin your personal collection of approaches, models, and techniques to be implemented with your students with different needs.

In this first chapter, we provide you with the foundational understanding you need to explore the different categories of exceptionality and to effectively support and teach students with exceptionalities. We first explain how exceptional students are defined and how many exceptional students are being served in the schools. This leads to an explanation of the meaning and intent of special education and related services. Next, we provide an overview of the history of the treatment and education of individuals with exceptionalities. We then discuss the litigation and legislation that defines special education today, and that will, in many cases, outline your responsibilities in the classroom. We conclude this chapter by introducing you to three issues in special education that we will revisit throughout the text: (1) the overidentification of students from culturally and linguistically diverse backgrounds in many categories of disability, (2) the need for early intervention and transition of young children with disabilities, and (3) the important role of the general education teacher.

Who Are Exceptional Students?

In the simplest terms, an **exceptional student** is one whose educational needs are not met by traditional educational programs so that a *special* education program is necessary. An exceptional student may have a disability, such as a learning disability, or a significant gift or talent. Many terms are used in the field of special education, some that you probably are familiar with and others that you might not be. Before we go any further, we will make a distinction between three important terms that are sometimes incorrectly used interchangeably: *impairment*, *disability*, and *handicap*.

An **impairment** refers to a loss or abnormality of a psychological, physiological, or anatomical structure or function. For example, Devon, who had a diving accident and is paralyzed below his waist, has an impairment. A **disability** is a limitation that is inherent in the individual as a result of the impairment, whereas a **handicap** is caused when an individual encounters a situation based on external factors. For example, Devon has a *disability* due to a lack of mobility caused by his paralysis. Devon would also have a *handicap* if he wanted to enter a building that has stairs but no ramp for his wheelchair. A person with a disability does not have to have a handicap. In fact, it should be a goal to ensure that no person with a disability also has a handicap. For example, some universities, through their Office of Students with Disabilities, make sure that the courses attended by students who use wheelchairs are offered on the first floor of buildings in case the elevators break down. The Individuals with Disabilities Education Act of 1990 (IDEA), an earlier version of the current federal law, first recommended that the term *disability* replace the term *handicap*, which had been used in previous legislation. To be consistent with the recommended terminology, we use the term *handicap* when referring to legal information prior to 1990 and the term *disability* for information after 1990.

Another recommendation made by IDEA was the use of "person-first" terminology that emphasizes the individual first and then the disability. For

exceptional student A student whose educational needs are not met by traditional education programs. An exceptional student can have a disability or can have gifts and talents.

impairment A loss or abnormality of a psychological, physiological, or anatomical structure or function.

disability A limitation that is inherent in an individual as a result of the impairment.

handicap A problem an individual encounters based on external factors.

 Relevant CEC Standards
▶ Issues in definition and identification of individuals with exceptional learning needs, including those from culturally and linguistically diverse backgrounds (CC1K5)
▶ Similarities and differences of individuals with and without exceptional learning needs (CC2K5)

A person with a disability does not have to have a handicap.

example, prior to IDEA an individual might be referred to as "a learning disabled student" or "an orthopedically impaired child." Now, the appropriate terminology is "a student with a learning disability" and "a child with an orthopedic impairment."

Students are defined as having a disability, and in need of special education, based on criteria outlined in the most recent federal law, the Individuals with Disabilities Education Improvement Act of 2004, referred to as the Individuals with Disabilities Education Act of 2004 (IDEA 04), which guides today's special education practices. This law is discussed in depth later in this chapter and will be referred to throughout the text. IDEA 04 identifies the following specific types, labels, or categories of students who are considered as having a disability:

> A child evaluated . . . as having mental retardation,* a hearing impairment (including deafness), a speech or language impairment, a visual impairment (including blindness), a serious emotional disturbance (referred to . . . as "emotional disturbance"),* an orthopedic impairment, autism, traumatic brain injury, an other health impairment, a specific learning disability, deaf-blindness, or multiple disabilities, and who by reason thereof, needs special education and related services.

IDEA 04 also states that, as a result of the disability, the student must need special education and related services to qualify for funding and services. For example, Sara, a student with diabetes, has a medical condition included under the other health impairment category. However, her diabetes is controlled through insulin shots administered at home, and she is having no particular difficulties academically. Therefore, she would not qualify for IDEA 04 funding and services.

Parts 2 and 3 of this text contain chapters that provide foundational and practical classroom information related to children classified with disabilities by each of these categories outlined by Part B of IDEA 04, which focuses on the education of school-aged children. Additionally, Part 4 of this text explores three areas of exceptionality not specifically identified in Part B of IDEA 04—students who are at risk, students with attention deficit/hyperactivity disorder (AD/HD), and students with gifts and talents. Students who are at risk have a high probability of being classified into an IDEA 04 category in the future if certain problems cannot be resolved through intervention. They may be eligible for services under Part C of IDEA 04. Students with AD/HD are often provided services through the IDEA 04 category of other health impairments or may receive educational accommodations under Section 504 of the Vocational Rehabilitation Act of 1973 (discussed later in this chapter). These students also frequently have another disability, such as a learning disability, and might receive services under that category. Even though gifted and talented students are not included under IDEA 04, they are acknowledged and supported through the Jacob Javits Gifted and Talented Education Act, most recently reauthorized in 2001.

Check Your Understanding

1. What is the definition of an exceptional student?
2. What is the difference between an impairment, a disability, and a handicap?
3. Students with which disabilities are served under IDEA 04?
4. Students with which exceptionalities not served under IDEA 04 are teachers likely to encounter in their classrooms?

---

*Although IDEA 04 uses the term *mental retardation,* we have chosen to use the term *intellectual disability* in this text. Intellectual disabilities is considered a less derogatory term by many parents and professionals. We will refer to mental retardation when discussing it as an IDEA 04 category and when referring to historical information such as early research and court cases. Similarly, the term *emotional* or *behavioral disorder* will be used in place of *emotional disturbance* whenever appropriate as this term better reflects the nature of the category.

How Many Exceptional Students Are There?

Two terms are typically used when describing the number of exceptional students. **Incidence** refers to the number of individuals identified as falling into a particular category for the first time during a specific period. The period of time used to determine incidence figures can vary, although one year is frequently used. We might find, for instance, that the number of individuals with emotional disturbance, ages 6 through 17 years, identified for the first time during 2009 was 9,500. **Prevalence,** on the other hand, refers to the total number of individuals who are in a given category at a particular point in time. For example, we might find that the total number of individuals ages 6 through 17 years with emotional disturbance in 2009 was 500,000. Prevalence is often expressed as a percentage of the total population in a particular category. In our example, if the total population of individuals ages 6 to 17 years was 50 million in 2009, the prevalence of individuals with emotional disturbance in that age range would be 1%. Incidence and prevalence rates are not interchangeable. As an example, Grossman (1983) pointed out that in underdeveloped countries, the *incidence* of mental retardation is relatively high because of problems such as poor nutrition and lack of prenatal care. However, because of the high mortality rate of these children, the *prevalence* is relatively low. For practical purposes, prevalence is more useful than incidence because it gives an indication of the total number of individuals who are actually receiving special education services; therefore, we report prevalence figures rather than incidence figures in this text.

Although prevalence rates are often estimates that have remained relatively consistent over the years, the most pragmatic method of determining the prevalence figures is to identify the percentage of individuals who are actually identified and receiving special education services. In 2004–2005, the percentage of the total number of school-aged students (ages 6–17) who received special education services under IDEA was 11.6%, or approximately 6 million students (United States Department of Education [U.S. DOE], 2006). This number does not include gifted and talented students. Reports indicate that more than 2.3 million students received services for gifts and talents in 2001–2002 (Council of State Directors of Programs for the Gifted, 2003). Although data from these two studies come from different years, they suggest that exceptional students make up approximately 15% of the school-aged population.

Figure 1.1 shows the percentage of students ages 6–17 receiving services in each category of disability as reported by IDEA as a function of the total population and of all students with disabilities. Almost half of all students ages 6–17 with disabilities fall into the learning disability category. In fact, 9 out of 10 students with disabilities (90.3%) fall into one of five categories: learning disabilities (45.3%), speech or language impairments (19%), other health impairments (9.3%), mental retardation (8.9%), and emotional disturbance (7.8%).

The percentage of students in different categories receiving special education has changed over the years. Figure 1.2 shows the increases and decreases in the various categories of disabilities between 1993 and 2005. Interestingly, only three categories—other health impairment, autism, and traumatic brain injury—show relative increases over that time period. The increase in the other health impairment category may be largely attributed to some states' use of this category to provide services for students with attention deficit/hyperactivity disorder, which itself is rapidly growing. The probable reason for the increases in autism and traumatic brain injury is that they were not considered as disability areas under federal law until 1990. Substantial interest and awareness, as well as improved diagnostic procedures, have resulted in more students being identified.

Interestingly, the category that showed the largest relative decrease between 1993 and 2005 was learning disabilities, which historically has been the fastest growing category. One possible explanation for this decrease may be related to the corresponding increase in the other health impairment category. In other words, students who may previously have been identified as having a learning disability might now be identified as having an attention deficit/hyperactivity disorder and are being served under the other

incidence The number of individuals identified as falling into a particular category for the first time during a specific period (such as a year).

prevalence The total number of individuals who are in a given category at a particular point in time.

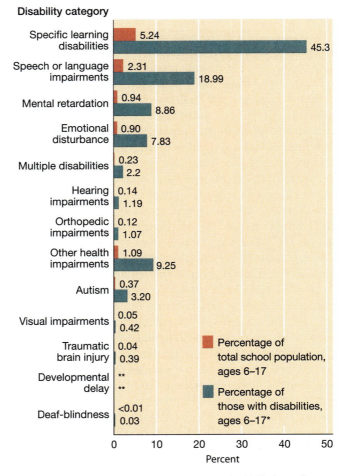

Disability category

Specific learning disabilities: 5.24 / 45.3

Speech or language impairments: 2.31 / 18.99

Mental retardation: 0.94 / 8.86

Emotional disturbance: 0.90 / 7.83

Multiple disabilities: 0.23 / 2.2

Hearing impairments: 0.14 / 1.19

Orthopedic impairments: 0.12 / 1.07

Other health impairments: 1.09 / 9.25

Autism: 0.37 / 3.20

Visual impairments: 0.05 / 0.42

Traumatic brain injury: 0.04 / 0.39

Developmental delay: ** / **

Deaf-blindness: <0.01 / 0.03

■ Percentage of total school population, ages 6–17

■ Percentage of those with disabilities, ages 6–17*

0   10   20   30   40   50
Percent

* Determined by dividing each disability percentage by 11.59, the total percentage of all students ages 6–17 with disabilities.

** Not reported because the category does not include students exclusively between the ages of 6–17.

FIGURE 1.1 Percentage of Students Ages 6–17 by Disability Category Receiving IDEA Part B Services in the Fall 2005 School Year

Source: www.ideadata.org/28th/ar_1-13.htm

health impairment category. These data do not mean that fewer students are receiving services in the categories that have shown decreases over time. In fact, the total number of students receiving services in *all* disability categories increased over the 1991–2005 period. For example, a little over 2.4 million students ages 6–21 received services for learning disabilities in 1991, but more than 2.7 million did so in 2005, although the number actually peaked in 2000 at over 2.8 million (U.S. DOE, 2006).

Prevalence figures vary from state to state, probably due, in part, to the different definitions and criteria used. Federal data indicated the following percentages (from low to high) for the five most prevalent disability categories in the 2004-2005 school year: learning disabilities: 2.2% (Kentucky) to 7.7% (Iowa); speech or language impairments: .47% (Hawaii) to 4.3% (West Virginia); other health impairments: .14% (Iowa) to 2.42% (Rhode Island), mental retardation: .34% (New Hampshire) to 2.96% (West Virginia); and emotional disturbance: .17% (Arkansas) to 2% (Vermont) (U.S. DOE, 2006). Prevalence rates for specific categories are also related to gender and ethnic background. For example, many more males are identified as having a learning disability, autism, and AD/HD than females; and more African American students are identified as having an intellectual disability or an emotional or behavior disorder than those in other racial groups. These differences are discussed in depth in subsequent chapters that focus on these specific exceptionalities.

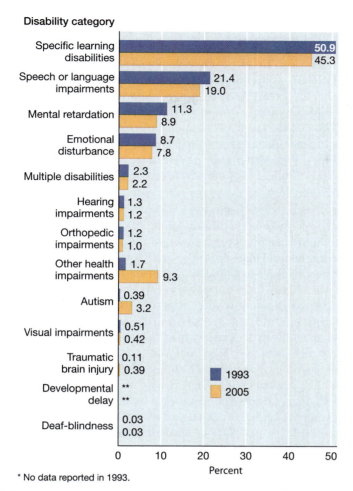

Disability category

Specific learning disabilities — 50.9 (1993), 45.3 (2005)
Speech or language impairments — 21.4 (1993), 19.0 (2005)
Mental retardation — 11.3 (1993), 8.9 (2005)
Emotional disturbance — 8.7 (1993), 7.8 (2005)
Multiple disabilities — 2.3 (1993), 2.2 (2005)
Hearing impairments — 1.3 (1993), 1.2 (2005)
Orthopedic impairments — 1.2 (1993), 1.0 (2005)
Other health impairments — 1.7 (1993), 9.3 (2005)
Autism — 0.39 (1993), 3.2 (2005)
Visual impairments — 0.51 (1993), 0.42 (2005)
Traumatic brain injury — 0.11 (1993), 0.39 (2005)
Developmental delay — ** (1993), ** (2005)
Deaf-blindness — 0.03 (1993), 0.03 (2005)

■ 1993 ☐ 2005

Percent: 0 10 20 30 40 50

* No data reported in 1993.

FIGURE 1.2 Percentage Increase/Decrease of Students with Disabilities Ages 6–21, from 1993 to 2005

Source: www.ideadata.org/docs/PARTBTRENDDATA/B2A.html

Check Your Understanding

1. What is the difference between incidence and prevalence?

2. What is the prevalence of students with all exceptionalities (ages 6–17) actually receiving services?

3. What is the most prevalent exceptionality? Approximately what percentage of the school-aged population falls into this category?

4. Why has the prevalence of some categories increased so dramatically?

What Are Special Education and Related Services?

IDEA 04 specifies that students with disabilities are entitled to a free, appropriate public education that addresses their individual educational needs. It also defines what constitutes *special education* and specifies that *related services* must be provided to allow students to have access to their special education program. In this section, we will discuss special education and related services separately, and share interviews with two special education teachers and a related services practitioner (a speech/language pathologist) to give you an idea of their roles and responsibilities.

 Relevant CEC Standards

▶ Models, theories, and philosophies that form the basis for special education practice (CC1K1)

▶ Relationship of special education to the organization and function of educational agencies (CC1K3)

Special Education

The reasons that a student's educational needs are not being met in the usual educational program can vary. These can include physical, sensory, health, or intellectual limitations; emotional or psychological problems; learning problems; communication deficits; or intellectual, academic, or creative gifts or talents. **Special education** is instruction specifically designed to meet the individual needs of these exceptional students. IDEA 04 defines special education as "specially designed instruction, at no cost to parents, to meet the unique needs of a child with a disability, including instruction conducted in the classroom, in the home, in hospitals and institutions, and in other settings, and includes instruction in physical education."

Components of Special Education

Special education involves many different components. For example, special education could include the use of a curriculum that focuses on functional life skills for a student with an intellectual disability, or it could involve the use of a specific learning strategy to teach math skills to a student with a learning disability.

In this text, we address four components of special education, each of which should be considered when working with exceptional students. The first component is *instructional content*, or what is taught to the student. The functional life skills curriculum for the student with an intellectual disability is an example of this component. The second component is *instructional procedures*, or how the content is taught to the student. The use of the learning strategy to teach math skills to the student with learning disabilities is an example of this. One commonly implemented instructional design procedure is the use of accommodations. An accommodation is a change in a lesson or procedure that is made to help a student learn the material or complete the task. For example, a student who has difficulty taking notes might be allowed to tape the lectures. Another student, who, because of his disability, works very slowly, might be given additional time to complete his class assignments. In later chapters, we provide a list of specific accommodations for students who teachers are most likely to work with—those with learning disabilities, intellectual disabilities, and emotional and behavioral disorders.

The third component of special education is the *instructional environment*, which not only includes where the instruction takes place (for example, in the general education classroom or in a separate classroom), but also involves adaptations to the instructional environment that facilitate learning. For example, a student with autism might need a structured, predictable classroom with a consistent schedule. The final component of special education we address is the *instructional technology* that is used to help support learning. Included in this component is the use of **assistive technology devices.** IDEA 04 defines an assistive technology device as "any item, piece of equipment, or product system whether acquired commercially off the shelf, modified, or customized, that is used to increase, maintain, or improve functional capabilities of a child with a disability." Assistive technology devices can range from something "low tech," such as a pencil grip for a student with a physical disability, to something "high tech," such as a voice synthesizer activated through the use of a computer for a nonverbal student.

Universal Design

What each of the above components of special education has in common is that they encompass the concept of **universal design** emphasized in IDEA 04. Universal design is a term borrowed from architecture that refers to the development of environments that are accessible to everyone. For example, following the concept of universal design, a school would be designed so that it would maximize accessibility for everyone. In addition to allowing easy entrance into the school for everyone, the application of universal design would affect the design of the classrooms, bathrooms, and the kitchen.

IDEA 04 indicates that universal design is the concept or philosophy that products and services should be designed and delivered around so that they can be used by individuals with the widest range of capabilities. Although universal design is obvious in the physical environment, it can also apply to instructional and assessment modifications.

special education Instruction specifically designed to meet the individual needs of an exceptional student.

assistive technology device Any item, equipment, or product system that is used to increase, maintain, or improve functional capabilities.

universal design The concept that environments, instruction, and assessments should be designed to be accessible to all individuals.

TABLE 1.1 Elements of Universal Design

CLASSROOM ELEMENT	APPLICATION
Inclusive classroom population	Design all classroom materials with the end user (diverse student population) in mind.
Precisely defined information	Remember the information that you are trying to teach or test. Avoid irrelevant materials that may be teaching or testing nontargeted behaviors or information.
Accessible, nonbiased materials	Accessible, nonbiased materials are those that consider the diversity of all students and do not present material that may be offensive or may give one group an advantage over another.
Amenable to accommodations	Even the best-designed tests and materials may need to be adjusted through accommodations. Avoid language or diagrams that cannot be converted to Braille, translated, or read aloud.
Simple, clear, and innovative procedures	Tests and materials should be clear and understandable. Tests are invalid if students cannot understand what the teacher expects. Students more clearly understand what is expected if they receive frequent feedback.
Maximum readability and comprehensibility*	Language should be clear, simple, and direct.
Maximum legibility	Font size should be large and familiar enough for students with visual difficulties to read. Overly enlarged text, however, may cause difficulty for some readers. For these readers, staggered right margins, white space around text, sans serif fonts, and space between lines increase legibility.

*These elements of universal design overlap with graphic design principles.

Source: Adapted from Acrey, C., Johnstone, C., & Millgan, C. (2005). Using universal design to unlock the potential for academic achievement of at-risk learners. *Teaching Exceptional Children, 38,* 22–31 (Table 1, p. 24). Copyright © 2005 by The Council for Exceptional Children. Reprinted with permission.

Teachers can implement universal design by planning lessons that *all* students can access. Mandlawitz (2006) in her summary of the implications of universal design in IDEA 04, noted:

> With few exceptions, children with disabilities are expected to meet the same high academic standards as children without disabilities using the general education curriculum. The dearth of instructional materials and assessment tools that are accessible, valid, and appropriate for use with children with a broad range of disabilities has made this goal more difficult. The concept of universal design is incorporated throughout the amendments of the law. (p. 7)

Mandlawitz goes on to remind us that IDEA 04 allows states to use funding to support technology using universal design principles; encourages research toward how to incorporate the principles in the development of curricula, instructional materials, and assessment tools; and requires, where feasible, that assessments be developed and administered using these principles. Table 1.1 shows some elements of universal design and how they can be applied in the classroom when designing tests and instructional materials.

In summary, two points regarding universal design are important. First, it is a philosophy that should be the guiding force in developing educational programs. Second, each of the four components of special education should be considered when developing a program that reflects the concept of universal design. In other words, each component should ensure that all students, with or without disabilities, have access to an appropriate educational program.

Where Special Education Is Delivered

Special education of exceptional students can occur in a number of settings. A special education program can potentially take place totally within the general education classroom, partially within the general education classroom, in a separate classroom for students with disabilities within a public or private school, or in a separate school that includes just students with disabilities. More restrictive settings such as residential facilities or home/hospitals may be used by a very small number of students with severe or unique needs. These placement options are discussed in depth in the next chapter. It should be emphasized, however, that the special education program should be carried out in the general education classroom whenever possible, and the student should participate in the general education curriculum to the maximum extent possible.

Who Delivers Special Education

A special education program can be implemented by any number of professionals including a special education teacher specifically trained to support students with disabilities or a general education teacher who teaches in a classroom that includes children with and without disabilities. In the latter situation, the special education teacher and other specialists will collaborate with the general classroom teacher to plan and assist in instruction. To illustrate the roles and responsibilities of special education teachers, we interviewed two teachers. The first teacher, Jamie, is a special education teacher who works in an inclusive setting, meaning that her students are primarily taught in the general education classroom. The second teacher, Carla, teaches students who are pulled from their home schools into a segregated setting. We asked them about their school's philosophies and practices, and about their roles and responsibilities.

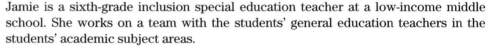

▌ Meet Jamie Worrell

Jamie is a sixth-grade inclusion special education teacher at a low-income middle school. She works on a team with the students' general education teachers in the students' academic subject areas.

1. **What is your school's philosophy regarding inclusion?** All students with mild disabilities should be included in the general education setting on a daily basis. The goal is to successfully have all special education students meet the minimum grade-level expectations in order to move on to the next grade.
2. **Describe how general education teachers, special education teachers, and related service personnel collaborate at your school.** Every Monday the general education teachers give me a set of lesson plans for the upcoming week. I then meet with each teacher on my team once a week to go over the lessons we are co-teaching. The general educators and I also meet on a weekly basis for 30 minutes to discuss any changes in the lesson plans or schedule for the week and any priority issues that directly relate to the special education students. The majority of the collaboration between general educators, special educators, and related service personnel takes place on a daily basis through e-mail. General education teachers will e-mail me for resources for a particular lesson or to let me know if a student performed well or poorly on an assignment or a test. Teachers will also e-mail me if they think any student needs to be re-taught a specific lesson or concept.
3. **What are your top three responsibilities?**
   - To maintain an open line of communication with the general education teachers on my team so that we can successfully collaborate on a daily basis
   - To maintain a trusting, open, and equal relationship with each special education and general education student so that when I am in a classroom I am seen as just another teacher and not the "Special Education Teacher"
   - To provide resource support to the general education teachers
4. **Describe a typical day.** After teaching two periods of language arts to my special education students, I go into the math, science, social studies, or reading class, depending on the day. As the general education teacher is giving a lecture, I walk around the classroom making sure the students are on the correct page and actively participating in the lesson either by asking questions, taking notes, or reading. Occasionally during the lecture, I intervene to clarify a concept or emphasize a

main point by stating it verbally and writing it on the board. Many times during math lectures, after the general education teacher finishes her lesson, I'll teach the class the same lesson, but in a different way and using manipulatives.

During my planning period, I check my e-mail. There are usually at least one or two messages from each general education teacher on my team. Most of the e-mails are to alert me to upcoming quizzes/tests, a particular student who needs help grasping a concept, or a change that has arisen in the lesson plans. I make the modifications I need to and work on modifying assignments for the different subject areas for the following week. When my planning is over, I go back to the classroom I was previously in to assist for the remainder of the periods.

▌ Meet Carla A. Rody

Carla Rody is a high school special education science teacher. Her students have severe emotional or behavioral disorders and have been removed from their home schools by the school district or court system. When students meet their therapeutic or behavior goals, they may return to their home school.

1. **What is your school's philosophy regarding inclusion?** Our belief is that most of our students will be able to return to their home schools through appropriate interventions. We have been very successful in this endeavor over the past three years. There are a few students, however, who will not be able to be successful within an inclusive setting and will remain in the center.
2. **Describe how general education teachers, special education teachers, and related services personnel collaborate at your school.** We have individualized education program (IEP) teams to develop the student's educational program, and multidisciplinary child study teams to identify modifiable behaviors, and to do such things as tutor for the statewide assessment. Also, district personnel observe students who are preparing to return to their home school. That team usually consists of the special education teachers from our school, a general education teacher and a disability specialist from the home school, our disability specialist and guidance counselor, and a district administrator.
3. **What are your top three responsibilities?**
    *   To make sure my students understand what they are learning
    *   To provide the types of differentiated instruction that will help my students be successful in class
    *   To provide a positive, consistent model to address my students' emotional and behavioral needs
4. **Describe a typical day.** I am in my classroom between 7 and 7:30 a.m. and set out lab materials for the three, 90-minute blocks of science; read the school's e-mails; and check my grade book. Our team meetings are from 8:30–8:50 a.m., and my first class is 9th grade Earth Science. I do an advance graphic organizer to set up the lesson and follow it with a hands-on lab to connect the reading and writing to real-world applications. My second block is 8th grade Earth Science. Because these students have not been exposed to the content and are behind in science concepts, they get more hands-on and one-on-one interventions to help connect the concepts into their world. My third block is a 10th–12th grade Biology class. My planning period is fourth block, and I use that time to meet with peers, do computer work, record grades, and set up the lab materials for the next day.

There are many similarities in Jamie's and Carla's situations. They both are very student oriented and take pride in their students' achievements. They spend time preparing for class, assessing student work, and teaching. Their philosophies regarding including students in the general education classroom are also similar although their educational settings result in different practices. Jamie spends most of her day planning and teaching collaboratively with the general education teachers. Carla spends most of her day teaching her students in isolation. Collaboration at Carla's school primarily involves the mutual development of the students' educational programs and preparing for their return to their home school.

The role of a special education teacher will vary based on the school and students' needs. The second half of each chapter in Parts 2–4 includes specific information to help prepare you to teach exceptional students. Whether you plan to be a special education teacher or a general education teacher, you will need a strong foundation of the components of special education to effectively plan and deliver your instruction.

Related Services

Related services are those activities or supports that enable a child with a disability to receive a free, appropriate, public education, and to benefit from the special education program. IDEA 04 lists the following related services that a student might receive.

- Transportation
- Speech-language pathology and audiology services
- Interpreting services
- Psychological services
- Physical and occupational therapy
- Recreation (including therapeutic recreation)
- Early identification and assessment
- Counseling services (including rehabilitation counseling)
- Orientation and mobility services
- Medical services for diagnostic or evaluation purposes
- School health services and school nurse services
- Social work services
- Parent counseling and training

Necessary related services are determined by the team responsible for developing a student's individualized education program (IEP), an overall plan for the student's education that is required by IDEA 04 and introduced later in the chapter. The following are brief descriptions of the roles of each of the related services identified by IDEA 04.

Transportation

Special transportation is a related service provided to many students, often those with more moderate to severe disabilities. If a student cannot get to school, she cannot receive an appropriate education. Particularly for students with physical disabilities, special transportation that includes a wheelchair lift may be needed. Also, because some programs may include students from outside the school's neighborhood, such as a special class for all students who are deaf in a district, special transportation is needed because the school attended is in a different location than the student's neighborhood school.

Speech-Language Pathology and Audiology Services

Speech and language pathologists provide a variety of related services. These specialists may perform assessments and evaluations, and provide intervention for a variety of speech and language disorders (Sunderland, 2004). In some instances, speech and language pathologists may also focus on other issues such as swallowing difficulties. These specialists can make recommendations for interventions related to the development of communication and literacy skills.

Audiology services can involve assessment of hearing for both degree and type of hearing loss. Audiology specialists can also fit, adjust, and maintain assistive listening devices such as hearing aids. In some cases, audiologists may provide counseling to individuals who have experienced hearing loss as well as make recommendations for adaptations and assistive technology that can aid the student. Audiologists can make recommendations to teachers on how best to arrange the physical and instructional environment and to communicate with a student to make maximum use of any residual hearing.

Interpreting Services

Interpreters are related service personnel that can work with those whose hearing loss is so severe that they cannot hear sufficiently to learn in the classroom. Generally, in this case, the student uses sign language as the primary means of communication. Interpreters usually accompany a student in all environments as needed, providing a bridge between the student and others who may not use sign language.

Psychological Services

School psychologists are related services providers who are frequently involved in assessment activities, especially those associated with the identification of students for eligibility for special education. In this capacity, they serve as data collectors and administer individual assessments. For example, they may observe a student's performance in a classroom setting or administer intelligence and achievement tests. Psychologists may also devise and implement behavioral interventions, and provide counseling as well as other services as needed. Psychologists can assist teachers in many ways including how to manage student behavior, how best to assess students, and by providing a source of data for educational decision making.

Physical and Occupational Therapy

Physical therapists perform individual and ongoing assessments of physical functioning, make recommendations for physical therapy interventions, provide direct treatment, and supervise the work of physical therapy assistants who may be providing direct services (Neal, Bigby, & Nicholson, 2004). Physical therapists usually focus on large muscle groups and functioning such as walking, posture, and positioning of the body. For example, a student with cerebral palsy may need assistance from a physical therapist in walking and other areas. Occupational therapists typically focus on smaller muscle groups and their use in daily activities (Neal et al., 2004). For example, they may help a student with the use of hands for writing, eating, and dressing. Occupational therapists provide initial and ongoing assessments as well as direct services and supervision of assistants.

Recreation

Some students with disabilities need related services for special recreational opportunities and instruction. For example, students who use wheelchairs may need an adapted program to develop and maintain good physical health and wellness. There are specialists who focus in this area, but these services are also provided by a variety

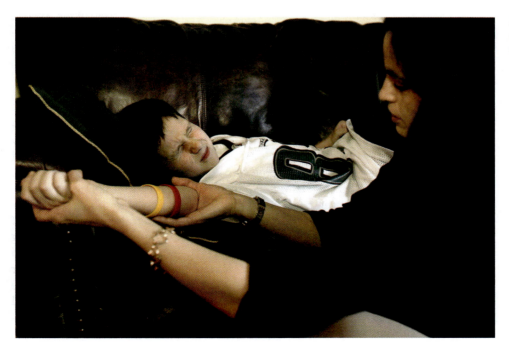

Physical therapists often work on developing a student's muscle tone.

of team members including teachers, parents, and community agencies (such as the YMCA). These services can include assessing recreation and leisure interests and preferences, provision of therapeutic services (such as therapeutic swimming/water activities), adaptation of activities and equipment, and identification of recreational resources and facilities (Downing, 2004).

Early Identification and Assessment

The related services of early childhood screening and assessment are often provided by community agencies, such as a local health service agency. These services include developmental screening to determine if individual assessments are needed, and the individual assessments themselves. These services can also involve monitoring overall development to determine whether important milestones are being achieved, such as walking and talking at an appropriate age (Downing, 2004). Medical professionals are also involved in this type of screening and assessment. These services are important in establishing the need for and implementation of interventions, whether medical, therapeutic, or educational, which can mediate the effects of an existing disability or reduce or eliminate the risks associated with other conditions, such as malnourishment or low birth weight.

Counseling Services

Counseling services might include academic counseling, emotional counseling, and rehabilitation counseling. Rehabilitation counselors provide assessments of a student's career/vocational attitudes, abilities, and needs; vocational guidance and counseling; training in career/vocational knowledge and skills; and identification of job sites and placements (Downing, 2004). These specialists can be especially helpful to teachers, students, and families in the transition from school to adult living.

Orientation and Mobility Services

Orientation and mobility specialists teach students with vision losses how to navigate within environments and from one environment to another. They would teach, for example, how to move within the classroom and how to navigate around the overall school environment. They assist students in traveling independently and can work with students on the use of canes, guide dogs, wheelchairs, and public transportation (Neal et al., 2004). These specialists are helpful to teachers, students, and families as they have special knowledge and skills to train individuals with vision losses to function in a variety of settings.

Medical Services for Diagnostic or Evaluation Purposes

Medical services for diagnostic purposes, for example, to assist in the identification of attention deficit/hyperactivity disorder, are included as a related service under IDEA 04. However, other medical services, such as prescribing medication and performing routine physical examinations, are not covered. On the other hand, health services such as dispensing medication and monitoring its effects at school are considered related services (Downing, 2004).

School Health and School Nurse Services

Some students with health-impairing conditions or multiple disabilities need monitoring and special services such as tube feeding and catheterization. School nurses may be involved in the provision of services or may train classroom personnel to carry out such services when special medical knowledge and training is not needed. For example, catheterization has been established as a related service that does require training, but neither special medical knowledge nor training pertinent only to medical professionals. Teachers and aides can be trained to perform this service.

Social Work Services

Social work services can include preparing developmental or social histories of a child, group and individual counseling for a student or the family, working with families on interventions at home and in the community, identifying and mobilizing community resources and agencies, and assisting in developing positive behavioral interventions (Downing, 2004). Social workers can be a great asset to teachers by serving as a bridge among the school, family, and community. For example, social workers can assist families in obtaining food stamps, housing, and other assistance from various agencies, which, in turn, help the student and family to meet needs that are critical to being prepared to learn and thrive.

Parent Counseling and Training

Counselors are available to assist parents with the many needs and concerns that they might face as a result of having a child with a disability. This might involve addressing parents' feelings of guilt or anger. Also, particularly with parents of young children, specific training may be necessary to assist them in areas such as early intervention services that could be implemented in the home.

Speech and language therapy is the most widely used related service. We interviewed a speech and language pathologist who provides services through a "pull-out" program. We asked her the same questions we asked Jamie and Carla about her school's philosophies and practices and about her roles and responsibilities.

▌ Meet Kim DiLorenzo

Kim DiLorenzo is a speech-language pathologist at a very large elementary school (1,150 students/100 faculty). She is one of four speech-language pathologists in her school and currently has a caseload of 61 students in grades 1–5.

1. **What is your school's philosophy regarding inclusion?** Because of the size of our school, inclusive practices are difficult. Students from general education classes receive "pull-out" services from special education teachers and speech-language clinicians.
2. **Describe how general education teachers, special education teachers, and related services personnel collaborate at your school.** General and special education teachers participate in weekly collaborative planning sessions. Special education teachers and speech-language pathologists are assigned to grade levels, and they attend the general education grade-level meetings as well as department and faculty meetings. Related service personnel such as physical therapists, occupational therapists, and counselors participate in IEP and parent meetings.
3. **What are your top three responsibilities?**
   - To implement IEP goals and document progress toward those goals
   - To provide educationally relevant therapy by combining individual speech and language goals with state standards
   - To provide IEP updates and meet with parents and classroom teachers to discuss progress/needs
4. **Describe a typical day.** My day begins at 7:30 a.m. with bus duty, unless I have a parent conference or an IEP meeting. The rest of the day is broken up into 30- to 45-minute blocks in which I see different groups of students for speech or language therapy. I have a block of time in the middle of the day when I complete diagnostic testing. Most of my meetings (parent conferences, IEP updates, and collaborative planning) are scheduled for the afternoon.

Under IDEA 04, every student with a disability is entitled to a special education program and any related services that are necessary. In this text, we focus on four components of special education: instructional content, instructional procedures, the instructional environment, and instructional technology. Important in all four components is the concept of universal design, or making sure all content and services are accessible for all students regardless of their capabilities and limitations.

Check Your Understanding

1. What is special education?
2. What are the components of special education?
3. What is universal design?
4. What are related services? What are some related services that students with disabilities might receive?

What Is the History of Special Education?

Relevant CEC Standard
▶ Historical points of view and contribution of culturally diverse groups (CC1K8)

To fully appreciate how far we have come in teaching exceptional students in recent years, one must look at the history of special education, which has had a dramatic impact on our current thinking and educational practices. Over the last several hundred years, there has been an evolution from intolerance to treatment to education of individuals with disabilities. As you will see, special education as a formal profession is relatively new. A general history of disabilities is provided here; histories of specific disabilities are presented in the relevant chapters in Parts 2–4.

Early History

Documentation of individuals who have disabilities, as well as those individuals with great gifts and talents, has been provided since the beginning of recorded history. The early treatment of individuals with disabilities varied from kindness and pity to cruelty and even barbarism. Sheerenberger (1983) noted, for example, that in ancient Egypt, children who would now be considered as having an intellectual disability were treated by priests using spiritual healing, amulets, and incantations. In Sparta, however, children with disabilities would be brought before a board of elders to determine their fate, and they were frequently thrown into the Eurotes River or abandoned in the wild. Sheerenberger pointed out that such practices were widespread until the fourth century when Christianity began to have a positive influence. On the other hand, early societies valued individuals who helped further societal goals with their gifts and talents. In Sparta, for instance, gifted individuals were those who were considered strong leaders and warriors (Colangelo & Davis, 2003). These individuals were perhaps the first exceptional students, being chosen for Plato's Academy primarily based on intelligence and physical ability. Treatment of individuals with disabilities began to improve during the Middle Ages, Renaissance, and Reformation. With advances in medicine, European physicians began to influence the way in which individuals were treated.

The 17th through 19th Centuries

Although there was some interest in deaf and blind individuals in the 17th century and the beginning of the 18th century, the treatment of individuals with disabilities during this time is best described as uncaring and inhumane. In Europe, individuals with disabilities were largely confined to hospitals and prisons, where the death rate was high. At one time in the United States, many exceptional individuals were thought to be witches, and were often persecuted and sometimes executed (Hickson, Blackman, & Reis, 1995). Real attempts made to treat exceptional individuals in a humane fashion were not made until the middle of the 18th century and continued in the 19th century. The influence of European physicians spread, and eventually interest and attention were paid to the abilities, rather than the limitations, of exceptional

TABLE 1.2	Individuals Making Significant Contributions to Special Education in the 18th and 19th Centuries
Jacob Periere	Taught individuals who could not hear or speak to use simple sign language in the mid-1700s
Phillippe Pinel	Freed patients from their chains in two insane asylums in Paris in the mid-1700s
Samuel Gridley Howe	Founded the New England Asylum for the Blind in 1832 (now the Perkins School for the Blind)
Thomas Hopkins Gallaudet	Founded the American Asylum at Hartford for the Education of the Deaf and Dumb in 1819 (now the American School for the Deaf)
Edouard Seguin	One of the first to work with individuals with intellectual disabilities in the United States

individuals. These efforts were carried to the United States by physicians and other professionals (see Table 1.2).

One person, Jean Marc Itard, is generally accepted as having the most influence during this time period. He is best known for working with Victor, the wild boy of Aveyron, a child who had been found wandering naked in the woods and reportedly had been raised by animals. Victor was taken to the Institution for Deafmutes in Paris in 1800, where Itard was on the medical staff. Itard implemented an intensive training program that lasted for 5 years. Although Itard was not completely successful, he did teach Victor to identify objects and letters of the alphabet, as well as to understand the meaning of several words (Kanner, 1964). Also of significance was Victor's progress in social development. When others saw the progress that Victor had made, interest in the possibility of teaching individuals who had been previously considered unteachable was stimulated.

Although the first public school was established in 1839, the first special education class was not introduced until almost 30 years later. In 1867 a class for deaf students commenced at the Horace Mann School for the Deaf in Boston. Several more classes for students with disabilities were formed over the latter part of the 19th century and beginning of the 20th century. These classes, however, were not legally sanctioned, and for the most part money to support them was negligible (Winzer, 1993).

Itard was best known for educating Victor, the Wild Boy of Aveyron (shown below).

The 20th Century

Negative attitudes by many toward individuals with disabilities continued in the early 1900s. These negative feelings were reinforced by Goddard's (1912) research that implied that low intelligence and deviant behavior were hereditary, a point that resulted in discrimination and more negative stereotypes. In fact, forced sterilization and segregation were popular solutions at that time. The negative attitude toward individuals with disabilities was perhaps exemplified best by the movie *The Black Stork*. This movie, shown in public theatres in 1917, told the story of Dr. Harry Haisenden, a Chicago physician who supported euthanasia for children with disabilities and refused to perform surgery on "deformed babies."

There were, however, some positive advances during the early 20th century. Grace Fernald, Samuel Orton, and others were making contributions to the field of special education, becoming actively involved in developing remedial approaches for individuals with reading problems. Also, the first professional organization, the International Council for the Education of Exceptional Children, was founded (see An Important Event).

The Black Stork *was a movie that encouraged euthanasia of babies with disabilities.*

In the 1930s, parents of children with disabilities began grassroots movements to push their agenda of advocacy. In the 1940s, Alfred Strauss and Heinz Werner created additional interest in special education by suggesting and researching a neurological basis for learning problems. Although their work initially focused on individuals with mental retardation, it was later applied to other areas and greatly affected the field of learning disabilities.

During the 1950s and 1960s, the civil rights movement helped to raise interest in equality, resulting in grassroots efforts of parents and organized advocacy groups such as the National Association of Retarded Children (now the ARC) and the United Cerebral Palsy Association. Also during this time, more favorable economic conditions prevailed, and the existing politics provided a positive attitude and more available funding for educational programs such as Head Start, an early intervention program for young children living in poverty. At the same time, research based on the work of Strauss and Werner continued, particularly after Samuel Kirk coined the term "learning disability" in 1963. In the 1970s, litigation and legislation began to have a significant impact on the field of special education. In a sense, the decades of the 1960s and 1970s were the beginning of the formal field of special education as it was recognized, and eventually funded, by federal legislation.

Check Your Understanding

1. Describe how individuals with disabilities or gifts were treated prior to the 18th century.

2. Which historical figures had an impact on special education in the 18th and 19th centuries in Europe and in the United States?

3. What were some positive and negative events or occurrences related to special education in the 20th century?

How Has Litigation and Legislation Affected Special Education?

As special education became more of a formal, identifiable professional field in the latter part of the 20th century, parents and other advocates sought the best programs possible for all exceptional students and wanted to ensure that their rights were not violated. Many students with disabilities were still being excluded from school or were participating in inferior educational programs. This dedication to the education of students with special needs resulted in several noteworthy court cases in the early 1970s that focused on the issue of exclusion of students from special education programs. Ironically, litigation also addressed discrimination issues at this time, claiming that minority students who were receiving special education programs were inappropriately identified as needing them. All of these cases eventually led to legislation that significantly affected special education practices. The most significant legislation was PL 94-142, the Education for All Handicapped Children Act, which initially defined and funded special education practices in the United States and guides its practice today through its current incarnation as the Individuals with Disabilities Education Act of 2004 (IDEA 04).

Early Court Cases

The early court cases related to special education revolved around exclusion and discrimination. Two court cases of the early 1970s are representative of litigation related to the exclusion of exceptional students from appropriate educational programs. The first was *Pennsylvania Association for Retarded Citizens (PARC) v. Commonwealth of Pennsylvania* (1971), a class action suit filed on behalf of a group of students with mental retardation who were not receiving appropriate educational programs. The result of the litigation was the mandate for a free, public education for students with mental retardation. The second case, *Mills v. Board of Education of the District of Columbia* (1972), was similar to the *Pennsylvania* case but broadened the right to a free, public education to include students with all disabilities.

The discrimination cases during this period primarily dealt with assessment issues that led to the possible erroneous labeling of minority students as having mental retardation (see Table 1.3). Specifically, these cases examined the possible inappropriate use of intelligence tests in assessment. In some cases, the cultural bias of the tests was called into question. Of the court cases listed in Table 1.3, the one that has had the greatest impact is *Larry P. v. Riles* (1972). This case addressed the question of whether or not intelligence tests are biased against African American students. It ultimately resulted in a ban on the use of intelligence tests with African American students in California. Inevitably, litigation and court battles such as these result in legislation. During the past 50 years, there have been considerable advances in the laws that govern special education.

Early Legislation Affecting Special Education

The earlier laws of the 1950s and 1960s related to special education (see Table 1.4) paved the way to the more significant legislation of the Rehabilitation Act of 1973

Relevant CEC Standard

▶ Issues, assurances, and due process rights related to assessment, eligibility, and placement within a continuum of services (CC1K6)

TABLE 1.3	Representative Court Cases Focusing on Discriminatory Assessment Practices
Hobson v. Hansen (1967)	Ruled that standardized testing was biased against African American and disadvantaged students.
Diana v. California State Board of Education (1973)	Ruled that tests must be administered in the native language of the student; also indicated that students could not be placed into special education on the basis of culturally biased tests.
Guadalupe v. Tempe (Arizona) Board of Education (1979)	Decision was similar to *Diana* ruling requiring the use of culturally nonbiased assessment.
Larry P. v. Riles (1972)	In perhaps the most well-known and controversial assessment case, the plaintiff argued that intelligence tests (the Wechsler Intelligence Scale for Children in particular) were biased against African American children. The case resulted in the banning of intelligence tests with African American students in California.
PASE v. Hannon (1980)	A case similar to the *Larry P.* case. The court, however, ruled that intelligence tests were not biased against African American students.

(Section 504, Public Law 93-112) and the Education for All Handicapped Children Act (Public Law 94-142). These two acts, particularly PL 94-142, provided the basis for many of the special education practices in place today. Specifically, the current special education legislation, the Individuals with Disabilities Act of 2004, evolved from the basic premises of PL 94-142. Before we discuss these laws, we want to let you know what the hyphenated number means in a public law. The first part of the number identifies the congressional session in which the law was passed. The second part of the hyphenated number refers to the number of the law passed within that congressional session. Thus PL 93-112 was the 112th law passed by the 93rd Congress, and PL 94-142 was the 142nd law passed by the 94th Congress.

TABLE 1.4	Early Laws Affecting the Field of Special Education

LEGISLATION	YEAR	SCHOOL PROGRAMMING AFFECTED
National Defense Education Act PL 85-926	1958	Provided funding to train special education teachers of students with mental retardation
Special Education Act PL 87-276	1961	Provided funding to train special education teachers of deaf students
Elementary and Secondary Education Act (ESEA) PL 89-10	1965	Provided funding to develop programs for economically disadvantaged students
Amendment to Title 1 of ESEA PL 89-313	1966	Provided funding for state-supported schools and institutions for students with disabilities
ESEA Amendments of 1966 PL 89-750	1966	Established first federally funded program for students with disabilities at the local school level
Vocational Education Amendments of 1968 PL 90-576	1968	Mandated that 10% of the funds for vocational education be earmarked for students with disabilities
ESEA Amendments of 1970 PL 91-230	1970	Resulted in the acceptance of exceptional students as a unique population with special educational needs

Rehabilitation Act of 1973 (PL 93-112, Section 504)

The Rehabilitation Act was passed in 1973 as an attempt to end education and job discrimination on the basis of a person's disability. Similar legislation had already been passed to prevent discrimination on the basis of sex, ethnic background, and religion. Essentially, this law stated that no otherwise qualified handicapped individual in the United States could be excluded from participation in any program or activity receiving federal financial assistance based solely on his or her handicap. Prior to this legislation, an employer of a university, hospital, U.S. government agency, or any other business or organization receiving federal funding could deny employment of an individual based solely on his or her disability. After the law passed, this practice was no longer acceptable if the individual had the necessary qualifications to meet the job requirements. The Rehabilitation Act also resulted in the development of "504 Plans," which allow for instructional accommodations for students who do not qualify for special education services under IDEA 04 but who, nonetheless, need additional help. For example, 504 Plans are often used with students with attention deficit/hyperactivity disorder, which is not considered a disability category under current federal law. This legislation also was the basis for the passage of PL 94-142, which expanded these concepts with many specific educational mandates and provided funding for special education services.

Education for All Handicapped Children Act (PL 94-142)

Passed in 1975, PL 94-142 is the most significant piece of legislation related to special education to date. PL 94-142 and its subsequent amendments and reauthorizations have provided guidelines, requirements, and funding for the education of exceptional students. PL 94-142 mandated six major principles to guide the education of individuals with disabilities:

1. Provision of a *free, appropriate public education* (FAPE) for all handicapped students (referred to as *zero reject*)
2. Use of *nondiscriminatory evaluation*
3. Development of an *individualized education program* (IEP)
4. Education of the student in the *least restrictive environment* (LRE)
5. Implementation of *due process* procedures
6. Right of *parental participation*

These and other principles and requirements will be addressed in depth later in this chapter in the discussion of IDEA 04, the most recent legislation related to PL 94-142.

After the passage of PL 94-142 in 1975, several court cases, some heard by the Supreme Court, focused on the interpretation of the new law. This litigation further defined and strengthened legislation related to special education (see Table 1.5).

Post–PL 94-142 Legislation

After PL 94-142 had been implemented for a number of years, several major amendments were made to respond to litigation regarding its interpretation, to provide additional funding for exceptional individuals, to extend the rights of students with disabilities, and to change terminology used in the special education field. These acts, briefly summarized in Table 1.6, include the Education of the Handicapped Act Amendments of 1986 (PL 99-457), the Individuals with Disabilities Education Act (IDEA; PL 101-476), and the 1997 reauthorization of IDEA (IDEA 97; PL 105-17). Additional legislation was passed that provided safeguards against discrimination of individuals with disabilities, the Americans with Disabilities Act, and that encouraged accountability for student progress, the No Child Left Behind Act. These pieces of legislation directly or indirectly affected the current law, the Individuals with Disabilities Education Act of 2004, which guides current special education practices.

Relevant CEC Standards

▶ Rights and responsibilities of students, parents, teachers, and other professionals and schools related to exceptional learning needs (CC1K4)

▶ Issues, assurances, and due process rights related to assessment, eligibility, and placement within a continuum of services (CC1K6)

▶ Laws, policies, and ethical principles regarding behavior management planning and implementation (CC1K2)

TABLE 1.5 — Significant Post–PL 94-142 Litigation

COURT CASE	ISSUE	RESULT
Board of Education of the Hendrick Hudson Central School District v. Rowley (1982)	Meaning of "appropriate" within FAPE	Although a school district must provide an appropriate education, it does not have to provide an optimal education.
Luke S. and Hans S. v. Nix et al. (1984)	Timely assessment	There should be more assessment before a referral to avoid a backlog of referrals.
Irving Independent School District v. Tatro (1984)	Related services	Clean intermittent catheterization was considered a related service for a student who needed it to attend school.
Burlington School Committee v. Department of Education of Massachusetts (1985)	Private school placement	The school district must pay for private school placement if the public school program is deemed inappropriate.
Honig v. Doe (1988)	Discipline	A student whose misbehavior is related to his disability cannot be denied a public school education.
Timothy W. v. Rochester School District (1988)	Educability	The school district must provide an educational program for a student with profound disabilities even if the district feels he is uneducable.

Americans with Disabilities Act (PL 101-336)

Enacted in 1990, the Americans with Disabilities Act (ADA) is essentially a civil rights act for individuals with disabilities. Among the provisions of the ADA are:

- Employers (for any business with 15 or more employees) cannot discriminate against those with disabilities. In other words, employers cannot use an individual's disability as a reason for not hiring him or her. In addition, employers must provide reasonable accommodations (e.g., modification of equipment), if necessary. Implementation of the ADA does not necessarily mean undue expense for the employer; there is language in the law that addresses the issue of excessive expenses. In addition, employers can be creative. For example, rather than replace a water fountain that is out of reach for an employee in a wheelchair, an employer could simply provide paper cups.

TABLE 1.6 — Amendments and Reauthorizations of PL 94-142 Leading to the IDEA 04

LAW	YEAR	PRIMARY CHANGES
EHA Amendments PL 99-457	1986	Required states to provide services for children ages 3–5; required states to provide services for infants and toddlers from birth through age 2.
Individuals with Disabilities Education Act PL 101-476	1990	Changed the name from EHA to IDEA. Changed term "handicap" to disability and added person-first language; added autism and traumatic injury as disability categories; required an individualized transition plan by age 16.
Reauthorization of IDEA 1997 PL 105-17	1997	Students with disabilities must participate in statewide or districtwide assessments or take an alternate assessment. Students must participate in the general education curriculum to the maximum extent possible.

- Public accommodations (e.g., hotels, restaurants) must have appropriate building codes to allow free access for individuals with disabilities (e.g., ramps for individuals in wheelchairs).
- All public transit authorities must have vehicles that allow accessibility for individuals with disabilities.
- Companies offering usual telephone services must also provide similar services for individuals with disabilities. For example, a large corporation with an employee with a hearing impairment must have a telecommunication system such as a relay service in which a caller dials a special number to reach an interpreter who, in turn, contacts the employee. This allows the caller and the employee to communicate through the interpreter.

Take a look around your college or university. Do you see signs of the ADA such as Braille room numbers and wheelchair ramps? The ADA has had, and will continue to have, a major impact on the lives of those with disabilities.

No Child Left Behind Act (PL 107-110)

The 1965 Elementary and Secondary Education Act was reauthorized in 1994 as the Improving America's Education Act, and again in 2002 as the No Child Left Behind (NCLB) Act. One of the main provisions of NCLB is an emphasis on standards and accountability, requiring annual assessments to demonstrate that students are making adequate yearly progress. Data indicated that prior to IDEA 97, students with disabilities were frequently being excluded in these types of assessments (Thurlow & Ysseldyke, 1997). The passage of NCLB made it clear that *all* students should be held accountable for their academic achievement. This meant that students with disabilities could not be excluded from districtwide or statewide assessments. As noted in Table 1.6, however, IDEA 97 allowed appropriate test accommodations, and in some cases, an alternate assessment from the mandated test. These allowances remained in the law in the most current legislation, IDEA 04. In fact, considerable effort was made to align the provisions of IDEA 04 with those of NCLB. At the time of the completition of this text, the NCLB was scheduled to be reauthorized in 2007.

Current Legislation: Individuals with Disabilities Education Act (PL 108-446)

The Individuals with Disabilities Education Act of 2004 (IDEA 04), the latest reauthorization of IDEA, was passed on November 19, 2004, and signed into law by George W. Bush on December 3, 2004. Congress made several statements justifying the rationale for reauthorizing IDEA. They acknowledged that the implementation of PL 94-142 and subsequent legislation resulted in improved services for children with disabilities and their families. But they also noted that efforts have been impeded by low expectations and a lack of focus on applying methods based on replicable research (considered scientifically based instruction).

The two parts of IDEA 04 that have the most relevance for teachers are Part B and Part C. Part B includes guidelines and funding for providing special education for students ages 3–21, although if a state does not provide public education for children without disabilities ages 3–5 and/or 18–21, it is not required to provide services for students with disabilities in those age groups. Part C provides funding and guidelines for early intervention services for infants and toddlers with disabilities or who are at risk for developing a disability from birth through age 2, and their families. IDEA 04 stipulates several requirements and provisions that serve as its backbone. Many of these evolved from the six principles first noted in PL 94-142. Others are the result of litigation and philosophical changes. We will discuss the provisions of IDEA 04 that have the most relevance to you as a future teacher: free appropriate public education, Child Find, individualized education programs, the least restrictive environment, procedural guidelines, evaluation procedures, transition from Part C to preschool programs, and participation in assessments. How these requirements and provisions fit into the overall special education process is discussed in greater depth in Chapter 2.

Provisions and Requirements of IDEA 04

Free Appropriate Public Education (FAPE). Originally mandated in PL 94-142, free appropriate public education means that all children with disabilities between the ages of 3 and 21, including children with disabilities who have been suspended or expelled from school, must receive a free, appropriate, public education. The issue of FAPE was addressed by the Supreme Court in the *Rowley* case (see Table 1.5), specifically asking the question, "Does *appropriate* education mean *optimal* education?" The Court found that it does not. Let's consider this issue with an example. Parents of most students with disabilities could argue that their children would benefit from having their own laptop computer. Does this mean that all those students must be provided with one? The decision is based on the unique needs of each individual student. If a student could participate in the educational program without a computer, even though the educational program might be enhanced by the addition of a computer, the answer is probably no. If, however, a student with a severe writing disability needed the computer to participate in the educational program, then the answer would probably be yes.

In a sense, IDEA 04 requires that the school district "level the playing field" so the student with a disability is not put at a disadvantage and an "appropriate" education is provided. In an interesting analogy, Bateman and Linden (1998) described this situation as: "The IDEA sets a Chevrolet standard, not a Cadillac standard. Be careful, though, not to mistake this for a Yugo standard. An IEP need not provide a superior education, but it must offer real educational benefit" (p. 145). In other words, every attempt must be made to give students everything they require based on their unique educational needs. In fact, many states have laws that require schools to provide programs that exceed the standards set by federal law. IDEA 04 also specifically states that educators must maintain high expectations for students with disabilities, implying that more than minimal educational programs should be provided.

Child Find. This mandate of IDEA 04 requires that all children with disabilities, including those who are homeless, wards of the state, and who attend private schools, be identified and evaluated to determine if they need special education services. This has been accomplished through community awareness efforts advertising that special education programs exist and resulting in many large-scale screening programs. Child Find applies to children who have all levels of disabilities and those who are at risk for having a disability.

The Individualized Education Program (IEP). IDEA 04 states that all children identified with a disability must have an individualized education program (IEP). An IEP is a statement of the student's specific educational program written by a multidisciplinary team that includes, among other things, the student's goals, any related services necessary, and how the student will participate in accountability assessments. An IEP must be developed for all students with a disability beginning at age 3. For infants and toddlers, an individualized family service plan (IFSP) must be developed, reviewed, and revised. An IFSP is also a written statement of the child's educational program, but includes the role of the family as well.

The Least Restrictive Environment (LRE). The least restrictive environment mandate requires that students with disabilities be educated with children without disabilities to the maximum extent appropriate. In other words, students with disabilities should be segregated from their peers without disabilities to the least extent possible. In addition, it states that students should be removed from the general education environment only when the nature or the severity of the disability is such that education in that setting with the use of supplementary aids and services cannot be achieved satisfactorily. This means that the students should be taught in the general education classroom unless their disability is significant enough that they need more intensive instruction that cannot be delivered in that setting (e.g., a student with profound intellectual disabilities who needs to work on independent living skills).

Procedural Guidelines. A considerable number of procedural safeguards are built into IDEA 04 that specify the rights and responsibilities of both the parents of the child with the disability and the local educational agency (LEA). For example, parents have the opportunity to:

- Examine all records relating to their child
- Participate in meetings involving the identification, evaluation, and educational placement of their child
- Obtain an independent educational evaluation if they so choose

A safeguard system, **due process,** provides a mechanism to ensure that decisions regarding the educational program for a student with a disability are fair and just. If there is a disagreement between the parents and the LEA, a due process hearing can be called. This brings in a neutral third party (called a hearing officer) who mediates and determines if procedural errors resulted in (1) the student not receiving FAPE, (2) the parents not being able to participate in decision making regarding their child's FAPE, or (3) deprivation of the student's educational benefits. Because of the costly and time-consuming nature of due process hearings, additional safeguards have been included in IDEA 04 that are designed to avoid due process hearings if possible. These include the option of requesting mediation prior to filing a due process complaint and the addition of a dispute resolution process called a "resolution session." This session must be convened prior to a due process hearing unless both the LEA and the parents agree to waive it. The intent is to develop a written, binding settlement to the dispute in question. See the Classroom Suggestions feature for some "do's" and "don'ts" related to procedural guidelines.

due process A safeguard system to ensure that decisions regarding a student's educational program are fair and just.

Classroom Suggestions Do's and Don'ts Regarding Procedural Guidelines

DO'S: PROCEDURAL SAFEGUARDS

❑ **Do** send parents prior written notice of proposed actions regarding their child. Parents are entitled to notice any time a district proposes or refuses to initiate or changes anything about the child's identification, evaluation, program, or placement. Notice must explain the district's proposed action, inform parents of their rights, and be provided in a form that parents can understand.

❑ **Do** give parents a complete procedural safeguards notice when (1) their child is referred for evaluation, (2) an IEP meeting is scheduled, (3) the child needs reevaluation, and/or (4) a parent requests a due process hearing. Make sure this notice is provided in the parents' native language, and avoid the use of jargon.

❑ **Do** make mediation available in order to resolve disputes between parents and schools in a nonadversarial fashion.

❑ **Do** provide parents with a genuine opportunity to participate in all meetings relating to their child.

❑ **Do** notify parents and student in advance if state law provides for the transfer of parental rights to the student when he or she reaches the age of majority as defined by state law.

DON'TS: PROCEDURAL SAFEGUARDS

❑ **Don't** take any action regarding a child's identification, evaluation, program, or placement without sending written notice to parents in advance.

❑ **Don't** put pressure on parents to use mediation, and don't use mediation to delay or deny the parents' right to a due process hearing or to any other rights.

❑ **Don't** restrict parents' access to their child's education records. Parents have a right to examine all their child's records, including student response forms for all tests.

Source: Bateman, B., & Linden, M. (1998). *Better IEPs: How to develop legally correct and educationally useful programs* (3rd ed.), pp. 20–21. Reprinted with permission, Sopris West, Inc.

Procedural guidelines are in place for parents and school personnel to settle any disputes.

Evaluation Procedures. Several guidelines relating to evaluation are included in IDEA 04. An initial evaluation is required within 60 days, or within a state's established time frame, of receiving parental consent for the evaluation to determine if a child has a disability. The evaluation should also determine the educational needs of the student. The law specifies that a reevaluation must be conducted if the LEA determines that it is necessary or if the parents or teacher requests one. However, a reevaluation *cannot* be conducted more frequently than once a year unless the parent and the LEA agree, and it *must* be conducted at least once every 3 years unless both the parent and the LEA agree that it is not necessary. IDEA 04 also outlines appropriate guidelines that should be followed when assessing students including the following:

- Use of a variety of assessment tools and strategies to determine whether the child has a disability.
- Determine the content of the IEP, including information showing how the student will be involved in the general education curriculum.
- The evaluation cannot be a single measure or assessment. In other words, multiple measures or procedures must be used in determining eligibility and IEP content. Technically sound instruments also must be used.

Nondiscriminatory evaluation procedures first specified in PL 94-142 are embedded in this section of the law as well. These include the requirement that assessments and other evaluation materials (1) are selected and administered so as not to be discriminatory on a racial or cultural basis, (2) are provided and administered in the language and form most likely to yield accurate information on what the child knows and can do academically, developmentally, and functionally, unless it is not feasible to do so, (3) are used for purposes for which the assessments or measures are valid and reliable, (4) are administered by trained and knowledgeable personnel, and (5) are administered in accordance with any instructions provided by the producer of such assessment. Students must also be assessed in all areas of suspected disability.

Transition from Part C to Preschool Programs. IDEA 04 ensures that infants and toddlers from birth through age 2 participating in early intervention programs (covered under Part C) have a smooth and effective transition to preschool programs (covered under Part B). For example, the Part C service coordinator or other professional working with the infant or toddler and family members will also be on the child's initial IEP team when the transition occurs at age 3. This provision is discussed in depth later in this chapter.

Participation in Assessments. Originally mandated in IDEA 97, the participation in assessments provision requires that all children with disabilities be included in all general, state, and districtwide assessments. If possible, students with disabilities should participate in the same required assessment program designed for all students, although accommodations can be provided. Accommodations might include increased time to take the assessment, a different setting, different response type (such as oral vs. written), or revised formats (such as enlarged print). In some instances, it might not be appropriate for a student to participate in the assessment, even with accommodations. For example, if a student's disability is severe enough that the assessment would not provide meaningful information regarding educational progress, the student would not need to participate in the required assessment. In this situation, an alternate assessment must be administered that more appropriately measures the content of the educational program.

Controversial Issues Addressed by IDEA 04

IDEA 04 addressed two controversial areas that have implications both for students with disabilities and the teachers who work with them. The first issue has to do with the procedural guidelines involving the discipline of students with disabilities. The second has to do with the concept of "highly qualified" when considering the credentials of special education teachers.

Discipline of Students with Disabilities. The issue of discipline, initially addressed in IDEA 97, has to do with change of educational placement. Regardless of the behavioral incident requiring discipline, the student must continue to receive educational services that address IEP goals. Several interrelated factors are involved in decisions regarding the change of placement. These are (1) the nature of the incident requiring disciplinary action, (2) the determination of whether the incident was caused by or was related to the student's disability, and (3) the authority and rights of both the parents and the LEA. Let's look at each of these factors separately.

1. *Nature of the Incident.* If the incident requiring discipline involves weapons or drugs, or results in serious bodily injury to others at school, on school premises, or at a school function, the student may automatically be placed in an interim educational placement, not to exceed 45 school days. These incidents involve what is known as **zero tolerance,** meaning that the infraction automatically results in the disciplinary action without considering extenuating circumstances. Zero tolerance policies have received criticism by some when they are used with students with disabilities. Is it fair never to consider the circumstances? What if an elementary student with an intellectual disability brings a knife in his lunch box that his mother accidentally left when she was cutting his apple that morning? The National Association of School Psychologists (2002) noted that "rather than increasing school safety, zero tolerance often leads to indiscriminate suspensions and expulsions for both serious and mild infractions. Studies have shown that minorities and students with disabilities constitute a disproportionately large percentage of expulsions and suspensions. Yet 95% of students in special education suspended and expelled did not exhibit the violent or aggressive behaviors that are the intended targets of zero tolerance policies" (p. 2).

2. *Relationship of Incident to Student's Disability.* If a decision is made to change a student's placement, a **manifestation determination** must be conducted within 10 school days to determine if the incident was caused by, or related to, the student's disability or if the incident was caused by the LEA's failure to implement the IEP. If either of these two criteria is met, the LEA must conduct a **functional behavior assessment (FBA)** and develop a **behavior intervention plan (BIP),** if they have not already been implemented. An FBA involves the determination of the function or purpose that a negative

zero tolerance Disciplinary action taken without considering extenuating circumstances.

manifestation determination Procedures used to determine if a behavior requiring disciplinary action is caused by, or related to, the student's disability.

functional behavior assessment The determination of the function or purpose that a behavior serves.

behavior intervention plan An educational program that emphasizes the development of positive behaviors that will serve the same purpose as a negative behavior.

If a behavioral incident is related to a student's disability, a functional behavior assessment must be conducted and a behavior intervention plan must be developed.

behavior serves and leads to the development of a BIP, which emphasizes the development of positive behaviors that will serve the same purpose as the negative behavior. The LEA must also modify the BIP if one has already been developed and return the student to the original placement (unless the LEA and parents agree otherwise). A manifestation determination is not necessary if the incident in question meets the criteria of the zero tolerance policy described in item 1.

3. *Authority of the LEA.* The LEA is given considerable latitude under IDEA 04. For example, the LEA can consider unique circumstances on a case-by-case basis when making a decision about changing a student's placement. The LEA also has the authority to change placement on an interim basis for no more than 10 school days. Finally, if the incident is found *not* to be related to the student's disability, the LEA can use the same disciplinary procedures used with students without disabilities (although FAPE must still be provided).

Highly Qualified Teachers. The second controversial issue in IDEA 04 has to do with the criteria of highly qualified teachers, a requirement that all teachers must meet per the legislation. This requirement was first outlined in the No Child Left Behind Act for general education teachers, although IDEA 04 identified the criteria for highly qualified special education teachers. There are three requirements for public elementary or secondary special education teachers to be considered highly qualified under IDEA 04:

1. Full state certification as a special education teacher (including certification through alternative routes) or have passed the state special education teacher licensing examination. Teachers in charter schools must meet the requirements of the state's public charter school law.
2. The special education certification or licensure requirements have not been waived on an emergency, temporary, or provisional basis.
3. At least a bachelor's degree.

Requirements for special education teachers working with students meeting alternate achievement standards, as well as for those teaching multiple subjects, are also specified.

Professionals in the special education field have vehemently opposed these criteria for "highly qualified." Specifically, there is concern that highly qualified defined by the law actually means less qualified. In other words, someone who has never taken a special education course or interacted with a student with a disability could become a "highly qualified" special education teacher by passing the state's licensing exam. This is analogous to allowing an individual to practice medicine who has passed the Medical Board exam but has never taken a medical course or seen a patient.

Check Your Understanding

1. What are three early court cases that had an impact on the field of special education?
2. What are the six principles of PL 94-142 that are still relevant in IDEA 04?
3. What court cases focused on the interpretation of PL 94-142? Which principles did they address?
4. What are the requirements of the Americans with Disabilities Act?
5. Describe the eight provisions of IDEA 04 that are most relevant to teachers.
6. What are two controversial issues addressed by IDEA 04?

What Are Some Current and Future Issues in Special Education?

Philosophical movements, historical events, and the impact of litigation and legislation have all resulted in issues in special education that are important today and will undoubtedly remain so in the future. Three of these issues in particular are the overrepresentation of students from culturally and linguistically diverse (CLD) backgrounds, the emphasis on education and transition of infants and toddlers with disabilities, and the important role of the general education teacher.

Overrepresentation of Students from Culturally or Linguistically Diverse Backgrounds

One of the significant concerns of professionals in the special education field is the overrepresentation of students from culturally or linguistically diverse backgrounds in certain categories of disabilities, particularly mental retardation and emotional disturbance. **Culturally diverse students** are those who come from backgrounds that are not primarily Western European. This population of students is rapidly growing. Based on several sources, Sadker, Sadker, and Zittleman (2008) reported these statistics:

- By 2012 the western United States will become a "minority majority," with no single ethnic or racial group having a majority.
- About 6 million Americans claim multiracial heritage with two or more races indicated on Census 2000.
- By 2030 the number of U.S. residents who are nonwhite or Hispanic will be about 140 million or about 40% of the U.S. population.

Linguistically diverse students are those whose primary language is not English. They are sometimes referred to as English language learners (ELLs) or as having limited English proficiency (LEP). IDEA 04 stated that the LEP population is the most rapidly growing population in our nation (IDEA, 2004). Estimates are that 15 to 20% of the school population speaks a language other than English in the home (Avoke' & Wood-Garnett, 2001). In some states, such as Florida, Texas, and California, students from non-European or non-English-speaking backgrounds already comprise more than 50% of the school population.

In IDEA 04, Congress acknowledged the significance, yet difficulty, of addressing the educational needs of students from culturally and linguistically diverse backgrounds, citing the following information:

- In 2000, 1 of every 3 persons in the United States was a member of a minority group or had limited English proficiency.
- Studies have documented apparent discrepancies in the level of referral and placement of limited English proficient children in special education.
- More minority children continue to be served in special education than would be expected from the percentage of minority students in the general school population.
- In the 1998-99 school year, African American children represented just 14.8% of the population aged 6 through 21 but comprised 20.2% of all children with disabilities.
- African American children are identified as having mental retardation and emotional disturbance at rates higher than their white counterparts.

As evidence of this final point, the Council for Exceptional Children (2002) reported that African American students are almost three times more likely to be identified as having mental retardation than their white counterparts. Similarly, they are almost twice as likely to be identified as having an emotional disturbance. The issue is complicated further when one considers that many students from culturally or linguistically diverse backgrounds come from low socioeconomic backgrounds. Poverty is considered a hidden demographic variable associated with academic achievement (Parrish, 2004).

In response to the data that indicate the overrepresentation of students from CLD backgrounds in certain categories of special education, IDEA 04 acknowledged that greater efforts are needed to prevent the intensification of problems connected with mislabeling and high dropout rates among minority children with disabilities. It also encouraged recruitment efforts for increasing the number of teachers from minority backgrounds to act as appropriate role models, provided funding for training personnel in effective teaching strategies and positive behavior interventions, and provided supports to prevent overidentification and misidentification of students. In the chapters in Parts 2 through 4,

culturally diverse students
Those students who come from backgrounds that are not primarily Western European.

linguistically diverse students
Those students whose primary language is not English. Sometimes referred to as English language learners or as having limited English proficiency.

 **Relevant CEC Standards**
▶ Issues in definition and identification of individuals with exceptional learning needs, including those from culturally and linguistically diverse backgrounds (CC1K5)
▶ Use and limitations of assessment instruments (CC8K4)

overidentification, or underidentification in the case of gifts and talents, of CLD students is discussed when it occurs. Additionally, specific concerns or conditions related to identification, instruction, and working with families of CLD students are addressed.

Education and Transition of Infants and Toddlers

Part C of IDEA 04 focuses on the education and transition of infants and toddlers, including the role of the family in their child's educational program. Recent available data indicated that the number of infants and toddlers with disabilities served under Part C increased almost 70% from 1992 to 2004 (U.S. DOE, 2005). Responding to this increase, IDEA 04 made several recommendations and suggestions for improving Part C.

Part C requires that the state provide a "statewide, comprehensive, coordinated, multidisciplinary, interagency" system that provides early intervention services for infants and toddlers with disabilities and their families. Among the services required by the state are (1) a rigorous definition of "developmental delay," (2) a comprehensive, multidisciplinary evaluation of the infant or toddler and an identification of the needs of the family, and (3) an individualized family service plan (IFSP) that also identifies the service coordinator who will be primarily responsible for the delivery of the IFSP. The service coordinator is a professional from the discipline most immediately relevant to the content of the IFSP.

Several mandates are included in Part C that affect children from birth to age 5. Many of these have to do with ensuring that there is a smooth transition for infants and toddlers served under Part C into Part B (beginning at age 3). Two points regarding transition are worth noting. First, the IFSP must indicate the steps to be taken to support the transition of the toddler to preschool or other appropriate services. Second, if the toddler is transitioned to a Part B program, the service coordinator or other representative from the Part C program is invited to the initial IEP meeting to assist with the transition from the IFSP to an IEP.

Another option may be available for parents when their child reaches age 3. IDEA 04 includes a new, optional state program. This program, if developed by a state, allows the toddler to continue to receive Part C services until he or she enters kindergarten. The program must include an educational component that promotes school readiness and that incorporates preliteracy, language, and number skills. Parents would be given the option to receive these services or to transition to Part B. Although this seems like a nice option, there are some concerns regarding its implementation because no additional funding was appropriated for this program.

An important addition to the IDEA 04 Part C requirements is that states that are applying for funding must include a description of the policies and procedures in place to ensure compliance with the Child Abuse Prevention and Treatment Act (CAPTA). Specifically, the state must show that a child under 3 will be referred for early intervention if (1) he or she is involved in a substantiated case of child abuse or neglect or (2) is affected by illegal substance abuse or has withdrawal symptoms from prenatal drug exposure.

Chapter 13 includes in-depth information on infants and toddlers including those who have disabilities or are at risk for developing a disability. Each chapter in Parts 2–4 includes discussion of early childhood considerations, particularly for children ages 3–5. Due to the importance of early intervention for many disabilities, it is important that special education teachers have strong knowledge of this area. Although most general classroom teachers will not be involved in early intervention, understanding its components and how to best transition

It is important to ensure that toddlers have a smooth transition from Part C services to Part B services.

children from early intervention programs into elementary school classrooms is important. In addition to including the preceding information on the transition from early childhood to elementary programs, this text also provides integrated coverage of transition from high school into higher education, employment, or simply adulthood.

Role of the General Education Teacher

An important issue in special education today is the increasingly important role of the general education teacher. When PL 94-142 was passed, stating that education for students with disabilities should occur in the least restrictive environment, the general education teacher became, in a way, an unsuspecting, and in some cases unwilling, participant in special education. For the most part, general education teachers were given neither appropriate training nor support that would help them in their new role of being a part of the special education process. Even knowing what their exact role should be was unclear. Misunderstandings of the term *LRE* worsened the situation. In a certain sense, however, general education teachers' fears of what might happen were worse than the eventual reality. For whatever reasons, the years following passage of the law created some dissonance between general and special educators. Many general education teachers resented being asked to teach students they were not trained to teach. Many special education teachers thought movements such as the Regular Education Initiative (discussed in Chapter 2) were an attempt to eliminate their jobs. Today, both sides have moved toward the realization that each has a very important role in the process of educating exceptional students. It is imperative that general education teachers are prepared to teach exceptional students in their classrooms, both through creating a positive and supportive classroom and through collaboration.

Creating a Positive and Supportive Classroom

In a positive and supportive classroom, an ideal classroom for students with all types of disabilities, individual differences are accepted and valued. In addition, there is ongoing assessment and evaluation of each student's progress to improve the match of students' needs and desires with the curriculum. More than two decades ago, Adelman and Taylor (1983) described what they called the "personalized classroom," which is more relevant now than it was then with the increase of students with disabilities being taught in the general education classroom. Such an environment includes these essential features:

- Teachers guide students to value and accept personal responsibility for their own learning.
- Teachers promote both independent and cooperative functioning as well as problem solving among all students.
- Learner differences and needs regarding all facets of the environment and programming are accepted and valued.
- A wide variety of options are offered to motivate each child and provide developmental matches. Many opportunities for success are provided.
- A continuum of structure is available, including independent and small group work. Grouping is flexible. Routines are clear and predictable.
- Teachers communicate respect and trust to their students, particularly when enforcing rules. Rules are well defined and clearly reflect classroom expectations.
- Informal and formal conferences are held with students to focus on their strengths as well as their needs. Specific praise and feedback are ongoing.
- Direct instruction is used, and cognitive and metacognitive strategies are taught as an integral part of the curriculum.

For these recommendations to be effectively implemented, it is absolutely imperative for general education and special education teachers to work and plan together, providing support for each other and their students.

collaborative consultation The mutual responsibility of general and special education teachers in planning an educational program.

cooperative teaching Special and general education teachers sharing in classroom planning and teaching.

Collaboration

The need for general education teachers and special education teachers to work collaboratively cannot be minimized. Careful planning and implementation of educational programs that are coordinated by all teachers are an absolute prerequisite for success. Two approaches receiving considerable attention in recent years are collaborative consultation and cooperative teaching. **Collaborative consultation** is the mutual responsibility by both general and special education teachers in the planning of the educational program for students with disabilities. This is a shared responsibility, with teachers in each discipline acting as equal partners. **Cooperative teaching** takes the relationship one step further as special and general education teachers share classroom teaching and planning. Colleges and universities need to offer the necessary additional training of these and other approaches, and school districts need to provide the appropriate resources and administrative flexibility to support these models.

At the core of this text is the concept that both general and special education teachers need to be thoroughly prepared to teach and support exceptional students. To do this as effectively as possible, they must work together. The foundational and instructional coverage in each chapter in Parts 2 through 4 is written for both the general and the special education teacher. Collaboration between these teachers and specialists is then integrated within the chapters as relevant. As a final piece, each of these chapters concludes with a section on the general education classroom that introduces future general education teachers to specific considerations and future special education teachers to specific challenges that their partners may face.

In summary, the field of special education has been, and continues to be, affected by a number of factors, including philosophical, historical, and legal factors. As a future educator, it is important to acknowledge these factors and continue to monitor changes that will affect your role in the classroom.

Check Your Understanding

1. Who are culturally and linguistically diverse students? What are the existing and projected demographics for these groups in the United States?

2. What recommendations or provisions does IDEA 04 include to address the problem of overrepresentation of culturally and linguistically diverse students in special education?

3. What provisions does Part C of IDEA 04 make for serving infants and toddlers? What steps are taken to help transition toddlers from Part C to Part B?

4. What initial concerns did general education teachers have after the passage of PL 94-142?

5. What are some characteristics of a positive and supportive classroom?

6. What is collaborative consultation? Cooperative teaching?

Chapter Summary

Go to the text's Online Learning Center at **www.mhhe.com/taylor1e** to access study resources, Web links, practice quizzes, and extending materials.

Who Are Exceptional Students?

- An exceptional student is one whose educational needs are not being met by a traditional program so that a special education program is necessary.
- An exceptional student can have a disability or have significant gifts and talents.
- The terms *handicap*, *impairment*, and *disability* are not synonymous.

How Many Exceptional Students Are There?

- Prevalence refers to the number of individuals who are in a particular category at a specific point in time and is expressed as a percentage. Incidence refers to the number of individuals identified in a particular category within a specific time frame (generally a year).
- The prevalence rate for exceptional students is approximately 15% or about 8 million students from kindergarten through grade 12.

- Over 90% of students identified under IDEA fall into the categories of learning disabilities (45.2%), speech or language impairments (19.9%), other health impairments (9.4%), mental retardation (8.1%), and emotional disturbance (7.8%).

What Are Special Education and Related Services?

- Special education refers to instruction specifically designed to meet the needs of exceptional students.
- Special education involves four components: instructional content, instructional procedures, the instructional environment, and instructional technology.
- Each component should emphasize the concept of universal design.
- Related services are those activities or services that enable a child with a disability to receive a free, appropriate public education and to benefit from the special education program.

What Is the History of Special Education?

- Documentation of the existence of exceptional individuals has been provided since the beginning of recorded history.
- Attempts to provide humane treatment were not made until the 18th and 19th centuries, primarily by European physicians such as Jean Marc Itard.
- In the mid-1800s, attempts to educate individuals with visual impairments, hearing impairments, and mental retardation began in the United States.

- In the 1900s, parent advocates, professionals, and eventually litigation and legislation furthered the cause of individuals with disabilities.

How Has Litigation and Legislation Affected Special Education?

- Important early court cases related to special education include *PARC v. Pennsylvania* and *Mills v. Board of Education of District of Columbia*.
- Important legislation includes PL 94-142 and its various amendments and reauthorizations.
- The Americans with Disabilities Act and the No Child Left Behind Act have had an impact on individuals with disabilities.
- The special education law that guides current practice is the Individuals with Disabilities Education Act of 2004 (IDEA 04).
- Key provisions of IDEA 04 are free, appropriate public education, Child Find, individualized education programs, the least restrictive environment, procedural guidelines, evaluation procedures, transition from Part C to preschool programs, and participation in assessments.

What Are Some Current and Future Issues in Special Education?

- Issues in special education include the overidentification of students from culturally and linguistically diverse backgrounds, the emphasis on the education and transition of infants and toddlers with disabilities, and the important role of general education teachers.

Reflection Topics

1. Why is it important to make a distinction between a disability and a handicap?
2. Gifted and talented students are not served under IDEA 04, even though they are considered exceptional students in need of special education. What do you think the pros and cons would be of including them under the law?
3. Do you think incidence figures or prevalence figures are most useful for reporting and planning purposes? Why?

4. Why do you think there were such negative attitudes toward individuals with disabilities at the beginning of the 20th century?
5. If you were a parent of a child with a disability, how much would you want to be involved in developing your child's education program?
6. If you were a parent of a toddler with a disability, would you want to transition your child to Part B at age 3 or wait until he or she was age 6? What do you think are the pros and cons of each decision?

Application Activities: For Learning and Your Portfolio

1. Interview someone with a disability. Ask, specifically, about the importance of distinguishing between a disability and a handicap, as well as the importance of using "person-first" terminology.
2. (*Portfolio Possibility*) Determine what accommodations your university provides to comply with the Americans with Disabilities Act. Make a list by disability area (e.g., ramps for physical disabilities, Braille room numbers for visual impairments).
3. Research Itard's work with Victor. What teaching procedures did he use? How effective were they?

4. Trace the impact of PL 94-142 on later legislation and how it currently affects special education services.
5. (*Portfolio Possibility*) Write a one-page paper that addresses the pros and cons of using a zero tolerance policy for students with disabilities.
6. (*Portfolio Possibility*) Visit an inclusion classroom. Interview both the general education teacher and special education teacher and make a list of (1) their roles and responsibilities performed individually and (2) their roles and responsibilities performed collaboratively.

CHAPTER 2

The Special Education Process

From Initial Identification to the Delivery of Services

INTRODUCING SAMMY

Sammy is a 7-year-old boy who just started second grade in a new school. His teacher, Ms. Gonzalez, noticed that Sammy is struggling academically, particularly in the areas of reading and language arts. He is having difficulty with his phonics skills, and both his handwriting and spelling are below the level expected for his age. He is considerably slower completing assignments than his peers and often has to work individually because he can't keep up. He has to go at his own pace, even when Ms. Gonzalez works with him in a small group.

Sammy is absent from school quite often and misses valuable instructional time, which affects his academic progress. In addition, Sammy is starting to display some behavior problems. He is occasionally overly aggressive with his peers, pushing and shoving his classmates and calling them names. Ms. Gonzalez describes Sammy's behavior as "explosive" and "unpredictable." Attempts by Ms. Gonzalez to have a parent conference have been unsuccessful because Sammy's parents have not responded to her messages. She requested to see the records and files from his previous school. Although the records were incomplete, they did indicate that Sammy had some of the same problems the previous year in first grade. His attendance was very sporadic, and he barely passed his academic subjects to allow promotion to second grade. Ms. Gonzalez now wonders whether Sammy should be referred for special education.

Take a moment to think about Sammy. Throughout this chapter, we'll ask you questions as you consider Sammy's situation in relation to the special education process. Similar cases and revisit questions are included in all subsequent chapters. ■

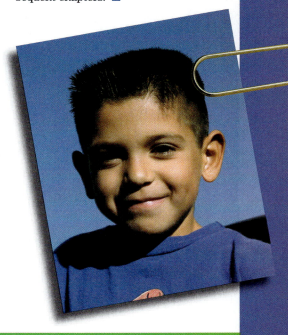

Ms. Gonzalez is obviously concerned about Sammy's lack of progress in her classroom. Sammy persistently struggles in academic areas such as reading and language arts, and displays behavior problems, such as aggression, that warrant attention. Based on her observations, Ms. Gonzalez thinks it is possible that Sammy has some type of disability that would require special education. In their careers, general education teachers will see a variety of indicators that may make them suspect that special education is needed for some of their students. Exceptional students are those whose educational needs are not being met in general education so that some type of "special" education program is necessary. In this chapter, we discuss the steps that ultimately result in the determination of which students receive special education. We also discuss the process of developing special education programs once students are identified. The steps in the special education process are initial identification, the prereferral process, the referral process, determination of eligibility for special education, and development of the student's special education program.

Although parents or physicians usually identify children with severe disabilities prior to their reaching school age, children with mild disabilities are often not identified until they are in the general education classroom. The general education teacher often makes the initial identification of a potential problem and is responsible for instituting a prereferral intervention program to provide immediate assistance and to determine whether the problem can be successfully addressed in the general education classroom, thereby avoiding a referral to special education. If a referral is needed, it is usually the general education teacher who initiates it. If the student is evaluated and meets the criteria for a given disability category, the general education teacher works closely with the special education teacher and others to plan for the student's educational program to assure that he or she is participating to the maximum extent appropriate in the general education curriculum.

The special education teacher may assist the general education teacher in developing a prereferral intervention program and definitely will become involved when the student is referred for evaluation for special education. If the student is identified as having a disability, the special education teacher will play an important role in developing the student's individualized education program (IEP) and ultimately delivering instruction.

This special education process is used for the majority of individuals who fall into an IDEA 04 disability category (those described in Parts 2 and 3 of this text). For the other exceptionalities discussed in this text (those in Part 4), similar processes unique to these exceptionalities are used.

How Are Exceptional Students Initially Identified?

Relevant CEC Standard

▶ Screening, pre-referral, referral, and classification procedures (CC8K3)

The first step in the special education process is to identify an individual as having a potential exceptionality. A number of individuals, including physicians, parents, and teachers, could be involved in this identification process. A variety of methods, from informal observation to formal screening tests, are used to identify a child who may need special education.

Initial Identification of Infants, Toddlers, and Preschool Children

Most individuals with severe intellectual disabilities or physical or sensory impairments are initially identified as needing a special education program early in life by their parents or physicians. In fact, this realization might even occur before the birth of the child based on prenatal testing. All infants, toddlers, and preschool children who have a disability or are at risk for developing a disability are entitled to special education services. Thus teachers of young children should identify those with mild problems or who are at risk for developing problems. This early identification of all children with disabilities is consistent with the Child Find provision of IDEA 04. Some parents might begin to notice that their preschool child's developmental skills, such as speech or language skills, seem to be lagging behind those of other children of the same age. In fact, for those preschool children ages 3–5, the most prevalent category of disability is speech or language impairments. In

Speech or language impairments are the most prevalent disability among preschool children.

2005, approximately 47% of all children in this age range receiving services under IDEA were receiving speech or language services (U.S. DOE, 2006).

Many school districts have large screening programs to determine whether further evaluation is needed. One screening test used in such programs is the Developmental Indicators for the Assessment of Learning–3 (DIAL–3; Mardell-Czudnowski & Goldenberg, 1998). The DIAL–3 consists of items measuring the areas of language, concepts, motor skills, self-help development, and social development. Cutoff scores determine whether additional evaluation is needed. If a potential problem is identified through the screening tests, the child is referred for further evaluation. Similarly, the DIAL–3 could be used to identify young children who might be gifted.

Initial Identification of School-Aged Students

Most children with mild disabilities are not identified as having a potential disability until they start school and begin to fall behind their classmates academically in areas such as reading or math, or demonstrate behavior problems such as withdrawal, aggression, or lack of compliance. The general education teacher frequently makes the determination that a significant difference is evident based on classroom performance. Another means of identifying potential problems is through the results of routine districtwide or statewide testing administered for accountability purposes and for monitoring student academic performance. A recent approach has been the use of the response to intervention (RTI) model, in which the entire class (or school) is screened to see who is at risk of having a disability and needs additional help.

Once a teacher, parent, or physician identifies a student as potentially having a disability, the decision about whether or not to refer the student for special education services must be made. The decision to refer a student for evaluation, however, should not be made lightly because the referral itself is a good predictor of special education placement. One way to clarify referral decision making is to initiate *prereferral assessment* and *prereferral intervention procedures* before making an official referral. Also, if the RTI model is used, those students identified as at risk will receive several levels of more intensive support. If a student doesn't respond to these interventions, it usually results in a referral.

SAMMY REVISITED What types of information did Ms. Gonzalez use to initially identify Sammy as a student who was having difficulty and might need to be referred for special education services?

What Are the Prereferral Process and the Referral Process?

♣ **Relevant CEC Standard**

▶ Screening, pre-referral, referral, and classification procedures (CC8K3)

When a student is initially identified as potentially having a need for special education, a decision must be made concerning whether or not to refer him for evaluation and consideration for special education services. If the student has a severe problem, the referral is usually made immediately. If the problem is mild in nature, the student often will go through the prereferral process. Based on information obtained in the prereferral process, a decision is made whether or not a referral for special education is necessary. As mentioned, a related decision-making model is the response to intervention (RTI) approach, which is suggested by IDEA 04 for the identification of learning disabilities.

The Prereferral Process

The prereferral process is undertaken when a disability is suspected but is not severe enough to warrant a referral without further investigation. Use of the prereferral process is considered best practice although it is not a legal requirement of IDEA 04. Nonetheless, almost 75% of the states either require or recommend it (Buck, Polloway, Smith-Thomas, & Cook, 2003).

prereferral assessment
Gathering information, usually informally, before a referral is made.

prereferral intervention
A program, designed from the prereferral assessment information, that is implemented before a formal referral is made.

The prereferral process includes both prereferral assessment and prereferral intervention. **Prereferral assessment** involves gathering information, usually informally, to help develop a **prereferral intervention** program, instructional changes designed to address a student's learning and/or behavior problems. The goals of using these procedures are to provide immediate help to the student and to determine whether changes in the student's current educational program will successfully address the student's problem and thus avoid the need for a referral for special education services. In other words, instead of teachers immediately referring students who begin to demonstrate problems in school, they make a systematic change to the educational program (prereferral intervention) based on information obtained about the students (prereferral assessment). Although the prereferral intervention program is sometimes developed by the general education teacher, it frequently is developed by a school-based team that might include the general education teacher, a special education teacher, and related service personnel (depending on the nature of the student's problem). Table 2.1 lists some examples of commercial products that can assist in the prereferral process. Figure 2.1 shows a model of the prereferral intervention process.

TABLE 2.1	Commercial Products to Assist in the Prereferral Process
NAME OF PRODUCT	**DESCRIPTION**
Academic Competence Evaluation Scales (DiPerna & Elliott, 2000)	Allows teachers to summarize their observations of areas such as academic and study skills
Academic Intervention Monitoring System (Elliott, DiPerna, & Shapiro, 2000)	Helps teachers develop interventions and identify and evaluate goals
Prereferral Intervention Manual and Prereferral Intervention Checklist (McCarney, 1993)	Provides intervention strategies and activities for common academic and behavior problems; also available as software

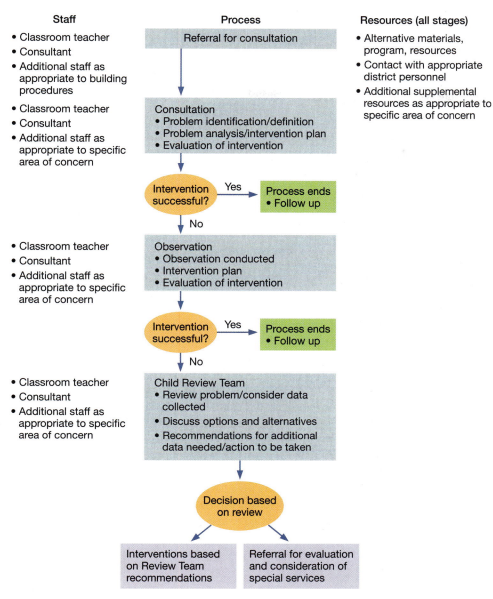

Staff

- Classroom teacher
- Consultant
- Additional staff as appropriate to building procedures

- Classroom teacher
- Consultant
- Additional staff as appropriate to specific area of concern

- Classroom teacher
- Consultant
- Additional staff as appropriate to specific area of concern

- Classroom teacher
- Consultant
- Additional staff as appropriate to specific area of concern

Process

Referral for consultation

Consultation
- Problem identification/definition
- Problem analysis/intervention plan
- Evaluation of intervention

Intervention successful? — Yes → Process ends • Follow up

No

Observation
- Observation conducted
- Intervention plan
- Evaluation of intervention

Intervention successful? — Yes → Process ends • Follow up

No

Child Review Team
- Review problem/consider data collected
- Discuss options and alternatives
- Recommendations for additional data needed/action to be taken

Decision based on review

Interventions based on Review Team recommendations

Referral for evaluation and consideration of special services

Resources (all stages)

- Alternative materials, program, resources
- Contact with appropriate district personnel
- Additional supplemental resources as appropriate to specific area of concern

FIGURE 2.1 Model of a Prereferral Intervention

Source: Graden, J., Casey, A., & Christenson, S. (1985). Implementing a prereferral intervention system: Part. 1. The model. *Exceptional Children, 51,* p. 380. Copyright © 2005 by The Council for Exceptional Children. Reprinted with permission.

To illustrate the prereferral process, we offer the following example involving Ms. Jones, a third-grade teacher. Ms. Jones has 30 students in her class and, therefore, has to rely heavily on large group instruction. She is concerned about the academic progress of three of her students, Latisha, Patricia, and Connor. Their scores on math tests have been consistently low during the first grading period. Additionally, she has observed that all three are beginning to have behavior problems, primarily during math time, and is concerned that these students will interrupt the entire class. Her first impulse was to refer them for special education, particularly since their math performance was getting progressively worse and their behavior was starting to disrupt the rest of the class. Her thinking was that they might be better served by receiving individual assistance in math from a special education teacher. However, her school district has a policy based on the state's recommendation that requires prereferral intervention for students suspected of having a mild disability before a referral is made. Therefore, the first thing Ms. Jones did was to observe the three students during math time and to analyze their performance on in-class math tests and math worksheets. Here is a summary of the specific steps Ms. Jones took and what she discovered.

Latisha was having problems in math computation. Ms. Jones collected the following examples from her most recent math worksheet.

$$
\begin{array}{ccccc}
74 & 53 & 92 & 81 & 68 \\
+\ 68 & +\ 24 & +\ 49 & +\ 63 & +\ 27 \\
\hline
1312 & 77 & 1311 & 144 & 815 \\
\end{array}
$$

After a careful analysis of Latisha's answers, Ms. Jones noted a specific error pattern. Although Latisha was correctly adding the various number combinations, she was adding the ones and tens columns independently and apparently did not understand the concept of renaming (carrying). Ms. Jones began a prereferral intervention program designed to teach her the renaming concept. After specific instruction on this skill, Latisha "caught on," and both math performance and behavior, apparently caused by frustration, improved. No referral was necessary, and Latisha remained in the general education classroom with Ms. Jones.

Patricia was having more significant problems than Latisha. In addition to computation deficits, Patricia was struggling with math concepts. For example, she often did not know whether to add or subtract when she was given a practical problem to solve. Ms. Jones noticed that, unlike Latisha, Patricia had no pattern in her computation errors; it seemed everything was just a guess. Patricia's behavior problems continued, and she became more and more distractible, frequently leaving her seat. Ms. Jones observed that she could not, or would not, stay seated for more than 2 or 3 minutes at a time. Based on this information, Ms. Jones implemented both an alternative instructional strategy for the math skills and a behavioral program using positive reinforcement for staying in her seat. After 6 weeks, Patricia's math skills and behavior had not changed appreciably. Ms. Jones documented her intervention attempts and referred Patricia for further evaluation for consideration to receive special education services.

Ms. Jones observed that Connor was distracted by Patricia, staying off task by talking to her and passing her notes. He frequently would wait until the last minute to complete his math work. When he was tested individually without distractions, Connor actually performed quite well on his math tasks. He apparently knew the math information but was not paying enough attention for the work to be completed adequately. Ms. Jones tried an alternate seating arrangement and the problem was solved. No referral was necessary, and Connor stayed in the general education classroom.

Prereferral assessment and prereferral intervention are used to try to avoid a referral for special education.

The prereferral process plays a significant role in the overall special education process as evidenced by the important decisions that were made in these examples. Because of Ms. Jones's prereferral intervention program, only one of the three students was ultimately referred even though she initially suspected that all three might need special education services. The prereferral interventions used with Latisha and Connor resolved the problems they were having. The interventions used with Patricia confirmed for Ms. Jones that further assessment was needed. It is important that teachers organize and monitor the steps of the prereferral process.

Ms. Jones used observation and error analysis to gather information to help her develop prereferral intervention programs for her three students. General education teachers routinely use these and other informal techniques, such as criterion-referenced testing and curriculum-based assessment, to help determine whether students need extra educational support. In addition to their use in assisting in the development of a prereferral intervention program, these informal techniques provide valuable information to document the need for a referral for special education services if one is necessary. Special education teachers also can use these valuable approaches to make instructional decisions for students if they are found eligible for those services.

Observation

Observation, although seldom used systematically, is perhaps the most widely used form of assessment. Put another way, teachers are always observing their students but often do not systematically collect observational data on which to base important decisions. Ms. Jones used observation to help her make important decisions, but she could have used a more systematic observational model for Patricia's out-of-seat and Connor's off-task distractible behavior. For example, a four-step model of carefully identifying a target behavior, recording the target behavior, making an instructional change, and continuing to record the target behavior would result in an objective evaluation of the effectiveness of the prereferral intervention program. Taylor (2009) provided a thorough discussion of observational assessment, including this four-step observational model.

To implement the four-step model with Conner, Ms. Jones could have carefully defined the target behavior (on-task behavior) as keeping his eyes on his math worksheet. Note that Ms. Jones would target the increase of a *positive* behavior rather than the decrease of a *negative* one (off-task behavior). Next, for several days, she would record the number of minutes out of a 10-minute period that Conner was on task. Ms. Jones would collect these **baseline data** prior to a change in the instructional/behavioral program. Once Ms. Jones instituted the change of seating for Connor, she would continue to collect data on his on-task behavior. Figure 2.2 visually depicts how the effect of the intervention might be evaluated.

baseline data Data collected prior to a change in an intervention program.

In this example the *duration* of the behavior was recorded. Other types of recording procedures might be more appropriate with other types of behavior or the conditions under which they are exhibited. For instance, there may be times when the *frequency* of a behavior, such as the number of words read correctly in a 5-minute period, would be more appropriate.

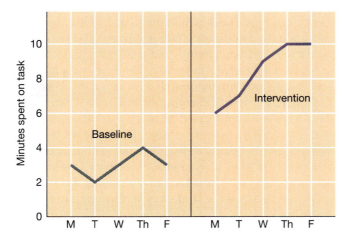

FIGURE 2.2 Effects of an Intervention on a Target Behavior

Source: Taylor, R. (2006). *Assessment of exceptional students: Educational and psychological procedures* (7th ed.). Boston: Allyn & Bacon. (Fig. 4.4) Copyright © 2006 by Pearson Education. Reprinted by permission of the publisher.

Criterion-Referenced Testing

Criterion-referenced tests (CRTs) are helpful in determining what specific skills to teach a student. CRTs can be developed by the teacher, although there are commercially published CRTs as well. Unlike **norm-referenced tests,** such as standardized achievement tests, which provide an indication of *how much* a student knows in comparison to others, a CRT focuses on the student's *mastery of content,* what the student does and does not know. Assume that Ms. Jones developed a CRT for Latisha to determine her instructional objectives in math computation. She could have implemented the following steps (Gronlund, 2006; Taylor, 2009):

1. *Identify the skill area to be measured.* For Latisha, Ms. Jones chose "Addition of two-digit numbers with carrying."
2. *Perform a* **task analysis** *or the identification of a sequential list of objectives within that skill area.* For example, a list of objectives could include the addition of one-digit numbers, addition of two-digit numbers without carrying, and addition of two-digit numbers with carrying.
3. *Develop test items that measure each objective.*

   a.
   $$8 \quad 4 \quad 5 \quad 7 \quad 6$$
   $$+4 \quad +9 \quad +6 \quad +5 \quad +3$$

   b.
   $$33 \quad 42 \quad 68 \quad 84 \quad 71$$
   $$+56 \quad +34 \quad +21 \quad +13 \quad +27$$

   c.
   $$48 \quad 66 \quad 89 \quad 27 \quad 75$$
   $$+37 \quad +65 \quad +19 \quad +58 \quad +25$$

4. *Determine standard of performance (criteria).* This indicates the percentage of items (e.g., 80%) that Latisha must pass to assume that she has "mastered" each objective.
5. *Administer and interpret the test.* Assume the following answers were given:

   a.
   $$8 \quad 4 \quad 5 \quad 7 \quad 6$$
   $$+4 \quad +9 \quad +6 \quad +5 \quad +3$$
   $$\overline{12} \quad \overline{13} \quad \overline{11} \quad \overline{12} \quad \overline{9}$$

   b.
   $$33 \quad 42 \quad 68 \quad 84 \quad 71$$
   $$+56 \quad +34 \quad +21 \quad +13 \quad +27$$
   $$\overline{89} \quad \overline{76} \quad \overline{89} \quad \overline{96} \quad \overline{98}$$

   c.
   $$48 \quad 66 \quad 89 \quad 27 \quad 75$$
   $$+37 \quad +65 \quad +19 \quad +58 \quad +25$$
   $$\overline{715} \quad \overline{1211} \quad \overline{918} \quad \overline{715} \quad \overline{910}$$

Using this procedure, Ms. Jones would find that Latisha could successfully perform one-digit plus one-digit addition (100% accuracy) and two-digit plus two-digit addition without carrying (80% accuracy), but that she could not successfully complete two-digit plus two-digit addition that required carrying (0% accuracy). These data indicate that Latisha might need practice on two-digit addition without carrying but that two-digit addition with carrying should be the instructional objective.

Although the previous example used an academic skill as the basis of the CRT, nonacademic skills can also be used. For example, if independent dressing is a goal for a student with a severe intellectual disability, the skill of putting on a shirt could be task analyzed to develop a list of sequential objectives. Observation then could be used to evaluate the student's performance in addressing each objective. Once you determine where in the sequence the student is performing, subsequent instructional objectives are identified.

Curriculum-based Assessment

In the past two decades, the concept of **curriculum-based assessment** (CBA) has received considerable attention. CBA is the measurement of a student's achievement level in terms of the *expected curricular outcomes of the school* (Tucker, 1985). In

other words, the teacher evaluates skill acquisition and very closely monitors a student's progress based on the curriculum being used. This approach has taken on added significance with the IDEA 04 requirement that students with disabilities participate in the general education curriculum to the maximum extent possible.

CBA can involve a number of different types of procedures, some that are informal and some that are more formal and standardized. The more informal type of CBA is similar to criterion-referenced testing and is sometimes referred to as **criterion-referenced curriculum-based assessment** (CR-CBA). CR-CBA involves the previously described steps of criterion-referenced testing with the content of the test based on the student's curriculum. For example, instead of Ms. Jones identifying the specific skill to task analyze, as she did in criterion-referenced testing, Ms. Jones could choose a portion of Latisha's math curriculum that includes that skill, which then could be used as the content of a CR-CBA to determine what specific skills she has demonstrated and what teaching objectives would be most appropriate.

The more formal type of CBA, developed in the 1980s by Deno and his associates at the University of Minnesota, is called **curriculum-based measurement (CBM)** (Deno, 1985; Deno & Fuchs, 1987). Within the CBM model, items for a test are drawn from an entire school year's curriculum. For Latisha, representative math computation items from the entire third-grade curriculum would be randomly chosen to develop a series of tests. Latisha would take a test on a weekly basis. Ms. Jones would graph the results to ensure that Latisha is making appropriate progress and would make instructional decisions based on these data. For example, if Latisha was not making sufficient progress in meeting a predetermined goal, an instructional change would be necessary. On the other hand, if Latisha's progress exceeded expectations, the goal date could be moved up.

criterion-referenced curriculum-based assessment A criterion-referenced test using the content of the student's curriculum as the basis for the items.

curriculum-based measurement A formal type of curriculum-based assessment that uses standard methodology.

Error Analysis

One invaluable source of information often overlooked is an analysis of the types of errors students make in their schoolwork. This can be particularly helpful when a written product is available, such as math computation problems or a writing sample for spelling, punctuation, and capitalization. Information from an error analysis can provide some idea of "how to teach" a student. When error analysis is used with CRTs and CR-CBA that give an indication of "what to teach," and with CBM that is helpful in monitoring progress, a comprehensive informal assessment package is available.

Suppose a teacher, Mr. Romick, is concerned with the spelling ability of one of his students, Marty. He analyzes the errors on her spelling tests and notes that Marty is transposing vowel combinations (e.g., freind for friend, baeutiful for beautiful). By teaching Marty specific spelling rules (including the sayings "usually 'i' before 'e' except after 'c'" and "usually when two vowels go walking, the first one does the talking") (Taylor, 2009), Mr. Romick was able to significantly improve Marty's spelling scores.

Latisha's work sample provided an example of how error analysis can be useful for math computation. Suppose, however, that Mr. Romick had a student, Julio, who was having difficulty in math computation, but when Mr. Romick tried to analyze the errors on problems like the following, no pattern was immediately obvious.

$$52 \qquad 63$$
$$\underline{\times 7} \qquad \underline{\times 9}$$
$$424 \qquad 727$$

think-aloud procedure A diagnostic procedure that allows the student to talk his or her way through the solution of a problem so the teacher can determine the incorrect procedures that are being used.

In this situation, it might also be helpful to use the **think-aloud procedure** in which a student "talks his or her way through" the solution of the problem. When Julio was asked to solve the first problem verbally, his error pattern became clear. He responded, "I multiplied 2 times 7 and got 14. I put the 4 below the 7 and brought the 1 over and added it to 5. Then I multiplied 6 times 7, got 42 and put it at the bottom." It is obvious that he was adding the 1 to the 5 and then multiplying 6 times 7 instead of multiplying 5 times 7 and then adding the 1. One instructional strategy that might be used is to teach him the saying "*My Dear Aunt Sally*" where the first letter in each word represents the order of math operations (multiplication, division, addition, subtraction) in solving math problems. Thus, he would know to multiply before adding.

Response to Intervention Model

As noted earlier, the response to intervention (RTI) approach was recommended in IDEA 04 specifically to help in determining the presence of a learning disability. The RTI model takes into account a student's response to a scientific, research-based intervention program. However, the philosophy and suggested models imply that RTI can also be used as a schoolwide model of screening and decision making. For example, a multitiered model has been described (IRIS Center, 2006) in which all students are initially screened (universal screening). Those who are struggling academically remain in the general education classroom but are targeted for more intensive or different instruction by the general education teacher (Tier 1). The prereferral procedures previously described would fit nicely into Tier 1. Those who still don't respond then receive even more intensive instruction that might include the special education teacher or other specialists (Tier 2). If this intervention is not successful, a referral is made (Tier 3). Alternatively, a student's failure at Tier 2 might, in and of itself, result in an identification of a learning disability depending on the criteria used. RTI is discussed in greater depth in Chapter 4.

SAMMY REVISITED What prereferral assessment procedures could Ms. Gonzalez use with Sammy? Why are these the most appropriate?

The Referral Process

Based on the prereferral assessment information that is collected, appropriate prereferral intervention strategies are developed and implemented. If these intervention attempts fail or if the problem is serious enough to warrant immediate attention, a formal referral is made for evaluation to determine eligibility for special education. At this point, parents must be notified and give their consent for the evaluation. A new requirement in IDEA 04 is that if the parents refuse to consent or fail to respond after repeated attempts, the local education agency (LEA) does not have to provide a special education program for their child.

The decision to refer a student for possible special education services should not be made lightly because once a student is referred, he or she will more than likely be found eligible for special education. In one study, 70% to 74% of students evaluated for special education services over a 3-year period were found to be eligible for those services (Ysseldyke, Vanderwood, & Shriner, 1997). There are several possible reasons for this phenomenon. Of course, there is the possibility that the student does, in fact, have a disability. However, other factors could influence the eligibility decision. For example, there is ambiguity among many of the definitions of, and the criteria used for, the different categories of disabilities. For instance, there are different criteria of what constitutes a learning disability, a term that is frequently used for students with a wide variety of school-related problems. Ysseldyke, Algozzine, and Epps (1983) highlighted the importance of the referral in an article combining two studies. In the first study, the authors identified 17 different criteria that could be used to label a student as having a learning disability. They subsequently tested 248 3rd-, 5th-, and 12th-grade students from general education classrooms who had not been referred for any learning problem and found that 85% met one or more of the criteria. In the second study, they found that 88% of low-achieving 4th-grade students could have been identified as having a learning disability. The results indicated the importance that the referral itself has on the identification of students who have disabilities because of the ambiguities of many definitions of the disability categories.

Other factors that could affect the eligibility decision are related to the limitations of tests used to identify students with disabilities, as well as factors related to the assessment process itself. Many tests used for identifying disabilities are technically inadequate and have been characterized as being culturally biased (Taylor, 2009). In addition, several factors could affect test performance and subsequent decisions based on those results. These can include student anxiety or lack of motivation, inappropriate test administration, or an examiner's scoring errors, just to name a few. If students perform poorly on the tests for any of these reasons, they will likely be found eligible for special education even though they might not have a disability.

Prereferral assessment and prereferral intervention can be very helpful and, if the intervention is successful, can be used to avoid a referral for special education. The prereferral process should not be used, however, to delay special education services for students whose problems are more severe. On the other hand, you should make sure that a referral is not made lightly because the student will probably be found eligible for special education.

> **SAMMY REVISITED** Do you think Ms. Gonzalez should refer Sammy for evaluation to determine possible eligibility for special education services? What information should she consider in making this decision?

Check Your Understanding

1. Why are both prereferral assessment and prereferral intervention important?
2. What informal assessment procedures are available?
3. What is an appropriate use for criterion-referenced testing? Curriculum-based assessment? Error analysis?
4. Describe the response to intervention model.
5. What are some possible reasons so many students who are referred for special education are found eligible?

How Do Students Become Eligible for Special Education?

The special education process formally begins once a child is referred for special education. IDEA 04 specifies that a child must be evaluated within 60 days of receiving parental consent or within any time frame established by the state (frequently less than 60 days). Students must meet certain eligibility criteria to receive special education services through IDEA 04. A student must first meet eligibility requirements for one (or more) of the following disability categories: mental retardation, hearing

Relevant CEC Standards
▶ Basic terminology used in assessment (CC8K1)
▶ Screening, pre-referral, referral, and classification procedures (CC8K3)
▶ Use and limitations of assessment instruments (CC8K4)

impairments (including deafness), speech or language impairments, visual impairments (including blindness), serious emotional disturbance, orthopedic impairments, autism, traumatic brain injury, other health impairments, specific learning disabilities, deaf-blindness, or multiple disabilities. IDEA 04 also allows the use of the term *developmental delay* for children ages 3–9 at the discretion of the state and local education agency. Most states have programs for gifted and talented students who must also meet eligibility criteria before receiving those services, but these students are not subject to IDEA 04 regulations.

It should be noted that IDEA 04 includes a special rule for eligibility determination. That rule states that a child cannot be considered to have a disability if the determining factor is a lack of appropriate instruction in reading, including in the essential components of reading instruction; a lack of instruction in math; or limited English proficiency. In other words, these factors must be ruled out as being the primary determinant of the child's difficulties in school.

Before discussing evaluation procedures used to determine if a child meets the criteria of an IDEA 04 disability category and warrants special education, we discuss the general issue of labeling students. The categories of disabilities, often referred to as "labels," have been a source of considerable controversy in the area of special education. In fact, the pros and cons of labeling students has led to one of the most heated discussions within the field of special education.

The Use of Labels

Some people feel that the use of disability labels, such as saying that a student has a learning disability or an emotional disturbance, is inappropriate and can result in negative consequences such as lowered expectations by the student and the teacher, peer rejection, and poor self-concept. IDEA 04 noted that a disproportionate number of children from culturally or linguistically diverse backgrounds receive a disability label, particularly mental retardation and emotional disturbance. This raises questions about the accuracy of the assessment information that results in these labels. Regardless of the criticisms of labels, they are nonetheless required to receive the funding from IDEA 04 that is necessary to provide the special education programs that students with disabilities need. Theoretically, labels are used to group students with similar characteristics so that goals and expectations can be determined. Labels do provide some general idea of the needs of the student. For example, the label *deaf-blindness* presents a different educational picture than the label *learning disability*. Unfortunately, the labeling process is not that easy, and a label rarely provides specific information about a student's educational needs. Concerns with labeling include inaccurate labels because of problems in validly assessing children from diverse cultural or linguistic backgrounds, problems defining many of the labels, not recognizing the variability of characteristics of individuals with the same label, and not acknowledging the overlap of characteristics of individuals with different labels (Taylor, 2009).

Problems Identifying Students from Culturally or Linguistically Diverse Backgrounds

Relevant CEC Standards

▶ Issues in definition and classification of individuals with exceptional learning needs, including those from culturally and linguistically diverse backgrounds (CC1K5)

▶ Legal provisions and ethical principles regarding assessment of individuals (CC8K2)

As just noted, there is concern about the overidentification of students from culturally and linguistically diverse (CLD) backgrounds as having disabilities such as mental retardation and emotional disturbance. In fact, one of the most significant challenges in special education is that of accurately evaluating and identifying those from CLD backgrounds.

If a student's primary language is not English, an examiner is faced with an array of concerns regarding test selection, test translation, and the meaningfulness of the results that are obtained. Even if the examiner speaks and understands the student's language, he might not be familiar with differences in dialect (Wolfram, 1990). As noted in Chapter 1, there has long been a legal mandate for nondiscriminatory assessment practices, although they are not that easy to implement. The Council for Exceptional Children (1997) identified four barriers to the continuing attempts at nondiscriminatory evaluation:

1. Few tests are published in languages other than English and therefore they have to be translated.
2. Translated tests are not always equivalent to the original because of language and dialect differences.
3. Most tests are standardized based on North American culture, making comparisons to individuals outside that culture difficult at best.
4. The use of interpreters can create problems. For example, the interpreter might not translate properly, or certain words might not have an equivalent in another language.

There are also concerns about evaluating students from culturally diverse backgrounds. The cultural orientation of students might dramatically affect how they perform on a test. For example, poor test performance of Hispanic and African American students has been noted when they are evaluated by an unfamiliar examiner (Fuchs & Fuchs, 1989). As another example, students from some cultures are taught to work independently from an early age. If they are confronted with a testing situation that they do not understand, they might be hesitant to ask for clarification or help, thinking that they should be able to "figure it out" on their own. It is absolutely imperative that individuals involved in the assessment process be sensitive to cultural differences.

Challenges to assessing linguistically diverse students to determine eligibility for special education include test selection, test translation, and the meaningfulness of the results.

Another issue that has received a great deal of attention is the accusation that tests, particularly intelligence tests, are inherently biased against individuals from culturally diverse backgrounds. This controversial area resulted in the *Larry P.* court case, banning the use of intelligence tests with African American students in California. Although there is ample evidence that the tests in question are not inherently statistically biased (e.g., Reschly, 1978, 1979; Taylor & Ziegler, 1987; Taylor, Ziegler, & Partenio, 1985), there also is considerable evidence that children from culturally diverse backgrounds do score lower, as a group, on intelligence tests. The result has been the overrepresentation of these children in certain categories, such as mental retardation, and underrepresentation in other categories, such as gifted. CEC (2002) identified several possible reasons for the "disproportionality" of minority students in certain categories of special education. These include two that are particularly germane to this discussion: (1) inequities associated with special education referral and placement procedures, and (2) misidentification and the misuse of tests. CEC recommended that some of these problems could be addressed by making better use of the prereferral intervention process previously discussed. Clearly, we must be aware of the data indicating disproportionality and attempt appropriate prereferral interventions. IDEA 04 also requires that states have policies and procedures in place to prevent inappropriate overidentification or disproportionate representation by race and ethnicity.

Problems with Definitions and Eligibility Criteria

Contributing to the concern about the use of labels is that many of the definitions and eligibility criteria used to label students are somewhat subjective. The same student might be identified as having a disability by one multidisciplinary team but not by

Students with the same label, such as emotional disturbance, often display very different characteristics.

another. Definitions and eligibility criteria also vary from state to state. In one study, Denning, Chamberlain, and Polloway (2000) surveyed all 50 states and the District of Columbia to determine the definition/criteria for determining eligibility for the mental retardation category. They reported a general lack of consistency, implying that a student might be found eligible in one state and not in another.

Variability of Characteristics

Another concern with the use of labels is that students who are given the same label do not necessarily have the same, or in some cases even similar, characteristics. For example, students identified as having emotional disturbance may have characteristics ranging from severe *internalizing* behaviors (e.g., withdrawal) to severe *externalizing* behaviors (e.g., aggression). Similarly, a student identified as having a learning disability may have any combination of a number of characteristics such as reading problems, language problems, writing problems, memory problems, or math problems. Trying to provide a specific educational program based solely on a label is thus a difficult and inappropriate endeavor.

Overlap of Characteristics

There is an increasing awareness that students who are given different labels might, in fact, have many similar characteristics. Much information is available that indicates that the similarity of students' educational needs is more a function of the severity of a disability rather than of the specific category of the disability. For example, students with mild intellectual disabilities and students with learning disabilities have more similar instructional needs than students with mild intellectual disabilities and students with severe intellectual disabilities. We note the similarities of characteristics and instructional needs of students from different categories in several chapters (e.g., learning disabilities, intellectual disabilities, emotional and behavioral disorders, attention deficit/hyperactivity disorder). In other words, it might make more educational sense to group students with mild and moderate disabilities together and those with severe and profound disabilities together. Such a generic approach, referred to as cross-categorical or noncategorical, has received a good deal of attention. In fact, many states have moved to the use of this approach for special education teacher certification.

Evaluation Procedures

Relevant CEC Standard
► Legal provisions and ethical principles regarding assessment of individuals (CC8K2)

Once a child is referred for special education, evaluation procedures are implemented to determine if eligibility criteria are met. As noted previously, most students with severe disabilities or with physical/sensory disabilities such as cerebral palsy, blindness, or deafness are typically identified prior to school age by parents or physicians. Other disabilities, such as communication disorders, are often identified by related services personnel. Although IDEA 04 now includes guidelines that allow consideration of a child's response to scientifically based instruction in the identification of a learning disability, the majority of students with mild disabilities are administered educational and psychological tests. Traditionally, norm-referenced tests are used to help make eligibility decisions, although there is still heavy reliance on informal measures with preschool children. Also, depending on the category of exceptionality, other procedures such as interviews, developmental histories, and the use of checklists and behavior rating scales might be required.

For the most part, the areas evaluated will be dependent on the eligibility criteria used, and the specific tests used to measure those areas might vary. Two areas frequently evaluated for a student suspected of having a mild disability are intelligence and achievement. Intelligence tests are used to determine an individual's IQ, which in turn is used to help make the decision regarding the most appropriate disability category (if any) for a student if the category includes IQ as a criterion. Achievement test scores are often used as one eligibility criterion and typically are used to document the student's educational performance level in a number of areas. Other areas of testing are explored if a student is suspected of having a specific type of problem. For example, some type of behavior rating scale might be administered for students referred for emotional or behavioral problems. Similarly, a diagnostic reading or math test might be used for students who are referred for problems in those areas. The specific methods of identifying exceptional students are discussed in the chapters in Parts 2–4 that focus on specific exceptionalities. Because intelligence and achievement testing are relevant for most exceptional students, a discussion of these follows.

Intelligence Testing

Intelligence testing has had a stormy and somewhat controversial history. There has been considerable debate regarding the nature of intelligence, and, subsequently, what intelligence tests should measure and what they actually do measure. Early professionals provided many theories about the nature of intelligence. Some, for example, have argued that it is a general ability (Spearman, 1927), whereas others envision it as having many components (Guilford, 1967). A quick look at the various available intelligence tests indicates that intelligence is defined in a number of ways and that intelligence tests measure a wide range of skills such as verbal ability, analytical thinking, and memory. Some tests, called single-skilled tests, measure only a narrowly defined concept of intelligence, such as reasoning or vocabulary, whereas others, called multiskilled tests, measure a variety of different areas. Some intelligence tests have even been developed for use with individuals with physical or sensory impairments or those who are nonverbal (Taylor, 2009).

The "grandfather" of intelligence tests is the Stanford-Binet Intelligence Scale (see An Important Event). Originally published in 1908, the Stanford-Binet is now in its fifth edition (Roid, 2003). This test includes both verbal and nonverbal measures in the areas of fluid reasoning, knowledge, quantitative reasoning, visual-spatial processing, and working memory. However, the intelligence test used most often in the schools to help determine eligibility for special education is the Wechsler Intelligence Scale for Children–IV (WISC–IV; Wechsler, 2003). The WISC–IV measures verbal comprehension, perceptual reasoning, working memory, and processing speed.

AN IMPORTANT EVENT

1908—Alfred Binet Develops the Stanford Binet Intelligence Scale

In 1904, Alfred Binet, a French psychologist, was commissioned by the Minister of Public Instruction in Paris to develop an instrument to help detect slow learners in the schools. His first attempt was published in 1905 in collaboration with one of his colleagues, Theodore Simon. He continued refining the scale and began working with Lewis Terman, who extended Binet's work to the United States. The result was the Stanford-Binet Intelligence Scale, completed in 1908, which was a catalyst for a boom in intelligence testing for the rest of the century. The Stanford-Binet remains one of the most frequently used tools for measuring intelligence today.

REFLECTION Do you think intelligence tests that measure both verbal and nonverbal skills should be used with students from culturally or linguistically diverse backgrounds? Why or why not?

Achievement Testing

Another area routinely evaluated when a student is referred for an academically oriented concern is achievement, typically in the areas of reading, mathematics, written language, and oral language, or in the mastery of content-area information. As noted previously, students must demonstrate an educational need before they are eligible for special education. For students with mild disabilities, in particular, this is often accomplished by showing that a student is falling behind in one or more achievement areas. Scores from achievement tests are also used in more sophisticated ways. For example, historically they were used in combination with scores from intelligence tests to determine whether a significant discrepancy exists, such as an IQ higher than achievement. Such a discrepancy was central in the identification of a learning disability for a number of years although IDEA 04 no longer requires it. The various uses of achievement tests are discussed in subsequent chapters that focus on specific exceptionalities.

A number of group-administered achievement tests are sometimes routinely administered to all students in general education settings. In more recent years, statewide achievement tests (e.g., the Florida Comprehensive Assessment Test) have also been used in **high-stakes assessment** that make decisions about retention, graduation, and even teachers' pay. To assist in special education eligibility decisions, however, some type of individually administered achievement test is usually employed. These include the Kaufman Test of Educational Achievement–II (KTEA–II; Kaufman & Kaufman, 2004b) and the Wechsler Individual Achievement Test–II (WIAT–II; Psychological Corporation, 2001). Both the KTEA–II and the WIAT–II measure the areas of reading, math, written language (expression), and oral language (expression).

high-stakes assessment
Large-scale assessment in which important decisions such as retention and graduation are made.

Using Test Information for Decision Making

In addition to intelligence and achievement tests, many other types of tests are frequently given to students who are referred for special education. To a large extent, the type of tests administered depends on the nature of the referral as well as the eligibility criteria used for the different exceptionality categories. For example, a student referred for a behavioral problem might be administered a behavior rating scale, and a student referred for an intellectual disability might also be given an adaptive behavior scale. Similarly, a student thought to be gifted might be administered a creativity test. After a battery of tests is administered, the pattern of test scores and other gathered information, such as observations and the family history, are analyzed to determine whether a student meets eligibility criteria for a specific category. As noted previously, eligibility criteria may differ from state to state or even school district to school district. Also, determining specific labels is not an exact science due to the numerous factors just discussed. Nonetheless, it is a process that is usually necessary to receive funding for the education of the students. The Classroom Suggestions feature summarizes several do's and don'ts related to evaluation.

SAMMY REVISITED Assuming that a referral for special education was warranted for Sammy, what evaluation procedures might be used?

Although there are many concerns about the use of labels, they are very much in use. Teachers should understand what they are and why they are necessary. That said, teachers should also keep the controversies regarding the use of labels in mind. Knowing the limitations of labels is an important part of using them. Students must meet certain eligibility criteria before they can receive special education services, and the eligibility criteria are different for each exceptionality. For the majority of students who are suspected of being exceptional, norm-referenced tests, particularly intelligence tests and achievement tests, are usually administered.

DO'S: EVALUATION AND IDENTIFICATION

❑ **Do** notify the child's parents about the proposed evaluation and obtain their written consent before conducting an initial evaluation, administering any new test as part of a reevaluation, or other circumstances as required by state law or district policy.

❑ **Do** ask parents to participate in the evaluation and identification process and consider their input as evaluation data.

❑ **Do** inform parents that they have a legal right to an independent educational evaluation at public expense if they disagree with the district's evaluation.

❑ **Do** consider requesting a due process hearing or mediation if a child's need for special education is clear but parents refuse consent for evaluation or reevaluation.

❑ **Do** use a variety of assessment materials and strategies that provide sufficient information to (1) judge whether the child fits into one of the IDEA eligibility categories; (2) decide if the child, because of the disability, needs special education; and (3) assess the child's educational needs and determine the content of the child's IEP.

❑ **Do** administer tests and other assessment materials in the child's native language or other appropriate mode of communication.

DON'TS: EVALUATION AND IDENTIFICATION

❑ **Don't** single out a child for testing, interviewing, or overt observation without notice to parents. Beware of "prereferral intervention" programs that have the effect of delaying an eligible child's special education evaluation or IEP.

❑ **Don't** equate evaluation with testing. Evaluation should also include observations, work samples, interviews, information provided by parents, cumulative files, etc. No one test comes close to being an adequate evaluation, legally or professionally.

❑ **Don't** rely on any standardized battery of assessments, and most definitely don't select tests solely from those "tabled" for use in a formula or for any other purpose.

❑ **Don't** rely exclusively on any formula or quantitative guidelines to determine eligibility. The more elaborate the formula, the sillier it will appear to a judge. The law requires the exercise of professional judgment.

❑ **Don't** ask a professional, such as a physician or psychiatrist, whether a child has a particular disability. Instead, provide the IDEA disability definition, and ask whether the child fits that definition.

❑ **Don't** use evaluation methods that discriminate on the basis of race, culture, or native language. Evaluation that discriminates on the basis of sex is forbidden by other federal laws (ESEA, Title IX), but the well-known fact that roughly twice as many boys as girls are in special education suggests that this prohibition is widely disregarded.

Source: Bateman, B., & Linden, M. (1998). *Better IEPs: How to develop legally correct and educationally useful programs* (3rd ed.) pp. 10–11. Reprinted with permission, Sopris West, Inc.

Check Your Understanding

1. Why is labeling students controversial? Why is labeling a student usually necessary?

2. What are some problems teachers confront when identifying students with disabilities from culturally or linguistically diverse backgrounds?

3. What types of instruments are typically used to identify students with mild disabilities?

4. What are the names of two intelligence tests and two achievement tests?

How Is an Exceptional Student's Educational Program Developed?

Once a child is identified as having a disability, a plan for his or her education is developed. Central to the philosophy of IDEA 04 is the development of the individualized education program (IEP) for all students ages 3–21 who have a disability. For infants and toddlers (birth–age 2) who have a disability or are at risk, an individual family service plan (IFSP) must be constructed. Among other things, an IFSP must indicate specific objectives for the early intervention program, a summary of the family's strengths and needs, and a list of strategies to be used.

An important consideration in planning for the education of a student with a disability is the placement or educational setting that is most appropriate for implementing the IEP. IDEA 04 mandates education in the least restrictive environment although the movement toward full inclusion of all exceptional students in the general education classroom has created some controversy.

The Individualized Education Program

As indicated in Chapter 1, an individualized education program (IEP) is a statement of a student's educational program written by a multidisciplinary team. The creation of an IEP is a requirement for any student ages 3–21 receiving funding under IDEA 04. In a very real sense, the IEP is the most distinguishing component of IDEA 04. Initially mandated by PL 94-142 in 1975, the IEP has reinforced the importance of looking at every student with a disability as an individual and not simply as a member of a category. IDEA 04 specifically indicates who should be involved in the development of a student's IEP as well as what content the IEP must include.

The IEP Team

The IEP is developed by a multidisciplinary team that includes, but is not limited to, the parents; at least one general education teacher (if the student is, or may be, participating in the general education classroom); at least one special education teacher; and a representative of the local education agency (LEA) who is qualified to provide specially designed instruction, is knowledgeable about the general education curriculum, and is knowledgeable about the availability of resources. Others who could be involved are individuals who can interpret the instructional implications of evaluation results, individuals with knowledge or special expertise regarding the child (including related services personnel), and, whenever appropriate, the student with the disability. IDEA 04 provides guidelines indicating that members are not required to attend the IEP meeting when their input/participation is not relevant for the student or they are unable to attend but can provide written input. In both instances, the parents and the LEA must agree that the attendance of these individuals is not necessary.

Who leads the discussions in IEP meetings? Martin et al. (2006) observed more than 100 IEP meetings for middle and high school students to determine the percentage of time each team member spent talking. Over half of the time, special education teachers were talking, followed by the parents (15%), general education teachers and administrators (9% each), and support staff (6%). Students were involved only 3% of the time. Martin et al. emphasized the need to involve students more in the development of their educational programs, particularly in the area of transition goals. In a survey of general education teachers, the majority reported that IEPs were helpful for curriculum preparation although they voiced the need for additional training (Lee-Tarver, 2006). Perhaps, this latter finding might help explain the limited role that general education teachers sometime take in IEP meetings.

Content of the IEP

IDEA 04 identifies several components that must be included in an IEP. The current requirements clearly indicate the intent of having students with disabilities be involved in the general education curriculum, participate in regular assessments, and interact with students without disabilities. Congress's suggestion to reduce paperwork resulted in the elimination of IEP objectives and benchmarks required in previous legislation, except for those students whose goals are aligned with alternate achievement standards. This change was made, in part, because of criticisms by

The IEP should clearly promote the student's participation in the general education curriculum.

teachers about the tremendous amount of paperwork that was required. The current requirements for IEPs include the following:

(a) General

(1) A statement of the child's present levels of academic achievement and functional performance, including—
    (i) how the child's disability affects the child's involvement and progress in the general education curriculum;
    (ii) for preschool children, as appropriate, how the disability affects the child's participation in appropriate activities; and

(2) (i) A statement of measurable annual goals, including academic and functional goals, designed to—
        (A) meet the child's needs that result from the child's disability to enable the child to be involved in and make progress in the general education curriculum, and
        (B) meet each of the child's other educational needs that result from the child's disability.
    (ii) For children with disabilities who take alternative assessments aligned to alternate achievement standards, a description of benchmarks or short-term objectives.

(3) A description of
    (i) how the child's progress toward meeting the annual goals will be measured; and
    (ii) when periodic reports on the progress the child is making toward meeting the annual goals (such as through the use of quarterly or other periodic reports, concurrent with the issuance of report cards) will be provided.

(4) A statement of the special education and related services and supplementary aids and services, based on peer-reviewed research to the extent practicable, to be provided to the child, or on behalf of the child, and a statement of the program modifications or supports for school personnel that will be provided to enable the child—
    (i) to advance appropriately toward attaining the annual goals;
    (ii) to be involved in and make progress in the general education curriculum and to participate in extracurricular and other nonacademic activities; and
    (iii) to be educated and participate with other children with disabilities and with nondisabled children.

(5) An explanation of the extent, if any, to which the child will not participate with nondisabled children in the regular class.

(6) (i) A statement of any individual appropriate accommodations that are necessary to measure the academic achievement and functional performance of the child on State and district-wide assessments.

(ii) If the IEP team determines that the child must take an alternate assessment instead of a particular State or district-wide assessment of student achievement, a statement of why—

(A) the child cannot participate in regular assessment; and

(B) the particular alternate assessment selected is appropriate for the child.

(7) The projected date for the beginning of the services and modifications, and the anticipated frequency, location, and duration of those services and modifications.

(b) Transition services. Beginning not later than the first IEP to be in effect when the child is 16, or younger if determined appropriate by the IEP team, and updated annually thereafter the IEP must include

(1) appropriate measurable postsecondary goals based upon age appropriate transition assessments related to training, education, employment, and, where appropriate, independent living skills;

(2) the transition services (including courses of study) needed to assist the child in reaching those goals; and

(c) Transfer of rights at age of majority. Beginning not later than one year before the child reaches the age of majority under State law, the IEP must include a statement that the child has been informed of the child's rights under this title, if any, that will transfer to the child on reaching the age of majority.

Transition goals are incorporated in the IEP and are not part of a separate individualized transition plan required in some previous legislation. The goal of transition is to help the student move from school to postschool activities including postsecondary education, vocational education, integrated employment (including supported employment), continuing and adult education, adult services, independent living, or community participation. Transition services include instruction, related services, and community experiences, and also involve the development of employment and other postschool adult living objectives. When appropriate, it also involves the acquisition of daily living skills and functional vocational evaluation.

In general the IEP team meets and discusses each of the preceding points, paying close attention to the student's strengths, the parents' input, and the results of recent evaluations, including the student's performance on statewide or districtwide tests. Particular care should be given to determine what information should be included in the IEP that will help the student make progress toward the annual goals, participate in the general education curriculum, and be included with students without disabilities to the maximum extent possible. Many states are also developing "standards-based IEPs" in which the student's goals are aligned with the state's accountability standards. The text appendix includes the model IEP form recommended by IDEA 04. The decisions about the specific information included in the IEP are based on several considerations, most notably the unique educational needs of the student. The four components of special education described in Chapter 1—instructional content, instructional procedures, instructional environment, and instructional technology—should all be considered.

SAMMY REVISITED If Sammy were identified as having a disability, to what extent do you think he should participate in the general education curriculum? In the statewide assessment program? Explain your reasoning. What additional information would help you make these decisions?

The Individual Family Service Plan

For infants and toddlers with disabilities, an individual family service plan (IFSP) must be developed in one or more of the following areas: physical development, cognitive development, communication development, social or emotional development, and adaptive development. The content of the IFSP must contain the following:

1. A statement of the child's present level of performance in the previously noted developmental areas based on objective criteria.
2. A statement of the family's resources, priorities, and concerns relating to enhancing the child's development.
3. A statement of the measurable results or outcomes expected to be achieved for the child and family, including preliteracy and language skills as developmentally appropriate for the child. In addition, the criteria, procedures, and timelines used to determine whether progress is being made and whether modifications or revisions of the results, outcomes, or services must be identified.
4. A statement of specific early intervention services based on peer-reviewed research, to the extent practicable, necessary to meet the unique needs of the child and family, including the frequency, intensity, and method of delivering services.
5. A statement of the natural environments in which early intervention services will appropriately be provided, including a justification of the extent, if any, to which the services will not be provided in a natural environment.
6. The projected dates for initiation of services and the anticipated length, duration, and frequency of the services.
7. The identification of the service coordinator from the profession most immediately relevant to the child's and family's needs who will be responsible for implementation of the plan and coordination with other agencies and persons, including transportation services.
8. The steps to be taken to support transition of a toddler with a disability to preschool or other appropriate services.

There are several areas in which an IFSP differs from an IEP. These include the identification of outcomes targeted for the family and not just the child; encouragement of service delivery in natural environments, including the home and community settings; and provision of services from multiple agencies (Bruder, 2000). Table 2.2

TABLE 2.2	Services Provided as Part of a Child's Individual Family Service Plan

- Family training, counseling, and home visits
- Special instruction
- Speech-language pathology and audiology services, and sign language and cued language services
- Physical therapy
- Psychological services
- Service coordination services
- Medical services only for diagnostic or evaluation purposes
- Early identification, screening, and assessment services
- Health services necessary to enable the infant or toddler to benefit from the other early intervention services
- Social work services
- Vision services
- Assistive technology services
- Transportation and related costs that are necessary to enable an infant or toddler and the infant's or toddler's family to receive another service

lists the specific services that must be provided (if appropriate) as part of the IFSP according to IDEA 04. Components of an IFSP are presented in Chapter 13.

Decisions about Program Placement

Part of the IEP process is determining where students will receive their special education. A continuing debate exists regarding the most appropriate educational setting in which exceptional students should be taught, most notably whether all students, regardless of the type or severity of their disabilities, should be taught in the general education classroom. As you learned in Chapter 1, there is a legal requirement that students with disabilities should be taught in the least restrictive environment (LRE), but this requirement does not make the decision any easier. The decision to remove a student from the general education classroom should be made only if the nature or severity of the disability precludes success in that environment, even with the addition of supplementary aids and services. Interestingly, there is also a debate about where gifted and talented students should be taught.

The Least Restrictive Environment

The concept behind the least restrictive environment is that students with disabilities should be educated with students without disabilities to the maximum extent appropriate. There are two key issues related to the concept of LRE. The first involves the interpretation of the phrase "should be educated." When the mandate for the LRE was first made in PL 94-142, many individuals felt that placing a student with a disability with their peers without disabilities during lunch or recess was conforming to this legal mandate. It must be stressed, however, that the operative word is *educated* in the LRE, not simply *placed* in the LRE. Current legislation is much clearer about the fact that a student with a disability must be exposed to the general education classroom and curriculum unless it is not appropriate to do so. Another key issue involves the interpretation of the phrase "the maximum extent appropriate." In general, this means that the unique needs of an exceptional student must be taken into account. For example, it might not be educationally advantageous for a student with a severe intellectual disability to be placed into a general education classroom for the entire day. It is possible, however, for that student to spend portions of the day in that classroom. The extent of a student's integration into the general education classroom is a decision that is usually made by the IEP team based on the student's educational needs. One set of guiding questions used in some states is referred to as the Holland Test. This "test" is based on the 1994 court case *Sacramento City Unified School District v. Rachel H.* Rachel Holland was an elementary student with an IQ of 44. Her parents felt that she could be taught in the general education classroom if she were given the appropriate supports. The court identified three criteria to be considered when determining an appropriate educational placement:

1. What are the educational benefits of placing the student in the general education classroom with supplemental aids and services versus the educational benefits of placement in a special education classroom?
2. What are the noneducational benefits of having the student interact with students without disabilities?
3. What effect will the student's presence in the general education classroom have on the teacher and on the other students?

Unfortunately, although these questions might help guide the decision making, their answers still require subjective judgments. Also, other states use different "tests" based on other court cases. As a result, placement in the LRE may vary for a student depending on his or her geographic residence (Douvanis & Hulsey, 2002).

Proponents of the LRE support the concept of providing a continuum of service options for students with disabilities. In keeping with the philosophy of the LRE, the decision regarding placement on the continuum is made on an individual basis considering the specific educational needs of the student. One of the earliest models of this

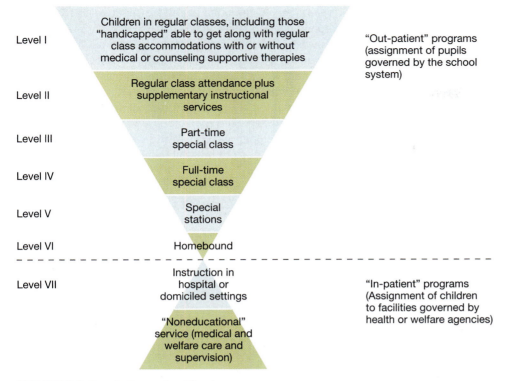

Level I — Children in regular classes, including those "handicapped" able to get along with regular class accommodations with or without medical or counseling supportive therapies

"Out-patient" programs (assignment of pupils governed by the school system)

Level II — Regular class attendance plus supplementary instructional services

Level III — Part-time special class

Level IV — Full-time special class

Level V — Special stations

Level VI — Homebound

Level VII — Instruction in hospital or domiciled settings

"In-patient" programs (Assignment of children to facilities governed by health or welfare agencies)

"Noneducational" service (medical and welfare care and supervision)

FIGURE 2.3 Deno's Cascade of Services

Source: Deno, E. (1970). Special education as developmental capital. *Exceptional Children, 37,* 230. Copyright © 1970 by the Council for Exceptional Children. Reprinted with permission.

continuum was the "cascade of services," proposed more than 25 years ago (Figure 2.3). Although some of the terms have changed, the model still serves as a basis for current placement options. In this model, Level I refers to a situation in which a student is taught in the general education classroom for the entire day. In this environment, the primary responsibility for the student's educational program would be placed on the general education teacher. At Level II, the student is still placed in the general education classroom although some of the direct instruction might come from special education personnel. Level III refers to the so-called resource room. Students at this level spend a portion of the day in the general education classroom, but also spend time in a special education classroom, the type of class and amount of time being dependent on the student's needs. Level IV involves placing the student in a special education classroom, although the classroom is located within the regular school. Level V refers to special education schools in which the students are segregated from their peers without disabilities. A student who must receive instruction at home, perhaps because of a medical problem, would be placed in Level VI. Level VII is reserved for those students whose problems are severe enough that they need constant attention or medical treatment and, therefore, must be served in residential settings. Overall, the concept of LRE implies that a student should be placed in as low a level (closest to Level I) as is both possible and appropriate.

The U.S. Department of Education keeps track of the number of students with disabilities who are served in various educational environments. In 2005, approximately 54% of the students with disabilities ages 6–21 were being served outside the regular classroom less than 20% of the time (spending at least 80% of the time in the general education classroom), about 25% were served outside the regular classroom between 20 and 60% of the time (spending 40% to 80% of their time in the general education classroom), and only about 17% were served outside the classroom greater than 60% of the time (spending less than 40% of their time in the general education classroom). This latter statistic includes both students served totally within a special education classroom (spending no time in the general education classroom) and those spending up to 39% of their time in the general education classroom. Thus it is difficult to determine the percentage of students who spend at least some of the day in the general education classroom, but it is likely in the range of 85% to 95%. Only 4% were served in public or private separate or residential facilities or home/hospital environments (U.S. DOE, 2006).

The traditional view of LRE assumes that the student's needs must be assessed and then "matched" to the environment that can best meet those needs. However, in the 1980s proponents of a movement known as the **Regular Education Initiative** (REI), which proposed that general education and special education teachers work collaboratively with students in the same classroom and that all students who need additional services receive them without the need for a label. As a result, the adaptive learning environments model was developed (ALEM; Wang & Birch, 1984; see An Important Event). This led, in part, to the current interest in inclusion.

Regular Education Initiative
A movement that supported the education of all students with special needs without the need for labels through the collaboration of general education and special education teachers.

AN IMPORTANT EVENT

1984—An Alternative Service Delivery Model for Special Education Is Suggested

Wang, M., & Birch, J. (1984). Comparison of a full-time mainstreaming program and a resource room approach. *Exceptional Children, 51*, 30–40.

In 1984 Wang and Birch published their proposal for the use of the adaptive learning environments model (ALEM), developed at the University of Pittsburgh. In this model, emphasis is shifted from determining the most appropriate setting, such as the general education classroom, resource room, or separate classroom, to placing a child to maximize learning (the least restrictive model), and toward investigating more creative settings that might be appropriate for students with different ability levels. This would involve such modifications as describing educational needs using instructional rather than labeling terms, implementing multiage grouping of students based on instructional needs, and changing staffing patterns to allow a greater interface between general education teachers and special education teachers. This model, which was implemented at several sites across the United States, was supported by proponents of the Regular Education Initiative (REI) but also was met with some criticism (e.g., Anderegg & Vergason, 1988). For example, issues such as cost and personnel shortages were mentioned. The REI had a significant impact on special education practices, which led, in part, to the current interest in inclusion.

REFLECTION Does the philosophy of the ALEM make sense? What problems can you see regarding its implementation?

Inclusion

Over the past two decades, the concept of inclusion has been popularized. Inclusion means that the IEPs for students with disabilities will be implemented primarily by the general education teacher in the general education classroom. Inclusion was not mandated by IDEA 04, but it is seen as a positive option by many professionals. It should also be pointed out that inclusion should be considered a philosophy, not simply a placement option (Baglieri & Knopf, 2004). Unfortunately, many educators feel that simply changing the location of instruction will make the instruction more effective (Mock & Kauffman, 2005).

Some professionals make the distinction between partial inclusion and full inclusion. **Partial inclusion** refers to a situation in which students with disabilities receive most of their instruction in the general education classroom but are also taught in another instructional setting, such as a resource room, when appropriate. A more radical approach is **full inclusion.** Proponents of full inclusion feel that all students, regardless of type or severity of their disability, should be taught in the general education classroom. Their essential argument is that students with disabilities represent a minority group and that placing them in any environment other than the general education classroom is a form of discrimination (e.g., Stainback & Stainback, 1992). This philosophy differs from the continuum of services model previously presented because it assumes that the LRE for all students with disabilities is the general education classroom. Critics point this out and

partial inclusion The philosophy that suggests that students with disabilities should receive most of their instruction in the general classroom but also be taught in other instructional settings when appropriate.

full inclusion The philosophy that all students with disabilities receive all of their instruction in the general education classroom regardless of their level or type of disability.

TABLE 2.3	Desirable Characteristics of Teachers in Inclusive Settings

What competencies do general education teachers and special education teachers need to be competent and inclusive teachers?

❏ Ability to problem solve, to be able to informally assess the skills a student needs (rather than relying solely on standardized curriculum)

❏ Ability to take advantage of children's individual interests and use their internal motivation for developing needed skills

❏ Ability to set high but alternative expectations that are suitable for the students; this means developing alternative assessments

❏ Ability to make appropriate expectations for each student, regardless of the student's capabilities, to allow all students to be included in a class and school

❏ Ability to determine how to modify assignments for students, how to design classroom activities with so many levels that all students have a part, how to design activity-based rather than seat-based teaching

❏ Ability to value all kinds of skills that students bring to a class, not just the academic skills, and make it explicit that in their classrooms they value all skills, even if that is not a clear value of a whole school

❏ Ability to provide daily success for all students and to counteract the message all students get when certain students are continually taken out of class for special work

Other competencies that will help general education teachers in an inclusive environment include:

❏ Realizing that every child in the class is their responsibility. Teachers need to find out how to work with each child rather than assuming someone else will tell them how to educate a child.

❏ Knowing a variety of instructional strategies and how to use them effectively. This includes the ability to adapt materials and rewrite objectives for a child's needs.

❏ Working as a team with parents and special education teachers to learn what skills a child needs and to provide the best teaching approach.

❏ Viewing each child in the class as an opportunity to become a better teacher rather than a problem to be coped with or have someone else fix.

❏ Maintaining flexibility and a high tolerance for ambiguity.

Source: The Interstate New Teacher Assessment and Support Consortium (INTASC) standards were developed by the Council of Chief State School Officers and member states. Copies may be downloaded from the Council's Web site at http://www.ccsso.org. Council of Chief School Officers (1992) Model standards for beginning teaching licensing, assessment, and development: A resource for state dialogue. Washington, DC: Author. http://www.ccsso.org/content/pdfs/corestrd.pdf. Used with permission.

suggest that the general education classroom may not always be the best environment to exclusively teach all students and that options should be available. However, as noted in Chapter 1, there needs to be a good reason for a student not to be taught in the general education classroom. As a result, the vast majority of students with disabilities spend at least a portion of the day in that setting working with both general education and special education teachers. It is important, however, that all teachers working in an inclusive setting be aware of the challenges they will face. Table 2.3 provides a list of desirable teacher characteristics for working with students in an inclusive setting.

Many researchers have noted the positive effects of including students with disabilities in the general education classroom. These positive effects have been found in the areas of academic achievement (Freeman & Alkin, 2000), adaptive behavior (McDonnell et al., 2003), social development (Simons, 1998), and classroom work skills (Dore, Dion, Wagner, & Brunet, 2002). Not surprisingly, there are also researchers who have found a lack of positive effects, and in some cases, the negative effects of inclusion. These include lower self-concepts of students with disabilities when they spend more time in the general education classroom (Wigle & DeMoulin, 1999) and a lack of individualized programming focusing on their true educational needs such as functional skills or vocational skills (Chesley & Calaluce, 1997). Others have even argued that integrating students in the general education classroom does not give them the opportunity to identify with the disability culture (Hall, 2002). This debate is not confined to inclusion practices in the United States. Inclusion has also been practiced in other countries for a number of years. In one recent, radical response to inclusion in England, the National Union of Teachers called for the end of inclusive practices (Halpin, 2006). This decision was based on a report from Cambridge University that indicated that inclusion was harming students with disabilities, was undermining the education of other students, and was exhausting the teachers.

A related area that has been studied extensively is the attitude toward inclusion. For example, students with disabilities have been reported to voice a preference for inclusion, noting that without it they remain isolated and feel like second-class citizens (Jarry, Castro, & Duff, 2006). One area that has been particularly targeted is teachers' attitudes toward inclusion. In one study Cook, Cameron, and Tankersley (2007) reported that "inclusive teachers" reported higher ratings of concern, indifference, and rejection of the students with disabilities than the students without disabilities. Idol (2006) evaluated the inclusionary practices in eight schools. She found that educators, including administrators, teachers, and staff were generally positive about teaching students with disabilities in the general education classroom although they were not sure about the best way to do it. They did prefer that the special education teacher or instructional assistant be present in the general education classroom. Several underlying themes regarding general education teachers' perceptions might explain some of their attitudes. These include concerns about the lack of appropriate training to work with students with disabilities (Wolery, 1995), the time required to implement inclusionary practices effectively (Mclean, 2001), and the need for additional support personnel (McNally, Cole, & Waugh, 2001). Special education teachers, on the other hand, seem to have a slightly more positive view of inclusion, although experienced special education teachers still have several reservations (Taylor, Richards, Goldstein, & Schilit, 1997), suggesting that their knowledge of its actual implementation gives them some reservation.

We hope that adequate resources and appropriate training of teachers needed to make inclusion successful will increase. Future research should continue to study inclusion objectively rather than fragmenting the special education field along philosophical lines. One possible area to study is the effectiveness of different methods of instruction within the full inclusion model. For example, should the general education and special education teachers work with all students, or should the special education teacher work only with students with disabilities and the general education teacher work only with the other students? In fact, the issue of collaboration between general education and special education teachers is an important one, regardless of the placement of the students. This issue is addressed in depth in Chapter 3.

Current Thinking on the Least Restrictive Environment

Taylor, Richards, and Brady (2005) summarized the status of the issue of placement. They pointed out that IDEA 04 requires that an explanation be provided in a student's IEP if the student is not participating with students without disabilities in the general education classroom. As noted earlier, IDEA 04 stipulates that placing a student in a separate class or separate school, or removing the student from the general education environment, should occur only when education in regular classes, even with supplemental aids and services, cannot be achieved satisfactorily. Even though this does keep the door to a continuum of services open, it provides a subtle but powerful distinction between this and earlier interpretations of the LRE. This interpretation assumes that the student will be taught in the general education classroom and that documentation must be provided if it is determined that he or she cannot perform in this environment. In the past, many professionals' first assumption was that a more restrictive placement was appropriate and that movement toward inclusion in the general education classroom should be made

SAMMY REVISITED If identified as having a disability, does Sammy seem to be a good candidate for an inclusive setting? Why or why not?

DO'S: PLACEMENT

❑ **Do** remember that program appropriateness is the primary IDEA mandate, and LRE is secondary. As a federal district court judge has explained:

Nowhere in the Act is a handicapped child required to sink or swim in an ordinary classroom. . . . Congress certainly did not intend to place handicapped children in a least restrictive environment and thereby deny them an appropriate education. (*Visco v. School District of Pittsburgh,* 1988)

❑ **Do** make available a continuum of various alternative placements, including resource rooms, special classes, and special schools, so children with disabilities can learn in the environment that is appropriate for them based on their individual needs.

❑ **Do** determine each child's placement at least annually and individually, basing the decision on the child's IEP.

❑ **Do** ensure that each placement decision is made by a group of persons, including parents, who are knowledgeable about the child, the meaning of the evaluation data, and the placement options.

❑ **Do** consider any potential harmful effects on the child or on the quality of services when selecting the LRE.

❑ **Do** make sure each child is educated and otherwise participates nondisabled children without disabilities to the maximum extent appropriate.

❑ **Do** place each child in the school he or she would attend if nondisabled unless the IEP requires some other arrangement.

DON'TS: PLACEMENT

❑ **Don't** remove a child with a disability from the regular classroom environment unless the disability is such that education in regular classes cannot be achieved satisfactorily, even with the use of supplementary aids and services.

❑ **Don't** substitute a policy of "full inclusion" for the continuum of various alternative placements required by the IDEA.

❑ **Don't** exclude parents from placement decisions.

❑ **Don't** forget to follow all the procedural requirements for all "changes of placement" including suspension of more than 10 days, expulsion, graduation, and significant program changes.

❑ **Don't** place a student on the basis of his or her disability category. Regardless of disability category, placement must be based on the student's IEP.

Source: Adapted from Bateman, B., & Linden, M. (1998). *Better IEPs: How to develop legally correct and educationally useful programs* (3rd ed.), 16–17. Reprinted with permission, Sopris West, Inc.

carefully. The Classroom Suggestions feature summarizes several do's and don'ts related to placement decisions that emphasize the LRE.

In summary, special education can be thought of as a process that begins when an individual is initially thought to have a potential problem. Depending on the severity of the suspected problem, most students are then given an immediate intervention prior to making a formal referral for special education. If this intervention is unsuccessful, the student is referred and evaluated to determine eligibility for special education services. If the student is found to meet criteria for a disability category, an educational program is developed and implemented.

Check Your Understanding

1. Who are the potential members of the IEP team?
2. What are at least four areas that must be addressed in a student's IEP?
3. What must an individual family service plan include?
4. What is the least restrictive environment?
5. What is a continuum of services? What are the pros and cons of offering a continuum of services?
6. What is inclusion? What are the pros and cons of inclusion?

Chapter Summary

Go to the text's Online Learning Center at **www.mhhe.com/taylor1e** to access study resources, Web links, practice quizzes, and extending materials.

How Are Exceptional Students Initially Identified?

- Children with severe disabilities are usually identified early in life.
- Individuals with mild disabilities might not be identified until they start having problems in school.

What Are the Prereferral Process and the Referral Process?

- The prereferral process involves both prereferral assessment and prereferral intervention, which are initiated to determine and remediate a problem in the student's current educational placement.
- The response to intervention paradigm provides an alternative model for prereferral decision making.
- If necessary, a formal referral is made for an evaluation to determine if the student is eligible to receive special education services.

How Do Students Become Eligible for Special Education?

- For a student to receive special education services, he or she must meet certain eligibility criteria outlined by IDEA 04.

- IDEA 04 lists 12 categories of disabilities for which a student might be eligible for services.
- Depending on the suspected category, the evaluation for a disability may include intelligence and achievement testing as well as the use of other tests and assessment procedures.

How Is an Exceptional Student's Educational Program Developed?

- Every school-aged student receiving services under IDEA 04 will have an individualized education program (IEP) determined by a multidisciplinary team.
- Infants and toddlers receiving services under IDEA 04 will have an individual family service plan (IFSP) designed for them and their families.
- One important decision is the educational placement in which the IEP will be implemented. Proponents of teaching students in the least restrictive environment support a continuum of services option. Proponents of full inclusion argue that this should always be the general education classroom.

Reflection Topics

1. As a general education teacher, why would you want to engage in the prereferral process? Do you see any drawbacks?
2. Why would you collect baseline data before initiating an intervention program? Why not just initiate the program and see if the student improves?
3. IDEA 04 allows the use of the term *developmental delay* for children ages 3–9. Would you prefer to use this term rather than *learning disability* or *emotional disturbance* for a kindergarten student? Why or why not?
4. The overrepresentation of children from culturally and linguistically diverse backgrounds in certain categories of disabilities is well documented. With this in mind, why do you think IDEA 04 requires that students be labeled?
5. Do you think it was a good idea for IDEA 04 to eliminate the requirement of short-term objectives and benchmarks for the IEPs of most students? Why or why not?
6. Do you believe that all students should be fully included in the general education classroom? Why or why not?

Application Activities: For Learning and Your Portfolio

1. Interview a general education teacher and ask what types of prereferral assessment procedures and intervention strategies are used in his or her school.
2. (*Portfolio Possibility*) Perform an error analysis on the following math problems from two students. Based on the results what would you do instructionally?

$$\begin{array}{r} 48 \\ -29 \\ \hline 21 \end{array} \qquad \begin{array}{r} 68 \\ +31 \\ \hline 37 \end{array}$$

3. Contact your local school district to find out what specific individually administered intelligence tests and achievement tests are recommended for eligibility determination.

4. (*Portfolio Possibility*) Make an annotated bibliography of five articles about problems in assessing culturally or linguistically diverse students. Are there any general themes?
5. Interview several experienced special education teachers to find out if they think it was a good idea or a bad idea to eliminate short-term objectives and benchmarks in the IEPs of most students with disabilities. What advantages are there? Disadvantages?
6. (*Portfolio Possibility*) Develop a position statement that supports the concept of the continuum of services model. Then write a position statement supporting full inclusion. Assume that these will be presented to a group of parents of students with severe disabilities.

SUMMARY

School, Family, and Community Collaboration

CHAPTER OUTLINE

INTRODUCING JOHN

John is an 8-year-old second grader recently identified as having an intellectual disability. More specifically, John's reading and written expression abilities have been assessed at a beginning first-grade level. He is able to recognize the alphabet and some common sight words (for example, his name, *boys*, *girls*), but has difficulty applying phonetic skills to unknown words. Because his reading is not fluent, he also has difficulty remembering important parts of passages such as who, what, when, and where, even when he receives reading assistance from one of his teachers. His intellectual level, as measured by an individual intelligence test, is significantly below average (IQ of 65). John's mathematics achievement is also below average, even when the tasks involve computation only. The introduction of word problems has created significant difficulties for him. Socially, John fits in well with his peers and family. He presents no behavioral issues and is generally well liked by the other students in school and in his neighborhood.

John's initial IEP team, consisting of his parents, a general education teacher, a special education teacher, a speech and language pathologist, the school psychologist, and the principal, determined that his educational placement would continue to be in his general education second-grade class. The team also decided that John should receive instruction from a special education teacher, Mr. Doss, who is already co-teaching and collaborating with John's general education teacher, Ms. Waring. He will also receive services from a speech and language pathologist, Ms. Everett, who will consult with both teachers and John's family concerning development of his language skills. Because John has no behavioral issues, the school psychologist's role is limited to assessment for eligibility. Until there is a reevaluation, the school psychologist is not likely to be involved with John. The principal, Ms. Avery, will ensure that John's teachers have time to co-plan their instruction. Ms. Avery will also ensure there is time for Ms. Everett ▶

to consult with John's teachers and his parents. Finally, Ms. Avery has established a regular bimonthly meeting for all team members to coordinate their instruction and assessment of John's progress.

John's parents, while cooperative, are still somewhat in shock over John's identification for special education and related services, and are unsure of what they can or should be doing. They would like for the teachers and the speech and language pathologist to help them better understand how to assist John with homework and other academics he can practice at home. ■

After John was identified with an intellectual disability, John's parents, several educators, and specialists met to determine the best education program for him. Two co-teachers—his general education teacher and a special education teacher—then implemented this plan with help from a speech and language pathologist, and the support of the principal. John's parents are also involved in helping John at home when they can.

Each student's education program will differ based on the individual's needs. What will not differ is the need for collaboration. In John's case, his parents, a general education teacher, a special education teacher, a speech and language pathologist, a school psychologist, and the principal created his IEP. In other cases, a different combination of teachers and specialists may be involved. A student with a hearing loss might receive support from an audiologist. A student with vision loss might receive services from an orientation and mobility teacher. Older students, who are transitioning from school, might work with vocational rehabilitation personnel, a transition specialist, and other adult services providers attending and participating in the IEP meeting and subsequent transition programming.

Whether you plan to be a general or special education teacher, being able to effectively collaborate is an important skill in supporting and teaching your students with special needs. The general education teacher, who may be the student's primary teacher, needs to work closely with a special education teacher and the student's family, in addition to, in some cases, specialists and community agencies, to create and present an effective curriculum and learning experience. For special education teachers, whether teaching students in a resource classroom, working in a general education classroom as a co-teacher, or spending individual time with students in and out of their classrooms, being able to collaborate with general education teachers and related services personnel is necessary to provide all of the support needed by the student.

With emergence of the concept of inclusion and the shift away from segregation and toward full integration of students in school and society, a majority of students with special needs are educated in the general education classroom (U.S. Department of Education, 2003b). With this shift, the need for collaboration has also emerged as a necessary and empowering process for making inclusion successful. Collaboration is critical in planning and programming for students with disabilities because federal law requires collaboration in IEP development and implementation. Most teachers today rely on collaborative efforts to plan and implement instruction through teaming. Collaboration facilitates and supports inclusion, is important in a changing and increasingly complex society, and is a critical component of special education in today's multicultural context (Duke, 2004). In this chapter, we discuss the many facets of collaboration as they affect students, families, teachers, and other professionals involved in the education and treatment of students with disabilities.

What Is Collaboration?

Friend and Cook (2000) defined **collaboration** as "a style for direct interaction between at least two coequal parties voluntarily engaged in shared decision making as they work toward a common goal" (p. 6). Welch (2000) described collaboration as

collaboration Process in which two or more equal parties work toward a common goal.

"a dynamic framework for efforts that endorse interdependence and parity during interactive exchange of resources between at least two partners who work together in a decision-making process that is influenced by cultural and systemic factors to achieve common goals" (p. 74). From these definitions, we can identify several key components of collaboration:

- two or more parties work together
- parties collaborate as equal partners
- participation is voluntary
- responsibility is shared among the parties
- parties work toward a common goal
- process is influenced by factors (such as school climate and culture) other than the parties themselves
- can be either a planned, formal process or a spontaneous, informal process
- resources are shared among parties
- leads to community building

In addition to these components, the uneven distribution of work is, at times, also a component of collaboration. Keeping these components in mind, what collaboration looks like will vary based on the student's needs and the individuals involved. For example, a high school student with a learning disability could be involved exclusively in general education classes during the day. His teachers will need to collaborate with each other to ensure they are all familiar with the accommodations the student needs and how to implement the student's accommodations. This team of teachers would meet on a regular basis, either weekly or monthly, to revisit how this student and other students are progressing in their academic programs.

Another example would be a general and special education teacher co-teaching a science class. The general education teacher would take primary responsibility for planning the curriculum, as she is the expert in that content area, but both teachers would plan and deliver the instruction. The general education teacher could focus on the science content, and the special education teacher could focus on teaching students how to take notes, outline, develop study skills, and how to use specific reading strategies like scanning for answers to questions at the beginning of the chapter and learning boldface terms. Each teacher would occasionally assume the other's role so that each is aware of the challenges and issues the other must overcome. The teachers would communicate daily to reflect on and improve their co-teaching efforts. They would have more extensive weekly meetings to plan for the next week's lessons.

A third example would be a student with more severe disabilities who spends a majority of his day with his special education teacher and a paraprofessional. The special education teacher also consults and collaborates with a sixth-grade general education teacher, the physical education teacher, and the music teacher to ensure the student is included as often as is appropriate. A physical therapist works with the student twice a week. She collaborates primarily with the special and physical education teachers who, in turn, share with the others strategies to enhance the student's physical participation in activities. The special education teacher and the paraprofessional communicate daily on how to meet the student's needs, what instructional strategies are working, and when progress is or is not being made. The special education teacher and paraprofessional communicate informally with the other teachers on a daily basis. At least quarterly, the team meets to review progress and communicate to the parents how the student is doing.

In all three examples, the school administrator ensures that all parties involved have adequate time and resources to fulfill their collaborative roles. The administrator, as a school leader, should promote the sense of community that establishes the importance of collaboration, the parity among team members, and the shared responsibility for decision making and outcomes. All parties are working toward a common goal of providing an individualized and appropriate education for the student.

A Brief History of Collaboration

Collaboration has always been present in schools, but it has emerged over the past 25 years as a more specific and well-defined process used to ensure an appropriate education for students with and without disabilities. Collaboration in the schools in the 21st century is, at least in part, a reflection of the theme of collaboration occurring in major disciplines and endeavors in business, social services, and technology, among others (Friend, 2002). Friend noted that "The importance of collaboration for schools is also a pragmatic matter: In this day and age there is simply too much for any one educator to know in order to effectively meet the needs of all his or her students" (p. 224).

Historically, special education teachers and related services personnel tended to use more "pull-out" services in which students with mild disabilities went to a resource room or special class to receive individualized or small group instruction for a portion of their school day (Pugach & Johnson, 1995). For students with more moderate to severe disabilities, educational services were often delivered in self-contained classes or special schools. During the 1970s, as the special education profession developed, consultation with general education teachers emerged as a means by which special education teachers could work with general education teachers in assisting students in the general education classroom. However, one problem with this model of service delivery was the tendency for the special educator or related services professional to prescribe interventions for the general educator to implement. For example, a special education teacher might have told a general education teacher that she needed to modify tests for a student by reducing the number of items

Teachers may communicate and meet informally or formally to ensure their collaborative efforts are successful.

and types of items. However, the general education teacher may have been left largely on her own to accomplish this task. This led at times to a one-sided, hierarchical approach to collaboration wherein the general education teacher was not on a level of parity with special education personnel (Pugach & Johnson, 1995).

Eventually, the collaborative consultation model evolved. In this model, general and special education teachers, and other professionals, were perceived to be equal partners working together to plan and implement programs for students. Additionally, models of collaborative teams were better defined. These teams involved groups of teachers (for example, by grade level or content area taught) working together to plan, teach, and solve problems occurring in one another's classrooms (Pugach & Johnson, 1995).

Future teachers should recognize that collaboration is not a one-dimensional process, but occurs along a continuum. In some cases, experts may still provide prescriptive interventions for students, but in most cases, school personnel and professionals work together and with families to find solutions to problems and to engage in learning that prepares students for life in an inclusive society (Pugach & Johnson, 1995). Collaboration is the process by which the goals of schools, including building community, responding to pressures from society, staff development, and creating positive and supportive environments for learning, are achieved (Friend, 2002).

Key Concepts of Collaboration

Relevant CEC Standard
▶ Models and strategies of consultation and collaboration (CC10K1)

Beyond the definition of collaboration are several key concepts that ultimately determine its success. The key concepts of collaboration are volunteering, sharing resources,

Teachers involved in collaboration should recognize the need for their partnership and that responsibility for collaboration must be shared.

sharing responsibility, sharing decision making, achieving common goals, community building, parity, recognizing that roles can involve different levels of work, planning a formal process, and collaborating spontaneously and informally (Friend & Cook, 2000). Each of these contributes to the success, or failure, of a collaborative effort.

Volunteering

Individuals, whether they are teachers, other professionals, community members, family members, or others concerned with the provision of educational services, should come to the process because they want to contribute their knowledge and skills to the issues being addressed. Friend and Cook (2000) noted that it is not possible to legislate or force individuals to interact in a particular manner. Some people may be unwilling to work with others and, therefore, will not be interested in collaboration. However, even in the absence of a mandate, people in schools, families, and the community may still wish to work together. It should be recognized that collaboration may be part of a job description for some, but for others it is not and to be involved means volunteering. Collaboration should be encouraged but never forced on the individual or a group in the absence of a job requirement (McIntrye & O'Hair, 1996).

Sharing Resources

Resources can be scarce in schools, families, and communities. Time, financial resources, and materials are all valuable assets to individuals and schools. Welch (2000) pointed out that those involved in collaboration must be willing to give others a "slice" of their resource pie in order to reach a common goal. For example, a teacher may need to give some of her time to meet with parents after school, and parents may need to give some of their free time to attend.

Sharing Responsibility

Sharing responsibility is an important part of collaboration for at least two reasons. First, sharing responsibility verifies that each party assumes a stake by working toward the goals of the process. Two teachers, who are each planning and delivering instruction to a class of students, must each share responsibility for the outcome as each will be affected if the instruction succeeds or does not. Second, sharing responsibility also means each party is willing to be held accountable for the effort, good or bad (Friend & Cook, 2000). These same two teachers should not point fingers blaming the other if the instruction is not successful; rather, they assume joint responsibility and together plan changes to the instructional format to be more successful. Accountability is a watchword in today's schools, and shared accountability is needed for successful collaboration.

Sharing Decision Making

To share responsibility, each party must be involved in and be able to contribute to the decisions made in the process. Although complete agreement with each decision is not necessary, it is important that each party accept any group decision, be willing to compromise as needed, and abide by decisions arrived at through a fair and collaborative effort. Friend (2002) pointed out that collaboration is "not about working with like-minded people. Collaboration is about trust and respect. It's about working together to create better outcomes" (p. 226).

Achieving Common Goals

Duke (2004) emphasized that the agendas of general and special education teachers can differ, creating a barrier to collaboration. General education teachers may be concerned with teaching the material to be covered to improve the overall class's performance on a yearly standards-based assessment. The special education teacher may be less concerned with this goal and more concerned with the progress of specific students with disabilities in the class. However, general and special education teachers do often work together on teams, presumably to achieve the overall goals of successful progress for all students. Beginning with commonly agreed-upon goals and then proceeding to negotiate more specific goals for a collaborative effort is one means by which professionals can begin the process of identifying and achieving common goals.

Community Building

Establishing and maintaining professional, collaborative relationships can be a difficult task (Niles & Marcellino, 2004). If trust and respect are present, these are reinforcing to most professionals and therefore encouraging to the collaborative process, even when it is difficult. Also, professional experience and growth can be outcomes of collaboration that reinforce participation and strengthen each party involved (Westling & Fox, 2004).

Parity

Parity suggests that in each collaborative situation, each person is equally valued as a contributor to the effort. It is also important to recognize that parity in a collaborative situation does not necessarily mean parity exists in all situations (Friend & Cook, 2000). For example, a paraprofessional who works with a student in an inclusive general education classroom may have excellent ideas concerning how to better accommodate the student. The student's special education teacher would likely collaborate with this paraprofessional along with the general education teacher concerning the student's successful inclusion. Later in the same day, the special education teacher has to provide feedback to the paraprofessional concerning tardiness in arriving at school. In the first situation, there is parity as each contributes equally to the programming ideas, whereas in the second situation there is not parity.

Differing Levels of Work

In collaborative work, not all parties necessarily share equally in the actual tasks involved in accomplishing the agreed-upon goals. For example, principals and other administrators often participate in IEP team meetings, sharing ideas, responsibility, and accountability for the outcomes. However, they are less likely to be involved in the daily activities necessary to make the effort a successful one. Rather, the principal provides the support necessary to make those activities happen. Each party is engaged in the achievement of the common goals, but each is not necessarily equally involved in carrying out the work.

In some cases, one party may be the only one capable of accomplishing a task. For example, if an IEP team decided a student needed to be assessed with an individual intelligence test, only a team member who was trained and licensed to give such a test could do so. However, the more the work can be divided equally, the less potential there is for conflict or resentment regarding how the goals are accomplished.

Planning a Formal Process and Collaborating Informally and Spontaneously

Collaboration is typically conceived as a planned, thoughtful, and formalized process in which the goals are identified and the roles of parties are determined in how best to accomplish the goals (Friend & Cook, 2000). Meetings are scheduled at mutually agreeable times, and negotiations among parties concerning the various aspects of the collaboration may be ongoing. Still, it is important to recognize that collaboration can be informal and spontaneous, especially when formal structures to encourage it are not in place. Teachers may collaborate among themselves, in the hall, in the teachers' lounge, or after school in each other's classrooms. Teachers may collaborate with parents through home–school communication or through informal meetings when students are being picked up or dropped off at school. Formal structures are more likely to establish and maintain collaboration, but informal collaboration can solve many issues and provide a growing sense of community through trust and respect.

Each of these key concepts, while important for successful collaboration, also serves to illustrate some of the issues that can arise that discourage or thwart collaboration. There are many barriers to collaboration, but they can be avoided or eliminated.

Barriers to Collaboration

Along with the key concepts for collaboration, future teachers should understand the potential barriers to collaboration. These barriers may not be evident in every collaborative effort, but they are likely to be encountered at some point in one's teaching career. Being aware of their existence and knowing that others have found ways to overcome these barriers can help teachers remain positive and focused on the goals to be achieved. Welch (2000) outlined several barriers to collaboration including conceptual barriers, pragmatic barriers, attitudinal barriers, and professional barriers.

Conceptual Barriers

Conceptual barriers can emerge when the collaboration in some way conflicts with the existing school culture or the "way things are done." For example, this type of barrier may emerge based on roles people play and typical expectations (Welch, 2000). Teachers develop and grow into their roles in their schools. A special education teacher may be very comfortable in her resource room, serving students with disabilities throughout the day, and collaborating through occasional consultation with general education teachers. This same special educator could be uncomfortable with assuming a new role that requires greater collaboration through co-teaching and serving her students directly in their general education classes rather than in her present resource room. Niles and Marcellino (2004) pointed out that developing new skill sets and personal capabilities takes time and that collaboration skills emerge and improve over time.

Pragmatic Barriers

Pragmatic, or logistical, barriers are sometimes considered the most significant in collaboration. Examples of these factors include scheduling, large caseloads, and competing responsibilities (Welch, 2000). For example, some teachers are willing to work extra hours after school to collaboratively plan when no time is provided during the school day or week. Other teachers may not be willing to do so. Some related services personnel, such as a speech and language pathologist, may serve a large number of students in different schools. This professional may find her caseload, the travel time, and the fact she serves three different schools as a major barrier to attending meetings for planning and programming that are not mandatory.

Many of these barriers can be addressed by the school and district administration. In a review of the literature concerning the roles of principals in supporting special education, DiPaola and Walther-Thomas (2003) found that building-level support from the principal and general education colleagues was crucial in valuing and supporting special education teachers. This support should be evident in the school culture. They summarized that

> effective leaders are committed to the success of all students and collaborate with others to achieve this aim. . . . Skillful principals invest the time necessary to devise policies and procedures that facilitate classroom support (e.g., specific human and material resources, relevant information, role flexibility, shared leadership opportunities, decision-making power) . . . effective principals foster collaboration and classroom communication by ensuring classroom teachers and specialists have regularly scheduled common planning time. (pp. 9–10)

Attitudinal Barriers

It is not unusual for teachers and administrators to express anxiety over working collaboratively. In the United States, adults, including teachers, are often socialized to seek individual achievement and therefore may be cautious about team or joint ventures and projects (Niles & Marcellino, 2004). Welch (2000) noted that as educators develop a more ecological perspective, looking at the interconnectedness of the various participants in a school setting, the need to collaborate, and what resources are available to make collaboration effective, becomes more evident.

Professional Barriers

A final barrier to collaboration is concerned with professionals themselves. Because future and current teachers may have varying experiences, have been trained differently, and have been introduced to different philosophies, it is natural that there may be disproportionate skills in, and experience with, collaboration. It is important that educators share and be willing to accept the expertise of one another. It is also critical that each participant understands that collaboration does not necessarily equate to congeniality but that it should equate to trust and respect (Welch, 2000).

Although barriers do exist, collaboration occurs in one form or another in most schools. It may be informal or spontaneous, but often it is a formalized, structured endeavor. In these cases, the formal endeavors frequently take the form of teamwork.

Particularly for inclusive education, teams mandated by law must be in place to serve students with disabilities. In other instances, the teams may serve specific functions particular to a school or district. These could be schoolwide discipline teams, grade-level teams, curriculum teams, or any number of other teams devoted to a particular function or need.

Role of Teams in Collaboration

Several types of teams are required as a part of the special education process, including prereferral intervention (or child study) teams, multidisciplinary evaluation teams, and IEP teams, as discussed in Chapter 2. Each of these teams, by necessity, requires a collaborative effort that is integral to the successful planning and implementation of inclusive educational programs.

Teams, like the collaborative process itself, have issues related to their effectiveness. Variables that promote team effectiveness include clearly stated goals, team cohesion built on trust and respect, good team communication, clearly defined roles and responsibilities, flexibility in team leadership responsibilities, and flexibility in setting schedules and meeting agendas (Fleming & Monda-Amaya, 2001). However, it is most important for future teachers to be prepared to respond to any of the potential barriers that affect collaboration and, in turn, effective teaming.

Ryndak and Pullen (2003) noted several important components of collaborative teams. As you can see, these are quite similar to the key concepts for effective collaboration.

- Team purpose is linked clearly to and defined by the needs of the students.
- Team accomplishments, or the failure to accomplish goals, are accepted by the team as a whole.
- Expanded role release means team members share expertise and skills so that other team members learn from one another and can carry out instruction or services that might be traditionally provided by other team members.
- Services are provided in natural settings including the student's general education classroom, home, and community, as needed.
- Equal partnership among team members requires that all members reflect the belief that their expertise should be viewed in relation to its relevance to the student's overall functioning.

Special education teachers have expertise in individual interventions, but the general education teacher may have the most in-depth understanding of a student's overall level of performance when that student is included in the general education classroom (Ryndak & Pullen, 2003). Parents know the most about their child at home and in the community. Each member's knowledge of the student, and the student's self-knowledge, allows that member to contribute to the team's efforts and to bring an equally valuable viewpoint (Ryndak & Pullen, 2003).

A lack of training about teaming and a lack of attention and value placed on team members' perceived needs are issues that can result in teachers not being invested in the teaming process (Malone, Gallagher, & Long, 2001). Conversely, good time management, positive and strong communication, willingness to work together, organization of team activities, and training in and effective use of good teaming strategies are factors that result in a positive collaborative teaming experience (Malone et al., 2001).

JOHN REVISITED What components of collaborative teams could be vital in helping John's parents with their concerns about his education?

Because collaboration is so common in schools today, future teachers need to have a firm understanding of what it means to collaborate with others. Collaboration can lead to enriching and empowering relationships and roles, successful outcomes beyond what any individual could ever accomplish, and growth in professional and interpersonal skills and communication.

1. What are the key elements of collaboration?
2. Historically, when and why did collaboration emerge as a powerful and necessary process for effective programming for students with disabilities?
3. What are the key components of collaboration?
4. What are possible barriers to collaboration?
5. What are some characteristics of effective teams?

What Are Best Practices for Collaboration between Schools and Families?

IDEA 04 stresses the importance of involving the student and his or her family in the educational process. Federal regulations include provisions for state and local education agencies to provide Parent Training and Information Centers and Community Parent Resource Centers. These centers offer services to parents and families in assisting their student with a disability and in working with state and local education agencies (for example, in IEP conferences or in understanding their legal rights and responsibilities under IDEA 04). Such centers might assist families in navigating through due process and mediation procedures if there is a dispute with a school agency about the appropriateness of the education of their student (*Federal Register*, 34CFR300.506(b)(t)(i)). However, special education teachers might acknowledge that family involvement is sometimes limited, sometimes virtually nonexistent, and, in the worst cases, sometimes discouraged, even if done so indirectly. There are many possible reasons for limited or no involvement. Sometimes family members may be so concerned with employment, other children, and simply surviving day to day that involvement in the IEP process may seem a lower priority. Other times, students and families may be intimidated by the IEP process and simply allow the professional members of the team to make decisions and plan programs, fearing they lack the expertise to be meaningful participants. Sometimes school personnel may use inaccessible language, such as educational jargon, disregard the concerns of parents, and adopt an attitude that they know what is best for a student in all circumstances. All these instances may lead to little or no meaningful collaboration between schools and families.

Future teachers should be aware of processes that encourage successful collaboration with families. Often, formal collaboration occurs during the IEP process, which is the primary focus in this section of the chapter. The collaborative efforts can focus on involving the student and/or family members more, resolving conflicts, and ensuring that cultural/ethnic values and beliefs are recognized and respected. Working with students and their families is one of the more important aspects of the teaching profession.

Relevant CEC Standards

▶ Roles of individuals with exceptional learning needs, families, and school and community personnel in planning of an individualized program (CC10K2)

▶ Concerns of families of individuals with exceptional learning needs and strategies to help address these concerns (CC10K3)

Increasing Student Involvement

The actual numbers of students with disabilities who are directly involved in developing their own IEPs is unknown. However, a recent study indicated that among students 14 years or older, 70% attended their IEP meetings (Martin, Marshall, & Sale, 2004). Survey results from 393 IEP team meetings and more than 1,600 participants indicated that students felt less competent as participants compared to parents, teachers, administrators, and related services personnel. These results suggest that there is a need to improve student involvement in the IEP process (Martin et al., 2004).

Some ways in which student participation can be enhanced include the following:

1. Ensuring parents know their child is invited to attend and participate
2. Providing students with background knowledge concerning the IEP and the process, as well as training in skills for participating (for example, asking questions, expressing one's thoughts) as appropriate to their age

3. Focusing on student strengths, gifts, and talents rather than only on skill or knowledge deficits
4. Increasing student responsibility for developing and implementing their plans
5. Involving peers and community members who are supportive of the student (Clark, 2000; Keyes & Owens-Johnson, 2003)

One specific method of involving students is **person-centered planning (PCP)** (further discussed in Chapter 5). Using this approach, professionals can better focus on the student and thereby encourage student participation, even if indirectly. PCP is used as means to help students achieve goals and desires while avoiding their fears (Callicott, 2003; Forest & Pearpoint, 1992). Person-centered planning places the values and desired outcomes of the student and his or her family at the center of the collaborative efforts. Professionals do not dictate what the outcomes should be. Professionals don't relinquish their responsibility to contribute to the process, but they do recognize that, ultimately, the student and the family will bear the effects of the collaborative effort more prominently than professionals. PCP places the student and family, not professionals, at the center of team planning.

The Making Action Plans (MAPs) method is one way for developing PCPs (Forest & Lusthaus, 1990; Keyes & Owens-Johnson, 2003; Vandercook, York, & Forest, 1989). In this method, team members contribute to the planning process as equal team members, but the student's and family's desired outcomes are a central focus of the process. Examples of steps/questions involved in MAPs and PCP are presented in Table 3.1. As you can see, the steps/questions guide team members as they meet to discuss future programming and how to achieve the most appropriate education.

Increasing Family Involvement

Family members are important in the collaboration necessary to develop effective programming for students. It is difficult to separate participation of families and that of their child in collaborative efforts. In fact, it has been suggested that families can assist the participation of their child by explaining the IEP process, teaching the child IEP terminology and the different roles participants play, and helping their child with the skills to actively participate (Martin et al., 2004). However, some family members may be less confident in their abilities to perform these and other collaborative functions. Parents

TABLE 3.1	Steps/Questions Used in Making Action Plans (MAPs) and Person-Centered Planning

❑ Invite parents, students, and other identified nonschool personnel who can contribute meaningfully (for example, peers, relatives, community members) in addition to professionals.

❑ Introduce all participants.

❑ Begin with probing questions such as:
  ❑ What is the student's history? Who is the student?
  ❑ What are the student's dreams and nightmares?
  ❑ What are the student's strengths, gifts, and talents?
  ❑ What does the student need right now?
  ❑ What would an ideal day look like that stresses achieving the dreams and avoiding the nightmares?
  ❑ Where would be the ideal settings?
  ❑ What goals and objectives can be included in the IEP that will assist in creating the ideal day in the ideal settings?
  ❑ Who will be responsible for each goal and objective?
  ❑ How and when will the goals and objectives be evaluated?
  ❑ How does each participant feel about the IEP and the MAPs process?

Source: Keyes, M. W., & Owens-Johnson, L. (2003). Developing person-centered IEPs. *Intervention in School and Clinic, 38,* 145–152.

Families should be encouraged to become meaningful and full participants in planning their student's education.

and family members may participate in different ways and at different levels. Fiedler, Simpson, and Clark (2007) identified four levels of parent and family participation. Each level builds on the skills and knowledge acquired in previous levels of involvement.

1. *Awareness, attendance, and basic participation.* At this level, family members receive information and become familiar with school and community programs and with their student's educational programs and services; they have opportunities to receive and provide information about their student's progress.
2. *Ongoing communication, information sharing, and basic program involvement.* At this level, family members and professionals are engaged in a free-flowing exchange of information and ideas (for example, through a daily log/journal sent between home and school).
3. *Advocacy and collaborative program involvement.* At this level, family members are directly involved in goal identification, analyses of strategies used, actual program implementation, and analyses of progress. Parents become advocates for their children.
4. *Collaboration and partnership participation.* At this level, family members have learned the knowledge and skills (for example, through in-service training provided by the school professionals) and possess the motivation to provide independent and joint programming with school personnel. Family members may also assume greater advocacy roles that involve other parents and children, conduct parent and student support groups, serve on district or school advisory boards, and provide training to school personnel and other families in specific skills and strategies to be used with other students (Fiedler et al., 2007).

The Classroom Suggestions feature on the next page presents a number of strategies identified by Taylor (2004) that can promote parent and family involvement in schools.

Conversely, parent and family involvement can be discouraged by not listening or involving family members in decision making, by not requiring important personnel to attend meetings, by presenting irrelevant information and/or only information that paints the student in a more negative light, by using too much technical language or educational jargon, and by not inviting parents to be involved even if they decline at times (Taylor, 2004).

Seligman (2000) identified three basic rules for effective communication between teachers and families. First, teachers should assume a relaxed and natural posture, leaning forward and remaining in a comfortable position, which conveys a willingness

JOHN REVISITED What strategies could John's teachers use to encourage participation of John's parents in the educational process?

Source: Taylor, G. R. (2004). *Parenting skills & collaborative services for students with disabilities.* Lanham, MD: ScarecrowEducation.

to listen and a sense of well-being. Second, teachers should make eye contact and maintain varying eye contact at an appropriate level. Staring for long periods of time can be uncomfortable to the speaker. Varying eye contact shows interest and that the teacher is listening. Third, the teacher should make comments to family members that follow from what the family members have been saying. Teachers can show they are listening, encourage open discussion, and ensure they are understanding what family members are expressing by using comments and questions directly related to what the teacher has heard from the family.

Increasing Sibling Involvement

Siblings of students with disabilities can be affected in both positive ways, such as learning advocacy and empathy skills, and in negative ways, such as hearing negative comments about their sibling and feeling that the sibling with a disability receives more attention and help (Fiedler et al., 2007). Fiedler et al. noted that siblings can be supported by providing them with information about their sibling's disability, providing opportunities to observe and talk with school personnel about their sibling, providing support from school and community personnel (for example, counseling), creating opportunities to interact with others who have siblings with a disability, and providing ways to participate in educational decision making such as in MAPs or IEP meetings.

Conflict Management

Conflict may arise from parental feelings of anger that emerge from feeling fear, hurt, frustration, or a sense of injustice (Martin, 2005). Parents may be afraid of the future or the implications of a diagnosis of disability. They may be hurt by comments about their child that are negative. They may be frustrated when their concerns or wishes appear to go unheard or unheeded. Parents may feel a sense of injustice if they are "blamed" for the problems of their child: for example, if they hear "He doesn't turn in homework because no one supports him at home." Martin suggested that good communication skills are critical in avoiding and resolving conflicts when they arise with parents. Parents and family members are integral to collaboration because most students with disabilities spend more time at home and in the community with their families than they do at school. The impact of the learning that occurs during these hours is critical to the adaptation and success of the student as she or he moves forward in life and into adulthood (Martin, 2005).

With any collaborative effort, conflicts are a possibility, and when they do arise, they should be managed in a fair and thoughtful manner. This is especially true when the conflict involves school personnel and the student and family. IDEA 04 includes provisions for mediation of issues and other due process procedures (see Chapter 2). Teachers and administrators can and should take measures to resolve conflicts before they become legal matters.

Increasing Involvement of Diverse Families

Teachers should find working with diverse families interesting and rewarding. However, if the teachers and other school personnel have different cultural/linguistic backgrounds from that of family members, communication among team members may present challenges. Effective communication techniques open the door to collaboration and positive relationships (Friend & Cook, 2000). Callicott (2003) provided these suggestions for teachers working with culturally or linguistically diverse families:

Relevant CEC Standard

▶ Culturally responsive factors that promote effective communication and collaboration with individuals with exceptional learning needs, families, school personnel, and community members (CC10K4)

- Use culturally responsive feedback and methods of communication. Some families would consider it insulting to launch into a conversation about their child without first having a more social conversation that explained the history, background, and dreams of the family.
- Show appreciation for and include cultural diversity in the curriculum and school activities, as well as during meetings with the family. Demonstrating they belong to the school can be very helpful in building collaborative relationships.
- Ensure that policies, procedures, and activities are in place to reduce the likelihood of prejudice. For example, including advocates in IEP meetings who are aware of and sensitive to a cultural/ethnic group can be helpful when none of the teachers are reasonably familiar with the family's background, language, and culture.

Meyer, Bevan-Brown, Harry, and Sapon-Shevin (2004) also pointed out that teachers and professionals involved in the special education process are more likely to be white and from a middle-class background whereas many students receiving special education and related services may be from different cultural backgrounds. Teachers need to be aware of their own cross-cultural competence. Meyer et al. stressed some ways teachers can improve delivery of special education to diverse students and families:

- Recognize that all students and families have multiple facets to their lives and personalities. One facet is defined by race and ethnicity but others are defined by their experiences.
- Support students based on their individual identities and not due to a single dimension such as race or ethnicity.
- Incorporate learning about other races and ethnic groups and families in the classroom activities.
- Model for peers without disabilities how to appropriately interact with those students with disabilities, both academically and socially.

Future teachers have many challenges in learning how to establish, build, and maintain collaborative relationships with students and families. The increasing diversity of the population, the laws, the curriculum, and technology make teaching ever more complex as well. Yet at the heart of education remains a critical foundation for learning human relationships. Learning to work with students, families, professionals, and the community is the centerpiece of effective education.

1. What practices can increase student involvement in collaboration?

2. What practices can increase family involvement in collaboration?

3. What practices can increase sibling involvement?

4. What conflicts might emerge between families and school personnel? How can these be handled?

5. What are some strategies that demonstrate respect for diversity when working with families?

What Are Best Practices for Collaboration among School Personnel?

Relevant CEC Standard
▶ Effective management of teaching and learning (CC5K3)

Research supports a number of characteristics and best practices concerning collaboration among school personnel. These characteristics and best practices are associated with types of collaboration between teachers (specifically, co-teaching models and collaborative consultation) and also are found in the roles and contributions of administrators, paraprofessionals, and related services personnel.

Co-teaching

One way teachers typically collaborate in the classroom is through co-teaching. In co-teaching, general and special education teachers collaborate as teams to make accommodations or modifications to assist students with and without disabilities (Fennick, 2001). Co-teaching currently represents a major aspect of the collaborative efforts among teachers working with students with disabilities in inclusive settings. It can be successfully implemented with students with mild to severe disabilities, and with young children as well as with students at the secondary level. Proponents stress that co-teaching takes advantage of the unique knowledge and skills each teacher brings to the classroom (Weiss & Lloyd, 2003). Like collaboration in general, there are important components necessary for a successful co-teaching relationship to occur. Interpersonal communication, agreement on the physical arrangement of the classroom, joint familiarity with the curriculum goals and modifications, agreed-upon instructional planning and presentation, classroom management procedures, and assessment plans all play into effective collaboration (Gately & Gately, 2001). Each of these components can affect the success of co-teaching, regardless of the model used. However, some models would necessarily place greater emphasis on some components and less emphasis on others.

Co-teaching has received increased attention as inclusive models of education have stressed maintaining students with disabilities in the general education classroom and legislation has emphasized access to the general education curriculum. Several models of co-teaching have been proposed, including six models identified by Friend and Cook (2000). In the following sections, we summarize possible emphases and applications of these six models.

One Teach, One Observe

In the one teach, one observe model, one teacher teaches and the other observes during instructional times (Friend & Cook, 2000). The teachers can switch these roles as needed. The observing teacher may be gathering data on the performance or behavior of a particular student. For example, while one teacher instructs the students in social studies and administers a weekly test, the other observes a student with a learning disability to see if she is paying attention, is on task, taking notes, and able to work through the test without assistance. In another situation, the observing co-teacher might be focused more on the other co-teacher. For example, the observing teacher could, on request, observe the instructing co-teacher to gather data on who is being called on to answer questions, how much time is being spent on each learning activity, and whether the instructing co-teacher is providing clear examples of concepts being taught. The one teach, one observe

Co-teaching can involve several different models, but all models depend on the collaboration of the teachers.

model involves less planning, less communication, and less collaboration between the co-teachers than some of the other models (Friend & Cook, 2000).

One Teach, One Drift

The one teach, one drift model also places less emphasis on co-planning, communication, and collaboration than some of the other models. This model is similar to the one teach, one observe model in that one of the co-teachers assumes the greater responsibility for planning and delivering instruction. The drifting co-teacher may move about the classroom to manage student behavior, observe students' work, and provide assistance to students as needed. In this model, co-teachers share the same space and students, but also share more classroom management responsibilities than in the one teach, one observe model. For example, the drifting teacher may be involved in ensuring students are on task, following directions, and completing assignments. There may also be a need on the drifting teacher's part to communicate with the co-teacher concerning the curriculum, instruction, and assessment of students. These first two models may be most comfortable for co-teachers as they embark on the collaborative process. They require less commitment, but still provide opportunities to build trust, respect, and a sense of community (Friend & Cook, 2000).

Station Teaching

The station teaching model involves the co-teachers planning and instructing a portion of the lesson content in stations that the students move through. For example, in a lesson instructing students on addition with carrying, one co-teacher may instruct her students on the use of manipulatives to solve the problem while the other co-teacher instructs her students on how to write down the mathematical computations for the problems. A third station may allow students to engage in a mathematics game that reinforces prior learning. As each co-teacher concludes her portion of the lesson, the groups of students at each station move to the next station so all students complete the activities in each station. In this model, co-teachers must communicate to co-plan the lesson and the instructional content, materials, and strategies each will use. They share the same space and students, are familiar with the curriculum and goals, and must share in classroom management and in determining how students are assessed. This model represents a significant leap in the collaborative process because the co-teachers must truly work together to be successful (Friend & Cook, 2000).

Parallel Teaching

The parallel teaching model involves each co-teacher planning and instructing students on the same material. Each teacher presents information to a smaller heterogeneous group of students in the class. The smaller teacher–student ratio created by two learning groups allows for greater discussion and interaction and closer supervision. Parallel teaching is best used for review of learning rather than initial instruction. For example, each co-teacher could review with her group for an upcoming test, going over key concepts and definitions and reviewing notes. This model requires co-teachers to be comfortable with the content and to plan together what and how the material will be taught (Friend & Cook, 2000).

Alternative Teaching

The alternative teaching model involves each co-teacher planning and instructing the students. In this model, each teaches a separate heterogeneous group of students. While one co-teacher works with a group for a specific purpose, the other co-teacher works with the remainder of the class. For example, one co-teacher might take a group of students who have fallen behind due to absences and re-teach material missed while the remainder of the class works on another activity under the other co-teacher's supervision. As another example, the first co-teacher could take her group and pre-teach material the whole class will be learning in the next lesson or day. When using this model, it is important that one of the groups does not become a homogeneous group of students with disabilities who are regularly pulled aside for remedial instruction, particularly when taught exclusively by a special education teacher. This is important so that the teachers do not create a static, "special education group" in the classroom, discouraging inclusive education. In this model, co-teachers must co-plan the instruction and materials for each group. They should be sharing the same space and the same students over time, both managing the classroom, both familiar with the curriculum and goals, and both sharing how students are assessed (Friend & Cook, 2000).

Team Teaching

In team teaching, co-teachers take equal responsibility for all aspects of the classroom: management, planning, preparing materials, delivering instruction, and assessing student learning. This model is the most collaborative. In team teaching, students may not distinguish between which co-teacher is a special educator and which is a general educator as the co-teachers regularly change roles, each taking the lead or jointly sharing teaching responsibilities (Friend & Cook, 2000). The Classroom Example includes a sample teaching plan for co-teachers using this model.

JOHN REVISITED Given John's current level of performance, what challenges might co-teachers face in including John in the general education classroom? Do you think one model of co-teaching might be preferable over another to address those challenges? If so, which one? If not, why not?

Teachers select the models of co-teaching with which they are comfortable and that are appropriate for their students. Initially, comfort level may be an important consideration. Future teachers should note that the models co-teachers use can change over time, particularly as they increase their knowledge, skills, and comfort level in working with another teacher in the classroom. For example, team teachers could use the other models as the students' needs indicate. Similarly, co-teachers who begin with a less collaborative model may experiment with or move on to more collaborative models over time, occasionally trying a new model while at other times using one with which they are familiar and comfortable (Friend & Cook, 2000).

Role of Administrators in Collaboration

Another set of best practices for collaboration among school personnel involves the contributions of participants who are not teachers. One of these participants is the school administrator. As a member of a collaborative team, a district or building-level administrator may serve in the role of facilitator. The facilitator is perhaps the most

The Plan

Learning Goal: Students will be able to use place values concepts to represent whole numbers and decimals using numerals, words, expanded notation, and physical models (Ohio Content Area Standards: Grade Three Mathematics: Numbers and Number Systems).

Lesson Objective: Students will be able to describe the multiplicative nature of the number system (e.g., 2520 can be represented as $2 \times 1000 + 5 \times 100 + 2 \times 10 + 0 \times 1$).

IEP Objectives (as appropriate): John will be able to apply principles of multiplication to solve computational and word problems with 90% accuracy.

Instructional Grouping: Students will be in one large group for initial instruction (one teach, one assist), followed by students being divided for smaller group instruction (parallel teaching), and finally divided into one smaller homogeneous group and one large homogeneous group (alternative teaching).

Instructional Activities

1. Ms. Waring (general education teacher) will provide direct instruction through modeling of the multiplicative nature of the number system (45, 168, 1355, 9021). Students will be asked to verbally describe the steps used in each problem as they progress through four additional problems (24, 198, 1222, 8706).

2. Mr. Doss (special education teacher) will observe John and two other students (Holly and James) to monitor whether they are able to state the steps.

3. Students will be divided into two prearranged heterogeneous groups. Each teacher will take one group of 10 students and continue to work on problems using guided practice. Students should be able to state the steps of how to solve the problem as well as write the problems on paper. Each teacher will observe and provide corrective feedback to his or her students. Each teacher will note any student having substantial difficulty with the problems.

4. At the end of the parallel teaching, the whole group will be re-formed to review the steps used in the lesson. Ms. Waring will lead the review, and Mr. Doss will assist individual students.

5. Following the review, students identified during parallel teaching as having difficulty will form a small group to receive additional direct instruction from Mr. Doss. The remainder of the students will continue independent practice and review of the lesson and previous learning (multiplication word problems using two- and three-digit numerals) with Ms. Waring.

Assessment

1. The large group in alternative instruction will be formally assessed through written products completed during independent practice: 90% accuracy should be achieved on the 10 problems presented for consideration of mastery. Ms. Waring will record the percent correct for each student.

2. Students in the smaller group in alternative instruction will be assessed through systematic observation using a checklist of each step used in the problems. Mr. Doss will record the step(s) with which each student is struggling, if any, by the end of the lesson.

important member of the collaborative team when it involves multiple members, such as on multidisciplinary evaluation teams and IEP teams. Facilitators are expected to maintain a positive atmosphere and cohesiveness within the team. They also organize group activities, foster a communicative environment, and synthesize the contributions of team members and the outcomes of the collaborative project (Pugach & Johnson, 1995). The ability to resolve conflicts and promote compromise and rapport are other useful skills of the facilitator (Westling & Fox, 2004). The leadership of collaborative teams should ensure a coherent vision for the team, comprehensive planning, adequate resources, sustained implementation efforts over time, continual evaluation, and improvement (Walther-Thomas, Korinek, & McLaughlin, 1999). Administrative support at the district level can facilitate communication within the schools, the system, and the larger community and can evaluate team efforts from a wider perspective than team members who are located in a single school.

To be effective leaders, particularly for co-teaching, Villa, Thousand, and Nevin (2004) suggested that administrators must believe the following:

- All students are capable of learning.
- All students have a right to be educated with their peers in neighborhood schools.
- Responsibility is shared for every child's learning.
- Co-teaching is a strategy for organization and instruction that benefits students and teachers alike.

Administrators are not always well prepared for their critical role in a collaborative general and special education partnership and may need in-service training themselves (DiPaolo & Walther-Thomas, 2003). Teachers must encourage a sense of community, trust, and mutual respect for administrators to be effective in their roles.

Role of Paraprofessionals in Collaboration

Relevant CEC Standard

▶ Roles and responsibilities of the paraeducator related to instruction, intervention, and direct service (CC7K5)

Teachers in inclusive settings often collaborate with paraprofessionals, sometimes referred to as paraeducators or teacher aides. Paraprofessionals typically are hired to provide specific support in the classroom or to a specific student or students. Federal regulations require that state educational agencies establish qualifications for paraprofessionals so that they are properly trained to assist in the delivery of special education and related services. In some situations, a significant portion of a student's instruction may be delivered by a paraprofessional (Giangreco & Broer, 2005). For example, when a paraprofessional is hired to work with a specific student, that paraprofessional will go with that student to all classes and activities, and will provide guidance, assistance, encouragement, and instructional support throughout each school day. Paraprofessionals are significant in the education and delivery of services to students with disabilities. Some of the many roles they may play are included in Table 3.2.

Most paraprofessionals are supervised by special education teachers or related services providers. As a teacher, it is important for you to know that those paraprofessionals

TABLE 3.2	Roles Assumed by Paraprofessionals

A paraprofessional may typically:

- Provide instructional support for small group work

- Give one-to-one instructional assistance

- Modify and adapt materials

- Administer adapted tests

- Implement behavioral intervention plans

- Monitor the school environment, such as in hallways and the cafeteria

- Collaborate with teachers and families

- Collect data for progress monitoring and other purposes

- Provide personal care assistance

- Job coach and train at community worksites

- Translate from English to other languages

Source: SPeNSE Fact Sheet. (2001). *The role of paraprofessionals in special education.* (ERIC Document Reproduction Service No. ED 469 294.)

Classroom Suggestions Suggested Procedures for Training Paraprofessionals

- ❏ Make training convenient for the paraprofessionals.
- ❏ Focus the content of training on those issues that are most relevant to the paraprofessionals.
- ❏ Evaluate paraprofessionals' performance.
- ❏ Identify their roles and responsibilities.
- ❏ Communicate effectively with paraprofessionals.
- ❏ Integrate the paraprofessional into the instructional and school setting.
- ❏ Manage and supervise the activities of the paraprofessional.
- ❏ Involve the paraprofessional in collaboration.

Sources: Warger, C. (2002). Supporting paraeducators: A summary of current practices. ERIC Reproduction Number ED 475 383; Westling, D. L., & Fox, L. (2004). *Teaching students with severe disabilities* (3rd ed.). Upper Saddle River, NJ: Pearson Prentice Hall.

who spend time in collaborative efforts, such as planning, curriculum development, counseling students, and evaluating programs, tend to feel more confident in their own ability to implement special education programs than those who do not. Collaborating in school, district, or community meetings enhances this confidence (SPeNSE Fact Sheet, 2001). Encouraging this collaboration can improve the support students receive.

Some paraprofessionals have reported feeling that they are not valued or trusted, and are underpaid. These factors may inhibit their ability to connect and collaborate within the school setting (Chopra, Sandoval-Lucero, Aragon, Bernal, De Balderas, & Carroll, 2004). Paraprofessionals may need staff development to fulfill their critical functions in schools. They may need training in delivering consistent discipline, in how to encourage students to use study strategies, or how to communicate effectively with a student with limited speech and language skills. Unfortunately, some research suggests they do not always receive the feedback, assistance, and training they might need (Rueda & Monzo, 2002). Possible procedures for training paraprofessionals are listed in the Classroom Suggestions feature above.

Future and current teachers will rely on paraprofessionals. Learning how to interact, supervise, and collaborate with them will be an asset in planning and implementing programs, working with students and their families, making connections to the community, and in building trust and respect among all team participants. Teachers must also have knowledge and skills in working with related services personnel who are involved with IEP teams, as well as in the programming of students with disabilities.

Role of Related Services Personnel in Collaboration

Both special and general education teachers will almost certainly collaborate with related services personnel. Related services are not typically provided by the classroom teacher but are necessary for a student with disabilities to benefit from his or her special education program (see Chapter 1, p. 12). They are necessary for students to receive an appropriate education, particularly as they relate to progress in the general education curriculum (Kochhar, West, & Taymans, 2000). Although IDEA does include a list of related services, the federal regulations assert that the list is not exhaustive and that related services should be identified by the IEP team at no cost to parents. As related services providers, bus drivers, school nurses, physical and occupational therapists, speech and language pathologists, and assistive technology specialists, among others, become integral in designing and supporting an appropriate educational program for many students with disabilities.

Future teachers might, at first, assume that any type of service can be a related service. In fact, many services, such as job coaches at a worksite, family and student counseling, and crisis intervention, can be considered related services for a particular student. Unfortunately, most states do not provide specific criteria for related services (Downing, 2004). Often, the key determinant is whether or not the service is needed in order for the student to benefit from special education and receive an appropriate education. Therefore, it is not always clear what is or is not a related service for any individual student. The related services personnel may themselves conduct evaluations to be shared with IEP team members to determine whether a service is recommended (Richards & Russell, 2003).

In general, teachers need not be concerned as much with what qualifies as a related service as in how to collaborate with these personnel to ensure an appropriate education. IDEA 04 includes language to ensure that such supplementary and related services can be delivered in a general education setting rather than in a pullout one. Therefore, related services should be considered in determining the student's least restrictive environment (Downing, 2004; Richards & Russell, 2003). Many related services personnel serve many or all students in various schools within a district. For example, an orientation and mobility specialist would likely serve a number of students with vision loss in the elementary, middle, and high schools within a school district. This can be a barrier to collaboration as their time and resources are stretched across students and schools (Martin, 2005).

JOHN REVISITED Currently, John receives services from a speech and language pathologist. Based on the case example and the Collaborative Plan for Working with John, what types of services does Ms. Everett provide for John? How can these help John in school?

In some situations, collaboration with related services personnel will primarily occur during an IEP meeting and perhaps through consultation throughout the school year. In other situations, the related services personnel will be involved with the teacher and student during the school day and share with teachers what he or she is doing to help the student. Related services personnel may also be directly involved with students while simultaneously providing consultation and collaboration with teachers and families to ensure everyone is able to address a student's needs throughout the day. The Classroom Example illustrates a team plan for working with John.

Collaboration among school professionals is complex and can involve a wide variety of individuals and service providers. Future and current teachers are most frequently involved in collaborating with one another and with administrators, but they also interact with paraprofessionals and related services personnel. The optimal inclusion of so many specialists in planning, programming, and assessment activities in a collaborative manner requires a team approach. This involves increasing and developing the knowledge and skills of all team members, building trust and respect among team members, meaningfully involving the student and family, and distributing the responsibility of providing an appropriate education across a wider number of individuals.

Related services personnel, like this speech pathologist, are important team members in the collaborative process of providing an appropriate education to students with disabilities.

Check Your Understanding

1. What are the characteristics of and procedures for the six co-teaching models discussed?

2. How can administrators support collaboration in their schools and district?

3. What can teachers do to ensure paraprofessionals are effectively, appropriately, and collaboratively involved in educating students with disabilities?

4. Who are some of the related services personnel a teacher might encounter in schools, and what roles can they play in team collaboration?

IEP Objective: John will speak in complete sentences when relating a story or answering questions requiring more than a one-word response in four of five opportunities over five consecutive assessments.

Team Training: Ms. Everett (speech and language pathologist) will work with the general and special education teacher, along with John's parents, in teaching techniques to encourage John to speak in complete sentences. Mr. Doss and Ms. Waring will each share information and techniques they have discovered that are effective. John's parents will discuss John's communication skills at home and in the community and when he is more likely to use complete sentences.

Team Assessment Plan

General and Special Education Teachers: Ms. Waring, the general education teacher, and Mr. Doss, the special education teacher, will assess John's use of complete sentences once weekly. One of the teachers will ask John five comprehension questions regarding a passage read in a text or trade book and record the number of complete sentences, if any, John uses. They will also record the number of responses that are not complete sentences. Note: "I am not sure." "I don't remember." are acceptable complete sentence responses. John will also be assessed once weekly on his ability to retell a story from a passage or book using complete sentences. Once weekly, after having read a passage, John will answer five comprehension questions and retell a story, and one of his teachers will record his responses.

Speech/Language Pathologist: Ms. Everett will assess John's ability to relate a story (an event from his own life) in complete sentences at least once every two weeks. John must use at least four complete sentences in relating his story with no more than one additional response of an incomplete sentence. Ms. Everett will also monitor John's use of complete sentences in his general education classroom as assessed by Ms. Waring and Mr. Doss.

John's Parents: John's parents will monitor his storytelling in complete sentences. They, individually or together, should record at least once every two weeks whether he is able to relate a story using the same method as Ms. Everett. They will report to Ms. Everett how John is progressing.

Data Compilation: Once every two weeks, Mr. Doss will compile data from all three sources and share the results with John, Ms. Waring, Ms. Everett, and John's parents.

What Are Best Practices for Collaboration between Schools and Communities?

Future teachers should be able to identify the characteristics and best practices associated with collaboration among school personnel and community personnel as these types of collaboration are common in two general types of situations: (1) when students transition from early intervention to preschool to school-aged programs, and (2) when students transition from school to adult life. Community personnel can include early childhood educators, health service professionals, higher education professionals, and other community agency employees such as social services workers, employers, and vocational rehabilitation workers. When we think of a truly successful educational experience for a student with special needs (or any student), we should envision a relatively seamless series of transitions from year to year, teacher to teacher, school to school, and program to program across the student's life span that result in fulfilling and rewarding school and life experiences. To make this happen, collaboration is an essential ongoing process across the individual's life span and involving various teams of people working together to achieve these goals.

**Relevant
CEC Standard**

▶ Relationship of special education to the organization and function of educational agencies (CC1K3)

Best Practices for Collaboration in Early Childhood

Collaborative teams in early childhood programs can involve many different individuals including medical and social service personnel (such as nurses and social workers), related services personnel (such as speech and language pathologists and physical therapists), early childhood program personnel (such as early intervention special

IDEA 04 mandates transition services be delivered to ensure a smooth transition from early intervention into preschool programs.

education teachers), school-aged personnel (such as general and special education teachers), and family members. All team members should be prepared to provide the best and most inclusive program for children. To accomplish this, a number of best practice activities should occur in preparation of the inclusion of a child with disabilities in a preschool program (Horn, Thompson, Palmer, Jenson, & Turbiville, 2004):

- Assess past experiences, past training, and existing needs for learning for team members to be effective in their respective roles.
- Involve participants in delivery of information and teaching skills so that team members are both delivering and receiving knowledge and skills training.
- Involve family members as a part of the team also delivering and receiving information.
- Evaluate the effectiveness of training and revise as necessary (Horn et al., 2004).

To promote a collaborative context, each team member should have a positive attitude toward change, take initiative to work together, be flexible in planning and service delivery so compromise can be achieved as needed, and develop both formal and informal communication strategies to build strong bonds among team members (Horn et al., 2004).

The interagency teams—groups made up of representatives of various organizations that are providing the child with services—involved in service delivery in early childhood programs are particularly important when the needs of the student and family extend beyond the abilities of any one agency (Walther-Thomas et al., 1999). For example, a family may have housing, counseling, nutritional, health care, and educational needs. Many states have adopted a comprehensive team services approach that involves different agency personnel in community-based service provision that enables families to access a wide variety of specific services tailored to the needs of their child (Walther-Thomas et al., 1999). Some communities also have created **full-service schools**. Full-service schools include an array of services for students and families such as before and after school care, recreation, health services, and counseling in a "one-stop" shopping approach to service identification and delivery (Walther-Thomas et al., 1999).

Early intervention and preschool programs form the foundation for school-aged programs and can reduce or eliminate the need for special education and related services by school age. Future teachers should be aware of the characteristics of interagency teams and procedures to facilitate their development and implementation.

full-service schools Schools that include an array of services for students and families such as after and before school care, recreation, health service, and counseling in a "one-stop" shopping approach to service identification and delivery.

Similarly, as students with disabilities transition from school programs to adult living, collaboration among schools and communities is critical for success.

Best Practices for Collaboration for Transition to Adult Living

The transition from school to adult living is a critical period recognized in IDEA 04. IDEA 04 mandates that transition planning begin no later than age 16 (Federal Register, 34CFR300.320(7)(b)), though many schools begin prior to that age (for example, when a student enters high school). Collaboration between school and community during this period in a student's life involves coordinated team efforts to ensure a seamless transition from school support services to adult support services. Adult services provided in the community may include support in obtaining employment, independent living, and participation in community life such as voting or in recreation and leisure programs. They can also be provided in postsecondary educational institutions such as vocational training programs, community colleges, and four-year colleges and universities. The coordination of these efforts often is guided by interagency agreements.

Future teachers may not be directly involved in the transition process if they teach younger students or primarily students without disabilities. Still, it is helpful to understand, at any grade level, what processes should be in place when a student is leaving school. The quality of adult outcomes for students with or without disabilities should have influence on how schools prepare students throughout their school years. Information about a long-term study concerning the transition outcomes for youths with disabilities is presented in An Important Event.

AN IMPORTANT EVENT

2005—The National Longitudinal Transition Study–2

The National Longitudinal Transition Study–2 (NLTS–2) prepared for the Office of Special Education and Rehabilitation Services in the U.S. Department of Education is a significant resource for understanding the characteristics of students with disabilities transitioning from school to adult life (Wagner, Newman, Cameto, & Levine, 2005). The NLTS–2 provides information on the adult outcomes for two cohorts of youths, the first from 1987 and the second from 2003, two years following their transition to adult living. Examples of the information available include school completion rates, household living arrangements, participation in postsecondary education programs, employment outcomes, and how students with different disabilities fared in adult life (Wagner et al., 2005). In general, the study showed improvement in transition between 1987 and 2003.

REFLECTION How might the transition to adult living be affected if students with disabilities and their families were left to their own resources only to determine outcomes in employment, postsecondary education, residential options, and community participation?

Transition Services

Transition services under IDEA are coordinated activities for a student, within an outcome-oriented process, that promote transition from school to adult activities and can include the following:

- employment
- postsecondary education
- vocational training
- continuing and adult education
- adult services
- independent living
- community participation (Palmer, Miles, Schierkolk, & Fallik, 2002)

transition services
Coordinated activities for a student within an outcome-oriented process that promote transition from school to adult life.

For example, students may need to have vocational interests and skills assessed, assistance in obtaining and maintaining a job, help in developing a budget and learning how to maintain a bank account, assistance in selecting and applying to colleges, or encouragement to participate in community recreational and leisure opportunities. The set of coordinated activities should take into account the interests and preferences of the student, including community experiences, employment development and development of other adult living activities, acquisition of daily living skills as needed, and functional vocational evaluation as needed (Palmer et al., 2002). The teacher may be involved in any or all of these activities, or may largely be a consultant to related services personnel who provide such services. In either case, teachers should understand the transition needs of a student and how classroom learning and activities can support those needs.

Planning and Programming

Many possibilities exist in planning and programming for the transition process. Clearly, to make this process successful, a coordinated set of activities will require a coordinated effort by a collaborative team. The collaborative team includes members of the IEP team, but may be expanded to include others such as vocational rehabilitation counselors, vocational evaluators, school counselors, local businesspeople, adult service providers (for example, organizations providing residential living options, employment services, and recreational/leisure opportunities), and family members.

Powers et al. (2005) outlined several ways in which IEP teams did not effectively plan for transitions. Goals were generally described with only minimal detail. Students' interests were not always taken into account, and a substantial number of students (24%) did not sign their own IEPs. General education teachers, transition specialists, and vocational rehabilitation staff were not involved in many planning meetings. Self-determination for students was not a common focus of activities. Students with developmental disabilities tended to be less involved in the IEP process, did not have their interests taken into account, and were placed in jobs or work experiences inconsistent with their wishes more than peers with other disabilities (Powers et al., 2005). Despite limitations in this study, it does illustrate that collaboration between schools, students and their families, and communities can be restricted.

Westling and Fox (2004) suggested some procedures that enable teams to collaborate more effectively for transition planning and programming:

1. Identify personnel who will be on the team.
2. Identify adult service agencies that will provide services and ensure their attendance.
3. Identify skills needed by the student and how they benefit the student.
4. Schedule meetings at convenient times including follow-up meetings to track progress.
5. Discuss with the student and family the options available for education and training as well as for living arrangements and community participation. Ensure the students' and family members' interests and preferences are heard.
6. Identify on the transition plan the services provided by specific agencies prior to and after leaving school, skills to be learned, who is responsible for carrying out specific tasks, a timeline for completing tasks, and a system for monitoring progress.
7. After follow-up meetings have been scheduled, make arrangements for an exit-from-school meeting with all team members and make arrangements to follow up with the student and family within six months of exiting school.

The collaboration efforts of the IEP team also can be promoted through interagency agreements.

TABLE 3.3	Essential Features of Interagency Agreements

- Staff in the various agencies assume responsibility for the development, revision, and ongoing implementation of the agreement. No one agency is solely responsible for this task.

- Directors of all participating agencies are committed to the agreements and their effectiveness.

- Direct service staff have input into the agreement.

- Agency staff have regular opportunities to collaborate on the agreement and to develop relationships.

- Agency staff are open to learning the missions of other agencies and to how each agency can complement the efforts of others.

- Agency representatives are actively involved in strategic planning for overall efforts of the interagency team.

- Determining impacts and outcomes of the plan, in addition to decisions developed from those impacts and outcomes, are data driven.

- Direct service staff have knowledge and understanding of the agreement and its provision.

- Technical assistance is available to direct service staff in implementing the provisions of the agreement.

Source: Crane, K., Gramlich, M., & Peterson, K. (2004). Putting interagency agreements into action. *Issue Brief. Examining Current Challenges in Secondary Education and Transition, 3*(2). Retrieved September 2004 from http://www.ncset.org

Interagency Agreements

An **interagency agreement** is a written agreement that agencies commit to that outlines their shared responsibilities for student learning and the participation of school, community, and family in achieving positive outcomes for students with disabilities (Crane, Gramlich, & Peterson, 2004). Interagency agreements can be at local or state levels and are required under IDEA 04. These formal agreements among schools and other service providers in the collaborative process are overseen by the state educational agency (Federal Register, 34CFR300.154). Schools may, in fact, invite other agency personnel to attend IEP meetings when transition planning and programming will be discussed. Although the contents of agreements may vary from district to district and state to state, Crane et al. (2004) listed essential features of effective interagency agreements, which are included in Table 3.3. Plans are developed as needed to ensure collaboration among agencies and to clearly define roles and responsibilities.

Interagency agreements enable agencies with sometimes competing interests to collaborate and function more effectively (Crane et al., 2004). For example, school districts and agencies wish to hold down costs to the degree appropriate. An interagency agreement might specify that a school district will provide students with vocational assessments that identify their interests, aptitudes, and present skills. In turn, a vocational rehabilitation agency may then provide assistance in obtaining and maintaining employment in an identified area. The school saves by having employment services provided by the vocational rehabilitation agency and, in turn, the vocational rehabilitation agency saves by not having to provide vocational assessment services. The student benefits because the work of each agency is part of a coordinated effort. The shared responsibilities for service provision, costs, monitoring progress, and continued follow-up eases the burden that might be placed on any one agency and provides a safety net such that students are less likely to "fall through the cracks" at the transition from school to adult living.

Future and current teachers should be aware of transition services, how teams can collaborate more effectively, and how interagency agreements help to ensure

interagency agreement A formal written agreement that provides commitment of shared responsibility for student learning and a plan on which the school, community, and family collaborate.

better collaboration. Although many teachers may not be directly involved in this transition process, the effectiveness of their school district is judged, at least to some extent, by its results. Understanding the process and the challenges faced by those involved, including the student and his or her family, helps all teachers to understand the importance of curriculum and instruction from early childhood through exiting school.

In this chapter, we have discussed how collaboration should occur between schools and families, among school personnel, and between schools and community service providers. Teachers are parties in both formal and informal collaboration. They are involved in teams mandated by law and established to meet specific school or district needs, and in teams created informally to support individual students. General and special education teachers frequently must work closely together in an inclusive educational environment to provide access to the general education curriculum for all students. Collaboration is a necessary component of professional life for teachers. Due to its importance, we will continue to address collaboration throughout the text as it pertains to the needs of students with various disabilities and their teachers.

Check Your Understanding

1. What are the general considerations for ensuring collaboration among schools and communities?

2. What are the characteristics of and best practices for effective early childhood program collaboration?

3. What are the characteristics of and best practices for effective transitions from school to adult living?

4. What are interagency agreements, and how do they affect the transition from school to adult living?

Chapter Summary

 Go to the text's Online Learning Center at **www.mhhe.com/taylor1e** to access study resources, Web links, practice quizzes, and extending materials.

What Is Collaboration?

- Collaboration has always been a part of school environments and cultures, but it has only been emphasized as a critical aspect of education for students with disabilities in the last 25 years.
- Collaboration consists of individuals working together toward a common goal. Definitions of collaboration share common elements of voluntariness; sharing resources, responsibility, and decision making; achieving common goals; community building; parity; levels of work; and planned or spontaneous processes.
- Conceptual, pragmatic, attitudinal, and professional barriers to collaboration can exist.
- Several types of collaborative teams may exist in the special education process. Team processes and outcomes are important in the collaborative process.

What Are the Best Practices for Collaboration between Schools and Families?

- Student involvement in IEP planning can be encouraged by ensuring parents know their child is invited to attend, providing students with background knowledge, focus-

ing on strengths rather than deficits only, increasing student responsibility for planning, and involving peers and community members involved in the student's life.

- Person-centered planning and MAPs are methods that focus on the student and encourage greater involvement of the student, peers, and other parties aside from educators in planning and programming.
- Parents can have differing levels of involvement in planning from basic awareness and participation to being fully participating team members. Professionals should respect these different levels while encouraging increased parent involvement.
- Siblings of students with disabilities can be encouraged to participate by receiving information, providing opportunities to observe and talk with school personnel, becoming involved with other siblings of students with disabilities, and directly participating in decision-making meetings.
- Parents and educators can come into conflict. Parents' wishes should not be ignored; they should not be blamed for their child's problems. Educators need to recognize the important role parents play in the education of the student.

SUMMARY

- Culturally diverse families' participation can be encouraged through using culturally responsive methods of communication, showing appreciation for their diversity, and ensuring policies, procedures, and activities reduce the likelihood of prejudice.

What Are the Best Practices for Collaboration among School Personnel?

- Co-teaching can be described using a variety of models including one teach, one observe; one teach, one drift; station teaching; parallel teaching; alternative teaching; and team teaching.
- Administrators may serve as the facilitators of collaboration and as educational leaders. Administrators may need training themselves in developing collaboration skills and encouraging it among teachers.
- Paraprofessionals may provide specific support in a classroom or to a specific student or students. Paraprofessionals need training and supervision, and should not be expected to fulfill the role of a teacher.
- Involving related services personnel in planning and programming is essential to ensure a comprehensive approach to education.

What Are the Best Practices for Collaboration among Schools and Communities?

- Collaboration among service providers in early childhood programs is necessary as personnel from a number of agencies may be involved.
- Full-service schools that provide an array of services such as before and after school care, recreation, health services, and counseling can be one method by which families can gain access to a collaborative approach to service delivery.
- Transition to adult living services requires a coordinated set of activities that include outcomes related to employment, postsecondary education, independent living, and community participation. Coordinating these activities requires a collaborative team approach and should encourage students to develop self-determination skills.
- Interagency collaborative teams, established by interagency agreements, outline the shared responsibilities among educational and community agencies in working with students and families in transition planning and programming.

Reflection Topics

1. What key concepts of collaboration do you think are most important for inclusion to succeed? Why?
2. Why would involving students in their own IEP meetings and other team decisions be important in their development?
3. As a teacher, how would you try to resolve any conflicts that arise with parents of one of your students concerning the most appropriate educational approach to be used?
4. Which model(s) of co-teaching is/are more appealing to you and why?
5. What type of administrative support do you think teachers need to be successful in collaborating with each other and families?
6. Do you believe full-service schools are beneficial for teachers and families as well as for the community? Why or why not?

Application Activities: For Learning and Your Portfolio

1. Interview one or more teachers who co-teach. Determine which model(s) of co-teaching is/are used. Ask each teacher what he or she believes is most important in making co-teaching work.
2. *(Portfolio Possibility)* Place yourself in the role of the general education teacher or special education teacher. Develop a learning objective in a content or specialty area. Develop a lesson plan to teach the objective that includes a model of co-teaching. Collaborate with a peer to accomplish this task, each of you assuming the role of general education teacher or special education teacher. If you have not yet learned lesson planning, find an existing lesson plan (many are available on the Internet) and discuss how it might be modified to meet the needs of John or other students with disabilities.
3. Role-play a situation in which you put yourself in the place of the parents, a student, and teachers involved in a meeting. Assess which behaviors and attitudes tend to encourage collaboration and which tend to discourage collaboration. Possible role-playing topics could be the identification of a child as having a learning disabil-

ity, the need to place a student in a more restrictive setting such as a resource room or self-contained classroom, or the need to plan for the transition of a student from school to adult living.
4. *(Portfolio Possibility)* Develop or participate in a MAP with a student in public school or with a college-aged peer. Evaluate the plan and the process in terms of the outcomes identified and the feelings of the participants.
5. Visit a community agency that serves infants and toddlers with disabilities. Inquire how the agency interacts with other service providers and how the agency plans for transitions of children to preschool programs. Hospitals, child-care centers, and home-based service providers might be agencies that would be involved with infants and toddlers.
6. Visit a community agency that serves adults with disabilities. Inquire how the agency interacts and collaborates with school personnel and family members. Vocational rehabilitation agencies, nonprofit employment agencies, and agencies that provide social services would be possibilities.

SUMMARY

Students with Learning Disabilities

CHAPTER OUTLINE

FOUNDATIONS

What Are the Foundations of Learning Disabilities?

A Brief History of Learning Disabilities
Definitions of Learning Disabilities
Prevalence of Learning Disabilities

What Are the Causes and Characteristics of Learning Disabilities?

Causes of Learning Disabilities
Characteristics of Students with Learning Disabilities

How Are Students with Learning Disabilities Identified?

Response to Intervention
The Use of Standardized Testing

PRACTICE

What and How Do I Teach Students with Learning Disabilities?

Instructional Content
    Types of Content Knowledge
    Areas of Instructional Content
    Transition Planning
Instructional Procedures

What Are Other Instructional Considerations for Teaching Students with Learning Disabilities?

The Instructional Environment
Instructional Technology

What Are Some Considerations for the General Education Teacher?

INTRODUCING JUSTIN

Justin is a 7-year-old boy who is currently in the second grade. His mother reports that she had a difficult pregnancy with Justin, who was born a month prematurely. She also states that Justin was somewhat delayed in language skills and milestones compared to her memory of his older brother's development. For example, Justin's brother said his first word right before his first birthday whereas Justin didn't say his until he was almost 18 months old. Justin received speech therapy for an articulation problem beginning at age 4 that continued through kindergarten. In the first grade he struggled with reading but stayed on grade level with the help of a tutor.

Justin's second-grade teacher, Ms. Phillips, initially noted that Justin was having difficulty with phonics skills and that his handwriting was not legible. She also reported that he is disorganized, often losing or mis-placing his assignments. When Justin does do his work, he loses interest part way through and usually does not finish it. When he stops doing his work, he will often tap his pencil and make mouth noises, distracting the other students.

Justin's school implements the response to intervention (RTI) model schoolwide. Subsequently, early in the school year all second-grade students were given a brief screening. In Ms. Phillips's class, three students, including Justin, were targeted as needing additional instruction. Although this was successful for one student, Suzie, Justin and the other student, Carlos, continued to struggle. The special education teacher, Mr. Mayer, consulted with Ms. Phillips and suggested some research-supported learning strategies for her to implement. Carlos responded favorably to the strategies, but Justin didn't. At that point, Mr. Mayer came into the

classroom and worked directly with Justin. This also proved to be unsuccessful, and based on this information Ms. Phillips decided that a referral for special education services was warranted. Justin's parents have expressed a preference for keeping him in the general education classroom. ■

Ms. Phillips is faced with a question that many teachers must ask—when is a student just temporarily struggling academically and when are the school problems a result of a disability? In Justin's case, the RTI approach demonstrated that Justin struggled through several stages of intervention, which helped answer that question. As you will see, Justin displays many characteristics of a student with a learning disability, such as problems with reading and writing. However, there is no prototype for a child with learning disabilities. For example, Ginny, a fourth grader, is an avid reader but has great difficulty in mathematics. Brandon, who just started middle school and is a member of the math team, is having problems in written expression and frequently turns in short written products with numerous errors in spelling, punctuation, and capitalization. Ginny and Brandon both have been identified as having a learning disability.

The majority of students with learning disabilities are taught in the general education classroom. As a general education teacher, you may be involved in helping to identify a learning disability or in ruling one out through a prereferral program. As a special education teacher, you will most likely collaborate with the general education teacher to provide learning supports to any students with learning disabilities. You might also work with them in a pullout program for part of the day or, less likely, teach them in a separate classroom. For both special and general education teachers, we want to emphasize that many of the instructional considerations and suggestions provided in this chapter can be applied to students identified with other disabilities or students who are not identified with a disability but who may need some additional instructional support.

This chapter follows a format you will find in each of the remaining chapters. The first half of the chapter focuses on the basic information about the exceptionality that you as a teacher need to understand: the history, definition, prevalence, causes, characteristics, and identification procedures. The second half explores the educational implications and offers suggestions in the areas of instructional content, instructional procedures, the instructional environment, and instructional technology. Finally, we identify some special considerations for the general education teacher.

What Are the Foundations of Learning Disabilities?

Although the term *learning disabilities* was not used until the early 1960s, the historical roots of learning disabilities go back more than 200 years. It is important to look at these historical roots to see how the disability has evolved from being considered a medical to an educational condition. Along with the development of an understanding of learning disabilities has been the evolution of its definition. There has been considerable debate about what a learning disability actually is. Frequently, in fact, a learning disability is defined by what it is *not*, such as a learning problem *not* due to sensory deficits or environmental disadvantage. Learning disabilities is currently the most prevalent disability, with almost half of all students receiving services under IDEA 04 being identified with a learning disability. You will most likely work with many students with learning disabilities during your teaching career.

A Brief History of Learning Disabilities

Relevant CEC Standards

▶ Historical foundations, classical studies, and major contributors in the field of learning disabilities (LD1K1)

▶ Philosophies, theories, models, and issues related to individuals with learning disabilities (LD1K2)

The history of what we now call learning disabilities began more than two centuries ago and was firmly implanted in a medical model. Wiederholt (1974), in a classic chapter about the history of learning disabilities, identified four distinct periods in how learning disabilities have been understood. The *foundational phase* (1800–1930) emphasized basic scientific research related to the brain. During this period, the relationship of injury to specific areas of the adult brain and the corresponding loss of specific functions, such as language skills or perceptual skills, was investigated. Researchers such as Kurt Goldstein, who studied World War I head injury patients,

FIGURE 4.1 Example of a Perceptual Shift

found that many patients displayed characteristics that would later be associated with learning disabilities. These characteristics include perseveration, in which an individual starts an activity but has difficulty stopping or changing it; hyperactivity; and figure/ground problems, in which an individual is unable to perceptually shift from foreground to background as when viewing the classic picture of the vase and the faces (Figure 4.1). The early conceptions of learning disabilities developed during this period emphasized their perceptual nature.

The *transition phase* (1930–1960) marked the application of brain research to the study of children. In the early 1940s, for example, Heinz Werner and Alfred Strauss began to bring the field of neurology into education. They noticed similarities between some of the characteristics of children who were having learning problems and those of adults who had suffered brain injury. This observation led to terms such as *minimal brain injury* and *minimal brain dysfunction*, which were early labels used for learning disabilities.

The *integration phase* (1960–1974) included coining the term *learning disability* (see An Important Event) and recognition of learning disabilities within school programs. Emphasis was placed on perceptual skills and their role in children's learning in the early stages of the integration phase through the work of researchers such as William Cruickshank, Newell Kephart, and Marianne Frostig. Although the views developed during this period emphasized the perceptual nature of learning disabilities, which later proved to be flawed, they did stimulate more research about, and interest in, the nature of learning disabilities.

AN IMPORTANT EVENT

1963—Dr. Sam Kirk Coins the Term *Learning Disabilities*

On April 6, 1963, Dr. Sam Kirk delivered a speech sponsored by the Fund for Perceptually Handicapped Children to a group of parents. Ironically, the message Dr. Kirk wanted to deliver was that labeling children with terms such as *perceptually handicapped, brain injured,* or *autistic* was satisfying for caring adults but did little to actually help the child. He argued that labels were classification terms that added little diagnostic information that would assist in "treatment, management, or remediation." He went on to say, however, that he had recently been using the term *learning disabilities* to refer to children who were experiencing problems in language, speech, reading, and communication skills. (Kirk had coined this term in his introductory

(continued)

special education textbook published in 1962; this meeting, however, popularized it.) He further stated that these children were neither blind nor deaf, nor did they have mental retardation. His statements had a significant effect. That evening, the parent advocacy organization eventually known as the Learning Disabilities Association of America (LDA), was founded. Dr. Kirk was appointed Chair of the Advisory Board. He, in turn, appointed to the board some of the major leaders in what was to become the field of learning disabilities.

REFLECTION Why do you think Dr. Kirk's speech had such an impact on the parents at that meeting?

Finally, the *current phase* (1975 to the present) is a time of emerging and future directions in the field of learning disabilities. We now emphasize interventions focusing on academic, behavioral, cognitive, and language areas. The majority of research today is on what strategies and supports can be provided to help students with learning disabilities achieve academically within the general education curriculum.

Definitions of Learning Disabilities

Relevant CEC Standards

▶ Impact of legislation on the education of individuals with learning disabilities (LD1K3)

▶ Current definitions and issues related to the identification of individuals with learning disabilities (LD1K5)

The development of learning disabilities as a category of disability was initially a reaction to the existence of a large number of children who were having a broad range of problems progressing academically, but who otherwise had no observable disabilities. The current federal definition of learning disabilities outlined in IDEA 04 is the most widely used, although the definition proposed by the National Joint Committee on Learning Disabilities (NJCLD) is commonly referenced. The definition used in practice varies from state to state.

The IDEA 04 Definition

Since the time of Kirk's influential speech, the definition of a learning disability has been constantly analyzed. Currently, the definition of learning disabilities originally proposed by the National Advisory Committee on Handicapped Children in 1968, updated by the federal government for PL 94-142 and, most recently, revised for the Individuals with Disabilities Education Act of 2004 (IDEA 04), is the most widely accepted. That definition is as follows:

> General—Specific learning disability means a disorder in one or more of the basic psychological processes involved in understanding or in using language, spoken or written, that may manifest in an imperfect ability to listen, think, speak, read, write, spell, or to do mathematical calculations including conditions such as perceptual disabilities, brain injury, minimal brain dysfunction, dyslexia, and developmental aphasia.

> Disorders Not Included—Specific learning disability does not include learning problems that are primarily the result of visual, hearing, or motor disabilities, of mental retardation, of emotional disturbance, or of environmental, cultural, or economic disadvantage.

This definition is sufficiently broad so that a variety of students might be considered as having a learning disability. It also includes both *inclusion* criteria, for example, the disability includes conditions such as brain injury or dyslexia, and *exclusion* criteria, such as the disability cannot be due to emotional disturbance or environmental disadvantage.

The NJCLD Definition

In addition to the IDEA 04 definition of learning disabilities, teachers should be aware of the definition proposed by the National Joint Committee on Learning Disabilities (NJCLD, 1997), an organization consisting of 13 professional organizations including the Council for Learning Disabilities and the International Reading Association. The NJCLD definition is frequently used and has both similarities to and differences from the federal definition. Both the NJCLD and IDEA define learning disabilities as involving deficits in a number of academic and cognitive areas. The NJCLD definition eliminated the psychological processing deficit requirement and redefined the exclusion aspect of the IDEA definition by stating that a learning disability cannot be the result of other disabilities or extrinsic factors, but that they can coexist. Although the NJCLD definition was not adopted by Congress, it represents the concerns that professionals had, and still have, with the federal definition.

JUSTIN REVISITED What aspects of the current federal definition of learning disabilities are consistent with Justin's characteristics? What aspects are inconsistent? What aspects are unknown?

Prevalence of Learning Disabilities

Approximately 5% of school-aged children have been identified as having a learning disability. In the 2005 school year, 5.24% of all students ages 6–17 received learning disabilities services under IDEA 04 (Office of Special Education Programs [OSEP], 2006). Learning disabilities is the largest area of disability, constituting over 45% of all students served under IDEA 04, and it has demonstrated considerable growth over time, probably due to increased awareness and the reclassification of students with other disabilities, such as mental retardation, into the learning disability category. Thinking about this information practically, in a typical class of 30 students, one or two will be identified as having a learning disability.

Factors such as gender, ethnic background, and geographic region appear to affect the prevalence rate of learning disabilities. It is generally accepted that more boys are identified with learning disabilities than girls, with three to four times more boys receiving services for learning disabilities than girls. Regarding ethnic background, several states have shown a rather dramatic underrepresentation of African American students with learning disabilities (Colarusso, Keel, & Dangel, 2001), but these same states have an overrepresentation of African American students identified with having intellectual disabilities.

The prevalence rate of learning disabilities, in general, also varies according to geographic region. Recent IDEA 04 data indicated that the percentage of students with learning disabilities by state ranged from 2.12% to 7.7% for students ages 6–17 (OSEP, 2006). It is unclear why this variability exists, but it is probably due to the different criteria used for identification.

Check Your Understanding

1. What are the four historical periods of learning disability research/education and their characteristics?
2. What was the focus of early research on what would eventually become the field of learning disabilities?
3. What is the IDEA 04 definition of learning disabilities?
4. How does the NJCLD definition differ from the IDEA 04 definition?
5. Approximately what percentage of the school population has a learning disability? What percentage of all students with a disability have a learning disability?
6. What factors appear to affect the prevalence of learning disabilities?

What Are the Causes and Characteristics of Learning Disabilities?

There is no consensus on the specific cause or causes of learning disabilities. In fact, the range of characteristics leads to a variety of possible causes. While the broadness of the learning disabilities definition has led to a range of possible causes and characteristics, this section focuses on those most often identified.

Causes of Learning Disabilities

The search for causes of learning disabilities has, and most likely will continue to have, very broad parameters. The causes most often recognized and researched today can be grouped into neurological, genetic, and environmental factors. Although these areas do not represent every possible cause, they provide a solid foundation for understanding identified causes.

Neurological Causes

Implicit in the IDEA 04 definition of learning disabilities is that the problem is in some way neurological in nature; in other words, it is related to a deficit in the central nervous system. These deficits could be due to brain injury, brain development, or brain structure. Minimal brain injury, one of the early terms used for learning disabilities, suggested a loss of brain functioning due to damage. Research in the mid-20th century proposed that learning disabilities are caused by *lags* in neurological development as opposed to the *loss* of neurological function. In other words, the problems are due to a slowly developing brain, not an injured one.

More recently, researchers have been interested in the structural brain differences between individuals with and without learning disabilities. For example, there is evidence that individuals with dyslexia, a severe reading disability, have a smaller planum temporale, a section of the temporal lobe of the brain, than do individuals without dyslexia (Miller, Sanchez, & Hynd, 2003). Advances in medical technology, such as the development of functional magnetic resonance imaging (*f*MRI), which makes it possible to determine which part of the brain is actively engaged when an individual is involved in a learning task, have led to improved techniques to search for neurological causes. For example, research has shown that individuals with reading and language disabilities show different brain activation patterns during specific tasks than do individuals without disabilities (Richards, 2001).

Genetic Causes

One often-debated issue is the possibility of a genetic basis of learning disabilities. As early as 1905, Hinshelwood noted a familial relationship of individuals with learning problems. There is, in fact, some evidence of this from twin studies. For example, reading problems have been more frequently reported between identical twins than between fraternal twins (Wadsworth, Olson, Pennington, & DeFries, 2000). There have also been reports that the prevalence of dyscalculia, a severe math disability, is 10 times higher in families of individuals with the problem than would be expected from the general population (Shalev et al., 2001) and that word recognition problems have a primarily genetic basis (Harlaar, Spinath, Dale, & Plomin, 2005).

Environmental Causes

Research has also provided evidence that environmental factors can cause learning disabilities. These environmental factors are grouped into those that occur prenatally, perinatally, and postnatally. *Prenatal* factors known to harm a fetus include maternal drug use, alcohol consumption, and smoking during pregnancy. Maternal use of drugs and alcohol during pregnancy is usually associated with more severe problems than learning disabilities, such as fetal alcohol syndrome. However, their use can result in various degrees of disability, depending on the amount of alcohol or other drugs consumed, and when or how long they were consumed during the pregnancy. Mothers who smoke during pregnancy are more likely to have smaller babies (under 5 pounds) who are subsequently at risk for a number of problems including learning disorders (National Institute of Mental Health, 2001).

Perinatal factors that cause learning disabilities occur at birth or very shortly thereafter. Complications during child delivery, such as the umbilical cord becoming twisted, could lead to **anoxia,** the loss of oxygen, which in turn may lead to a learning disability. It is also possible that some slight injury may occur to the brain as the child passes through the birth canal. Again, these factors can lead to more severe problems as well.

anoxia Loss of oxygen that can affect a newborn child.

TABLE 4.1	Controversial and Unsubstantiated Theories Regarding the Cause of Learning Disabilities

- Hyperactivity and associated learning problems are caused by artificial coloring and salicylates, a chemical found in a number of foods, particularly fruit (Feingold, 1975).

- Reading problems of many adults are attributed to their inability to process full spectrum light (scotopic sensitivity syndrome) that requires the use of colored, filtered lenses (called Irlen lenses) when reading. (Irlen Institute, n.d.).

- Learning problems are caused by hypoglycemia, or low blood sugar (Runion, 1980).

- Learning problems are caused by nutritional deficits (Simopoulos, 1983).

- Learning disabilities are caused by food allergies, particularly from sugar, eggs, wheat, and chocolate (Crook, 1983).

Postnatal factors that cause learning disabilities occur after the child is born. Several postnatal factors have been linked to learning disabilities. Essentially, any factor that can cause neurological problems can cause learning problems. These include medical conditions such as meningitis, as well as the ingestion of certain substances, such as lead-based paint, known to cause brain damage. Although lead-based paint is now banned, lead is still found in some water pipes, with estimates that as many as 890,000 young children develop lead poisoning each year (Cohen, 2001). In 2007, there was a large recall of toys by a major company because of their lead content. Some of the more controversial causes suggested in the early history of the field were related to postnatal factors (Table 4.1). We mention these because you might hear about them, but there is little to no research to support their influence.

Although environmental, cultural, and economic disadvantage are excluded as causes of learning disabilities in the IDEA 04 definition, a few states have eliminated this exclusionary component (Kidder-Ashley, Deni, & Anderton, 2000). It is thus likely that many students are identified as having a learning disability whose problems are at least associated with these factors. For example, low socioeconomic status and poverty have long been linked to learning problems (Arends, 2007).

Characteristics of Students with Learning Disabilities

There have been many attempts to identify the major characteristics of students with learning disabilities. One of the earliest studies in this area was made in 1963 by a task force that was assembled on the recommendation of the federal government and concerned agencies. The task force identified 10 commonly exhibited characteristics of minimal brain dysfunction/learning disability: (1) hyperactivity, (2) perceptual-motor impairments, (3) emotional lability, (4) general coordination deficits, (5) disorders of attention, (6) impulsivity, (7) disorders of memory and thinking, (8) specific learning disabilities, (9) disorders of speech and hearing, and (10) equivocal neurological signs (Clements, 1966). The task force findings reinforced the neurological basis of learning disabilities. Notice that none of the 10 listed characteristics specifically addressed academic skill deficits. Today both academic and nonacademic characteristics are associated with learning disabilities. These include characteristics related to reading, mathematics, written expression, expressive and receptive language, cognition (including attention, memory, and metacognition), and social/emotional areas. It is important to remember that not all students identified as having a learning disability will have all of these characteristics or display problems in all of these areas.

Characteristics Related to Reading

Many people are under the impression that the terms *learning disability* and *reading disability* are interchangeable. The reality is that some students with learning disabilities do not have difficulty reading. However, a reading problem is the most

Relevant CEC Standards

▶ Psychological, social, and emotional characteristics of individuals with learning disabilities (LD2K2)

▶ Impact learning disabilities may have on auditory and information processing skills (LD3K3)

▶ Typical language development and how that may differ for individuals with learning disabilities (LD6K1)

Many students with learning disabilities struggle with reading and writing.

phonological awareness The recognition that words, syllables, or sounds exist in spoken language and the ability to manipulate them by deleting, adding, substituting, and transposing.

rapid automatic naming Quickly naming stimuli such as digits, letters, or names of simple objects; related to early reading ability.

frequently reported academic problem for those with learning disabilities with estimates as high as 90% (Bender, 2004). Needless to say, reading is a very important skill that is directly related to overall academic performance. It is no wonder that so much attention has focused on this area. Students with learning disabilities manifested in reading ability may also have problems with phonological awareness, rapid automatic naming, reading recognition, and reading comprehension.

One of the most severe reading problems linked to learning disabilities is dyslexia. Dyslexia is described as having a neurological basis (International Dyslexia Association, 2002) and being resistant to remediation (Hynd, 1992). Therefore, when a child is labeled as having dyslexia, even informally, it suggests some type of biologically based reading problem that cannot be remediated or is difficult to remediate. In reality, reading problems can occur from a variety of causes, and the incidence of "pure" dyslexia is not very high. Bender (2004) stated that fewer than 1% of individuals with learning disabilities have dyslexia and that the terms *reading disability* and *dyslexia* should not be used interchangeably. He further pointed out that the vast majority of reading problems can be effectively remediated.

Problems in reading that might indicate a learning disability related to early reading skills include phonological awareness and rapid automatic naming. **Phonological awareness** is the recognition that words, syllables, or sounds exist in spoken language and can be manipulated by deleting, adding, substituting, and transposing. It manifests itself in the ability (or lack of ability) to break down speech into smaller parts such as sounds or syllables. An individual with a problem in this area might not recognize that "dog" is actually made up of three sounds, d/o/g. Lewis, Frebairn, and Terry (2000) followed a group of 4- and 6-year-old children with phonological processing problems into the third and fourth grades. They found that these children developed problems in reading decoding (sounding out words), reading comprehension, and spelling. Another important early reading skill is **rapid automatic naming (RAN),** the ability to quickly name stimuli such as digits, letters, or pictures of simple objects. Research has indicated that young children who have difficulty with RAN also have deficits in reading ability (Bowers & Ishaik, 2003). Research on phonological awareness/processing and RAN is very important because there also is evidence that children who experience reading problems early in life continue to have problems and rarely catch up. The "Matthew effect," the phenomenon that good readers become better readers and poor readers become poorer readers, has been observed for years (Stanovich, 1986). The Matthew effect reinforces the extreme importance of early reading intervention, one of the goals of the No Child Left Behind Act.

Two areas in reading in which students with learning disabilities often have problems are in word recognition and reading comprehension. As a group, students with word recognition problems can display a number of characteristics either in isolation or in combination. These include mispronunciations; skipping, adding, or substituting words; reversing letters or words; and difficulty blending sounds together.

While many students with learning disabilities eventually learn word recognition skills, they may still have problems in comprehension. Problems in reading comprehension, understanding what is read, can be due to a number of possible factors including lack of background knowledge, difficulty understanding text structure, and vocabulary deficits (Ehren, 2005; Joshi, 2005). It also follows that a

Story #1: With Substitutions

Note: Answer the comprehension questions after reading each story.

Jim went out to the car to get his fourteen airport. It was a middle plan that he had made with his further. He took it with him everywhere he went. He was ready upset when he find that one of the wings had been off. His dad, house, sad not to worry between they would buy animal plant tomorrow.

Story #2: Without Substitutions

Jim went out to the car to get his favorite airplane. It was a model plane that he had made with his father. He took it with him wherever he went. He was really upset when he found that one of the wings had broken off. His dad, however, said not to worry because they would build another plane together.

Comprehension Questions

1. What is a good title for this story?
2. What did Jim leave in the car?
3. Why was Jim upset?
4. Why did Jim's father tell him not to worry?

FIGURE 4.2 Effects of Word Substitutions on Reading Comprehension

word recognition problem can cause a comprehension problem (Williams, 2003). For example, if a student comes across unfamiliar vocabulary words and substitutes incorrect words for them, the meaning of the passage will be difficult to determine. Figure 4.2 provides an example of the effects of word substitution on reading comprehension.

Characteristics Related to Mathematics

Mathematics is another area in which a student with learning disabilities might experience problems. It is estimated that approximately 25% of students with learning disabilities receive services for mathematics (Miller, Butler, & Lee, 1998; Rivera, 1997), and that math problems frequently persist into adulthood (Patton, Cronin, Bassett, & Koppel, 1997). Areas in which students with learning disabilities have been reported as having difficulties include calculation, knowledge of math facts, understanding of math concepts, and problem-solving skills (Smith, 2004). Related areas include difficulty with word problems (Bryant & Dix, 1999), math anxiety (Baloglu & Kocak, 2006), and retrieving math information from long-term memory (Geary, 2003).

Writing and Written Expression Characteristics

Students with learning disabilities might have problems with handwriting, spelling, and written language/written expression, such as punctuation, vocabulary, and sentence structure. They also might have problems in more than one of the areas, as they seem to be interrelated. Figure 4.3 on the next page shows a writing sample that includes all of the previously mentioned problems.

Handwriting. Poor handwriting, a characteristic of some students with learning disabilities, may be related to a number of underlying causes, including poor fine-motor skills, faulty visual perception of letters and words, lack of coordination, the inability to transfer the input of visual information to the output of fine-motor movement, and difficulty remembering visual impressions (Lerner & Kline, 2006). Also, if handwriting is difficult for a student, writing may take longer (Hallahan, Lloyd, Kauffman, Weiss, & Martinez, 2005).

Spelling. Spelling is an area in which many students with learning disabilities have considerable difficulty. Some emphasis has been placed on determining the type of spelling

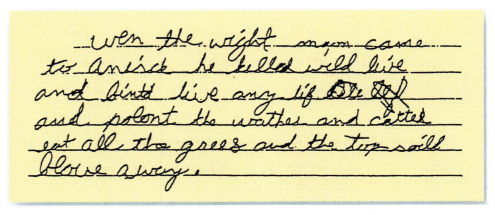

FIGURE 4.3 Writing Sample Showing Problems with Handwriting, Spelling, Punctuation, Vocabulary, and Sentence Structure

problem that students demonstrate. For example, Berninger and Amtmann (2003) identified several types of error patterns, each with its own suggested instructional procedures. These included phonological processing errors (*pincess* for *princess*), spelling conventions errors (*busyer* for *busier*), and letter production errors (*maq* for *map*).

Written Expression. Many students with learning disabilities display problems in the overall area of written language or written expression. Problems with handwriting and spelling often lead to difficulty in composing written products (Berninger & Amtmann, 2003; Graham, 1999), and it appears that many students with learning disabilities have more difficulty with compositional writing than with writing single words or sentences (Mayes, Calhoun, & Lane, 2005). Compositional writing involves aspects such as capitalization and punctuation, vocabulary, organization, and theme development. For example, a student with a learning disability in this area might write a story that is short; is not well thought out; and has numerous capitalization, punctuation, and spelling errors.

Expressive and Receptive Language Characteristics

The importance of language in the field of learning disabilities is well appreciated. In fact, many states have programs specifically for students with language learning disabilities (LLD). Students with learning disabilities in this area might have problems in expressive language (producing language), receptive language (understanding language), or in both. Although students with learning disabilities have problems in both areas compared to normally achieving students, research generally supports the fact that they have greater difficulty with expressive language than with receptive language (Hallahan et al., 2005). It is important to identify language problems because they are directly related to academic areas, particularly reading and written expression. Problems in language at age 5 might show up as reading problems at age 8 and writing problems at age 14 (Lerner & Kline, 2006). Students with learning disabilities can have problems with any of the components of language (discussed in depth in Chapter 7). It should be noted, however, that some students with learning disabilities have strong verbal skills. These students might be identified as having a nonverbal learning disability.

Cognitive-Related Characteristics

The federal definition of learning disabilities mentions deficits in "thinking." The general area of thinking, or cognition, is complex and includes a number of specific subareas. The subareas particularly relevant to a discussion of learning disabilities are attention, memory, and strategy use. Another related area is metacognition, an individual's ability to think about the thinking process. Note that a distinction is made between cognition and intelligence. The IQs of students with learning disabilities vary considerably, from low average to quite high, even into the gifted range.

Attention. There are several types of attention problems that students with learning disabilities might demonstrate. A student might have difficulty focusing attention on the task at hand or not be able to attend to the important aspects of a task. A related characteristic that is frequently noted is distractibility. In effect, however, children with attention problems might attend to very little, whereas children who are distractible might attend to too many things.

Memory and Strategy Use. Memory is a sequential process that has several components. Sousa (1999) provided an excellent description of this process. First, an individual must perceptually register information presented. This information is then immediately stored in short-term memory. Next, an individual uses his or her working memory to keep the information while it is processed. The information is then sent to long-term memory for storage. Later, through the process of retrieval, the information can be reused.

Research has indicated that many students with learning disabilities have problems with both visual and, particularly, auditory short-term memory (Swanson & Saez, 2003). These students also have difficulty in the area of working memory (Siegel, 2003; Swanson, Cooney, & McNamara, 2004). Attention, in fact, has been turned to this area because of the important role of working memory in reading recognition and reading comprehension (Seigneuric & Ehrlich, 2005; Siegel, 2003). For example, when reading a word, a student must simultaneously recognize the visual configuration of letters, note the order of the letters, and break the word into individual sounds. The student with a working memory deficit might have difficulty retaining this information while synthesizing and blending the letter sounds to recognize the word (Young, 2000).

There is evidence suggesting that the memory problems are related to the difficulty or failure to use strategies that facilitate remembering, and that the teaching of strategies can help an individual remember and learn new information. In one significant early study, Torgesen (1977) observed strategies used by both accomplished and poor readers to memorize different material. The accomplished readers recalled more information and consistently used more organized and active techniques to help them remember. More important, when the groups were given instruction on the use of efficient strategies, the poor readers' memory scores improved to the point that there were no significant differences between the two groups. Put another way, students with learning disabilities are considered to be passive learners who do not use strategies as skillfully as their peers without learning disabilities and therefore need specific instruction in this area.

Metacognition. **Metacognition** is how one thinks about one's own thinking and the ability to use and regulate strategies and other organization skills. Not only do students with learning disabilities have difficulty developing effective cognitive strategies, but they also may have problems with metacognition, knowing when and how the strategies should be employed. For example, a student might learn a specific strategy to remember information when reading a textbook and might not realize that that same strategy could be used in helping to remember other information as well.

metacognition Regulation of the awareness and use of strategies to learn new information.

Social and Emotional Characteristics

Research indicates that many students with learning disabilities have some type of problem in social and emotional areas. There are estimates that one-third of all students with learning disabilities have social skills deficits (Bryan, 1997) and that these students might also have problems relating to others (Haager & Vaughn, 1997). There is some evidence that students with learning disabilities are more likely to be socially rejected by their peers than their peers without learning disabilities (Kuhne & Wiener, 2000; Wong & Donahue, 2002). Similarly, many students with learning disabilities have fewer friends and less social status than their peers and thus should be provided with a supportive environment to enable them to meet others (Whitehouse, Chamberlain,

& O'Brien, 2001). Other behavior problems that have been associated with learning disabilities are depression, anxiety disorders, and antisocial personality disorder (Sundheim & Voeller, 2004). This should not be interpreted to mean that all, or even most, students with learning disabilities will display these characteristics, but you should be aware that they may exist.

Low self-concept, including academic, social, and general self-concept, has been reported for many students with learning disabilities (Elbaum & Vaughn, 2003). A related well-documented characteristic is **learned helplessness.** This refers to a situation in which individuals have inaccurate insight into the nature of their behavior, attributing their successes to external factors such as luck and attributing their failures to internal factors such as a lack of effort or ability.

JUSTIN REVISITED What characteristics does Justin have that are consistent with the research on learning disabilities?

learned helplessness
Individuals attribute their successes to external factors out of their control and attribute their failures to internal factors.

As discussed in this section, there are many potential causes and a wide variety of characteristics of learning disabilities. What implications do these findings have for you? First, for the most part, the specific cause of learning disabilities will not be known, and probably has little relevance to what you would do instructionally. Second, the variability of characteristics suggests that you must be prepared to address any number of academic and nonacademic areas when planning and implementing instruction. In other words, instruction must be based on the specific characteristics of the student with a learning disability, not based on the general label of learning disability.

Check Your Understanding

1. What are some neurological and genetic causes of learning disabilities that have been suggested?

2. What prenatal, perinatal, and postnatal environmental factors have been associated with learning disabilities?

3. What types of characteristics of learning disabilities were reported by the 1963 task force?

4. What types of reading, mathematics, and written expression characteristics might a student with learning disabilities exhibit?

5. What types of problems might a student display in the area of cognition? Language? Social or emotional areas?

How Are Students with Learning Disabilities Identified?

Relevant CEC Standards

▶ Impact learning disabilities may have on auditory and information processing skills (LD3K3)

▶ Terminology and procedures used in the assessment of individuals with learning disabilities (LD8K1)

▶ Factors that could lead to misidentification of individuals having learning disabilities (LD8K2)

The first step in the assessment process that leads to eligibility for learning disability services is the initial identification of the student as having a possible learning disability. This initial identification is often made by the general education teacher, but it could also be made by others, including the parents. Usually, informal procedures such as observation and classroom performance are used initially to identify a student. It is also possible that results from statewide or districtwide assessments might be used.

After a student is identified as having a possible learning disability, he or she is evaluated to determine whether eligibility criteria are met. Federal regulations related to learning disabilities include specific guidelines to help clarify the identification process. One of the guidelines in earlier regulations was that the student have a severe discrepancy between intelligence and achievement in one or more of the following areas: oral expression, listening comprehension, written expression, basic reading skills, reading comprehension, mathematics computation, or mathematics reasoning. In other words, a student would be identified as having a learning disability if his or her standardized test scores fell below what would be expected based on the student's IQ score. Although there were those who strongly supported the concept of this aptitude-achievement discrepancy (e.g., Kavale, 2002), there were also critics who pointed to several problems with this model. One major argument against the discrepancy model was that it makes early identification of a learning disability difficult. In other words, using the discrepancy model means that students must "wait to fail" before they can receive services. Partially as a result of this and other arguments, IDEA 04 changed the guidelines associated with the identification of learning disabilities to eliminate the need for a severe discrepancy.

IDEA 04 also introduced the response to intervention (RTI) process, which determines whether or not a child responds to "scientific, research-based intervention" and indicated that this information could be used to help make a diagnosis of learning disability. Historically, there has been a heavy reliance on standardized testing. Depending on the specific eligibility criteria used and the nature of the student's problems, tests measuring intelligence and achievement, processing skills, and language and academic abilities are frequently used. Ideally, determination of eligibility is made using multiple sources of information. Recommendations have been made that both RTI and standardized tests be used in identifying learning disabilities and that the exclusive use of either is inappropriate (Wodrich, Spencer, & Daley, 2006).

Response to Intervention

Response to intervention (RTI) is a process to determine possible learning disabilities based on the student's response to scientific, research-based interventions. This procedure was designed as a multilevel approach to identify students who are experiencing academic problems before they fall too far behind. Several different models have been proposed; here are the steps in the RTI process as described by Fuchs, Mock, Morgan, and Young (2003, p. 159):

1. Students are provided with "generally effective" instruction by their classroom teacher.
2. Their progress is monitored.
3. Those who do not respond get something else, or something more, from their teacher or someone else.
4. Again, their progress is monitored.
5. Those who still do not respond either qualify for special education or for special education evaluation.

RTI is often thought of as a three-tiered model (Figure 4.4). The following example demonstrates the use of this model.

> All first grade students at John F. Kennedy elementary school are administered the first grade reading list of 20 words from an informal reading inventory (Universal Screening). In Ms. Jenkins class of 30 students, six students, Teddy, Clarence, Ginny, Sue, Billy, and Joey, met the criterion indicated in the inventory for frustration level, thus indicating that they were struggling in the area of oral reading. These six students remained in the general education classroom and received direct instruction on phonics skills. Their performance was evaluated and monitored weekly using standardized word lists (Tier 1). Teddy, Clarence, Sue, and Joey failed to make appropriate gains and were given a more intense intervention program that included collaboration with a special education teacher. Monitoring of the oral reading continued (Tier 2). Teddy and Sue responded to the intervention but Clarence and Joey still were not making adequate progress. Clarence and Joey received an even more intensive program in which the reading specialist worked on a one-to-one basis with each student, and the monitoring continued. After several weeks, Clarence finally "caught on," but Joey did not. Joey would now be considered for eligibility for a learning disability (Tier 3). Depending on the individual state's eligibility criteria, Joey's lack of response to intervention might be enough for identification, or, more likely, he may be recommended for an evaluation that will probably include standardized testing.

Two approaches to RTI are typically used—the problem-solving approach and the standard treatment protocol approach. In the *problem-solving approach*, a team of professionals decides the nature of the intervention that will be used with a specific

response to intervention
Relatively new criterion indicating that a student's lack of response to a scientific, research-based intervention can be considered in identifying a learning disability.

UNIVERSAL SCREENING: All students are given a screening measure. Students at risk for academic failure are identified.

Tier 1

Students receive effective instruction in the general education setting, using validated practices. Student progress is monitored on a weekly basis. (In some approaches, universal screening is considered part of Tier 1.)

Tier 2

Students whose progress is less than desired receive different or additional support from the classroom teacher or another educational professional. Student progress continues to be monitored.

Tier 3

Students whose progress is still insufficient in Tier 2 may receive even more intensive instruction, which can be provided in a variety of ways. Then, depending of a state's or district's policies, students may qualify for special education services based on the progress monitoring data or they may receive either an abbreviated or a comprehensive evaluation for the identification of learning disability.

FIGURE 4.4 Three-tiered Response to Intervention (RTI) Model
Source: iris.peabody.vanderbilt.edu/rti01_overview/rti01_03.html

student so that no single intervention is used schoolwide. The *standard treatment protocol*, on the other hand, uses one universal, validated intervention for all students receiving extra help (IRIS Center, 2006). Although each approach has its strengths, the standard treatment protocol has been recommended because of the consistency of the intervention, particularly when RTI is used in place of standardized tests for identification (Fuchs & Fuchs, 2006).

The RTI approach has many advantages in identifying students with learning disabilities including the supplemental provision of instruction to a large number of at-risk students and ongoing progress monitoring. This approach also allows identification of a learning disability *before* the student begins to have significant problems (Vaughn et al., 2003). Other advantages are the potential reduction of bias during the identification process, and the emphasis on a risk model rather than a deficit model (Vaughn & Fuchs, 2003). The use of RTI could improve schoolwide achievement because all students would be monitored to determine who needs additional help (VanDerHayden, Witt, & Barnett, 2005).

There are several unanswered questions about the RTI process. How long should the intervention be in place? How intense should the instruction be? What criteria will be used to determine responsiveness and unresponsiveness? What actually constitutes scientific, research-based instruction? How is RTI different from prereferral intervention? Compton (2006) raised additional questions that relate to who should receive the additional intervention and by whom the intervention should be applied. Vaughn and Fuchs (2003) questioned whether or not the lack of response to intervention in and of itself should be considered a learning disability. Several models have been suggested in which RTI is used in combination with low achievement (Fletcher, Francis, Morris, & Lyon, 2005) and with reading growth rates (Burns & Senesac, 2005). Should additional diagnostic information such as IQ be used to distinguish between a learning disability and an intellectual disability? Undoubtedly, these and other questions will be addressed as RTI is tested and refined.

The Use of Standardized Testing

Standardized testing historically has been the major approach used to determine whether a student meets eligibility criteria for learning disabilities. Because a number of characteristics are associated with this category, it is not surprising that many different types of tests are used. Intelligence and achievement tests are the most routinely administered. Other instruments that are frequently used are tests measuring process skills, primarily if a deficit in that area is required for eligibility, as well as tests measuring language and academic skills.

Even though the presence of a severe discrepancy between intelligence and achievement is no longer required by the federal definition of learning disabilities, they remain important areas to evaluate. As the category of learning disabilities typically excludes those individuals whose measured IQ is below approximately 75, it is important to obtain a valid estimate of a student's intelligence. In addition, many states and districts designate an IQ cutoff (e.g., above 80 or above 90). Achievement tests are administered to document that an educational need exists and to indicate the general level of performance in a wide variety of academic areas (an academic profile of strengths and weaknesses).

A somewhat controversial issue is the use of **process tests,** those designed to measure how well individuals integrate and understand information. According to the IDEA 04 definition of learning disabilities, a student with a learning disability has difficulty with psychological processing. One problem in assessing processing skills is determining what processing really means and what aspect of processing to measure. Perceptual processing tests were once quite popular and are still used in some states. These tests measure such skills as copying geometric figures. Other processing tests that are used include those in the areas of memory and, more recently, phonological processing.

process tests Instruments that purportedly measure how well a person processes information.

Depending on the specific type of language or academic problem a student exhibits, a variety of instruments are available. For language problems there are tests that measure several components of language as well as specific language components such as semantics or pragmatics. Academic tests are available in reading, math, and spelling/written language. The choice of the instruments will depend on the individual characteristics of the student. In some instances, these types of instruments might be used to help make eligibility decisions. In others, they may be used to provide more information for instructional purposes.

JUSTIN REVISITED What procedures should be used to assess Justin for a learning disability?

Teachers play an important role in the overall identification of students with learning disabilities. As a general education teacher, you may be involved in the initial identification and will be involved if the RTI approach is used to help determine eligibility. As a special education teacher,

The type of test administered depends on the characteristics of the student.

you might administer some of the standardized tests, primarily the achievement and academic tests, and also might be involved in the RTI approach.

Check Your Understanding

1. What steps are usually taken before a student is referred for a learning disability?
2. What is the response to intervention model? What are the pros and cons of this model?
3. Why are intelligence tests and achievement tests frequently used?
4. What are some problems with assessing processing skills?

What and How Do I Teach Students with Learning Disabilities?

 Relevant CEC Standards

▶ Effects of phonological awareness on the reading abilities of individuals with learning disabilities (LD3K2)

▶ Impact learning disabilities may have on auditory and information processing skills (LD3K3)

▶ Methods for guiding individuals in identifying and organizing critical content (LD4K5)

▶ Relationships among reading instruction methods and learning disabilities (LD7K1)

▶ Sources of specialized curricula, materials, and resources for individuals with learning disabilities (LD7K2)

There is considerable overlap in the instructional needs of students with mild/moderate disabilities across the categories of learning disabilities, mental retardation/intellectual disabilities, and behavioral and emotional disorders. These instructional needs may include academic instruction, functional and life skills instruction, and behavioral and social skills instruction. Generally, students with learning disabilities need highly intensive instruction in both the process of learning and the content of learning (Miller, 2002). The focus of instruction is determined by the individual student's cognitive, social, and emotional needs, not by his or her category of exceptionality. Because the most prominent characteristic of students with learning disabilities is difficulty in academic learning, this chapter presents an overview of current educational programs and techniques for teaching academics to students with learning disabilities. Just as the instructional considerations in this chapter may apply to students with mild/moderate intellectual disabilities and/or emotional and behavioral problems, instructional considerations in Chapters 5 and 6 may also apply to some students with learning disabilities who may need a more functional curriculum and/or social skills focus in their educational programs. Keep this overlap in mind as you read all three chapters.

A vast array of techniques and materials is available for teaching academics, as well as other goal areas, to children, adolescents, and adults with learning disabilities. In selecting the appropriate program design, materials, and teaching techniques, teachers must fully assess each individual's unique educational needs. A critical determinant of the type of program to implement is the age of the students (Lerner & Kline, 2006). Final consideration in program planning for an individual with learning disabilities of any age is to provide as much opportunity as possible for that student to interact with peers without disabilities. In this part of the chapter, we focus specifically on the content areas in which students with learning disabilities may need additional instruction, including transition skills, and specific instructional procedures that have proven successful with many students with learning disabilities.

Instructional Content

Most students with learning disabilities will be taught within the general education curriculum with additional support when needed in the areas of reading, written language, mathematics, and study skills. Another area that demands consideration in content planning for secondary students is transition. You may find that you need to implement a functional skills or social skills curriculum with some students with learning disabilities. These curricula are discussed in Chapters 5 and 6.

Types of Content Knowledge

Three different subprocesses of knowledge must be addressed when considering instructional content for students with learning disabilities: declarative knowledge, procedural knowledge, and conditional knowledge (Meichenbaum & Biemiller, 1998). **Declarative knowledge** is knowledge of the facts that must be learned: in other words, the "what" part of learning. This will likely come from the general education curriculum goals. For example, declarative knowledge is knowing the three branches of the government or the names of the state capitals. This is the type of knowledge that is typically the focus of educational instruction and assessment. The two other types of knowledge, which are significant in teaching students with learning disabilities, are **procedural knowledge,** or the "how" of learning, and **conditional knowledge,** or the "when and why" of learning. For example, the student needs to learn that making a word or sentence out of the first letters of a list will help him or her remember the list (procedural knowledge) but will not be useful for learning the content of a full chapter (conditional knowledge). Declarative knowledge may be lacking in students with learning disabilities due to a deficit in procedural or conditional knowledge. For example, a student may be failing history tests because he or she may not know how and when to study the chapter. For students with learning disabilities to learn the same content as students without disabilities, an array of procedural and conditional strategies should become part of the content taught (e.g., Gersten, 1998). Procedural knowledge involves the use of cognitive strategies, and conditional knowledge involves the use of metacognitive strategies. Both of these will be covered under the section titled Instructional Procedures.

Areas of Instructional Content

The areas of content that are most often affected by learning disabilities are reading, written language, mathematics, and study skills. Which areas need to be addressed will be determined by the individual student's needs.

Reading. Reading requires skills in the broad areas of both decoding and comprehension. Decoding is translating print into oral language, and comprehension is understanding the language of the text once it is decoded (Carnine, Silbert, & Kameenui, 1997). After a very comprehensive examination of reading research, the National Reading Panel (2000) identified five essential components of effective reading instruction: phonological awareness training, phonics instruction, fluency instruction, vocabulary instruction, and comprehension instruction. Students with learning disabilities may experience difficulty in any of these areas.

Phonological awareness is a skill that has come to the forefront of literacy education. Because spoken language is a continuous stream of sound, it is not until children begin to read that they must learn to segment language in the way that it is done in written language (Smiley & Goldstein, 1998). Students with problems in phonological awareness will need extra support in developing an understanding of how words, syllables, and sounds construct words. Fortunately, research shows that young children can develop phonological awareness through specific instruction and that such teaching can have a positive effect on overall reading achievement (Armbruster & Osborn, 2001; Torgesen, 2000). Typically, instruction in phonological awareness focuses first on spoken language and includes structured activities in rhyming, blending, and segmenting sounds and then moves to teaching alphabetic principles of how letters relate to the sounds in speech (phonics). A list of programs that have been developed for teaching phonological awareness and alphabetic principles is available in Online Appendix A at the Online Learning Center.

Some students with learning disabilities may need phonics instruction, or sound-symbol (letter) correspondence. The Direct Instruction (DI) method of teaching reading, designed in the late 1960s by Engelman and his associates, is one specific curriculum program with a very heavy phonics emphasis available to teach reading to students with learning disabilities. DI is a structured, teacher-directed program that should not be confused with the more general direct instruction approach to teaching discussed in the Instructional Procedures section. DI is based on the principle of teaching sequences of skills designed to minimize error, providing ample practice, and giving immediate feedback and positive reinforcement. Its emphasis is on the

declarative knowledge The "what" of learning: knowledge of the facts, concepts, or definitions that must be learned.

procedural knowledge The "how" of learning; cognitive strategy knowledge.

conditional knowledge The "when and why" of learning; metacognitive strategy knowledge.

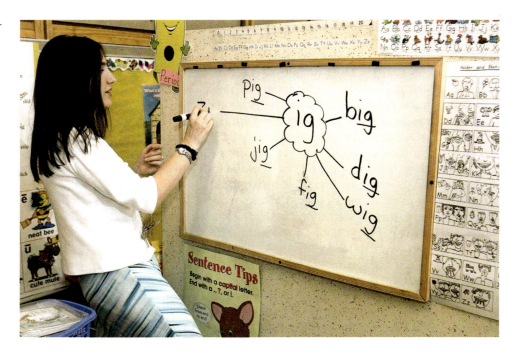

Some students with learning disabilities may need instruction in phonological awareness and phonics.

antecedents of instruction, such as teacher directions, instructional statements, and prompts. Curriculum design is a critical element of the DI program (Stein, Carnine, & Dixon, 1998; Tarver, 1999). The DI approach teaches a series of carefully sequenced phonics skills. Children are taught in small groups, with teachers following a rigidly prescribed, fast-paced script that involves hand signals (one finger up for response time), auditory signals (such as clapping), verbal signals (such as "say it slow" and "say it fast"), and includes many opportunities for unison group responses. There is ongoing evaluation and continual regrouping according to demonstrated competencies or weaknesses. DI has been the focus of considerable validation and feasibility research and a high level of effectiveness has been reported (Carnine, Silbert, Kame'enui, & Tarver, 2004; Ellis, 2001; Tarver, 1999). Another exemplary program for students with language-based learning disabilities in the middle grades is the Wilson Reading System (Moats, 1998; Shaywitz, 2003). This structured program includes instruction in phonemic segmentation, sight word fluency, vocabulary, oral expressive language development, and comprehension.

fluency The ability to read quickly and accurately.

Fluency is the ability to read quickly and accurately and is, by its nature, related to reading comprehension, for if a reader takes too long to decode a sentence or passage, the beginning of what was read is lost before the end is reached. Students with problems with fluency will need extra help in learning to decode more quickly and accurately. Repeated readings, in which students are asked to read the same material repeatedly, is one strategy that has been found to be effective in building fluency (Kuhn & Stahl, 2003). In this approach, students are given one minute to read a passage. Then the number of words read accurately within that time frame is recorded; corrective feedback is often provided. Students are then asked to read the passage again to determine if they can accurately read more words within the minute. The passage is repeatedly read until students are reading 100 or more words accurately within a minute (DeVault & Joseph, 2004). Corrective feedback may include teacher modeling, direct instruction, and positive comments or suggestions (Conderman & Strobel, 2006).

Students with learning disabilities in the area of reading may display problems in vocabulary development. Repeated readings may also enhance vocabulary if corrective feedback includes information about new words and word meanings (National Reading Panel, 2000). Also promising in promoting vocabulary learning are interventions that engage students interactively with memory devices and graphic depictions (such as mnemonics and semantic mapping discussed later in the chapter) paired with direct instruction and practice (Bryant, Goodwin, Bryant, & Higgins, 2003; Jitendra, Edwards, Sacks, & Jacobson, 2004).

Reading comprehension, creating meaning from words, is critical to independence and success in school and in much of life. Reading comprehension can be increased for students with learning disabilities through the development of cognitive and metacognitive strategies (Armbruster & Osborn, 2001; Boulineau, Fore, Hagan-Burke, & Burke, 2004; Vaughn, Gerstsen, & Chard, 2000). Examples of strategies with demonstrated success in reading comprehension at various age levels, including story mapping, collaborative strategic reading (CSR), and peer-assisted learning strategies (PALS), can be found in Online Appendix A on the Online Learning Center. Repeated silent readings have also been used to improve comprehension rates of secondary students with learning disabilities (Freeland, Skinner, Jackson, McDaniel, & Smith, 2000).

Written Language. Students with learning disabilities may require support in developing written language skills. An effective way of supporting writing development is by focusing on writing as a process rather than a product. In the mid-1980s, Graves (1983, 1985) presented the idea that writing is a not just a product but is a process of cognitive activity. This process involves question asking, decision making, problem solving, and feedback with the overall purpose to communicate ideas to others. The process of written composition occurs over time and includes several stages.

Teaching the writing process involves showing students how to write in overlapping and recurring stages, which include prewriting, drafting, revising, editing, and creating a final draft. In a recent analysis of research-based instructional interventions for teaching written expression to students with learning disabilities, three components of instruction stood out as reliably and consistently leading to improvement in teaching expressive writing: adhering to a basic framework of planning, writing, and revision; explicitly teaching critical steps in the writing process; and providing feedback guided by the information explicitly taught (Gersten, Baker, & Edwards, 1999). Teachers should remember that writing is a process that occurs over time and that it should be taught accordingly. Students with learning disabilities will typically need to be taught writing strategies within each component of the process. For example, in the stage of editing, students may need to learn to use the error monitoring strategy COPS (Schumaker, Deshler, Nolan, Clark, Alley, & Warner, 1981) to remind them to check for **C**apitalization, **O**verall Appearance, **P**unctuation, and **S**pelling. Both elementary and secondary students with learning disabilities have been found to write more reflective, complex, and well-written essays when explicitly taught writing strategies (Chalk, Hagan-Burke, & Burke, 2005; De La Paz, Owen, Harris, & Graham, 2000; Saddler & Graham, 2005; Schumaker, & Deshler, 2003). Online Appendix A includes descriptions of effective strategies.

Mathematics. Students with learning disabilities who lack awareness of skills, strategies, and resources that are needed to perform tasks and who fail to use self-regulatory mechanisms to complete tasks will undoubtedly have problems with mathematics (Miller & Mercer, 1997). As noted earlier, math disabilities are second only to reading disabilities as academic problem areas for students with learning disabilities. Fortunately, effective instruction in self-regulation and cognitive strategies use can improve both computation and conceptual problem-solving skills in students with math disabilities (e.g., Maccini & Hughes, 2000; Miller et al., 1998; Montague, 1997). Students with learning disabilities will often need learning strategies in both computation and story problem solving. For example, Big, Bigger, Borrow can prompt a student to borrow if the second numeral is bigger than the first. Online Appendix A includes some additional examples of successful math strategies.

Study Skills. Some study skills that students with learning disabilities may need to be taught include listening, note taking, time management, comprehension, textbook usage, memory strategies, and test taking. Many students with learning disabilities lack the organizational skills that are essential to learning. For example, their note taking

PRACTICE

may be so random or filled with inessential details that it does little to help them study. Or due dates and directions may be lost in a notebook that has no logical order of pages. Some students may become so discouraged that they stop trying and end up failing in school (Johns, Crowley, & Guetzloe, 2002). However, substantial gains in content learning have been reported with strategy instruction (e.g., De La Paz & MacArthur, 2003;

JUSTIN REVISITED What specific content area(s) does Justin need help in? What would you suggest to help him in these areas?

Mastropieri, Scruggs, & Whedon, 1997; Pressley et al., 1995). For example, a passing grade in science may result when a student learns a strategy to help determine what points in a lecture and a chapter are essential. The acquisition of study skills may be the key to independence all through school and life for many individuals with learning disabilities. Learning a strategy such as using a planner book to keep track of due dates (or meeting dates and times) may eventually lead to better performance on a job. See Online Appendix A for additional study skill strategies.

Transition Planning

A key area of instructional content for secondary students with learning disabilities is in the area of transition. Although the majority of students with learning disabilities transition directly into employment (Gerber & Price, 2003), the IDEA mandate for education in the least restrictive environment has resulted in increasing numbers of students with learning disabilities being enrolled in academic coursework that should better prepare them for postsecondary education (Brinckerhoff, McGuire, & Shaw, 2002). In fact, more students with learning disabilities are enrolling in postsecondary education than in the past, and the full-time employment, employment benefits, and salary earned by graduates are both competitive with the general workforce and exceed those of adults with learning disabilities who are not college graduates (Madaus, 2006).

For students going into the workforce, goal setting and self-advocacy skills are important so that they will know what assistance or information they want or need, and can speak for themselves in the job setting. Specific vocational training programs may be necessary for success as well. Other areas that need to be addressed are independent living or life skills, vocational education, and community-based instruction. All of these are discussed in Chapter 5.

For students with learning disabilities going on to postsecondary settings, in addition to developing learning strategies in reading, writing, and study skills, transition plans should assist them with the development of goal setting and self-advocacy skills so that they can initiate services needed at the postsecondary level (Miller, 2002; Taymans & West, 2001). The secondary-level teacher of students with learning disabilities and the student should work closely with service providers at local postsecondary institutions to identify necessary services for students with disabilities. Some student experiences may include identifying the desirable characteristics of a college; understanding his or her legal rights; finding out what documentation is required to receive accommodations at his or her college of interest; enrolling in summer precollege courses or at least exploring to get to know the campus, the library, the study strategies, and time management skills that may need sharpening; learning and using strategies to investigate specific classes before enrolling (Taymans & West, 2001); and developing self-advocacy plans (Lock & Layton, 2001; Skinner, 1998). Students who have been identified as having a learning disability should come into the postsecondary setting fully aware of the strategies, accommodations, and devices that work for them and be able to advocate for their use. The use of assistive technology should also be included in transition programs as it is essential to success in postsecondary education (Mull & Sitlington, 2003) as well as in employment, social, and recreational/leisure activities. Technology, including word processing, text messaging, and iPods or MP3s, exist in all of these settings today.

Instructional Procedures

Structure is an important part in planning instructional programs for students with learning disabilities. A structured program is one in which all students know the

**Relevant
CEC Standards**

▶ Strategies to prepare for and take tests (LD4K1)

▶ Methods for increasing accuracy and proficiency in math calculations and applications (LD4K3)

▶ Methods for teaching individuals to independently use cognitive processing to solve problems (LD4K4)

▶ Enhance vocabulary development (LD6K4)

▶ Teach strategies for spelling accuracy and generalization (LD6K5)

▶ Teach methods and strategies for producing legible documents (LD6K6)

▶ Teach individuals with learning disabilities to monitor for errors in oral and written communications (LD6K7)

daily routines and expectations; understand the rules; are presented the curriculum in an organized, sequential fashion; and are focused on learning tasks rather than extraneous stimuli. These concepts apply to programming for all age groups of students with learning disabilities. Developing a structured program takes a great deal of planning based on a sound foundation of knowledge of effective instructional strategies. Two teaching approaches that have been shown to be particularly effective with students with learning disabilities, which you may want to use with all of your students, are task analysis and direct instruction. Other approaches that may work well with students with learning disabilities emphasize an analysis of the unobservable cognitive behaviors that occur during a task. These cognitive approaches include cognitive and metacognitive strategies training and the use of mnemonics. Finally, this section concludes with some considerations for teaching students who are both English language learners and have a learning disability.

Task Analysis

One approach to organizing and sequencing curriculum used by teachers of all students that has been found to be especially effective for students with learning disabilities and that has been endorsed by many educators is the task analytic approach (Taylor, 2009). As you may recall from Chapter 2, task analysis involves breaking down a task, skill, or objective into simpler components. The task analysis begins when a teacher chooses a learning task appropriate for the child to master and states the terminal objective in behavioral terms that emphasize observable, measurable tasks. The terminal objective is then broken down into incremental steps arranged in order of complexity, with each step being a prerequisite for the next one, until the terminal goal is reached. It is important for teachers to state behavioral objectives clearly and concisely, being sure to specify what the student is expected to do as a result of instruction. The following might be a simple terminal objective for the elementary student:

> Given problems requiring the subtraction of a one-digit number from a two-digit number with renaming, the student will write the correct answers.

A task analysis of this terminal objective would provide the following steps for teaching it:

- Given problems requiring the subtraction of numbers 1–10 from the numbers 1–10, the student will provide the correct answers.
- Given problems requiring the subtraction of 0 from the numbers 1–10, the student will provide the correct answers.
- Given problems requiring the subtraction of a one-digit number from a two-digit number without renaming, the student will provide the correct answers.
- Given problems requiring the subtraction of a one-digit number from a two-digit number with renaming, the student will provide the correct answers.

The task analysis method does not tell the teacher how to teach; it merely clarifies what the student should be taught. If the student has difficulty at any one step in the task, it is up to the teacher to provide additional procedures or develop smaller incremental steps for achieving the objective. While this strategy can be used with any student, it works particularly well with students with learning disabilities as it provides a logical and sequential structure for learning the skill and ensures that prerequisites are met.

Direct Instruction

A complementary effective instructional procedure to consider using with students with learning disabilities is direct instruction. **Direct instruction** is based on Rosenshine and Stevens's (1986) model of explicit, effective instruction, which has taken many forms but maintains several fundamental and sequential components of effective instruction. These include daily review, presentation, guided practice,

direct instruction An instructional procedure that maintains several fundamental and sequential components of effective instruction: daily review, presentation, guided practice, independent practice, and weekly and monthly reviews.

independent practice, and weekly and monthly reviews. Although they do have many basic principles of learning in common, direct instruction differs from Direct Instruction (DI), introduced in the Instructional Content section, in that it is a general teaching method, not a specific program. Research consistently demonstrates that explicit, direct instruction enhances the achievement of students with learning disabilities (Swanson & Hoskyn, 1998) because it presents skills or information in explicit steps to ensure that information is understood before the next step is taken.

Daily Review. A well-planned direct instruction lesson begins with a review of the previously presented material to check to be sure that students have retained the material and to serve as an introduction and linkage to the new presentation. Questions are generally an appropriate format for review, particularly as this allows more opportunity for student rehearsal.

Presentation. Second, the teacher presents new material. A good presentation contains several components:

- *An advance organizer.* A short statement of the objectives and an overview of the lesson plan should begin the lesson.
- *A rationale.* Programming for generalization begins here with presenting to, and eliciting from, students some examples of why they need to know this and where they will use it other than in this class (i.e., other classes and real life, both work and social).
- *Presentation of the skill or strategy.* Lessons should be clearly presented, well-sequenced, and well-organized (Swanson, 1999a). Characteristics include concise and clearly understood explanations, highlighted key concepts, sufficient illustrations and concrete examples, and many questions to check for understanding. A key aspect of this component should be actual demonstration and modeling of the skill or strategy by the teacher while "thinking aloud."

Guided Practice. Third, in this teacher-guided, interactive step, students demonstrate what the teacher has modeled, including the think aloud procedure, explaining any problems they are having, making decisions, and evaluating their own performance. Additional explanations and examples are given and, again, many questions are asked by the teacher to check for understanding. Whenever feasible, all students should have a chance to respond and participate as well as receive feedback, both positive and corrective. The teacher provides support, or **scaffolds,** until the student is ready to assume control. If incorrect or incomplete responses are given, prompts are provided, and students should be encouraged to evaluate their own responses. Guided practice is usually continued until a success rate of 80% or its equivalent is reached.

scaffolds Support provided by the teacher until the student is ready to assume control of learning.

Independent Practice. Next, independent practice should be assigned that is directly related to both the presentation and guided practice as determined by the objective. The teacher should guide students through the first few examples, then, if possible, actively monitor their independent practice. If students are truly ready for independent work, the teacher will have to respond only to minor questions or give cues as reminders. If the teacher finds that he or she is basically re-teaching the information, this is an indication that not enough time was provided in presentation or guided practice and that a return to the appropriate step is necessary. To be sufficient, independent practice needs to continue beyond the level of mastery (overlearning). Homework assignments should always be independent practice of skills that have already been directly taught in the classroom.

Weekly and Monthly Reviews. Finally, there should be a systematic review of material to ensure that the learned material has been maintained. Generalization checks are also needed to ensure students are using learned skills or strategies in other settings with other people. Prompting or re-teaching may be necessary. All of these components may be included in one lesson, or several lessons may be spent on one or more of the components. An example of a lesson plan using the direct instruction approach is shown in Online Appendix A.

A significant component of direct instruction is modeling while "thinking aloud."

Cognitive and Metacognitive Strategies Instruction

Research consistently has indicated that many individuals with learning disabilities do not know how to learn, need instructional strategies that can command attention, and frequently exhibit poor motivation. The cognitive model of instruction addresses these obstacles through an approach to instruction that adds an emphasis on learning *how to learn*. Instead of analyzing only the observable, measurable aspects of a task, the teacher should also consider the cognitive aspects of how a learner thinks when performing a task. For example, when a student is subtracting a three-digit number from a three-digit number, the teacher might instruct him or her to verbalize the steps required to perform the task while asking the questions, "What do I do next?" "Does that seem right?"

A sizeable research base exists that demonstrates the usefulness of the *strategies instruction approach*, directly teaching students how to use cognitive and metacognitive strategies to acquire skills and information (Sturomski, 1997). In an analysis of instructional components across a range of intervention studies, results support a combination of the components of direct instruction and strategy instruction as the best model for teaching academics to students with learning disabilities across diverse samples, classroom settings, and ages (Swanson, 1999a). Effective strategy instruction usually includes cognitive strategies, metacognitive strategies, the Learning Strategies Curriculum, use of mnemonics, and attribution retraining.

Cognitive Strategies. **Cognitive strategies** are deliberate, planned activities used to acquire information, such as rehearsing a phone number or highlighting a chapter. This instructional procedure focuses on teaching students procedural knowledge, or how to learn and how to control their own learning. Examples of cognitive strategies include procedures in reading, such as self-questioning, constructing representational images, activating prior knowledge, and rereading difficult-to-understand sections of text; in writing, such as planning, drafting, reviewing, and revising; and in memorizing, such as repetition and relating to previously acquired, associated material (Pressley et al., 1995). One caution in teaching students with learning disabilities how to use cognitive strategies is to not let strategic behaviors become the end goal of instruction, but to teach them as tools to use to solve problems and acquire information. That is, simply learning the steps of a strategy for how to study is not the end goal; rather, using that strategy to increase grades in social studies should be the goal.

cognitive strategies Deliberate, planned activities used to acquire information.

Metacognitive Strategies. Students with learning disabilities who have a deficit in metacognition are not aware of what variables affect their cognitive performance and thus do not plan and regulate their performance. **Metacognitive strategies** enable individuals to come up with a plan to direct, monitor, evaluate, and regulate their own behavior. For this reason, metacognitive strategies are often referred to as self-regulatory strategies (Sturomski, 1997). Good strategy instruction must include metacognitive strategy instruction, or conditional knowledge, to make students aware of the purposes of cognitive strategies, how they work, why they work, when they work, and where they can be used. For example, rehearsing information (saying it to oneself) will work for basic information like a phone number but will not work for a whole chapter.

metacognitive strategies Used for planning (deciding what strategy to use), monitoring (checking during use to be sure strategy is working), and checking outcomes of learning (checking after use to be sure strategy worked).

Teaching metacognitive strategies involves three important areas of the learning process: planning, monitoring, and checking outcomes (Reid, 1988). During the *planning* phase, the teacher encourages the learner to decide which cognitive/learning strategy should be applied by predicting the outcomes of using different strategies to address the task requirements. The teacher should next teach the student to *monitor* his or her learning by self-questioning while using a strategy to see if it is working and,

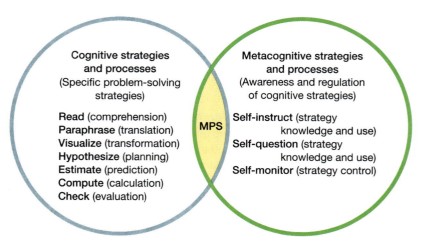

FIGURE 4.5 Cognitive-Metacognitive Model of Mathematical Problem Solving (MPS)
Source: From Montague, M. (1997). Cognitive strategy instruction in mathematics for students with learning disabilities. *Journal of Learning Disabilities, 30*(2), 164–177. Copyright 1997 by Pro-Ed, Inc. Reprinted with permission.

if necessary, revising the original plan. Finally, the student should be taught to *check the outcomes* after learning and determine if the strategy has worked. An example of these processes for the task of studying a chapter follows:

> *Planning:* The student plans to use highlighting, graphic organizers, or outlining to study, based on whether the exam will be essay or multiple-choice, and how much information is in the chapter.

> *Monitoring:* While studying the chapter, the student asks, "Am I understanding this? Am I remembering this?" "Is this strategy working?" If not, he or she may have to reread or decide on another strategy for remembering.

> *Checking the Outcomes:* The student may read and answer the questions at the end of the chapter just studied and decide whether to re-study, perhaps with a new plan, or congratulate him- or herself on a job well done.

For an example of cognitive and metacognitive processes applied to mathematical problem solving, see Figure 4.5.

Learning Strategies Curriculum. Instructional programs that include both metacognitive and cognitive aspects of the strategy being taught have achieved the most success with students with learning disabilities (Deshler, Ellis, & Lenz, 1996). The Learning Strategies Curriculum (LSC), developed by the University of Kansas Center for Research on Learning (see An Important Event), is an example of a very comprehensive curriculum for the secondary level that has an emphasis on both of these areas (Deshler, Warner, Schumaker, & Alley, 1983). The curriculum consists of a collection of learning strategy instructional packets that have been field tested extensively with positive results. The LSC is very structured and provides teachers with consistent, step-by-step procedures for teaching specific learning strategies to students with learning disabilities in both academic learning and social interaction. The strategies in academic learning are related to reading, storing and remembering information, expressing information, demonstrating competence, and mathematics. Strategies in social interaction include community building strategies, cooperative thinking strategies, a self-advocacy strategy, and a class participation strategy. The teaching model incorporates all components of effective instruction discussed earlier in the direct instruction approach to teaching. The University of Kansas Center for Research on Learning has also developed teacher-focused Content Enhancement Routines, which are techniques for teaching academically diverse students in general education content-area subjects by helping them identify, organize, comprehend, remember, and attend to important concepts presented in lessons or textbooks (Bulgren & Lenz, 1996). All of the routines promote direct explicit instruction. The manuals and materials for both the Learning Strategies Curriculum and the Content Enhancement Routines are available to the public only through training delivered by certified instructors.

Mnemonics. Mnemonics is a cognitive strategy that may be useful to students with learning disabilities to help them remember information. **Mnemonics** are devices, such as rhymes or songs, used to aid memory. They are often used to help students remember the steps in a cognitive or metacognitive strategy or specific information. Individuals with learning disabilities, mild intellectual disorders, and behavior disorders across a wide age range can be taught to use mnemonic strategies independently and to generalize their use (Fulk, Mastropieri, & Scruggs, 1992; Greene, 1999; Levin, 1993; Mastropieri & Scruggs, 1991, 1998). Some of the most commonly used mnemonics include the "first letter" strategies of acronyms and acrostics. In an **acronym,** each letter represents the first letter in a word or sentence to be remembered. A well-known example of this is HOMES for the names of the Great Lakes (**H**uron, **O**ntario, **M**ichigan, **E**rie, and **S**uperior). A teacher-developed example is presented in the Classroom Example feature with each letter in LETTER representing the first letter in a series of steps for writing a friendly letter. This could also be used or adapted for a business letter. In an **acrostic,** a sentence is devised for letter retrieval. A familiar example is "**E**very **g**ood **b**oy **d**oes **f**ine" to remember the musical notes on the lines of the treble clef (E, G, B, D, F).

The cues provided by the first letter of each word of an acronym are minimal and may not be sufficient for some learners. When the to-be-recalled material is unfamiliar, keywords may be preferable (Brigham & Brigham, 2001; Uberti, Scruggs, & Mastropieri, 2003). The **keyword method** works to enhance recall by linking unfamiliar information to more familiar information. It is effective because it is concrete and meaningful and closely ties new information to students' prior knowledge (Scruggs & Mastropieri, 2000). Mastropieri and Scruggs (1991) presented the following "three Rs" of the keyword method:

1. *Reconstruct* the term or word to be learned into an acoustically similar, already familiar, and easily pictured concrete term—select a keyword (to learn barrister is a lawyer, the keyword selected is bear).

mnemonics Devices such as acronyms, acrostics, rhymes, or songs used to aid memory.

acronym A word in which each letter represents the first letter in a word or sentence to be remembered.

acrostic A sentence in which the first letter of each word represents the first letter in a word or sentence to be remembered.

keyword method A method to enhance recall by linking unfamiliar information to more familiar information.

Purpose: To aid students in writing a friendly letter.

Population: Elementary

LETTER

Lead off with date and greeting.

Express my thoughts and ideas in the body.

Terminate with closing and my name.

Take time to proofread.

Edit and revise if necessary.

Realize that I am a good letter writer.

Source: Provided by Ellen Karger (1998), South Florida teacher of students with learning disabilities.

JUSTIN REVISITED Are there some metacognitive or cognitive strategies that might help Justin learn better? If yes, in what areas? If not, why do you think these would not help him?

2. *Relate* the keyword to the to-be-learned information in an interactive picture, image, or sentence (e.g., the interactive sentence to be pictured is "a bear pleading a case in court").

3. *Retrieve* the appropriate response: when asked what the response is (what is a barrister?): first, think of the keyword ("bear"); second, think back to the interactive picture and what was happening in that picture ("a bear pleading a case"). Finally, give the desired response ("a barrister is a lawyer").

attribution retraining A procedure to retrain an individual's attributions of success or failure. Possible attributions include ability, effort, task difficulty, and luck.

Attribution Retraining. Students are more likely to use effective cognitive strategies when they attribute their learning success to the use of these strategies (Meltzer & Montague, 2001). Many students with learning disabilities may need to be taught to do this. Successful **attribution retraining** requires first teaching students to make statements that reflect attributions of effort, then teaching them to attribute difficulties to ineffective strategies, and finally, arranging for them to experience success with effective strategies (Ellis, Lenz, & Sabornie, 1987). Examples of positive self-statements that attribute success to effort and not to luck include: "I can probably do this problem because I've done similar ones successfully." "I'm usually successful when I work carefully and use the learning strategy correctly." "If I make a mistake, I can probably find it and correct it." (Corral & Antia, 1997, p. 43).

The overriding goal of attribution retraining is to teach individuals that through effort and appropriate selection of strategies, they can be in control of their own learning and can be successful. Students must believe that making the effort to use strategies is worthwhile and will result in improved academic performance (Meltzer, Katzir-Cohen, Miller, & Roditi, 2001).

Effective Instruction for English Language Learners

As more than one-third of students in public school may be from culturally and linguistically diverse backgrounds (Ford, 2000), you may very well have students in your class who are English language learners and also have learning disabilities. Many of the strategies you would consider for any of your students with learning disabilities will work as effectively with a student who is also an English language learner. Some of the instructional practices especially effective for English language learners, summarized in an examination of existing research and analyses of discussions with professional work groups by Gersten, Baker, Marks, and Smith (1999), include the following:

- Using visuals to reinforce concepts and vocabulary
- Utilizing cooperative learning and peer tutoring
- Making strategic use of the native language by allowing students to organize their thoughts in their native language
- Providing sufficient time and opportunities for students to use oral language and writing in both formal and informal contexts
- Focusing on rich and evocative vocabulary words during lessons and using these as vehicles for teaching literary concepts

Other practices to consider are providing lectures that are simplified, appealing, and multisensory; adapting textbooks and assignments; evaluating their textbooks and assignments for appropriateness; and using supplementary materials (Sheppard, 2001). Research on the characteristics of effective teachers of students with cultural and linguistic diversities indicates that effective teachers have high expectations of their students, see themselves as members of a community, believe in diversity and meeting individual needs, are confident in their ability to teach diverse students, recognize the diverse languages in their classrooms as valuable, and acquire a few words from each. They also communicate directions clearly, pace lessons appropriately, involve the students in decisions, monitor students' progress, and provide feedback (Bos & Vaughn, 2006).

Check Your Understanding

1. What three types of knowledge need to be included in content teaching?
2. What are some major areas of content where students with learning disabilities may have special needs?
3. What should transition programs for students with learning disabilities in academic preparation programs include?
4. What is task analysis?
5. What are the fundamental and sequential components of effective instruction that are included in direct instruction?
6. What are cognitive and metacognitive strategies? What are some mnemonic devices that can be used successfully in teaching strategies? What is attribution retraining?
7. What are some strategies that are particularly effective with English language learners who have learning disabilities?

What Are Other Instructional Considerations for Teaching Students with Learning Disabilities?

In addition to planning for instruction, the teacher of students with learning disabilities should give careful thought to the instructional environment and how instructional technology will be used. The instructional environment can play a significant role in the successful performance of students with learning disabilities. It is important to plan for both structure and organization in the environment and to give careful thought to how students are grouped. Instructional technology has many uses with students with learning disabilities from preschool through postsecondary settings. For some students, it is essential for success.

The Instructional Environment

In general, organizing the instructional environment is a critical component of effective teaching and successful learning (Miller, 2002). It can play an important role by introducing order into the often chaotic lives of students with learning disabilities (Lerner & Kline, 2006). Major considerations in making decisions about the instructional environment involve two interrelated topics: determining the physical arrangement of the classroom and selecting the best option in grouping students for instructional purposes.

The Physical Arrangement

Despite the lack of uniformity in behavioral and educational characteristics among individuals with learning disabilities, certain environmental considerations have proven helpful with the vast majority of these students. In fact, most educators find that certain basic principles benefit all students whether or not they have learning problems. These principles include reducing congestion in high-traffic areas, making sure the teacher can see all students, making frequently used materials and supplies easily accessible, and ensuring that all students can see whole class presentations (Santrock, 2008). All of these contribute to helping students, with or without learning disabilities, stay on task and avoid distractions.

The Preschool Classroom. Over half of preschoolers with disabilities receive their education totally or primarily in general education classrooms (U.S. Department of Education, 2006). Overall, the preschool environment should be well designed and structured, and should be arranged to promote efficiency, accessibility, and independence. The materials and equipment should be arranged so that personnel and students can move quickly from one activity to another without undue delays. The arrangement of the classroom communicates the teacher's expectations for participation and interaction in the classroom. The importance of developing language and pre-literacy skills, including positive experiences with oral and written language materials, should be evident in the arrangement of the classroom. This would include areas for language stimulation, phonological awareness centers, and centers where the students are read to, where students can handle books, and where students can make picture books. Also apparent should be centers and areas where students are introduced to alphabetic principles.

Elementary and Secondary Classrooms. Organization is a key component of achieving structure in classrooms for elementary and secondary students with learning disabilities (Muyskens & Ysseldyke, 1998). Any instructional equipment and materials should be organized and ready to use to avoid any "dead time" in which the student is left alone without instruction. Students should have definite places to put their class work and homework assignments, as well as their personal belongings and books. If a classroom is well organized, students with learning disabilities are more likely to behave appropriately and engage in instruction readily.

The classroom should have both tables and desks for individual work, large and small group work, peer tutoring, and cooperative learning, and areas that minimize distractions and promote student engagement (Olson & Platt, 2004). A work carrel is one option that provides a less-distracting environment for individual students with learning disabilities who seem to be overly distractible (Polloway, Patton, & Serna, 2005). The purpose of the carrel should be carefully explained, however, to make sure students do not view the isolation as punishment (i.e., timeout). Other ways to modify space are through the use of partitions, screens, special rooms, and quiet corners. The goal is to slowly increase the amount of space and number of distractions with which the student must contend (Lerner & Kline, 2006).

Instructional Grouping

Grouping is an instructional factor that can powerfully influence the levels of individual student engagement (Maheady, 1997). With increased numbers of students with

**Relevant
CEC Standard**

▶ Methods for ensuring individual academic success in one-to-one, small-group, and large-group settings (LD4K2)

learning disabilities receiving education in the general education classroom, both special education and general education teachers need to consider grouping practices that are effective for meeting these students' needs (Vaughn, Hughes, Moody, & Elbaum, 2001). In addition to individual student needs and abilities, the content being covered should influence the choice of grouping options as some instructional material is better suited to a particular grouping option. Frequently used groupings for students with learning disabilities include one-to-one instruction, small group, whole class, and peer tutoring.

One-to-One Instruction. In one-to-one instruction, students work alone with a teacher, a paraprofessional, or a computer with well-sequenced materials at their own level (Friend & Bursuck, 2006). Though one-to-one instruction has been a highly prized instructional procedure for students with learning disabilities, special educators report that the following factors impede their ability to implement one-to-one instruction: (1) heavy caseloads; (2) increased time to work collaboratively with classroom teachers, which reduces their time for providing instruction directly to students; and (3) ongoing and time-consuming paperwork that facilitates documentation of services but impedes implementation of services (Moody, Vaughn, & Schumm, 1997; Vaughn, Moody, & Schumm, 1998). Fortunately, although one-to-one instruction may be appropriate or even necessary in certain circumstances, such as catching up a student who has been absent from school, it is neither required for individualization of instruction nor has it been found to be superior to small group instruction (Polloway, Patton, & Serna, 2005; Thurlow, Ysseldyke, Wotruba, & Algozzine, 1993).

Small Group Instruction. Small group instruction may take place with homogeneous (similar skills) or heterogeneous (varied skills) groups of students, depending on the instructional objective. Individualizing instruction is more easily accomplished in small groups than in large ones; therefore, small groups are appropriate when teachers present different material to different students, and they are frequently used to teach the acquisition of a specific skill (Polloway et al., 2005) or to re-teach a skill to a small number of students who need more instruction. For example, small groups are appropriate when students are using different reading materials, need more

PRACTICE

opportunities to respond to questions, or have fallen behind other students. Group formation should be flexible and should be determined by such criteria as students' skills, prior knowledge, or interest levels (Vaughn, Hughes, Moody, & Elbaum, 2001). Use of flexible grouping strategies has been shown to improve achievement and self-esteem (Johnson & Johnson, 1991; Slavin, 1995) and to satisfy preferences of students with learning disabilities for working with a variety of classmates rather than with the same students all the time (Vaughn, Schumm, Klingner, & Saumell, 1995).

Whole Class Instruction. Although there are times when more individualized instruction in small groups is preferred for students with learning disabilities, there are other times when whole class instruction is effective (Elbaum, Schumm, & Vaughn, 1997). For example, large group instruction can be used effectively for brainstorming discussions, social studies or science content common to all, game playing, video watching, or numerous other classroom activities (Mercer & Mercer, 2005). Introduction and presentation of a strategy and guided practice may be provided for the whole class (Lewis & Doorlag, 2006). Large group instruction may be helpful to students with learning disabilities as they make the transition from special to general education settings where whole class instruction is the most commonly used practice (Bos & Vaughn, 2006).

Peer Tutoring. Peer tutoring has been shown to be effective for students with learning disabilities in elementary and secondary grades for both tutors and tutees (Elbaum, Vaughn, Hughes, & Moody, 1999; Topping & Ehly, 1998). Peer tutoring increases academic performance for students with learning disabilities in reading, spelling, math, learning social studies facts, and punctuation and capitalization in language arts. It has also been shown to improve social attitudes and attitudes about school learning, and to promote positive interactions among tutor, tutee, and content. However, for any peer tutoring experience to be effective, it must be carefully structured, with tutors trained, materials prepared, and an appropriate location designated. Friend and Bursuck (2006) suggest topics for training peer tutors, including the development of positive relationships with tutees and the development of effective communication and interaction skills. Students with learning disabilities should have the opportunity of being both tutor and tutee.

A version of peer tutoring that combines whole class instruction, peer tutoring, and cooperative learning, **classwide peer tutoring (CWPT)** (Greenwood, Maheady, & Delquadri, 2002), has been shown to be effective at both the elementary and secondary levels for students with learning disabilities (Olson & Platt, 2004). In CWPT, each student is paired with another student for tutoring in academics and can earn points, and bonus points, for following all the rules. This allows all students in the classroom to be actively engaged in learning and to practice in a motivating game format. This highly successful technique for grouping, which is great for inclusive classrooms, is discussed more in depth in Chapter 14.

classwide peer tutoring (CWPT) A combination of whole class instruction, peer tutoring, and cooperative learning.

Instructional Technology

Although technology has been used for some time with individuals with sensory or physical impairments, it is only in recent years that technology has been used with students with learning disabilities (Bryant & Bryant, 1998). Technology for teaching academics to students with learning disabilities generally falls under the umbrella term *assistive technology.* As mentioned in Chapter 1, an assistive technology device is defined by IDEA 04 as any item, piece of equipment, or system that is used to maintain or improve functional capabilities of individuals with disabilities. Appropriate assistive technology for students with learning disabilities can include, but is not limited to, computers, video cameras, laser videodiscs, taped books, software programs, spellers, tape recorders, readers, scanners, calculators, electronic mail, and electronic date books. These devices, or equipment, may be high tech, using sophisticated electronics, or low tech, such as an abacus for math computation (Learning Disabilities Association [LDA], 1995). For many students with learning disabilities, assistive technology adaptations are imperative for success (Bryant & Bryant, 2003). For example, word processors and software for creating graphic organizers can make it possible for students with learning disabilities who have trouble composing and writing on paper at the same time to create reports and essays that are equivalent to or better than those of their peers without disabilities. Speech recognition programs can help students write better because they can get their thoughts down on paper—something they were unable to do successfully before—by first dictating what they want to write. Computer-assisted instruction can provide the extra practice students with learning disabilities may need to master basic math facts. Use of necessary assistive technology should be written into an individual student's IEP. It is then the responsibility of the school district to provide assistive technology devices and services identified in the IEP (LDA, 1995).

Finally, when considering the use of technology, the student's family background should be kept in mind. Family decisions involved in the use of technology are often influenced by cultural and linguistic backgrounds (Parette, 1998; Parette & McMahan, 2002). For the best results in assistive technology implementation, teachers must be sensitive to these issues. Different cultures view the use of technology differently. For example, Euro-American families may want to be taught how to teach their children to use the devices whereas Asian American families may prefer that professionals assume responsibility for training (Parette, 1997, cited in Parette, 1998).

Use of Instructional Technology with Preschool Students with Learning Disabilities

Many assistive technology devices considered standard in classes for older students with learning disabilities can also be used with preschoolers if the children are carefully supervised. These include tape recorders, language masters, overhead projectors, and computers. Children even younger than 3 years of age can learn to operate a computer safely and effectively. Interactive software based on good children's literature and appropriate content is increasingly available (Hutinger & Johanson, 1998) and helps the child to maintain attention longer and screen out outside distractions. Practice with computer programs designed to build skills in phonological awareness has been shown to positively affect the skills of preschool and kindergarten children (Foster, Erickson, Foster, Brinkman, & Torgesen, 1994).

Children even younger than 3 years of age can learn to operate a computer safely and effectively.

In Practice Meet Educator Michael Woods and His Student Kathy

I teach learning strategies at an urban high school in one of the nation's largest school districts. I have taught for over 14 years, primarily at the high school level, though I have worked with students at all levels. My area of expertise is postsecondary transition and independent living skills. I was honored to receive the 2004 Teacher of the Year Award in my school district.

My student Kathy is an 11th grader who has been receiving services for

learning disabilities since the 4th grade. She was in a pullout resource room setting through middle school. She was gradually included more and more in general education and now, with the exception of her learning strategies class, attends all classes in an inclusive general education setting. She is working on a standard diploma, and her IEP goals are directed at teaching her learning strategies to support her success in the inclusive environment.

Kathy has experienced success in her elective courses (art, physical education, cooking). However, she requires extensive support in her academic courses. These supports include teaching her cognitive and metacognitive learning strategies in reading comprehension, study skills, essay and short answer test taking skills, and report writing. Additionally, Kathy needs to develop self-advocacy skills. She shows some limitations when it comes to communicating her needs and/or questions to her general education teachers. She describes talking to her teachers as "difficult." When asked why, she replies, "I don't want to feel stupid … there are only a few teachers I am good at talking with."

I had to help her feel more positive about her ability to meet these requirements. I pointed out that she could be successful if she tried hard and applied the strategies she learned in her strategies class.

Instructional Content and Procedures

Like many students with learning disabilities, Kathy and the students in my learning strategies course require ongoing instruction in organizational strategies, study skills, self-advocacy, and written expression. For that reason, whole group lessons have been created to provide both support and reinforcement of these activities. I have taught Kathy to use graphic organizers to better understand her reading assignments. She has learned to attend to the text organization patterns (for example, chronological, compare-contrast, or cause-effect) and to select a graphic organizer that she can apply to that particular chapter or text. She has also learned to attend to the visual cues in each of her texts, including bold print and marginal notes. As another example, I focus on note taking and

Use of Instructional Technology with Elementary and Secondary Students with Learning Disabilities

A creative teacher uses assistive technology in a variety of ways to enhance the educational programming for elementary and secondary students with learning disabilities. When used appropriately, assistive technology can make initial teaching presentations, as well as subsequent drill, exciting to students with learning disabilities who are often turned off by traditional class work. For example, *Number Heroes* (Edmark, Inc.) presents basic math concepts and problem-solving skills with the help of Fraction Man, Star Brilliant, and other math superheroes (Bryant & Bryant, 2003). Assistive technology should be chosen with the students' needs in mind. Students who are highly distractible may attend to a learning task more easily when they put on earphones and listen to a tape recorder or, better yet, listen to and interact with a language master. The overhead projector can also make a lesson more enjoyable for students with learning disabilities and allows

study skill habits. While most special education classes teach these skills throughout the lower and middle grades, this skill becomes critical in the high school setting. To help with this, we required Kathy to continue taking notes, so she can develop this skill, in addition to asking the instructor for a copy of his or her notes so she is sure to have all of the information.

Much of the content in my learning strategies class is tailored to events that are happening within the general education classroom. For example, if a science teacher requires students to complete a report on the "Planets," instruction within my classroom focuses on how to glean information from various resources on planets as well as how to create an organized, comprehensive report. Although students learn many of these skills in other academic courses, such as English, the generalization to other settings can be quite difficult for students with learning disabilities.

Instructional Environment and Technology

My learning strategies class that Kathy attends is conducted every other day for 100 minutes, on a block schedule. I also support Kathy and my other students in the general education classroom through observations and student–teacher reports. The learning strategies class is a mixed-grade-level class; students in grades 9 through 12 attend. This setting lends itself well to peer support and tutoring, especially for students who have successfully completed courses in which other students require assistance. However, this mixed setting sometimes makes it difficult to meet the instructional needs of all students. The utilization of whole group lessons—I provide direct instruction of specific learning strategies from the University of Kansas curriculum—can be of great assistance when trying to ensure instructional momentum within the class. However, I still do a tremendous amount of more intensive individualized instruction with each student applying the strategies to his or her own specific texts.

The utilization of technology can be of great assistance for my students, particularly when they are writing research reports. Many young high school students are very computer savvy. What they often lack, however, is the ability to discern which information is important and which is extraneous. In my learning strategies course, I teach students to transfer skills they use for text-based readings to the online setting. For example, the same use of graphic organizers to comprehend text chapters can be applied to reading material online and taking notes on it for writing a research paper.

Collaboration

I find it very necessary to stay in close communication with Kathy's general education teachers. I try to meet face to face with each teacher at least once a week, but if time constraints do not allow this, I communicate with them through written reports or questions in their school mailboxes or e-mail. I have encouraged their use of peer tutoring and cooperative learning techniques within their general education courses. I have pointed out how techniques such as these benefit both general education and special education students and help engage all students in learning. I also share articles from some of my journals that relate to what they are teaching. Collaborating requires some finesse, as building communicative, productive relationships with teaching peers can be challenging. In Kathy's situation, she initially wanted me to intervene with her teachers to assist in her success. It was important for me to cooperate with her teachers rather than to appear threatening or judgmental. Later in the year—and after some coaching and instruction—Kathy was able to intervene (using her newly developed self-advocacy skills) on her own behalf. By intervening on her own behalf, Kathy was able to eventually learn to address her own questions in a more expedient manner.

the teacher to maintain eye contact with the students. The traditional teacher-at-the-overhead lesson can be interspersed with students being asked to come forward and write answers on the transparency, thus keeping students physically as well as visually engaged.

The use of computers in classrooms is no longer an exception; it has become the general rule. Computers can be used in direct instruction of academics to students with learning disabilities in various ways such as drill and practice, tutoring, instructional games, research, writing, and problem solving. Computer work is most useful for independent practice after extensive direct instruction and guided practice. Educational game software can be used to provide practice on previously taught skills and is often self-correcting. For example, after the teacher has introduced algebraic ratios, the students may use *Astro Algebra* (Edmark, Inc.) software to travel through the galaxy practicing ratios (Bryant & Bryant, 2003). These programs combine video graphics and audio effects with academic skill practice and are designed to be fun and motivate students to practice. Teachers need to monitor such programs to be sure the student is practicing the skill and not simply activating various game stimuli (Miller, 2002).

Computer software is available in a number of areas in which students with learning disabilities often need extra support. Several computer programs have been developed to support phonological awareness skills and letter-sound correspondence practice for elementary-level students (Torgesen, 1999). The scope of reading skills covered by reading software programs may include word identification, vocabulary, fluency building, and comprehension (Bryant & Bryant, 2003). In the area of writing, technological tools can make the process easier as well as more motivating for students with learning disabilities (Graham, Harris, & Larsen, 2001). For example, SOLO, a widely used software toolset from Don Johnston, Inc. that includes Write Outloud, Co-writer, and Draft Builder, develops learning skills in reading, writing, planning, organizing, revising, and editing for students in grades 3 to 12. Another widely used program is Inspiration, which students can use to create graphic organizers and expand topics into writing. In Kidspiration, K–5 students can build graphic organizers by combining pictures, text, and spoken words to represent thoughts and information. In mathematics instruction, computer-aided instruction has been shown to be an effective tool (Okolo, Bahr, & Reith, 1993). Students who use appropriate technology persist longer, enjoy learning more, and make gains in math performance. Instructional software for computation, time, money, measurement, algebra, and word-problem solving is widely available. Students with poor organizational skills, memory deficits, or illegible handwriting may benefit from using personal digital assistants (PDAs) to keep track of assignments, make to-do lists, take notes, cue themselves to perform a particular task with the alarm or paging system, access and remember task sequences, or organize important information (Bauer & Ulrich, 2002; Matthews, Pracek, & Olson, 2000; Miller, 2000; Salend, 2005). A significant advantage of handheld PDAs is their portability and their universal use.

The Selection of Technology

Technology has great potential for improving performance of students with learning disabilities on general education expectations (Maccini, Gagnon, & Hughes, 2002),

---

Classroom Suggestions Tips for Software Selection

When selecting software, make sure:

❑ Content is free of gender, cultural, and racial stereotypes.

❑ Content is interesting, engaging, and encourages exploration and imagination.

❑ Activities require decision making and judgments.

❑ It has a high degree of interactivity.

❑ The screen is not cluttered. The less clutter on the screen, the better.

❑ Procedures and goals match those being taught in school.

❑ Directions are simple to read or have images or speech to guide use.

❑ Software is modifiable (e.g., speed, quantity of problems, levels).

❑ Programs contain more than one activity.

❑ There are small increments between levels.

❑ Only a limited number of incorrect responses are allowed per problem.

❑ There are built-in instructional aids (e.g., virtual manipulatives in math).

❑ There are minimal keyboard skill requirements and easy-to-understand icons.

❑ There are praise and helpful feedback provisions.

❑ It has a built-in review.

❑ Real-life solutions are simulated.

❑ It has good record-keeping capabilities.

And

❑ Remember software is a learning tool—not the total solution!

Source: Adapted from Lee (1987), Babbitt (1999), Hutinger and Johanson (1998).

but teachers must take care to choose well-designed, time-efficient programs. They must also avoid using the computers to simply keep students occupied without relating the computer work to their educational needs. Assistive technology must be carefully matched to the needs of the student and the environment in which the learning will take place (Beigel, 2000).

With valuable instructional time limited, teachers should carefully select appropriate, time-efficient software that meets the needs of students and incorporates best practice in instructional design and curriculum (Bryant & Bryant, 2003). Several characteristics of software that result in efficient use by students with learning disabilities are presented in the Classroom Suggestions feature on the opposite page.

The need for assistive technology does not end with education, but persists in employment, social, and recreational/leisure activities (Raskind & Bryant, 2002). Whether it is writing a letter to a friend at home with the assistance of a word processor, checking for spelling errors in a memo to a coworker, or using a calculator to help keep score in a card game, assistive technology devices may provide the needed support to enable individuals with learning disabilities to be effective in a variety of contexts and settings.

Check Your Understanding

1. What are two key elements in physical arrangement of the instructional environment for students with learning disabilities?

2. Describe some instructional grouping options for students with learning disabilities.

3. What is assistive technology? What assistive technology is appropriate for preschool children with learning disabilities? How can assistive technology be used with elementary and secondary students with learning disabilities? What are some characteristics of well-designed, time-efficient software programs?

What Are Some Considerations for the General Education Teacher?

Instruction for students with learning disabilities typically takes place in a general education classroom, with or without direct special education support, although some pullout classes may be necessary. In fact, almost all students with learning disabilities spend at least a portion of their day in general education settings (U.S. Department of Education, 2006). The role of the special education teacher is most often that of a collaborator or team teacher working with the general education teacher. The educational goals for students with learning disabilities will usually be derived from the general education curriculum. The high frequency of this occurrence is likely affected by the IDEA 04 requirement that students with disabilities be included in statewide assessment programs. Some ways to provide access to the general education curriculum for students with learning disabilities include the use of accommodations, adaptations, parallel outcomes, and overlapping curriculum.

An **accommodation** is a change based on the student's needs in how information is presented by the teacher or how understanding is demonstrated by the student (King-Sears, 2001). Accommodations may be provided in instructional methods and materials, such as think aloud models and graphic organizers; assignments and tests, such as varying formats and step-by-step instructions; time demands and scheduling, such as extended time for tests and early assignments; and the learning environment, such as in the use of a closed study carrel to complete work (Beech, 2003). For example, a student with a learning disability may need extended time to answer essay questions given in a history class, or the student may be

Relevant
CEC Standard
▶ Co-planning and co-teaching methods to strengthen content acquisition of individuals with learning disabilities (LD10K1)

JUSTIN REVISITED

Justin's general education teacher is concerned about his progress. Do you think Justin should remain in a general education classroom? Why or why not?

accommodation A change in the input or output method used by the teacher or the student related to the intended instructional outcome without changing the content or conceptual level.

Classroom Suggestions Accommodations That Can Be Made in the General Education Classroom for Students with Learning Disabilities

DIFFICULTY	EXAMPLES OF ACCOMMODATIONS
Understanding lectures, discussions	❑ Introduce new vocabulary before the lesson. ❑ Provide overview of content at beginning. ❑ Use advance organizers on what will be included.
Following directions	❑ Use prearranged signal to gain attention. ❑ Change tone of voice to alert student. ❑ Give student agenda or schedule for each day. ❑ Repeat and simplify directions. ❑ Combine oral directions with pictures or diagrams. ❑ Assign a study buddy.
Completing assignments	❑ Break long-term assignments into parts with earlier due dates. ❑ Use a kitchen timer. ❑ Give student individual responsibility checklist.
Confused by complex materials	❑ Block sections on paper for each response by drawing lines or folding. ❑ Use color coding. ❑ Use uncluttered, clearly formatted tests and worksheets.
Organizing or locating materials	❑ Let student use special folder or binder. ❑ Give student compartmentalized container. ❑ Give student a checklist for each class to be kept in binder. ❑ Let student keep one copy of school materials at home and another at school.
Handwriting	❑ Place a dot on starting place. ❑ Let student use a word processor. ❑ Let student dictate to a teaching assistant or classmate. ❑ Let student use audio or video recording. ❑ Reduce length of assignment or allow more time.

Source: Adapted from Beech (2003).

allowed to present the information in the form of a graphic organizer rather than an essay. Many accommodations also help students without disabilities, but they are *necessary* for some students with learning disabilities to benefit from the general education curriculum (Bigge & Stump, 1999). See the Classroom Suggestions above for other examples of accommodations.

Beyond accommodations, some types of curriculum changes may be considered in teaching students with learning disabilities in general education classrooms (King-Sears, 1997, 2001; Switlick, 1997). First, an **adaptation** is a change made to the curriculum that keeps the academic content the same as for other students but slightly changes the conceptual level required. For example, if most students are required to define 20 terms, a particular student with a learning disability may need only match the definitions and terms, while another student with a different learning disability may be required to learn fewer terms. Second, a **parallel curriculum** is a curriculum change in which all students study the same content, but what is to be learned within that curriculum differs for a student with a learning disability. For example, whereas most students in the math class are working on basic addition facts, the student with a learning disability may be working on one-to-one correspondence. Finally, an **overlapping curriculum** plans for a student to participate in both a shared curriculum and a supplementary curriculum based on his or her specific needs, allowing a student with a learning disability to be involved in the general education curriculum while also working on very different content or curriculum goals (King-Sears, 2001). For example, a student may work on the same general science goals as the rest of the class while also being assigned the overlapping goals of ask-

adaptation A change made to the curriculum that keeps the academic content the same but slightly changes the conceptual level required of the student.

parallel curriculum The content is the same as for most students but major changes in the outcome are made within that content.

overlapping curriculum A student is involved in the general education curriculum while also working on very different content or curriculum goals.

ing for help and accepting criticism in a social skills curriculum. In summary, as most students with learning disabilities spend at least part of their day in general education classrooms, the general educator must be prepared to work with these students, both on his or her own and in collaboration with the special education teacher.

Check Your Understanding

1. What is an accommodation?

2. What are some ways in which the general education curriculum may be adapted to meet the needs of students with learning disabilities?

3. What is a parallel curriculum? What is an overlapping curriculum?

PRACTICE

Practical Considerations for the Classroom

Learning Disabilities is an IDEA 04 category. IDEA defines learning disabilities as "a disorder in one or more of the basic psychological processes involved in understanding or in using language, spoken or written, which may manifest in an imperfect ability to listen, think, speak, read, spell, or do mathematical calculations." Disorders included are perceptual disabilities, brain injury, minimal brain dysfunction, dyslexia, and developmental aphasia. Disorders not included are learning problems that are primarily the result of visual, hearing, or motor disabilities; mental retardation; emotional disturbance; or environmental, cultural, or economic disadvantage.

Identification Tools: The general classroom teacher often makes the initial identification based on classroom observation and performance, and state- or districtwide assessments. *Prereferral Assessment and RTI Approaches:* Possibly uses criterion-referenced testing, curriculum-based assessment, and criterion-referenced measurement. *Formal Identification:* Several sources are used for identification. They may include intelligence and achievement tests, tests measuring process skills, and language and academic tests. The response to intervention approach may also be used.

Characteristics	Indicators You Might See
Related to Reading	May have problems with phonological awareness or processing; rapid automatic naming; word recognition (mispronunciation; skipping, adding, or substituting words; reversing letters or words; difficulty blending sounds together); and comprehension (due to lack of background knowledge, difficulty understanding text structure, and vocabulary deficits).
Related to Mathematics	Possible problems with basic number facts, calculation, application, language of math, problem solving, oral drills and worksheets, word problems, math anxiety, and retrieving information from long-term memory.
Writing and Written Expression Characteristics	Possible problems with handwriting, spelling, or written language/written expression (punctuation, vocabulary, and sentence structure).
Expressive and Receptive Language Characteristics	Possible problems with producing and understanding language.
Cognitive-Related Characteristics	Possible problems with attention, memory, strategy use, and metacognition.
Social and Emotional Characteristics	Possible social skills deficits, and problems with social cognition and relationships with others. May have fewer friends and less social status than peers. Possible behavioral problems include depression, anxiety disorders, and antisocial personality disorder. May also display learned helplessness.

	Methodologies and Strategies to Try	**Considerations for the General Classroom and Collaboration**
lities will participate in the general ost likely need intensive instruction in content of learning. o include declarative knowledge, ional knowledge. gram for reading. (phonological awareness, decoding uage (teaching writing as a process), oblem solving), and study skills (such agement, comprehending textbook the development of goal setting and program with daily routines and m presented in an organized, sequential isks rather than extraneous stimuli. nd when to teach; provide activities for ; organize and pace the curriculum; and direct instruction. acognitive strategies instruction. ing Strategies Curriculum would be of ocial interaction. Consider attribution ELLs include using visuals to reinforce cooperative learning and peer tutoring, language by allowing students to ve language, providing sufficient time e oral language and writing in formal and n rich vocabulary words during lessons to terary concepts. Also consider providing lectures; adapting textbooks and entary materials. : areas, make sure you can see all naterials and supplies easily accessible, whole class presentations. ronment should be structured and independence, and functionality. It nd literacy development. tudents, the environment should be " Structure and routine are important. dividual work, large and small group work, arning. Decrease possible distractions. le one-to-one instruction, small group, classwide peer tutoring. r interactive software as well as other der students. tudents, consider how the computer can oring, instructional games, research, chnology is available to help develop nizational skills. ulture in mind when recommending	• Task Analysis (p. 113) • Direction Instruction (p. 113) • Cognitive Strategies (p. 115) • Metacognitive Strategies (p. 115) • Mnemonics (p. 117) • Attribution Retraining (p. 118)	Instruction generally occurs in the general education classroom. The general education teacher should: • Establish a positive climate that promotes valuing and accepting personal responsibility for learning. • Consider accommodations such as modified instructional methods or materials, assignments and tests, time demands and scheduling, and the learning environment. • Consider adapting the academic content. • Consider a parallel or overlapping curriculum. **Collaboration** General and special educators should consult on: • Determining the curriculum • Developing accommodations • Choosing procedures and strategies • Planning the physical environment • Planning for assistive technology

Chapter Summary

Go to the text's Online Learning Center at **www.mhhe.com**/taylor1e
to access study resources, Web links, practice quizzes, and extending materials.

What Are the Foundations of Learning Disabilities?

- The history of learning disabilities can be viewed in four distinct periods: the foundational phase, the transition phase, the integration phase, and the current phase. In the current phase, the focus is on the academic, behavioral, cognitive, and language aspects of learning disabilities.
- The IDEA 04 definition of learning disabilities, which includes both inclusion and exclusion criteria, is most frequently used although the NJCLD definition has received support.
- About 4% to 5% of school-aged children are identified as having a learning disability, representing almost half of all students identified as having a disability under IDEA 04. Prevalence seems to be affected by gender, ethnic background, and geographic region.

What Are the Causes and Characteristics of Learning Disabilities?

- Possible causes of learning disabilities are grouped into neurological; genetic; and environmental, including prenatal, perinatal, and postnatal factors.
- Learning disabilities represent a wide range of characteristics, and no one individual will display all of them.
- Frequently reported characteristics related to learning disabilities include problems in the areas of reading, mathematics, written expression, expressive and receptive language, cognition, and social and emotional skills.

How Are Students with Learning Disabilities Identified?

- IDEA 04 now allows the use of response to intervention to help in the identification process.
- Identification of a learning disability typically involves the measurement of intelligence and achievement and, in some states, testing psychological processing.

What and How Do I Teach Students with Learning Disabilities?

- Most students with learning disabilities participate in the general education curriculum. In planning for content, teachers should consider types of content knowledge and whether extra instruction is needed in the areas of reading, written language, mathematics, or study skills.
- Students with learning disabilities may go on to postsecondary settings or move directly into the workforce. Transition services to prepare for either of these routes needs to be a part of the curriculum.
- Instructional procedures found to be particularly effective for students with learning disabilities include task analysis, direct instruction, and cognitive and metacognitive strategies instruction. English language learners with learning disabilities may require additional accommodations to fully benefit from instructional procedures.

What Are Other Instructional Considerations for Students with Learning Disabilities?

- Structure and organization are key aspects of the environment for students with learning disabilities and need to be considered in planning the physical arrangement of the classroom.
- Grouping options that should be considered when teaching students with learning disabilities include one-to-one instruction, small groups, whole class, and peer tutoring. Which option is used will depend on the individual student and what is being taught.
- The use of technology to assist students with learning disabilities can be valuable from preschool through the secondary level. Technology is often used with students with learning disabilities to make the presentation of information more interesting and clear, to provide additional practice with concepts, and to provide supports needed to complete tasks.

What Are Some Considerations for the General Education Teacher?

- The general education teacher may adjust assignments or lessons through accommodations and adaptations to the curriculum.
- Parallel curriculum outcomes or an overlapping curriculum may be used to aid inclusion of students with learning disabilities in the general education classroom.

Reflection Questions

1. Do you think that a severe discrepancy between ability and achievement should still be used as a criterion for the identification of learning disabilities? Why or why not?
2. As noted in this chapter, the specific cause of a learning disability is frequently unknown. Given this fact, do you think students from low-socioeconomic environments should be excluded from the learning disability category even though that might be associated with their academic problems? Why or why not?
3. Does the response to intervention model make sense for identifying students with learning disabilities? Why or why not? Should it be used by itself to identify these students, or should other assessment information also be included? Why?

g disabilities be included
and be required to meet
ate in state assessment pro-
d cons of doing so?
to provide accommoda-
dents with learning disabili-

ties because they feel it is unfair to the other students.
How would you justify the need for accommodations
for the reluctant educator (other than that it is required
by law)?

6. Do you think there are transitions at the elementary level
that should be addressed? If so, what are some of them?

ities: For Learning and Your Portfolio

termine what accommoda-
or students with learning
y. Also find out if there is
a student who thinks he or
sability to be evaluated for
the accommodations that
used for identifying a pos-

or writing" simulates what it
bility. Try this activity.
ite your name on a piece of
directly at the paper. Think
and what your handwriting

here are many different
isorders of psychological
t, if any, procedures/tests
ol district to measure pro-
columns on a sheet of

paper. In one column, indicate the various aspects of
psychological processes that are evaluated. In the
other, list the corresponding test(s) that are used.

4. In the direct instruction approach described in this
chapter, programming for generalization in the form of
a rationale begins early in the lesson. Present three
examples (one in-school and two out-of-school) for students on why they need to learn to alphabetize: *street*,
short, *state*. Design a homework assignment that would
provide further generalization.

5. Create a list of six mnemonics that you remember from
your earlier days in school.

6. (*Portfolio Possibility*) Discover how services are provided to students with learning disabilities at your college
or university. Is there an office for students with disabilities? Or are services provided through another mechanism? Is there any assistive technology available? If so,
what? Are there support personnel? How does this compare to the secondary school services in your district?

SUMMARY

CHAPTER 5

Students with Mental Retardation/Intellectual Disabilities

...TRODUCING JANETTA

...e sec- ...t her ...w up ...has ...many ...anet- ...aca- ...local ...al ser-

...on- ...g ...he gets ...of ...

...y all ...nsis- ...en ...ers. ...ut ...rds. ...cting ...nath

Janetta is able to count to 20 and can add single digits if she has manipulatives or uses her fingers. She has not learned to tell time. She also has difficulty sustaining her attention when Ms. Scott reads stories of some length. Sometimes Janetta doesn't follow directions, such as lining up when told to do so or getting out materials in a timely manner. Ms. Scott feels this occurs because Janetta doesn't process the message as quickly or clearly as do other children. Janetta sometimes needs help in art, where she has trouble following directions during instruction and completing her work on time; in the cafeteria, where she has difficulty making choices among food options; and on the playground, when learning rules for games. Janetta appears to be less independent than most of her classmates. For example, Janetta needs help to button her coat

correctly and when washing her hands. Janetta tries very hard at whatever she does and enjoys Ms. Scott's positive attention.

Ms. Scott used a variety of teaching techniques and materials unsuccessfully during prereferral intervention. ▶

Case Studies

She had a peer buddy demonstrate how to follow directions and complete tasks, maintained proximity to Janetta to allow closer monitoring, and used visual aids to help Janetta when she had trouble processing information presented orally. Ms. Scott is having trouble finding the time to give Janetta the amount of support she needs. The prereferral intervention team engaged Janetta's mother in this prereferral process, seeking suggestions for how Janetta might learn best and what types of activities she might find reinforcing. ■

Janetta does not appear to have any physical or sensory disabilities, but she is having difficulty learning skills at the same pace as her peers. Her life experiences could explain some of her delays in development, but the fact that she has repeated kindergarten and still is not mastering the skills at that level suggests there may be other problems that could represent an intellectual disability. If ultimately diagnosed with an intellectual disability, Janetta will most likely be classified as having a milder disability rather than a more severe one. Most students with intellectual disabilities do exhibit mild to moderate disabilities (Batshaw & Shapiro, 2002). That is, their developmental delays may be less noticeable until they reach school age where the demands of learning academic skills make their challenges more evident. A much smaller group of students with intellectual disabilities have severe disabilities. They are discussed in Chapter 12. Although some people may envision a student with Down syndrome when they think of a student with an intellectual disability, most students with intellectual disabilities do not have Down syndrome or possess physical characteristics that make them appear "different" from other students. They may appear typical in every respect but have difficulty adapting to ever more demanding school, home, and community environments. Some students, like Janetta, have greater difficulty with academic and more abstract learning but function reasonably well in everyday routine activities. Some individuals need supports academically as well as in daily living routines. It is important to remember that there is considerable variation in the characteristics, abilities, and needs of students with intellectual disabilities. Labels such as intellectual disabilities or mental retardation may tend to conjure up images of incompetent or dysfunctional people, so future teachers should be aware that many people in this disability category can and do function quite well with needed supports.

What Are the Foundations of Mental Retardation/Intellectual Disabilities?

You may be most familiar with the disability that is discussed in this chapter being referred to as mental retardation. However, throughout this chapter we use the term *intellectual disabilities* based on its recent adoption by many in the field. After an overview of the history of intellectual disabilities, we share the development of this new terminology and then explore how both definitions and terminology have changed to reflect shifts in thinking about what an intellectual disability is and how educators should think about students who are identified within the IDEA 04 category of mental retardation, the term used in the law. Also included in this section of the chapter are an overview of the classification systems you may encounter in your future schools and information on the prevalence of this disability.

A Brief History of Mental Retardation/Intellectual Disabilities

Historically, social reactions to people with intellectual disabilities have ranged from positive, such as eliciting caretaking responses, to rather negative, such as prompting rejection (Berkson, 2004). For example, early histories of Western society depicted people with diminished cognitive abilities and different behavior as demonically possessed, leading to less regard for their treatment and welfare (Braddock & Parish, 2002). This ambivalent attitude toward people with disabilities continued in the emergence of American society. The 19th and 20th centuries ushered in an age during which special hospitals and institutions were constructed to provide care and treatment for people who would now most likely be identified as having intellectual disabilities. It was apparent as the 20th century began that there was concern for the treatment of individuals with intellectual disabilities, albeit tempered with less than favorable attitudes about the origins of the condition. Some professionals believed intellectual disabilities were punishment for violating natural laws of moral behavior (Braddock & Parish, 2002).

These less than favorable attitudes of the early 20th century were perhaps most evident in the rise of eugenics, born of social Darwinism, which established itself as a movement concerned with genetics and its impact on race and humankind. Eugenicists believed that natural selection and "survival of the fittest" principles could be applied to humans and that people with intellectual disabilities should be segregated from society and even sterilized to prevent reproduction (Trent, 1994). Even the professionals charged with care and treatment of the "feeble-minded" were often concerned with describing, explaining, and ultimately controlling a segment of society they believed was responsible for a variety of social problems including crime, pauperism, alcoholism, and prostitution (Elks, 2004). As the 20th century progressed, eugenicists lost favor and concern for civil rights emerged. The National Association for Retarded Children (now simply called the ARC to avoid the use of the term "retarded") was formed in the 1950s and was dedicated to advocacy and service provision to those with intellectual disabilities. In the 1960s the movement to deinstitutionalize individuals who had been housed in state institutions also grew in accordance with advocacy for policy change by President Kennedy's Panel on Mental Retardation in 1962 (Braddock & Parish, 2002). "Normalization," providing as typical a life in home and community settings as possible, became a guiding principle in advancing services for people with intellectual disabilities (Wolfensberger, 1972). By the 1970s, there was movement across the country toward more and improved educational and community services, culminating in the passage of PL 94–142.

Today, IDEA 04, Section 504 of the Rehabilitation Act of 1973, and the Americans with Disabilities Act secure and safeguard the rights of individuals with intellectual disabilities to equal opportunity and equal protection under the law. Perhaps most important in the historical perspective of intellectual disabilities was the success of parents and families, in particular, in organizing an advocacy movement that pushed the nation toward recognition of and legislation guaranteeing the needs and rights of individuals with intellectual disabilities (Braddock & Parish, 2002). Teachers are among the more influential members of society. How we perceive, treat, educate, and promote respect for students with intellectual disabilities will influence how students and other adults without disabilities respond to and include those individuals.

Definitions of Mental Retardation/Intellectual Disabilities

When considering the definition of intellectual disabilities, it is important to remember that individuals with intellectual disabilities are unique as individuals. The two definitions of intellectual disabilities most relevant to educators are the IDEA 04 and American Association on Intellectual and Developmental Disabilities (AAIDD) definitions: the former because of its use in the law, and the latter because it was developed by an organization that influences professional dialogue and thought.

Despite questions regarding the appropriateness of the term *mental retardation* and its negative connotations in society and for the individual, this term has been and continues to be used in legislation (Smith, 2003). IDEA 04 did not change the definition from earlier reauthorizations and maintains the use of the term *mental retardation*. The U.S. Department of Education saw no compelling reason to change the term or the definition as these were considered sufficiently broad for identification of these students (Federal Register, 34CFR 300.8(c)(6)). The Division on Mental Retardation

Relevant CEC Standards

▶ Definitions and issues related to the identification of individuals with intellectual disabilities/ developmental disabilities (MR1K1)

▶ Continuum of placement and services available for individuals with intellectual disabilities/ developmental disabilities (MR1K3)

and Developmental Disabilities, a division of the Council for Exceptional Children, voted in 2002 to eliminate mental retardation from its name and is now called the Division on Developmental Disabilities. As of January 1, 2007, after some debate, AAIDD members voted to change the organization's name from the American Association on Mental Retardation (AAMR). The AAIDD changed its name in the belief that the terms *intellectual* and *developmental* disabilities were less stigmatizing than the term *mental retardation* (AAIDD, 2007). Some experts prefer the term *developmental disabilities* to either mental retardation or intellectual disabilities as it may better reflect the wide variety of conditions resulting from myriad causes that lead to disabilities that emerge between birth and 18 years of age, the developmental period (e.g., Smith, 2003).

One aspect of identifying students with intellectual disabilities under IDEA 04 is that educational performance must be adversely affected.

The IDEA 04 Definition

IDEA 04 defines mental retardation as "significantly subaverage general intellectual functioning existing concurrently with deficits in adaptive behavior and manifested during the developmental period, that adversely affects a child's educational performance." This definition includes four key components:

- the individual has subaverage general intellectual functioning, often measured as an IQ of 70–75 or below (or about 2 standard deviations or more below the mean on an individual intelligence test);
- the individual displays concurrent deficits in adaptive behavior, meaning problems in adapting to everyday life in school, home, and/or the community;
- the disability is manifested during the developmental period, meaning it is present prior to 18 years of age; and
- the disability adversely affects educational performance.

This definition is often used in public schools, but IDEA 04 does allow states to consider using terminology other than mental retardation and to emphasize current functioning rather than just focusing on the four above components (Federal Register, 34CFR300.8(c)(6)), which reflects more recent thought about the use of the term *mental retardation*.

The AAMR's Definition

In 2002 the AAMR published the most recent edition of *Mental Retardation: Definition, Classification, and Systems of Support* (Luckasson et al., 2002) (note the organization had not yet changed its name to AAIDD), which includes its definition of what they still called mental retardation. This definition reads:

> Mental retardation is a disability characterized by significant limitations in both intellectual functioning and adaptive behavior as expressed in conceptual, social, and practical adaptive skills. This disability originates before age 18. (Luckasson et al., 2002, p. 1)

However, the AAMR also places prominent emphasis on the student's present functioning and the impact that supports can have on functioning. The AAMR definition also emphasizes identification of strengths as well as limitations. These emphases reflect a changing perception of intellectual disabilities as a condition that is not solely one of limitations and that improvement may occur whatever the existing limitations may be (Luckasson et al., 2002).

JANETTA REVISITED Based on the IDEA 04 and AAIDD definitions, does Janetta appear to have challenges evident in the definition of intellectual disabilities? What leads you to your conclusion?

IDEA 04 and the AAMR both stress that an important purpose in identifying anyone with a disability is to also identify how to best help that individual grow and improve in knowledge and skills. Regardless of the definition applied to identify students with intellectual disabilities, future teachers should understand that the students in this disability category are not all alike. Smith (2006) pointed out, "Maybe it will be someone who needs constant care, or maybe it will be someone much like yourself but who needs help with academic skills. Maybe it will be someone with severe physical disabilities, or maybe it will be someone you would pass on the street without notice" (p. 201).

Classification of Individuals with Intellectual Disabilities

Luckasson et al. (2002) pointed out that classification systems for describing levels of intellectual disabilities may be used for a variety of purposes and may be based on the needs of individuals and their families, researchers, and practitioners. Classification could be based on intensities of needed supports, etiology, levels of measured intelligence, or levels of assessed adaptive behavior. Perhaps the more important aspects of classification for teachers may be for determining eligibility, organizing information about the individual, and planning effective educational programs. For eligibility determination, schools may classify students by severity or degree of disability.

Classification by Severity or Degree. AAMR introduced a classification system developed around the severity of mental retardation in the 1980s (Luckasson et al., 2002). This classification system, based on four levels of intellectual disabilities, remains in use today:

mild (IQ range of 50–55 to 70–75)

moderate (IQ range from 35–40 to 50–55)

severe (IQ range from 20–25 to 35–40)

profound (IQ below 20–25)

This system is the subject of criticism for its emphasis on IQ as the determinant of a person's abilities and because of the arbitrary nature of cutoff scores such as an IQ of 70–75 (Greenspan, 2006).

Classification by Levels of Support Needed. The 1992 AAMR definition of mental retardation presented a new system of classification based on level of supports needed (Luckasson et al., 1992). This system of classification places less emphasis on measured intelligence and focuses on the present level of functioning of the individual. This concept of supports needed was maintained and refined in the 2002 manual. Supports needed are categorized into four different levels: intermittent, limited, extensive, and pervasive (Luckasson et al., 1992). These levels of support, which can change over time, are summarized in Table 5.1.

A student who needed limited supports (such as job training and support to secure and maintain employment) at one point in time could become more independent and

TABLE 5.1	American Association on Mental Retardation (AAMR) Levels of Support, 2002	
LEVEL	**DESCRIPTION**	**EXAMPLE**
Intermittent	Provided on an as-needed basis; short-term or episodic in nature	Assistance needed while recovering from a serious illness
Limited	Time-limited but more consistent than intermittent	Transition services needed when moving from school to adult life
Extensive	Regular or daily support in some environments	Daily supervision in maintaining living arrangements needed
Pervasive	Consistent, high-intensity supports	24-hour nursing care needed involving more than one staff member each day

Source: Luckasson, R., Borthwick-Duffy, S., Buntinx, Wil H. E., Coulter, D. L., Craig, E. M., Reeve, A., Schalock, R. L., Snell, M. E., Spitalnik, D. M., Spreat, S., & Tassé, M. J. (2002). *Mental Retardation: Definition, classification, and systems of supports* (10th ed.). Washington, DC: American Association on Mental Retardation.

require only intermittent supports at a later time (support staff periodically check on the person's job performance) because the earlier supports have led to improved performance. The 2002 manual stresses that "although the concept of supports is by no means new, *what is new is the belief that the judicious application of supports can improve the functional capabilities of individuals with mental retardation*" (Luckasson et al., 2002, p. 145). The AAIDD publishes a Supports Intensity Scale that allows professionals to measure the support needs of individuals with intellectual disabilities in 57 life activities in areas such as home living, community living, lifelong learning, employment, health and safety, socializing, protection and advocacy, as well as 28 behavioral and medical areas such as skin care, respiratory care, prevention of emotional outbursts, and maintenance of mental health treatments (Thompson et al., 2007).

The term *mental retardation* may conjure perceptions about the immutability and power of IQs, and a deficit-oriented concept of an individual's ability (Greenspan, 2006). However, current thinking emphasizes that intellectual disabilities are multifaceted in how and where they affect people; how supports can alter a student's adaptation at school, home, and community; and that these disabilities may be better defined by how much help a student needs than by an IQ (Luckasson et al., 2002).

Prevalence of Mental Retardation/Intellectual Disabilities

Relevant CEC Standards

▶ Factors that influence overrepresentation of culturally/linguistically diverse individuals (MR1K2)

▶ Trends and practices in the field of intellectual disabilities and developmental disabilities (MR1K5)

According to the U.S. Department of Education (2006), .94% of students, ages 6–21 years, are classified as having mental retardation (using the IDEA category name). Based on this prevalence estimate, every teacher in a typical public school will engage students with intellectual disabilities at some point in his or her career. However, some experts believe that this prevalence rate is low as some students who may have been identified as having a mild intellectual disability in the 1970s may now be served in the learning disabilities category or not served at all (Smith, 2006). This may be due, at least in part, to school personnel deciding on the use of a learning disability label in preference to a label of intellectual disability and the use of an IQ cutoff score of 70 (Donovan & Cross, 2002).

Prevalence rates have indicated that a larger proportion of African Americans receiving special education are identified as having mental retardation than any other racial/ethnic group (U.S. Department of Education, 2003b). Oswald, Coutinho, Best, and Nguyen (2001) found that whereas the overall prevalence rate of mental retardation was about 1%, the prevalence rate among African Americans was slightly higher than 1%. The *25th Annual Report to Congress* stressed that African American students were nearly three times more likely to be identified as having mental retardation than students in other racial/ethnic groups (U.S. Department of Education, 2003b).

Of importance to all teachers is that we believe schools and educational systems should be inherently fair places where all students are treated equally. Overrepresentation in special education could easily be perceived as a serious threat to the fairness we all believe should exist in our schools. Why this overrepresentation exists and how it can be eliminated has not yet been resolved. In a review of the literature, Green (2005) suggested that overrepresentation may be due to lack of effective instructional programs that address the needs of African American students; ineffective identification procedures and processes; assumptions and beliefs of professionals who dominate the field; teachers' attitudes and perceptions; lack of or inappropriate learning opportunities; a disconnect in race, culture, and class among students and school personnel; reliance on high-stakes assessments; and a disconnect between school personnel's view of child behavior and a cultural/familial perspective.

Unequal representation has also been identified between males and females. Males tend to be identified as having mental retardation more often than females (Oswald et al., 2001), with the *25th Annual Report to Congress* specifying that for students 6–17 years of age, about 56% are male (U.S. Department of Education, 2003b). This may be in part due to the fact that intellectual disabilities are associated with some genetic disorders, such as Fragile X syndrome, which occur more frequently in males than females.

Check Your Understanding

1. How have people with intellectual disabilities historically been treated by society? What improvements in treatment occurred during the latter portion of the 20th century and in the early 21st century?

2. What is the IDEA 04 definition of mental retardation? The AAMR definition of intellectual disabilities? How are these definitions different from one another? How are they similar?

3. How does the levels of support classification system differ from classification by levels of severity?

4. What is the prevalence of mental retardation/intellectual disabilities?

5. What group is overrepresented in the IDEA 04 category of mental retardation?

What Are the Causes and Characteristics of Mental Retardation/Intellectual Disabilities?

The future teacher is often unaware of or not familiar with the specific or suspected cause of a student's intellectual disability. In fact, a specific cause is frequently not actually known. When a specific cause is known, it may help the teacher better understand some of the characteristics that emerge as a result of that specific cause.

Causes of Mental Retardation/Intellectual Disabilities

Taylor, Richards, and Brady (2005) discussed two major categories of causes of intellectual disabilities: genetic and chromosomal causes, and environmental causes. Causes can be prenatal, perinatal, or postnatal in origin. In addition, psychosocial factors may not always lead to an intellectual disability, but one or more of these factors may place a child at risk for an intellectual disability (Taylor et al., 2005).

Genetic and Chromosomal Causes

The 2002 AAIDD classification manual (Luckasson et al., 2002) lists examples of disorders associated with genetic and chromosomal causes. Table 5.2 lists conditions linked to chromosomal and genetic factors that result in an intellectual disability. Knowledge of the role of genetics and chromosomal disorders has implications for prevention and treatment of intellectual disabilities as well as genetic counseling for potential parents (Warren, 2002b).

Relevant CEC Standards

▶ Causes and theories of intellectual disabilities and implications for prevention (MR2K1)

▶ Medical aspects of intellectual disabilities and their implications for learning (MR2K2)

TABLE 5.2	Examples of Chromosomal and Genetic Causes of Intellectual Disabilities
CONDITION	**POSSIBLE PROBLEMS/RESULTS**
Tuberous sclerosis	Tumors in nervous system may lead to ID
Phenylketonuria (PKU)	Inability to metabolize the enzyme phenylalanine; can result in ID if untreated
Hurler syndrome	Inability to break down various carbohydrates; usually results in mental and physical disabilities and early death
Tay-Sachs disease	Abnormal buildup of lipids within body tissue results in physical and mental disabilities and early death
Fragile X syndrome	Possible ID; communication, behavioral, and attention disabilities
Down syndrome	Can result in ID and physical features; usually milder disability and features

Source: Taylor, R. L., Richards, S. B., & Brady, M. P. (2005). *Mental retardation. Historical perspectives, current practices, and future directions.* Boston: Pearson.

TABLE 5.3	Examples of Environmental Causes of Intellectual Disabilities

CONDITION	ORIGIN	POSSIBLE PROBLEMS/RESULTS
Infections		
Toxoplasmosis	Protozoic infection that can be carried in raw meat or cat feces	ID can occur particularly if infection occurs in first two trimesters of pregnancy
Rubella	German measles infection	ID and sensory disabilities can result especially during first trimester of pregnancy
Radiation	Exposure to radiation in utero; effects vary depending on time and degree of exposure	Can result in ID
Malnutrition	Pre- or postnatal lack of adequate nutrition	Can result in ID; may be among the leading causes in developing countries
Maternal Factors		
Maternal health	Poor prenatal care	Increases risk for conditions (e.g., prematurity) that can lead to ID
Drug and substance abuse	Exposure in utero	Increases risk for conditions (e.g., prematurity) that can lead to ID, including fetal alcohol syndrome
Blood type incompatibility	Rh blood factor incompatibility between mother and fetus	Can result in ID if untreated

Source: Taylor, R. L., Richards, S. B., & Brady, M. P. (2005). *Mental retardation. Historical perspectives, current practices, and future directions.* Boston: Pearson.

Environmental Causes

Environmental factors that occur prenatally, perinatally, and postnatally can result in biological or medical problems that affect the individual's growth, development, and functioning. An example of a prenatal cause of intellectual disabilities is a maternal infection during pregnancy, such as rubella (German measles). Anoxia, the loss of oxygen, to the baby during childbirth is an example of a perinatal cause. Anoxia could occur, for example, if the umbilical cord wraps around the baby's neck, cutting off breathing. An example of a postnatal cause is encephalitis, resulting from being bitten by a mosquito infected with a virus leading to a high fever and brain damage (Taylor et al., 2005). Table 5.3 presents examples of environmental factors related to the prenatal, perinatal, and postnatal causes of intellectual disabilities.

Psychosocial Factors

Psychosocial factors may not always cause disabilities but may place an individual at risk for developing an intellectual disability (Taylor et al., 2005). As Byrne (2000) noted, the precise biological origins of many intellectual disabilities are not easily identified; therefore, intellectual disabilities might be viewed as a social category of disability as much as a scientific or medical category. Attempts have been made to determine factors that may be *related* to intellectual disabilities in addition to factors that *cause* them.

About 24% of elementary and middle school students and 25% of high school students with disabilities live in poverty compared to 20% of students without disabilities (U.S. Department of Education, 2003). Living in poverty in and of itself might be sufficient for identifying a child *at risk* for developmental difficulties that can lead to disability (Guralnick, 1998). For example, lack of proper nutrition and health care are variables affecting many children living in poverty (Baroff, 1999; Reichard, Sacco, & Turnbull, 2004). If malnutrition has occurred, the condition must be addressed by age 2 for the child to catch up in growth and development (Baroff, 1999). If a child receives inadequate health care, the child may be at greater risk for having conditions that go untreated (e.g., high fever), which can ultimately affect the child's growth and development. The precise interaction of psychosocial factors with other factors that lead to intellectual disability is not known, but the presence of both biological conditions (e.g., a genetic condition) and one or more of these factors (Batshaw & Shapiro, 2002) may result in intellectual disabilities.

Future teachers should not equate the presence of conditions in a child's life, such as living in poverty, as being the specific cause of a child's intellectual disability. These psychosocial factors do create *risk* for developmental problems and therefore may contribute to an intellectual disability, but the specific cause of some intellectual disabilities is not known and may result from an interaction of factors (Luckasson et al., 2002).

Prevention of Intellectual **Disabilities**

Efforts have been made over time to reduce the prevalence of intellectual disabilities through prevention. These preventive efforts take many forms. Some are focused on genetic causes, and others on environmental causes and psychosocial factors.

With advances in medicine and technology, we are now able to identify more conditions that are associated with intellectual disabilities at the prenatal stage. The Human Genome Project has provided a wealth of genetic knowledge with the potential for affecting the field of intellectual disabilities. Knowledge of human genetics could prove useful not only in early identification but also in the prevention and treatment of some disorders that cause intellectual disabilities (Capone, 2001).

The development of methods such as magnetic imaging and computer tomography has proven helpful in identifying such problems as neural tube defects and hydrocephalus (H. Alexander, 2000), and the isolation and analysis of fetal cells found in the mother's blood is useful in identifying chromosomal disorders prior to birth (D. Alexander, 2000). Amniocentesis, sampling of amniotic fluid prior to birth, and chorionic villi sampling, removal of and testing a small amount of placental tissue, help in early diagnosis but not necessarily in prevention of a condition leading to intellectual disabilities. Continued research in human genetics, fetal surgery, fetal therapy, and other medical technologies may provide more preventive techniques, although the ethical considerations in such treatments may raise debate (Taylor et al., 2005). Knowing a child will be born with a disability can raise difficult questions for would-be parents and families.

Good prenatal and neonatal care are important in the prevention of intellectual disabilities. Infectious agents, exposure to drugs and alcohol in utero, and malnutrition are examples of environmental causes that can be avoided. Early intervention services are critical in these efforts. One such important effort that demonstrated the effectiveness of early intervention through educational and other services was the Carolina Abecedarian Project (see An Important Event).

AN IMPORTANT EVENT

The Carolina Abecedarian Project

Ramey, E. T., & Campbell, F. A. (1984). Preventative education for high-risk children: Cognitive consequences of Carolina Abecedarian Project. *American Journal of Mental Deficiency, 88,* 515–523.

The Carolina Abecedarian Project was designed to determine whether interventions during early childhood could prevent intellectual disabilities (Ramey & Campbell, 1984). Children included in the Carolina Abecedarian Project came from low-socioeconomic status environments. Half of the children were exposed to a "prevention-oriented" intervention program that began during infancy, as

(continued)

early as 6 weeks of age, and continued to the age of 5 years. Cognitive and language development were major goals of this educational intervention. All children received nutritional services, pediatric care, and related benefits, including medical and social worker input. This was to ensure that the only major difference between the groups was the intervention program itself. The results of the Carolina Abecedarian Project indicated that prevention of poor intellectual outcomes through intensive, systematic early intervention, combined with nutritional and health care, was indeed possible (Ramey & Ramey, 1992). Teachers should be aware that the use of early intervention services can reduce or eliminate the need for special education services at school age.

REFLECTION What impact might the addition of early educational interventions have on the overall growth and development of young children?

Characteristics of Students with Mental Retardation/Intellectual Disabilities

Relevant CEC Standards

▶ Theories of behavior problems of individuals with intellectual disabilities/developmental disabilities (MR1K6)

▶ Medical aspects of intellectual disabilities and their implications for learning (MR2K2)

▶ Psychological, social/emotional, and motor characteristics of individuals with intellectual disabilities/developmental disabilities (MR2K3)

▶ Impact of multiple disabilities on behavior (MR3K3)

Perhaps the most general distinguishing characteristic of students with intellectual disabilities is that they experience *difficulties in learning* due to deficits in intellectual functioning and adaptive behavior skills. Intellectual functioning involves many abilities, including acquiring new skills or knowledge, knowing how to use the various skills or knowledge in appropriate situations, and learning to use abstract thought and language. Students with intellectual disabilities, in general, also share several social, personal, and adaptive behavior skill characteristics.

Intellectual and Academic Characteristics

For ease of discussion, we have separated characteristics of intellectual disabilities into the major areas of attention, academic, memory, transfer and generalization, and language.

Attention Characteristics. In general, students with intellectual disabilities have problems attending to tasks. Findings related to attention include the following:

- Individuals with intellectual disabilities, as a group, may desire more personal feedback from others and, therefore, may pay more attention to people rather than to task requirements (Krupski, 1977).
- Direct training on all attention requirements of discrimination tasks can significantly improve the performance of students with intellectual disabilities (Ross & Ross, 1979). It also appears that using teaching materials and environments that are relevant to the individual's life (e.g., real coins and bills versus pictures on worksheet papers) may enhance attention.
- Attention difficulties of students with intellectual disabilities should be addressed in early intervention as well as subsequent schooling (Serna & Carlin, 2001).

Attending skills can be improved through instruction. Also, keep in mind that variables such as motivation and interest in the learning task can affect attention (Hodapp & Zigler, 1997). The more interesting the task is to an individual, the more likely the individual is to devote his or her attention to it.

Academic Characteristics. In school, learning is often viewed in terms of academic performance. Students with intellectual disabilities tend to have reading, especially comprehension, and mathematical skills well below grade level. Nearly 75% of students with mental retardation scored in the lowest possible range (below the 21st percentile) on measures of passage comprehension, letter/word identification, mathematical calculation, and applied problem assessments (U.S. Department of Education, 2003). Katims (2001) noted that although overall reading comprehension skills, oral reading, and writing skills were often commensurate with primer or early grade levels, many students showed improvement over time. Also, students with mild intellectual disabilities perform as well academically in inclusive educational settings as in pullout or resource settings, suggesting that academic skills can and do improve in inclusive classrooms (Cole, Waldron, & Majd, 2004). However, these same students are among those in special education more likely to be educated outside the most inclusive environments (U.S. Department of Education, 2003). Finally, it is important to remember that while about half of all students with a low IQ score will receive similar or lower academic achievement scores, about half will have the same or better achievement scores as their IQ score (McGrew & Evans, 2003).

Memory Characteristics. Although differences of opinion do exist, difficulties in memory do not appear to involve these students' ability to remember for a long period of time once information is committed to memory (Taylor et al., 2005). Information moves into long-term memory only when there is sufficient exposure and repetition of storage in short-term memory. For example, remembering a person's name without writing it down generally requires the learner to hear the name and repeat it several times, perhaps associating the name with the person's face. Numminen, Service, and Ruoppilla (2002) suggested that the research literature shows that individuals with intellectual disabilities have problems specifically with **working memory,** the part of the memory that holds information for short periods. Working memory could be considered the part of the memory that allows one to hold information in memory while working on a task. Repeating the name several times while also looking at the person's face allows one to store it in short-term memory so it can be used in conversation within the next minute. Long-term memory requires repeatedly using the name in association with the person's face, probably over a period of time, to be able to remember the name more or less permanently. Students with intellectual disabilities tend to perform and score more poorly on working memory tasks than their peers without disabilities (Henry & MacLean, 2002). However, Baldi (1998) found that memory training could improve the performance on a name-memorizing task in a majority of adolescent students with intellectual disabilities.

working memory Individual's ability to hold information for usage for short periods of time.

Transfer and Generalization Characteristics. Students with intellectual disabilities tend to have deficits in the ability to *transfer* information; apply learning to new, yet similar situations; and to *generalize*, or apply learning in different situations based on past learning. For example, a student might learn to use addition and subtraction with a calculator quite effectively in the classroom yet still need additional instruction on how to use that skill while shopping in the community. To ensure transfer and generalization, different situations and settings must be incorporated in instruction (Alberto & Troutman, 2006). Transfer and generalization problems lead to a need for supports in more environments or situations (Luckasson et al., 2002).

Language Characteristics. There is considerable evidence that many students with intellectual disabilities follow the same basic order of language development as do students without intellectual disabilities. However, language development, as a whole, may be delayed for this group (Tager-Flusher & Sullivan, 1998). For example, students could experience delays in learning vocabulary or engaging adequately in the give-and-take of conversation. Difficulties in memory may contribute to this problem, affecting the ability of some students to construct more complex verbal messages (Hesketh & Chapman, 1998). For example, a child may not adequately remember the events of two days ago to be able to tell others what was occurring at that time in the proper order and without omission of events. In addition, speech disorders might accompany language delays. Various studies indicate the presence of significant speech problems in students with intellectual disabilities, including articulation, voice, and fluency problems (Taylor et al., 2005).

Quality of life is linked to the quality of interpersonal relationships for students with intellectual disabilities.

Social and Personal Characteristics

The two areas of social and personal characteristics that we will focus on are personal expectations and social relationships. The social and personal characteristics of students with intellectual disabilities often reflect their own expectations of themselves, which are frequently based on their past experiences with failure or success (Taylor et al., 2005; Thomas & Patton, 1986). For example, a student with an intellectual disability who repeatedly fails in learning to read adequately may begin to believe he is unable to learn to read, as well as begin to believe he is unable to learn in other areas. Conversely, a student who believes he is capable of reading may work very hard in learning the vocabulary and reading skills necessary to obtain and maintain a job. Unfortunately, the expectations of personal failure are high for many of these students. Expectations may be based to some extent on whether students are internally motivated (they pursue tasks for the pleasure of solving problems, because the task is of interest, or are self-guided learners) or are extrinsically motivated (they are more concerned with the rewards or punishments associated with completing or failing to complete a task) (Woolfolk, 2001). Switzky (1997) stressed that individuals with intellectual disabilities probably experience both types of motivation, depending on the situation and circumstance, but there is evidence that many individuals with intellectual disabilities do exhibit extrinsic motivation (Hodapp & Zigler, 1997). Further evidence indicates that some students with intellectual disabilities also suffer from poor self-images or self-concepts (Taylor et al., 2005).

Another social-personal characteristic of students with intellectual disabilities involves relationships with peers who have no disabilities. Nearly half of parents of children with intellectual disabilities surveyed reported that their child rarely received phone calls from friends with only a quarter reporting frequent calls (U.S. Department of Education, 2003). One early finding that has received considerable support is that students with intellectual disabilities, if rejected by peers, tend to be rejected based on their *behavior* rather than on their having been labeled as having intellectual disabilities (Gottlieb, 1974). The quality of life people with intellectual disabilities enjoy is linked to the development of interpersonal relationships (Bonham et al., 2004; Storey, 1997). Relationships may develop and mature when common interests are shared among the participants (Green, Schlein, Mactavish, & Benepe, 1995). Development of appropriate social behaviors is a key to the acceptance of students with intellectual disabilities by those who have no disabilities. It should be emphasized that students with intellectual disabilities can and do make friends. Additionally, educating those without disabilities about their peers with intellectual disabilities can enhance acceptance and encourage development of social skills and relationships (Polloway, Patton, & Serna, 2005).

Adaptive Behavior Characteristics

Students with intellectual disabilities have limitations in adaptive behavior skills, the skills needed to function in different environments. Adaptive behavior skills are grouped into conceptual (or cognitive), social, and practical abilities and can cover a wide range of behavior and learning. Examples of adaptive skills include interpersonal skills, language skills, daily living skills, maintaining a safe environment, and being self-diected, among others. Limitations in adaptive behavior skills can include an acquisition deficit, not knowing how to perform a skill; a performance deficit, not knowing when to use a skill; or other motivational circumstances affecting whether or not a skill is used (Luckasson et al., 2002).

Community living and participation is another area of adaptive skill acquisition and performance. Overall, individuals with intellectual disabilities tend to live at home longer, be more dependent on social services, and be less well integrated in the workforce than their peers without disabilities (Blanck, 1998). However, individuals with milder intellectual disabilities may be significantly more likely to obtain competitive employment than those with more severe disabilities (Moore, Harley, & Gamble, 2004). There may, though, be more limited opportunities and training, in particular, for those with severe/profound levels of disability than for those with milder intellectual disabilities (Moore et al., 2004).

General discussion of the characteristics of individuals with intellectual disabilities tends to focus on knowledge and skill limitations, with less emphasis on strengths and abilities. The future teacher should be aware that these strengths do exist in each individual. Many students with intellectual disabilities are capable of learning academics and developing communication and other skills. Most individuals with intellectual disabilities are able to live, work, and function within the larger society with supports. Teachers can support these strengths by creating a supportive learning environment that develops motivation to learn rather than encouraging learned helplessness.

JANETTA REVISTED What characteristics does Janetta display that might lead a teacher to suspect she may need to be referred for assessment for eligibility for special education and related services?

Check Your Understanding

1. What are examples of known genetic and biomedical causes and environmental factors that can lead to intellectual disabilities?

2. What are some ways in which intellectual disabilities can be prevented?

3. What are the intellectual and academic characteristics of students with intellectual disabilities?

4. What are the social and personal characteristics of students with intellectual disabilities?

5. What are the adaptive behavior skill characteristics of students with intellectual disabilities?

How Are Students with Mental Retardation/ Intellectual Disabilities Identified?

The major purpose of identifying individuals with intellectual disabilities is to provide them with appropriate education and related services. We have discussed how some of the causes of intellectual disabilities can be identified prenatally, perinatally, or postnatally. However, many students with intellectual disabilities, primarily those for whom a clear cause of their disability is not detectible, are not identified until school age (Batshaw & Shapiro, 2002). At this point, intelligence testing, adaptive behavior skills assessment, and academic skills assessment are the more common methods used in identification. The focus of this section is on the identification of mild

 Relevant CEC Standards

▶ Definitions and issues related to the identification of individuals with intellectual disabilities/ developmental disabilities (MR1K1)

▶ Specialized terminology used in the assessment of individuals with intellectual disabilities/ developmental disabilities (MR8K1)

▶ Environmental assessment conditions that promote maximum performance of individuals with intellectual disabilities/ developmental disabilities (MR8K2)

▶ Adaptive behavior assessment (MR8K3)

intellectual disabilities. Identification of those with more severe intellectual disabilities is discussed in Chapter 12.

The diagnosis of intellectual disabilities is typically made when (1) the individual's IQ is approximately 70–75 or below, (2) an individual displays significant limitations in adaptive skills, and (3) the age of onset is below 18 years (Luckasson et al., 2002). Logically, then, identification of students suspected of having intellectual disabilities is typically based on assessments of their intelligence and their adaptive skill competencies. In addition, as IDEA 04 requires that educational performance be adversely affected, academic ability is also evaluated. Luckasson et al. (2002) stressed that identification is only the first step of any assessment process. Although it is important to first determine whether a student has intellectual disabilities, it is just as important to determine what supports a student might require to address his or her needs as well as to assess the impact of those supports once provided. Levels of support needed can be determined by designing educational programs and supports and then evaluating whether the programs and supports result in improved outcomes. The Supports Intensity Scale, mentioned previously, is intended for use in identifying the needed supports of an individual. A student having great difficulty in literacy skill development could be provided with one-on-one assistance that includes regular assessments to evaluate whether his or her skills are increasing.

Intelligence Testing

The AAMR stresses that general functioning can be measured by one or more individually administered and standardized tests of intelligence, although IQ should not be construed as a permanent and unchanging measure nor as an indicator of all facets of intelligence (Luckasson et al., 2002). The more widely used tests are the Stanford-Binet Intelligence Scale–Fifth Edition (Roid, 2003) and the Wechsler Intelligence Scale for Children–IV (Wechsler, 2003). (Revisit Chapter 2 for descriptions of these assessments.) Each could be used, depending on the age of the individual, to determine his or her IQ. Again, the power of and overreliance on IQ testing has been questioned: as much as 50–60% of a person's achievement is related to variables beyond intelligence (McGrew & Evans, 2003).

Adaptive Behavior Skills Assessment

Adaptive behavior skills assessments measure the student's ability to perform skills needed for everyday life. Assessments of adaptive behavior typically used to determine deficits in adaptive skills include the AAMR Adaptive Behavior Scales–School Edition: 2 (Lambert, Nihira, & Leland, 1993), the Vineland Adaptive Behavior Scales–II (Sparrow, Balla, & Cicchetti, 2005), and the Scales of Independent Behavior–Revised (Bruininks, Woodcock, Weatherman, & Hill, 1996). These scales often rely on interviewing an adult familiar with the individual with suspected intellectual disabilities to rate overall adaptive skill abilities. These assessments measure such everyday skills as dressing, table manners, handling money, and telling time among many others. However, direct observation of the student's behavior may prove especially useful in comparing how he or she functions compared to his or her peers.

Academic Skills Assessment

The student's academic skills are also evaluated to help determine whether he or she has intellectual disabilities. As described in Chapter 2, general achievement tests such as the Kaufman Test of Educational Achievement–II (Kaufman & Kaufman, 2004b) and the Wechsler Individual Achievement Test–II (The Psychological Corporation, 2001), as well as the Woodcock-Johnson–III (Woodcock, McGrew, & Mayer, 2001; normative update 2006) are frequently administered to assess these skills. When appropriate, specific academic areas such as reading or math can be evaluated using both norm- and criterion-referenced testing including curriculum-based assessments. Teachers commonly use direct observation and samples of a student's actual work to assess academic skills. When all skill areas are assessed, a multifactor evaluation team of educational personnel determines whether the student is eligible to receive special education and related services.

General education teachers are frequently involved in initially bringing concerns to a child study team that the student is not performing well in class. Also, general education teachers may be involved in administering some assessments such as an adaptive skills assessment or direct observation of behavior and skills during the identification process. It is important that all educators be aware of the overrepresentation of African Americans in this category and safeguard against bias that might be present that could influence the identification process.

Check Your Understanding

1. Which level of intellectual disabilities are typically identified prior to school age, and which are typically identified after the student enters school?

2. What are the three characteristics that lead to a diagnosis of an intellectual disability?

3. What role does intelligence testing play in identification?

4. What role does adaptive behavior skills assessment play in identification?

5. What types of academic skills assessments are used?

What and How Do I Teach Students with Mental Retardation/Intellectual Disabilities?

Today, most students with intellectual disabilities will spend at least part of their schooling in general education classrooms, particularly in the earlier grades. In selecting the appropriate programs, materials, and teaching strategies for students with intellectual disabilities, teachers must consider each individual's unique educational needs keeping in mind a long-term goal of maximum independence. Just as the instructional content and procedures in Chapter 4 may also apply to students with intellectual disabilities and/or emotional and behavioral problems, the information on instructional content and procedures in this chapter may apply to students with learning disabilities and/or emotional and behavioral problems, especially those students who need a more functional curriculum.

An important consideration when making instructional decisions for the student with intellectual disabilities has to do with the age of the student and the level of schooling. The same instructional components appropriate for a preschool student will not necessarily be appropriate for an adolescent. Current programs for students with intellectual disabilities typically fall into three age categories: preschool (including infant programs), elementary, and secondary (including middle school programs).

Instructional Content

National school reform has resulted in increased access to general education and basic academic skill learning for students with intellectual disabilities; however, at some point, other skills instruction may need to replace or overlap the general education curriculum. Most students with intellectual disabilities will require a combination of academic and other skills if schooling is to have an impact on their lives (Taylor et al., 2005). Which content and skill development is emphasized will depend on each individual student's capabilities and need for supports, and should be decided through person-centered planning. **Person-centered planning** makes the individual

Relevant CEC Standards

▶ Trends and practices in the field of intellectual disabilities/developmental disabilities (MR1K5)

▶ Specialized materials for individuals with intellectual disabilities/developmental disabilities (MR4K1)

▶ Model programs for individuals with intellectual disabilities/developmental disabilities including career/vocational transition (MR7K1)

person-centered planning Educational planning that makes the individual the most important part of the planning; involves family and friends and takes into consideration the abilities and aspirations of the individual.

the most important part of the planning, involves family and friends in the planning, and takes into consideration the abilities and aspirations of the individual (Butterworth, Steere, & Whitney-Thomas, 1997).

Very often students with intellectual disabilities need a more functional curriculum, including life skills development, to prepare them for a successful adult life (Bouck, 2004; Goldberg, Higgins, Raskind, & Herman, 2003; Miller, 2002). A functional curriculum will often focus on functional academics, independent life skills, and self-determination and self-advocacy. Additionally, to be adequately prepared for the adult world, students with intellectual disabilities typically need community-based instruction (Bouck, 2004; Miller, 2002) and comprehensive transition planning.

Basic Academic Skills

Concern with basic academic skill development is certainly not new to educators, but in the past decade there have been a number of mandates to teach these to all students in a general education classroom. Students with intellectual disabilities may learn basic academic skills, such as reading and mathematics, through the general education curriculum. It is well documented that students with intellectual disabilities can learn to read and write (Browder & Xin, 1998; Katims, 2000, 2001) and do benefit from the academic content taught in the general classroom. Westling and Fox (2004) suggest that individuals within the traditional range of moderate mental disabilities and above be included in learning academics. They caution that the learning potential of an individual with intellectual disabilities should never be underestimated.

All children with mild or moderate intellectual disabilities should be taught specific academic skills, content, and skill sequences as long as there is a high probability that they can acquire them. Some modifications in instructional procedures, such as embedding words into pictures, in the general education classroom setting can lead to success in acquiring basic fundamental reading and math skills most often emphasized in programs for elementary-aged students. These skills can be practiced later in natural settings or embedded with other functional skills being taught in appropriate contexts. For example, the student could be asked to find the reading words in the grocery store or recreational facility. Successful instruction of basic academic skills involves the teacher's careful analysis of the objectives for the student and the development of an appropriate program based on those goals. Decisions about a student's

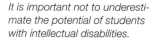

It is important not to underestimate the potential of students with intellectual disabilities.

involvement in the general curriculum should be made within the context of ensuring success and progress (Wehmeyer, Lattin, & Agran, 2001).

Whereas the academic abilities of younger students with intellectual disabilities are closer to their peers without disabilities, older students with intellectual disabilities tend to be further from their peers and thus require more functional skill development (Westling & Fox, 2004). Unfortunately, no clear-cut guidelines suggest the age at which it is desirable to shift the emphasis from basic academic skills to functional skills. Westling and Fox suggest that the general education academic curriculum is most likely to be successful at K–3 grade levels. A parallel adapted curriculum that includes some areas of the general education curriculum with an emphasis on selected components may be more appropriate for students in the early to mid-elementary levels. Adaptations may be made in task complexity, task requirements, or task presentation. At later elementary through secondary grade levels, a functional or limited academic curriculum may become more appropriate, particularly at the secondary level, and may either overlap or circumvent the general education curriculum. Curriculum overlapping is primarily used to embed functional, practical skills into learning activities across the curriculum (Salend, 2008). For example, the student with intellectual disabilities could use words learned in a reading class to follow a recipe in a life skills class.

Beyond age and grade level, considerations for the appropriateness of a traditional academic curriculum should include the amount of success the student has had thus far in learning academics, the type of academics that are needed for functioning in relevant life activities, the relative value or significance of academic skills in increasing independence when compared to other skills, and the wishes of the student and the student's parents (Westling & Fox, 2004).

Instructional materials or programs used to teach basic academic skills to students with intellectual disabilities can be those that are used for students without disabilities or those that have been specially designed for students with intellectual disabilities. Because of their lower skill levels, teachers frequently use reading books for students with intellectual disabilities that are designed for much younger students who have no disabilities. Unfortunately, however, such material is often not motivating for older students with intellectual disabilities as the topics are designed to appeal to younger children. Reading programs that emphasize basic skills development have been created specifically for students with various disabilities, including those with intellectual disabilities. An example is the Direct Instruction (DI) method of teaching reading, designed in the late 1960s by Engelman and his associates to teach beginning reading skills through the use of phonics or sound–symbol relationships. The program uses direct instruction, high levels of student response, error correction, and other forms of teacher feedback to improve students' reading comprehension (Sexton, 2001). See Chapter 4 for more information on the DI reading program.

JANETTA REVISITED Do you think Janetta should be removed from an academic program at this point in time? Why or Why not?

Functional Academics

Basic academic skills are important; however, it is typically instruction in functional academics that is most needed by students, particularly older ones, with intellectual disabilities (Bouck, 2004). **Functional academics** are practical, everyday problem-solving skills that will serve the individual in his or her current and future life. Functional academics may include everyday literacy skills, such as reading recipes, ordering from a menu, catching the right bus, or writing notes to ourselves or others; and everyday number skills, such as counting out money to pay for lunch, telling time so as not to be late for work or miss favorite TV shows, balancing a checkbook, or using a debit card (see Table 5.4). Functional academics may also be applied for personal enjoyment: reading magazines, newspapers, or tabloids; keeping a diary; or keeping score in bowling (Westling & Fox, 2004). The teacher should place the greatest emphasis on teaching the meaning of words that occur in the student's natural

functional academics Practical, everyday problem-solving skills that will best serve the individual in his or her current and future life.

TABLE 5.4	Literacy Skills: What Should Students Learn to Read?

High frequency words identified by sight and read in many environments

Lesser emphasis:
Fry's list (1957, 1972)
Dolch words (1950)
Lists from reading instruction texts

Greater emphasis:
Words on signs and labels
Words on schedules
Words in listings such as Yellow Pages
Words in stores and other community settings
Words in directions and recipes
Words on job applications
Words found in ecological inventory of a student's environment

Arranged and taught in sets of 2–10 words.

Source: Adapted from Westling & Fox (2004).

environment. As previously mentioned, for many students with intellectual disabilities, functional academic skills may be taught in the traditional setting of the general education classroom and later applied to more natural settings. Sight word vocabulary in the general education setting may be taken from the grocery store, cookbooks or recipes, or food labels.

Independent Life Skills

life skills Life management skills that relate to community access, daily living, budgeting and finances, independent living, transportation, and social relationships.

In addition to functional academics, the majority of students with moderate disabilities, and many with mild disabilities, require instruction in **life skills,** or life management. Life skills are those skills needed to thrive in today's society, such as using a telephone, participating in leisure activities, grocery shopping, and preparing meals. Many life skills are learned incidentally by general education peers through simple observation and participation in school, home, and community activities and experiences. Students with intellectual disabilities may require specific and systematic instruction to learn these same skills (Bigge & Stump, 1999). The life skills curriculum is a viable addition or modification to the general education curriculum. Other components of this curriculum include community access, daily living, budgeting and finances, independent living, transportation, and social/relationships (Patton, Cronin, & Jairrels, 1997). The general education curriculum may support the development of social skills needed by students with intellectual disabilities to interact appropriately with their environment. Leisure skills may be introduced through physical education, sporting events, and school clubs (Bigge & Stump, 1999). It is becoming increasingly clear that the inclusion of content that is functional is relevant for all age groups. In other words, the goal of special education from early childhood across grades should be to prepare the student with intellectual disabilities to function outside the school environment.

Selecting which functional life skills to emphasize with a particular student depends on the student's individual needs and age. For a preschool student, this might involve a discussion with the family to determine which functional skills, such as eating, dressing, or communicating, are high priorities. A necessary functional skill for an elementary-aged student might be improved social or affective skills, or prevocational skills such as being on time and completing assigned work. In high school, this might be academic training using learning strategies to assist a student who plans to continue his or her education in a postsecondary setting. Approximately 2.5% of students with intellectual disabilities go on to college (Kaye, 1997), and most of these students attend technical schools or other programs where life skills such as reading a class schedule and eating in a cafeteria are needed. On the other hand, prevocational or vocational training might be

chosen for the student who wants to become gainfully employed immediately after high school. When assessing existing life skills to plan a curriculum, it is important to realize that an individual's experiences and opportunities in activities such as shopping, hygiene, use of eating utensils, and communication vary across cultures (Bigge & Stump, 1999). Each student's curriculum should be based on his or her specific goals, needs, and background and not driven by the label of intellectual disability.

Self-Determination and Self-Advocacy Skills

The changing view of disabilities during the 20th century, along with numerous follow-up studies identifying a need for improved postschool outcomes of special education programs, and an increased focus on active learner participation, have led to a call for the inclusion of self-determination skills in the curriculum for students with intellectual disabilities. In a comprehensive follow-up study of students with intellectual disabilities one year after they had graduated, aged out, or dropped out of school, Wehmeyer and Schwartz (1997) found that students with intellectual disabilities who rated high on self-determination were more likely than their peers who were not self-determined to be happy and to have achieved more positive adult outcomes, including being employed at a higher rate and earning more per hour, and living outside the home.

Self-determination, a combination of skills, knowledge, and beliefs that enable a person to engage in goal-directed, self-regulated, autonomous behavior (Field, Martin, Miller, Ward, & Wehmeyer, 1998), has become a hallmark of providing full and complete special education services (Karvonen, Test, Wood, Browder, & Algozzine, 2004). Self-determined people know how to exercise choices and make decisions in their own lives. Essential components of a self-determination curriculum include self-awareness, self-evaluation, choice making, decision making, problem solving, goal-setting, and goal attainment. For example, to make realistic choices about future goals, the student must be aware of his or her own interests and abilities, both strengths and limitations.

The importance of self-determination in the transition planning process has been designated as one of the most critical issues for students with intellectual disabilities (Thoma, Nathanson, Baker, & Tamura, 2002) as there is wide acceptance that becoming more self-determined is critical to successful transition from school to adult life (Agran, Blanchard, & Wehmeyer, 2000; Field et al., 1998; Wehmeyer &

self-determination A combination of skills, knowledge, and beliefs that enable a person to engage in goal-directed, self-regulated, autonomous behavior.

PRACTICE

Palmer, 2003; Wehmeyer & Schwartz, 1998). The development of self-determination skills should be infused into daily instruction and practice (Thoma et al., 2002; Wehman & Kregal, 2004; Wehmeyer, 2002) and can be implemented in inclusive environments (Field et al., 1998). This can be as simple as allowing the student with an intellectual disability to choose his or her own lunch items or writing implements. It is imperative that educational programs in self-determination reflect the beliefs, values, and expectations in the student's culture and be flexible and culturally responsive enough to support the best interests of the student and the family (Frankland, Turnbull, Wehmeyer, & Blackmountain, 2004). For example, the age at which children are allowed or expected to make decisions about their own lives varies in different cultures, and this information must be considered when planning an educational program in self-determination, preferably through collaboration with the family.

Although transition planning is not required to begin until age 16 for students with disabilities, children with intellectual disabilities between the ages of 9 and 11 can begin to set goals and use these goals to determine their actions and correct those actions when needed. Students with intellectual disabilities over the age of 12 can make decisions, generalize problem-solving skills to other environments, set and focus on long-term goals, and evaluate and change plans as needed to achieve their goals (Doll, Sands, Wehmeyer, & Palmer, 1996). Therefore, programming for successful postschool outcomes can and should begin early, and IEP goals and objectives should both reflect this programming and involve students in the development of these goals. Examples of goals designed to promote self-determination may include "I will learn more about my particular learning needs," or "I will learn to make better decisions" (Wood, Karvonen, Test, Browder, & Algozzine, 2004).

Individuals who are self-determined know what they want and can use their self-advocacy skills to get it (Martin, Huber Marshall, & Maxson, 1993). **Self-advocacy** is the ability to support and promote one's own interests. Self-advocacy skills allow individuals with intellectual disabilities a chance to speak for themselves and others. This may include asking for required accommodations, assistance when needed, and the help of others (Bigge & Stump, 1999). Younger students with intellectual disabilities may work on self-advocacy for asking a friend to share a toy, play a game, or find a lost pencil. Some specific areas requiring self-advocacy instruction for older individuals with intellectual disabilities include education and transition planning, legal and civil rights, adult service acquisition, personal safety, home living, employment rights and responsibilities, social relationships, and family planning.

self-advocacy Skills that enable individuals with disabilities to speak for themselves and others.

JANETTA REVISITED Do you think it is too early to begin teaching Janetta self-determination skills? Why or why not? Is there any indication that she may need some help in this area? If so, what should she be taught?

Community-based Instruction

community-based instruction Vocational and independent living areas within the community are the actual classrooms.

Community-based instruction involves teaching skills in natural environments such as worksites, shopping malls, and restaurants (Wehman, 1992). The focus of this instruction can move from training to actual employment as students with intellectual disabilities near completion of secondary education (Wehman & Targett, 2004). For example, a student might start by cleaning cafeteria tables under the direction of a teacher and then move to working at a fast-food restaurant, cleaning tables with the teacher serving as a job coach and providing training and support. Secondary-level vocational training and work-study programs typically include some community-based instruction (Lerner & Kline, 2006). Vocational training may be delivered through general or special classes (Polloway et al., 2005). Career-related work experience in conjunction with the completion of student-identified transition goals has been associated with improved graduation and employment outcomes (Wehmeyer & Schwartz, 1997).

Instruction may take place in a natural environment such as a worksite, grocery store, or restaurant.

PRACTICE

A necessary component of high school preparation for students with intellectual disabilities who are employment bound following graduation may be paid work experiences in a natural setting or apprenticeships (Polloway et al., 2005). Students should acquire work experience or a work history prior to graduation, and services should be in place to ensure transition to employment and adult living. Other work experiences might include a mentoring program or job shadowing in which secondary-level teachers of students with intellectual disabilities provide instruction in skills needed to be successful in the workplace as well as other employability skills. The key is that there be a match between classroom curricula and workplace skills. For example, social skills objectives should match the expectations in the workplace; and vocabulary lessons should incorporate the words needed on the job. The more a student generalizes academic, social, and life skills from school to nonschool settings, the less time will need to be spent on community-based instruction. The less a student generalizes, the more time is needed (Olson & Platt, 2004).

Transition Planning

Educators have become increasingly aware of the need for transition programming and instruction geared toward preparing students with intellectual disabilities for out-of-school adjustment. However, training for community living must occur well before transition from school to adult living (Sitlington, Clark, & Kolstoe, 2000). Without adequate, appropriate programming, students with intellectual disabilities have considerable problems adjusting to both employment and independent living in the community, lead extremely segregated social lives, are isolated from peers, and have considerable difficulty in participating in various community functions (Blackorby & Wagner, 1996; Patton et al., 1997; U.S. Department of Education, 1998). Given these findings, there has been an increased call for focusing transition programming not only on employment and postsecondary education but also on establishing more student independence and training in accessing community services leading to increased community involvement and satisfactory personal and social relationships (Sitlington et al., 2000). The transition plan of a student with an intellectual disability will be based on his or her individual strengths and needs, but it will most likely include development of functional academics, independent life skills, and self-determination and self-advocacy skills.

Instructional Procedures

Instructional procedures used with students with intellectual disabilities should increase opportunities for learning, reduce errors in learning made by the student, and be easily implemented by teachers to assist students in the acquisition, maintenance, and generalization of skills (Maciag, Schuster, Collins, & Cooper, 2000). If they are to have a chance at mastering the skills needed to be successful in school and in the future, most students with intellectual disabilities will require direct/explicit instruction that includes clear objectives, advance organizers, presentation and demonstration with a think aloud model, guided practice, independent practice, and post organizers (see Chapter 4 for a review of the direct instruction model). Two aspects of direct instruction should be particularly considered when teaching students with intellectual disabilities: learning sequence, and presentation and practice. Special attention to task analysis and the sequencing of learning objectives is necessary to ensure that the lesson moves from simple tasks to more complex ones. Extra consideration needs to be paid to the presentation and practice components because students with intellectual disabilities often need to spend additional time at this stage. A direct instruction lesson that was taught as part of a sequence on ordering food at a restaurant is located in Online Appendix A.

Learning Sequence

In teaching a direct instruction lesson to students with intellectual disabilities, the teacher must ensure through task analysis that he or she is beginning with simple tasks before moving to more complex ones. The teacher should actively target specific skills and then systematically teach them to the students. For example, if teaching how to summarize a paragraph, the teacher might start by teaching students to find the main idea and then details and then how to paraphrase them, or put them in their own words, to summarize the paragraph. This process can be enhanced in both task presentation and response requirements by considering and systematically manipulating three hierarchical levels of difficulty: recognition, recall, and reconstruction levels. **Recognition** requires only that the student select the response from multiple choices. Difficulty may vary depending on the number of choices from which the correct answer is to be selected. For example, consider the differences in difficulty level when asked to point to the word "girl" when shown two different words, four different words, or six different words. Of course, there may also be varying degrees of difficulty within one level. Consider the difference in these tasks found in one commercially produced language arts workbook. On page 14, students are asked to underline the words in each sentence that have opposite meanings. Example: My dirty hands needed washing to be clean (underline "dirty" and "clean"). On page 15, students were asked to circle the two words in each box that have opposite meanings. Example: happy sad forgot (circle "happy" and "sad"). Although both of these tasks are at a recognition level, an analysis of what is required for each response should lead us to question the order of presentation. On the second page, the student only has to consider three words. On the first page, the student has to choose between eight words presented in a sentence format. At the next level, **recall** requires that the student remember the response and provide it without any choices. When shown the word "girl," the student is asked, "What is this word?" At the **reconstruction** level, the student must recall the information and must also produce it, as in "write the word 'girl'." A transition from recall to reconstruction may be created by asking for only partial reconstruction, as in "complete the word: '_ _ rl'." Another example would be the sequence of selecting which response is a complete sentence when shown sentences (recognition); telling what a complete sentence must include (that is, a subject and verb) (recall) and then writing the verb in a complete sentence given the subject (partial reconstruction); and, finally, writing a complete sentence (reconstruction). An example of a learning sequence for naming coins that considers these levels of difficulty is provided in the Classroom Example.

recognition A level of difficulty that requires only that the student select the response from multiple choices.

recall A level of difficulty that requires the student to remember the response and give it without any choices.

reconstruction A level of difficulty that requires the student not only to recall the information but also to produce it.

Objective: The student(s) will name a penny and a nickel.

Subobjectives: The student will:

1. Point to a penny following a model. (This is a penny, show me a penny.)

2. Point to a penny when asked. [Recognition with one choice]

3. Name a penny following a model. (This is a penny, what is this?)

4. Name a penny when asked. [Recall]

5. Point to a nickel following a model. (This is a nickel, show me a nickel.)

6. Point to a nickel when asked. [Recognition with one choice]

7. Name a nickel following a model. (This is a nickel, what is this?)

8. Name a nickel when asked. [Recall]

9. Point to a penny and a nickel following a model. (This is a penny and this is a nickel, show me a penny and nickel.)

10. Point to a penny and a nickel when asked. [Recognition with two choices]

11. Name a penny and a nickel following a model. (This is a penny and this is a nickel, what is this?)

12. Name a penny and a nickel when asked. [Recall]

Presentation and Practice

Students with intellectual disabilities often need more repetition and examples in presentation, more coaching and support in guided practice, and more opportunities for independent practice than do their peers without disabilities.

One important support procedure is the use of prompts. A **prompt** is an additional stimulus or cue that will increase the chances of a correct response being given. For example, teachers can instruct students by using prompts such as verbal directions, graphic and symbolic stimuli (written symbols), gestures (hand waving or pointing), physical assistance (hand-over-hand assistance to a gentle tap), modeling, or pictorial displays.

Within each of these types of prompts, a continuum of degree of assistance exists, and the appropriateness of the prompt must be judged based on the skills and needs of the student (Kennedy & Horn, 2004). For example, "Pick up your shirt" provides more assistance than "What should you do with your shirt?" For students with intellectual disabilities, selecting a prompt that is functional for assisting the student in answering correctly is crucial, as is systematically fading the prompt to less and less assistance until the student can respond independently to the natural cues to the task, such as the fact that the shirt is on the floor. There is also a continuum of degrees of assistance between the types of prompts. For example, a physical assistance prompt, such as taking the student's hand and guiding the formation of the letter *b*, provides more assistance and is more intrusive than a verbal prompt, such as "Draw a stick and a ball to form the letter *b*." Use of prompts must be systematically planned to assure correct responses on the part of the student and lead to the greatest degree of independence possible for the student. Prompt types may also be paired to provide more assistance at first to ensure a successful response. For example, while physically guiding the student's hand in forming the letter *b*, the teacher says, "I draw a stick and a ball to form the letter *b*." Prompts are typically ordered into a hierarchy that can be delivered in a most-to-least or least-to-most sequence (Kregel, 2004). Figure 5.2 presents an example of prompts from least to most intrusive to be used in teaching a student to write his name. To be most

prompt An additional stimulus or cue that will increase the chances of a correct response being given.

1. Cue Prompt: Write your name.
2. Verbal Prompt: Write your name, J-U-A-N.
3. Verbal Prompt plus Graphic Product Prompt: Write your name, J-U-A-N, below where I have written it.

   Juan

4. Verbal Prompt plus Modeling Prompt: Watch me write your name, J-U-A-N. Now you write it.
5. Verbal Prompt plus Physical Assistance Prompt: Write your name, J-U-A-N (teacher provides hand-over-hand guidance).

effective, prompts should focus the student's attention on the task, not distract from it; prompts should be as weak, or nonintrusive, as possible; prompts should be faded out as rapidly as possible; and unplanned prompts should be avoided (Alberto & Troutman, 2006). Based on these guidelines, examples of ineffective prompts during instruction might include using illustrations in a preprimer to help with reading, thus distracting the student's attention from the words; physically guiding a student's hand when writing the answers to double-digit multiplication problems, hiding the full problem from view; allowing extended use of a printed multiplication table; or providing facial or verbal intonations indicating the appropriate answer to a reading comprehension question so that the student learns to simply read the facial or verbal cues.

Generalization

generalization When a behavior endures over time, occurs in a variety of settings, or occurs across a set of related behaviors.

Given the problems that students with intellectual disabilities have in generalization, the ability to apply information or skills to different settings, an extremely important aspect of teaching students with intellectual disabilities, must be systematically planning for and promoting this ability. Without generalization programming, a student with intellectual disabilities may learn addition and subtraction skills at school but not be able to apply them when shopping. **Generalization** has occurred when a behavior endures over time, occurs in a variety of settings, or occurs across a set of related behaviors (Kregel, 2004). To be effective, teaching of generalization should occur before, during, and after teaching. Common procedures used by effective teachers include using many examples during initial instruction, linking instruction throughout the lesson to the real-world use of the skill through applications, and using the same or similar learning materials from a lesson in a real-world situation later (Taylor et al., 2005).

Check Your Understanding

1. What are some skills that might be included in functional academics? What are some independent life skills that may need to be taught directly to students with intellectual disabilities? When should these skills be taught?

2. What is self-determination? What are self-advocacy skills?

3. What is community-based instruction?

4. What should be considered in transition planning for students with intellectual disabilities?

5. What components of direct/explicit instruction may need special consideration in teaching students with intellectual disabilities? What are some ways this may be accomplished in each?

6. Why is it important for students with intellectual disabilities to be taught generalization skills? What are some ways this can be done?

What Are Other Instructional Considerations for Teaching Students with Mental Retardation/Intellectual Disabilities?

Just as planning and implementing instructional content and procedures based on individual needs are important to the success of students with intellectual disabilities, the structure of the instructional environment and the use of technology may also have a significant impact on their education. The environment can support the goal of normalization, and technology can aid the development of independence.

The Instructional Environment

The environment within which education is provided to students with intellectual disabilities has long been considered a crucial component of success. In the not-too-distant past, before the inclusive education movement began, these students were taught in different instructional environments, or classrooms, than their peers without disabilities. The predominant belief was that because the instructional needs of students with intellectual disabilities were so divergent from those without disabilities, there was a need for their education to be distinctly different. With the adoption of principles of normalization, integration, and inclusion, along with a developing database of research supporting these principles, it has become quite clear that separate educational environments may not be necessary or appropriate for most students with intellectual disabilities, especially those with mild intellectual disabilities. In addition, most modifications of the physical environment needed for these students can be made within general education classrooms. Whether students receive special education instructional services in general education classrooms or in special classrooms within the general education school for all or part of the day, considerations such as the physical arrangement of the classroom and grouping of students are vital components of a successful school program.

Relevant CEC Standard

▶ Approaches to create positive learning environments for individuals with mental retardation/developmental disabilities (MR5K1)

The Physical Arrangement

The physical arrangement of the classroom should allow students with intellectual disabilities to experience a "normalized" environment to help them meet instructional goals as well as to develop age-appropriate social and communication behaviors. Students with intellectual disabilities should be physically included within a general education classroom, not seated on the side or at a special table. As there does not seem to be one best way to organize a classroom, teachers may need to be flexible enough to change the classroom from time to time to address the various student needs (Miller, 2002). In general, all furniture and materials should be arranged attractively, appropriately, and neatly (Schloss, Smith, & Schloss, 2001). Some elements of the physical arrangement should be planned for based on students' ages.

The Preschool Classroom. A number of physical environment considerations must be addressed when developing programs for preschool students with intellectual disabilities. To start, services for young children with intellectual disabilities must be provided in natural environments (IDEA, 2004). A **natural environment** is the setting where the child would be if he or she did not have a disability. Natural environments include preschool programs, as well as grocery stores, restaurants, and shopping malls (Olive & McEvoy, 2004).

The actual physical arrangement of the classroom, including the placement of materials, must be planned to ensure social interaction with other students; highly structured routines need to be determined to promote acquisition of specific information; and scheduling that engages students must be developed. The arrangement of the preschool classroom can actually assist students in acquiring necessary skills and in

natural environment The setting where the child would be if he or she did not have a disability.

generalizing those skills to other environments. Providing natural environments can increase the infant's or young child's control, participation, and interaction (Noonan & McCormick, 1993). Optimally, different areas of the classroom, or learning centers, should be arranged so that a student realizes a particular behavior is expected or required in each area. Otherwise, students with intellectual disabilities may produce behaviors that interfere with learning because they are confused about what they should be doing in a particular area. By placing certain play materials in one area of the classroom, for example, students can begin to associate that area with free play. In contrast, a television set sitting on a table where students are required to display certain pre-arithmetic skills would certainly not be an appropriate physical arrangement. The concept of providing natural or functional environments requires that teachers be aware not only of the materials in each of the areas but also of how these items can naturally affect the learning that takes place. The classroom arrangement should also encourage and support play and communication among children to facilitate peer acceptance and provide age-appropriate models (Westling & Fox, 2004). Quiet areas with plenty of space for mats or cots should be provided for naptime and for children who just need a break. When it is time for more active play, carefully arranged outdoor space and appropriate equipment should enhance the children's physical development and provide a break from indoor activities. Providing the student with an intellectual disability with a particularly interesting toy on the playground, such as a giant bubble wand or a shovel and bucket, may encourage interaction with other students (Westling & Fox, 2004).

The Elementary Classroom. Physical environment concerns for elementary-aged students with intellectual disabilities are very similar to those for preschool students. A structured environment, particularly the classroom and classroom routines, is very important. In structuring the environment, physical factors, such as the placement of desks or carrels and materials, should be considered to promote interaction between peers with and without intellectual disabilities. An environment that is sensitive to individual needs provides each student with intellectual disabilities with a comfortable space, interesting scenery, opportunities to engage in age-appropriate and functional activities, and choices (Alberto & Troutman, 2006). For those students with intellectual disabilities who are in the general education curriculum, the physical arrangement in the typical general education classroom and any decisions about the arrangement of the classroom, for example, placement of desks, carrels, tables, or materials, may be determined by the general education teacher in consultation with the special education teacher.

The Secondary Classroom. One of the major goals of teaching secondary-level students with intellectual disabilities is to prepare them for life outside the classroom. Teaching secondary-level students involves attempting to make all instruction immediately relevant for out-of-school adjustment. With this in mind, classroom arrangement should indicate that this is a place of business and should be neat and uncluttered (Schloss et al., 2001). Transition programming philosophy emphasizes that the best educational sites for out-of-school adjustment may be in the student's community. Consequently, community-based instruction has become the benchmark for many educational programs for adolescents with intellectual disabilities; in other words, vocational and independent living areas within the community are the actual classrooms. For example, to learn a specific job skill, such as office or clerical support, the student should become aware of all of the natural stimuli associated with that skill, such as office personnel and machinery. Such natural stimuli can be found within the community, so instruction of that skill should take place within the community. In the case of these placements, collaboration between the special educator and a community agency is generally necessary.

Instructional Grouping

An important consideration in teaching students with intellectual disabilities is grouping. One-to-one instruction is frequently provided. However, one-to-one instruction should not be viewed as the only possible method of teaching students with intellectual disabilities. With careful planning, individualization of instruction can happen even in small groups. When each student is being taught at his or her own level, individualization is occurring no matter how many students are present. In fact, a one-to-one teaching situation may actually interfere with learning to respond in other situations. For example, even if the student performs a task successfully in a one-to-one situation with the teacher present, he or she may not perform the same task correctly when operating in a small group. In this case, the student may have incidentally learned that successful task completion or performance is possible in one-to-one situations with the teacher, but not in small groups. The student has become a passive learner depending on the teacher's presence and direction. Advantages of small group instruction are that peer models can be used and that students can experience instruction in a less restrictive environment. It also enables the teacher to maximize the time of instruction and minimize the time when little learning is taking place (Browder & Snell, 2000). In addition to one-to-one and small group instruction, cooperative learning, peer tutoring, and whole group instruction have been shown to be effective in teaching students with intellectual disabilities. All of these groupings work well across all age groups for students with intellectual disabilities.

Cooperative Learning. A specific type of teaching procedure conducted in small group environments that has received support in its use with students with disabilities, including those with intellectual disabilities, is **cooperative learning.** Cooperative learning is a teaching method in which students of various abilities work together and are responsible for both their own learning as well as the group's reaching specific goals. Certain components, such as group rewards, specified tasks that contribute to the attainment of group goals assigned to each individual in the group, and accountable performance of each individual on his or her own task are included in this procedure. Students need not have the same levels of ability, nor do they need to be working on the same skill as long as they are working together toward a mutual goal (Westling & Fox, 2004). For example, if the group is working on a report for class, the student with an intellectual disability may be asked to illustrate the report through drawing or cutting and pasting clipart. Aside from the established educational benefits from such an approach, considerable data indicate that cooperative learning can produce positive social and emotional effects and is relevant across age groups (Qin, Johnson, & Johnson, 1995; Stevens & Slavin, 1995). For example, the student who has been assigned to be the illustrator of a report can realize his or her part in the positive interdependence that is required to complete the task. Furthermore, students from families and cultures that emphasize interdependence in working together to reach goals will feel very comfortable in a cooperative learning group. In a review of research- and field-based guidelines, Miller (2002) provides several guidelines for implementing cooperative learning (see the Classroom Suggestions).

cooperative learning A grouping arrangement in which students of various abilities work together and are responsible for both their own learning and the group's reaching specific goals.

PRACTICE

Classroom Suggestions Guidelines for Implementing Cooperative Learning

- ❑ Place students with disabilities in groups with students who are willing and able to help.
- ❑ Ensure that group goals and individual accountability are clear.
- ❑ Provide students with specific training in interpersonal, social, and cooperative skills.
- ❑ Monitor group functioning.
- ❑ Resist the temptation to interrupt groups to help students with disabilities.
- ❑ Keep assignments similar in length for all students.
- ❑ Establish an ethic of cooperation in the class.

Source: Miller, S. P. (2002). *Validated practices for teaching students with diverse needs and abilities.* Boston: Allyn & Bacon. Copyright © 2002 by Pearson Education. Adapted by permission of the publisher.

What Are Other Instructional Considerations for Teaching Students with Mental Retardation/Intellectual Disabilities? **161**

Peer Tutoring. Peer tutoring, particularly classwide peer tutoring (CWPT) (Greenwood, Delquadri, & Carta, 1997) and peer-assisted learning strategies (PALS), introduced in Chapter 4 and further discussed in Chapter 14, are also successful grouping arrangements for students with intellectual disabilities. In each of these grouping strategies, a student with an intellectual disability would work directly with a peer. In a study that compared CWPT to teacher-led instruction in a general education classroom that included students with intellectual disabilities, it was found that both spelling accuracy and academic engagement were better during CWPT for both students with intellectual disabilities and students without disabilities (Mortweet et al., 1999). Another way for students to work in dyads is the **buddy system** in which a student is assigned a buddy who will give him or her support by doing such things as going over instructions, explaining rules, or answering questions. Paraeducators could also provide support in these areas, although the buddy system is a more natural situation for the setting. Both buddies and paraeducators should be trained on the appropriate amount of assistance to provide to ensure that students with intellectual disabilities do not become overly dependent on them.

Whole Group Instruction. Whole group instruction is the most common arrangement in general education classrooms. The demands of such an arrangement can be very difficult for students with intellectual disabilities who have difficulty maintaining attention, particularly in a room with so many students and materials that seem much more interesting than what the teacher is presenting. Students with intellectual disabilities often need to be taught self-regulation strategies for remaining attentive to what is being presented (Bigge & Stump, 1999). For example, using a teacher-prepared outline for note taking may help keep the student focused on the main ideas, or an individual desk tape recorder that quietly beeps on a regular basis can remind a student to attend. It is also important for the teacher to actively engage students with intellectual disabilities on a high-frequency basis, such as by using many checks for comprehension. One technique for increasing participation of all students in a large or small group is through the use of **response cards.** Response cards may be laminated cards or signs with preprinted answers on them (for example, Singular and Plural, or True and False) that all students will hold up after a question is asked so the teacher can see their responses. Or response cards may be blank chalkboards or white boards (cut-up shower board from a home improvement store works) on which students write their answers before holding them up on cue. Response cards not only engage all students but also allow the teacher to observe the level of understanding of individual students. This information can guide the teacher in asking individual students to give their answers aloud with an explanation for them, thus providing any necessary repetition for students with intellectual disabilities.

To sum up, in relation to grouping, what is most important is that teachers ensure that all students with intellectual disabilities are presented with avenues through which to participate and that grouping

buddy system A student is assigned a buddy who will give him or her support by doing such things as going over instructions, explaining rules, or answering questions.

response cards May be laminated cards or signs with preprinted answers on them or blank white boards written on with dry-erase markers that all students will hold up so the teacher can see their responses.

Response cards can increase student participation and provide feedback to the teacher.

GROUPING ARRANGEMENT	POSSIBLE ACCOMMODATIONS
Whole group instruction and practice	Let student sit next to an aide, volunteer, or trained classmate who can help maintain attention and understanding.
	Give the student a preview of what is going to happen during the class.
	Provide a balance of different kinds of activities within the lessons.
	Provide follow-up instruction individually, as needed.
Small group instruction and practice or cooperative learning activities	Make sure student has communication and social skills needed for group interaction.
	Assign a specific role and responsibility to the student when working in a group.
	Let student work with a trained classmate to help him or her stay on task.
	Allow partial participation in cooperative groups.

Source: Beech, M. (2003). *Accommodations: Assisting students with disabilities.* Tallahassee, FL: Florida Department of Education, Bureau of Instructional Support and Community Services.

arrangements are structured to meet their individual needs (Bigge & Stump, 1999). Some students with intellectual disabilities may require accommodations to the grouping arrangements discussed. Several suggestions for such accommodations are presented in the Classroom Suggestions above.

JANETTA REVISITED What grouping arrangements may be most responsive to Janetta's needs? Explain why you think she would benefit from the ones you select.

Instructional Technology

Technology plays a significant role in teaching students with intellectual disabilities (Westling & Fox, 2004). The use of assistive technology can increase the independence, productivity, self-esteem, self-reliance, and self-determination of individuals with intellectual disabilities (Davies, Stock, & Wehmeyer, 2002; Wehmeyer, 2002). Assistive technology recommended for students with intellectual disabilities can provide benefits at two levels: removing barriers and adapting the curriculum (Wehmeyer, Lattin, & Agran, 2001). If assistive technology allows the removal of a barrier, then a curriculum adaptation may not be necessary. For example, if a video presentation of content rather than a print presentation requiring reading skills is possible, then the curriculum content may not need to be adapted. As another example, software that makes a mouse pointer more visible or an expanded keyboard with large letter keys and a more spacious overall layout may allow a student to participate in general education activities on the computer. When considering any type of assistive technology, it is important to be culturally sensitive to the student's family and consult with them to ensure that they support the use of technology.

Technology That Removes Barriers

A range of technologies can remove barriers for students with intellectual disabilities. The use of graphics or a web-based presentation, films, or videos rather than a textbook can facilitate the presentation of materials. Computer software can offer immediate spelling assistance and aids in paper revision by reading the paper aloud to the student (Williams, 2002). Assistive technology can also allow for an adaptation of student engagement or response through the use of artwork, photography, or videos. Although many students with intellectual disabilities are able to perform arithmetic calculations, the speed with which they complete these calculations may be somewhat slow. Calculators can be used to compensate for such a speed deficit. Other ways to remove barriers through technology include using the digital clock for students who have trouble telling time with a typical analog clock and word processing for students who have difficulty with writing skills.

Technology That Adapts the Curriculum

The introduction of computers into the classroom made many more sophisticated types of programs available for individualized instruction. In addition, many software programs allow teachers to make adjustments based on student needs, such as pacing, level of difficulty, amount of practice, and feedback options (Miller, 2002). In this case, a student with intellectual disabilities could use the same software program as his or her general education peers but with teacher-implemented adaptations that make it easier for him or her to use. For example, in a drill-and-practice program, if a student with intellectual disabilities gives a wrong response, the program can be adjusted so that it does not automatically present the same problem again but branches into other types of problems or questions based on the type of difficulty the student is having. The computerized version of the Edmark Reading Program, available in both English and Spanish, is an example of this type of program. In addition, the Internet has considerable potential for curriculum adaptation and augmentation of curriculum (Wehmeyer, 2002). For example, narrative content from a textbook can be put into text and HTML format, with hyperlinked key concepts or words that take students to another Web page that defines the concept and provides more background.

Although the major purpose of using equipment for individualized instruction is to meet specific educational needs, other purposes can be served as well. For example, all students with intellectual disabilities who are too uncomfortable to fully participate in their IEP meetings may display their strengths, interests, skills, and goals through an electronic portfolio presentation (Glor-Scheib & Telthorster, 2006). Video technology can be used to supplement community-based education by simulating worksites and work tasks, allowing more realistic practice while in the classroom (Mechling & Ortega-Hurndon, 2007).

Still another advantage relates to how the student may be perceived by others. Gardner and Bates (1991) provided data indicating that students with intellectual disabilities were viewed more favorably by others when those students were able to demonstrate that they could use sophisticated technology.

Technology can also play a significant role in enhancing life beyond school such as providing ways to make social contact, access business and consumer resources, participate in recreation and leisure activities, and conduct career exploration (Male, 2002). A Best Buddies International program called e-Buddies provides individuals with intellectual disabilities an opportunity to develop new e-mail friendships while acquiring and practicing needed computer skills. Handheld computers have great potential in

Other students view students with intellectual disabilities more favorably when they can use sophisticated technology.

assisting individuals with intellectual disabilities in independent time management and personal scheduling (Davies, Stock, & Wehmeyer, 2002). Tape-recorded auditory prompt systems using verbal commands and cues to direct completion of a specific task may serve as a "ticket to work" for many individuals with intellectual disabilities by increasing the amount of time on task while wearing a socially acceptable portable player with a headset (Post, Storey, & Karabin, 2002).

JANETTA REVISITED What benefits can assistive technology provide Janetta?

Consideration of Diverse Families in Technology Decisions

Miller (2002) reminds us that it is critically important to demonstrate cultural sensitivity when working with families in the selection of assistive technology that promotes independent functioning of students with intellectual disabilities. She cautions that the Western values of independence and self-sufficiency are not necessarily the values of family members from all cultures. Dependence on families throughout life may be expected and valued (Hourcade, Parette, & Huer, 1997). Furthermore, some communities of minority populations may prefer not to use technological devices that draw attention to the family (Parette, 1998).

Recognizing the importance of family involvement in assistive technology decision making and the overrepresentation of minority groups in special education programs, the Division on Mental Retardation and Developmental Disabilities (now the Division on Developmental Disabilities) published a strong statement in 1997 regarding devices and services, emphasizing the importance of cultural sensitivity (Parette, 1997). To increase participation of minority families in assistive technology decision making and to elicit their support in the use of technology, professionals need to identify family needs for training, support, and information (Kemp & Parette, 2000). Recommendations for facilitating minority family involvement suggested by Kemp and Parette include the following:

- Schedule home visits that are sensitive to the parent's work schedule.
- Provide alternative forms of communication if there is no telephone in the home.
- Provide child care, transportation, and meals for events held at the school.
- Disseminate user-friendly materials in formats amenable to the diverse family.
- Provide stipends to families to cover costs for registration, lodging, and meals when participating in conferences, seminars, and training programs.

The importance of family involvement and commitment to the successful use of technology cannot be overstated. This is particularly true for minority families, and every effort should be made to involve them.

Check Your Understanding

1. What are some ways that physical arrangement of the instructional environment can support normalization?
2. What are some instructional grouping options that can be used in teaching students with intellectual disabilities? What are some techniques that can enhance self-regulation and rates of student engagement?
3. Assistive technology recommended for students with intellectual disabilities can be important at two levels: removing barriers and in adapting the curriculum. Give an example of each.
4. How can technology play a significant role in enhancing life beyond school?
5. What are some ways professionals can attempt to increase participation of minority families in assistive technology decision making?

PRACTICE

In Practice Meet Educator Juliana Berry and Her Student Helen

I teach reading, language, and math in a resource setting at a low-socioeconomic inner-city school in the largest district in the city. I have taught for three years at the elementary level, though I have experience with students at all levels. I have expertise in the areas of reading and technology and combine those content areas in all subjects. I am currently seeking a masters' degree in Education Leadership with certification to be a principal.

My student is Helen, a fourth grader who has been receiving services for mental retardation since the second grade. There is no history of learning or intellectual disability in her family. Helen's oral language skills are below average in both receptive and expressive areas. She is also rated below average in decoding skills in reading, reading comprehension, and thinking/information processing. She does follow directions well, but overall Helen's working memory is poor. This skill is needed in all academic areas, especially in the area of math. Her memory for general information is another area of weakness. She seems to be alert to details in numbers and in pictures, recognizing subtle differences and omitted items. Helen's in-school and out-of-school social-emotional behaviors do not appear to interfere with her learning. Her intelligence test scores, verbal ability score of 49, performance of 61, and her adaptive behavior score of 64 indicate she is eligible for services for students with mild mental retardation.

Helen's general education class experience has been limited. She participated in a general education class during her primary grades but lagged behind in sound/symbol correspondence and vocabulary. Her primary

teachers worked very closely with Helen to increase her working memory and processing speed with songs, rhymes, and using familiar text, numbers, and games. When I first met Helen, she was quiet and unresponsive to any instruction I provided, so I began to ask her for help with classroom activities such as 1-2 step tasks like counting and taking down calendar numbers and then putting up the new calendar. After a few weeks, she participated in classroom activities with guided practice. Her interest in the lesson and skills was evident. I knew that if she was going to succeed I needed the support of her family. I spoke with the family and provided a plan of action I was going to initiate and asked for their assistance. It has been my experience that students with mental retardation are much like students with learning disabilities or students without disabilities; they want to please and receive attention, and these are factors a teacher may utilize during instruction.

Instructional Content and Procedures

Helen's individualized education plan is based on her needs in reading, language, math, and social skills. In all

What Are Some Considerations for the General Education Teacher?

The number of students with intellectual disabilities being served in general education classes has steadily increased over the last decade (U.S. Department of Education, 2006), and the students who have access to the general education classroom are more likely to have access to the general education curriculum (Wehmeyer, Lattin, Lapp-Rincker, & Agran, 2003). The role of the general educator in providing educational services for students with intellectual disabilities has too often focused primarily on addressing possible social interactions that might accompany inclusion for these students. With movements toward full inclusion,

content areas, she is functioning at a mid-kindergarten level, and her goals are concentrated in reading, language, math, and increasing her memory skills. In reading, we work together on both sight words and phonics, and I encourage her to use context clues using self-questions I have taught her. To increase comprehension, whole group read alouds emphasize who, what, when, where, and why questions to find specific details and place them on a graphic organizer. Helen's reading goals also include reading environmental print such as signs, schedules, and labels. In math, Helen works on number meaning, one-to-one correspondence, and simple math facts of addition and subtraction with/without regrouping. I use concrete items and experiences for solving math problems, such as wicky sticks or bears (her favorite) to form groupings in addition and subtraction. Her math goals also include calculator skills for survival. All of the content in my resource classroom mirrors the content she receives in her general education classes. For example, during the read alouds, my students in the resource room use the same book as the general education classroom. This provides extra modeling and guided practice that allows my students to better participate in general education classroom discussions about the book. This is also the case in math. In general education, Helen's accommodations provide her with more time for written assignments, opportunity for oral responses, and repeated instructions and directions for comprehension.

Instructional Environment and Technology

Helen attends my resource class every day. She receives three 45 minute classes on a block schedule. I also support Helen and my other students in the general education classroom during whole group instruction. The resource classes are mixed-grade-level classes; students are in grades K–5th. I schedule my students according to their grade level block content assignments. For example, Helen receives 45 minutes of reading resource and 45 minutes of general education during a 90 minute reading block in the morning. Most of my students come to me during the first part of a content block because general education teachers instruct whole group on grade level during the first part, and many special needs students have difficulty participating. For my instructional content, I use the district-mandated curriculum for reading and math and supplement with instructional and test preparation books and games developed to ensure student mastery of state curriculum standards and success on state assessment tests through interactive software tutorials that guide students through the learning process. Technology use in my classroom is a vital piece of Helen's academic career. I use Web quests, digital storytelling for language, Write: Outloud programs, and a variety of literature websites for reading skills and activities. The use of technology is highly motivating for my students and provides them with skills for their future.

Collaboration

Collaboration is a key part of my instruction. I collaborate daily with my students' general education teachers about my lessons and activities and accommodations needed for their lessons. We plan lessons together in which our students work in groups. For example, for language, Helen and some of my other students worked with a fifth-grade class on a school newspaper. We teachers meet daily and communicate via e-mail and after school. I am fortunate enough to have a strong and positive relationship with my fellow teachers, which allows me to call them at night and discuss upcoming lessons. Collaboration has provided me with the opportunity to observe and learn how my students work in their grade level while functioning at a low level. It has also lead to my using more grade-level fiction books, which keep their interest and increase their listening comprehension and vocabulary skills. This does take work on my behalf, but it is well worth it.

however, the general educator will more often assume the majority of instructional control. Different models of teacher support, ranging from consultation to collaboration with special educators, have been shown to be valuable in the general education setting that supports students with intellectual disabilities. The fact remains that, without the collaboration and assistance of general educators, successful integration and inclusion of students with intellectual disabilities is highly unlikely. A fundamental step in achieving success is to ensure that general and special educators approach students with intellectual disabilities with high expectations for success (Cushing, Clark, Carter, & Kennedy, 2005; Wehmeyer, 2002). Inclusion of students with intellectual disabilities may require accommodations and adaptations of the classroom curriculum based on a student's IEP, but it does not require that the student perform at the same level as peers without

TABLE 5.5	Cascade of Integration Options	
OPTION	**DESCRIPTION**	**CONDITION(S)**
Unadapted participation in general education	Same activities, same setting	Student can complete activities as planned for general education. Lesson objectives match student's IEP.
Adaptations to the general education curriculum	Same activities, different but related objectives, same setting	Student can meet general education objectives with minor modifications (time, response mode).
Embedded skills with the general curriculum	Similar activity, different but related objectives, same setting	Components of activity can be met by student and match an IEP component.
Functional curriculum in the general education classroom	Different activities, different but related objectives, same setting	Class activities are mostly unrelated to student's IEP, but some IEP objectives can be met in the same setting.
Functional curriculum outside the general education classroom	Different activities, different unrelated objectives, different setting	Class activities are mostly unrelated to student's IEP. IEP objectives are better met in a different setting (require equipment, repetition, etc.).

Source: Adapted from Wolfe, P. S., & Hall, T. E. (2003). Making inclusion a reality for students with severe disabilities. *Teaching Exceptional Children, 35*(4), 56–61. Copyright © 2003 by The Council for Exceptional Children. Reprinted with permission.

intellectual disabilities. Wolfe and Hall (2003) provided a cascade of integration options based on the work of many researchers (Table 5.5). This cascade illustrates a range of accommodations, from unadapted participation in general education to a functional curriculum outside the general education classroom, any of which may be appropriate for an individual with intellectual disabilities in an inclusive education environment.

The results of extensive research repeatedly indicate that all students benefit from well-designed and explicitly taught skills (Hall, 2002). There are also aspects of a curriculum for students with intellectual disabilities that could benefit students without intellectual disabilities. For example, encouraging self-determination skills for all youth could help them be more successful in their educational programs as well as help them develop lifelong success skills (Field, 1997). There are many ways in which self-determination can be supported throughout general education. For example, inclusion in the curriculum, the way in which discipline is conducted, and the manner in which student scheduling is completed can encourage self-determination (Field et al., 1998). All students may also benefit from life skills preparation, as many general education students are unprepared for life after school (Benz, Lindstrom, & Yovanoff, 2000; Conley, 2002).

inclusive service-learning An approach that allows students with and without disabilities to integrate and apply knowledge and skills learned in school to address needs in their schools and communities through community service activities.

Inclusive service-learning is one approach to allowing students with and without intellectual disabilities to integrate and apply knowledge and skills learned in class to address needs in their schools and communities through community service activities (Kleinert et al., 2004; Kluth, 2000; Yoder, Retish, & Wade, 1996). Service-learning is linked to the curriculum and, for students with intellectual disabilities, to IEP objectives. In service-learning, students with and without intellectual disabilities work together from planning to implementing to monitoring and evaluating a service project. Benefits to students with intellectual disabilities include increases in attendance, academic skills, social skills, and social relationships (Brill, 1994). High school peers without intellectual disabilities who participate in collaborative service-learning have been shown to demonstrate significantly more positive attitudes toward students with intellectual disabilities, and all disabilities, than students who participated in service activities directed to helping students with disabilities, such as the Special Olympics (Burns, Storey, & Certo, 1999). Inclusive

Working together on service-learning projects can increase positive attitudes of peers without disabilities toward students with intellectual disabilities.

service-learning can be applied to all age groups from elementary through postsecondary and all severity levels from mild to profound.

Check Your Understanding

1. What is the most significant variable in promoting successful integration and inclusion of students with intellectual disabilities in general education?

2. What are some accommodations that may be provided for individuals with intellectual disabilities in an inclusive education environment?

3. What are some aspects of teaching procedures and curriculum adaptations for students with intellectual disabilities that could benefit all students, with or without disabilities?

4. What is inclusive service-learning?

PRACTICE

Practical Considerations for the Classroom

What IDEA 04 Says about Mental Retardation: Mental Retardation is an IDEA category. The IDEA definition of mental retardation is: "Mental retardation means significantly subaverage intellectual functioning, existing concurrently with deficits in adaptive behavior and manifested during the developmental period, that adversely affects educational performance." However, the term "intellectual disabilities" is preferred by many experts and teachers over the term "mental retardation."

Identification Tools: Severe mental retardation is typically identified at birth or shortly thereafter by a physician. Identification of mild mental retardation is typically done through intelligence testing and adaptive behavior and academic skills assessment. *Intelligence Testing:* Stanford-Binet Intelligence Scale and the Wechsler Intelligence Scale for Children–IV. *Adaptive Behavior Skills Assessment:* AAMR Adaptive Behavior Scales–School Edition: 2, Vineland Adaptive Behavior Scales–II, Scales of Independent Behavior–Revised. *Academic Skills Assessment:* Kaufman Test of Educational Achievement–II and the Wechsler Individual Achievement Test–II, and direct observation and consideration of sample work.

Characteristics	Indicators You Might See
Intellectual	Difficulty in learning, holding attention, memory (retention and retrieval), and transfer and generalization of learning.
Academic	Reading (especially comprehension) and math skills below grade level, deficits in memory, problems with transfer and generalization, and delayed language development and possible speech disorders (specifically showing articulation, voice, or fluency problems).
Social-Personal	Problems adapting properly to the environment, often creates expectations for self based on past experiences, possibly suffers from poor self-image or self-concept, if rejected by peers without disabilities, assumes it is based on behavior rather than having intellectual disabilities.
Adaptive Behavior Skills	Limitations in adaptive behavior skills may be in conceptual, social, or practical abilities.

Students with Mental Retardation/ Intellectual Disabilities

Teaching Implications

Instructional Content

- Determine whether functional academics, independent life skills, and/or self-determination and self-advocacy skills need to be taught.
- When teaching basic academic skills, consider using both modified general education materials and those created for students with intellectual disabilities.
- Consider community-based instruction.
- Transition planning can begin between the ages of 9 and 11 by starting to set goals and using goals to determine actions. Transition planning should focus on employment and/or postsecondary education, student independence and training in accessing community services, and positive personal and social relationships.

Instructional Procedures

- Choose procedures that increase opportunities for learning, reduce errors in learning made by the student, and can be easily implemented.
- Use direct/explicit instruction that includes clear objectives, advance organizers, presentation and demonstration with a think aloud model, guided practice, independent practice, and post organizers.
- In direct instruction lessons, use task analysis to move from simple tasks to more complex. Target specific skills and systematically teach them by considering the levels of difficulty of recognition, recall, and reconstruction.
- Allow for more repetition and examples in presentation, more prompting and support in guided practice, and more opportunities for independent practice.
- Place emphasis on the analysis and application of prompts.
- Teach generalization before, during, and after instruction.

Instructional Environment

- Consider whether the student would learn best in the general classroom or a special classroom.
- For preschool children, the environment should be planned, include highly structured routines to promote acquisition of specific information, and include scheduling that engages students.
- For elementary students, plan a structured environment that includes comfortable space, interesting scenery, opportunities to engage in age-appropriate and functional activities, and choices.
- For secondary students, the teaching environment should be neat and uncluttered. Instructional environments may include nonschool settings.
- Consider one-on-one instruction, collaboration, peer tutoring, and whole group instruction.

Instructional Technology

- Consider the use of technology to remove barriers.
- Consider the use of technology to adapt the curriculum by adjusting pace, level of difficulty, amount of practice, feedback options, and so forth.
- Consider the use of technology to help enhance life skills beyond school.
- In choosing technology, be sure to consider family preferences.

Methodologies and Strategies to Try

- Learning Objectives Sequence (p. 156)
- Using Prompts (p. 157)
- Promoting Generalization (p. 158)
- Inclusive Service-Learning (p. 168)

Considerations for the General Classroom and Collaboration

Instruction could occur in the general classroom, in a special program, or in a combination of the general classroom and a special program.

The general education teacher should:

- Have high expectations for success of students.
- Know that inclusion may require accommodations, but does not require that students perform at the same level as same-age peers without intellectual disabilities.
- Remember that many skills needed by students with intellectual disabilities can benefit other students as well (such as self-determination skills).
- Consider using inclusive service-learning.

Collaboration

General and special educators should consult on:

- Curriculum content and materials
- Procedures and strategies used
- Accommodations and adaptations to be provided
- The physical environment
- Choosing instructional technology

Chapter Summary

Go to the text's Online Learning Center at **www.mhhe.com**/taylor1e
to access study resources, Web links, practice quizzes, and extending materials.

What Are the Foundations of Mental Retardation/Intellectual Disabilities?

- Trends in the education and treatment of individuals with intellectual disabilities have shown both progress and regression over time. A focus on education of individuals with intellectual disabilities emerged during the later half of the 20th century, fueled by advocacy organizations.
- The term *mental retardation* has been recently replaced by the term *intellectual disabilities* by major organizations in the field, although *mental retardation* is still used in the federal definition of the disability.
- The IDEA 04 definition of mental retardation contains four key components: subaverage intelligence, deficits in adaptive behavior, emergence of characteristics before the age of 18, and resulting in an adverse effect on academic performance.
- A definition published by the American Association on Mental Retardation is also widely used by the field. It states that mental retardation is a disability that emerges before the age of 18 that is characterized by limitations in intellectual functioning and adaptive behavior.
- Common classification systems used are classification by severity or degree and classification by levels of needed support.
- According to IDEA 04 data, the prevalence of mental retardation is .94%.
- There is an overrepresentation of African Americans in this category. In general, there are more males identified in this category than females.

What Are the Causes and Characteristics of Mental Retardation/Intellectual Disabilities?

- Chromosomal and genetic causes can be prenatal, perinatal, or postnatal in origin.
- Environmental causes can also occur prenatally, perinatally, or postnatally and include such factors as infections, anoxia, and disease among others.
- Psychosocial factors include low-socioeconomic status, which can lead to other factors such as poor nutrition and health care. In many cases these factors may interact with other biological factors to contribute to intellectual disabilities rather than being the clearly identifiable cause.
- Prevention of intellectual disabilities may occur through better understanding and treatment of human genetic conditions, prenatal testing, and early intervention.
- Intellectual characteristics of students with intellectual disabilities affecting learning and adjustment include attention, academics, memory, transfer and generalization, and language. Students may have difficulty with categorization skills that help them make sense of the world.

- Academic skills are often well below that of peers without disabilities, but can be learned, especially when used in functional skill activities.
- Working and short-term memory deficits affect learning more prominently than do long-term memory deficits; however, students can improve memory skills with instruction.
- Transfer and generalization make the application of knowledge and skills to new situations a challenge. Teaching skills in a variety of settings and situations can help with transfer and generalization.
- Language skills are often delayed. Speech disorders are also more common than among students without disabilities.
- Many students with intellectual disabilities tend to be more extrinsically than intrinsically motivated although all students are likely to experience both types of motivation.
- Students with intellectual disabilities may have limited social relationships with peers without disabilities. A social network is important to quality of life. Relationships can be encouraged through interactions and education of both students with intellectual disabilities and those without disabilities.

How Are Students with Mental Retardation/Intellectual Disabilities Identified?

- Intelligence tests are still frequently used to identify students with mental retardation/intellectual disabilities despite the limitations associated with IQ scores. IQs are not permanent and do not include all variables that affect growth and achievement.
- Adaptive behavior scales are used to establish how well a student with mental retardation/intellectual disabilities adjusts at school, at home, and in the community.
- Academic skills are assessed because identification of mental retardation/intellectual disabilities requires that the condition adversely affect educational performance.

What and How Do I Teach Students with Mental Retardation/Intellectual Disabilities?

- Whether a student is participating in the general curriculum or not, basic academic skills, functional academics, independent living skills, and self-determination and self-advocacy skills may need to be taught.
- Community-based instruction may be used, and transition planning should be incorporated.
- Students with intellectual disabilities learn best through direct instruction that is systematically sequenced, taking into account prompts in instruction, and generalization needs of the students.

SUMMARY

What Are Other Instructional Considerations for Teaching Students with Mental Retardation/ Intellectual Disabilities?

- Normalized environments based on age level are very important in teaching students with intellectual disabilities.
- Preschool children with intellectual disabilities should be taught in a natural environment. Elementary students should be taught in a structured environment that encourages interaction. Secondary students may participate in community-based instruction.
- One-to-one instruction, cooperative learning, peer tutoring, and whole group instruction are grouping options that should be considered. Many grouping options may be successfully used, particularly with accommodations.
- The use of assistive technology is important in removing barriers to the general education curriculum and in adapting the curriculum.
- Technology may also be valuable in enhancing life beyond school.

- Family involvement is important in implementing assistive technology, especially in the families of children who are culturally or linguistically diverse.

What Are Some Considerations for the General Education Teacher?

- Increasing numbers of students with intellectual disabilities are spending at least part of their schooling in general education, particularly at younger ages.
- A cascade of integration options should be considered when including students with intellectual disabilities in the general education classroom.
- Different models of teacher support, ranging from consultation to collaboration with special educators, have been shown to be valuable.
- Service-learning has been found to be an effective method for including students both with and without intellectual disabilities.
- A fundamental step is to ensure that general and special educators approach these students with high expectations for success.

Reflection Topics

1. Do you believe an intellectual disability is a permanent condition or one that could change over time? Why?
2. What do you think might be a better term than "intellectual disabilities"? Is a term needed at all? Defend your choice or position.
3. Should students with intellectual disabilities be in neighborhood schools? Why or why not?
4. Should students with intellectual disabilities be included in general education classrooms? Justify your response.
5. At what point do you think an overlapping curriculum would become appropriate for a student with intellectual disabilities in a general education curriculum? When would an alternative program be considered appropriate?
6. Are there any aspects of a functional or life skills curriculum that you believe would benefit students in general education? What about self-determination skills? How?

Application Activities: For Learning and Your Portfolio

1. (*Portfolio Possibility*) Determine if there is a local chapter of the ARC or Best Buddies International, Inc. in your location. If so, participate in one or more activities sponsored by the organizations or similar organizations (e.g., Special Olympics, Very Special Arts Festival). Examine how individuals with intellectual disabilities are more like you than different from you. Document your experience.
2. (*Portfolio Possibility*) Attend an IEP meeting for a student with intellectual disabilities at a local school as permitted. Reflect on the process and the outcomes of the meeting. Describe the roles the various participants assumed in the meeting.
3. Investigate the demographics of local school districts. What percentage of students in the schools are identified as having intellectual disabilities? What percentage of those students are African American, white, Hispanic, or from other ethnic/racial groups?

4. (*Portfolio Possibility*) Go to your curriculum library or the Web site for the Center on Self-Determination and examine a copy of a self-determination curriculum for a particular age level. Describe the skills included in the curriculum. Might these skills be beneficial for other students? Why or why not?
5. List at least three prompts from least to most intrusive that might be used for this addition problem:

    25
    +12

6. (*Portfolio Possibility*) Go to the e-buddies Web site and download the lesson plans and teacher's guide provided there. Reflect on the information being taught, and explain how this program might contribute to more than the social relationships of an individual with intellectual disabilities. Consider signing up to be an e-buddy.

SUMMARY

CHAPTER 6

Students with Emotional or Behavioral Disorders

CHAPTER OUTLINE

INTRODUCING BOBBY

Bobby is an eighth-grade student who lives in a large city with his mother and sister. Bobby began displaying behavior problems when he was about 4 years old when he started being aggressive with his 3-year-old sister and hurting animals. His mother took Bobby to a screening held by the local school district and voiced concerns about his behavior. He was evaluated and placed in a preschool program for at-risk children where his teacher worked with Bobby on anger management. Bobby continued to display aggressive behavior in kindergarten and at that time starting seeing the school counselor on a weekly basis.

By the time Bobby was in the second grade, it became apparent that he needed some additional help controlling his aggression. He was constantly disrupting the class, becoming aggressive when he didn't get his way, and talking back to his teacher, Mrs. Phelps. Both his mother and Mrs. Phelps described his behavior as "explosive" and couldn't predict what would push him over the edge. He also started missing school, frequently complaining of headaches and stomachaches, and his grades began to suffer. It was suggested that Bobby would benefit from a class with more structure and fewer students. He was referred for special education toward the end of the second grade and met the state's criteria for emotional disturbance.

Now in the eighth grade, Bobby, according to his middle school teachers, frequently challenges authority, talks back, and is defiant and noncompliant. Academically, he is struggling in virtually every content area and is reading at the fourth- to fifth-grade level. He has also become somewhat of a loner with no friends. ■

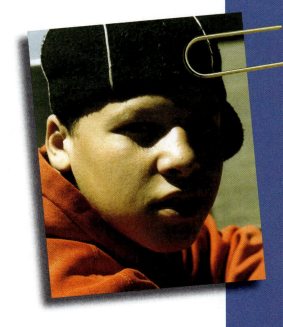

Students like Bobby provide a significant challenge to teachers and parents alike. Behaviors such as aggression, defiance, and noncompliance can be very upsetting to teachers and very disruptive in the classroom, which perhaps influences why students with emotional or behavioral disorders are taught in segregated settings more often than students with other disabilities.

Although Bobby displays several negative behaviors, other students with emotional or behavioral disorders may display very different types of characteristics. For example, Sylvia is very quiet, withdrawn, and is frequently depressed, and Brad is very anxious and doesn't interact with his peers. Both Sylvia and Brad, however, could be considered as having an emotional or behavioral disorder. Most students with emotional or behavioral disorders, like Bobby, also have academic problems that must be addressed alongside their emotional or behavioral needs.

Although students with emotional or behavioral disorders are taught outside the general education classroom more than students with other high-incidence disabilities, the trend toward including them in the general classroom has steadily increased. Both general education and special education teachers will often be involved in their education. Perhaps more than any other disability area, the need for collaboration is an absolute must. These students need to be given a consistent, structured environment. Collaboration helps to ensure that consistency.

What Are the Foundations of Emotional and Behavioral Disorders?

Individuals with emotional or behavioral problems have been present since the beginning of recorded history. However, the education of these individuals really only began in the 20th century. Currently, one of the active discussions in the field is in regard to the definitions of emotional and behavioral disorders, both about the best term to use to describe students with these disorders and the best way to define the category. Another concern in the field is that although the actual number of students receiving special education services due to emotional or behavioral disorders is below prevalence estimates, there appears to be an overrepresentation of students from low-socioeconomic status and culturally diverse backgrounds.

A Brief History of Emotional and Behavioral Disorders

Relevant CEC Standards

▶ The legal, judicial, and educational systems serving individuals with emotional/ behavioral disorders (BD1K4)

▶ Organizations and publications relevant to the field of emotional/ behavioral disorders (BD9K1)

Evidence of the early recognition of individuals with emotional or behavioral problems was provided by Greek philosophers and educators, who described conditions consistent with schizophrenia as early as 1400 BC (Winzer, 1993). However, society's attempts to improve the lives of individuals with emotional or behavioral disorders are a relatively recent phenomenon. As late as the 1600s, these individuals were segregated from the rest of society in hospitals and asylums. The first asylum, St. Mary of Bethlehem, was established in London in 1547. St. Mary of Bethlehem was eventually referred to as Bedlam, a term that now means uproar or confusion. Although asylums cared for the individuals' physical needs, they largely ignored their emotional and psychological needs.

In the 1700s and 1800s, more humane treatment of individuals with emotional or behavioral problems was advocated. As an example, in 1793 Philippe Pinel, a French physician, ordered that the mental patients at Bicetre, a male asylum, be removed from the chains that held them (Sheerenberger, 1983). Later, individuals such as Dr. Benjamin Rush, known as the father of psychiatry in the United States, and Dorothea Dix, who was responsible for the establishment of more than 30 mental hospitals, began addressing the needs of these individuals (Coleman & Webber, 2002). It wasn't until the late 1800s, however, that interest in the emotional and behavioral problems of children began to surface. Prior to that time, attention was focused on adults (Winzer, 1993).

In the 20th century, a number of important events occurred that resulted in more appropriate education and treatment of individuals with emotional or behavioral problems. The development of professional organizations such as the Council for Exceptional Children and the American Orthopsychiatric Association provided strong advocacy. Also, comprehensive programs such as Project Re-Ed (Hobbs, 1966) and Achievement Place (Phillips, 1967) began to show that intensive, collaborative efforts could make a difference in the lives of children with emotional or behavioral problems. Research investigating ways in which these individuals could be better served also increased, and efforts to improve the education and mental health services for individuals with emotional or behavioral problems continue today. Currently, students with emotional or behavioral disorders are given the same rights as any other student, even though they are sometimes taught in a more restrictive environment.

Definitions of Emotional and Behavioral Disorders

The choice of definition used for students with emotional or behavioral disorders is an area of considerable debate. In fact, there even is controversy over the term that should be used to describe these students. The term *emotional disturbance* is currently used in the IDEA 04 definition. Technically, this term implies that only students with emotional problems, not those with behavioral problems, are included in the category. As a result, other terms, such as *behavior disorders*, have been suggested as being more descriptive of the types of students actually identified in educational settings. The term *emotional or behavioral disorders*, which is used in this chapter and endorsed by many professionals, implies that a student could display either type of problem. In fact, the use of the federal term *emotional disturbance* is not supported by many states. Muller and Linehan (2001) surveyed the 50 state education agencies and five nonstate jurisdictions to determine their use of the federal terminology of the various disability categories. They found that the agencies were less likely to use the federal term for emotional disturbance than the federal term for any other disability category.

Relevant CEC Standard

▶ Educational terminology and definitions of individuals with emotional/behavioral disorders (BD1K1)

The IDEA 04 Definition

The Individuals with Disabilities Education Act of 2004 (IDEA 04) defines emotional disturbance as:

(1). A condition exhibiting one or more of the following characteristics over a long period of time and to a marked degree that adversely affects a child's educational performance.

   (a). An inability to learn which cannot be explained by intellectual, sensory, or health factors.

   (b). An inability to build or maintain satisfactory interpersonal relationships with peers and teachers.

   (c). Inappropriate types of behavior or feelings under normal circumstances.

   (d). A general pervasive mood of unhappiness or depression.

   (e). A tendency to develop physical symptoms or fears associated with personal or school problems.

(2). Emotional disturbance includes schizophrenia. The term does not apply to children who are socially maladjusted unless it is determined that they have an emotional disturbance.

Controversial Aspects of the IDEA 04 Definition

The federal definition of emotional disturbance has been referred to as "vague and internally inconsistent" (Simon, 2006), "nebulous, often illogical, and self-contradictory" (Gresham, 2005), and "vague and incomplete" (Theodore, Akin-Little, & Little, 2004). One obvious omission in the IDEA 04 definition, as well as earlier federal definitions, is any specific mention of negative behaviors such as aggression, disruption, or acting out as possible characteristics. One might argue, however, that these types of behaviors fall under point (B), which addresses interpersonal relationships. Some of the harshest criticism of the IDEA 04 definition has focused on the omission of students with social maladjustment from the emotional disturbance category (Merrell & Walker, 2004). One concern is that social maladjustment is not clearly defined so it is difficult to discriminate between emotional disturbance and social maladjustment. Some have suggested that the two should be combined into an emotional disturbance/social maladjustment category (Kehle, Bray, Theodore, Zhou, & McCoach, 2004), which would have the same effect as simply eliminating the exclusion clause. Forness and Kavale (2000) pointed out that the criterion of "inability to build or maintain satisfactory relationships with peers or teachers" (Point B) actually describes social maladjustment. Needless to say, the exclusion of these students remains a controversial issue.

Another controversial aspect of the IDEA definition noted by Kauffman (2005) is the requirement that the disorder adversely affect educational performance. He argued that this may contribute to the exclusion of services for students with certain types of emotional or behavioral disorders. Suppose a student, Tina, is severely depressed and has poor peer relationships but is performing average in achievement. Since educational performance is often considered academic achievement, Tina might not qualify for needed services. In addition, Forness and Kavale (2000) argued that the phrase "inability to learn which cannot be explained by intellectual, sensory, or health factors" might confuse the definition of emotional disturbance with the definition of a learning disability. Finally, there is a concern about the subjectivity involved in determining what is meant by "a long period of time" and "to a marked degree." The relative frequency or intensity of the various behaviors is important because most children display some of these characteristics some of the time.

An Alternative Definition

As a result of concerns about the IDEA definition of emotional disturbance, various alternatives have been proposed. The one proposed by a task force appointed by the National Mental Health and Special Education Coalition, which represented 30 professional and advocacy organizations, has received the most attention.

From the coalition's findings, Forness and Knitzer (1992) proposed that a new term, *emotional or behavioral disorder* (EBD), replace the term *serious emotional disturbance* used in IDEA. The proposed new definition of EBD was as follows:

I.   The term emotional or behavioral disorders means a disability that is characterized by emotional or behavioral responses in school programs so different from appropriate age, culture, or ethnic norms that they adversely affect educational performance, including academic, social, vocational, or personal skills, and which:
(a) is more than a temporary, expected response to stressful events in the environment;
(b) is consistently exhibited in two different settings, at least one of which is school-related; and
(c) is unresponsive to direct intervention applied in general education, or the child's condition is such that general education interventions would be insufficient. Emotional and behavioral disorders can coexist with other disabilities.
II. This category may include children or youth with schizophrenic disorders, affective disorders, anxiety disorders, or other sustained disorders of conduct or adjustment when they adversely affect educational performance in accordance with section I. (p. 13)

Although the coalition's recommendations were not incorporated into federal law, as we have said, we believe emotional or behavioral disorder is the most appropriate term that represents the heterogeneous group of students identified under this category.

Classification of Individuals with Emotional or Behavioral Disorders

The subjective nature of the various definitions of individuals with emotional or behavioral disorders, and the similarities and differences among the individuals they attempt to define, have resulted in a number of classification systems that try to provide meaningful categorization. Some of these systems are more educationally oriented whereas others are more medically oriented.

Educational Classification

In a very real sense, we might think of students with emotional or behavioral problems as falling into one of two categories: those who are, in fact, "disturbed," and those who are primarily "disturbing to others." These two categories, which have received considerable support, have been referred to as internalizing and externalizing disorders (e.g., Merrill & Walker, 2004). **Internalizing disorders** are those in which the individual himself is "disturbed" and include behaviors such as personality problems, anxiety, and depression. **Externalizing disorders** are those in which the individual is disturbing to others and include behaviors such as aggression, acting out, and disobedience.

Students are also sometimes classified using the **dimensional classification system** (Quay & Peterson, 1996). This system includes six categories or dimensions of behavior problems:

- *Conduct disorder:* Includes physical aggression, anger, disobedience, and oppositionality.
- *Socialized aggression:* Involves behaviors such as stealing or using drugs around others, lying, school truancy, and gang membership.
- *Attention problems-immaturity:* Includes short attention span, problems in concentration, distractibility, and impulsivity. It also includes passivity and childishness.
- *Anxiety-withdrawal:* Includes internalizing disorders such as generalized fearfulness and anxiety, fear of failure, poor self-esteem, and hypersensitivity to criticism.
- *Psychotic behavior:* Includes speech disturbances, delusions, and impaired reality testing.
- *Motor tension excess:* Involves behaviors such as overactivity, restlessness, and tension.

Medical Classification

The primary medical classification system used for individuals with emotional or behavioral disorders is based on the *Diagnostic and Statistical Manual of Mental Disorders, Fourth Edition, Text Revision* (*DSM-IV-TR*), published by the American Psychiatric Association (2000). The *DSM-IV-TR* consists of 16 major categories, including mood disorders, anxiety disorders, and schizophrenia, all discussed later in this chapter. Another medical classification system is provided by the *International Classification of Diseases, 10th Edition* (World Health Organization, 1999). It includes a chapter called Mental and Behavioural Disorders, which lists disorders similar to the *DSM-IV-TR* such as schizophrenia and mood disorders.

Prevalence of Emotional and Behavioral Disorders

The prevalence estimates for students with emotional or behavioral problems used by the U.S. Department of Education has been 2% for more than two decades. Estimates from various other sources indicate that between 3% and 6% of the school-aged population exhibit significant emotional or behavior problems requiring special education (Kauffman, 2005). In one classic study, Rubin and Balow (1978) reported that more than 7% of the students they observed were reported by teachers as having significant behavior problems.

Cullinan and Epstein (1995) proposed a "rule of one-third" for identifying students who have emotional or behavior problems. They suggested that one-third of all students in a particular year might display behavior problems that concern teachers. Of that third, about one-third—approximately 10% of all students in a given year—need to have some type of modification of the educational program. Finally, of that third, one-third—approximately 3 to 4% of all students in a given year—will require special education or other services to deal with their problems.

Relevant CEC Standard
▶ Factors that influence overrepresentation of diverse individuals in programs for individuals with emotional/behavioral disorders (BD2K4)

Regardless of these estimates, the actual number of students ages 6–21 being identified and served under the IDEA 04 category of emotional disturbance is only 0.72%, or less than half of the U.S. Department of Education estimated 2% figure and considerably lower than other estimates. This still makes emotional disturbance the fourth-largest IDEA 04 disability category with 8% of students with disabilities having the emotional disturbance label (U.S. Department of Education, 2006). Perhaps one reason the number of students being identified and served is significantly below the number estimated to actually need services is that the stigma often associated with the emotional disturbance label results in fewer referrals, particularly for younger children. Also, exclusion of students who are socially maladjusted may add to the underrepresentation.

BOBBY REVISITED What behaviors does Bobby exhibit that are consistent with the IDEA 04 definition of emotional disturbance? What category or categories of the dimensional classification system best include Bobby's behavior?

Gender and Age Factors

Both gender and age have been found to be related to prevalence figures. More boys than girls are identified as having emotional or behavior problems. Additionally, there is some evidence that suggests that males are more likely to have externalizing disorders, such as antisocial behavior or aggression, and that females are more likely to have internalizing disorders, such as anxiety or depression (Romano, Tremblay, Vitaro, Zoccolillo, & Pagani, 2001; Sachs-Ericsson & Ciarlo, 2000). One reason that more boys are identified may be that a teacher is more likely to notice and refer a student who is exhibiting externalizing behaviors than one displaying internalizing behaviors.

Prevalence figures also indicate that older students are more likely to be identified than younger children. For example, in 2005 fewer than 6,000 children ages 3–5 received services for emotional disturbance. That number rose to almost 132,000 for students ages 6–11 and to more than 311,000 for students ages 12–17. This could be due to two reasons. First, parents and teachers might be more hesitant to formally label a younger child as having an emotional or behavioral disorder. Second, the nature of the problem behaviors changes with age. For instance, a first-grade student might display aggression verbally whereas a fifth-grade student might be physically aggressive. The teacher probably would be less tolerant of physical aggression.

Socioeconomic Status and Ethnicity Factors

Other variables that affect the prevalence of emotional and behavioral disorders are socioeconomic status and ethnicity. It appears that poverty actually doubles the risk of being identified (Costello, Messer, Bird, Cohen, & Reinherz, 1998). Further, even when sociodemographic variables, such as poverty, are controlled, gender and ethnicity make a big difference (Coutinho, Oswald, Best, & Forness, 2002). For example, Coutinho et al. found that whereas 0.75% of the population they studied had emotional disturbance, the prevalence ranged from 0.07% (Asian females) to 1.7% (African American males). African American males were 5.5 times more likely to be identified than white females. The overrepresentation of African American students identified as having an emotional or behavioral disorder has been recognized for decades (Olmedo & Kauffman, 2003). This overrepresentation issue was noted as an area of concern in IDEA 04.

The history of emotional and behavioral disorders indicates that although attention to the emotional, behavioral, and educational needs of these students really did not begin until the 20th century, great progress has been made. As a teacher, you should be aware of the term and definition used in your state to describe students with emotional or behavioral problems. You should also be aware of the various factors that affect prevalence. For example, you should be sensitive to students who display characteristics such as anxiety and depression in addition to those who are disruptive and aggressive.

Check Your Understanding

1. Who were some advocates in the 1700s and 1800s that helped make the treatment of individuals with emotional or behavioral problems more humane?

2. What events occurred during the 20th century that improved the education of individuals with emotional or behavioral problems?

3. What is the IDEA 04 definition of emotional disturbance? What are some criticisms of this definition?

4. What are some classification systems used for individuals with emotional or behavioral disorders?

5. What is the estimated prevalence rate of emotional and behavioral disorders? The percentage of the student population actually identified and receiving services? What factors are related to the prevalence rate?

What Are the Causes and Characteristics of Emotional and Behavioral Disorders?

There is some debate about what causes emotional and behavioral disorders, although evidence indicates that both environmental and genetic factors play a role. Students with emotional or behavioral disorders display a large range of characteristics, from severe withdrawal to extreme aggression to psychotic behavior. These characteristics can vary as a function of gender, age, and ethnicity. In general, a set of externalizing, internalizing, intellectual, and academic characteristics is recognized.

Causes of Emotional and Behavioral Disorders

The discussion of the causes of emotional or behavioral problems focuses on the long-held debate regarding environmental versus genetic determinants. Although there are strong supporters of each position, it is generally accepted that both the environment and genetics play a role.

Relevant CEC Standard
▶ Etiology and diagnosis related to various theoretical approaches in the field of emotional/behavioral disorders (BD2K1)

Environmental Causes

Environmental factors are important in determining an individual's behavior and emotional well-being. Although controversial factors, such as exposure to television violence, have been suggested as direct causes of emotional or behavioral disorders (Huesmann, Moise, & Freedman, 2005), there is more consensus about the effect of family, school, and community factors. Family factors could include parental discord, inconsistent or extreme punishment, and lack of emotional support (Reid & Eddy, 1997). Becvar and Becvar (1988) identified several characteristics of emotionally healthy families. The absence of these family characteristics increases the risk of a child developing problems. These characteristics include the following:

- A legitimate source of authority, established and supported over time
- A consistently enforced rule system
- Stable and consistent nurturing behavior
- Effective child-rearing practices
- Common family goals
- Flexibility to adapt

Family factors, including a consistently enforced rule system, can affect an individual's emotional and behavioral development.

School factors, such as negative school experiences and unrealistic teacher expectations, and community factors, such as gang involvement, can also play a role in the development of an emotional or behavioral disorder. It is important, however, to put the role of the environment in causing emotional or behavioral problems in perspective. Does a child coming from an abusive or neglectful family have a higher risk of developing emotional or behavioral problems? Probably so. Does this mean that the child will develop such problems? Not necessarily. The same can be said about school factors and community factors.

Genetic Causes

Research indicates that some emotional and behavioral problems, particularly more severe problems, have a genetic basis. In discussing the genetic–environment issue, Rutter and Silberg (2002) stated, "Any dispassionate review of the evidence indicates that there are substantial genetic effects on psychopathology, including emotional and behavioral disturbance" (p. 464). In one study, parents of identical and fraternal twins rated their children's problematic behavior. Slightly over one-third of the behaviors were attributed to genetics and slightly more than half were attributed to the shared environment (Loeber, Novak, & Lynam, 2000). Other research based on investigations of the degree of mental illness occurring within families suggests that schizophrenia, in particular, has a genetic basis (Gottesman & Reilly, 2003; Sawa & Kamiya, 2003). Sanjuan et al. (2006) found that a mutation of a specific gene was highly associated with individuals with schizophrenia who had auditory hallucinations.

Combined Causes

The professional consensus is that the causes of emotional and behavioral disorders are both environmentally and genetically influenced, particularly considering the wide range of individuals who fall into this category. Rutter and Silberg (2002) contend that because data indicate that both factors are involved in the determination of emotional and behavioral problems, it only follows that the interaction of the genetic and environmental factors should be considered. In other words, an emotional or behavioral problem may be due to environmental factors, to genetic factors, or perhaps, to a combination of the two.

Characteristics of Students with Emotional or Behavioral Disorders

Three points need to be emphasized when discussing the characteristics of students with emotional or behavioral disorders. First, students in this category have a wide variety of characteristics, making it difficult to create a "typical" list of characteristics. Second, there is evidence that problem behaviors are related to both gender and age (Achenbach & Edelbrock, 1991). This means that different characteristics are displayed in boys and girls, and that characteristics might change as the student ages. Table 6.1 presents characteristics that are typically associated with males and with females, and Table 6.2 on page 184 lists behaviors that typically decrease and increase with age. Third, there is evidence that problem behaviors are related to a student's ethnicity. Cullinan, Evans, Epstein, and Ryser (2003), for instance, found that European American children with emotional disturbance displayed significantly more relationship problems, depression/unhappiness, and physical symptoms/fears than their African American counterparts.

Though students with emotional or behavioral disorders display a range of possible characteristics, the majority of these fall into the categories of externalizing, internalizing, intellectual, and academic characteristics.

Externalizing Characteristics

Externalizing characteristics of emotional or behavioral disorders are those that directly affect others and are easy to observe. These include hitting and fighting with others, refusing to comply, and destroying their own and others' belongings.

Relevant CEC Standard
▶ Social characteristics of individuals with emotional/behavioral disorders (D2K3)

TABLE 6.1	EBD Characteristics in Males and Females

HIGHER PREVALENCE IN MALES	HIGHER PREVALENCE IN FEMALES
PROBLEM BEHAVIOR	**PROBLEM BEHAVIOR**
Clinic males equal to or moderately higher than nonclinic males	**Clinic females equal to or moderately higher than nonclinic females**
Shows off	Overweight
Bragging	Bites fingernails
Teases a lot	Behaves like opposite sex
Disobedient in school	Easily jealous
Can't concentrate	Fears
Destroys own things	Nightmares
Impulsive	Worrying
Cruel to others	Shy and timid
Attacks people	Self-conscious
Threatens people	Moody
Temper tantrums	Too dependent
Steals outside home	Thumb-sucking
Hangs around with children in trouble	Runs away from home
Prefers older children	Headaches
Encopresis	Skin problems
Clinic males much higher	**Clinic females much higher**
Sets fires	Cries a lot
Swearing	Feels unloved
Fighting	Stomachaches, cramps
Hyperactive	Aches and pains
Poor school work	Lonely
Cruel to animals	Unhappy, sad, or depressed
Vandalism	Sulks a lot
	Screams a lot
	Sexual preoccupation
	Overeating

Source: S. Pfeiffer. *Clinical child psychology: Introduction to theory research.* Published by Allyn & Bacon, Boston, MA. Copyright ® 1990 by Pearson Education. Reprinted by permission of the publisher.

Other behaviors that are considered externalizing include acting out and aggression. Students with higher levels of aggression have both more intense and more frequent episodes. In addition, they have more difficulty identifying the cause of their aggression (Bohnert, Crnic, & Lim, 2003). Students with externalizing behaviors typically are referred for special education more often than are students with other types of problem behaviors because of their effect on others.

One *DSM-IV-TR* classification category that is considered as externalizing is **conduct disorders.** Individuals with conduct disorders have a repetitive and persistent pattern of behavior that violates age-appropriate societal norms or rules, or the basic rights of others. There are four major groupings of these behaviors: (1) aggressive behavior that causes or threatens physical harm to people or animals, (2) nonaggressive behavior that causes property loss or damage, (3) deceitfulness or theft, and (4) serious rule violations. Because of the exclusion of social maladjustment in the definition of emotional disturbance, many students with conduct disorders are not identified as having emotional or behavioral disorders, particularly because the courts and many states define social maladjustment as a conduct disorder or oppositional/defiant behavior (Slenkovich, 1992).

conduct disorder A disorder that involves a repetitive and persistent pattern that violates age-appropriate societal norms or the basic rights of others.

What Are the Causes and Characteristics of Emotional and Behavioral Disorders? **183**

DECREASE WITH AGE	INCREASE WITH AGE
PROBLEM BEHAVIOR	**PROBLEM BEHAVIOR**
Large decrease	*Large increase*
Whining	Use of alcohol and drugs
Wets bed	Truancy
Too dependent	Poor school work
Demands attention	Hangs around with child in trouble
Cries a lot	Secretive
Fears	Swearing
Nightmares	
Picking	*Moderate increase*
Encopresis	Runs away from home
Speech problem	Headaches
Thumb-sucking	Overweight
Does not eat well	Dizzy
Talks too much	
Destroys own things	*Small increase*
Shows off	Unhappy, sad, depressed
	Sleeps too much
Moderate decrease	Underactive
Prefers younger children	Likes to be alone
Easily jealous	Sexual preoccupation
Hyperactive	
Plays with sex parts in public	
Plays with sex parts too much	
Unusually loud	
Poor peer relations	
Destroys others' things	
Attacks people	
Disobedient at home	

Source: S. Pfeiffer. *Clinical child psychology: Introduction to theory research.* Published by Allyn & Bacon, Boston, MA. Copyright ® 1990 by Pearson Education. Reprinted by permission of the publishers.

Internalizing Characteristics

Internalizing characteristics are those that directly affect the individual with the emotional or behavioral problem. Although students with emotional or behavioral disorders who exhibit internalizing characteristics can have debilitating problems, they are not identified as frequently as those with externalizing problems because their behaviors typically do not affect others. One of the most common internalizing problems is anxiety. A related characteristic associated with some students with emotional or behavioral problems is social withdrawal. The degree of withdrawal can vary in intensity from a disinterest in making friends and engaging in conversation to severe withdrawal.

    Another category of internalizing problems is referred to as **mood disorders.** This category includes manic disorders, depressive disorders, and bipolar disorder, characterized by periods of fluctuating manic and depressive states. Childhood depression is recognized as a serious mental health problem that can even ultimately lead to suicide. Clearly, teachers must take a student's depression and any suicide threats seriously.

    The IDEA 04 definition of emotional disturbance specifically states that individuals with **schizophrenia** are considered to have an emotional disturbance. Schizophrenia is a psychotic disorder characterized by delusions, hallucinations, disorganized speech, and disorganized or catatonic behavior. Other characteristics include a lack

mood disorders A class of disorders that includes manic disorders, depressive disorders, and bipolar disorders.

schizophrenia A condition characterized by delusions, hallucinations, and disorganized speech and behavior.

of emotional expression and a lack of goal-directed behavior (American Psychiatric Association, 2000).

Intellectual and Academic Characteristics

One of the criteria included in the IDEA 04 definition of emotional disturbance is "an inability to learn which cannot be explained by intellectual, sensory, or health factors." This implies that these students should score within the average range of intelligence or higher on IQ measures. Kauffman (2005) noted, however, that as a group, students with emotional or behavioral disorders typically score in the low-average range of intelligence, with more students scoring in the lower IQ levels and fewer scoring in the upper levels than students without emotional and behavioral problems. The severity of the emotional or behavioral problem is shown to influence IQ. Those with more severe problems tend to have lower IQs.

> **BOBBY REVISITED** What externalizing and internalizing characteristics does Bobby exhibit?

A related area is language. There is considerable evidence that students identified as having an emotional or behavioral disorder are much more likely to have language deficits than those students without emotional or behavioral problems. Benner, Nelson, and Epstein (2002) reported that approximately three out of four students identified with an emotional or behavioral deficit also have language problems. Nelson, Benner, and Cheney (2005) also reported moderate to large language deficits, particularly related to externalizing behaviors.

Although some early research indicated that more children with emotional disturbance were above average academically than below average (Tamkin, 1960), this does not appear to be the case. Most students with emotional or behavioral problems also have academic difficulty (Trout, Nordness, Pierce, & Epstein, 2003), and IDEA 04 indicates that a student's educational performance must be adversely affected to be identified as having an emotional disturbance.

There are many characteristics and possible causes of emotional and behavioral disorders. Acknowledgment of the wide variety of characteristics, in particular, has important implications for both general and special education teachers. It is important that general education teachers look for students with signs of emotional or behavioral problems that typically go unnoticed, such as withdrawal or depression. For all teachers working with these students, it is important that they be prepared to address a wide range of academic, emotional, and behavioral needs.

Check Your Understanding

1. What are some environmental factors that might cause emotional or behavioral problems?
2. What evidence is available that certain emotional and behavioral disorders have a genetic basis?
3. What are some examples of externalizing characteristics of emotional and behavioral disorders? Internalizing characteristics?
4. What intellectual characteristics may students with emotional and behavioral disorders display? Academic characteristics?

How Are Students with Emotional or Behavioral Disorders Identified?

The area of emotional and behavioral disorders, perhaps more than any other area discussed in this text, has a multidisciplinary foundation. Professionals from a number of disciplines—education, psychology, and psychiatry—all could be involved in identification of these disorders. Decisions about the emotional or behavioral status of a student should only be made based on multiple sources of information. This includes interviews with parents and teachers and the use of academic testing in addition to techniques such as observation and the use of behavior rating scales, behavior assessment systems, personality inventories, and projective tests.

 Relevant CEC Standards

▶ Etiology and diagnosis related to various theoretical approaches in the field of emotional/behavioral disorders (BD2K1)

▶ Policies and procedures involved in the screening, diagnosis, and placement of individuals with emotional/behavioral disorders including academic and social behaviors (BD8K2)

▶ Types and importance of information concerning individuals with emotional/behavioral disorders from families and public agencies (BD8K3)

Observation is used primarily by teachers to initially identify a student and to provide objective information to help make the eligibility decision. Behavior rating scales and behavior assessment systems, also used by teachers, address the question, "How significant is this student's emotional or behavioral problem compared to other students?" Personality inventories, used primarily by psychologists and psychiatrists, also compare the student to other students. Finally, projective tests, also used by psychologists and psychiatrists, have limited value although they are still administered by some professionals. Gresham (2005) suggested that the response to intervention model described in Chapter 4 would be very appropriate to help identify students with emotional or behavioral disorders.

Observation

The measurement or recording of *observable behavior*, a procedure widely used by teachers, is an excellent screening method for students with behavior or emotional problems and is usually the first way a student is identified as having a potential problem. The observational model provides very objective, precise information but still requires subjective decision making. One attempt to address this issue focuses on the comparison of observational data between the target student and a control student. Using this approach, the teacher would specifically define the behavior and would choose another student with a similar background, such as same age and gender, as the target student. She would then observe and record the behavior for both students and note the differences between the two students. This provides some idea of how much the behavior of the target student deviates from his peers.

Observation can be used to help document the type, frequency, and duration of the problem behaviors. Although it should not be used exclusively, observation can provide valuable additional information to help make eligibility decisions. Observation is inexpensive, easy to do, and can be done in natural settings, such as the classroom. It also requires no subjective interpretation about the *meaning* of the behavior (e.g., John is shouting at his teacher because he has latent hostility toward authority figures). Observation can also be helpful in conducting a functional behavior assessment (FBA). As described in Chapter 1, a functional behavior assessment typically involves an analysis of what happens immediately before the behavior occurs (antecedents) and what happens immediately after the behavior occurs (consequences) to develop a hypothesis about the purpose for the behavior. In the previous example, it might be observed that John typically shouts at his teacher during math time and that the teacher places John in time-out whenever he shouts at her. Thus the hypothesis might be that the purpose of the shouting is task avoidance during math time. Although the FBA does not lead to eligibility decisions, its use in developing behavioral intervention plans is significant and is discussed later in this chapter.

Relevant CEC Standard

▶ Characteristics of behavior rating scales (BD8K1)

Teachers are often asked to complete behavior rating scales.

Behavior Rating Scales

Behavior rating scales are used to document the presence and degree of certain behavior characteristics. For the most part, the formats of different behavior rating scales are similar; they are composed of a list of behavior characteristics such as "Has temper tantrums" and "Shows signs of depression" that are grouped together to measure different behavioral areas such as aggression, withdrawal, and depression. Each item is rated using a system specified in the rating scale, such as the behavior never, occasionally, or frequently occurs. Use of behavior rating scales has been shown to reliably differentiate students with and without behavior problems (Hinshaw & Nigg, 1999) although some problems of agreement have arisen when more than one informant is used (Synhorst, Buckley, Reid, Epstein, & Ryser, 2005). An example of a behavior rating scale is the Devereux Behavior Rating Scale–School Form (DBRS-SF; Naglieri, LeBuffe, & Pfeiffer, 1993). The DBRS-SF has two forms, one for ages 5–12 and one for ages 13–18. It is designed to be used by either the general education or special education teacher. It includes 40 items that are grouped according to four factors: interpersonal problems, inappropriate behaviors/feelings, depression, and physical symptoms/fears. These are the same areas included in the IDEA 04 definition.

Behavior Assessment Systems

Behavior assessment systems have multiple components, including behavior rating scales. For instance, they might include a teacher rating scale, a parent rating scale, a peer rating scale, a self-report scale, an observational component, and an interview component. The advantage of behavior assessment systems is that they provide ratings of the student from multiple informants in multiple settings. Frequently used behavior assessment systems include the Achenbach System of Empirically Based Assessment (ASEBA; Achenbach, 1991, 1997, 2000, 2003) and the Behavior Assessment System for Children–II (BASC–II; Reynolds & Kamphaus, 2004). The ASEBA measures areas such as anxious/depressed, thought problems, and aggression. The BASC–II includes areas such as depression, interpersonal relations, and attention problems.

Personality Inventories

Most personality inventories have the following characteristics in common: (1) they are designed primarily for use with adolescents and adults, (2) they typically use a true/false format, and (3) they measure a large number of personality characteristics or factors such as paranoia, reality distortion, and psychological discomfort. Personality inventories have been criticized for a variety of reasons. For example, their use for most school-aged children is limited, although some attempts have been made to develop appropriate objective inventories for younger students (Taylor, 2009). A second criticism focuses on the self-report format used in many of these instruments. Specifically, there is some question of the "truthfulness" of the information provided by an individual. Partially as a result of the self-report format, most inventories include validity scales designed to determine whether the individual is giving truthful responses. Finally, the instruments primarily use medical rather than educational terminology. Therefore, the results are not particularly useful for teachers. Two popular personality inventories are the Minnesota Multiphasic Personality Inventory–2 (Butcher, Dahlstrom, Graham, & Kaemmer, 1989) and the Personality Inventory for Children–2 (Lachar & Gruber, 2001). The latter instrument was designed for younger students and requires a parent to provide the responses.

Projective Tests

Projective tests, based primarily on psychoanalytic theory, assume that a student will "project" his or her feelings, emotions, and personality characteristics when a relatively abstract stimulus is presented. For example, the Rorschach Ink Blot Test (Rorschach, 1932) requires the individual to "interpret" ink blots. Thematic picture tests such as the Thematic Apperception Test (Murray & Bellak, 1973) and the Children's Apperception Test (Bellak & Bellak, 1991) present pictures or photographs designed to elicit certain themes that subsequently are interpreted by the examiner to determine personality dynamics. In other projective techniques, such as the Draw-a-Person Screening Procedure for Emotional Disturbance (Naglieri, McNiesh, & Bardos, 1991) or the Kinetic Drawing System for Family and School (Knoff & Prout, 1985), the examiner interprets drawings made by the student.

Projective testing is one of the most controversial areas in educational and psychological assessment. School psychologists reported that they are the least

Projective tests have been criticized for a number of reasons, yet they are frequently used.

useful assessment technique to evaluate students with emotional disturbance (Cheramie, Griffen, & Morgan, 2000). Nonetheless, they are one of the more frequently used approaches (Irgens, 2001). They are particularly used frequently in clinical settings. Wood, Nezworski, Lilienfeld, and Garb (2003) pointed out that the Rorschach Ink Blot Test is still widely used even after a half century of research that is largely negative regarding its utility. Projective tests, in general, have been criticized for being time-consuming and lacking adequate psychometric properties (Petot, 2000). There is also a great deal of subjectivity in the scoring and interpretation of these tests (Salvia, Ysseldyke, & Bolt, 2007; Taylor, 2009). Teachers should not use projective tests and techniques, but teachers should be aware of their uses and limitations in case they see the test results. If they are used at all, they should be administered and interpreted by someone, usually a psychologist or psychiatrist, who is specifically trained in this area.

BOBBY REVISITED What assessment instruments might have been administered to Bobby? How could the results be used?

Although some identification procedures, such as personality inventories and projective testing, are administered by psychologists/psychiatrists, teachers still play an important role in the identification of students with emotional or behavioral disorders. They are frequently asked to provide observational data, complete a behavior rating scale, or contribute information for the appropriate component of a behavior assessment system. The assessment information provided by these procedures is helpful for all teachers who work with these students in terms of monitoring progress and, to a certain extent, the development of instructional programs.

Check Your Understanding

1. How are students with emotional or behavioral disorders typically identified?
2. What are the strengths and limitations of observation?
3. What is a behavior rating scale? What are the names of some behavior rating scales?
4. What is a behavior assessment system? What is the advantage of using a behavior assessment system?
5. What is the difference between behavior rating scales and personality inventories?
6. What is a projective test? What are the limitations of projective tests?

What and How Do I Teach Students with Emotional or Behavioral Disorders?

Teaching students with emotional or behavioral disorders is a challenging process requiring commitment and knowledge on the part of the teacher. The specific approaches used in classes for students with emotional or behavioral problems may vary widely. Intervention must fit the characteristics of the student, the settings in which they take place, and the skills, willingness, and perseverance of the teacher (Nelson, 2004). Teachers should look for what is best suited to a particular situation or student and not feel the need to adhere solely to a particular educational approach. Typically, students with emotional or behavioral problems need intensive educational programs that include academics, behavioral training, and social development (Kauffman, 2005; Miller, 2002). The degree of severity of a student's emotional or behavioral problems as well as a student's age influence decisions concerning the choice of the appropriate educational program and instructional procedures.

Instructional Content

Curricula for students with emotional or behavioral disorders, whether they are in a general or separate classroom, generally focus on academic and social skills. The academic curriculum will often be the general curriculum with accommodations made to fit the individual students' emotional or behavioral needs. The social/behavioral skills area is particularly emphasized in the curriculum for these students who often struggle with self-control and social interaction. Service-learning activities can be very effectively used to meet both academic and social needs of these students. Transitional programming may vary greatly as do the needs of students with emotional or behavioral disorders.

Academic Skills

It has long been established that there is a relationship between academic underachievement and emotional and behavioral disorders (Wehby, Falk, Barton-Arwood, Lane, & Cooley, 2003). This may be caused in part by the misconception held by some educators that students must behave appropriately before academic learning is possible (O'Shaughnessy, Lane, Gresham, & Beebe-Frankenberger, 2003). In fact, the reality is quite the opposite. Increased academic learning can improve classroom behavior (Kauffman, 2005), and ineffective instruction in academics may actually exacerbate emotional and behavioral disorders (e.g., Gunter & Denny, 1998; Johns, Crowley, & Guetzloe, 2002). Effective instruction is thus a form of classroom management based on the premise that fewer behavior problems occur when students are engaged in learning (Newcomer, 2003).

The academic curriculum is also important for students with emotional or behavioral disorders because academic achievement is fundamental to emotional and social adjustment (Kauffman, 2005). At least a moderate level of success in academics is necessary for children to develop healthy self-images. Academically unsuccessful children are often shunned or rejected by their peers (Kauffman, Mostert, Trent, & Hallahan, 2002), which could lead to even more severe emotional or behavioral disabilities. It is, therefore, mandatory that academics be effectively taught to these students. Another reason for an emphasis on the academic curriculum of students with emotional and behavioral disorders is the increasing federal requirements for academic standards. These standards, to which students with emotional or behavioral disorders are often held accountable, are typically tied to the successful completion of school and can influence future social and economic opportunities. For positive outcomes in academic programs to occur for these students, behavioral learning and classroom instruction in academics need to be linked (Tonelson & Butler, 2000). Instructional intervention must be sustained, flexible, positive, collaborative, culturally appropriate, and continually monitored (Levy, Coleman, & Alsman, 2002).

Relevant CEC Standards

▶ Sources of specialized materials for individuals with emotional/behavioral disorders (BD4K1)

▶ Resources and techniques used to transition individuals with emotional/behavioral disorders into and out of school and post-school environments (BD4K3)

▶ Model programs that have been effective for individuals with emotional/behavioral disorders across the age range (BD7K1)

PRACTICE

Social Skills

Students with emotional or behavioral disorders often lack the social competence skills that influence peer acceptance, school success, self-confidence, and employment success (Gresham, 1997, 1998; Kauffman et al., 2002; Malloy & McMurray, 1996). Thus, development of social and personal problem-solving skills needs to be an integral part of any curriculum provided to students with emotional or behavioral disorders (Johns, 2000) and should be incorporated as early as possible (Hune & Nelson, 2002; Walker, Ramsey, & Gresham, 2004). The social curriculum will often focus on the development of problem-solving skills. Teaching problem-solving skills involves teaching students *how* to think rather than *what* to think, and provides them with ways to identify and implement appropriate behavioral responses in the presence of various stimuli (Robinson, Smith, & Miller, 2002). Depending on the nature of the social skills problem, an intervention may be specific and quick to implement, or it may require an extensive curriculum. In either case, it is important that the student with the emotional or behavioral disorder become a self-regulated, strategic user of social skills. To reach this goal, it is critical that social skills instruction be embedded in daily instruction (Mathur & Rutherford, 1996).

BOBBY REVISITED What content areas do you think need to be addressed in order for Bobby to be successful in later life? Explain.

Social skills are typically taught through sequencing and generalization. Sequencing entails breaking a social skill down into its component parts and teaching it step-by-step. For example, students may learn the steps of accepting negative feedback through discussing and practicing SLAM (McIntosh, Vaughn, & Bennerson, 1995): **S**top what you are doing, **L**ook the person in the eye, **A**sk the person a question to clarify what he or she means, and **M**ake an appropriate response to the person. Furthermore, intervention strategies that promote social skills generalization outside the training sessions should be implemented to better ensure the ability of the student to apply what he or she has learned to other situations (e.g., Gresham, 2002; Kauffman et al., 2002; Mathur & Rutherford, 1996). To promote this generalization, it has been recommended that social skills be taught in the natural environment using real-life examples and incidental learning, such as the teachable moment (Gresham, Sugai, & Horner, 2001). For example, SLAM may be cued and practiced before the teacher returns a less than perfect paper to the student. The social skills strategy STOP, presented in Online Appendix A, may be used during actual group instruction activities.

Complete social skills training programs have been developed for students who may need more extensive instruction at the preschool, elementary, or secondary level. These may be used in an overlapping curriculum that allows a student to be involved in the general education curriculum with social skills curriculum goals targeted concurrently (King-Sears, 2001). For example, a student might be working on general science goals with overlapping goals in asking for help and class participation from a social skills curriculum. The examples of social skills programs that follow represent just a few that have been used successfully with students in preschool, elementary, and secondary programs in different settings. Before beginning any social skills instruction, the teacher should investigate the student's cultural and linguistic background to assure that the skill being taught appropriately reflects the student's background. For example, firm handshakes or direct eye contact may not be condoned in the student's background culture (Lee & Cartledge, 1996).

Commonly used social skills programs include the skillstreaming programs available for preschool children (McGinnis & Goldstein, 1990), elementary-aged children (McGinnis & Goldstein, 1997), and adolescents (Goldstein & McGinnis, 1997). Each program includes a comprehensive list of social skills, such as apologizing and responding to teasing, that are broken down into small steps and then taught through a five-step instructional procedure that includes modeling, role playing, practice, feedback, generalization, and reinforcement. The generalization is built in through structured homework assignments (see the Classroom Example). Other popular social skills programs are included in Table 6.3 on page 192.

HOMEWORK REPORT 1

Name: *Sam*   Date: *October 15*

SKILL: *Responding to teasing*

STEPS:
1. *Stop and count to five.*
2. *Think about your choices:*
   a. *Ignore the teasing.*
   b. *Say how you feel.*
   c. *Give a reason for the person to stop.*
3. *Act out your best choice.*

With whom will I try this? *The kid in fifth grade.*

When? *Recess.*

What happened? *I kept playing. The kid teased me more.*
Then he stopped.

How did I do?   ☺   😐   ☹

Why did I circle this? *I forgot to stop and count to five.*

Source: McGinnis & Goldstein (1997).

Service-Learning Programs

Service-learning activities, structured community service activities through which students apply skills learned in school to address needs in their schools and communities, can be very effective as a method for enhancing the curriculum to meet the academic, social, and emotional needs of students with emotional or behavioral disorders (e.g., Frey, 2003; McCarty & Hazelkorn, 2001). According to Muscott (2001), service-learning programs have the potential to meet three important goals: (1) promote self-esteem and self-worth through the completion of socially important projects; (2) engage disenfranchised students in school-related activities and curriculum; and (3) revise other people's pessimistic views of students' worth and ability to contribute to society. Students have reported a feeling of empowerment by providing services to the community, and both teachers and students have reported extreme satisfaction with service-learning programs (Muscott, 2000, 2001).

Transition Planning

The strengths and needs of students with emotional or behavioral disorders vary greatly, so transition plans will be different for each student. Transition programming

TABLE 6.3	Representative Social Skills Curriculum Programs		
PROGRAM	**AGE/GRADE LEVEL**	**DESCRIPTION**	**SKILLS FOCUS**
Social Skills Intervention Guide (SSIG) (Elliot & Gresham, 1991)	Preschool, elementary, and secondary levels	Delivers content through small group instruction and individualized tutoring, instruction, coaching, and debriefing. Tied directly to a Social Skills Rating System (SSRS; Gresham & Elliot, 1990)	Five domains: cooperation (e.g., helping others), assertion (e.g., asking others for information), responsibility (e.g., caring for property or work), empathy (e.g., showing concern), and self-control (e.g., taking turns).
Aggression Replacement Training: A Comprehensive Intervention for Aggressive Youth (ART) (Goldstein, Glick, & Gibbs, 1998)	Ages 3–18	A cognitive behavioral intervention with training on each of three components. Runs concurrently for an hour a day, lasting approximately 10 weeks. May be conducted as a pullout or integrated program. Parent involvement ranges from mandatory participation to daily homework-based contact.	(1) A behavioral component, Skillstreaming, to enhance prosocial skills; (2) an emotional component, Anger Control Training, which teaches antisocial behavior inhibition; and (3) a values component, Moral Education, centered on dilemma discussion groups.
Second Step: A Violence Prevention Curriculum (Seattle Committee for Children, 1992)	Preschool/ kindergarten through grade 9	An award-winning program that teaches social and emotional skills for violence prevention. Lessons are easy to teach, flow sequentially, and require minimal teacher preparation time. Integration activities tie the lessons to academic learning requirements in health, science, math, social studies, and language. Second Step is one of the most tested, effective, and user-friendly social skills curricula available (Walker, Ramsey, & Gresham, 2003/2004a, 2004).	Three essential competencies: empathy, impulse control and problem solving, and anger management.

requires thoughtful planning to create a curriculum that is relevant, engaging, and useful to students (Johns et al., 2002). Areas of transition planning include vocational and life skills for some students, and preparation for postsecondary educational experience for others. Other transition concerns may include transition from juvenile detention and transition from homelessness to school.

Vocational and Life Skills. Early preparation for the work world is an appropriate focus of school for some students with emotional or behavioral disorders. It has been suggested that the elementary years should include content such as job sampling and work concepts (Gajar, Goodman, & McAfee, 1993). Middle school would then focus on work habits, specific vocational skills, and decision making. Stuart (2004) reminded us that it is particularly important to ensure that girls with emotional or behavioral disorders practice problem-solving skills to help them feel empowered enough to assume active decision-making roles in vocational planning. At the secondary level, students participate in actual work experiences. Critical job-related social skills should be addressed in transition plans as adolescents with emotional or behavioral disorders are often lacking in the social skills and perception of what is needed to maintain competitive employment in a specific workplace (Carter & Wehby, 2003). Participating in real work experiences provides a setting for teaching these skills. The benefits of work experience may be increased through including job tours, job shadowing, guest speakers (same gender, race, or disability as students) from the community, and forming strong connections with families by inviting them to chaperone a worksite visit and meeting with them individually or as a group to familiarize them with the program (Stuart, 2004).

Postsecondary Education. As is the case with learning disabilities, the number of students with emotional or behavioral disorders who continue with postsecondary education has been increasing (Frank & Sitlington, 1997) since the IDEA requirements for transition planning led to the increase in support services available at postsecondary institutions. Successful transition to postsecondary education institutions often relies on coordination between academics and study skills instruction, participation in extracurricular activities, and a program for social skills and self-advocacy skills (Edgar & Siegel, 1995; Rogers & Rogers, 2001). The student should be guided in obtaining information about various colleges and what special programs or support they each offer. Visits or interviews with college representatives should be planned. The student should also determine what documentation is required for services at his or her targeted institution and should be prepared to take that information to the initial orientation session.

Reintegration from Juvenile Detention. In a *CEC Today* article, Peter Leone, of the National Center of Education, Disability, and Juvenile Justice, stated that a current national survey indicated that between 30 and 40% of those in the juvenile justice system in the United States are children with disabilities (Cosmos, 2002). Nearly half of these children have emotional or behavioral disorders (Quinn, Rutherford, Leone, Osher, & Poirier, 2005). Beyond the obvious need for preventive measures in the schools, transition needs for successful reintegration of many of the currently incarcerated students as they return to the school system must be addressed. Students reentering a school system from a juvenile detention center are typically moving from a highly structured environment to a much more open one. This change in structure and attention may itself contribute to disruptive behaviors in students when they return to their community schools (Stephens & Arnette, 2000). Planning for transition back into the community school should involve community-based school staff participating in cooperative meetings with educational staff from the detention center, inservice workshops, and correctional school visits to better understand the students' educational environment prior to returning to the community (Barclay, Roberts, & Rutherford, 2003).

Homelessness. About half of the population of homeless students have some type of disability. These students very often have pervasive physical, academic, and emotional or behavioral needs, and emotional/behavioral disorders, identified or unidentified, are more prevalent than any other type of disability (Wilder, 2003; Zima, Forness, Bussing, & Bernadette, 1998). Some of these children live with their families and others live alone. Wilder suggests that IEP and transition plans for these students should include counseling services, extensive social skills training, and visits to environments where students are likely to live, work, or attend school to observe behavioral expectations in that environment. Curriculum should address sexual issues, including dating, rape, sexual abuse, and prostitution; marriage and family relationships and responsibilities; gang prevention; consequences of drug addiction and conflict resolution; problem-solving skills; and self-advocacy (Wilder, 2003; Zionts, Zionts, & Simpson, 2002). Service-learning experiences may be valuable for these students (Muscott, 2000) as this ties the school curriculum directly to the needs of the community. Free breakfasts and lunches, a place to put personal belongings, and a place to shower and wash clothes should help a homeless student with emotional or behavioral problems feel safer, more accepted, and less stigmatized at school (Wilder, 2003). Sensitive transition specialists can help the many resilient homeless students survive and be successful in a more inviting world.

Instructional Procedures

The type of teaching procedures used with students with emotional or behavioral disorders will depend on the content and the behavior(s) being targeted in intervention

Relevant CEC Standards

▶ Advantages and limitations of instructional strategies and practices for teaching individuals with emotional/behavioral disorders (BD4K2)

▶ Prevention and intervention strategies for individuals at risk of emotional/behavioral disorders (BD4K4)

programs. The earlier the intervention is implemented, the better the outcome. Because students with emotional or behavioral disorders by definition have behavioral change as a goal, many procedures, such as cognitive behavioral intervention and behavioral management intervention, are designed for this purpose. There are also procedures that have been found to be successful in facilitating academic skill acquisition and developing social skills. Some procedures may be used for more than one purpose. For example, effective teaching strategies themselves have been shown to contribute to reducing disruptive behavior in a classroom. The ultimate goal of any procedure in teaching students with emotional or behavioral disorders is for the student to become an independent, self-regulated learner. Self-regulation has been discussed in previous chapters and includes skills such as self-monitoring, goal-setting, strategy selection and implementation, and self-evaluation/self-reinforcement. In this following section, we specifically explore early intervention, direct instruction, cognitive behavioral interventions, and behavioral management intervention. For additional suggestions of teaching strategies, revisit Chapter 4. Many of the instructional strategies for teaching academics to students with learning disabilities are also appropriate for teaching academics and social skills to students with emotional or behavioral disorders, although students with emotional or behavioral disorders will need more behavioral support than do their peers with learning disabilities or mild mental retardation/intellectual disabilities (Sabornie, Evans, & Cullihan, 2006).

The Importance of Early Intervention

An accumulating body of literature presents a compelling rationale for early intervention with children with emotional or behavioral disorders (Kendziora, 2004). Without early intervention, many disruptive behaviors and noncompliance in young children, well documented in preschool and kindergarten (Henry, Gordon, Mashburn, & Ponder, 2001), can become lifelong concerns. Social and emotional factors measured in preschool are more powerful predictors of school dropout than later intelligence or achievement scores (Jimerson, Egeland, Sroufe, & Carlson, 2000). Behavioral measures in early childhood have been shown to be predictive of later difficulties in academics, peer relationships, school expulsion, and general learning (Kendziora, 2004), and those behaviors evident in early childhood become progressively more resistant to intervention as the child ages (Lane, 1999). A recent national survey indicated that kindergarten teachers feel that compliance with reasonable adult requests predicts a successful transition into school (Rimm-Kaufman, Pianta, & Cox, 2000). Even in early intervention classrooms, behavior management skills will be necessary if teachers are to prepare these children for future success in school. Treating noncompliance at an early age may prevent the development of more destructive behavior (Walker, Ramsey, & Gresham, 2003/2004a), and the most effective early preventive intervention programs have been those subscribing to behavioral and cognitive behavioral methods (Durlap & Wells, 1997, 1998). Furthermore, parental participation in any school-based intervention effort is essential (Conroy & Brown, 2004; Walker, Ramsey, & Gresham, 2004).

BOBBY REVISITED Was Bobby a good candidate for early intervention? If so, what qualified him? What do you think an early intervention program would have done for Bobby?

Walker et al. (2003/2004a) noted that research has demonstrated that the best way to intervene at school is to start with an inexpensive schoolwide intervention and then add on more intensive interventions for the most troubled children. An intervention that is used as a general schoolwide or whole classroom strategy for all students with and without disabilities is referred to as a **universal intervention**. A universal intervention might be classwide or cafeteria-wide social skills training. Universal interventions improve all students' behavior, have the greatest impact on students who are just beginning to be aggressive or defiant, and offer daylong support for students who may be receiving more intensive intervention during only part of the day (Walker et al., 2003/2004a). In fact, more intensive interventions for selected students are more effective if implemented within the

universal intervention An intervention that is used as a general schoolwide or whole classroom strategy for all students with and without disabilities.

context of a universal intervention (Eddy, Reid, & Curry, 2002; Sugai, Horner, & Gresham, 2002). For example, a universal intervention recommended by Brown, Musick, Conroy, and Schaeffer (2002) to teach young children compliance with reasonable adult requests involves a five-step process employed consistently throughout the day by all adults in the school setting. This five-step process is based on empirically validated behavioral strategies (e.g., Walker & Walker, 1991).

Step 1: Make reasonable and clear requests while children are paying attention.
Step 2: Following reasonable adult requests, give children 5 seconds to begin to comply.
Step 3: Employ descriptive praise for child compliance.
Step 4: Following instances of child noncompliance, restate requests in a firm voice and give children 5 seconds to begin to comply.
Step 5: Following instances of child noncompliance with second follow-up requests, physically assist children in completing or partially completing requests.

Direct Instruction

A key to reducing inappropriate behavior in students with emotional or behavioral disorders and providing effective instruction is to increase instructional time and task engagement. With its emphasis on engaged learning time, structure, sequencing, frequent feedback, and practice, the direct instruction approach to teaching academics has been shown to be effective with this population of students (Landrum, Tankersley, & Kauffman, 2003; Yell, 1992). Several guiding principles for teaching students with emotional or behavioral problems using direct instruction have been suggested (Newcomer, 2003).

- Skills taught must be relevant and meaningful to students.
- The number of examples, illustrations, and models employed should be sufficient to ensure concept development and skill acquisition as well as demonstrate relevancy to the student's life.
- Teachers should plan examples and models carefully and regularly evaluate the effectiveness of the instruction.
- Materials should be varied in form and in content, as well as difficulty level. Positive feedback should be used to encourage student participation and success.

Appropriately planned direct instruction can lead to increased academic achievement and improved classroom behavior in students with emotional and behavioral disorders. An example of the use of direct instruction to teach the strategy STOP and promote generalization of the strategy is presented in Online Appendix A. The strategy and procedures in this example were developed by a teacher to meet a specific need observed in her students.

Cognitive Behavioral Intervention

Cognitive behavioral strategies, through which students learn how to learn, and metacognitive behavioral strategies, through which students learn how to plan and monitor their learning, can help students with emotional or behavioral problems be successful in school. Cognitive behavioral intervention involves teaching concepts of self-instruction, self-monitoring, self-evaluation self-regulation, and self-attribution, so that students may become independent learners in control of their own behavior. For example, using self-instruction, the teacher may model for the student by speaking aloud—"I am going to think of how I am going to act if someone cuts in front of me in a line." The teacher then works with the student to simultaneously and overtly talk his or her way through the task or problem. Next, the student overtly talks his or her way through the task with teacher feedback. Finally, the student fades overt speech and relies on internal dialogue to work through the task. Generalization training is necessary to teach the student to use this internal dialogue across settings, situations, types of problems, and so forth (Meichenbaum, 1980). Cognitive behavioral strategy training has been used to increase attending skills, reflective behaviors, and social and academic skills. It has also been found to foster self-regulation and self-management skills. Students who have these skills are much more likely to display appropriate behaviors in a variety of settings (Coleman & Webber, 2002).

Mnemonic strategies, described in Chapter 4, have also been shown to improve academics and increase positive social behaviors for students with emotional or behavioral disorders (Cade, & Gunter, 2002; Lloyd, Forness, & Kavale, 1998; Scruggs & Mastropieri, 2000). For example, ZIPPER (Zip your mouth, Identify the problem, Pause, Put yourself in charge, Explore choices, and Reset) was successfully used as a component in an intervention to improve social behavior by promoting recall of the cognitive behavioral strategy to reduce "angry behavior" and aggression (Smith, Siegel, O'Connor, & Thomas, 1994).

Behavioral Techniques Intervention

A number of procedures can be used to manage behavior, but the most widely implemented fall under the category of applied behavior analysis. **Applied behavior analysis** is the systematic application of behavioral principles to change socially significant behavior (Alberto & Troutman, 2006). These behavioral techniques, when effectively applied, lend themselves well to individual student and classroom management. The key concept in behavior and classroom management is *consistency*. Teachers must know in advance what they may and may not do in assigning consequences for increasing or decreasing student behaviors. If classroom rules are not consistently enforced and students cannot predict and expect the consequences for their behavior, then a behavioral approach may become more damaging than helpful. With thoughtful implementation, however, the teacher can achieve an effective and efficient classroom management program.

Behavioral Intervention Plan. As mentioned earlier, a functional behavior assessment (FBA) is frequently used to determine the function or purpose of behavior. FBAs are increasingly being used to develop effective intervention plans for students with emotional or behavioral disorders who demonstrate problem behaviors (Fox, Conroy, & Heckaman, 1998; Heckaman, Conroy, Fox, & Chait, 2000; Kern, Hilt, & Gresham, 2004). Through direct observation, interviews, questionnaires, rating scales, and anecdotal reports, it is determined whether there is a pattern of events or behaviors that consistently precedes (antecedent events) or follows (consequences) the occurrence of the behavior (Barnhill, 2005). Alberto and Troutman (2006) note six common functions of behaviors: (1) to gain attention, (2) to obtain a tangible object or activity, (3) to gain sensory stimulation (e.g., body-rocking or hand flapping), (4) to escape attention from or interaction with a peer or adult, (5) to escape a task or activity, or (6) to escape internal stimulation that is painful or uncomfortable (e.g., a bruise on one's behind that hurts when seated). Based on the functional assessment results, a systematic **behavioral intervention plan** can be developed. A positive behavioral intervention plan contains the details of the strategies to be used in intervention and the assessment methods that will be used to evaluate progress (Shippen, Simpson, & Crites, 2003). The plan may be skill-based, antecedent-based, and/or consequence-based, depending on the functional assessment results, and should include an alternative appropriate behavior (that is, a replacement behavior) to accomplish the same function. Earlier in the chapter, an example was given that depicted a student's shouting at the teacher for the function, or purpose, of escaping a task (math). Another example of a function of a behavior follows. Whenever the teacher asks a question, Tamara yells the answer out in class without raising her hand. Through direct observation, it is determined that each time this occurs, the teacher stops, turns to Tamara, and sternly reminds her that she needs to raise her hand. Since the teacher scolds Tamara each time she yells out, and she continues to yell out, it appears that the function of the behavior is to gain the teacher's attention, and Tamara is receiving the attention she wanted. In other words, the yelling out in class has achieved its purpose, or function, and will continue unless the only way that Tamara receives attention from the teacher is through the use of an alternative behavior, such as raising her hand. This analysis begins the development of a positive intervention plan.

applied behavior analysis The systematic application of behavioral principles to change socially significant behavior.

behavioral intervention plan A written plan that contains the details of the strategies to be used in intervention and the assessment methods that will be used to evaluate progress.

Both the functional behavioral assessment and the positive intervention plan should include consideration of different cultural perspectives and culturally appropriate replacement behaviors (Salend & Taylor, 2002). For example, if a student is from a culture that shows appreciation of a speaker through participatory behavior such as choral responses, a plan should incorporate this information. The student would first need to be taught that different rules for what is appropriate participation apply to different settings. The teacher may then allow spontaneous choral responding in some situations, such as story time, and require a replacement behavior of raising one's hand in another, such as during social studies. It would be necessary to make the rules of participation very clear for each setting while a student learns another way of participating in another setting. Many behavioral techniques can be incorporated into a behavioral intervention plan.

> **BOBBY REVISITED** Bobby's teachers and parents describe him as "explosive" and state that they couldn't predict what would bring on this behavior. How could his teacher determine what is causing Bobby's explosions at school? Briefly describe the process.

Techniques to Increase Behaviors. Methods used to increase desired behaviors include positive and negative reinforcement, token economies, contingency contracting, and the Premack Principle. All these procedures have one common element— reinforcement of appropriate behavior. **Positive reinforcement** is the contingent presentation of a consequence following a student response to increase that response. The consequence, which sometimes is referred to as a "reward," may be tangible or social, immediate or delayed. For example, the reinforcement may be either stickers or praise awarded immediately after each correct response or at the end of a designated period of time. Reinforcers must be individualized for a particular student, as what may be reinforcing to one student may not be for another. This can be determined only by observing what happens to the behavior it follows. It is important to note that appropriately used reinforcers have not been found to decrease intrinsic motivation (McGinnis, Friman, & Carlyon, 1999). Also, it is possible to positively reinforce undesirable responses and therefore increase their frequency. For example, giving attention for misbehavior that results in an increase in the misbehavior, as in the case of Tamara discussed previously.

Giving specific praise can be a very effective and simple strategy for positively reinforcing many appropriate behaviors and establishing a positive classroom environment (Sutherland, Copeland, & Wehby, 2001). Research has found that praise is greatly underutilized, particularly with students with emotional or behavioral disorders (Mayer & Sulzer-Azaroff, 2002; Walker et al., 2003/2004a). Teachers need to increase the use of praise, and students may need to be taught how to recruit teacher praise (see An Important Event). Praise should be immediate, frequent, enthusiastic, descriptive, and varied and should involve eye contact (Walker et al., 2003/2004a).

positive reinforcement The contingent presentation of a consequence following a student response to increase that response.

AN IMPORTANT EVENT

Does Praise Have an Effect on Behavior in the Classroom?

Madsen, C. H., Becker, W. C., & Thomas, D. R. (1968). Rules, praise, and ignoring. Elements of elementary classroom control. *Journal of Applied Behavior Analysis, 1,* 139–150.

A study by Madsen, Becker, and Thomas (1968) was the first to establish a relationship between teacher praise and disruptive behavior of students. The researchers demonstrated that when teachers praised appropriate behavior, students' disruptive behavior decreased. Specifically, they found that (1) rules alone have little effect on classroom behavior, (2) ignoring inappropriate behavior and showing approval for appropriate

(continued)

behavior together were very effective in improving classroom behavior, and (3) showing approval for appropriate behavior is probably the key to effective classroom management.

REFLECTION What implications does this research have for teachers' instructional planning?

negative reinforcement The presentation of an aversive stimulus and then its removal as a consequence of the student's behavior resulting in an increase of the behavior.

Negative reinforcement is the removal of an aversive stimulus as a consequence of the student's behavior. When negative reinforcement is appropriately applied, the desired behavior is increased, not decreased. A common example is canceling a homework assignment, assuming homework is undesirable to the students, if all in-class work is completed correctly. Negative reinforcement is generally considered more intrusive than positive reinforcement because some aversive stimulus must be present. Again, it is also possible to negatively reinforce undesirable responses and increase their frequency, as in the case with John who yelled at the teacher when confronted with math time, resulting in his being sent to time-out, or, in other words, the removal of the aversive stimulus, math.

token economy The contingent presentation of something tangible that can be exchanged later for some preferred reinforcer.

A **token economy** involves the contingent presentation of something tangible, such as a check mark, a poker chip, or a ticket, which can be exchanged later for some preferred reinforcer, such as free time or computertime. Token systems have been used in both general and special education, with children with mild to severe disabilities, with preschoolers through adults, and with social and academic behaviors (Kazdin, 2001). A token economy is one of the more commonly used and adaptable behavioral intervention strategies. Token systems can be effective in increasing on-task and academic behaviors and in generating positive changes in behaviors other than those targeted (for example, attendance may increase as the result of rewards for academic performance). In addition, token economies can provide immediate reinforcement (the token) when the preferred reinforcer cannot be easily delivered. By establishing "reinforcement menus," the teacher is able to provide a wide variety of rewards for students who can "purchase" their own preferences. It is important when using a token economy that students continue to improve performance, the requirements for obtaining tokens become more demanding as the student improves, and that eventually the token system is phased out altogether (Kerr & Nelson, 2006).

One disadvantage of token economies is that they are subject to the dangers of monetary systems. Some of the problems that may be encountered include theft of tokens, extortion, an overabundance of tokens, insufficient supply of reinforcers, borrowing tokens, and students' performing favors for tokens from other students (Kazdin & Bootzin, 1972). Therefore, the teacher must be careful in establishing the rules governing economies as well as specifying the contingencies governing the award of tokens. One way of avoiding some of these problems is to individualize tokens so only the person who has earned them can use them, for example, by simply having students write their names on their tokens. Although token economies can be extremely useful in classroom management, it should be noted that not all students will respond to them, and they should not be considered a panacea.

contingency contract An agreement, usually in writing, that specifies consequences for desired performances.

Like token economies, behavioral contracting systems, or contingency contracts, are used widely in the schools to support positive behavior (Hester & McCarvill, 2000). **Contingency contracts** are agreements, usually in writing, that specify consequences for desired performances. The contract may spell out what the students as well as the teacher must do. Contingency contracts, also referred to as behavior contracts, are one way of providing an individualized program of reinforcement without using tokens. Kazdin (2001) listed several advantages of using contingency contracts:

- They allow for student input in determining reinforcement contingencies.
- They are not usually aversive and generally do concentrate on building appropriate behaviors.

CONTRACT

I, _____ , agree to do the following

behaviors:

1. _____

2. _____

3. _____

When: _____

How well: _____

If I am successful, I will receive _____ ,

given by _____ , on _____ .

Bonus clause _____

Penalty clause _____

_____

(Student signature)	_Date_
(Teacher signature)	_Date_

PRACTICE

- They are flexible because different kinds of contingencies might be encompassed (e.g., behavioral and academic improvement).
- They can be renegotiated at any time.
- They provide a written and explicit record of what the contingencies are.
- They help to structure the student–teacher relationship by more clearly defining roles, expectations, and outcomes.

Another advantage of behavior contracts is that they help students develop self-management techniques. For example, a student may not be ready to assume total responsibility for task completion but may still experience a sense of pride and satisfaction in planning, defining, and accomplishing goals leading to that end. Goal-setting is an important strategy for use with students with emotional or behavioral problems and may be incorporated into contingency contracts. (The Classroom Example illustrates the components of a contingency contract.)

One of the most common secondary reinforcers, a reinforcer that is not food or drink, used by teachers is activities (Alberto & Troutman, 2006). The systematic use of activity reinforcers is referred to as the **Premack Principle.** This simple but effective positive reinforcement procedure capitalizes on students' preferences (Premack, 1959). The

Premack Principle Positive reinforcement procedure that uses student-preferred activities as reinforcers for performing less preferred activities.

What and How Do I Teach Students with Emotional or Behavioral Disorders? **199**

teacher uses student-preferred activities as reinforcers for performing less preferred activities (i.e., if you do X, you may then do Y). For example, students might receive an extra 10 minutes of computer use for completing seat assignments on time. This procedure may be used to increase the strength, frequency, and duration of the less preferred responses.

Techniques to Decrease Behaviors. Building adaptive responses and increasing positive behaviors should be the teacher's primary focus. When maladaptive behavior occurs, however, there may be a need to decrease behaviors. Methods for decreasing behaviors include differential reinforcement of other behaviors or incompatible behaviors, time-out, response cost, extinction, and punishment.

Differential reinforcement is positive reinforcement that involves rewarding students for performing behaviors other than targeted undesirable ones. The teacher rewards the student for engaging in any appropriate behavior other than the undesirable behavior (for example, rewarding any appropriate behavior other than hitting), or the teacher rewards behaviors that are incompatible with, or in direct conflict with, the performance of the undesirable response (for example, the teacher rewards in-seat behavior to reduce out-of-seat behavior). In both cases, the teacher should also develop a contingency plan for dealing with the inappropriate response when it does occur. These methods are less intrusive than some other procedures for reducing undesirable behaviors and can be used with intervention plans based on a functional assessment that includes a replacement behavior. However, it is generally recognized that behavior change may take some time.

Another procedure for misbehavior is time-out from positive reinforcement, simply referred to as **time-out.** Time-out refers to the contingent removal of the student from a positively reinforcing environment for some predetermined amount of time, usually 5 to 15 minutes. There are three types of time-out: (1) contingent observation where the child can still see and hear what is being taught and appropriate behavior being reinforced but is ineligible for reinforcement, such as standing a few feet away from a group receiving instruction; (2) exclusionary time-out wherein the student cannot see but can hear what is being taught, such as sitting a student at a desk behind a screen in an area of the room; and (3) seclusionary time-out, which involves removing the student to a specially designed time-out room. It is the latter of the three that many professionals may think of as time-out, but it is clearly the most intrusive form. Also, because time-out assumes that the environment from which the student is being removed is positively reinforcing, seclusionary time-out use may work against the teacher. If the teaching environment is actually undesirable, students may misbehave to "escape" into time-out. Similarly, the teacher must ensure that the time-out area is not rewarding so that students will not misbehave to attain that environment. The teacher must ensure that the learning environment is rewarding, and the levels of time-out and the procedures to follow must be carefully planned (Alberto & Troutman, 2006; Kerr & Nelson, 2006). Walker et al. (2004) recommended that time-out be used sparingly, as a last resort, and be avoided with older students.

A procedure for decreasing behavior that may be easily incorporated into a token economy is referred to as **response cost,** or the withdrawal of specific numbers of reinforcers contingent on a behavior's occurrence. Kazdin (2001) described response cost as a mild form of punishment that generally does not elicit the undesirable side effects of more intrusive punitive procedures. When using response cost, as with all management systems, students must clearly understand the rules and penalties beforehand (Alberto & Troutman, 2006). Daily review is usually necessary. Response cost is much easier to manage than time-out (Walker et al., 2004). It should be used in conjunction with positive reinforcement procedures that increase appropriate behavior, and the subtraction of points should never be punitive or personalized. When response cost contingencies are used, the student should never be in a "deficit" situation. That is, should the student engage in responses that cost him or her tokens, the cost should never exceed the number of tokens in the student's possession. In addition, giving students the opportunity to earn tokens back, contingent on emission of appropriate behavior, may lessen the punishing impact of response cost and encourage positive behavior. If a student has lost all tokens with no chance of recovery, what motivation is there to continue to behave or work?

differential reinforcement Positive reinforcement in which the teacher rewards students for performing behaviors other than, or behaviors that are incompatible with, targeted undesirable ones.

time-out The contingent removal of the student from a positively reinforcing environment for some predetermined amount of time.

response cost The withdrawal of specific numbers of reinforcers contingent on a behavior's occurrence.

Extinction can also be used to decrease behaviors. **Extinction** is withholding positive reinforcement for a previously reinforced response. This procedure can be quite effective for relatively minor misbehavior, such as occasional talking out of turn. Extinction typically involves ignoring the undesirable response when it has been previously reinforced by attention. However, the teacher should be aware that it is not unusual for an undesirable response to actually worsen at the onset of an extinction procedure as the student doubles up efforts to obtain the reinforcement that was previously available. For example, a student who is ignored for talking out may initially talk out even more before a decrease in behavior is observed. Typically, extinction of a response takes some time, particularly if the response has been reinforced over a long period. It is also more effective if it is paired with positive reinforcement for an incompatible behavior. In the previous example, this would mean reinforcing with attention when the student is being quiet. It is worth noting that teachers may unintentionally extinguish desirable behavior if they fail to provide reinforcement on an intermittent basis, such as forgetting to praise a student who has previously been praised for completing seatwork.

Finally, **punishment,** another means to decrease behaviors, may range from a mild reprimand to a derisive remark to a very intrusive procedure such as manual restraint (to prevent injury of self or others). Punishment refers to contingently applying an aversive consequence following a behavior to reduce the behavior. Although punishment can be effective in suppressing behavior, it may not eliminate the behavior. Punishment may not teach the student what the appropriate behavior is, only what is inappropriate. Punishment may also generate a host of undesirable side effects. People tend to avoid or escape situations involving punishment. Therefore, the use of punishment may result in students' avoiding contact with the person or location identified with the punishing situation. The teacher who administers punishment may become associated with punishment, evoking unpleasant feelings in the student rather than positive ones. Also, punishment can provide a model of aggression, or it may lead to excessive anxiety, thereby interfering with learning. For all these reasons, many professionals agree that the use of punishment should generally be avoided. Simpler, less intrusive, nonaversive behavioral interventions (e.g., differential reinforcement) have grown in popularity as alternatives to the use of aversive procedures as many professionals and parents condemn the use of seriously aversive procedures altogether. Alberto and Troutman (2006) stressed that physical or other strong aversive consequences are a last resort to be used only after positive alternatives have been used and failed, and only under the most extreme instances of inappropriate behavior. For example, procedures such as differential reinforcement may not be appropriate for self-injurious or dangerously aggressive behavior, as they tend to be slow in eliciting change.

Nonbehavioral Intervention Techniques

Although most programs for students with emotional and behavioral disorders include some behavioral intervention, there are also some effective nonbehavioral techniques that are generally more concerned with a student's internal feelings and expressions about them. These approaches could be used as adjuncts to behavioral intervention programs or as sole support systems for students with emotional or behavioral disorders who do not need or no longer need behavioral intervention. Included in these approaches are creative dramatics, play therapy, bibliotherapy, and pharmacological treatment.

Drama as a therapeutic intervention is based on the premise that individuals gain understanding of society and its influences on their behavior if they act out significant scenes from their lives (Newcomer, 2003). **Creative dramatics,** or dramatic improvisation, refers to an improvised drama created by the players (Beyda, 2002). Creative dramatics has been shown to have positive effects on academics, language, and social skills; it has improved self-concept and has promoted positive attitudes of general education students toward students with emotional or behavioral disorders (Buege, 1993; de la Cruz, Lian, & Morreau, 1998). Creative dramatics, including role-reversal, perspective-taking, and working with peers, differs from direct role playing in that situations and characters may be slightly removed from real life (Beyda, 2002).

extinction Withholding positive reinforcement for a previously reinforced response.

punishment Contingently applying an aversive consequence following a behavior to reduce the behavior.

creative dramatics An improvised drama created by the players.

PRACTICE

play therapy The use of a child's play for self-expression and the exploring of feelings to work through troubling experiences, fears, and anxieties.

bibliotherapy The use of literature to help people solve problems and deal with feelings, to teach about a particular disability, or to promote social awareness and acceptance of differences.

pharmacological treatment The use of medication to help in controlling some emotional or behavioral disorders.

Play therapy capitalizes on the idea that a child's play is a strong medium for self-expression and lends itself to exploring feelings and working through troubling experiences, fears, and anxieties. Therapists from every major psychological orientation have successfully used play therapy to treat children with emotional or behavioral disorders (Kaduson & Schaefer, 2000). Newcomer (2003) reported on successful case studies in the areas of stress disorders due to violence, abuse, natural disasters, plane crashes, and war; loss through death; repeated foster placements or divorce; and fears and phobias.

Bibliotherapy involves the use of books and stories to help people solve problems and deal with feelings, to teach about a particular disability, or to promote social awareness and acceptance of differences. Solving problems through literature is a familiar process in school and is considered both noninvasive and child friendly (Sullivan & Strang, 2002/2003). By learning a problem-solving strategy and applying it to children's literature, students can become more independent and effective problem solvers (Forgan, 2002). Additional benefits may include positive effects on students' self-concepts and behavior (Sridhar & Vaughn, 2000). Bibliotherapy can be used routinely or to deal with a specific problem or as a preventative measure; it can be used individually, in small groups, or as a universal intervention in whole class teaching (Maich & Kean, 2004); and it can be used well with culturally diverse populations. For example, storytelling has always been an important part of Native American cultures, and Robbins (2002) has illustrated how culturally sensitive stories can be used to help American Indian youth examine their lives. One overall caution should be heeded in the use of bibliotherapy: topics that may concern parents or the community, such as abortion or birth control, should be avoided unless approved by your school administration.

Pharmacological treatment, the use of drugs to control behavior of students with emotional or behavioral disorders, is becoming more common, systematic, and effective, and medications can be extremely helpful to some students in controlling emotional or behavioral disorders (Kauffman, 2005). However, teachers do not and should not presume to determine when medication is needed, although they may make a referral for an evaluation to other professionals. If medication is prescribed, the teacher's role becomes central to this treatment by carefully monitoring the effects of any medication on the classroom behavior of students during their continued academic and social skills programs. The teacher may provide essential feedback to the parents and other professionals in determining whether the medication is working, needs to be discontinued, or needs a dosage adjustment. The goal is to obtain maximum benefits with

Books and stories can be used to help children solve problems and deal with feelings.

minimum side effects. Teachers should educate themselves about the effects, dosages, and possible side effects of any drugs that have been prescribed for their students (Konopasek, 2004; Konopasek & Forness, 2004). This treatment is not a separate, discrete intervention and will be further discussed in Chapter 14.

Check Your Understanding

1. What content is generally included for students with emotional or behavioral problems? Describe some programs that exist for students who may need more extensive instruction in social skills. How can service-learning activities contribute?

2. What two major areas of transition planning are typically included for students with emotional or behavioral disorders? What other transition needs may exist for this population of students?

3. What should most early intervention efforts focus on? How important is family involvement?

4. What aspects of direct instruction are particularly relevant for students with emotional or behavioral disorders? What is the ultimate goal of cognitive and metacognitive strategy instruction for students with emotional or behavioral disorders?

5. What are some techniques used to increase desired behavior in the classroom? What are some techniques used to decrease inappropriate behavior in the classroom?

6. What are some nonbehavioral techniques that may be used in classrooms for students with emotional or behavioral disorders?

What Are Other Instructional Considerations for Teaching Students with Emotional or Behavioral Disorders?

Motivating students and creating an atmosphere that is free of threat and conducive to learning is very important in teaching students with emotional or behavioral disorders. Specific physical arrangements in the classroom and grouping options can make this more likely to occur. In addition, many aspects of instructional technology are particularly relevant for motivating students with emotional or behavioral disorders and increasing the probability of their success in school and later life.

Relevant CEC Standards

▶ Advantages and disadvantages of placement options and the continuum of services for individuals with emotional/behavioral disorders (BD5K1)

▶ Functional classroom designs for individuals with emotional/behavioral disorders (BD5K2)

The Instructional Environment

Debate continues about the benefits of inclusion, but it is apparent that students with emotional or behavioral problems are likely to continue to gain increased exposure to general education classroom settings. About 21% of students with emotional or behavioral disorders were served in general education classes in 1989, but by 2004, a little more than 32% were served in general education classrooms. In 2006, more than 82% spent some time in general education, and 35% spent more than 80% of their time there. In addition, 15% of students with emotional or behavioral disorders are served in separate educational facilities, in residential facilities, and in homebound or hospital settings (U.S. Department of Education, 2005). Whether a student with emotional or behavioral disorders is receiving services in a general education or separate special education classroom, there are important considerations related to the physical arrangement of the room and grouping options.

The Physical Arrangement

The physical arrangement and attributes of the room may have significant effects on the social and motivational climate of a class, regardless of whether children with emotional or behavioral disorders are present. The way in which a teacher chooses to set up the classroom is especially important for students with emotional or behavioral problems. For example, a disorganized, chaotic classroom is likely to foster disorganization and chaos in students, leading to classroom management problems. Placement of desks and chairs should take into consideration the need for positive classroom socialization and interactions as well as the need for positive peer modeling opportunities. If in-class time-out is to be used, this needs to be considered in the classroom arrangement as well. Finally, the classroom environment should reflect and augment the teacher's particular teaching style and the types of skills to be taught.

The Preschool Classroom. Key words in the consideration of the physical arrangement of the preschool classroom with students with emotional or behavioral disorders are *structure* and *consistency.* For example, it has been demonstrated that the level of aggression in young boys can be affected just by the orderliness of the classroom (Walker et al., 2003/2004a). The teacher needs to carefully organize the classroom, keeping in mind the old adage "a place for everything and everything in its place." This rule should continue to operate throughout the school year. A consistent and orderly schedule should be established and followed. Children should be able to predict what is next, and any necessary changes should be appropriately introduced. Classroom arrangement should promote socialization and should include classroom materials, such as sand and blocks, that promote sharing and that have been found to increase opportunities for social interactions.

Elementary and Secondary Classrooms. Elementary and secondary classroom environments should be structured, consistent, and designed to maximize academic engagement and social interactions. Ideally, classrooms for students with emotional or behavioral difficulties include an observation room. This room can function as an office for the teacher, but it also enables the teacher or other staff, such as a psychologist making behavioral observations, to watch the class. In addition, such a room can be used for private conversations about or with students. The physical location of the classroom in the school is important. For example, if the classroom does not have its own bathroom and sink, it should be located relatively close to them. A long trip to the bathroom or sink can lead to many opportunities for disruptive outbursts or noncompliance with rules. If the class is a self-contained special education classroom, the most important aspect of the classroom's location is whether or not it provides for interaction with peers without disabilities.

How students feel physically in their immediate environment—that is, restricted or free to move about—may influence how they behave. The use of space is an important consideration when designing the classroom. Utilizing circular tables for a group discussion may foster more openness than would restrictive and separate work desks. Similarly, designing an area for conversation may help students understand where conversational behavior is appropriate. There also needs to be a supervised "safe space" within the school for those times when the student must leave the classroom for a period of time (Johns et al., 2002).

Positive behavior support techniques can result in classroom environments that encourage high rates of student success and avoidance of common behavior problems (Scott, Payne, & Jolivette, 2003). **Positive behavior support** (PBS) is a behaviorally based systems change approach to redesigning the environment to minimize problem behaviors. The change may occur on a schoolwide, classwide, or individual basis. In this technique, areas or arrangements that cause problems to the student with emotional or behavioral disabilities, or the class as a whole, are analyzed. For example, the area surrounding the pencil sharpener may lead to negative interactions between two students who arrive there at the same time. PBS in the classroom is developed, implemented, and monitored by the classroom teacher in collaboration with any other adults working in the room and with input from students. It is conducted mostly through observations and interviews to track problems and where they occur. Once problem areas, such as at the pencil sharpener, sink, doorway, or behind the teacher's desk, have been identified by all, they are further analyzed to determine when and why they are a problem, and then a plan is devised to correct the problem. The teacher and her collaborators may prescribe specific rules, routines, and physical arrangements to decrease or prevent problem behaviors. This may also occur at the school level, such as in the cafeteria, in the hallways, or on the playground. Positive behavior support systems on a schoolwide basis are universal interventions and can be extended downward for use with young children (Conroy &

positive behavior support A behaviorally based systems change approach to redesigning the environment to minimize problem behaviors.

TABLE 6.4 Summary of Stakeholders' Proposed Strategies for Positive Behavior Support, Rejected and Accepted Examples

PROBLEM CONTEXT	PROPOSED STRATEGIES	
	REJECTED	**ACCEPTED**
Coat rack: beginning of school and after recess	Put in new coat rack area, one student at a time in the area, keep coats at desk	Remove portable barricade, revise routine to allow smaller number in area at one time, teach expectations for coat hanging
Doorway: transition times		Revise line-up routine to bring students into line in smaller groups, teach expectations for line-up process
Sink: clean-up time	No students allowed at sink	Teach sink and clean-up expectations, draw physical lines on floor to direct wait line areas
Teacher's desk: work times	Have a help desk at the back of the room	Revise routines so students raise hand to get assistance rather than approaching desk, teach hand raising
Art table: independent work time	Remove art table from room	Devise a sign-up sheet for using the art table
Individual student: academic times	Separate work area, one-to-one assistant	Try classroomwide strategies and monitor individual students

Source: Scott, T. M., Payne, L. D., Jolivette, K. (2003). Preventing predictable behaviors using positive behavior support. *Beyond Behavior 13*(1) 3–7. Used with permission by Council for Children with Behavioral Disorders.

Brown, 2004). Table 6.4 provides a summary of problem areas noted in one classroom, along with rejected and accepted proposals for correcting them.

Instructional Grouping

Several grouping options can be used effectively for students with emotional or behavioral disorders. Peer tutoring is particularly suitable for use with students with emotional or behavioral disorders because it provides practice in skills and strategies in academics and also emphasizes social and communication skills (Bos, Coleman, & Vaughn, 2002). **Cross-age tutoring** has been demonstrated to be a successful approach to teaching reading to students with emotional or behavioral disorders (Burrell, Wood, Pikes, & Holliday, 2001), particularly when African American males with behavioral disorders and low achievement tutor younger same-race students with behavioral disorders (Cochran, Feng, Cartledge, & Hamilton, 1993; Coleman & Vaughn, 2000). When compared to same-age tutoring, cross-age tutoring has been found to result in greater social gains for students with emotional or behavioral disorders (Durrer & McLaughlin, 1995). Students with emotional or behavioral disorders have also shown increases in both academic learning and appropriate social behaviors in **reverse-role tutoring,** wherein the student with the disability is the tutor, and in **reciprocal tutoring,** wherein students trade off the roles of tutor and tutee (Tournaki & Criscitiello, 2003). Peers may also, through careful training and supervision, learn to give social reinforcers very effectively in naturally occurring peer interactions and may be helpful in initiating social interactions with socially withdrawn students (Kauffman et al., 2002). For example, middle school students have successfully trained their classmates in social skills (Cartledge, Wang, Blake, & Lambert, 2002). The Peer-Assisted Learning Strategy (PALS) supplemental reading program found in Online Appendix A and the classwide peer tutoring (CWPT) program described in Chapter 4 have been demonstrated to be effective with students with emotional or behavioral disorders (e.g., Falk & Wehby, 2001; Landrum et al., 2003; Wehby et al., 2003).

The use of socially intensive cooperative learning strategies may be successfully employed with students with emotional or behavioral problems when cooperative learning skills are taught and each group member is accountable for contributing to

cross-age tutoring The tutoring of younger students by older students.

reverse-role tutoring A form of tutoring in which the student with the disability is the tutor.

reciprocal tutoring A form of tutoring in which students trade off the roles of tutor and tutee.

PRACTICE

In Practice Meet Educator Joanne Bennett and Her Student Robert

I have taught students with disabilities for nearly 25 years. I have a master's degree and am certified to teach students with emotional/behavior disorders, as well as elementary-aged students without disabilities. I have taught in a variety of settings, including the general education classroom, resource room, separate day school, and hospital/homebound settings at both the elementary and secondary levels. Furthermore, I have taught in urban and suburban neighborhoods. I currently teach elementary-aged

students with disabilities in a center-based school.

When I met Robert, he was an eighth-grade student with a primary classification of emotional/behavior disorder. He was verbally and sometimes physically aggressive toward others. Having been retained twice in elementary school, Robert was much larger than his classmates. He bullied students who were smaller and more introverted. His aggression, noncompliance, acting out, and verbally abusive behavior limited his exposure to the students and staff in inclusive environments and interfered with his academic progress. He was placed in my self-contained classroom to provide maximum support in a regular school setting.

Instructional Content and Procedures

To address Robert's academic needs, I conducted informal assessments and developed an assessment portfolio. I did not give graded assignments but circled incorrect answers and then gave him an opportunity to self-correct or problem solve with me to achieve mastery. Robert was very frustrated with academic work. His self-esteem was very poor and he often called himself dumb. Through my assessments, I

discovered that Robert had major gaps in his knowledge of specific content areas. He had problems with memory, math skills, problem-solving skills, and organizational skills as well.

An individualized program was developed for Robert to address each area of deficit in a systematic manner using direct instruction. Organizational skills, test taking skills, study skills, and social skills were integrated throughout the day. An intensive, highly structured social skills program was implemented during homeroom in the morning and a social skills class before dismissal. These sessions became time for teaching and discussing life lessons, school survival skills, debriefing sessions, and a time to transition to the general population or the community.

The structured social skills program taught self-determination, self-monitoring, and goal-setting. Robert developed short- and long-term goals that were incorporated into his personal contracts. Robert's focus shifted from day-to-day positive and negative interactions in each class to his future in school and his career. His driving force was no longer dropping out of school at the end of the year to "set myself free" from the agony of school and his failure in the school system. By the end of the school year Robert had increased his

the group (Sonnier-York & Stanford, 2002). Students should be strategically grouped, taking into account both academic achievement and social skills, because a group's success is related to its members' abilities to interact in a positive, productive manner (Farmer, 2000; Sutherland, McMaster, & Marshall, 2003). Cooperative learning uses a combination of **independent** and **interdependent group contingencies.** Group members work under contingencies in which their individual, or independent, improvement, as well as their combined, or interdependent, performance is evaluated and rewarded. If carefully managed, group contingencies can encourage positive peer pressure (Kauffman et al., 2002; Kerr & Nelson, 2006; Popkin & Skinner (2003).

Instructional Technology

Technology subsumes a range of universal equipment in most students' lives, including calculators, video cameras, VCRs, DVDs, personal computers, printers, software,

independent group contingencies An instructional grouping method in which group members' individual improvement is evaluated and rewarded.

interdependent group contingencies An instructional grouping method in which group members' combined performance is evaluated and rewarded.

math level by three years and his reading by two years. He was self-confident, exhibiting socially appropriate behavior, and was working as a media assistant in the school media center.

Instructional Environment and Technology

My colleague in general education and I proposed a program to the administration that incorporates a team teaching model. This model gives students with emotional or behavioral disorders the opportunity to transition from class to class in a highly structured manner, very much like other students in the school. I saw Robert for homeroom, math, science, and social skills. My co-teacher saw him for language arts, reading, and social studies. Robert was mainstreamed during lunch, physical education, and the arts.

Before the start of the year, Robert's former teacher and I devised a program that would meet the needs of Robert and the other students through a positive behavior support system. We set up five classroom rules that were stated in a positive manner. The students helped develop the rules that would facilitate a safe school environment. Robert was very active in the development of these rules. During the first two weeks of school, we reviewed the rules and consequences and even role-played.

In addition to the class rules, there was a tiered system of structured positive consequences. This consisted of a system with five levels that gave the students the ability to attain increasing numbers of privileges. These reinforcers consisted of tangible items in the class store, activities, game day, or field trips. The students selected all the items used as reinforcers. Points could be earned for positive behavior, completed classwork, completed homework, and for parents' signatures. At the end of the day, the total points were graphed. On Fridays, students' points were tallied and their status on the level system was determined. Afterward, they had an opportunity to trade their points for items or activities. Robert enjoyed jumbo pens, computer games, and feeding the fish. Later in the year, Robert's choices of reinforcers shifted from tangible items to activities that exposed him to the students and the staff of the general school population.

We saw an increase in appropriate behavior and a decrease of inappropriate behavior almost immediately. A great deal of the "junk behavior" that Robert displayed, such as foot stomping, verbal outbursts, and walking around the room, were no longer functional. Instead, more appropriate and socially acceptable behavior began to emerge. Robert, who was once the leader of classroom disruption and a bully, became a role model and peer counselor.

Collaboration

Critical to the implementation of Robert's educational program was the collaboration of all the parties involved. The week before school started, program goals and procedures were developed, approved, and a written plan was made. Everyone not only communicated but was involved in brainstorming sessions, actively participated in the program goals, and took responsibility for their assigned tasks. The administration provided support, administrative approval, adaptations to school discipline procedures, and assigned an assistant principal to work with us. The special education team, consisting of an exceptional student education specialist, the co-teacher, and I, communicated daily. The general education staff communicated on a daily basis through a mini check sheet I devised for elective classes. I met with the general education teachers weekly for instructional planning and discussed any concerns. Support staff, a crisis management teacher, resource officer, cafeteria staff, media center teacher, and an assistant, were seen on an as-needed basis. Robert's parents were important players in Robert's educational program and were involved in developing and following the guidelines of the behavior intervention plan. They participated through individual contracts, weekly letters, phone contacts, and the check sheet system. The highly structured system of behavioral intervention and strong focus on collaboration gave Robert access to the entire school campus, the community, and its resources.

telecommunication networks, scanners, and much more (Udvari-Solner & Thousand, 1996). It is important that students with emotional or behavioral disorders be able to access these to fit into today's world (Johns, 2000). Recent research indicated that students with emotional or behavioral disorders may improve their behavior to increase their access to computer use, and that use of computers can have positive effects on academic achievement, attitudes, and self-esteem (Diem & Katims, 2002; Keyes, 1994; Mayer & Leone, 2002; Murray, 2002; White & Palmer, 2003). Furthermore, students with emotional or behavioral disorders have been shown to benefit from self-monitoring and graphing their own social and academic behaviors on the computer (Gunter, Miller, Venn, Thomas, & House, 2002). Young children with emotional or behavioral disorders involved in computer-based activities demonstrated increased levels of cooperative and social play outside the computer setting

BOBBY REVISITED Do you think there are any benefits for Bobby in assistive technology? If so, what are they?

(Howard, Greyrose, & Beckwith, 1996). When working with students with emotional or behavioral disorders in computer labs, teachers need to establish simple but firm computer lab rules from the start, remind students of the rules as necessary, and have a regular schedule that includes working on an assigned task and free time (White & Palmer, 2003).

Check Your Understanding

1. What two aspects of the physical arrangement of the instructional environment are most important in facilitating positive behavior support and social interactions for students with emotional or behavioral disorders?

2. What two instructional grouping options are particularly relevant for students with emotional or behavioral disorders?

3. How can computers be used to promote self-regulation of behavior for students with emotional or behavioral disorders? What added benefit has been found to occur with young children working in computer-based activities?

What Are Some Considerations for the General Education Teacher?

Relevant CEC Standard

▶ Strategies for integrating student initiated learning experiences into ongoing instruction for individuals with emotional/behavioral disorders (BD4K5)

▶ Collaborative and consultative roles of the special education teacher in the reintegration of individuals with emotional/behavioral disorders (BD10K3)

Unfortunately, perhaps due to the fact that teachers report being less prepared for dealing with behaviors than academics (Davies & Ferguson, 1997), children with emotional or behavioral disorders have been found to be the least welcome in general education classrooms (Guetzloe, 1993; Johns et al., 2002). However, as stated previously, effective instruction in academics is itself effective classroom management, and for the majority of students with challenging behaviors, effective interventions can be efficiently applied in general classroom environments (Lewis & Sugai, 1999; Nelson, 1996; Scott & Nelson, 1999). Within the previously discussed use of universal approaches to positive behavioral supports and intervention for students with emotional or behavioral disorders, all students—with and without disabilities, in the classroom or in the school—are targeted to the same degree and in the same manner, and thus all students should benefit. As for student concerns, general education students from four different ethnic groups and students with emotional or behavioral disorders have agreed that what they want in the classroom is for teachers to be fair and to respect them, listen to what they say, build teacher–student relationships, be sensitive to their feelings, help them solve problems, assign relevant class work, and learn different ways to teach them (Bacon & Bloom, 1994; Sheets & Gay, 1996).

In efforts to merge general and special education, it is necessary to ensure that the school does not contribute to emotional or behavioral difficulties. Kauffman's (2005) discussion of this concern leads to some implications for the general education teacher which include (1) being sensitive to students' individuality while maintaining clear and positive expectations for academic performance, (2) ensuring and convincing students that the classroom instruction in both academics and social skills is relevant to their futures, (3) providing the appropriate reinforcement for desirable behaviors to all students, and (4) modeling desirable behaviors in work ethics and classroom interactions. Furthermore, behavior problems may actually be exacerbated if any of the following conditions exist in a classroom: expectations are too high or too low, students cannot predict adult responses to behavior, a fully academic approach to instruction is applied to students who clearly need to learn vocational and community living skills, children are given frequent attention for noncompliance, desirable behavior is rarely praised, or the teacher does not treat academic work seriously or is disrespectful in dealings with students.

Teachers need to ask themselves questions about their own behavior in the classroom and act accordingly. Kauffman et al. (2002) suggested the following questions for teachers who wish to be positive and supportive of appropriate behavior:

Classroom Suggestions Accommodations for a Student Who Has Difficulty with Self-Control

- ❑ Give student a copy of class rules and expectations. Let student role-play examples on a regular basis.

- ❑ Give student positive reinforcement for replacement behaviors or for following class rules.

- ❑ Establish and regularly use a hierarchy of consequences for rule infractions. Make sure student understands expectations and consequences.

- ❑ Monitor student's compliance with class rules and communicate regularly with the student, the family, and others.

- ❑ Use a regular routine for transitions in the class. Establish system of alerts and procedures to follow to get ready to start a lesson, to change classes, to complete an activity, to go to lunch, or to go to another area in the school.

- ❑ Identify a quiet area in the classroom where student may go when necessary.

Source: M. Beech, 2003. Copyright ® Florida Department of Education, Bureau of Exceptional Education and Student Services. Used with permission.

- How frequently do I offer praise or other positive evaluations (e.g., smiles, pats, approval) of my students' appropriate behavior?
- Do I ignore most minor misbehavior?
- Do I emphasize positive outcomes of desirable behavior rather than avoidance of negative consequences for inadequate performance?
- Am I able to avoid getting drawn into power struggles and other forms of negative interactions with students?
- Do students like being in my classroom?
- Are my students learning academic and social skills at a level commensurate with their abilities?

Responsible inclusion decisions should consider educational needs and curriculum outcomes that best ensure successful progress for the student (Webber, 1998). With accommodations, some students with emotional or behavioral disorders will be able to function successfully in a general education classroom. Examples of accommodations that may help in providing a positive and supportive classroom for students who have difficulty controlling their own behavior are presented in the Classroom Suggestions feature. Some students will need curriculum delivery or expectation changes beyond accommodations or in combination with them.

To conclude, teaching practices that contribute to successful inclusion programs for students with emotional or behavioral disorders include (1) collaborative co-teaching by a general education and special education teacher, (2) commitment by co-teaching team to make adaptations and modifications of what is taught and how it is presented for the entire class, (3) the use of student peer facilitators, (4) carefully planned cooperative learning activities with special attention to social skills and group dynamics, (5) flexibility in scheduling and grading for all, and (6) integration of social skills instruction into the curriculum (Johns et al., 2002).

Check Your Understanding

1. Who benefits from universal approaches to positive behavioral supports and intervention?

2. What do both general education students and students with emotional or behavioral disorders want in a classroom teacher?

3. What are some ways a teacher can ensure that the school does not contribute to emotional or behavioral difficulties?

4. What are some teaching practices that contribute to successful inclusion programs?

IDEA 04 uses the *term emotional disturbance* for this disability. It defines emotional disturbance as (1) a condition exhibiting one or more of the following characteristics over a long period of time to a marked degree that adversely affects a child's educational performance: (a) an inability to learn which cannot be explained by intellectual, sensory, or health factors; (b) an inability to build or maintain satisfactory interpersonal relationships with peers and teachers; (c) inappropriate types of behavior or feelings under normal circumstances; (d) a pervasive mood of unhappiness or depression; (e) a tendency to develop physical symptoms or fears associated with personal or school problems; (2) emotional disturbances include schizophrenia. The term does not apply to children who are socially maladjusted unless it is determined that they have an emotional disturbance

Identification Tools: It is recommended that multiple sources of information be used to assess students. Source include observation of a student, including a functional behavioral assessment; behavior rating scales such as the Devereux Behavior Rating Scale–School Form; behavior Assessment Systems such as the Achenbach System of Empirically Based Assessment and the Behavior Assessment System for Children–2; objective inventories such as the Minnesota Multiphasic Personality Inventory–2 and the Personality Inventory for Children–2; projective tests such as the Rorschach Ink Blot Test and the Thematic Apperception Test.

Characteristics	Indicators You Might See
Externalizing	Hitting and fighting, refusing to comply, destroying own and others' belongings, acting out, general aggression, and characteristics of a conduct disorder.
Internalizing	Anxiety, social withdrawal (from disinterest in making friends to severe withdrawal), characteristics of mood disorders, schizophrenia (delusions, hallucinations, disorganized speech, and disorganized or catatonic behavior).
Intellectual and Academic	Low-average IQ, language deficits, academic problems.

Students with Emotional or Behavioral Disorders

Teaching Implications

Instructional Content

- Students are typically held to national or state academic standards so must participate in an academic curriculum.
- Social skills curriculum helps with the development of social and personal problem-solving skills; the focus is on *how* to think rather than *what* to think.
- Use sequencing and generalization to teach social skills.
- Popular social skills programs include: Skillstreaming, the Social Skills Intervention Guide, Aggression Replacement Training, and Second Step.
- Service-learning activities can be effective additions to the curriculum.
- In terms of transition, consider vocational and life skills, postsecondary education, and change from juvenile detention and homelessness.

Instructional Procedures

- At the preschool level, begin with a schoolwide intervention and add more intensive interventions as needed.
- Remember that effective instruction decreases behavioral problems and increases learning.
- Strategies to consider include direct/explicit instruction, cognitive behavioral intervention, behavioral management intervention.
- To increase behaviors, use positive reinforcement, negative reinforcement, token economies, contingency contracts and the Premack Principle.
- To decrease behaviors, use differential reinforcement of other behavior or incompatible behavior, time-out, response cost, extinction, and punishment.
- Nonbehavioral intervention techniques include creative dramatics, play therapy, bibliotherapy, and pharmacological treatment.

Instructional Environment

- Organize classroom to encourage positive classroom socialization and interactions.
- For preschool classrooms, arrange the classroom to encourage structure and consistency.
- For the elementary and secondary levels, classrooms should be structured, consistent, and designed to maximize academic engagement and social interactions.
- Consider using positive behavior support techniques.
- Consider peer tutoring (cross-age tutoring, reverse-role tutoring, and reciprocal tutoring) and cooperative groups.

Instructional Technology

- Contingent use of technology leads to improved behavior.
- Consider using a computer to allow students to self-monitor and graph their own behaviors.
- Consider technologies used with students with learning disabilities such as computers, video cameras, and so forth.

Methodologies and Strategies to Try

- Universal Intervention (p. 194)
- Direct/Explicit Instruction (p. 195)
- Cognitive Behavioral Intervention (p. 195)
- Behavioral Intervention Techniques (p. 196)
- Behavioral Intervention Plan (p. 196)
- Positive Reinforcement (p. 197)
- Negative Reinforcement (p. 198)
- Token Economies (p. 198)
- Contingency Contracts (p. 198)
- Premack Principle (p. 199)
- Differential Reinforcement (p. 199)
- Time-Out (p. 199)
- Response Cost (p. 200)
- Extinction (p. 200)
- Punishment (p. 200)
- Creative Dramatics (p. 200)
- Play Therapy (p. 202)
- Bibliotherapy (p. 202)
- Pharmacological Treatment (p. 202)

Considerations for the General Classroom and Collaboration

Effective instruction leads to fewer behavioral problems. With accommodations, students with EBD can succeed in a general classroom.

The general education teacher should:

- Be sensitive to students' individuality while maintaining clear and positive expectations for academic performance.
- Ensure and convince students that the classroom instruction in both academics and social skills is relevant to their futures.
- Provide appropriate reinforcement for desirable behaviors for all students
- Model desirable behaviors in work ethics and classroom interactions (Kauffman, 2005).

Teaching practices that contribute to successful inclusion programs include:

- Co-teaching with a special education teacher
- Commitment of co-teacher team to make adaptations in what is taught and how it is presented to the entire class
- Use of student peer facilitations
- Carefully planned cooperative learning activities with special attention to social skills and group dynamics
- Flexibility in scheduling and grading for all
- Integration of social skills instruction into the curriculum (Johns, Crowley, & Guetzloe, 2002)

Collaboration

General and special educators should consult on:

- Identifying students with a possible emotional or behavioral disorder
- Choosing and emphasizing the academic curriculum
- Selecting and implementing a social skills curriculum
- Planning for transition from non-school environments
- Implementing behavioral interventions
- Planning the instructional environment
- Planning for the use of instructional technology

Chapter Summary

Go to the text's Online Learning Center at **www.mhhe.com**/taylor1e to access study resources, Web links, practice quizzes, and extending materials.

What Are the Foundations of Emotional and Behavioral Disorders?

- Although individuals with emotional or behavioral problems have been recognized throughout history, only relatively recently have attempts been made to address their emotional, behavioral, and educational needs.
- There is considerable controversy over the term that should be used to describe this category of disability. IDEA 04 uses the term *emotional disturbance;* however, *emotional or behavioral disorders* is endorsed by many professionals.
- IDEA 04 defines an emotional disturbance as an inability to learn that is not accounted for due to intellectual, sensory, or health factors; problems developing relationships with others; inappropriate behaviors or feelings; an overall unhappy or depressed mood that is pervasive; and a tendency to have physical symptoms caused by personal or school programs. One can have one or several of these characteristics. The characteristics must be present over a long period of time and to a degree that negatively affects educational performance. Schizophrenia is also included in this definition.
- Controversies regarding the IDEA 04 definition include the lack of mention of negative behaviors, the exclusion of social maladjustment, the requirement that educational performance has to be affected, and how long the characteristics must be displayed.
- The IDEA 04 definition is most often used, but other definitions, such as that by the Council for Children with Behavioral Disorders, have been proposed.
- Individuals with emotional or behavioral disorders may be classified by whether they have an internalizing or externalizing disorder, the dimensional classification system, or by the system offered through the *DSM-IV-TR.*
- Although estimates indicate that 2% of the school-aged population have emotional or behavioral disorders, the actual number of students receiving services has been around 1% for at least the last decade. Boys are more likely than girls to have an emotional or behavioral disorder. For those identified, boys are more likely to have an externalizing disorder and girls an internalizing disorder. Older children are more likely to be identified than younger children. Poverty appears to increase the risk of identification. Prevalence rate is also affected by ethnicity. For example, African American students are overrepresented.

What Are the Causes and Characteristics of Emotional and Behavioral Disorders?

- Environmental factors, genetic factors, and a combination of the two have been suggested as causes of emotional or behavioral disorders.
- Students with emotional or behavioral disorders may display externalizing or internalizing characteristics.

- Students with emotional or behavioral disorders may display characteristics of lower intelligence or lower academic achievement than their peers.

How Are Students with Emotional or Behavioral Disorders Identified?

- Professionals from several areas may be involved in identifying emotional or behavioral disorders.
- Identification procedures include the use of direct observation, behavior rating scales, behavior assessment systems, personality inventories, and projective tests.

What and How Do I Teach Students with Emotional or Behavioral Disorders?

- Typically, students with emotional or behavioral problems need intensive educational programs that include academics, behavioral training, and social development. Social skills programs and service-learning opportunities may be used to deliver a curriculum that supports social development.
- Transition planning may include preparation for vocational training or postsecondary education. Transition may also need to be planned for reintegration from juvenile detention or a homeless situation.
- Early intervention has been found to be very effective with students with emotional or behavioral disorders.
- Effective instructional procedures for students with emotional or behavioral disorders include direct instruction, cognitive behavioral intervention, behavioral intervention techniques and nonbehavioral intervention techniques. Behavioral intervention can include techniques to both increase and decrease behaviors.
- Effective instruction is a form of classroom management, and fewer behavior problems occur when students are engaged in learning.

What Are Other Instructional Considerations for Teaching Students with Emotional or Behavioral Disorders?

- The physical arrangement of the room and grouping options may have significant effects on the climate of a class and the quality of instruction. Structure and consistency should be focused on in preschool classrooms. These should also be a major part of elementary and secondary classrooms, though these environments should also be designed to maximize academic engagement and social interactions.
- Peer tutoring and cooperative learning have been found to be particularly effective with students with emotional or behavioral disorders.
- Computer usage can have positive effects on achievement, attitudes, and self-esteem.

SUMMARY

What Are Some Considerations for the General Education Teacher?

- Some students with emotional or behavioral disorders will be able to function successfully in a general education classroom with accommodations.

- Many students with emotional or behavioral disorders taught in the general education classroom will need curriculum delivery or expectation changes beyond accommodations, or in combination with them.

Reflection Topics

1. Do you think students who are socially maladjusted should be excluded from the IDEA 04 definition of emotional disturbance? Why or why not?
2. What are the pros and cons of the alternative definition of emotional and behavioral disorders proposed by the national coalition? Would you support a recommendation to Congress to adopt the definition?
3. What should be done to raise teachers' awareness of internalizing problems, which are often overlooked?
4. Many professionals are concerned that services for students with emotional or behavioral disorders are not provided until problems in academics are present. What are the pros and cons of this practice? Do you think this is appropriate?
5. Should all students with emotional or behavioral disorders be placed in general education classrooms, or should we maintain a continuum of services? Why? If your answer is the latter, explain what students might be exceptions and what kind of programs might be justified.
6. Do you think there is any legitimacy to the concern that schools might actually contribute to children's emotional or behavioral disorders? Explain your answer.

Application Activities: For Learning and Your Portfolio

1. (*Portfolio Possibility*) Develop your own behavior checklist that includes specific behaviors you would look for that might indicate that a student has an emotional or behavior problem. Make sure the behaviors are *observable*. For example, don't include terms like "withdrawal"; rather, include statements such as "prefers to be by himself rather than interacting with peers."
2. Research several available behavior rating scales to determine the types of items they include and to see the type of rating system that is used.
3. (*Portfolio Possibility*) Research the pros and cons of identifying a preschool child as having an emotional or behavioral disorder. Write a short paper that addresses both sides of the issue.
4. Observe either a classroom for students with emotional or behavioral disorders, or an inclusion classroom with students with emotional or behavioral disorders in it and describe ways that the teacher keeps students engaged during instructional and transition times.
5. Observe either a classroom for students with emotional or behavioral disorders or an inclusion classroom with students with emotional or behavioral disorders in it and describe any examples you see of the teacher's use of techniques to increase or decrease behaviors. Describe each. Does it appear to be working?
6. (*Portfolio Possibility*) Locate several books, stories, and videos/DVDs that deal with personal problems or disabilities and are appropriate for use in bibliotherapy. List the books with the recommended age group and the topic or purpose for which they could be used.

CHAPTER 7

Students with Communication Disorders

CHAPTER OUTLINE

INTRODUCING KATHLEEN

Kathleen is an 8-year-old third grader who has a communication disorder. She lives with both her parents and an older sister in an upscale suburban neighborhood. Kathleen's 12-year-old sister, who is in a program for gifted children, had some problems with "r" articulation that were cleared up by age 8. Kathleen was first evaluated for articulation problems at age 6, with errors reported in articulating "l," "r," "s," "z," "ch," and "j" sounds. Kathleen's hearing was tested and found to be within the normal range. A language evaluation was conducted using both standardized tests and natural speech samples. It was reported that Kathleen had problems forming plurals and past tenses, and had difficulty using pronouns. She spoke in very simple sentences and demonstrated below-average vocabulary although her intelligence scores were well within the normal range.

Kathleen is now receiving individual speech and language services in a pull-out therapy room for 30 minutes twice a week. Ms. Lewis, a speech-language pathologist, works with her on articulation of the identified sounds of words using modeling and imitation. She uses picture cards to address plurals and past tense markers. The pictures for these exercises are expanded as new vocabulary words are mastered. Unfortunately, Kathleen misses most of her classroom science instruction due to her pullout instruction and feels embarrassed and different when she returns to her classroom.

Kathleen's current classroom teacher, Ms. Klein, reports that Kathleen has difficulty expressing her ideas and becomes very frustrated when she is not understood. As her speech is often unintelligible in conversation, she is frequently frustrated. Kathleen's articulation of "r" has improved greatly, but she continues to have trouble with the other sounds reported earlier and still speaks in very simple sentences. Her teacher has also noted that Kathleen is falling behind in reading comprehension and is becoming less and less social, often avoiding interactions with her peers. To address these problems, Ms. Klein has recommended that Kathleen receive support services from Ms. Lewis within the general education class rather than through a pullout program. ■

uman communication is an ordinary everyday event that is often taken for granted and frequently appears to be so effortless that little thought is given to how it is accomplished. Indeed, most people are able to communicate quite easily even though they have little conscious awareness of how they communicate. Human communication is, in fact, a complex process that is not easily mastered by all individuals. Communication overlaps with so many cognitive and emotional processes that difficulties in communication may affect an individual's world knowledge, academic and social skills development, relationship building, self-concept, and even employment. As is often the case, Kathleen's communication problems are beginning to cause problems in academics. In addition, her level of frustration at being so often misunderstood is leading to socialization problems. Kathleen's teacher and the speech-language pathologist will need to work together to prevent her communication problems from becoming pervasive.

Some students with communication disorders may have characteristics similar to Kathleen's; others may have different communication problems and characteristics. For example, Gary, age 16, speaks in well-formulated, well-articulated sentences. However, when and what he chooses to say are often seen as bizarre and inappropriate for the setting or situation. Furthermore, his affect is flat, and his speech is often delivered in a monotone. Tangela, age 12, has cerebral palsy. She speaks at a very low volume due to her lack of muscular control, which makes it difficult for others to hear what she is saying. Darby, age 10, has an age-appropriate language structure but speaks with a lisp (e.g., Lewith for Lewis). She has no problems with academic learning but is embarrassed to speak in a classroom setting. And Keith, age 9, has a very severe stutter but is doing quite well in school. He is fortunate enough to have a teacher and classmates who wait for him to speak without interrupting him, so he is very willing to speak in class. The majority of students with communication disorders are educated in the general education classroom, and they work with a speech-language pathologist either in the classroom or through a pullout program.

What Are the Foundations of Communication Disorders?

Relevant CEC Standards

▶ Models, theories, and philosophies that form the basis for special education practice (CC1K1)

▶ Historical points of view and contribution of culturally diverse groups (CC1K8)

▶ Issues in definition and identification of individuals with exceptional learning needs, including those from culturally and linguistically diverse backgrounds (CC1K5)

With the expansion of knowledge in the area of communication development in the last 40 years has come a greater emphasis on the importance of communicating effectively. In response, emphasis on both the identification of and intervention for communication disorders has moved from focusing only on speech disorders to including the more prevalent language disorders. Communication disorders are now classified as either speech or language disorders, and a student may exhibit either one or both of these disorders. Definitions for communication disorders are provided by both IDEA 04 and the American Speech-Language-Hearing Association (ASHA). Students with communication disorders are found in both special education and general education classrooms. The likelihood of every teacher coming in contact with students with communication disorders is very high.

A Brief History of Communication Disorders

The nature of communication has been the subject of speculation and debate for centuries. Despite years of accumulated research, some aspects of the communication process are still not clearly understood. One focus of this research has been investigating speech and language impairments. These impairments range from relatively minor deficits in speech, such as the mispronunciation of one sound, to severe disorders, such as having no verbal language.

The advent of school-based speech and language services occurred nearly 100 years ago when 10 "speech correctionists" were hired in the Chicago public schools. These services have undergone many fundamental changes in scope and focus since that time (Whitmire, 2002). In the 1950s, "speech correctionists" worked with as many as 150 to 250 primarily elementary school children with mild to moderate speech impairments in articulation, fluency, and voice (ASHA ad hoc Committee, 1999). In the 1970s, as knowledge of language development increased, "speech therapists" learned to identify and treat language impairments as well. In 1979, the American Speech-Hearing Association (ASHA), the professional organization for speech-language pathologists, added "language" to its name, becoming the American Speech-Language-Hearing Association, but it maintained the acronym ASHA (Hulit & Howard, 2002). At this time, speech-language pathologists typically worked to "correct" speech and language impairments by pulling students out of the classroom to work in groups in a separate therapy room. However, with the passage of IDEA in 1975, and subsequent legislation, the practice of providing services in isolated settings came under fire. It was also becoming evident that naturalistic context and spontaneity in speech and language are related to successful evaluation and intervention in speech and language programs.

Today, the speech-language pathologist works as an educational team member and collaborator to provide services and support in the general education environment for students with communication disorders to facilitate their successful participation in socialization and learning. ASHA (1993) recommended a maximum caseload of 40 children per speech-language pathologist, depending on the time requirements included in the IEPs and IFSPs. Both assessment and intervention have become more contextually based and educationally relevant. This means that the general education and special education teacher must work closely with the speech-language pathologist to best serve the needs of students with communication disorders rather than the pathologist working independently with the student. Collaboration allows for observation of a greater range of language-related skills. In addition, decisions on intervention based on classroom success add authenticity to the programs and objectives (Dohan & Schulz, 1998).

Definitions of Communication Disorders

Human communication begins with the conceptualization of ideas in thought. **Communication** is the process by which one individual expresses those ideas, feelings, opinions, or messages to others and receives and understands ideas, feelings, opinions, or messages from others. Communication involves at least two people and includes, among other aspects, language and speech. Without identification and appropriate intervention, problems with language and speech can lead to learning and socialization problems.

communication The process by which one individual relates ideas to another. It includes, among other aspects, language and speech.

Language and Speech

Very simply put, **language** is a rule-governed system of arbitrary symbols that stand for meaning. Language is the system we use to communicate ideas and includes both *expressive language*, through which we send messages, and *receptive language*, through which we receive and understand messages. **Speech** is the physical production of that system. Thus, when expressing an idea verbally, the idea is first conceptualized (thought), then formulated into the code (language), and finally, produced as a series of audible sounds (speech). Of course, language can also be expressed through manual means such as using American Sign Language (ASL), and communicative intent can be demonstrated without words. In this chapter we focus on communication disorders in spoken language.

language A code in which arbitrary symbols stand for meaning, and the rules that govern that code.

speech The physical production of language.

Structurally, speech can be viewed as consisting of four systems: *respiration*, the breathing that supports speech; *voicing*, the sound powered by the vocal folds/chords; *resonance*, the means by which sound is changed as it travels through the cavities of the neck and head; and *articulation*, the formulation of speech sounds by the lips, tongue, and other structures. More specifically, it is the integration of these four systems that is needed for the production of normal speech. An element that is important to everyday speaking is the forward flow of speech. Fluent speech is rhythmic and smooth, lacking pauses, repetitions of speech units, or any other interruptions of speech flow. Still another aspect of everyday speech is the ability to utilize elements such as stress, pitch, timing, and loudness to impart meaning. For example, in American English there is generally a rise in pitch at the end of a question.

Spoken languages are generally considered to have five components: phonology, morphology, syntax, semantics, and pragmatics. In typical language development, all of these aspects of language develop simultaneously in fairly predictable sequences. **Phonology** deals with the system of speech sounds and the rules governing their use. These are the rules that indicate what sounds occur, what sound combinations are acceptable, and where those sounds and combinations of sounds may occur for a specific language. The smallest significant unit of sound is the **phoneme.** The phoneme is significant in that if it were to be replaced with another phoneme in a word, the meaning of the word would change. For example, the following words are the same except for the beginning phoneme in each: *bat, cat, hat, that.* All of these words are made up of three phonemes, or sounds, which are not necessarily the same as the number of letters, or graphemes, used to represent these three sounds. Each word has only one differing phoneme, and yet each word has a different meaning. The unit of sound that changed is significant. Although humans are capable of making more than a hundred speech sounds, only about 44, depending on one's dialect, are used in American English. Children must learn both individual speech sounds and the rules that govern their use. For example, in English they learn that words do not begin with the sounds of "m" and "b" together, although this may be common in other languages. The production of most phonemes is mastered in the first few years of life (see Table 7.1). This occurs in spite of the fact that children only hear language in long streams of sound. Language is not segmented into sounds, words, or syllables until children enter school where language is also presented in written form.

Morphology involves the rules governing the use of the smallest significant unit of meaning, the **morpheme.** Morphemes may be free or bound. Free morphemes have meaning on their own and may not be broken into smaller units and still maintain that meaning: for example, *cat.* A bound morpheme has meaning only when attached to another morpheme. For example, *s* alone has no meaning, but when attached to *cat,* as in *cats,* it acquires the meaning of more than one. Or consider *er,* which has a different meaning when attached to *teach* (*teacher*) than when attached to *big* (*bigger*). The meaning of a bound morpheme can only be determined when it is attached to another morpheme. Morphemes allow for the creation of new words that may be added to one's vocabulary. Children's first utterances are primarily free morphemes. The addition of bound morphemes is acquired in a specific sequence. For example, from about age 2 to about age 4, a child goes from saying *Daddy go* to *Daddy going* to *Daddy's going.* As children are learning morphological rules, they often overgeneralize them to irregular words. For example, a child may say *I falled down and I hurted my foots.* By school age, children may use their morphological knowledge to comprehend unfamiliar vocabulary. For example, a child seeing the word "bellowed" in context can deduce, if nothing else, that the word is a verb because it ends with the suffix -ed, which is a past tense morpheme.

Syntax refers to the rules of word function and word order. It encompasses the rules for forming phrases, clauses, and different kinds of sentences. For example, it governs how we change the declarative sentence, *You are going to the movies,* to the interrogative

phonology The system of speech sounds and the rules governing their use.

phoneme The minimally significant unit of sound.

morphology The rules governing the use of minimally significant units of meaning.

morpheme The minimally significant unit of meaning.

syntax The rules of word function and word order.

Communication involves both expressing and receiving information.

TABLE 7.1	Consonant Phoneme Acquisition for Standard English Speakers
PHONEME	**AGE RANGE IN YEARS FOR CORRECT PRODUCTION**
p, h, w, m, n	2–3
b	2–4
d, k, g	2–4
f, y	2½–4
t, ng	2–6
r, l,	3–6
s	3–8
sh, ch, z	3½–8
j	4–7
v	4–8
th with no voice (*thin*)	4½–7
th with voice (*then*)	5–8
zh (middle of measure)	6–8

Source: Adapted from Sander (1972).

sentence, *Are you going to the movies?*—or, in the case of the past tense declarative sentence, *You went to the movies*, to the interrogative sentence, *Did you go to the movies?* By age 3, children begin to combine words into subject-verb-object sentences and then move on to develop questions and negatives. For example, they go from *I no want it* or *I not want it* to *I don't want it.* By the fourth year of life, children are embedding and combining clauses: *I don't want you read that book* or *I show you the ball I got.* As children's language systems mature, more complex uses of these rules are learned. Full mastery of some rules may still be developing in elementary school, such as the use of *because, although,* and *unless* to conjoin sentences.

Semantics is a system of rules governing the meaning of words and word combinations. Included in this component are multiple meanings of words such as *run* (as in being a candidate for election and moving quickly) and the figurative meanings of words such as *yellow* (cowardly). Other figurative language usage, such as idioms (*spill the beans*), metaphors (*the eye of a needle*), similes (*eats like a pig*), and proverbs (*don't put the cart before the horse*), are also semantic aspects of language. Semantics rules dictate that a woman is short or tall, but a skirt is short or long. In the second year of life, a toddler learns to associate phonological patterns with actions and objects, such as saying *uh-oh* when something falls or saying *baba* for bottle. During initial acquisition, young children may overextend in their vocabulary use. For example, if they have inferred that the word *doggie* is used for an animal with four legs, they may demonstrate overextension by calling all animals with four legs *doggie.* As children develop, they learn what the features of a dog are that distinguish it from a horse. Children's vocabulary increases rapidly from about 50 words at 18 months to around 2,600 at age 6, and continues to increase rapidly through adolescence (Owens, 2005). As vocabulary increases, children must move from learning general concepts to more specific concepts, such as learning the difference in meaning between *tell* and

semantics A system of rules governing the meaning of words and word combinations.

ask. During the school years, children learn to use and understand words that are used figuratively, such as *March comes in like a lion* or *She felt so blue.*

pragmatics A system of rules governing the use and function of language.

Whereas phonology, morphology, and syntax relate to the form of language, and semantics relates to the content of language, **pragmatics** is the use of language. Our communicative intents, such as requesting objects, requesting actions, commenting, and acknowledging, are governed by rules of pragmatics. Socialization skills, such as conversation, are governed by rules of pragmatics as well. For example, the rules of effective conversation require that the speaker wait for his or her turn to speak and then speak about something that is related to the previous speaker's comments. For a child to be an effective communicator, he or she must learn to use language to express a wide variety of communicative intents.

Some nonlinguistic cues may also be included in our knowledge of the use of language. Requesting a favor has nonlinguistic (e.g., smiling nicely) as well as linguistic components. These components include both *kinesics* (gestures, body posture and movement, eye contact, and facial expressions) and *proxemics* (the physical distance between communicators) and will vary from culture to culture. Effective communication requires a good match between linguistic and nonlinguistic components of language.

Also of interest is children's knowledge of classroom pragmatics, the rules governing the use of language in school settings. The school environment may place different academic and social language demands on the child than does the home. For example, the rules for asking questions in school, which include raising the hand, can be quite different than at home. The school-age years are characterized by growth in all aspects of language, but the most prevalent development appears to be in pragmatics and semantics. For example, 3-year-olds sustain the topic in a conversation only 20% of the time; 4-year-olds can remain on a topic when explaining something but still cannot sustain dialogue (Owens, 2005). Throughout school, there is a growing adherence to maintaining the topic in a conversation. Increasingly, research in language acquisition, language disorders, and education has demonstrated that speech and language development and disorders should not be assessed or treated in isolation from the naturalistic contexts in which they occur. Furthermore, no communicative act should be interpreted without consideration of context, conversational style of the participants, the interaction of these styles, and the cultural and linguistic background of the communicators (Tannen, 1994).

To function successfully in communication, the rules of all of these components of language must be mastered to some degree. There are, as we have seen, age-appropriate aspects to this mastery, and there are also cultural and subcultural differences in the rules. Speaking out when a teacher is talking can be indicative of appreciation or agreement in the culture of some African American children who are taught to be members of a participative audience (in church, for example), not a passive audience. Not making eye contact with an authority figure, particularly when being reprimanded or questioned, may be a show of respect for some Native Americans and African Americans. Too often, mainstream teachers interpret this as disrespect or guilt: "He won't even look me in the eye when I ask him about it!" If a speaker has not mastered the rules of his or her home culture, he or she may be experiencing a language delay or disorder and may need assistance in replacing some of his or her language behaviors with more age-appropriate usage. If a speaker has mastered a different set of rules, that is, the rules of another culture or subculture, he or she does not have a language disorder but may need assistance in acquiring an additional set of rules to be used in specific contexts. For example, the child may need to learn that in Ms. Arlington's class eye contact is expected when the teacher is talking. This may include teaching the student an eye contact strategy and practicing it by role playing.

IDEA 04 and ASHA Definitions of Communication Disorders

speech or language impairment According to IDEA, this is a communication disorder, such as stuttering, impaired articulation, a language impairment, or a voice impairment, that adversely affects a child's educational performance.

IDEA 2004 defines a **speech or language impairment** as a communication disorder, such as stuttering, impaired articulation, a language impairment, or a voice impairment, which adversely affects a child's educational performance. A more specific and more often used definition of communication disorder is that of the American Speech-Language-Hearing Association (ASHA ad hoc Committee, 1993). This definition includes both speech disorders and language disorders. ASHA defines a **speech disorder** as an impairment of the articulation of speech sound, fluency, and/or voice. ASHA defines a **language disorder** as the impairment or deviant development of comprehension and/or use of spoken, written, and/or other symbol system. The disorder may involve (1) the *form* of language (phonology, morphology, and syntax), (2) the *content* of language (semantics), and/or (3) the *function* of language in communication (pragmatics) in any combination. See An Important Event for an overview of the origin of these terms. ASHA further differentiates a communication disorder from a communication difference/dialect, which reflects shared regional, social, or cultural/ethnic factors. A regional, social, or cultural/ethnic variation of a symbol system should not be considered a disorder of speech or language.

AN IMPORTANT EVENT

1970s—Form, Content, and Function of Language Are All Recognized as Important

Prior to the 1970s, research and definitions of language focused almost exclusively on its form or structure. Some explanations of language focused on use to the exclusion of form and content. In the early 1970s, Lois Bloom argued for the importance of content with examples from her research of how many different forms of structure may exist in the telegraphic statement "Mommy sock." Its structure depends on its context and meaning. Is it a statement of possession as in "This is Mommy's sock"? Is it a command as in "Mommy, give me the sock"? Or is it one of the many other interpretations one might place on this utterance? In their book on language disorders, Bloom and Lahey (1978) pointed out that language has three major components: content, form, and use. "Language consists of some aspect of *content* or meaning that is coded or represented by linguistic *form* for some purpose or *use* in a particular context" (p. 11). These three components are integrated, and the interaction of all three must be considered. This three-dimensional view of language was presented as necessary to a basic understanding of both language development and language disorders. Although the term "use" has since been changed to "function" in ASHA's definition, this three-dimensional view has become the only acceptable way to view language development and the basis for defining language disorders.

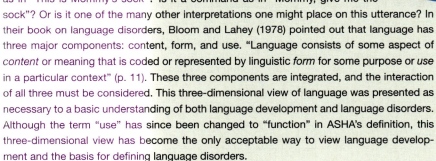

REFLECTION How do you think this newer view of language development would affect a teacher's classroom practices?

As a teacher, you should be familiar with the IDEA 04 definition of communication disorders because it is used to determine whether services are provided, and you should be familiar with the ASHA definition because it is commonly used by specialists in the field of communication disorders. A working understanding of language and speech will help you support your individual students.

Prevalence of Communication Disorders

IDEA reports that in the 2005 school year, approximately 2.3% of students ages 6 to 17 received services for speech and language impairments (U.S. Department of Education, 2006). The actual number of students receiving services for communication disorders is much higher than these data indicate because they do not include students who have communication disorders secondary to other disabilities. IDEA 04 counts students only once, and that is in their primary disability area. If a student with a learning disability also receives speech and language services, he or she is only counted under learning disabilities and not under speech and language impairments. About half of children receiving services under IDEA 04 for another primary disability also have speech-language disabilities; thus the overall prevalence of students with communication disorders is higher than reported by IDEA (Hall, Oyer, & Haas, 2001). Almost 22% of all children who received services for disabilities under IDEA Part B in Fall 2002 received services for speech or language disorders (ASHA, 2007).

ASHA (2007) reports that approximately 7% of children entering school have a specific language impairment. Many of these students with language impairments will later be identified as having learning disabilities as the literacy requirements in school increase, and thereafter learning disability will be their primary disability. It is difficult to accurately report the different types of speech and language disorders for which students were receiving services because the ASHA figures combine articulation, language, voice, and fluency disorders into one number. Finally, it should be noted that, as with several other disabilities, prevalence varies with gender. Approximately two-thirds of students receiving speech and language services are boys (Hall et al., 2001).

When one considers what is required to learn language and how early and rapidly it is learned, it is not surprising that so many children have communication disorders. In fact, it is somewhat amazing that so many children have learned to communicate without any problems.

Check Your Understanding

1. When did the focus on language disorders in addition to speech disorders begin?
2. How have speech and language services changed over time?
3. What are the two types of communication disorders?
4. What are the major components of language? Give an example of each.
5. What are the IDEA 04 and ASHA definitions of communication disorders? How do they differ?
6. What is the prevalence of communication disorders? How does it vary based on primary and secondary disability consideration?

What Are the Causes and Characteristics of Communication Disorders?

Relevant CEC Standard
▶ Typical and atypical human growth and development (CC2K1)

There are many causes of communication disorders, particularly when considering both primary and secondary disabilities. However, as is true for many disabilities, in most cases, the causes are difficult to discern. Characteristics will vary depending on the component of language or speech that is affected and whether the communication disorder is a primary or secondary disability.

Causes of Communication Disorders

Knowledge of the causes of communication disorders is important in their treatment in some cases and may lead to prevention in others. Speech and language disorders can be *congenital*, ones that the child is born with, as in a communication disorder associated with cerebral palsy; or *acquired*, when the onset is after birth, as in a communication disorder related to a traumatic brain injury. In addition, speech and language disorders can be classified as organic or functional. *Organic* communication disorders may result from an aberrant structure or a neuromuscular malfunction in the speech organs, such as a cleft palate. Organic causes may be related to heredity, factors during pregnancy, birth trauma, accidents, or diseases (Hall et al., 2001). Other speech and language disorders may be *functional*, with no organic cause identified to explain the disorder; currently they are presumed to be the result of learning, psychological, or environmental factors (Hulit & Howard, 2002). In practice, the cause of a particular speech or language disorder is rarely easy to determine. Factors associated with communication disorders include lack of adequate prenatal care, substance abuse during pregnancy, premature birth, poverty, craniofacial anomalies, lack of stimulation in childhood, genetics, and hearing loss (Hall et al., 2001).

Causes of Language Disorders

The cause of primary language disorders for many students appears to be functional and nonorganic, as they exist in the absence of any other developmental disability or obvious structural or neurological problems. This type of language disorder is called a **specific language impairment (SLI).** Children with SLI comprise the greatest number of those receiving language intervention services. Researchers have attempted to pinpoint the cause and nature of SLI for decades without a great deal of success. Certain environmental factors, such as poverty and limited language input, have long been known to increase the risk of SLI. Recent evidence has pointed to biological or genetic factors that predispose some individuals to SLI. About 20% to 40% of children with SLI have a sibling or a parent with a language disorder (Justice, 2006).

In addition to those children identified as having SLI, others receiving language services in the schools have disabilities such as cognitive, motor, or sensory limitations as their primary disability. These disabilities frequently result in secondary communication disorders. For example, language disorders are common in children with developmental disorders such as intellectual disabilities and autism. Children with these secondary language disorders each present a unique profile of language difficulties and etiologies.

specific language impairment (SLI) A child language disorder that exists in the absence of any other developmental disability or obvious structural or neurological problems.

Causes of Speech Disorders

Some causes of articulation, voice, and fluency disorders have been identified. Articulation disorders may be due to organic causes such as structural malformations in or around the mouth, or functional causes. This distinction becomes important because if a malformation does exist, it needs to be corrected or compensated for before speech intervention can be successful (Hulit & Howard, 2002). For example, **a cleft palate** is an organic structural defect caused by the failure of the parts of the mouth and/or lips (cleft lip) to fuse appropriately during fetal development. This may leave a child with a hole in the roof of the mouth that can lead to numerous speech problems. The causes of clefts include heredity, oxygen deprivation, maternal diet, and medications taken by the mother during pregnancy. Until the organic defect is corrected through plastic surgery or compensated for by the insertion of an obturator to close the hole in the palate, the child will not be able to control air in the mouth to correctly form many speech sounds. For example, the "b" sound requires that air be held in the mouth before being released between the lips. Without correction, the child with a cleft palate will not be able to hold the air in the mouth. In fact, since air often escapes through the nasal cavity, the speech of someone with a cleft palate tends to be hypernasal, sounding as if the speaker is talking through his or her nose. The outcome today for most children with clefts is very good, and successful surgery can usually be done at a very young age. The need for correction also applies to other cases where defects of the tongue and teeth may be present. Even though corrections may be made for some defects, speech therapy will still be necessary to correct the speech habits that have formed before the surgical or dental correction.

cleft palate An organic structural defect caused by the failure of the parts of the mouth or lips (cleft lip) to fuse appropriately during fetal development.

Voice disorders may be caused by any number of interacting organic and functional factors, such as structural differences, neuromuscular problems, or wrongly learned breathing patterns. Hearing loss, psychological deficits, and growths on the vocal folds/chords have all been associated with changes in voice. So, too, have behaviors that are abusive to the vocal folds, such as smoking and drinking or, in school-aged children, shouting or making car noises. Many students with the primary disability of cerebral palsy have secondary voice disorders due to lack of neuromuscular control of respiration. For example, weak respiration might lead to a voice that is not loud enough.

Neurological damage and psychological factors, among other causes, can lead to fluency breakdowns. The cause of stuttering, the best-known fluency disorder, is unknown. Several theories based on organic causes have been proposed, usually

Even after repair of structural malformations, speech therapy will be needed.

FOUNDATIONS

centering on the neurological system or on the respiratory, voicing, or articulatory aspects of the speech system. Some have argued that stuttering is a learned behavior. Recent studies suggest that genetic factors play a role and that many, if not most, individuals inherit traits that predispose them to develop stuttering. These genetic traits impair the ability to string together the various muscle movements necessary to produce fluent sentences (ASHA, 2006b). After stuttering has developed, other factors, such as frustration, anxiety, and listeners' responses, may maintain or exacerbate dysfluencies.

Characteristics of Students with Communication Disorders

Relevant CEC Standards

▶ Educational implications of characteristics of various exceptionalities (CC2K2)

▶ Similarities and differences of individuals with and without exceptional learning needs (CC2K5)

▶ Similarities and differences among individuals with exceptional learning needs (CC2K6)

▶ Effects of cultural and linguistic differences on growth and development of individuals with exceptional learning needs (CC6K1)

▶ Characteristics of one's own culture and use of language and the ways in which these can differ from other cultures and uses of languages (CC6K2)

▶ Ways of behaving and communicating among cultures that can lead to misinterpretation and misunderstanding (CC6K3)

Language may be considered impaired when it is significantly different from the language of others of the same age, gender, or regional, social, or cultural/ethnic background. Van Riper and Erickson (1996) suggested that speech is impaired when it deviates so far from the speech of other people that it calls attention to itself, interferes with communication, or provokes distress in the speaker or listener. In other words, impaired speech is conspicuous, unintelligible, and unpleasant. Although this definition is much too subjective to easily use, it gives us a good picture of the general characteristics of both language and speech impairments.

Characteristics of Language Disorders

Characteristics of language disorders are largely determined by whether they are primary or secondary language disorders. Characteristics of primary language disorders may appear in one or several of the five components of language. Characteristics of secondary language disorders are strongly associated with the identified primary disability.

Primary Language Disorders. As noted previously, children who have difficulty acquiring the rules of spoken or written language may be exhibiting a specific language impairment (SLI), a language-learning disorder with no known origin. Children with SLI may have language problems primarily in one component of language, or they may have difficulties across several components of language: phonology, morphology, syntax, semantics, and pragmatics. Language disorders are the most common type of communication impairment affecting children (Justice, 2006).

Children with disorders in phonology comprise a large number of the cases receiving speech and language services in the public school setting. These disorders fall into two categories: articulation disorders and phonological processing disorders. Misarticulation is the term generally used to describe children who have difficulty in the physical production of speech sounds. A child who substitutes the sound of "w" for "r," as in saying *wabbit* for *rabbit*, and has no other sound errors would be considered to have an articulation disorder. As misarticulation is a physical production problem, it is placed under speech disorders in this discussion. A **phonological processing disorder** refers to difficulty in learning the rules for producing speech sounds in the absence of any obvious physical limitations. A phonological disorder is characterized by the use of **phonological processes,** rules that simplify adult speech forms, beyond the normal period of using these processes. Unlike an individual with an articulation disorder, an individual with a phonological disorder may be able to articulate a phoneme but does not use it in all words. For example, the individual with a phonological disorder may omit consonant sounds at the ends of words but articulate them in the beginnings of words (e.g., *ca* for *cat*, but *two* is *two*). An individual may substitute a particular phoneme for all beginning phonemes that have similar articulatory features (e.g., saying *tin* for *thin, sin, fin*, and *shin*). Or, he or she may articulate a phoneme correctly in one word but not in another word (e.g., say *sip* for *ship*, and then say *share* for *chair*). If an individual persists in the use of any of these phonological processes beyond the typical age of 4 when they disappear in normal development, the child may require speech-language intervention.

phonological processing disorder Difficulty in learning the rules for using speech sounds in the absence of any obvious physical limitations.

phonological processes Rules that simplify adult speech forms.

An individual with a **morphological disorder** may omit or misuse specific morphemes beyond the typical age to do so (for example, *saying two mouse* or *two mouses* for plural, or *I fall down* or *I falled down* for the past tense). Some children may communicate orally but not exhibit language difficulties until they reach school age when they are required to use more complex syntactical structures, such as embedded clauses. An individual with a **syntactic disorder** may persist in using simple sentences when he or she should be using more complex structures or may continue to confuse word order when forming sentences or using more complex structures (for example, saying *Where the truck is?* or *I not want to go*).

An individual with a **semantics disorder** may know a limited number of vocabulary words, use the wrong vocabulary word, create a new word, have trouble retrieving a word when it is needed, or have trouble with multiple meanings and figurative language. For example, the child may imagine a bright blue person when told that someone is blue today. Some children may not exhibit such language difficulties until they reach school age and are required to understand more abstract semantic concepts, such as metaphoric language and words with multiple meanings.

In order to maximally use language, children must learn how to initiate a conversation, maintain a conversational topic, appropriately change topics, and close a conversation. Some nonlinguistic cues may also be included in our knowledge of the use of language. For example, accepting criticism has nonlinguistic (e.g., nodding) as well as linguistic components. Pragmatics has been called the area of most important language growth during school-age and adult years (Lue, 2001). The individual with a **pragmatics disorder** may have significant difficulties fitting into social settings due to difficulties in language use. It has been reported that in conversations with peers, children with SLI talk less, are addressed less, and collaborate less than their peers (Brinton, Fujiki, Spencer, & Robinson, 1997). The child with SLI in pragmatics may show difficulties understanding listener perspective, identifying themes or concepts, and using humor. He or she may also have trouble maintaining the topic of a conversation. Examples of language disorders in each of the areas of form, content, and function are illustrated in Table 7.2.

As there are regional, social, and cultural/ethnic variations in each of these language components, the student's background must be considered when analyzing anything that appears unusual in his or her language. For example, in morphology, a child may have learned to mark the possessive with the "s" sound only in the absence of word order. That is, when asked, "What do you have?" the student may respond "John hat" because in his or her dialect, word order indicates that the hat belongs to John. However, in response to "Whose hat is that?" the same student may respond "John's" because now there is no word order to mark the possessive, so the possessive marker is required. Any difference in language use that can be observed in a child's background community is not to be considered a disorder of language. The student has learned language; he or she has simply learned a different set of rules, or a first language may be interfering. Of course, it is possible to have a language disorder in one's first dialect or language that makes it even more difficult to learn a second. Careful observation and analysis will be necessary to determine what the appropriate intervention should be. The teacher and clinician must also differentiate the child with limited language skills due to limited exposure to English from the child who has had exposure to English but still has difficulties.

The presence of SLI has significant educational implications. Difficulty with spoken language may have an impact on all areas of academic performance. Although SLI has been primarily considered a disorder of oral language, many children with SLIs may exhibit reading and writing difficulties. A child with difficulties in phonology may also have problems understanding the sound-symbol associations necessary to encode and decode written words or segment words into syllables. In the domain of semantics, the expressive writing of students with SLI may include circumlocution (talking around a topic), or reliance on nouns or overuse of specific words. The ability to read more complex material requires understanding the perspective of the writer (pragmatics), identifying central concepts (semantics and pragmatics), and using

morphological disorder Omitting or misusing specific morphemes beyond the typical age to do so.

syntactic disorder A disorder in which one uses simple sentences when more complex structures should be used or confuses word order when forming sentences or using more complex structures.

semantics disorder Difficultly in vocabulary development.

pragmatics disorder Difficulty in using language appropriately based on the setting.

TABLE 7.2	Examples of Language Disorders	
Phonology	Nicholas, 6½-year-old with phonological disorder, illustrating final consonant deletion	da <u>ca</u> <u>caw</u> da <u>mou</u> (The cat caught the mouse).
Morphology	Mikey, 7-year-old with learning disabilities, overgeneralizing rule for regular third person singular present tense to an irregular verb	He <u>doos</u> (do + z) it all the time like that!
Syntax	Mikey, illustrating problem with rule requiring a verb particle to be moved when used with a pronoun	My mom is picking <u>up</u> me today.
Semantics	Melissa, a 10-year-old with learning disabilities and language disorders, illustrating problems with word retrieval	*Teacher:* What kinds of things do they have there? *Melissa:* They have, let's see, they have a game like it's a big table and air blows up and you have like a little circle thing and you can move it across. (Melissa shows the shape of a circle with her hands.) *Teacher:* Oh, OK, And can you tell me the name of the game? *Melissa:* And if they get it across the other person wins. *Teacher:* Do you know what the name for that game is? *Melissa:* Uh, uh: . . . I think it's called . . . Ping Pong! No . . .
Pragmatics	Leo, a 7-year-old, English language learner with speech and language disorders, and hyperactivity, illustrating difficulty with maintaining a topic in conversation	*Teacher:* I want you to tell me all about your little brother. *Leo:* He's really good, but um he's 5 months. And I got this new jacket from Brazil from my Dad. *Teacher:* Did you get it for Christmas? *Leo:* No, it's not from Christmas. It's because um I think it was because my birthday, because he's he's going to Brazil. He's already in Brazil with his father and his um brother. And. you saw my Dad once didn't you?

Source: Smiley, L. R., Goldstein, P. (1998). *Language delays and disorder: From research to practice.* Reprinted with permission of Delmar Learning, a division of Thomson Learning, www.thomsonrights.com. Fax 800-730-2215.

metaphoric language (semantics). The ability to write more complex material requires the pragmatic ability to understand the needs of the reader in order to include the information necessary to communicate effectively.

Secondary Language Disorders. Some children may have difficulty learning and using spoken language as a result of another disability such as an intellectual disability, an emotional or behavioral disorder, a learning disability, or an autism spectrum disorder. Individuals with intellectual disabilities have a broad continuum of skills in areas of development, including speech and language. Because language and cognition are strongly linked, the speech and language skills of an individual with *intellectual disabilities* will generally be influenced by his or her cognitive abilities or by the underlying syndrome, such as Down syndrome, Williams syndrome, or Fragile X. Individuals with intellectual disabilities may go through the same stages of language acquisition in the same sequence as normally developing children but progress at a slower rate, and they may not attain the same level of language development. Many students with intellectual disabilities will have delays in morphological and syntactic development, with particular difficulty in more advanced forms. The vocabulary of students with intellectual disabilities may be more concrete but not necessarily lower than others. Interpreting idiomatic expressions can be particularly difficult. Individuals with intellectual disabilities may also exhibit weaknesses in pragmatic skills such as maintaining and adding to the topics of a conversation and repairing conversations that break down (Kuder, 2003). These weaknesses tend to limit opportunities for exposure to language and use of language skills. Children with *emotional* or *behavioral disorders* may have difficulties in all language areas that may interfere with the educational process (Hyter, Rogers-Adkinson, Self, Simmons, & Jantz, 2001). They often experience expressive and significant pragmatic disorders, have fewer opportunities to interact with others, and possess fewer tools for appropriately participating in the interactions they do have (Westby, 1998). Students with *learning disabilities* may have underlying language problems in one or more of the components of language. Many will have problems in phonological awareness, morphological endings, understanding and using syntax, semantic concepts, word finding, figurative language, and pragmatic skills (Kuder, 2003).

Children exhibiting *autism spectrum disorders* (ASD) have marked deficits in using communication for social interaction. Primarily, these deficits affect the ability to establish meaningful relationships with other people. Students with ASD may exhibit strengths in some areas of language, such as articulation and syntax, but exhibit weaknesses in semantics and pragmatics. They tend to have difficulty using language for social functions and sharing experiences. They often have poor eye contact, flat affect, use greetings infrequently, and are delayed in symbolic play. They may use communication to request objects or actions but rarely to comment. Children with ASD who speak may exhibit any or all of the following: echolalia, exact repetition of an utterance spoken to the child; a tendency to comment off topic; poor repair skills; avoidance of social interactions; use of "you" when 'I' is meant; and abnormalities of pitch, stress, rate, rhythm, and intonation.

Characteristics of Speech Disorders

Characteristics of speech disorders relate to voice, articulation of speech sounds, and fluency. A **voice disorder** is the atypical production of voice quality, pitch, or loudness. The voice differs significantly from that of a person of a similar age, gender, cultural background, and racial/ethnic group (Stemple, Glaze, & Gerderman, 1995). It draws attention and detracts from performance in school, home, community, or work (Justice, 2006). Examples of students with voice disorders include a student who has a particularly hoarse voice, a student who speaks in an extremely high-pitched voice, a student who speaks in a monotone with no changes in pitch, and a student who speaks excessively loudly or softly.

voice disorder Atypical production of voice quality, pitch, or loudness.

An **articulation disorder** is the atypical production of speech sounds. It may include the *substitution* of one sound for another (e.g., *Tham Thmiley* for *Sam Smiley*), the *distortion* of a sound (e.g., a whistling "s" in *soup*), the *addition* of an extra sound (e.g., *sumber* for *summer*), or the *omission* of a sound (e.g., *yeterday* for *yesterday*). An individual with an articulation disorder typically has difficulty with only one or two specific sounds. The most common sounds misarticulated by children are "r" (including the syllabic consonant "er") and "s"/"z."

articulation disorder The atypical production of speech sounds.

A **fluency disorder** is the atypical flow of verbal expression, characterized by impaired rate and rhythm, such as stuttering. A fluency disorder is manifested in behaviors that interrupt or prevent the forward flow of speech. Specifically, these behaviors include interjections (*I um need to ah see*), revisions (*I have I need to see*), incomplete phrases (*I need and then—*), broken words (*I n-[pause]-eed to see*), prolonged sounds (*I neeeeed to see*), and repetitions (*I nnnnneed to see*) of sounds, syllables, words, and phrases. Certain breakdown patterns can be used to identify different disorders of fluency. The most common and best-known fluency disorder is stuttering, also referred to as developmental stuttering. Although different definitions of stuttering exist, nearly all include part-word repetitions (that is, repetition of sounds or syllables) and prolonged sounds as primary speech characteristics. Each repetition and prolongation is referred to as a *dysfluency*, a term

fluency disorder The atypical flow of verbal expression, characterized by impaired rate and rhythm.

meaning disordered fluency. Conditions that enhance fluency for some developmental stutterers include singing, acting from a script, and choral reading. In addition to dysfluencies, individuals who stutter nearly always display struggle behaviors coinciding with their speech breakdowns. Examples of such behaviors are foot taps, arm swings, and eye blinks. These are attempts to avoid or escape dysfluencies. Fluency disorders affect children most between 2 and 10 years of age. Three to four boys are affected for every girl (Craig, Hancock, Tran, Craig, & Peters, 2002; Justice, 2006).

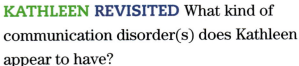

KATHLEEN REVISITED What kind of communication disorder(s) does Kathleen appear to have?

Sometimes, determining the cause in cases of organic etiology may lead to medical correction or modification that can be very important to the effectiveness of communication and intervention. However, in most cases of speech and language disorders, knowing the cause does not determine the educational needs of the child. It is only by identifying each student's characteristics and needs that an appropriate intervention plan can be developed.

Check Your Understanding

1. What are congenital versus acquired causes of communication disorders? Organic versus functional disorders?

2. What is a specific language impairment? What are its causes?

3. What are some of the possible causes of a speech disorder?

4. Describe the characteristics of specific language impairments in each of the five components of language.

5. What are some disabilities that may have secondary language disorders? What are some of the characteristics of secondary language disorders?

6. What are the most common characteristics of the three major types of speech disorders?

How Are Students with Communication Disorders Identified?

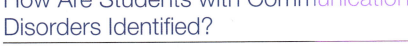

Relevant CEC Standards

▶ Issues in definition and identification of individuals with exceptional learning needs, including those from culturally and linguistically diverse backgrounds (CC1K5)

▶ Screening, prereferral, referral, and classification procedures (CC8K3)

▶ Use and limitations of assessment instruments (CC8K4)

Although school-aged children will likely be screened for communication problems in the early grades, screening will not identify all existing problems. Also, because some disorders are variable, they may not be evident at the time of a screening or even during an evaluation. For these reasons, classroom teachers should be prepared to refer students whose speech or language is unique or unusual. If, for example, a teacher is concerned that a child's fluency or voice sounds abnormal, or that the child's language seems immature, the teacher should refer the student for prereferral activities or evaluation.

Identification of students with communication disorders should consider information from several people and several types of procedures in several settings. Although the student's presenting characteristics will determine the specific evaluation needed, some general procedures are typically included. Individuals involved should minimally include the general classroom teacher, the parent, the speech-language pathologist, and usually an audiologist. Other professionals, such as an occupational therapist or physical therapist, may be relevant.

Identification of Language Disorders

Language assessment is an information-gathering process requiring the speech-language pathologist (SLP) to rely on standardized, norm-referenced tests; informal measures; and the perceptions and concerns of those who are significant in the child's life. The SLP is often required to use more than one measure to determine eligibility for services. A family history is an essential initiation into the evaluation process. In the case of a full evaluation, most school districts or states have guidelines regarding which standardized assessments may be used. The evaluation should include tests of expressive and receptive language skills using standardized tests as well as an analysis of spontaneous language. The speech-language pathologist may use informal measures, such as observational checklists and teacher reports. Interviews with the student, as appropriate, and any person having personal knowledge of the student can provide essential information. SLPs also frequently obtain a language sample, which is an analysis made of elicited conversational speech. This is generally done while playing or talking with the child or by having the child tell some type of story. The language sample allows the SLP to observe how the child uses all domains of expressive language and conversational abilities in spontaneous utterances. In addition, the SLP consults other members of the multidisciplinary collaboration team, such as caregivers, teachers, and a psychologist, to obtain a better picture of how the communication disorder may affect aspects of the child's life. It is likely that he or she will observe the child in the classroom to assess the impact the communication disorder has on the child's ability to learn and to identify the potential for intervention within the classroom setting. The SLP may also observe the child on the playground; during other therapy, such as physical therapy; and may make a home visit. The specific assessment procedures depend on the child's age, the aspect of language being assessed, and requirements by the school district or state.

The speech-language pathologist may use a norm-referenced test to identify a language disorder. Two issues associated with such tests are that they are based on standard American English and that they are typically devoid of context. As most speech and language assessment materials are based on standard American English, the SLP and classroom teacher must be careful in the interpretation of test scores when using them to make placement decisions for students who are not native speakers of American English or who speak a nonstandard dialect of American English. Another issue is that few, if any, tests sample behavior in real-life contexts. In fact, most formal language tests are devoid of naturalistic context and often rely on elicited imitation of a model (Lund & Duchan, 1993). Children may fail to imitate, without context, what they produce spontaneously. In fact, Bloom and Lahey (1978) found that Peter, very much an imitator in natural speech, could not fully imitate his own spontaneously produced sentences when presented to him the next day. For example, on Day 1, Peter, trying to fit a colt's feet into a barrel said, *I'm trying to get this cow in here.* When asked to imitate this same sentence

A naturalistic language sample may be obtained while playing a game.

the next day, Peter repeated only, *Cow in here*. Missing from this situation were both context and intention to speak. On the other hand, short sentences may be imitated correctly by a child who has no ability to produce them in spontaneous language.

As the limitations of standardized assessment procedures are many, it has become more apparent that naturalistic context and spontaneity are necessary to obtain a true sample of a student's language. A valid assessment of all components of language in a naturalistic context is needed for determining intervention programming goals and for obtaining frequent, repeated measurements regarding the effects of intervention. The importance of analyzing the spontaneous language of children and adolescents in order to prevent or minimize other problems and to integrate this knowledge into classroom intervention has been well established. A good assessment will clearly indicate what needs to be taught or increased and should make the transition to intervention a smooth one (Hegde & Maul, 2006). Classroom-based assessment and intervention are commonly and successfully used by SLPs in collaboration with classroom teachers (Dohan & Schulz, 1998).

Identification of Speech Disorders

Procedures used in the identification of a speech disorder may include an articulation test, the evaluation of a student's ability to produce speech sounds in isolation and in words, sentences, and spontaneous speech; a measure of auditory discrimination, the ability to tell the difference in different sounds; the determination of whether the child hears the difference in a correct speech sound and the sound he or she makes; an evaluation of fluency; an evaluation of voice; a hearing test; a case history obtained from the parents and the student, if appropriate; an examination of samples of the student's work; and checklists or scales completed by parents and those who work with the child in the educational setting (Hall et al., 2001).

Speech-language pathologists are specially trained to assess, diagnose, and treat fluency disorders. The teacher also plays an important role in the identification of students who stutter by referring to the SLP every student for whom abnormal fluency is suspected. A commonly held myth is that stuttering nearly always disappears on its own. Although spontaneous recovery does sometimes occur, the majority of children presenting stuttering tendencies may not recover without intervention.

Evaluation of Students Who Are Linguistically Diverse

The evaluation of a possible language or speech disorder of nonstandard English speakers must be done carefully. As mentioned previously, most speech and language assessment materials are based on Standard American English (SAE). If this type of assessment is used, the child may be assessed for use of Standard American English rather than the ability to use language and speech. An awareness of the existing rule-governed differences in speech and language between the Standard American English speaker and the African American English speaker is necessary for an accurate assessment to occur (see An Important Event). A phonological assessment by an SLP of the speaker of African American English must take into account the differences between the sounds of Standard American English and African American English. A failure to take dialect differences into account substantially increases the likelihood of misdiagnosing normally speaking African American children as having articulation disorders (Cole & Taylor, 1990). The same can be true for morphological and syntactic differences, as well as semantic and pragmatic differences. For example, the stories of working-class African American children are usually personal, with less chronological sequencing and few formulaic openings or closings (Battle, 1996). The stories include many judgment statements about the characters and their behaviors, and are very expressive, with the inclusion of a variety of cues such as loudness, stress, intonation, exclamations, and repetitions to enhance the story or the characters. Listeners not accustomed to African American storytelling style may have difficulty identifying the topic and may ask poorly timed questions that interrupt the flow of the narrative and throw the speaker off balance. The result may be perceived as an expressive language disorder when actually it is the child trying to deal with interruptions in narrative style.

AN IMPORTANT EVENT

1997—Linguistic Society of America Passes a Resolution on African American English

Most American dialects are free from stigma, especially the many regional dialects, but one dialect has been a victim of prejudicial ignorance. This dialect, or actually a collection of closely related dialects, has been variously referred to as Black English (BE), Black Vernacular, African American English (AAE), and more recently, Ebonics (from ebony and phonics). Not only is this the most publicized and stigmatizing dialect in schools today, it is also the dialect that has been most studied. In the 1960s, BE/AAE became the focus of national attention with the onset of the civil rights movement. In the 1970s, pioneer sociolinguists Dillard (1972) and Fasold and Wolfram (1978) identified the rule-governed linguistic features that differ in BE and SAE. In 1996, the Unified School Board of Oakland, California, adopted a resolution that recognized Ebonics, or BE/AAE, as a system to be taken into account when teaching Standard English. In this way, schools respect and use students' linguistic competence as a resource rather than a deficit (Wolfram, Adger, & Christian, 1999). Their intention was neither to eradicate Ebonics nor to teach it. In 1997, the Linguistic Society of America passed a resolution to make it known that Ebonics by any of its names is systematic and rule-governed, and any characterizations of it as slang, lazy, defective, ungrammatical, or broken English are incorrect and demeaning.

REFLECTION How do you think knowing that a dialect is different, not deficient, would influence assessment and intervention?

The assessment format and procedures themselves may be biased against nonstandard English speaking or culturally diverse children. To begin with, Crago (1992) pointed out that the evaluation situation may have components that are unfamiliar. For example, in some cultures, adults do not ask children questions to which the adults already know the answer; in other cultures, children are not expected to be alone with adults. If the child is used to communicating mostly with peers, the testing situation may be very uncomfortable, resulting in incorrect conclusions. The teacher and clinician need to know the cultural situations, interactions, and caregivers in a child's life to effectively structure the situation and the participants in the process. Many sources of assessment should be used, including naturalistic observations in keeping with the child's linguistic and cultural community. For example, if the teacher or clinician is aware that Native American children talk more with peers than with adults, the procedure may be structured to include other children as the communicative partners (Crago, 1992).

For students with limited English proficiency (LEP), information about native language and English language proficiency is needed to first determine whether they should be assessed in the native language (Ortiz, 1997). In addition, efforts should be made to obtain information from parents on whether their presenting problems are

basic interpersonal communication skills (BICS) Conversational abilities that LEP students may master quite easily.

cognitive academic language proficiency (CALP) The more complex, abstract language use related to problem solving, evaluating, and inferring.

also evident in the home and community. Finally, in assessing language proficiency, it is important to determine both **basic interpersonal communication skills** (BICS) and **cognitive academic language proficiency** (CALP) (Cummins, 1984) in both the first language and the second language. BICS are conversational abilities that LEP students may master quite easily. CALP entails the more complex, abstract language use related to problem solving, evaluating, and inferring. Students who are learning a second language generally acquire conversational skills in one to two years, but may need five to seven years to achieve academic language ability. Students who have CALP proficiency in their first language will master critical literacy in a second language more easily and quickly than students who do not possess CALP in a first language (Westby, 1995). It is important to ensure that limited academic language proficiency is not misinterpreted as a learning disability (Ortiz, 1997). Westby suggested that it is problematic to diagnose students who have had less than five to seven years of learning school language as having a learning disability or communication disorder.

Most all individuals who assess language assess children from a culture different from their own (Carter et al., 2005). A variety of alternative techniques have been proposed for assessing culturally and linguistically diverse students for whom English is a second language (Saenz & Huer, 2003). These include norming a test for the specific population being tested, using dynamic assessment techniques to determine a child's response to intervention, using other nonstandardized measures such as parent interviews or checklists, and modifying standardized tests. Each of these techniques has advantages and disadvantages that need to be considered when determining the least biased language assessment procedures for bilingual students.

Whatever tests, alternative assessments, or other measures are used for identification of students with communication disorders, the teacher should be an integral part of the assessment process. The classroom teacher may best know the student's speech and language in the classroom and any affects on other cognitive and social behavior that a communication disorder may be having. Specific information requested of the teacher by the speech-language pathologist is likely to include the nature of the problem, its consistency, and awareness of the problem on the part of the student and his or her peers.

Check Your Understanding

1. What will generally be included in a full evaluation of language?
2. Why is a language sample analyzed whenever possible?
3. What are some issues in the use of norm-referenced tests to evaluate language?
4. What might be included in an evaluation of speech disorders?
5. What are some ways that a different dialect may affect assessment?
6. What are BICS and CALP, and how do they play a role in assessment of students for whom English is a second language?

Relevant CEC Standards

▶ Use strategies to facilitate integration into various settings (CC4S1)

▶ Select, adapt, and use instructional strategies and materials according to characteristics of the individual with exceptional learning needs (CC4S3)

▶ Use strategies to facilitate maintenance and generalization of skills across learning environments (CC4S4)

▶ Use strategies that promote successful transitions for individuals with exceptional learning needs (CC4S6)

▶ Social skills needed for educational and other environments (CC5K5)

What and How Do I Teach Students with Communication Disorders?

For teachers and other professionals serving students with disabilities, an understanding of communication disorders and intervention is paramount for three basic reasons: (1) language ability is related to academic success, (2) there is a strong relationship between students with disabilities and language deficiencies, and (3) language deficits may be the earliest indicator of other problems. Students with communication disorders will participate in the general curriculum. Additional content taught will most likely focus on communication intervention, including social-emotional communication skills,

Annual Goal

Victor will demonstrate grade-appropriate vocabulary understanding and use and apply them in his third-grade reading program.

Objectives

- Given multiple-choice answers, Victor will select with 80% accuracy the correct definition of vocabulary within a story he reads.

- Victor will correctly define vocabulary within a story he reads with 80% accuracy.

- Victor will correctly use new vocabulary from a story he has read to answer Wh- comprehension questions with 80% accuracy.

- Victor will correctly use, with 80% accuracy, new vocabulary from a story he has read to retell the story using a story graph.

Annual Goal

Victor will correctly produce initial /r/ and syllabic consonant "er" in various positions in words, spontaneous sentences, and connected discourse in his third-grade language arts class.

Objectives

- Victor will correctly produce the initial /r/ in words and spontaneous sentences in his speech therapy group with 80% accuracy.

- Victor will correctly produce the initial /r/ in words and spontaneous sentences in his third-grade language arts class with 80% accuracy.

- Victor will correctly produce syllabic consonant "er" in words and spontaneous sentences in his speech therapy group with 80% accuracy.

- Victor will correctly produce syllabic consonant "er" in words and spontaneous sentences in his third-grade language arts class with 80% accuracy.

- Victor will correctly produce /r/ and syllabic consonant "er" in words and spontaneous sentences, and connected discourse in his third-grade language arts class with 80% accuracy.

PRACTICE

and on supporting academics affected by the communication disorder, particularly literacy development. Effective instructional procedures will depend on the type of communication disorder.

Instructional Content

When planning instructional content for students with communication disorders, the main consideration is related to speech and/or language interventions. The implications of the communication disorder on educational achievement, social behavior skills, and occupational success should be addressed. A language disorder may result in poor problem-solving abilities and poor information storage and retrieval, which could significantly affect academic success. In addition, a child's language abilities may affect social outcomes such as peer relations, family relations, and later employment. For example, new vocabulary and knowledge of appropriate interactions in a specific occupational context may need to be taught. If teachers and speech-language pathologists understand language and its manifestations in social and academic tasks, they can implement programs that are language integrated and beneficial to students with communication disorders.

An area that will most likely be a focus is literacy. There is increasing evidence that early instruction that focuses on language and communication skills can enhance the academic success of children with communication disorders, especially in reading (Moats, 2001). Without intervention, communication disorders may have serious far-reaching consequences. Since reading is dependent, for hearing individuals, on spoken language, it is not surprising that children who have difficulty learning language often have difficulty with reading and other language arts skills.

Goals and objectives for students with communication disorders should be designed in the context of the general education curriculum to support content learning and to take advantage of the social-communication context of the classroom (Dodge, 2004). It has become more and more evident that naturalistic context and spontaneity in speech and language are related to successful intervention in speech and language programs. Goals such as "Increase expressive vocabulary" were common when speech and language intervention plans were written and implemented in isolation but are no longer appropriate (Whitmire, 2002). Instead, goals need to be integrated into the IEP and implemented in the classroom. The Classroom Example includes authentic goals and objectives. At the secondary level, the SLP may provide, in consultation with the teacher, curriculum-relevant language support with the appropriate combination of skill and strategy objectives based on the individual needs of students (Ehren, 2002).

Depending on the needs of the individual student, the teacher and the SLP may rely on commercially available materials, develop their own, or adapt an item or activity that is not designed for language. Intervention might focus on directly enhancing speech and language skills. For students with more severe impairments, intervention should focus on enhancing communication skills rather than development of speech intelligibility and language. This requires functional assessment of the environment to determine the communication needs of the child. The focus of intervention should be functional, teaching the child the skills necessary to participate fully within the environments in which he or she lives, works, and spends leisure time.

To assist in the development and implementation of language intervention, there are many materials and computer software programs available in all areas for students of all ages. One of the best-known curricula for language development is the Peabody Language Development Kits-Revised (Dunn, Smith, Dunn, & Horton, 1981). This curriculum includes pictures, puppets, shapes, and other materials to enhance oral language skills in children from preschool to 7 years old. Materials are also commercially available that focus on specific speech sounds, such as flashcards that contain specific phonemes or specific language concepts. For example, the Fokes Sentence Builder (DLM Teaching Resources) uses sentence strips designed to help students in grades 1 to 6 develop increasingly longer and more complex sentences. The Nonverbal Language Kit (Linguisystems) provides a curriculum for grades 2 to 11. The Pragmatic Activities for Language Intervention (Communication Skill Builders) involve real conversational language in a variety of activities for students ages 2 through 12, including crafts, role playing, puppetry, and more.

KATHLEEN REVISITED Are there areas other than speech and language that need to be addressed in Kathleen's program? If so, what are they?

Educating individuals with communication disorders is truly a team effort, and communication development is best achieved through collaboration of all members of the team, including family members. In addition, the teacher and SLP should focus on social communication skills to facilitate inclusion with peers without disabilities. Intervention efforts should include teaching these children how language is used to interact with other persons. In other words, the emphasis should be on increasing communicative competence. Programming for all students with communication disorders should provide opportunities for interactions across a variety of communication contexts and communication partners.

Instructional Procedures

Procedures for teaching speech and language targets to students with communication disorders will vary based on both the specific problem and the individual. What the instructional procedures for this group of students have in common is that they should all be taught as they would naturally occur in conversation. To help with this, the classroom should be designed to encourage verbal participation, ideally through engaging students with exciting materials and activities. Historically, in an attempt to emphasize and isolate a language target, unnatural discourse had been encouraged. Consider the following interaction, in which the teacher is attempting to have the child produce the present progressive form of the verb.

> Teacher: (*Shows a picture of a boy riding his bike.*) What's the boy doing?
> Student: Riding the bike.
> Teacher: Use a complete sentence.
> Student: The boy is riding the bike.

The student's first response is the natural way to answer such a question. However, with the teacher's interest in practicing the "is + ing" form, the student is required to respond in an unnatural way (Smiley & Goldstein, 1998). Intervention in a natural environment such as the child's classroom provides many opportunities to practice language in its natural form.

In addition to the classroom teacher and SLP, peers and family members can serve as important agents for language intervention. Any communicative act can potentially enhance communication skills. Parents may choose to take a more direct role in speech and language intervention by serving as tutors or helping the child with homework. The optimal language intervention strategy for a child utilizes a combination of formats. With a phonological disorder, for example, the SLP could begin intervention with individual sessions to develop specific skills, and then work in collaboration with the classroom teacher and parents to facilitate generalization of the newly learned skill.

Procedures for Students with Language Disorders

Many effective teaching strategies presented in other chapters may be applied to oral language development, including direct instruction, cognitive and metacognitive strategies, and graphic organizers, all introduced in Chapter 4. The interactive use of language, modeling, guided practice, active engagement, and feedback in these procedures make them very appropriate for students with language disorders. A direct instruction lesson in teaching sight words is presented in Online Appendix A. In this example, the teacher and the SLP have collaboratively decided on the sight word selections and are focusing on word meaning as well as reading .

All too often, the development of language comprehension is slighted in favor of language expression, although both understanding and expression must be taught. Language comprehension may be enhanced through modeling before, during, and after a targeted construction is taught. The teacher should make an effort to frequently use a form or structure or vocabulary word that is being taught. For example, if the irregular past tense is being practiced, the teacher could make many comments such as *Marlon put his work in the* box; *Diego went to speech class.* To practice production, the teacher could incorporate many questions or comments throughout the day or class period, such as *What did you do during lunch?* or *What did you learn in Math class today?*

Relevant CEC Standards
▶ Teach individuals to use self-assessment, problem solving, and other cognitive strategies to meet their needs (CC4S2) (Replaces CC4.S12)
▶ Use procedures to increase the individual's self-awareness, self-management, self-control, self-reliance, and self-esteem (CC4S5)

PRACTICE

Techniques that can be used to stimulate both comprehension and production in language development include the following (Hall et al., 2001):

Modeling: Restating what the student has said in a slightly more advanced manner. For example, correcting a verb tense or irregular plural.

Expansion: Restating with the addition of information to a child's utterance so that language or vocabulary is slightly more advanced. For example, adding an adjective, adverb, because clause, or more information. The teacher or clinician may follow Andrew's comment that "Wilbur was Charlotte's friend" with the elaboration, "Yes, Wilbur was Charlotte's friend and Templeton, Avery, and Fern were Charlotte's friends too."

Using Self-Talk: Talking about what you are doing as you are doing it and perhaps why you are doing it. For example, if the future tense is being worked on, the teacher may use think aloud statements such as, "Let's see, I will need paper for the printer to finish my last draft. Where did I put my paper? Oh yes, I will have to go to the supply closet. That's where I put it yesterday." This example also made use of the past tense, which was an earlier goal (Smiley & Goldstein, 1998).

Using Parallel Talk: Talking about what the student is doing while he or she is doing it. For example, if subordinating clauses are being focused on, "Syrynthia will put two tablespoons of butter in because we are doubling the recipe."

Cloze Procedure: Starting the utterance and letting the child complete it. For example, targeting specific vocabulary, "Another name for a car is ____."

All of these techniques can be used in naturally occurring classroom situations, turning them into language teaching opportunities, or incidental teaching.

Games and activities may be developed to focus on particular forms, structures, or vocabulary. For example, playing the game Jeopardy in Social Studies is an excellent way to practice Wh- question development. Plural Bingo, Vocabulary Concentration, or a game board requiring the conjoining of two sentences in order to move can be both fun and beneficial. The vocabulary involved in teaching and learning, such as the language of directions, the language of rules, and the language of problem solving, may need to be taught. It may also be beneficial to teach vocabulary commonly used in peer interactions. Owens and Robinson (1997) have developed a list of young children's books and specified their potential uses within the classroom to target specific language skills (see Online Appendix A). They suggested that the literature be selected based on speech and language goals of the classroom and individual children with communication disorders. For example, *Do You Know What I'll Do?* (Zolotow) might be used for future tense, or *Airplanes* (Barton) for vocabulary and categorization.

Procedures for Students with Speech Disorders

Procedures for working with students with speech disorders will vary depending on the type of disorder and the specific student's needs. The speech-language pathologist and the teacher will need to collaborate often. Goals for speech improvement need to be emphasized or reinforced in the general education classroom even if the student is in pullout therapy, perhaps even more importantly if this is the case.

Voice Disorders. Prior to therapy with the SLP, the student identified with a voice disorder should be assessed by a physician to identify the cause of the disorder. Generally, therapy for voice disorders involves teaching a vocal behavior that is not currently present, substituting a new, appropriate vocal behavior for an inappropriate one, or strengthening weak or inconsistent vocal behaviors (Andrews & Summers, 2002). The special or general education teacher can be of great assistance to the SLP in the management of the voice problem. If the disorder is the result of vocal abuse (for example, shouting), speech therapy will first focus on identification of where and when the abusive behavior occurs and then on instruction of new alternate behaviors. The role of the teacher might involve reinforcing those behaviors learned in voice therapy or modeling the appropriate vocalization. If the problem is more severe, such as laryngitis, the teacher can allow the student to rest his or her voice in class.

Misarticulations. The goal in articulation therapy is for a child to produce correct speech sounds in all speaking situations (Hall et al., 2001). This typically involves a gradual progression from less to more difficult and lengthy contexts such as moving from producing a sound in isolation, to then producing a sound in syllables, to using sounds in words, to using them in short sentences, to using them in longer sentences. In order to generalize this production from speech therapy settings to all settings, collaboration between the SLP who is administering the therapy and other professionals and family members in the student's environment is necessary. All individuals should be aware of the targeted sounds and contexts, and should provide models and opportunities to practice this sound in both academic and spontaneous communication. For example, the teacher could select a storybook to use in language arts that includes many words with the targeted sound. For instance, Owens and Robinson (1997) suggest that *Itchy, Itchy Chicken Pox* (Maccarrone) might be used for "ch" words.

Fluency Disorders. In general, stuttering therapies can be divided into two types. The first of these is *stuttering modification.* With stuttering modification approaches, the person who stutters learns to regulate or control his or her dysfluency. That is, the tense, uncontrolled dysfluencies common to stuttering are replaced by breakdowns in fluency that are easier for the individual to control. For example, a speaker who typically produces long, physically tense dysfluencies learns to modify these dysfluencies to more fleeting, relatively effortless breaks in speech (ASHA, 2006b). The therapist provides positive fluency models during comfortable, well-paced interactions and uses games focused on rhythm and timing during talking, such as chanting familiar rhymes (Justice, 2006).

The other major approach to stuttering treatment is *fluency shaping.* The idea behind fluency shaping is that by using new and different techniques, speech can be stutter free. In other words, if a person learns to speak in a fluency-enhancing manner, dysfluency will not occur. For example, the speaker may begin by practicing smooth, fluent speech at rates that are much slower than typical speech, using short phrases and sentences. Over time, speakers learn to produce fluent speech at progressively faster rates, in progressively longer sentences, and in progressively more challenging situations (ASHA, 2006b). Sometimes SLPs employ a therapeutic plan that utilizes elements of both approaches. Both types of stuttering treatment techniques are first practiced in therapy sessions and then practiced in real-life settings. Day-to-day fluency management is hard work and requires a great deal of mental energy. Often, particularly with young students, stuttering management is indirect; that is, dysfluencies are not addressed with formal therapeutic techniques. Instead, recommendations center on altering the environment of the child who stutters. When this occurs, the parents and the teacher play significant roles. The student may require a slow, easy speech model. Parents, teachers, and others in the child's environment are asked to model a simple and deliberate speaking pattern. Changes may also be implemented in the way typical family activities are carried out. For example, increased turn taking is a means by which family conversations can be made less stressful for a child.

Most children who stutter are fluent when reading aloud in unison with someone else, so having the class read in pairs can be a valuable procedure to use during oral reading time (Trautman, 2006). In general, students with fluency problems should be given the same materials and responsibilities as other children, and the SLP and the classroom teacher should discuss specific goals. The same quality and quantity of work should be expected of the student who stutters as from the one who does not.

Several specific suggestions for teachers in promoting fluency at all ages are presented in the Classroom Suggestions feature above.

Check Your Understanding

1. What areas of development other than speech and language may need to be addressed in a program for students with a communication disorder?

2. Why should students with communication disorders receive instruction in natural environments?

3. What are some procedures that can be used with students with language disorders?

4. What are some procedures that can be used with students with speech disorders? What is the role of the teacher in voice therapy? Misarticulation therapy? Fluency therapy?

What Are Other Instructional Considerations for Teaching Students with Communication Disorders?

Relevant CEC Standards

▶ Basic classroom management theories and strategies for individuals with exceptional learning needs (CC5K2)

▶ Effective management of teaching and learning (CC5K3)

▶ Teacher attitudes and behaviors that influence behavior of individuals with exceptional learning needs (CC5K4)

▶ Demands of learning environments (CC5K1)

▶ Social skills needed for educational and other environments (CC5K5)

▶ Adaptation of the physical environment to provide optimal learning opportunities for individuals with disabilities (GC5K2)

Environment is very important in the use of speech and language, and it must be considered in intervention. Both the physical arrangement and grouping will have an impact on the communication of a student with communication disorders. In addition, the use of technology, through alternative and augmentative communication, and technology to support fluency, should be planned for as it can be used to enhance communication.

The Instructional Environment

With a focus on naturalistic and spontaneous speech and language use, it is essential to evaluate how the student's communication skills affect his or her ability to interact across conversational partners and environments. In inclusive schools, instruction for communication skills occurs in heterogeneous groups in general education or special education classrooms, and in other school settings; or, as in the case of functional and vocational communication skills, instruction takes place in nonschool environments such as vocational or community settings (McCormick, 2003a). Whenever possible, language instruction should take place in the environment that the child is most likely

to use it in because communication is influenced by the setting in which it takes place. For example, storytelling, conversation, and classroom participation have different rules for participation, so any language intervention involving these events should take place as they occur in the student's everyday physical location (Owens, 2004).

ASHA (1993, 1996) noted that it is essential that time be made available in the SLP's weekly schedule for collaboration/consultation with parents, general educators, special educators, and other service providers. Included in the collaboration/consultation should be decisions about the setting's physical arrangement and the instructional grouping in terms of the individual student's communication needs.

The Physical Arrangement

The physical environment of the classroom determines the degree to which a student's communication ability is taxed. Communication can be facilitated by adapting the environment or providing strategies that are relevant in a particular environment (Dohan & Schulz, 1998). Some aspects of the environment may be influenced by age and by communication needs.

The Preschool Classroom. The physical environment of a classroom has a powerful effect on the quality and the quantity of young children's oral language experiences. The arrangement of the environment is the single most essential element of language intervention in inclusive preschools (McCormick, 2003b; Roskos & Neuman, 2002). Roskos and Newman identified four key spatial elements in classrooms that facilitate language learning and use: open space; clearly identified areas of the classroom; the availability of a variety of materials that encourage creativity and problem solving; and authentic, functional, dramatic play settings such as pretend restaurants and grocery stores. Materials and settings should be rotated regularly.

The classroom should be a language-rich environment in which children are exposed deliberately and recurrently to high-quality verbal input among peers and adults, and in which adult–child verbal interactions have high levels of adult responsiveness (Justice, 2004). Content-rich, student-centered, integrated language programs promote an environment that is also sensitive to special linguistic and cultural needs of English language learners (Poon-McBrayer & Garcia, 2000). Children should

Classroom Suggestions Environmental Arrangement Strategies for Increasing Communication

STRATEGY	DESCRIPTION	EXAMPLE
Materials of interest	Make available materials, objects, and activities that interest the student to elicit requests for them.	Place the student's favorite toy in the classroom.
Within view, out of reach	Place desired materials within student's view, but out of his or her reach to elicit request for help.	Place a favorite toy on an out-of-reach shelf.
Assistance	Provide materials that the student needs to ask for assistance to operate.	Give the student an unopened milk carton, a pencil that needs sharpening, a toy that needs winding up, or another object, as appropriate to her abilities.
Out of context	Offer materials or objects out of context to elicit comments or protests.	Hand a lunchbox to the wrong student, or hang a picture upside down.
Inadequate portions	Provide small portions so student will need to request additional material.	Give a student a small portion of juice with instructions to ask for more if desired.
Sabotage	Fail to provide needed objects or materials to elicit requests for them.	Forget to put out crayons for a coloring activity.
Silly situations	Create a situation that violates a student's expectations to elicit comments or protests.	Jokingly reach for the paste when the student has requested crayons.

Source: Adapted from Ostrosky & Kaiser (1991).

experience many different word types (content), grammatical constructions (form), and ways that language is used for social and functional purposes (use) (Bunce, 1995).

Some teachers may actually unintentionally preempt naturally occurring opportunities for language interaction by arranging the environment so that children can acquire whatever they want by themselves or by providing children with what they want without requiring any communication (Phillips & Halle, 2004). This can be avoided by intentionally structuring the environment to encourage communication through the use of oral language or augmented communication systems, such as manual signing. Ostrosky and Kaiser (1991) suggested some specific environmental arrangement strategies to increase the number of opportunities for communication in preschool (see the Classroom Suggestions). McCormick (2003b) added two cautions that must be considered when using these strategies. One is to be sensitive to children's tolerance for frustration and not to upset them with too many communication demands. The second relates to fostering independence—these environmental arrangement strategies should only be used at times when communication objectives are a higher priority than independence objectives.

The Elementary Classroom. The classroom arrangement for elementary students with communication disorders also needs to enhance communication. Furniture should be arranged to make it possible for students to easily interact with each other; this means large tables, interactive learning centers, and computer centers with space for interactive problem solving. The teacher should provide opportunities and activities that encourage communication in these places. Language arts activities provide a natural environment for targeting communication skills of students with language disorders. For example, students may work together to create storybooks using large tables for planning and writing, and computer centers for the final production.

The Secondary Classroom. Delivery models at the secondary level must take into account the setting demands of the school. Often, the secondary student with a communication disorder will be in a general education consultation program with or without some pullout services for language, study skills, or social skills classes. Ehren (2002) suggested that the SLP provide direct services to address the underlying language concepts and structures of the content areas of science, social studies, and math. Some direct services may be delivered in a separate class that is counted as an elective toward graduation. For example, the production of an illustrated study guide with graphic organizers for science may be developed in a language and learning disabilities class and used for an elective in art. Other secondary students with more severe language impairments may be taught in a community environment that may be a vocational training setting, and the SLP might provide direct services to address the underlying language concepts and structures of the student's vocational training and community setting.

Instructional Grouping

Optimal instructional grouping for students with communication disorders depends on the delivery system used. The choice of service delivery option will depend on the needs of the student and how those needs may best be met. Whatever option is selected, it will more than likely change over time as the student's communication skills develop. The SLP may work directly with the student with communication disorders or consult with others in the student's environment, such as the caregiver, teacher, or instructional aide, to assist them in helping the child improve his or her communication skills. ASHA (2000) recommended seven service delivery options, which are presented in Table 7.3 with

 Relevant CEC Standards
▶ Methods for ensuring individual academic success in one-to-one, small-group, and large-group settings (GC5K3)

TABLE 7.3	ASHA Service Delivery Options
Monitoring	The speech-language pathologist sees the student for a specified amount of time per grading period to monitor or "check" on the student's speech and language skills. Often this model immediately precedes the termination of services. Typical general education grouping will be used.
Collaborative consultation	The speech-language pathologist, regular, and special education teacher(s), and parents/families work together to facilitate a student's communication and learning in educational environments. This is an indirect model in which the speech-language pathologist does not provide direct service to the student but rather consults with the teacher. Instructional grouping decisions are made by the collaboration team.
Classroom-based program	This model is also known as integrated services, curriculum-based, transdisciplinary, interdisciplinary, or inclusive programming. There is an emphasis on the speech-language pathologist providing direct services to students within the classroom and other natural environments, such as the playground. Team teaching by the speech-language pathologist and the regular or special education teacher(s) is frequent with this model. Instructional grouping decisions are made by the collaboration team.
Pullout program	Services are provided to students individually or in small groups within the speech-language resource room setting. Some speech-language pathologists may prefer to provide individual or small group services within the physical space of the classroom.
Self-contained program	The speech-language pathologist is the classroom teacher responsible for providing both academic/curriculum instruction and speech-language intervention. This model is generally used with students who have more severe or multiple communication problems. Instructional grouping decisions are made by the SLP.
Community-based program	Communication services are provided to students within the home or community setting. Goals and objectives focus primarily on functional communication skills in a natural environment. In the case of the home setting, the SLP works with individuals. In other community settings, such as the workplace, grouping may be possible.
Combination	The speech-language pathologist provides two or more service delivery options (for example, provides individual or small group treatment on a pullout basis twice a week to develop skills or pre-teach concepts and also works with the student within the classroom).

Source: American Speech-Language-Hearing Association Ad Hoc Committee on Service Delivery in the Schools. (1993). Definitions of Communication Disorders and Variations. *ASHA, 35* (Suppl. 10), 40–41. Used with permission.

PRACTICE

implications for instructional grouping. Pullout service delivery and delivery of the collaborative consultation model are two frequently used options. Within the classroom, group work and peer interaction are effective grouping strategies.

Pullout Service Delivery. The pullout service delivery option has the advantage of giving students intensive practice in speech and language skills. Group sessions allow children to observe feedback given to others, and there may be less stigma associated with receiving services in the group setting as students discover that others among their peers also have communication problems. Disadvantages to the pullout model are that the student misses classroom instruction time and that he or she is singled out as different and may therefore feel socially stigmatized. The greatest disadvantage, however, is that the child is not provided with the opportunity to learn to use the skills in real-life situations, thereby limiting generalization. Collaboration with the classroom teacher on targeted skills can help alleviate this disadvantage.

The Collaborative Consultation Model. Speech-language pathologists are increasingly entering into collaborative settings with classroom teachers to support children with communication disorders. The rationale for this approach is that language is not a skill that can be isolated from other areas of academics. Rather, it is the foundation on which all learning occurs. Further, the function of language is to engage in interactions with other people, and it is best learned in interactive, naturalistic contexts.

There are many advantages to using a collaborative consultation approach. The most important is that the general education classroom is usually the least restrictive academic environment. Also, the SLP and classroom teacher may benefit from each other's expertise and unique perspective about the child and thus be able to provide even greater support. The SLP may provide insight about the relationship between oral language skills and reading, and the teacher can provide insight regarding the student's learning strengths and weaknesses. This approach has the added benefit of employing materials the student is already using, thereby enhancing learning and increasing generalization. Furthermore, students with speech and language problems are exposed to peers who serve as models for pragmatic skills as well as other areas of language. Another advantage of the collaborative consultation model is that students remain in the classroom. They do not miss valuable class time, nor are they identified as being "different." Similarly, the classroom-based model provides a more natural environment, and carryover of what has been taught may be more quickly and easily achieved than in a pullout model (Hall et al., 2001). In this model, students are grouped with others who have similar goals and objectives. For some subjects, such as social studies, the teacher and SLP may co-teach the entire class.

Group Work and Peer Interaction. With the exception of the self-contained program option, all service delivery options include or may include time spent in the physical space of the classroom or community setting where the student is receiving his or her education. Within these settings, group work may be particularly appropriate because of the social interaction in a group (Hall et al., 2001). Peer support strategies may also be particularly relevant because language impairment has a significant negative impact on peer interactions (McCormick, 2003a).

Children learn language from more advanced language users during reciprocal social interactions (McCormick, 2003b). Individuals with communication disorders who can most benefit from opportunities to interact with peers to increase and practice their language skills are often avoided by their peers who find them uncomfortable to be around or too "weird" to play with. McCormick recommends four **peer support interventions** for preschoolers to increase peer interactions between children with and without communication disorders: (1) teaching peers to initiate interactions with their classmates with disabilities, (2) teaching peers to respond to their classmates with disabilities, (3) peer modeling, and (4) cooperative learning practices. Initiations taught to willing peers may include organizing play, sharing, physical assistance, and affection. Peer responses, which may be taught to peers without disabilities, include attending to,

peer support interventions
Procedures used to increase peer interactions between children with and without communication disorders.

commenting on, and acknowledging the behavior of classmates with disabilities in mutual activities, such as when playing a game. Peer modeling includes prompting a "model" to remind a classmate with a disability what the rules are for a game on the playground or what to say in the lunch line. These techniques to increase interactions may be adapted for older students to apply within peer tutoring and buddy systems in which older students work together on their class assignments.

Cooperative learning groups can also promote communication since the emphasis in this arrangement is on fostering cooperative interactions in an often heterogeneous group. This not only provides opportunities for practicing interactive skills but also provides good models for communication. Classwide peer tutoring (first introduced in Chapter 4), which combines peer teaching and cooperative learning, can be a very effective group arrangement.

Instructional Technology

Knowledge of language development has increased greatly in recent years. This knowledge, paired with the 1997 strengthening of IDEA requirements for considering assistive technology and services, has resulted in an astonishing growth in the number of available augmentative and alternative communication systems, and technology to support fluency.

Augmentative and Alternative Communication Systems

Augmentative and alternative communication (AAC) systems are generally considered when speech is inadequate for a person to communicate effectively (Bryant & Bryant, 2003). **Augmentative communication** includes methods and devices that supplement existing verbal communication skills to enhance the communication skills that the individual already exhibits. **Alternative communication** refers to techniques that substitute for spoken communication for those individuals who appear unable or unlikely to develop spoken language skills. While initially there was concern that the use of such devices might interfere with the acquisition of spoken language, there is now substantial literature indicating that this is not the case. In fact, when speech is used with AAC, users have demonstrated positive gains in speech production and comprehension, attention span, task orientation, school performance, social skills, feelings of self-worth, and job opportunities (ASHA, 2006a; McCormick, & Wegner, 2003). Alternative communication strategies are best used in natural environments while doing purposeful activities (Lue, 2001).

The use of an AAC system may be the secondary system (augmentative) of communication for an individual, or it may be the primary system (alternative) of communication. Successful use of AAC to support academic and social gains must involve collaboration among the AAC user, the caregivers, and all professionals involved in the student's education. All training should occur in naturalistic settings and use of AAC must occur across settings.

AAC systems may be unaided or aided. Unaided AAC systems require no external devices. The most commonly used unaided AAC systems are gestures and manual signs. Aided systems use equipment or devices to provide the user with a means of communication. This equipment may be "low tech" such as picture, word, or letter boards with the user simply pointing to the appropriate symbol to communicate his or her needs. A

KATHLEEN REVISITED Do you think speech and language services are being delivered in the most effective manner for Kathleen? If yes, explain your response. If no, explain and suggest an alternative approach. Are there specific grouping techniques you would recommend?

Relevant CEC Standard
▶ Augmentative and assistive communication strategies (CC6K4)

augmentative communication Methods and devices that supplement existing verbal communication skills to enhance the communication skills that the individual already exhibits.

alternative communication Techniques that substitute for spoken communication for those individuals who appear unable or unlikely to develop spoken language skills.

For individuals with little or no voice, augmentative and alternative communication systems, and voice output communication aids (VOCAs) are useful.

In Practice Meet Educator Jamie Mendelsohn and Her Student Victor

I have recently completed a dual master's degree in special and elementary education and am currently teaching in an inclusive classroom, with a co-teacher, as the general education provider. Located in a metropolitan area, the school has students who come from diverse cultures and countries and are widely varied in socioeconomic status, race, and abilities.

My student Victor is in second grade and has been identified with a communication disorder in both speech and language. Victor's communication disorders often interfere

with his social and academic involvement in the classroom community. Victor lacks the articulation and vocabulary to share his opinions and express his needs verbally. This challenge often results in verbal outbursts in order to gain attention. I have been looking for ways to bridge the gap between his unspoken thoughts and the need for verbal expression. Victor is pulled out of the classroom twice a week for speech services in a group of three children. He also works twice a week with an occupational therapist, where the focus of therapy is on strength and agility in gross motor coordination and on handwriting and pencil grip in fine motor control.

Instructional Content and Procedures

All instructional content is based on state standards and citywide curricular calendars. It is differentiated in the classroom through presentation, materials, and grouping. Overall unit goals and comprehensive unit skills attainment are assessed on a daily basis through observation and conferences. Individualized goals are modified so that each child can achieve success. The modifications made

support the students' strengths as well as areas of weakness.

Within our literacy curriculum, we are working on writing stories. Victor has always followed the writing workshop procedures. When asked to share what he has written, he often has difficulty reading his work and making sense of what he has written. While he observed classroom routines and integrated socially and physically within the community, he was not producing any work toward achieving the curricular goals for the second-grade school year. The goal that I have implemented for Victor for the past few months has been for the development of meaningful and purposeful writing through direct instruction.

Through observations, interviews, student work, and even casual conversation, teachers get to know what will help their students feel successful and how the students learn best. With Victor, it was important for me to note how he interacted with students in the classroom, what structures he relied on, and, most important, the successes, though tiny, he experienced. Verbal positive reinforcement from the teachers, school personnel, and his guardians went a long way. It became clear that Victor was proud of the work he was completing.

pointing device may be positioned on the user's head if the student is unable to use his or her hands or fingers for pointing. AAC systems may also be "high tech," incorporating some electronic equipment. Voice output communication aids (VOCAs), visual tracking devices, and communication equipment utilizing keyboards are becoming more common in the management of severe communication disorders. Whether electronic or not, learning to use an AAC system can be challenging and must be carefully planned for and supported by all communication partners, including teachers, parents, and classmates. AAC users tend to be passive communication partners. To be successful communicators, the users must learn not only the symbols/vocabulary and their meanings but also how to use them in an interactive way (McCormick & Wegner, 2003).

Technology That Supports Fluency

Over the years, a variety of instrumentation has been utilized to treat disorders of fluency. Metronomes and similar devices have been used to impel persons who stutter

I began to give Victor responsibilities, academic and social, to further motivate and strengthen his enthusiasm to participate as a community member. Victor loves to hold the door for the class as they pass into the hallway. This duty is earned through his attention to hallway rules and helps Victor feel valued as a community member. Victor's passion for art is obvious in art class as well as in the classroom, so when he completes his work, he has permission to draw or color on paper for the remaining time in that activity. During many read alouds, he will stop and sketch a picture to gain a deeper understanding of the text. By becoming aware of his passions, we are able to teach through his strengths and motivate him to participate. Since September, Victor's attitude and participation throughout daily activities has grown. Victor is now engaging in much more meaningful conversation and appropriate discourse.

Victor's reading level remains below grade level. In the beginning of the week, I present Victor with a challenging book that he is unable to read on his own. I then spend 10 minutes going through the book, providing a strong book introduction and a picture walk, reviewing advanced words and complex vocabulary, and engaging him in a plot discussion. This allows Victor's enthusiasm toward reading to spike, while strengthening his skills and increasing his reading and vocabulary abilities. Victor rereads the book throughout the week, in addition to reading books at his independent level. This balance keeps interest, engagement, and enthusiasm at high levels.

Instructional Environment and Technology

Children enter our room in the morning and work throughout the day at their own pace and diligence. Many of the students prefer to work on the rug during writing or reading, or sit cross-legged in the corner of the room. They know it is their responsibility to complete their work and make smart choices. There is a strong sense of independence in their completion of activities and tasks, and an even stronger sense of collaboration as the students work with one another during many points of the day. Victor has taken on many academic roles and responsibilities in his daily routine. For example, he finds success in math more easily than others, and, at times, will act as a math coach for other students. Victor also enjoys leading the class in a clapping game, a form of copycat, in which students follow the clapping pattern that he chooses. His expressions indicate that this experience leaves him with feelings of importance and ownership from his participation in the lesson.

In inclusive classrooms, grouping structures are formed around common needs—groups of children who need more or less experience with certain skills or strategies are placed together to receive specialized instruction in this area. With two teachers in the room, there is opportunity for many, varied grouping situations. Many of the lessons are taught in a parallel teaching model, with both teachers teaching the same lessons simultaneously. The student–teacher ratio is about 12:1, making the experience of a group lesson smaller and more intimate, with opportunities for all to participate. This helps Victor focus, creating a more conducive learning environment for him. We also use station teaching. Students move through the stations for a designated time period, learning new things at each station. Two stations have teacher-directed instruction and two contain independent learning activities that support different learning styles.

Collaboration

There is a strong sense of collaboration within the school community that includes consistent and systematic communication among teachers, related service providers, and parents. I am in constant communication with Victor's service providers, working with them to implement individualized academic, social, and behavioral goals. This communication is critical in order to maintain a cohesive work environment and reinforce one another's goals. I truly enjoy the conversations with the specialists who work with Victor because they help me gain deeper knowledge about how I can include other techniques in my regular classroom practice.

into rhythmic speech patterns. Visual feedback has been found to be helpful in eliminating behaviors that hamper fluent speech. Finally, delayed auditory feedback equipment has been found to aid the fluency of some who stutter. This instrumentation plays speech back to the speaker with a short delay interval (about a quarter of a second). Other auditory feedback that may be helpful to some includes having the voice played back at higher or lower pitches, or playing white noise in the speaker's ear while he or she is speaking.

Using Technology in the Classroom

Teachers should attend training sessions on any form of instructional technology used with their students with communication disorders. The most important use of communication technology is in the natural environment, so teachers will need to be knowledgeable of both the purpose and use of the system. Other students will be curious about any technology, and the teacher will need to explain and discuss the system. SLPs and the student with the communication disorder, if he or she so desires, may be included in this discussion. It is also the responsibility of the teacher to assess the effectiveness of the AAC device in the development of communication skills needed for academics, vocational skills, or social interactions (Polloway, Smith, & Miller, 2004).

Check Your Understanding

1. Why is the natural environment important to speech and language intervention?

2. What are some environmental arrangement strategies used to promote the use of language and speech at the preschool, elementary, and secondary levels?

3. What are some recommended service delivery options for students with communication disorders?

4. How can group work be an effective grouping strategy for students with communication disorders?

5. What is augmentative communication? What is alternative communication? How does AAC use effect the acquisition of spoken language? What are aided and unaided AAC systems? Give some examples of each. What is the role of the teacher in the use of AACs?

6. How is technology used in stuttering therapy?

What Are Some Considerations for the General Education Teacher?

Relevant CEC Standard
▶ Barriers to accessibility and acceptance of individuals with disabilities (GC5K1)

The majority of students with communication disorders will be taught in the general education classroom and receive speech and language services within the classroom through collaboration or consultation with the speech-language pathologist. In fact, in 2005 almost 90% of 6- to 21-year-old students receiving speech and language services in the schools spent more than 75% of their time in the general education environment (OSEP, 2005). Examining students' communication needs, designing objectives, and implementing an intervention plan to meet those needs are joint responsibilities of the teachers and the SLP with the involvement of other specialists, administrators, support staff, and parents, as appropriate (Dohan & Schulz, 1998). This collaboration ensures that accurate information about both the curriculum and the disorder are considered, and that collaboration continues beyond planning into intervention. The general education classroom is often the most appropriate setting for the implementation of therapy goals and the transfer of new skills. Peers and family members may provide communicative enrichment by serving as models of appropriate speech, language, and social skills, and they can provide positive communication experiences. The more the student interacts with others, the more opportunities he or she has to practice speech and language skills. Naturalistic settings provide the best settings for intervention for the student with a communication disorder. The view of the SLP as a specialist who exclusively diagnoses and treats speech and language disorders in an isolated setting is no longer a reality (Dohan & Schulz, 1998). The most relevant intervention plans are those written by a team (Whitmire, 2002).

Collaboration between teachers and SLPs becomes even more important in light of the ever-increasing evidence that literacy problems are very often language based. As you recall from Chapter 4, the National Reading Panel (2000) identified five essential components of effective reading instruction, at least one of which, phonological awareness training, is directly related to oral language instruction. Vocabulary instruction and comprehension instruction may also be related to oral language instruction. In a recent survey, early childhood educators agreed that classroom teachers and SLPs should share responsibility for serving children with oral language problems and difficulty in learning to read and write (Shaughnessy & Sanger, 2005). Ehren (2000) suggested that while sharing the responsibility of intervention at any grade level, the teachers should be considered the experts in curriculum content and knowledgeable about language, whereas the SLP should be considered the expert in language and knowledgeable about curriculum content.

Hall, Oyer, and Haas (2001) described the following overall responsibilities of a general education teacher when working with students with communication disorders:

- Be a good speech model.
- Create a classroom atmosphere conducive to communication.
- Accept the student with communication disorders.
- Encourage classmates to accept the student with communication disorders.
- Consult and collaborate with the speech-language pathologist.
- Detect possible communication disorders and make appropriate referrals to a speech-language pathologist.
- Contribute to the student's motivation.
- Reinforce the goals of speech therapy.
- Help the student remember therapy appointments.
- Help the student catch up on anything that is missed while in speech therapy.

In light of the importance of context in the development and use of communication, the general education classroom is often the most appropriate setting for the student with a communication disorder and for intervention of specific language impairments. This will require close collaboration between the teacher and the speech-language pathologist.

Check Your Understanding

1. Where are the majority of students with communication disorders served?
2. Who is responsible for responding to the communication needs of a student in general education? How is this done?
3. What is typically the best setting for the intervention of communication disorders?
4. What are some ways a teacher can be positive and supportive in the classroom?

PRACTICE

Practical Considerations for the Classroom

Characteristics	Indicators You Might See
Primary Language Disorders	May have language problems primarily in one area of language or across several areas (phonology, morphology, syntax, semantics, and pragmatics).
Phonological Processing Disorder	Difficulty learning rules for using speech sounds in the absence of obvious physical limitations and beyond the age-appropriate time.
Morphological Disorder	Omits or misuses specific morphemes beyond the typical age to do so.
Syntactic Disorder	Uses simple sentence when more complex structures should be used, or confuses word order when forming sentences or using more complex structures.
Semantic Disorder	Knows a limited number of vocabulary words, uses the wrong word, may create a new word, may have trouble retrieving a word when it is needed, or may have trouble with multiple meanings or figurative language.
Pragmatics Disorder	May have problems fitting into social settings due to difficulties in language use.
Secondary Language Disorders	Difficulty using language due to another disability.
Mental Retardation/ Intellectual Disabilities	May have delays in morphological and syntactic development. Vocabulary may be more concrete, but not necessarily lower than others. Interpreting idiomatic expressions may be difficult. May show a weakness in pragmatic skills.
Emotional or Behavioral Disorders	May have difficulties in all language areas. Often have expressive and significant pragmatic disorders, have fewer opportunities to interact with others, and possess fewer tools to successfully interact.
Learning Disabilities	May have underlying problems in one or more components of language.
Autism Spectrum Disorder	May have deficits in using communication for social interaction. May have strengths in some areas of language.
Speech Disorders	Difficulty in voice, articulation of sounds, and fluency.
Voice Disorder	Atypical production of voice quality, pitch, or loudness.
Articulation Disorders	Atypical production of speech sounds. May include substituting one sound for another, the distortion of a sound, the addition of an extra sound, or the omission of a sound.
Fluency Disorders	Atypical flow of verbal expression, characterized by impaired rate and rhythm. Could include interjections; revisions; incomplete phrases; broken words; prolonged sounds; and repetitions of sounds, syllables, words, and phrases.

Students with Communication Disorders

Teaching Implications

Instructional Content

- Supports for literacy, educational achievement, social behavior skills, and occupational success should be considered.
- Goals and objectives should be designed within the context of the general education curriculum.
- Commercially available resources that support communication development should be considered.
- Intervention for students with severe impairments should focus on enhancing communication skills rather than the development of speech intelligibility and language.
- Consider a focus on social communication skills to facilitate inclusion with peers without disabilities.
- Programming should always provide opportunities for interactions across a variety of communication contexts and communication partners.

Instructional Procedures

- Speech and language targets should be taught as they would naturally occur in language.

  Language Disorders
  - Focus on both language comprehension and language expression.
  - Consider creating games and activities based on particular forms, structures, or vocabulary.
  - Select literature based on specific targeted language skills.

  Speech Disorders
  - Reinforce speech improvement goals in the general education classroom if the student is in pullout therapy.
  - Voice Disorders: Reinforce behaviors learned in voice therapy or model appropriate vocalization.
  - Misarticulations: Provide models and opportunities to practice targeted sounds in academic and spontaneous communication.
  - Fluency Disorders: Support the SLP's stuttering modification or fluency shaping.

Instructional Environment

- Design the classroom to encourage verbal participation.
- Ensure language instruction occurs in a natural environment.
- Instructional grouping options to consider are pullout service delivery, the collaboration consultation model, and group work with peer interaction.
- At the preschool level, consider open space; that areas of the classroom are clearly identified; that materials encourage creativity and problem solving; and that there are authentic, functional, dramatic play areas. Classrooms should be language-rich environments. Children should experience many different word types, grammatical construction, and ways language is used for social and functional purposes.
- At the elementary level, the arrangement should enhance communication. Furniture should be arranged to encourage interaction. Activities should encourage communication.
- At the secondary level, planning for the environment should take into account the setting demands of the schools.

Instructional Technology

- Consider using augmentative communication and alternative communication systems.
- Consider using technology that supports fluency.
- Attend training sessions for any of these technologies you will use with your students.

Methodologies and Strategies to Try

- Direct Instruction (p. 119)
- Cognitive and Metacognitive Strategies (p. 122)
- Modeling (p. 236)
- Expansion (p. 236)
- Self-Talk (p. 236)
- Parallel Talk (p. 236)
- Cloze Procedure (p. 236)

Considerations for the General Classroom and Collaboration

The general education teacher should:

- Encourage interaction between students with and without communication disorders.
- Work closely with the SLP, other specialists, parents, and administrators to support speech and language skills.
- Model good speech and language.
- Collaborate with SLP on literacy instruction.

Collaboration

General and special educators should consult on:

- Planning the classroom environment
- Determining the general education curriculum
- Adapting procedures and strategies used
- Planning to reinforce skills learned with the SLP in the general education classroom
- Planning for assistive technology

Chapter Summary

Go to the text's Online Learning Center at **www.mhhe.com**/taylor1e to access study resources, Web links, practice quizzes, and extending materials.

What Are the Foundations of Communication Disorders?

- School-based speech-language services have existed for the last 100 years. Since the 1950s, many significant changes have occurred in these services. Today, speech-language pathologists collaborate with teachers to support communication development.
- Communication encompasses both language and speech. Speech is the integration of the four systems of respiration, voicing, resonance, and articulation. Language is made up of phonology, morphology, syntax, semantics, and pragmatics.
- IDEA defines a speech or language impairment as a communication disorder, including stuttering, impaired articulation, a language impairment or a voice impairment, that adversely affects a child's educational performance.
- The American Speech-Language-Hearing Association (ASHA) defines a speech disorder as an impairment of the articulation of speech sound, fluency, or voice. It defines a language disorder as the impairment or deviant development of comprehension or use of spoken, written, and other symbol systems.
- About 2.3% of students ages 6 to 17 receive services for speech and language impairments under IDEA. Communication disorders is the second largest category of primary disabilities under IDEA 04. Almost 22% of all children who received services for disabilities under IDEA received services for speech or language disorders.

What Are the Causes and Characteristics of Communication Disorders?

- Causes of communication disorders may be congenital or acquired, organic or functional.
- Causes of primary language disorders are typically functional and nonorganic. A primary language disorder that is functional, nonorganic is called a specific language impairment. Research shows that environment and biological factors may be related to its cause.
- Articulation disorders may be caused by organic factors. Voice disorders may be caused by a large number of interacting organic and functional factors. Fluency disorders may be caused by neurological damage or by psychological factors.
- Characteristics of primary language disorders, or specific language impairments, differ with the components of language involved. Cultural or regional language differences are not disorders.
- Characteristics of secondary language disorders vary based on the associated primary disability.
- Characteristics of speech disorders are related to the type of disorder—articulation, fluency, or voice disorders.

How Are Students with Communication Disorders Identified?

- Identification of students with communication disorders involves gathering information from several individuals and several types of procedures in several settings.
- Language disorders are usually identified using standardized, norm-referenced tests; informal measures; and the observations of those with whom the child interacts.
- Speech disorders may be identified using an articulation test, the evaluation of a child's ability to produce speech sounds in different situations, a measure of auditory discrimination ability, the determination of whether a child hears differences in speech, an evaluation of fluency, an assessment of voice, a hearing test, a case history, an examination of the child's work, and checklists or scales.
- Evaluation of children who are linguistically diverse may be affected by the fact that identification tools use Standard American English. When assessing children with limited English proficiency, basic interpersonal communication skills (BICS) and cognitive academic language proficiency (CALP) should be considered.

What and How Do I Teach Students with Communication Disorders?

- Most students with a communication disorder will need speech and language intervention as well as attention paid to their academic and social skills.
- Goals and objectives for students with communication disorders should be designed for the general education classroom.
- The instruction of students with communication disorders should take place in natural environments.
- For students with language disorders, both language comprehension and expression should be taught.
- Instruction for students with speech disorders will depend on the specific disorder. Goals for speech disorders should be stressed in the general education classroom even if the student participates in pullout therapy.
- Instructional procedures for students with communication disorders typically involve support services from and collaboration with speech-language pathologists to ensure that targeted goals in speech and language are being addressed in the natural environments.

What Are Other Instructional Considerations for Teaching Students with Communication Disorders?

- The physical environment should encourage communication.
- There are several service delivery options for students with communication disorders. The most frequently used are the pullout service delivery model and the collaborative consultation model.

- Within the classroom, group work and peer interaction can support language and speech development for students with communication disabilities.
- Augmentative and alternative communication devices may assist students with communication disorders. These may be unaided or aided systems. In addition, several technologies are available to assist students with fluency disorders. The teacher should be well acquainted with any communication technology used both to assist the student and to explain its use to the rest of the class.

What Are Some Considerations for the General Education Teacher?

- Most students with communication disorders will spend all or some of their time in the general education classroom.
- Educational planning needs to be a collaborative effort involving teachers and speech-language pathologists.

Reflection Topics

1. Why do you think the ASHA definition of communication disorders is the most widely used definition? Relate your answer to the IDEA 04 definition.
2. What do you see as logical arguments for serving students with communication disorders in the general education classroom? What role do you think collaboration plays in the success of such a program?
3. Why do you think a communication disorder can affect academic and social development?
4. Why do you think it is important to distinguish between a language disorder and a language difference? What are the implications for intervention?
5. How might having a stutter affect your adjustment in school and in the community?
6. Do you think it would be better to use an augmentative or alternative device if there is an option? Why?

Application Activities: For Learning and Your Portfolio

1. Talk with a preschooler, kindergartner, first grader, and second grader who have no identified speech problems. Listen for the sounds of "r," "sh," "ch," and "j" in their speech. Note any differences that you may detect, illustrating with examples of words where the sounds were correctly or incorrectly articulated. Is there a difference based on age? Did you notice a trend?
2. Interview a speech-language pathologist who works in a public school setting. Ask the SLP what techniques are used to ensure that therapy is naturalistic and contextual.
3. (*Portfolio Possibility*) Develop a game or activity that could be used to help students with a specific aspect of one of the language components (for example, semantics: word retrieval). Include specific directions for playing and examples of items to be included.
4. Visit a special education or inclusive classroom for two hours. During this time, listen closely to the students' language and write down anything that sounds "incorrect" or "different." Note how you may use these examples to help in identification of a student with a speech or language impairment.
5. Go to your school district's Web site or district procedures manual to determine how your school district or state defines a communication disorder. How does it compare to the IDEA 04 and ASHA definitions? How does your district or state identify a communication disorder? Does it include recognition of naturalistic settings?
6. Visit the Office of Students with Disabilities (or its equivalent) at your university. Ask to observe or use any augmentative or alternative technology that they may offer.

SUMMARY

CHAPTER 8

Students Who Are Deaf or Hard of Hearing

CHAPTER OUTLINE

INTRODUCING ALLISON

Allison is a 6-year-old girl who has just started the first grade. She has a hearing loss resulting from repeated and severe ear infections in infancy and throughout her early childhood. The infections resulted in a bilateral conductive hearing loss. Her loss is mild to moderate—she does not hear clearly until sounds reach a 40 decibel level. She experiences this hearing loss across all frequencies of sound detectable by the human ear. Prior to entering school, Allison received early intervention services at home from an audiologist and early childhood special educator. Because of her frequent illnesses, she only sporadically attended a center-based preschool program. With time, medical interventions greatly reduced the infections and their severity.

Allison uses hearing aids that make it possible for her to learn using her auditory channel. Her speech and language skills are delayed, likely the result of not hearing adequately in early childhood. Her parents are concerned about her literacy skills development as she begins school. Because she qualified for early intervention, the school and Allison's parents developed an IEP for her. She receives speech and language services regularly. An itinerant teacher for students who are deaf or hard of hearing provides consultation to her general education teacher. The team did not feel they should "pull out" Allison for resource room services if her literacy skills, which will be monitored and assessed frequently, can be developed in her general education class. Also, an audi-

ologist will provide consultation to Allison's parents, teachers, and speech and language pathologist to ensure her hearing aids are working properly, are being maintained, and are being used as effectively as possible. ■

Allison's abilities are typical of a student who is hard of hearing. That is, while she does have a significant hearing loss, she is able to use her residual hearing for learning in much the same way that hearing students do. When a student is deaf, additional considerations must be addressed in order to provide an appropriate education in the least restrictive environment. Students with hearing losses are a heterogeneous group with differences in degree and type of hearing loss, cognitive abilities, literacy backgrounds, need for technology, and preferred communication method (Stewart & Kluwin, 2001). Teachers need to understand how to help students with hearing losses learn effectively and efficiently because these students will assume important roles in schools and in life (Moores, 2001). As I. King Jordan, the first deaf president of Gallaudet University, stated, "Deaf people can do anything except hear" (Shapiro & Valentine, 2006).

What Are the Foundations of Deafness and Hard of Hearing?

It is important for future teachers to understand that even though deafness and hard of hearing are low incidence disabilities, it is likely that they will interact with students or adults who have hearing losses. Understanding the foundations that underpin the unique perspectives regarding how best to educate these students can help to alleviate misunderstanding among those who are hearing toward students who learn, but do not hear. Before we discuss the history, definitions, and prevalence of deafness and hard of hearing, we want to introduce some related terminology.

The terms used to describe those with hearing problems can stir controversy. The following is summarized from Easterbrooks (1999) and Frasu (2004). **Deaf with a capital "D"** can be used as a specific term to refer to members of the Deaf community and Deaf culture. Deaf community members most likely identify American Sign Language (ASL) as their first or primary language even if they do use speech to communicate. We discuss Deaf culture at length later in this chapter. **Deaf with a small "d"** can be used to refer to people who have significant hearing loss but do not necessarily identify themselves as being members of the Deaf community and culture. There is not universal agreement as to what is or who belongs to the Deaf community and culture. The term *deaf* can also be used to refer to an individual's audiological status. That is, it can be used to describe the level of hearing loss. **Hard of hearing** refers to those with mild to severe hearing losses who probably use speech for communication, will need educational and technological support, and may or may not identify with the Deaf culture. **Hearing impairment,** the term used in federal legislation, refers to a medical condition that leads to hearing loss. However, some people with hearing loss consider this term offensive as they would the terms "deaf-mute" or "deaf and dumb." In general, the term *hearing impairment* is not used to refer to an individual (e.g., hearing impaired student). **Hearing** is a term used to refer to people who have no hearing loss (e.g., hearing peers) (Easterbrooks, 1999; Frasu, 2004). We will use the term *manual communication* to refer to all aspects of communication that are visual (e.g., fingerspelling, ASL, gestures, facial expressions) and *sign language* for ASL or variations of ASL. Finally, throughout this text we have stressed the use of person-first language, but the term *deaf people* is commonly used in texts concerning and by authors in the Deaf community, and thus we will divert from the person-first language in this respect at various points in this chapter.

A Brief History of Deafness and Hard of Hearing

Not much is known about the experiences of those who were deaf or hard of hearing in early history. According to Lang (2003), there is little information about the roles of signs, gestures, or oral language in the lives of deaf people. Overall, however,

Deaf with a capital "D" Refers to members of the Deaf culture and community.

deaf with a small "d" Refers to any group of people whose audiological status places them in that range of hearing loss.

hard of hearing Refers to individuals with mild to severe hearing losses.

hearing impairment An impairment in hearing, whether permanent or fluctuating, that adversely affects a child's educational performance.

hearing Refers to individuals with no identified hearing loss.

Relevant CEC Standards

▶ Issues and trends in the field of education of individuals who are deaf or hard of hearing (DH1K4)

▶ Major contributors to the field of education of individuals who are deaf or hard of hearing (DH1K5)

individuals who were deaf were denied legal and human rights as well as education and equality in participating in the mainstream of society throughout much of early history (Lee, 2004).

In 1816, American Thomas Hopkins Gallaudet visited Europe to learn about educating deaf people and later cofounded the American School for the Deaf. Gallaudet's son, Edward, would later become the first president of Gallaudet University. The Important Event feature relates the story of the founding of Gallaudet University.

AN IMPORTANT EVENT

The Founding of Gallaudet University

In 1857, Edward Miner Gallaudet was approached by a prominent businessman to become superintendent of a school for children with sensory losses, which became the Columbia Institution for the Deaf, Dumb, and Blind. In 1864 President Abraham Lincoln authorized the school to grant college degrees in liberal arts and sciences, which resulted in the school changing its name to the National Deaf-Mutes College. Later, the school became Gallaudet College and finally Gallaudet University (Marschark, Lang, & Albertini, 2002). Gallaudet University continues to be the premier American higher education institution that extensively incorporates American Sign Language in the classroom and as part of its academic culture.

REFLECTION Why do you think some students who are deaf might prefer to attend a university where the majority of students are deaf?

The "oralist" movement, which originated in Europe, reached the United States late in the 19th century (Burch, 2002). Oralists believed that because oral speech was the primary mode of communication in schools and the world, teaching children who were deaf to speak and use oral language was preferable to using sign language. Oralists attempted to integrate marginalized communities in the United States, establish English as the common spoken language, and tie speech to normality. If deaf people learned speech, they would be more integrated into "normal" society (Burch, 2002). Edward Gallaudet and Alexander Graham Bell were at the forefront of the debate over whether the use of manual communication, oral language, or a combination of the two was in the best interest of educating children who were deaf. The National Association for the Deaf was founded in the United States to strengthen the political influence of the Deaf community and to advocate that how a Deaf person should communicate was an individual choice and should not be imposed by educational institutions (Lang, 2003). Concern about which method of communication should be stressed in a child's education still exists today.

Prior to the passage of the IDEA, most students who were deaf were educated in residential or special day schools (Moores, 2001). The passage of PL 94-142 mandated educational services for students who were deaf and hard of hearing. Today, most students with hearing losses are educated in schools that include their hearing peers (Moores, 2001). The Americans with Disabilities Act, passed in 1990 with the intention of breaking down employment barriers, specifically provided for telephone relay systems, enabling 24 hours a day, 365 days a year telephone communications through written words. Closed captioning also became more widely available during the 1970s and 1980s (Marschark et al., 2002). The emergence of these services was the result of organized advocacy by and on behalf of those who were deaf and hard of hearing to gain access to and participation in the economic and social mainstream of society (Humphries, 2004). Awareness of deafness and American Sign Language (ASL) have expanded in recent years (Moores, 2001).

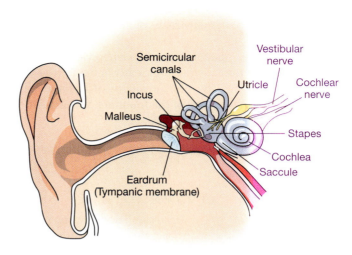

FIGURE 8.1 The Outer, Middle, and Inner Ear

Definitions of Deafness and Hard of Hearing

As already noted, terminology related to deafness and hard of hearing can carry multiple connotations. In this section, we focus on clinical and educational definitions of deaf and hard of hearing rather than on cultural perspectives.

Clinical Definitions of Deaf and Hard of Hearing

Clinical definitions of deaf and hard of hearing are based on the type and degree of hearing loss. To understand these clinical definitions, it is first necessary to examine aspects of the hearing system and sound. Figure 8.1 provides a diagram of the outer, middle, and inner ear. For a person to hear adequately, sound waves must be conducted from the outer ear, through the middle ear, and into the inner ear. In the inner ear, the cochlea converts the energy transmitted through the outer and middle ears into electrical energy. This generates a nerve impulse that is transmitted along the auditory pathway, which includes the auditory nerve, to the brain where it is interpreted as sound. The inner ear is also important in our vestibular system, which affects balance and our sense of body position in space.

loudness Refers to the intensity of a sound and is measured in decibels.

frequency Refers to the measurement of sound waves and is expressed in cycles per second or hertz.

Sound can be described in terms of loudness and frequency. **Loudness** refers to the intensity of a sound and is measured in decibels (dB). The larger the dB number, the louder the sound. Zero dB represents the lowest level of sound that a typically hearing person can perceive (Herer, Knightly, & Steinberg, 2002). The **frequency** of sound waves is measured in cycles per second, or hertz (Hz). The human ear can detect frequencies from 20 Hz to 20,000 Hz, but most human speech occurs in the 300 to 6,000 Hz range with the majority occurring between 300 and 3,000 Hz (Herer et al., 2002; Woodcock & Aguayo, 2000). Table 8.1 lists degrees of hearing loss expressed in terms of decibels.

Teachers need to understand that hearing losses are not easily described (Woodcock & Aguayo, 2000). A person could have different decibel losses at different frequencies. Two people with the same overall average decibel loss can hear the world quite differently and have different needs because their losses are also at different frequencies. For example, one student could have a 70 dB loss at 500, 1,000, and 2,000 Hz, whereas another student who has a 30 dB loss at 500 Hz may have an 80 dB loss at 1,000 Hz and a 100 dB loss at 2,000 Hz (Woodcock & Aguayo, 2000). Hearing loss can be described in relation to the type of hearing loss, the degree of hearing loss, and the age of onset.

sensorineural loss A hearing loss caused by a problem directly associated with auditory nerve transmission.

Types of Hearing Loss. The type of hearing loss is usually associated with and described by some problem with the actual physiological or neurological transmission of sound. **Sensorineural hearing loss** is caused by a problem directly related to

TABLE 8.1	Hearing Loss Expressed in Decibels (dB)
LEVEL OF SOUND	**SIGNIFICANCE FOR HEARING**
0 dB	Softest sounds heard by humans
0fi20 dB	Normal hearing level even if a slight loss
20 dB	Soft or low volume speech
20–40 dB	**Mild hearing loss**
40 dB	Sound of a fan
40–60 dB	**Moderate hearing loss**
60 dB	Typical loudness of conversation
60–80 dB	**Severe hearing loss**
80 dB	Sound of a vacuum cleaner
90 dB or greater	**Profound hearing loss**
90 dB	Sound of a motorcycle
100 dB	Sound of a semi-truck going by

Source: Herer, Knightly, & Steinberg (2002); American Speech-Language-Hearing Association. (n.d.). *Type, degree, and configuration of hearing loss.* Retrieved June 20, 2005, from www.ASHA.org

auditory nerve transmission; it is a problem associated with the inner ear or auditory nerve that may result in deafness (Falvo, 2005). For example, if there is an actual defect in the operation of the cochlea, a sensorineural loss may occur. A **conductive hearing loss** is caused by a problem directly associated with the transmission of sound waves from the outer ear through the middle ear that prevents at least some sound waves from reaching the cochlea in the middle ear (Falvo, 2005). Excessive wax buildup in the auditory canal, a punctured eardrum, middle ear infections, or calcification of the series of bones in the middle ear can all cause this type of hearing loss. Conductive hearing losses tend not to diminish the clarity of sound but rather the loudness of sounds heard. These losses tend to be mild to moderate and can often be improved with amplification (Falvo, 2005). A **mixed hearing loss** results when an individual experiences both a conductive loss and a sensorineural loss (Herer et al., 2002). Hearing losses can be unilateral, affecting only one ear, or bilateral, affecting both ears. The impact of the hearing loss is influenced by variables such as "severity, age at onset, age at discovery, and age at intervention" (Herer et al., 2002, p. 200).

conductive hearing loss
A hearing loss caused by a problem associated with transmission of sound waves from the outer through the middle ear.

mixed hearing loss A hearing loss that results when an individual experiences a conductive loss in one ear and a sensorineural loss in the other ear.

Degree of Hearing Loss. The level of hearing loss is an important issue in classification. Therefore, degree of hearing loss has been established as a common type of measure. Students who are deaf or hard of hearing can be described as having a mild, moderate, severe, or profound hearing loss.

As a rule, an individual who has a decibel loss greater than 26 dB, but less than approximately 70 dB, a mild to moderate hearing loss, is considered hard of hearing. An individual with a loss greater than 70 dB is considered to have a severe to profound hearing loss. Some consider the 90 dB level the one that separates deaf individuals and those that are hard of hearing (Blamey, 2003). Again, it is important for teachers to remember that audiometric descriptions of hearing loss (dB and Hz) do not adequately describe how well a student might be able to use his or her residual (remaining) hearing for learning, especially if amplification is helpful and if the loss does not interfere with hearing human speech.

ALLISON REVISITED Why would Allison's hearing loss be considered mild to moderate? Would she be considered deaf or hard of hearing?

congenital hearing loss Hearing loss acquired prior or at to birth.

adventitious hearing loss Hearing loss acquired after birth.

prelingual hearing loss Hearing loss occurring prior to the development of speech and language.

postlingual hearing loss Hearing loss occurring after the development of speech and language.

Age of Onset. Individuals may also have their hearing loss described by the age of onset. Those with **congenital hearing loss** had the hearing loss at birth. Those with **adventitious hearing loss** acquired their hearing loss after birth. **Prelingual hearing loss** occurs prior to the development of speech and language. **Postlingual hearing loss** occurs after the development of speech and language (Falvo, 2005). Performance in speech and oral language environments can be influenced by age of onset, severity and type of hearing loss, family language environment, and exposure to manual or spoken language (Bernstein & Auer, 2003).

The IDEA 04 Definition

Under IDEA 04, *deafness* means a hearing impairment that is so severe the child is impaired in processing linguistic information through hearing, with or without amplification, and that adversely affects a child's educational performance. *Hearing impairment* means an impairment in hearing, whether permanent or fluctuating, that adversely affects a child's educational performance but that is not included under the definition of deafness. Under federal law, the primary consideration for eligibility for services is that the hearing loss has an adverse effect on the student's educational performance. A second consideration is whether with or without amplification a student is able to process linguistic information through hearing. Students who are considered deaf may not be able to process linguistic information through hearing, whereas those with hearing impairments are able to do so although they may need assistive devices. Also note that a student may be considered to have a hearing impairment when a hearing loss is fluctuating. We use the term *hard of hearing* to refer to those students who would typically be labeled as having a hearing impairment under IDEA 04.

For educators, there are at least two important considerations involving the definitions of deafness and hard of hearing. First is whether the student is able to process and use oral speech and language. Clearly, if a student is not able to process and use oral speech and language, educational adaptations and modifications will vary, at least to some degree, from those for students who are able to do so. Second, deaf students may have wishes, strengths, needs, and sensibilities of which the typical hearing person initially may have little awareness.

Prevalence of Deafness and Hard of Hearing

The prevalence of hearing loss in the general population is considerably greater than the prevalence among school-aged children and adolescents. Hearing losses occur in older people over time; therefore, the overall prevalence of hearing loss in the population is greater than that for school-aged individuals. An overall estimate of hearing loss in the population is about 10%, or 23 million Americans. Of that number, about 1.5 million are deaf in both ears (Marschark et al., 2002). In contrast, about .14% of all school-aged children were served in the IDEA 04 category (U.S. Department of Education, 2006). As we can see from these data, the category of hearing impairments has a very low incidence, representing only a small percentage of school-aged students in special education. Not all students who may appear to have a hearing loss will qualify for services. For example, 10–15% of school-aged children may fail hearing screenings at school, but the majority of these children have transient hearing losses that may not adversely affect their educational performance (Herer et al., 2002).

Future teachers, who may encounter a student who has a severe hearing loss, may find they do not understand the nature of the challenges the student faces and how to provide an appropriate education. Understanding the foundations of hearing loss provides some background for initial understanding of hearing loss. Certainly, all teachers, in school or in their private lives, are likely to encounter individuals with hearing losses.

Services for students who are deaf or hard of hearing have improved considerably although improvements can still be made. Because the definition of deafness and hard of hearing can vary based on age and severity, it is not easy to know the exact prevalence. Hearing impairments, the category used in IDEA 04, is a low incidence disability.

Check Your Understanding

1. What were important issues in the development of educational programs for students who are deaf or hard of hearing?
2. What terms are used to refer to people who are deaf or hard of hearing? What does each of the terms imply?
3. What are the different types of hearing loss? What are the different degrees of hearing loss?
4. What are the IDEA 04 definitions of deafness and hearing impairments?
5. What is the overall prevalence estimate of school-aged children who are deaf or hard of hearing?

What Are the Causes and Characteristics of Deafness and Hard of Hearing?

The causes of hearing losses are myriad, and specific causes are not always identifiable. Causes can be examined in terms of whether they result in conductive, sensorineural, or mixed hearing loss, as well as by their point of origin in the outer, middle, or inner ear. Hearing loss can also be discussed based on whether it is caused by genetic or environmental factors. Characteristics of students can vary by degree and type of hearing loss, as well as the age of onset.

Relevant CEC Standard

▶ Etiologies of hearing loss that can result in additional sensory, motor, and/or learning differences (DH1K3)

Causes of Hearing Losses

Hearing losses may be conductive, sensorineural, or mixed. Generally, but not exclusively, conductive losses are associated with the outer and middle ears. Sensorineural losses are associated with the inner ear mechanisms.

Causes Associated with Conductive Hearing Loss

A conductive hearing loss, one that appears when limited sound waves reach the cochlea, is most often caused by an abnormality in the pinna or small bones within the middle ear, some type of blockage, or a perforated eardrum. If the pinna, the cartilage formation that is the visible portion of the outer ear, is either very small, absent, or extremely misshapen, a conductive hearing loss can occur as one of the pinna's functions is to help localize sound into the auditory canal. The middle ear consists of the eardrum, or tympanic membrane, and a series of three small bones: the malleus, incus, and stapes (Falvo, 2005). Falvo noted that abnormalities in the small bones can result in a hearing loss as can blockages of the auditory canal caused by growths or the presence of foreign bodies or if excessive cerumen (earwax) is allowed to build up.

The most common hearing problems are associated with some type of fluid buildup in the ear canal (Falvo, 2005). This general condition is referred to as **otitis media** and is especially prevalent in young children. About three out of four children experience otitis media by 3 years of age although certainly not all experience a permanent or significant hearing loss (Herer et al., 2002).

otitis media Middle ear infections that can lead to either temporary or permanent hearing loss.

There are two types of otitis media (National Institute on Deafness and Communication Disorders [NIDCD], 2002). In *acute otitis media*, a short-term inflammation of the eardrum develops. Usually, the inflammation initially results from some type of bacterial or viral infection that is then aggravated by a buildup of fluid in the middle ear. Parts of the ear can also become swollen. This condition can be quite painful. In *otitis media with effusion* (fluid), the same conditions as above exist, except that the condition is relatively long-term and continuous. Fluid remains in the ear after the infection is over. In both types, the infection often happens as a result of another illness such as a cold. In otitis media with effusion, hearing loss may be significant and permanent (NIDCD, 2002). Table 8.2 lists several possible signs that a child might be experiencing otitis media.

TABLE 8.2	Signs a Child Might Be Experiencing Otitis Media

A child may be experiencing otitis media if she or he experiences any of the following:

❑ Chronic pain or fever

❑ Fluid draining from ear

❑ Unusual or recent trouble sleeping

❑ Problems with balance

❑ Rubbing, pulling, or scratching of ears as if irritated or while crying

❑ Unexplained or recent irritability

❑ Inattention to sounds in the environment

❑ Wanting television, radio, or speech to be louder than normal

❑ Not hearing or following directions that would typically be heard and followed

❑ Lack of energy or listlessness

Source: National Institute on Deafness and Other Communication Disorders (2002); American Speech-Language-Hearing Association (n.d.).

myringotomy Placing small tubes inside the ears to allow air to vent inside the ear and prevent fluid buildup while relieving the existing pressure.

Consistent and appropriate treatment of cases of otitis media is necessary. Antibotics might be prescribed for bacterial-related infections. **Myringotomy,** placing small tubes inside the ears to allow air to vent inside the ear and prevent fluid buildup while relieving the existing pressure, may also be used (NIDCD, 2002).

Finally, a perforated eardrum, the tympanic membrane, can result in temporary hearing loss or permanent loss if accompanied by an infection. Perforations usually heal themselves within a few weeks (American Academy of Otolaryngology, n.d.).

Causes Associated with Sensorineural Hearing Loss

Sensorineural loss may stem from both genetic and environmental causes (Herer et al., 2002). They may result in pre- or postlingual hearing loss.

About 30% of all cases of prelingual deafness have genetic origins (Smith & Robin, 2002). Because prelingual deafness occurs prior to the acquisition of oral speech and language, it has implications for how a child will initially acquire language and what type of language (oral or manual). In many cases, prelingual deafness is caused by a specific syndrome that leads to sensorineural hearing loss.

Usher syndrome is the most common condition that can result in both hearing and vision problems. Three to 6% of children who are deaf may have Usher syndrome. In the most severe cases, children may experience profound deafness and have severe balance problems. Milder cases may result in normal hearing that worsens over time to severe hearing loss with normal to near-normal balance (NIDCD, 2003). Other genetic syndromes associated with hearing losses are Pendred syndrome and Waardenburg syndrome (Herer et al., 2002; Smith & Robin, 2002).

The most prevalent environmental cause of sensorineural hearing loss is maternal rubella, a German measles virus that has its most devastating effect on an unborn child during the first three months of pregnancy. A mother who contracts rubella during the first trimester of pregnancy has about a 30% risk of bearing a child with a severe to profound sensorineural hearing loss (Herer et al., 2002).

Prenatal and perinatal maternal viruses or infections, such as cytomegalovirus, toxoplasmosis, and syphyilis infections can also cause sensorineural hearing loss (Herer et al., 2002).

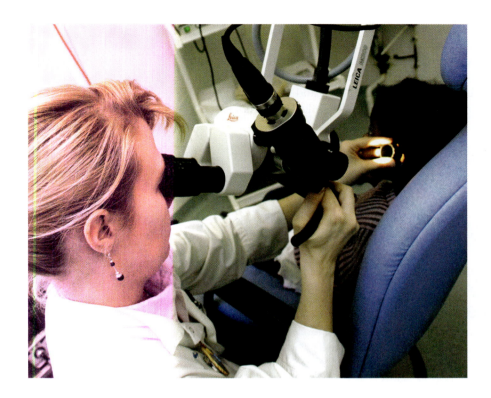

Finally, mixed hearing losses can result from conditions that cause a combination of conductive and sensorineural hearing losses. It is possible that a conductive hearing loss could be medically treated or improved with amplification while the sensorineural loss remains. The degree of hearing loss is significantly affected by the degree and type of sensorineural damage (Falvo, 2005).

Characteristics of Deaf Students and Those Who Are Hard of Hearing

Characteristics of students who are deaf or hard of hearing can vary considerably based on the age of onset of the hearing loss, the degree and type of hearing loss, the family's primary language (ASL or spoken English), and the early developmental experiences of the student. Another important variable that affects a student's characteristics is whether the student and her or his family are members of the Deaf community and culture. In this section we focus specifically on cultural, intellectual, academic, speech and language, and social-emotional characteristics.

Cultural Characteristics

From a cultural perspective, "deafness constitutes a difference, not a deficiency, that it is part of the human condition, and that it places no limits on social, emotional, intellectual, and academic development" (Moores, 2001, p. 1). The Deaf community meets the following criteria of a distinct culture (Deafculture.com, n.d.):

- A distinct language (ASL)
- A distinct folk tradition encompassing performing arts and storytelling in ASL and Deaf history
- Distinct social institutions (e.g., churches or sports teams for Deaf people)
- Distinct schools
- To some extent, distinct social protocols (e.g., using touch more extensively to gain attention, notifying other Deaf people when one leaves the room so that people know where you are)

Padden and Humphries (2005) noted that while Deaf culture is defined by its history and traditions, it is primarily defined by the use of sign language in everyday life.

Relevant CEC Standards

▶ Cognitive development of individuals who are deaf or hard of hearing (DH2K1)

▶ Impact of the onset of hearing loss, age of identification, and provision of services on the development of the individual who is deaf or hard of hearing (DH2K2)

▶ Cultural dimensions of hearing loss that may impact the individual (DH3K2)

▶ Influence of families on the overall development of the individual who is deaf or hard of hearing (DH3K3)

▶ Impact of hearing loss on learning and experience (DH3K4)

They stressed that the use of ASL distinguishes the Deaf culture from that of hearing people and also from other deaf people and those who are hard of hearing who primarily use other forms of communication. Deaf culture can include those who are not "legally" deaf but who use ASL as a primary means of communication and those who self-identify as Deaf (Woll & Ladd, 2003). The Important Event feature describes one movement that was a major influence on the empowerment of Deaf people.

AN IMPORTANT EVENT

The Deaf President Now Movement

In 1987 the President of Gallaudet University resigned and the process began to identify a new one. The Deaf community had expressed a desire for the university to hire, for the first time, a Deaf president. In March 1988 the board of trustees once again hired a hearing president, although two of the three finalists were Deaf. The "Deaf President Now" movement went into full swing through letters, calls, telegrams, and protests. The campus was shut down for a week with protesters making the following demands: the resignation of the newly hired president and her replacement with a Deaf president, the resignation of the board president and a restructuring of the board to create a 51% majority of members who were Deaf, and that there be no reprisals against the protesters. By week's end, the board agreed to all the demands, and I. King Jordan became Gallaudet University's first Deaf president. (Jankowski, 1997)

In 2006 students again disagreed with the selection of a new president, staging protests and voicing their concerns. It was evident nearly 20 years later that Deaf people considered themselves empowered to influence events and institutions.

Sources: Marschark, Lang, & Albertini, 2002; http://www.aslinfo.com/trivia.cfm; retrieved 6/14/2005.

REFLECTION If you were a student at Gallaudet University in 1987, do you believe having a Deaf president would have been important to you? Why or why not?

It should be acknowledged that deaf persons do not all agree that a Deaf community and culture exist, and if it does exist, they do not agree on whether it is beneficial to deaf persons. However, the perceptions of those who consider themselves to be members of the Deaf culture can and do affect how they view themselves, regardless of how others might view them. Children and youths who are deaf or hard of hearing must find their own identities, which may be rooted in association with a group. For example, "a deaf person who has attended hearing schools may absorb the standard view of deafness as a disability, while, in contrast, the culture within the school for the deaf may facilitate the construction of identity as a culturally Deaf person" (Andrews et al., 2004, p. 171; Bat-Chava, 2000). Students who are deaf may also assume a bicultural identity in which they are comfortable with both hearing and Deaf cultures (Andrews et al., 2004).

Also, important can be the perception of others, particularly teachers who are not familiar with hearing loss and Deaf culture. An educator unfamiliar with ASL might view a child whose primary language is ASL as being deficient in or lacking language skills (Liddel, 2003), which is not the case. ASL and other sign languages are legitimate and distinct human languages. ASL can be analyzed and studied linguistically as can vocally produced languages. It has distinct grammar and conventions. This recognition as a distinct language was a watershed for Deaf people (Liddel, 2003).

Some individuals who are hard of hearing may find themselves not quite fully members of a hearing or Deaf community. Such a dilemma may be avoided by educating

ALLISON REVISITED What are some issues Allison might encounter in developing her own sense of identity in school as a result of her hearing loss?

individuals who are hard of hearing as bilingual-bicultural students, focusing on both ASL and English communication skills, and actively promoting both Deaf and hearing cultures (Grushkin, 2003). It is equally important to recognize that those who consider themselves members of the Deaf culture may perceive their particular characteristics quite differently from those who are hearing.

Intellectual Characteristics

In years past, the cognitive abilities of deaf people were thought to be lower than those of hearing people. However, this may have been due to how cognitive ability was assessed (Maller, 2003). Because of difficulties in using assessment instruments designed for hearing persons with those with significant hearing loss, it is somewhat challenging to assess the intellectual characteristics of deaf students (Simeonsson, Wax, & White, 2001). Deaf and hearing people score similarly on nonverbal tests of intelligence (Maller, 2003). Also, studies have indicated that children who are deaf or hard of hearing who are tested on performance IQ scales and are given directions both verbally and through manual language score better than those who received instructions verbally, through pantomime, and visual aids (Simeonsson et al., 2001).

A majority of studies have indicated that in terms of perception, learning, and memory, there are no significant differences between hearing children and those who are deaf (Moores, 2001). In fact, Moores pointed out that most professionals with experience with deaf children "rely more heavily on their own experiences and insights than on the reports of scientists who assess a limited range of behaviors . . . without bothering to acquaint themselves with the field or to acquire the communication skills necessary to interact fluently with deaf children and adults" (p. 166). It is clear that, as a group, students who are deaf are not intellectually deficient (Moores, 2001).

Academic Characteristics

Standardized testing remains the single most commonly used method for assessing and comparing the achievement of students with hearing losses to that of hearing peers (Moores, 2001). In their review of the literature on achievement testing, Karchmer and Mitchell (2003) found that deaf students and those who were hard of hearing score lower than hearing peers in achievement. However, such analyses of overall achievement may not adequately account for other variables such as gender, socio-economic class, and language proficiency (Karchmer & Mitchell, 2003).

Of considerable importance in school and later in life are the abilities to read, store what is read, retrieve that information, and use it in meaningful ways. Low reading comprehension is a problem area for many deaf students although this does not mean deaf students cannot learn to read or comprehend grade-level material (Kelly, 2003). Learning to read and write is a greater challenge for most students who are deaf than for hearing students (Moores, 2001). Children who grow up with ASL as their first language may find themselves learning another language (English) while simultaneously learning to read and write—not an easy task (Andrews et al., 2004).

Many students with hearing losses maintain at or above grade-level work, and the functional reading and writing abilities of students who are deaf or hard of hearing are likely higher than standardized achievement tests detect (Moores, 2001). It is also important to understand that literacy development is linked to language development and that early exposure to both ASL, if appropriate based on hearing loss, and English provides the strongest foundation for the development of literacy skills (Marschark et al., 2002). With early intervention, children who are deaf or hard of hearing can learn the prerequisite skills necessary for acquiring reading and writing skills at school age (Andrews et al., 2004). Literacy instruction is likely to be a major emphasis for students with hearing losses in the 21st century (Stewart & Kluwin, 2001).

Mathematic skills can also be a problem area for some students who are deaf or hard of hearing. Any difficulties are more likely the result of delays in language, knowledge and skills in mathematical procedures, and experience rather than cognitive delays. Language comprehension is recognized as having a pivotal role in mathematics comprehension as well (Hyde, Zevenbergen, & Power, 2003). Another reason

FOUNDATIONS

math difficulties may be present is that students who are deaf may spend less time in math instruction, as well as in other content areas such as science, than do hearing children, as literacy development is often a major focus (Moores, 2001).

Speech and Language Characteristics

Speech and language characteristics can vary widely among students who are deaf or hard of hearing. These are affected by variables such as the age of onset of the hearing loss, type and degree of hearing loss, and language experiences at home and in school. A student who has congenital deafness and whose parents are deaf may have very different speech and language characteristics than another student whose deafness is acquired postlingually and whose family uses spoken language as the primary mode of communication.

Speech Characteristics. Blamey (2003) concluded that the spoken language of some students who are deaf or hard of hearing may be delayed in comparison to that of hearing students. This may be, at least in part, due to delays in being fitted for assistive listening devices such as hearing aids and cochlear implants. However, because assistive listening devices do not provide "normal" hearing in many instances, direct intervention in speech skills is necessary if these are to be developed. Overall, through early intervention, direct instruction, and the use of listening aids, many students who are deaf or hard of hearing can and do achieve intelligible and age-appropriate speech (Blamey, 2003).

Language Characteristics. Language is the means by which we communicate, learn from others, and access much of the information we need to succeed in school and life. Marschark et al. (2002) pointed out that language development is influenced by the early home/language environment. Many children who are deaf are born to nonsigning, hearing parents and may be exposed primarily or exclusively to spoken language that they cannot perceive. If not exposed to a fully accessible language during the early critical developmental period, children who are deaf or hard of hearing may develop language delays and be less well prepared for learning to read and write upon entering school (Marschark et al., 2002). Compounding the issue is a lack of knowledge and skill in assessing and working with families with cultural and linguistic differences; these families may use a spoken language other than English as well as ASL or other forms of manual communication (Hwa-Froelich & Vigil, 2004). For a child to develop the readiness skills to succeed when

Although lower reading skills can be an issue, many students who are deaf and hard of hearing are at, or above, grade level academically.

entering school, language development requires consistent exposure to a language that is accessible, either manually or orally (Marschark et al., 2002). It should be emphasized that ASL is a natural language that children who are deaf acquire in a typical and predictable fashion and that those who do acquire ASL at an early age may perform better academically than deaf students who do not learn ASL at an early age (Drasgow, 1998).

Social and Emotional Characteristics

Individuals who are deaf "run the gamut from those who are psychologically healthy, with positive self-perceptions and strong identities, to those who struggle" (Andrews et al., 2004, p. 199). Teachers should consider the strengths of these students and how well they learn to cope in complex school and community environments. Calderon and Greenberg (2003) noted that some children who are deaf may demonstrate deficits in the mastery of social-emotional skill development, which can lead to poor outcomes including low academic achievement, underemployment, and higher rates of problems with drug and alcohol abuse, as well as psychological issues. As language is necessary to mediate and negotiate social situations and to handle emotions, lack of language skills may contribute to any deficits in social-emotional skills. The lack of these language skills could result in impulsivity and less well developed emotional regulation (Calderon & Greenberg, 2003). Providing guidance to parents on how to establish an appropriate and supportive environment for young children who are deaf is a challenge for professionals because an adequate research base establishing best practices in this area is lacking (Traci & Koester, 2003). Calderon and Greenberg (2003) stated that children with hearing losses who are experiencing difficulties "can become socially and emotionally competent if given the same opportunities as hearing children to develop self-awareness, independent thinking, and good problem-solving skills over the course of their development" (p. 186).

Future teachers need to understand the diversity of characteristics among students who are deaf or hard of hearing, be aware of problem areas that may exist, and understand that these students possess strengths and abilities that allow them to be successful in both Deaf and hearing cultures. Of particular importance are understanding cultural differences and developing language skills. Because language skills are so critical in all aspects of life, establishing what skills a student has and needs is paramount in providing an appropriate education. Academics, cognitive skills, social skills, and emotional regulation are all influenced by the adequacy of language skills, whether they are English or ASL skills.

Check Your Understanding

1. What are the main types of causes of hearing losses?
2. Which causes tend to produce conductive, sensorineural, or mixed hearing losses?
3. What is the Deaf culture and what role does it play in the lives of many individuals who are deaf or hard of hearing?
4. What are the intellectual, academic, speech and language, and social-emotional characteristics of students who are deaf or hard of hearing?

How Are Students Who Are Deaf or Hard of Hearing Identified?

Identification of hearing problems is typically made by a medical professional. Identifying newborns and young children may require special assessment procedures. The identification of older children is typically done through an audiometric evaluation. Whenever a child is identified as being deaf or hard of hearing, parents may want to consider genetic testing and counseling to learn more about their child's condition. However, such testing may not be desirable to members of Deaf culture. Also, genetic testing and counseling can reveal unwanted information. It may be best used as a means to confirm a condition that leads to hearing loss (Arnos, 2002; Smith & Robin, 2002).

Identification of Newborns and Young Children Who Are Deaf or Hard of Hearing

Relevant CEC Standards

▶ Specialized terminology used in assessing individuals who are deaf or hard of hearing (DH8K1)

▶ Specialized procedures for evaluation, eligibility, placement, and program planning for individuals who are deaf or hard of hearing (DH8K2)

If a child is deaf or severely hard of hearing, preliminary identification, confirming that some kind of hearing problem does in fact exist, is usually done by parents or pediatricians. Once a hearing problem is suspected, professionals may use certain procedures to aid in identification that involve observing the child's responses to sounds in controlled environments, the use of electroencephalogram readings in response to sounds, and evaluating the cochlea responses to sounds transmitted inside the ear (Cone-Wesson, 2003; Herer et al., 2002). Assessing speech perception is also important (Cone-Wesson, 2003).

Identification of School-Aged Students Who Are Deaf or Hard of Hearing

For those children who have less severe hearing losses, preliminary identification may be delayed until they go through a screening program in school or begin to experience difficulty with schoolwork. Certain symptomatic behaviors can indicate that a child may have a hearing loss or problem. These include the following:

1. Complaints by the child about the ears
2. Frequent infections of the ear, nose, or throat
3. Speech articulation problems
4. Embarrassment about participating in oral interactive school activities
5. Frequent requests by the child to have a verbal message repeated or said more loudly
6. Problems attending to the normal conversation of others (Stephens, Blackhurst, & Magliocca, 1982)

When a hearing loss is suspected, medical evaluations may point to treatment. Along with a medical evaluation, an audiometric evaluation can be used to determine the type and degree of hearing loss as well as the ability to understand speech (Falvo, 2005). Falvo outlined four types of testing used in an audiometric evaluation. In terms of initial testing, pure-tone tests are usually conducted once a hearing loss is suspected. Pure-tone tests help to determine the degree and type of hearing loss present. Two types of tests are possible. In a pure-tone air test, or pure-tone audiogram, sounds of different pitches and different loudness levels are transmitted, usually through earphones, directly into the ear. This test is often used to determine if there may be a conductive, sensorineural, or mixed hearing loss. Speech reception threshold and speech discrimination threshold tests help to determine at what decibel level a student can hear speech and, once loud enough, how well the student can understand the speech. That is, a student with a hearing loss could perceive speech but still not understand some or all of it (Falvo, 2005). Audiologists, personnel trained in the assessment and remediation of hearing loss, conduct audiometric evaluations and are also helpful in identifying what, if any, type of amplification device a student may need.

Assessment of the Effect on Educational Performance

Because identification of students under IDEA 04 requires evidence that the hearing loss adversely affects educational performance, assessment of intellectual and academic abilities should occur in addition to validation that a hearing loss exists. Maller (2003) outlined several potential problems in testing:

- Translating test directions or items without following special procedures.
- Administering any test without evidence of the test's validity for the purpose intended.
- Using tests for deaf students who have additional disabilities that interfere with their performance.
- Reporting verbal intelligence scores within the body of a psychological report. There is a lack of evidence that these scales are valid for use with deaf students.

- Using verbal intelligence test scores as predictors of academic achievement in deaf students.
- Not considering diversity issues in test administration.
- Analyzing test profiles of deaf students in the absence of normative comparison groups. Some tests, such as the Stanford Achievement Test, do have norms available for deaf children (Stewart & Kluwin, 2001; Maller, 2003).

There continues to be a lack of research into the psychometric properties and validity of norm-referenced testing for deaf students. In general, when tests are used to obtain information about a deaf student, administration and interpretation of results are best done by a deaf practitioner or one very familiar with the population (Brice, 2002).

It is also important to note that students who are hard of hearing may have unique needs as well. Although from an educational perspective these students should be able to process linguistic information through hearing, it may be unwise for an evaluator to assume the student is able to hear and process all information sufficiently to perform her or his best on an assessment. Therefore, some techniques, such as the use of gestures or combinations of sign and spoken English, may be necessary for some students (Moores, 2001).

ALLISON REVISITED What might be some important considerations in administering assessment instruments to Allison?

Check Your Understanding

1. What types of hearing assessments are used with younger children?
2. How can genetic testing and counseling be used? What are some issues that arise from such procedures?
3. What are the components of an audiometric evaluation?
4. What are potential problems in administering assessments to students who are deaf or hard of hearing?

What and How Do I Teach Students Who Are Deaf or Hard of Hearing?

As noted previously, whether a student and her or his family consider themselves to be members of the Deaf community and culture can have some bearing on what and how a student who is deaf or hard of hearing is taught. Future teachers should remember that one can assume a medical model approach, meaning students are viewed as deficient and disabled, or one can assume a cultural approach, wherein students are viewed as different but capable and successful (Moores, 2001).

Relevant CEC Standard
▶ Models, theories, and philosophies that provide the basis for educational practice for individuals who are deaf or hard of hearing (DH1K2)

Instructional Content

It is important that an IEP team make individualized decisions concerning how best to educate a student who is deaf or hard of hearing. As team members, teachers will work with students, families, and related services personnel such as an audiologist or an itinerant teacher of students who are deaf or hard of hearing in determining what is an appropriate education. Most students will be learning the same curriculum as hearing students but still may need alternative educational objectives and procedures (Stewart & Kluwin, 2001). Content area subjects, literacy skill development, and transition are all important areas of consideration in determining curriculum.

Content Areas

The need to effectively communicate with others, socially interact, and to use those skills to build satisfying childhood, adolescence, and adult lives is a major consideration in developing an appropriate education for students who are deaf or hard of hearing.

Most students who are deaf or hard of hearing learn the same curriculum as hearing students, though some may need differentiated educational objectives.

Literacy skill development is a critical area to develop these abilities (Stewart & Kluwin, 2001). However, content areas such as science, math, and social studies should also receive emphasis (Moores, 2001). "Effective curriculum design for this group requires consideration of a wide range of learning characteristics that, in turn, determine specialized and individualized curriculum objectives. The goal of such differentiated objectives is not to achieve differentiated objectives but to ensure achievement of the same overall learning outcomes as all other students" (Power & Leigh, 2003, pp. 48–49).

It is important for teachers to expand the curriculum objectives in traditional content areas to include objectives related to cognitive and language development (Stinson & Kluwin, 2003). Stinson and Kluwin offered several considerations for instruction in the traditional content areas. Teachers should not rely on rote skill development, such as in math, but more on constructivist approaches that challenge students to think and apply skills and learn relationships among different curriculum areas. Adult-mediated, highly interactive learning in authentic contexts will aid students who lack the experiential background that hearing peers may possess (Stinson & Kluwin, 2003). The Classroom Example shows how objectives for a mathematics lesson might be modified for a student with a significant hearing loss.

Literacy

Literacy skill development should occur within the larger context of life (Marschark et al., 2002). Bowe (2002b) pointed out several areas that can assist in literacy development. Students who are deaf or hard of hearing need early intervention. Adults should use the child's interests to help in this early literacy development. For example, playing with a block could lead to the use of words and signs such as *hand*, the color of the block, *square*, and *hard*. Also, parents or teachers could use self-talk, explaining what they are doing and how they make decisions, to provide models of language use. Students in school need instruction and experiential opportunities in vocabulary development that emphasize how vocabulary is linked to everyday life. They need repeated opportunities for reading aloud, or signed reading, to build fluency. Teachers should use miscue analysis of students' language usage to determine what rules they use to construct messages and express ideas. Teachers can then analyze how students use word attack skills. Instruction in phonics and phonemic awareness can be helpful, but must be considered as supplemental for some students who are deaf and unable to hear the sounds of human speech. Students also need instruction in how to comprehend what they have read, remember that information, and communicate the information to others when needed

Standard: Geometry and Spatial Sense

1st Grade Level Indicators: Spatial Relationships

Overall Unit Objectives:

The typical student will be able to:

1. Extend the use of location words to include distance (such as near, far, close) and directional words (such as left, right).
2. Copy figures and draw simple two-dimensional shapes from memory.

The student with a significant hearing loss will be able to:

1. Use location signs in ASL to indicate distance (such as near, far, close) and direction (such as left, right).
2. Be able to identify written English words indicating distance and demonstrate understanding of those words.
3. Following a model and directions given in ASL, copy figures and draw simple two-dimensional shapes from memory.

Other Accommodations

The student's tasks will focus on functional activities in addition to typical learning activities (such as indicating distance of a speaker and whether it is necessary to move closer); being able to draw the shapes of road signs needed later for navigating a neighborhood (yield sign/triangle).

Assessment Accommodations

Performance-based assessments will be used to demonstrate understanding of concepts as well as any paper-pencil assessments or assessments in ASL. For example, the student will physically demonstrate distances from a speaker such as near, far, and close.

(Bowe, 2002b). The Classroom Suggestions feature on the next page lists questions to consider when planning instruction for students who are deaf or hard of hearing.

Deaf Studies

Another area of importance can be that of Deaf studies. While there is more than one approach to Deaf studies, Stewart & Kluwin (2001) emphasized that an integrated approach can address deaf, hard of hearing, and hearing students' learning. Deaf studies can assist in developing community, self-image, and recognition of diversity (Stewart & Kluwin, 2001). In an integrated approach, all students learn about hearing loss, Deaf culture, and sign language as appropriate in various curriculum areas (Stewart & Kluwin, 2001). For example, students could learn about the use of technology to assist students with hearing losses in science; learn about ASL in literacy classes; and learn about the history of Deaf culture in social studies.

Finally, Stewart and Kluwin (2001) describe several areas important in the curriculum for students who are deaf or hard of hearing:

- Authentic experiences, particularly in language development, to help make connections to the real world. Students who are deaf or hard of hearing may not have had the same experiential background as hearing students.
- Vocabulary development addressed in context and words that are taught as part of everyday life, in conversation, and in developing concepts.
- Self-expression opportunities "to practice elaborate verbal skills . . . [and] for definition and refinement of ideas" (p. 13).
- Deaf role models to provide positive images about deaf adults and to provide a model of success and achievement rather than one of limitations.

❑ How does the student communicate? If communication skills are not developing appropriately, then the IEP team may need to reconsider placement, language, and mode of communication.

❑ To what does the student respond? The student should be able to respond to both oral and visual information adequately.

❑ What were the student's early communication experiences? If a child did not experience adequate communication early in life, then this may have repercussions for overall development as well as how the student is taught.

❑ How can educators make communication visually accessible to the student? Use of visual materials can ensure the student is receiving accurate content information in clear and comprehensible ways.

❑ Does the student interact with peers? The student should be able to express thoughts, feelings, and needs, as well as to interact socially with peers.

❑ Will the family be able to do the same things at home that are done at school? Mismatches in the language use at home and school can delay language development. Parents may need assistance in learning techniques used in school if they choose to defer to the choices made by educators.

❑ What are the expectations of the family for the student? The cultural and overall family aspirations for the student should be taken into account in the IEP and instructional procedures.

❑ Do the student's teachers have the necessary skills to instruct the student? Because communication skills are so important, all parties involved need to be prepared for the language and mode of communication that the IEP team determines is most appropriate for the student.

Source: Easterbrooks, S. R., & Baker, S. K. (2001). Enter the matrix! *Teaching Exceptional Children, 33*(3), 70–76.

Transition Planning

As discussed throughout this text, the period of transition from school to adult life is a crucial one. This is especially true for those with significant hearing losses. Adjustment to postsecondary education or to employment can present new and different challenges. Recent studies suggest as many as 25,000 deaf students and those who are hard of hearing attend U.S. colleges and universities (Schroedel, Watson, & Ashmore, 2003). Although accommodations should be available as mandated by the Americans with Disabilities Act and vocational rehabilitation legislation, students who are hard of hearing do not always seek them, perhaps due to denial of their hearing loss, particularly if it is a relatively mild one.

Bonds (2003) identified several key factors in establishing curricula to better prepare students who are deaf or hard of hearing for college or work:

- The curriculum available to general education students should be accessible to those with hearing losses.
- Assessment of areas such as achievement levels and social-emotional adjustment should be done in reliable and valid ways.
- Career interests and aptitudes need to be adequately assessed. Student interests are a key component of transition and career planning.
- Career fairs and field trips should be used.
- Opportunities for career education should allow students to study all aspects of a career or industry.
- Internships and apprenticeships should be available to students with professionals in the community.
- Expectations should be kept high, and there should be a focus on students being self-motivated.
- A sense of reality should be maintained. Effort should be recognized, but students need to understand the competitive and challenging nature of postsecondary life.

Instructional Procedures

There are various approaches to providing instruction to students who are deaf or hard of hearing. Future teachers should be aware of these approaches and why students and their families may prefer one approach to another. There are three types of instructional approaches differentiated by the communication modes used in each: oralism, bilingual-bicultural, and total communication. Each has its merits and challenges.

Oralism is an approach that emphasizes the development of speech, speechreading, and listening with amplification. **Speechreading,** sometimes referred to as lipreading, involves the ability to consider the situational context, facial expressions, gestures, body language, and lip and tongue movements to try to determine what a speaker is saying. ASL is not emphasized in oralism; the development of language skills in English and the use of English in instruction and communication are dominant (Fiedler, 2001). Advocates of this approach might stress that learning and using oral language promotes social integration in a hearing society (Marschark et al., 2002). This approach may be preferred for some students who can hear adequately with amplification or cochlear implants. Developing the sounds of speech is a significant challenge for students who are congenitally deaf and who may not have "fully intelligible" speech even after extensive training (Marschark et al., 2002).

Another option for students and families is the *bilingual-bicultural* approach, sometimes referred to as the bi-bi approach, which emphasizes the early use of ASL as the deaf child's natural language (Fiedler, 2001). In school, ASL is the language of instruction, and English is taught through reading and writing. **Fingerspelling** may also be used with ASL. Fingerspelling involves the use of 26 different finger/hand positions denoting each letter of the alphabet. Users of ASL fingerspell words for which there is no sign or the sign is unknown. Both ASL and English are valued as languages as are Deaf and hearing cultures (Fiedler, 2001). Some experts believe that "sign language can play a positive role in the educational, social, and personal development of most deaf children" (Marschark et al., 2002, p. 104). English is a second language for these students. This approach could also incorporate cued speech and signed English (Pittman & Huefner, 2001). **Cued speech** is supplemental to spoken English as many sounds in the language look quite similar on the lips. Cued speech involves the use of 36 different manual cues to aid in distinguishing between the 44 sounds in oral English. There are manual cues for vowels and consonants and their combinations (Marschark et al., 2002). **Signing Exact English** (SEE) was developed to aid deaf students in learning English. It combines existing ASL signs with new signs specifically to create a manual code to aid in understanding English. This manual code represents English on the hands (Pittman & Huefner, 2001). SEE is also an important tool in the third instructional approach, total communication.

Finally, the *total communication* approach focuses on using the student's preferred mode of communication. It can include oral and auditory approaches as well as speechreading, sign language, and other manual systems (Fiedler, 2001). In school, instruction may involve the simultaneous use of ASL and spoken English, as well as the use of amplification as appropriate. Deaf students might benefit from other aspects of this approach after first having become proficient in ASL as their primary language (Marschark et al., 2002).

Fiedler (2001) pointed out that there is no single best educational approach and that family history and characteristics may influence which approach is preferred. For example, most deaf students have hearing parents. These parents might prefer the oral or total communication approaches because of their significant emphasis on learning spoken English. Similarly, families that use both ASL and English for communication might prefer the total communication method. Also, families who have opted for cochlear implantation might prefer a method that stresses oral language skills. Families in the Deaf culture might prefer the bilingual-bicultural approach (Fiedler, 2001). A collaborative team of professionals, the student, and the student's family should determine which approach is preferable from instructional and cultural perspectives.

 Relevant CEC Standards

► Instructional strategies for teaching individuals who are deaf or hard of hearing (DH4K3)

► Communication features salient to the individual who is deaf or hard of hearing that are necessary to enhance cognitive, emotional, and social development (DH6K1)

► Components of nonlinguistic and linguistic communication used by individuals who are deaf or hard of hearing (DH6K4)

speechreading The process of considering the situational context, facial expressions, gesture, body language, and lip and tongue movements to try to determine what a speaker is saying.

fingerspelling Uses 26 different finger/hand positions to denote each letter of the alphabet.

cued speech Uses 36 different manual cues to aid in distinguishing among the 44 sounds of oral English. Cues can represent vowels, consonants, or a combination.

signing exact English Combines existing ASL signs with new signs to create a code to help deaf students learn English. This code represents oral English through hand movements.

PRACTICE

What Are Other Instructional Considerations for Teaching Students Who Are Deaf or Hard of Hearing?

Relevant CEC Standards

▶ Processes for establishing ongoing interactions of individuals who are deaf or hard of hearing with peers and role models who are deaf or hard of hearing (DH5K1)

▶ Learner opportunities for interaction with communities of individuals who are deaf or hard of hearing on local, state, and national levels (DH5K2)

Both the instructional environment chosen and instructional technology used are critical in the delivery of services to students who are deaf or hard of hearing. Deaf cultural beliefs and values can have a significant impact on where and with whom students are educated. Regardless of whether students are educated in a separate or general education classroom, certain environmental arrangements can assist student learning. The use of technology to aid listening and communication, as well as to access visual information, can support student learning. Teachers should be aware of how to use such technology when students are included or when teaching in a special class or school for students who are deaf or hard of hearing.

The Instructional Environment

The consideration of the least restrictive environment can take on a new dimension due to the emphasis on Deaf culture among some students who are deaf or hard of hearing. Different preferences than the typical inclusive classroom may emerge for particular students and their families. We discuss these possible preferences along with benefits of inclusion and those of special schools for those who are deaf. We also explore special environmental arrangements for students who are deaf or hard of hearing. The need to access information aurally or visually makes arrangement of the environment an important consideration.

The Least Restrictive Environment

When an IEP team is deciding the least restrictive environment for students who are deaf or hard of hearing, there are several considerations (Stinson & Kluwin, 2003). First, the team must consider whether the student should be included in the general education classroom with appropriate accommodations and collaboration among general and special education teachers, and related services personnel. Second, the team must consider whether the student should attend a special class for students who are deaf or hard of hearing or receive services in a resource room in a neighborhood school. Another possible placement option is co-enrollment classes, which "include both deaf and hearing students, ideally in equal numbers, and a curriculum taught in both sign language and the vernacular" (Stinson & Kluwin, 2003, p. 54). Finally, students could be placed in a special school for students who are deaf or hard of hearing. Advantages in residential schools include the provision of role models who are deaf or hard of hearing, peers who are fluent in ASL and can use the language for social engagement, and accommodations and adaptations for students who are deaf or hard of hearing are standard fare (Marschark et al., 2002).

Fiedler (2001) outlined several overall considerations in determining the least restrictive environment for deaf students or those who are hard of hearing:

- The communication needs of the student including use of residual hearing, communication mode, and what the student needs to communicate
- Language and the communication mode, including proficiency in spoken and written English as well as manual communication

- Academic level, including current skill levels and whether the student is able to work at the same level as hearing peers
- Other needs, including socialization and academic development as well as the student's current developmental level
- Opportunities for instruction in the student's language and communication mode, including whether the student can effectively communicate with adults and peers

Student and Family Preferences

Parents face difficult decisions as team members considering the best placement options for their child. These decisions can have implications for long-term achievement and adult success (Marschark et al., 2002). Some have suggested that sufficient research is lacking to summarily conclude that the inclusion of deaf students fosters their integration into the larger mainstream of hearing society (Marschark et al, 2002). This does not mean that such placements might not be preferable. To date, differences among deaf students in achievement have not been adequately explained simply by comparing the type of placement in which students were educated (Stinson & Kluwin, 2003). It may be that students who prefer particular programs, such as special schools or inclusive classrooms, possess certain characteristics that make such programs a good match, confounding researchers in determining whether one environment is preferable over another (Marschark et al., 2002). Finally, a review of studies examining differences between deaf students placed in segregated classrooms versus inclusive classrooms suggested no specific conclusion can be drawn regarding which environment might lead to better developmental and academic outcomes (Kluwin, Stinson, & Colarossi, 2002).

Environmental Arrangements

Educators must consider the degree and type of hearing loss and how this could affect the student's physical placement in the classroom. Collaboration among all team members, possibly including an audiologist, interpreter, general and special education teachers, as well as the student and family, is critical in ensuring that the environment will support the student who is deaf or hard of hearing. Student and parent preferences can influence the decision concerning what is the least restrictive environment. The Classroom Example on the next page features a checklist that an older student with a hearing loss might use to determine how well he or she can access the learning activities in the classroom.

Luckner, Bowen, and Carter (2001) provided specific suggestions for use of materials and the physical environment to assist students who are deaf or hard of hearing. These suggestions place important emphases on use of visual cues, organization, and routines to assist students in understanding what is happening in the classroom and what is being learned:

- Choose visuals the students will easily recognize.
- Use larger-size materials with younger students.
- Use a variety of visual materials such as line drawings, detailed pictures, written words, and photographs among others.
- Post classroom rules.
- Keep posted classroom job choices and menus.
- Use transition time cards/charts to establish and maintain routines.
- Keep task organizers posted or available that outline steps needed to complete tasks.
- Post or give students daily schedules.
- Use and teach students to use Internet resources.
- Provide graphic organizers for content.
- Show hierarchical, conceptual, sequential, and cyclical patterns in learning.

Of some importance as well is the use of interpreters in the classroom environment. Stewart and Kluwin (2001) suggested consideration of where the interpreter will be located, whether the teacher and students will be stationary or moving about, how well each party can see the others, and whether interpreters should have advance knowledge about the educational activities and content.

9 Weeks Grading Period _____

Location of Classroom _____

Teacher's Name _____

Content Area Class _____

As a student, please check each area for each content area class and teacher.

	Yes	No
I have explained to my teacher that I have a hearing loss.	_____	_____
I have communicated with my teacher regarding accommodations I need.	_____	_____
I have explained how I best communicate.	_____	_____
My seat provides me with the best access to visual materials.	_____	_____
My seat provides me with the best access to oral presentations.	_____	_____
My seat provides me with the best access to peers' contributions.	_____	_____
I have obtained access to all technology I need for this class.	_____	_____
I have ensured maintenance of any personal technology (e.g., hearing aid).	_____	_____
I have communicated with my interpreter as needed regarding assistance.	_____	_____
I have communicated with my note taker as needed regarding assistance.	_____	_____
I understand the assignments expected of me for this class.	_____	_____

ALLISON REVISITED What would be some considerations for Allison's general education and itinerant teacher (who provides services to students at different schools) in providing accommodations during instruction?

Schick (2004) pointed out that providing a good education to students who are deaf or hard of hearing means more than just providing an interpreter. The general education and special education teachers must work with the interpreter as a team member to ensure learning is occurring. The interpreter is not likely to have training in assessing student learning but can provide information based on his or her observations. The teachers should ensure active participation of the student, not leaving it to the interpreter to make the connections alone. The teachers should collaborate with the interpreter to promote integration of the student in the classroom and to determine to what extent the student feels a part of the class culture and activities. Finally, school personnel should ensure that any interpreter is trained and qualified. A student's learning difficulties could be the result of the limitations of an inadequately trained interpreter (Schick, 2004)).

Instructional Technology

Relevant CEC Standard
▶ Strategies for stimulating and using residual hearing (DH6K8)

The use of instructional technology has significant implications for students who are deaf or hard of hearing. The use of technology for these students can be conceived as having at least three major facets. First, technology use can be motivating as well as entertaining. Second, technology use can support, but does not guarantee, better learning. Third, technology is likely to be used by students in the future (Stewart & Kluwin, 2001). Students need to learn about the available technology as well as how to use it (Stewart & Kluwin, 2001). In general, technology can be viewed as a means to improve hearing and listening or to improve visual communication (Harkins & Bakke, 2003). In addition, computer technologies can be used to directly support student learning.

Hearing Technologies

A range of technologies has been developed to improve individuals' abilities to hear. The technologies most frequently used are hearing aids, loop systems, and cochlear implants.

Hearing Aids. A hearing aid is an electronic device powered by a battery that amplifies and changes sound. Hearing aids receive sound through a microphone, convert the sound waves to electrical signals, and then amplify the signals and send the sound to the ear through a speaker. Hearing aids do not restore normal hearing, nor do they eliminate all background noise. Some issues hearing aid users might encounter include noise reduction, loudness control, and feedback reduction. More modern digital hearing aids can be especially helpful in dealing with these problems (Harkins & Bakke, 2003). Adjusting hearing aids for successful use in school and the community takes time and patience (NIDCD, 2007a). Table 8.3 summarizes the four basic styles of hearing aids as well as the three types of circuitry available in hearing aids.

Some students who are deaf or hard of hearing may need interpreter services in their classrooms. Interpreters are important team members but should not be responsible for ensuring a student is comprehending all material.

TABLE 8.3	Types of Hearing Aids and Circuitries
TYPES OF HEARING AIDS	
Behind the ear	Fits behind ear; often used with younger children; uses an ear mold that fits into the ear canal to transmit amplified sounds
In the ear	Fits completely in the outer ear; must be replaced as child grows older so is more often used with older children and adults; more difficult to remove and adjust
In the canal	Fits in the ear canal itself; inconspicuous but must also be replaced as ear grows; more difficult to remove and adjust
Implantable hearing aid	Are implanted and can be helpful for individuals with chronic ear canal or middle ear problems; can aid when other hearing aids are less helpful due to chronic ear problems (such as otitis media)
TYPES OF CIRCUITRIES	
Analog/conventional	Audiologist determines volume and other specifications such as pitch adjustments; least expensive type of circuitry
Analog/programmable	Audiologist uses a computer to program the hearing aid; can be programmed such that child can change program to adjust to different listening conditions
Digital/programmable	Audiologist uses a computer to program the hearing aid; can be adjusted for sound quality and response time for the individual; most flexible and adjustable, as well as most expensive type of circuitry

Source: Alexander Graham Bell Association for the Deaf and Hard of Hearing (n.d.).

PRACTICE

Hearing aids can be selected with the help of an audiologist. The audiologist will take into account the individual's hearing ability, school and home activities, physical challenges, medical issues, and cosmetic preferences. Cost can be a factor as well as whether the individual needs a single aid or two hearing aids (NIDCD, 2007a). The degree of hearing loss and the loss at various frequencies are important considerations in achieving a best-fit hearing aid for an individual (Harkins & Bakke, 2003). Teachers who have students with hearing aids should have some understanding of their use and adjustment.

Many students with a hearing loss will use a hearing aid or other amplification system.

A problem area in the use of hearing aids is their maintenance. Malfunction rates can be quite high among students who may lack information about hearing aids and their use and maintenance. Intervention programs to correct these problems have been successful (Most, 2002).

Loop systems allow teachers to speak into a microphone and directly transmit their speech to the student with a hearing loss.

Loop Systems. Loop systems, also known as FM systems, are used in classrooms throughout the country (Marschark et al., 2002). A loop system is a closed circuit system that allows FM signals from an audio system to be sent to an electronic coil in a hearing aid. The receiver in the hearing aid picks up the signals and sends the sounds to the listener. Loop systems can be especially useful in large classrooms, lecture halls, or other situations with substantial background noise or where there may be distance between a speaker and listener (Marschark et al., 2002). The teacher wears a microphone that picks up her or his voice, and the FM signal created is transmitted to the hearing aid user, making speech more intelligible in the presence of competing environmental sounds.

Cochlear Implants. Cochlear implants have had tremendous impact in the treatment of sensorineural hearing losses (Eisen, 2006). Unlike hearing aids, cochlear implants bypass the hearing mechanisms in the ear itself and directly stimulate the auditory neurons of the inner ear (Harkins & Bakke, 2003). A cochlear implant consists of a microphone, a speech processor, a transmitter, and an internal receiver/stimulator connected to an electrode array in the inner ear. The microphone, which collects sound, is mounted on the user's head, behind the ear. In turn, the signal is passed on to the speech processor, also worn on the body. This processor is essentially a computer designed to convert the audio signals into a set of instructions for transmission to the internally worn receiver/stimulator for stimulating the electrodes in the inner ear. This processor must be individually fitted and adjusted. The devices can use different speech-processing strategies based on the preference of the individual or on what appears to work best in the case of younger children (Harkins & Bakke, 2003). Cochlear implants can aid understanding of speech alone or in conjunction with speech reading, although such outcomes are not guaranteed. The implants can also aid users in perceiving and understanding environmental sounds (Marschark et al., 2002).

Robbins (2003) suggested that the use of cochlear implants in profoundly deaf children younger than 3 years of age could yield benefits in communication development. The benefits derive from children experiencing an auditory environment at approximately the same age as a hearing child would, enabling the deaf child to develop communication skills at a similar age as hearing children. However, Robbins also pointed out that such early implantation presents challenges. From a medical standpoint, the use of anesthesia, the surgical techniques themselves, and the anatomy of young children present issues. From an audiological perspective, the clinician should determine that hearing aids are insufficient and the implant is needed. Accurately assessing the hearing of very young children can be problematic. After implantation, the audiologist must also be able to document the benefits of the device. From a parental viewpoint, making a decision for such an invasive procedure may be difficult, particularly if the child has recently endured a severe illness or if the parents are grieving following a diagnosis of deafness (Robbins, 2003). Cochlear implantation requires a team approach involving teachers, related services personnel, and medical personnel in determining the outcomes and management of the device (Archbold, 2006).

The availability of cochlear implants may appear to be a wonderful opportunity for hearing parents and their children with a hearing loss. If the implantation occurs early in life, proponents claim the child will more likely derive greater benefit (Archbold, 2006). Within the Deaf culture, however, questions have arisen about the appropriateness of such procedures. Some Deaf parents believe that deafness is not a disability but leads to differences in culture and language. Such parents point out that the evidence is not unequivocal that prelingually deaf children who receive implants greatly improve their speech and language development (Brice, 2002). There are also considerations regarding the invasiveness of the procedure, the need for extensive follow-up and therapy, and costs (Marschark et al., 2002). Some in the Deaf culture suggest that life with a cochlear implant leaves the individual neither fully hearing nor deaf, perhaps leading to issues in self-identity and one's place in the world. Although parents who are hearing might be less likely than Deaf parents to consider such issues in making a decision about implantation, it is important to note that hearing parents may not fully understand what it means to be deaf and that life as a Deaf person with identity in a Deaf culture is not simply life without hearing (Marschark et al., 2002).

Visual Communication Technologies

As we stated earlier, some uses of technology are intended to bypass the need for hearing and make information available visually. These can take several forms, including closed captioning, telecommunications relay services, faxes, instant messaging and e-mail, and Internet technology.

Closed Captioning. *Closed captioning* involves having spoken language in a video program typed along the bottom of a television screen so that an individual can read what is being said. Television manufacturers are now required to include a captioning decoder chip in all TV sets larger than 13 inches. Closed captioning can be turned off and on as desired. Closed captioning can be "built into" recorded programs or be available in real time for live programming (Harkins & Bakke, 2003).

Telecommunications Relay Service. Telecommunications Relay Service (TRS) uses an operator to facilitate communication primarily between deaf and hearing people (Harkins & Bakke, 2003). When an individual has a text telephone (TTY), he or she can call a central number and be connected to an operator. The operator places

PRACTICE

In Practice Meet Educator Carol Elder and Her Student Katie

I am an Early Childhood Special Education teacher in a preschool classroom and have been teaching preschool for 18 years. My educational background is Child Development and Interdisciplinary Early Childhood Education. Our preschool program is a collaborative effort that serves my state's at-risk 4-year-old population, 3- and 4-year-old children with disabilities, 3- and 4-year-old Head Start eligible children, and a small percent of 3- and 4-year-old children whose families pay tuition. We are located in a rural public elementary school setting, and our preschool classrooms are a blend of all four categories of preschoolers. The children with disabilities receive specially designed instruction within the regular classroom. There is no distinction between the children regardless of how they qualify for the program, and the classroom environment is truly an inclusive setting.

My student Katie is a 4-year-old child who has a hearing loss. Her developmental history reveals several neonatal risk factors for hearing loss. Unfortunately, her hearing loss was not diagnosed until her mother brought her to preschool for a developmental screening at age 3. Through collaboration with our speech-language pathologist (SLP), we concluded that she was not hearing us during screening. At that time, we suggested that her family seek the advice of an audiologist. His examination tions indicated a moderate to moderately severe loss. Further assessments indicated she had severe hearing loss in her right ear and a mild loss in her left ear. She was fitted for hearing aids at that time. These findings were quite difficult for Katie's family. We continued with our assessments to determine her current level of performance. The speech-language pathologist used the Preschool Language Scale to determine auditory comprehension and expressive language skills. Her family provided information about her communication development through parent language surveys, and I completed behavioral observations on her as she played in the preschool classroom. Time was crucial for the school and family to work together to "bombard" her with as much language as possible because the hearing loss appeared to be progressive.

Instructional Content and Procedures

In determining the instructional content and learning objectives for Katie, I used

the call and relays the conversations by typing the spoken words of a hearing person to the TTY of the deaf person and orally speaks the typed messages of the deaf person to the hearing person (Harkins & Bakke, 2003). The Americans with Disabilities Act of 1990 requires that this service be available 24 hours a day, 365 days a year.

TTY technology is being incorporated into personal computers, but this is not yet universally available. Computer technology would allow the user to create a call-management system that would allow for storage of directories, automatic dialing, storing of conversations, and other valuable options (Harkins & Bakke, 2003).

Fax Machines. Facsimiles of documents can be transmitted over telephone lines. This can be useful for both personal and other types of communication (e.g., legal information, forms) and is especially valuable when TTYs are not available, as may be the case in other countries (Harkins & Bakke, 2003).

Instant Messaging and E-mail. Instant messaging and e-mail have grown increasingly popular for both home use and in the workplace. This technology helps bypass the need for an operator in using a relay service. It also allows those communicating to interact more freely than with a relay service, and tends to be a faster form of communication (Bowe, 2002a).

the assessment results to determine appropriate goals for her. Then I connected these to the Early Childhood Standards that our state developed for use in the preschool programs. A long-term goal for her is to be able to speak/sign using appropriate forms, conventions, and styles to communicate ideas and information to different audiences for different purposes with 80% accuracy as evidenced by progress data, teacher observation, and standardized tests by the annual review date.

Short-term objectives are that she will

- hear and repeat separate sounds in words and play with sounds to create new words.
- use sentences averaging at least five to six words per utterance to express ideas and feelings.
- follow directions with more than two steps.
- answer questions with details.

Instructional procedures include the use of gestures, signs, and facial expressions as well as verbal language when communicating with Katie. I use music, songs, finger plays, books, puppets, props, and photos to teach many new concepts and American Sign Language. She is quite expressive herself and eager to learn many new signs daily. To assist her in successfully hear-

ing and repeating separate sounds in words, I use a sound/symbol program that incorporates sounds of letters with a picture of something that begins with that sound and ASL for the letter that makes the sound. She is learning these quickly and always attempts to make the sign and the sound of the letter presented. Pre- and postteaching communication skills with verbal language and signs are other strategies that have benefited her in the area of language comprehension. I use the Creative Curriculum to monitor continuous progression of skills.

Instructional Environment and Technology

In our preschool classroom, children are actively engaged in learning activities that are, for the most part, child directed, with certain portions of the day in teacher-directed activities. Katie enjoys the exploratory nature of our classroom and has learned the routine of our day. She often interacts with other children and also enjoys playing alongside others. Adaptations that have been made for Katie include the use of a personal FM system that is attached to her personal hearing aids. This enables her to attend to the speaker/teacher's voice as well as reduce background noises. Other modifications

include the use of sign labels on materials and other objects in the classroom and sign language instructional videotapes and computer software. As a team, we are working to make Katie's school and home environments places where she can be successful in learning to communicate with others.

Collaboration

Two deaf educators from the state's School for the Deaf visited our classroom as well as Katie's home, made recommendations, and gave us materials to use in teaching American Sign Language. Also, there are Web sites that give the sign in ASL and these are quite helpful. One, www.aslpro.com, offers free American Sign Language dictionaries, games, and other materials as well as materials for purchase.

I collaborate with the SLP and speech therapy is conducted in my classroom. The SLP conducts circle time two days per week and small group time four days a week in my classroom. This collaboration has proven to be most effective in improving the communication skills of the preschoolers in our program. It is also a wonderful opportunity for me to identify specific techniques and strategies to use with all the children in our program, and especially with those with communication disorders.

PRACTICE

Computer Technologies That Support Learning. Computer usage in general has great potential in helping students produce work and materials. The following computer programs can aid students who are deaf or hard of hearing (Stewart & Kluwin, 2001):

- Word processing programs can be of considerable assistance to students and teachers in the learning process. Grammar and spell check functions help students to produce written work with few errors. Word processors can also be useful for producing newsletters.
- Databases and spreadsheets can help teachers and students explore numerical concepts in visual ways. They help in organizing, analyzing, and presenting data visually. Students can create their own data sets and think about how to store, retrieve, and structure information for current and future use.
- Computer publishing software can assist students in creating finished written products for grading and presentations, as well as for personal use, such as a family calendar of events (Stewart & Kluwin, 2001).

Future teachers need to have the knowledge and skills to understand and maintain technology that is available to students who are deaf or hard of hearing. As the complexity and array of technology increase, this will be a demanding area in which to maintain that knowledge and those skills.

1. What are possible instructional environments for students who are deaf or hard of hearing?

2. What are some considerations for determining the least restrictive environment? What might affect a Deaf student's and his or her family's preference for a least restrictive environment?

3. What environmental arrangements can be made to maximize accessibility and learning for students who are deaf or hard of hearing?

4. What types of hearing technologies are available? What are some concerns with cochlear implants?

5. What visual communication technologies are available?

6. How can technology improve the productivity of students who are deaf or hard of hearing?

What Are Some Considerations for the General Education Teacher?

Relevant CEC Standard

► Roles and responsibilities of teachers and support personnel in educational practice for individuals who are deaf or hard of hearing (DH9K1)

Although there are special schools and classes for deaf students, many deaf students and those who are hard of hearing are integrated into general education classrooms. Most students who are deaf or hard of hearing spend at least some of their day in general education classes (Office of Special Education and Rehabilitative Services, 2005).

It is important, therefore, that general educators be aware of procedures that enhance inclusive education for these students. Luckner and Muir (2002) offered a number of suggestions based on a survey and observation of successful students who are deaf who received most of their educational services in general education settings. Respondents, which included teachers and paraprofessionals as well as parents, identified a number of factors that can affect successful inclusive education. We summarize some of their findings and suggestions:

- Active family involvement is very helpful. Teachers can assist by ensuring that materials for parents are translated appropriately. The use of class newsletters and social events can also promote interaction. Finding ways for parents to volunteer in school and participate in school-sponsored sign language lessons are other ways to promote family involvement.
- Early identification and early intervention are critical in establishing good relationships with parents.
- Development of self-determination is important for students who are deaf or hard of hearing. Ultimately, students should be able to make decisions, take control of their own lives, and assume meaningful roles in adulthood.
- Extracurricular activities can be used to promote socialization and interaction among students. Help students identify activities in which they are interested and then facilitate participation.
- Helping deaf and hard of hearing students interact with hearing peers is critical to building a social network and social skills. Activities and lessons intended to nurture peer support and friendships can be considered in educational planning.
- Students should learn to be self-advocates. They need to learn to recognize when they need help and when and how to request help. They should also understand appropriate accommodations for them. Students should be active participants in their IEP planning and understand their legal rights. Students need to learn to set goals and identify their needs to meet those goals, as well as how to express those needs effectively.
- Teachers need to collaborate and consult with other IEP team members. This is critical in assisting the general educator in making appropriate adaptations in the classroom and to the curriculum.

Firstly, establish how the deaf person communicates. If they are asking you a question using their voice, it is safe to assume that they will be expecting to lip-read your reply.

❏ Face the person directly; if you look away the deaf person cannot see your lips.

❏ Speak clearly at a normal pace.

❏ Do not shout.

❏ Make sure there are no bright lights behind you that could make it difficult to see your face.

❏ Use whole sentences rather than one word replies, lip-reading is 70% guess work and many words look the same. Using sentences gives contextual clues.

❏ Be patient. If you are asked to repeat something, try changing the sentence slightly; it may make it easier to understand.

❏ Do not give up. If you cannot make yourself understood then try writing it down.

Source: From www.royaldeaf.org.uk. Used with permission by The Royal Association for Deaf People.

- Teaching approaches that can be helpful include preteaching and postteaching strategies. As students grow older and there is increasing emphasis on retention of knowledge in academic content areas, preparing the student for the content (e.g., teaching new vocabulary and concepts) and reviewing the content (e.g., key concepts, clarifying misconceptions) can help reinforce and expand student learning.
- Teachers should have high but realistic expectations for students. High expectations tend to lead to better performance. Involving students as active participants in their learning and rewarding them appropriately are two ways teachers can help. They also can help show students how learning is relevant to their lives, use students' interests and curiosity, and show an interest in students' lives and experiences.

Most hearing people and general education teachers are not proficient in ASL. Therefore, many students who are deaf and are included may rely on speechreading techniques to understand oral messages, especially in the absence of an interpreter. The Classroom Suggestions feature provides some suggestions for hearing peers and teachers to use when communicating with students who are deaf or hard of hearing.

Teachers should perceive themselves as members of a team on which special educators, related services personnel such as audiologists, and general educators collaborate to ensure students who are deaf or hard of hearing have accommodations that meet their needs. General educators need to understand they should not be "going it alone." Understanding basic strategies to enhance learning and promote socialization among students is possible without extensive training in special education.

ALLISON REVISITED What are some ways Allison's general education and special education teachers can encourage Allison's inclusion in the general education classroom?

Check Your Understanding

1. What strategies can be used in the general education classroom to promote listening, learning, and the development of social relationships?

2. What can teachers do to promote student involvement in understanding their own challenges and how to overcome those?

PRACTICE

Practical Considerations for the Classroom

What IDEA 04 Says about Hearing Impairments: Hearing impairment means an impairment in hearing, whether permanent or fluctuating, that adversely affects a child's educational performance but that is not included under the definition of deafness. Deafness means a hearing impairment that is so severe that the child is impaired in processing linguistic information through hearing, with or without amplification, that adversely affects a child's educational performance.

Identification Tools: Initial identification is typically made by parents or the pediatrician. Identification tools with infants include observing behavior in response to sound. Audiometric evaluation is used with older children and students, which may include the pure-tone air test, bone conduction threshold test, and hearing and speech threshold tests.

Characteristics	Indicators You Might See
Intellectual and Other Cognitive	Research on intellectual characteristics suggests that hearing loss does not equate to diminished cognitive ability.
Academic	Tend to score lower on achievement testing, though many maintain grade-level or better work. Special areas of difficulty may be literacy and math. Lower achievement may be due to the tests themselves, lack of instruction or experiential knowledge base, and language issues.
Speech and Language	Speech and language ability will depend on age of onset, type and degree of hearing loss, and language experiences at home and at school. Spoken language tends to be delayed.
Socioemotional Characteristics	Characteristics range from being well adjusted to having difficulties. Communication issues and lack of trained professionals knowledgeable about deafness may contribute to problems.
Deaf Culture	Possesses a cultural perspective of deafness. Uses ASL, has own history and culture, and view selves within different norms rather than having a deficit.

A Reference for Teachers

Teaching Implications

Instructional Content

- Select a curriculum or adaptations based on the perspective of the student and his or her family, and on his or her individual needs.
- Consider content area and literacy skill development as well as Deaf studies when planning the curriculum.
- Consider the need for interpreters and the limitations of interpreters as a means of access to the curriculum.
- Plan a transition curriculum.

Instructional Procedures

- First, decide, with the child, his or her family, and your other team members, the instructional approach (oralism, bilingual-bicultural, or total communication) that is the best option for that individual.
- Determine accommodations or adaptations needed to make content accessible to students.

Instructional Environment

- The least restrictive environment should be based on the communication needs of the student, academic level, socialization needs, and opportunities for instruction in the student's primary language.
- In planning the instructional environment, choose visuals students will easily see, use larger-sized materials with younger students, post information about the classroom the student will need to know, and provide graphic organizers for content.
- If an interpreter works with the student, plan for his or her involvement.
- If the child has residual hearing, seat him or her so that it can be best used.

Instructional Technology

- Be aware students may use hearing aids, loop systems, or cochlear implants. Become familiar with their operation and any specific support needed from you.
- Consider closed captioning, telecommunications relay service, fax machines, instant messaging, and e-mail to help with communication.
- Consider the use of computer technology to help students create work.

Methodologies and Strategies to Try

- Oralism (p. 271)
- Bilingual-Bicultural (p. 271)
- Total Communication (p. 271)

Considerations for the General Classroom and Collaboration

Students who are hard of hearing are typically taught within the general education classroom. Students who are deaf may be taught in the general education classroom, resource room, or special classroom or school.

The general education teacher should:

- Have high expectations for the student.
- Encourage active family involvement.
- Support early identification and intervention.
- Promote self-determination and self-advocacy.
- Promote socialization.
- Use preteaching and postteaching strategies to support student learning.
- Discuss with students how to participate in classroom discussions.
- Plan group work to be sure the student with a hearing loss can interact.
- Make lessons hands-on and visual.

Collaboration

General and special educators should consult on:

- Curriculum content
- Procedures and strategies used
- The physical environment
- Working with interpreters
- Supporting any assistive technology used to improve access to sound and communication

Chapter Summary

Go to the text's Online Learning Center at **www.mhhe.com**/taylor1e
to access study resources, Web links, practice quizzes, and extending materials.

What Are the Foundations of Deafness and Hard of Hearing?

- The terms "Deaf," "deaf," "hard of hearing," "hearing impairments," and "hearing" all have specific implications related to perceptions concerning differences versus disabilities and membership in the Deaf culture.
- Education of students who are deaf or hard of hearing was formalized in the United States in the 19th century. The oralist movement began the debate of what language individuals who are deaf or hard of hearing should use.
- Clinical definitions of deafness and hard of hearing focus on describing hearing loss in terms of type and degree. Types of hearing losses include conductive, sensorineural, and mixed.
- Hearing losses can be congenital, adventitious, prelingual, or postlingual.
- The IDEA 04 definition states deafness means a hearing impairment that is so severe that the child is impaired in processing linguistic information through hearing, with or without amplification, that adversely affects a child's educational performance. Hearing impairment means loss in hearing, whether permanent or fluctuating, that adversely affects a child's educational performance.
- Hearing impairments is a low incidence category of disability. Less than 1% of school-aged children are served under the hearing impairments IDEA category.

What Are the Causes and Characteristics of Deafness and Hard of Hearing?

- Hearing losses can result in conductive, sensorineural, or mixed hearing losses. Causes of conductive losses tend to be in the outer and middle ears and include blockage of the ear canal, otitis media, and perforated tympanic membrane. Causes of sensorineural losses tend to be in the inner ear or the auditory nerve.
- Genetic causes of sensorineural losses account for only a small percentage of cases of deafness and include Usher syndrome.
- Environmental causes of sensorineural losses include infections such as rubella.
- Deaf community and culture can have a major impact on an individual's perceptions about his or her own characteristics.
- Intellectual capabilities of students who are deaf or hard of hearing are difficult to assess because IQ tests tend to include many verbal performance items, but nonverbal tests indicate no significant differences between students who are deaf or hard of hearing and hearing students.
- Reading and comprehension skills tend to be delayed compared to those of their hearing peers.
- As a group, students who are deaf tend to have lower achievement than hearing peers although many are on or above grade level.

- English speech and language skills tend to be lower in students who are deaf or hard of hearing; this is affected by age of onset, type and degree of hearing loss, and language experiences at home and school.
- As a group, students who are deaf can develop appropriate social and emotional skills.

How Are Students Who Are Deaf or Hard of Hearing Identified?

- Hearing losses are typically identified by medical professionals. Identification of newborns and infants requires special audiological techniques.
- Identification of older children usually occurs through screening followed by standard audiological assessments that establish the degree and type of hearing loss. The effects on educational performance is the primary concern of teachers.

What and How Do I Teach Students Who Are Deaf or Hard of Hearing?

- Academics should include all subject areas although literacy may be of particular importance. Constructivist approaches that challenge students are preferable to rote memory learning.
- Literacy skills should be emphasized from early childhood. Students should be able to comprehend, remember, and communicate information from reading.
- Deaf studies is an area of learning for both students with hearing losses and hearing peers. Information about technology use, Deaf culture, and ASL could be incorporated into traditional curriculum areas such as science, social studies, and language arts.
- Transition planning should include key factors such as access to the general education curriculum, assessment of career interests, internships, and high expectations for success.
- Oralism is an approach that focuses on speechreading and other techniques to emphasize the development of oral English speech and language over ASL. This approach is controversial among some people within the Deaf culture.
- The bilingual-bicultural approach emphasizes ASL as the first and natural language with English language being taught as a second language.
- Total communication involves using both oral English speech and language along with ASL during instruction so that skills in both areas may be developed or used by students. The student's preferred mode of communication is emphasized.

What Are Other Instructional Considerations for Teaching Students Who Are Deaf or Hard of Hearing?

- Determining a student's least restrictive environment should consider communication mode, academic level, and socialization needs.

- Deaf culture considerations may influence student and family preferences as to the least restrictive environment.
- Environmental arrangements should include consideration of such factors as visual materials, posting of rules and class jobs, and using cards and charts to establish schedules and routines.
- Interpreters should be trained and collaborate with the teacher, but not be responsible for ensuring student learning.
- Hearing aids are commonly used to amplify sounds and it is important to know how they work and should be maintained.
- Loop or FM systems also aid listening and are helpful in large or noisy environments.
- Cochlear implants can aid listening in students with sensorineural losses, but their implantation is invasive and may not be preferred by Deaf culture members.
- Closed captionings produce typed words on a television screen to accompany what is being said orally.

- Telecommunication relay services allow a person with a hearing loss who has a text telephone to communicate through an operator with hearing persons who have traditional telephones.
- Instant messaging and e-mail can bypass the need for telecommunication relay services.
- Word processing, databases, spreadsheets, and computer-based publishing programs can aid students in producing written products.

What Are Some Considerations for the General Education Teacher?

- Most students are educated in general education settings at least part of their day.
- Teacher awareness of the impact of hearing loss and teacher attitudes can affect successful inclusion.
- Teachers should promote family involvement especially during early childhood.
- Self-determination skills are important as are activities to promote social skill development.

Reflection Topics

1. Do you believe there is a need for a Deaf culture? What might be gained or lost by people identifying with a Deaf culture?
2. Do you believe special residential schools offer students who are deaf unique opportunities?
3. How might being hard of hearing affect your adjustment in school and in the community? How might the experience differ from being deaf?

4. If you were a hearing parent with a child with congenital deafness, do you think you might want him or her to have a cochlear implant? Why or why not?
5. Do you think learning American Sign Language for those who are hearing should be accepted to meet a foreign language requirement in high school or college?
6. If you were the hearing parent of a deaf child, would you want the child to use ASL as a primary language or want your child's education to focus on oral skills?

Application Activities: For Learning and Your Portfolio

1. (*Portfolio Possibility*) Construct a brief lesson in your content or licensure area. Then reconsider the lesson in light of having a student who would be using a loop system in class. Include accommodations needed to ensure participation in the lesson's activities.
2. Invite an interpreter to speak to your class or professional group. Devise a list of questions in advance about what the role of an interpreter is, how and why the person learned sign language, and what opportunities exist for training in ASL.
3. (*Portfolio Possibility*) View a television-based lesson (e.g., Arts and Entertainment Channel Classroom or History Channel Classroom) with the sound turned off and using only closed captioning. Reflect on the effects this has on your note taking and ability to comprehend the information being transmitted.

4. Make a list of activities or skills to be carried out by students in your class. Pair students and have one try to teach the activity or skill using modeling and gestures only. Reflect on how this affected each member of the pair.
5. (*Portfolio Possibility*) Place ear muffs over one or both ears so that you can hear, but not clearly. Participate in a learning activity. Consider how being hard of hearing affected your comprehension. Make a list of tips that might assist a student who is hard of hearing who was participating in the activity.
6. Make a list of questions and interview an audiologist. Consider such questions as what types of hearing problems she or he most frequently encounters in children and youths, how she or he assesses those problems, and what types of assistive devices can help.

CHAPTER 9

Students with Blindness or Low Vision

CHAPTER OUTLINE

INTRODUCING ROBERT

Robert is a 16-year-old, 11th-grade student with a vision loss that is believed to have been present since birth. His parents first suspected he had a problem when, in early infancy, he did not seem to respond to their faces but did react to their voices. Also, he did not seem very interested in the toys and objects they placed in and around his crib unless he could touch them and had little interest in learning to crawl. At 9 months of age, Robert was examined by an ophthalmologist who confirmed that Robert had a vision loss. He was enrolled in an early intervention program, and an orientation and mobility specialist helped Robert learn to move safely about the home. An early intervention teacher helped Robert's parents understand how to develop his other senses as well as how to use what vision he did possess. His parents were encouraged to read to him and support his development of language skills and early literacy skills. By school age, it was confirmed that Robert's vision was 20/200 in his best eye even when wearing glasses.

When he started school, Robert's school district provided services to him through a teacher of students with blindness and low vision. Robert's special education teacher taught him early keyboarding skills, assessed his needs for assistive technology and learning media to aid access to the curriculum, further developd his listening skills, and helped him to learn to function in school and the community with his vision loss. Robert spent much of his school days in the general education classroom. Robert gained ground academically as he learned to use his residual vision, compensated for his vision loss, and developed learning strategies that helped him acquire and retain the information and skills he was taught. Robert was also taught time management, money management, and other skills needed for independent living.

Robert enjoys talking with other students and participating in after-school functions and extracurricular activities, but he is friendly with only a few peers. Many of the sighted students ignore him because they do not know how to react to someone with a serious vision loss. They have difficulty comprehending how someone can live a "normal" life without fully functioning vision.

Robert is now fully included in his high school classes and receives some transition planning support. He plans to attend college, and he hopes to study counseling. Because of his own disability, he believes he could be very empathetic to others with the same or similar challenges. ■

R obert's vision loss was diagnosed early in his life. Early intervention can be helpful by providing children with corrective lenses or other therapies (Miller, Menacker, & Batshaw, 2002). Most children with a vision loss can function fine in schools with corrective lenses. For a very small percentage, the loss is so significant that, even with corrective lenses, their educational performance is adversely affected. Even students considered legally blind usually do possess some residual vision that can be of use to them (Chaudry & Davidson, 2001).

Some students with blindness or low vision may attend special classes and even special schools for students with vision loss. Others, like Robert, are immersed in the general education curriculum, often receiving related services supports. Students in both placements may go on to college and be employed in a variety of fields. Many teachers will have students with some degree of vision loss that affects how the students perform in the classroom. Thus it is important for all teachers to understand how to ensure equal access and equal learning opportunities for these students.

Students with blindness or low vision may also have other disabilities (Miller et al., 2002), but our focus is on those students with vision loss as their disability under IDEA 04. Students with deaf-blindness and students with multiple disabilities are discussed in Chapter 12.

What Are the Foundations of Blindness and Low Vision?

Relevant CEC Standards

▶ Historical foundations of education of individuals with blindness or low vision (VI1K3)

▶ Role models with blindness or low vision and their importance (VI5K2)

▶ Organizations and publications relevant to the field of visual impairment (VI9K1)

Future teachers should learn about the historical trends in the education of students with blindness or low vision as they still affect service provision today. Teachers should understand the definitions of blindness and low vision as they pertain to IDEA 04, but also how other definitions of vision loss affect obtaining services such as job services assistance. We also discuss the prevalence rates of blindness and low vision.

A Brief History of Blindness and Low Vision

Early history has included stories of talented individuals with blindness or low vision who have made remarkable contributions to society. For example, Homer wrote *The Illiad* and *The Odyssey*; Nicholas Saunders was a professor of mathematics at Cambridge University in the late 1600s and early 1700s; Maria Theresia von Paradis was a pianist and teacher in Vienna into the early 1800s. By 1834, Louis Braille had established a system of raised dots that could be used by individuals with blindness or low vision for reading, writing, and music, creating a great stride in education (Hatlen, 2005). Each of these important contributors had a vision loss.

Formal educational efforts for students with blindness or low vision in the United States have been evident since the early 19th-century, and inclusive public school programming options have been available since 1900 (American Foundation for the Blind, 2006). Prominent among the early 19th century schools was the New England Asylum for the Blind. Later, Samuel Gridley Howe, a Harvard-educated physician, became involved in the school, which eventually became the Perkins School for the Blind. In 1837 the first school for students with blindness or low vision supported with state funds was established in Ohio (Hatlen, 2005). As other states founded similar schools, the need for accessible books and materials was evident. The American Printing House (APH) for the Blind was established in 1858 and continues to produce accessible materials for individuals with blindness or low vision using state-of-the-art technology (American Printing House for the Blind, 2004).

At the beginning of the 20th century, Chicago established day school classes for students with blindness or low vision. In 1913 the first classes for "partially seeing" students were established in Roxbury, Massachusetts, and Cleveland, Ohio. Books from the APH became available to public school students with blindness or low vision in 1912 (Hatlen, 2005). However, the physical integration of students with blindness or low vision did not guarantee assimilation into adult society. Advocacy organizations such as the National Federation of the Blind and the American Council of the Blind advocated for legislation that encouraged a more accepting attitude toward people with blindness or low vision among society in general (Tuttle & Tuttle, 2004). Public school programs continued to grow over time until the passage of IDEA in 1975 established the right of all children and youth with disabilities to educational opportunities (Sacks, 1998). The Rehabilitation Act of 1973 (Sec. 504), the Americans with Disabilities Act (ADA), and IDEA 04 all increased educational opportunities for students with vision losses.

In the 1990s advocates and professionals established the National Agenda, an expanded common core curriculum for students with blindness or low vision, which stated that students with blindness or low vision have educational needs that are specific to their disabilities. The goals included in the National Agenda are outlined in An Important Event.

AN IMPORTANT EVENT

1995—Establishment of the National Agenda for the Education of Children and Youth with Visual Impairments, Including Those with Multiple Disabilities

From A. L. Corn, K. M. Huebner, F. Ryan, and M. A. Siller, *Journal of Visual Impairment and Blindness.* Copyright 1996 American Foundation for the Blind (AFB). Reproduced with permission of the AFB.

During the 1990s, the American Foundation for the Blind established a steering committee to create a process for developing the national agenda for the education of individuals with visual impairments. The committee identified 19 goal statements that were eventually pared down to 8 following input from parents, persons with visual impairments, and professionals. These 8 goals were considered to be those that would have high impact on students' education and high likelihood of occurrence (Hatlen, 2005). Corn, Hatlen, Huebner, Ryan, and Siller (1996) listed these goals:

1. Students and their families will be referred to an appropriate education program within thirty days of identification of a suspected visual impairment.
2. Policies and procedures will be implemented to ensure the right of all parents to full participation and equal partnership in the education process.
3. Universities, with a minimum of one full-time faculty member in the area of visual impairment, will prepare a sufficient number of educators of students with visual impairments to meet personnel needs throughout the country.
4. Service providers will determine caseloads based on the needs of students and will require ongoing professional development for all teachers and orientation and mobility instructors.
5. Local education programs will ensure that all students have access to a full array of placement options.
6. Assessment of students will be conducted, in collaboration with parents, by personnel having expertise in the education of students with visual impairments.
7. Access to developmental and educational services will include an assurance that instructional materials are available to students in the appropriate media and at the same time as their sighted peers.
8. Educational and developmental goals, including instruction, will reflect the assessed needs of each student in all areas of academic and disability-specific core curricula.

REFLECTION Considering the goals of the National Agenda, what do you think were some possible problems associated with educating children and youth with blindness or low vision?

Definitions of Blindness and Low Vision

Relevant CEC Standard

▶ Educational definitions, identification criteria, labeling issues, and incidence and prevalence of figures for individuals with blindness or low vision (VI1K3)

Teachers should be familiar with both the legal and IDEA 04 definitions of blindness and low vision. They should also be aware of different terms and definitions that might be used in their state. For example, various states use terms such as *educationally blind*, *low vision*, and *functionally blind* to describe children who may need instruction in the use of braille for reading and writing (Corn & Koenig, 1996). Finally, while we use the terms *blindness* and *low vision* in this text, some individuals associate negative connotations with the term "blind." Therefore, some prefer the IDEA 04 term "visual impairment" to describe all students with vision loss in need of special education and related services (Huebner, 2005).

The Legal Definition

visual acuity How sharp visual images are perceived.

Legal or clinical descriptors can be used to differentiate between individuals who are blind and those who have low vision. These descriptors are most closely associated with **visual acuity,** or how sharp visual images are perceived (Falvo, 2005). Typically, a standard distance of 20 feet is used as a base measure of visual acuity. An individual being tested must discriminate letters or forms being shown at that distance, with 20/20 vision designated as normal visual acuity. This means that the tested individual can see at 20 feet what a sighted individual should be able to see at 20 feet. Visual acuity of 20/100 would mean that the individual was seeing at a distance of 20 feet what a typically sighted individual would see at 100 feet. For defining the terms of low vision and blindness, the acuity measure takes into account the best possible correction (i.e., use of corrective lens) in the best eye (i.e., the eye with the best vision with corrective lens use). **Low vision** typically refers to vision of 20/70 up to 20/200, and **legal blindness** refers to vision of 20/200 or worse in the best eye with the best possible correction (Falvo, 2005). Individuals with low vision are generally able to use printed materials in learning whereas those who are blind are generally taught using tactile materials and braille or through other assistive technology (Harley, Lawrence, Sanford, & Burnett, 2000). Legal definitions are more useful for determining eligibility for government services than for educational purposes (Huebner, 2005).

low vision Vision of 20/70 to 20/200 in the best eye with the best possible correction.

legal blindness Vision of 20/200 or worse in the best eye with the best possible correction.

visual field The scope of what one can see without turning the head or moving the eyes.

The individual's **visual field,** the scope of what one can see without turning the head or moving one's eyes, is another descriptor that may be used to classify an individual as legally blind (Falvo, 2005). This visual field limitation is sometimes called "tunnel vision" although some conditions (for example, macular degeneration) affect the central field of vision, not peripheral vision. If the visual field is no greater than 20 degrees in width, the individual can still be classified as blind, even though visual acuity is not within the range of blindness (20/200 in the best eye with correction). Table 9.1 summarizes descriptors used in defining students with blindness or low vision.

Teachers should be aware that legal blindness does not equate to total blindness. For example, a student with 20/200 vision in the best eye with the best possible correction would be considered legally blind, but the student may still use printed materials through compensatory strategies and assistive technology. Factors such as motivation, cognitive skills, and how well a student has learned to use his or her vision can affect visual performance in school (Huebner, 2005). Most people who are "blind" do have perception of movement and/or light. Those who are *functionally blind* have little or no usable residual vision (Harley, Lawrence, Sanford, & Burnett, 2000).

TABLE 9.1	Clinical Descriptors for Low Vision/Blindness
TERM	**ACUITY/FIELD OF VISION**
Low vision	20/70 to 20/200 in best eye with best possible correction
Legal blindness	20/200 or greater in best eye with best possible correction
Legal blindness	Field of vision restricted to 20 degrees or less regardless of visual acuity

The IDEA 04 Definition

IDEA 04 defines visual impairments, including blindness, as "vision that, even with correction, adversely affects a child's educational performance. The term includes both partial sight and blindness." Note that the term *partial sight* is used instead of the now more commonly used term *low vision*. Most experts define blindness and low vision based on the effects of vision loss on an individual's ability to use any residual vision, if there is any. IDEA 04 emphasizes visual impairment that adversely affects educational performance. From an educational perspective, emphasis is placed on how individuals with vision loss use their vision. In fact, two students with the same visual acuity and field of vision may not perceive visual stimuli in the same way (Huebner, 2005). In general, but with exceptions, students with low vision use their vision for learning with accommodations (such as large print books) while students with blindness must have accommodations and modifications that rely on other senses, such as touch.

ROBERT REVISITED Do Robert's academic challenges suggest that he would meet the IDEA 04 definition for a visual impairment: that is, a vision loss that adversely affects educational performance? If Robert were performing at least at an average level in content area classes, would he qualify?

Prevalence of Blindness and Low Vision

Visual impairment is considered a low prevalence IDEA 04 category. In the 2005 school year, estimates of the overall prevalence was .04% for children 6–21 years of age, or about 4 students in 10,000. During the same period, more than 25,000 students with blindness or low vision were receiving special education and related services in the United States (U.S. Department of Education, 2006). Some students may have vision losses but do not experience an adverse effect on their education because they use corrective lenses. It is also reasonable to assume the number of students who are legally or educationally blind is smaller than the number who have low vision and are able to use printed materials. The American Foundation for the Blind (2002) reports that 90% of all individuals with visual impairments have some functional vision.

Future teachers will almost certainly encounter students with significant vision losses. Many of these students will use corrective lenses and will thus experience no significant difficulties in using their vision for learning; others will experience some difficulties. Legal and educational definitions differ, and the former does not always tell teachers how the student can use his or her residual vision. Once teachers understand how vision is affected, they can work with other professionals, the student, and the family to plan and implement an appropriate educational experience.

Check Your Understanding

1. Historically, when did efforts to educate students with blindness and low vision emerge in the United States?

2. What are the legal definitions of low vision and blindness?

3. What is the IDEA 04 definition of visual impairments? How does it differ from the legal definitions?

4. What is the overall prevalence of blindness or low vision among school-aged children? Is the prevalence of those with blindness or low vision greater?

What Are the Causes and Characteristics of Blindness and Low Vision?

Blindness and low vision have many possible causes that can affect various parts and functions of the eye. It is helpful to understand some of the major causes of vision loss and how the eye functions. Similarly, the possible characteristics emerging as a result of a vision loss can be quite diverse.

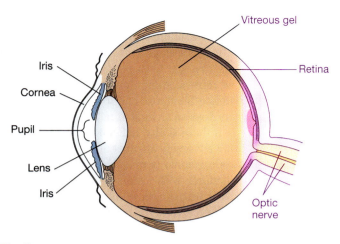

Vitreous gel

Iris

Cornea

Pupil

Lens

Iris

Retina

Optic nerve

FIGURE 9.1 The Eye

Relevant CEC Standards

▶ Basic terminology related to the structure and function of the human visual system (VI1K4)

▶ Basic terminology related to diseases and disorders of the human visual system (VI1K5)

▶ Development of the human visual system (VI2K1)

refraction The focusing of light as it passes through the components of the eye.

myopia Nearsightedness; distant objects appear out of focus but near objects are in focus.

hyperopia Farsightedness; near objects appear out of focus but distant objects are in focus.

astigmatism Difficulties in focusing at any visual range.

Causes of Blindness and Low Vision

The eyes are complicated and are vulnerable to a number of different types of vision loss. These can be classified as optical defects, ocular motility defects, and external and internal problems of the eye (Harley et al., 2000). Before learning about these causes of blindness or low vision, an understanding of how the eye works is needed.

The abilities to see and to interpret what is being seen are based on the interaction between the eye and the brain. Figure 9.1 shows the internal structure of the eye. Visual stimuli enter the eye through the cornea, which is the front, transparent portion of the eyeball. The pupil, the central dark opening of the eye, opens or closes depending on the brightness of the environment. This opening and closing is controlled by the iris, the colored portion of the eye, which surrounds the pupil. Directly behind the iris and pupil is a lens. The lens can change shape to take what is being seen and focus it onto the very back of the eye, called the retina. Within the retina are receptors, rods and cones, which take the light energy and translate it into neurological messages to be conveyed along the optic nerve to the occipital lobe of the brain where the impulses are interpreted (Falvo, 2005).

Optical Defects

The major optical defects are refraction problems including myopia, hyperopia, and astigmatism. These are problems in refraction (Harley et al., 2000). **Refraction** involves the focusing of light as it passes through different components of the eye. In **myopia**, or nearsightedness, the individual can see well at close range, but has trouble seeing visual stimuli at far distances (Falvo, 2005). Students with myopia might have problems copying from images on an overhead or on a board at the front of the room without corrective lenses. In **hyperopia**, or farsightedness, the opposite is the case; the student can see at far distances but not well at close range (Falvo, 2005). These students may have poor attention or difficulty with problems requiring near vision such as seatwork or individual reading. They may gaze out the window to rest their eyes from time to time (Harley et al., 2000). With **astigmatism**, the individual experiences focusing problems, regardless of whether the visual stimulus is near or far away. Images may appear partially in focus and, at the same time, partially blurred. Astigmatism is usually present at birth; myopia and hyperopia tend to emerge during childhood (although many individuals with typical vision do eventually develop hyperopia as they grow into middle age or older). Headaches, nausea, or tired eyes may occur when the eyes are used for prolonged periods as a result of these problems (Harley et al., 2000). Refraction problems can usually be controlled by the use of corrective lenses or surgery.

Ocular Motility Defects

Ocular motility involves the coordinated use of two eyes simultaneously to achieve binocular vision. Because the eyes are separated in space, each sees objects from a slightly different angle, which results in two different images being formed on the retinas. The brain blends or fuses these images to create a coherent image (Harley et al., 2000). If problems of coordination of eye movements are experienced, the student will find seeing a clear image problematic (Miller et al., 2002). If such difficulties are not corrected, serious problems can result, including blindness in an affected eye.

Common problems of ocular motility include nystagmus, strabismus, and amblyopia. In **nystagmus,** the eyes tend to move abruptly in continual jerky types of involuntary motion even though the eyes are fixed in terms of direction (Falvo, 2005). Nystagmus can cause a student to tilt or turn his or her head to see better, but it may cause no visual disturbance to the individual (Falvo, 2005). **Strabismus** refers to any deviation in the alignment of the eyes as a result of muscle imbalance or a neurological condition (Falvo, 2005). Although one eye alone can be affected, with strabismus, both eyes tend to converge either inward or outward. Students with strabismus that is not corrected may develop diplopia (double vision) or lack stereopsis (maximum level of depth perception). If the brain is unable to fuse the two images into a coherent single image, it may suppress the image from one eye, resulting in amblyopia. **Amblyopia,** commonly referred to as "lazy" eye, is the suppression of images resulting from strabismus or any disorder, such as an uncorrected refractive error. Amblyopia can be treated if detected early (National Eye Institute, 2006).

Types of External Eye Problems

External problems of the eye can affect many parts of the eye including the orbit, eyelids, and cornea. Orbital problems can include protruding, recessed, or abnormally small eyeballs (Harley et al., 2000). Abnormalities of the eyelids include drooping of the upper eyelids, outward or inward rolling of the eyelids, eyelids that do not close completely, and inflammation of the lids or glands around the eye, among others (Harley et al., 2000). One can also experience corneal problems. Growths, thinning of the cornea, inflammation of the cornea, and other problems can lead to problems with vision, pain, and tearing of the cornea (National Eye Institute, 2007).

Types of Internal Eye Problems

A number of conditions can affect the internal components of the eye. These include problems with the retina and cortical visual impairment. **Retinopathy of prematurity** (ROP) results from vascular damage to the retina as a complication of premature birth and is the most common cause of retinal damage in infants. Higher oxygen levels critical to sustaining life needed by premature infants also increase the likelihood that retinal damage will occur (Miller et al., 2002).

Other types of problems associated with the retina are pigment degeneration, or retinitis pigmentosa; retinal degeneration, or macular degeneration; and a detached retina. Retinitis pigmentosa leads to gradual loss of peripheral vision and can ultimately result in total loss of vision (Falvo, 2005). Macular degeneration results in loss for seeing fine detail and ultimately in central vision, but does not necessarily result in total blindness (Falvo, 2005). The first two conditions typically have a genetic cause, and in both conditions visual difficulties usually progress in severity (Sacks, 1998). A detached retina may result from various causes, including injuries and hemorrhaging due to complications from diabetes, and vision loss may develop suddenly or progress over time (Falvo, 2005). If not treated quickly, a detached retina can cause permanent loss of vision in the eye (Sacks, 1998). **Cortical visual impairment** is a type of vision loss in which the physical components of the eye are normal or nearly so, and therefore the vision loss results from damage to the parts of the brain dedicated to interpreting and responding to optic nerve impulses (Miller et al., 2002).

This discussion of causes of blindness and low vision is by no means exhaustive. Interested readers might wish to consult the Web site of the National Institutes of Health (www.nih.gov), which includes a wealth of information on various diseases and disorders of the eye.

nystagmus Abrupt, jerky movements of the eyes.

strabismus Any deviation in the alignment of the eyes as a result of muscle imbalance.

amblyopia A generally correctable vision defect caused by the suppression of images resulting from strabismus or other eye disorders that causes blurred images in either or both eyes. Also referred to as lazy eye.

retinopathy of prematurity Vision loss resulting from high oxygen levels given to sustain life in infancy.

cortical visual impairment Loss of vision resulting from brain damage or other conditions.

Relevant CEC Standards

▶ Effects of visual impairment on development (VI2K3)

▶ Impact of visual impairment on learning and experience (VI2K4)

▶ Psychosocial aspects of visual impairment (VI2K5)

▶ Effects of visual impairment on the family and the reciprocal impact on the individual's self-esteem (VI3K1)

The characteristics of students with blindness or low vision vary according to the individual, but some generalizations can be made. *Age of onset* can have considerable impact on a student. A student who has congenital blindness (who is blind at birth) may have distinctly different characteristics from a student who is adventitiously blind (who becomes blind after birth). Also, a student with low vision versus one with blindness may have distinctly different characteristics. In addition, students with the same visual acuity and field of vision could still perceive visual stimuli differently due to experience, motivation, cognitive ability, and use of residual vision, among other possible factors (Huebner, 2005). Students with blindness or low vision can and do achieve academic success and success in life with the proper supports and modifications as individually needed (Algozzine & Ysseldyke, 2006). In this section, we explore the intellectual characteristics, play and social interaction skills, language and concept development, academic achievement, perceptual abilities, and psychological and social adjustment of students who are blind or have low vision.

Intellectual Characteristics

The general consensus is that the ability to see may have little or no effect on one's general intelligence. What must be considered, however, is that tests used to measure intelligence in this population may not adequately measure intelligence because most tests are designed for sighted children. The degree to which intellectual ability in students with blindness or low vision can be measured by standardized instruments is not fully understood (Miller & Skillman, 2003). Teachers should not consider low vision or blindness as indicative of lowered intelligence.

Play and Social Interaction Skills

Play and social interaction skills may be delayed in children with blindness or low vision. These children may display significant delays in several types of play skills including exploratory-sensorimotor and symbolic play (Hughes, Dote-Kwan, & Dolendo, 1998). For example, children with congenital blindness do not have the vision that encourages them to explore the environment to obtain or examine familiar or novel objects of interest by crawling or walking to the objects. Vision influences development for young children by providing reasons for movement, estimation of space, stimulation of coordination and control, stimulation of exploration, incentives for communication and cognitive development, and help in concept development (Ferrell, 2005). It is important to understand that adult mediation and opportunities for integration with peers without disabilities may be key to developing these and other skills (D'Allura, 2002; Hughes et al., 1998).

Language and Concept Development

Although speech and language delays, such as preverbal skills like looking at a speaker, may occur due to a child's difficulty in seeing (Miller et al., 2002), most children with blindness or low vision do not display any crucial differences in language development when compared with sighted children. This is due to the fact that most language learning relies on hearing and speech, which are typically unaffected. Children may have problems with the pragmatics of language, nonverbal communication signals and skills, due to lack of ability to "read" and learn the body language of others. Although typical oral language skills are used by most students with blindness or low vision, they may not use the same physical gestures or facial gestures, and they may use gestures differently than do sighted children (Frame, 2000).

Children with blindness may have problems associating words with concepts and generating various word meanings (Ferrell, 2005). For example, children with blindness may have greater difficulty than sighted children in understanding the concept of a "bird" without hands-on interaction. Although a child with blindness may be able to describe a bird and what it does with the appropriate terms, he or she may not have the same understanding as a sighted child who has seen birds flying, as well as seen their feathers, beaks, and feet and how these are used by the bird. However, research suggests that children with vision losses do develop concepts. This appears to be the result of opportunities to learn from early childhood onward and the fact that there are no other disabilities, such as deafness, present that further impede concept development (Ferrell, 2005).

Academic Achievement

The comparison of academic achievement between sighted students and students with blindness or low vision should be made with caution because the methods of evaluation may be quite different. For example, literacy might be assessed through the use of braille versus printed, standardized tests (Katsiyannis & Maag, 2001). It is commonly assumed that, in general, the academic achievement of individuals with blindness or low vision is affected by the severity of the vision loss and the age of onset. However, with proper supports, students with blindness or low vision should be able to access and succeed in the general education curriculum. There is evidence that students with blindness or low vision succeed in academics and enter higher education at rates similar to those of their sighted peers (Wolffe, 2005). One statewide study indicated that 77% of all students with blindness or low vision who read print or braille read at or above grade level (Craig, Hough, Churchwell, & Schmitt, 2002).

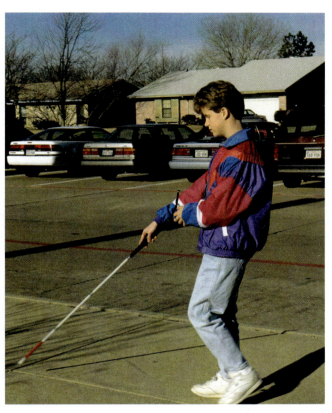

Students who are blind may need to learn orientation, mobility, and wayfinding skills.

Perceptual Abilities

One important perceptual ability relates to use of vision. Visual perception is the capacity to interpret or give meaning to what is seen with the eyes in respect to the individual's developmental level (Wolffe, 2005). These can include such skills as discriminating forms, people, objects, pictures, letters, and numbers. It also includes visual memory, such as looking for a missing object; figure-ground discrimination, such as finding a hidden object within a picture; visual closure, such as recognizing an object that is partially hidden; and eye-hand coordination.

With students with blindness or low vision, perceptual development also involves consideration of tactile (touch) and auditory development as well as the fullest use of residual vision. Students who are blind may have a distinct disadvantage in "seeing" the totality of objects if touch is the primary mode of perception. The world of the child or adolescent with a vision loss may quite literally be at his or her fingertips; these students may also be challenged in developing a "whole picture" perspective as a result of having limited sensory input when perceiving objects (Wolffe, 2005).

Another type of perceptual ability that is affected in students with blindness or low vision is spatial perception (Bouchard & Tetreault, 2000). This has to do with the child's ability to perceive his or her own body in space and in relation to surroundings. It should not be surprising that individuals with blindness can experience difficulty in this area. Even children born with low vision may go through the stages of motor development with a compromised or imprecise visual sense of space (Bouchard & Tetreault, 2000).

This imprecise sense of one's position in space and in one's surroundings accounts for the problems that some individuals may have in orientation and mobility. Some students can be disoriented by activities such as taking a walk in the neighborhood (Ambrose, 2000). Orientation and mobility skills are very important. **Orientation** is the process of using sensory input and information to know one's position in an environment; **mobility** is moving about an environment safely and efficiently (Hill & Ponder, 1976). **Wayfinding** is the outcome of good orientation and mobility skills. Wayfinding involves learning a route through an environment

orientation The process of using sensory input and information to know one's position in an environment.

mobility Moving about an environment safely.

wayfinding Learning a route through an environment and being able to retrace it from memory.

What Are the Causes and Characteristics of Blindness and Low Vision?

and being able to retrace it from memory (Blades, Lippa, Golledge, Jacobson, & Kitchin, 2002). Individuals with blindness or low vision can successfully learn orientation, mobility, and wayfinding skills when training is provided beginning in early childhood (Blades et al., 2002; Wolffe, 2005).

Psychological and Social Adjustment

Family and friendship support is critical and valued in the psychological and social development of children and adolescents with blindness or low vision. Some parents have expressed concern about their children's social isolation and lack of opportunities to participate with others in extracurricular and community activities (Leyser & Heinze, 2001). Huurre and Aro (2000) found that adolescents with congenital blindness or low vision may have more problems in relationships with friends than do sighted adolescents. They may spend more time alone than sighted individuals and may have to work harder to establish and maintain friendships. Individuals with blindness or low vision may not be able to see actions, objects, or events occurring that provide context for social conversations and interactions (Tuttle & Tuttle, 2005). For example, attending a sporting event and conversing about the event relies to some extent on seeing the action. However, social contacts, networks, and support have positive effects on social adjustment (Kef, 2002). It is important to understand that the difficulties in social adjustment experienced by some individuals with blindness or low vision may also be influenced by the negative perceptions of sighted peers and the need for peers to learn to react positively to human differences (Huurre & Aro, 2000). Peers may assume the student is unable to hear or comprehend what is said, ask a companion about the student's interests or feelings rather than posing direct questions, or display pity or condescension resulting from an inappropriate view of vision loss (Tuttle & Tuttle, 2005).

ROBERT REVISITED Robert has typical intellectual abilities. What might be some reasons he may have few friends at school?

Future teachers will likely encounter some students with vision loss, even if the loss does not reach the threshold for requiring special education or related services. Knowledge of the causes of vision problems and the resulting characteristics helps teachers to understand how and what to teach students with blindness or low vision, as well as how to arrange the environment to optimize use of residual vision and other senses for learning.

Check Your Understanding

1. What are some optical and ocular motility defects that cause vision loss?

2. What are some common external and internal problems of the eye that may cause vision loss?

3. How are intellectual development and social skills development affected by vision loss?

4. How is language and concept development affected by vision loss?

5. How are academic and perceptual skills affected by vision loss?

6. What are some issues regarding psychological and social adjustment?

Relevant CEC Standards
▶ Specialized terminology used in assessing individuals with blindness or low vision (VI8K1)

▶ Ethical considerations, laws, and policies for assessment of individuals with blindness or low vision (VI8K2)

How Are Students with Blindness or Low Vision Identified?

Typically, congenital vision losses are identified at a young age through a variety of medical procedures. In school-aged children, vision losses are identified through many of the same procedures used with younger children but can also use procedures (for example, Snellen chart) when students can report what they see and follow directions for a visual task. A student's functional visual abilities should be assessed comprehensively through a variety of components to determine how the student will learn best and function in everyday life.

Various professionals are involved in identifying vision loss and treating vision problems. **Ophthalmologists** are medical doctors who identify and treat eye problems, prescribe drugs, and perform surgery. **Optometrists** examine eyes for defects and problems in refraction and prescribe corrective lenses. **Opticians** make or deal in optical devices and instruments. A **low vision specialist** is an ophthalmologist or optometrist who further specializes in assessment, prescription, and use of low vision devices (Harley et al., 2000). Overall, three types of assessment are routinely conducted when evaluating vision: refractive power, ocular motility, and visual fields.

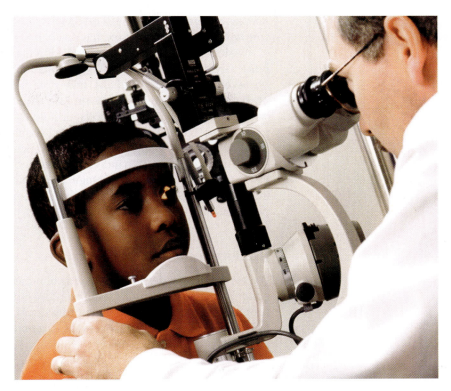

Identification of a vision loss may begin with a medical examination.

Identification of Blindness or Low Vision in Infants and Toddlers

When appropriate screening and medical care are provided, most children with blindness or low vision are identified before 4 months of age (Chen, 2001). In infants and young children, parental reporting may be the best means of first identifying a suspected vision problem (Miller et al., 2002). Parents may notice behaviors such as a lack of visual fixation on the parents' faces or interesting objects, abnormal eye movements, an eye gaze that always seems to go in one direction, or a lack of blinking or reaction to a threatening gesture or bright light shone in the eyes (Miller et al., 2002). Visual acuity in infants does not approach 20/20 until about 6 months of age (Harley et al., 2000), and infants do not respond to stimuli such as a Snellen chart, the chart with letters varying in size on each row indicating various levels of visual acuity, as can older children. Therefore, other techniques are used in identifying vision loss in young children.

Taking a family history is important because congenital blindness and low vision can be genetic, and other factors, such as trauma, can affect a child's vision. Because of the challenges in assessing young children, the pediatric ophthalmologist may assess behavioral responses, such as the reaction to the presentation of a toy, to determine if the child has central, steady, and maintained visual behavior (Miller et al., 2002). Many children identified with a vision loss prior to age 3 have legal blindness and other disabilities in addition to a vision loss (Hatton, 2001).

Identification of Blindness or Low Vision in School-Aged Children

Because vision plays an extremely important role in school programs, vision screening is often a mandatory part of early school assessment. For most people, the screening procedure is the familiar Snellen chart, in which the individual reads rows of letters from a distance of 20 feet (Harley et al., 2000). Most people are familiar with this type of screening or a similar process, often used when obtaining a driver's

ophthalmologists Medical doctors who identify and treat eye problems.

optometrists Eye doctors who examine eyes for defects and problems in refraction and prescribe corrective lenses.

opticians Individuals who make or deal in optical devices and instruments.

low vision specialist An ophthalmologist or optometrist who further specializes in assessment, prescription, and use of low vision devices.

 **Relevant CEC Standards**

▶ Specialized procedures for screening, prereferral, referral, and identification of individuals with blindness or low vision (VI8K4)

▶ Alternative assessment techniques for individuals with blindness or low vision (VI8K5)

license, where one is expected to view rows of letters in a viewfinder and read the row with the smallest letters that one can view clearly.

Vision screening should be considered a less precise assessment of visual capability. Given the nature of the typical screening procedures, it is recommended that observers, especially teachers, take note of behaviors that might indicate a vision problem including frequent eye rubbing, squinting at visual stimuli, tilting of the head when looking at objects or books, or holding objects or books unusually close to the eyes. If a problem is suspected, referral should be made to a qualified individual, such as an ophthalmologist, who can complete an in-depth assessment and prescribe necessary interventions. This individual may not only confirm that a visual acuity, field of vision, or depth perception problem exists but will also be able to determine if muscle imbalance problems, problems associated with convergence of the eyes, or other problems are present.

Comprehensive Assessment

Once a student is identified as having blindness or low vision, the student may need a comprehensive assessment. Heinze (2005) outlined that comprehensive assessment should include the components of functional vision, learning media assessment, cognitive ability, academic achievement, orientation and mobility skills, and social skills and independent living skills.

Assessment of Functional Vision

Vision utilization, the use of residual vision to obtain information from the environment, is important in every skill area (Spungin & Ferrell, 2007). For example, a student with a vision loss may use residual vision to the extent that he or she is able to read printed materials with magnification and to navigate environments safely. Assessing how well students can use that residual vision in functional ways is a critical aspect in providing services to students with blindness or low vision. Under IDEA 04, a student receives services for a visual impairment only if the vision loss adversely affects educational performance. A functional vision assessment occurs after the student has been assessed by medical and other vision specialists for diagnosis and treatment of existing eye conditions. Functional vision refers to how well a student uses his or her vision in daily activities in various settings (Harley et al., 2000). If these assessments indicate a need for special education services, the student's functional vision, or how well the student can use his or her eyesight to take in material visually and learn, should also be assessed (Harley et al., 2000). Functional vision assessment can address needs related to lighting, print size, how well one can use pictures and print in testing, and types of devices needed to access print materials (Heinze, 2005). Overall questions the assessment specialist should consider are listed in Table 9.2. Functional vision assessments are conducted with the student using his or her corrective lenses or low vision aids, such as a magnifying glass. The educational implications of the outcomes for each question can benefit teachers in providing access and accommodations in the classroom.

Students can also benefit from additional and periodic assessment of the medical condition of the eye, near and distance vision, color vision, contrast sensitivity, and visual field (Koenig, Holbrook, Corn, DePriest, Erin, & Presley, 2005). Such assessments can be helpful in prescribing optical techniques, such as corrective lenses, and indicate areas of instruction in the use of assistive technology, such as learning to use computer software programs.

Learning Media Assessment

A learning media assessment (LMA) is used by educational teams to make "deliberate and informed decisions on the total range of instructional media needed to facilitate learning for students with visual impairments" (Koenig & Holbrook,

TABLE 9.2	Considerations in Planning for Assessment of Functional Vision

Does the student:

❑ understand and follow verbal directions?

❑ respond verbally by matching, pointing, nodding, or eye gaze?

❑ read and write adequately?

❑ require a special means for communication?

❑ require special positioning in order to access the visual environment?

❑ tire quickly or have a short attention span?

❑ need to have modeling or practice items provided?

❑ require special motivation?

❑ wear corrective lenses or use a prescribed low vision device?

Other Considerations

❑ Will the examiner need assistance with assessment?

❑ Is the student following a developmentally sequenced early childhood curriculum, a functional life skills curriculum, or an expanded core curriculum?

❑ What areas of the functional vision assessment are or are not appropriate when considering the student's age, abilities, and communication skills?

Source: Harley, R. K., Lawrence, G. A., Sanford, L., & Burnett, R. (2000). *Visual impairment in the schools* (3rd ed.). Springfield, IL. Courtesy of Charles C. Thomas Publisher, Ltd.

1995, p. 2). Koenig and Holbrook outlined three areas of information gathered in an LMA:

1. *Efficiency in using sensory channels.* Use of vision, touch, and hearing in learning and living tasks are assessed.
2. *Types of general learning media used.* This aspect of the LMA can involve assessing use of materials such as objects, models, and diagrams as well as methods such as imitation, prompting, and listening. Overall, the purpose of this information is to make recommendations "concerning the visual, tactual, and auditory learning media which will ensure continuous progress in learning" (p. 6).
3. *Literacy media used for reading and writing.* Once a primary sensory channel for learning is established, the educational team should make an initial decision as to which channel is best for reading and writing and what media will aid the student. For example, some students will use printed materials, perhaps with modifications (such as enlarged print), and others may use braille.

Also, the LMA can help the team identify specific reading and listening skills that should be assessed, as well as how well the student uses assistive technology (Heinze, 2005). The LMA involves ongoing assessment, which is necessary to continually evaluate whether the preferred media should be changed or modified (Koenig et al., 2005). The following questions should be answered in this ongoing assessment process (Koenig, 1990; Koenig & Holbrook, 1989):

- Is there any new information available from ophthamological or functional vision evaluations that might alter the preferred media?

FOUNDATIONS

- Is the student successful in academic tasks with the current media?
- Does the student comprehend what he or she reads?
- Can the student read his or her own handwriting?
- Can projected career goals be accomplished with current reading and writing skills?
- Is there any new technology available that could enhance the student's academic performance?
- Even if a student uses braille, would he or she benefit from developing a basic level of print reading skills if sufficient functional vision permits?

Literacy skill development for students with blindness or low vision is critical to school, daily living, and career success, be it using media to access print, braille, or a combination of the two (Corn & Koenig, 2002).

Assessment of Cognitive Ability

It is important that academic or psychological testing take into account whether the student can respond to visual stimuli. Assessors of students with blindness or low vision have mixed ratings of satisfaction with various instruments for assessing cognitive ability and intelligence that were developed for sighted individuals (Miller & Skillman, 2003). Another concern is that students with blindness or low vision may have limited background experience, which penalizes them in terms of performance on many standardized norm-referenced tests (Heinze, 2005). There are higher satisfaction ratings for tests designed specifically for individuals with blindness or low vision, such as the Oregon Project for Visually Impaired and Blind Preschool Children (Dial, Mezger, Gray, Massey, Chan & Hull, 1990). Multiple sources of data including test results, developmental inventories, observation, and other sources should be used.

Assessment of Academic Achievement

It may be possible to assess a student with blindness or low vision's academic skills similarly to those of sighted students if the student is familiar with and can use printed materials. Otherwise, braille, listening, or a combination of the two may be necessary in academic assessments of students with blindness or low vision (Harley et al., 2000). Computer-based testing with a synthesized voice may become more available, more useful, and preferred over human readers of tests (Hansen, Lee, & Forer, 2002).

This area should include assessment of the student in the expanded core curriculum, discussed in detail later in this chapter, such as reading, math, and special compensatory skills such as braille literacy (Heinze, 2005). Again, multiple sources of data, such as observations, work samples, and an LMA, should be used along with test results.

Assessment of Orientation and Mobility Skills

Assessment in the area of orientation and mobility skills addresses concepts such as body image, spatial orientation, special physical education needs, and how familiar the student is with the classroom, school, home, and community settings. A special orientation and mobility skills teacher may also assess use of special devices, such as a cane for moving around the school, and independence in travel skills. Gross motor skills including coordination and balance are also important areas (Heinze, 2005).

Assessment of Social Skills and Independent Living Skills

Social skills can be assessed through formal tests such as the Vineland Adaptive Behavior Scales–II. However, informal techniques such as observation and interviewing people familiar with the student are useful. How well a student is able to eat, dress, groom, prepare food, clean, and manage money are important areas to evaluate for independent living skills. Assessment of these skills can be very important for goal development as social skills are frequently learned through observation, which may be difficult for students with vision loss (Heinze, 2005).

Future teachers should be **aware of how students** with blindness or low vision are **identified and what procedures can be helpful in that** process. In some cases, teachers may be the first persons to suspect that a child is having vision problems. To be **prepared for the possible identification of students** with blindness or low vision, it is most important for **teachers to understand their role in the screening process and how the comprehensive assessment can be used to plan and implement an appropriate educational program.**

ROBERT REVISITED What types of information might an IEP team wish to obtain about Robert's functional vision skills?

Check Your Understanding

1. How are students with blindness or low vision identified in early childhood?
2. How are students with blindness or low vision identified at school age?
3. What are the components of a comprehensive assessment?
4. What is the assessment of functional vision, and why is it crucial to delivery of services to a student?

What and How Do I Teach Students with Blindness or Low Vision?

IEP teams must consider two **major issues in determining what and how to teach** students with blindness or low **vision. First, students with blindness or low vision will** likely participate in the general **education core curriculum accessed by all students,** but they may also need to learn skills in an expanded core curriculum that address needs specific to their vision loss. This is not to suggest there are two curricula for students with blindness or low **vision; rather, these students may need to learn some** skills that typical students would not, such as how to manage money when one cannot read denominations and how to use braille. Second, they may require instructional accommodations and special procedures that assist in accessing the expanded core curriculum (Hatlen, 1996).

Instructional Content

For preschool and younger children with blindness or low vision, an early intervention curriculum should be developed. For school-aged students, skills needed in the core curriculum taught to students without disabilities and skills in the expanded core curriculum should be addressed.

Instructional Content for *Young Children and Their Families*

As soon as an infant or toddler is diagnosed with a vision loss, caregivers should become involved in an early intervention program (Miller et al., 2002). Hatton, McWilliam, and Winton (2002) identified several issues specific to early interventionists working with infants and toddlers and their families. First, parents may experience depression at the realization their child has a vision loss. Also, if the child exhibits a lack of eye contact, the attachment process between child and parent could be inhibited. Parents need to learn to interpret their child's behaviors, like crying and reaching, and to adapt the environment by bringing objects to the child to touch and explore physically to promote effective reception of sensory input for the child. Parents also need to learn about their child's diagnosis and prognosis. Because some conditions, such as premature birth that leads to retinopathy, may present other complications, such as low birth weight, medical issues may be the primary priority for a family. Finally, early interventionists need to understand typical child development and the impact of vision loss on development (Hatton et al.,

Relevant CEC Standards

▶ Attitudes and actions of teachers that affect the behaviors of individuals with blindness or low vision (VI3K3)

▶ Relationships among assessment, individualized education plan development, and placement as they affect vision-related services (VI7K1)

▶ Strategies for assisting families and other team members in planning appropriate transitions for individuals with blindness or low vision (VI10K1)

Young children with blindness or low vision may need early intervention services to ensure appropriate development. Use of touch can be an important skill area.

2002). Bishop (2005) noted that motor, social, cognitive, and language development can be impeded if parents are not taught how and encouraged to use techniques to encourage their child's growth. Chen (2001) identified several other important areas in early intervention; these are included in Online Appendix A.

Vision losses affect children from all ethnic/cultural groups. Chen (2001) outlined a number of considerations for working with diverse families of young children with blindness and low vision. Many of the suggestions could also be applicable to families with children with other disabilities as well. These are also listed in Online Appendix A.

Accessing the Expanded Core Curriculum for School-Aged Children

Most students with blindness and low vision have no cognitive disabilities and are quite capable of working within the general core curriculum. They may learn much or all of the same knowledge and skills taught to students without disabilities. Each state determines its general core curriculum, which is explained in the standards, benchmarks, and indicators provided in the various content areas such as mathematics, science, language arts, social studies, fine arts, and physical education. Most students with blindness or low vision also benefit from participating in the expanded core curriculum.

The expanded core curriculum, introduced in 1996 through the "National Agenda for the Education of Children and Youths with Visual Impairments, Including Those with Multiple Disabilities," includes skills that are needed particularly by many students with blindness or low vision, such as visual efficiency skills and orientation and mobility skills. Some skill areas in the expanded core curriculum, such as independent living skills and recreation and leisure skills, may be included in the general core curriculum for all students, but not to the degree needed by many students with blindness and low vision (Hatlen, 1996). The major areas included in the expanded core curriculum include compensatory skills, literacy and braille, listening, orientation and mobility, social interaction, independent living, recreation and leisure, career and transition, and visual efficiency skills (Hatlen, 1996).

Compensatory Skills. Compensatory skills are skills needed by students with blindness or low vision to gain access to and succeed in the general core curriculum. Compensatory skills could include listening skills, organizational skills, and spatial understanding and communication skills (Hatlen, 1996). Communication skills are particularly important given the literacy needs of students with blindness or low vision.

Visual Efficiency Skills. As students with blindness or low vision exhibit considerable variation in visual acuity, it is important that their use of any existing residual vision be encouraged (Hatlen, 1996). Personal traits such as age of onset of the vision loss, expectations of family and others, presence of role models, availability of instruction, and cognitive factors such as level of concept development and communication skills can influence visual efficiency (Corn, DePriest, & Erin, 2005). Learning to focus attention on relevant tasks and stimuli in an environment are important skills for these students.

Some students who are blind rely on learning to read and write with braille as they are not able to use residual vision for printed materials.

Literacy and Braille Skills. Braille, one of the communication systems for those with blindness or low vision, is a system of reading and writing that relies on touch rather than vision, utilizing a series of raised dots representing various letters of the alphabet. Knowledge and skills in this area include the mechanical aspects of reading and writing braille; spatial orientation; use of the braillewriter and the slate and stylus; and the use of decoding, comprehension, and encoding strategies for braille reading and writing (Koenig & Holbrook, 2000). Braille mathematics, braille music, the computer braille code, and foreign language braille codes are other possible areas for braille instruction. Additional learning in receptive and expressive oral language, the use of communication boards, manual communication, and other augmentative devices can help students develop communication skills (Koenig & Holbrook, 2000).

Braille requires some time and effort to learn and should begin in early childhood with an emphasis on tactile perception and hand movement, or **prebraille skills** (Koenig & Holbrook, 2005). It is important that parents and teachers also gain familiarity with braille. Prebraille skills serve as the foundation for being a good braille reader later. Parents should read to their child, expand his or her experiences in the world, encourage oral language skills, and support fine motor skill development (Koenig & Holbrook, 2005). When the student enters school, formal instruction in braille literacy should begin and continue to include use of print media, as appropriate, in conjunction with braille, and the use of braille as a tool for learning other content. As the student becomes more proficient, he or she should be taught to use the various types of slate and styli available for braille writing, advanced skills in the use of computer braille, and any emerging technologies (Koenig & Holbrook, 2000). Students who do not receive substantial training (one to two hours per day) in braille literacy skills and who do not receive instruction from qualified personnel in the use of braille are at risk for entering later academic years with insufficient skills for mastering the content area knowledge required (Koenig & Holbrook, 2005).

In general, professionals have become concerned that braille literacy is on the decline and that students who can benefit from braille literacy skills may not be receiving adequate instruction (Koenig & Holbrook, 2000). There have also been difficulties cited, such as the lack of funding and production, and inefficient management in the timely delivery of braille and large print textbooks and materials to schools and students (Emerson, Corn, & Siller, 2006). Students in middle and high school may continue to need specialized instruction to increase their fluency in braille reading and writing and the use of braille literacy skills in content subject areas; to use reference materials, such as dictionaries; in traditional methods of braille writing, like the Perkins braillewriter, slate and stylus; as well as in new computer technologies and using skills in everyday contexts such as signing one's name or word processing (Koenig & Holbrook, 2005).

prebraille skills The tactile perception and hand movements that will be needed to develop Braille literacy skills.

Writing in braille can take several forms. The slate and stylus procedure uses braille paper inserted into a slate. The slate is composed of two hinged plates of metal or plastic. The top plate, which fits over the paper, has slight indentations that correspond to each of the notches of the top plate. By using the notches as guides, the student inserts the stylus onto the top of the paper and presses the stylus down into the indentations. In actuality, the bottom of the paper will become the reading portion, given that the dots will be raised by the use of the stylus. Although this writing procedure is portable, it can be an extremely time-consuming process.

Another readily available writing procedure uses the Perkins Brailler, sometimes referred to as a braille typewriter or braillewriter. It operates very much like a typewriter except that there are only six keys. Each key produces one of the six dots in their different positions. By depressing a certain number of keys at the same time, the individual can produce desired single-cell, raised-dot combinations. Finally, the Mountbatten Brailler is an electronic device used for producing braille writing and note taking.

Listening Skills. Students with blindness or low vision may need support becoming proficient using listening skills. Because so much learning occurs through the auditory channel, students with blindness or low vision should be taught to use their listening skills to obtain, organize, and store information. Younger children need to learn skills such as awareness and attending to sounds, localizing sounds, developing auditory memory, and auditory closure ("filling in" portions of a speaker's message that may not have been heard clearly). As students get older, they can listen to gather information from speakers, obtain information from recorded sources, and learn strategies for directing their own listening activities (Koenig & Holbrook, 2000).

Orientation and Mobility Skills. Important to some students with blindness or low vision is learning to navigate the school and other environments. These skills enhance students' enjoyment and learning in life as they develop greater independence (Hatlen, 1996). The educator should consider a variety of factors in orienting students to both indoor and outdoor environments. The Classroom Suggestions

Classroom Suggestions Checklist for Environmental Arrangement Considerations for Students with Blindness or Low Vision

❑ Is the student familiar with bus loading zones, procedures, and safety?

❑ Is the student familiar with the playground, boundaries, and safe use of equipment?

❑ Is the student familiar with the community environment that must be navigated and procedures in coming and going to school?

❑ Does the student know the locations and purposes of all the offices, rooms, and potential hazards in the school building?

❑ Does the student know the physical arrangement of her or his classroom(s) and has the environment been made navigable and safe?

❑ Does the student know the location of areas within the classroom such as a sink, restroom, or learning centers?

❑ Is the student familiar with the media center and procedures for using the materials and equipment there?

❑ Is the student familiar with the cafeteria and the procedures involved in obtaining, eating, and disposing of food?

Source: Cox, P., & Dykes, M. (2001). Effective classroom adaptations for students with visual impairments. *Teaching Exceptional Children, 33*(6), 68–74.

provides a checklist educators can use when considering environmental challenges for students with blindness or low vision.

Cox and Dykes (2001) pointed out that educators should also be aware that for the student to understand the physical arrangement of the school and classroom, and to use what is available there, as well as to access curriculum materials, the student will need tactile and kinesthetic learning opportunities that involve hands-on activities and materials. The environment should be reasonably consistent in its setup so students can develop a mental map of the room's layout to avoid injury from colliding with or falling over furniture or objects. Auditory input is critical, but educators should not assume that students with a vision loss will understand verbal input as might a sighted student. For example, just because a student may be able to hear a group discussion on local geography does not mean the student will truly understand that geography. Virtual models of classrooms and schools can be constructed so that students can use tactile input to better construct a mental map of the layout of physical environments prior to actually navigating them. Teachers should be involved in supporting a student's navigation, but an orientation and mobility teacher can be especially helpful in developing skills in this area (Cox & Dykes, 2001).

Orientation and mobility (O&M) teachers provide consultation to educators as well as direct services to students. These teachers can conduct individual assessments to determine a student's present levels of performance and participate in the development of IEPs. In terms of direct instruction, O&M teachers help students learn mobility skills when moving with a sighted guide, protective techniques, indoor and outdoor cane skills, how to cross streets, and the use of transportation. The use of a cane enables individuals to move reasonably safely in both indoor and outdoor environments. A cane also can serve to alert drivers and others that the individual has a significant vision loss. O&M teachers may also provide inservice to teachers, other personnel, and family members (Griffin-Shirley, Kelley, & Lawrence, 2006).

Social Interaction Skills. People with typical vision learn many social skills by observing the behavior and appearance of others. Students with blindness or low vision do not learn these skills incidentally (Hatlen, 1996). These students may need the special education teacher to work with parents to encourage early social interactions, assess social competence, provide direct and targeted instruction in social skills, provide accurate and constructive feedback, construct opportunities for experiential learning at school and in the community, and ensure these skills are included in a student's IEP. It may also be important for these students to have opportunities to interact with and gain mentoring from other individuals with blindness or low vision to prevent a sense of isolation and to help develop an identity as a person with a vision loss (Sacks & Silberman, 2005).

Independent Living Skills. Traditional classes in the area of independent living skills, such as family and consumer sciences, may be inadequate for students with blindness or low vision (Hatlen, 1996). Activities of daily living that lead to independence in everyday functioning, such as dressing, grooming, personal hygiene, food preparation, money management, time monitoring, and organization, may need to be taught directly to students (Hatlen, 1996). Also, teachers should be sensitive to cultural values regarding independence, as some families may place greater value on interdependence within the family and culture than on individual independence (Kelley & Smith, 2005).

Recreation and Leisure Skills. The typical core curriculum tends to stress physical fitness, individual and team games, and athletics, many aspects of which can be appropriate for students with blindness or low vision. Students with blindness or low vision may need to develop other skills and activities they can enjoy throughout their lives (Hatlen, 1996). In general, special education teachers and adaptive physical education teachers should expose students to a variety of activities so that they may choose those that match their interests, provide direct instruction in the necessary skills, consult with community personnel to ensure participation outside of school, and link recreation and leisure to the typical core curriculum: for example, swimming can involve understanding time and distance (McGregor & Farenkopf, 2005).

It is important that adults not make summary judgments about which activities are appropriate for students with blindness or low vision. People with blindness and low vision engage in downhill skiing, bowling, scuba diving, and hiking and camping as well as special sports such as beep baseball, which is specifically designed for those with blindness or low vision (McGregor & Farenkopf, 2005).

Career and Transition Skills. As students move through their school years, career education and transition planning and programming become increasingly important. Prior to the transition from high school to adult life, students with blindness or low vision should receive career education and vocational counseling. Career education may be similar to that afforded students without disabilities, but it should also include community-based experiences, assessment of individual abilities and interests, and opportunities to interact with adults with blindness or low vision who are employed (Spungin & Ferrell, 2007). Access to technology skill development and assistive technology devices can be critical in developing employment options because many individuals will require assistive technology to perform their job duties (Butler, Crudden, Sansing, & LeJeune, 2002). The Classroom Example presents a sample form for analyzing a potential work environment for a student with a vision loss.

Because discrimination does exist, it is important that students with blindness or low vision learn self-advocacy skills. They must also set personal goals and develop plans to achieve those goals. Development of self-determination skills, such as making choices and decisions about one's present and future, are an important curriculum area from early in schooling to the transition process. Nagle (2001) also suggested that employers and others in the community be educated to improve attitudes toward those with blindness and low vision, and to improve social support networks that could enhance the transition process. Summer or part-time employment can also be helpful in preparation for the transition from school to adult living (Nagle, 2001).

The expanded core curriculum is an important focus for the instructional content for students with blindness or low vision. Still, depending on how services are delivered, such as through an itinerant model with limited time spent with a special education teacher or other low vision specialists, many students may not be receiving the quality and quantity of instruction in these important areas that may benefit them (Wolffe, Sacks, Corn, Erin, Huebner, & Lewis, 2002). Future teachers should be aware of the expanded core curriculum and the need for students with blindness or low vision to have access to the instructional content and procedures that lead to the acquisition of the important skills embedded in that curriculum.

Instructional Procedures

In choosing instructional procedures to use with students with blindness or low vision, one consideration is how procedures need to be modified to ensure students can fully access materials and activities. For the most part, students with blindness or low vision should engage in the same tasks and learn the same information as students without disabilities, although more time may be needed to complete assignments (Holbrook & Koenig, 2005). Adaptations may be needed due to specific issues related to blindness or low vision, as well as general classroom procedures to ensure access to learning activities. Holbrook & Koenig suggested that adaptations be individualized and be based on the functional impact of the student's vision loss on his or her education, need for assistive technology to access materials, the student's adaptive skills, including listening-comprehension skills, personal preferences of the student, and the goals of each assignment.

Name of Student _____

Name of Potential Employer _____

Location of Employer _____

Date of Analysis _____

Name of Person Completing Analysis _____

Check the appropriate space and provide comments:	**Yes**	**No**
1. Does the job require use of residual vision in performance of job duties?	_____	_____
Explain:		
2. Will the student need extensive mobility and orientation training?	_____	_____
Explain:		
3. Is transportation to work available through public transit or coworkers?	_____	_____
Explain:		
4. Will the student need specialized assistive technology on the job?	_____	_____
Explain:		
5. Will the student have access to job training through the employer?	_____	_____
Explain:		

Complete the following:

1. List accessibility issues if any:

2. List typical activities or work tasks:

3. List people within the environment with whom the person will interact:

4. List any special considerations for the climate and culture of the environment:

5. List benefits or special accommodations available:

Source: Adapted from Sitlington, P. L., & Clark, G. M. (2004). *Transition education and services for students with disabilities* (4th ed.). Boston, MA: Allyn & Bacon.

PRACTICE

Adaptations for Specific Issues Related to Blindness or Low Vision

This section discusses adaptations and suggestions related to specific physical and perception issues that a student may experience due to blindness or low vision. Collaboration among teachers, related services personnel, the family, and the student is crucial in determining which specific procedures will work best for the individual.

Physical Issues. Physical manifestations and characteristics may affect the classroom experience of a student with blindness or low vision (Harley et al., 2000). If a student's eyes have an abnormal appearance, counseling may be necessary to deal with reactions from others. Care for a prosthetic eye may also be necessary. If unusual or persistent mannerisms such as weaving of the head or rocking emerge, cognitive and behavioral interventions may be necessary (Estevis & Koenig, 1994). If the eyes have unusual movement or responses, it may be necessary to explain these to the general education teacher because these movements can affect visual attention, focusing, and eye fatigue (Harley et al., 2000).

Perception Issues. How students with blindness or low vision perceive what they can see should be considered when planning their educational experiences (Harley et al., 2000). Some students may need training in using their residual vision more effectively. For example, a student with a recently acquired vision loss may need assistance in learning how to use his or her residual vision to continue reading printed materials with magnification. Some students develop loss of vision or very weak vision in one eye. These students should be seated in the part of the room (left, center, or right side) that best accommodates their low vision. Students with convergence problems may need extended time to complete reading assignments because near reading ability is affected. Students with depth perception difficulties may need to be taught eye-hand coordination and distance recognition skills. Teachers need to know that some students with distant visual discrimination problems may not respond to visual or facial expressions and may need oral directions in locating materials (Harley et al., 2000).

Several adaptations should be considered for students with color or visual discrimination problems. Students with color discrimination problems may need to have objects labeled that are normally identifiable by their color, such as colored paper or crayons. These students can also benefit from use of contrast and controlled lighting. Finally, they may also need to be taught skills used in everyday life, such as responding to traffic signals, which are dependent on color discrimination (Harley et al., 2000).

General Classroom Procedures

General classroom procedures can support the learning of students with blindness or low vision. Classroom teachers can provide a student with a copy of teacher or class notes, read aloud while writing on a board or overhead, supply audiotapes of print materials as needed, allow a student to orally record responses rather than writing them, enlarge print materials distributed to the class, and provide hands-on learning. Teachers should keep in mind that students with blindness or low vision need direct instruction in areas where incidental learning may not occur, such as in learning names of peers and building relationships (Cox & Dykes, 2001).

Students with blindness or low vision may also benefit from the use of models and manipulatives that allow them to experience hands-on learning. For example, the use of a three-dimensional model of the classroom and school could aid the student in developing a mental map of the environment (Budd & LaGrow, 2000). Tactile diagrams and graphs and the use of real objects in the classroom can also be helpful (Kumar, Ramasamy, & Stefanich, 2001). The Classroom Suggestions feature lists additional procedures that may be used by the teacher of students with blindness or low vision.

❏ Ensure that the student has all educational materials in the media form best suited to her or him.

❏ Ensure that the student is trained in the use of and has access to all necessary and technological devices.

❏ Use direct instruction in developmental skills and academic strategies and any other area requiring modification, adaptation, or reinforcement.

❏ Recommend seating placement and modifications in the environment as well as facilitating movement.

❏ Ensure that others fully understand the student's unique needs.

❏ Suggest accommodations in assignments or assessments.

❏ Collaborate with others in including the student in routine learning and social activities.

❏ Act as a catalyst in helping the peers and classmates without disabilities, as well as family members, to understand the vision loss and its implications.

Source: Spungin, S. J., & Ferrell, K. A. (2007). *The role and function of the teacher of students with blindness or low vision.* Retrieved July 3, 2007, from http://www.cecdvi.org/Postion%20Papers/RevisedRole&FunctionofTVI2006.doc

Check Your Understanding

1. What considerations should be made when working with infants, toddlers, or preschool children who have blindness and low vision?

2. Which areas of skill development should be considered when planning the expanded core curriculum for students with blindness or low vision?

3. What transition issues should be considered in planning for postsecondary life or education?

4. What are some general adaptations for physical manifestations and perceptual characteristics of vision problems?

5. What instructional procedure adaptations can be made when working with students with blindness or low vision?

What Are Other Instructional Considerations for Teaching Students with Blindness or Low Vision?

Of considerable importance in delivering services to students with blindness or low vision are the instructional environment and the use of technology. Access to the content of the general education curriculum is often dependent on the arrangement of the classroom or learning space and the use of assistive devices. Additionally, hardware and software can make visual materials and learning more accessible. Knowing how to arrange the classroom and which technologies are available and helpful can enhance the achievement of students with blindness or low vision.

Relevant CEC Standard
▶ Impact of visual impairment on learning and experience (VI2K4)

The Instructional Environment

Today, the tendency is to recommend placement of students with blindness or low vision in settings with opportunities to interact with peers without disabilities (Miller et al., 2002), whether in the general education classroom or in a special classroom in a neighborhood school. We can think of the instructional environment in at least two ways.

Students with blindness or low vision will need access to the physical environment, materials, and learning activities. Hands-on learning activities can be helpful.

First, it is the least restrictive environment (LRE) in which the student can learn and interact with others. Second, regardless of which environment is determined to be least restrictive, certain adaptations can be made to enhance learning and skill acquisition.

Placement Options

There are several important points that may influence the decision of what constitutes the LRE for a student with blindness or low vision.

- Learning may need to occur through touch and sound more than through vision.
- Specialized skills and equipment may be needed.
- Direct instruction of skills learned incidentally by others through observation and modeling may be required.
- Individualized instruction, such as learning braille literacy skills, may be needed at times.
- Equal access to the core curriculum is a key goal.
- Provision of services by appropriately certified personnel, such as by an O&M specialist, may be required. (Huebner & Koenig, n.d.)

It is possible that the LRE for a child with blindness or low vision will change over the years. A child learning to read and write in braille may need considerable individualized instruction initially but may require much less once those literacy skills are mastered. Although inclusion is a popular movement in schools today, the Division on Visual Impairments of CEC supports the continuing existence of placement options including special schools and classes for students with blindness or low vision. Special schools, once residential in nature, now provide outreach services such as direct itinerant services, inservice training for teachers and families, sites for professional practica, early intervention, assessment and diagnostic services, technical assistance to local education agencies, production and dissemination of special materials, and support groups (Huebner & Koenig, n.d.).

One consideration in determining student placement is the support available from a special education teacher or related services provider. As visual impairment is a low incidence disability category, some school districts, especially rural or smaller districts, may lack the "critical mass" of students with blindness or low vision needed to provide all necessary services from within the district's own resources or within a particular school in a district. In these cases, itinerant teachers of students with blindness or low vision may provide direct instruction, consultation to general education and other special education teachers, assistance in assessing students' skill development, curriculum modification, and use of technology (Huebner & Koenig, n.d.). Itinerant teachers should serve students with few special education needs and whose overall educational needs can be met by general education teachers or other special education teachers. It is important that IEPs not be written based on the amount of time or services available from an itinerant teacher but on the individual needs of the student (Lewis & Allman, 2005).

Resource rooms may provide some advantages. First, special education teachers are able to view a student's functioning and adjustment in a variety of school settings such as the classroom, cafeteria, and gym. Second, special education teachers may be more available to assist in the inclusion of students with blindness or low vision than would be the case in an itinerant model (Lewis & Allman, 2005).

Residential schools served many students with blindness or low vision in the United States prior to IDEA (Hatlen, 2005), and many states continue to support these special residential schools. Lewis and Allman (2005) pointed out several possible advantages of these schools. They provide an environment where all the adults involved understand the challenges and strengths of students with blindness or low vision. Learning activities and materials are specifically designed for these students, which results in increased academic engagement time— students with blindness or low vision do not have to wait through instruction designed for students with typical vision and then receive special adaptations or instruction. Because they are residential, instruction can easily extend beyond the six-hour school day and into the living areas and community. Most residential schools do not lead to complete segregation of students with blindness or low vision from others without disabilities, but they can lead to a degree of separation from families because of their residential nature.

ROBERT REVISITED What benefits is Robert likely to derive from being in the general education environment versus a special school or classroom? What benefits might he derive from a special school or classroom?

Arranging the Instructional Environment

Future teachers should be aware that the environment and materials used in general or special education classes will need to be adapted for students with blindness or low vision. Many adaptations can be made without significant effort (for example, reducing glare or adjusting brightness). The key is that students with blindness or low vision should be learning much of or the same material as those without disabilities. There are at least two ways to plan the arrangement of the instructional environment for students with blindness and low vision. First, educators should address adaptations in the environment itself that can aid access and learning. Second, educators should consider how to make instructional environments most conducive to the use of the student's functional vision.

Classroom Adaptations. Particularly for students with low vision, making the environment as conducive as possible for use of functional vision in learning is an important facet of planning and instruction. Harley et al. (2000) note that visual performance is affected by brightness, contrast, time, distance, complexity of tasks, and the size of images. Ways to plan for these areas are summarized in the Classroom Suggestions.

Modifying Materials for Students with Blindness and Low Vision. Access to print is critical for those students with functional vision for its use. To support access, the teacher should consider whether and how classroom materials need to be modified. Some students will be able to access materials through larger print. Overall, large print readers outnumber braille readers by better than a 4:1 ratio (Wall & Corn, 2002). In addition to making materials accessible through large print, the student may also need materials in braille, recorded on tape or CD, or read by a human reader to fully access the curriculum.

For some students, increasing the actual size of the printed word or image determines whether they can read the material. These students may require that you increase the size of fonts on materials you use in class and make available large print books so that they can more easily discriminate the letters and words. Although some students may be able to read regular print texts by holding the page very close to their eyes, this may cause fatigue and can adversely affect their reading rate. Large print books are by nature more cumbersome than regular print books, so if a student can use regular print

Brightness. Although it might stand to reason that most students with blindness and low vision benefit from a brighter environment, some students will not benefit because of the distinct characteristics of their visual impairment. For example, certain types of visual-motor tasks (like typing or word processing) probably require increased lighting, whereas gross-motor tasks such as walking do not. The teaching environment, therefore, must allow for adjustments in brightness. In addition, some students are sensitive to too much light.

Glare may result from unwanted light coming from the chalkboard, floor, or the pages of a book. By using reflective control colors for chalkboards and floors and nonglossy reading book pages, glare can be considerably reduced. The student might also be positioned to reduce glare.

Contrast refers to the degree that a visual task (or an object/symbol that is being looked at) is visually discrete or different from the background of the task. Increasing contrast increases visibility of materials for many students. For example, the contrast between black letters on white paper (or vice versa) seems appropriate for most students with blindness and low vision although other color contrasts can also be helpful.

Size refers to the use of devices with enlarged letters and numbers. For example, telephones, timers, and other devices can be used that are designed for those with vision losses. Optical devices (for example, magnifying devices) can also be used.

Sources: Corn, A. L., DePriest, L. B., & Erin, J. N. (2005) Visual efficiency. In Holbrook, M. C. & Koenig, A. J. (Eds.), *Foundation of education: Volume II instructional strategies for teaching children and youths with visual impairments* (2nd ed., chap. 13); Harley, R. K., Lawrence, G. A., Sanford, L., & Burnett, R. (2000). *Visual impairment in the schools* (3rd ed.). Springfield, IL: Charles C Thomas.

materials, this is advisable (Gardner & Corn, n.d.). Frank (2000) reported that several factors could affect access to large print materials including the length of time needed to obtain the materials, the quality of copies, the amount of information about what was available and rights to the materials, and emotional responses to the potential difficulties in obtaining the materials. Similarly, braille books are larger—a typical print textbook may come in several volumes in braille—and more cumbersome as well.

Holbrook and Koenig (2005) provide examples of how materials may be modified:

1. Decrease visual clutter. For example, remove unnecessary elements from a printed task to focus student attention on the relevant characteristics.
2. Make materials tactile. For example, translate the material into braille, and make graphics such as maps in three dimensions.
3. Convert materials to auditory form for large quantities of written material where reading itself or locating information in a text are not the goals of the assignment.
4. Have another student describe or narrate what is taking place visually when using videos in teaching,
5. Use real objects to substitute for the pictures when possible when using pictures in teaching.

Instructional Technology

Relevant CEC Standard

▶ Strategies for teaching technology skills to individuals with blindness or low vision (VI4K6)

It is critical that students with blindness or low vision have access to technology to enhance independence and efficiency in learning. According to the Division on Visual Impairments of CEC, technology instruction that is tailored to individual needs should be a fundamental part of the curriculum for these students (Mack & Koenig, n.d.). Table 9.3 includes examples of assistive technology available in three critical areas: speech, scanned materials, and braille. Programs for magnifying computer screen text and graphics to make regular print materials accessible through enlargement are also available (Kapperman & Sticken, 2005). Decisions about which technologies may be most beneficial for a student should be based on the results of a comprehensive evaluation, including the learning media assessment (Kapperman & Sticken, 2005).

The primary advantage of assistive technology is that it allows users to access the printed word in a manner that suits their functional vision ability and skills. The use of assistive technology can provide less expensive access to printed materials than either braille or large print materials. This technology also provides access to the Internet and allows for better productivity in school and on a job (Kapperman & Sticken, 2005).

Although not really technology as we typically think of it, guide dogs are used by some individuals with blindness or low vision to enhance safe movement in community environments. Because some level of maturity is expected from the human

TABLE 9.3	Assistive Technology Hardware and Software for Students with Blindness or Low Vision

TALKING WORD PROCESSORS	SPEECH SYNTHESIZERS	SCANNED MATERIAL ACCESS
Intellitalk Software Suite—Talking word processing program that allows students to hear the letter, word, sentence or phrase as it is entered into the computer.	Software versions—Works in the Windows 2000, XP, Vista environment with a SoundBlaster compatible sound card. Examples include AT&T Natural Voices, DECaccess 32, Eloquence, and Microsoft SDK.	Open Book—Uses a scanner to take a picture of the page, which it sends to your PC, translates the picture into understandable text, and then speaks the text aloud or outputs to Braille.
Write: OUTLOUD—Allows the student to set background and font colors, and then save the configuration.		Expert Reader—An easy-to-use stand-alone reading machine that offers improved levels of speed, accuracy, and ease of use.
		Kurzweil 1000—Software that works on your personal computer and a scanner to convert the printed word into speech.

BRAILLE TRANSLATION SOFTWARE	BRAILLE EMBOSSERS	BRAILLE DISPLAYS	PORTABLE DEVICES
Braille2000—Braille editing tool that handles all kinds of direct entry Braille tasks with automated page layouts to aid the production of literary, textbook, and music Braille.	Braille Embossers are printers whose output is braille instead of print. Examples include Braille Blazer, Braillo, Everest, Index Basic, Juliet, Marathon, Romeo, Thomas, and Viewplus.	Braille displays utilize what is called refreshable Braille cells to allow the computer screen to be read line by line in braille. Examples include Braille Connect, Braillex, Braille Wave, Brilliant, Focus.	PacMate BNS or Voice Note BT—Have a Braille keyboard layout and speech output.
Duxbury—Grade 2 braille editing and translation software.			Braille Wave—Braille keyboard, refreshable Braille.
Megadots—Allows you to create, edit and format text and to perform all the basic functions of a standard word processor.			PacMate TNS or VoiceNote QT—Have a Qwerty keyboard and speech output.
NFB-Trans—Freeware translation program available from the National Federation of the Blind.			PacMate QX or BrailleNote QT—Have a Qwerty keyboard layout, speech output, and refreshable Braille.
			Mountbatten—Braille keyboard; speech, and paper braille output.
			PacMate BX or BrailleNote BT—Have braille keyboard, speech output and refreshable braille.

Source: Overview of technology for visually impaired and blind students. Taken from www.tsbvi.edu/technology/overview.htm. Used with permission.

PRACTICE

partner, many students are age 16 or older before they have a guide dog. According to Guide Dogs for the Blind (2006), about 10,000 people in the United States and Canada use guide dogs. Guide dogs may go anywhere a person goes. The public should remember that guide dogs are working animals, and one should always seek permission from the human partner before approaching, petting, or allowing one's own dog to interact with a guide dog. Guide dogs are often initially trained by puppy-raiser families before beginning their formal training at a special school. Guide dogs are not just well-trained pets; they undergo thousands of hours of training to prepare for their duties. Guide dog and human must also be trained in tandem to build the working relationship. Typically, dogs meet their human partners when the dogs are 1 to 1.5 years old, and training the two together takes two to four weeks. Special schools for training guide dogs rely on funding sources rather than requiring individuals with blindness or low vision to pay for the services (Guide Dogs for the Blind, 2006).

Check Your Understanding

1. What are some considerations in determining the LRE for a student with a visual impairment? What are possible educational placements?

2. How can the instructional environment be adapted to aid learning through the use of functional vision? How can materials be modified to improve access?

3. Why are technology and technology skill development fundamental to a student's curriculum?

4. What are some types of technology available to support students with blindness and low vision?

What Are Some Considerations for the General Education Teacher?

If the LRE for a student with blindness or low vision is part- or all-day placement within the general education setting and working within the general education curriculum, the general education teacher, along with the rest of the IEP team, should collaborate to consider two primary areas. How can the environment be prepared for the student? How can the student be accommodated in the learning and other activities within the classroom?

The inclusion of students with blindness or low vision begins with how the environment is prepared to accept and allow access for the student. Researchers in one national study identified both inhibiting and facilitating factors for access to the general curriculum (Smith, Geruschat, & Huebner, 2004). The first inhibiting factor was the assumption by general education teachers and parents that large print materials are easy to obtain or create, and that bigger is always better. Second, general and special education teachers lacked training in the use of optical devices and computer software, and parents sometimes felt that optical devices were stigmatizing. Third, itinerant services, rather than having fully qualified teachers and other professionals available in a school, were considered less desirable for allowing access to the general education curriculum. In rural areas in particular, the availability of qualified personnel, such as low vision specialists, can be a problem in determining which services optimize functional vision. The study found that facilitating factors included a philosophy that the students should be prepared for lifelong learning and that large print materials are not always best when other computer technologies allow access to regular print materials. Another facilitating factor was a core group of individuals committed to providing excellence in services.

Generally, peers and students with blindness or low vision may need some preparation and ongoing encouragement to establish relationships. Researchers have found that simply placing students in classes with sighted peers does not necessarily result in successful socialization. Each group needs support in developing interaction skills. In addition, time should be allowed for unsupervised interactions, such as on the playground (McGaha & Farran, 2001). Preparation of teachers, students, and parents for the challenges and benefits of inclusive education are important for each group to interact successfully with the other.

Classroom Suggestions Suggestions for Including Students with Blindness and Low Vision in the General Education Classroom

Cox and Dykes (2001) and Smith and Luckasson (1992) offered several suggestions for including students with blindness or low vision in the general education classroom:

❑ Provide visual cues such as posting and reading a daily schedule and have time cues (e.g., easily readable clock or verbal cues) available to help students stay on track.

❑ Plan for regular consultation with the vision specialist.

❑ Make materials as tactile as possible (e.g., make models three dimensional, or if two-dimensional models are used, raise lines so their outlines can be felt). Be consistent in the placement of materials so that students know where particular items are located.

❑ Check for understanding of verbal directions and input on a regular basis.

❑ Develop auditory cues or signals for getting and paying attention.

❑ Provide extra space for organizing equipment or technology.

❑ Place the child's desk close to the teacher, the chalkboard, and the door (but not so close as to warrant undue attention).

❑ Reduce distracting glare by placing the child's desk facing away from the light source but in a well-lighted area.

❑ Allow the child to move closer during presentations or demonstrations.

❑ Remove dangerous obstacles and clutter from the room.

❑ Open or close doors fully, as half-opened doors can be dangerous obstacles.

❑ Reduce unnecessary noise.

❑ Speak in normal tones.

❑ Although it is important to provide extra time for completing assignments in many instances, a reasonable due date should be established.

❑ Do not allow the student's disability to become an excuse for poor or unacceptable performance.

❑ Tell the student when you are leaving the room. It is a good idea as well to inform a student who is blind when you enter a room or are offering some materials or items to the student.

Sources: Cox and Dykes (2001); Smith and Luckasson (1992).

Students with vision loss have reported that support for their emotional and learning needs, being listened to and cared for, being encouraged to excel, and receiving assistance with problem solving were all important teacher variables that affected their adjustment in school (Chang & Schaller, 2002). Therefore, teachers should acknowledge the support needs of the student and build in time for encouragement, have high but realistic expectations, demonstrate caring, and be willing to listen to and help solve problems.

General education teachers typically provide feedback in written form for most students punctuated with auditory feedback. However, for some students with blindness or low vision, written feedback may be of little use. They may relay primarily on auditory feedback. Holbrook & Koenig (2005) pointed out three ways to provide auditory feedback to students regarding assignments and their performance. First, although this is a time-consuming process, a teacher could discuss the work directly with the student in a way that also allows for clarification as needed. Occasional conferences may be more realistic. Second, feedback can be provided via an audiotape. Third, a student who uses computer technology may also prefer feedback via a computer disk or flash drive.

General education teachers should maintain high expectations academically and socially for students with blindness or low vision. Students need to understand that employers often apply the same standards of competence as with any employee (Holbrook & Koenig, 2005).

In Practice Meet Educator Ingrid Huisman and Her Student Darin

I teach math in a multicultural, low-socioeconomic high school. I am currently enjoying my 24th year of teaching. As a member of the special education department, I teach applied math. This is a resource math class for ninth graders who do not take algebra because their math skills are two or more years behind their peers. The students in my classes have a variety of math levels due to disabilities such as learning disabilities, emotional disabilities, autism, other health impairments, traumatic brain injuries, speech impairments, and visual impairments. In one class I may have students whose math levels range from third grade to seventh grade. My challenge is to

design curriculum that will meet each student's needs and increase their math abilities. Some of my students will go on to take pre-algebra and then algebra in the 11th grade, making it possible for them to get on a college track. Some of my students will continue to take practical math courses that focus on functional math that is needed in daily applications.

My student Darin qualifies for special education with a learning disability and visual impairment. Darin is legally blind and has received special education services since he was in first grade. Darin can navigate his way around the school without assistance, and he can see and recognize his friends and teachers when they are about five feet from him. Darin's difficulty with learning comes to a large degree from his learning disability, which is compounded by his blindness. His learning disability is in the areas of reading comprehension, written expression, and math reasoning. Darin has glasses and can read what is written on paper if he holds his eyes very close to it. This makes it difficult to read because he can only see a few words or numbers at a time. He works with the specialist in visual impairments who helps him with strategies for coping with his blindness.

Instructional Environment and Technology

Darin's math class has nine other students in it. For Darin to be successful,

most of his work needs to be enlarged. If the students are expected to take notes, Darin must sit right next to the screen where the notes are being projected, then he can follow along with the rest of the class. Additionally, I give him a copy of the notes rather than require him to copy them. My assistant or I will read tests, quizzes, and daily work to Darin and other students who have difficulty with reading. Through this accommodation, his math learning is not impeded by his reading difficulties, and he is more successful getting started and gaining momentum. Another accommodation that is made for Darin is to decrease the number of items on assignments or allow him to answer orally instead of writing his response. Although my room is equipped with three student computers, Darin does not use the computer very much. He is unable to see the details of the entire screen. I hope new technology will offer Darin better opportunities for learning in the future using computer technology.

Instructional Content and Procedures

Each student in my class has an IEP that lists his or her math goals and accommodations. My district does not have a predetermined curriculum for the students enrolled in applied math classes. I am free to create lessons and find activities that can be adapted. Many times a problem-solving task can be solved in a variety of ways,

Future teachers are responsible for ensuring that all students are included in the classroom to allow for meaningful participation in learning and development of satisfying and appropriate social relationships. General education teachers set the tone in the inclusive classroom that leads to achievement and acceptance. Special educators should be able to assist general educators with suggestions and specific strategies to promote successful inclusion of students with blindness or low vision.

using different levels of math ability. I may give the following problem to my students knowing that some of my students are going to approach it with varying levels of background knowledge and skills in math.

Pencils are on sale at the discount store. You can buy 4 pencils for 3 dollars. You have 18 dollars. How many pencils can you buy?

Darin frequently will demonstrate frustration with problem solving. I encourage him to use a strategy that makes sense to him. I may give the students mock money and pencils and have them act out the problem.

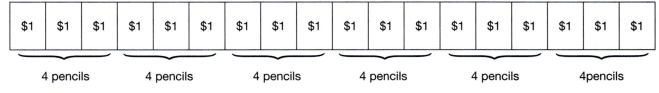

4 + 4 + 4 + 4 + 4 + 4 = 24 pencils

Although Darin needs to start out solving this problem with a visual, he can learn to use a table such as this one. Darin uses the multiplication chart or calculator to complete the table.

Number of dollars	3	6	9	12	15	18	21	24			
Number of pencils	4	8	12	16	20	24					

Some of my students are able to use a proportion to solve this same problem.

$$\frac{\text{number of dollars}}{\text{number of pencils}} \quad \frac{3}{4} = \frac{18}{?}$$

To use this strategy, Darin must understand that the ratio of dollars to pencils is 3 to 4. Then he must recognize that the number of pencils will increase proportionately with the number of dollars. I encourage all my students to choose a strategy that fits their own unique learning style.

Collaboration

Each special education student at my school is assigned a case manager, a special education teacher who serves as a contact person and confidant for the student. At the beginning of the year Darin's case manager introduced herself to Darin and encouraged him to come to her if he had any concerns or questions. Darin's mom was also contacted and assured that Darin was being monitored. This system gives families one person to call if they have a question about anything. Darin's case manager makes contact with all of his other teachers to gather information about him and to give information when needed.

In preparation for the annual review of Darin's IEP, Darin's case manager gathers information concerning strengths and weaknesses from all his teachers and asks the teachers to make suggestions about his placement in classes for the next year. Each of Darin's teachers responds to a checklist of accommodations that they feel Darin needs to be successful. Darin is present in the meeting with his parent, and they can request additional accommodations. His specialist in visual impairments, an administrator, and a general education representative are also present at this meeting. Darin is supported by an entire team of people who care about him. By focusing on his strengths, Darin's support team helps him to be successful.

Check Your Understanding

1. How should the environment be prepared, physically and socially, for the student with blindness or low vision?

2. How can teachers support and involve students with blindness or low vision in learning activities and the general education curriculum?

3. What are some simple procedures to increase the likelihood of more successful inclusion of the student with blindness or low vision?

Practical Considerations for the Classroom

What IDEA 04 Says about Visual Impairments: IDEA defines a visual impairment as blindness or a loss of vision that adversely affects educational performance.

Identification Tools: Congenital vision losses are typically identified during infancy by a doctor or vision specialist. Less severe vision losses may not be identified until the child reaches school age. *Identifying Young Children:* Parental reporting, the family history, and behavioral responses may be used to identify blindness or a vision loss. *Identifying School-Aged Children:* A Snellen chart may be used in school screening. A comprehensive assessment that examines functional vision use, learning media, cognitive ability, academic achievement, orientation and mobility skills, and social and independent living skills is most helpful to teachers.

Characteristics	Indicators You Might See
Intellectual Ability	Blindness and low vision generally have no effect on general intelligence. Students may have difficulty with the "big picture" if they must learn through hearing and touch and cannot see objects in their wholeness.
Play and Social Interaction Skills	Play and social interaction skill development may be delayed, especially in exploratory-sensorimotor and symbolic play; early intervention is necessary.
Language Development	No crucial differences in language development from that of those without blindness or low vision. Individuals may use different physical or facial gestures. Individuals may have problems with the pragmatics of language.
Academic Achievement	Academic achievement may lag slightly behind that of sighted students due to gaps in knowledge created by limited visual input, experience, or slower development. Most students should be able to achieve academically.
Perceptual Abilities	Includes tactile and auditory development, as well as any residual vision. May have difficulty with spatial perception affecting orientation, mobility, and wayfinding skills.
Psychological and Social Adjustment	May have social skill issues due to social isolation or due to negative reactions of peers.

Students with Blindness or Low Vision

Teaching Implications

Instructional Content

- Early intervention should be planned for young children identified with a visual impairment. Family involvement should be planned for.
- Many students with visual impairments will participate in the general curriculum.
- The expanded core curriculum includes skills not in the general core curriculum as well as skills that are included but not to the degree needed, such as the following:
  - Compensatory skills for their vision loss
  - Visual efficiency skills
  - Literacy and braille skills
  - Orientation and mobility skills
  - Social interaction skills
  - Independent living skills
  - Recreation and leisure skills
  - Career and transition skills

Instructional Procedures

- In selecting instructional procedures, consider how they need to be modified to allow students to fully access the learning activities and materials.
- Consider adaptations needed for physical issues.
- Consider adaptations needed for perceptual issues.
- Determine what additional materials, such as large print, auditory, models, and manipulatives can be provided to the student to improve learning and access to the curriculum.

Instructional Environment

- Remember that a student's least restrictive environment is individualized but is frequently in the general education classroom with adaptations and consultation.
- Some students may attend special schools.
- Plan an environment that supports the student's orientation and mobility. Ensure that the environment is consistently designed.
- Consider making a model of the classroom for the student to create a mental picture from.
- Consider the effects of brightness, contrast, time, distance, complexity of tasks, and the size of images when planning the environment.

Instructional Technology

- Assistive technology should be based on individual needs and a learning media assessment.
- Access to information can be supported through optical devices, speech and scanned print software, and braille access software.
- When integrating high technology aids, consider accessibility, affordability, availability, compatibility, portability, usability, and trainability.
- Guide dogs may be of assistance to their human partners.

Methodologies and Strategies to Try

- Many instructional techniques used with sighted students are applicable although some modifications may be needed to the materials and activities.
- Direct intervention by or consultation with a teacher specifically trained to work with these students may be necessary to ensure proper accessibility and accommodations are made.
- The use of technology and braille literacy programs can be beneficial.
- Providing role models for students with vision loss can help in mentoring students in career development and transitions.
- Behavioral interventions can be helpful in reducing unusual mannerisms (such as head weaving) as well as to help students learn how to care for themselves (for example, caring for a prosthetic eye).
- Provide emotional and social supports and involve the family and peers in the student's education.

Considerations for the General Classroom and Collaboration

The general education teacher should:

- Be sure that the classroom environment is properly prepared for the student.
- Become familiar with the type of materials or aids (large print, optical devices, computer software) the student needs to access information and perform tasks.
- Plan accommodations for all lessons, activities, and classroom resources.
- Encourage social interaction between students with visual impairments and other students in the class.
- Give feedback in person, auditory form, or by computer as needed.
- Maintain high expectations for learning and performance.

Collaboration

General and special educators should consult on:

- Planning the classroom environment
- Determining the skills needed in the expanded core curriculum
- Developing adaptations
- Planning for assistive technology
- Working with orientation and mobility teachers, vision specialists, and any other related service professionals

Chapter Summary

Go the text's Online Learning Center at **www.mhhe.com/taylor1e** to access study resources, Web links, practice quizzes, and extending materials.

What Are the Foundations of Blindness and Low Vision?

- Special institutions and schools for teaching students with blindness and low vision emerged in the United Stated in the 1800s. Public school programs emerged in the 20th century. During the 1990s, experts and advocates developed a National Agenda for improving educational programming for students with blindness and low vision.
- Legal blindness is defined as visual acuity of 20/200 or worse in the best eye with the best possible correction. Legal blindness can also be defined as field of vision restricted to 20 degrees. Using the legal definition, low vision is defined as visual acuity of 20/70 to 20/200 in the best eye with the best possible correction and generally being able to read printed materials. Functional blindness is defined as having little or no residual or functional vision and requiring learning through tactile, auditory strategies, braille, or other assistive technologies rather than directly through printed materials.
- The IDEA 04 definition of a visual impairment focuses on vision loss that adversely affects educational performance and includes both blindness and low vision. Determining how a student is able to use any residual vision is more important for teachers than the legal definitions.
- The overall prevalence rate of students with blindness or low vision in schools is estimated to be .04%, although this figure may be low. More students are identified as being able to use print materials than are those who use only braille or auditory strategies for learning.

What Are the Causes and Characteristics of Blindness and Low Vision?

- Problems with vision are classified as optical defects, ocular motility defects, and external and internal problems of the eye. Optical defects are problems with refraction and refractive mechanisms in the eye. Ocular motility defects involve problems with binocular vision. External problems of the eye can affect the orbit, eyelids, and cornea. Internal problems of the eye include retinopathy of prematurity (ROP), which results in damage to the eye associated with complications from premature birth. Cortical visual impairment results from brain damage that affects the reception and interpretation of auditory nerve impulses. The actual components of the eye are normal or nearly so.
- Characteristics of students with blindness or low vision may depend on age of onset, whether the students are blind or low vision, and the specifics of the problem.
- Intellectual ability is generally unaffected in students with blindness and low vision. Play and social interaction skills can be delayed. Language development is generally typical, but some students have difficulty with nonverbal communication because they do not see these important aspects of communication. Academic achievement can lag, but most students should be able to achieve at least at average

levels. Perceptual abilities are affected, resulting in the need for the development of orientation and mobility skills and wayfinding skills. Psychological and social adjustments are not uniquely affected by blindness and low vision, but peer relationships and friendships may be affected. The effect may stem from less sophisticated social skills on the part of a student with blindness or low vision or from negative reactions from peers.

How Are Students with Blindness or Low Vision Identified?

- Children with congenital and severe impairments are generally identified through medical procedures by 4 months of age.
- Routine visual screening is typically done when children enter school. Snellen chart procedures are often used for screening at this time.
- A comprehensive assessment is needed that includes functional vision assessment, learning media assessment, assessment of cognitive ability, academic achievement, orientation and mobility skills, and social and independent living skills.

What and How Do I Teach Students with Blindness or Low Vision?

- Early intervention is important for children identified with vision loss for typical development to occur. Family involvement should be considered and family members included in intervention efforts.
- Students with blindness and low vision generally learn the same academic content as peers. However, they may need to learn some skills not included in the general core curriculum or skills that are included in that curriculum, but not to the degree needed.
- Students with blindness or low vision should learn skills included in the expanded core curriculum including compensatory skills, literacy and braille skills, orientation and mobility skills, social interaction skills, independent living skills, recreation and leisure skills, career transition skills, and visual efficiency skills.
- Instructional procedures may need to be modified to ensure students with blindness and low vision can access learning activities and materials.
- Physical issues that may need to be addressed or planned for include physical appearance of the eyes, care for the eyes, unusual mannerisms, and the responses of others.
- Perceptual issues that may need to be addressed or planned for include learning how to use residual vision, seating arrangement, accommodating for depth perception, visual discrimination, and color discrimination problems.
- Teachers can provide copies of notes, read aloud, supply audiotapes of print materials, and provide for hands-on learning activities. The use of models and manipulatives may also be helpful.

SUMMARY

What Are Other Considerations for Teaching Students with Blindness or Low Vision?

- The LRE for students with blindness and low vision is often the general education classroom with special adaptations and consultation from a special education teacher. Itinerant models of service delivery may be used in some school districts. Some students may attend special residential schools that are specifically designed for students with blindness and low vision.
- The physical environment of the classroom may need to be adapted to maximize use of functional vision.
- Materials may need to be adapted to suit both print readers and braille users. Teachers can modify visual materials by removing visual clutter, making materials tactile, converting them to auditory form, having narration for videos and other visual presentations, and using real objects as substitutes for pictures.
- Assistive technology should be chosen based on individual need and learning media assessment. A variety of technologies are available including software that allows for better access to print and scanned materials and to braille access software.
- Guide dogs can be of assistance in mobility.

What Are Some Considerations for the General Education Teacher?

- Factors that inhibit inclusion of students who are blind or have low vision are the belief that large print materials are always easily produced and that bigger is better, lack of training in optical device and computer software use, and a lack of available appropriately trained special education personnel.
- Factors facilitating inclusion of students who are blind or have low vision include a philosophy that students should be prepared for lifelong learning, the understanding that computer technologies may allow access to regular print materials, and a core group of individuals committed to excellence in service provision.
- The general education teacher may need to make adaptations in the physical environment, the teaching materials and activities, and in the assignments given. Planning should be done to support social relationships with peers.
- Feedback may need to be given in person, by recording, or by computer as some students will not be able to read written feedback from their teachers.
- General education teachers should maintain high expectations for learning and performance.

Reflection Topics

1. How do you think the varying definitions of low vision and blindness affect the individual? How do you think these definitions affect educators?
2. What do you think your reaction might be as a parent if you were informed in the first few months of your child's life that she or he had a severe vision loss? What would you want to know or learn?
3. What challenges might be involved in assessing the academic abilities of a student with blindness or low vision?
4. What implications are there for placing students with blindness or low vision in a neighborhood school?
5. In what ways might common classroom materials need to be adapted for a student with low vision who can access enlarged printed materials?
6. If you had a student who was blind in your general education class, what information would you want to know in order to enhance her or his inclusion?

Application Activities: For Learning and Your Portfolio

1. (*Portfolio Possibility*) Look at the materials and resources, such as large print textbooks or technology, available in the local district or in your state for students with blindness or low vision. Create a list of resources and materials available and sources from which they can be obtained.
2. Interview an individual who has blindness or low vision. Ask what challenges that person has encountered in everyday life, in school, and in employment (if appropriate).
3. (*Portfolio Possibility*) Take a lesson from a school-adopted content area text (e.g., language arts, mathematics, science) appropriate to the grade/age level or content area for which you will be certified/licensed. Adapt that lesson to meet the needs of a student with low vision. Consider the physical environment, content and learning objectives, activities, grouping, materials, and assessment procedures. Develop a plan for differentiating instruction for someone who cannot read printed materials or see visually presented information.
4. Examine the classroom and building in which you are taking this course. How is it or could it be adapted for a person with blindness? Create a list of recommendations.
5. Work with one or more peers in trying to perform simple, everyday tasks such as washing your hands and pouring a beverage with your eyes covered. Determine how you might teach a child with blindness to perform these skills.
6. Go through a portion of your college class with your eyes covered. Make a list of challenges you face in accessing the learning and how your access could be improved.

SUMMARY

CHAPTER 10

Students with Physical or Health Disabilities

INTRODUCING MARTA, ANDRE, AND BEN

Marta is a 7-year-old girl who lives in a large urban area. She was born a month premature in a difficult delivery and was diagnosed soon after as having cerebral palsy. Her muscle tone is very tight, and she has problems controlling her voluntary motor movements. Although her arms are affected, her legs are affected more, requiring the use of a wheelchair.

To complete her school assignments, Marta needs to use a computer with an adapted keyboard. Although her speech is relatively understandable to those who know her, individuals meeting her for the first time have difficulty comprehending what she says. Because of her motor limitations, it is difficult to assess Marta, but it appears that her intelligence is in the normal range.

Andre was 9 years old when he had his first seizure. He was sitting in his fourth-grade classroom when he suddenly lost consciousness. His head hit the desk, and he started to jerk and shake. His teacher, Ms. Carothers, recognized that Andre was having a seizure. She helped him out of his desk and laid him gently on the floor, placing his head to the side on a rolled up towel. After the seizure ended, Andre slept for about 10 minutes, waking up groggy and disoriented. He was taken to the nurse's office where he rested until his father picked him up and took him home. Ms. Carothers explained Andre's situation to his classmates, who were frightened by the incident. ▶

Andre is now in the sixth grade. His seizures are somewhat controlled by

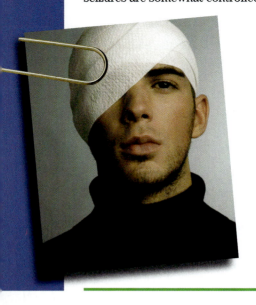

medication although on average he still has one a month. Andre says that he has a funny taste in his mouth before the seizure starts, and he tells his teacher when he notices this.

Ben is a 17-year-old high school student. One night at the beginning of his senior year he went to a party with several of his friends. On the way home, distracted by the joking around in the car, the driver ran a red light and hit another car. Ben was riding in the passenger seat and wasn't wearing his seatbelt. He hit the windshield and immediately lost consciousness. He regained consciousness in the hospital two days later and remained there for two weeks, being evaluated and monitored. Ben's physician determined that he had a severe brain injury. When Ben returned to school, his teachers observed that he had lost many of his academic skills, had short-term memory problems, and was easily frustrated and agitated. Both Ben and Ben's parents are having difficulty accepting the changes that they have seen. ■

The types of conditions Marta, Andre, and Ben have are extremely diverse, yet all three are described as physical or health disabilities. In this chapter, we discuss three separate categories recognized under IDEA 04 that can be grouped collectively as physical or health disabilities: orthopedic impairments (OI), other health impairments (OHI), and traumatic brain injury (TBI). An individual with spina bifida who uses a wheelchair (orthopedic impairment), an individual with diabetes (other health impairment), and an individual who has brain damage as a result of a diving accident (traumatic brain injury) would all be considered to have a physical or health disability.

What Are the Foundations of Physical and Health Disabilities?

Individuals with physical or health disabilities have a wide variety of medical conditions, each with its own unique history. We have grouped them together in this chapter, but IDEA 04 considers orthopedic impairments, other health impairments, and traumatic brain injury as separate categories.

A Brief History of Physical and Health Disabilities

Relevant CEC Standard
▶ Historical foundations related to knowledge and practices in physical and health disabilities (PH1K2)

Each of the physical and health disabilities has its own unique history. Therefore, a discussion of the histories of all the disabilities included in this chapter is not possible. It should be pointed out that the majority of these disorders have been present since the beginning of recorded history, but understanding these conditions did not come until much later. For example, prior to the 19th century, people with epilepsy who had seizures were thought to be possessed and were shunned or, in some cases, exorcised to release the evil spirits (Weinstein, 2002). The first known description of epilepsy was around 350 BC, but the first real understanding of epilepsy was not shared until the 1800s when a physician, John Hughlings Jackson, provided a basic foundation of the neurology of epilepsy based on his observations (Epilepsy Foundation, 2005). Similarly, cerebral palsy was not formally described until a 19th-century English surgeon, William Little, wrote about a disorder that occurred early in life and resulted in stiff, spastic muscles in the legs, and to a lesser extent, in the arms. He noted that the condition resulted in difficulty crawling and walking, and neither improved nor got worse as children grew older. This condition, which was called Little's disease, is now known as spastic diplegia cerebral palsy. Other conditions, such as acquired autoimmune deficiency disorder (AIDS), are relatively recent phenomena. Suffice it to say that regardless of when these disorders were first described, education of individuals with these disorders is a relatively recent practice.

Definitions of Physical and Health Disabilities

Although there are many different types of physical and health disabilities, each one in some way affects the educational functioning of the individual and thus requires special education or related services. As noted, IDEA 04 provides a definition for orthopedic impairments, other health impairments, and traumatic brain injury—all considered to be physical or health disabilities.

Relevant CEC Standard

▶ Issues and educational definitions of individuals with physical and health disabilities (PH1K1)

> An **orthopedic impairment** (OI) is one caused by congenital anomaly, such as clubfoot or the absence of some member; by disease, such as poliomyelitis and bone tuberculosis; and by other causes, such as cerebral palsy, amputations, and fractures or burns that cause contractures.

orthopedic impairment An impairment caused by a congenital anomaly, disease, or other causes such as cerebral palsy.

These conditions need to adversely affect educational performance to be considered as OIs by IDEA 04.

> An **other health impairment** (OHI) is a disorder resulting in limited strength, vitality, or alertness, including a heightened alertness to environmental stimuli, which results in limited alertness with respect to the educational environment that
> (i) is due to chronic or acute health problems such as asthma, attention deficit disorder or attention deficit hyperactivity disorder, diabetes, epilepsy, a heart condition, hemophilia, lead poisoning, leukemia, nephritis, rheumatic fever, Tourette's syndrome, and sickle cell anemia; and
> (ii) adversely affects a child's educational performance.

other health impairment An impairment affecting an individual's vitality, strength, or alertness.

> **Traumatic brain injury** (TBI) is an acquired injury to the brain caused by an external physical force, resulting in total or partial functional disability or psychosocial impairment, or both, that adversely affects a child's educational performance. The term applies to open or closed head injuries resulting in impairments in one or more areas, such as cognition, language, memory, attention, reasoning, abstract thinking, judgment, problem solving, sensory, perceptual, and motor abilities, psychosocial behavior, physical functions, information processing, and speech. The term does not apply to brain injuries that are congenital or degenerative, or to brain injury induced by birth trauma.

traumatic brain injury An acquired injury to the brain caused by an external force.

Although the categories of OI, OHI, and TBI represent disabilities with a variety of causes, to qualify for services under IDEA 04 students must share one common criterion—the condition must adversely affect educational performance.

Prevalence of Physical and Health Disabilities

Physical and health disabilities are considered low incidence disabilities under IDEA 04. Only .99% of school-aged students, ages 6 to 21, received services for physical or health disabilities in the 2005 school year (U.S. Department of Education, 2006). The percentages reported for services under IDEA for the specific disabilities were .10% for orthopedic impairments, .85% for other health impairments, and .04% for traumatic brain injury.

The prevalence of TBI could be much higher, but it is difficult to determine the exact number of students with this disability. One factor that may affect the reported prevalence is poor transition services from hospital to school settings, which may result in the school being uninformed about the TBI itself. In addition, TBI is often diagnosed as another disability, such as AD/HD or a learning disability (Bullock, Gable & Mohr, 2005). Nonetheless, the prevalence of TBI in the schools has increased steadily. For example, only about 200 students with TBI received services under IDEA in 1991, a year after it was recognized as a disability category. That number had increased to almost 23,500 by 2005 (U.S. Department of Education, 2006).

Another interesting trend is the rapid increase in the number of students with OHI served in the past decade. In the 1991 school year, just over 58,000 students received services under this category. That number had increased to more than 557,000 students by the 2005 school year. In fact, OHI is now the third-largest category of disability under IDEA 04, recently surpassing mental retardation and emotional disturbance. When compared to the prevalence of OI, in which approximately 51,000 received services in 1991 and just under 63,000 in 2005, the magnitude of the increase in OHI services is particularly visible. The increase in the number of students receiving OHI is most probably due to increased identification of students with attention deficit/hyperactivity disorder under this category.

Although relatively few students receive services under the three categories of physical or health disabilities in IDEA 04, particularly OI and TB, the prevalence rates of those who have these medical conditions is relatively high. For example, 10% to 12% of the population will develop asthma by the age of 18, and approximately 7% of the population has diabetes. Remember, however, that the number of students who receive special education and related services is affected by the specific eligibility criteria stated in IDEA 04. Many students who have physical or health disabilities may never receive special education services per se because their disability does not adversely affect their educational performance. Many of these students are taught within the general education school program without any curricular modifications. For example, consider Cindy, a student with diabetes who receives insulin injections at home to control her high blood sugar. Cindy is a good student, and her diabetes does not directly affect her school performance and does not require any related service. Although Cindy technically has a medical condition considered an OHI, she would not qualify for services under IDEA 04 because her diabetes does not adversely affect her educational performance. It is still very important, however, that teachers be familiar with the signs and characteristics of the disabilities. Cindy's teacher, for instance, should know the signs of low blood sugar and high blood sugar, both of which are possible with diabetes, and alert her parents and the school nurse if she sees them.

The area of physical and health disabilities represents a heterogeneous group of medical conditions with different histories, definitions, and prevalence rates. Although the number of students who receive special education and related services under these three categories is slightly below 1% of the school-aged population, it is highly probable that many other students with physical and health disabilities will be taught by general education teachers. Even though these students are not officially receiving services under IDEA 04, it is imperative that all teachers be aware of these conditions.

Check Your Understanding

1. Why is the history of physical and health disabilities more difficult to describe than the histories of other disabilities, such as learning disabilities?

2. Which three separate categories under IDEA 04 comprise the area of physical and health disabilities?

3. What are the definitions of OI, OHI, and TBI? What criterion do the IDEA 04 categories of OI, OHI, and TBI have in common?

4. Approximately what percentage of the school population is being served as students with a physical or health disability under IDEA 04?

5. What is one possible reason the prevalence rate of OHI is increasing rapidly?

What Are the Causes and Characteristics of Physical and Health Disabilities?

Physical and health disabilities have a wide variety of causes and characteristics. Students with orthopedic impairments often experience deficits in motor movement that stem either from some type of central nervous system (CNS) damage or from loss of a limb or appendage. Students with health impairments, on the other hand, suffer from illnesses or diseases that normally influence the operation of various organs of the body. Students with TBI may have a variety of characteristics depending on factors such as the type, location, and severity of the injury.

Orthopedic Impairments

Teachers of students with orthopedic impairments are most likely to encounter those with cerebral palsy, spina bifida, and muscular dystrophy. Each of these has different causes and, more important, have different characteristics that teachers need to recognize and address.

Cerebral Palsy: Causes and Characteristics

Cerebral palsy is caused by damage to different parts of the brain that results in problems in muscle tone and muscle movement. The damage, which typically occurs before, during, or shortly after birth, is not progressive, or deteriorating. It can affect a broad range of both gross and fine motor movements. Although all forms of cerebral palsy are the result of brain damage, there can be various reasons for the damage itself. It was once thought that the majority of cases of cerebral palsy were caused by interruption of either blood flow or oxygen to the baby during the birth process. Now the prevailing thought is that problems related to prematurity and intrauterine development are the most common causes (Croen et al., 2001). For example, there is evidence that cerebral palsy is caused by abnormal fetal cell development during early pregnancy (National Institute of Neurological Disorders and Stroke [NINDS], 2006a). Problems during the birth delivery are common for children with cerebral palsy but "seem to be related to preexisting brain abnormalities rather than the cause of them" (Pellegrino, 2002, p. 444).

There are four types of cerebral palsy, which are based on the location of the brain damage. These types of cerebral palsy are typically described by the effect the damage has on muscle tone, the amount of tension exhibited by muscles, which then affects movement and motor development. The four types are spastic cerebral palsy, the most common type, athetoid cerebral palsy, ataxia, and mixed cerebral palsy (Table 10.1).

Cerebral palsy is often described in terms of its effect on the functioning of different areas of the body. The following terms are used to describe the areas of the body that are affected.

- Monoplegia: Affects only one arm or one leg
- Hemiplegia: Affects the arm and leg on one side of the body
- Double hemiplegia: Affects the arms primarily with some involvement of the legs
- Diplegia: Affects all limbs but both legs are more adversely affected
- Paraplegia: Affects both legs but there is no involvement of the arms
- Triplegia: Affects three limbs
- Quadriplegia: Affects the functioning of the torso and all four limbs, with no observable difference in involvement among the limbs

Relevant CEC Standards

► Medical terminology related to physical and health disabilities (PH2K1)

► Etiology and characteristics of physical and health disabilities across the life span (PH2K2)

► Secondary health care issues that accompany specific physical and health disabilities (PH2K3)

► Types and transmission routes of infectious and communicable disease (PH2K4)

Many students with cerebral palsy will need to use a wheelchair.

TABLE 10.1	Types of Cerebral Palsy and Their Effects
TYPE	**EFFECTS**
Spasticity	Difficulty initiating voluntary movements, increased muscle tone with tight muscles and stiff joints; difficulty walking, grasping objects, writing; speech often affected
Athetoidosis	Involuntary movement of the limbs with muscle tone quickly changing from tight to loose; arms flailing; walking and speech problems
Ataxia	Muscle coordination problems affecting balance and gait
Mixed	More than one type of cerebral palsy is present (e.g., spasticity in some limbs, athetosis in others)

The types of cerebral palsy range in severity from mild, in which there is very little effect on motor movements, to severe, in which the individual is almost totally unable to move voluntarily at all. Aside from the basic motor limitations, children with cerebral palsy often experience other types of associated conditions, including seizures; vision problems, such as crossed eyes; hearing loss; and eating, feeding, and speaking problems. Approximately one-half to three-fourths of individuals with cerebral palsy will also have intellectual disabilities. However, because of motor and in some cases speech impairments, it is often difficult to accurately measure intelligence (Pelligrino, 2002).

MARTA REVISITED What type of cerebral palsy do you think Marta has? Why? Think about both her motor characteristics and the areas that are affected.

Because of the different types and severity of cerebral palsy, it is important that teachers collaborate closely with a variety of related services personnel. For example, a physical therapist would be able to assist in positioning the student to minimize the motor problems and maximize the learning environment; and a speech therapist might provide helpful suggestions regarding the student's communication skills.

Spina Bifida: Causes and Characteristics

Spina bifida is a congenital disorder that results when bones surrounding the spinal cord do not close or grow together. This can cause an opening or hole to form in the back. Although the cause of this problem is still not known, there is evidence that genetic factors interact in some way with the early intrauterine environment. There is no cure for spina bifida, although there is strong evidence that mothers who take folic acid, a type of B vitamin, before and during pregnancy reduce the risk of having a baby with spina bifida. Since 1998, certain foods, such as bread, have contained folic acid, but it is still necessary to use supplements (Liptak, 2002).

spina bifida occulta A condition in which an opening exists in one or more of the vertebrae in the spinal column.

meningocele A type of spina bifida in which the membranes surrounding the spinal cord protrude through a hole in the vertebrae forming a sac.

myelomeningocele The most severe type of spina bifida in which the spinal cord protrudes through a hole in the back that can result in paralysis of the lower limbs.

There are three types of spina bifida. In **spina bifida occulta,** an opening exists in one or more of the vertebrae of the spinal column, but there is no damage to the spinal cord itself. Estimates are that approximately 10% (Liptak, 2002) to 40% (National Information Center for Children and Youth with Disabilities [NICHCY], 2004) of all Americans may have this condition, but because there are very few symptoms, it is often left undiagnosed.

The second type of spina bifida is called **meningocele,** in which the membranes surrounding the spinal cord, called meninges, protrude through a hole in the vertebrae, causing the development of a sac (the meningocele). As with spina bifida occulta, the meningocele does not damage the spinal cord. Surgery can repair this condition with typically very few, if any, long-term effects.

The most severe and commonly diagnosed type of spina bifida is **myelomeningocele,** in which the spinal cord itself protrudes through the back so that the nerves themselves are exposed (see Figure 10.1). Depending on where this sac is located,

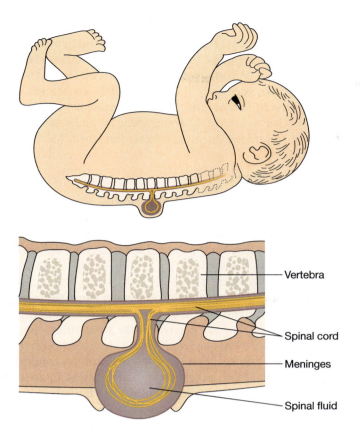

FIGURE 10.1 Child with a Myelomeningocele

various degrees of neurological problems can result. The higher the sac is formed, the more serious the neurological problem. For example, if the sac develops high on the spinal cord and nerve damage occurs, total paralysis of the lower limbs is probable. However, approximately 85% of individuals with a myelomeningocele have a chance of walking with or without assistance (Shutack, 2005). Neurosurgery is performed to close the sac while trying to preserve the nerves.

It is important that teachers be aware of the many problems that may accompany the paralysis caused by a myelomeningocele, including loss of bowel and bladder control, difficulty breathing and swallowing, and seizures. Hydrocephaly, an enlarged head caused by a buildup of cerebrospinal fluid, is a common accompanying condition. It is estimated that 70% to 90% of those with a myelomeningocele will also have hydrocephaly (NICHCY, 2004). In these cases, it is necessary to surgically insert a **shunt,** a valve that diverts the cerebrospinal fluid away from the brain and into the bloodstream.

Muscular Dystrophy: Causes and Characteristics

Muscular dystrophy is a class of disorders typically characterized by a general and progressive weakening of muscles. Although there are various forms of the disorder, **Duchenne muscular dystrophy** is the most prevalent type. Duchenne muscular dystrophy is usually inherited from the mother who has a defective gene that regulates dystrophin, which is responsible for the maintenance of muscle fiber. The gene is located on the X sex chromosome, so primarily males will inherit the disorder in this fashion because females have another X chromosome with a normal gene that will make enough of the protein to avoid the disorder. It is also possible that the disorder could be caused by a gene mutation rather than inheritance of the defective gene (NINDS, 2006b).

Duchenne muscular dystrophy usually begins to develop during the preschool years, with muscle weakening first occurring in the lower leg area. This muscle weakness progresses upward through the muscles of the body, resulting in the need for the

shunt A surgical procedure for hydrocephaly in which a valve is implanted that directs cerebrospinal fluid from the brain into the bloodstream.

Duchenne muscular dystrophy The most prevalent type of muscular dystrophy; it primarily affects males. It involves progressive muscle weakness and usually results in death in the early 20s.

Labels on figure: Vertebra, Spinal cord, Meninges, Spinal fluid

individual to use a wheelchair by the age of 8 to 10, a respirator by age 20, with death usually occurring in the early 20s (NINDS, 2006b). Outward symptoms of Duchenne muscular dystrophy include frequent falls, large calf muscles, and difficulty getting out of a chair or bed. School performance of a student with Duchenne muscular dystrophy will usually decline, especially during the adolescent years, as the muscle weakening produces severe fatigue. Inactivity can make the condition worse, and physical therapy can be very helpful. Unfortunately, at the present time there is no known cure or therapy to prevent the progression of the disorder.

Other Health Impairments

Several health conditions can result in the need for special education and/or related services, including epilepsy, asthma, cystic fybrosis, diabetes, and autoimmune deficiency syndrome (AIDS). Students with attention deficit/hyperactivity disorder (AD/HD), discussed in Chapter 14, are also frequently provided services under this category.

Epilepsy: Causes and Characteristics

A person is diagnosed with epilepsy when he or she has recurrent seizures. A seizure results in problems with consciousness, movement, and/or sensation. Although there are several types of seizures, they are caused by the same thing—an electrical dysfunction, or an abnormal electrical discharge, in the brain. Although the exact cause of a seizure is usually not known, it can result from various conditions, including developmental brain abnormalities, infections, and brain injury. Interestingly, seizures caused by brain injury might not occur for months after the injury (Schacter, 2004). Individuals who have seizures experience a considerable range of possible behavioral effects, which depend on the location and severity of the brain involvement. Seizures are more prevalent in those individuals who also have other disabilities such as cerebral palsy and intellectual disabilities. Approximately half of individuals who have both of these disabilities will also have seizures (Epilepsy Foundation, 2005a).

Epilepsy is identified by the type of seizures that the individual experiences. Although the following seizure types are discussed separately, there is considerable overlap in their characteristics. Also, it is not uncommon for children to experience different types of seizures, both over time as well as simultaneously.

Seizures are often categorized as having a *generalized onset* or a *partial onset*. Generalized seizures simultaneously affect large regions in both hemispheres of the brain, whereas partial seizures start in one specific area of the brain and may or may not spread (Weinstein, 2002). Examples of generalized seizures are the generalized tonic-clonic seizure and the absence seizure. Examples of partial seizures are the simple partial seizure and the complex partial seizure.

The **generalized tonic-clonic seizure,** formerly called the grand mal seizure, is considered one of the most serious types of seizures. In the first phase of the seizure, the tonic phase, the individual becomes extremely rigid as muscles tighten, loses consciousness, and falls to the ground. The second phase, the clonic phase, begins when the individual displays violent and almost rhythmic jerking of the body, including the arms and legs. Injuries often occur when an individual has this type of seizure, so the immediate environment must be made as safe as possible. For example, all nearby furniture and objects should be removed. It is also important to lay the individual down and turn the head to the side to help prevent breathing problems and let any saliva drain; and it is a good idea to put a soft, folded object, such as a towel or jacket, under the head to avoid any head injuries that might be caused by the jerking movements. One common misconception is that the person will swallow his tongue and choke. It is unnecessary and dangerous to insert a tongue depressor, or any object, into the mouth. Table 10.2 provides some additional suggestions for teachers when a student has a generalized tonic-clonic seizure in their classrooms. After a few minutes, the seizure terminates and the individual usually rests or sleeps for a period of time. If the seizure lasts longer than five minutes, medical attention should be sought (Devinsky, 2004b). Given the unconscious nature of the generalized tonic-clonic seizure, the person will not remember the incident.

generalized tonic-clonic seizure An abnormal electrical discharge in the brain in which the individual becomes extremely rigid, loses consciousness, and displays rhythmic jerking.

TABLE 10.2	Suggestions for Managing a Student with a Generalized Tonic-Clonic Seizure

1. Keep calm and reassure other people who are nearby.
2. Don't hold the person down or try to stop his or her movements.
3. Time the seizure with your watch.
4. Clear the area around the person of anything hard or sharp.
5. Loosen ties or anything around the neck that may make breathing difficult. Don't attempt artificial respiration except in the unlikely event that the person does not start breathing again after the seizure has stopped.
6. Stay with the person until the seizure ends naturally.

Source: Adapted from *First aid for generalized tonic clonic (grand mal) seizures.* © 2007 Epilepsy Foundation of America, Inc. Reprinted with permission.

Absence seizures, formerly called petit mal seizures, result in the individual experiencing a momentary loss of consciousness, usually for only a few seconds. These lapses can occur rather frequently, but due to their brevity they may not be noticeable to an observer. During the seizure, the child is usually very still, the eyes may blink, or there might be very slight movements of facial or arm and leg muscles. Typically, the child will not be aware of the seizure. It is important that teachers be familiar with this type of seizure because many students experiencing them are thought to be daydreaming, not paying attention, or "zoning out." Also, during the seizure the student might be able to do simple tasks, such as walking, but be unable to perform more complex activities, such as reading (Weinstein, 2002). If the teacher notices that a student has periods of rapid blinking, it is important to tell the parents, particularly if the student has not been diagnosed.

In a **simple partial seizure,** the symptoms will vary depending on the site in the brain that is affected. The person remains alert and remembers the incident. This type of seizure might result in abnormal muscle movement and/or sensory sensations. For example, the person may experience a ringing in the ears or some different type of taste, smell, or touch sensation. When the seizure only results in unusual sensory sensations, it is referred to as an **aura** (Weinstein, 2002). Because simple seizures can spread and cause other types of seizures, it is important that individuals who experience an aura warn others that a seizure might be coming. Given the loss of consciousness that occurs with some varieties of seizures, this warning can be useful in making sure that the environment is made safe. Simple partial seizures usually last less than two minutes.

Complex partial seizures, formerly called psychomotor seizures, usually last up to five minutes. One of the outward signs sometimes associated with this type of seizure activity is agitation and aberrant behaviors and, more rarely, aggression (Weinstein, 2002). Other symptoms of this type of seizure include eye blinking, facial grimacing, lip smacking, repetition of movements, and odd behavior such as disrobing or laughing or crying for no reason. As Devinsky (2004a) noted, a person who experiences a complex partial seizure will appear to be awake and alert, but in reality "nobody's home."

As a general rule, seizures are controlled through the use of medication, primarily anticonvulsant drugs. As with all drugs, the side effects must be considered. Even if a drug controls seizure activity, it is possible for it to have an effect on something else such as alertness or awareness. Also, given the biochemical changes that constantly occur in developing bodies, changes in medication may be needed as a child grows older. Although it was once thought that children with seizures should stay on medication for life, this practice is now questioned. The current thinking is that medication should be stopped after a seizure-free period of time, such as two years.

absence seizure An abnormal electrical discharge in the brain in which the individual experiences a momentary loss of consciousness.

simple partial seizure An abnormal electrical discharge in the brain in which the individual might have abnormal muscle movements or sensory sensations such as a certain taste or smell.

aura A seizure that only results in a sensory sensation, such as a certain taste or smell. Auras can be used as a warning that a more serious seizure might occur.

complex partial seizure An abnormal electrical discharge in the brain in which the individual displays behaviors such as agitation, eye blinking, facial grimacing, and occasionally aggression.

ANDRE REVISITED What type of seizure does Andre have? What did Ms. Carothers do during Andre's seizure that was appropriate?

Asthma: Causes and Characteristics

Asthma is a respiratory condition that results in breathing difficulties. It is caused by an inflammation of the airways or by the tightening of the muscles around the airways. Asthma typically results from the child being exposed to any number of environmental conditions, including viral infections, allergy provoking substances (e.g., pollen, animal hair, and certain foods such as peanuts or shellfish), or emotional stress. There is some evidence, however, that also points to the possibility that asthma may have a genetic basis (Holgate, Davies, Powell, & Holloway, 2005), although it is considered a complex disorder in which several genetic and environmental factors need to occur (Eder & von Mutius, 2005).

The general symptomatic behaviors seen in children with asthma are wheezing, coughing, tightness in the chest, and difficulty breathing, especially in exhaling air from the lungs. It is considered the most common lung condition of children. Although it most often begins in the early childhood years, onset can be considerably later.

Generally, most cases of asthma can be treated effectively with medication or the use of bronchodilators (inhalers) that relax the muscles surrounding the airways, making breathing easier. Given the numerous environmental causes, however, efforts are commonly geared toward prevention of an asthma attack by making the student aware of those causes and controlling exposure to them. It is also important that teachers be aware of the allergies that students have that might provoke an asthma attack and ensure that they are not exposed to them. For example, a student who is allergic to animal hair should avoid the petting area on a field trip to the zoo.

anaphylactic reaction A severe allergic reaction that can be potentially life-threatening. It sometimes occurs with asthma.

Asthma can lead to what is known as an **anaphylactic reaction,** a severe allergic reaction that poses a potentially life-threatening situation. Individuals who have severe asthma might use an adrenaline kit such as EpiPen®, an injection that can be self-administered. Teachers should be familiar with the administration of these kits as well, particularly for younger children who have severe asthma.

Cystic Fibrosis: Causes and Characteristics

Cystic fibrosis is an autosomal recessive genetic disorder. Both parents must be carriers of the defective gene, called the cystic fibrosis transmembrane conductance regulator gene, for the condition to occur. This gene normally makes a protein that controls the movement of salt and water in and out of the cells (National Heart, Lung, and Blood Institute [NHLBI], n.d.a). When this gene is defective, mucus, which is usually watery and moistens certain body organs, becomes thick and sticky. Cystic fibrosis is a degenerative disorder with no known cure. Some advances in gene therapy that could eventually result in the defective gene being replaced by a working gene are being explored (Lee et al., 2005).

Symptoms of cystic fibrosis include persistent coughing, frequent episodes of pneumonia, dehydration, and a large appetite with no subsequent weight gain. Although problems associated with cystic fibrosis start within the pancreas, the organ responsible for secreting substances to break down various food products, many other organs of the body are also affected. In fact, most of the debilitating problems have to do with the lungs. In its late stages, the mucus present within the lungs becomes so thick that normal respiratory functioning is impossible. Cystic fibrosis usually results in digestive problems, such as fatty stools, and also causes a person to lose excessive salt in his or her sweat, which can disrupt the mineral balance in the blood.

Problems associated with cystic fibrosis are usually apparent during the first year of life. Children with the disorder are highly susceptible to pneumonia. With each incident, more and more damage to the lungs occurs through the continued overproduction of abnormal mucus. The most common cause of death is respiratory failure. Although there is still no known cure, medical science has established regimens dealing with the symptoms of the disorder. These include medication such as mucus thinning drugs; chest physical therapy, in which the chest and back are pounded to dislodge the mucus; and aerobic exercise. These intensive practices have had a positive effect. Until the 1980s, death usually occurred in childhood or adolescence. Today, the life expectancy has increased to 35 years old (NHLBI, n.d.b).

Diabetes: Causes and Characteristics

Diabetes is a disorder in which the body does not produce or effectively use insulin, a hormone necessary for transporting specific sugars to body cells. There are two types of diabetes. Type 1 diabetes usually has its onset in childhood, whereas Type 2 diabetes typically emerges in adulthood. The exact etiology of diabetes is still not known, although it appears that in both types risk factors must be inherited from both parents, creating a genetic *predisposition*, and certain environmental factors must be present. One such environmental factor is diet. For example, infants who are breast-fed and those who eat solid foods at later ages are less likely to have Type 1 diabetes. Those having a greater risk of Type 2 diabetes have diets that are too high in fat and too low in protein and carbohydrates (American Diabetes Association, n.d.b). Other factors that contribute to Type 2 diabetes are obesity and lack of exercise.

In Type 1 diabetes, formerly called juvenile diabetes, the body does not produce the insulin that is needed to carry sugar from the blood to the cells for energy. The more common type of diabetes, Type 2, is caused when the body produces too little insulin or uses the insulin ineffectively. In both types, the result is high blood sugar that results in damage to the eyes, kidneys, heart, and nerves if left untreated. Unfortunately, high blood sugar, and subsequent low sugar in the cells, makes the body sense a sugar "crisis" and, instead of stopping the production of sugar, accelerates the production. If this vicious cycle is not stopped, a life-threatening condition arises. Therefore, in many cases of diabetes, the individual must receive insulin injections. In less severe cases, diet management and exercise are used.

Teachers should be familiar with diet restrictions for their students with diabetes and need to recognize the signs of both low blood sugar, hypoglycemia, and high blood sugar, hyperglycemia. Hypoglycemia, which occurs when the student gets too much insulin, results in symptoms such as increased hunger, perspiration, nervousness, sleepiness, and dizziness. Hyperglycemia is more serious and is caused when the student does not get enough insulin. The symptoms include increased hunger, thirst, urination, blurred vision, dry mouth, and dry or itchy skin.

Acquired Immunodeficiency Syndrome: Causes and Characteristics

Over the past three decades, more and more attention has been given to children who have acquired immunodeficiency syndrome (AIDS), caused by the human immunodeficiency virus (HIV), which is transmitted sexually, through the blood, or is passed from mother to child. About 90% of pediatric AIDS cases are caused when an infected mother transmits the virus to her unborn child and can be diagnosed by 1 month of age for most infants and by 6 months for the vast majority (Spiegel & Bonwit, 2002).

There is still considerable misunderstanding and misconception about AIDS and how it is transmitted. For example, AIDS is not transmitted through saliva, urine, or vomit unless blood is present. Clearly, it is important that teachers who work with students with AIDS be knowledgeable of the disease and that the information be shared with others. This includes the use of universal precautions. **Universal precautions** are a set of guidelines published by the Centers for Disease Control that are designed to prevent exposure to blood-borne pathogens. These include using protective gloves when exposure to bodily fluids is possible, cleaning surfaces and objects that may have been contaminated thoroughly with a bleach solution, and using tweezers or a broom and dust pan to pick up sharp objects such as broken glass.

universal precautions A set of guidelines designed to prevent exposure to blood-borne pathogens.

The symptoms of HIV in children include swelling of the lymph nodes, enlargement of the liver and spleen, and a predisposition to viral and bacterial infections. In the classroom, problems that will likely become apparent in the majority of children with HIV include cognitive deficits, motor functioning problems, speech and language deficits, and problems with memory and attention. The onset of these problems does not occur in a consistent manner; some children will display rapid deterioration and others a gradual loss of skills (Conlon, 1992). When the presence of the HIV virus leads to AIDS, the child is very susceptible to infections (Spiegel & Bonwit, 2002). In general, the concern is that the child will become chronically ill.

Fortunately, there have been many advances made in AIDS screening and treatment. For example, in the United States voluntary HIV screening has been encouraged in routine prenatal care. This has resulted in a decrease of the transmission of mother-to-child HIV from 25% to 1–2% in the United States and other developed countries (Lindegren, Steinberg, & Byers, 2000). The discovery of new drugs and use of drug therapy, called highly active antiretroviral therapy, has made quite a difference. For example, the mortality rate from AIDS decreased 80% from 1995 to 1998 in the United States and other developed countries (Spiegel & Bonwit, 2002).

Traumatic Brain Injury

A traumatic brain injury (TBI) is an acquired head injury caused by an external force. There can be many causes of the brain damage, and the characteristics of TBI depend on, among other factors, the severity and location of the injury. TBI is a disability that can affect all aspects of an individual's life. It is now clear that we must consider all of these aspects when developing educational programs for these students, recognizing the range and interdependence of skills necessary for classroom performance, and not just focusing on specific skill development and recovery (Stavinoha, 2005). The sudden onset of TBI, which has an effect on the entire family, can shatter a student's hopes and dreams and replace them with fear and uncertainty (Bullock et al., 2005).

Causes and Characteristics of Traumatic Brain Injury

Major causes of TBI include motor vehicle accidents, falls, violence-related injuries (e.g., gunshot wounds), and sports injuries (National Institutes of Health, 1998). IDEA 04 refers to both open head injuries and closed head injuries. An **open head injury** is one in which the skull is penetrated so the area of the brain that is affected is exposed, causing problems in the behavioral functions that the area controls. A **closed head injury** does not result in specific penetration but can result in serious consequences.

Although TBI is usually associated with accidents, it, unfortunately, is also frequently caused by intentionally inflicted injuries, particularly for young children. This phenomenon is sometimes referred to as shaken baby syndrome or shaken impact syndrome when the child's head actually impacts a surface such as the floor or wall.

The characteristics of TBI are varied and depend on the type and location of the injury, the severity of the injury, and the age of the individual when the traumatic event occurs.

Type and Location of the Injury. Some general characteristics are typically associated with TBI, although not all individuals will display all of them. For example, an individual who is involved in an automobile accident in which the brain injury is generalized might display more of these characteristics than an individual who receives an injury such as a bullet wound in a very specific area of the brain. Because brain functions are associated with certain brain areas (see Figure 10.2), particularly in adolescents and adults, a specific injury might result in a very predictable consequence, such as the loss of reasoning and planning (frontal lobe), loss of perception (parietal lobe), visual problems (occipital lobe), or auditory problems (temporal lobe). The general characteristics associated with TBI fall into four broad categories: physical, cognitive, social/behavioral, and academic.

Physical characteristics often associated with TBI include problems with coordination, walking, vision, speaking, hearing, and sustaining energy level (Bullock et al., 2005). Other more serious physical problems that can occur include paralysis, muscle contractions/tightening (spasticity), and seizures (NICHCY, 2006). The physical repercussions of TBI can also interfere with the child's educational program. For example, headaches, fatigue, dizziness, and sleep problems that may accompany TBI might negatively affect a student's school performance (Stavinoha, 2005).

Cognitive characteristics include changes in IQ as well as specific problems in areas such as attention and memory. The change in IQ of an individual with TBI is dependent on the degree and type of injury. Although there is some post injury IQ recovery, this can be somewhat misleading because many cognitive areas such as information processing and attention are not necessarily adequately measured by standardized intelligence tests (Stavinoha, 2005). In other words, areas not reflected in intelligence tests may be affected.

open head injury A brain injury in which the skull is penetrated and a portion of the brain is exposed.

closed head injury A brain injury in which the skull is not penetrated.

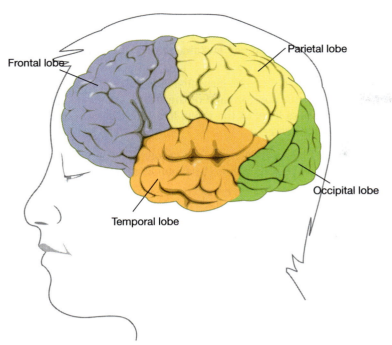

FIGURE 10.2 Lobes of the Brain

The following cognitive-related areas may be affected by a TBI:

- Language comprehension, word finding skills, and oral language fluency (Stavinoha, 2005)
- Concentration, organizational skills, and judgment (NICHCY, 2006)
- Attention, mental processing speed, and language comprehension that place a ceiling on how much information the individual is able to remember, store, and retrieve (Stavinoha, 2005)

Changes in cognitive ability including memory, reasoning, understanding, and organization may affect short-term and long-term skills (Bullock et al., 2005) although short-term functions seem to be more affected. For example, a student might remember information prior to the injury but may have difficulty remembering new information presented after the brain injury.

Behavioral, social, and emotional changes are often seen in students with TBI. Behavioral changes include temper outbursts, irritability, aggressiveness, lack of self-control, and hyperactivity (Bullock et al., 2005). Angry outbursts and impulsivity, which are often accompanied by attention deficits, memory deficits, and self-organization problems have also been reported (von Hahn, 2003). Social changes include the development of inappropriate sexual behavior (von Hahn, 2003) and difficulty maintaining conversations (American Speech, Language, and Hearing Association [ASHA], 2005b). Emotional changes following TBI might involve mood changes and loss of emotional control resulting in inappropriate laughing or crying (NINDS, 2006c). Some of the deficits in these areas may be due to the injury itself, whereas others may be due to the individual's emotional response to the injury.

Although there are a limited number of studies evaluating students' *academic functioning* following TBI, there is evidence that students will have persistent problems in academic areas such as word decoding, reading comprehension, spelling, arithmetic, and written language (Stavinoha, 2005). Problems in short-term memory also result in difficulty learning new material (ASHA, 2005). The results of brain injury in younger children may lead to academic deficits at a later point in life. For example, Mike was involved in a serious bicycle accident when he was in the first grade. Although he had some problems with memory and language skills that immediately affected his academics, his major problems did not begin to occur until five years later. Mike's injury primarily affected his higher cognitive skills such as problem solving, abstract thinking, and cognitive flexibility, all of which were required for academic success during middle school. Parents and teachers might not even be aware that school problems at a later age may be due to an injury sustained much earlier in life.

Severity of the Injury. TBI can be classified as mild, moderate, or severe. Although there is no universal definition for each of these terms, the level of severity is often tied to the consciousness level of the individual following the injury. The following criteria have been suggested:

> *Mild TBI.* Individuals remain conscious or lose consciousness and have amnesia for a short period of time (less than 30 minutes).
>
> *Moderate TBI.* Individuals lose consciousness or have amnesia between 30 minutes and 24 hours.
>
> *Severe TBI.* Individuals lose consciousness or have amnesia for longer than 24 hours.
>
> *Very severe TBI.* Individuals lose consciousness or have amnesia for more than a week (von Hahn, 2003).

Injury of all degrees of severity can result in problems in areas such as attention, concentration, memory, and thinking although those with moderate or more severe TBI will likely have additional characteristics such as repeated vomiting, seizures, and dilation of the eye pupils (NINDS, 2006c)

Age When Injury Is Acquired. Because specific areas of the mature brain are associated with specific functions, the site of the injury is a predictor of the type of deficit an older person will have. This is not as true in children, however, because their brain is still developing and often other brain regions will compensate for the deficits ordinarily associated with the damaged brain area. For example, an injury to the temporal lobe of the left hemisphere that would result in some type of language impairment for an adult might not be as evident in a younger person whose right hemisphere might take over these functions. However, depending on how much the injury affects the child's future brain growth, the same injury ultimately might have more of an effect on children than it does on adults (von Hahn, 2003). In other words, although younger children might be able to reorganize certain functions after damage better than older individuals, they tend to have more significant cognitive impairment and poorer outcomes in the long run (Stavinoha, 2005).

BEN REVISITED What general characteristics does Ben display that are consistent with TBI?

The types of characteristics displayed also can be roughly grouped based on the age of the individual with TBI. For example, more severe attention problems appear to be associated with brain injury occurring at a younger age (Stavinoha, 2005). Mayfield and Homack (2005) noted that preschool and elementary students typically display hyperactivity, distractibility, impulsivity, and temper tantrums, whereas older students show impatience, irritability, agitation, and inappropriate comments.

Check Your Understanding

1. What are the types and characteristics of the various types of cerebral palsy? Spina bifida?

2. What is the typical progression of Duchenne muscular dystrophy? What causes the disorder?

3. What are the names and characteristics of the different types of seizures?

4. What are the characteristics and possible causes of asthma?

5. What effect does cystic fibrosis have on an individual's body? What causes cystic fibrosis?

6. What are the characteristics of both Type 1 and Type 2 diabetes?

7. What are the major causes of TBI? What factors affect the characteristics that a person with TBI will experience?

How Are Students with Physical or Health Disabilities Identified?

The vast majority of students with orthopedic impairments or other health impairments are identified through the use of medical diagnostic procedures, with physicians and other related specialists, such as physical or occupational therapists, providing critical data. In some cases, observable physical characteristics are used as indicators of the disorder, such as wheezing and tightness in the chest for asthma. In other situations, laboratory or medical tests are used, such as a blood test to identify Duchenne muscular dystrophy. Many times, both procedures are used. Laboratory diagnostic procedures are also available that can detect the presence of many atypical conditions in utero. For example, *amniocentesis*, the removal of a small amount of amniotic fluid; *chorionic villus sampling*, the removal of tissue samples from the placenta; and an *ultrasound*, the bouncing of sound waves off of the fetus to produce a "picture" are all prenatal procedures that can detect various problems of the fetus. Identification of traumatic brain injury is made through medical procedures such as brain imaging, as well as by observing the physical symptoms the person exhibits.

Identification of Orthopedic Impairments

The medical conditions that result in orthopedic impairments are usually diagnosed based on observable characteristics and laboratory or medical tests. An example in which the observable characteristics are primarily used for identification is cerebral palsy. The status of the child's developmental reflexes, muscle tone, strength, and sensory capabilities are all considered. Early signs include lethargy, abnormal crying, trembling of the arms and legs, abnormal reflexes, hand held in tight fist, and feeding difficulties such as poor sucking or swallowing. Children with cerebral palsy are also slow to meet developmental milestones such as crawling and sitting. Medical tests may be conducted to rule out other conditions such as nerve or muscle problems.

Prenatal identification of many physical and health disabilities is possible using a variety of techniques.

Another disorder primarily diagnosed through observation is spina bifida, where the diagnosis is made at birth based on an examination of motor and sensory functions and the presence of a protruding meningocele or myelomeningocele. Prenatal diagnosis also can be made using amniocentesis to determine whether there are high levels of alpha-fetoprotein (AFP) in the amniotic fluid. If there is an opening in the fetal spinal cord, AFP will leak into the amniotic fluid and can be detected (Liptak, 2002).

Laboratory or medical tests are used to diagnose orthopedic impairment for Duchenne muscular dystrophy. First, there will be elevation of the creatine phosphokinase (CPK) enzyme in the blood. Electromyography (EMG) will determine that the weakness is due to muscle damage rather than nerve damage. Finally, a muscle biopsy can determine that the muscle weakness is due to muscular dystrophy rather than to some other muscle disease. An ultrasound can also be used to detect muscle abnormalities. In addition, a simple blood test can be used now to detect Duchenne muscular dystrophy in over 95% of the cases (Flanigan et al., 2003). Before this test was developed, most individuals had to have a muscle biopsy, a relatively invasive procedure, to confirm the diagnosis.

Identification of Other Health Impairments

Those conditions that are considered other health impairments are usually identified through various laboratory and medical procedures designed to evaluate the unique nature of each disorder. The diagnosis of epilepsy is commonly made using an electroencephalograph (EEG), which measures the brain's electrical activity and can indicate which part of the brain is

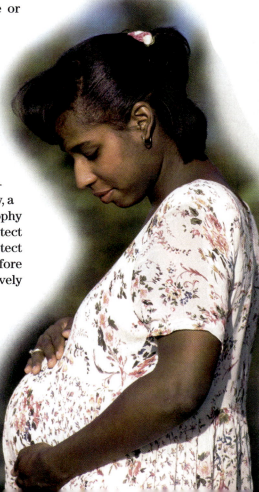

TABLE 10.3	Procedures for Identifying Other Health Impairments

IMPAIRMENT	PROCEDURES
Cystic fibrosis	Sweat test to determine if salt level is high
	Blood tests to look for defective CTFR gene
	Chest X rays
	Lung function tests
Diabetes	Fasting blood glucose test
	Oral glucose tolerance test
AIDS	HIV screening using a procedure such as enzyme immune assay
	Western blot is used to confirm

affected. Brain imaging techniques include computerized tomography (CT scan), computerized axial tomography (CAT scan), magnetic resonance imaging (MRI), and positive emission tomography (PET scan). In some cases, spinal taps may be used to help determine the cause of the seizures (Weinstein, 2002).

A physical exam is used to identify asthma. Procedures include the use of a stethoscope to listen to the breathing and physically checking the skin and inside of the nose for signs of allergies. Spirometry testing, in which the person blows into a hose to measure the vital capacity or how much air the lungs are producing, is often used. In addition, a **challenge test** is sometimes implemented. This involves the person taking a spirometry test, followed by either the inhalation of an airway-constricting chemical or cold air or engagement in extensive physical exercise. After this, the spirometry test is taken again to determine how much the lung capacity is reduced. More recently, nitric oxide, a chemical marker in asthma, has been measured in exhaled air (Mayo Foundation for Medical Education and Research, 2005). Table 10.3 lists the types of procedures used to diagnose a range of other health impairments.

challenge test A test used to determine the reduction of lung capacity to help diagnose asthma.

Identification of Traumatic Brain Injury

Most children sustain some type of mild head trauma that does not necessarily need medical attention as they go through life. However, if a child has severe headaches, significant bleeding from the wound, repeated vomiting, or has a concussion where the loss of consciousness is more than momentary, medical attention should be sought (Reece & Sege, 2000). The brain imaging procedures previously mentioned often are used to determine the location and degree of the brain injury.

When it is necessary to evaluate the seriousness or severity of the head injury, one frequently used instrument is the Glasgow Coma Scale (GCS). The GCS is given within six hours after the injury and measures the individual's level of response in three areas: eye opening, best motor response, and verbal response. Another method of assessing brain injury severity is the amount of amnesia following the trauma.

As noted previously, to qualify for services under IDEA 04, it is necessary to document not only that a brain injury has occurred but also that it adversely affects educational performance. This usually involves a multidisciplinary team approach to get a broad picture of the student's functioning. Keyser-Marcus et al. (2002) recommended that five sources be considered: neuropsychological assessment, prior school records, academic testing, observational data, and self-reports from the student. These sources of data provide information on the location of the brain injury, both pre- and postinjury academic performance, and both objective documentation of behaviors and the student's perceptions of the effects of the injury.

1. What diagnostic criterion is required for all students to receive services for a physical or health disability under IDEA 04?

2. What prenatal procedures can be used to identify many physical and health disabilities?

3. What observable characteristics are used to help identify cerebral palsy? Spina bifida? Duchenne muscular dystrophy?

4. What laboratory tests are used to identify Duchenne muscular dystrophy? Diabetes? AIDS? What brain imaging techniques are used to determine TBI?

5. After a student is identified as having a TBI, what other information needs to be gathered?

What and How Do I Teach Students with Physical or Health Disabilities?

What and how to best teach students with physical or health disabilities presents several considerations for teachers. The combination of physical, health, and learning needs often requires that a number of professionals be involved with these students. In the following sections, we focus on collaborative teaming, which requires professionals to engage in role release, giving up their professional "turf," and being willing to train and be trained by others to provide integrated instruction and related services. General and special education teachers, along with therapists and specialists, work with the student and the family to meet the student's needs. The collaborative teaming approach encourages less use of pullout services to special clinics or therapy rooms and emphasizes that services and content be delivered in the natural and least restrictive environments of the school, home, and community.

Relevant CEC Standards

▶ Instructional practices, strategies, and adaptations necessary to accommodate the physical and communication characteristics of individuals with physical and health disabilities (PH4K1)

▶ Specialized health care interventions for individuals with physical and health disabilities in educational settings (PH5K2)

Instructional Content

The instructional content that students with OI, OHI, or TBI should learn will most likely include the general education curriculum with any adaptations as needed, special content addressing their particular health and physical needs, life skills, social skills, self-determination development, and skills and knowledge needed for transitioning to adult life.

Access to the General Education Curriculum

Access to the general education curriculum for students with OI, OHI, or TBI can be accomplished, in part, through universal design. Universal design, introduced in Chapter 1, suggests that curricula and materials should be accessible, interactive, and enable all students, with or without disabilities, to achieve progress. In addition, materials and activities should accommodate a wide variety of conditions including physical, health, sensory, and other disabilities. The adaptations needed should be as unobtrusive as possible (Bauer & Kroeger, 2004). For example, providing wheelchair tables and materials that are easy to grasp and hold can assist individuals with physical or health disabilities.

It is important to note that students with TBI may have emerging and changing curriculum and learning needs. Given the possible variations in individuals in recovery from their injury, performance can be highly variable in and across academic subjects, and performance can change over time. Teachers need to be flexible and innovative in their curriculum and teaching approaches; what is appropriate at the beginning of a school year or when a student reenters school can change within months (Michaud, Semel-Concepcion, Duhaime, & Lazar, 2002). For example, a student could reenter school with losses in speech and language skills and visual-motor integration problems that make communication difficult, using a pen or pencil problematic, and processing orally presented information a challenge. The student could have significant challenges in learning language arts skills at this time because of the emphases on speaking, writing, listening, and reading. However, the student could recover these abilities over time, making it possible for him or her to use these skills in learning and interacting with others more effectively. Trying to fit a child or adolescent with TBI into the existing curriculum rather than adjusting the curriculum to the student can lead to frustration and a sense of failure for the student and teachers alike (Semrud-Clikeman, 2001).

Students with physical and health disabilities may also be served using Section 504 Plans, initially discussed in Chapter 1, which are required under the provisions of the Rehabilitation Act of 1973 and its subsequent reauthorizations even though the student may not qualify for special education. These plans are intended to provide students with physical and health disabilities accessibility to the general education curriculum so that they have equal opportunities to learn (Best, 2005). Accommodations could include "removal of architectural barriers, provision of information in accessible formats (such as computer-based math problems, use of augmentative communication, or low-tech academic materials adaptations), provision of accessible test and other evaluation materials, a shortened day to accommodate fatigue, and many other possibilities" (Best, 2005, p. 10). Section 504 Plans are intended to provide equal access to the general education curriculum and the school environment.

Special Health Care Content

Students with physical and health disabilities often have special health care issues, and they may need to learn how to manage their conditions to the extent appropriate (Demchak & Greenfield, 2003). For example, a student with diabetes should learn to monitor blood sugar levels and insulin management; a student with a physical disability who uses a wheelchair should learn how to transfer to sitting in a chair, the bed, and the toilet if the student is able. In turn, this promotes independence.

Teachers may also need to obtain special knowledge and skills when they have students with disabilities in their classes (Demchak & Greenfield, 2003). This is most relevant to special education teachers and related services personnel because they

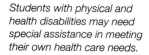

Students with physical and health disabilities may need special assistance in meeting their own health care needs.

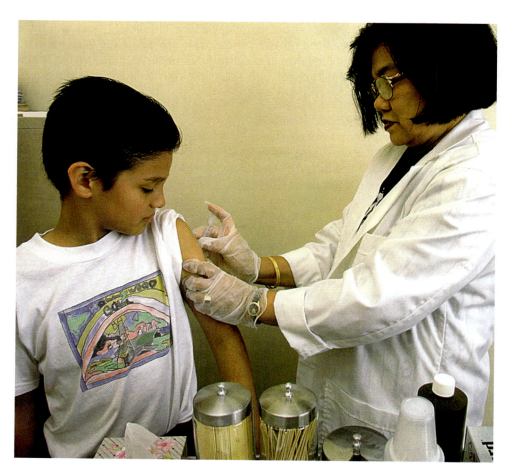

often provide direct services, such as assistance with eating, toileting, and other activities of daily living, to students during the school day, but it could also be relevant to general education teachers who should be aware of and monitor students with physical or health disabilities in their classes.

Life Skills Curriculum

The life skills curriculum approach emphasizes preparation for accomplishing the activities and routines of everyday life. Bowe (2000) noted that students with physical or health disabilities may need to learn skills such as using money; consumer skills, such as shopping for food and eating in a restaurant; using public transportation; and other skills such as job skills, following directions, and performing specific job tasks. Also, some students may be so physically challenged by their disabilities that learning how to assist others in helping them accomplish these tasks may be a focus of a life skills curriculum (Bowe, 2000). For example, a student may be unable to eat independently, but the student could still make choices as to which food item to eat, when he or she is ready for another bite or needs a drink, and when the student is no longer hungry. Others have suggested that life skills, such as citizenship skills like voting, can be infused in and complement the general education curriculum (Stump & Bigge, 2005).

Social Skills

Of some importance, especially for students with TBI, is social adjustment (Dykeman, 2003). Being accepted by peers, building a network of social relationships, and developing friendships are all key in establishing self-esteem. Because of the injuries they suffer and the subsequent rehabilitation, students with TBI may experience considerable time away from the school setting and their peers. Similarly, students with physical or health disabilities may be hospitalized or have home-based instruction for periods of time, also reducing the opportunities for social interaction that contributes to self-esteem.

Dykeman (2003) pointed out that students with TBI may experience a lowered sense of self-efficacy due to problems learning age-appropriate skills and difficulties interacting with others in social settings. Including structured opportunities for social interaction, rehearsal of skills, and the use of scripts and role playing in the curriculum and learning activities can be of benefit. For example, an adolescent male student who has difficulty interacting with female students could engage in role-playing activities, scripting (such as how to ask a girl on a date), and engaging in conversations (such as asking about the girl's interests, taking turns in the conversation).

Self-Determination

The basic premise behind the development of self-determination skills is that students should learn to share in and make decisions, make choices, set goals for themselves, and self-advocate (Fiedler, Simpson, & Clark, 2007).

Clark and Bigge (2005) pointed out several self-adaptability skills that are important for students with physical or health disabilities to acquire:

- Decision making: for example, selecting a career choice
- Independent performance: for example, self-regulating performance in school or on a job, such as working without supervision
- Self-evaluation: for example, evaluating one's punctuality at school or on a job
- Autonomy: for example, recognizing areas in need of improvement and making adaptations to conform to school or work norms

The acquisition of these skills can promote self-determination and self-advocacy. Self-advocacy involves learning skills that focus on knowledge of self; helpful information about the school, such as what type of equipment is accessible, and how the environment contributes to adjustment; personal care management; responsibilities; and community access (for example, knowing how to get homework done, and knowing what type of part-time job one would like) (Clark & Bigge, 2005). The ability to make decisions and advocate for oneself are critical in developing independence and a fulfilling adult life (Fiedler et al., 2007).

PRACTICE

Student Name: Andre Anders

Type of Seizures Experienced: Generalized tonic-clonic

Medication Needed: Tegretol for seizure control

Frequency of and What Happens During Seizures: Andre's seizures are generally controlled, but they still occur as often as once a month. He experiences an aura (a sensation) and reports this to his teacher, indicating a seizure is likely to follow. Andre will lose consciousness and experience severe convulsions. He may also lose bowel or bladder control. The duration of the seizure is typically less than one minute. He may sleep for a few minutes to an hour or longer following the seizure. He will be disoriented upon waking and may be embarrassed because of the loss of bowel or bladder control.

What May Lead to a Seizure: Triggers are not known, but the seizures tend to occur in the afternoons during periods of noise and activity.

Teacher and Staff Response: If Andre reports he is about to have a seizure, have him lie down. If the seizure occurs unexpectedly, gently lower him to a lying position unless he is secure in a seated position. Move objects that could cause injury away from him. Place a towel or soft object (such as a pillow) beneath his head and turn his head to the side. LET THE SEIZURE RUN ITS COURSE. DO NOT ATTEMPT TO HOLD HIM DOWN OR CONTROL HIS CONVULSIONS. Contact the nurse and Andre's parents immediately. Allow Andre to sleep. If he awakens, monitor him and allow him to change clothes if needed. Be sure to record the date, time of day, and length of the seizure.

Restrictions: Monitor Andre during periods of high activity (for example, physical games, loud and busy assemblies). Be sure he can notify you if he experiences his aura. Avoid an abundance of activity in the classroom during afternoons to the degree possible.

Source: Adapted from Demchak, M., & Greenfield, R. G. (2003). *Transition portfolios for students with disabilities. How to help students, teachers, and families handle new settings.* Thousand Oaks, CA: Corwin Press.

Transition Planning

Transition considerations for students with OI, OHI, or TBI can take two major forms. First is the transition from school to adult living. This type of transition and the curriculum content would not differ significantly for these students from that of students discussed in previous chapters, so long as individual needs, such as for assistive technology or support for health care needs, are addressed. For example, a student whose physical limitations require adult assistance in many activities of daily living may need the IEP team to spend considerable time planning for a residential living option that provides for maximum independence but still includes necessary care.

A second type of transition to consider is the transition from a hospital or rehabilitation setting, such as after initial recovery from a TBI, or within school settings or delivery systems (Semrud-Clikeman, 2001). In these cases, transition portfolios can be useful in assisting students, parents, and teachers. Transition portfolios may consist of personal data (name, age, parents' names, address, telephone, emergency contacts), medical information, educational programming information (such as summary of IEP goals and objectives), adaptations needed (such as accommodations included on the IEP), communication needs (such as use of assistive technology for oral and written communication), and reinforcement strategies (such as likes in terms of activities, objects, and praise) (Demchak & Greenfield, 2003). The Classroom Example above includes a sample of medical information that might be included in a student's transition portfolio as he moves from a hospital to school setting.

Instructional Procedures

Once curriculum goals and objectives are identified, general and special education teachers, along with other IEP team members such as the student, parents, and related services personnel, must determine what instructional procedures should be used. In this section, we focus on general procedures teachers need to know to address the physical, health, and social needs of these students. These include areas that could be addressed in individualized health plans and strategies for behavioral and social skill development. Because of the challenges parents may face in caring for and promoting the independence of students with OI, OHI, or TBI, educators should consider special supports for them as members of a collaborative team.

Individualized Health Plans

Students with physical or health disabilities may have an **individualized health (care) plan,** or IHP (Heller, Forney, Alberto, Schartzman, & Goeckel, 2000). IHPs provide teachers with information about the student's health care status and prescribed health care procedures or physical management procedures. IHPs are not required but are recommended as part of the IEP development. IHPs contain general information such as the history and diagnosis of the student's condition, assessment information, and procedures. The Classroom Example regarding Andre's seizures could be included as part of an IHP. Heller et al. (2000) noted the following broad areas that should be addressed in an IHP:

- *Communication skills.* For example, students with cerebral palsy that severely affects their oral-motor functioning may not be able to speak clearly and may need to learn to communicate using alternative or augmentative communication systems.
- *Medications and their administration.* Many students will need to learn when, how much, and how often to take medications as well as possible side effects.
- *Lifting, carrying, and transferring.* Students who use wheelchairs may need to learn to transfer themselves from the chair to a toilet and back. Some students may not be able to lift or transfer themselves but can learn how to offer assistance to those who are primarily doing the lifting and transferring.
- *Handling and positioning.* Students may need to learn how to best position themselves to allow them to hear, see, and manipulate materials. They may need to be able to communicate this to others if they cannot position themselves (see the Classroom Suggestions for additional information about positioning students).
- *Mobility.* Students need to learn to orient themselves in their environment and know how to navigate environments. They must learn how to be mobile in each environment as well as remember how to get from one environment to another. A student with TBI may have both physical issues (for example, hemiplegia) and memory issues that could make finding his or her way difficult.
- *Eating and feeding.* Some students will need to be tube fed or learn to manage their own feeding. Some students with cerebral palsy may need to learn the use of adaptive equipment as well as special techniques for improving their own eating skills. For example, a student may need to use a spoon with a built-up handle and a plate with a nonslip bottom as well as how to most effectively use the spoon to reduce spillage.
- *Toileting and ostomy management.* To be independent, as well as to maintain self-esteem and personal dignity, it is helpful for students to be able to manage these very personal needs to the degree possible.
- *Catheterization.* Similar to toileting and ostomy management, students who need catheterization who can learn to manage this task will enjoy greater independence and privacy. Still, teachers and paraprofessionals as well as health care aides may be involved in toileting, ostomy management, and catheterization.
- *Respiratory management.* Students with compromised breathing or oxygen intake may need to learn to take care of their tracheostomies or oxygen intake. Again, school staff may also be involved.
- *Ventilator management.* Ventilator management will likely be managed by someone other than the student. Students with Duchenne muscular dystrophy, for example, may have muscles and nerves affected such that they need a ventilator to manage breathing and oxygen intake. School nurses or health care aides may be closely involved with the education and in-school care of students with severe physical and health disabilities (Heller et al., 2000).

individualized health (care) plan A plan developed to provide teachers with information about the health care status, prescribed health care procedures, and the physical management procedures for a student.

PRACTICE

Classroom Suggestions Positioning of Students

- ❑ Proper positioning affects muscle tone and posture, provides alignment and body support, provides for effective use of the upper body, promotes stability, which can help students feel secure and safe, and it can reduce deformity.

- ❑ Change positions frequently. This avoids pressure sores, redness, and discomfort. Sitting and lying (lying supine, prone, or on either side) are the most commonly used positions.

- ❑ Sidelyers, which support the back and trunk while lying on one's side, allow students a change in position, and the student can still use his or her arms and hands to manipulate materials or objects.

- ❑ Wedges are used for lying prone, on one's front side, and elevate students slightly so that materials can be read, observed, and manipulated when placed below the head and shoulder position.

- ❑ When lying supine, on one's back, ensure students are supported on either side so they don't fall or roll over, support knees and ankles, and provide for the use of the arms and hands to manipulate materials placed above the student. Students can also be supported so knees are bent and feet are flat on the floor.

- ❑ Seating includes ensuring the pelvis is at a neutral, 90 degree angle, not slanted forward or backward, rotated to the left or right.

- ❑ Feet should be level and supported by the floor or wheelchair foot pedals.

- ❑ The trunk and shoulders should be supported, usually by straps. This provides for better posture and head control.

- ❑ Pommels, padded cylindrical supports, on the shoulders may also provide for better head control.

- ❑ Leg separators or abductors can be used to prevent involuntary crossing of the legs and to maintain symmetry.

Source: Best, S. J., Reed, P., & Bigge, J. L. (2005). Assistive technology. In S. J. Best, K. W. Heller, & J. L. Bigge, *Teaching individuals with physical or multiple disabilities* (5th ed.). Upper Saddle River, NJ: Pearson.

One might conclude that students who have very personal hygiene and management needs would be best served in a more private and restrictive setting, such as in a special classroom. However, this may not be the conclusion of many teachers and parents. Mukherjee, Lightfoot, and Sloper (2000) found that both teachers and parents felt inclusive education had benefits for both students with disabilities and those without, but that school staff needed additional assistance to make inclusion successful. These areas of assistance included (1) obtaining health-related information; (2) making sure this health-related information is passed on between and within schools; (3) ensuring medical care is available in schools; (4) taking responsibility for coordinating support for these students; and (5) providing emotional support. With these types of support, along with an IHP that promotes student independence and self-management, inclusive education can be realized for many students.

Strategies for Behavioral and Social Skills Development

Particularly for students with TBI, who may experience emotional adjustment and behavioral issues due to their injuries, social skills development and support can be very important. Students with TBI may experience behavioral and personality changes and may need assistance with peer relationships (Michaud et al., 2002). A variety of strategies have been useful in promoting appropriate social behaviors including positively reinforcing students for appropriate behavior, prompting, providing corrective feedback as needed, and using behavioral contracts (Dykeman, 2003). For example, students having difficulty with impulse control, such as disrupting class by making inappropriate comments, could be praised for gaining attention by raising their hand and in other appropriate ways, or be verbally cued or visually prompted to raise their hand or remain silent. Students could be corrected and redirected when the behavior occurs and enter into a contract that provides incentives for overall reductions in the inappropriate disruptions and an increase in the appropriate alternatives. Modeling appropriate behaviors and having peers also model appropriate behavior could be helpful.

Cognitive strategies (such as being able to monitor and adjust one's attention level) can also be helpful as students gain increased cognitive and memory skills. Learning to self-monitor and self-manage behavior is important in learning greater independence and social competence (Dykeman, 2003).

Supporting Parents of Students with Physical or Health Disabilities

Parents are integral members of the collaborative team. Semrud-Clikeman (2001) offered several suggestions for teachers and related services personnel of students with TBI in providing support for parents. We summarize those suggestions in the following paragraphs. Some suggestions could also be helpful for teachers.

First, provide current and practical information about the student, but do not overwhelm parents with more information than could be reasonably processed. Details about how the child's disability affects school performance in the classroom, socially, and psychologically are important. Parents may be less likely to understand the types of educational or medical jargon that teachers or related services personnel might use among themselves. For example, discussing a child's physical limitations in terms related to abduction, adduction, pronation, or supination may be confusing and intimidating to some parents. When parents are still upset about the disability, information should be provided in small amounts and repeated as needed. Parents should be given frequent opportunities to ask questions.

Second, keep in mind that in large meetings, the number of teachers and other professionals can be intimidating for parents. A premeeting with a teacher to explain what will occur, who will be present, the roles of team members, and some of the major findings or discussion points can help parents. The school psychologist, in particular when working with a student with TBI, and other professionals should also be knowledgeable about the nature of the injury and be able to translate that information for parents into educational and social recommendations.

Third, ensure parents understand that recovery takes time, that skills do not emerge or reemerge at the same time, and that some skills may never be recovered. Parents should also understand that the student may be resistant to the efforts of team members, confrontational, and easily upset by his or her circumstances. Parents should be encouraged to find means for respite from their child and to take care of their own emotional health as students with these types of disabilities can require extensive supports at home that add stress to parents (Semrud-Clikeman, 2001).

Students with physical and health disabilities may need special equipment to gain access to the environment and learning activities.

PRACTICE

BEN REVISITED How can Ben and his parents be supported in coming to an understanding of Ben's injuries and their impact on his academic, social, and behavioral skills?

Check Your Understanding

1. What special health care content might be included in the curriculum?

2. Why are life skills important to include in the curriculum?

3. Why is social skills development so important for students with TBI?

4. What may transition planning include for students with physical or health disabilities?

5. What are individualized health care plans, and how can they help teachers?

6. What strategies can be helpful in developing behavioral and social skills?

7. In what ways can teachers provide support to parents of students with physical and health disabilities?

What Are Other Instructional Considerations for Teaching Students with Physical or Health Disabilities?

Relevant CEC Standards

▶ Sources of specialized materials, equipment, and assistive technology for individuals with physical disabilities (PH4K2)

▶ Communication and social interaction alternatives for individuals who are nonspeaking (PH6K1)

Other areas of instructional consideration for students with physical and health disabilities include the environment and the use of assistive technology. The instructional environment requires two primary considerations: the continuum of services needed and how the classroom can be arranged to accommodate the physical and health needs of students. The use of technology requires consideration of both adaptive equipment and assistive technology.

The Instructional Environment

Students with physical and health disabilities have unique needs that require services to be delivered in a variety of settings. For example, a student with TBI may need hospitalization followed by a rehabilitation facility placement before returning to the school environment. Once in the school environment, the IEP team must then decide whether a full-time special class, part-time special class, or full-time general education class placement with supports, or some other placement is most appropriate (Semrud-Clikeman, 2001).

The Continuum of Services

Because of the need for a continuum of services, described and discussed in Chapter 2, IEP teams must work collaboratively with students and families in determining the least restrictive environment for students with physical or health disabilities. Parents want assurances that their children's unique needs can and will be met in more inclusive settings (Cook & Swain, 2001). It is important, therefore, that parents be members of a collaborative team that ensures appropriate education and related services (Fiedler et al., 2007).

A student with asthma may rarely need hospitalization and may be in a full-time general education classroom throughout his or her schooling. However, a student with muscular dystrophy may thrive in a full-time general education classroom initially but require services in more specialized placements such as a special classroom, home, or in a hospital, as the condition worsens over time. Many students with physical and health disabilities will need related services, such as physical and occupational therapy, that may have to be provided in a special room or setting. Some may take advantage of distance learning. A continuum of services is needed in terms of the environments in which these students will be educated, but provision of services in a less restrictive, inclusive environment is still desirable for most students during their schooling (Heller et al., 2000).

Classroom Arrangements

When students are educated in their neighborhood schools, Best (2005) suggested that general and special education teachers consider the following factors:

- *Architectural barriers.* These may need to be modified or overcome. For example, it will need to be ensured that entries are wide enough for students using wheelchairs.
- *Tangible barriers.* Logistical problems in obtaining equipment when it is needed and repairing equipment in a timely manner can be challenges. Young children grow quickly. If equipment designed specifically for his or her age/size is not delivered or repaired punctually, the child may not get maximum benefit from its use.

- *Failure to schedule and deliver services.* General and special education teachers must work collaboratively along with related services personnel to ensure that the goals of the general education curriculum and those of the IEP are being met and that the services needed to achieve those aims are provided.
- *Material portability.* Augmentative communication systems, physical and occupational therapy equipment, special furniture, and mobility devices such as walkers may have to be moved from one environment to another or duplicated in multiple environments.
- *Accessibility in movement.* All areas of the classroom should be physically accessible, and students should have access to the learning activities in each environment.
- *Competing philosophies.* If teams do not work collaboratively and achieve consensus on the curriculum, goals and objectives of the IEP, and determination of the least restrictive environment, effective education may be thwarted.
- *Appropriate training.* All teachers and staff will need training and consultation in providing accessible, safe environments, adapting materials and learning activities as needed, and collaborating to provide related services to benefit students (Best, 2005).

> **MARTA REVISITED** How could Marta's teachers address her physical disabilities in the typical elementary classroom? What changes might need to be made to the classroom?

Distance Learning

Distance learning, also referred to as distance education, involves students being taught outside of the school environment, such as from home or a hospital, possibly without face-to-face interaction with a teacher (Simonson, Smaldino, Albright, & Zvacek, 2006). It can involve print media, such as textbooks; or telecommunications, such as e-mail, Internet-based learning, and online course technologies; or both print and telecommunications. Teachers who use distance learning for students need training in effective strategies, to have carefully designed courses and adequate support systems, to interact with the learner electronically or in person, and to determine how to assess learning outcomes (Simonson et al., 2006). A student in a rehabilitation facility may be able to use e-mail and Internet resources to access course materials and instruction online and to communicate with a teacher on a regular basis, even if face-to-face visits are very limited in number. Instruction can also be offered through a school site–based telephone system (Best, Reed, & Bigge, 2005).

Scherer (2004) developed recommendations for teachers of distance learning courses. These recommendations can also be considered when evaluating whether a distance education class is appropriate for a student. Those recommendations we consider more relevant to students with physical or health disabilities include the following:

- Plan for periodic face-to-face meetings to achieve personal involvement.
- Ensure students understand that they may have minimal contact with peers.
- Make materials available early, and give students opportunities for training in using the technology.
- Pick the right technology for the learning goals. Some goals, such as drafting and editing a personal narrative, may be easily done by e-mail. Other goals, such as researching causes and effects of earthquakes, will likely require students to have electronic access to materials via e-mail and the Internet (Scherer, 2004).

Instructional Technology

Instructional technology for students with physical and health disabilities includes two major components—adaptive equipment, such as the positioning equipment described earlier, and assistive technology. An Important Event on the next page describes a legislative initiative that outlines what is considered assistive technology.

The environment may need to be arranged to provide access for students who use special equipment.

Assessment for the Use of Instructional Technology

Instructional technology should be selected based on individual need because students with the same disability can have different needs (Demchak & Greenfield, 2003). Assessment for the use of technology must take into account student variables such as those outlined in Table 10.4, as well as others such as appearance, comfort, performance, cost, and availability (Scherer, 2004). For example, an augmentative communication system could be reasonably effective but odd in appearance to others and large in size, making it conspicuous and less desirable to some students. Some technology devices are more reliable in performance than others. Devices that are in need of frequent repair can defeat the purpose of their use. Some technology is more readily available. If it will take months for special technology to be available, IEP teams should consider alternatives that will achieve the desired purposes that are more readily available. Once assessments have been conducted, the team is likely to consider the need for both adaptive equipment and assistive technology.

Use of Adaptive Equipment

adaptive equipment Specialized devices designed and used to help a student perform some function.

Adaptive equipment is defined as specialized devices designed and used to help a student perform some function (Heller et al., 2000). Adaptive equipment can be used for physical management and self-help skills as well. Physical management equipment includes positioning devices such as sidelyers and wedges, which were discussed earlier. Such devices are necessary to promote health as well as achieve positioning that allows students to access learning activities. A child who is prone positioned (on his chest) on a wedge can use his hands and arms to interact with materials. Other devices can be used to aid mobility and movement, such as motorized wheelchairs and prosthetic limbs, or a leg brace to provide support and proper limb alignment. Without mobility devices such as prostheses and orthoses, some students would be less independent and, perhaps, completely dependent on others to move from one location to another. A **prosthesis,** such as a prosthetic leg, replaces a body part, and an **orthosis,** such as a leg brace, enhances the use of a body part

prostheses Equipment that replaces a body part.

orthoses Equipment that enhances the use of a body part.

NEEDS, CAPABILITIES, AND PREFERENCES

❑ What does the student need to do in the classroom?

❑ What are the student's strengths, interests, and learning styles?

❑ Does the student possess the requisite skills to use the technology for maximum benefit?

PRIOR EXPOSURE TO AND EXPERIENCES WITH TECHNOLOGY

❑ Is the student receptive to the use of technology?

❑ What is the student using now?

❑ What has worked well and not worked well in the past?

MOTIVATION AND READINESS

❑ What are the student's dreams and aspirations?

❑ Does the use of technology fit into and with those dreams and aspirations?

❑ Does the student recognize that technology can be assistive in overcoming any discrepancies between the current and desired situation?

EXPECTATIONS, MOOD, AND TEMPERAMENT

❑ What are the student's expectations academically and socially?

❑ What is the student's overall and typical mood (for example, sad, anxious, happy)?

❑ What level of support from others does the student have and desire?

❑ Does the student's physical status (for example, energy level and mood) lend itself to the use of technology?

LIFESTYLE

❑ What are the student's typical routines throughout the day in school, home, and community?

❑ What are peers, family, and other significant persons doing during these routines?

Source: Adapted from Scherer, M. J. (2004). *Connecting to learn. Educational and assistive technology for people with disabilities.* Washington, DC: American Psychological Association.

PRACTICE

(Bowe, 2000). Prostheses and orthoses can benefit a student's health but can also be important for appearance. For example, a prosthetic leg may allow a student to wear pants or slacks without any noticeable difference from peers without disabilities. Such devices also help students achieve greater participation in activities, such as walking or running, and allow greater independence.

Self-help skills equipment includes devices such as nebulizers to administer medication, adaptive toilets, adaptive eating tools (for example, spoons with built-up handles for easier gripping; lunch trays with nonslip bottoms to provide stability), and health care equipment such as colostomy bags or tube feeding equipment (Heller et al., 2000).

Falling within the category of adaptive equipment are alternative or augmentative communication devices, equipment that allows individuals to communicate in ways other than orally. Picture boards or symbol boards that allow a student to point to items that indicate needs or wants are examples of alternative communication devices. For example, a very young student with severe cerebral palsy who is unable to communicate orally could have a board with pictures of food, water, a toilet, and other items that might be needed. Such a board could also include symbols such as happy or sad faces to

In Practice Meet Educator Barbara Gejer and Her Student Kyle

I am a Resource Specialist teacher for grades three through five at a suburban elementary school in a 25,000-student unified school district. I have been teaching special education for seven years and was part of the implementation team for the Learning Center model in our district. I also hold a multiple-subjects creden-

tial and have experience teaching general education. In 1998 I was recognized as one of the district's employees of the year.

Kyle is a fifth-grade student with cerebral palsy. He needs a walker to help him keep his balance; he uses a DynaMyte (augmentative communication) system as his voice; and he requires a one-to-one paraeducator to facilitate his inclusion in the general education classroom. He has difficulties with fine and gross motor control. The muscles in his throat are also affected, and he cannot swallow well nor produce speech other than open vowel sounds. He is virtually blind in one eye and wears glasses to correct the vision in his other eye. Kyle also suffers from an intellectual disability. Recent evaluations indicate that he functions in the moderate range.

Kyle receives speech therapy, physical therapy, and occupational therapy in the school setting, as well as adaptive P.E., assistive technology support, and resource specialist program services. He also receives private speech services, clinic-

based physical therapy, inclusion support consultative services, and home-based services. Kyle has a caseworker from the Regional Center and a low-incidence specialist from the County Offices of Education who also provide consultative support.

Kyle likes being a part of his class. With significant modifications and accommodations, he is able to participate in science, social studies, math, and language arts. His report card grades reflect his progress toward his IEP goals rather than meeting state-determined content standards.

Instructional Content and Procedures

Kyle's instructional content is based on the same district-adopted curriculum used by all fifth-grade students. However, it must be modified to a level he can access, and activities must be adapted to meet his cognitive and physical needs. Kyle listens on tape to grade-level core literature books such as *Charlie and*

indicate emotions and feelings. Augmentative communication devices are used to expand the individual's ability to communicate orally through speech. Early devices were similar to the communication boards just described but might have included electronic pads that activated verbal requests. For example, the student touches the pad and a recorded voice states, "I am thirsty. Could I have some water, please?" (Bowe, 2000). Augmentative communication devices can be quite sophisticated today, using computer technology to produce synthesized speech that enables students to express themselves as ably as individuals without disabilities in terms of the complexity and length of messages. Augmentative communication devices may be slower than orally produced speech, and the equipment can be quite expensive, costing thousands of dollars. A student could need special training to use these devices, and maintenance and repair can be issues as the devices become increasingly complex. Still, the ability to communicate with others when a condition limits or prohibits oral production of speech can be one of the more important uses of equipment for the adjustment and well-being of the individual (Bowe, 2000).

Use of Assistive Technology

Scherer (2004) noted several assistive technology developments that can improve students' access and their instruction. Computer monitors can be set to make text larger,

the Chocolate Factory, often in an abridged version with a slightly lower vocabulary. To assess Kyle's reading levels, I have him read a graded passage "with the voice in his head" while I track his good eye following the words. I then present comprehension questions on index cards with the answers presented in a multiple-choice format. Kyle must read not only the questions but also the answer choices before he points to his selection. On the most recent assessment using this procedure, Kyle was able to select the correct answer to four out of the five questions presented for each passage.

In math, Kyle's classmates are currently learning least common multiple and greatest common factor in order to add and subtract unlike fractions. Kyle is just learning that a fraction represents equal shares of a whole. This concept is reinforced with software programs that he can use with the computer on his desk.

The fifth-grade social studies book began with a chapter on landforms. While the rest of the class was creating a map of a fictional country with various landforms, I had Kyle matching words to pictures: *mountain* to a picture of Mt. McKinley, *desert* to a picture of Death Valley, *river* to a picture of the Mississippi, and *ocean* to a picture of the Pacific Ocean. I had the paraeducator program Kyle's DynaMyte with the vocabulary words and associate them with scanned pictures for Kyle to use for independent practice. When the lesson taught longitude and latitude, I had Kyle color a picture of a globe: green for the continents and blue for the oceans. Kyle then traced over the equator with a black crayon.

For the science unit on plant cells and structures, I had Kyle match vocabulary words to pictures of the stem, roots, leaves, and flower while the rest of the class discussed stamen, pistil, and ovaries. During a group presentation, he was able to point to "his" parts of the plant on a drawing while he used his DynaMyte to "speak" for him.

His classmates high-fived him, making Kyle feel very much a part of his fifth-grade classroom.

Instructional Environment and Technology

In keeping with the philosophy of full inclusion, I provide all my services to Kyle in the general education classroom. He receives 45 minutes of Resource Specialist services five times a week. He sits at a double desk at the side of the room so that he has access to his paraeducator and room for his assistive technology: a laptop computer, scanner, printer, DynaMyte, and a variety of software programs. Although I have had extensive training in the use of the assistive technology devices, I feel that my time with Kyle is best spent in direct instruction and modeling curriculum modifications. I collaborate with the paraeducator about specific content that should be programmed into the DynaMyte and discuss what software is best used to reinforce specific concepts.

Collaboration

To best address Kyle's unique needs, I collaborate with the other professionals who have expertise in areas I do not have. We hold monthly team meetings with all service providers, the classroom teacher, and the parent to discuss Kyle's progress and plan specific strategies and techniques. The school-based team also collaborates informally on an as-needed basis. This collaborative effort has been expanded to include the middle school team to discuss placement options and transition activities. We meet annually to review Kyle's IEP as well.

PRACTICE

magnify items, allow slides to be viewed more easily through an attached microscope, and provide voice output that guides the user as he or she navigates through folders, programs, and other icons on the desktop. Touchscreens provide access by directly touching the screen rather than using a keyboard or mouse. For inputting information, voice recognition software can be helpful for those who cannot use a mouse or keyboard at all. Special keyboards, such as those with enlarged letters and numbers, and keyboards with a limited number of keys relevant only to an individual's needs, can provide better access. Pointers, joysticks, touchpads, and roller balls are methods by which students can access mouse functions. For example, students with very limited use of their arms and hands could use a pointer attached to their head to strike keys or a touchscreen. Eye-gaze systems can be used to allow students to use their eye movements to activate computer functions, and some mice can be activated by the feet. Switch systems can also be used for students who have little motor control or ability but can move a single body part, such as moving their elbow up and down. Sophisticated switch systems are available for students able to control their breathing. Sip and puff switches allow students to create a Morse code by pushing air out through a switch or breathing air in through the tube; this code can be translated by computer software and used to activate the computer functions (Scherer, 2004).

Finally, assistive technology can be used to address accessibility for instruction through environmental and object modification. Best, Reed, and Bigge (2005) suggested some factors to keep in mind:

1. Make sure materials are accessible. For example, use storage areas at the appropriate height so students can easily take things out or drop them in.
2. Arrange the environment to allow access for wheelchairs or other adaptive equipment.
3. Ensure work surfaces such as tabletops or wheelchair trays are adjustable for height and angle. Having work surfaces that provide stability for both arms, such as ones that allow a student to rest his or her elbows on the surface, can also be helpful.
4. Make sure objects can be modified to be more stable. For example, use clamps for attaching them to work surfaces, masking tape to secure items, textured paper.
5. Ensure objects can be designed with boundaries. For example, add a rim or edge on a work surface so a student with poor motor control cannot easily push an item off the surface accidentally.
6. Make available grasping aides such as a special cuff to hold crayons or pencils, Velcro on toys and on a palm glove to aid in picking objects up, or gloves with magnets for picking up metal objects.
7. Keep in mind that manipulation aids can help students activate parts of toys. Parts can be enlarged or have extensions or knobs attached that make manipulation easier. Tongue depressors placed between book pages will allow some students to turn pages when they lack the fine motor ability to do so.
8. Consider modifying the environment. Appliances activated by a computer rather than traditional hand controls can be used to enhance accessibility in the home.

The possibilities for the use of adaptive equipment and assistive technology are extensive and should be individualized. For general and special education teachers, related services personnel such as occupational therapists, physical therapists, and speech and language pathologists can be important members of the collaborative team in assessing, selecting, and maintaining such equipment.

Check Your Understanding

1. Why is the continuum of services so necessary for students with physical and health disabilities?

2. What are some considerations in arranging the physical environment of the classroom?

3. How can distance learning assist students?

4. What are some considerations in assessing a student for the use of instructional technology?

5. What are adaptive equipment, prostheses, and orthoses, and how can they assist students?

6. How do alternative or augmentative communication devices assist students?

What Are Some Considerations for the General Education Teacher?

Relevant CEC Standard

▶ Roles and responsibilities of school and community-based medical and related services personnel (PH10K3)

In one study, a majority of general education teachers expressed concern over their ability to meet the needs of students with physical and health disabilities and felt they needed more training (Singh, 2001). Many also expressed an interest in learning more about adaptive equipment and indicated some awareness of the environmental adaptations students with these types of disabilities might need. General education teachers who teach students with physical or health disabilities will need to work collaboratively with special education teachers and related services personnel to better utilize special equipment and technology and to provide accommodations and modifications to the physical environment and learning activities. There are three major areas for general education teachers to develop skills in working with students with physical or health disabilities.

First, teachers should work to make students safe and the environment and equipment accessible. To accomplish this, they can do the following (Dugger, Wadsworth, & McKnight, 1999; Mukherjee et al., 2000):

1. Work with medical and related services personnel to ensure awareness and understanding of medical and health-related issues and how these should be handled. For example, teachers should become familiar with universal precautions, emergency care plans, and routine treatment plans. Teachers should obtain information about the student and understand the confidential nature of such information.
2. Learn how to make the physical environment safe and accessible as discussed earlier.
3. Learn how to use and adjust assistive equipment as appropriate. Some equipment, such as special wheelchairs, may need a specialist for adjustments or repairs.

Second, general education teachers should make instructional adaptations including the following (Dugger et al., 1999):

1. Schedule instructional times to ensure medical concerns and related services can be provided, as well as special education as needed.
2. Make seating arrangements that allow for use of assistive technology and equipment while allowing access to water, electricity, appropriate lighting, and so forth with minimum disruption to other students.
3. Adapt materials to accommodate special needs of students. Teachers may want to use enlarged print, books on tape, or computer software. Teachers should be prepared to modify assignments and assessments as needed. For example, they may allow students to take tests orally or provide extra time for students to complete assignments.

Third, general education teachers should support the social and emotional development of students with physical or health disabilities. To accomplish this, they can do the following (Mukherjee et al. 2000):

1. Ensure students can take part in extracurricular activities as appropriate or participate in field trips and other school-related activities.
2. Help students develop relationships with peers. Also, provide assistance and guidance in explaining a student's condition to peers as appropriate.
3. Be sympathetic and a person the student can talk to about concerns. Many of these students have good reason to be worried about their health and medical issues and may need someone to listen to their concerns. Teachers may also wish to consult with counselors or school nurses about such concerns and how to provide emotional support to students with serious medical issues.

Although the needs of students with physical or health disabilities can be complex, the general education teacher should be aware of how to ensure students' health and medical needs are accommodated, especially in emergencies; how to adapt instruction and materials; and how to provide for the social and emotional support of students. General education teachers should seek and expect the collaboration of special education teachers, related services personnel, parents, and students themselves in the provision of these accommodations.

Check Your Understanding

1. In what ways can general education teachers work to make students safe and the environment and equipment accessible?
2. What are some instructional adaptations general education teachers can make?
3. How can general education teachers support the social and emotional development of

PRACTICE

Practical Considerations for the Classroom

Characteristics	Indicators You Might See
Orthopedic Impairments	
Cerebral Palsy	Damage to muscle tone that affects movement and motor development. May experience difficulty making voluntary movements and controlling involuntary movements. Muscles may be tight and joints stiff. May have difficulty walking and grasping objects. Speech may be impaired. May affect only one arm or leg or multiple areas. Half to three-quarters may also have intellectual disabilities.
Spina Bifida	Nerve damage in spinal cord may result in paralysis that could lead to difficulties in bowel and bladder control, breathing, and swallowing. May have seizures and/or hydrocephalus.
Duchenne Muscular Dystrophy	Generally begins with muscle weakness in the lower leg area. May fall frequently, have large calf muscles, and have trouble getting out of a chair or bed.
Other Health Impairments	
Epilepsy	Has seizures. During a generalized tonic-clonic seizure, the student initially becomes rigid, loses consciousness, and falls to the ground; then, displays rhythmic jerks; finally, after seizure ends, individual will rest or sleep for a period of time. In an absence seizure individual loses consciousness for a few seconds; these may not always be noticeable. Complex seizures may result in eye blinking, facial grimacing, lip smacking, and odd behaviors. Individuals may experience a sensory sensation (e.g., ringing in the ears or taste in the mouth) before a seizure called an aura.
Asthma	May experience wheezing, coughing, tightness in the chest, and difficulty breathing.
Cystic Fibrosis	Results in mucus in the lungs that makes respiratory functioning difficult. May result in digestive problems and disrupt the individual's mineral balance.
Diabetes	Leads to high blood sugar, which can damage organs. Symptoms of high blood sugar include hunger, thirst, blurred vision, increased urination, dry mouth, and dry or itchy skin.
Acquired Immunodeficiency Syndrome	Symptoms include swelling of the lymph nodes, enlargement of the liver and spleen, and a predisposition to viral and bacterial infections. May have cognitive deficits, motor functioning problems, speech and language deficits, and problems with memory and attention.
Traumatic Brain Injury	
Physical	May have problems with coordination, walking, vision, speaking, hearing, and sustaining energy level. May also have paralysis, spasticity, and seizures. May have headaches, fatigue, dizziness, and sleep problems.
Cognitive	May have a change in IQ and problems with attention and memory. May have problems with language functions as well as concentration, organization skills, and judgment.
Behavioral, Social, and Emotional	Behavioral changes may include temper outbursts, irritability, aggressiveness, lack of self-control, and hyperactivity. Social changes may include inappropriate sexual behavior and difficulty maintaining conversations. Emotional changes may include mood swings and loss of emotional control.
Academic Functioning	May have problems with word decoding, reading comprehension, spelling, math, and written language.

Students with Physical or Health Disabilities

Teaching Implications

Instructional Content

- Students should have access to the general curriculum. Many students, especially with physical and health disabilities, will have no cognitive problems.
- Use universal design in planning the curriculum.
- Consider using learning strategies, study skills, and other approaches that increase comprehension, storage, and retrieval of information with students with physical and health disabilities.
- Consider what assistive technology should be used.
- Consider incorporating content on how to manage the physical or health condition.
- Consider including life skills, self-determination, and self-esteem development in the curriculum.
- Determine whether social skills should be incorporated in the curriculum.
- Keep in mind that students with TBI will have evolving curriculum and learning needs.
- Support planning for transition, whether to adulthood or from a hospital or rehabilitation setting.

Instructional Procedures

- Develop an individualized health care plan.
- Consider using positive reinforcement, prompting, providing corrective feedback, and using behavioral contracts with students who need behavioral support.
- Consider whether strategies should be developed to support cognitive and memory skills or for understanding social cues and situations.
- Keep parents in mind when planning and implementing instruction. Ensure positive and open communication.
- Teach life skills using everyday materials and activities.
- Teach social skills directly as needed.
- Prepare students without disabilities for the conditions of peers with disabilities.
- Use distance learning as needed.

Instructional Environment

- Consider the continuum of services when planning placement and support for students.
- Plan the classroom to avoid physical barriers and to encourage mobility.
- Ensure accessibility of materials and learning activities.

Instructional Technology

- Consider the use of both adaptive equipment and assistive technology.
- Start by assessing what instructional technology can support student learning whether through physical comfort, communication, or direct learning.
- Assess the best way to acquire needed technology.
- Ensure students know how to use their adaptive equipment or assistive technology.

Methodologies and Strategies to Try

- Create an individualized health plan (p. 343).
- Position students as needed (p. 344).
- Positively reinforce behavior (p. 344).

Considerations for the General Classroom and Collaboration

The general education teacher should:

- Learn as much about using adaptive equipment as possible.
- Work closely with special education teachers and related services personnel.
- Make students safe and the environment, activities, and equipment accessible.
- Make instructional adaptations as needed.
- Support the social and emotional development of students.

Collaboration

General and special educators should consult on:

- The individualized health plan
- Coordinating and supporting the work of related services personnel
- Planning the classroom environment
- Determining the curriculum
- Developing accommodations
- Adapting procedures and strategies used
- Assessing what the role of instructional technology should be and developing a plan based on this

Chapter Summary

Go the text's Online Learning Center at **www.mhhe.com/taylor1e** to access study resources, Web links, practice quizzes, and extending materials.

What Are the Foundations of Physical and Health Disabilities?

- Students with a wide variety of medical conditions are considered to have a physical or health disability. Because of this, rather than one general history of physical and health disabilities, each specific disability has its own history.
- Three separate categories under IDEA 04 are considered physical or health disabilities: orthopedic impairments (OI), other health impairments (OHI), and traumatic brain injury (TBI). In each case, the disability must adversely affect educational performance to warrant services under IDEA 04.
- According to the most recent IDEA data, only slightly under 1% of the school-aged population receive services in these categories, mostly in the OHI category.

What Are the Causes and Characteristics of Physical and Health Disabilities?

- The causes and characteristics of students with OI and OHI vary significantly, depending on the medical condition. Causes range from brain damage to genetics to viruses. The characteristics of each condition are unique.
- Because the cause of TBI is head trauma, the characteristics depend on a number of factors such as the type, location, and severity of the injury.

How Are Students with Physical or Health Disabilities Identified?

- Identification procedures vary depending on the nature of the medical condition.
- For OI and OHI, identification of the physical characteristics of the condition and the use of medical tests such as blood tests and biopsies are involved.
- For TBI, brain imaging procedures can be used.
- For all students, the effect of the medical condition on educational performance must be evaluated.

What and How Do I Teach Students with Physical or Health Disabilities?

- Students should have access to the general education curriculum.
- Learning to manage their own health care needs can also be important for those with physical disabilities.
- Life skills, social skills, self-determination, and transition are also important learning areas.
- Individual health care plans may be implemented to provide teachers with important information and to outline management procedures for a student's condition.
- Students with TBI, in particular, can benefit from behavioral and cognitive strategies. Teachers may need to support parents in understanding and managing their student's condition and educational status.

What Are Other Instructional Considerations for Teaching Students with Physical or Health Disabilities?

- A continuum of service delivery placements is important as students may receive services in a variety of settings.
- Classrooms must be arranged for accessibility and safety. Distance learning may be necessary for students with extended stays at home or in medical facilities.
- Adaptive equipment can be used for positioning and assisting students with everyday tasks.
- Alternative or augmentative communication systems can aid students who have difficulty with speech production.
- Assistive technology can be helpful in allowing better access to learning activities and materials.

What Are Some Considerations for the General Education Teacher?

- Safety and accessibility are important environmental considerations.
- Instructional adaptations to schedules, seating arrangements, and materials may be needed.
- Support in emotional and social development can facilitate the inclusion of students with physical and health disabilities.

Reflection Topics

1. Suppose you are a secondary-level teacher and have a student in your class with a degenerative disease, such as Duchenne muscular dystrophy. How would you prepare yourself and your students for the possibility that the student might die during the school year?

2. If you had a student with epilepsy in your class who had recurrent generalized tonic-clonic seizures, would you prepare your other students for what to expect if a seizure occurs? If so, how would you do so?

3. If you had a student with AIDS in your classroom, what, if anything, would you tell the rest of the students?

4. When a student with a physical or health disability requires assistance in self-help skills such as toileting and eating, what do you think a teacher's role should be?

SUMMARY

5. How would you address the situation if a student without a disability in your class complained he was bothered by the appearance of a student with a physical disability?

6. Should teachers be required to continue learning about new technologies in order to benefit students who may need special hardware and software?

Application Activities: For Learning and Your Portfolio

1. Suppose you have a student with cerebral palsy in your class. Make a list of questions that you would want answered by a physical therapist that would help you plan the student's educational program.

2. (*Portfolio Possibility*) Research the use of folic acid and its role in the prevention of spina bifida. Write a two-page paper that summarizes the research.

3. Interview a teacher who works with a student with traumatic brain injury. Find out all the areas that the teacher must address and the various professionals with whom she or he collaborates.

4. (*Portfolio Possibility*) Assume you are arranging a classroom and school building for a student who uses a wheelchair. Review the layout of the classroom and determine what changes would be needed to make the classroom and building safe and accessible.

5. Visit a classroom, rehabilitation facility, or hospital setting that includes students with physical or health disabilities. Determine what types of adaptive equipment and assistive technology are available and what their uses are.

6. After obtaining permission from a cooperative individual, interview a student with a physical or health disability at your college or university or in a local school district. Ask the student questions such as what are some challenges she or he faces? What changes would make the person's education easier or more accessible? How would the person prefer others to react to her or his condition?

SUMMARY

CHAPTER 11

Students with Autism Spectrum Disorders

CHAPTER OUTLINE

FOUNDATIONS

What Are the Foundations of Autism Spectrum Disorders?

A Brief History of Autism Spectrum Disorders
Definitions of Autism Spectrum Disorders
Prevalence of Autism Spectrum Disorders

What Are the Causes and Characteristics of Autism Spectrum Disorders?

Causes of Autism Spectrum Disorders
Characteristics of Autism Spectrum Disorders

How Are Students with Autism Spectrum Disorders Identified?

Early Screening
Diagnosis

PRACTICE

What and How Do I Teach Students with Autism Spectrum Disorders?

Instructional Content
Instructional Procedures
    Direct Instruction
    TEACCH
    Applied Behavior Analysis
    Social Stories
    Unsupported Methods

What Are Other Instructional Considerations for Teaching Students with Autism Spectrum Disorders?

The Instructional Environment
Instructional Technology

What Are Some Considerations for the General Education Teacher?

INTRODUCING ALEX

Alex is a 6-year-old boy who was first diagnosed as having autism by his pediatrician a short time before his third birthday. His parents initially became concerned about Alex when his language and other developmental skills started to lag behind those of his fraternal twin, Alan. Alex's parents had noticed that he also had feeding and sleep problems, and that he was not overly social. He preferred to play alone, fixating on one toy, a miniature truck. Alex rarely made eye contact and did not like to be held. Due to his lag in language development compared to his brother and because he did not respond when his name was called, Alex's parents initially thought that Alex had a hearing problem. They turned to Alex's pediatrician, who referred them to an audiologist. The audiologist tested Alex to find that his hearing was within normal limits. Alex's pediatrician reached a diagnosis of autism based on direct observation, a thorough developmental history, and

results from intelligence and language testing conducted by a psychologist.

After being diagnosed with autism, Alex immediately began receiving special education services under Part C of IDEA 04. His individualized family service plan (IFSP) emphasized development of communication and social skills, and his parents were involved in his program. When he turned 3, Alex was transitioned into a preschool program under Part B of IDEA 04. His individualized education program continued to focus on communication and social skills, and his family's involvement in his education also continued.

Alex is now in first grade at his local public elementary school in a general education class. His teacher, Mr. Runyon, runs a highly structured classroom with a very stringent schedule and routine. He feels that this helps all of his students, not just Alex. One of the areas Alex needs particular help with is communication. His special education teacher, Ms. Dunn, works

with Alex one hour a day, frequently implements applied behavior analysis, and uses the Picture Exchange Communication System to help Alex communicate. Alex has made slow, but steady progress in Mr. Runyon's classroom. He cooperates with other children, though he does not initiate interactions, and can only speak in three-word sentences. ■

Like most children with autism, Alex was diagnosed with the disorder early in life. In fact, the most widely used definition of autism requires that an individual *must display* the characteristics before the age of 3, although this does not mean that the diagnosis has to be made prior to age 3. Alex's diagnosis was based on the fact that he demonstrated many of the characteristics associated with autism, including problems in communication and socialization. Autism is just one, though the most prevalent, of the disorders on the autism spectrum. Autism spectrum disorders (ASD), also known as pervasive developmental disorders, include five specific disorders: autistic disorder (autism), Asperger syndrome (also referred to as Asperger disorder), Rett syndrome (also referred to as Rett disorder), childhood disintegrative disorder, and pervasive developmental disorders not otherwise specified (PDD-NOS). Although each of these disorders results in social, communication, and/or behavioral deficits, they each have unique characteristics. For example, Rosie, a 14-month-old girl with Rett syndrome, developed normally during her first year, but soon started to avoid eye contact, lose her muscle tone, and have difficulty walking. Jonathan, a 17-year-old boy with Asperger syndrome, has poor social skills and is preoccupied with current events, reading several newspapers and watching numerous news shows each day. There is also variability within categories. While Alex does use limited oral language, Ben, another child in his class with the same diagnosis of autism, does not speak at all and rocks back and forth constantly.

Because Alex is placed in a general education classroom, the special education teacher must collaborate closely with Mr. Runyon to assist him in using behavior analysis principles and training him in the use of the Picture Exchange Communication System. For this reason, it is equally important for future special education and general education teachers to have a strong understanding of the foundations of the disorder and of practical ways to support the learning of students with an autism spectrum disorder.

What Are the Foundations of Autism Spectrum Disorders?

Autism, recognized in the first part of the 20th century, was the first of the autistic spectrum disorders to be identified. The four other disorders also included in the spectrum were subsequently classified. Each of the five disorders has its own specific definition in the most widely used diagnostic system published by the American Psychiatric Association (2000). IDEA 04 provides a specific definition for autism, but not the other four disorders. Students with these other disorders are sometimes served in a different IDEA 04 category. For example, a student with Rett syndrome or childhood disintegrative disorder may be served under the category of mental retardation. The prevalence of autism, the most common of the five disorders, has increased dramatically in recent years. In fact, it has been one of the fastest-growing categories over the last few years.

A Brief History of Autism Spectrum Disorders

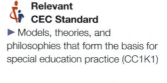
Relevant CEC Standard
▶ Models, theories, and philosophies that form the basis for special education practice (CC1K1)

Although individuals with autism spectrum disorders (ASD) have undoubtedly existed for many centuries, it was not until the mid-20th century that the disorders were recognized and labeled. The term *autism* was coined in 1911 when Eugen Bleuler, a Swiss psychiatrist, used it to describe a condition of self-absorption caused by poor social relatedness (Gupta, 2004). Attention was brought to the disorder when, in 1943, Leo Kanner described 11 children with what he termed "early infantile autism" (see An Important Event). Although Kanner did a remarkable job of describing the features of autism, diagnostic criteria for the disorder were not identified until 1956 (Kanner & Eisenberg, 1956).

1943—Leo Kanner Publishes His Classic Study on Early Infantile Autism

Kanner, L. (1943). Autistic disturbances of affective contact. *Nervous Child*, 2, 217–250.

"Early infantile autism" was first observed and labeled by Leo Kanner in 1943. In his report, Kanner described 11 children (8 boys and 3 girls) who had the disorder. These children had been brought to him at the Harriet Lane Home (now a part of Johns Hopkins School of Medicine) because of concerns by parents and physicians. The children displayed characteristics of unusual development such as lack of social skills, possible deafness, and feeding difficulties. Among the specific characteristics Kanner noted as evident in the children before age 6 were an inability to relate themselves to people and situations in a normal way; an excellent rote memory; echolalia (child repeating words spoken to him/her); a fear of loud noises; the insistence on sameness; and a desire to be left alone. Kanner's observations represented the first time that the multiple characteristics of autism were described.

REFLECTION What teaching implications can be made from Kanner's observations?

Autism was officially acknowledged as a disorder by the American Psychiatric Association (APA) in 1980 and first considered a disability under the Individuals with Disabilities Education Act in 1990. The four other disorders that fall within the autism spectrum began to be identified soon after autism was first recognized, though these were not officially recognized until the last portion of the century. In 1944, a year after Kanner's initial publication on autism, Hans Asperger, a German physician, independently described a form of autistic-like behaviors that he initially termed "autistic psychopathy," but was eventually called Asperger syndrome in the early 1980s (Wing, 1981). Asperger's original work was not translated into English for almost 50 years (Frith, 1991).

Rett syndrome, the third disorder on the autistic spectrum, was initially recognized in 1966 when an Austrian physician observed two girls in his waiting room displaying unusual hand mannerisms (Perry, 1991). It was not until almost 20 years later that Rett syndrome was identified as a specific disorder (Harris, Glasberg, & Ricca, 1996) after a report describing 35 girls with the same characteristics was published (Hagberg, Aicardi, Dias, & Ramos, 1983). The fourth and fifth disorders on the spectrum, childhood disintegrative disorder and pervasive development disorder not otherwise specified, were added to the fourth edition of the *Diagnostic and Statistical Manual* in 1994 (APA, 1994).

Definitions of Autism Spectrum Disorders

Each of the five autism spectrum disorders has its own specific definition based on the diagnostic criteria specified in the *Diagnostic and Statistical Manual of Mental Disorders 4th ed. text revision* (*DSM-IV-TR*) published by the American Psychiatric Association (2000).

Relevant CEC Standard

▶ Issues in definition and identification of individuals with exceptional learning needs, including those from culturally and linguistically diverse backgrounds (CC1K5)

Autistic Disorder (Autism)

Autism, meaning "living in self" in Greek (Gupta, 2004), is characterized by behavioral deficits in three broad categories: social interaction, communication, and restrictive or repetitive behaviors (see Table 11.1). The *DSM-IV-TR* states that an individual with

TABLE 11.1	*DSM-IV-TR* Criteria for Autistic Disorder (Autism)

A. A total of six (or more) items from (1), (2), and (3), with at least two from (1) and one each from (2) and (3):

  (1) Qualitative impairments in social interaction, as manifested by at least two of the following:

   (a) Marked impairment in the use of multiple nonverbal behaviors such as eye-to-eye gaze, facial expression, body postures, and gestures to regulate social interaction

   (b) Failure to develop peer relationships appropriate to developmental level

   (c) A lack of spontaneous seeking to share enjoyment, interests, or achievements with other people (e.g., by a lack of showing, bringing, or pointing out objects of interest)

  (2) Qualitative impairments in communication as manifested by at least one of the following:

   (a) Delay in, or total lack of, the development of spoken language (not accompanied by an attempt to compensate through alternate modes of communication such as gesture or mime)

   (b) In individuals with adequate speech, marked impairment in the ability to initiate or sustain a conversation with others

   (c) Stereotyped and repetitive use of language or idiosyncratic language

   (d) Lack of varied, spontaneous make-believe play or social imitative play appropriate to developmental level

  (3) Restricted repetitive and stereotyped patterns of behavior, interests, and activities as manifested by at least one of the following:

   (a) Encompassing preoccupation with one or more stereotyped and restricted patterns of interest that is abnormal either in intensity or focus

   (b) Apparently inflexible adherence to specific, nonfunctional routines or rituals

   (c) Stereotyped and repetitive motor mannerism (e.g., hand or finger flapping or twisting, or complex whole-body movements)

   (d) Persistent preoccupation with parts of objects

B. Delays or abnormal functioning in at least one of the following areas, with onset prior to age 3 years: (1) social interaction, (2) language as used in social communication, or (3) symbolic or imaginative play.

C. The disturbance is not better accounted for by Rett's disorder or childhood disintegrative disorder.

autism must display problems in social interaction, communication, or symbolic or imaginative play before the age of 3. Although autism can be diagnosed after the age of 3, the behaviors that constitute the disorder must have been evident before that age when using the *DSM-IV-TR* definition. The IDEA 04 definition of autism is similar to the *DSM-IV-TR* definition, although it does not specifically *require* that the problems occur before age 3. It reads:

> Autism means a developmental disability significantly affecting verbal and nonverbal communication and social interaction, generally evident before age three, that adversely affects a child's educational performance. Other characteristics often associated with autism are engagement in repetitive activities and stereotyped movements, resistance to environmental change or change in daily routines, and unusual responses to sensory experiences.

Asperger Syndrome

Asperger syndrome is sometimes mistakenly referred to as "mild autism." Individuals with this disorder have social interaction impairments and develop restrictive, repetitive interests, beliefs, and activities that impair social, occupational, or other areas of functioning. Unlike individuals with autism, those with Asperger syndrome do not have the accompanying communication impairments. Also, although individuals with autism often display cognitive deficits, individuals with

Asperger syndrome do not have a clinically significant delay in cognitive ability (APA, 2000).

Rett Syndrome

Rett syndrome, a rare disorder found virtually exclusively in girls, is a neurodevelopmental disorder in which the child usually develops normally until about 6 to 18 months of age, at which time the characteristics of the syndrome emerge. These characteristics include **hypotonia,** the loss of muscle tone; reduced eye contact; decelerated head growth; and disinterest in play activities. These changes are followed by rapid developmental regression, including hand wringing, unsteady walking, breathing irregularities, feeding and swallowing difficulties, severely limited expressive and receptive language development, and seizures.

hypotonia The loss of muscle tone.

Childhood Disintegrative Disorder

Also a rare disorder, childhood disintegrative disorder is one in which the child develops normally for the first two years of life, but starts regressing developmentally between the ages of 2 and 10. At least two of the following areas must be affected: expressive or receptive language, social skills or adaptive behavior, bowel or bladder control, or play or motor skills such as coordination. Individuals with childhood disintegrative disorder will also display communication deficits and behavior characteristics consistent with autism.

Pervasive Development Disorder Not Otherwise Specified

A pervasive developmental disorder–not otherwise specified (PDD-NOS) is diagnosed when a child displays some autistic behaviors and meets some, but not all, of the criteria for any of the other pervasive developmental disorders. Examples would be a child whose autistic behaviors began after the age of 3 or an individual who has severe impairments in social interactions and communication but who does not have restrictive and repetitive patterns of behavior.

ALEX REVISITED Why do you think Alex was diagnosed with autism and not Asperger syndrome?

Prevalence of Autism Spectrum Disorders

The National Institute of Mental Health (NIMH, 2004) reported that the prevalence estimates of autism spectrum disorders range from 2 to 6 per 1,000 children. A more recent study reported the prevalence to be 1 in 150 children (Centers for Disease Control, 2007). Although overall prevalence figures vary, there is agreement about some of the prevalence indicators of autism spectrum disorders.

First, it is agreed that autism is the most prevalent of the autism spectrum disorders. Fombonne (2002) reported that the prevalence of autism is 60 times greater than that of childhood disintegrative disorder (CDD). In a review of the available data, the following prevalence rates were reported: autism, 10 per 10,000; Asperger disorder, 2.5 per 10,000; Rett syndrome and CDD, fewer than 1 per 10,000 (Volkmar, Lord, Bailey, Schultz, & Klin, 2004). Volkmar et al. noted, without specifying a reason, that the prevalence rate of pervasive developmental disorder–not otherwise specified is rarely investigated. PDD-NOS, however, is the only autism spectrum disorder in which specific inclusion criteria are not identified. Some estimates regarding the prevalence of autism are even higher than 10 per 10,000, indicating that autism occurs in 1 of every 250 births (Autism Society of America [ASA], 2003). Still, only .25% of children ages 3–5 and .29% of individuals ages 6–21 received services under IDEA's autism category in the 2004-2005 school year (U.S. Department of Education, 2006).

A second agreement is that the prevalence of autism is increasing, with some even suggesting that autism has become an epidemic. It is one of the fastest-growing IDEA disability categories, with a 10% to 17% annual growth (ASA, 2003).

The number of students receiving services for autism increased from 0.39% of all students receiving IDEA services in 1993 to 3.20% in 2005 (U.S. Department of Education, 2006). Some of the reasons suggested for this increase include the following:

- Greater awareness of autism (Gillberg & Wing, 1999)
- Improved methods of identification (Croen, Grether, Hoogstrate, & Selvin, 2002)
- Increased awareness that autism can exist across all IQ levels (Wing, 1993)

Certainly, the fact that autism was included as a disability under IDEA in 1990 resulted in greater attention to the disorder and more efforts made in its identification. It is difficult to determine whether there is a true increase in autism or just an increased awareness of the disorder.

A third agreement regarding the prevalence of autism spectrum disorders is that there is a connection between the disorders and gender. Approximately four times more males than females have autism, and there is a 9:1 ratio of males to females with Asperger syndrome (National Autistic Society, 2005). Childhood disintegrative disorder also occurs more frequently in males. As noted earlier, Rett syndrome occurs virtually exclusively in females.

Whether you plan to be a special education teacher or a general education teacher, the increased prevalence of students with autism in particular will most likely be reflected in your classroom. It is important that you know how each of the disorders is defined so that you can prepare to teach any child who enters your classroom with a diagnosis of an autism spectrum disorder.

Is the number of individuals with autism actually increasing, or are we just more aware of the disorder and have improved identification procedures?

Check Your Understanding

1. What five disorders make up the autism spectrum disorders?

2. What are the definitions of each of the autism spectrum disorders?

3. What is the range of estimated prevalence of autism spectrum disorders? What agreements do researchers have about the prevalence of autism?

4. What are some of the possible reasons the number of individuals identified as having autism is increasing?

5. Which of the disorders are more prevalent in boys and which one is more prevalent in girls?

What Are the Causes and Characteristics of Autism Spectrum Disorders?

With the exception of Rett syndrome, the causes of autism spectrum disorders are unknown but are thought to be neurological, or brain-based, in nature. Each of the disorders on the spectrum is characterized by different degrees of communication skills impairment; social interaction deficits; and/or restrictive, repetitive, and/or stereotyped behavior such as rocking back and forth and hand flapping. Although this chapter includes information on all of the autism spectrum disorders, the main focus in this and the remaining sections is on autism because teachers are most likely to encounter students with this disorder in their classrooms.

Causes of Autism Spectrum Disorders

Research on the causes of autism spectrum disorders, particularly autism, has increased as the disorders have become more prevalent, but researchers are still unable to point to a specific cause. The one exception to this is Rett syndrome. Researchers have identified a mutation of a specific gene, MeCP-2, as being responsible for this syndrome. Exploration of the causes of the other autism spectrum disorders, particularly autism, has focused on the brain and both genetic and nongenetic causes. Before we explore the most likely causes of autism, let's examine the controversial theories that you may have heard about as causing autism.

Controversial Theories Regarding Causes of Autism

Several controversial theories of the cause of autism have been proposed. When Kanner first described autism, he hypothesized that it might be caused by a lack of warmheartedness in the family (Gupta, 2003). This theory of poor parenting eventually became known as the "refrigerator mom" theory, suggesting that the child's autism was caused by a cold, uncaring mother (Bettleheim, 1967). Besides being a rather sexist theory, there is no support that bad parenting is a cause of autism. A strong challenge to the poor parenting theory came when Rimland (1964) wrote a book suggesting that autism was due to biological, not psychological, factors. Kanner recanted his position that autism is caused by family factors at a 1969 meeting of the National Association of Autistic Children (Gupta, 2003).

A more recent controversial theory of the cause of autism revolves around a common childhood vaccine. Based on research conducted at the Royal Free Hospital in London, Wakefield et al. (1998) suggested that autism is caused by the MMR (measles, mumps, rubella) vaccine routinely administered to children at an early age. Wakefield and his associates contended that the measles virus present in the vaccination caused a bowel inflammation that allowed toxins to leak into the brain, thus causing autism (Fitzpatrick, 2004). The Wakefield et al. study immediately drew criticism. First, there was a volatile critique by Chen and DeStefano (1998) indicating that the MMR vaccine had been used safely for more than three decades, and expressing concerns that parents would shun the vaccination, thus resulting in more diseases. Large-scale studies of the MMR–autism link show that there is no cause-effect relationship (e.g., Honda, Shimizu, & Rutter, 2005).

Other vaccines, specifically those that contain the preservative thimerosal, have also been suggested as a cause of autism. Thimerosal contains mercury, which is known to be a nerve-cell poison (Cook, 2005). Although studies have not supported the relationship of exposure to thimerosal and autism (e.g., Jick & Kaye, 2004), recommendations have been made that research continue in this area (ASA, 2004).

The Brain and Autism

In investigating possible causes of autism, researchers have primarily focused on the role of the brain. As just noted, as early as 1964, a biological basis of autism was suggested. It now is generally accepted that autism is a result of abnormalities in brain structure or brain function (ASA, 2004). Research has indicated that some of these abnormalities may be caused by genetic factors and others, perhaps, by environmental triggers.

One way researchers have explored possible causes of autism is by studying the brains of individuals with autism. Research in this area has uncovered several differences in the brains of those with and without autism ranging from the physical size of the brain to differences in various areas of the brain.

Abnormally large heads of individuals with autism have been observed for a number of years (Kanner even reported it in his 1943 study). Neuroimaging techniques have helped document that brain size in young children with autism may be as much as 10% larger than in those without autism (e.g., Sparks et al., 2002). The difference is not as large as the child ages, and in adolescents and adults "the size of the effect is diminished to a few percent at most" (Volkmar et al., 2004,

p. 146). It is possible that this abnormal brain development, called the "growth dysregulation hypothesis," is caused by genetic defects in brain growth factors (NIMH, 2004).

Several areas of the brain have been reported to be involved in individuals with autism. Two that have been particularly studied are the limbic system, which plays a role in emotion and the formation of memories (Boeree, 2002), and the cerebellum, which regulates attention, sensory modulation, emotional modulation, and motor and behavior initiation (Mesibov, Adams, & Klinger, 1997). In addition, decreased blood flow has been reported in individuals with autism in the left hemisphere of the brain, which is responsible for language functions (Bragdon & Gamon, 2000).

Genetic Causes of Brain Abnormalities

The brain abnormalities found in individuals with autism are thought to be genetically based, at least in part. This assertion is supported by twin studies. It has been reported that an identical twin of an individual with autism has a 60% chance of also having autism, whereas only 5% of fraternal twins of an individual with autism will also have autism (Ozonoff & Rogers, 2003). Although these data support a genetic cause, they also suggest that autism is not solely genetically based because 40% of identical twins do not share the disorder. Other evidence of a genetic basis for autism is that a family with a child with autism has a much higher than usual chance (1 of 20) of having another child with autism (National Institute of Neurological Disorders and Stroke, 2005).

Although a genetic cause is suspected, only a few genes that seem to be associated with autism have been isolated. Genes in a specific area on chromosome 15 (Veltman et al., 2005) and chromosome 7 (Ozonoff & Rogers, 2003) have been suspected as possible causes of autism. It is likely that autism is a complex disorder that results from multiple gene abnormalities (Polleux & Lauder, 2004).

Nongenetic Causes of Autism

Autism is a condition that an infant is born with or develops early in life. This latter point suggests that some factor might "trigger" the disorder in some children. In particular, it seems that environmental factors might interact with genetic susceptibility during vulnerable periods of development (Lawler, Croen, Grether, & Van de Water, 2004). To date, no single environmental factor has been identified, but, as previously mentioned, we do know that it does not result from poor parenting. Some factors that have been considered are problems during pregnancy and delivery (e.g., oxygen deprivation at birth), viral infections, and metabolic imbalances (ASA, 2004). Seizures in infants can also trigger the development of autism (Gillberg & Coleman, 2000).

Characteristics of Autism Spectrum Disorders

Relevant CEC Standards

▶ Educational implications of characteristics of various exceptionalities (CC2K2)

▶ Similarities and differences of individuals with and without exceptional learning needs (CC2K5)

▶ Similarities and differences among individuals with exceptional learning needs (CC2K6)

As outlined by the *DSM-IV-TR*, each of the five autism spectrum disorders has specific associated characteristics (Table 11.2). There does, however, seem to be some general overlap of characteristics among the autism spectrum disorders. Gillberg and Coleman (2000) refer to these as the *triad of social impairments*. The characteristics included within this triad are (1) difficulty interacting with other people in a social context; (2) difficulty communicating with others, both verbally and nonverbally; and (3) rigid and restrictive behavioral repertoire and imaginative skills, including the need for elaborate routines, insistence on sameness, restricted play patterns or interests, and motor stereotypes such as rocking back and forth. It must be remembered, however, that autism spectrum disorders represent five distinct categories and not all individuals with an autism spectrum disorder will have all of these characteristics. A student with Asperger syndrome, for example, might have good communication skills, whereas a student with autism might not. The National Research Council (2001) pointed out that "Even though there are strong and consistent commonalities, especially in social deficits, there is no single

TABLE 11.2	*DSM-IV-TR* Characteristics of the Autism Spectrum Disorders

DISORDER	CHARACTERISTICS
Autistic Disorder	Impairments in social interaction; impairments in communication; restricted, repetitive, and stereotyped patterns of behavior, interests, and activities
Rett's Disorder	Apparently normal initial development; subsequent loss of purposeful hand skills and social engagement; poorly coordinated gait or trunk movements; severely impaired receptive and expressive language.
Childhood Disintegrative Disorder	Apparently normal development for at least the first two years; loss of skills in two of the following areas before age 10: language, social skills or adaptive behavior, bowel or bladder control, play or motor skills, resulting in impairments in social interaction and/or communication, and/or restrictive patterns of behavior
Asperger's Disorder	Impairment in social interactions; restricted, repetitive, and stereotyped patterns of behavior, interests, and activities; no delay in language or cognitive development
Pervasive Developmental Disorder–Not Otherwise Specified	Severe impairments of social interactions, communication, and/or stereotyped behavior, interests, and activities although criteria are not met for any other disorder

Source: Reprinted with permission from the *Diagnostic and Statistical Manual of Mental Disorders,* 4th edition, text revision (copyright 2000). American Psychiatric Association.

behavior that is always typical of autism or any of the autism spectrum disorders and no behavior that would automatically exclude an individual child from diagnosis of autism spectrum disorder" (p. 2).

By far, the most information about characteristics of the autism spectrum disorders is reported on individuals with autism. As noted previously, the three major characteristics of autism are impairments in social interactions; impairments in communication; and repetitive patterns of behavior, interests, and activities. In this section, we address these characteristics of autism as well as the important area of cognition. Remember that not all individuals will display all of these characteristics.

Social Characteristics of Autism

Difficulty with social interaction is one of the main characteristics of individuals with autism. In early life, this is apparent when a child appears to dislike cuddling and physical affection (Bragdon & Gamon, 2000). Later, this is often manifested as a difficulty in establishing relationships with others, which results in a lack of friends (Gillberg & Coleman, 2000; NIMH, 2004).

One social interaction characteristic of individuals with autism is a problem in joint attention, which results in a limited ability to share interests or achievements with others (Johnson, 2004). For example, a child and his mother would have difficulty focusing on, and playing with, a toy at the same time. In addition, many individuals with autism display decreased facial recognition of others and may not make eye contact. All of these social interaction problems are found in individuals of various ages and IQ levels (Lord & Volkmar, 2002). Problems are also seen in the area of social responding, such as a lack of response to parents' voices when they call the child's name, and an apparent unawareness of other children, even those who show signs of distress (Bragdon & Gamon, 2000). For example, a child with autism might ignore another child in the same room who is crying.

Communication Characteristics of Autism

Deficits in communication skills are very common in individuals with autism. Because of the importance of communication in developing social relationships, it is actually difficult to separate the two areas. For example, a child with autism who is unable to communicate as expected with peers might have a very difficult time establishing friendships with them. Communication deficits in individuals with autism can be divided into two categories: deviations in language development and specific deficits related to communicative intent.

Deviations in Language Development. Children with autism generally display several deviations in language development. Often they may use a few to several words by age 2, but then stop speaking for one or more years, and in some cases, may never speak again (Gillberg & Coleman. 2000). One language characteristic displayed by many children with autism is **echolalia,** the "parroting" or repeating of words and phrases said to them. For example, if a child is asked "How are you today?" she may respond with the same phrase, "How are you today?" Echolalia can be either *immediate*, as in the previous example, or *delayed*, in which the child repeats a previously heard word or phrase hours, days, or weeks later (Johnson, 2004). Other less prevalent language characteristics are **palilalia,** when the child repeats his or her own words; **echopraxia,** the repetition of others' gestures and movements (Gillberg & Coleman); and using made-up words called **neologisms.** Another common language characteristic is that individuals with autism may refer to themselves by their name instead of "I" or "me." For example, "Brandon want the toy" rather than "I want the toy" (NINDS, 2005).

Deficits in Communicative Intent. The primary function of language is communication. Many individuals with autism have deficits in communication intent or conveying the intended meaning. Even if normal language patterns are intact, communication problems can exist. For example, Rubin and Lennon (2004) noted that although some individuals with high-functioning autism develop relatively sophisticated language abilities, such as vocabulary skills and knowledge of grammatical structure, their ability to use language for communication in real-life situations is sometimes masked. For example, a student with autism who is having difficulty understanding the intent of a peer's conversation might use good vocabulary, but what is said may be totally unrelated to the peer's comments. Speech problems, such as unusual intonation or rhythm, might also lead to difficulties in conversational skills (Bragdon & Gamon, 2000). In addition, children with autism frequently do not use nonverbal communication skills, such as gesturing, that are used by others to help convey meaning (Gillberg & Coleman, 2000).

One specific communication characteristic that can result in problems is the tendency for individuals with autism to comprehend or interpret information very literally. Gillberg and Coleman (2000) provided the following example:

> An example of this literal interpretation is provided by a 10-year-old girl with autism, with a full-scale IQ of 100, who appeared panic-stricken when a nurse about to do a simple blood test said: "Give me your hand, it won't hurt." The girl calmed down immediately when another person, who knew her well, said: "Stretch out your index finger." The girl had understood, at the first instruction, that she was required to cut off her hand and give it to the nurse. (p. 14)

Behavioral Characteristics of Autism

The primary behavioral characteristics of autism are repetitive and stereotypic behavior, an extreme need for routine, an unusual preoccupation or interest in certain objects or activities/facts, and abnormal sensory and motor functions. A less frequent, but often publicized characteristic is the uncanny talents exhibited by individuals with autism who have what is known as savant syndrome. **Savant syndrome** occurs in up to 10% of individuals with autism and usually involves spectacular abilities in areas such as music, art, mathematics, calendar calculating, and mechanical/spatial skills (Treffert, 2005). This condition was popularized in the 1988 movie *Rain Man* in

echolalia The repetition of others' words or phrases.

palilalia The repetition of one's own words.

echopraxia The repetition of others' gestures and movements.

neologisms Made-up words. Students with autism sometimes use them.

savant syndrome A condition occurring in approximately 10% of individuals with autism in which extraordinary abilities in areas such as art, music, and mathematics are displayed.

which Dustin Hoffman portrayed a man with autism who had remarkable mathematics skills, allowing him to calculate betting odds in Las Vegas.

Repetitive and Stereotypic Behavior. Individuals with autism frequently engage in **motor stereotypies,** or repetitive motor movements. These could include behaviors such as hand flapping, hand wringing (acting like they are constantly washing their hands), and rocking back and forth. A related behavior found in some individuals with autism is self-injury (Handen & Lubatsky, 2005). This might take the form of pinching, scratching, or hitting themselves. A child with autism might also spend hours repeating the same activity, such as spinning a wheel on a tricycle.

Extreme Need for a Routine. Another behavioral characteristic of individuals with autism, which has direct implications for instruction, is the need for a routine or the insistence on "sameness." Frequently, if a routine is interrupted, it will result in frustration and temper tantrums. As a teacher, you will need to ensure that consistent schedules and routines are used if you have a student with autism in your class. For example, the order in which the student's IEP goals are taught should be the same each day. Many individuals with autism have difficulty regulating their emotions and might cry in class or have verbal outbursts, particularly when they are in a strange environment or are frustrated (NIMH, 2004). The following scenarios are extreme examples of the need for routine.

Many individuals with autism have an unusual preoccupation with objects.

> One 6-year-old child insisted that his mother had to put the frying pan on the stove and heat some butter in it before he would have his breakfast. This "show," as it was, had to be put on every morning or he would scream for hours, refusing to eat altogether. Another boy would eat only if one of the legs of his father's chair was one inch away from one leg of the table and his mother had one elbow on the table. (Gillberg & Coleman, 2000, pp. 16, 18)

A less extreme, but educationally important example is a student who throws a temper tantrum when his teacher changes his seat or schedule.

motor stereotypies Repetitive motor movements such as hand flapping.

Unusual Preoccupation with Objects or Activities. Individuals with autism might have strong attachments to objects such as stones or pieces of plastic toys, particularly objects that spin, glitter, or are round (Gillberg & Coleman, 2000). In addition to a preoccupation with objects, there is also preoccupation with activities. For example, Johnson (2004) pointed out that children with autism often will play with typical toys in unusual ways such as turning a miniature truck over and spinning the wheels repeatedly rather than "driving" it as other children might. This is often referred to as preoccupation with parts of objects. Other examples of preoccupation are an obsession with football or baseball statistics and an interest in all there is to know about topics, such as the *Titanic* or dinosaurs.

Specific Sensory and Motor Characteristics. Individuals with autism may also display characteristics related to sensory and motor functions. These include the following:

- Abnormal response to sensory stimuli, including response to sound
- Reduced sensitivity to pain, heat, or cold

- Abnormal activity levels (hyperactivity or hypoactivity)
- Abnormal eating and sleeping behaviors (Gillberg & Coleman, 2000)

For example, a person with autism might display an underresponsiveness or an overresponsiveness to certain noises. In particular, many individuals with autism are overresponsive to certain textures such as clothing made of wool. These unusual sensory and motor behaviors provide a particular challenge for teachers who must address these areas in addition to the student's educational objectives.

Cognitive Characteristics of Autism

Although not mentioned among the diagnostic criteria in the *DSM-IV-TR*, certain cognitive deficits and strengths are associated with autism. These include low IQ, difficulties in executive functioning, deficits in theory of mind, and strengths in visual skills.

Low IQ. For a number of years, many professionals thought that autism coexisted with an intellectual disability. We now know that this is not the case, although the estimate of individuals with autism who have an intellectual disability is close to 70% (La Malfa, Lassi, Bertelli, Salvini, & Placidi, 2004). There is, of course, the question of whether the lower IQs that result in a diagnosis of mental retardation reflect true deficits or are a function of behaviors that make traditional intelligence testing difficult.

Difficulty in Executive Functioning. There is evidence that individuals with autism have problems in executive functioning, which involves planning, shifting attention, and using working memory, among other cognitive functions. Deficits in these areas could lead to the characteristics that these individuals frequently exhibit such as repetitive behaviors, lack of flexibility of thought, and problems in novel or ambiguous situations that affect routine or well-learned tasks (Hughes, 2001). For example, problems in planning might lead to difficulty in reacting to ambiguous situations, and difficulty shifting attention might result in preoccupation with a single activity.

theory of mind The ability of an individual to see the world from the perspective of others.

Deficits in Theory of Mind. Perhaps considered more a cause of many cognitive characteristics rather than a characteristic itself, is a deficit in theory of mind. **Theory of mind** has to do with "mentalizing" or seeing the world from the perspective of others. Most children by age 4 are able to make first-order attributions (e.g., "I think that he thinks that . . ."). A child with autism may never develop this skill or might not develop it until adolescence (Bragdon & Gamon, 2000). By age 7 most children are able to make second-order attributions (e.g., "I think that he thinks that she thinks that . . ."). For most individuals with autism, this skill is "totally lacking" (Bragdon & Gamon, 2000). The following is an example of a theory of mind task:

> Pete and Jackie are sitting at a kitchen table, each with a spoon in front of them. Jackie has to leave the room and puts her spoon under a napkin. When she is out of the room, Pete replaces the spoon under Jackie's napkin with a fork.
> *What did Jackie think was under her napkin when she came back into the kitchen?*

Children with autism will often say that Jackie thinks a fork is under the napkin because they will not realize that she was unaware of the switch when she was out of the room. This type of deficit could lead to some of the characteristics seen in autism such as a lack of empathy or compassion, problems with pretend play, and deficits in social interactions. Although this phenomenon has been studied for more than 20 years, there are those (e.g., Tager-Flusberg, 2001) who question its relevance, particularly since some individuals do pass the tasks. In fact, Downs and Smith (2004) reported that some children with high-functioning autism could develop advanced theory of mind abilities.

Strengths in Visual Skills. Although development of cognitive skills is uneven, it is generally accepted that individuals with autism are stronger in visual processing skills than verbal processing skills (Ruble & Gallagher, 2004). In fact, individuals with autism perform better than most people on tasks such as that in Figure 11.1 in which

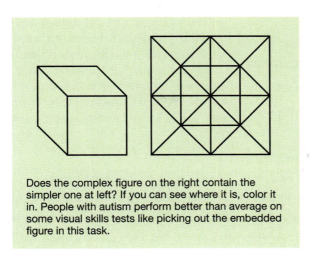

Does the complex figure on the right contain the simpler one at left? If you can see where it is, color it in. People with autism perform better than average on some visual skills tests like picking out the embedded figure in this task.

FIGURE 11.1 Example of a Visual Processing Task.

Source: From Bragdon, A., and Gamon, D. *Games That Work a Little Bit Differently,* p. 45. New York: Bragdon Publishers. Used with permission.

the objective is to find the figure on the left that is embedded in the figure on the right. Can you find it?

Some people with autism say that they "think" visually. Temple Grandin, a university professor who has autism, frequently lectures about living with the disorder. Here are her words regarding her thinking process. "As a young child I used visualization to help me understand the Lord's Prayer. The 'power and glory' were high tension electric towers and a blazing rainbow sun. The word 'trespass' was visualized as a 'No Trespassing' sign on the neighbor's tree" "(Grandin, n.d.). She also pointed out how visual thinking is an asset in her career as a livestock equipment designer because she can visualize a video of a finished piece of equipment and can test it to see if it works. Table 11.3 lists several cognitive strengths and weaknesses of individuals with autism.

TABLE 11.3	Possible Cognitive Strengths and Weaknesses of Individuals with Autism
RELATIVE STRENGTHS	**RELATIVE CHALLENGES**
Visual discrimination	Expressive and receptive language
Visual spatial processing	Disengaging and/or shifting attention
Capacity to focus or sustain attention for static visual information	Shifting attention between response modalities (e.g., auditory to visual) Making rapid changes to task expectations
Ability to immediately recall information of a rote nature	Recalling information in the absence of contextual or semantic cues
Recall of discrete information versus more complex or conceptual information	Organizing information
Associative learning (e.g., stimulus-response learning, paired learning)	Recalling aspects of a learning episode that are not explicitly targeted
Procedural learning (e.g., calculations, reproduction of music, and drawing)	Coping with new information due to cognitive inflexibility, incomplete understanding of implicit concepts, or problems in strategy generation

Source: Tsatsanis, K. 2004. Heterogeneity in learning style in Asperger Syndrome and high-functioning autism. In *Topics in Language Disorders,* 24, p. 262. Used with permission by Lippincott Williams & Wilkins.

ALEX REVISITED What social, communication, behavioral, and cognitive characteristics, if any, did or does Alex display that are consistent with autism?

The characteristics of autism and the other autism spectrum disorders are varied. It is important to recognize that autism spectrum disorders represent a wide range of functioning levels; subsequently, a stereotype should not be formed. As a teacher, it will be most important for you to learn what the individual characteristics are of any students you have with autism spectrum disorders.

Check Your Understanding

1. What are some controversial theories about the cause of autism?
2. What evidence is there that autism is caused by abnormal brain structure or brain function?
3. What have results of twin studies suggested regarding the genetic basis of autism?
4. What are possible environmental factors that might cause or trigger autism?
5. What is the triad of social impairments characteristic of autism spectrum disorders?
6. What are some social, communication, behavioral, and cognitive characteristics of autism?

How Are Students with Autism Spectrum Disorders Identified?

Relevant CEC Standards

▶ Issues in definition and identification of individuals with exceptional learning needs, including those from culturally and linguistically diverse backgrounds (CC1K5)

▶ Screening, prereferral, referral, and classification procedures (CC8K3)

▶ Use and limitations of assessment instruments (CC8K4)

The majority of individuals with autism spectrum disorders are diagnosed before they enter the classroom. Even so, although teachers are typically not involved in the initial diagnosis, they should know how the identification process works to better understand the autism spectrum disorders and be able to support their students with the diagnosis. The complexity of autism spectrum disorders results in the need for a multidisciplinary evaluation for identification that involves the parents and professionals including psychologists and medical personnel. Identification might include neurological, cognitive, and language testing as well as audiological screening (NINDS, 2005). Parents provide valuable information about their child's development that will document the presence of certain characteristics that may lead to identification. For instance, parents can confirm that the characteristics of autism are/were displayed before the age of 3. In addition to a medical examination and the administration of cognitive and language tests, rating scales specifically designed to help identify children with autism are also used. It should be noted that children can be identified as needing special education under IDEA 04 without having a medical diagnosis.

Early Screening

Parents are usually the first to initially identify that their child is behaving differently, in a way that might be consistent with a diagnosis of an autism spectrum disorder. Sometimes this behavior is noticeable from birth; other times the behaviors appear suddenly in a child who has been developing normally. Some of the first symptoms seen in infants with autism are nonspecific characteristics such as hyperactivity, lack of initiative, and sleep and feeding problems (Gillberg & Coleman, 2000). Parents are generally accurate in identifying developmental problems in their children, although they might not understand the nature or extent of the problems. It is important, however, to document the age at which certain characteristics were displayed. Reviewing baby albums and videotapes can help parents remember when developmental milestones were reached (NIMH, 2004).

For autism, screening instruments have been designed to help identify young children before the age of 2 who warrant further attention. Examples are the Symptoms of Autism Before Age 2 Checklist (Dahlberg & Gillberg, 1989) and the Checklist for Autism in Toddlers (Baron-Cohen, Allen, & Gillberg, 1992). In addition, informal checklists such as the one in Figure 11.2 can be completed.

What are the signs of autism?

- Spins objects
- Sustained odd play
- Little or no eye contact
- Severe language deficits
- Insistence on sameness
- Uneven gross-fine motor skills (may not kick a ball but can stack blocks)
- Laughs, cries, or shows distress for no apparent reasons
- Noticeable physical over-activity or extreme under-activity
- Difficulty expressing needs; gestures or points instead of speaking
- Not responsive tp verbal cues; acts as if deaf but tests in normal range
- Echolalia (repeats words or phrases in place of normal responsive language)
- Inappropriate attachments to objects
- May not want cuddling or act cuddly
- Unresponsive to normal teaching methods
- Oversensitivity or under-sensitivity to pain
- Aloof manner; difficulty mixing with others

FIGURE 11.2 Informal Checklist of Autism Characteristics.

Source: From Assistive Technology for Children with Autism by Susan Stokes, Autism Consultant. Written by Susan Stokes under a contract with the CESA7 and funded by a discretionary grant from the Wisconsin Department of Public Education. Used with permission by the Autism Society of America.

Diagnosis

The diagnosis of an autism spectrum disorder requires that the criteria for the specific disorder be met. This is usually determined by physicians or psychologists. The advantages of early diagnosis, such as immediate access to intervention services, are numerous (Goin & Myers, 2004). For autism, diagnosis usually cannot be made confidently until the child is about 30 months of age (Stone et al., 1999). Until then, it is difficult to judge behaviors associated with autism such as poor peer relationships and limited conversational skills (Gillberg & Coleman, 2000). Estimates are that 40% of all children with autism wait at least three years after initial identification until a clear diagnosis is made (National Autistic Society, 2005).

The actual diagnosis of autism is typically made based on information from a variety of sources. The first step in diagnosis is generally a thorough medical examination. Because the symptoms of autism are similar to those of other developmental disabilities, it is first necessary to "rule out" other conditions such as a communication disorder, a hearing impairment, or an intellectual disability. Other sources of information that could be used to help make a diagnosis include a developmental history, parent (and teacher) reports, direct observation of the child, and formal testing of communication and intellectual functioning (Charman & Baird, 2002). In a very real sense, the diagnosis of autism is one that is largely based on clinical judgment. "Unlike conditions such as mental retardation or learning disorders, where the disability is defined by objective criteria and performance on quantitative measures, the diagnosis of autism requires developmentally informed clinical judgment" (Ozonoff & Rogers, 2003, p. 17).

The child's developmental history should include the areas of physical factors, family factors, language/communication, social behavior, and education (Plotts & Webber, 2001–2002). Intelligence tests such as the Stanford-Binet Intelligence Scale–Fifth Edition (described in Chapter 2) may be administered by psychologists, and communication instruments such as the Preschool Language Scale–4 (Zimmerman,

Steiner, & Pond, 2002) may be given by speech and language clinicians. The actual tests that are used will largely depend on the age of the individual when they are given. There are also rating scales designed specifically to help identify individuals with specific autism spectrum disorders, such as autism (Childhood Autism Rating Scale [Schopler, Reichler, & Renner, 1988] and the Gilliam Autism Rating Scale–2 [Gilliam, 2006]), although a diagnosis should never be made using just the results of these instruments.

ALEX REVISITED What behaviors did Alex's parents notice that led to the ultimate diagnosis of autism?

The screening and diagnosis of autism spectrum disorders is a multidisciplinary endeavor. Although oftentimes these children are identified in their preschool years, teachers still might play an important role in their identification, particularly for those with high-functioning autism who might not be diagnosed early in life.

Check Your Understanding

1. Who is usually involved in the screening and diagnosis of autism spectrum disorders?
2. What are some methods of early screening for autism spectrum disorders?
3. What screening procedures are typically used?
4. Why is a medical evaluation important?
5. What areas are typically evaluated for a diagnosis of autism?

What and How Do I Teach Students with Autism Spectrum Disorders?

Following the establishment of autism as a separate category of disability under the Individuals with Disabilities Education Act, and an increase in identification of children with autism spectrum disorders, there has come a surge in the attention given to instructional considerations for students with an autism spectrum disorder. In recent years, a variety of promising programs and procedures have been developed for working with students diagnosed with one of the autism spectrum disorders, particularly autism, in the areas of communication, social skills, cognitive functioning, and behavior change. Areas of consensus across programs include the need for early intervention, intensive and extensive instructional programming, and one-to-one and small group instruction to meet individualized goals (National Research Council, 2001).

Whether you plan to be a special education or general education teacher, the content and procedural suggestions in the following section should be used to form the basis for how you teach your student or students with autism spectrum disorders. Effective programs are based on the unique needs and abilities of each individual student and the needs of the family. With this in mind, the content areas and specific procedures introduced here should be considered the information, guides, and tools with which to start the foundation for your own knowledge of best practices for teaching students with an autism spectrum disorder. You will need to select an appropriate curriculum and choose instructional procedures based on each individual student's needs. As the characteristics and abilities of students with autism spectrum disorders cover a wide range, so must your teaching knowledge and tools. As explained in the beginning of the chapter, we focus mainly on students with autism because it is the most common of these disorders.

Relevant CEC Standards

▶ Use strategies that promote successful transitions for individuals with exceptional learning needs (CC4S6)

▶ Social skills needed for educational and other environments (CC5K5)

▶ Strategies for crisis prevention and intervention (CC5K6)

Instructional Content

For some students with autism spectrum disorders, the general education curriculum with some modifications will be appropriate. For others, major adaptations, such as a more functional academic approach, may be needed (Iovannone, Dunlap, Huber, & Kinkaid, 2003). No one program will meet the needs of all students on the autism spectrum. However, based on the characteristics of students with autism spectrum disorders, most programs for these students will include goals in functional communication, social skills, and/or cognitive skill development. Additionally, it is essential that intervention in these areas begin as soon as a diagnosis is made or suspected, that planning be family-centered, and that transition planning be included in the student's curriculum.

The Need for Early Intervention

Early intervention plays an extremely important role in the future success of individuals with autism spectrum disorders. The value of early intervention for children with autism was first shown through the results of the UCLA Young Autism Project (Lovaas, 1987). See An Important Event for more information on this project. It has since been demonstrated that intensive intervention beginning by 3 years of age results in a significantly better outcome for children with autism than intervention beginning after 5 years of age (Harris & Handeleman, 2000). Furthermore, the earlier the intervention begins (that is, before age 3), the better the outcome (McGee, Morrier, & Daly, 1999). According to the National Research Council (2001) report, the features that are considered critical to preschool programs for children with autism spectrum disorders include the following:

Appropriate curriculum and instructional procedures for working with students with autism are based on individual students' needs and abilities.

- entry into an intervention program as soon as an autism spectrum diagnosis is seriously considered
- intensive instructional programming year-round for five full school days a week
- repeated, planned teaching opportunities with sufficient amounts of adult attention in one-to-one and very small group instructional sessions
- inclusion of a family component, including parent training
- low student–teacher ratios (no more than two young children with autism spectrum disorders per adult in the classroom)
- ongoing program evaluations and student progress assessments with results translated into adjustments in programming

The report also states that functional, spontaneous communication should be the primary focus of early education.

AN IMPORTANT EVENT

1987—Ivar Lovaas Reports the Findings of the Young Autism Project

Lovaas, O. I. (1987). Behavioral treatment and normal educational and intellectual functioning in young autistic children. *Journal of Consulting and Clinical Psychology, 55*, 3–9.

Pioneering work in the education and treatment of children with autism has been conducted by Ivar Lovaas and colleagues since the 1970s. In 1987, Lovaas reported on the long-term effects of the Young Autism Project, a highly

(continued)

PRACTICE

structured early intervention behavioral treatment project. This program was initiated with children under 4 years of age and was conducted throughout each day by all significant persons (e.g., teachers, parents) across different environments for more than 40 hours of individual treatment per week for two years. Treatment in the second year was extended into community settings in mainstream preschool programs. On average, the children in the early intervention group made significant advances in achievement and showed increases in IQs over a comparison group of similar children who did not receive the early intervention. Lovaas noted that although treatment was intensive, the potential savings between providing intensive early intervention versus lifelong support is substantial. This project represents one of the longer, more intensive, and clearly more effective programs reported in the literature, and it emphasizes the importance of early intervention for children on the autism spectrum. It also offers parents and teachers hope and encouragement for the successful education of children with autism.

REFLECTION Do you think such a time-consuming, intensive intervention makes sense? What are some logistical barriers to such an approach?

Initially opening in 1982 as a federally funded demonstration program, one of the first early intervention programs in the country to include children with autism with typical children was Learning Experiences, an Alternative Program for Preschoolers and their Parents (LEAP). LEAP's scientifically based individualized curriculum addresses social, emotional, language, adaptive behavior, cognitive, and physical developmental areas. LEAP blends a behavioral approach with developmentally appropriate practices (Strain & Hoyson, 2000). It focuses on enhancing the skills of children with autism in interaction and play with typically developing peers. The curriculum is well known for its peer-mediated social skill interventions (National Research Council, 2001). Typical peers are trained to respond promptly and appropriately to initiations by their peers with autism throughout the day. They are also taught how to initiate interactions and maintain a conversation with their peers with autism. For example, typical peers are taught to begin a conversation with a specific peer with autism through gaining attention in a way that is acceptable to the child with autism and then producing a favorite toy of the child's to discuss. LEAP also includes a behavioral skill-training program for parents.

A newer promising model program for providing effective inclusive services for young children with autism is Project DATA (Developmentally Appropriate Treatment for Autism) out of the University of Washington. Project DATA combines the best practices of applied behavior analysis and early childhood special education (Schwartz, Sandall, McBride, & Boulware, 2004). Children with autism are integrated into a university-based comprehensive early childhood program where their successful interactions with peers, activities, and materials are facilitated by a family-centered, developmental-behavioral approach to instruction and curriculum (Allen & Schwartz, 2001). Although the preschool program is the primary component of the overall program, an additional extended-time component was added for the children with autism. During this extended time, highly individualized intensive instruction focuses on enhancing children's abilities to access the preschool environment and benefit from embedded curriculum and naturalistic teaching strategies. For example, for a child who needs to learn how to imitate, a very explicit program in hand clapping may be initiated one-on-one in extended-time and then systematically move step-by-step to demonstrating these imitation skills at a circle-time activity in the general education

ALEX REVISITED Do you think Alex will be successful in school? What variables in his educational history lead you to this prediction?

preschool classroom. Recently, this project has been extended to include Baby DATA, which provides services to infants and toddlers with autism and related disorders.

Functional Communication

As verbal and nonverbal communication difficulties are central to a diagnosis within the autism spectrum, helping a child develop functional communication skills is a key element in the curriculum. Without any conventional means of communicating, children with autism spectrum disorders often develop their own unconventional and inappropriate means of communicating that may include self-injurious behaviors and temper tantrums. For example, if a child sees an item he or she wants and cannot express this desire verbally, the frustration may lead to expressing the desire through yelling, kicking, or head banging. Although communication abilities of individuals on the autism disorder spectrum range from totally nonverbal to highly verbal, the need for teaching more conventional communication skills to express one's needs and desires often exists.

Communication, whether verbal, gestural, or pictorial, is the key to independent functioning and should be a fundamental component of any educational program for students with autism (Scott, Clark, & Brady, 2000). The level of communication competence reached by individuals with autism has been found to be an important predictor of educational outcome (McEachin, Smith, & Lovaas, 1993). That is, the higher the level of communication competence, the more likely the student is to experience educational success. There is now a large body of research that supports using naturalistic teaching methods that are initiated by the child and focus on the child's interests to support functional communication skills. For example, rather than trying to elicit a set response from a student in an isolated setting, the teacher should use systematic teaching during situations that arise in the natural classroom setting, such as the preschooler's asking for a snack. These methods should be interspersed with and embedded in the natural environment, such as a classroom, and use natural reinforcers, such as a snack, that follow what the child is trying to communicate (National Research Council, 2001). Table 11.4 presents some guidelines for supporting the development of communication skills in some children with autism spectrum disorders.

Social Skills

Even the most capable individuals with autism spectrum disorders often experience difficulty in social situations (Kuoch & Mirenda, 2003). For example, a child with Asperger syndrome may be functioning above grade level in academic subjects but may have no idea how to interact with peers, constantly making inappropriate, seemingly insensitive remarks, such as "that shirt looks like someone spilled nasty brown mustard

TABLE 11.4	Guidelines for Developing Communication Skills

1. Make communication an integral part of a child's life in and out of school.

2. Communication, rather than rote response, should be the goal.

3. Emphasize spontaneous speech, whether pictorial, gestural, or verbal.

4. Give the child many opportunities to communicate in all settings.

5. Any socially acceptable attempt to communicate should be reinforced in all settings.

6. Communication goals should be part of any plan to change maladaptive behavior.

7. Initial communication goals should target obtaining items and activities that the student finds reinforcing.

8. Communication goals should be developmentally and chronologically appropriate.

9. Work together with all significant people in the student's environment to make the communication training as consistent as possible.

Source: Scott, Clark, & Brady, 2000.

all over it." Or a high functioning student with autism may work well in structured group settings in the classroom but sit alone and apart from other children in the cafeteria. Without social interaction enhancement training, students with autism spectrum disorders are vulnerable to rejection and isolation that could lead to failure in educational programs (Myles & Simpson, 2001). Enhanced social skills can benefit students not only in school but also throughout their lives (Safran, Safran, & Ellis, 2003). To be most effective, instruction in the area of social skills should be delivered throughout the day in various settings and use specific activities to meet age-appropriate, individualized social goals (National Research Council, 2001). For example, incorporating a child's obsessive interests into instructional activities has proven to be an effective method to enhance engagement in activities, including social activities (Iovannone et al., 2003). So, if a student with autism whose social goals include working cooperatively with others is currently obsessed with trains, he or she may be placed in a cooperative learning group that has been assigned a report on the development of the railway system.

hidden curriculum The unwritten social conventions of a school or class that typical students intuitively comprehend.

One important social skill that is too often neglected is awareness of the **hidden curriculum,** or the unwritten social conventions that peers intuitively comprehend (Bieber, 1994). Every school, classroom, and society contains a hidden curriculum. This hidden curriculum includes the many unwritten rules of how to act, how to talk, how to dress, and so on that most people know and take for granted, but which may cause major difficulties for students with autism spectrum disorders. The hidden curriculum includes being aware of teacher expectations; developing teacher-pleasing skills; knowledge of which students to interact with and which to avoid; and which behaviors attract negative attention and which attract positive, and in what situations (Myles & Simpson, 2001). A hidden curriculum in high school is that if a school dance begins at 7:30 p.m., no self-respecting teenager arrives before 8 o'clock. In elementary school, a student carries his or her books to school in a backpack—not a briefcase. The hidden curriculum often needs to be directly taught to and interpreted for students with autism spectrum disorders. Videotapes, pictures, cartoons, role playing, and peer-mediated assistance can be useful in direct instruction. For example, looking at and discussing contrasting pictures of elementary school students going to school in backpacks and adults going to work with briefcases may help a student understand why he was teased for carrying his books in a briefcase as his mother does every day when she goes to work.

Cognitive and Academic Skill Development

As crucially important as communication and social skills are for children with autism spectrum disorders, so too is the acquisition of academic skills (Broun, 2004). Although academics are often a relative strength and may serve as a bridge to the social world for students with Asperger syndrome (Safran et al., 2003), most students with autism spectrum disorders will need support in the development of cognitive skills. Instruction for cognitive skill development should take place in the context in which the skills are to be used, with generalization and maintenance in natural contexts as important as the acquisition of new skills (National Research Council, 2001). For example, once figuring percentages has been mastered in class, students could be assigned to apply this to the sale of a favorite item advertised in the paper at 15% off. They could also be asked to report on any other instances in their lives when they come across the need to figure percentages, for example, at a restaurant. Cognitive characteristics that may result in academic difficulties include poor problem-solving and organizational skills; concrete, literal thinking; difficulty differentiating relevant and irrelevant information; interests that are obsessive and narrow; and low social standing among their peers (Barnhill, Hagiwara, Myles, & Simpson, 2000). For example, poor organizational skills may lead to failure to turn in homework because the student does not put it in or near his or her backpack when it is finished. As another example, a student obsessively interested in planets may so focus on the presence of planets in a math problem that the question being asked is missed. Concrete literal thinking once led to a student's being dismissed from reading class day after day for standing up and moving about the room with his reading book each time the teacher stated that the class was going to "go around the room reading" a specific passage.

Family Involvement

One of the most universally beneficial supports for children with autism spectrum disorders and their families is a commitment to comprehensive and family-centered support (Dunlap & Fox, 1999; Ozonoff & Rogers, 2003). A family-centered support system addresses the needs and desires of individual families rather than simply providing predefined services (National Research Council, 2001). Parents are seen as valuable sources of information and partners in the education of their child. They are active participants in developing their child's educational plan and may be very involved in their child's treatment. In a family-centered support system, parents are trained in essential behavioral principles or specific teaching techniques used at school and may become very effective tutors. They may also be co-assessors in the functional behavioral analysis approach to determine the function of a behavior in the natural setting of the home. Parent involvement may occur at various levels including communicating through daily home notes, participating in parent visits and observations, and serving as trained volunteers in the school (Scott et al., 2000). A comprehensive program will also facilitate networking with other parents and provide support groups for both parents and siblings.

Transition Planning

The range of expectations for adult life is wide when considering students on the autism spectrum. Some students may plan to go on to higher education and will need transition plans that contain important skills to facilitate success in college (Williams & Palmer, 2006). These plans should include understanding his or her learning needs and types of accommodations that are helpful; developing self-advocacy skills; and confirming daily living and independence skills that will be needed to function in the dorms, cafeterias, and other areas of campus life. For example, a student with Asperger syndrome may need to learn cues for determining when it is or is not appropriate to interrupt a roommate, and when it is time to stop talking. The components of self-determination, which include choice-making skills, self-advocacy skills, positive perceptions of control and efficacy, and self-knowledge and awareness (Wehmeyer, Agran, & Hughes, 2000), are not only relevant for the college-bound student but are also essential for the student who will be pursuing a job after graduation. For these students, the transition plan will also need to include work experience and development of job-related skills and skills for leisure and recreation. For others, the focus of the transition plan may be on community-based training and self-care. A transition plan for an employment-bound student with autism may include rotating through several work experiences to determine which suit him best. Assessment of the job environment, as well as job skills, would be included in the plan to help him match his own characteristics to those of the workplace. For example, this student is very sensitive to sounds, so a noisy shop setting may not be the best place of employment, but he has a high tolerance for repetitive activities, so assembly line work may be a good match. Interview skills will also need to be learned and practiced.

Instructional Procedures

There is no single universally effective method of teaching all children and youth with autism spectrum disorders (Simpson, 2005), and determining appropriate interventions for children with autism spectrum disorders is a complex issue (Kabat, Masi, & Segal, 2003). Effective practices are those that are scientifically validated and match the needs of the individual, the setting, and the family. A review of research on techniques used in intervention for children with autism identified six common elements of effective interventions (Iovannone et al., 2003). Effective interventions include the following:

- individualized support and services for students and families
- systematic instruction
- clear, structured environments
- specialized curriculum content focusing on characteristics of autism
- a functional approach to problem behaviors
- family involvement

Relevant CEC Standards

▶ Use strategies to facilitate integration into various settings (CC4S1)

▶ Teach individuals to use self-assessment, problem solving, and other cognitive strategies to meet their needs (CC4S2)

▶ Select, adapt, and use instructional strategies and materials according to characteristics of the individual with exceptional learning needs (CC4S3)

▶ Use strategies to facilitate maintenance and generalization of skills across learning environments (CC4S4)

▶ Use procedures to increase the individual's self-awareness, self-management, self-control, self-reliance, and self-esteem (CC4S5)

Some effective practices include direct instruction, TEACCH, and several applied behavior analysis programs, including discrete trial intervention, pivotal response teaching, and incidental teaching. Also promising is the use of Social Stories. Some aspects of these different programs may be combined to meet the needs of individual students. In fact, some experts suggest it is actually desirable to be "eclectic" (Prizant & Wetherby, 1998). However, teachers and families must be careful, as many available procedures have not been validated.

Direct Instruction

Direct instruction is an effective procedure for teaching students with autism spectrum disorders. As you should recall from other chapters, this approach uses a highly structured, step-by-step procedure with frequent questioning, modeling, and guided and independent practice, all based on a careful analysis of the task to be taught. It also allows for high levels of student engagement, which is a key aspect of successful programs for students with autism spectrum disorders (Iovannone et al., 2003). Direct instruction can be used to teach communication, social skills, and cognitive skills.

TEACCH (Treatment and Education of Autistic and Related Communication Handicapped Children)

Developed in the early 1970s by Eric Schopler, the TEACCH approach is to develop a program around skills, interests, and needs of the student with autism (Mesibov, 2005). It allows for implementation of a variety of instructional methods, but a primary tenet of this approach is to respect the culture of autism and change the environment to adapt to the needs of children with autism by making the environment highly structured and predictable. An "autism-friendly" environment is one in which students are less exposed to the kind of stimuli, such as a high noise level or unexpected events, that can lead to behavior problems (Mesibov, Shea, & Schopler, 2005). Creating an autism-friendly environment involves organizing the physical environment, developing schedules and work systems, making expectations clear and explicit, and using visual materials that allow students with autism to use these skills independently without adult prompting and cuing (Mesibov, 2005).

Although the specifics of the classroom are based on individual student needs, a typical classroom using the TEACCH approach will be large, include a bathroom, and have only one exit. It will be located far away from the smells of the cafeteria and the noises of the gymnasium. It will have ample storage space, perhaps built-in cabinets, and many well-marked work or play areas. These areas should be marked with masking tape on the floor or partitions. Each area should have easily accessible materials and be clearly marked with visual icons denoting what activity is to occur there. Students' tables and desks should face blank walls, and the window should be covered with a shade. Each student should have a cubbyhole or locker for personal items.

Capitalizing on the typical strength of students with autism spectrum disorders, visual cues are incorporated throughout the TEACCH procedure. For example, visual schedules are used to help with sequential memory and organization of time. This helps students better understand what is expected of them, which lessens their anxiety level and assists them in independent transitions from one activity to another. Schedules can be designed using a variety of formats, depending on the needs of the individual (Stokes, 2006). A general schedule with visual cues should be posted on the wall. Each student should have an individual schedule with visual cues such as drawings or photographs.

Applied Behavior Analysis

Applied behavior analysis (ABA) techniques are the most widely scientifically validated procedures used to bring about behavior change in students with autism spectrum disorders. In contrast to TEACCH, one aim of ABA is to change the individual with autism to adjust to the environment, rather than adjusting the environment to the individual,

Visual schedules should be arranged in a "top-to-bottom" or "left-to-right" format and include a way for students to indicate that an activity is finished.

and to blend in with his or her peers (Jennett, Harris, & Mesibov, 2003; Kazdin, 2001). Teachers using this approach focus on teaching students skills they do not have, such as a conventional means of communicating desires. Teaching will generally consist of a request to perform an action ("Tell me what you want."), a response from the child ("blue crayon"), followed by a reaction by the teacher ("Good talking! Here's the blue crayon."). Techniques used with students with emotional or behavioral disorders to increase or decrease behaviors discussed in Chapter 6, such as positive and negative reinforcement, extinction, and time-outs, are also useful in teaching students with autism spectrum disorders. Another procedure presented in Chapters 6 and 14 that can lead to effectively reducing or eliminating inappropriate behaviors such as hitting or screaming is functional behavior assessment (FBA). FBA is used to determine the function or purpose of a behavior by systematically analyzing the antecedents of the behavior—that is, when and where it is occurring. Based on the assessment results, a systematic behavioral intervention plan is developed that contains the details of the strategies to be used in intervention. For example, if screaming is likely to occur more often when the student has been sitting in one place for longer than 15 minutes, planned breaks may be scheduled to prevent the occurrence of the behavior. Three types of applied behavior analysis often used with students with autism are discrete trial teaching, pivotal response teaching, and incidental teaching.

One of the most utilized highly structured ABA approaches to teaching students with autism spectrum disorders is the **discrete trial** method of teaching first initiated by Lovaas in the 1970s as an approach to teaching children with autism. A discrete trial is a set of acts that contains a stimulus or antecedent, a behavior, and a consequence. One discrete trial is comprised of giving a cue, observing the student's response, and presenting a correction or reinforcer. During the pause between intervals, or trials, the teacher records data on the correctness of the responses to use in planning the next steps. As the child's response becomes more reliable, the prompts are withdrawn until he or she responds independently. Traditionally, a discrete trial is implemented one-on-one at a table with speech as the primary communicative mode, beginning with vocal imitation and followed by word imitation. The teaching is highly structured and involves detailed planning of the requests, timing, wording, and the teacher's reaction to the student's response (Prizant & Wetherby, 1998). However, discrete trials can be embedded into naturalistic classroom activities (McBride & Schwartz, 2003). For example, turn taking can be taught one-on-one at a table using "My turn, your turn" verbal cues until the student can anticipate the other person's turn. Then, a third person may be

discrete trial training Highly structured adult-directed applied behavior analysis approach to teaching students with autism spectrum disorders using massed trials.

Discrete trials are typically implemented one-on-one at a table.

brought into the group using the same verbal cues and then "Whose turn?" may be added to elicit verbal or gestural responses.

Emphasis in the 1980s on communicative intent led to the development of other more naturalistic behavioral approaches such as pivotal response teaching and incidental teaching (Prizant & Wetherby, 1998). **Pivotal response teaching** (PRT) uses a modified discrete trial format. Rather than relying on massed trials using adult-selected materials and arbitrary reinforcement, PRT relies on interspersed mastery trials using more natural reinforcement and child-selected materials (Koegel, Koegel, Harrower, & Carter, 1999). For example, instead of going to a private space at specific times to work one-on-one with an adult to respond to "What is this?" with "blue cup" and earn a raisin, Marcia will be asked at snack time, "What do you want?" and after responding "cup" will be asked "which cup?" When she responds "blue cup," she will be given a cup of apple juice. She will also be asked to describe other objects as "blue" throughout the day. The pivotal behaviors that PRT focuses on are responding to multiple cues, motivation, self-management, and self-initiation. For example, Marco, age 8, learned the sequence of using the toilet and then washing and drying his hands at home, but he could not do so in a public restroom because he did not understand that paper towels served the same purpose as the cloth towels he used at home. Thus, for Marco the first pivotal area for intervention is responding to multiple cues, in this case cloth towels and paper towels (Koegel et al., 1999).

Motivation is addressed in a number of ways in pivotal response teaching, such as incorporating choices and reinforcing students with naturally occurring rewards. For example, if the student says the name of the object of desire, he receives it. Self-management involves teaching the students to be aware of inappropriate behaviors, collect data on them, and reinforce themselves or ask for reinforcement from someone else in the environment. For example, a student will be taught to follow directions and then record each time she follows directions in group time to earn a self-selected reinforcer for each time she follows directions and then at the end of the activity. Finally, self-initiation involves teaching students to spontaneously, without prompting, ask questions such as "What's that?" or "Where is it?" to gain information (Koegel et al., 1999).

Incidental teaching applies ABA to preacademic skills taught within typical early childhood activities in preschools or home settings instead of sitting face-to-face with the child at a table in a clinical setting (McGee et al., 1999). Teachers arrange the learning environment by placing preferred toys or activities within sight, but not within reach. Once the child shows an interest by gesturing or requesting, the teacher prompts an elaboration. For example, if the student reaches and says "truck," the teacher asks, "What color truck do you want?" Once the student has said "red truck," he or she is allowed to play with the truck for a set time. Both generalization and social interaction are promoted through incidental teaching. The basic concept of structuring learning objectives around everyday activities can be modified and applied to learners at any age.

Social Stories

A promising intervention used to address the social skills deficits in individuals with autism spectrum disorders is the use of Social Stories, as developed by Carol Gray (1993). **Social Stories** are short stories with simple sentences and optional illustrations about specific, commonly encountered situations. Social Stories make use of visual information, such as line drawings, pictures, or photographs, along with written words, or written words alone, to improve understanding of various social situations and to teach specific behaviors to use when interacting with others. Social Stories can be used to introduce changes and novel events in home and school, and to explain social concepts and situations (Gray & Garand, 1993). For example, providing a Social Story about a field trip or the place being visited before a field trip occurs may relieve a child's anxiety and assist him or her in behavior control (Welton, Vakil, & Carasea, 2004). Social Stories are written in the first person and are individually written for each child for various difficult social situations, such as waiting in the lunch line in the cafeteria. Social Stories must be

pivotal response teaching A modified discrete trial format that relies on interspersed mastery trials using natural reinforcement and child-selected materials.

incidental teaching Method of instruction that uses applied behavior analysis to teach preacademic skills within typical early childhood activities in preschools or home settings instead of sitting face-to-face with the child at a table in a clinical setting.

Social Stories Short stories with simple sentences and optional illustrations about specific, commonly encountered social situations.

At my school, students eat lunch in the cafeteria.

The cafeteria can be very crowded at lunch.

When I go to the cafeteria, I get my tray and stand at the end of the line. I stay in line and wait with everyone else to get my lunch.

When I have to wait I can think of other things. I can think of a song or my favorite book.

Soon it will be my turn and I can choose my lunch.

Waiting in line is hard but I try my best to wait calmly. Everyone feels good when people wait their turn.

Source: Crozier, S., & Sileo, N. M. (2005). Encouraging positive behavior with social stories: An intervention for children with autism spectrum disorders. *Teaching Exceptional Children, 37*(6), 26–31. Copyright © 2005 by the Council for Exceptional Children. Reprinted with permission.

written at the child's cognitive developmental level. They generally include four types of sentences (Gray, 1997): *descriptive sentences* describe a social setting and the behavior displayed by individuals in the setting; *perspective sentences* show the reaction of others to the situation; *affirmative sentences* explain an opinion or value; and *directive sentences* help guide the individual to appropriate behaviors while in a specific setting or situation. The recommended ratio of sentences is approximately two to five of the first three types of sentences to every zero to one directive sentence (Gray, 1997). The Classroom Example shows a Social Story with picture cues.

Unsupported Methods

Desperate parents may search for treatment or a cure for their child who has an autism spectrum disorder. In this search, they may be willing to try anything and are vulnerable to the many costly therapies, many of which are not supported by scientifically based research, they come across in their search. As Kacy Dolce, the parent of a 4-year-old child with autism stated in an interview for *Newsweek*, "We don't know enough yet to say no. I'll do anything to help our child" (Kalb, 2005). And, unfortunately, many unsupported or as yet unstudied complementary or alternative treatments purporting to eradicate the cause of the problems are available for unsuspecting, well-meaning families (Kalb, 2005; Levy & Hyman, 2005). Concerns are that families may spend thousands of dollars on these treatments in lieu of validated treatments. Examples of popular unsupported programs include facilitated communication, dolphin therapy, hormone therapy, and diet.

There is now a large body of research indicating that **facilitated communication** (FC) does not have scientific validity (National Research Council, 2001). FC is a form of communication in which the "facilitator" physically supports the child's hand, wrist, elbow, or forearm as the child constructs messages either by typing on a keyboard or pointing to letters on a keyboard or alphabet board. After a time of great rejoicing by parents and some professionals at the heights of literacy through which these previously uncommunicative subjects were now able to communicate, it was found that the facilitators, not necessarily deliberately, were influencing the

facilitated communication An alternative means of communication in which students are given physical and emotional support to type on an electronic keyboard or point at letters on an alphabet board.

PRACTICE

output. At this point in time, FC is not recommended for use with students with autism spectrum disorders (Simpson, 2005). However, this does not preclude other research and practice into the use of keyboarding, literacy learning, and augmentative alternative communication devices as avenues of communication (National Research Council, 2001).

Another unsupported treatment that has gained popularity with the public is dolphin therapy. In this treatment, when the child makes a correct response to a target question or exhibits a specific skill, the child is taken into the water by an adult who stays close while the child is allowed to swim with or ride the dolphins. It is purported that the unique bonding with these "sensitive creatures" leads to gains in learning rates for students with autism. There is no evidence that anything more than the value of the reinforcer (dolphins) is involved in any success of this program (Scott et al., 2000).

Yet another unfounded treatment is the administration of secretin, or hormone therapy. Secretin is a gastrointestinal hormone primarily administered for diagnostic purposes during an endoscopy. It came into demand as a treatment for autism spectrum disorders after television and print media published results of a series of case studies by Horvath et al. (1998) in which three children with autism who underwent diagnostic endoscopies subsequently reported changes in behavior. After this publicity, thousands of children received intravenous secretin treatments. However, after an unparalleled number of adequately powered, well-designed clinical studies, no efficacy in this treatment for children with autism spectrum disorders has been demonstrated (Levy & Hyman, 2005). Currently being investigated are theories that the characteristics of autism may be related to gluten (protein and other cereals) and casein (protein from milk) intolerance, leading to the belief that autism may be controlled by diet. This proposal has not yet been subjected to the rigors of full scientific scrutiny (Shattock, 2006).

Evidence, not the marketplace, should be the source of information for families and teachers when determining treatment for children with autism (Levy & Hyman, 2005). It is essential that professionals in the field stay up-to-date on the research surrounding the many therapies being recommended to both parents and professionals. The National Research Council's (2001) report, *Educating Children with Autism*, is an example of literature that can help both parents and professionals in evaluating programs and procedures for children with autism spectrum disorders.

Check Your Understanding

1. Why is early intervention considered crucial for the success of individuals with ASD?

2. What three content areas are most often included in programs for students with ASD?

3. What are some areas of transition that may need to be included in plans for students with autism spectrum disorders?

4. Describe some instructional strategies that have proven successful with students on the autism spectrum.

5. Name and describe some applied behavioral analysis techniques that have been successfully used with students with autism spectrum disorders. What is a Social Story? What are some unsupported methods of treatment for students with autism spectrum disorders?

What Are Other Instructional Considerations for Teaching Students with Autism Spectrum Disorders?

Whatever approaches or combination of approaches are selected for the educational program of a student with an autism spectrum disorder, there will be other factors to consider. One will be the instructional environment, including both physical arrangement and grouping, and another will be the use of instructional technology. The almost certain objectives in communication and socialization for students with autism spectrum disorders should influence your decisions in planning your classroom environment. Communication needs may also influence the technological features of your classroom. Most of these decisions are best made by special education and general education teachers in collaboration with each other, families of students, and other appropriate personnel such as the speech and language pathologist or occupational therapist.

The Instructional Environment

Structure and routine are key to the positive influence of an instructional environment on students with autism spectrum disorders. Many students with autism spectrum disorders are very attuned to structure and routine and are extremely affected by changes in the environment such as previously unannounced schedule changes or rearrangement of the furniture, even the movement of one computer. It is well established that children with autism spend much less time in focused and socially directed activity when in unstructured situations than do other children (National Research Council, 2001). For example, on a playground, a child with autism is unlikely to join in any activity in which other children are participating; he or she is more likely to spend the time alone and unfocused, perhaps turning in circles. A program is structured when the activities, schedule, and environment are clear to both the students and educational personnel. If a program is structured, observing the students in the classroom for 10 minutes should enable the observer to identify what each of the students is supposed to be doing (Iovannone et al., 2003). Teachers should specifically consider structure in planning the physical environment and grouping strategies for working with students with autism spectrum disorders.

The Physical Arrangement

In planning the physical arrangement of the classroom, the teacher should consider both the characteristics of the students with autism spectrum disorders and the individual students' IEPs. How the environment should be arranged will also be influenced by the student's age. Classrooms for younger children with autism spectrum disorders should focus on providing a natural environment, and those for older students should focus on providing as much structure and routine as possible.

The Preschool Environment. At the preschool level, the most important aspect of the instructional environment is that it is a natural environment. Learning in natural environments, where the child would typically spend time, appears to be the most effective intervention approach in increasing initiation of spontaneous communication and generalization for young children with autism spectrum disorders (National Research Council, 2001). A natural environment for children under age 3 is generally the home, but there are other potential natural environments for children this young. Examples include child-care centers, nursery schools, "Mother's morning out" activities, and organized recreation classes (Woods & Wetherby, 2003). Providing intervention in natural environments allows children to learn functional and meaningful skills within daily caregiving, play, and social interactions, with caregivers mediating the process as it occurs (Woods & Wetherby, 2003). For example, an intervention targeting communication may take place at the home during morning playtime with the caregiver. For young children over age 3, the preschool setting is a natural environment. The environment should be arranged to prompt or cue a child to initiate social interaction and should allow the child to access natural reinforcers, objects, or events that the child desires (Woods & Wetherby, 2003).

Relevant CEC Standards

▶ Demands of learning environments (CC5K1)

▶ Basic classroom management theories and strategies for individuals with exceptional learning needs (CC5K2)

▶ Effective management of teaching and learning (CC5K3)

▶ Teacher attitudes and behaviors that influence behavior of individuals with exceptional learning needs (CC5K4)

▶ Social skills needed for educational and other environments (CC5K5)

▶ Adaptation of the physical environment to provide optimal learning opportunities for individuals with disabilities (GC5K2)

PRACTICE

Elementary and Secondary Classrooms. Elementary and secondary classroom environments should be designed keeping in mind the fact that students with autism spectrum disorders often thrive on structure and routine and are stressed by the lack of it. Teachers need to take this into account and plan the classroom environment and time with as much structure and routine as possible. For example, schedules should not vary without warning. Transitions between activities might be preceded with two-minute warnings. Outside the classroom, the child should be directed to participate in well-structured activities or clubs where his abilities might counterbalance his social deficiencies (Saffran, 2002). For example, a student who is particularly skilled and knowledgeable in the use of computers might join the Technology Club. However, unstructured times do exist in school. Some problem times, particularly in middle and high school, include bus rides, changing classes, lunch, physical education, study hall, and before and after school. During these times, social demands become more complex, the rules for acceptable behavior are less clear, and many students with autism spectrum disorders need more support (Adreon & Stella, 2001). See the Classroom Suggestions for some ways to provide support during these unstructured periods.

Visual schedules, charts, and cue cards capitalize on the strengths of most students with autism spectrum disorders and can be used to help support learning in the classroom. Scott, Clark, and Brady (2000) suggest that the structure of the classroom and the learning tasks should visually answer the following questions:

- Where do you want me to go?
- What do you want me to do?
- How will I know when I'm done?
- What do I do then?
- What happens if I do it?
- What happens if I don't do it?
- What happens if I don't know how to do it?

Some behavior problems in the classroom may be related to noise sensitivity. A child's placement in a classroom should take this into account by sitting him or her

Classroom Suggestions Supports for Unstructured Times for Students with Autism Spectrum Disorders

UNSTRUCTURED TIME	PROBLEM	SUPPORT OPTIONS
Bus rides	Novel experience; increased social demands	❏ Adult supervision at bus stop ❏ Peer buddy ❏ Bus monitor ❏ Preferential seating
Changing classes	Respond poorly to stress of being rushed; multiple social and sensory challenges	❏ Peer buddy ❏ Alternate changing time
Lunch	Social and sensory demands of large, crowded cafeteria	❏ Assigned seating away from problem peers ❏ Adult supervision ❏ Alternate lunch location ❏ Allowing student to leave area once lunch is eaten
Physical education	Poor gross motor skills; difficulty grasping "team mentality"	❏ Assign a specific role such as score keeper or equipment manager ❏ Teams selected by teacher, not peers

Source: Adreon, D., & Stella, J. (2001). Transition to middle and high school: Increasing the success for students with Asperger syndrome. *Intervention in School and Clinic, 36*(5), 266–271.

away from any potentially bothersome noises such as air conditioning fans, water pipes, timers, buzzers, or other electronic noises (Grandin, 1995). Even the hum of a florescent light may be very distracting to some students with autism spectrum disorders (Moreno & O'Neal, 2006). Listening to an iPod to mask noises may be helpful and may reduce humming or repetitive stereotypic behavior used by the child to screen out noxious noises. An assembly, pep rally, or unstructured recess time can also be very difficult for these students. Earplugs or headphones may help screen out the noise, or the teacher may want to consider an alternative to attending these events (Safran, 2002).

An alternative that may be useful for many students is establishment of a **home base.** A home base is a place in the school where the student can go to (1) escape the stress of the teacher, peer, and instructional demands; (2) prevent tantrums, rage, meltdowns or shutdowns; or (3) regain control after a tantrum, rage, or meltdown (Linn & Myles, 2004). This is not a time-out; it is a positive experience. It is not an escape from work; the student takes the work with him or her. The location may be a counselor's office, the speech-language pathologist's room, or a resource room.

The physical arrangement of the classroom may also be influenced by the use of positive behavior support (PBS). As you may recall from Chapter 6, PBS is a behaviorally based systems change approach to redesigning the environment to minimize problem behaviors. This may occur on a schoolwide, classwide, or individual basis.

> **home base** A place in the school where the student can go to escape stress; prevent tantrums, rage, meltdowns or shutdowns; or regain control after a tantrum, rage, or meltdown.

Instructional Grouping

Group instruction provides an excellent environment for generalization and maintenance of skills that may have first been taught individually to students with an autism spectrum disorder (National Research Council, 2001). Group assignments need to be carefully structured so that the student with the autism spectrum disorder is not seated in close proximity to known bullies or aggressive students, but may, in fact, be seated next to a "peer buddy" who could even serve as a social translator (Hughes, Guth, Hall, Presley, Dye, & Byers, 1999; Saffran, 2002). Peer buddies can take on many roles in the student's academic and social life in school. They can be used as recess buddies, bus companions, peer tutors, physical education partners, computer buddies, lunchtime partners, after-school friends, or homework companions (Moyes, 2001).

> **Relevant CEC Standard**
> ▶ Methods for ensuring individual academic success in one-to-one, small-group, and large-group settings (GC5K3)

Interactions established between children with autism spectrum disorders and adults do not easily generalize to peers. How a child responds to or makes requests of his or her caregiver is not—or should not be—the same as when speaking to peers. Students with autism spectrum disorders may have problems seeing this distinction. However, typical peers have been shown to be effective tutors when taught specific strategies to elicit social, play, and communicative responses from a child with an autism spectrum disorder (National Research Council, 2001). Tutors need to be briefed on characteristics of autism spectrum disorders displayed by their partners (Simpson, Myles, Sasso, & Kamps, 1997). Classwide peer tutoring (CWPT), discussed in Chapters 4, 5, 6, and 14, has been used successfully with students with autism (Maheady, Harper, & Mallette, 2003). As you may recall, in CWPT, students are taught particular skills by peers who are trained and supervised by classroom teachers. The students work in teams, earning points, while the teacher's role changes from "deliverer" of instruction to facilitator and monitor of peer-teaching activities.

Instructional Technology

Instructional technology is most often used with students with autism spectrum disorders to support communication. Computers offer a way for students with autism spectrum disorders who prefer visual communication to learn visually. For students with autism spectrum disorders who have problems with verbal communication, a range of technologies are available to help them communicate and to augment or replace more conventional means of communication. Augmentative and alternative

In Practice Meet Educator Toby Honsberger and His Student Madison

I am an exceptional student education teacher and behavior analyst at a charter school for children diagnosed with autism. The school educates 50 children ranging in ages from 3 to 13. I have been working with children with autism and other developmental disabilities in different facets for eight years. After receiving a master's degree in Teaching Students With Intensive Special Needs, I completed the requirements to become a Board Certified Behavior Analyst. In addi-

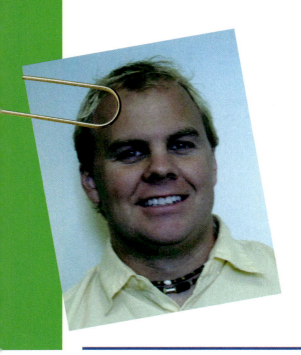

tion to my role as a special educator, I am also responsible for the development and monitoring of individualized behavior plans within the school.

Madison is a 6-year-old girl with a primary diagnosis of autism. Madison's parents chose to enroll her in our school after her public school placement was deemed no longer an appropriate setting at this time due to the excessive challenging behaviors she was exhibiting. She became the eighth student in a classroom of six boys and two girls. One special educator and two assistants manage Madison's classroom.

When enrolled at 5 years old, Madison was nonverbal and did not exhibit any appropriate, functional communication skills. She did not initiate or reciprocate any appropriate social interactions with her peers; adult interactions were limited to rudimentary requests for food or toys that consisted of reaching and screaming. Madison displayed little eye contact, engaged in repetitive stereotypic hand movements, and exhibited tantrum behavior that included screaming, crying, and aggression. Functional behavioral assessments were conducted to determine why Madison engaged in many of her challenging behaviors. The results of these assessments suggested that gaining access to

toys or foods as well as getting attention from others maintained these interfering behaviors.

Instructional Content and Procedures

Due to her lack of communication skills as well as the results of her functional assessment, instruction with Madison began with teaching her to request preferred items and activities. A variety of communication methods were explored including an electronic augmentative communication device, American Sign Language (ASL), and the Picture Exchange Communication System (PECS). Madison showed the most interest and early success with the PECS program, and consequently it was the medium chosen for her communication instruction. PECS is designed for individuals with limited speech abilities to communicate via pictures of representative objects, activities, or concepts. The goal of PECS is for an individual to independently and spontaneously utilize these pictures to communicate effectively and efficiently with others. It was the goal of Madison's educational team for her to utilize this communication tool to convey her wants and needs rather than her communicative attempts via challenging behaviors.

communication technology often used with students with autism spectrum disorders includes the Picture Exchange Communication System and Voice Output Communication Aids.

Computer Technology

Children with autism spectrum disorders typically process visual information more easily than auditory information (Stokes, 2006). With this in mind, the computer can be a very attractive and powerful tool for students who prefer visual information or for those who have difficulty with interpersonal contacts. For example, using activity schedules on the computer, enhanced with sound and video, can be an effective way

Madison worked within small groups consisting of one or two other students in the classroom. A combination of discrete trials and incidental teaching were utilized to teach Madison the skill of using pictures to communicate her wants and needs. Discrete trials sessions consisted of Madison working with me in groups of one or two other students. Madison's favorite activities and/or foods were shown to her along with pictures of these items. When Madison expressed a desire to have one of the items by pointing or reaching, she was provided with physical prompts to choose the picture of the item and hand it over to her teacher; in return, the teacher would give her the pictured object or activity. This process was repeated many times until Madison was using the pictures to make requests independently.

Incidental teaching took place across Madison's school day. The teacher's assistants or I would follow Madison's lead as to what she wanted, and then use graduated physical cues to encourage her to use her pictures to request and obtain the desired items or activities.

After mastering requesting via pictures, Madison was introduced to more abstract concepts such as taking a break, social greetings, and academic skills. These new concepts have opened the door for age-level academic instruction including pre-reading, math, and social skills. As Madison became fluent in the use of her pictures to express her wants and needs, the challenging behaviors that had posed the biggest barrier to her

success at school decreased to near zero levels.

Instructional Environment and Technology

Pictures of common items have been posted throughout Madison's classroom to facilitate comprehension of picture-to-object correspondence. For example, a picture of the toilet is posted on the bathroom door, pictures of foods are posted on the refrigerator door, and a picture of pencils, crayons, and markers is posted on the art cabinet. A book containing Madison's common pictures is kept with her at all times, lending itself to spontaneous communication. As Madison began to communicate more effectively, classroom groupings were rearranged to have her take part in a social group with three of her peers in the classroom where social interactions between the students are encouraged and facilitated.

As Madison has become fluent in her use of pictures to communicate, instruction has started to move toward teaching her to use an augmentative voice output communication aid. This device will provide Madison with more items and concepts to communicate and will also give her an audible voice. When pictures on the screen of the small computer-like system are touched, a prerecorded voice "says" aloud what is being communicated.

Collaboration

Madison's major obstacles to appropriately and effectively accessing her

educational environment have been her challenging behaviors and her lack of communication. Efforts to overcome these barriers have been a collaborative effort from all members of her educational team, including the speech-language pathologist (SLP), her parents, and me. The SLP has worked closely with teachers and assistants, consulting on the usage and application of the PECS curriculum while continuing to work on Madison's emerging speech development. Madison's parents were integral in the decision-making process to choose PECS as Madison's initial mode of communication, and they played a large role in continuing the PECS instruction at home. Regular communication among the SLP, Madison's parents, and me enabled us to discuss successful strategies, identify potential problems, and remain consistent with instruction and expectations for Madison. Having everyone working on the same page has been an invaluable piece to Madison's successes.

After almost a year as a member of our classroom, Madison's communication has developed and flourished, and as a result, her challenging behaviors have been replaced by appropriate interactions with others. Members of her educational team have recently developed a transition plan to move Madison to a less restrictive environment. Madison's new educational goal is to be participating within an inclusion classroom by the beginning of the next school year.

PRACTICE

to teach students to manage their work, play, and skill-building activities independently (Stromer, Kimball, Kinney, & Taylor, 2006). Video clips of peers without disabilities engaged in examples and nonexamples of targeted social skills may be embedded in computer programs (Simpson, Langone, & Ayres, 2004). Digital video delivered by computer offers many possibilities for teaching both social and functional skills (Ayres & Langone, 2005). The affinity for computer technology that students with autism spectrum disorders often have should certainly be capitalized on. However, Saffran (2002) cautions that students' time on computers should be limited to avoid encouraging a potential obsession and allowing the computer to become a substitute for human contact.

Augmentative and Alternative Communication

For children with autism spectrum disorders who do not acquire functional language or have difficulty processing spoken language, augmentative and alternative communication (AAC) technology can be a useful component of an educational program (National Research Council, 2001). As you recall from other chapters, augmentative communication is the use of any aids or techniques that supplement existing vocal or verbal communication skills, and alternative communication refers to communication techniques that take the place of vocal or verbal communication skills. For example, a speech synthesizer may be used as an alternative to vocal communication. AAC often incorporates the use of visual language systems that capitalize on the visual processing strengths of many students with autism spectrum disorders. Sign language and picture boards are two types of low-tech communication systems taught as alternative communication for students who are unable to speak or as augmentative communication for students who have limited functional communication. Pictures on picture boards can be words, photographs, or line drawings and have the advantage of not only being visually processed but also requiring minimal fine motor skills, and being easily understood by all. Boardmaker (from PCI Educational Products) is a popular software package for generating pictures for communication symbols as it allows teachers and parents access to more than 3,000 picture symbols that can be viewed and printed in several languages.

The most widely used picture communication system, the **Picture Exchange Communication System** (PECS), is a systematic behavioral program that teaches children to use pictures to communicate their needs and desires by approaching a communication partner and exchanging a symbol for the real thing (Frost & Bondy, 1994). The symbol could be a picture of juice or a symbol for "help" that the student would give to the teacher or a peer. The pictures may be computer generated or cut out of magazines, and they represent categories such as clothing, foods, and feelings. The program includes procedures for expanding single words (a picture of a pizza) to multiple words (using a sentence strip *I want* placed before the picture of the pizza) and increasing communicative functions from requesting to labeling and commenting (*I see* placed before the picture of the pizza). There is evidence that PECS may enhance the development of spoken language (Bondy & Frost, 1994: Charlop-Christy, Carpenter, Le, Leblanc, & Kellet, 2002).

Finally, there is also growing evidence that both dedicated voice output communication aids (VOCAs) and computers with communication software can be used effectively in school by some students with autism (Mirenda, 2003). VOCAs are portable electronic devices that produce synthetic or digitized speech output. Graphic symbols can be used with VOCAs to represent messages that are activated when an individual selects a symbol from the display. Many children with autism are motivated to communicate by use of these devices, particularly by the auditory feedback immediately given as they use the device (Stokes, 2006). However, it is important that parents, special and general education teachers, and the speech-language pathologist all know how to program any communication devices and collaborate on the most effective uses of them (*CEC Today*, 2002).

Picture Exchange Communication System A systematic behavioral program that teaches children to use pictures to communicate their needs and desires through approaching a communication partner and exchanging a symbol for the actual object.

Check Your Understanding

1. How should the instructional environment be designed for young children with autism spectrum disorders? For school-aged students? What are some ways that the need for structure can be planned for in the classroom?

2. Describe the benefits of students with autism spectrum disorders working in groups and in pairs. What are some effective pair-grouping techniques?

3. What are some advantages and cautions in the use of computer technology with students with autism spectrum disorders?

4. How is AAC used with students with autism spectrum disorders? Describe the Picture Exchange Communication System. What is a VOCA, and how is it used with students with autism spectrum disorders?

What Are Some Considerations for the General Education Teacher?

Relevant CEC Standard
▶ Barriers to accessibility and acceptance of individuals with disabilities (GC5K1)

Almost half of students with autism spectrum disorders ages 6 to 21 are spending 40% or more of their time in general education classrooms (U.S. Department of Education, 2006). The National Research Council (2001) report on educating students with autism recommends that children receive specialized instruction in settings in which ongoing interactions occur with typically developing children whenever compatible with educational goals. Temple Grandin (1995), the college professor with autism mentioned earlier in the chapter, points out that meaningful contact with children who have typical social behavior is essential if a child with autism is to learn social skills.

The trend toward inclusion noted, inclusion of students with autism spectrum disorders takes very careful planning and collaboration between the general education teacher, special education teacher, specialists, and the family. As Steven Shore, an author, doctoral student, and special educator with Asperger syndrome, reminds us, a child doing his own thing in the back of the classroom while the other students are doing something completely different is not an example of inclusion (Brownell & Walther-Thomas, 2001). One model that offers guidelines and supports to facilitate success in inclusion is the autism spectrum disorder inclusion collaboration model (Simpson, de Boer-Ott, & Smith-Myles, 2003). This model has five major interwoven components and emphasizes shared responsibility and decision making among general educators, special educators, and other support personnel. Each of the following five components affects the others, and all must be present for success.

1. *Environmental and curriculum modifications:* availability of appropriately trained support personnel, reduced class size, collaborative problem-solving relationships, continued inservice training for general education teachers, implementation of appropriate instructional methods, availability of paraeducators, and adequate teacher planning time.
2. *Attitudinal and social support:* strategies to create an accepting environment for students with disabilities, supportive administrative personnel, positive teacher attitudes, supportive parents, dissemination of information about inclusion and autism spectrum disorders to peers and adults, and best-practices social interaction training methods.
3. *Coordinated team commitment:* shared responsibility with clearly defined roles of all service delivery personnel, effective communication, and shared decision making.
4. *Recurrent evaluation of inclusion practices:* determining strengths and weaknesses of curriculum delivery and reception, environmental arrangements, interaction amounts and types, participation level of students, and attitudes of the general education teacher, paraeducators, and peers.
5. *Home–school collaboration:* meaningful individualized parent participation, suitable administrative support, and parent training in the educational and inclusion process.

Individual characteristics and needs of each individual student with an autism spectrum disorder will need to be considered when planning instructional strategies. The Classroom Suggestions on the next page offers some general strategies for increasing the success of students with autism spectrum disorders in general education classes. Remember, also, that the classroom considerations presented earlier in the chapter are applicable to the general education classroom as well as to the special education classroom.

ALEX REVISITED Could Alex be included in a general education class? If yes, full or part time? What would be the benefits for Alex? If no, explain why not.

Classroom Suggestions Tips and Strategies for Teaching Students with Autism Spectrum Disorders in General Education Classes

CHARACTERISTIC	SUGGESTIONS
Insistence on sameness	❑ Provide predictable and safe environment ❑ Minimize transitions ❑ Offer consistent daily routine ❑ Avoid surprises; prepare the student for all environmental changes in routine; use a written or visual schedule to prepare him or her ❑ Allay fears of unknown by exposing him or her to new activity, teacher, class, school, camp beforehand and as soon as possible after informing student (to avoid obsessing) ❑ Ensure consistent treatment and expectations from everyone
Impairment in social interactions	❑ Protect from bullying and teasing ❑ Educate peers on social problems as true disability ❑ Emphasize student's strengths in cooperative learning settings ❑ Teach the student what to say and how to say it ❑ Teach the student why an action or comment was inappropriate ❑ Utilize a buddy system by providing a sensitive peer to look out for student ❑ Encourage active socialization and limit time spent in isolated pursuit of interests ❑ Do not take misbehavior personally; misbehavior is usually an effort to survive confusing, disorienting, or frightening experiences
Restricted range of interests	❑ Limit relentless discussion of fixations by providing specific times when the topic may be discussed and questions asked ❑ Praise student for simple, expected social behaviors such as allowing others to speak ❑ Set firm expectations for completion of class work outside his or her area of interest; provide opportunities to pursue interests at another time ❑ Give assignments that link interests to the subject being studied; use fixation to broaden interests
Poor concentration	❑ Break assignments into small units with frequent feedback and redirection ❑ Time work sessions to help students organize themselves; unfinished work must be finished during own time (e.g., during special interest time) ❑ Provide time with support to do homework ❑ Seat student at front of the class and direct frequent questions to him or her ❑ Plan a nonverbal signal with the child for times he or she is not attending ❑ Sit buddy next to student to remind him or her to attend ❑ Actively encourage student to leave inner thoughts and fantasies behind and refocus on real world
Academic difficulties	❑ If student is not learning, break task into smaller steps or present it in several ways (e.g., visually, verbally, physically) ❑ Provide a highly individualized academic program engineered to offer consistent successes ❑ Do not assume that the student understands something he or she can parrot back ❑ Offer expanded explanations and try to simplify abstract concepts; use visual cues ❑ Provide strategies for remembering deadlines or materials (e.g., a picture of a pencil on his notebook); praise student when he or she remembers something previously forgotten ❑ Set firm expectations for quality of work ❑ Provide a great deal of practice and repetition of newly learned skills ❑ Use mnemonic devices ❑ Allow student to use keyboarding when writing or allow alternatives to writing ❑ Use graphic and visual organizers; highlight critical information
Emotional vulnerability	❑ Prevent outbursts by offering a high level of consistency; prepare student for changes in daily routine ❑ Teach student how to cope; help him or her make a list of steps that can be followed when upset ❑ Be calm, predictable, and matter-of-fact in interactions with student, while clearly indicating patience and compassion ❑ Be alert to changes in behavior that may indicate depression; do not expect student to acknowledge that he or she is sad or depressed; report to student's therapist or make a referral (adolescents are especially prone to depression) ❑ Identify a support staff member with whom the student checks in at least once daily ❑ Provide a "safe-place" or "safe-person" for highly stressful events

(continued)

CHARACTERISTIC	SUGGESTIONS
Communication problems	❑ Use and interpret speech literally; avoid idioms, double meaning, sarcasm, nicknames, and cute names (Pal, Buddy, Wise Guy)
	❑ Remember that facial expressions and other social cues may not work
	❑ Avoid verbal overload; be clear; use shorter sentences if student is not understanding
	❑ Interrupt repetitive verbal arguments and/or repetitive verbal questions; logical responses or arguing seldom stops this behavior as it is usually the result of uncertainty about something or someone in the environment. Try requesting that student write down question or argument; write your reply or you write it and ask that he or she reply.
	❑ Do not rely on student to relay important messages to parents. Frequent and accurate communication between teacher and home is very important. Phone calls work best.

Source: Williams, K. (2001). Understanding the student with Asperger syndrome: Guidelines for teachers. *Intervention in School and Clinic, 36*(5), 287–292; Moreno, S., & O'Neal, C. (2006). *Online Asperger syndrome information and support (OASIS): Tips for teaching high functioning people with autism.* Retrieved January 30, 2006, from http://www.udel.edu/bkirby/asperger/moreno_tips_for_teaching.html; Marks, S. U., Shaw-Hegwer, J., Schrader, C., Longaker, T., Peters, I., Powers, F., & Levine, M. (2003). Instructional management tips for teachers of students with autism spectrum disorder (ASD). *Teaching Exceptional Children, 35*(4), 50–55.

Check Your Understanding

1. How can inclusion aid students with autism spectrum disorders in developing social skills?

2. Describe some environmental and curricular modifications for students with autism spectrum disorders.

3. Describe some attitudinal and social support strategies.

4. What does coordinated team commitment mean?

5. What does the recurrent evaluation of inclusion practices involve?

6. What does home–school collaboration involve?

7. What are some specific tips for successful inclusive classrooms?

PRACTICE

Practical Considerations for the Classroom

What IDEA 04 Says about Autism Spectrum Disorders: Autism is an IDEA 04 category. Other ASDs may be covered in other IDEA categories, such as mental retardation.

Identification Tools: Identification may include neurological, cognitive, language, and behavioral testing. A developmental history, parent and teacher reports, and direct observation may also be used. *Under Age 2 Screening Instruments:* Symptoms of Autism Before Age 2 Checklist, and Checklist for Autism in Toddlers. *Intelligence Test:* Stanford-Binet Intelligence Scale–Fifth Edition. *Communication Instrument:* Preschool Language Scale–4. *Rating Scales:* Childhood Autism Rating Scale, and Gilliam Autism Rating Scale.

Characteristics	Indicators You Might See
Common Characteristics Across All Autism Spectrum Disorders	Communication skills impairment; social interaction deficits; and restrictive, repetitive, and/or stereotyped behavior.
Characteristics of Autism	
Social	Possible problems in joint attention, facial recognition of others, making eye contact, and social responding.
Language Development	May display deviations in language development, echolalia, palilalia, echopraxia, or use neologisms. May refer to self by name rather than "I."
Communication	May display deficits in communication intent such as interpreting information literally.
Behavioral	May show repetitive and stereotypic behavior, have an extreme need for routine, show strong interest in certain objects or activities/facts, and display abnormal sensory and motor functions.
Cognitive	May have a low IQ, difficulty in executive functioning, strong visual skills, and deficits in theory of mind.

A Reference for Teachers

| |

Instructional Content

- Early intervention is extremely important and should include year-round five-day-a-week programming; repeated, planned teaching opportunities with one-to-one and small group sessions; family involvement; low student-to-teacher ratios; and ongoing program and student progress evaluations.
- The general education classroom with modifications may be appropriate for many students.
- Functional communication skills may need to be taught, ideally in natural settings.
- Social skills need to be developed in various settings using specific activities to meet individual, age-appropriate goals. The hidden curriculum should be especially considered.
- Cognitive skills may need to be developed. Support may be needed in developing problem-solving and organizational skills; reduction of concrete, literal thinking; and differentiating relevant and irrelevant information.
- Transition programs should help develop an understanding of individual needs, self-advocacy skills, and daily living skills.

Instructional Procedures

- Use scientifically validated procedures to meet the individual needs of the student.
- Consider using direct instruction to teach communication, social, and cognitive skills.
- Consider using a TEACCH program that revolves around the student's skills, interests, and needs.
- Determine whether applied behavior analysis, including discrete trials, pivotal response teaching, and incidental teaching, would be beneficial.
- Consider using Social Stories.
- Avoid unsupported instructional procedures and methods such as facilitated communication.

Instructional Environment

- Provide as much structure and routine as possible in all aspects of the classroom (instruction, schedule, physical arrangement, etc.).
- For preschool children, instruction should take place in a natural environment. Arrange environment to prompt the child to initiate social interaction and to have access to natural reinforcers.
- For elementary and secondary students, focus especially on structure and routine. Incorporate visual information and cues to capitalize on this typical strength. Consider creating a home base for the student at school. Provide extra support for the student during unstructured times.
- Avoid seating students with ASD next to bullies or aggressive students. If possible, seat them next to peer buddies.
- Encourage peer tutoring, such as classwide peer tutoring.

Instructional Technology

- Technology is most often used to support communication.
- Computer technology can support students who prefer visual information and have difficulty with interpersonal contacts. Video clips can be used as examples and for teaching different skills. Computer time should be limited to avoid encouraging any obsessive behavior and replacing human interaction.
- Augmentative and alternative communication can be used to help students who do not have functional language or who have difficulty processing spoken language.
- The Picture Exchange Communication System can allow students to use pictures to communicate.
- Voice output communication aids and computers with communication software can also help some students communicate.

Methodologies and Strategies to Try

- Direct Instruction (p. 380)
- TEACCH (p. 380)
- Discrete Trials (p. 381)
- Pivotal Response Teaching (p. 382)
- Incidental Teaching (p. 382)
- Social Stories (p. 382)
- Classwide Peer Tutoring (p. 382)

Considerations for the General Classroom and Collaboration

Students with autism spectrum disorders may be taught in a special school, a dedicated classroom, or, increasingly, in the general education classroom.

The general education teacher should:

- Consider the Autism Spectrum Disorder Inclusion Model.
- Determine environmental and curriculum modifications needed.
- Support social interactions between students.
- Continuously evaluate inclusion practices to determine strengths and weaknesses of the delivery and reception, environmental arrangement, interaction amounts and types, participation level, and attitudes of teachers and student peers.
- Implement specific strategies and supports based on individual student characteristics and needs.

Collaboration

General and special educators should consult on:

- Curriculum content
- Procedures and strategies used
- Training peer buddies
- The physical environment
- Any assistive technology used to support communication

Chapter Summary

 Go the text's Online Learning Center at www.mhhe.com/taylor1e to access study resources, Web links, practice quizzes, and extending materials.

What Are the Foundations of Autism Spectrum Disorders?

- Although the term *autism* was coined in 1911, it was not until 1943 when the characteristics of 11 children with "early infantile autism" were reported that interest in the disorder began. The four other disorders on the spectrum were identified over the next 50 years.
- Autism was officially recognized as a disorder in 1980 and considered a disability under IDEA in 1990.
- Autism spectrum disorders include autistic disorder, Asperger syndrome, Rett syndrome, childhood disintegrative disorder, and pervasive developmental disorder–not otherwise specified, each defined based on the *DSM-IV-TR*. Autism also is specifically defined by IDEA 04.
- Autism is characterized by behavior deficits in social interaction, communication deficits, and restrictive or repetitive behaviors. These characteristics must be evident before the age of 3 per the *DSM-IV-TR* definition. The IDEA 04 definition does not have this requirement.
- Asperger syndrome is defined by social interaction impairments and the development of restrictive, repetitive interests, beliefs, and activities that impair functioning.
- Rett syndrome is a neurodevelopmental disorder in which characteristics of hypotonia, reduced eye contact, decelerated head growth, and disinterest in play activities emerge between the ages of 6 and 18 months. The syndrome then results in rapid developmental regression.
- Childhood disintegrative disorder is defined by a developmental regression in at least two of the following areas: expressive or receptive language, social skills or adaptive behavior, bowel or bladder control, or play or motor skills. The disorder is also marked by communication deficits and behavior characteristics consistent with autism.
- Pervasive developmental disorder–not otherwise specified is indicated when a child displays some autism spectrum behavior and meets some, but not all, of the requirements for the other autism spectrum disorders.
- Prevalence estimates for autism spectrum disorders vary from 1 to 3 per 500 children. More recent data indicates 1 in 150.
- Autism is the most prevalent autism spectrum disorder, with estimates from 1 in 250 to 1 in 1,000 persons having the disorder. It is the fastest-growing IDEA 04 category.
- Autism Asperger syndrome, and childhood disintegrative disorder occur more frequently in males. Rett syndrome appears almost exclusively in females.

What Are the Causes and Characteristics of Autism Spectrum Disorders?

- Although there is no known cause for the majority of the autism spectrum disorders, it is generally accepted that they are neurologically based.
- Overall, research does not support the controversial proposals that poor parenting or vaccines cause autism spectrum disorder.
- Research suggests both genetic and environmental causes.
- Individuals with autism spectrum disorders exhibit a number of social, communication, and behavioral deficits.
- Communication deficits may include those in communicative intent and deviations in language development.
- Behavioral characteristics may include repetitive and stereotypic behavior, an extreme need for routine, an unusual preoccupation with objects or activities, and specific sensory and motor characteristics.
- Cognitive abilities in those with autism spectrum disorders will vary. Individuals with ASDs may have low IQs, difficulty in executive functioning, and deficits in theory of mind. They may also have strengths in visual skills and strong cognitive abilities.

How Are Students with Autism Spectrum Disorders Identified?

- Most students with autism spectrum disorders are identified before they enter the classroom.
- Early screening is possible, though effective diagnostic tests to identify children under age 2 have not been developed.
- Multiple sources of information are used to identify individuals with autism spectrum disorders, including medical, intellectual, and communication evaluations.
- Parents provide valuable information based primarily on their observations.

What and How Do I Teach Students with Autism Spectrum Disorders?

- Individuals with autism spectrum disorders greatly benefit from early intervention. Early intervention programs should ideally contain family-centered support.
- Students with autism spectrum disorders typically need instruction in functional communication skills, social competence, and cognitive functioning.
- Transition plans for students with autism spectrum disorders may vary greatly from preparing for college attendance to developing independent living skills.
- Decision making on how to teach students with autism spectrum disorders must be highly individualized and is often very complex.
- Some effective scientifically validated practices include direct instruction; TEACCH; and applied behavior analysis programs such as discrete trial intervention, pivotal response teaching, and incidental teaching. Also promising are Social Stories.
- Many procedures exist for teaching students with autism spectrum disorders that have no scientific validation and should thus be avoided.

SUMMARY

What Are Other Instructional Considerations for Students with Autism Spectrum Disorders?

- Many students with autism spectrum disorders are very attuned to routine and are extremely affected by changes in the environment.
- Preschool children with autism spectrum disorders should be taught in natural environments. These environments should encourage social interaction and allow access to natural reinforcers.
- Elementary and secondary classrooms should encourage structure and routine. Visual schedules, charts, and cue cards; a home base; and the use of positive behavior support may also help make the classroom a supportive environment.
- Carefully structured group assignments can be very beneficial to students with autism spectrum disorders. Class-wide peer tutoring may also be effective.
- Computer technology is often beneficial for students with autism spectrum disorders. However, it is important that computer technology not be allowed to take the place of human contact.

- Both high-tech and low-tech versions of augmentative and alternative communication devices are useful in helping students with autism spectrum disorders communicate.

What Are Some Considerations for the General Education Teacher?

- Increasing numbers of students with autism spectrum disorders are being educated in general education classes.
- Plans for this inclusion must be carefully developed and implemented with the collaboration of general education and special education teachers.
- Five considerations in planning an inclusive environment for students with autism spectrum disorders include environmental and curriculum modifications, attitudinal and social support, coordinated team commitment, recurrent evaluation of inclusion practices, and home–school collaboration.

Reflection Topics

1. Why do you think the prevalence estimates of autism spectrum disorders vary so much? What is your position as to the reason the prevalence of autism is increasing so rapidly?
2. What frustrations do you think parents of children with autism experience on a daily basis?
3. Do you think children as young as age 2 should be identified as having autism? Why or why not?
4. Consider the differences in the TEACCH program and ABA techniques. Should we change the environment to adapt to the needs of children with autism or do we change children with autism so they will adjust to the environment? Why?

5. What do you think a teacher should do if a parent comes in and very excitedly says that she has just heard of this great diet that may cure autism and is considering putting her child on it? This teacher has just read an article stating that this diet has no scientific research to support it.
6. What do you see as logical arguments for including students with autism spectrum disorders in the general education classroom? What role do you think collaboration plays in the success of such a program?

Application Activities: For Learning and Your Portfolio

1. (**Portfolio Possibility**) Many individuals are fascinated with savant syndrome. Do some Internet research on the topic and write a short paper about its characteristics and possible causes.
2. Conduct some research on thimerosal, the preservative used in some vaccinations. Do you think it could play a role in the development of autism?
3. Try using the theory of mind task on page 370 with typical preschool children of different ages (e.g., ages 4, 6, and 8). What did you find?
4. Select two specific social skills targets for a specific student age and develop social skills stories using the description on page 382.

5. Consider various aspects of campus life (for example, dorm, cafeteria, laundry, library, and campus setup) to figure out possible obstacles for high-functioning students with autism or Asperger syndrome. Write guidelines or checklists for using these areas.
6. All personnel working with a student with an autism spectrum disorder using technology should know how to use the devices. Write some reasons and specific situations that make this important.

SUMMARY

Students with Severe Disabilities

INTRODUCING DAVID

David is a 14-year-old, eighth-grade student with severe and multiple disabilities. David has cerebral palsy, likely caused by an infection with high fever his mother contracted early in her pregnancy. David has had several surgeries to improve his ability to walk without falling, which has been affected by his cerebral palsy. He also has epilepsy as a result of the brain damage that led to his cerebral palsy. He takes medication to control his seizures. David was enrolled in home-based early intervention services in infancy. His parents have managed to raise David and two siblings despite the emotional and financial stresses. David's IQ is not known because David is nonverbal, but is estimated to be in the 40s. Cerebral palsy has dramatically affected David's ability to control his lip and tongue movements in speaking. David can walk now, but he has poor fine motor skills and has trouble with many school activities, such as holding a pencil, writing legibly, and

using a calculator. However, because of his education and life experiences, he is able to do many things comparable to his chronological peers including riding his bicycle (an adult 3-wheeler), interacting on the computer, listening to popular music, reading books at his level, and doing chores around the house. David seems much like his peers in many respects and is generally happy and adjusted to his life.

David has been included with his general education peers for his schooling. He receives physical and occupational therapy and speech and language services, which sometimes result in him being "pulled out" from his general education class. In the general education classroom, David needs considerable modification in the curriculum being learned by his peers without disabilities. He has no significant behavioral issues and is able to communicate effectively with an alternative/augmentative communication system using symbols, pic-

tures, and word "buttons" that produce synthesized speech. Some students, several of whom have attended school with David since kindergarten, enjoy helping David in the classroom and around the school. Other students largely ignore him although they do not display any hostility toward him. David's peers invite him to sports events and other after-school activities from time to time. ▶

The IEP team is considering transition planning and programming in preparation for David's entrance into high school. This planning has resulted in debate among team members as to how David's education should proceed. David expresses that he enjoys being with his friends and that he would like to live away from home someday like his older siblings. Some professional team members believe David should continue in his inclusive classes, despite the major curriculum modifications needed, so he can continue his relationships with his peers. Other team members believe David should be educated using a more community-based approach that stresses functional and career/vocational skill development although it would involve spending much time outside of the school environment. David's parents are unsure what to do. ■

In many ways, David is a typical student with severe disabilities who has had a good educational experience. Despite having severe disabilities, David has been able to develop socially and academically alongside his peers. His school district's commitment to inclusive education and his teachers' abilities to modify the general curriculum to meet his needs have enabled him to participate in the general education classroom. However, as he grows older, questions arise as to whether an inclusive education might focus more on community-based instruction rather than on classroom-based instruction. Some students with severe disabilities have greater limitations than David; some are unable to walk, have very limited communication abilities, and have significant behavioral issues such as self-abusive behaviors. Still others have better physical abilities than David, are able to use oral speech and language adequately, and ultimately live and work with at least some degree of independence. Students with severe disabilities are more like everyone else than they are different, and they can be quite varied in both abilities and disabilities.

The term *severe disabilities* is an encompassing one. To educators, individuals with severe disabilities typically have multiple disabilities including intellectual, developmental, physical, sensory, behavioral, health-impairing, communication and/or other disabilities; or are deaf-blind.

What Are the Foundations of Severe Disabilities?

The foundations of severe disabilities are somewhat unique in that various disabilities and combinations of disabilities are included. The historical foundations are similar to those with intellectual disabilities. The definitions include two IDEA categories, multiple disabilities and deaf-blind. Classification may be based on the levels of support the individual needs for daily living. Severe disabilities is a low incidence category.

A Brief History of Severe Disabilities

Relevant CEC Standard

▶ Historical foundations, classic studies, major contributors, major legislation, and current issues related to knowledge and practice (IC1K2)

Historically, one could trace the history of people with severe disabilities along the path of those with intellectual disabilities. Treatment could be humane but often included segregation or marginalization from society. In the 18th and 19th centuries, institutions were established to provide for the education and treatment for those with severe disabilities. By the beginning of the 20th century, however, institutions became places of custodial care rather than for treatment or education (Braddock and Parish, 2002).

A rubella outbreak in the United States in the 1960s resulted in a larger number of cases of dual sensory losses. Rubella, or German measles, is highly contagious and, when contracted by a pregnant woman in the first trimester, poses great risk for sensory and cognitive disabilities. The large number of cases of deaf-blindness resulting from this outbreak led to federal legislation establishing regional centers for individuals identified as deaf-blind (Sacks, 1998). Also in the 1960s, a movement in the United States to

TABLE 12.1	Organizations Concerned with the Education and Treatment of Individuals with Severe Disabilities or Deaf-Blindness

TASH Formerly The Association for Persons with Severe Handicaps, it is now known only by its acronym. TASH serves professionals, individuals, and families. TASH conducts annual conferences and publishes the professional journal, Research and Practice for Persons with Severe Disabilities. TASH is known for its advocacy on behalf of people with severe disabilities.

ARC Formerly the Association for Retarded Citizens, the ARC is now known only by its acronym. This organization is for professionals, but in particular, for individuals and families. The ARC is active in providing programs and advocacy services in many communities. The ARC has a long history of involvement in obtaining civil rights and a free, appropriate education for all children with disabilities.

American Association of the Deaf-Blind (AADB) The American Association of the Deaf-Blind is dedicated to promoting the welfare, independence, and integration of people with both vision and hearing losses. It is an organization of, by, and for people with deaf-blindness. The organization conducts annual conferences and also publishes a quarterly journal, The Deaf-Blind American.

Helen Keller National Center for Deaf-Blind Youths and Adults (HKNC) The Helen Keller National Center for Deaf-Blind Youths and Adults is located in New York State and has regional offices across the country. The center provides rehabilitation services at its primary location and through field services in other areas of the country. The overall mission of the center is to promote choice and independent living and working for individuals with deaf-blindness.

Sources: HKNC (http://www.hknc.org/AboutUsMAIN.htm); TASH (http://www.tash.org); ARC (http://www.TheARC.org); AADB (http://www.aadb.org).

deinstitutionalize individuals with severe disabilities gained momentum and culminated with the passage of PL 94-142 in 1975 (Braddock and Parish, 2002). The Individuals with Disabilities Education Act established multiple disabilities and deaf-blindness as federal categories of disability. Since 1975, advocacy organizations have continued their efforts to gain access to life in the mainstream of society for people with severe disabilities.

Whether possessing multiple disabilities or deaf-blindness, many people with severe disabilities continue to struggle for an inclusive education and equal participation as members of society. Words on a page only go so far in ensuring rights for an individual and the opportunity to function and participate in society. Advocacy organizations play a major role in ensuring access and equal opportunity for individuals with severe disabilities. TASH (formerly known as The Association for Persons with Severe Handicaps), in particular, is a well-recognized and prominent organization that includes people with and advocates for those with severe disabilities. Table 12.1 lists some of the organizations actively supporting individuals with severe disabilities today.

History teaches us many lessons. One lesson of considerable importance is the need for advocacy on the part of individuals with severe disabilities. Teachers are advocates for students with severe disabilities. Both special and general education teachers play important roles in modeling acceptance of students with severe disabilities for students without disabilities. This modeling includes creating an atmosphere recognizing and valuing human differences, human dignity, and the right to education of all students.

Students with severe disabilities may still spend considerable time with their special education teachers, but they are included in general education learning and activities. They may also be included in other settings, such as recreation and leisure or job sites. All teachers should expect that students with severe disabilities may be present in their schools and quite possibly in their classrooms.

Definitions of Severe Disabilities

There is no universally accepted definition of severe disabilities, in part because it is not a specific disability category under IDEA 04. Different educators and the public

Relevant CEC Standard
▶ Definitions and issues related to the identification of individuals with disabilities (IC1K1)

itself may perceive what is "severe" in quite different ways. For example, a general education teacher may perceive any student who is unable to read adequately as having a severe disability. In contrast, a special education teacher who serves students with multiple disabilities is likely to have a different perspective. However, IDEA 04 does include definitions of the two relevant categories that are the focus of this chapter—multiple disabilities and deaf-blindness.

The IDEA 04 Definition of Multiple Disabilities

IDEA 04 defines multiple disabilities as meaning "concomitant impairments (such as mental retardation-blindness, mental retardation-orthopedic impairment, etc.) the combination of which causes such severe educational needs that they cannot be accommodated in programs solely for one of the impairments. The term does not include deaf-blindness." This definition emphasizes the presence of multiple disabilities requiring increased special education and related services. Students with deaf-blindness are not included because this is a disability category in and of itself.

DAVID REVISITED Do you think David qualifies as having multiple disabilities under the federal definition? Why or why not?

The IDEA 04 Definition of Deaf-Blindness

According to IDEA 04, deaf-blindness is "hearing and visual impairments, the combination of which causes such severe communication and other developmental and educational problems that they cannot be accommodated in special education programs solely for children with deafness or children with blindness." A student need not be both legally blind and legally deaf to qualify for services as deaf-blind. For example, a student could have a visual impairment, such as 20/100 in best eye with the best possible correction, and a hearing loss, such as at 50 decibels, which affects his daily functioning although neither loss reaches the thresholds for legal blindness or legal deafness. The combination of the two sensory losses, however, increases the educational needs of the student such that he could be considered as having deaf-blindness.

Teachers need to be aware that knowing a student has severe disabilities does not provide precise information about the student's physical or medical condition or her or his strengths and needs. For example, one student could use a wheelchair, have severe physical and health issues, and intellectual disabilities, but have functional communication skills. Another student could have intellectual disabilities with no significant physical or health issues, but have severely limited communication skills. Knowing a student has severe disabilities informs the teacher that the student is likely to need considerable support to succeed and that this need is likely to be ongoing in one or more environments. Therefore, planning the inclusion of students with severe disabilities requires knowledge of the individual more than the label.

Classification of Individuals with Severe Disabilities

Perhaps the best way to view classification is through the lens of the American Association on Mental Retardation's (AAMR) levels of support system introduced in Chapter 5. This classification system reflects the level of support needed to adapt adequately: intermittent support, time-limited support, extensive support, or pervasive support (Luckasson et al., 2002). Students with severe disabilities are likely to need extensive or pervasive supports. A student requiring *extensive support* needs intensive supports in one or more environments on a regular basis, such as needing an aide who provides assistance throughout the day in a general education classroom. A student requiring *pervasive supports* needs intensive assistance in more than one setting on an ongoing basis. For example, the student may need to be monitored by a school nurse, require a special aide in the classroom, and be dependent on special transportation. The need for one of these levels of support might help classify a student as having a severe disability, but there is no uniform method for classifying individuals with severe disabilities (Collins, 2007).

Teachers should be aware that extensive or pervasive supports can take many forms, such as medical care, physical therapy, or increased time with a special education teacher, and do not necessarily equate to additional requirements of general education teachers. All teachers can view their role as that of collaborators involved in a support team as opposed to being the person solely responsible for meeting a student's extensive or pervasive needs.

Prevalence of Severe Disabilities

The estimated percentage of students in the United States, ages 6–21 years, served under the category of multiple disabilities in 2005 was 0.23% or about 1 student in 500. The prevalence of deaf-blindness has been estimated to be very low, less than 0.01% of the student population. Because there is no specific federal category of severe disabilities, it is difficult to make a truly accurate prevalence estimate. However, it is reasonable to state that, overall, severe disabilities are a low prevalence disability (less than 1% of students) when the prevalence of multiple disabilities and deaf–blindness are considered in combination.

Check Your Understanding

1. What is the history of educating students with severe disabilities in the United States?

2. What two federal categories can be considered as severe disabilities? What are their definitions?

3. Which levels of support under the AAMR classification system are closely associated with severe disabilities?

4. What is the prevalence of severe disabilities?

What Are the Causes and Characteristics of Severe Disabilities?

The causes and characteristics of severe disabilities differ from individual to individual. In this section, we address a number of these, but do not provide an exhaustive discussion due to the number of possibilities. Prospective teachers should understand that a label of "severe disabilities" is likely to tell us only that a student has some serious challenges. Such a label does not identify in any specific way the challenges that person faces or the strengths that person might possess.

Relevant CEC Standards
▶ Current issues related to knowledge and practice (IC1K1)
▶ Etiologies and medical aspects of conditions affecting individuals with disabilities (IC2K3)

Causes of Severe Disabilities

The causes of severe disabilities are many and varied. Like intellectual disabilities discussed in Chapter 5, severe disabilities are thought to be caused by genetic or biological factors, such as fetal alcohol syndrome, and by environmental factors, such as trauma at birth. Additionlly, some environmental variables, including poisoning and accidents, can cause severe disabilities (McDonnell, Hardman, & McDonnell, 2003). Other environmental variables do not directly cause severe disabilities, but they can contribute to them. For example, an individual could have a mild/moderate disability that becomes severe in an impoverished or abusive environment. A child may have cerebral palsy that involves serious physical difficulties but less severe cognitive ones. If the child does not receive appropriate nurturance, health care, early intervention, and encouragement to develop motor, communication, social, and cognitive skills during the critical developmental period from birth to 6 years, then the child could develop a severe disability. This child could develop more physical disabilities, such as contractures that result from untreated unusually high muscle tone; a deficiency in social and communication skills if oral-motor skills go untreated; and more severe cognitive disabilities if the child fails to acquire readiness skills needed to begin linguistic and arithmetic literacy development.

In addition, several syndromes can result in severe disabilities. Table 12.2 lists eight syndromes that can cause severe disabilities, however, this list is not exhaustive. Many other rare conditions and syndromes can lead to severe disabilities. In part, the rarity of many of these syndromes and conditions helps explain why severe disabilities are so low in incidence.

As we mentioned earlier in this chapter, Rubella is a viral infection that can cause visual and hearing losses as well as other problems in children when contracted by

TABLE 12.2	Syndromes That May Result in Severe Disabilities	
SYNDROME	**CAUSE**	**RESULTS**
Hurler syndrome	Lack of an enzyme	• Severe mental retardation • A number of distinctive physical features • Early death
Tay Sachs disease	Occurs primarily in Ashkenazi Jews (of eastern European descent)	• Causes progressive neurological problems • Severe mental retardation • Early death
Lesch-Nyan syndrome	A genetic disorder	• May lead to serious self-injurious behavior • Aggression • Neurological problems • Mental retardation
Rett syndrome	A genetic disorder	• Regression in development beginning around 6 to 18 months • May result in loss of speech, motor, and social functions • Mental retardation
Wolf-Hirschhorn syndrome	A chromosomal disorder	• May cause distinctive physical features • Microcephaly (abnormally small skull) • Seizures • Heart problems • Profound mental retardation
Cri-du-Chat syndrome	A chromosomal disorder	• Physical disabilities • High pitched cry (hence the name of the syndrome which means "cry of the cat") • Microcephaly • Severe mental retardation
Cornelia De Lange syndrome	A chromosomal disorder	• Physical disabilities • Health impairing conditions • Severe mental retardation • Self-injurious behavior
Angelman syndrome	A chromosomal disorder	Severe problems with • Speech and language • Balance and gait • Seizures • Microcephaly • Significant mental retardation

Source: Taylor, R. L., Richards, S. B., & Brady, M. P. (2005). *Mental retardation. Historical perspectives, current practice, and future directions.* Boston: Pearson.

the mother during pregnancy. Encephalitis, an infection of the brain and/or its lining, can also cause severe disabilities (Taylor et al., 2005).

Deaf-blindness can also result from a variety of factors that cause vision loss in combination with other factors that cause hearing loss (Sacks, 1998). An individual could have two conditions, each of which leads to a sensory impairment (Heller, Alberto, Forney, & Schwartzman, 1996). For example, an individual could experience a congenital hearing loss, a hearing loss at birth as a result of genetics, and then contract an infectious disease that causes a vision loss. Many of the causes for vision and hearing losses are discussed in Chapters 8 and 9, respectively.

DAVID REVISITED Does knowing the cause of David's disability help in determining what services he needs? Does it help a teacher to know how to best teach David?

Characteristics of Students with Severe Disabilities

In our discussion of the characteristics generally found among persons with severe disabilities, we will focus on those possessed by students who have multiple disabilities with one of those characteristics being diminished cognitive functioning. We acknowledge this would not be the case for every individual. For example, an individual could have severe physical and health-impairing disabilities but still have average or above average cognitive abilities. Our discussion of the characteristics of individuals whose disabilities are primarily physical or health-related is included in Chapter 10.

In general, individuals with severe disabilities can have significant delays in development (Heller et al., 1996). That is, individuals may display significantly slower development than their chronological peers in many areas. For example, a student may pass through the typical stages of speech and language development, but exhibit the abilities associated with each stage at an age later than one would typically expect. At times, students with severe disabilities may display characteristics that indicate significant differences from peers without disabilities. For example, some students with severe disabilities may not develop speech at all, indicating more significant differences in development. There are several areas in which delays and differences might be displayed including abstract thinking/conceptual thinking, learning, attention, memory, transfer/generalization, communication, social-personal, behavioral, and physical delays or disabilities. In addition, while students with deaf-blindness have their own set of possible characteristics similar to those of students with multiple disabilities, they also possess some specific to their sensory disabilities.

Relevant CEC Standards

▶ Impact of sensory impairments, physical and health disabilities on individuals, families, and society (IC2K2)

▶ Psychological and social-emotional characteristics of individuals with disabilities (IC2K4)

▶ Impact disabilities may have on auditory and information processing skills (IC3K2)

▶ Impact of multiple disabilities on behavior (IC3K3)

Abstract Thinking/Conceptual Characteristics

In human development, we generally move from first understanding the concrete (things that are real in our environment such as people, animals, and objects) to representational thinking (such as that a picture of a person represents the real person) to abstract thinking/concept development (such as contemplating how DNA determines our individual human traits). Individuals with severe disabilities may have difficulty learning information that is abstract/conceptual (Taylor et al., 2005). Some students may have difficulty with representational thinking as well. This characteristic has enormous implications for determining curriculum and instruction. For example, a student who has difficulty with representational thinking should probably learn money-handling skills by using actual money rather than pictures of money or "fake" money. A student who has trouble with abstract thinking/concept development would likely have difficulty understanding why taxes are taken out of a paycheck for purposes such as Social Security.

It is important to understand that it is difficult to assess the conceptual development and actual learning potential of many students with severe disabilities because they do not respond well to the traditional types of tests used to assess this area. More dynamic assessment procedures may provide more reliable information about general

Students with severe disabilities may be challenged when tasks are more abstract or conceptual in nature.

cognitive abilities and whether some individuals might achieve a level of abstract reasoning and learning beyond what is typically expected (Hessels-Schlatter, 2002). These procedures are discussed later in the chapter.

Learning Characteristics

In general, those with severe disabilities will learn fewer skills and gain less overall knowledge than their peers without disabilities. Typically, it takes them longer and requires more opportunities/repetitions to learn than their peers without disabilities. Also, the more complex learning becomes, the greater the learning challenges (Brown et al., 1983). For example, a young student without disabilities may learn to write her name with only occasional practice to ensure retention. A young student with severe disabilities might require the entire school year to learn to write her name. Including writing the date on papers compounds the learning difficulties and amount of time needed. These learning difficulties may occur due to problems with abstract thinking/concept development, attention, memory, transfer and generalization of learning, and developing academic skills that lead to more advanced learning, such as using reading skills to learn more about history, literature, science, and math. Additionally, individuals with severe disabilities often have problems with learning language skills that form the foundation for communication that is so important in learning from others, such as the ability to ask questions or to seek clarification, and basic self-care and safety skills (Taylor et al., 2005).

Attention Characteristics

Individuals with severe disabilities may exhibit problems with attending to tasks for sustained periods of time as well as focusing on the aspects of a task that are relevant for learning to occur (Taylor et al., 2005). For example, students with severe disabilities may be unable to maintain their attention to an activity, such as when having a book read to them, as long as do their peers without disabilities. Additionally, these students may not focus on what the teacher, parent, or peer is emphasizing. In teaching a young child with severe disabilities the concept of a circle, the teacher might mistakenly use only a picture of a red circle, comparing it to a blue triangle and a purple square. As a result, the child might perceive that anything "red" is a circle and not learn the actual shape. Supporting the development of attention skills in early childhood may ultimately help students with severe disabilities to better maintain and focus attention. In turn, this may lead to improved learning outcomes including the ability to remember information and skills, and eventually to transfer that learning to new environments and situations (Serna & Carlin, 2001).

Memory Characteristics

Individuals with severe disabilities often have deficient working and short-term memories. Working memory refers to our ability to hold information long enough to gather all the data immediately needed for a task (Swanson, 1999b). For example, a student must be able to recall and remember a phone number long enough to successfully dial the number. These deficiencies, in turn, can affect long-term memory and retrieval; that is, being able to remember the phone number indefinitely and being able to state it or write it as needed (Taylor et al., 2005).

It is important to recognize that students with severe disabilities do remember people, events, knowledge, and skills. Long-term memory may be less affected than working and short-term memory. In other words, once information or a skill is learned, the material or skill may be retained permanently or for long periods of time just as it would be for an individual without severe disabilities. One of us recently had the occasion to visit a school taught at some years prior. Learning that a former student with severe disabilities was currently in a supported employment arrangement a few miles away, a decision was made to pay a visit. The student, spying his former teacher from 50 yards or so away, dropped everything in his hands, shouted his teacher's name, and came running at full speed with a hearty greeting. His supervisor commented on his surprise that the student remembered the teacher even though it had been several years (with intervening teachers) since the two had shared a classroom. In fact, one study demonstrated that individuals with severe disabilities recognized faces with an ability comparable to that of individuals without disabilities, but that short-term memory difficulties were still evident (Bonnaud, Jamet, Deret, & Neyt-Dumesnil, 1999).

transfer/generalization The ability of an individual to take new learning and use it in a new environment or situation, or to apply the learning in some manner that was not directly taught.

Transfer/Generalization Characteristics

The **transfer/generalization** of skills, as introduced in Chapter 5, refers to the ability of an individual to take newly learned knowledge and skills and use them in a new environment or situation (transfer) or to apply the learning in some manner that was not taught directly (generalization). For example, consider a student who learns to use money in a simulated store at school. The student shows transfer and generalization of these skills when she goes to the cafeteria and uses those same money skills to purchase lunch, and then later uses them to purchase an item at a convenience store in the community. The ability to transfer/generalize skills is critical to expanding one's learning, increasing one's adaptation in many environments, and to overall successful living in an increasingly complex society (Hamill & Everington, 2002).

Individuals with severe disabilities have difficulty with transfer/generalization (Taylor, Collins, Schuster, & Kleinert, 2002). Skills may need to be taught in each environment in which they are used. Additionally, students may need to be shown how to apply the same skills in new and different ways (Hamill & Everington, 2002). For example, a student with severe disabilities could be taught how to ride a tricycle in the school gym. When the student visits her grandparents and is given her own tricycle, she may need some direct instruction on the new tricycle before riding it. Later, she may have greater difficulty than peers without disabilities in generalizing the skills of pedaling and steering the tricycle to riding a bicycle. She might again require more direct instruction to accomplish the task.

Students with severe disabilities may need more direct instruction to learn skills than do peers without disabilities, due to difficulties with the acquisition, transfer, and generalization of skills.

Generalization of skills, then, is often the direct result of the use of particular instructional strategies. These include using multiple teachers, so students attend to the relevant task dimensions rather than the particular teacher; multiple settings, so students adjust to different materials, backgrounds, and different problems that arise; and natural reinforcement, so students do not become dependent on a specific reinforcer for doing a task (Farlow & Snell, 2006).

Communication Characteristics

Communication is an important tool in learning. Much of our learning in schools and everyday life is verbally mediated. That is, speech and language are important in how we receive information, directions, and feedback about our performance that helps us to do things better and of increasing developmental complexity. It is also the medium by which most people seek assistance and approval from teachers and others, and engage in social relationships. Speech and language problems for students with severe disabilities may include articulation, language use, language comprehension, and pragmatics (Fossett, Smith, & Mirenda, 2003). Some students acquire atypical or delayed speech and language (Heller et al., 1996). Some individuals with severe disabilities develop quite functional speech and language. Still others need augmentative or alternative communication systems to assist them in communicating with others.

Lack of communication skills has an enormous impact on adaptation in everyday life. In fact, special educators are taught to consider that problem behavior among those with severe disabilities may first and foremost be a problem with communicating effectively with others (Kennedy, 2004). For example, if an individual cannot linguistically express pain, anger, frustration, or other emotions, then the outcome may be behavior that appears aggressive ("Leave me alone!"), withdrawn ("I don't feel good!"), or self-stimulating such as rocking back and forth ("I'm bored!"). Because of the central role that communication plays in our lives, deficiencies in speech and language skills are a major area of concern for individuals with severe disabilities. Many students with severe disabilities must be explicitly taught communication skills in order to develop social skills and relationships (Westling & Fox, 2004).

Social and Personal Characteristics

The need for family supports, friendships, and community participation are important for people with severe disabilities (McDonnell et al., 2003). Many individuals with severe disabilities are less well equipped communicatively than their peers without disabilities to form social networks and friendships given their multiple disabilities. Still, it may be that having *opportunities* to develop friendships and common interests are more important in forming social relationships than are physical abilities and limitations (Westling & Fox, 2004).

Research has suggested that the opportunities afforded by inclusive school settings do provide for improvements in social competence for students with severe disabilities (Fisher & Meyer, 2002). Similarly, community placement has been shown to provide for improved integration over institutional settings (Spreat & Conroy, 2001). Another study indicated that college student engagement in service learning with individuals with severe disabilities can positively affect peers without disabilities' perceptions about the individual specifically and those with disabilities in general (Smith, 2003). It would appear that quality of life is also linked to the development of social relationships (Storey, 1997).

Finally, it is worth noting that the area of human sexuality remains a largely unfulfilled need in this population. Barriers from family and professionals, as well as institutional policies, can inhibit the development of sexual identity and intimacy (Bambara & Brantlinger, 2002).

Behavioral Characteristics

As with other areas of disabilities, the behavioral characteristics of students with severe disabilities can vary considerably. We noted earlier that behavioral issues may emerge due to communication challenges. It would be an error to assume that all, or even most, individuals with severe disabilities display the problem behaviors discussed here. Still, the presence of problem behaviors is evident in the overall population.

Stereotypical behavior includes repetitive, apparently nonpurposeful movements that tend to be physically harmless yet interfere with adaptation to the environment. Examples include rocking, flapping of fingers or hands, or idiosyncratic movements of an individual, such as flapping a piece of string. The overall prevalence of stereotypical behavior is not known. These behaviors may emerge due to drug therapy effects or be non–drug induced. It is assumed that the non–drug induced behavior may emerge from a lack of social and environmental engagement (Newell, 1997). Individuals with high levels of stereotypical behavior tend to have lower adaptive behavior scores and are limited in expressing thoughts, understanding others, taking care of themselves, building relationships, and engaging in functional or enjoyable activities when alone or with other people (Matson, Kiely, & Bamburg, 1997).

Students with severe disabilities may display self-injurious behavior, apparently nonpurposeful movement that inflicts harm on the individual. Examples include the banging of one's head or arm, gouging fingers in one's eye, scratching, biting, and other forms of self-abuse. Again, prevalence levels are not known, but this type of behavior does occur more frequently in those with severe disabilities than in peers without disabilities and peers with milder disabilities (Kahng, Iwata, & Lewin, 2002). Self-injurious behavior is amenable to treatment, but intervention efforts should focus on prevention as well (Kahng et al., 2002).

Physical Characteristics

In general, people with severe disabilities are not in good health (Westling & Fox, 2004). Because so many individuals with severe disabilities have multiple disabilities, it is important to gain some understanding of the physical characteristics of these persons. As noted earlier in this chapter, a number of syndromes lead to health impairments as well as physical disabilities. Health impairments, including heart and respiratory problems, as well as orthopedic disabilities, can sap the vitality and energy of an individual to the extent that he or she is less able to participate in and learn during the normal routines of a day. These physical disabilities can also be progressive and lead to diminishing ability and early death. Additionally, physical disabilities can compromise a student's ability to interact with the environment and other people. These disabilities might also affect the services delivered as students may need nursing care, health monitoring, and physical and occupational therapy.

Characteristics of Students with Deaf-Blindness

Some students with deaf-blindness have no intellectual disabilities. However, as with the discussion of individuals with multiple disabilities, our focus is on students who have deaf-blindness and intellectual disabilities. Students with deaf-blindness and intellectual disabilities have varied characteristics, although some generalities can be made. First, many of the characteristics evident in students with severe disabilities are also present in those with deaf-blindness who have intellectual disabilities. Communication issues are common. Also, students with deaf-blindness have characteristics related to their sensory needs, learning, mobility, social interactions, and academics that should be addressed through assessment and instruction (White, Garrett, Kearns, & Grisham-Brown, 2003).

Another important characteristic of students with deaf-blindness is related to social adjustment and behavior. Because of deficits in communication and lack of sensory input in hearing, seeing, and imitating appropriate models and standards of behavior, these students may develop challenging behaviors or need to have their own communication behaviors interpreted by those around them (Prickett & Welch, 1998; White et al., 2003). Clearly, how well students are able to use and interpret

TABLE 12.3	Characteristics of Students with Deaf-Blindness Based on Age of Onset of Sensory Losses
DISABILITY	**CHARACTERISTICS**
Congenital or early deaf-blindness	This is a rare occurrence. Individuals use touch as a primary learning sense. Taste, smell, and movement are also critical sources of sensory input. Concept development may be significantly delayed.
Congenital or early vision and hearing loss	Most individuals in this category do retain some vision, hearing, or both. Distance sensory information may be available as well as some other vision and/or hearing input. Individuals may be able to learn things at close range with adaptations. The distance sensory input can be helpful in learning and communication development although early intervention is critical.
Early loss of one sense with later loss of the other	Individuals who lose one sense after their early years of development can use their intact senses for concept development and learning. Those born with hearing losses use vision as a primary source of input although literacy skills may still be affected. Those with vision loss early in life use hearing and touch as primary senses of input. If hearing is intact, literacy skills may develop although braille, large print, or auditory materials may be needed.
Progressive deaf-blindness	This occurs when either or both senses are lost progressively possibly causing fluctuating sensory input from day to day and a steady decline over time. When the losses occur later in childhood, students may have had the opportunity to acquire basic academic skills as did their peers without disabilities. When one sense is lost and the other progressively worsens, the student is challenged with finding new ways to access sensory input.

Source: Prickett, J. G., & Welch, T. R. (1998). Educating students who are deafblind (pp. 139–159). In S. Z. Sacks & R. K. Silberman (Eds.), *Educating students who have visual impairments with other disabilities.* Baltimore: Paul H. Brookes.

sensory information, from any or all senses, has a major impact on their understanding of what is occurring in an environment and the subsequent characteristics they develop (White et al., 2003). A final consideration in understanding the characteristics of students with deaf-blindness is that they are often influenced by the age of onset of either or both sensory losses (Prickett & Welch, 1998). Table 12.3 includes a brief summary of these characteristics.

The causes of severe disabilities result in many different characteristics. These characteristics present a range of challenges and tend to be lifelong, affecting the individual in multiple environments (Heller et al., 1996). Future teachers working in inclusive environments will likely have students with severe disabilities in their classrooms. Perhaps the most important consideration is not to prejudge a student's abilities and potential for learning. When you encounter someone whose speech and language is limited, who uses a wheelchair, and perhaps has some physical or sensory disabilities along with intellectual disabilities, you might be inclined to wonder, "How could this person participate in the typical routines of a classroom or school?" If your mind is open to possibilities and a belief that the person is more than the sum total of his or her disabilities, you may find yourself surprised at what such a student can do, as well as enjoy.

Check Your Understanding

1. What are the causes of severe disabilities?
2. What are possible cognitive characteristics of students with severe disabilities?
3. What social-personal characteristics might a student with severe disabilities have?
4. What behavioral characteristics might a student with severe disabilities display?
5. What are some possible physical characteristics of individuals with severe disabilities?
6. What unique characteristics are more evident in students with deaf-blindness?

How Are Students with Severe Disabilities Identified?

The presence of more than one disability and the need for lifelong supports tend to make the identification of individuals with severe disabilities less problematic than that of some other disabilities, such as learning disabilities. In fact, severe disabilities, especially those disabilities that are congenital, may be identified at birth or shortly thereafter. For example, an individual with severe physical and intellectual disabilities would almost certainly be identified shortly after birth. However, some conditions, such as Tay Sachs, take time to emerge and may not be evident immediately. In some cases, a physical or sensory disability could eventually lead to secondary disabilities, such as cognitive and communication disabilities, if not treated properly. In such instances, the presence of multiple and severe disabilities may also emerge over time.

Physicians typically diagnose the presence of physical, health-impairing, and/or sensory disabilities (Heller et al., 1996). Communication disorders may be identified by licensed speech and language pathologists prior to or after entering school. Severe communication and intellectual disabilities can make assessment difficult as most assessment instruments are designed for those with intact hearing and vision, the physical ability to respond to tasks, and the communication skills to understand what is said and to respond orally (Taylor et al., 2005).

What is usually more important in the identification process of students with severe disabilities is determining present levels of performance, strengths and learning needs, and the services required to meet IEP goals and objectives. This assessment focus yields information that is useful to teachers and families for planning for everyday activities. Still, medical diagnoses also can yield important information about ongoing treatment such as physical or occupational therapy and medication needs (Hamill & Everington, 2002).

Relevant CEC Standards

▶ Definitions and issues related to the identification of individuals with disabilities (IC1K1)

▶ Specialized terminology used in the assessment of individuals with disabilities (IC8K1)

DAVID REVISTED How has David's early identification aided both David and his family?

Early Childhood Assessments

Various assessment procedures can be used to identify young children with severe disabilities. Haring and Lovett (1997) discussed a number of these. Assessments in early childhood include neonatal screening, medical evaluations, developmental assessment batteries, and scales to assess family functioning. Such assessments could be formal, such as developmental batteries, or informal, such as observations or interviews. In either case, the assessment specialist working with younger children must be able to communicate effectively and work collaboratively with families. Family needs should be assessed and could include employment and financial resources, home and neighborhood safety, domestic workload, child-care workload, child play opportunities, marital roles, social support systems, family supports, and cultural/ethnic concerns. Other areas for assessment include communication skills, especially between caregivers and the child, and sensitivity to the child's overall biological state (e.g., agitated, crying, alert, drowsy). Still other possible areas of assessment include the extent of developmental delays, symptoms and behaviors, and overall developmental history. Assessments of young children are often done using a transdisciplinary approach in which professionals work together, assessing the child's functioning as a team, rather than providing separate individual professional assessments. Play-based assessment may be incorporated in which caregivers and professionals engage the child in a sequence of play activities that enable the team to assess various developmental skills (Haring & Lovett, 1997).

Assessments Used with School-Aged Students

Once a child reaches school age, several other assessments can be used to identify severe disabilities. An individually administered intelligence test is often included as a measure of cognitive ability. However, the use of IQ tests with students with severe disabilities may have limited value because students may lack the verbal, motoric, sensory, and other skills needed to respond meaningfully to the items on such tests. The usefulness of IQ scores in understanding abilities and needs of students with severe disabilities is also questionable (Collins, 2007). Adaptive behavior scales may be more useful than IQ tests in understanding strengths and needs. Adaptive behavior deficits typically would be more pronounced in students who need more extensive or pervasive supports (Luckasson et al., 2002). Increased occurrence of maladaptive behaviors, such as stereotypical or self-injurious behavior, could also be an indicator of a more severe disability.

A potentially promising area is **dynamic assessment.** Dynamic assessment usually involves a test-teach-retest paradigm that places greater emphasis on how well the student learns than on the product of learning (Taylor et al., 2005). Dynamic assessment may be useful in evaluating learning potential in students who do not respond well to traditional IQ tests. One such method is the Analogical Reasoning Learning Test (ARLT; Hessels-Schlatter, 2002). Other assessments that can be helpful in identifying and evaluating knowledge and skill development include ecological inventories, individualized curriculum-based assessment, functional assessment of behavior, assessment of student preferences and choices, adult/transition outcomes, and quality of life, as well as program quality (Brown, Snell, & Lehr, 2006). The focus on the assessment of students with severe disabilities is frequently on how well the person functions in various environments, what knowledge and skills are lacking that inhibit that functioning, means available for compensating for deficit areas (for example, alternative or augmentative communication systems to compensate for deficits in speech and language skills), and what knowledge and skills still need to be learned to enhance independence and overall adjustment.

Teachers are most often engaged in the identification process through more dynamic assessment methods. Standardized assessments may not yield valid results for students with limited capacity to understand or respond to typical assessment items such as reading or listening to a statement and providing a written or oral response. Therefore, teachers attempt to determine what the student knows and can do through observing and engaging the student in various activities in multiple environments. The activities could be academic, such as recognizing the letters in one's own name, or involve everyday life skills such as making a bed or loading a dishwasher. With younger children, teachers are involved in determining learning potential as well as present levels of performance as the child's disabilities may "mask" the student's true abilities.

dynamic assessment A test-teach-retest paradigm that places greater emphasis on how well the student learns than on the product of learning, and is useful for evaluating learning potential.

Students with severe disabilities may need frequent assessments through various methods to determine what they have learned.

Identification of Individuals with Deaf-Blindness

Vision and hearing losses are diagnosed by specialists in these fields. Significant vision loss is considered to occur when visual acuity is no better than 20/70 in the best eye with the best possible correction or the field of vision is severely restricted, for example, to 20 degrees or less (Falvo, 2005). To be diagnosed with a significant hearing loss, an individual would have a loss at 40 decibels or greater (Falvo, 2005). It is important to remember that a student need not be legally blind and deaf to qualify as having deaf-blindness. Rather, the presence of significant losses in both sensory areas can qualify an individual under this category (Heller et al., 1996).

Check Your Understanding

1. When are most students with severe disabilities identified? Why is this?

2. What are some ways severe disabilities are identified in young children? What areas of family functioning might need to be assessed?

3. What are some ways severe disabilities are identified in school-aged students? Why are dynamic assessment methods often more useful for teachers than standardized assessments?

4. What are some specific areas of assessment important for identifying students with deaf-blindness?

What and How Do I Teach Students with Severe Disabilities?

Relevant CEC Standard
▶ Strategies for integrating student initiated learning experiences into ongoing instruction (IC4K3)

Students with severe disabilities can have many instructional needs. They typically do not learn as much content or develop as many skills as their peers without disabilities. Often, they require more time or increased time and repetition to acquire knowledge and skills. Transfer and generalization issues may make it necessary to conduct instruction in environments other than the school classroom. Finally, because of speech and language disabilities, as well as behavioral issues, students with severe disabilities may need direct instruction in areas many teachers would assume students should learn incidentally such as listening to a story or learning to play with other children.

Instructional Content

Selecting instructional content for students with severe disabilities can be a more complicated decision than it might initially appear. States often have curriculum standards for learning in the general curriculum, but teachers may find themselves having to adapt and modify those curriculum standards to plan and provide an appropriate education for these students.

Access to the General Education Curriculum

The research literature supports the inclusion of students with severe disabilities in the general education classroom over segregated models of service delivery (Falvey, 2004). Access to the general education curriculum is important at both the preschool and primary/secondary school levels for students with severe disabilities. Access in early childhood is important because the learning potential of the student may not be established and teachers do not want to "sell short" a student's capabilities for learning. At later ages, students with severe disabilities need opportunities to interact with and learn from peers without disabilities (Falvey, 2004). It is also worth noting that students without disabilities can learn knowledge and skills by interacting with students with severe disabilities (Ohtake, 2003). Inclusion in the general curriculum is important, but it often requires adapting learning goals and objectives to ensure access and appropriate instructional content.

Access to the General Education Curriculum in Early Childhood. Many children with severe disabilities are identified early in life and become eligible for services at that time (Heller et al., 1996). Early childhood services can be home-based, delivered to the child and/or family in the home, or center-based, delivered at an educational center with other children. Despite the possible severity of their disabilities, it is in infancy and early childhood that the achievement gap between these children and those without disabilities is most narrow. All young children are learning self-care, cognitive, communication, social, play, and readiness skills among others. However, young children with severe disabilities will likely need some special instructional procedures and targeting of specific skills to progress in their development (Hamill & Everington, 2002).

Developmentally appropriate practice is the method used in many programs for young children, with or without severe disabilities. This practice assumes children develop at different rates and involves engaging each child in activities appropriate to her or his current developmental level to build on skills to learn increasingly higher-level developmental skills (Hamill & Everington, 2002). Learning is student-centered rather than teacher-centered with educators often serving as facilitators of learning. However, students with severe disabilities will learn fewer skills and need a longer time to learn skills. In early childhood programs, developmentally appropriate practice may include special education strategies including individual interventions, a focus on functional skill development, adult-directed learning, and transition planning that enable children to function in present and future environments (Hamill & Everington, 2002).

Horn, Thompson, Palmer, Jenson, and Turbiville (2004) suggested the following possible strategies for improving access to the general education curriculum for young children with severe disabilities:

- Alter the physical, social, or temporal aspects of the environment to allow for participation and engagement in learning and other activities.
- Adapt materials.
- Use special equipment (such as special scissors or pencils) to enhance participation.
- Use children's preferences to increase engagement.
- Simplify activities by task analysis or changing or limiting the number of steps learned.

- Use adult and peer supports for learning and engagement.
- Embed specific skills in the general classroom activities that are fun and motivating.
- Include families in the process.

Access to the General Education Curriculum for School-Aged Students. Students with severe disabilities can be and are taught within the general education curriculum despite their learning challenges. However, what and how these students are taught needs to be carefully considered in order to meet all of their needs. Major tasks for the teacher are to adapt learning objectives and standards, and to identify which skills to teach directly and which to embed in other instruction.

Janney and Snell (1997) examined the inclusion of students with moderate to severe disabilities in five elementary classrooms and found a frequent adaptation to be that of modifying academic learning objectives. This study did not, however, uncover a universal process or format used by the teachers to determine how to adapt objectives and other aspects of instructional content. Learning objectives in lesson plans can be adapted for students with severe disabilities in several ways including limiting the number of objectives taught, focusing on only the most important objective(s), or providing an alternate objective. These types of adaptations accommodate students in short-term planning. Examples of adaptations to a general curriculum standard, benchmark, and indicator are included in Table 12.4. Long-term planning adaptations are also an important consideration.

A common way for adapting the general curriculum to include students with severe disabilities in long-term planning is to modify the use of the standards that support the general curriculum. McGregor (2003) pointed out that IEPs can be standards referenced as opposed to standards driven. In a *standards referenced approach*, planning still begins with the individual student's needs. Once specific goals and objectives are determined, they are referenced to existing general curriculum standards. That is, teachers modify the wording and subsequently the learning that is included in the standards, benchmarks, or indicators in the general education curriculum to more closely match what the student with severe disabilities needs to actually learn. In a *standards driven approach*, teachers select specific standards, benchmarks, and indicators to be taught from the general curriculum guidelines. A standards driven approach becomes increasingly difficult as students grow older and the learning included in the general curriculum becomes increasingly complex and abstract. By using a standards referenced approach, the IEP continues to be

TABLE 12.4	Adaptations to General Education Curriculum Standards/Benchmarks Referenced Learning Objectives

1. Example of Modification of a Standards Referenced Lesson Objective.

K–3 English Language Arts Standard: Reading Applications: Informational, Technical, and Persuasive Text

Benchmark: Identify the central ideas and supporting details of informational text.

Lesson Objective: Given a silently read passage, students will correctly identify the main idea and two supporting details in each paragraph without assistance.

Modified Objective for Student with Severe Disabilities: Given an orally read passage by an adult or peer, the student will correctly identify one idea in a paragraph without assistance.

2. Example of Modification of a Standards Referenced IEP Objective.

K–3 English Language Arts Standard: Phonemic Awareness, Word Recognition, and Fluency

Benchmark: Demonstrate fluent oral reading using sight words and decoding skills, varying intonation and timing as appropriate for text.

Modified IEP Goal for Student with Severe Disabilities: Given functional sight words, the student will be able to correctly identify the requested word without assistance.

Modified Benchmark/Short-Term Objective: When presented with functional word choices in the school environment (for example, boys/girls on the restroom doors), the student will make the correct choice without assistance.

individualized. It remains important that the goals and objectives outlined in the IEP be linked to meaningful outcomes. The outcomes of the standards referenced approach should focus on the development of skills that are used in a variety of daily activities and settings, improve opportunities to interact with others, increase problem solving, and help students to live better and be contributors in their lives (McGregor, 2003). Sometimes, even with adaptations, students with severe disabilities are not able to fully accomplish typical learning objectives or daily activities, such as getting their lunch, independently.

In some cases, students might benefit from practicing already learned skills (transfer and generalization) in different environments and activities rather than learning new skills (Hamill & Everington, 2002). Enrichment skills that enhance an activity, but that are not part of the core skills, could also be taught. Social and communication skills expand activities but are not always mandatory to their completion. The Classroom Suggestions above lists strategies for ensuring the long-term access for students with severe disabilities to the general education curriculum.

As children with severe disabilities become older, they will need to learn skills that are chronologically age-appropriate. Although a student's overall level of development may be lagging, an educator should not continue teaching skills and using activities and materials only appropriate for children at that younger developmental level. For example, it would be age-inappropriate for a 14-year-old student to continue working on assembling puzzles designed for 3- to 5-year-olds even though the student may need to continue to develop eye-hand coordination. It has been suggested for many years now that students with severe disabilities should be taught using chronologically age-appropriate curriculum objectives and activities (Brown et al., 1977). Therefore, educational teams must make decisions on what is to be learned based on many variables including age, functionality of skills, benefits of inclusion, student and family preferences, and general curriculum standards.

Using Assessments to Choose Curriculum Objectives

Assessment procedures used to determine curriculum objectives for students with severe disabilities typically involve systematic observation of skill development rather than paper-and-pencil activities. Ecological inventories and functional behavior

Domain:	Functional academics/social skills
Environment:	School
Subenvironment:	Cafeteria
Activity:	Obtain lunch
Skills:	Enter and wait in line
	Select cutlery, napkin, tray
	Select desired food items
	Select desired beverage
	Pay for lunch
Additional Skills:	Greet workers, peers
	Use "please" and "thank you"
Activity:	Eating
Skills:	Select desired seat and sit down
	Eat using appropriate manners
	Dispose of leftovers
	Place cutlery and tray in
	appropriate area
Additional Skills:	Converse with peers
	Ask for help if needed

assessments are useful both in selecting the knowledge and skills in the curriculum to be taught and in documenting progress in learning.

Ecological Inventories. Ecological inventories have been in use for some time to identify the functional skills needed for students with severe disabilities. Ecological inventories are used to delineate chronologically age-appropriate skills and functional skill curriculum content students need to function in various environments including school, home, community, and workplace (Brown et al., 1979). Ecological inventories involve examining the student's environments and creating a weekday and weekend schedule for the student, interviewing the student and significant others about the activities that occur and who is present, and observation of the student. Various sub-environments, such as the school cafeteria, the home kitchen, or the community bus stop, are also identified. Next, activities that occur in each environment are identified: for example, selecting items for lunch in the cafeteria, loading the dishwasher in the kitchen, or identifying the correct bus and getting on it at the bus stop in the community. Once all the possible activities are identified, the educational team must select those that are most important to learn. This selection could be based on variables such as how often the activity occurs, its usefulness in future environments, its effect on inclusion in other activities, student and family preferences, and safety. Once activities have been identified for instruction, the specific skills needed to complete each activity are identified. Task analysis is a useful strategy in this process. Instructional strategies are then planned, implemented, and revised to teach the skills needed. Finally, other skills such as social skills—saying "Please" and "Thank you" in the cafeteria, greeting the bus driver—can be identified to enrich and enhance the learning of the activity-specific skills (Falvey, 1989; Westling & Fox, 2004). A sample ecological inventory for a school environment is presented in the Classroom Example above.

Functional Behavior Assessment. A functional behavior assessment can be useful in identifying skills for instruction. As we pointed out earlier, a lack of communication skills can lead to challenging behavior on the part of the student as a means of meeting his or her own needs. The overall purpose of a functional behavior assessment is to gather data, make hypotheses about the reason certain behaviors are occurring, design interventions to test those hypotheses, and teach more adaptive skills (Ryan, Halsey, & Matthews, 2003). The basic considerations in a functional behavior assessment include the following tasks:

- Assess the environment including antecedents, consequences, and setting events (earlier events that may increase the likelihood of the occurrence of the behavior).
- Consider what functions the behavior serves. Two basic categories of functions, particularly relevant to students with severe disabilities (six possible functions are discussed in Chapter 6), include obtaining something desirable, such as others' attention, or escaping or avoiding something undesirable, such as avoiding performing a task. (Ryan et al., 2003)

Functional behavior assessment is especially important in understanding the possible communication functions of behavior exhibited by students with severe disabilities who have no or very limited verbal language (Kennedy, 2004). For example, a student who pushes the teacher away whenever the teacher approaches could be communicating she doesn't like the activity the teacher is beginning and thus is attempting to escape or avoid the activity. However, the student could also be communicating she doesn't feel well or is tired or bored with the activity.

Functional behavior assessment allows a team of educators to look for patterns of behavior in various situations and to hypothesize what function or purpose the behavior serves for the student. Suppose the team believes the student is communicating that she doesn't like the activity (for example, washing her hands) she is learning. If the activity is an important functional skill that she definitely needs to learn, the team might decide to use the Premack Principle (Chapter 6) to encourage the student to stay on task. Using the Premack Principle, the student will be allowed to participate in a high-preference activity (looking at favorite books) when she has completed the lower-preference activity (washing her hands). The teacher task analyzes washing hands and uses a series of verbal and sometimes gentle physical prompts to teach the student to complete washing hands. When she is done, she is allowed a brief period of time to select a book of her choice. The team records the student's progress on washing hands and the frequency of pushing the teacher away. If the former improves and the latter decreases, the hypothesis is likely correct and the intervention successful. If no progress is realized, the team may need to consider another hypothesis and intervention. Whenever inappropriate responses are targeted for reduction, it is important to remember that more appropriate behaviors must be taught. The Classroom Example presents a sample functional behavior assessment in which an inappropriate behavior is targeted.

Alternate Assessment

When students with severe disabilities access the general education curriculum, it is likely they will not be learning the *exact* same knowledge and skills that their peers without disabilities will be learning. Therefore, state and district assessments allow students with the most severe disabilities to take alternate assessments rather than participate in traditional high-stakes paper-and-pencil tests. Common alternate assessments include portfolios of student work, direct observation of student performance, review of progress toward IEP goals and objectives, video observations of performance, and performance assessments or the application of a skill in a given situation such as being able to cross a street safely as opposed to being able to verbally state the procedures for safe crossing (Taylor et al., 2005; Ysseldyke & Olsen, 1999). Alternate assessment can potentially enhance expectations for students with severe disabilities and increase awareness of their needs in determining public policy. However, it also could potentially lead to inordinate time spent gathering data of questionable value (Browder et al., 2003a).

Antecedent(s)	Behavior(s)	Consequence(s)	Frequency
• Working on tasks	• Throwing objects randomly	• Teacher allows student to quit working	Ranges between 0–8 episodes per day with 4 episodes being average. Does not occur every day and occurs with high frequency on others.
• Teacher says, "It's time to get to work," or something very similar	• Throwing objects at teacher	• Teacher says, "Okay, but you will have to go to work in a few minutes."	

Hypothesis: Student is aggressive to escape or avoid work; student may be experiencing physical discomfort from health problems.

Goal: Reduce throwing objects to a zero frequency.

Intervention: Ensure no physical reasons for behavior. Assuming no known physical cause, reinforce with praise working or going to work; teach student to communicate, "I need to stop," and "I'm not feeling well," by use of picture board. Reinforce communication. Do not respond orally to throwing objects. Do not engage in physical confrontation; redirect student if he throws an object.

Monitor Progress: Record frequency of throwing objects and antecedents and consequences; record and reinforce use of picture board. Evaluate progress in 2 weeks.

PRACTICE

Teachers may be required to complete extensive paperwork indicating how the student's learning is related to content area standards rather than producing a positive impact on the individual's life (Browder et al., 2003a).

Browder et al. (2003b) examined alternate assessment performance indicators across multiple states. Overall, they found that alternate assessments still had an academic curriculum context, particularly in the areas of reading and math. These researchers pointed out that while alternate assessments have the benefit of increasing expectations for academic skill achievement, they could also lead to a lack of emphasis on assessment of functional skill development. Educators should not be inclined to automatically eliminate or avoid academic skill instruction, but should focus on ways to expand the concept of functional academics, the instructional options for teaching them, and their application and assessment (Browder et al., 2003b).

Transition Planning

Of considerable concern to educators, students, and families are the adult outcomes of schooling. How students with severe disabilities will successfully transition to postsecondary life should be a major emphasis in planning and programming as the student grows older. The overall requirements for transition planning and programming for students with severe disabilities are not different from those of any other student served under IDEA 04. However, although the law requires that planning begin no later than age 16 years, planning for these students should be considered in their early years and continue throughout adolescence and young adulthood. Because the need for support services tends to be extensive or pervasive, the planning and programming to ensure services are in place and that the student is achieving his or her maximum level of independence and self-determination

Students and adults with severe disabilities can be engaged in meaningful job training and employment.

supported employment Can involve the use of job coaches who provide individual help to individuals in learning new job skills and continue monitoring; supported employment can also involve more extensive supervision through the employment of small groups of individuals who work in a business or perform jobs in the community.

DAVID REVISTED What should the educational team be considering in planning and programming for David's transition to postsecondary life? Can David's aspirations to be with his friends and to learn the skills necessary for more independent living be accommodated through his IEP?

should begin early. Transition planning and programming can have a direct impact on the overall quality of life for these students. Kraemer, McIntyre, and Blacher (2003) studied a number of transition variables associated with students' quality of life and report that young adults with moderate to severe intellectual disabilities were found to have higher quality of life when they also had good adaptive skills. Paid work was also associated with quality of life for this group.

Family involvement in the transition process is important because it is more amenable to positive changes, even at later points in the process, than would be overall changes in the student's physical or cognitive abilities. In other words, as students prepare to transition to postsecondary life, families can be armed with the knowledge and skills for self-advocacy that will enhance adult outcomes (Kraemer et al., 2003).

A final note concerning transition planning and programming has to do with what types of outcomes might be expected. Over time, the historical perspective that students with severe disabilities can only be expected to live in institutions or group homes and be employed in sheltered workshops has been altered. Individuals with severe disabilities are now involved in more independent living arrangements. Some students attend postsecondary educational programs for further training and programming appropriate to their abilities. Others are involved in full-time, competitive employment. Still others are involved in supported employment.

Supported employment has made paid work possible for those individuals who may not be able to work, at least initially, independently in a competitive community job (Pierangelo & Guiliani, 2004). **Supported employment** can involve the use of job coaches who provide help to individuals learning new job skills and continue to check on the individuals across time. Supported employment can also involve more extensive supervision through the employment of small groups of individuals who work in a business (assembling parts or packaging products in a factory), employment of small groups who perform jobs in the community (such as cleaning or landscaping services), and employment of individuals within a business that employs both individuals with and without disabilities (such as repairing boats and marine engines) (Pierangelo & Guiliani, 2004). A review of the literature suggests that while there have been very positive outcomes of supported employment and general satisfaction by consumers using supported employment services, individuals who achieve competitive employment versus supported employment tend to earn higher wages and receive better job benefits (Tashjian & Schmidt-Davis, 2000). Supported employment emerged as an effort to improve outcomes for those with severe disabilities, but individuals with other types of disabilities have become eligible in recent years, resulting in underrepresentation of those with severe disabilities in such programs (Taylor et al., 2005).

Instructional Procedures

Instruction for students with severe disabilities should be planned to meet both short- and long-term objectives. Strategies should focus on teaching in natural settings and emphasize functional skill development. It is critical that teachers plan to collaborate with both paraprofessionals and families. Teachers should have particular sensitivity to the needs of culturally and linguistically diverse families. The partnership among family members and teachers is critical for all children, but is especially important for those with severe disabilities. Without collaborative partnerships, what is being learned at home or in school may not be emphasized and reinforced in the other environment, compounding the challenges in knowledge and skill acquisition.

Specific Instructional Strategies

Several specific strategies have proven to be effective with students with severe disabilities. Teachers can use strategies for teaching specific target behaviors, naturalistic teaching, and embedded skill instruction and partial participation.

Teaching Specific Target Behaviors. Teaching specific target behaviors, such as addition with a calculator or telling time, frequently relies on systematic instruction, use of prompts, and task analysis. A commonly used strategy for teaching specific target behaviors is discrete trial teaching. Discrete trial teaching is discussed fully in Chapter 11, but we mention it here as it is effective with students with severe disabilities. Discrete trial teaching is a highly structured, adult-directed, applied behavior analysis approach to teaching using massed trials. With students with severe disabilities, errors in acquiring and performing skills are frequent. Therefore, having strategies to handle errors is critical in the use of systematic instruction such as discrete trial teaching.

Students with severe disabilities also tend to learn well through **chained behaviors.** Chained behaviors include a series of discrete behaviors that are sequenced and combined to complete a larger, single behavior. For example, a student with severe disabilities could be taught how to make a bed independently through the acquisition of smaller steps—putting on the sheets, pillows, and bedspread—that result in learning a complete task (Collins, 2007).

Massed trial teaching and distributed trial teaching also can be effective with these students. In **massed trial teaching,** the educator has the student practice skills repeatedly in the same teaching session. This makes reinforcement of the acquisition of the skill frequent and may aid in overcoming some of the challenges associated with working and short-term memories. An example of massed trial teaching would be to have a student practice writing her or his name several times each teaching session. However, some skills do not logically lend themselves to this type of teaching. For example, it would be very artificial to have a student practice putting on and taking off a pullover shirt numerous times in a single teaching session. In this case, distributed trial teaching is more appropriate. In **distributed trial teaching,** the skill is taught at naturally occurring times and to natural cues in the environment such as when getting ready for school, when one's shirt is dirty, or when one is changing into clothing for physical education class.

Naturalistic Teaching Strategies. Naturalistic teaching strategies are implemented whenever appropriate

Relevant CEC Standard
▶ Methods for ensuring individual academic success in one-to-one, small group, and large group settings (IC5K4)

chained behaviors A series of discrete behaviors that are sequenced and combined to complete a larger, single behavior.

massed trial teaching An instructional strategy that involves practicing skills repeatedly in the same teaching session.

distributed trial teaching An instructional strategy that involves teaching a skill at naturally occurring times and to natural cues in the environment.

One-on-one instruction may be required in some learning activities such as discrete trial teaching.

occasions in everyday interaction emerge, and they help support communication skills. Sometimes referred to as enhanced milieu teaching strategies, these approaches include modeling by the teacher. For example, the teacher could say "water" when the student looks at the water play table during an ongoing activity. A second approach is the mand-model strategy. In this method, the teacher says to the student, "You want to play . . ." (the mand) followed by the teacher saying "water" (the model) if the student does not respond within an interval of time. Incidental teaching then expands on these learning opportunities. If the child says "water," the teacher then replies, "Tell me 'play water.'" Finally, the use of a time delay can be incorporated. The teacher waits for the student to make a response, "play water," before continuing with the activity (Collins, 2007; Kaiser & Grim, 2006). Overall, enhanced milieu teaching uses everyday communication situations: (1) to respond to the meaning of a student's communication while simultaneously providing a model of more elaborate communication; (2) to provide supportive prompts for this elaborated communication within social interactions; and (3) to support functional outcomes for students' attempts at communication (Kaiser & Grim, 2006). These procedures have been used effectively with children in early intervention programs and have been successfully taught to parents of children with disabilities to encourage their children's language development (Kaiser, Hancock, & Nietfield, 2000; Kaiser & Hester, 1994). These strategies are designed to encourage generalization of communication attempts because the communication interaction is functional and provides naturally reinforcing consequences (Kaiser & Grim, 2006).

behavior chain interruption strategy A learning strategy that involves interrupting a task analysis of sequenced or chained steps to encourage communication skill development.

Another variation of naturalistic teaching is **behavior chain interruption.** In this strategy, a task analysis of sequenced steps, which is "chained" to form a complete skill, is interrupted during instruction. For example, a student could be learning to load a dishwasher step-by-step. At the point he needed to add detergent, the teacher could ask him, "What do you need? Can you tell me what it is called?" This adds the element of learning language to the skill of loading a dishwasher. The interruption is planned by the teacher and typically involves encouraging communication skill development. Interruptions could involve something missing that the student needs to request from the teacher, or an interruption in which the student needs consent or assistance to continue, or to obtain feedback and reinforcement (Carter & Grunsell, 2001). This is a robust technique for increasing requesting and has been widely applied, but such interruptions in tasks can be distressing for some students (Carter & Grunsell, 2001). The Classroom Suggestions includes specific strategies for the use of this teaching strategy.

Classroom Suggestions Strategies for Teaching Behavior Chains to Students with Severe Disabilities

The following are strategies for the use of teaching behavior chains:

❏ Give feedback to the student indicating a need to pause and providing another opportunity to perform the skill using more intrusive prompting such as a full physical prompt as needed.

❏ Gently stop a student making an error and redirect the student's attention to what aspect of the skill needs correcting using prompts as necessary.

❏ As learning progresses, wait to see if the student will self-correct and then provide prompts as needed to correct the error.

❏ Adapt or simplify skills that are consistently performed incorrectly. For example, a teacher could have the markings on a washing machine dial color coded if the student seems unable to respond to the markings used by most people.

❏ Gently interrupt when an error occurs and give several opportunities at that point to correct the error. Reinforce self-corrections and prompted corrections.

Source: Adapted from Snell, M. E., & Brown, F. (2006). Designing and implementing instructional programs (pp. 111–169). In M. E. Snell & F. Brown, *Instruction of students with severe disabilities* (6th ed.). Upper Saddle River, NJ: Merrill.

Embedded Skill Instruction. Embedding skills to be learned by students with severe disabilities in general education routines and learning activities is crucial in inclusive education (Taylor et al., 2005). For example, while peers without disabilities are learning scientific concepts related to combustion, a student with severe disabilities may be learning about fire safety and hazards at greater depth than others and learning much less about the associated scientific principles. Specific strategies for embedded instruction are numerous but rely on two basics. First, collaboration is critical among general and special education teachers, related services personnel, and other IEP team members so that everyone working with a student is aware of these various skills to be embedded in the routine activities of the day. This includes collaboration in planning, delivering instruction, assessing student performance, and evaluating instructional effectiveness. The second is adapting instruction and/or materials.

Snell and Brown (2006) noted that instructional adaptations fall into two primary categories. First, teachers may adapt the level of difficulty or amount of input given the student (for example, basic household fire hazards) or the output required of the student (identifies only hazardous materials while other students also identify procedures for storing or disposing of such materials). Second, teachers may vary the modality of input (for example, viewing real hazardous materials rather than viewing pictures of them) or the output (pointing to the actual materials rather than saying the names of hazardous materials). Sometimes teaching materials themselves may also be adapted (for example, questions put on tape rather than in written form) to meet the student's input needs or to assist the student in output (having someone scribe oral responses rather than writing responses) (Snell & Brown, 2006).

Partial Participation. **Partial participation** was initially designed to allow individuals to partially engage in an activity rather than deny or delay their involvement because prerequisite skills had not been learned or demonstrated (Baumgart et al., 1982). What meaningful participation is may be questioned by some, but the principle should be considered in determining whether a student can or should be engaged in everyday activities. One guide to implementing partial participation is whether the student enjoys the role assigned in the activity and if the role is a preference of the student, family, and peers. For example, a student may not be able to prepare his own lunch independently, but he can perform some steps in the process. Baumgart et al. (1982) first defined the principle of partial participation, and their ideas are explored in An Important Event.

partial participation Individuals are allowed to partially engage in an activity rather than deny or delay their involvement because prerequisite skills have not been learned or mastered.

AN IMPORTANT EVENT

1982—The Principle of Partial Participation Is Identified

Baumgart, D., Brown, L., Pumpian, I., Nisbet, J., Ford, A., Sweet, M., Messina, R., & Schroeder, J. (1982). The principle of partial participation and individualized adaptations in educational programs for students with severe handicaps. *Journal of The Association for Persons with Severe Handicaps, 7(2), 17–27.*

Baumgart et al. (1982), explored the question, "How can I involve a student with such severe disabilities that she/he will never be able to complete the activity on her/his own?" Their response is a convincing argument for partial participation. Baumgart et al. begin by offering a definition of the principle of partial participation that

(continued)

asserts that students with severe disabilities "can acquire many skills that will allow them to function, at least in part, in a wide variety of least restrictive school and non-school environments and activities" (p. 19). Individual adaptations and how they can be used to generate functional curriculum skills are discussed and recommended with the goal of the student functioning as independently as possible in everyday routines of life. Accommodations can include changing rules and routines in an activity, changing materials, or changing the way an activity is performed. Partial participation is now a common consideration in determining accommodations that affect decisions about a student's least restrictive environment and a student's capacity for engaging in daily activities and routines.

REFLECTION Have you ever engaged in activities in which you may never be independent (for example, working with a parent in repairing a car or carpentry work in your house)? Did the fact you would not be independent make the activity less enjoyable? Do you think students with severe disabilities might enjoy activities that they cannot do independently?

Working with Paraprofessionals

Students with severe disabilities will very often receive supports from paraprofessionals. As introduced in Chapter 2, paraprofessionals, sometimes referred to as paraeducators, engage in a wide variety of roles in serving students with disabilities, including (1) sharing information about students with teachers, (2) attending relevant meetings, and (3) participating as collaborative team members (Carroll, 2001). Carroll also noted that when working with students, paraprofessionals modify materials, take and record data, facilitate social interactions, manage small and large groups, facilitate social interactions among students, assist students with daily living skills, and teach community and home-living skills. Although teachers retain the overall responsibility for instruction, there has been a trend for paraprofessionals to assume greater responsibility for the delivery of instructional services to students with severe disabilities. This trend raises some concerns as to who is ultimately responsible for a student's educational program (Giangreco & Doyle, 2002).

This concern can be mediated by employing the following strategies:

- Clarify the role of the paraprofessional (instructional, health care aide, etc.)
- Align that role with the paraprofessional's skill development
- Provide orientation, training, and supervision in carrying out that role
- Determine when paraprofessionals need supports (teachers should be working in unison with paraprofessionals to meet student needs)
- Do not rely solely on paraprofessionals to conduct teacher-level learning activities and make teacher-level decisions (Giangreco & Doyle, 2002)

Teachers bear the responsibility for providing training, setting up regular meetings, providing feedback, and evaluating paraprofessionals (Carroll, 2001). Teachers should recognize the significant role these individuals can assume in delivery of services, but balance that with their own responsibility to ensure quality instruction and to be engaged with students.

Working with Families

As you might hypothesize, some parents of children with severe disabilities experience higher levels of stress than parents of children without disabilities. Possible contributing factors include child characteristics such as challenging behavior, intellectual disabilities, physical disabilities, and self-care and social skill deficits. Concerns about the prognosis of the child and the stigma of having a child with a disability are also potential contributors to parental stress levels. Therefore, one primary concern for educators is to be aware of parental stress. Teachers or other professionals can provide or suggest to parents services that they may need to cope successfully with the family stress so that they can fully participate in the educational process in the manner and to the level at which they desire (Lessenberry & Rehfeldt, 2004). It is important for educators to remember that families do manage life in different ways and that not all parents will wish for the same level of involvement. Less involvement than expected should not, however, be interpreted to mean a parent does not care about the education or welfare of the child (Poston, Turnbull, Park, Mannan, Marquis, & Wang, 2003).

It is also a mistake to assume that all families of children with severe disabilities have great difficulty in coping or adjusting to life. Having a child with a severe disability should not be perceived as an overall negative experience of sorrow and woe (Rieger, 2004). Some researchers have suggested that the long-held belief that a child with disabilities introduces significant marital stress is not as pervasive an effect as one might assume. Also, the belief that virtually all families are significantly stressed by a child with disabilities may not be true, although significant problems can exist in some families (Risdal & Singer, 2004). Clearly, more research is needed to determine which families adapt well and which families may do less well.

Best practices in working with culturally and linguistically diverse families of children with severe disabilities have not been fully addressed by educators. This may be the result of a false assumption that the needs of the child are so great that culture and language do not matter. However, for educators to interact successfully with these families, each party needs to respect, listen, and learn about the other's culture, language, and beliefs (Park & Lian, 2001). For example, researchers in one study found that hospital practices in a neonatal intensive care unit differed from the caregiving beliefs of Mexican immigrant families. The families in this study reported communication and cultural barriers as stressors. The need for improved access to trained translators, informational audiotapes, and printed materials in Spanish were cited (Denney, Singer, Singer, Brenner, Okamoto, & Fredeen, 2001).

Another study conducted with Korean American parents suggested that the cultural beliefs of diverse families vary considerably and that no one method to encourage parental participation in the educational process is suitable for all. Trust, caring, respect, professional expertise, and a focus on children's strengths facilitated partnerships between Korean American families and professionals (Park, Turnbull, & Park, 2001).

Check Your Understanding

1. What are some ways to promote access to the general education curriculum for preschool children and school-aged students with severe disabilities?

2. What assessments can be used to help determine curriculum objectives for students with severe disabilities?

3. What are three useful assessment strategies for students with severe disabilities?

4. What are some transition considerations of students with severe disabilities?

5. What are some specific instructional strategies that can be used with students with severe disabilities, and how are they applied?

6. What are some important roles for paraprofessionals in working with students with severe disabilities, and how can teachers support them in those roles?

7. What are some important considerations in working with families of students with severe disabilities?

What Are Other Instructional Considerations for Teaching Students with Severe Disabilities?

Both the instructional environment and uses of instructional technology need to be carefully planned to best support students with severe disabilities. In terms of the instructional environment, the first question to address is where the student should be taught. Once this is determined, the possibility of community-based instruction should also be considered. Use of instructional technology should be considered based on the individual student's needs. For students with severe disabilities, assistive technology might be particularly useful in enhancing communication or compensating for a disability.

The Instructional Environment

Relevant CEC Standards

▶ Barriers to accessibility and acceptance of individuals with disabilities (IC5K2)

▶ Adaptation of the physical environment to provide optimal learning opportunities for individuals with disabilities (IC5K3)

To provide an appropriate education for students with severe disabilities in the least restrictive environment, educators must consider the physical environment as much as what is taught and how students need to be taught. Despite our discussion of the severity and multiplicity of the disabilities of such individuals, it would be incorrect to assume that these students cannot be and are not served in general education classrooms for part or all of their school day. Particularly with younger children, the developmental delays or differences of the individual with severe disabilities may be less pronounced than with older students who are learning more abstract and complex skills. The primary consideration in choosing a learning environment is evaluating where a student will learn best. Another consideration, especially with older students, is that inclusive educational environments can be extended into the community with peers and other people without disabilities through community-based instruction (Falvey, 1989). Learning job skills, how to use a public transportation system, or shopping in the community are taught in inclusive environments. Students who are deaf-blind have very specific needs in their environment that the teacher will need to plan for. Finally, extended school year services may provide students with severe disabilities additional instruction and support they need to be as successful as possible.

Placement Options

Where students with severe disabilities should be taught has been long debated. Brown, Wilcox, Sontag, Vincent, Dodd, and Gruenewald (1977) posited that the least restrictive environment for students with severe disabilities should include opportunities for long-term interactions with peers without disabilities. These interactions are essential to developing the knowledge and skills needed to function in school and adult life.

Although differences of opinion on where students with severe disabilities should be educated persist, most educators agree that integrating students with severe disabilities into general education school campuses is preferable to isolating them in special centers. Integration, in this case, means either establishing special classrooms within the general education school or having students with disabilities receive special education instructional services in general education classrooms.

A number of benefits of inclusion of students with severe disabilities have been identified (Alper, 2003). Inclusion provides opportunities for social interactions not available in more segregated settings, which in turn can improve communication as well as social skills. Friendships can develop between students with and without severe disabilities. Inclusion with peers without disabilities can also provide models of appropriate behavior that can be imitated rather than relying only on models of behavior of other people with disabilities. General education teachers may develop higher learning expectations for students with severe disabilities and increased expectations for conduct for all students. Age-appropriate functional skills linked to the general education curriculum can be taught. Finally, inclusion in school environments may enhance the likelihood that students will be included in the community and throughout life (Alper, 2003). Alper also summarized benefits of inclusion for peers without disabilities. These benefits include learning tolerance of individual differences and exceptionalities, learning about the abilities of students with disabilities rather than just their areas of difficulty, and learning about different professions and roles of professionals in the schools.

The following is a modified list of guidelines presented by Westling and Fox (2004) for including students with severe disabilities in general education settings:

- Students with severe disabilities should attend their neighborhood school.
- Supports should be provided in general education classes to avoid the student having to attend a special class because that is where supports are provided.
- If a student should need special classes during any part of the day, the home-room should be a general education one.
- The ratio of students with severe disabilities to those without disabilities should be natural, or less than 1% of the school population.
- A number of teaching tactics and approaches should be applied to promote learning and inclusion, not just assigning a unique paraprofessional to provide one-to-one instruction.
- If specific classes are selected for inclusion, then hands-on instruction and activity-based learning may be most appropriate. When students with severe disabilities participate in more community-based instruction, including peers without disabilities is desirable.
- If students must be placed in special classes for most of the day, they should still have opportunities to participate and interact with peers without disabilities during specials, extracurricular activities, and other appropriate times (e.g., during lunch).
- Educators should collaborate to promote learning and social interaction.
- Peers without disabilities can volunteer to play a variety of roles (e.g., classroom helper, bus companion, tutor, cooperative learning group member).
- The general educator should participate in IEP development and meetings.
- Administrators must also be supportive in the process.

Community-based Instruction. The greatest difference of opinion regarding the inclusion of students with severe disabilities in general education classes may occur when the curriculum and instructional adaptations required for learning are so pronounced that the student's ability to engage in the same learning activities with peers without disabilities could be significantly diminished. In general, but not exclusively, this occurs at the secondary level of schooling. For example, it is unlikely that a student with severe disabilities would derive meaning from Shakespeare's tragedies and might not be best placed solely in an inclusive classroom. However, this student has functional literacy needs that must be addressed. **Community-based instruction** (CBI) can overcome the problem of an apparent lack of inclusive educational practices in some situations. CBI involves teaching students skills in the community environments in which the skills will be used (Falvey, 1989). For example, the student might be taught functional literacy skills such as reading labels on grocery items or the signs in grocery store aisles in the community. This practice helps avoid issues related to transfer and generalization of skills from the school environment to the community (Falvey, 1989). CBI provides an inclusive education because it involves meaningful and regular interaction with people without disabilities in the community

DAVID REVISTED If you were on David's IEP team, what concerns might you express about involving him in community-based instruction?

community-based instruction Involves teaching students skills in the community environments in which the skills will be used.

Students with severe disabilities can benefit from learning in general education classrooms with appropriate support.

(for example, grocery clerks, bus drivers) and learning meaningful knowledge and skills needed to be successful to live, work, or use leisure time in integrated community environments. Owens-Johnson and Hamill (2002) suggest that CBI can provide for functional life skills instruction and practice but must also:

- Be systematic and organized and based on the IEP.
- Occur regularly such as daily or at least weekly. It is not a "field trip" model of instruction.
- Involve active student participation that is planned, scheduled, consistent, and implemented over time.
- Involve only small groups of students at a time.
- Be paid for by the school district with appropriate precautions taken for liability.

Environmental Considerations for Students with Deaf-Blindness

Because of their sensory disabilities, the environment for students with deaf-blindness must be organized to maximize the sensory abilities they have and help them to compensate for their sensory losses. Prickett and Welch (1998) identified several important considerations, gleaned from research literature, for constructing a learning environment for deaf-blind students. First, simulating the deaf-blind experience can help the teacher understand the challenges the student may face in the classroom. A teacher could attempt to perform some of the expected routines and tasks in her or his classroom while wearing a blindfold, ear plugs, or other simulation devices to gain insight into how the physical environment hinders or aids a student with deaf-blindness. Keeping this in mind, educators should:

- Evaluate the environment based on student needs and consider lighting, positioning, seating, acoustics, and location of materials and furniture.

- Adjust materials as needed to meet the particular needs of a student.
- Seek help in obtaining and maintaining any adaptive or assistive technology present.
- Structure group activities that take into account the fact that the student will need assistance with social interactions (Prickett & Welch, 1998).

Extended School Year Services

A final consideration in the instructional environment for all students with severe disabilities involves extended school year services, typically during summers when many schools are not in session. These services are allowed under IDEA 04 but may be limited to particular categories of disability as well as limited in the duration, amount, and type of services provided (Etscheidt, 2002). Eligibility for extended school year services can be and is based on various factors, depending on the state, district, and IEP teams. However, it is probably best that such services be determined by use of a multifactored evaluation that can address such issues as whether the student is likely to regress significantly, whether goals can be achieved or maintained, and whether other circumstances merit extended school year services (Etscheidt, 2002).

Instructional Technology

Many students with severe disabilities have multiple disabilities. Different types of assistive technology, therefore, are often necessary to enhance communication skills and compensate for other disabilities such as physical ones. Assistive technology can be quite simple in design or somewhat complicated and require specific training in its use. However, a general rule for selecting assistive technology is to choose the technology that helps the individual perform the desired skills in the most effective and efficient manner. Generally, it is desirable, although not mandatory, for assistive technology to be easily understood by others who interact with the individual with disabilities. For example, a student could use a communication device that uses synthesized speech that can be understood by any listener. A communication device that involves the student pointing to symbols that represent words or concepts may have to be learned by the listener to be understood. Among a range of considerations, the selection of assistive technology used must take into account a variety of factors including cost, reliability, and functionality. Keep in mind that related services personnel, such as occupational therapists and speech and language pathologists, may be involved in the creation, selection, and training in the use of assistive technology.

Adaptive equipment, discussed at some length in Chapter 10, helps the individual student adjust more easily to certain instructional and life situations. Some adaptive equipment, such as bolsters or wedges, can help support a student in a better sitting position. Other items can assist the student to perform certain tasks more independently. For example, large-handled spoons allow for easier gripping and special tables may help a student to stand or sit and be able to use her or his hands.

Communication technology can be particularly useful. Assistive technology can be applied to provide for either augmentative communication or alternative communication aids or systems. Alternative/augmentative communication (AAC) aids are also discussed in Chapter 7 and are typically used by students who cannot communicate to others through oral language or whose oral language is so difficult to understand or is lagging such that listeners have difficulty comprehending the oral message (Best, Heller, & Bigge, 2005). These aids range from rather simple indicator devices (pressing buttons results in a light that signifies "yes" or "no") to more complicated systems that use pictures or symbols arranged on a board. Some AAC aids or systems can be used to produce spoken language. Generally more complex in use and in the hardware, these aids and systems have the advantage of using the communication medium (spoken language) that is understood by the

Relevant CEC Standard
▶ Communication and social interaction alternatives for individuals who are nonspeaking (IC6K2)

PRACTICE

In Practice Meet Educator Amanda Norris and Her Student Nathaniel

I am a special education teacher at an elementary school in eastern Kentucky. I have four years' experience in this school district. Although I am classified as a resource teacher, I collaborate in the general education classroom. Like many school districts in the state, large portions of the population live below the poverty line. Our school is well known in the state because of our efforts to make education accessible to all students, including those with the most severe disabilities.

My student, Nathaniel, is a 12-year-old boy who has been identified as having multiple disabilities including autism and an intellectual disability. Nathaniel needs considerable help at school with washing, changing clothes, eating, and even cutting his hair. Our philosophy is that his potential for learning is greatest when his basic needs are first met.

Nathaniel was identified as having special needs at age 3. He has been receiving special education and related services from a speech therapist, an occupational therapist, a paraeducator, and a special education teacher. Nathaniel is currently in the fifth grade. He is fully included.

However, as the special education teacher, I remain primarily responsible for implementing his educational needs and providing him with access to the general curriculum. Either a paraeducator or I accompany him in content classes to ensure that he receives the necessary attention to be an active contributor to the classroom.

Throughout the course of Nathaniel's education I have watched him grow from an impulsive child into a young man who fully participates in each class. His frequent violent outbursts, temper tantrums, and unwillingness to participate in areas outside his interests have been replaced with self-restraint and reasoning. His academic skills have also improved dramatically. He excels in math and can read picture symbols independently. He is now able to self-monitor his work and highlight the number of words he can identify and check his mathematics with a calculator.

general public. Those AAC aids and systems that do not rely on the use of spoken or written language can usually be understood with little training but may require some familiarity on the part of those communicating with the individual with severe disabilities.

Kaiser and Grim (2006) made several suggestions for consideration in the selection of assistive technology to support communication:

- The selection should be based on recent assessments of the student, environment, and equipment.
- Students may need practice or training to learn to use a system, but this should not preclude using the system in naturalistic teaching opportunities during training.
- Communication partners may also need training in the use of the system as well as how to expand the use of the system and model these new uses.
- Using an alternative communication system does not reduce a student's opportunity to learn speech, especially when used in combination with oral language.

Some systems can be costly. If damaged or lost, replacement may take some time, leaving the individual without adequate communication. Additionally some systems may require more maintenance and troubleshooting. Finally, if the system is purchased by the school district, it may be available for use only during the school day or until the individual graduates or leaves the district. Again, there are advantages and disadvantages to the use of either low or high assistive technology.

Instructional Content and Procedures

Although he participates in the Kentucky Alternate Assessment Program, Nathaniel is included in the general education setting and participates in the curriculum identified by the Department of Education in the Kentucky Core Content Document. To ensure that Nathaniel receives the most from each instructional class, he works with a special education teacher or an instructional assistant who provides services to a small group of students. The special education teacher works with students identified with special needs and also helps other students who may require extra assistance on an assignment.

Nathaniel struggles with reading, so most of his assignments are modified with text-to-picture software. This software pairs pictures with words so the student can read using the picture cues if he is unable to read the text. Nathaniel is very proficient in completing assignments that have been modified in this way. He also utilizes text-to-speech software in which scanned text can be highlighted and read to him. He is cur-rently using this program with teacher guidance, but we are working toward independent use with this program also.

Math instruction requires very little modification. Nathaniel excels in this area and can complete the same assignments as his peers. He can do mental mathematics as well as manipulate objects to solve problems. However, an instructional assistant or special education teacher is present because Nathaniel can get frustrated and off task if he has difficulty with a problem.

Instructional Environment and Technology

Nathaniel is a member of a fifth-grade homeroom and attends classes with his peers. Each teacher is aware of his special needs and receives a copy of his IEP at the beginning of the year. The school day is divided by block scheduling, and students go to different classrooms for reading, mathematics, social studies, science, and activity classes.

Nathaniel's use of text-to-graphic software and text-to-speech software is documented on his IEP and is based on his need for supported reading. These software programs also allow him to work more independently.

Collaboration

As a collaborative teacher, I work closely with Nathaniel's general education teachers. I meet with each of them at least once a day. They provide me with their lesson plans a week in advance, which gives me time to modify the work for Nathaniel.

To build a good working relationship with his general education teachers, I also volunteer to assist in their classrooms grading papers, watching their classrooms while they attend meetings, and so forth. We also team teach. While I instruct the entire classroom, the general education teacher provides specialized assistance to the students under my supervision.

This close relationship between his teachers benefits Nathaniel. He is welcomed in each classroom, and each educator is aware of the supports necessary to enhance his learning. Through collaboration I also have gained content knowledge and teaching strategies from other professionals that enhance my work.

PRACTICE

Some students with severe disabilities may need alternative/augmentative communication aids to effectively interact with others.

What Are Other Instructional Considerations for Teaching Students with Severe Disabilities? **431**

1. What are some ways that educators can encourage the integration of students with severe disabilities into an inclusive environment at school or in the community?

2. What are the possible benefits of inclusion for students with severe disabilities and peers without disabilities?

3. What is community-based instruction, and why might it be implemented?

4. What factors are important in considering how to organize the best possible physical environment for students with deaf-blindness?

5. What are important considerations in the selection of alternative/augmentative communication systems?

What Are Some Considerations for the General Education Teacher?

Relevant CEC Standard

▶ Models and strategies of consultation and collaboration (CC10K1)

The role of the general education teacher in providing educational services for students with severe disabilities has expanded over time from being involved in instruction when students were occasionally mainstreamed into specific activities such as art or music, to playing a key role in the development of IEPs and daily planning and programming for students. Different models for teacher support, ranging from consultation to collaboration with special education teachers, have proven to be invaluable. The fact is, without the cooperation and assistance of general education teachers, full integration and inclusion of students with severe disabilities is highly unlikely. Prater (2003) outlined a number of suggestions for general education teachers to consider when including students with disabilities. We have modified these recommendations in some instances to more specifically address the needs of students with severe disabilities.

- Show concern for the student and the student's success.
- Adjust the classroom and learning environment. The acronym CRIME can help, which signifies curriculum, rules, instruction, materials, and environment.
- Write down and refer to the student's strengths and limitations.
- Include with those skills, learning preferences, and behaviors.
- Compare what you have written down with a list of student and classroom characteristics that facilitate, hinder, or are neutral to the student's success.
- List a few skills or characteristics you could teach the student or modify in your classroom.
- Select and implement adaptations and instruction to meet the goals of the team-designated interventions as well as those you may have chosen that may affect all students (such as a new seating arrangement).
- Use teaching procedures that are effective with all students. Although special teaching procedures can be useful, many procedures used with students without disabilities are also helpful.
- Collaborate with special education teachers when special procedures, materials, or other adaptations are needed.

- Change as needed. Don't give up on the use of some procedure or adaptation too quickly, but do change them when assessment indicates progress is lacking.
- Assess student performance and teaching effectiveness regularly.

This list is not exhaustive, but it does summarize basic principles useful in including students with severe disabilities. General education teachers should remember that they are not or should not be "going it alone" in including students with severe disabilities. They are part of a team with the special education teacher, paraprofessionals, related services personnel, the student's family, and possibly others. Collaboration is the key to ownership, understanding, and success.

It is logical for a general education teacher to ask, "What about the other students? How is their education affected?" Research has indicated that there is little if any negative impact on the achievement of students without disabilities by the inclusion of those with severe disabilities. Peck, Staub, Gallucci, and Schwartz (2004) surveyed parents of students without disabilities concerning the impact of inclusion of students with severe disabilities on their children. These researchers found that parents generally indicated they felt good about inclusion and that it increased their child's appreciation for the needs of others and increased acceptance of differences. The majority of parents also stated that they thought it unlikely that their child's academic progress was affected. Fifteen percent of parents believed their child's progress had actually improved. Of course, not all parents in this survey responded positively, but overall results suggest that our fears as educators regarding potential negative impacts of inclusion may not be well founded. Finally, although this discussion focuses on general education teachers, it is important to note that special education teachers can have fears concerning their role in inclusive classrooms, the impact on the learning of their students, and the need to learn new content and skills. With a team approach, these fears and students' challenges can be overcome.

DAVID REVISTED If David was to be included in your general education classroom, what types of information and support would you request from his special education teacher?

Check Your Understanding

1. How has the role of the general education teacher changed over time in working with students with severe disabilities?

2. What are the key considerations for general education teacher in including students with severe disabilities?

3. How does the presence of students with severe disabilities affect the learning of peers without disabilities?

Practical Considerations for the Classroom

Characteristics	Indicators You Might See
Cognitive	Problems with abstract/conceptual thinking, learning, attention, memory, and transfer/generalization.
Communication	Limited speech and language skills, atypical or delayed speech or language, use of augmentative or alternative communications systems.
Social-Personal	May have limited skills for developing social networks and friendships.
Behavioral	Self-stimulatory behavior such as repetitive, seemingly nonpurposeful movements such as rocking, flapping of fingers or hands, or idiosyncratic movements; self-injurious behavior such as banging of one's head or arm, gouging fingers in one's eye, scratching, biting, or other forms of self-abuse.
Physical	Poor health and multiple disabilities are common.
Deaf-Blind	Some may have no cognitive disabilities but many do have significant challenges, communication problems, sensory needs, challenging behaviors.

A Reference for Teachers

Teaching Implications	Methodologies and Strategies to Try	Considerations for the General Classroom and Collaboration

Instructional Content

- Improve access to the general curriculum for early childhood students by altering the environment to allow for participation and engagement, adapt materials, use special equipment to increase engagement, simplify activities by task analysis, use adult and peer supports, embed specific skills in the general classroom activities, include families in the process, focus on functional skills.
- Adapt learning objectives by limiting the number of objectives taught, focusing on only the most important objectives, or providing an alternative objective.
- Modify the use of the standards that support the general curriculum.
- Implement partial participation and allow students to be involved in activities to the extent they are able.
- Use assessments such as ecological inventories, functional behavior assessments, and alternative assessments to help choose curriculum and evaluate learning.
- For students with deaf-blindness, work to interpret their communication system and use systematic strategies to promote social relationships.
- Include transition planning and programming.

Instructional Procedures

- Teach specific target behaviors using discrete trial teaching, massed trial teaching, or distributed trial teaching.
- Implement milieu and naturalistic teaching and the modified approach of behavior chain interruption strategy.
- Embed skills instruction using collaboration and adapting instruction and/or materials.
- Instigate partial participation.
- Keep parental stress in mind.

Instructional Environment

- Consider whether the student would learn best in the general classroom or a special classroom.
- Consider community-based instruction.
- For deaf-blind students, evaluate the environment based on assessment of student needs, incorporate assistive technology, structure group activities to account for assistance needed for social interactions.
- Consider extended school year services needed.

Instructional Technology

- Use technology to compensate for physical disabilities and enhance communication skills.
- Consider cost, reliability, and functionality when choosing technology.
- Use adaptive technology to allow student to adjust to certain instructional/life situations.
- Consider alternative/augmentative communication aids.
- Allow time for training of student and teacher on new technology.
- Base selection of assistive technology on recent assessments of the student, environment, and equipment.

Methodologies and Strategies to Try

- Discrete Trial Teaching (p. 421)
- Massed Trial Teaching (p. 421)
- Distributed Trial Teaching (p. 421)
- Enhanced Milieu Teaching Strategies (p. 422)
- Behavior Chain Interruption Strategy (p. 422)
- Embedded Skill Instruction (p. 423)
- Partial Participation (p. 423)

Considerations for the General Classroom and Collaboration

Instruction could occur in the general classroom, a special program, or in a combination of the general classroom and a special program.

The general education teacher should:

- Show concern for the student and his or her success; believe in yourself and the student.
- Adjust the classroom and learning environment as needed.
- Select and implement adaptations and instruction to meet the goals of the team-designated interventions as well as those you may have chosen that may affect all students.
- Use teaching procedures that are effective with all students.

Collaboration

General and special educators should consult on:

- Collaborate with special education teachers when special procedures, materials, or other adaptations are needed.
- Change as needed. Don't give up on the use of some procedure or adaptation too quickly, but do change when assessment indicates progress is lacking.
- Assess student performance and teaching effectiveness regularly.

435

Chapter Summary

 Go the text's Online Learning Center at **www.mhhe.com/taylor1e** to access study resources, Web links, practice quizzes, and extending materials.

What Are the Foundations of Severe Disabilities?

- The history of individuals with severe disabilities closely mirrors that of individuals with intellectual disabilities. Until the early to mid-20th century, many individuals with severe disabilities were institutionalized. The last 50 years have seen a focus on advocating for the treatment and education of those with severe disabilities.
- There is no universally accepted definition of severe disabilities. Typically those with severe disabilities are served within the IDEA 04 categories of multiple disabilities or deaf-blindness.
- IDEA 04 defines multiple disabilities as the coexistence of impairments that results in severe educational needs that educational programs for the individual impairments cannot support.
- IDEA 04 defines deaf-blindness as the existence of both a hearing and a visual impairment that requires more educational support than programs for either individual impairment could provide.
- The prevalence of severe disabilities is estimated to be less than 1%. It is a low prevalence disability.

What Are the Causes and Characteristics of Severe Disabilities?

- The causes of severe disabilities are varied and can be caused by genetic, biological, or environmental factors. Several syndromes have been identified as often leading to severe disabilities.
- Students with severe disabilities may or may not have intellectual disabilities. Characteristics include difficulties in abstract reasoning/concepts, attention, memory, learning, and the transfer/generalization of skills.
- Students with severe disabilities may display problems in communication and in the social-personal arena.
- Behavioral characteristics of students with severe disabilities may vary considerably. Students may display stereotypical repetitive, nonpurposeful movements or self-injurious behaviors.
- Students with severe disabilities may be in poor health.
- Students who are deaf-blind may or may not have intellectual disabilities. They will often have communication problems as well as display characteristics related to their sensory needs. Deaf-blind students may also have issues with social adjustment and behavior due to deficits in communication and lack of sensory input. Specific characteristics are often influenced by the age of onset of the sensory losses.

How Are Students with Severe Disabilities Identified?

- Severe disabilities are often identified at birth.
- Individual disabilities that contribute to multiple disabilities are identified by professionals in related fields.

- Identification of severe disabilities in early childhood is often done through neonatal screening, medical evaluations, and developmental assessment batteries and scales to assess family functioning. A transdisciplinary approach is often used.
- Identification of severe disabilities in school-aged students often includes IQ testing, adaptive behavior scales, and dynamic assessments. A focus of assessment is on how well the individual functions in different environments.
- The identification of deaf-blindness is typically done by specialists in each field. The individual needs only to have significant losses, rather than being both legally deaf and blind, in both areas to be considered deaf-blind.

What and How Do I Teach Students with Severe Disabilities?

- Students with severe disabilities may participate in the general curriculum. Developmentally appropriate practice should guide the curriculum choices for young children with severe disabilities being taught in an inclusive environment.
- The general education curriculum for school-aged students with severe disabilities can be made accessible through the adaptation of learning objectives and standards and carefully selecting skills to be developed.
- Ecological inventories and functional behavior assessments are useful in determining functional curriculum objectives for students with severe disabilities.
- Alternate assessments may be more effective with students with severe disabilities than traditional assessment tools.
- Transition planning for students with severe disabilities should start early and heavily involve the student's family. Transition planning may include preparing students for postsecondary education programs, full-time competitive employment, or supported employment.
- Some instructional strategies to consider using with students with severe disabilities are teaching specific target behaviors, using naturalistic teaching strategies, implementing embedded skill instruction, and planning for partial participation.
- Students with severe disabilities will often be supported by paraprofessionals. Teachers should work closely with paraprofessionals to define and support the services they provide.
- Teachers should plan to work closely with parents of students with severe disabilities and be aware that culturally and linguistically diverse families may have different views and needs.

SUMMARY

What Are Other Instructional Considerations for Students with Severe Disabilities?

- Students with severe disabilities should be educated in natural, inclusive environments when possible. Inclusion can support communication and social skills as well as provide benefits to general classroom peers.
- Community-based instruction allows students with severe disabilities to learn skills within the inclusive environment of the community at large.
- The classroom environment for students with deaf-blindness must be planned for with both sensory limitations in mind.
- Extended school year services should be considered for students with severe disabilities.

What Are Some Considerations for the General Education Teacher?

- Many general education teachers are involved in the IEP development and daily instruction of students with severe disabilities.
- Collaboration between general education teachers, special education teachers, paraprofessionals, related services personnel, families, and others is needed for the successful inclusion of students with severe disabilities.
- Research shows that the inclusion of students with severe disabilities does not negatively affect the learning of other students in general education classrooms.

Reflection Questions

1. How do you think people with severe disabilities are perceived in society today? On what do you base your opinion? Do you think perceptions are improving or worsening?
2. Should individuals with severe disabilities be encouraged to have an active social life that might include sex and marriage? Why or why not?
3. Should public schools go to additional expense to provide community-based instruction and supervision for students with severe disabilities? Do improved adult outcomes justify such expense?
4. Should students with severe disabilities be excluded from some environments (e.g., school cafeteria) because other students might make fun of them or be disturbed by their presence (e.g., a student who drools)? Why or why not?
5. What do you think the role of general education teachers should be in promoting inclusive education for students with severe disabilities?

Application Activities: For Learning and Your Portfolio

1. (*Portfolio Possibility*) Examine your state's guidelines for the use of alternative assessments in statewide assessments mandated under the No Child Left Behind Act and the Individuals with Disabilities Education Improvement Act. Construct guidelines for a teacher of a student like David for the types of assessment activities and materials that might be gathered to provide evidence of student learning.
2. Visit a classroom that serves students with severe disabilities or an inclusive classroom that has one or more students with severe disabilities. Consider the learning objectives and activities being taught to those with disabilities and to students without disabilities. Compare and contrast how they are alike and how they are different.
3. (*Portfolio Possibility*) Construct a lesson plan in your certification/licensure area and for your grade/age level. Include adaptations and accommodations that might be needed for either a student like David or like one of the students with severe disabilities you observed in a school setting.
4. Visit a typical classroom in a school or use your own college classroom. Devise a plan for arranging the physical layout of the classroom for a student with deaf-blindness.
5. Interview a parent of a student with severe disabilities. Ask the parent how the student's disabilities have affected the student and the family. Ask the parent what his or her dreams for the student are.
6. (*Portfolio Possibility*) Create a directory of adult service providers with contact persons, phone numbers and addresses, and services provided to adults with severe disabilities. Provide sufficient information that families of students with disabilities could use this directory to assist them in obtaining services and planning for the transition of their student to adult living.

SUMMARY

CHAPTER 13

Students Who Are At Risk: Early Identification and Intervention

INTRODUCING RICKY, CODY, AND MARGARET

Ricky was born to 16-year-old LaKendra, who dropped out of school after she gave birth. LaKendra's pregnancy and delivery were smooth even though she received no prenatal care. Ricky's father, Ricky Sr., was a little older than LaKendra and tried to maintain a relationship with his son while contributing what he could to the household, including an apartment that LaKendra shares with her same-age cousin, Sharon, who also had dropped out of high school. Both cousins work part-time as servers in a nearby restaurant, and Sharon usually stays with Ricky while LaKendra is at work. Ricky Sr. and LaKendra had not been in a long-term relationship when she became pregnant, and he eventually moved across the state to be with a girlfriend who was finishing college. Starting at age 2, Little Ricky was often left home alone at night while his mother and Sharon went out to clubs. He did not have bedtimes, mealtimes, or other structure in his life. LaKendra's mother tried to help out, but she worked full-time and often put in hours at night.

When Little Ricky was 4, LaKendra's mother called Ricky Sr. to tell him that the Department of Children and Family Services was removing Ricky from the home because someone had reported LaKendra for leaving Ricky alone. Ricky Sr. picked up Little Ricky and took him across the state to live with him and his wife. Ricky Sr. and his wife welcomed Little Ricky into a supportive and structured home life and enrolled him immediately in a structured and supportive preschool program.

Cody is a 6-year-old kindergartener who is being held back from first grade because he lacks basic readiness skills such as knowing his numbers, alphabet, address, and full phone number. His mother is several years older than his father, and they divorced two years after adopting Cody. Very little is known about Cody's birth parents' genetic back-ground or medical history, but his development seemed to be on target, and he was highly verbal and very imaginative from early on. He has a good vocabulary, as evidenced by his comments, "Grand-dad, you are a scientist, so why don't you know about dinosaurs?" and "You know, Granddad, T. Rex was a carnivore." ▶

Ricky

His father, John, is a successful attorney living two hours away from where Cody's mother, Faith, moved after the divorce. John provides full financial support for both Faith and Cody. John and his parents see Cody as often as they can. They take him on trips when Faith allows, provide him with many stimulating activities, and are very responsive to him. They have found that Cody loves computer games and activities, but Faith will not allow a computer in her home.

When told of the problems that Cody was having in kindergarten, Faith said she just wants Cody to be a free spirit and cares little that Cody is having difficulties with academics because she feels that that can come later. Right now she wants him to develop his creative side. John and his parents are having Cody tested and are asking for recommendations to help Cody develop his basic readiness skills. Faith has refused to participate because, in her words, "Cody is fine, he's just not interested in reading right now; this is just something John and his family have cooked up."

Margaret is a 2-year-old twin. During her mother Isabella's pregnancy, a sonogram indicated that one baby was not receiving enough blood supply and nutrition, was too small, probably had abnormal brain ventricular development (filled with cerebrospinal fluid), and would probably have heart and lung problems. Isabella's doctor recommended that she see a perinatologist, a specialist in obstetrics who cares for high-risk babies before birth. Isabella, her husband Stanton, and her mother drove to a specialist in the next state. After viewing the sonogram, the specialist gave Isabella and Stanton three choices: (1) terminate the smaller baby, (2) do a laser procedure to separate the placental blood flowing between the two babies, or (3) do nothing. He thought there was a high probability that the smaller baby would have an intellectual disability if carried to term or would die in utero. The problem with the third choice, doing nothing, was that if the small baby died before birth, toxins could affect the larger baby. This would not be the case with the second option because the twins would be given separate blood flows. Isabella and Stanton saw this as the best option, and Isabella went almost immediately into laser surgery. After the surgery, the larger baby looked good, and the smaller baby looked no worse. For the next six weeks, a sonogram each week indicated that both baby girls were growing. At 32 weeks, the larger baby (4+ lbs.) was still growing, but the smaller baby (3 lbs.) was not. A Caesarian section was scheduled for the next day, and Isabella delivered two healthy babies breathing on their own. They stayed in the hospital for two to three weeks, and Isabella visited several times a day to learn how to feed and care for them. Stanton and both of Isbaella's parents were there almost as often. Both babies were on oxygen, under lights, and being fed with a tube. The smaller baby, Margaret, also received physical therapy. The larger baby, Lila, was removed from the supports and allowed to go home before Margaret was. Margaret was allowed to go home when she weighed in at just over 4 lbs.; her sister was then 5 lbs. 14 ozs. Once home, Margaret was taken back to the hospital for regular monitoring, and her physical therapy continued. Margaret continued to have problems with her ventricle development. Once she was strong enough, she underwent an MRI to determine if she needed surgery to fix this problem. Fortunately, Margaret did not need surgery, but she continued to be closely monitored. Lila developed normally. Margaret did the same things as Lila, but at a slower pace. For the next several months, Margaret continued to grow and catch up with Lila. Slowly, with the help of regular visits from the physical therapist, Margaret learned to walk. At 2½ years of age, Margaret is almost the same size as Lila and developmentally lags behind her less and less.

At 2½, Margaret could be considered developmentally delayed and is thus receiving early intervention. Ricky and Cody are "at risk" for developmental delays or later school failure unless they receive early intervention services. Cody is already old enough to enter school and is showing developmental delays in some areas. Providing intervention and/or special education services *after* children have experienced failure for two or three years may not be effective. By this time the child is likely to have developed low motivation, a poor self-concept, and/or disruptive behavior problems (O'Shaughnessy, Lane, Gresham, & Beebe-Frankenberger, 2002). The early signs of learning and behavior problems are evident during the preschool years, and early identification and intervention may prevent failure for many children who are at risk for school failure.

This chapter describes who children at risk are, what factors contribute to this problem, and how educators can help alleviate the impact of the risk factors and prevent later failure. Many children remain at risk for failure as they enter school, and some may later become at risk for dropping out of school. Although the major emphasis of this chapter is on infants and toddlers who are at risk for developmental delays as defined by IDEA 04, Part C, and 3- to 5-year-olds who may be served under IDEA 04, Part B, intervention at school age and adolescence is also important for many students who are still, or are just becoming, at risk. For example, consider Jorge, an English language learner who has just started first grade with no kindergarten experience, no exposure to books, and no computer access. He is still struggling to learn English and has trouble sitting in his seat and listening to his teacher. Allie is a fourth grader who comes to school hungry and tired because her parents keep her up most of the night with loud music and partying. She has trouble staying awake, much less concentrating on reading. Furthermore, she has learned that if she picks on other children, she may get sent to time-out where she has found that she can fall asleep with no one noticing. Ronnell is in ninth grade and has had to take a job at night to help support his siblings; he is finding that going to school and maintaining his job are becoming more and more difficult. He is considering dropping out or taking a job as a drug runner, which will pay a lot more for less work time. Then there's Laurel, an 11th grader who is in an abusive relationship, just like her mother's. Laurel's boyfriend threw her birth control pills away, and she now fears she is pregnant. Laurel is so afraid of what her stepfather will do to her if this is the case that she cannot concentrate on school and is considering running away—or just ending it all.

What Are the Foundations of At-Risk Conditions?

When did the recognition of and focus on at-risk children begin? Who are children at risk, and what are the factors that put them at risk? Why are early education programs so important to this group of children? We explore these questions in this section to prepare you for the second half of the chapter, which discusses what you as a teacher can do to support children who are at risk. It is important for all educators to recognize that many children may need preventive intervention to help ensure success in school and keep them from needing special education services.

A Brief History of At-Risk Conditions

The term *at risk* has been used in educational policy and programs since the 1980s; however, the concept of educational programs for children at risk had its start much earlier. J. McVicker Hunt's 1961 book, *Intelligence and Experience*, led psychologists and educators to acknowledge the importance of the environment on the development of humans (Bricker, 1986). Soon after, in 1965, the Operation Head Start program

Relevant CEC Standards

▶ Models, theories, and philosophies that form the basis for special education practice (CC1K1)

▶ Historical points of view and contribution of culturally diverse groups (CC1K8)

was launched to serve young children at risk of school failure, then referred to as "disadvantaged," as a result of living in low-income family environments (see An Important Event).

In the last decade, substantial research has been done on the potential long-term harm of at-risk conditions. The Carnegie Foundation of New York's 1994 report, *Starting Points*, highlighted the critical importance of the first three years of life and identified several major factors contributing to what it called a "quiet crisis" facing families, and infants and toddlers, in the United States. Specific factors identified included low prenatal care and immunization rates, the rising incidence of child abuse and neglect, and disturbing trends in family stability. The 2000 report, *From Neurons to Neighborhoods: The Science of Early Childhood Development* (Shankoff & Phillips, 2000), released by the National Research Council and the Institute of Medicine of the National Academies, added to the growing knowledge of how crucial the early childhood years are to healthy development. From these reports grew an ever-increasing focus on education for young children who are at risk for failure in school.

The Definition of At Risk

At risk has an official definition for children 5 years of age and younger through IDEA 04, and a generally used definition or understanding related to school-aged children and adolescents. Under IDEA 04, Part C, Early Intervention Program for Infants and Toddlers with Disabilities, participating states and jurisdictions must provide services

Relevant CEC Standard

▶ Issues in definition and identification of individuals with exceptional learning needs, including those from culturally and linguistically diverse backgrounds (CC1K5)

to young children, birth through age 2, who are currently experiencing developmental delays, and to those who have a diagnosed mental or physical condition that has a high probability of resulting in developmental delay. In addition, states are *encouraged* to serve children under age 3 who are at risk of developmental delays. Under IDEA 04, an **at-risk infant or toddler** is an individual under age 3 who would be likely to experience a substantial developmental delay if early intervention services are not provided. As you will recall from Chapter 1, under Part B of IDEA 04, preschoolers, ages 3 to 5, some of whom may have been served under Part C, are entitled to special education services if they have developmental delays in physical, cognitive, communication, social-emotional, or adaptive development. The focus of many of these services is prevention of further delays.

Only infants and toddlers can be defined by IDEA 04 as at risk, even though some of these infants and toddlers continue to be at risk throughout their school years and still other children become at risk for developmental delays or academic problems as they move through preschool and school. In school, being at risk of school failure often means the student scored below a designated level on the statewide assessment instrument. Taking a broader view, being at risk means that a child is exposed to certain factors, such as an unsettled home life or poverty, that increase the chances of academic struggle or failure. As children enter adolescence, some remain at risk or become at risk of behaviors such as dropping out of school, drug use, or pregnancy.

To support children at risk, schools with large populations of students from low-income or immigrant families qualify for additional federal funding under Title I of the Elementary and Secondary Education Act (ESEA) of 1965. According to Title I, the purpose is "to ensure that all children have a fair, equal, and significant opportunity to obtain a high-quality education and reach, at a minimum, proficiency on challenging state academic achievement standards and state academic assessments" (Sec. 1001). Schools that do not qualify for Title I funds need to ensure that the same opportunities exist for their students who at risk. Some of these children in both types of schools will not have been involved in early intervention or prevention programs.

Prevalence of Students Who Are At Risk

The number of children at risk is growing. At the end of 2005, IDEA, Part C, was serving 256,416 infants and toddlers (U.S. Department of Education, 2006). This is an increase in the number of children served since 1995 by more than 48%. In 2005, 2-year-olds were the largest proportion, representing well over half of the children served under Part C. Infants less than one year old comprised 16% of all infants and toddlers served. Overall, Part C served 1 in 40 of the birth through 2-year-old population in 2005. In 2005, more than 700,000, or 1 in 15, children ages 3 through 5 were served under Part B.

According to the 16th annual *KIDS COUNT Data Book* (Annie E. Casey Foundation, 2005), national trends in child well-being are no longer improving as they had been in the late 1990s. In fact, there are many negative trends on the rise including the 4 million children (up one million from 2000) who live with parents facing persistent unemployment that is often accompanied by domestic violence, depression, substance abuse, and prior incarceration that makes entering the workforce especially difficult. This represents a third of American children, with a range from 23% in Nebraska to 41% in Mississippi. Child poverty, perhaps the most global of all well-being indicators and a major at-risk factor, had increased in the United States to 18% (12.7 million children) in 2003. At this time, the poverty line determined by the U.S. Office of Management and Budget was $14,824 for a family of one adult and two children; however, many children from families living above the technical poverty line may still be at risk due to family income. Among the states, the child poverty rate ranged from a low of 8% in New Hampshire to a high of 30% in Louisiana. Another major risk factor is teen pregnancy. In 2003, the teen birth rate was 10% for females ages 15–19; the percentage of births to teens who were already mothers was 20%.

at-risk infant or toddler Defined by IDEA 2004 as an individual under age 3 who would be likely to experience a substantial developmental delay if early intervention services are not provided.

Considering these risk factors for school failure, which are discussed in the next section of this chapter, these data do not bode well for the number of children who may be at risk in today's schools.

Children of all ages my be at risk for school failure, but it has become clearer over time that the younger we identify these children and provide services to them, the more likely they are to be successful in school. Whether using IDEA 04's definition of at-risk younger children or a broader definition that encompasses all school-aged students, it is important for educators to recognize the influence of and increase in at-risk conditions. Recognizing that a child is at risk and planning interventions can prevent the need for special education services and/or failure in school.

Check Your Understanding

1. When did the concept of educational programs for children who are at risk begin? What term for children at risk was typically used at that time?

2. When did the term *at risk* come into use in educational programming? What brought this about?

3. How do Part C and Part B of IDEA 04 define *at risk*? Who else might be considered at risk?

4. Overall, what percentage of infants and toddlers are served under Part C of IDEA according to the latest data? Part B?

5. What is the child poverty rate in the United States? What other negative trends are on the rise?

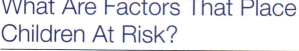

What Are Factors That Place Children At Risk?

Relevant CEC Standards

▶ Typical and atypical human growth and development (CC2K1)

▶ Educational implications of characteristics of various exceptionalities (CC2K2)

▶ Similarities and differences of individuals with and without exceptional learning needs (CC2K5)

▶ Similarities and differences among individuals with exceptional learning needs (CC2K60)

risk factors Those elements of life that can contribute to the probability of developmental delays if no intervention is provided.

Children who are at risk for school failure come from all economic, racial, ethnic, cultural, and linguistic backgrounds, although children living in poverty tend to be at higher risk than children from other economic backgrounds (*Getting Ready*, 2005; National Research Council, 2001). It is important to recognize that students are not inherently at risk; rather, they are placed at risk for developmental delays or educational failure by many factors (CRESPAR, 2006). **Risk factors,** or causal factors as they are sometimes called, are not causes per se but can contribute to the probability of developmental delays if no intervention is provided. The greater the number of risk factors, the greater the risk of a developmental delay. And the effects are not just additive, they are multiplicative, doubling or tripling the risk as they accumulate (Kauffman, 2005). As educators, we must reduce and eliminate as many of the risk factors as possible by providing parent training and supports, school-based prevention and intervention, and effective collaboration among schools, families, and communities (Walker & Sprague, 1999). Three categories of risk for developmental delay from birth through 2 years of age are frequently described by states in identifying infants and toddlers who are at risk of developmental delay: established risk, biological/medical risk, and environmental risk (Shackelford, 2006). In our discussion of these areas of risk, we address factors for children under the age of 5 who might be served under IDEA 04 and factors for older students. A range of protective factors may support children at risk, and there is no typical child at risk.

Conditions of Established Risk

IDEA 04 requires that states provide services to children with conditions for which risk for developmental delay has been established whether there is currently a delay present or not. For those with no developmental delay present, IDEA 04 includes them if they have a "diagnosed physical or mental condition which has a high probability of resulting in developmental delay." These conditions include, but are not limited to, chromosomal abnormalities; genetic or congenital disorders; severe sensory impairments, including hearing and vision; inborn errors of metabolism; disorders reflecting disturbance of the development of the nervous system; congenital infections; disorders secondary to exposure to toxic substances, including fetal alcohol syndrome; and severe attachment disorders. Congenital and chromosomal anomalies include, for example, Down syndrome, Fragile X, Klinefelter's syndrome, and Turner's syndrome. Inborn errors of metabolism include phenylketoneuria (PKU). Fetal alcohol syndrome, a result of a mother's heavy drinking during pregnancy, is strongly linked to intellectual disabilities. Several states have included other conditions, and many states use the phrase "but is not limited to" in order to allow flexibility in including other conditions (Shackelford, 2006).

Conditions of Biological/Medical Risk

States may also serve, under the optional category of at risk, children under 3 years of age who have a history of biological or medical conditions or events that result in a higher probability of developmental delay or disability. Examples that states have listed include low birth weight, intraventricular hemorrhage at birth, chronic lung disease, and failure to thrive (Shackelford, 2006). Of course, not all children with a history of any of these conditions are delayed in development. Unfortunately, some of these risks may come hand in hand with other risks, particularly environmental risks. For example, low birth weight is often related to poverty conditions that may lead to a lack of prenatal care, poor nutrition during pregnancy, and preterm birth. In 2000, 13% of black infants, 7% of white infants, and 6% of Hispanic infants had a low birth weight (Barton, 2004). The more premature the infant, the lower the birth weight and the greater the risk of developmental delay.

Conditions of Environmental Risk

Some children's caregiving circumstances and current family situation place them at greater risk for delay than the general population. As with biological or medical risk conditions, states may choose to include these children under the optional category of at risk. Examples of environmental risk factors include parental substance abuse, family instability, poverty, homelessness, violence in the home, and teen pregnancy.

The basic needs of children in homes with substance-abusing parents often go unmet.

IDEA 04 requires that children involved in substantiated child abuse or neglect, or affected by illegal substance abuse or withdrawal symptoms from prenatal drug exposure must be referred for early intervention services. Inclusion of other factors is encouraged.

Parental Substance Abuse

Alcohol and other drug abuse by the mother during pregnancy can lead to mild to severe impairments in language/communication, social/behavioral, academic/cognitive, and adaptive behavior development (Miller, 2006; Roseberry-McKibbin, 2006). Furthermore, children born of substance-abusing parents are more likely to experience physical, sexual, or emotional abuse or neglect than children in non-substance-abusing homes (Child Welfare Information Gateway, 2003). The basic needs of children in these households, including nutrition, supervision, and nurturing, often go unmet. Neglect during early development can have a profound negative effect on a child's development, particularly in the area of language acquisition (Paul, 2001). Also, parental substance abuse may lead to students who themselves use alcohol and other drugs, further placing them at a higher risk of failing in school and later in life (Mastropieri & Scruggs, 2007). It is estimated that 9% of U.S. children live with at least one parent who abuses alcohol or other drugs (Office of Applied Studies, 2003).

Family Instability

Divorce, separation, or lack of marital status may result in parents having separate living accommodations with the children moving back and forth from one home to another. This situation can disrupt established routines or require children to master the rules and routines of more than one environment. Eating, sleeping, dressing, getting to school, studying, and completing other school assignments may lack stable structures or routines. The loss of a parent or a sibling may lead to depression and confusion. Many children experience only temporary reactions to these situations, but others may have problems in school as a result of them. Family mobility may also cause problems for children. For example, migrant children often have to move from region to region depending on where the work is available that season. This may result in an inability to "get into" an established structure or routine or form nurturing relationships with adults and peers at school. Children living in poverty and those from single-parent homes are reported to have the highest school-changing rates, and frequent school changers score lower on school tests (Metropolitan Housing Council, 2004). Any of these factors may put a child at risk for problems in school.

Poverty

Children who grow up in poverty are at high risk for failure in school and life for many reasons. To begin with, the prenatal care in the first trimester of the mother's pregnancy for women living in poverty is much lower than that of higher-income women. Mothers living in poverty are often malnourished, and their children tend to grow up malnourished as well (Brice, 2002). Children living in poverty may have responsibilities such as taking care of their siblings, running errands, or housecleaning beginning at an early age. Later these students may come to school without basic needs for food, clothing, shelter, or health care being met, and they may have no educational materials or computers at home. Typically, children living in poverty have not been far out of their neighborhood, so the background knowledge needed to more easily grasp many of the concepts with which they are presented at school are limited. Poor nutrition, lack of adequate sleep, and no access to health care are all correlates of poverty that can lead to children's being at risk for developmental delays as well as later school failure. Although lead poisoning, a known cause of developmental delays, can affect children from all social and economic levels, it is a much greater risk for children of low-income families who live in older housing (Barton, 2004; CDC, 2006). Low birth weight and premature birth occur at higher rates in families living in poverty, putting these infants at risk both medically and environmentally. Children of migrant workers and other low-income, culturally and linguistically diverse families may have limited access to health care resulting in frequent illness and absences from school.

Homelessness

The fastest-growing segment of the homeless population, currently a third of this population and growing, is families with children (National Coalition for the Homeless, 2006). In 2003, children under the age of 18 accounted for nearly 40% of the homeless population with 42% of these children under the age of 5 (National Law Center on Homelessness and Poverty, 2004). Deep poverty and housing instability are especially harmful during the earliest years of childhood (Homes for the Homeless, 1998). School-aged children who are homeless face barriers to attending school that include lack of transportation, residency requirements, lack of previous school records, and limited clothing and school supplies (National Coalition for the Homeless, 2006). The principal causes of family homelessness are poverty and lack of affordable housing. Domestic violence also contributes to homelessness among families. A lack of affordable housing and long waiting lists for assisted housing means that many women must choose between abuse and homelessness. In 2000, more than half the cities surveyed by the U.S. Conference of Mayors reported that domestic violence was the primary cause of homelessness (National Coalition Against Domestic Violence, 2006). And for those families who want to stay together, over half of the cities surveyed in 2004 reported that families had to break up in order to enter emergency shelters.

Violence in the Home

Witnessing domestic violence has resulted in adverse effects on cognitive, social, emotional, and behavioral functioning of children (O'Keefe & Lebovics, 2005). Specific problems include deficits in problem solving, low self-esteem, lack of empathy, poor academic performance, difficulties in concentration, and school phobia (Edelson, 1999). Multiple risk factors are often present in these homes. Other factors may include child physical and sexual abuse, parental alcohol and drug use, high levels of verbal conflict, poverty, parental psychiatric disorders, and child neglect (Wolfe, 1997).

Teen Pregnancy

Teenage pregnancy, or children having children, is a risk factor that continues at high rates and cuts across all racial, ethnic, and socioeconomic strata. Not only do many of these teenagers drop out of school, they also have little experience and are often too immature for the responsibilities of parenting. Furthermore, a recent study of 120 low-income pregnant and parenting teens found that nearly half had been pushed or shoved, close to 1 in 5 had been punched or hit with something that could hurt, and 1 in 25 had had a knife or gun used on them (Kennedy & Bennett, 2006). A strong relationship has also been reported between teen mothers on welfare and abusive control on the part of their male partners through work-related, school-related, or birth-control-related sabotage to better ensure their isolation and dependence on the male partner (Raphael, 2005).

Child Abuse or Neglect

Each state provides its own definitions of child abuse and neglect, but federal legislation provides a foundation for states by defining a minimum set of acts or behaviors to be included: (1) any recent act or failure to act on the part of a parent or caretaker that results in death, serious physical or emotional harm, sexual abuse or exploitation; or (2) an act or failure to act that presents an imminent risk of serious harm. Most states recognize four major types of mistreatment (Child Welfare Information Gateway, 2006). **Neglect** is failure to provide for a child's basic needs and may be physical (e.g., lack of food, shelter, or appropriate supervision), medical

neglect Failure to provide for a child's basic needs, which may be medical, educational, or emotional.

(e.g., lack of medical or mental health treatment), educational (e.g., lack of education or special education services), or emotional (e.g., lack of psychological care or protection from alcohol or other drug use). **Physical abuse** is physical injury as a result of punching, beating, kicking, biting, shaking, throwing, stabbing, choking, hitting, burning, or otherwise harming a child. Whether the physical harm is intended is a consideration. **Sexual abuse** includes activities such as fondling a child's genitals, penetration, incest, rape, sodomy, indecent exposure, or exploitation through prostitution or production of pornographic materials. **Emotional abuse** is a pattern of behavior that impairs a child's emotional development or sense of self-worth. This may include constant criticism, threats, or rejection as well as withholding love, support, or guidance. Emotional abuse is almost always present with other forms of abuse. The rate of child abuse in 2003 was 12.4 per 1,000 children, with children under 3 having the highest rates of victimization at 16.4 per 1,000 children (U.S. Department of Health and Human Services, 2005). Child abuse and neglect can have devastating effects on children's emotional and cognitive development. Child victims have an increased risk for adverse health effects such as smoking, alcoholism, drug abuse, eating disorders, severe obesity, depression, suicide, and sexual promiscuity (National Center for Injury Prevention and Control, 2005). The most severe consequence is, of course, death. In 2003, 1,169 children were reported to have died as a result of abuse or neglect (U.S. Department of Health and Human Services, 2005). Children with disabilities are at a higher risk for maltreatment than children without disabilities (Goldson, 2001). Table 13.1 summarizes possible physical and behavioral indicators of abuse.

School Factors

At school age, children at risk may be placed further at risk by entering a school that is unsupportive and unresponsive to students' needs and has low expectations for them. Failure in school at a young age often has lifelong consequences including many of the factors mentioned earlier, such as low self-esteem, teen pregnancy, drug and alcohol abuse, and unemployment (National Association for Bilingual Education [NABE], 2004). Having teachers with at least five years' experience is related to positive school achievement, yet minority and low-income students are more likely to be taught by teachers with three or fewer years of experience and to be in schools with higher teacher turnover (Barton, 2004). Students in high-poverty schools are much more likely to be taught by out-of-field teachers in larger classes. Many teachers in schools serving low-income, black children have been found to be too inflexible in their expectations (Ferguson, 1998). This is often due to a lack of understanding or acceptance of cultural differences and a lack of knowledge of the effects of risk factors on children. Beegle (2003) reports that in a survey of people who grew up in generational poverty and later achieved success through higher education, the respondents noted, among other things, that most elementary and high school teachers "didn't care" and perceived that they "didn't know what to do with kids like them." The atmosphere of the school, and the home, need to communicate the value of academics and create excitement about learning, and this would seem less likely to occur in the schools described above. Other risk factors in schools include daily schedules that are not followed, principals who are uninterested in curricula and uninvolved in teacher recruitment and professional development, lack of full use of libraries and other media resources, and few systems of public reward for students' academic excellence (Snow, Burns, & Griffin, 1998).

English as a Second Language

The stakes are especially high for children who are English language learners (ELLs), who must master academic content and a new language at the same time. The time it takes to learn a new language varies from child to child and depends on such factors as age, motivation, personality, knowledge of first language, and exposure to English (Santos & Ostrosky, 2003). Learning to read in a language in which the child is not proficient is an added risk factor for many children. In 2004, nearly 1 in 5 U.S. children

TABLE 13.1 Possible Physical and Behavioral Indicators of Abuse

TYPE OF ABUSE	PHYSICAL INDICATORS	BEHAVIORAL INDICATORS
Physical Abuse	• Injuries (bruises, welts, bite marks, etc.) not consistent with explanation of cause • Injuries in various stages of healing • Unexplained burns (cigarettes, scalding water, electric curler, etc.) • Delayed or inappropriate treatment of injuries • Regular occurrence of injuries after absence, weekend, vacation	• Runaway attempts, fear of going home, early arrival to school • Extremes of behavior—aggressive or withdrawn • Self-deprecating, self-destructive, sad, cries often • Abusive behavior and language in play • Wearing long sleeves or other concealing clothing inappropriate for weather • Overly compliant, eager to please
Physical Neglect	• Lags in physical development • Poor hygiene, consistent hunger, unattended medical needs • Regular absences or tardiness • Consistent lack of supervision	• Constant fatigue, listlessness, falling asleep at school • Depression, loneliness, demands for constant attention and affection • Begging or stealing food • Overly adaptive behavior • Irrational behavior, poor impulse control
Sexual Abuse	• Difficulty sitting or walking • Fatigue, sudden weight change • Unusual or excessive itching in genital or anal area • Suspicious stains, blood on underwear or clothing • Unexplained pregnancy in nonsexually active child • Repeated urinary infections, pain during elimination	• Unwillingness to change clothes for gym • Extremely passive or aggressive • Sophisticated or unusual sexual behavior or knowledge, excessive seductiveness • Low self-esteem, distrust or fear of adults, self-injurious behaviors • Poor peer relationships • Wears provocative clothing or layers of clothing
Emotional Abuse	• Bedwetting and/or diarrhea • Headaches, nausea, abdominal pain, severe allergies • Failure to thrive (physically, emotionally) • Substance abuse	• Antisocial, destructive behaviors • Fear of failure, overly high standards, excessive neatness • Severe depression • Poor peer relationships • Extreme attention-seeking

Sources: Child Prevention Website: www.safekidsbc.ca; The Crisis Call Center: www.crisiscallcenter.org/crisisweb/child_abuse_indicators.htm; Nova Scotia Department of Justice: www.gov.ns.ca/just/childAbuse.htm; State of Kentucky: http://ag.ky.gov/NR/rdonlyres/1A6EA72A-D081-4155-97DB-88638DF61510/0/AbuseIndicatorBrochure.pdf; Committee for Children: www.cfchildren.org/artriclef/flynn

ages 5 to 17 spoke a language other than English at home, and a reported 1 in 20 children had difficulty speaking English, ranging from 0% in Mississippi to 12% in California (Annie E. Casey Foundation, 2005). The need for strong interaction between parents of English language learners and the school is well recognized, and it is important that those interactions be culturally sensitive (Jordan, Reyes-Blanes, Peel, Peel, & Lane, 1998).

Protective Factors

Over time, particularly with no early identification, prevention, or intervention programs, risk factors can lead to negative, destructive outcomes. Figure 13.1 illustrates how a path from early exposure to one or more risk factors may lead to later destructive, longer-term outcomes. However, none of these risk factors invariably causes a

RICKY, CODY, AND MARGARET REVISITED Based on the three case studies at the beginning of the chapter, under which of the three categories frequently used by states to identify children for services under IDEA 04, Part C, might each of the children be eligible for services? Are any of these children in a required services category?

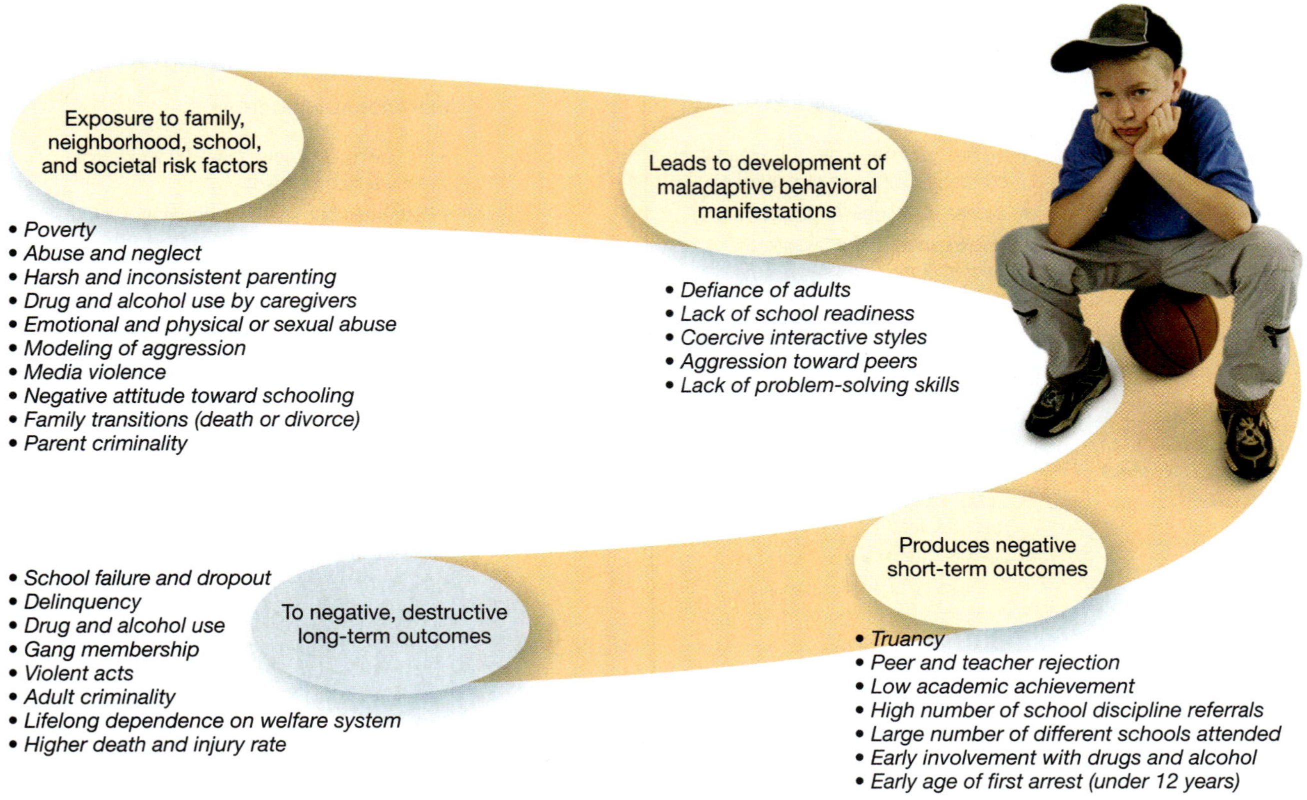

FIGURE 13.1 The Path to Long-Term Negative Outcomes for At-Risk Children and Youth

Source: Walker, H. M., & Sprague, J. R. (1999). *Intervention in School and Clinic, 35*(2), 67–73, fig. 1. Copyright 1999 by the Hammill Institute on Disability. Reprinted with permission.

protective factors Factors that may intervene with the harm caused by risk factors, explaining the resiliency of some children.

delay or disability. Although the addition of risk factors increases the risk, the concept of heightened risk is not a simple cause-effect relationship and may vary with each individual (Kauffman, 2005).

Protective factors, those that may help children be resilient enough to overcome risk factors, that may intervene include the child's temperament (low emotionality and high sociability), high self-esteem, school competence, good emotional relationship with at least one parent, and perceived social support (Levendosky, Huth-Boocks, & Semel, 2002; O'Keefe, 1998). In an in-depth study on the homeless, one trend emerged over all: education is a strong predictor of the stability of family structure *and* of a family's ability to rise out of poverty and become independent (Homes for the Homeless, 1995). Factors that may protect children from abuse and neglect include good health, an above-average intelligence, hobbies or interests, good peer relationships, an easy temperament, a positive disposition, an active coping style, positive self-esteem, good social skills, an internal locus of control, and a balance between seeking help and autonomy (Child Welfare Information Gateway, 2004). Table 13.2 presents a list of protective factors associated with antisocial and criminal behavior that operate across child, family, school, and community.

Profile of an At-Risk Child

There is no one profile of an at-risk child. The National Early Intervention Longitudinal Study (NEILS) of Part C of IDEA 04 early intervention programs found that although the children come from a diverse range of families, a disproportionately high number of the children being served are males from low-income families, children who are ethnic minorities, and those in foster care (Scarborough et al., 2004). Eligibility data for infants and toddlers showed 62% were eligible for IDEA 04, Part C,

TABLE 13.2	Protective Factors Associated with Antisocial and Criminal Behavior

CHILD FACTORS	FAMILY FACTORS	SCHOOL CONTEXT	COMMUNITY AND CULTURAL FACTORS
• Social competence • Social skills	• Supportive, caring parents • Family harmony	• Positive school climate • Prosocial peer group	• Access to support services • Community networking
• Above-average intelligence	• More than two years between siblings	• Responsibility and required helpfulness	• Attachment to community
• Attachment to family	• Responsibility for chores or required helpfulness	• Sense of belonging/bonding	• Participation in church or other community group
• Empathy	• Secure and stable family	• Opportunities for success at school and recognition of achievement	• Community/cultural norms against violence
• Problem-solving ability	• Supportive relationship with other adult	• School norms against violence	• Strong cultural identity and ethnic pride
• Optimism	• Small family size		
• School achievement	• Strong family norms and morality		
• Easy temperament			
• Internal locus of control			
• Moral beliefs			
• Values			
• Self-related cognitions			
• Good coping style			

Source: Walker, H. M., Ramsey, E., & Gresham, F. M. (2004). *Antisocial behavior in schools: Evidenced-based practices* (2nd ed.). Reprinted with permission of Wadsworth, a division of Thomson Learning: www.thomsonrights.com. Fax 800-730-2215.

services because of developmental delay, 22% because of diagnosed medical conditions, and 17% for reasons related to biomedical conditions and/or environmental factors placing them at risk of developmental delay. Nearly one-third of the children found eligible had low birth weight, 4 times the rate in the general population, and the infants and toddlers were 8 times more likely to be rated as having fair or poor general health. Children who were eligible because of developmental delays began services as toddlers, whereas those eligible because of diagnosed conditions or biological or environmental risk factors tended to begin in the first year of life. The variability of the data from NEILS indicates teachers need to keep in mind that there is no typical child in these early intervention programs.

Check Your Understanding

1. What are the three categories of risk for developmental delay frequently described by states for children from birth through age 2?

2. What are some conditions of established risk? Biological/medical risk?

3. What are the environmental risk factors for which IDEA 04 requires intervention? What are some other environmental risk factors for older students?

4. What is a protective factor? Give a few examples.

5. Who do data indicate is the typical child in early intervention programs?

How Are Children Who Are At Risk Identified?

Relevant CEC Standards

► Issues in definition and identification of individuals with exceptional learning needs, including those from culturally and linguistically diverse backgrounds (CC1K5)

► Screening, prereferral, referral, and classification procedures (CC8K3)

► Use and limitations of assessment instruments (CC8K4)

Age-old concerns about identifying students with early academic and behavioral problems still exist. Kauffman (2005) lists some beliefs and concerns related to early identification of behavior problems that are also applicable to early identification of learning problems resulting from at-risk conditions:

- Some people prefer to maintain "developmental optimism" in the face of signs that a young child is at high risk: "He'll grow out of it," "It's just a phase she's going through." *Research finds that learning problems tend to worsen as children age* (see An Important Event).
- Others worry about the stigma associated with any identification of deviance or risk status. *Their concerns about avoiding the stigma of identification may prevent intervention, not the development of the disorder.*
- Some people worry that to predict or anticipate something is to make it happen. *However, it is impossible to prevent what we do not anticipate.*
- Early screening, identification, and intervention are costly and one should not be provided without the other. *Early intervention can be expensive, but so are the prisons and necessary welfare support where some children at risk may end up without intervention.*

Kauffman states that early intervention is the essence of prevention and needs to occur before problems become very serious. Over time, the recommended age of early intervention for prevention has moved from early school grades, to preschool and kindergarten, to infants and toddlers.

AN IMPORTANT EVENT

1996—Longitudinal Study Answers the Question, "Do 'Late Bloomers' Catch Up?"

To investigate whether low-achieving children can catch up academically to their peers, Francis, Shaywitz, Stuebing, Shaywitz, and Fletcher (1996) tracked 403 students from 12 communities in Connecticut from grades 1 to 9. In third grade, students were designated as *low-achieving, reading disabled-discrepant,* or *not reading impaired,* depending on their reading scores. Reading scores were analyzed at each grade for evidence of either a developmental lag or a skill deficit. If the developmental lag theory were correct, students who were behind would eventually catch up. Data clearly demonstrated that, on average, neither the low-achieving nor the reading disabled-discrepant students ever caught up to their peers who were not reading impaired. This study finally put to rest the developmental lag theory: Students do not naturally "catch up" on their own.

REFLECTION What are the implications of this research for preventing future reading disabilities?

The Identification of Infants and Toddlers At Risk

Under Part C of IDEA 04, states must identify and provide services for children from birth through 2 years of age who are experiencing developmental delays, such as a 20-month-old who is not walking yet, and to those who have a diagnosed mental or physical condition with a high probability of developmental delays, such as a child who is born deaf or blind. In addition, *at their discretion,* states may choose to identify and serve infants and toddlers who are at risk of experiencing developmental delays.

The task of identifying children at the infant and toddler stage and providing services to their families has been a major challenge for states. Over the past few years, definitions and eligibility criteria have been narrowed by some states and expanded by others. The added challenge of serving children under age 3 who are at risk of developmental delays has resulted in fears of highly increased numbers of identified children and the related increases in cost. As of July 2005, only eight of the fifty states and six jurisdictions that participate in the Part C program were serving infants and toddlers who fall under the optional category of at risk for developmental delays (Shackleford, 2006). However, several states, including Mississippi and Idaho, indicate that they will monitor the development of these children and refer them for early intervention services as delays are manifested, and some states, including Alaska, are serving these children through collaboration with other programs such as Early Head Start. Michigan and some other states allow local service areas to choose whether to serve this population. A concern of many is that young children will develop well-established patterns of problem behaviors if not identified and served while they are still at a level of risk. The lack of early prevention intervention diminishes the effectiveness of later services (Conroy & Brown, 2004). It is anticipated that in the future many more states will be serving infants and toddlers who are at risk of developmental delays.

Part C of IDEA 04 specifies the developmental areas—physical, communication, cognitive, social or emotional, and adaptive—that are to be included in definitions of developmental delay for infants and toddlers, but each state must identify appropriate diagnostic instruments, procedures (including informed clinical opinion), and levels of functioning or other criteria used to determine eligibility. An example of an instrument that assesses all of these areas in children from birth to 8 years of age is the Battelle Developmental Inventory, Second Edition (BDI–2; Newborg, 2004). It is available in both English and Spanish.

A review of state eligibility definitions by Shackleford (2006) reveals many differences among states. Most states express quantitative criteria for identifying delays, such as differences in chronological age and actual performance level expressed as a percentage, or performance at a specified number of months or standard deviations below age mean; some use a more qualitative description of delay indicated by atypical development or observed atypical behaviors. For example, Indiana very specifically requires 2.0 standard deviations in one area or 25% below chronological age, or 1.5 standard deviations in two areas or 20% below chronological age in two areas; Colorado requires a significant delay in one or more developmental domains with "significant delay" meaning development determined by qualified personnel to be outside the range of "normal" or "typical" for a same-age peer. There is a wide range in the level of delay required by states that have quantitative criteria. Because there are so few reliable and valid instruments for the birth through 2 age group, and questionable predictive validity for available instruments, Part C requires that all states must include *informed clinical opinion* as a determination. Several states specify this option alone.

The Identification of Young Children At Risk

Nearly 7 in 10 infants and toddlers being served by Part C are eligible to transfer to Part B services when they turn 3. The number of children receiving services through Part B, serving children ages 3 to 5, has increased steadily since 1991 (U.S. Department of Education, 2003b). These children are often at risk of school failure for learning and/or emotional-social problems. Over the last two decades, much information has been accumulated on identifying in young children some key antecedents to later academic and behavioral problems (O'Shaughnessy, Lane, Gresham, & Beebe-Frankenberger, 2003). For example, inefficient phonological awareness skills in young children are highly predictive of later reading difficulties, and noncompliance and antisocial behavioral patterns are reliable predictors of later behavior problems, indicating that children who exhibit these characteristics are at risk for school failure.

Literacy Measures

Schools have many individually administered early screening assessments that are appropriate for students in kindergarten through third grade. In kindergarten, assessment covers early reading skills such as letter-name knowledge, phonemic awareness, letter-sound knowledge, and vocabulary. After reading instruction begins in first grade, the ability to read words accurately and fluently should be measured, and by the end of first grade, oral reading fluency should be measured (Torgesen, 2004).

As you may recall from Chapter 4, in 2000, the National Reading Panel reviewed a large number of studies and identified five key components of effective reading instruction: phonemic awareness, phonics, fluency, vocabulary, and text comprehension. Based on these findings, Reading First, part of the 2000 reauthorization of the Elementary and Secondary Education Act, provides funds to states to implement plans for improving reading achievement through research-based literacy instruction. Many instruments for kindergarten through third grade are designed to assess the five essential components of reading listed in the National Reading Panel report. Examples of instruments found to be sufficient for reading screening in the early years include the Dynamic Indicators of Basic Early Literacy Skills (DIBELS–5; Good, Kaminski, Smith, Laimon, & Dill, 2001), which identifies students at risk for failure to read by individually assessing fluency of phonological awareness, knowledge of letter names, and word attack skills in Pre-K to second grade, and the Early Reading Diagnostic Assessment, Second Edition (ERDA–Second Edition; Psychological Corporation, 2003),which evaluates all five essential components of reading in kindergarten through third grade and is also available in Spanish. Another instrument that meets the requirements of the Early Reading First and Reading First initiatives is the Pre-Reading Inventory of Phonological Awareness (PIPA; Dodd, Crosbie, McIntosh, Teitzel, & Ozanne, 2003), which is designed for use with children ages 4 through 6. It is an easy-to-administer inventory of phonological awareness skills including rhyme awareness, syllable segmentation, alliteration awareness, sound isolation, sound segmentation, and letter-sound knowledge. With the current mandates for reading proficiency, many instruments are becoming available to assess the literacy needs of young children at risk of failure in school.

Behavioral Measures

Early identification of children at risk for behavior problems is extremely important. The longer students are allowed to be aggressive, defiant, and destructive, the more difficult it is to change this behavior. Reaching just 8 years of age without preventative intervention may mean that bad behavior becomes a lifelong condition (Walker, Ramsey, & Gresham, 2003-2004). The Early Screening Project (Walker, Severson, & Feil, 1995) is a group-administered instrument used to identify Pre-K to kindergarten students at risk for externalizing or internalizing behavioral problems. It assesses these behaviors in structured and unstructured settings. The Systematic Screening for Behavior Disorders (Walker & Severson, 1990) has three "gates" for identifying the most troubled children in grades 1 to 6. Gates 1 and 2 identify both externalizing and internalizing behavior patterns through teacher ratings; at Gate 3, a school psychologist, school counselor, social worker, or another trained observer completes ratings to determine the appropriate intensive intervention.

Although there are concerns about early identification of children, research has indicated its grave importance. The sooner children are able to receive support for any problems, the more likely they are to be able to overcome them. However, some of these children, whether identified or not, will still be at risk of failure when they enter elementary school. Others will become at risk after they begin elementary or even secondary school. The identification of and support for these children continues to be important.

Check Your Understanding

1. What are some of the concerns about early identification? Have these concerns been justified?

2. In general, how are infants and toddlers who are at risk identified by most states?

3. What are the developmental areas that are to be included in definitions of developmental delay for infants and toddlers for IDEA 04, Part C?

4. What areas of assessment are included in identifying young children as being at risk?

What and How Do I Teach Students Who Are At Risk?

Although IDEA 04 defines children at risk as infants and toddlers, most research on best practices for young children who are at risk includes children ages 0 to 6, and thus that age range is the major focus of the content and procedures presented here. However, even with early intervention, follow-through studies have demonstrated that we need to continue programming for school-aged children and adolescents. Some of these students may have at-risk conditions that persist, and others may encounter new at-risk conditions as they age. For those children who are at risk of school failure or dropping out after they reach school age, many, if not most, of the procedures presented in other chapters will be relevant for prevention intervention before students are given a disability label. Some of these procedures include the direct instruction and cognitive strategies found in Chapter 4, functional skills in Chapter 5, behavioral management techniques in Chapter 6, and the self-regulatory techniques in Chapter 14.

Instructional Content

Children who are at risk will take part in the general education curriculum. Depending on individual needs, children at risk are likely to require additional support in the areas of language and literacy skills, mathematical skills, and social/behavioral control. In addition, it is essential that the teacher include family involvement to support the child.

Language and Literacy Skills

In 2005, almost two in five fourth graders scored below the basic reading level (Annie E. Casey Foundation, 2005). This is an alarming figure, particularly in light of the fact that nearly three-quarters of students who do not possess basic early literacy skills by the end of third grade will continue to struggle with reading throughout school and into adulthood (Bryant, 2003). Furthermore, possible negative outcomes associated with reading failure include school failure, teacher and peer rejection, substance abuse, and school dropout. The significance of the development of language and literacy in early childhood is very clear. Foundational skills that are key to kindergarten success in learning to read include language, such as understanding and using vocabulary; phonological awareness, or sensitivity to sounds and sound combining; and knowledge about print, including letter names and the realization that letters have sounds. If children receive appropriate exposure in these areas,

The significance of literacy development in early childhood is very clear.

as few as 5% may experience serious reading difficultly later (Snow et al., 1998). As children develop early language and literacy skills, the focus should move toward the other key components of the National Reading Panel report: phonics, fluency, vocabulary, and comprehension.

Mathematical Skills

With the current reading initiatives, we must remember to include math proficiency. Students' math skills are a little better than reading, but not much. More than one in five fourth graders scored below the basic math level in 2005, and just over a third scored at or above proficient math level (Annie E. Casey Foundation, 2005). The significance of math success is illustrated by the fact that when 62 high school dropouts in a West Virginia Job Corps program were asked what caused them to quit school, most answered "mathematics" (Viadero, 2005). Important early concepts in math include a heavy emphasis on number sense and vocabulary. These concepts should be included in programs that are attempting to increase a child's readiness for school.

Social and Behavioral Control

Factors that are associated with children's success in school include self-confidence, a willingness to try new things and persist at difficult tasks; an ability to develop and maintain relationships with peers and adults, and cooperate and participate in group settings; and an ability to communicate emotions (Bowman, Donovan, & Burns, 2000; Shonkoff & Phillips, 2000). In 2005, a study of almost 4,000 kindergarten classrooms revealed that prekindergarten students are expelled at a rate more than three times that of their older peers in grades K–12 (Gilliam, 2005). Most children with budding behavior problems begin to display them during the preschool years, placing them at risk for peer rejection, teacher rejection, limited opportunities for learning appropriate behavior in school, and continued problems as they get older (Kaufman, 2005; Walker et al., 2004). It is imperative that social and behavioral goals be a part of early childhood intervention for students who are at risk for school failure and need support in this area.

Family Involvement

There is ample research demonstrating that family involvement is an essential aspect of the success of programs that attempt to reduce the chance of school failure in children who are at risk (National Research Council, 2001; Weiss, Caspe, & Lopez, 2006). The current research base indicates that family involvement can be strengthened to bring about positive outcomes for young children's readiness for school through three family involvement processes (Weiss, Caspe, & Lopez, 2006). These include nurturing and responsive parent attitudes, values, and practices in raising young children (parenting); both formal and informal connections between the family and the educational setting (home–school relationships); and parental emphasis on activities in the home and community that promote learning skills (responsibility for learning). Practices associated with responsibility for learning, specifically home-based family involvement, have been shown to be perhaps the strongest predictor of child outcomes in motivation to learn, attention, task persistence, receptive vocabulary skills, and low conduct problems (Fantuzzo, McWayne, & Perry, 2004). These practices included reading to a child at home, providing a place for educational activities, and asking the child about school.

Raising a Reader is a successful home-based program developed for low-income families, which is supported by the nonprofit organization of Peninsula Community Foundation in San Mateo County, California. Raising a Reader engages parents in daily "book cuddling" with their children from birth through 5 years of age. Bright red bags filled with high-quality picture books bursting with bright artwork, age-appropriate

RICKY, CODY, AND MARGARET REVISITED What components of early intervention programs do you think will be most important for Ricky? What about for Cody? And Margaret? Explain each of your responses.

Name: Zack X

Date of Evaluation: 01-02-07

Date of Birth: 07-19-05

CA: 2y, 5m, 13d

Your Family's Outcomes

OUTCOME 1. What would you like to see happen for your child and family as a result of Early Steps supports and services?
Parents would like Zack to say daddy or mommy when he wakes up in the morning.

TIMELINES/CRITERIA FOR PROGRESS: When will we review progress toward this outcome, and what will progress look like?
Goal will be met when Zack is saying mommy or daddy by his 3rd birthday.

STRATEGIES: Who will do what within your child's everyday routines, activities, and places to achieve this outcome?
Speech therapist will educate family on age-appropriate development.
Speech therapist will evaluate Zack to determine needed services.
Speech therapist and family will create a reward system to motivate Zack.

LOCATION OF SERVICES: Home

Your Family's Outcomes

OUTCOME 2. What would you like to see happen for your child and family as a result of Early Steps supports and services?
Parents would like Zack to follow directions when parents instruct him to do something.

TIMELINES/CRITERIA FOR PROGRESS: When will we review progress toward this outcome, and what will progress look like?
Goal will be met when Zack is following adult-directed instructions by his 3rd birthday.

STRATEGIES: Who will do what within your child's everyday routines, activities, and places to achieve this outcome?
Special instructor will educate family on age-appropriate development.
Special instructor and family will create reward system to motivate him to follow directions.

LOCATION OF SERVICES: Home

Your Family's Outcomes

OUTCOME 3. What would you like to see happen for your child and family as a result of Early Steps supports and services?
Dad would like Zack to play with toys without putting them in his mouth.

TIMELINES/CRITERIA FOR PROGRESS: When will we review progress toward this outcome, and what will progress look like?
Goal will be met when Zack is playing with toys and not mouthing them by his 3rd birthday.

STRATEGIES: Who will do what within your child's everyday routines, activities, and places to achieve this outcome?
Occupational therapist will educate family on age-appropriate development.
Occupational therapist and family will work on attending and imitating.

LOCATION OF SERVICES: Home

Source: Provided by Early Steps Intervention Program, Palm Beach County, Florida, 2007.

PRACTICE

language, and multicultural themes are brought into the home on a weekly basis. Parents, even those with limited or poor reading skills or poor English proficiency, are taught read-aloud strategies to use with their children. The program has expanded into libraries, child-care centers, Head Start programs, teen mother programs, and home visiting nurse programs in many communities, many states, and other countries. Independent evaluations show that Raising a Reader has resulted in significant improvements in kindergarten readiness and family reading behavior.

Individual Family Service Plan

As you may recall from Chapter 2, the equivalent of an individualized educational program (IEP) for infants and toddlers with disabilities is an individual family service plan (IFSP). Among other things, this plan must indicate specific goals for the child in the early intervention program, a summary of the family's strengths and needs, and a list of strategies to be used. The IFSP often addresses the areas of language development, preliteracy skills, premathematical skills, and social/behavioral control and how the family will be involved in planning and implementing these goals. See the Intervention Example for a sample of goals of an IFSP at the infant/toddler stage.

Instructional Procedures

Without early intervention, many young children who are at risk may continue to be at risk throughout school. Family service components of early intervention programs are essential for success. Procedures for the development of language and literacy skills and social/behavioral skills will often need to be included in these early intervention programs.

Universal Design for Learning

All teachers, whether or not a child with exceptionalities or at-risk conditions has been identified in their class, should routinely design instruction and materials that can meet the needs of all students before they fail. An instructional planning philosophy that embraces this is Universal Design for Learning (UDL) presented in Chapter 1. This approach can facilitate prevention, a major goal in early intervention, although other levels of intervention may be necessary to meet the needs of all children. When using UDL, the teacher focuses on initially designing instruction that provides all learners with various ways of acquiring information and knowledge, alternatives for demonstrating what they know, and multiple means of engagement through tapping into learners' interests, offering appropriate challenges, and increasing motivation (Center for Applied Special Technology [CAST], 2006). This is an alternative to making accommodations for different learning styles only after they have been identified; in other words, it is intervention for prevention. UDL makes education more inclusive and effective for all. As you will recall from Chapter 6, a universal intervention is a schoolwide or whole classroom strategy used for all students with and without disabilities and from culturally and linguistically diverse backgrounds. Establishing progressive intervention levels can be an effective way for schools to coordinate general and special educators, provide intervention that ensures a match between instruction and a child's current level, and adjust intervention based on an individual's progress (O'Shaugnessy et al., 2003). Well-implemented universal interventions are successful for about 80% to 90% of all students who may be at risk for more serious behavior problems (Sugai, Horner, & Gresham, 2002).

Prevention

prevention An outcome of the process of intervention in an effort to avert learning and/or emotional and social disorders.

The goal for education of children at risk is prevention. **Prevention** is an outcome of the process of intervention in an effort to avert learning and/or emotional or social disorders. There are three types of prevention: *primary prevention*, with the goal of preventing harm; *secondary prevention*, with the goal of reversing harm; and *tertiary prevention*, more intensive work with the goal of reducing harm (Walker & Severson, 2002). At the primary or universal level of prevention, all young children and their families receive regular and adequate health care and guidance, screening and monitoring of development, parenting advice and support, high-quality early education and care, and guidance as the child begins to interact with others. Early educators should maintain predictable schedules, minimize transitions, provide visual reminders of the rules, give attention for appropriate behavior, provide choices, and maximize child engagement. In other words, a universal design should be in place. However, even at the infant stage and toddler age, some students will need secondary, or more intensive, prevention (Kauffman, 2005). Secondary prevention for students at risk may include community programs such as parenting classes; child development education through pamphlets or videos; resource support for families who have multiple risk factors; or professionally guided playgroups. Even when teachers implement these practices, a few children are likely to continue to display challenging behavior (Fox, Dunlap, Hemmeter, Joseph, & Strain, 2003), leading to the need for a third level of intervention. At the tertiary level, when children are at high risk and are showing evidence of the existence of delays in social and behavioral development, focused intervention efforts should be provided by home visitors who help families learn critical skills to support their children's development and by professionals who work with the children to model useful strategies and techniques for the family. Early educators collaborate with families to provide assessment-based positive behavior support (Fox, 2006a, 2006b). These interventions, which must consider the cultural context of the family, usually include teaching families interaction skills to assist infants and toddlers in coping with difficult situations, understanding routines, and supporting the child's language and social development (Fox, 2006b).

Early Intervention/Prevention Programs

Parents and caregivers from all backgrounds want their children to succeed in school (O'Shaugnessy et al., 2003), and early intervention is essential for children who are at risk. Without early intervention, many of these children will undoubtedly continue to be at risk throughout school. In a synthesis of research on early intervention/prevention for young children 0 to 6 years of age who are at risk or who have challenging behaviors, Smith and Fox (2003) report that effective early education prevention programs include both a child and family service component. They are center based and provide quality programs with low teacher–child ratios and well-trained staff. Effective intervention programs provide instruction to both parents and children. Intervention for children concentrates on appropriate social skills, compliance, self-regulation, and academic engagement. Programs for children 3 to 5 years of age were found to have positive effects, and the effects were maintained as the children grew older.

One example of a successful early intervention program is the Perry Preschool Project, which took place in Michigan between 1962 and 1967. The program was for

Effective early intervention programs include both child and family services.

3- and 4-year-old, mostly African American low-income children with no visible handicapping conditions who were considered at high risk of school failure (Weikert, Bond, & McNeil, 1978). Intervention involved a half-day preschool every weekday plus a weekly 90-minute home visit, both for eight months of the year for two years. The program group significantly outperformed the no-program group on various intellectual and language tests from their preschool years up to age 7, and on school achievement tests at ages 9 and 10. Graduates of the program have been followed for three decades. The intervention had positive effects on grades, high school graduation rates, and earnings, as well as negative effects on crime rates and welfare use at ages 27 and 40 and higher rates of employment, income, and home ownership for those in the intervention than those who were not. Another early model program was the Carolina Abecedarian Project for infants and children through age 5 that was conducted in North Carolina from 1972 to 1985 (described in Chapter 5). The Abecedarian Project, as you may recall, demonstrated that early prevention intervention can be successful. Furthermore, half the children in the treatment group received another three years' of follow-up intervention after school entrance. This program consisted of assigning a teacher to attend the school on alternate weeks to talk with the children's general education teacher and then visit the parents to provide them with learning activities to reinforce what was going on in the classroom. Those children who received both preschool and school-age services outscored the children who received preschool services alone on both intellectual and achievement measures.

Over time, research has indicated that the family service components of effective early intervention programs for parents concentrate on behavior management, increasing positive interactions, increasing children's prosocial behavior, and strategies to guide and support their children's development. Services and supports for families include parenting education and support groups, peer mentors, child care, respite care, and home visiting. Program staff assist in identifying and accessing community resources and coordinate and collaborate with these programs. Parents who receive services and intervention in positive interactions with their children are more emotionally supportive, less detached, and have more positive interactions with their children than parents who do not receive services (Dunst & Kassow, 2004; Love et al., 2002). Furthermore, a responsive, sensitive, and nurturing caregiver style by the parents, caregivers, and early educators has been found to have a positive influence on young children's cognitive and social-emotional development (Fox, 2006a; Trivette, 2003). Three skills are particularly important in teaching parents to become sensitive to their children's intent to communicate or interact: awareness/attentiveness to their children's attempts, accurate interpretation of cues, and timely and appropriate responsiveness to the children's behaviors. The use of videotapes to model sensitive interactions and to provide feedback to parents on their interactions enhances the effectiveness of parent training in positive interactions (Dunst & Kassow, 2004). The Intervention Example, in which early interventionist Dan Langley works with a first-time mother and father and their 7-month-old daughter, illustrates this practice. In this scenario, Dan is working with Marianne and Albert at the monthly parenting sessions sponsored by the neonatal intensive care unit of the hospital where baby Natasha was born five weeks prematurely.

Language and Literacy

After extensive research, Juel concluded in 1988 that if a child is a good reader in first grade, there is a nearly 90% probability the child will be a good reader in the fourth grade. Alternatively, if a child is a poor reader in first grade, there is a nearly 90% probability the child will still be a poor reader in the fourth grade. This finding is alarming and indicates that effective reading instruction needs to begin before the child enters school to prevent reading problems.

Literacy exposure has been linked to the acquisition of literacy skills, and literacy exposure in children from lower-income families is typically low. Because of this,

At their last third-Thursday session, the participants watched a video and discussed responsive parenting styles with infants and toddlers with Dan. The video included scenes of a variety of families modeling parental sensitivity as they went about daily activities with their young children. As a follow-up, Dan made arrangements for each family to videotape their own parent–child interactions during the next week in preparation for a scheduled video-viewing session with him in their individual homes. With Natasha tucked into her crib for the night, Marianne, Albert, and Dan settled in to watch the video. Dan briefly reviewed the characteristics of positive parental sensitivity before showing the video: "While we watch, try to focus on the elements of parenting sensitivity we talked about at our last group meeting. Speak up when you see yourselves, first, being aware of—that is, paying attention to—Tasha; second, correctly figuring out what Tasha's behavior means; and third, responding promptly and appropriately to her behavior."

After a few minutes of teasing and self-conscious laughter, the trio settle in to viewing and discussion. "I'm impressed," Marianne comments at the end of the evening. "I thought I really understood this concept, but there's nothing like seeing yourself in action to separate what you think you're doing from what you're really doing with your child!" Marianne identifies several places in the taped session when she appeared to be making a big effort to play with the baby and engage her attention while totally missing what Natasha's behavior was actually communicating about the baby's interests and feelings. "I kept trying to thrill her with the new rattle toy," the young mom explains, "but I can see now that Tash was turning her head away and becoming agitated, clear signs she'd rather get as far away as possible from that bothersome noise. I just didn't realize. . . ."

"The biggest lesson for me was seeing how I'd simply defer to Marianne, relying on her to figure out what Tasha's behavior meant," Albert says. "There were at least four times where I said something like, 'What does she want now, honey?' instead of looking up from the paper and figuring it out for myself. I'm gonna change that!"

Dan summarizes the session, reminding each of the parents of the many instances of sensitive responding captured on their tape. "We saw some really good stuff, and you found places ripe for improvement. Well, friends, I call that a good night's work!"

Source: Bottomlines, November 2004, 3(3), p. 2. Used with permission.

early shared reading provides one means of intervention to improve the early literacy skills of at-risk children, particularly those from lower-income families (Barton, 2004; Lonigan, Anthony, Bloomfield, Dyer, & Samwel, 1999). A review of research indicates that 2- and 3-year-old children experience remarkable gains in language development and school readiness through shared storybook reading with adults trained in the skills of dialogic reading, one form of shared reading (Cutspec, 2004). This is most effective when both parents and teachers in the children's care centers practice this technique, when it is implemented one child to one adult, and when the adult patiently waits for the child's responses. In dialogic reading, the adult is trained in eight key steps to use while reading:

- Ask "what" questions.
- Follow the child's answers with more questions.
- Repeat what the child says.
- Help the child as needed. If necessary, answer the question asked of the child and have him or her repeat what was said.
- Praise and encourage the child.
- Follow the child's interests.
- Slow down and give the child time to respond to questions.
- Allow the session to be fun!

When these practices are mastered and regularly incorporated into shared reading sessions, three additional techniques are added:

- Ask open-ended questions.
- Expand on what the child says.
- Emphasize fun in ways that will encourage continued interest in reading.

Shared book reading with 2- and 3-year-old children can result in gains in language development.

In the home, the child and a parent/caregiver should read together at least once a day, and in the day-care setting, the minimum reading time with the teacher or staff member should be three times a week.

As children reach preschool and school age, Foorman and Torgeson (2001) note that the components of effective reading practices are the same whether the goal is prevention or intervention. The five key components of reading identified by the National Reading Panel in 2000 still apply. Children most at risk of reading failure need instruction that is explicit and comprehensive, intensive, and emotionally and cognitively supportive in small group or one-on-one formats. Successful early literacy for students means that schools must establish a range of intervention and grouping options at different levels of student performance (Marston, Muyskens, Lau, & Canter, 2003; Moody, Vaughn, & Schumm, 1997; O'Shaugnessy et al., 2002).

When teachers use research-based instructional components of reading, almost all students can learn to read (Moats, 2001). For example, a federally funded model program, Project PRIDE (Preventing and Remediating Reading Problems Through Early Identification and Direct Teaching of Early Literacy Skills), effectively used a three-tiered system of evidence-based reading procedures in an attempt to prevent reading failure in at-risk children (Bursuck et al., 2004). Tier 1 was the general education reading program in kindergarten, grade 1, or grade 2, with some additional teaching methods such as the direct instruction components of advance organizers, modeling, guided and independent practice along with systematic error corrections, and a motivational system. Tier 2 consisted of extra practice in small ability groups on essential skills in the school reading series. The instruction took place in a pullout setting in kindergarten and grade 1 and in the general education class for grade 2. Small group sessions were taught by general education teachers, Title I teachers, special education teachers, and paraprofessionals using the same enhancements as Tier 1, but in smaller groups. Tier 3 was an intensive alternative reading program (*Reading Mastery*) conducted daily in small ability groups outside the general education class by Title I or special education teachers.

Implementing effective educational plans for students who are struggling with reading depends on the collaboration of researchers, teachers, teacher educators, and policy makers (Denton, Vaughn, & Fletcher, 2003). Committed special and general education teachers must work together to provide high-quality, research-validated instruction to all students in the most effective environment. Without preventative measures, children's small reading problems can spiral into devastating ones (Torgesen, 2004).

Social and Behavioral Skills

Emotional and social development of infants and toddlers provides the foundation for their future emotional, social, and cognitive development (Fox, 2000b). Problems that occur early are likely to be indicators of later, more difficult problems and thus need to be dealt with as soon as possible. Vaughn et al. (2003) report that social skills interventions for 3- to 5-year-old children with developmental delays often use the following: prompting of target behaviors, play-related activities, free-play generalization, reinforcement of appropriate behaviors, modeling of specific social skills, storytelling, direct instruction of social skills, and imitation of appropriate behaviors. In a Universal Design for Learning setting, many of these techniques will be applied to all children. There is very strong evidence for the success of positive behavior support (PBS), discussed in Chapter 6, as an intervention approach for young children. Establishing programwide PBS in preschool is both supportive and proactive (Stormont, Lewis, & Beckner, 2005). Behavior support interventions are planned for home, early education settings, and community environments by a team of educational staff, the child's family, and other professionals who may be involved in the child's education. The team completes a functional assessment to identity factors related to the child's challenging behavior, and this leads to the development

WHAT DO I "GET" OR "GET OUT OF" WHEN I USE CHALLENGING BEHAVIOR?

BEHAVIOR			
What happens just before the behavior?	**Describe exactly what the behavior looks like.**	**What do adults/siblings do when problem behavior occurs?**	**Why might he/she be doing this?**
Example:			**To get:**
He is told to go to the bathroom to take a bath.	*He screams, runs to the other end of the house and drops to the ground kicking.*	*Mom/Dad chase after him. When he drops and kicks we back off and wait him out.*	**To get out of:** *taking a bath until he is ready (delays going to take a bath)*
			To get:
			To get out of:
			To get:
			To get out of:

Source: Lentini, R., Vaughn, B. J., & Fox, L. (2005). *Creating Teaching Tools for Young Children with Challenging Behavior* [CD-ROM]. University of South Florida, Tampa, FL. www.challengingbehavior.org. Used with permission.

of a behavior support plan. A great deal of data demonstrate very clear and consistent effects of functional assessment and assessment-based intervention for preventing and dealing with challenging behaviors (Fox, Hemmeter, Smith, & Dunlap, 2003). A form for use in assessing functional behaviors is presented in the Intervention Suggestions. This form can serve as the basis for a positive support plan that should be shared with the parents, caregivers, and any other staff who may be involved with the intervention program and are, therefore, members of the intervention team. Appropriate behaviors, such as lining up and walking quietly, may be taught by teachers through modeling the specific behaviors in context, highlighting the occurrence of example behaviors in context with positive reinforcement, and supporting appropriate behaviors by using prompts and cues when children are first learning the behaviors and in particularly challenging settings (Stormont, Lewis, & Beckner, 2005).

Early intervention for infants and toddlers at risk for developmental delays and eventual school failure needs to occur as soon as possible. If implemented well, such programs can lead to a better outcome for many children who would eventually be labeled with a disability and then placed in special education. Successful programs focus on the development of literacy and social/behavioral skills, and, of necessity, include family involvement.

Check Your Understanding

1. What three content areas should be included in early intervention programs? Why?

2. What are some practices associated with responsibility for learning, specifically home-based family involvement?

3. What is Universal Design for Learning? Describe the benefits of its use.

4. Describe three types of prevention.

5. Describe the major components of effective early education prevention programs. What is usually the focus of the family service components of effective early intervention programs?

PRACTICE

6. What are some effective language and literacy intervention strategies?

7. What are some effective social skills interventions for 3- to 5-year-old children with developmental delays?

What Are Other Instructional Considerations for Students Who Are At Risk?

Relevant CEC Standards
▶ Demands of learning environments (CC5K1)
▶ Ways to create learning environments that allow individuals to retain and appreciate their own and each other's respective language and cultural heritage (CC5K8)
▶ Adaptation of the physical environment to provide optimal learning opportunities for individuals with disabilities (GC5K2)
▶ Methods for ensuring individual academic success in one-to-one, small-group, and large-group settings (GC5K3)
▶ Technology for planning and managing the teaching and learning environment (CC7K4)

Two instructional considerations for children who are at risk are the home and instructional environment and the use of technology. As the home environment is very often the educational environment for infants and toddlers who are at risk, it must be considered alongside any other intervention site. Based on the high rate of child poverty and its impact as a risk factor, many young children who are at risk will not have an opportunity to learn to interact with technology at home. It is thus even more important than usual to expose these children to the world of the Internet.

The Home Environment

The optimal location for intervention with young children is the natural environment, including home and community settings such as parks, child-care centers, or stores (Fox, 2006b). In 2005, almost 90% of infants and toddlers eligible under Part C of IDEA 04 were being served primarily in the home. In a synthesis of practice-based research, Trivette (2004) reports that a responsive home environment for young children provides positive and supportive interactions with adults as well as materials and activities that stimulate children. As described in the model early intervention programs discussed previously, parents, caregivers, and early childhood educators enhance a child's cognitive and social-emotional development when they consistently interact with the child in prompt, sensitive, responsive, and supportive ways in the home. The volume of speech, the speed of response, and the level of expressiveness or emotion should match the child's so that the response is easily received. Home environments of infants and toddlers should be arranged to encourage frequent interactions with responsive adults and should provide a variety of play materials as natural everyday occurrences. This arrangement need not be a financial burden as Toni, a 17-year-old single mother who is working part-time stocking supermarket shelves and studying to pass her GED, demonstrates in the Intervention Example of a responsive home environment. She has put into place what her child's child-care teacher has told her makes a good home environment.

RICKY, CODY, AND MARGARET REVISITED Based on the case studies, what might be some benefits for each child of having the home as the intervention setting?

The Instructional Environment

In 2006, 60% of Part B preschoolers (ages 3–5) received special education services in either early childhood settings or part-time early childhood/part-time special education settings. Only 3% were served primarily at home, and 4% were served in other settings, including residential facilities, separate schools, itinerant services outside the home, or reverse mainstream settings. The critical importance of the instructional environment in early childhood education, including adult–child interaction, has been well established (Dodge & Colker, 2002). Effective classrooms for young children with challenging behaviors are well organized, engaging, and include developmentally appropriate practices, activities, and materials (Alter & Conroy, 2006). In these classrooms, the physical arrangement should ensure visual monitoring of children

Let's take a look . . .

With Thomas seated by an open kitchen drawer where he's happily sorting through plastic food containers and lids, Toni offers a tour of what she describes as the "responsive home" she's created for her baby.

"Well, as you can see, we've set things up so that Thomas can handle all sorts of stuff that's interesting and safe for him to have. Not just here, but in the living room and bedroom too. When he pats on certain low drawers and doors and babbles at me, he knows I'll open 'em up, and he can play with what's inside. His toy shelves in our room are just cardboard boxes I brought from the market and covered with adhesive paper, just like the building blocks I made, but he loves them."

Toni keeps the row of brightly colored shelves filled with toys she borrows every month from a toy-lending library or discovers in "under-a-dollar" bins at yard sales. Her major baby equipment purchases were a folding stroller and a second-hand backpack carrier. "These make it easier for Thomas to come along with me everywhere, and I always have him interact in some way with store clerks, people in the park, bus drivers—same as I do!"

Toni encourages her younger brother, Darius, to play with Thomas and to bring his school pals home. "It's good for Thomas to interact with lots of people, and for them to notice and show interest in what he's doing," she explains. "It's being responsive, and it makes all the difference."

Source: Bottomlines, November 2004, 2(7), p. 2. Used with permission.

and smooth transitions among activities. Materials should be arranged to promote engagement, mastery, and independence. For example, increasing the accessibility and availability of toys and materials can increase independence. The interpersonal climate should include positive attention and positive feedback for appropriate behavior.

Effective classroom environments also include consistent daily schedules (Alter & Conroy, 2006). Schedules for young children should use photographs or pictures or even real objects. Schedules should be included within activities as well as across activities. For example, a visual schedule within an activity would indicate what to do first, next, and so on. Embedding choices in the schedule so that students select one activity or another may help decrease the probability of challenging behaviors. Classroom settings become more predictable when schedules are consistently followed, thus helping children feel more secure and comfortable, reducing behavior problems, and increasing rates of child engagement (Ostrosky, Jung, Hemmeter, & Thomas, 2003). Effective practices also include the provision of rules for preschool children, and rituals and routines at an even younger age (Alter & Conroy, 2006). This provides structure, consistency, and stability, and communicates values for all in the class. A routine is an event that is scheduled on a regular basis during which children learn about the sequence of activities, begin to predict what will come next, and work on becoming more independent (Ostrosky et al., 2003). A ritual may be a song, a rhyme, a game, or a movement to remind children of what is expected of them or to prompt them to make transition easier. Alter and Conroy offer the example of a ritual that reminds children of the rules when going to a quiet place such as a library: "Zip it, lock it, and put it in your pocket" This very catchy ritual is accompanied by representative actions—zipping zipper over the lips, turning a key at the end, and putting the key in their pocket. Of course, these rituals first need to be taught using small steps, with much feedback and practice.

Schedules, routines, and rituals can help in planning a positive support system for individual children in need of support. The positive support planning form shown in the Intervention Example on page 468 helps to determine

RICKY, CODY, AND MARGARET REVISITED Based on the case studies, what are specific needs, if any, of each child in terms of their instructional environments?

PRACTICE

In Practice Meet Educator Christine Honsberger and Her Student Sam

My name is Christine Honsberger, and I am a Board Certified Behavior Analyst. I obtained my undergraduate degree in psychology and a master's degree in applied behavior analysis. I currently work as part of a team of professionals that includes speech and language pathologists, special educators, and occupational and physical therapists. I work with children between the ages of 18 months and 3 years who exhibit social and communication delays.

Sam is a 24-month-old boy exhibiting communication and social delays. Sam first entered the program at 18 months. His mother, Lisa, was concerned that Sam was not using any words or babbling. At a playgroup they had been attending, Lisa observed that Sam did not seem to notice the other children. While other children would gather around a new toy, Sam would sit by himself in a different corner of the gym, seemingly uninterested in what the other children found so exciting.

The first conversation I had with Lisa and her husband, Matt, consisted of informing them of the importance of actively engaging Sam throughout the day. Together, we identified goals for his individual family service plan (IFSP). These goals were geared toward increasing Sam's communication and social skills and having Sam eat meals with his family. To create a developmentally appropriate and functional curriculum for Sam, I used a number of tools to gather the necessary information. This assessment included utilizing a standardized evaluation tool (the Battelle Developmental Inventory) and a tool geared toward identifying skill deficits for children with an ASD (Assessment of Basic Language and Learning Skills). In addition to these structured measurements, I observed Sam and spoke with Lisa and Matt to discuss successes and challenges at home.

Instructional Content and Procedures

Together, Sam's parents and I identified a skill, pointing, that Sam needed to learn to help him communicate his wants and needs. We then discussed using most to least prompting to help Sam point. Whenever Sam indicated he wanted something, either by reaching for it or using one of his parents' hands to obtain an item, Matt or Lisa would physically help him extend his pointer finger toward the item before he could make an error. To ensure that Sam was making progress toward the goal of pointing independently, Matt and Lisa recorded data on the level of prompting Sam needed, and we reviewed these data together at least once a week.

Our second goal was to increase Sam's eye contact during fun activities. Sam loved roughhouse activities. Matt and Sam often played together in this way in the evenings after Matt came home from work. Sam would laugh and often take his father's hands and put them back on his body indicating he wanted another tickle, but he very rarely made eye contact. Together we identified strategies Matt could use during these playtimes to encourage Sam to look at Matt's eyes to let him know he wanted the activity to continue. Matt would initiate the activity and engage in the activity for approximately 30 seconds, he would

which routines the child is having difficulty with and why that may be the case. Writing the support plan down increases the probability that all team members supporting the child will be consistent in plan implementation (Lentini, Vaughn, & Fox, 2004). Other examples may be found in Online Appendix A.

Instructional Technology

In 2000, nearly two in five children under age 18 lived in households without a computer (Annie E. Casey Foundation, 2005). This represents a range from nearly one in five in New Hampshire to more than half in Mississippi. Perhaps a worse

then wait for Sam to look toward his eyes before engaging in the activity again. If Sam did not look, Matt would bring his hands up to his eyes to encourage Sam to look up. As soon as Sam made eye contact, Matt would use behavior specific praise to let Sam know the exact behavior that was being rewarded (for example, "Good looking!"). We identified a way for Matt to track Sam's progress and criteria for increasing expectations (for example, maintaining eye contact).

Instructional Environment and Technology

As we began discussing Sam's communication skills, Lisa and Matt reported that most of what Sam wanted was consistently available. They regularly provided drinks and snacks, and most of his toys were on the floor of his playroom. If Sam wanted an item that was out of reach, he would seek out a parent; take him or her to the desired object, and push his or her hand toward the object.

We developed a plan to increase Sam's communication skills by capitalizing on the items that Sam regularly sought access to. We started by coming up with a list of Sam's most preferred foods, drinks, and activities. It was important to identify items and activities Sam would be motivated to obtain. We then discussed environmental modifications that were needed at home to encourage Sam to communicate with another person. Lisa and Matt agreed to put Sam's most preferred items in clear bins or out of his reach.

One of the goals Sam's parents wanted to target was mealtime behaviors, and I observed a mealtime and spoke with both parents to discuss the observation. During mealtimes, Sam was seated in his high chair and had access to books, toys, and an alphabet placemat. He often cried and threw food, after which Lisa would allow Sam to be "all done." She also reported that she was so scared he would be hungry she would give him some of his most preferred snacks soon after. We discussed the importance of limiting distractions during mealtimes and utilizing reinforcement for eating rather than free access to toys and activities.

We identified a number of strategies to be used during mealtimes to encourage Sam to eat more successfully and independently. We identified potential reinforcers to be used to motivate him to eat his meal from his preferred items list. We also wanted to incorporate choice into an activity that in the past was determined by his parents. We decided to use pictures to help Sam make a choice and to show him what he needed to do to earn access to a preferred item. We created a First-Then board to visually depict what Sam needed to eat and what he would earn when he was finished. Before the mealtime began, Sam would choose what he wanted to eat out of a field of two choices, and choose what toy he wanted to play with after he finished eating a specified amount. We also removed the toys that were available during mealtimes to encourage him to focus on eating his food and earning access to them after he was finished. His parents were encouraged to provide attention and behavior specific praise for taking bites and to ignore all other challenging behaviors (throwing food and crying.) Within one week Sam was sitting with his family during mealtimes and eating his entire meal. Matt and Lisa were thrilled and reported that they were able to go out to dinner as a family for the first time since Sam was a baby.

Collaboration

When working with children who are at risk, it is absolutely essential for professionals to collaborate with parents. An intervention is only as successful as the person implementing it, and creating an intervention that families feel comfortable with ensures that it will be practiced with fidelity. Creating a program targeting a range of communication, social, and self-help skills also benefits from collaboration between disciplines. To ensure this was done, all of the providers for Sam met weekly to discuss strategies and progress. In addition to weekly meetings, notes were written after every home visit and shared with all of Sam's providers and family members involved in following through with activities.

I have worked with this family for one year, and Sam has made tremendous gains. Matt and Lisa have done an amazing job incorporating teaching opportunities into their everyday lives. Every place they go or activity they do is an opportunity to teach Sam a new skill or generalize a skill into a new environment.

statistic in this day of Internet research is the fact that, on the average, more than half of children do not have access to the Internet at home (31% in New Hampshire to 68% in Mississippi lack access). As these children reach school age, they will certainly need more time at school using computers to catch up to other children who have home access. However, many schools in low-income areas have fewer computers than schools in high-income areas where parent organizations often add to the technology funds. This widens the Internet access gap (Barton, 2004), and all too often the available computers in low-income schools are used for basic skills drill-and-practice instead of for word processing, as research tools, or for problem solving.

TABLE ACTIVITIES/SMALL GROUP

Why might the child be doing this?	What can I do to prevent the problem behavior?	What can I do if the problem behavior occurs?	What new skills should I teach?
Child wants attention from other children and/or an adult	• Schedule "time" with friends/adult immediately following activity • Use a **visual schedule** to tell the child when he/she can play with friends/adults (e.g., center or special activity) • Allow child to sit next to favorite friends (if not too disruptive) • Teach other children to encourage the child and each other (e.g., clapping, thumbs up, high five) • Praise for participating • Use a **"raise hand" visual cue card** to prompt child to raise hand for attention	• Use **first-then visual:** "First do table activity, then play with friends/adult" • Show **visual schedule,** and remind of when the child can play with friends/adult • Remind with **visual cue card** to raise hand • Give words to say, like "Look what I did"	• Teach child to raise hand for teacher attention by prompting with **visual cue card** • Teach the child to gesture/say, "Look at me" or "This is fun" • Teach the child to choose a friend to go with to the activity • Teach the child to follow **visual first then** and/or **visual schedule**

Source: Lentini, R., Vaughn, B. J., & Fox, L. (2005). *Creating Teaching Tools for Young Children with Challenging Behavior* [CD-ROM]. University of South Florida, Tampa, FL. www.challengingbehavior.org. Used with permission.

Children at risk of developmental delays due to biological or medical reasons include children with physical and sensory disabilities. Educational and support technology discussed in Chapters 8, 9, and 10 is relevant for serving young children who are at risk for developmental delays. As you may recall from Chapter 4, children as young as 3 years of age can learn to operate a computer safely and effectively.

Check Your Understanding

1. What is the optimal location for intervention with young children?

2. Describe an effective home environment for infants and toddlers who are at risk.

3. Describe an effective instructional environment for infants and toddlers who are at risk.

4. Why is the use of computers so important to children who are at risk due to environmental factors?

What Are Some Considerations for the General Education Teacher?

Relevant CEC Standards

▶ Effective management of teaching and learning (CC5K3)

▶ Teacher attitudes and behaviors that influence behavior of individuals with exceptional learning needs (CC5K4)

Much of the responsibility of teaching children who are at risk and working with the families of these children falls on the general education teacher in collaboration with special education teachers and other staff who may be involved in the child's education. In early childhood programs, in particular, general education and special education services are merged. Although elementary and secondary teachers will not be involved in early intervention, risk factors do not end in early childhood. Throughout school, educators must work to alleviate risk factors as much as possible and to enhance protective factors that are school-related in any way to prevent school failure or dropping out of school. Universal educational techniques presented in earlier chapters should be implemented. For example, functional behavior assessment, positive behavior support, direct instruction, social skills instruction, and applied behavior analysis techniques are all options for supporting students at risk. Procedures for teaching the emerging English language learner are imperative for students who are not only struggling with learning English but who also have not had prior school experiences. They will need extra exposure to books, shared reading with their teachers and families, a great deal of engaged learning time, many language experiences, and extra time on the computer.

The following examples illustrate how a general education teacher might interact with students at risk. An alert, observant teacher will note that both 4th grader Allie, who is often tired and hungry; and 11th grader Laurel, whose boyfriend watches her like a hawk, are showing symptoms of neglect and abuse and may need to see a school counselor or a counselor from another social service agency. Laurel's depression needs to be dealt with immediately; more than 7% of 15- to 19-year-olds committed suicide in 2003 (National Center for Health Statistics, 2005). Both Laurel and Allie will need a positive and supportive environment in the classroom. A functional behavior assessment should indicate why Allie is picking on other students in the class and lead to the implementation of a positive behavior support plan. Legitimate time may need to be provided for Allie to nap in a nurse's office during recess or on arrival at school. Direct instruction and engaged learning time may help both Allie and Laurel concentrate better on their studies. Both Laurel and Ronnell, who is working nights and considering dropping out of school, may need to be taught strategies in problem solving, decision making, self-determination, and self-advocacy. Perhaps there is a job for Ronnell at school before and after hours that could provide a more positive and supportive environment within the school community and encourage him to stay in school. All of these students have special needs even though they are not labeled as having disabilities. Collaboration among general education teachers, special education teachers, and other school staff may help prevent these students and many others from being referred for special education services, failing in school, or dropping out of school.

Check Your Understanding

1. Who is usually responsible for intervention programs for school-aged students at risk of school failure or dropping out?

2. How can these intervention programs most effectively be implemented?

Practical Considerations for the Classroom

What IDEA 04 Says about Students At Risk: Under IDEA, children at risk are children ages birth through age 2 who are experiencing developmental delays or who have a diagnosed mental or physical condition that has a high probability of resulting in a developmental delay (served under part C); or children ages 3 to 5 who have developmental delays in physical, cognitive, communication, social-emotional, or adaptive development (served under Part B).

Identification Tools: *Infants and Toddlers:* The earlier at-risk conditions are identified, the better. There are no universal procedures or diagnostic instruments; these vary by state. May evaluate based on quantitative differences in chronological age and actual performance level, by a qualitative description of delay, or other measures. *Early Childhood:* Measures of literacy, including early reading skills. May use the Dynamic Indicators of Basic Early Literacy Skills, the Early Reading Diagnostic Assessment, Second Edition or the Pre-Reading Inventory of Phonological Awareness. Also measures of potential behavior problems. May use the Early Screening Project, or the Systematic Screening for Behavior Disorders.

Risk Factors	Indicators You Might See
Conditions of Established Risk	Chromosomal abnormalities; genetic or congenital disorders; severe sensory impairments, including hearing and vision; inborn errors of metabolism; disorders reflecting disturbance of the development of the nervous system; congenital infections; disorders secondary to exposure to toxic substances, including fetal alcohol syndrome; and severe attachment disorders.
Biological/Medical	Low birth weight, intraventricular hemorrhage at birth, chronic lung disease, and failure to thrive.
Environmental	Parental substance abuse, family instability, poverty, homelessness, violence in the home, teen pregnancy, child abuse or neglect, school factors, and speaking English as a second language.

Students Who Are at Risk

Teaching Implications

Instructional Content

- Plan to include the child in the general curriculum.
- Participate in development of an IFSP to document specific goals.
- Consider support needed in language and literacy.
- Determine whether support is needed in developing mathematical skills.
- Consider whether social and behavioral control skills need to be developed.
- Involve the child's family in curriculum planning and implementation; write an IFSP to document specific goals.

Instructional Procedures

- Use Universal Design for Learning when planning instruction.
- Consider what kind of prevention needs to be planned for.
- Work with parents to develop ability to support children's skill development at home.
- Use research-based literacy programs and strategies.
- To support social and behavioral skills, prompt target behaviors, use play-related activities, free-play generalization, reinforcement of appropriate behaviors, modeling of specific social skills, storytelling, direct instruction of social skills, and imitation of appropriate behaviors.
- Consider implementing a PBS program.
- Provide students at risk who are English language learners with more exposure to books, shared reading, engaged time, many language experiences, and extra computer time.

Instructional Environment

- Instruction should be in a natural environment, in many cases the home, community settings, and child-care centers.
- Encourage parents to work with children on skills at home.
- For children at risk for behavioral problems, instruction should be well organized, engaging, and include developmentally appropriate practices and materials.
- Arrange materials to promote engagement, mastery, and independence.
- Develop a consistent daily schedule.
- Establish predictable rules, routines, and rituals.

Instructional Technology

- Realize that many children at risk may not have access to technology at home.
- Consider whether technology can be used in instruction to help develop skills.

Methodologies and Strategies to Try

- Dialogic Reading (p. 461)
- Shared Reading (p. 461)
- Positive Behavior Support (PBS) (p. 462)
- Functional Behavior Assessment (p. 463)
- Direct Instruction (p. 469)
- Social Skills Instruction (p. 469)
- Applied Behavior Analysis Techniques (p. 469)

Considerations for the General Classroom and Collaboration

Instruction for children at risk typically occurs in the general classroom.

The general education teacher should:

- Develop a positive and supportive environment.
- Use Universal Design for Learning.
- Involve students' families.

Collaboration

General and special educators should consult on:

- Enhancing protective factors
- Alleviating at-risk factors
- Procedures and strategies used
- Involving families
- Using technology
- Developing an IFSP

Chapter Summary

Go to the text's Online Learning Center at **www.mhhe.com/taylor1e** to access study resources, Web links, practice quizzes, and extending materials.

What Are the Foundations of At-Risk Conditions?

- The focus on children who are at risk began in the 1960s with programs for the disadvantaged and has increased steadily since the change in terms to *at risk* in the 1980s.
- IDEA 04 uses the term *at risk* to define infants and toddlers who are at risk for developmental delays. Children birth through age 2 who are at risk for developmental delays are served under IDEA 04, Part C. Children ages 3 to 5 at risk for developmental delays are served under IDEA 04, Part B.
- Children may remain or become at risk for developmental delays or academic or social problems in preschool, at school age, and during adolescence. Some funding for this population, not served under IDEA 04, is available through Title I of the ESEA Act.
- IDEA 04, Part C, served 2.4% of the birth through 2-year-old population in 2005, and 5.8% of the 3- to 5-year-old population were served under IDEA 04, Part B. Overall, there has been a rise in conditions that put children at risk.

What Are Factors That Place Children At Risk?

- The factors that place children at risk of developmental delays and school failure are numerous. These factors are commonly grouped into established risk conditions, biological or medical conditions, and environmental risk factors.
- Conditions of environmental risk include parental substance abuse, family instability, poverty, homelessness, violence in the home, teen pregnancy, child abuse or neglect, school factors, and English as a second language.
- Protective factors are those that may help children be resilient to risk factors. Such factors include temperament, education, family structure, health, and intelligence, among many others.
- The characteristics of each child are unique; there is no typical child who is at risk.

How Are Children Who Are At Risk Identified?

- Early identification of children at risk allows for the greatest impact of early intervention services.
- Infants and toddlers may be identified by physical, communication, cognitive, social-emotional, and adaptive behaviors.
- Measures of literacy skills and behavioral measures are typically used to identify young children at risk.

What and How Do I Teach Students Who Are At Risk?

- Children at risk for developmental delays and school failure often need a focus on language/literacy skills, mathematical skills, and social/behavioral control.

- Family involvement plays an important role in the learning of children at risk. Three ways to strengthen family involvement are encouraging positive parenting, developing home–school relationships, and sharing with parents a responsibility for learning. An IFSP will establish collaborative goals for the family and the education providers.
- Using the Universal Design for Learning can help meet the needs of all children before they encounter learning problems.
- The goal for children who are risk should be prevention of school failure. The three levels of prevention are primary prevention, secondary prevention, and tertiary prevention.
- Successful early intervention programs include family involvement and focus on the development of social skills, compliance, self-regulation, and academic engagement.
- Literacy development should focus on developing early literacy skills in young children and phonemic awareness, phonics, fluency, vocabulary, and text comprehension in older children.
- Procedures that can help the development of social/behavior skills include prompting targeted behaviors, play-related activities, free-play generalization, reinforcement of appropriate behaviors, modeling of specific social skills, storytelling, direct instruction of social skills, and imitation of behaviors. Universal Design for Learning, positive behavior support, and functional assessments should be considered.

What Are Other Instructional Considerations for Students Who Are At Risk?

- The best intervention environment for young children is the natural environment—the home and areas in which they would typically interact. A responsive home environment provides positive and supportive interactions with young children.
- Effective instructional environments are well organized, consistent, and include well-established rules, rituals, and routines.
- Many children who are at risk have no computers or Internet access at home and will need extra time at school to catch up with peers.

What Are Some Considerations for the General Education Teacher?

- From early childhood on, much of the responsibility for serving children who are at risk falls on general education teachers in collaboration with special educators and other staff.
- Programs and teachers should work to alleviate risk factors and enhance protective factors for children who are at risk.

Reflection Topics

1. Why do some people think that early identification is not a good idea? How would you respond to someone expressing this belief?
2. What do you think is the significance of family involvement in early intervention programs for children who are at risk?
3. Do you think knowledge of protective factors can help educators reduce the number of children who fail in school? How?
4. What are the implications of each state deciding on identification criteria for infants and toddlers who are at risk?
5. Do you think more states should provide early intervention for infants and toddlers who are at risk of developmental delays due to environmental risk factors? Why or why not?
6. Do you think intervention in the natural environment is a good idea? Why or why not?

Application Activities: For Learning and Your Portfolio

1. Go to your own state department Web site on eligibility for at-risk services and determine which of the children in the case study examples at the beginning of this chapter would or would not be served in your state.
2. (*Portfolio Possibility*) Write a position paper that either supports or rejects the value of early identification of children who are at risk for developmental delays.
3. Interview a teacher who works in a program for infants and toddlers. Find out what role the teacher plays in family involvement, what the educational program focuses on, and who the other professionals with whom she works are.
4. Find a copy of an IFSP form used in your district or a local early intervention program. Note the ways in which family involvement is included.
5. Using the Classroom Example: Routine-based Support Planning Form, fill in some suggestions for a child who is bored or doesn't like table activities and wants to get out of the group.
6. Visit an early intervention center or classroom. Describe the instructional environment and any use of technology that is evident.

SUMMARY

Students with Attention Deficit/ Hyperactivity Disorder

CHAPTER OUTLINE

FOUNDATIONS

What Are the Foundations of Attention Deficit/Hyperactivity Disorder?

A Brief History of Attention Deficit/Hyperactivity Disorder
The Definition of Attention Deficit/Hyperactivity Disorder
Prevalence of Attention Deficit/Hyperactivity Disorder

What Are the Causes and Characteristics of Attention Deficit/Hyperactivity Disorder?

Causes of Attention Deficit/Hyperactivity Disorder
Characteristics of Students with Attention Deficit/Hyperactivity Disorder

How Are Students with Attention Deficit/Hyperactivity Disorder Identified?

Interviews
Questionnaires and Checklists
Rating Scales
Academic Testing
Direct Observation

PRACTICE

What and How Do I Teach Students with Attention Deficit/Hyperactivity Disorder?

Instructional Content
Instructional Procedures
Direct Instruction
Cognitive Behavior Modification
Precision Teaching
Behavioral Intervention
Medication as a Support for Learning
Early Multicomponent Interventions

What Are Other Instructional Considerations for Teaching Students with Attention Deficit/Hyperactivity Disorder?

The Instructional Environment
Instructional Technology

What Are Some Considerations for the General Education Teacher?

INTRODUCING ANDY

Andy is a 10-year-old boy who is currently in the third grade. He was retained in kindergarten for one year because of his immature behavior. For instance, he would run around the classroom bothering the other students and rarely participated in any of the classroom activities. Andy's kindergarten teacher had concerns that he might not be developmentally ready for first grade. Andy did struggle in the first grade and in the beginning of the second grade, but with the help of a tutor hired by his parents, he was able to make satisfactory grades.

By the end of the second grade, however, Andy's inattentiveness and lack of organizational skills were significant enough that his teacher, Ms. Gonzales, thought Andy needed to be referred to his pediatrician to determine whether he might have attention deficit/hyperactivity disorder (AD/HD).

Ms. Gonzales and Andy's parents completed several questionnaires and checklists requested by Andy's pediatrician. Their input indicated that Andy displayed behaviors such as making careless mistakes in schoolwork, not following instructions, and talking excessively. The pediatrician diagnosed Andy as having AD/HD and suggested that he receive medication. His parents decided against it, preferring to work with Ms. Gonzales to develop a collaborative communication system, thinking that a consistent approach should be used at school and at home. A notebook was sent back and forth between Ms. Gonzales and Andy's parents with daily notes regarding Andy's behavior. It also indicated what assignments he didn't complete at school that he needed to finish at home. This plan was implemented with only one month left before the school year ended, so it was difficult to determine if the program was successful. ▶

Andy's parents first met with his current teacher, Mr. Ziegler, to discuss and implement the program that was developed in the previous year. Mr. Ziegler soon noted that the program was not effective. Andy's parents were also overwhelmed because it often took three or four hours for him to complete his unfinished schoolwork and any homework. Andy is also very disorganized and frequently forgets to turn the homework in to Mr. Ziegler.

As a result of the lack of progress, Mr. Ziegler and Andy's parents had another conference and decided to provide some accommodations through a 504 Plan. This included letting Andy use a computer for his written work and allowing him extra time for tests. Although these accommodations (implemented for about two months) helped somewhat, Andy was becoming increasingly more frustrated and was starting to avoid doing any work at school. His parents were also getting frustrated over what they said was increasingly becoming a "homework battle." After discussions with his teacher and his pediatrician, Andy began receiving Ritalin twice a day. Mr. Ziegler will continue to implement Andy's 504 Plan accommodations and meet regularly with Andy's parents to evaluate the success of the plan. Both Mr. Ziegler and Andy's parents will carefully monitor the effects of the medication. ■

In some ways Andy sounds like a pretty typical 10-year-old student. After all, many children do not like to write or do homework, and they will occasionally avoid tasks. Similarly, many students have difficulty sitting still in class. What makes Andy's situation different is the degree to which he exhibits these behaviors and the fact that he displays them both in school and at home. Most children choose when to exhibit these behaviors, but students like Andy who have attention deficit/hyperactivity disorder (AD/HD) have little control over them. Students with AD/HD typically have problems paying attention and controlling their impulses and behavior. Some students with AD/HD may be similar to Andy; others may display different behaviors. For example, 5-year-old Bret is described by his parents as a "whirling dervish" who never seems to stop moving. On the other hand, Mike, who is 17 years old, is somewhat withdrawn and disorganized. He has difficulty planning ahead and often does not complete his assignments.

AD/HD is a controversial disability. There are many who believe that there is an epidemic of AD/HD and that too many individuals are being identified. Others believe the disorder does not exist at all; that it is more a learned behavior caused by poor parenting or poor teaching. The frequent use of medication to treat AD/HD adds to the controversy. Suffice it to say, however, that AD/HD *does* exist. The Attention Deficit Disorder Association (ADDA, 2005) noted that AD/HD is recognized as a disorder by the courts, the U.S. Department of Education, the Office of Civil Rights, and all major medical, educational, and psychological associations.

AD/HD is being diagnosed more and more often, and students with AD/HD are most often being taught in general education classes, requiring support from special education teachers and general education teachers alike. With this in mind, general education teachers must be prepared to recognize possible signs of the disorder and to provide a supportive instructional environment. If a child with AD/HD is placed in a general classroom, the special education and general education teachers will need to collaborate to plan for and implement instruction that will allow the student to learn to his or her potential.

AD/HD is *not* considered a separate disability under IDEA 04. However, students with AD/HD might qualify for services under IDEA 04 within the category of other health impairments (OHI). In fact, AD/HD is specifically listed as one of the conditions considered to be an OHI if certain criteria are met. Students with AD/HD also may qualify under the IDEA 04 categories of learning disabilities or emotional disturbance because they often have those disabilities along with their AD/HD. Students who do not qualify under IDEA 04 are allowed teaching accommodations under Section 504 of the Rehabilitation Act of 1973.

What Are the Foundations of Attention Deficit/ Hyperactivity Disorder?

Attention deficit/hyperactivity disorder was initially described at the turn of the 20th century, but it did not receive significant attention until the mid-20th century. In the 1960s, the American Psychiatric Association (APA) included an earlier term and definition for AD/HD in its diagnostic manual. Attention to AD/HD has increased significantly in recent years even though it is not considered a separate disability category under IDEA 04.

A Brief History of Attention Deficit/Hyperactivity Disorder

Attention deficit/hyperactivity disorder has gained considerable attention in recent years, but the condition was first described more than 100 years ago. In 1902, George F. Still, a British physician, presented a series of papers to the Royal College of Physicians in which he described children with a variety of characteristics including attention problems and hyperactivity. He believed that they had "defective moral control" due to their lack of inhibition to engage in certain behaviors such as hyperactivity. Interestingly, a deficit in behavioral inhibition is currently being researched and is considered one of the main characteristics of AD/HD. Interest in the area was heightened in 1918 with the outbreak of Van Economo's encephalitis, a Spanish influenza pandemic that resulted in individuals with characteristics such as hyperactivity, impulsivity, and aggressive behavior (Resnick, 2000).

In the mid-20th century, professionals began recognizing what would eventually become AD/HD as a specific disorder and that students with this disorder had unique educational needs. In the 1950s, William Cruickshank began his important work on the relationship of brain injury and hyperactivity and distractibility. Also during the 1950s, the terms "minimal brain dysfunction" (MBD) and "minimal brain injury" (MBI) were introduced to describe children with hyperactivity and distractibility. In other words, these children displayed behaviors associated with brain injury even though no physical evidence was present, hence the use of the term "minimal."

In the 1960s, the term *learning disabilities* was introduced and used to relabel many children with the MBD/MBI label. Cruickshank continued his research on brain injury and hyperactivity. In his 1967 book on brain-injured children he stated, "The first barrier to adjustment, and perhaps the most significant, is the characteristic of *hyperactivity*" (p. 30). He went on to describe two types of hyperactivity caused by brain injury. Sensory hyperactivity causes the child to respond to unessential or irrelevant stimuli. Cruickshank believed that this type was most associated with poor school achievement. The other type, motor hyperactivity, he described as leading to management problems at home and school. Interestingly, although the terms have changed, these descriptions are very similar to those currently being used: AD/HD, predominantly inattentive, and AD/HD, predominantly hyperactive-impulsive. Also in the 1960s, the American Psychiatric Association (1968), in the second edition of their *Diagnostic and Statistical Manual* (*DSM*), used and defined the term "hyperkinetic reaction disorder of childhood." In the 1970s, professionals shifted their research interests from hyperactivity to attention problems (Weyandt, 2001). This resulted in the introduction of the term "attention deficit disorder (ADD) with or without hyperactivity" in the third edition of the *DSM* (American Psychiatric Association [APA], 1980). In the 1987 revision of the *DSM*, the hyperactivity option was eliminated and replaced with "undifferentiated attention deficit disorder." In 1994, the current term, "attention deficit/hyperactivity disorder," was introduced and is maintained in the 2000 APA manual. As discussed in the next section, three types of AD/HD were also defined.

The Definition of Attention Deficit/Hyperactivity Disorder

Because AD/HD is not considered a disability under IDEA 04, there is no legal, federal definition. The American Psychiatric Association has been providing various terms

Relevant CEC Standards

▶ Models, theories, and philosophies that form the basis for special education practice (CC1K1)

▶ Historical points of view and contribution of culturally diverse groups (CC1K8)

Relevant CEC Standard

▶ Issues in definition and identification of individuals with exceptional learning needs, including those from culturally and linguistically diverse backgrounds (CC1K5)

and definitions of AD/HD for more than 40 years. Currently, the definition provided in the *Diagnostic and Statistical Manual, Fourth Edition-Text Revision* (APA, 2000) is the one most widely used. The APA states, "The essential feature of Attention-Deficit/Hyperactivity Disorder is a persistent pattern of inattention and/or hyperactivity-impulsivity that is more frequently displayed and severe than is typically observed in individuals at a comparable level of development" (p. 85). The definition indicates that an individual with AD/HD must display characteristics that are *persistent, frequent,* and *severe.* The *DSM-IV-TR* provides general diagnostic criteria as well as specific diagnostic criteria for three types of AD/HD: predominantly hyperactive/impulsive, predominantly inattentive, or combined (both hyperactive/impulsive and inattentive). Table 14.1 lists the criteria for these three types of attention deficit/hyperactivity disorders.

ANDY REVISITED Would you say that Andy's behavioral characteristics are considered hyperactive-impulsive, inattentive, or a combination of both?

Several important points about the APA definition of AD/HD and accompanying diagnostic criteria are worthy of note. First, the symptoms of AD/HD must be present for at least six months, and some of the symptoms must be initially displayed before the age of 7. This means that someone whose behavior is caused by a temporary situation, such as divorce or a death in the family, should not be diagnosed as having AD/HD. Similarly, an individual who first starts displaying AD/HD characteristics later in life might not be identified as having AD/HD, although some individuals are identified later in life after it is determined that they did initially display characteristics before age 7. Second, the impairment should be exhibited in multiple settings. For example, if a student is only exhibiting AD/HD characteristics at school, there may be another reason for the behavior such as peer pressure, boredom, or task avoidance. The requirement that the disorder impairs performance in social, academic, or occupational areas means that the AD/HD can affect an individual's life in a number of areas. Finally, the diagnostic criteria state that the symptoms persist to a degree that is maladaptive and inconsistent with the individual's developmental level. This means that the disorder has a significant effect on the individual's life.

The criterion that characteristics of AD/HD must be present by the age of 7 has proven controversial. Barkley and Biederman (1997) argued that this criterion has no empirical justification and should be eliminated or at least broadened to include onset throughout the childhood years. Murphy and Gordon (2006) recommended that onset of the AD/HD impairments by roughly 12 to 14 years of age should be sufficient. It should also be noted that many individuals are being diagnosed *for the first time* as having AD/HD as adults. This phenomenon has implications for meeting the eligibility criterion of exhibiting the AD/HD characteristics prior to age 7, frequently requiring the use of developmental histories and interviews.

Prevalence of Attention Deficit/Hyperactivity Disorder

Between 3% and 5% of school-aged children have AD/HD (APA, 2000), making it one of the most prevalent categories of exceptionality. Assuming general education class sizes of approximately 30–35 students, on average, about two students in each class will have AD/HD, particularly

Evidence supports the fact that AD/HD persists into adolescence and adulthood for many individuals. However, with supports tailored to individual needs, students with AD/HD can be academically successful.

TABLE 14.1   Diagnostic Criteria for AD/HD from the *DSM-IV-TR*

A. Either (1) or (2):

(1) six (or more) of the following symptoms of inattention have persisted for at least 6 months to a degree that is maladaptive and inconsistent with developmental level:

Inattention
(a) often fails to give close attention to details or makes careless mistakes in schoolwork, work, or other activities
(b) often has difficulty sustaining attention in tasks or play activities
(c) often does not seem to listen when spoken to directly
(d) often does not follow through on instructions and fails to finish schoolwork, chores, or duties in the workplace (not due to oppositional behavior or failure to understand instructions)
(e) often has difficulty organizing tasks and activities
(f) often avoids, dislikes, or is reluctant to engage in tasks that require sustained mental effort (such as schoolwork or homework)
(g) often loses things necessary for tasks or activities (e.g., toys, school assignments, pencils, books, or tools)
(h) is often easily distracted by extraneous stimuli
(i) is often forgetful in daily activities

(2) six (or more) of the following symptoms of hyperactivity-impulsivity have persisted for at least 6 months to a degree that is maladaptive and inconsistent with developmental level:

Hyperactivity
(a) often fidgets with hands or feet or squirms in seat
(b) often leaves seat in classroom or in other situations in which remaining seated is expected
(c) often runs about or climbs excessively in situations in which it is inappropriate (in adolescents or adults, may be limited to subjective feelings of restlessness)
(d) often has difficulty playing or engaging in leisure activities quietly
(e) is often "on the go" or often acts as if "driven by a motor"
(f) often talks excessively

Impulsivity
(g) often blurts out answers before questions have been completed
(h) often has difficulty awaiting turn
(i) often interrupts or intrudes on others (e.g., butts into conversations or games)

B. Some hyperactive-impulsive or inattentive symptoms that caused impairment were present before age 7 years.

C. Some impairment from the symptoms is present in two or more settings (e.g., at school [or work] and at home)

D. There must be clear evidence of clinically significant impairment in social, academic, or occupational functioning.

E. The symptoms do not occur exclusively during the course of a Pervasive Developmental Disorder, Schizophrenia, or other Psychotic Disorder and are not better accounted for by another mental disorder (e.g., Mood Disorder, Anxiety Disorder, Dissociative Disorder, or a Personality Disorder).

Code based on type:
314.01 Attention-Deficit/Hyperactivity Disorder, Combined Type: if both Criteria A1 and A2 are met for the past 6 months
314.00 Attention-Deficit/Hyperactivity Disorder, Predominantly Inattentive Type: if Criterion A1 is met but Criterion A2 is not met for the past 6 months.
314.01 Attention-Deficit/Hyperactivity Disorder, Predominantly Hyperactive-Impulsive Type: if Criterion A2 is met but Criterion A1 is not met for the past 6 months.

Coding note: For individuals (especially adolescents and adults) who currently have symptoms that no longer meet full criteria, "In Partial Remission" should be specified.

Source: American Psychiatric Association. Reprinted with permission from the Diagnostic and Statistical Manual of Mental Disorders, 4/e, text revision (copyright 2000).

in the elementary years. As with many categories of exceptionality, the prevalence of AD/HD appears to be gender related. There is a higher prevalence of boys with AD/HD than of girls. Although reports as high as a 9:1 ratio of males to females have been made (APA, 2000), a common ratio that is reported is 3:1 (e.g., DuPaul & White, 2004).

In addition to gender, age affects prevalence rates of AD/HD. Although only about 20% of all those with AD/HD have been reported to have the hyperactive-impulsive type, more than 75% of children ages 4 to 6 with AD/HD have that type (McBurnett, 1995). Many people think that children will "outgrow" their AD/HD, but the majority continue to display characteristics of this disorder into adolescence and adulthood (Weyandt, 2001). Research has indicated that more than 70% of children with AD/HD continue to have the disorder in adolescence, and up to 50% demonstrate symptoms into adulthood (ADDA, 2005). This suggests that although the overall prevalence decreases in older persons, AD/HD does not go away.

Although AD/HD is not tied to a specific ethnic group, many African American students with the disorder go undiagnosed (Hervey-Jumper, Douyon, & Franco, 2006). Among the reasons for this might be parents' lack of information about AD/HD or their unwillingness to have their child diagnosed. Daley (2006) pointed out the importance of increasing parents' understanding of AD/HD to encourage greater consent for their children's receipt of intervention as students with AD/HD. Another important point to note is that different cultural groups may define inattention differently (Roseberry-McKibben, 2007). This might affect the referral rate, which, in turn, could affect the prevalence.

Particularly in recent years, the prevalence of this disorder has been increasing at a rapid rate. It is highly likely that you will be involved in the instructional planning or teaching of a student with AD/HD. Because AD/HD is not considered a separate disability under IDEA 04, there is no funding for special education services per se, although a student might qualify under a different category such as other health impairment (OHI). If you are a general education teacher, you might address the student's needs either informally or through the use of a 504 Plan. If you are a special education teacher collaborating with the general education teacher, instructional/behavioral suggestions would be appropriate, particularly if the student qualifies for IDEA 04 services under another category.

Check Your Understanding

1. Who initially described individuals who displayed attention problems and hyperactivity?

2. What is the definition of AD/HD? What are some of the criticisms of the current definition?

3. What are some of the general criteria for AD/HD?

4. What are the three types of AD/HD?

5. Approximately what percentage of the school population has AD/HD?

6. How is AD/HD related to gender and age?

What Are the Causes and Characteristics of Attention Deficit/Hyperactivity Disorder?

A discussion of the causes of AD/HD is important for two reasons. First, if causes are identified, the fact that the disorder does, in fact, exist is strengthened. Second, if a neurological basis of AD/HD is established, it helps to justify why medication could be an important part of the overall educational/treatment program for students with this disorder. After discussing the possible causes of AD/HD, we will introduce the characteristics most often associated with it.

Causes of Attention Deficit/Hyperactivity Disorder

Although it is generally accepted that AD/HD is a neurologically based disorder, myths still persist regarding its cause. Popular misconceptions include that AD/HD is caused by any of the following:

- a poor diet
- food additives
- too much sugar
- too much television viewing
- fluorescent lights

Poor parenting or teaching has also been suggested as a cause of AD/HD. Although certain specific factors, such as an inconsistent or unpredictable environment, might make the behaviors associated with AD/HD increase, they do not *cause* the disorder.

Barkley (2006b) noted that there is no credible theory related to a social/environmental cause of AD/HD. However, research has suggested both prenatal and perinatal nongenetic causes of AD/HD (Spencer, Biederman, Wilens, & Faraone, 2002). Some of these factors include premature birth, maternal smoking and alcohol use, and exposure to lead (U.S. Department of Education, 2003a). So far, research into the cause or causes of AD/HD has focused primarily on the brain and genetic causes.

The Brain and AD/HD

AD/HD is thought to be a disorder related to neurological, or brain anatomy and brain operation, differences. However, not all individuals diagnosed with AD/HD have these differences, and these differences also exist in individuals who do not have AD/HD. In addition, the cause of these differences is still not clearly established. There is considerable research on the areas of the brain that are affected in AD/HD. These include the prefrontal lobe, the basal ganglia, and the cerebellum (Krain & Castellanos, 2006). The prefrontal lobe is responsible for a number of cognitive functions including problem solving, self-regulation (monitoring one's behavior), and response inhibition (reflecting on when a behavior should be emitted). The basal ganglia are associated with motor behavior and may play a part in the hyperactivity seen in some individuals with AD/HD. Similarly, the cerebellum also controls motor behavior. There is some evidence that AD/HD is caused by a lag in brain development, and in some children the gap closes in mid-adolescence (CBS News 2007).

Genetic Causes of AD/HD

Although AD/HD is thought to be neurologically based, the exact cause of the disorder is not known. In fact, Haslam, Williams, Prior, Haslam, Graetz, and Sawyer (2006) suggested that AD/HD exists on a continuum and is not a single entity; therefore, no specific cause can be attributed to it. There are both suspected genetic and nongenetic causes of AD/HD, but the majority of the evidence indicates that AD/HD is inherited (Barkley, 2006b; Larsson, Lichtenstein, & Larsson, 2006) and is probably the result of multiple interacting genes (Children and Adults with Attention Deficit Disorder [CHADD], 2003). There is also some indication that genes responsible for the regulation of neurotransmitters (Waldman & Gizer, 2006), particularly dopamine, may be involved (Faraone, Doyle, Mick, & Biederman, 2001; Galili-Weisstub & Segman, 2003). Willingham (2004–2005) estimated the heritability of AD/HD to be about 80% (the heritability of adult height is approximately 90%), with estimates that a child of an adult with AD/HD has approximately a 25% chance of having AD/HD (Eli Lilly and Company, 2005).

Like many other exceptionalities, the genetic basis for AD/HD is based largely on twin studies. Results of these studies indicate that an identical twin of someone with AD/HD is much more likely than a fraternal twin with AD/HD to have the disorder (Willingham, 2004–2005).

Relevant CEC Standard
▶ Typical and atypical human growth and development (CC2K1)

Characteristics of Students with Attention Deficit/Hyperactivity Disorder

The *DSM-IV-TR* definition of AD/HD includes diagnostic criteria that identify the specific characteristics an individual must possess to receive the diagnosis. Based on these characteristics, an individual can be predominantly inattentive, unable to get focused or stay focused on an activity or task; predominantly hyperactive-impulsive, very active and frequently acting without thinking; or a combination of the two. Other characteristics associated with inattention and hyperactivity/impulsivity are listed in Table 14.2.

TABLE 14.2	Characteristics Associated with Inattentive and Hyperactive/Impulsive Types of AD/HD
INATTENTIVE SYMPTOMS	**HYPERACTIVE/IMPULSIVE SYMPTOMS**
Failure to give close attention to details; prone to careless mistakes	Tendency to fidget and squirm when seated
Difficulty sustaining attention and in persisting with tasks until they are complete	Tendency not to remain seated when it is expected to do so
Often appears as if his or her mind is elsewhere	Engages in excessive running or climbing when it is inappropriate
Frequently shifts from one uncompleted activity to another	Difficulty playing quietly
Difficulty organizing tasks and activities	Appears to be often "on the go" or "driven by a motor"
Dislike and avoidance of activities that require sustained mental effort	Talks excessively
Disorganized work habits; materials necessary for tasks are scattered, lost, or carelessly handled	Difficulty delaying responses; tendency to blurt out answers before a question is completely stated
Easily distracted by irrelevant stimuli; frequently interrupts tasks to attend to trivial events easily ignored by others	Difficulty waiting one's turn
Forgetful in daily activities; for example, misses appointments	Frequently interrupting or intruding on others

Source: Willingham, D. (2004–2005). Understanding AD/HD. *American Educator, Winter,* p. 38. Reprinted with permission from the *American Educator,* the quarterly journal of the American Federation of Teachers, AFL-CIO.

The characteristics associated with AD/HD differ as a function of age. Preschool children will often show excessive gross-motor behavior such as running around, climbing on furniture, and moving from activity to activity. Elementary-aged children with AD/HD frequently are restless and fidgety, often working carelessly and not finishing their work. Adolescents might demonstrate withdrawal as a primary characteristic. In general, it appears that younger children are most associated with the hyperactive/impulsive type of AD/HD whereas older students are more likely to have the inattentive type (McBurnett et al., 1999) or the combined type of AD/HD (U.S. Department of Education, 2003a). Adults with AD/HD often are distractible, disorganized, have mood swings and short tempers, and have problems planning ahead (CHADD, 2001). Researchers have found that as a child ages, the hyperactivity/impulsivity characteristics tend to go away but the inattentive characteristics remain (Hinshaw, Owens, Sami, & Fargeon, 2006; Larrson et al., 2006). The characteristics of AD/HD that research has focused most on are in the areas of cognition, academic performance, and social-emotional behaviors, as well as its coexistence with other disabilities.

Cognitive Characteristics

executive functioning The activation, organization, planning, integration, and management of cognitive functions.

behavioral inhibition The difficulty inhibiting and/or monitoring behaviors.

Although most individuals with AD/HD have average intelligence, there is evidence that they do have deficits in **executive functioning.** In other words, they have difficulty activating, organizing, planning, integrating, and managing cognitive functions. Fuggetta (2006) reported differences in executive control functioning between individuals with and without AD/HD in a controlled study, and Barkley (1997, 2006c) theorized that problems in executive functioning are due to a deficit in **behavioral inhibition,** resulting in individuals with AD/HD having difficulty inhibiting and/or monitoring their behavior. Behavioral inhibition results in many of the typical characteristics such as impulsivity and difficulty in planning. Barkley's theory helps to explain why students with AD/HD often are impulsive, or act before they think, which has been reported to be the primary characteristic of AD/HD-combined type (Solanto et al., 2001). There is also neurological evidence that AD/HD is associated with problems in inhibition. Booth et al. (2005), using fMRI, reported less brain activity for children with AD/HD than for their peers without AD/HD when they performed an inhibition task. Behavior inhibition problems also result in deficits in motor control.

Other cognitive characteristics that have been reported in individuals with AD/HD are decreased time attending to a task (Lorch et al., 2004) and slower visual processing speed not attributed to inattention (Weiler, Bernstein, Bellinger, & Waber, 2002). This might result in a slower reading rate. In addition, although students with AD/HD are able to learn new words at the same rate as those without AD/HD, they have more difficulty recalling the words after a delay (Cutting, Koth, Mahone, & Denckla, 2003). This might be due to their lack of using rehearsal strategies.

Academic Characteristics

Students with AD/HD frequently do not achieve their academic potential. This results in a greater risk of grade retention and school dropout compared to their peers without AD/HD (DuPaul & White, 2004). Students with AD/HD spend less time academically engaged and more time off task than do their peers without AD/HD (Vile Junod, DuPaul, Jitendra, Volpe, & Cleary, 2006). Other characteristics of students with AD/HD that could affect school performance include the following:

- Difficulty attending to academic tasks
- Difficulty organizing academic tasks
- Not listening to directions or the instruction itself
- Making careless mistakes

These problems, such as difficulty with organizational skills, extend beyond the classroom and affect virtually every aspect of the student's life.

It appears that the more severe the AD/HD characteristics are, the more the disorder will affect school performance (Barry, Lyman, & Klinger, 2002). However, school problems are more than likely to be *performance-related* rather than *ability-related*, although a significant number of students with AD/HD also have a learning disability. For example, Julio might actually have good math computation skills, but his dislike of written assignments and his tendency to make careless mistakes could lead his teacher to believe he has math problems. On the other hand, Jack might also display problems with math, but they could be related to a learning disability in the area of math that coexists with his AD/HD.

ANDY REVISITED What academic difficulties does Andy have that might be attributed to AD/HD?

Although students with AD/HD of all ages can have school-related problems, secondary-level students seem to have more difficulties. DuPaul and White (2004) summarized several issues related to older students with AD/HD. First, high school students must learn the expectations of multiple teachers. This means that they must display good organizational skills to know which teacher requires what assignments. Second, they must coordinate a more complex schedule that involves changing classrooms. Third, there is more emphasis at the secondary level on independent, long-term assignments that require organizational skills. Finally, because of their impulsivity, many students with AD/HD focus on the present with little planning for the future. Subsequently, they are also less likely to seek postsecondary education.

Social and Emotional Characteristics

Given the nature of the behaviors associated with AD/HD, it is not surprising that there are social-emotional consequences. One problem area is difficulty with peer relationships. Students with AD/HD have been reported to have fewer close friendships

Relevant CEC Standard
▶ Educational implications of characteristics of various exceptionalities (CC2K2)

and greater peer rejection than their peers without AD/HD (Bagwell, Molina, Pelham, & Hoza, 2001). Unnever and Cornell (2003) found that because of the lack of self-control in some students with AD/HD, there is a greater tendency for them to display bullying behaviors. This undoubtedly would lead to problems in peer relations. Aggression is more likely seen in those with the hyperactive-impulsive type of AD/HD whereas those with the inattentive type of AD/HD are more likely to be withdrawn (U.S. Department of Education, 2003a). Kos, Richdale, and Hay (2006) reported that information about peer relationships was one area in which teachers specifically needed more knowledge about students with AD/HD. A related area in which students with AD/HD might exhibit characteristics is antisocial behavior. It appears that the severity and pervasiveness of the AD/HD are related to the student's level of antisocial behavior (Thapar, van den Bree, Fowler, Langley, & Whittinger, 2006).

Another area that has been studied in students with AD/HD is their motivation. A survey of parents, teachers, and the students with AD/HD themselves about the students' motivational style indicated that they had a preference for easy work, were less persistent, received less enjoyment from learning, and had more of a tendency to be motivated by external rather than internal factors (Carlson, Booth, Shin, & Canu, 2002). A comprehensive summary of the characteristics associated with AD/HD is presented in Table 14.3.

TABLE 14.3	Characteristics Associated with AD/HD

Cognitive

- Mild deficits in intelligence (approximately 7–10 points)
- Deficient academic achievement skills (range of 10–30 standard score points)
- Learning disabilities: reading (8–39%), spelling (12–26%), math (12–33%), and handwriting (common but unstudied)
- Poor sense of time, inaccurate time estimation and reproduction
- Decreased nonverbal and verbal working memory
- Impaired planning ability
- Reduced sensitivity to errors
- Possible impairment in goal-directed behavioral creativity

Language

- Delayed onset of language (up to 35% but not consistent)
- Speech impairments (10–54%)
- Excessive conversational speech (commonplace), reduced speech to confrontation
- Poor organization and inefficient expression of ideas
- Impaired verbal problem solving
- Coexistence of central auditory processing disorder (minority but still uncertain)
- Poor rule-governed behavior
- Delayed internalization of speech (30% delay)
- Diminished development of moral reasoning

Adaptive Functioning   (10–30 standard score points behind normal)

Motor Development

- Delayed motor coordination (up to 52%)
- More neurological "soft" signs related to motor coordination and overflow movements
- Sluggish gross motor movements

Emotion

- Poor self-regulation of emotion
- Greater problems with frustration tolerance
- Underreactive arousal system

School Performance

- Disruptive classroom behavior (commonplace)
- Underperforming in school relative to ability (commonplace)
- Academic tutoring (up to 56%)
- Repeat a grade (30% or more)
- Placed in one or more special education programs (30–40%)
- School suspensions (up to 46%)
- School expulsions (10–20%)
- Failure to graduate high school (10–35%)

Task Performance

- Poor persistence of effort/motivation
- Greater variability in responding
- Decreased performance/productivity under delayed rewards
- Greater problems when delays are imposed within the task and as they increase in duration
- Decline in performance as reinforcement changes from being continuous to intermittent
- Greater disruption when noncontingent consequences occur during the task

Medical/Health Risks

- Greater proneness to accidental injuries (up to 57%)
- Possible delay in growth during childhood
- Difficulties surrounding sleeping (up to 30–60%)
- Greater driving risks: vehicular crashes and speeding tickets

Source: Barkley, R. A., *Attention Deficit Hyperactivity Disorder: A Handbook for Diagnosis and Treatment.* © 1998 Guilford Press. Reprinted by permission.

Coexistence with Other Exceptionalities

The coexistence, or comorbidity, of AD/HD with other exceptionalities is well documented. Although AD/HD and giftedness do coexist (Leroux & Levitt-Perlman, 2000), the majority of exceptionalities that coexist with AD/HD are disabilities. The professional literature indicates that approximately half of students with AD/HD have some type of coexisting disability (U.S. Department of Education, 2003a). Approximately 20% to 30% of students with AD/HD also have a learning disability (Wender, 2002). This comorbidity adds to the difficulty that these students have in school. Some professionals have even suggested that, in the future, AD/HD and learning disabilities might be considered different manifestations of the same disability (Bender, 2004).

Another disability commonly coexisting with AD/HD is emotional disturbance, particularly conduct disorders, oppositional defiant disorder, and anxiety or mood disorders. Gresham, Lane, and Beebe-Frankenberger (2005) reported that students with both AD/HD and conduct problems have a higher risk for social, behavioral, and legal problems than students with just AD/HD or students with conduct problems only. Teachers must be aware of the implications of a student having more than one disability.

> **ANDY REVISITED** Based on Andy's description, does it seem possible that he might also have another disability? If so, which one(s)?

Resnick (2000) reported the comorbidity of AD/HD with anxiety disorders to be between 10% and 40%, and AD/HD with bipolar disorder to be 10%. The comorbidity between AD/HD and bipolar disorder appears to be particularly strong for adolescents (Masi et al., 2006). The coexistence with some conditions seems to have a genetic basis. Coolidge, Thede, and Young (2000) reported the results of a twin study that indicated that there was a substantial genetic overlap between AD/HD and conduct disorders, and between AD/HD and oppositional defiant disorder.

As a teacher, the cause of AD/HD for any of your students probably has little direct relevance, although a brain-based cause suggests that medication might be an appropriate part of the overall educational program. Of greater importance is knowing possible characteristics of students with AD/HD. Students with AD/HD can display a number of diverse characteristics including inattention, hyperactivity, and/or impulsivity as well as academic and social-emotional problems. These varied characteristics suggest that teachers will need to address a variety of each student's individual needs.

Check Your Understanding

1. What areas of the brain are thought to be involved in AD/HD?
2. What evidence is there that AD/HD has a genetic basis? What nongenetic causes have been suggested?
3. What cognitive characteristics are associated with AD/HD?
4. What academic problems do students with AD/HD often have? Are these related to lack of ability? What specific challenges do adolescents with AD/HD face?
5. What are the social and emotional characteristics of AD/HD?
6. What is the comorbidity of AD/HD with other exceptionalities?

How Are Students with Attention Deficit/ Hyperactivity Disorder Identified?

Relevant CEC Standards

▶ Issues in definition and identification of individuals with exceptional learning needs, including those from culturally and linguistically diverse backgrounds (CC1K5)

▶ Screening, prereferral, referral, and classification procedures (CC8K3)

The identification of individuals with AD/HD should be a comprehensive process that involves multiple persons, procedures, and settings. No single procedure or source of information, such as a parent or teacher, is sufficient to make the diagnosis (DuPaul & White, 2004), particularly since the diagnostic criteria require subjective interpretation.

The types of procedures that are used to address diagnostic questions include the use of interviews, questionnaires, and checklists; rating scales; academic testing; and direct observation. In addition, assessment procedures, such as intelligence and academic tests, used to identify students with other types of disabilities under IDEA 04 are sometimes administered. Although most students with AD/HD are diagnosed using the *DSM-IV-TR* criteria and receive any accommodations via a 504 Plan, some also might qualify for services under IDEA 04. Specifically, a student with AD/HD can qualify under three IDEA 04 categories: specific learning disabilities (SLD), emotional disturbance (ED), and other health impairment (OHI; Davila, Williams, & MacDonald, 1991). To qualify for SLD or ED, the student must meet the requirement for those categories. To qualify for OHI, students must have chronic or acute impairments that limit their alertness and thus negatively affect school performance (Weyandt, 2001).

When an individual is suspected of having AD/HD, the first step is usually a medical evaluation by a physician who is knowledgeable about AD/HD. This includes vision and hearing screening to rule out other medical problems that might be causing the inattention, hyperactivity, and/or impulsivity. As noted earlier, the overall identification process should involve multiple personnel and multiple sources of information. Personnel who might be involved include school and private psychologists, nurses, social workers, and physicians (including psychiatrists) (CHADD, 2001). The multiple sources of information involve the various procedures listed above. Many of these procedures, such as interviews, checklists and questionnaires, and rating scales, should be used with both parents and teachers. This helps to meet the *DSM-IV-TR* requirement that the behaviors occur in multiple settings.

Interviews

A popular way for evaluating an individual thought to have AD/HD is through the interview process. Interviews, which are considered by some to be the most important component of a comprehensive AD/HD evaluation (Barkley & Edwards, 2006), should be conducted with the child's parents and teacher(s) and, when appropriate, the individual him- or herself. Parent interviews can serve several purposes including obtaining valid and reliable information about the individual's current functioning, determining the individual's developmental, medical, cognitive, academic, behavioral, and social-emotional history, and gathering information about the family's history and current family functioning. The interviewer should remember that this could very well be a stressful time for the parents and thus should play a supportive role in addition to a fact-finding role.

Teachers are frequently the first who notice the AD/HD behaviors of a student in their classroom and often provide this information to the parents who might not have observed, or accepted, their child's AD/HD-related behavior. It is very important to obtain information from the teacher, in part, to help meet the *DSM-IV-TR* requirement that the behaviors occur in multiple settings. An interview is one method of obtaining input from the teacher about a number of school-related behaviors. Typical questions that might be asked are "How is the student performing academically?" "How long does the student attend to a task?" "Does the student display good work habits, such as completing and turning in homework assignments?" "How long does the student persist at a task before he gets bored?" and "What is the student's activity level in the classroom?" Teachers have the advantage of comparing the behaviors of the student in question with the behaviors of the other students in class.

When appropriate, the individual suspected of having AD/HD should be interviewed. This decision is largely based on the person's age. For example, interviewing a 4-year-old child might not provide a tremendous amount of information, whereas interviewing an adult would provide valuable information. Goals of interviewing the individual suspected of having AD/HD include gathering information about the individual's perspective regarding his or her problem behavior and observing the individual's appearance, behavior, and language skills (Weyandt, 2001).

Questionnaires and Checklists

Questionnaires and checklists are helpful in determining the presence of AD/HD. Most questionnaires are designed more for parent use, asking information about the child's health, developmental, and medical history. An example is the Childhood History Form (Goldstein & Goldstein, 1998), which includes questions related to areas such as complications in pregnancy, factors related to the delivery, and behavior during the postdelivery period and infant period. It also has questions about the child's temperament, medical history, developmental milestones, school history, and home behavior. Such questionnaires can be helpful because there is some evidence that certain characteristics seen in young children, such as accident proneness and a difficult temperament, are good predictors of AD/HD (Weyandt, 2001).

Checklists, both formal and informal, can be used with both parents and teachers to help document the types of behaviors that are exhibited at home and in school. Examples of items that a parent or teacher might simply check yes/no are:

- Becomes easily frustrated?
- Is in constant motion?
- Has difficulty attending to tasks?
- Has problems following directions?
- Has difficulty finishing tasks that child has started?
- Seems to act before thinking?

Many checklists are developed based on the characteristics listed in the *DSM-IV-TR* criteria (refer back to Table 14.1).

Rating Scales

Behavior assessment systems, general behavior rating scales, and AD/HD-specific rating scales are used to help identify students with AD/HD. Behavior assessment systems include forms that allow for parent rating, teacher rating, and self-rating. Examples are the Achenbach System of Empirically Based Assessment and the Behavior Assessment System for Children–II. General behavior rating scales such as the Devereux Behavior Rating Scale–School Form also include items that might be helpful in documenting AD/HD. These behavior assessment systems and general behavior rating scales were described in Chapter 6. Specific AD/HD-related instruments also have been developed with the primary purpose of assisting in the diagnosis of AD/HD. These include the Attention Deficit Disorders Evaluation Scale–2 (McCarney, 1995), the ADD-H Comprehensive Teacher's Rating Scale–2 (Ullmann, Sleator, & Sprague, 1991), the Attention Deficit/Hyperactivity Disorder Test (Gilliam, 1995), and the Conners Rating Scales–Revised (Conners, 1997).

Academic Testing

One of the *DSM-IV-TR* criteria is that the AD/HD behaviors exist in more than one setting. One of those settings, depending on the individual's age, is usually the school. Although a student's academic history is usually obtained from parent and teacher input and school records, the student's achievement is sometimes evaluated. Instruments such as the Kaufman Educational Achievement Test–II and the Wechsler Individual Achievement Test–II (described in Chapter 2) can be administered. This is particularly true if the student might qualify for special education services under IDEA 04 as having another disability such as a learning disability.

Direct Observation

Direct, systematic observation to document the individual's behavior can be an invaluable tool. This could involve determining the frequency of a behavior, such as the number of times a student gets out of his seat during his 20-minute math lesson. It could also involve determining the duration of a behavior, such as how long a student stays on task. There are also more formal observation systems. One that is particularly appropriate for AD/HD is the **TOAD system: T**alking out, **O**ut of seat, **A**ttention problems, **D**isruption (Goldstein & Goldstein, 1998). In this system, the observer records data for both the student suspected of having AD/HD, the target student, and a comparison student to determine the severity of the behaviors of the target student.

ANDY REVISITED What specific interview questions could have been asked of Andy's parents when the pediatrician made the diagnosis of AD/HD?

TOAD system An observational system that stands for Talking out, Out of seat, Attention problems, and Distraction.

Teachers play an important role in the identification of students with AD/HD. In many cases, they may be the first to note the inattention, hyperactivity, and/or impulsivity displayed by a student. They may be involved by being interviewed, completing a behavior rating scale or an AD/HD rating scale, and/or directly observing and documenting classroom behavior.

Check Your Understanding

1. Who should be involved in the identification of an individual with AD/HD?
2. What are the roles of the individuals involved in the identification process?
3. What techniques are available to assist in identification?

What and How Do I Teach Students with Attention Deficit/Hyperactivity Disorder?

Given the characteristic behaviors of students with AD/HD, teaching them can be a very challenging and interesting task. Typically, AD/HD behaviors interfere with academic learning and self-control, and intervention thus needs to focus on both of these areas. Medication often is combined with direct instruction and behavioral intervention techniques. Whatever content and procedures are chosen, parent involvement is essential to the success of educational programs for students with AD/HD.

Relevant CEC Standards
▶ Sources of specialized materials, curricula, and resources for individuals with disabilities (CC4K1)
▶ Strategies for integrating student initiated learning experiences into ongoing instruction (CC4K5)
▶ Basic classroom management theories and strategies for individuals with exceptional learning needs (CC5K2)
▶ Social skills needed for educational and other environments (CC5K5)
▶ Strategies for crisis prevention and intervention (CC5K6)
▶ Strategies for preparing individuals to live harmoniously and productively in a culturally diverse world (CC5K7)

Instructional Content

Many students with AD/HD also have characteristics and performance behaviors that qualify them for programs for students with learning disabilities or emotional or behavioral disorders. This being the case, many of the instructional content needs of students with AD/HD are similar to those of students with those disabilities. However, with or without the coexistence of another exceptionality, programs for students with AD/HD need to include instruction in academics and self-regulation skills as well as parent training and counseling components. In general, the goal of the program content is to improve attention, task completion, and academic achievement (Coleman & Webber, 2002).

Academics

Most students with AD/HD are required to meet the standards of the general education curriculum by passing the state's standardized assessment. As Minskoff and Allsopp (2003) pointed out, providing students with AD/HD with all the accommodations in the world while taking the test will not help if students have not learned the content of the general curriculum. Unfortunately, the characteristic problems in attention and self-regulatory behaviors often lead to difficulties in school, and when these problems persist, students with AD/HD are at significant risk for academic failure (Barkley, 2006a). To learn the content of the academic curriculum, students with AD/HD may need to be directly taught specific strategies to increase organizational skills and goal setting, improve listening and attending skills, and aid in following instructions. Mnemonic strategies, tricks to aid memory, such as ROY G BIV (red, orange, yellow, green, blue, indigo, violet) to remember the colors of the rainbow, and self-instruction, talking to oneself about the requirements of a task while performing it, are both effective approaches for helping students with AD/HD master academic content.

Self-Regulation

Recent theoretical work has conceptualized AD/HD as a deficit in self-regulated behavior (Barkley, 2004). **Self-regulation,** or self-control, is the individual's ability to influence his or her own behavior. Individuals with AD/HD may have the skills to perform desired behaviors, but they do not perform the behaviors consistently or maintain them over time due to a lack of self-regulation behaviors (Harris & Schmidt, 1997). Self-regulation procedures are usually aimed at increasing attention and decreasing impulsivity for students with AD/HD (Coleman & Webber, 2002; Reid, 1999). The student is taught a set of self-instructions or a sequence of problem-solving steps that are practiced overtly and then covertly. Self-regulation, which should be the goal of all programs for students with AD/HD, often needs to be directly taught.

Self-assessment and self-evaluation of behavior are fundamental to self-regulation (Reid, Trout, & Schartz, 2005). Students with AD/HD are taught to ask questions about their past behavior, such as "Did I complete the homework assignment as required?" "How well did I do?" and "Why do I rate myself that way?" Questions such as these allow a student to determine what behavior should occur in the future. Self-assessment processes are incorporated into **self-monitoring** strategies that can help the student with AD/HD learn how to attend, become more self-aware, and remain focused for longer periods of time (Weyandt, 2001). Self-monitoring strategies have been used to improve academic productivity, accuracy of work, and social behavior (Kauffman, 2005). Steps for implementing self-monitoring (Reid, 1999) are presented in the Classroom Suggestions.

Self-monitoring may be used with external reinforcement or with self-reinforcement. **Self-reinforcement** systems teach students to evaluate their own academic and social behaviors and then reinforce themselves accordingly (with positive statements, points, or other tokens). For example, the student may award herself with five stickers after determining that she has correctly used an appropriate strategy to ask for help five times in a two-hour period. These systems have been successful with students with AD/HD (Pfiffner, Barkley, & DuPaul, 2006). However, students with AD/HD still need some external reinforcement for displaying self-monitoring skills in order to

self-regulation Self-control that enables an individual to act in a manner that influences his or her own behavior.

self-monitoring The observation and recording of one's own behavior.

self-reinforcement Evaluating and reinforcing oneself.

PRACTICE

Classroom Suggestions Steps for Self-Monitoring for Students with AD/HD

STEPS	DESCRIPTION
Select a target behavior	Four considerations are: ❑ Must be well specified so student can accurately self-assess ❑ Should be a behavior the student is aware of and can easily observe ❑ Should be appropriate for the setting or task ❑ Should be a good personal match
Collect baseline data	Baseline data allow for assessment of effectiveness after self-monitoring begins
Obtain willing cooperation	Schedule a conference to address the problem areas frankly. Point out the benefits the student would derive by improving his or her behavior; frame self-monitoring as something that has helped a lot of other students with the same kind of problem.
Instruct in self-monitoring procedures	Four steps are involved: ❑ Teacher explains the procedure ❑ Teacher models the steps while verbalizing ❑ Teacher models the steps while the student verbalizes them ❑ Student models and verbalizes the steps
Provide independent practice	During first few times, teacher observes to be sure student follows the procedures consistently and appropriately. Reminders may be necessary during the first few sessions.

Source: Reid, R. (1999). Attention deficit hyperactivity disorder: Effective methods for the classroom. *Focus on Exceptional Children, 32*(4), 1–20.

maintain them. For example, the teacher may award points to the student for doing such a good job of self-monitoring. Self-reinforcement and self-monitoring programs that have incorporated goal-setting have also been successful with students with AD/HD (Barry & Messer, 2003; Codding & Lewandowski, 2003).

Parent Training

Due to the nature of the disorder, children with AD/HD are characteristically not very adept at thinking through the consequences of their actions (Anastopoulos, Rhoads, & Farley, 2006). Parents, who typically have extreme difficulty in dealing with a child with AD/HD at home, can benefit from training in systematic behavior management skills, which teach parents how to interact more positively and effectively with their children (Kauffman, 2005). These procedures are most effective when carried out both in the home and at school. Parents of children with AD/HD are usually trained to implement contingency-management programs (Pelham, Wheeler, & Chronis, 1998) that use very explicit, systematic, externalized, and compelling forms of rules, instructions, and consequences (Smith, Barkley, & Shapiro, 2006). Procedures may include token reinforcement systems to encourage appropriate behavior and response cost (withdrawing rewards) and time-out (brief social isolation) for inappropriate behaviors (Kauffman, 2005). As caregivers of children with AD/HD are subject to extreme levels of stress, training in dealing with stress is also essential (Pelham et al., 1998).

Counseling Services to Support Understanding and Transition

Adolescents with AD/HD invariably need counseling services to help them understand their disability (Pfiffner et al., 2006). Until they fully understand and accept their disability, they are unlikely to accept or request help from others. Most adolescents resist taking stimulant medication, so they may also need counseling on the benefits of starting or returning to medication to improve school performance and earn privileges such as driving (Robin, 2006). Counseling may also help students with emotional issues such as severe test anxiety or depression (Weyandt, 2001) and may complement classroom strategies.

AD/HD is a lifelong problem and 30% to 70% of children with AD/HD continue to display characteristics into their adult lives (Heiligenstein, Guenther, Levy, Savino, & Fulwiler, 1999). Adults may not appear as active as they did as children, having replaced their moving-around behavior with pencil tapping or leg swinging, but other characteristics, such as attention problems and distractibility, remain (Heiligenstein, Conyers, Berns, & Smith, 1998). Because of this, adolescents with AD/HD need to be taught coping strategies they can use across time (Robin, 2006). Career counseling may help the adolescent consider what type of work environment he or she may be best suited to. The counselor can help the student remain focused on his or her goals and reinforce the accomplishment of these goals.

Instructional Procedures

Different intervention techniques have been tried with students with AD/HD in both home and classroom settings. Many instructional procedures used to help regulate attention, hyperactivity, distractibility, and motivation in students with AD/HD are similar to those used with students with learning disabilities and emotional/behavioral disorders. Task analysis, clear consistent rules, repetitious verbal instructions, advance organizers, and learning strategies are among the procedures that may be effective with students with AD/HD (Reid, 1999). These procedures are all components of the direct instruction approach to teaching. Cognitive behavior modification and precision teaching may be useful in increasing both academic and behavioral performance. The use of combined procedures has become more popular in teaching students with AD/HD (Forness, Kavale, Sweeny, & Crenshaw, 1999; Reid, 1999). Behavioral instruction is a critical element of effective teaching for students with AD/HD. Medication may enhance learning for some students. The most common and successful combination of instructional procedures in early intervention is the use of stimulant medication along with training teachers and parents how to manage the student's behavior (Kauffman, 2005).

Direct Instruction

Based on their known characteristics, explicit direct instruction is required in teaching students with AD/HD. As you may recall from Chapter 4, major components of direct instruction include presentation (advance organizer, rationale for learning, demonstration), guided practice, and independent practice. Advance organizers for students with AD/HD need to be clear and explicit. During presentation to students with AD/HD, teachers need to repeat and highlight key concepts many times and include specific examples and prompts. During guided practice, students should obtain high levels of accuracy before moving on to independent activities. This step is very important for students with AD/HD, as they are more likely to be disruptive at levels of 75% accuracy than at 90% accuracy (DePaepe, Shores, Beck, & Denny, 1996; Reid, 1999). A post organizer at the end of a lesson or class should highlight important topics and give reminders about homework, exams, or other class business. A combination of the components of direct instruction and strategy instruction, found to be the best model for teaching students with learning disabilities, is most often also applicable to students with AD/HD.

Cognitive Behavior Modification

The strategies approach to self-regulation had its beginnings with **cognitive behavior modification** (CBM), an educational approach developed by Meichenbaum

cognitive behavior modification (CBM) An educational approach to help students internalize efficient learning strategies by actively involving them in the learning process using verbalization, modeled strategies, and a planned, reflective goal statement.

(1977; Meichenbaum & Goodman, 1971) to help students internalize efficient learning strategies by actively involving them in the learning process, using verbalization, modeled strategies, and a planned, reflective goal statement. The CBM procedure of self-instruction can be very useful in keeping students' attention focused on the task they are attempting to accomplish. A typical training sequence would include the following scenarios:

1. The teacher performs a task while verbalizing questions, self-guiding instructions, and self-evaluating performance.
2. The student performs the task while the teacher gives instructions.
3. The student performs the task while overtly verbalizing instructions.
4. The student performs the task while whispering instructions.
5. The student performs the task while verbalizing covertly.

This procedure led the field of special education into the contemporary emphasis on cognitive behaviors and has been successfully used for both academic and behavioral problems.

Precision Teaching

precision teaching A system of evaluating and improving instruction characterized by direct, continuous, and precise measurements of student progress using response rate.

Rather than being a specific method of instruction, **precision teaching** is a system of evaluating and improving instruction (Lindsley, 1971). It is characterized by direct, continuous, and precise measurements of student progress using response rate. The underlying principle is that a skill is mastered when it can be performed accurately and quickly (Olson & Platt, 2004). The steps of precision teaching are as follows:

1. Pinpoint a target behavior.
2. Evaluate pupil progress in daily timed exercises.
3. Graph data daily to set instructional goals.
4. Design the instructional program.
5. Analyze the data and make instructional decisions.

By observing and charting student behavior before and after a specific instructional program is presented, the teacher can see the effect of the program and make more accurate instructional decisions. For example, a teacher might measure the effects of repeated readings on a student's level of fluency by timing each reading and charting the best daily performance of reading rate and number of errors. This chart provides feedback to the teacher on the effectiveness of the instruction. Charted data also help students become aware of their progress toward instructional goals and can be used for self-monitoring when students observe and record their own behavior for purposes of self-regulation.

Behavioral Intervention

As we have discussed several times throughout this text, the use of functional behavior assessment (FBA) can help in clearly defining the target behaviors and the most effective intervention plan (Dupaul & Ervin, 1996). Behavioral intervention involves ensuring that rewarding consequences follow desirable behavior and that either no consequences or only punishing consequences follow undesirable behavior (Kauffman, 2005). As we have discussed several times throughout the text, functional behavioral assessment (FBA) can help in clearly defining the target behaviors and most effective intervention plan. Behavioral intervention programs can be embedded in teaching activities and should be considered a critical part of effective teaching of students with AD/HD. Furthermore, it has been demonstrated that skillful use of this procedure results in warm, caring relationships between students and teachers (Kauffman, 2005). As we have discussed several times throughout the text, functional behavioral assessment (FBA) can help in clearly defining the trarget behaviors and most effective intervention plan. Behavioral intervention techniques for use with students with AD/HD are the same as those prescribed earlier for students with emotional or behavioral disabilities, such as positive reinforcement, token economies, contingency contracting, and punishment, with the following caveats offered by Pfiffner, Barkley, and DuPaul (2006). Rules and instructions must be clear, brief, and delivered often through more visible and external modes of presentation. Consequences used to manage the behavior of students with AD/HD must be delivered swiftly, frequently, and more immediately than with typical students. These consequences should be more powerful than merely occasional praise or reprimands. Whereas the use of positive approaches should be emphasized, negative consequences are usually necessary. However, to be effective, punishment must remain in a relative balance with rewards, and should be implemented one to two weeks after the positive reinforcement system has been established. For example, in the case of time-out, removing a student from a setting in which the opportunity for reinforcement is low will most likely not be effective as it is not punitive. Furthermore, reinforcers, most particularly rewards, must be changed or rotated frequently as their effectiveness will be lost more rapidly than is normal because satiation seems to occur more quickly with students with AD/HD. This means, for example, that a menu of rewards in place for a token economy system must be changed every two to three weeks to remain powerful. However, with such a schedule of change or rotation, a token economy system may be maintained all year with minimal loss of power. Classroom rules and their consequences need to be reviewed and prompted often, particularly before transitions across classes or activities. Furthermore, teachers' knowledge of AD/HD and attitudes toward the disorder are critical to successful behavior management.

Behavior interventions may include a range of in-class consequences, home-based programs, self-management interventions, and modification of academic tasks and the classroom environment (Pfiffner et al., 2006). Consistent home and school communication is recommended to increase the educational success of students with AD/HD. **Home-based contingency programs,** in which contingencies are provided at home based on school performance, are among the most recommended behavioral interventions (Pfiffner et al., 2006). Reports, often referred to as report cards or home-school notes (Reid, 1999), are sent home to parents listing target behaviors along with quantifiable ratings for each behavior. These behaviors may include almost any school behavior, such as paying attention, turning in assignments, working independently, or getting along with peers (Walker, Ramsey, & Gresham, 2004). At first, reports are sent on a daily basis. As behavior improves, they are faded to a less frequent basis, although many students with AD/HD will need reports on a weekly basis throughout the year. The Classroom Example on the next page presents a home-based contingency program report card from Pfiffner, Barkley, and DuPaul (2006). Given that homework is a common problem for children with AD/HD, it is often good to include an update on this on all reports. In addition, including at least one or two positive behaviors that were displayed is recommended. After the parent or caregiver has inspected the report, discussed the positive ratings, and briefly, neutrally asked about any negative ratings, reports should be clearly and consistently translated into home consequences such as TV time, movie, special dessert, or a special outing. The child is then asked to formulate a plan in response to the ratings and the parent/caregiver reminds him or her about it the next morning. Programs may involve positive and negative consequences or rewards alone, particularly if parents tend to be overly coercive or abusive. Rewards may include praise and attention; however, tangible rewards or token programs are usually necessary as well.

home-based contingency programs Reinforcement is provided at home based on school performance.

ANDY REVISITED What are some instructional procedures that could be used to help Andy with completing and turning in his homework?

Medication as a Support for Learning

Medication has been used to treat AD/HD since 1937 when physician Charles Bradley, working with children with encephalitis, noted dramatic improvement in conduct and school performance after the administration of an amphetamine (Benezedrine). This observation led to studies in the use of medication to enhance the learning and behavior of students with attention problems and hyperactivity. The medications usually given are psychostimulants such as Ritalin, Dexedrine, Cylert, or Adderall, or a nonstimulant drug called Strattera. A summary of commonly

Name: _____   Date: _____

Please rate child in areas below according to this scale:

2 = Very good

1 = OK

0 = Needs improvement

Target Behavior	1	2	3	4	5	6
Participation						
Class work						
Handed in homework						
Interaction with peers						
Teacher's initials						

Total points earned: _____

Homework for tonight (list class period by assignment):

Comments:

Source: Pfiffner, L. J., Barkley, R. A., & DuPaul, G. J. (2006). Treatment of AD/HD in school settings. In R. A. Barkley, *Attention-deficit hyperactivity disorder: A handbook for diagnosis and treatment* (3rd ed., pp. 547–569). New York: Guilford Press.

paradoxical effect The mistaken notion that stimulant medications such as Ritalin have an opposite effect on individuals with AD/HD than on individuals without AD/HD.

prescribed medications and their pros and precautions can be found in Online Appendix A. The use of stimulants to decrease activity level is not, as once thought, a **paradoxical effect,** meaning that the effects of the drugs only occur in the specific group of individuals, in this case, those with AD/HD. The effects of the stimulants are the same as they are for individuals without AD/HD. Psychostimulants raise the level of arousal or alertness in the central nervous system by increasing concentrations of neurotransmitters, resulting in improved memory, cognition, and attention. The practice of medicating students with AD/HD is a controversial issue in the field of special education, especially as the focus on AD/HD increases. However, at this point in time, research clearly indicates that the correct dosage of the correct drug results in significant improvement in behavior and the ability to learn in about 90% of children with AD/HD (Crenshaw, Kavale, Forness, & Reeve, 1999; Kauffman, 2005; MTA Cooperative Group, 1999).

Most educators would agree that drugs should be used only after other procedures have been attempted and only if a valid diagnosis of AD/HD has been made. Academic problems existing before the administration of drugs generally continue after drug therapy is initiated. If drug therapy is used, it should be used in combination with behavioral and academic training programs, and with the willingness of the prescribing physician to collaborate with school professionals (Forness et al., 1999). Family education is crucial before beginning medication, particularly, with adolescents (Robin, 2006).

Hallahan and Kauffman (2006) and Kauffman (2005) noted that comprehensive reviews of the available research point to the following cautions in the use of drug therapy:

1. These drugs are very powerful, and the decision to medicate a student should not be made without physicians, parents, and teachers communicating effectively.
2. Psychostimulants do not affect all children in the same way, and a few do not respond favorably.
3. Optimal levels of dosage are extremely important for any benefits in academic performance and can sometimes be difficult to establish. A dosage that is too high may interfere with learning rather that facilitate it.
4. Taking medication may lead to undesirable motivational changes; children may come to rely on the medicine rather than themselves for behavior changes. Parents and teachers must be careful that children do not give up the responsibility for their behavior.
5. Medication alone is rarely, if ever, enough. Strong educational programming in academic training almost always needs to be provided in combination with drug therapy.

Adverse effects from stimulants include insomnia, decreased appetite, stomachaches, headaches, and jitteriness. These effects are generally mild, short lived, and responsive to dosage or timing adjustments (Connor, 2006; Goldman, Genel, Bezman, & Slanetz, 1998). If medication is prescribed, it is important for the physician, educators, and parents to monitor its effects carefully and maintain close communication to be sure that a correct dosage is being administered at the best time of the day to facilitate optimal effectiveness. In treatment guidelines published in the October 2001 issue of *Pediatrics*, the American Academy of Pediatrics recommended that the prescribing physician, parents, the child, and school personnel should specify goals related to the specific problems of the individual child (e.g., school performance, difficulty finishing tasks, and problems with interactions with schoolmates).

In the reauthorization of IDEA 04, school districts are prohibited from requiring a child to obtain a prescription for a substance covered by the Controlled Substances Act as a condition of attending school, receiving an evaluation, or receiving services. This provision further states, however, that this does not prohibit teachers and other school personnel from consulting or sharing classroom-based observations with parents or guardians regarding a student's academic and functional performance, or behavior in the classroom or school, or regarding the need for evaluation for special education or related service. In a letter to the Office of Special Education and Rehabilitation Services (OSERS), Honaker (2005), Deputy Chief Executive Officer and Chief Operating Officer of the American Psychological Association, stated that the organization believes the latter part of this language is imperative to ensure that the lines of communication between school personnel and parents remain open regarding the needs of the child.

ANDY REVISITED Do you think Andy might benefit from medication? Why or why not?

Early Multicomponent Interventions

Because of the nature of characteristics of AD/HD, preschool children with this disorder are often excessively active, uncooperative, frequently noncompliant with parental requests, defiant in response to authority figures, and already delayed in academic readiness skills (Smith et al., 2006). Without intervention, these behaviors may become severe enough to result in expulsion, thus denying these children the opportunity to develop preacademic skills, learn valuable social skills, and adjust to the structure of school (McGoey et al., 2002). Three primary approaches to intervention have been effective in reducing negative behaviors in young children with AD/HD: stimulant medication, parent training, and classroom behavior management (McGoey et al., 2002). Each of these programs needs to be individually tailored for the child based on the function of the target behavior. Brief functional assessment procedures are useful and time-efficient methods for determining the variables influencing the behaviors of preschoolers with AD/HD (Boyajian, DuPaul, Handler, Eckert, & McGoey, 2001). Components of successful behavioral interventions include positive reinforcement and response cost programs, giving effective directions and requests, teaching self-control, and using consistent methods of discipline. Linking the three intervention approaches of medication, behavior management, and parent training into one multicomponent intervention promotes collaboration among the parent, the school, and the child and is most likely to lead to a successful outcome (McGoey et al., 2002).

Check Your Understanding

1. What two content areas are often included in programs for students with AD/HD? What are some strategies students with AD/HD may need to be successful in academics? What is the goal of self-regulation?

2. What are parents generally taught in parent training programs? What is the purpose of counseling services for adolescents with AD/HD?

3. What overall instructional approach is needed to teach students with AD/HD? What are cognitive behavior modification, precision teaching, and behavioral intervention?

4. How can medication help the learning of students with AD/HD? What are some considerations that should be made if a student with AD/HD is using medication?

5. What combination of instructional approaches has been found to be most successful with students with AD/HD?

6. What are the three primary approaches to intervention with young children? What approaches to intervention have been effective in reducing negative behaviors in young children with AD/HD?

What Are Other Instructional Considerations for Teaching Students with Attention Deficit/Hyperactivity Disorder?

Relevant CEC Standards

► Demands of learning environments (CC5K1)

► Ways to create learning environments that allow individuals to retain and appreciate their own and each other's respective language and cultural heritage (CC5K8)

► Adaptation of the physical environment to provide optimal learning opportunities for individuals with disabilities (GC5K2)

► Methods for ensuring individual academic success in one-to-one, small-group, and large-group settings (GC5K3)

► Technology for planning and managing the teaching and learning environment (CC7K4)

Alongside the considerations of the content that should be taught to and procedures that should be used with students with AD/HD is planning for the classroom environment in which instruction takes place and for the use of instructional technology. Students with AD/HD are highly susceptible to any aspects of their environment that may distract them and direct their attention away from the task at hand. Specifically, how students with AD/HD are grouped can have a significant impact on their learning, as can technology that particularly supports the learning of students with AD/HD. This includes devices designed to focus the child's attention and software to facilitate drill-and-practice.

The Instructional Environment

Structure and routine, which are important factors in the instructional environment for students in many categories of exceptionalities, are of even greater importance for students with AD/HD. As Hallowell and Ratey (1992) noted, these students need their environment to structure externally what they cannot structure internally on their own. For students with AD/HD to be successful, the environment must be arranged to maximize attention on the teacher and lesson, and to minimize distraction from other students and objects in the classroom. Both the physical arrangement of the classroom and the grouping options need to take this into account.

The Physical Arrangement

Much attention has been given to developing guidelines for establishing the physical environment for students considered "hyperactive" or "distractible." In the early days of recognition of children with what is now termed AD/HD, Cruickshank, Bentzen, Ratzeburg, and Tannhauser (1961) stressed a reduction of all distracting stimuli in the classroom (see An Important Event). Although their approach was quite drastic, it is still recognized that attention problems may be exacerbated by the student's environment or aided by changes that create an AD/HD-friendly environment (Yehle & Wambold, 1998). Altering the classroom environment, or antecedents to behavioral problems, often results in a quick and significant change in behavior (Reid, 1999).

AN IMPORTANT EVENT

1959—A Sterile Classroom Is Proposed for Hyperactive Children with Limited Attention Spans

As part of an early demonstration pilot study dealing with the education of children who were hyperactive and brain-injured, an educational program was devised that included reduced environmental stimuli, reduced space, a structured school program, and an increase in the stimulus value of the teaching materials. It was suggested that an appropriate classroom environment for distractible children was a classroom as devoid of stimuli as possible. The color of the walls, woodwork, and furniture matched the floor; windows were opaque; bulletin boards and pictures were removed. There were no intercom systems, no pencil sharpeners, and walls were soundproofed. Only absolutely essential furniture was in the room, and the number of children was greatly reduced from that in the typical elementary classroom (Cruickshank et al., 1961).

The students each worked in three-sided cubicles with their desks affixed to the walls that were painted the same color as everything else in the room and remained blank. All learning experiences took place in this stimulus-free space. Results indicated that success varied with individuals.

REFLECTION Why would or wouldn't this classroom setup be possible or desirable in today's educational system?

The Preschool Classroom. Preschool children with AD/HD function best in a highly structured environment with specific, concise routines, directions, and demands (Kyle, DuPaul, Yugar, & Lutz, 1996). These youngsters are at a disadvantage in a wide-open free-play classroom. A physically structured classroom with walls and a door will block out distractions from the halls. Children with AD/HD should be seated away from the door and any other potential visual or auditory distractions. Preschool children with AD/HD will be even more active than typical preschoolers, but movement should be teacher-directed and nondisruptive whenever possible. Learning centers can be set up in three-sided carrels with interactive materials, and transition from one center to another can be scheduled to allow purposeful movement. In- and out-of-seat activities should be frequently alternated. Any changes in schedules or routines should be avoided, and the child should be prepared ahead of time if an unavoidable change is to take place.

Elementary and Secondary Classrooms. Children with AD/HD are at a disadvantage if the classroom is noisy, disorderly, or lacking in clear consistent routines, rules, and expectations (Reid, 1999). Therefore, physical modifications that may be helpful for elementary and secondary students with AD/HD include reducing unnecessary clutter in the classroom, having individual desks or study carrels available, clearly designating a space for the student to keep his or her materials, and decreasing auditory distractions by closing the door (Yehle & Wambold, 1998). Students with AD/HD should be seated in the front/middle of the room close to the teacher and away from distracting stimuli, such as bulletin boards or windows. Working in study carrels can greatly decrease distractions for a student with attention problems. Students with AD/HD should also be given legitimate opportunities to move around in the classroom, use the restroom, or get a drink of water (Beech, 2003). Additional desks may be provided so that a student could quietly take his or her work and move if the need arises (Carbone, 2001). See Figure 14.1 for a visual image of a possible

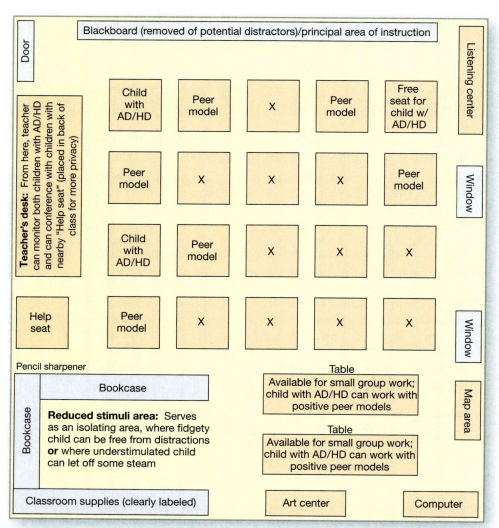

FIGURE 14.1 Classroom Model of Structural Interventions for Children with AD/HD

Source: Carbone, E. (2001). Arranging the classroom with an eye (and ear) to students with AD/HD. *Teaching Exceptional Children, 34*(2), 72–81. Reprinted with permission.

classroom arrangement as a structural intervention. Traditional row-seating patterns are used because this is the most structured and predictable option.

Instructional Grouping

Instructional grouping can significantly affect students with AD/HD because other students may distract them or unwittingly reinforce their inappropriate behavior (Reid, 1999). Most students with AD/HD spend at least some time in the general education classroom and therefore are involved in the many grouping options that exist in these classrooms.

Large Group Instruction. When in a large group, or working on independent work, most students with AD/HD do better when they are seated in individual, separated desks (Pfiffner et al., 2006). The young student's workspace may need to be defined, such as with masking tape when on the floor, when participating in large group activities (Yehle & Wambold, 1998). Attention to a lecture can be enhanced by delivering it in an enthusiastic, yet focused style, keeping it brief, and allowing frequent participation (Pfiffner et al., 2006). Other helpful strategies include tape-recording lectures for the student to listen to again, interspersing lectures with brief moments of physical exercise, and scheduling academic subjects in the morning when the activity levels and attentiveness of students with AD/HD are better controlled.

Peer Tutoring. Peer tutoring provides a learning environment well suited to the needs of students with AD/HD, in that it provides immediate, frequent feedback and active responding at the student's pace (DuPaul & Stoner, 2003). Peer tutoring is probably most effective when students with AD/HD are paired with well-behaved and conscientious students (Pfiffner et al., 2006). **Peer-mediated instruction** in reading, in which one partner reads to another who monitors and corrects errors and then switches roles with the partner, has also been shown to be effective in increasing on-task behavior. Teachers can also have peers assume roles as "behavior modifiers" who ignore disruptive, inappropriate behavior of their peers and praise or award tokens for positive behavior such as getting a good grade or helping another peer (Pfiffner et al., 2006). Peers seated next to students with AD/HD can prompt attention through subtle cues such as touching the student's back when attention lapses are noticed and report to the teacher when prompts are not effective (Mastropieri & Scruggs, 2007). Of course, these peer assistants will need to be chosen judiciously from students with strong interpersonal skills.

peer-mediated instruction
One partner performs while the other monitors and corrects errors and then roles are switched.

Classwide Peer Tutoring. Classwide peer tutoring (CWPT), which uses a combination of whole class instruction, peer tutoring, and cooperative learning, has been shown to be effective with students with AD/HD (DuPaul, Ervin, Hook, & McGoey, 1998; DuPaul & Henningson, 1993). In CWPT, students within the same class are trained in explicit presentation formats to work with each other while being monitored by the classroom teacher (Greenwood, Maheady, & Delquadri, 2002). After the teacher presents new material to the entire class, tutoring pairs, who are assigned to small groups or teams, take turns teaching each other, monitoring skills, and keeping points. The points earned by each tutoring pair are then awarded to their assigned team (Maheady, Harper, & Mallette, 2003). It has been recommended that the teacher start with simple drill-and-practice of spelling words, vocabulary definitions, or math facts to work out the logistics, for example, smoothly transitioning to pairs. Once students are proficient with the procedures, more challenging content may be added (Fulk & King, 2001). CWPT has been used successfully at both the elementary and secondary levels, in both basic skills and content areas (Mastropieri & Scruggs, 2007; Olson & Platt, 2004), and in both pullout and inclusive settings (Greenwood, 1996, 1999). It has also been used effectively to support language development in English language learners (Sheppard, 2001). CWPT has been shown to be superior to conventional forms of teacher-led instruction in improving pupils' academic outcomes (Greenwood, Arreaga-Mayer, Utley, Gavin, & Terry, 2001).

Peer-Assisted Learning Strategies. **Peer-assisted learning strategies** (PALS) borrows the basic structure of the classwide peer tutoring system, but expands the procedures to engage students in strategic reading activities (Fuchs, Fuchs, Mathes, & Simmons, 1997). Students are engaged in three strategic reading activities: *partner reading*, read-alouds with brief retellings; *paragraph shrinking*, summarization and main idea identification; and *prediction relay*, formulating and checking predictions. Although originally developed for grades 2 through 6, PALS programs have been extended downward to kindergarten and first grade, with activities focusing on phonological awareness, sound-letter correspondence, decoding and fluency; and upward to high school, using expository rather than narrative text (Fuchs et al., 2001; Fuchs, Fuchs, & Kazdan, 1999). There is also a PALS program for instruction in math. Both PALS and CWPT provide effective means of actively involving students with AD/HD in group interactions.

peer-assisted learning strategies (PALS) An expansion of the basic structure of the classwide peer tutoring system (CWPT) that engages students in strategic reading activities.

Instructional Technology

Many teachers have noted that students with AD/HD are much more attentive when working on computers or playing video games (Yehle & Wambold, 1998). Many positive aspects of computer usage are particularly relevant for students with AD/HD and can be used by teachers to their advantage. Computers motivate, increase attention, and provide immediate feedback. Time on the computer may be used as a reward, or the computer and the many software programs now available may be used as instructional

In Practice Meet Educator Varie Hudson Hawkins and Her Student David

I teach in a self-contained third-grade inclusion classroom in a Title I School of Excellence in one of the fastest growing school districts in southern Georgia. I am a National Board Certified master teacher with 19 years of teaching experience at the elementary level. I was recently inducted into my university's Academic Hall of Fame. I have a passion for learning and am currently working on the final chapter of my dissertation in Advanced K–12 Teaching and Learning. I teach all academic subjects: reading, writing, language arts, mathematics, science, and social studies. My school serves elementary students in kindergarten through grade 5. The school's student population is approximately 70% African American and 30% Caucasian and other.

I have 16 students in my self-contained third-grade classroom. Of these students, five have learning disabilities and are diagnosed with attention deficit/hyperactivity disorder (AD/HD). Two of these students attend occupational therapy and require special pencils and pencil grippers due to poor motor coordination. I collaborate with the special education teacher and two paraprofessionals to meet the unique needs of these students who all have varying abilities. Another student, David, qualified for special education services at the end of his second-grade year under other health impaired (OHI) due to AD/HD and failing grades in all academic areas the previous year. He reads on a preprimer/kindergarten level and poses special challenges to me.

David politely informed me on the first day of school that "I can't read, and you will have to find me some kindergarten books because I am special ed." David is outgoing and very inquisitive in his peer interactions. During direct instruction he frequently makes excuses for not doing his work and remarks that "I am stupid and don't know very much." I realized quickly that I have to provide him with some successes in learning to build his self-esteem.

Instructional Content and Procedures

Instructional content is based on state standards and is broken down into learning objectives for six weeks of instruction. To meet the needs of learners in mixed ability groups, I differentiate instruction, which means providing learners with multiple options for learning new concepts. I plan my instruction based on learner needs because I have to meet students where they are. Because of David's reading difficulties, most of his assignments are read to him or taped so he can listen and follow along. If someone reads the assignments to him, David will make above average scores, which tells me that he comprehends well.

devices. Many features inherent in technology are related to the characteristics of effective instruction (Xu, Reid, & Steckelberg, 2002):

- Computers may be used to introduce new material with graphics, words, and sound with game formats, animation, or color.
- Computers allow repeated trials, offer privacy, and organize content into smaller chunks of information.
- Software can provide step-by-step instruction, wait for responses, offer immediate feedback and reinforcement, and allow students to work at their own pace.

Computer-assisted instruction (CAI) has been shown to improve academic performance in math and reduce off-task behavior (Ota & DuPaul, 2002). Using a computer for written expression allows the student to concentrate on what is being written

One of David's goals is to increase his reading ability and vocabulary skills to at least the second-grade level. David does well with small group and individualized instruction. Students with AD/HD are often inattentive, cannot follow directions, have difficulty organizing tasks, are easily distracted, and are often forgetful of daily activities. Additionally, they are very restless, fidgety, impulsive, and are constantly out of their seats. David displays most of these characteristics so I vary his instruction. For example, we read together (I read to you, you read to me, we read some passages together), or he may be paired with another student and buddy read. His word identification and vocabulary development has grown, and his instructional reading level has increased to 1.5 (first grade, fifth month) from the beginning of the year.

Other modifications for David include reducing classroom distractions and surrounding him with students who are good role models who can assist him when he becomes frustrated. I maintain eye contact with him when providing direct instruction and request that he repeat the instructions back to me. I also write assignments in his home-school agenda in brightly colored ink. Instructional content focuses on capitalizing on the student's strengths, providing highly structured environments, variability of assignments, providing clear expectations, and a supportive atmosphere to assist in esteem building.

Instructional Environment and Technology

My instructional method consists of a blend of whole class, small group, and individualized instruction. My flexible groups are not fixed, but grouped based on content and assessment *of* and *for* learning. For example, if I find that a number of students are not grasping main idea/detail concepts, I work with them in small group settings until mastery is achieved. I also spiral the curriculum for continuous review of difficult concepts.

Assistive technology is a very useful tool and has helped me with David in his reading/language arts. Most of the books on his reading level are on the computer where he can listen with headphones. After reading the books there is a short comprehension/vocabulary quiz. He loves the computer stories and drills, and he also participates in the Accelerated Reader program. Word processing is a useful tool for my two students who attend occupational therapy; poor handwriting is no longer a concern when they are using the computer. Tape recordings of reading assignments and whisper phones so the students can hear themselves are very useful tools. When I use the overhead projector, I use different color pens to maintain interest and motivation.

Collaboration

For inclusive practices to work it takes time, effort, administrative support, and collaboration among teachers. A collaborative effort takes shared problem solving and planning, targeting problem areas, focusing on shared needs, and shared evaluation of outcomes. My grade level collaboratively plans integrated lessons along with the Title I and special education teachers. This shared planning has helped with cohesiveness and team building as we share materials and provide each other with feedback, suggestions, and fresh ideas.

When working with parents and families, it is helpful when they share their specific knowledge of the child's special needs with the teachers and team. It is extremely useful to know the child's preferences, strengths, and weaknesses. Parents need to be encouraged to share their goals and concerns for their child with the collaborative team. The special education teacher and I provide parents flexibility in scheduling, often meeting with parents during lunch, or before or after school. We keep parents informed of their child's progress on a daily basis using the home-school agenda or through phone calls. Honest, open communication between the team and parents is helpful in creating a successful student learning environment. After all, we share the same goal: the academic and emotional success of all children.

rather than the physical production of the symbols, and may increase attention and productivity (DuPaul & Eckert, 1998). Students with poor organizational skills, memory deficits, or illegible handwriting may benefit from using personal digital assistants (PDAs) to keep track of assignments, make to-do lists, take notes, cue themselves to perform a particular task with the alarm or paging system, access and remember task sequences, or organize important information (Bauer & Ulrich, 2002; Matthews, Pracek, & Olson, 2000; Miller, 2002; Salend, 2005). A significant advantage of handheld PDAs is their portability and their universal use.

Access to the Internet can provide the appealing activities of exploring many topics for research and answering questions with the most up-to-date information almost immediately. Two types of technology that have been found to be particularly relevant for students with AD/HD are those designed to help them maintain attention and those designed to facilitate drill-and-practice.

The sound of the soft tone reminds the student to ask, "Am I doing my work?" and check Yes or No on a self-monitoring sheet.

Attention Maintenance Technology

Several technologies are available to help students with AD/HD maintain attention. The **Attention Trainer** (available from Gordon Systems, DeWitt, NY) is a device that has received strong empirical support for decreasing off-task behaviors in students with AD/HD (Xu et al., 2002). This battery-operated device can be placed on a child's desk to keep track of point losses in response-cost systems. Teachers can decrease point values on the display with a remote transmitter that causes a red light to shine for 15 seconds as the point is deducted. The device is relatively unobtrusive and has not been found to result in negative social stigma or excessive peer attention, as is often the fear on the part of teachers. Its use can be phased out over four to six weeks and replaced with a less intensive class token system or a **tone-prompt system,** a small tape recorder with an earpiece for private monitoring, which intermittently plays soft tones to remind the student to check YES or NO on a self-monitoring chart in reference to paying attention. The teacher may also use a pocket-sized tape recorder or vibrating watch to remind himself or herself to attend to the student with AD/HD and provide an appropriate consequence (Pfiffner et al., 2006). Egg timers, alarm clocks, and wristwatch alarms, although more intrusive to the class, may be used to alert both the student and the teacher to determine state of attention.

Drill-and-Practice Programs

Attention Trainer A battery-operated device that keeps track of points or point losses.

tone-prompt system A tape recorder that intermittently plays soft tones to remind a student to monitor him- or herself.

Computer-assisted drill programs can result in positive gains by students with AD/HD if the terminal skill is acquired before the practice begins, the activity emphasizes rapid responding, and the software includes a management system that monitors student progress (Xu et al., 2002). Software packages that include game formats and animation may be even more effective (Pelham et al., 1998). Computer-assisted instruction provides immediate feedback, instant reinforcement, and many opportunities to respond to academic stimuli, all techniques that have been shown to improve the performance of students with AD/HD (Barkley, 1998). For example, one computerized reading program that has been shown to be effective in increasing oral reading fluency and task engagement in students with AD/HD is the Headsprout Early Reading Program (Clarfield & Stoner, 2005). This CAI program is relatively inexpensive, easy to use, and provides individualized, highly engaging teaching with many opportunities to respond, and high rates of reinforcement.

ANDY REVISITED What are some uses of technology that may be beneficial to Andy?

Check Your Understanding

1. Why is structure so important in the environment of students with AD/HD?

2. What are some seating arrangements that are beneficial to students with AD/HD? What are some ways teachers can accommodate the need for physical movement by students with AD/HD?

3. What are some accommodations that can be made in large group instruction?

4. What factors make peer tutoring particularly suitable for students with AD/HD?

5. What aspects of the use of computers make it an effective instructional approach to teaching students with AD/HD? How can technology be used to aid in decreasing off-task behaviors?

What Are Some Considerations for the General Education Teacher?

Relevant CEC Standards
▶ Effective management of teaching and learning (CC5K3)
▶ Teacher attitudes and behaviors that influence behavior of individuals with exceptional learning needs (CC5K4)

As the majority of individuals with AD/HD spend time in the general education classroom, most general education teachers will encounter these students in their classrooms. The role of the general education teacher in the success of a student with AD/HD is a significant one. A useful guideline for teachers to keep in mind is that the goal of educators "should not be to eliminate the disability known as AD/HD but to manage it as effectively as possible, recognizing that it is a chronic, disabling condition" (Kauffman, 2005, p. 279). With this in mind, many strategies and accommodations can help teachers effectively manage AD/HD in their classrooms.

First of all, to facilitate good discipline in the classroom, Guetzloe (*CEC Today*, 2004) suggests that teachers consider the following three Cs that are highly relevant for students with AD/HD:

- *Conditions in the classroom.* Are rules and routines clear and positively stated?
- *Curriculum.* Is it interesting or are you drilling and boring students? Are computers available and instruction enjoyable and easy to follow? If instruction is interesting, students are more likely to stay on task than cause trouble.
- *Consequences.* Do you use positive interventions and reinforcements or only aversive techniques like berating or excluding?

More specifically, teachers may help the student with AD/HD follow directions by calling attention to relevant information through color coding, highlighting, underlining, and increasing font size. Preparing and distributing an outline of the lesson, including objectives, can assist the student with AD/HD in note taking, homework, and studying for an exam. The use of a study buddy to repeat and explain directions can be valuable (Beech, 2003). When teaching students with AD/HD, clear expectations need to be established, posted, and reviewed regularly, including simple and clear classroom rules and consequences, as well as consistent and calm follow-through on consequences (Beech, 2003; Yehle & Wambold, 1998).

Students with AD/HD are more likely to misbehave when too much work is required at once, especially if the work is difficult or repetitious. Reid (1999) suggested that shortening assignments, interspersing different activities within assignments, and providing frequent breaks or alternative activities, making sure that all breaks are structured and occur only after the work is completed, can solve this problem. For example, the student may be assigned 10 math problems to do, then five spelling words to study, followed by oral reading. Another area that is particularly troublesome for students with AD/HD is homework. Too much homework, particularly when it is work that was too long or difficult to be completed in class, becomes another source of stress for both parents and students. Homework should be kept to the absolute minimum and should not be uncompleted class work (Reid, 1999). Additional responsibilities that the general education teacher may be asked to assume include keeping observational data, completing checklists, and monitoring side effects of medication manifested in the classroom (Coleman & Webber, 2002). See the Classroom Suggestions on the next page for some other teaching strategies and accommodations for students with AD/HD.

The 504 Plan

Some students with AD/HD who are not eligible for special education services may qualify for accommodations under Section 504 of the Vocational Rehabilitation Act of 1973. In fact, this has become the more global vehicle for accommodating children with AD/HD (Blazer, 1999). For these students, the general education teacher

Classroom Suggestions — Accommodations for Teaching Students with AD/HD

PROBLEM AREA	TEACHING STRATEGIES
Organizational skills	❑ Help student plan ahead and schedule blocks of time to complete tasks. ❑ Provide student with different colored notebooks or folders for each class. ❑ Ask student to wear a hip or back pack to carry essential information (e.g., identification, bus pass, lunch money, pens).
Following directions	❑ Foreshadow directions to students and point out importance of listening (e.g., "Listen, I am going to give the directions for the midterm project now."). ❑ Provide both written and oral directions. ❑ Repeat and paraphrase important directions two or three times.
Staying on-task during seatwork	❑ Avoid unnecessary repetition of practice items. ❑ Try to schedule a time when student is naturally more attentive. ❑ Modify seatwork requirements (e.g., answer orally into a tape recorder).
Unstructured transition times	❑ Foreshadow transition time and remind students of limitations (e.g., "Remember you have only five minutes to get to your next class."). ❑ Provide a plan; indicate a clear purpose (e.g., "Go to the library and check out a book on dogs."). ❑ Arrange for student to have a responsible partner to follow during transitions.
Completing worksheets and tests	❑ Teach student to use a blank sheet of paper to cover sections not being completed. ❑ Provide alternative, nonstimulating environment for work completion. ❑ Allow student to take breaks. ❑ Allow student extra time. ❑ Use simple borders and include no more pictures or other extraneous material than necessary.
Completing and turning in homework	❑ Coordinate a school-to-home monitoring system. ❑ Spend a few minutes at the end of the day reviewing and prioritizing assignments. ❑ Give parents an extra copy of textbooks.

Source: Yehle, A. K., & Wambold, C. (1998). An AD/HD success story: Strategies for teachers and students. *Teaching Exceptional Children, 30*(6), 8–13.

---

504 Plan A plan to determine what accommodations will be implemented in the classroom for a student who does not qualify for services under IDEA 04 as per the requirements of Section 504 of the Vocational Rehabilitation Act.

will be involved in writing a Section 504 Plan, or just a **504 Plan,** a plan that outlines what accommodations are needed and will be implemented in the classroom. Creating a 504 Plan should involve collaboration with the parent and student and all involved teachers and other school personnel. Physical, instructional, and behavioral accommodations should be considered. See the Classroom Example for a sample 504 Plan.

Collaboration between the General and Special Education Teachers

Communication and collaboration between general and special educators is extremely important for students with AD/HD who receive all or part of their education in general education settings. Research has shown that there is a relationship between the co-teacher (general and special education) relationship and program quality (McCormick, Noonan, Ogata, & Heck, 2001). Committed special and general educators must work together to provide high-quality research-validated instruction to all students in the most effective environment, and this means not losing sight of what Minskoff (1998) reminds us makes special education special—individualization based on a student's specific needs. Decisions about classroom environment, grouping options, and any accommodations or changes to the curriculum should be made together beginning with the IEP development. Sharing information regarding the student's patterns of performance as well as specific academic levels is essential to ensure that appropriate learning environments and programming continue to be

Student: _John Doe_   **Subject:** _____   **Date:**_____

Please use the following rating scale in your evaluation:

1 (very effective) **2** (effective) **3** (somewhat effective) **4** (not effective) **5** (not applicable)

I.   PHYSICAL ADAPTATIONS. Providing structured learning environment

    1. Classroom seating to minimize distractions 1 2 3 4 5
    2. Allow for movement, as needed, perhaps to a library corner or quiet spot in the room 1 2 3 4 5

II. INSTRUCTIONAL ADAPTATIONS. Enhancing comprehension and learning

    1. Directions/assignments in written form 1 2 3 4 5
    2. Extend time limit on tests 1 2 3 4 5
    3. Permit alternative assignments 1 2 3 4 5

III. BEHAVIORAL. Management techniques

    1. Use reward system; incentive chart 1 2 3 4 5
    2. Give tasks student can successfully complete 1 2 3 4 5

Additional Teacher Accommodations or Comments

*After analysis of teacher input, this form can be recompiled to state most effective strategies. Now form can be titled "Annual Classroom Accommodation Review Form" and inserted in student's permanent file. Rating scale should be omitted for annual compilation.

Signatures:

Teacher _____   Student _____

Teacher _____   Parent _____

Source: Blazer, B. (2006). Developing 504 classroom accommodation plans: A collaborative systematic parent-student-teacher approach. *Teaching Exceptional Children, 32*(2), 28–33. Copyright 2006 by the Council for Exceptional Children. Reprinted with permission.

PRACTICE

provided. Plans can also be made to provide consistency in behavior management strategies.

Most students with AD/HD will spend at least part of the day in the general education classroom. The general education teacher can be the determining factor in the success of these students as he or she plans and implements the physical, instructional, and behavioral characteristics of the classroom. Collaboration with a special educator should make this job easier and more satisfying as will observing the progress that most students with AD/HD can make in the right classrooms.

Check Your Understanding

1. Where are most students with AD/HD served?

2. What are the three Cs of discipline?

3. How can a teacher make homework more effective for students with AD/HD?

4. What additional responsibilities might a teacher have if she or he has a student with AD/HD in class?

5. What is a 504 Plan?

Practical Considerations for the Classroom

Characteristics	Indicators You Might See
Cognitive	Often have deficits in executive functioning, self-regulation, working memory, internalized speech, and analyzing and synthesizing behavior. Also, may have decreased time attending to a task and slower visual processing speed not attributed to inattention.
Academic	Frequently do not achieve academic potential. May have difficulty attending to and organizing academic tasks, difficulty listening to directions or instruction, and make careless mistakes.
Social-Emotional	May have difficulty with peer relationships and display bullying behavior. Aggression most likely seen in those with hyperactive-impulsive AD/HD. Those with inattentive AD/HD are more likely to be withdrawn. May have a lower self-concept and peer-relation concept than their peers.
Coexistence with Other Disabilities	May also be diagnosed with a learning disability or emotional disturbance (particularly conduct disorders, oppositional defiant disorder, and anxiety or mood disorders).

Students with Attention Deficit/Hyperactivity Disorder

Teaching Implications

Instructional Content

- If identified as having another disability as well, consider content with this in mind.
- Most students will participate in the general curriculum. To support academics, teach strategies to increase organizational skills and goal-setting, tricks to aid memory, and self-instruction.
- Consider accommodations to support the learning of academic content.
- Support the development of self-regulation through self-monitoring strategies and self-reinforcement systems.
- Consider parent training to encourage appropriate behavior at home.
- Consider student counseling for dealing with AD/HD and transition.

Instructional Procedures

- Instructional procedures should help regulate attention, hyperactivity, distractibility, and motivation.
- Consider using direct/explicit instruction, cognitive behavior modification, and precision teaching.
- Consider behavioral interventions including home-based contingency programs.
- Be aware of how medication may be used with students with AD/HD. If medication is used, it must be combined with behavioral and academic training programs.
- For preschool children, consider a combination of medication, parent training, and classroom behavior management.
- Successful behavioral interventions for preschoolers include positive reinforcement and response cost programs, giving effective directions and requests, teaching self-control, and using consistent methods of discipline.

Instructional Environment

- Remember that students with AD/HD are easily distracted. Plan a structured environment with this in mind.
- For preschoolers, avoid wide-open free-play spaces. Seat children away from the door and other possible distractions. Create learning centers that encourage scheduled, purposeful movement. Alternate in- and out-of-seat activities. Avoid changes in schedule or routine.
- For elementary and secondary students, reduce unnecessary clutter, provide individual desks or carrels, designate space for the student to keep materials, and decrease distractions. Seat students in front/middle of-the room close to the teacher. Allow for opportunity to move around the classroom.
- Effective instructional groupings include large groups, peer tutoring, classwide peer tutoring, and peer-assisted learning strategies.

Instructional Technology

- Remember that computers can motivate, increase attention, and provide immediate feedback.
- Consider attention maintenance technology.
- Consider drill-and-practice programs.

Methodologies and Strategies to Try

- Direct/Explicit Instruction (p. 491)
- Cognitive Behavior Modification (p. 491)
- Precision Teaching (p. 492)
- Behavioral Intervention (p. 492)
- Functional Behavior Assessment (p. 492)
- Home-based Contingency Programs (p. 493)

Considerations for the General Classroom and Collaboration

Instruction often occurs in the general education classroom.

The general education teacher should:

- Remember the 3 Cs: conditions in the classroom, curriculum, and consequences.
- Consider accommodations to help focus students' attention to relevant information and to control workload.
- Keep homework to a minimum.
- Be prepared to keep observational data, complete checklists, and monitor side effects of medication.
- Be prepared to contribute to a 504 Plan.

Collaboration

General and special educators should consult on:

- Determining the curriculum
- Developing accommodations
- Choosing procedures and strategies used
- The student's patterns of performance to determine future programming
- Behavior management strategies
- Planning the physical environment
- Planning for assistive technology

Chapter Summary

Go the text's Online Learning Center at **www.mhhe.com/taylor1e** to access study resources, Web links, practice quizzes, and extending materials.

What Are the Foundations of Attention Deficit/ Hyperactivity Disorder?

- The formal history of AD/HD dates back only to the beginning of the 20th century with the identification of the characteristics of attention problems and hyperactivity in children. Much of the research that would later lead to the description of AD/HD was conducted in the 1950s and 1960s. In 1994, the current term of attention deficit/hyperactivity disorder was introduced.
- The American Psychiatric Association's definition of AD/HD is the most widely used. It states that attention deficit/hyperactivity disorder is marked by inattention and/or hyperactivity-impulsivity that appears as a pattern of behavior and is more severe than behaviors in peers. AD/HD characteristics must be persistent, frequent, and severe. They must include inattention and/or hyperactivity-impulsivity. They must be present for at least six months and have appeared before the age of 7. The characteristics must be present in multiple settings. Finally, the disorder must be shown to have a significant effect on the individual's life.
- The APA has identified three types of AD/HD: predominantly hyperactive-impulsive, predominantly inattentive, and combined.
- Prevalence estimates of AD/HD range from 3% to 5% of the school-aged population.
- About three times more boys than girls are identified, and the prevalence decreases slightly with age.

What Are the Causes and Characteristics of Attention Deficit/Hyperactivity Disorder?

- It is generally accepted that AD/HD is a neurological disorder. Research has focused on differences in the prefrontal lobes, the basal ganglia, and the cerebellum. There is some evidence that AD/HD is caused by a lag in brain development.
- There is evidence that AD/HD may have a genetic basis, though some nongenetic factors, including premature birth, maternal smoking and alcohol use, and exposure to lead, have also been suggested.
- Younger children with AD/HD tend to display characteristics associated with the hyperactive/impulsive type of AD/HD. Older students most often show characteristics of the inattentive or combined type of AD/HD.
- Cognitive characteristics of AD/HD include deficits in executive functioning that lead to a deficit in behavioral inhibition, decreased ability to spend time on task, and slower visual processing speed. One theory that has received considerable attention is that the primary characteristics of AD/HD result from deficits in behavioral (response) inhibition and self-regulation that, in turn, lead to behavior such as impulsivity.
- Academic characteristics of AD/HD include difficulty attending to academic tasks, difficulty organizing academic tasks, not listening to directions, and making careless mistakes. Academic problems are most likely to be performance related rather than ability related.
- Social-emotional characteristics of AD/HD include difficulty with peer relationships and problems in motivation.
- AD/HD often coexists with other disabilities, most frequently a learning disability. Other disabilities that often coexist with AD/HD are emotional disturbance, oppositional defiant disorder, and anxiety or mood disorders.

How Are Students with Attention Deficit/ Hyperactivity Disorder Identified?

- Identification should involve multiple sources of information from multiple settings.
- A student being assessed for AD/HD may also be assessed for specific learning disabilities or emotional disturbance to determine whether he or she is eligible for services through these IDEA 04 categories.
- Individuals involved in the identification process may include physicians, psychologists, nurses, social workers, teachers, and parents.
- Identification procedures that may be used include teacher, parent, and student interviews, the use of questionnaires and checklists, the use of rating scales, academic testing, and direct observation.

What and How Do I Teach Students with Attention Deficit/Hyperactivity Disorder?

- Most programs for students with AD/HD include instruction in academics and self-regulation skills, parent training, and counseling services components.
- Effective instructional procedures for students with AD/HD include direct instruction, cognitive behavior modification, precision teaching, and behavioral intervention. Behavioral intervention may include home-based contingency programs.
- The use of medication may support the learning of students with AD/HD. The use of medication is controversial but supported by research. Medication is most effective when used in combination with behavioral and academic training programs.
- Primary approaches to early intervention programs with students with AD/HD include stimulant medication, parent training, and classroom behavior management. Most preschoolers with AD/HD will benefit from a combination of these approaches.

What Are Other Instructional Considerations for Teaching Students with Attention Deficit/ Hyperactivity Disorder?

- Structure and routine and designing the classroom environment specifically for students with AD/HD are extremely important.
- How students with AD/HD are grouped can have a significant effect on their success.

SUMMARY

- Both attention systems and drill-and-practice software can help students with AD/HD learn.

What Are Some Considerations for the General Education Teacher?

- Many accommodations can be helpful in effectively teaching and supporting students with AD/HD in the general education classroom.

- Many general education teachers will be involved in writing and implementing Section 504 Plans to accommodate students with AD/HD.
- Positive communication and collaboration between the general educator and the special educator are significantly related to success in the classroom for students with AD/HD.

Reflection Topics

1. Why do you think some people believe AD/HD is not really a disorder? How would you respond to someone expressing this belief?
2. Do you think AD/HD is being overdiagnosed, or do you think we are just more aware of it?
3. Would knowing a specific cause of AD/HD have implications for treatment? If so, what would the implications be?
4. What are the advantages and disadvantages of a direct interview of a student's teacher and parent?

5. There are individuals who are concerned that the use of psychostimulants with students with AD/HD is equivalent to "mind control" and is being overused and abused. What are your thoughts on this topic?
6. What are the advantages of placing most students with AD/HD in general education classes? Can you think of some disadvantages?

Application Activities: For Learning and Your Portfolio

1. (*Portfolio Possibility*) Write a position paper that either supports or rejects the statement that AD/HD should be a separate category under IDEA 04.
2. Interview a parent of a child with AD/HD and see how the disorder affects how he or she does homework.
3. (*Portfolio Possibility*) Research Barkley's theory on behavioral inhibition and write a reaction paper.
4. The first step in the cognitive behavior modification training sequence is as follows: The teacher performs a task while verbalizing questions, self-guiding instruc-

tions, and self-evaluating performance. Provide an example of this step for the problem:

$$\begin{array}{r} 25 \\ +42 \\ \hline \end{array}$$

5. Interview a general education teacher who has students with AD/HD in his or her class. Find out what strategies and accommodations have been helpful.
6. (*Portfolio Possibility*) Use the checklists found at http://www.ldonline.org/article/5885 to develop what you think would be a reasonable 504 Plan for Andy.

SUMMARY

CHAPTER 15

Students Who Are Gifted and Talented

CHAPTER OUTLINE

INTRODUCING JUANITA

Juanita is a 10-year-old, fourth-grade student who is often described by her family, friends, and teachers as intense, inquisitive, energetic, and imaginative. She has excelled in school since she moved to the United States from Brazil when she was 6 years old. Juanita is an independent learner, often preferring unstructured, independent tasks to teacher-directed or cooperative group activities. She prefers finding solutions to problems independently and, sometimes, in unconventional ways. Her favorite time of the year is prior to the Science Fair when she spends considerable time researching topics related to her projects. This year she did two projects because she is interested in both astronomy and plant biology. Juanita is sensitive to criticism, is particularly self-critical, and becomes easily frustrated when she makes mistakes.

Juanita's current teacher, Ms. Bertrand, notes that Juanita dislikes most routine practice tasks such as math drills. Achievement tests indicate that Juanita is well above average in reading; she enjoys reading most anything about her topics of interest: science and science fiction. However, she doesn't like her parents' and teacher's suggestion that she expand her reading to other areas. Juanita has a good grasp of mathematical concepts, but often makes careless computation errors by rushing through her assignments so she can do something else. Results from achievement tests indicate that she is above grade level in mathematics, although her classroom performance is lower than expected. Her parents often wonder if Juanita is just bored and not being challenged during class time. Socially, Juanita has a few close friends and is generally accepted by her peers. Her friends enjoy hearing about her favorite topic, UFOs, and are intrigued by her vivid imagination. A few students in her class call her "weird Nita" behind her back. ■

Juanita possesses many characteristics of a gifted and talented student. She is an independent learner, dislikes routine tasks, has a very vivid imagination, and has strong academic skills. These are not the only possible characteristics of gifted and talented students. For instance, Ted is an average sixth-grade student academically but is a talented musician who began composing his own songs at age 5. Max is an excellent ballet dancer who is attending a school for the performing arts. There is no single prototype for gifted and talented students.

Juanita's teacher, Ms. Bertrand, has an important task—to provide the supports and learning environment to help Juanita achieve her full potential and to nurture her personal and social growth. Should Juanita be considered an exceptional student? Does she require a special education program instead of a traditional education program? You could argue that her current educational program is not adequate and that she would benefit from a special education program that provides her with the opportunity and guidance to develop her superior skills. Therefore, she would meet the definition of an exceptional student we provided in Chapter 1—a student whose educational needs are not being met by traditional educational programs so that a special education program is necessary.

What Are the Foundations of Gifts and Talents?

Throughout the centuries, gifted and talented people have been recognized by their societies. Wolfgang Amadeus Mozart was known for his musical genius. Marie Curie became the first woman to receive a Nobel Prize for her research with Radium. Twentieth-century figures include Bobby Fischer, who became a grand master in chess at an early age, and Martin Luther King Jr., who was an inspired leader of the civil rights movement. Although gifted and talented people have been recognized and esteemed throughout history, the formal education of gifted and talented students did not emerge in the United States until the late 19th century. Gifted and talented students are not addressed by IDEA 04, which only includes students with disabilities, although funding has been available since 1988 under the Jacob K. Javits Act. In 2006, almost $10 million was appropriated under the act (Davidson Institute for Talent Development, 2007). Several federal definitions of gifts and talents have been proposed, but there is no clear consensus about which definition to use. Because of this, there is a range of working definitions for gifted and talented students that results, in part, in the difficulty of establishing how many gifted and talented students there really are.

A Brief History of Gifts and Talents

Relevant CEC Standard
▶ Historical foundations of gifted and talented education (GT1K1)

Gifted education in the United States did not begin until the end of the 19th century. At that time, the educational programs for students who would be considered gifted today were primarily modifications of, or additions to, the existing educational programs. For example, a tracking program was started in St. Louis in 1870 that allowed students to complete the first eight grades in fewer than eight years. In Cambridge, Massachusetts, students who were capable of accelerated work were provided with special tutors in 1891. At the turn of the century, specific programs for gifted students began to emerge. In 1902, the first special school for gifted children was opened in Worcester, Massachusetts, and special classes for gifted students were created in Los Angeles and Cincinnati in 1916. Several more were started across the country in the following years (Davis & Rimm, 2004). The interest in gifted education has had several peaks and valleys since the opening of the special schools for gifted students in the early 1900s (see Table 15.1). For the most part, political and philosophical issues continue to affect the area of gifted and talented education. There are both strong supporters and strong critics. Consider the following extremes. A new public school for students with IQs over 160, the Davidson Academy, was opened a few years ago in Reno, Nevada (Janofsky, 2005). Conversely, in

TABLE 15.1	Events Affecting Attitudes toward Gifted and Talented Education

YEAR	EVENT
1930	A period of low interest in the education of gifted and talented students began with the advent of the Great Depression and a focus on equity in the country.
1946	Interest rises as the American Association for the Study of the Gifted was established.
1957	Interest increased as the Russian rocket *Sputnik* was launched, sparking demands for educating gifted students in science and math.
1960	Concerns for equity reduced support for gifted education.
1972	Sidney Marland provided the first federal definition of gifted and talented, bringing attention to the field at the national level.
1981	Interest waned with the passage of the Education Consolidation and Improvement Act, which reduced federal funds for gifted and talented by 40%.
1988	Interest in the education of gifted and talented students again rose when the Jacob K. Javits Gifted and Talented Students Education Act was passed, increasing the funding and creating the National Research Center on the Gifted and Talented.

Source: Adapted from Clark, B. (2002). *Growing up gifted* (6th ed., pp. 11–12). Upper Saddle River, NJ: Merrill.

Montgomery County, Virginia, a group called the Equity in Education Coalition was formed to lobby for the elimination of the designation "gifted and talented," stating that it gives the students an unfair advantage over others (Aratani, 2005).

Definitions of Gifts and Talents

As with many definitions of exceptional students, the ones for gifted and talented students are somewhat subjective. Think about your family and friends. Do you know anyone that you consider to be gifted or talented? One might argue that almost all individuals are gifted or talented in some way. Several definitions of gifted and talented students have been proposed and are currently being used. These include various federal definitions and Renzulli's three-ring definition.

Relevant CEC Standard
▶ Issues in definition and identification of individuals with gifts and talents, including those from culturally and linguistically diverse backgrounds (GT1K5)

The Federal Definitions

The first federal definition of gifted and talented students was introduced in 1972 in a report called *Education of the Gifted and Talented* (Marland, 1972), issued by the U.S. Office of Education. In this report, the first federal definition was provided. The **Marland definition,** named for then Commissioner of Education Sydney Marland, who wrote the report, would eventually serve as the foundation for many of the definitions of gifted and talented students used today. Two requirements of the Marland definition were that gifted and talented students must need differential educational programs (specialized programs) and that they are capable of high performance. The definition further specified six areas in which students could demonstrate high performance or exhibit potential for high performance: (1) general intellectual ability, (2) specific academic aptitude, (3) creative or productive thinking, (4) leadership ability, (5) visual and performing arts, and (6) psychomotor ability.

Marland definition Definition of a gifted student stating that a gifted student should demonstrate high performance or potential in either general intellectual ability, specific academic aptitude, creative or productive thinking, leadership ability, visual and performing arts, or psychomotor ability.

Modified versions of the Marland definition were proposed by the U.S. Department of Education as part of the Gifted and Talented Act (Public Law 95-516) in 1978, and by the Education Consolidation and Improvement Act of 1981. These subsequent definitions were similar to the Marland definition but eliminated psychomotor ability (e.g., superior athleticism) as one of the possible criteria.

The most recent federal definition of gifts and talents was proposed in the 1993 report *National Excellence: A Case for Developing America's Talent*. This report, prompted by concerns about the underidentification of certain groups of individuals as gifted and talented, such as culturally and linguistically diverse students, offered the following definition:

> Children and youth with outstanding talent perform or show the potential for performing at remarkably high levels of accomplishment when compared with others of their age, experience, or environment. These children and youth exhibit high-performance capability in intellectual, creative, and/or artistic areas, possess an unusual leadership capacity, or excel in specific academic fields. They require services or activities not ordinarily provided by the schools. Outstanding talents are present in children and youth from all cultural groups, across all economic strata, and in all areas of human endeavor.

Of particular significance is the fact that the term "gifted" is not used in this definition. Perhaps as an attempt to change the perception that gifted and talented students are only those who have high IQs, the more generic term "outstanding talent" is used. Another important point is the continued inclusion of students who show *potential* for superior performance. This has led to a current emphasis on talent development by providing appropriate educational experiences to those who demonstrate potential, not just to those who have already demonstrated superiority.

Renzulli's Three-Ring Definition

Joseph Renzulli's (2003) "three-ring" definition states that gifted and talented students have a combination of three attributes: above-average ability, task commitment, and creativity. For example, Sue, an 11th-grade student who excels academically, is extremely motivated to learn as much as possible, and is interested in applying her knowledge in a meaningful, creative way, possesses these three attributes. The various combinations of these characteristics lead to high performance in a number of general and specific performance areas. Figure 15.1 illustrates the three rings and also lists both the general and specific performance areas.

General performance area

Mathematics	Visual arts	Physical sciences
Philosophy	Social sciences	Law
Religion	Language arts	Music
Life sciences		Movement arts

Specific performance areas

Cartooning	Demography	Electronic music
Astronomy	Microphotography	Child care
Public opinion polling	City planning	Consumer Protection
Jewelry design	Pollution control	Cooking
Map making	Poetry	Ornithology
Choreography	Fashion design	Furniture design
Biography	Weaving	Navigation
Filmmaking	Play writing	Genealogy
Statistics	Advertising	Sculpture
Local history	Costume design	Wildlife management
Electronics	Meteorology	Set design
Musical composition	Puppetry	Agricultural research
Landscape architecture	Marketing	Animal learning
Chemistry	Game design	Film criticism
etc.	Journalism	etc.
	etc.	

Above-average ability Task commitment Creativity

* This arrow should read as "brought to bear upon"

FIGURE 15.1 Renzulli's Three-Ring Definition of Giftedness

Source: Renzulli, J. (2003). "Conception of giftedness and its relationship to the development of social capital." In Colangelo, N., and Davis, G., *Handbook of Gifted Education,* 3/e. Published by Allyn & Bacon, Boston, MA. Copyright © 2003 by Pearson Education. Reprinted by permission of the publisher.

Currently Used Definitions

Because the area of gifted and talented does not have a federally mandated definition, states and school districts have considerable flexibility in choosing their definition. In a survey of all 50 states, Stephens and Karnes (2000) found the following:

- Most states were using some form of the 1978 federal definition.
- Three states were using the Marland definition that included psychomotor ability.
- One state was using Renzulli's three-ring definition.
- Only four states seemed to be using the most current federal definition.
- Five states reported no definition.

Stephens and Karnes also identified the number of states that name specific areas of high-performance ability in their definitions. *Superior intellect* was mentioned by 39 states and *specific academic skills* and *demonstrated high-performance achievement* were both mentioned by 33 states. On the other hand, other areas noted in the definitions, such as *leadership ability*, were mentioned by fewer states (18). Even though there is agreement among most professionals that giftedness should not be limited to those with intellectual and academic superiority, these findings indicate that they continue to be the most widely used criteria. These results also show a lack of consensus regarding an operational definition of gifted and talented.

Prevalence of Gifts and Talents

Determining the actual number of gifted and talented students in the United States is a difficult task. The prevalence estimate of 3–5% of the school population often is used and has not changed for a number of years. Other estimates are higher, suggesting that 6%, or about 3 million students, are gifted and talented (National Association for Gifted Children, 2005). Some have argued that a broader concept of gifted and talented should be used that would result in 10–15% of the school population being identified (Renzulli & Reis, 2003). The actual number of kindergarten through grade 12 students receiving gifted education is over 2 million (Council of State Directors of Programs for the Gifted, 2003), although there is considerable variability across states.

The true prevalence rate of gifts and talents is difficult to determine for several reasons. First, different definitions are being used. Second, not all schools have mandatory gifted programs, and not all states and local school districts collect information on the number of gifted and talented students served (*National Excellence*, 1993). Finally, the prevalence rate is obscured by the fact that several groups of students, such as underachievers, students with disabilities, females, and culturally and linguistically diverse learners, are typically underrepresented in gifted and talented programs. This factor is perhaps of greatest concern and will be discussed in more depth later in this chapter.

Relevant CEC Standards
▶ Incidence and prevalence of individuals with gifts and talents (GT1K6)
▶ Ways specific cultures are negatively stereotyped (GT5K1)

Underrepresented groups include females and students from culturally and linguistically diverse backgrounds.

JUANITA REVISITED Do you think Juanita should be referred for a gifted education program? Why might Juanita not be referred for a gifted education program?

Since gifted education began at the end of the 19th century, there have been both supporters and critics. Currently, each state has considerable latitude regarding its gifted programs. Because there are many definitions being used, it is important that you as a teacher determine what definition and eligibility criteria your state/school district uses to identify gifted and talented students, as well as what services are available once students are identified. This is particularly important because teachers are frequently the first to identify the early signs of gifts and talents.

Check Your Understanding

1. When did gifted education begin in the United States? What were some examples of early programs?

2. In the Marland definition, what six areas were included in which students could demonstrate or have the potential to demonstrate high performance?

3. What are the major features of the most recent federal definition of gifts and talents?

4. How does Renzulli's definition differ from the current federal definition? What are the similarities?

5. What definitions of gifted and talented are used by different states?

6. What is the prevalence of gifted and talented students? What are some reasons the actual number of gifted and talented students is difficult to determine?

What Are the Causes and Characteristics of Gifts and Talents?

Gifted and talented students can exhibit a range of characteristics. One gifted student may have a very high IQ, whereas another might have incredible artistic ability. Still another might be a world-class violinist at the age of 6. Researchers have made progress in identifying characteristics of students who are gifted and talented, both in terms of general characteristics and those that you, as a teacher, might be most interested in. Although researchers have not found concrete answers, they have learned more about possible causes of gifts and talents.

Causes of Gifts and Talents

Why is 8-year-old Bryce able to play a song on the piano after hearing it only once? What allows 13-year-old Olivia to understand math at such a level that she attends a university algebra course? In other words, what causes an individual's gifts or talents? Historically, these questions led to the nature–nurture debate about whether certain traits are inherited (nature) or due to environmental factors (nurture). This debate has largely centered on intelligence, the most widely used criterion for gifted and talented. However, this argument also has been extended to areas such as academic ability, artistic talent, and musical talent. Although current thinking is that the nature–nurture debate, particularly regarding the origin of intelligence, should be put to rest (Rutter, 2006; Sternberg, Grigorenko, & Kidd, 2006), a discussion of the genetic and environmental determinants and, most important, their interaction is warranted. It is currently believed that it is unlikely that intellectual superiority or any other gift or talent is caused by any single factor.

Genetic Origins of Intelligence

Interest in the hereditary nature of intelligence dates back to the early 1700s when Charles Darwin posited his theories on natural selection. Subsequently, Darwin's cousin, Sir Francis Galton, was one of the first who attempted to link "geniuses" to hereditary factors.

The role of heredity in determining intelligence has been empirically studied primarily through three types of studies. The first type compares the IQs of identical twins to those of nontwin siblings raised in the same environment. The second type of research compares the IQs of twins and siblings raised together versus those raised apart. The third type compares the IQs of adopted children to their adoptive and biological parents. In general, results from all three types of studies indicate that heredity plays an important part in determining an individual's intelligence, accounting for as much as 70% of intelligence (Bouchard, 1997).

Environmental Origins of Intelligence

The counterargument made to genetic proponents is that intelligence is determined by the environment in which a person lives (e.g., the amount, type, and degree of environmental stimulation a person receives). The relationship between socioeconomic status (SES) and IQ has long been established (e.g., Gottfried, 1984). As a group, children from low SES backgrounds score lower on intelligence tests than their peers from high SES backgrounds. Gottfried also noted that environmental factors, such as maternal involvement and the amount and type of play materials and stimulating activities, are related to IQ. More recently, Farah and Noble (2005) noted that factors associated with low SES, including health status, child-rearing practices, and the number of parents in the home, can have a significant effect on a child's intellectual development. They reported that there are neurocognitive differences in children from low SES backgrounds. Some researchers have reported that as much as 75% of student achievement, which is moderately correlated with intelligence, can be attributed to family environmental factors (Cleveland, Jacobson, Lipinski, & Rowe, 2000).

Are outstanding talents due to heredity or to the environment or a combination of the two factors?

Interactive Causes of Intelligence

That high intelligence, or any gift and talent, can be attributed to any single factor, whether it be genetic or environmental, is highly unlikely. Undoubtedly, intelligence is the result of an interaction of both of these factors (Plomin & Price, 2003). Four decades ago, Jensen (1969) provided an interesting, and somewhat controversial, model to attempt to explain this interaction. His **threshold hypothesis** suggested that heredity is important in setting the intellectual potential of an individual, and the environment determines how much of the potential is realized. For example, two children might be born with the same intellectual potential but one may excel more than the other because of environmental factors. More recently, Clark (2002) stated "the fact that development is a product of the effect of experience on the unfolding of genetic potential has now been supported by a wide range of studies over several decades" (p. 45). She, however, disagrees with the notion that genes "set the limits." In short, the current thinking is that there is a strong case for considering the interaction of genetic and environmental factors in the development of intelligence.

Characteristics of Students Who Are Gifted and Talented

Because of the heterogeneity of the population of gifted and talented students, it is impossible to list or discuss all of their characteristics. The characteristics of

threshold hypothesis The hypothesis suggesting that heredity is important in setting the intellectual potential of an individual and that the environment determines how much potential is realized.

Relevant CEC Standards
▶ Similarities and differences of individuals with and without gifts and talents and the general population of learners (GT2K2)
▶ Similarities and differences among individuals with gifts and talents (GT2K3)

individuals with gifts and talents that are most often investigated are intellectual, academic, creative, and social-emotional. It is clear that these students can possess superior capabilities in a number of areas, and an individual student might display any one or a combination of characteristics.

Before discussing the reported characteristics that these students *do* possess, we want to discuss the characteristics that these students *do not* have. Historically, there has been much misinformation about the characteristics of individuals who are gifted and talented, particularly regarding their personality. We want to break down these myths to eliminate some of the stereotypes associated with these students and to reinforce the notion that they should be viewed as individuals, not as a group.

Myths about Students Who Are Gifted and Talented

The popular perception used to be, and still is to some, that students who are gifted and talented are "different" in a negative sense. For many, hearing the term "gifted student" conjures images of geeks and nerds from movies like *Revenge of the Nerds*. Descriptions of these individuals frequently include the adjectives "neurotic," "socially inept," "odd," "unstable," and "lonely." Research, however, has not supported the presence of these characteristics for the majority of individuals with gifts and talents. This was initially addressed by what are now known as the Terman studies, a classic series of studies that took place over several decades in which Lewis Terman and his associates followed a group of highly gifted students to determine their outcomes in adulthood (see An Important Event).

AN IMPORTANT EVENT

1925–1959 The Terman Studies

Terman, L. (1925). *Genetic Studies of Genius.* Stanford, CA: Stanford University Press; Terman, L., & Oden, M. (1947). *Genetic Studies of Genius: Vol. IV. The Gifted Child Grows Up.* Stanford, CA: Stanford University Press; Terman, L., & Oden, M. (1959). *Genetic Studies of Genius: Vol. V. The Gifted Group at Midlife,* Stanford, CA: Stanford University Press.

In the 1920s, Lewis Terman and his associates began a study that would continue for more than 30 years of more than 1,500 gifted and talented individuals and their life outcomes (Terman, 1925; Terman & Oden, 1947, 1959). Contrary to the stereotypical characteristics of gifted and talented students, such as being lonely, socially inept students, the Terman data indicated that this group was well adjusted, had superior physical characteristics, and made successful transitions into the work world, frequently becoming leaders in their chosen profession. Considerable attention has been given to the Terman data, even five decades after their publication (e.g., Leslie, 2000; Zuo & Cramond, 2001). Terman was also known for being actively involved in the development of the original Stanford Binet Intelligence Scale. With his interest in intelligence, it was only natural that he would also be interested in studying a group who had superior IQs. The Terman studies are generally regarded as the most significant research about individuals who are gifted, although they did have some limitations. For example, the subjects were nominated by their teachers who many times choose children who are well behaved, attractive, conforming, and popular. In addition, the subjects were primarily white, middle-class individuals chosen on the basis of high IQs (IQs averaged about 150 with some as high as 190). As a result, some of the findings might *not* be relevant for minority children who are gifted or those whose gifts or talents lie in some area other than high intellect.

REFLECTION What implications should the Terman studies have on our perceptions of gifted students?

Intellectual Characteristics

There has been considerable interest in the intellectual characteristics of gifted and talented students. Despite efforts to encourage the consideration of multiple areas in which a student can be gifted and talented, a high IQ is still one of the major, and in some cases the only, criteria used to determine eligibility for gifted and talented programs (Richert, 1997). The IQ cutoff point often used for eligibility into gifted programs is 130, meaning that the individual scored higher than approximately 96% of the population.

It is important that we have a broad view of intelligence. Perhaps the most widely publicized model of intelligence is Gardner's theory of multiple intelligences, which he first introduced in his book *Frames of Mind* (Gardner, 1983). Gardner felt strongly that a single IQ was not an accurate indication of a person's potential/ability. As a result, he investigated several different types of intelligence, subjecting each to a stringent set of criteria. Currently, Gardner has identified eight types of intelligence— Verbal-Linguistic, Logical-Mathematical, Musical, Spatial, Bodily-Kinesthetic, Interpersonal, Intrapersonal, and Naturalistic, with a ninth, Existential, being evaluated. Table 15.2 on the next page provides the definition of each type along with examples of famous people who have/had each type.

Other intellectual characteristics that have been associated with students who are gifted include advanced logical thinking, such as questioning ability and problem-solving behavior; and early language development, including superior comprehension skills. Davis and Rimm (2004) described a second-grade student who deduced that there must be negative numbers because temperatures can go below zero. Some gifted children might start talking at 7 months of age; others might start later but advance in language areas rapidly (Davis & Rimm, 2004). Another cognitive-related characteristic is an accelerated pace of thought processes that might require an accelerated pace of instruction. Without an accelerated pace, the student might become frustrated. Also, these students might display flexibility of thought processes. This might require giving the student the opportunity to solve the problem in diverse ways. However, the student's penchant for doing things differently might lead to the perception that the student is being disruptive and disrespectful (Clark, 2002). Therefore, it is important that teachers both recognize that gifted and talented students might approach learning from a different perspective than other students and be tolerant of those differences.

Academic Characteristics

Academic superiority is perhaps the major reason students who are gifted and talented are initially identified, at least within the school setting. Superior academic performance, approaching tasks in a diligent manner, demonstrating superior study skills, and applying course content in a creative way quickly gain the attention of the classroom teacher. For example, Deon, a kindergarten student, frequently finishes his work before his classmates and asks for more to do. He also asks his teacher if he can bring a book to read while he is waiting for the rest of the class to finish their work. Other characteristics associated with academic superiority are self-reliance and spending considerable time engaging in leisure reading and working on homework assignments (Konstantopoulos, Modi, & Hedges, 2001).

Creative Characteristics

Students who are gifted and talented are often highly creative. Creativity has multiple meanings and can be defined using diverse descriptors such as having a good sense of humor, being sensitive, or frequently daydreaming. Paul Torrance, the author of a test called the Torrance Test of Creative Thinking, has conducted considerable research in the area of creativity. He identified a number of creative behaviors associated with giftedness, including originality and persistence in problem solving, being full of ideas, and finding ways to do things differently. He noted, however, that not all creative people possess all of these traits (Torrance, 1977, 1981). In addition, many students who are not gifted also display these characteristics.

Relevant CEC Standard
▶ Cognitive characteristics of individuals with gifts and talents in intellectual, academic, creative, leadership, and artistic domains (GT2K7)

Relevant CEC Standards
▶ Academic characteristics of individuals with gifts and talents (GT3K4)

FOUNDATIONS

| TABLE 15.2 | Gardner's Theory of Multiple Intelligences |

CATEGORY	CORE OPERATIONS	EXAMPLE
Verbal-Linguistic: Master sensitivity, desire to explore, and love of words, spoken, and written language(s).	Comprehension and expression of written and oral language, syntax, semantics, pragmatics	William Shakespeare Toni Morrison
Logical-Mathematical: Confront, logically analyze, assess and empirically investigate objects, abstractions, and problems, discern relations and underlying principles, carry out mathematical operations, handle long chains of reasoning.	Computation, deductive reasoning, inductive reasoning	Paul Erdos Isaac Newton
Musical: Skill in producing, composing, performing, listening, discerning, and sensitivity to the components of music and sound.	Pitch, melody, rhythm, texture, timbre, musical themes, harmony	Charlie Parker Wolfgang Amadeus Mozart
Spatial: Accurately perceive, recognize, manipulate, modify and transform shape, form, and pattern.	Design, color, form, perspective, balance, contrast, match	Leonardo da Vinci Frank Lloyd Wright
Bodily-Kinesthetic: Orchestrate and control body motions and handle objects skillfully to perform tasks or fashion products.	Control and coordination, stamina, balance, locating self or objects in space	Martha Graham Tiger Woods
Interpersonal: Be sensitive to, accurately assess, and understand others' actions, motivations, moods, feelings, and other mental states and act productively on the basis of that knowledge.	Ability to inspire, instruct, or lead others and respond to their actions, emotions, motivations, opinions, and situations	Virginia Woolf Dalai Lama
Intrapersonal: Be sensitive to, accurately assess, understand and regulate oneself and act productively on the basis of one's actions, motivations, moods, feelings, and other mental states.	Knowledge and understanding of one's strengths and weaknesses, styles, emotions, motivations, self-orientation	Mahatma Gandhi Oprah Winfrey
Naturalist: Expertise in recognition and classification of natural objects (i.e., flora and fauna) or artifacts (i.e., cars, coins, or stamps).	Noting the differences that are key to discriminating among several categories or species of objects in the natural world	Charles Darwin Jane Goodall
Existential*: Capturing and pondering the fundamental questions of existence; an interest and concern with "ultimate" issues.	Capacity to raise big questions about one's place in the cosmos	Søren Kierkegaard Martin Luther King Jr.

Note: *Unconfirmed ninth intelligence.

Source: Karolyi, C., Ramos-Ford, V., & Gardner, H. (2003). Multiple intelligences: A perspective on giftedness. In N. Colangelo & G. Davis (Eds.), *Handbook of gifted education* (3rd ed., pp. 100–112). Boston: Allyn & Bacon, p. 102.

Relevant CEC Standards

▶ Affective characteristics of individuals with gifts and talents in intellectual, academic, creative, leadership, and artistic domains (GT2K8)

▶ Affective characteristics of individuals with gifts and talents (GT3K5)

Social and Emotional Characteristics

Several social and emotional characteristics associated with gifted and talented students have been reported, including high motivation and task persistence, high levels of sensitivity, self-awareness, and idealism (Clark, 2002). Another characteristic that has been reported is perfectionism. Pfeiffer and Stocking (2000) pointed out that this characteristic can make gifted and talented students vulnerable to social and emotional problems. Parker (2000, 2002) distinguished between healthy, or adaptive, perfectionism, and unhealthy, or maladaptive perfectionism, each of which might lead to different consequences. The social-emotional characteristics that have been studied most are personal/social adjustment and self-concept. Two conflicting views of gifted and talented students' personal/social adjustment, their ability to make and maintain friendships, have emerged over the years. Some argue that gifted and talented students are more at risk for adjustment problems. Others argue the opposite, that they are better adjusted than their peers (Gallagher, 2003). Gallagher went on to state that there is little difference in adjustment between gifted students and their nongifted peers and also noted that any advantage might be in favor of gifted students, although these students are not immune to social and emotional problems. A related area is peer relations. Goshorn (2006), a gifted student herself, wrote that being in a gifted program negatively affected her relations with her high school peers.

Regarding gifted and talented students' self-concept, research generally has indicated that they have higher scores on measures of perceived self-importance and self-efficacy than do their nongifted peers (Merrell, Gill, McFarland, & McFarland, 1996) and that they show higher academic self-perceptions than the average student (McCoach & Siegle, 2003).

As a teacher, it is not really important to know the specific cause of a student's gifts and talents although acknowledgement of the interaction of both genetic and environmental factors is warranted. It is important to remember that it is not possible to come up with a prototype for a gifted and talented student. Each individual is unique and may possess one or many gifts and talents. Research has helped to shed some light on the characteristics of students with gifts or talents as a group, but individual students could possess a wide variety of characteristics.

JUANITA REVISITED What cognitive and academic characteristics does Juanita have that are consistent with being gifted and talented? Social-emotional characteristics?

Check Your Understanding

1. What role does genetics appear to play in determining gifts and talents? What role does the environment play?

2. Is it likely that gifts and talents are caused by an interaction of genetic and environmental factors? Why or why not?

3. What are intellectual characteristics of gifted and talented students? What are the types of intelligences included in Gardner's multiple intelligences model?

4. What kinds of academic characteristics do gifted and talented students frequently exhibit?

5. What are possible creative characteristics of gifted and talented students?

6. What does research tell us about the social and emotional characteristics of gifted and talented students?

How Are Students Who Are Gifted and Talented Identified?

The procedures used to identify gifted and talented students vary from state to state, and even from school district to school district. For example, some states use intelligence tests and either have an IQ cutoff point (e.g., 130) or specify a percentage of students who will qualify (e.g., those with IQs in the top 3–5%). Other states might take a much more liberal approach to identification. One example is the talent pool strategy in which 15–20% of the school population is identified using a wide variety of procedures (Renzulli & Reis, 2003). Identification procedures can include teacher nominations, peer nominations, rating scales and checklists, IQ and achievement tests, creativity tests, and a range of alternative assessments.

Because students can be gifted or talented in a variety of areas, multiple procedures and multiple criteria should be used in identification. Research has shown that no single method can accurately and effectively identify gifted and talented students.

Relevant CEC Standards
▶ Issues, assurances, and due process rights related to assessment, eligibility, and placement within a continuum of services (GT1K7)

▶ Screening, prereferral, referral, and identification procedures for individuals with gifts and talents (GT8K4)

Every effort should be made to ensure that those from traditionally underrepresented groups, such as students from culturally and linguistically diverse groups, be properly evaluated.

Before an individual's gifts and talents can be formally identified, someone must first notice that the individual in question has excelled in one or more areas. For young children, the parents are usually the first to identify early gifts and talents, frequently based on behavioral and developmental variables, such as starting to read at a very early age. Once a child starts school, the general education teacher is likely to initially identify a gifted student, frequently based on the student's academic performance. As we will discuss, teachers should also use other criteria when considering if a student might be gifted or talented.

Identification of Preschool Children with Gifts or Talents

A somewhat controversial issue is whether we can accurately identify gifted and talented preschool children, usually those ages 3–5. A related issue is whether we even *should* identify young gifted and talented children. Proponents of early identification argue that such identification allows for the early development of young children's gifts and talents and provides an argument for early school admission (Colangelo, Assouline, & Gross, 2004). Critics counter that by identifying children early in life, we are in danger of "stealing" their childhood and putting undue pressure on them to succeed. The number of preschool gifted education programs is fairly limited, and the criteria for admission differ with each program.

Parents are often the first to initially identify their preschool child as gifted or talented. What types of behaviors do parents look for in their children that would indicate giftedness? Rogers and Silverman (1998) surveyed parents of both gifted and nongifted children to determine what early indicators discriminated between the two groups of children. The gifted children displayed advanced vocabulary, extreme alertness, excellent memory, and a high degree of creativity. Parents of the gifted children also reported that their children had considerably more interest in puzzles and computers (not video games) than did the parents of the nongifted children.

Identification of School-Aged Students with Gifts or Talents

Most school-aged gifted students are initially identified by their teachers. Depending on the criteria used to determine eligibility, a teacher nomination for a gifted program might be sufficient for a student to be identified as gifted. In other instances, the teacher will refer the student who is then evaluated by the school system. Although most school districts still rely primarily on the use of standardized tests, such as intelligence, academic, and creativity tests, to identify students, other procedures, including peer nominations and rating scales and checklists, are sometimes used. Some alternative assessment procedures are also available.

Teacher and Peer Nominations

Teachers play an important role in the initial identification of students who are gifted and talented. Teacher nominations are frequently used as one aspect of the identification process, although there is some question about their accuracy, particularly in overidentifying students as being gifted (Gittman & Koster, 1999; Neber, 2004). On the other hand, Weston (2001) reported that almost 75% of the students nominated by teachers were identified as gifted. One concern is that teachers tend to focus more on academic performance and less on other gifted and talented attributes such as creativity and leadership skills (Siegle, 2001). It is important that teachers be aware of all the areas in which a student can be gifted or talented. Otherwise, it is likely that many students who are gifted and talented will not be identified.

Another potentially valuable source of information for the identification of gifted and talented students is peer nomination. Davis and Rimm (2004) pointed out that

How effective are teachers and peers at identifying gifted and talented students?

"Peers are very good at naming gifted and talented classmates. They are especially helpful in identifying minority or rural gifted students, or those who are culturally different, disadvantaged, or have a disability. Children know who's who" (p. 94). Some direct questions that might be asked to help indicate whether or not a classmate is potentially gifted and talented include: "Who is the smartest kid in class?" "Who always finishes his or her work first?" "Who tells great stories?" "Who has the most unusual ideas?" "Who could invent the most games with a box of stuff?" Another technique for eliciting a peer nomination is the disguised approach in which a hypothetical situation is set up. A teacher might ask the students the following questions: "A friendly alien is visiting your class. Who would ask the alien the most unusual questions? Who would remember the most about the alien?" (Davis & Rimm, 2004).

Gifted and Talented Rating Scales

Formal rating scales have been developed to help identify gifted and talented students. There is some evidence that training teachers to use rating scales will result in better prediction of students' gifted attributes (e.g., Hunsaker, Finley, & Frank, 1997). The Scales for Rating Behavioral Characteristics of Superior Students (SRBCSS; Renzulli, Smith, White, Callahan, & Hartman, 2001) is perhaps the most widely used rating instrument. The SRBCSS measures four major areas: learning characteristics, motivational characteristics, creativity characteristics, and leadership characteristics. Unfortunately, however, many rating scales are poorly constructed, and some are simply lists of behaviors with few criteria established as to how many traits a student must demonstrate to be considered gifted. There is also the recurring problem of their lack of cultural sensitivity. This reinforces the notion that multiple procedures should be used to identify gifted and talented students. Rating scales might provide valuable information, but they should not be used exclusively to identify these students.

Intelligence and Achievement Testing

Like many other types of exceptional students, individuals who are gifted and talented are frequently identified through the use of standardized, norm-referenced tests. As noted in Chapter 2, most students referred for special education are administered intelligence tests and achievement tests. This is true for most of those referred for gifted education as well, primarily because these instruments measure skills most often used to define giftedness (Stephens & Karnes, 2000). Initially, intellectual screening tests such as the Kaufman Brief Intelligence Test–II (Kaufman & Kaufman, 2004a) might be used, although more comprehensive, individually administered intelligence tests, such as the Wechsler Intelligence Scale for Children–IV, are usually required to identify individuals who are gifted. Nonverbal tests such as the Naglieri Nonverbal Ability Test (Naglieri, 2003) also have the potential to identify gifted students who might be overlooked using more typical, verbally based tests (Lewis, 2001). Most students identified as gifted perform well on tests of academic achievement, such as the Kaufman Test of Educational Achievement–II and the Wechsler Individual Achievement Test–II. This is expected because superior classroom performance frequently is the reason for initial referral of these students.

Creativity Testing

In addition to the areas of intelligence and achievement, creativity is sometimes evaluated when a student is suspected of being gifted or talented. However, creativity is very difficult to define and measure. Perhaps the most widely used creativity test is the Torrance Test of Creative Thinking (TTCT; Torrance, 2000a, 2000b). The TTCT has two forms: verbal and figural. The tasks require the student to do things such as suggest improvements in toys, name unusual uses for common objects, and complete unfinished pictures. Another instrument is the Profile of Creative Abilities (Ryser, 2007).

As popular as standardized tests are, they have significant limitations, particularly when their use is the only procedure employed. For one thing, they identify students based on a very narrow view of giftedness. This is not particularly an indictment of the tests themselves; rather, it's an indictment of the system that allows such a narrow interpretation of gifted and talented attributes.

Identification of Underrepresented Groups with Gifts or Talents

Several groups are typically underrepresented in gifted and talented education. These include underachievers, students with disabilities, females, and students from culturally and linguistically diverse backgrounds. It is imperative that special attention be paid to ensuring that these groups are given equal opportunity for identification.

Relevant CEC Standard
▶ Use and limitations of assessment instruments for students with gifts and talents (GT8K5)

Students Who Underachieve

Because high academic ability is often the primary criterion used by teachers when recognizing and referring students for gifted education, gifted underachievers are often overlooked. There are many possible reasons for the underachievement of students who are gifted, including (1) peer pressure to be like everyone else and not demonstrate special gifts or talents, (2) an underchallenging classroom environment, (3) anxiety and depression, (4) rebelliousness, and (5) problems in self-regulation (Reis & McCoach, 2002). Another reason might be that the student is bored and does not see the need to do what he or she views as meaningless work. Colangelo, Assouline, and Gross (2004) reported that some gifted students need to decide whether to risk social rejection for excelling academically. They noted that researchers have found that "the pressure to dumb down can start in the early years of elementary school" (p. 29). As with all the groups of underrepresented gifted and talented students, the teacher is the key to remedy the problem. In the case of underachievers, it is important that teachers consider the use of criteria other than academic performance.

Students with Disabilities

twice exceptional A student who is both gifted and has a disability.

Students with disabilities who are also gifted and talented are referred to as **twice exceptional**. In particular, the identification of gifted students who have learning disabilities has received considerable attention in recent years. Oftentimes, these students are identified neither as being gifted nor as having a learning disability because their exceptionalities "mask" each other. For example, Jane is a very bright 10-year-old student who is currently in the fourth grade. Because she is so bright, she is able to compensate for her learning disability by making average or slightly below average grades in school. Thus, she is not referred for either gifted education (remember that superior academic skills are often the basis for a referral) or a learning disability program (since she is not failing academically).

There are several possible reasons some students with disabilities are not identified as gifted and talented. Many of these students are identified by their disability alone, with their gifts and talents being overlooked (Baum, Rizza, & Renzulli, 2006). For example, Denise, a student with a visual impairment, also is a talented musician and might qualify for services as a gifted and talented student as well, although her talent might be overlooked because of her disability. Another reason for underidentification is that the disability might affect the validity of the assessment of certain skills. Jim, a student with severe cerebral palsy, is actually quite intelligent, but his test scores do not reflect this because he was administered an intelligence test that included the measurement of fine motor skills. Jim's situation emphasizes why it is important that when tests are used, the appropriate ones are selected or they are adapted so that the student's disability doesn't affect the test results.

Females

It may come as a surprise to many that females are often underrepresented as gifted and talented students because girls frequently develop and mature faster than boys and outperform them in classroom achievement (Kerr & Nicpon, 2003). Certain stereotypes and barriers to achievement presented by parents, schools, and the larger society affect the identification of girls as being gifted (Reis, 2002). For example, one common misconception is that girls are not good in science and math. This attitude might have two effects. First, teachers might not look for strengths in these areas, and second, the students themselves might not pursue these areas if they believe that they will probably fail. Teacher perceptions regarding gender differences have an important impact. For example, Powell and Siegle (2000) noted that the stereotype that boys do not like to read whereas girls do influences those who are eventually identified as gifted. In other words, voracious reading might be considered a common characteristic among girls, but might be considered a sign of giftedness in boys. It is important for teachers to avoid these stereotypes.

Students from Culturally and Linguistically Diverse Backgrounds

Gifted students from culturally and linguistically diverse (CLD) backgrounds are underrepresented, and the statistics are alarming. The percentage of African American, Hispanic, and American Indian children in gifted programs is roughly one-half of their percentage in the total population (Gallagher, 2003). The reason for this underrepresentation is debatable. Many point out that the criteria and assessment procedures are biased, whereas others argue that giftedness is not equally distributed across all demographic groups and the underrepresentation is thus expected (Gottfredson, 2004). McBee (2006) reported that teachers tend to refer more Asian and white students and fewer African American, Hispanic, and low-socioeconomic students. He suggested that the underrepresentation issue might be a referral problem rather than an assessment problem. There have been many suggestions that schools should aggressively locate and identify culturally diverse students who are gifted using techniques other than standardized tests. In other words, we must actively search this population for candidates using alternative approaches.

Alternative Approaches to Identification

Several alternative procedures have been recommended for use in the overall identification process of students with gifts or talents, including dynamic assessment, portfolio assessment, and performance assessment tasks. **Dynamic assessment** uses a test-train-retest model in which a student is pretested on a learning task, such as a visual analogies task, is provided direct instruction on how to solve the problem, and then is posttested to determine how rapidly and efficiently the task is learned. The use of dynamic assessment has resulted in the identification of culturally and linguistically diverse students for gifted programs that was consistent with the percentage of

Relevant CEC Standards
▶ Issues in definition and identification of individuals with gifts and talents, including those from culturally and linguistically diverse backgrounds (GT1K5)
▶ Ways specific cultures are negatively stereotyped (GT5K1)

dynamic assessment A test-train-retest model used to determine how quickly and efficiently an individual learns new material.

portfolio assessment A means of determining students' achievements and abilities using a collection of their work.

those students in the total school population (Lidz & Macrine, 2001) and has been strongly endorsed for school districts with large numbers of traditionally underrepresented groups (Kirschenbaum, 1998).

Portfolio assessment involves the collection of a student's work that provides an indication of the depth and breadth of his or her achievements and abilities. For example, a reading portfolio for a third-grade student might include an audiotape of oral reading and a list of books read, including the student's reactions and summaries. Using portfolios to identify gifts and talents is particularly helpful in areas such as artistic and creative ability and has been recommended as a supplementary procedure to standardized testing, observation, and self-identification (Schwartz, 1997).

Another alternative approach that has been used to help identify minority students and students from low-socioeconomic backgrounds is performance assessment. This involves the use of different verbal and nonverbal tasks designed to measure gifted abilities. VanTassel-Baska, Johnson, and Avery (2002) reported that their use of performance assessment resulted in the identification of an additional 14% low-income and 12% minority students who would not have been identified through traditional procedures.

JUANITA REVISITED What rating scales or tests would be appropriate to test Juanita for gifts or talents?

The ideal process to identify gifted and talented students includes the use of multiple measures and multiple criteria. However, the specific definition and eligibility criteria that a school district uses will largely dictate the identification procedures employed. For example, if gifted and talented is narrowly defined, such as by intellectual and/or academic superiority, then standardized tests will probably be used. If, however, a more liberal definition is used, then multiple procedures might be suggested. Both special education teachers and general education teachers should learn the identification procedures used in their school because they will play such an important role in them.

Check Your Understanding

1. Why is it important to use multiple procedures and multiple criteria when identifying gifted and talented students?

2. What are some procedures for identifying preschool children as gifted and talented? What are the pros and cons of early identification?

3. When identifying school-aged children as gifted and talented, what are some advantages and disadvantages of using teacher nominations?

4. What are the limitations of standardized testing when identifying gifted and talented students?

5. What groups are typically underidentified as gifted and talented? Why?

6. What alternative assessment procedures have been suggested for identifying gifted and talented students?

What and How Do I Teach Students Who Are Gifted and Talented?

Relevant CEC Standards
▶ Models, theories, and philosophies that form the basis for gifted education (GT1K2)
▶ Teacher attitudes and behaviors that influence behavior of individuals with gifts (GT1K14)
▶ Educational implications of various gifts and talents (GT2K4)

What types of educational programs are available for gifted and talented students? How many of these students have access to appropriate educational programs? How can these programs be improved? Unfortunately, the answers to these questions indicate that much more can and should be done to improve the available services. The *National Excellence* (1993) report on the status of education for gifted and talented students noted several problems, including that the general education curriculum was not challenging to gifted and talented students and that teachers made few accommodations to meet their learning needs. Some also have argued that the implementation of the No Child Left Behind Act, which focuses on all students meeting minimal standards, has, in fact, left gifted students largely ignored (Colangelo, Assouline, & Gross, 2004; Kaplan, 2004).

Fortunately, there is information about how we can improve the education of gifted children in our classrooms and gifted education programs in schools. In addition to the need to make resources for gifted students more available and accessible, there is a need to base the development of gifted programs, including any specialized curriculum, as well as the modification, or differentiation, of the general education curriculum, on what has been deemed successful in the past. One crucial component is the teacher, who should be trained and motivated, collaborative, and willing to try different ways to modify and teach the curriculum. Although some states have certification or endorsement programs for teachers of gifted and talented students, other states do not. In many cases it is left up to the general education teacher to differentiate the curriculum to address the needs of any gifted and talented students. A **differentiated curriculum** requires that the teacher adapt the standard curriculum to provide instruction at *every* student's appropriate level, consistent with the concept of universal design. This means varying the complexity and depth of the material presented based on students' instructional needs. Tomlinson et al. (2003) pointed out that this is becoming increasingly more difficult as the classroom includes more and more diverse learners. Differentiating a curriculum for a gifted student means more than simply having them do more of what they already know (Tomlinson, 1995). In this section, we discuss instructional content and instructional procedures that are appropriate to use with gifted and talented students. But first we want to talk about two popular approaches used with gifted and talented students—acceleration and enrichment.

differentiated curriculum An adaptation to the standard curriculum to provide instruction at the students' appropriate level.

Acceleration and Enrichment

Acceleration and enrichment are two approaches that provide the basic framework for teaching gifted and talented students. **Acceleration** involves moving the student through the curriculum at a faster pace. For example, students might skip a portion of the curriculum that they have already mastered or enroll in school at an earlier age than usual. **Enrichment** involves modifying or adding to the curriculum to make it richer and more varied, such as assigning additional research projects in specific areas related to students' gifts and talents. Enrichment also includes different program delivery services such as the use of field trips and summer programs. Most educational programs for gifted and talented students include some combination of the elements of both acceleration and enrichment. For example, a student might be working at a faster pace than her or his peers (acceleration) and also be involved in an academic competition (enrichment).

Relevant CEC Standard
▶ Acceleration, enrichment, and counseling within a continuum of service options for individuals with gifts and talents (GT5K4)

acceleration An educational approach that allows a student to cover the usual curriculum content faster.

enrichment An educational approach that involves the modification of, or addition to, the curriculum to make it richer and more varied.

Acceleration Approaches

Acceleration approaches are classified as being either *grade-based*, which shorten the number of years spent in school, or *subject-based*, which introduce content earlier than expected for age or grade level (Rogers, 2002). Examples of grade-based acceleration are early admission to school (or college) and skipping a grade. Subject-based approaches include advanced placement courses and the International Baccalaureate program. In the 1950s, the Ford Foundation started the College Board Advanced Placement (AP) program. The AP program provides first-year college courses in high school and can result in college credit, frequently allowing students to graduate in fewer than four years. There are 37 courses and exams available in 22 content areas such as American History and Calculus. Almost 2 million high school students took AP exams in 2004, making the AP program "the largest scale acceleration program in the country" (Colangelo et al., 2004, p. 31). Another alternative is the International Baccalaureate (IB) program, a rigorous, preuniversity two-year course of study that meets the standards for universities and colleges worldwide. Acceleration may be most relevant for intellectually and academically gifted students and less effective for students with creative and other talents. In fact, Colangelo et al. stated, "All acceleration requires high academic ability" (p. 8).

Acceleration has been studied extensively, and, in general, research has supported its use (Swiatek, 2002; Vialle, Ashton, Carlon, & Rankin, 2001). It has also been found that students in accelerated programs have higher self-esteem than students who do not participate in the programs (Gross, 2001). The advantages of using

TABLE 15.3	Advantages of Using Acceleration

✔ Acceleration is the most effective curriculum intervention for gifted children.

✔ Acceleration is a virtually cost-free intervention.

✔ Entering school early is an excellent option for some gifted students both academically and socially. High-ability young children who enroll early generally settle in smoothly with their older classmates.

✔ Gifted students entering college early experience both short- and long-term academic success, leading to long-term occupational success and personal satisfaction.

✔ Radical acceleration (acceleration by two or more years) is effective academically and socially for highly gifted students.

✔ Many educators have been largely negative about the practice of acceleration, despite abundant research evidence for its success and viability.

✔ Educational equity does not mean educational sameness. Equity respects individual differences in readiness to learn and recognizes the value of each student.

✔ The key question for educators is not whether to accelerate a gifted learner but rather how.

Source: Colangelo, N., Assouline, S., & Gross, M. (2004). *A nation deceived: How schools hold back America's brightest students.* Iowa City, IO: University of Iowa.

acceleration were touted by Colangelo et al. (2004), and some of their 20 important summary points are presented in Table 15.3.

Enrichment Approaches

Enriching a standard curriculum adds depth and makes it more varied for gifted or talented students. Possible enrichments include additional research projects, the use of learning centers, enrollment in summer programs, and participation in academic competitions. Gifted and talented students frequently are enrolled in enrichment programs that emphasize higher-level thinking skills or specific areas in which the student has superior talent. Enrichment fits well with the conceptual framework that acknowledges that the area of gifted and talented is multidimensional in that it can be designed for any area.

JUANITA REVISITED Would Juanita be a good candidate for an acceleration program? An enrichment program? Why or why not (for each)?

Instructional Content

Relevant CEC Standards

▶ Models, theories, and philosophies that form the basis for gifted education (GT1K2)

▶ Sources of differential materials for individuals with gifts and talents (GT4K1)

▶ Differential curriculum needs of individuals with gifts and talents (GT7K6)

Whether a gifted and talented student is taught within a separate gifted program or in a general education classroom, the major education goal, as with all students, is to help the student develop to her or his full potential. The content of the student's educational program will largely depend on the nature of the individual's gifts and talents. Although the majority of gifted programs are designed for individuals with intellectual and academic superiority, programs for those students who have other talents, such as significant creative or leadership skills, need to include content that reflects those particular strengths. Some areas that should be considered priorities for gifted and talented students include those as diverse as basic academic skills, computer skills, creative thinking and problem solving, and affective (social-emotional) development (Davis & Rimm, 2004). In the remainder of this section, we discuss the content areas of thinking, problem solving, and social-emotional skills, as well as how Bloom's taxonomy model and Gardner's theory of multiple intelligences can be used to help choose content for gifted and talented students, primarily those with intellectual and academic superiority.

Thinking Skills

When creating or differentiating a curriculum for gifted students, it is particularly important to plan for the development of thinking skills. Clark (1992) noted that gifted children between 1 and 4 years of age need to be placed in a stimulating, responsive environment in which vocabulary, curiosity, and intuition can be developed. For example, an environment with colorful, interesting, and interactive toys would foster thinking skills by providing an inviting, motivating opportunity to learn.

When a child who is gifted reaches school age, **divergent thinking skills,** being able to solve a problem in which there is no single correct response, should be encouraged. Divergent thinking tasks usually begin with words such as "imagine" or "suppose." For example, "Can you imagine ways that soccer typifies Mexican culture?" and "Suppose that Caesar never returned from Gaul. Would the empire have existed?" However, **convergent thinking skills,** which require the student to identify one correct answer when presented with a problem, should not be ignored. Convergent thinking tasks usually begin with words such as "why" or "how." "Why was Richard III considered an evil king?" "How does gravity differ from electrostatic attraction?" (Ciardiello, 1998).

Problem-Solving Skills

Another important content area to include when teaching gifted students is problem solving. Problem solving encourages the student to seek creative methods to answer important questions such as "What specific suggestions do you have that would help address the problem of hunger in third world countries?" Instructional programs have been developed to help develop these skills. As an example, the Future Problem Solving Program emphasizes *how to think* rather than *what to think.* Frasier, Lee, and Winstead (1997) described this program's goals as helping students to enhance their creative thinking, increasing their interest and awareness of the future, and developing communication and research skills.

Social and Emotional Skills

One often overlooked teaching content area is addressing the social and emotional needs of students who are gifted and talented. As noted previously, research indicates that these students frequently are well adjusted, although they sometimes receive considerable peer pressure from other students and many have feelings of perfectionism and loneliness. It is important for teachers to be aware of these areas and make sure that they are addressed. Another way to address social and emotional needs is through counseling, an area that has received considerable attention with the gifted and talented population (e.g., Colangelo, 2003; Moon, 2003).

Bloom's Taxonomy

Several educational models and theories can be used to select the instructional content for gifted students. A key example is Bloom's taxonomy (Bloom, 1956), a classic model that identifies six levels of cognitive understanding. The six levels, from lower-level thinking to higher-level thinking, are Knowledge, Comprehension, Application, Analysis, Synthesis, and Evaluation. Table 15.4 on the next page lists these levels along with common verbs that can be used by teachers to encourage the particular level of thinking. At the lowest level, the Knowledge level, a teacher would use words such as "define" or "name" to guide the student's interaction with the content. At the highest level, the Evaluation level, the teacher would ask the student to "compare," "conclude," or "justify." When teaching students who are gifted, a teacher should create objectives and ask students questions that emphasize the highest two or three levels—Analysis, Synthesis, and Evaluation—to challenge the students and keep them engaged. For example, in a history lesson about John F. Kennedy, rather than asking questions such as "name the Secretary of State and Defense Secretary during Kennedy's presidency," a teacher should ask questions such as "compare and contrast Kennedy's social policies with those of Lyndon Baines Johnson."

Gardner's Theory of Multiple Intelligences

Gardner's theory of multiple intelligences can also be used as a basis to develop content for a gifted and talented student. Gardner's theory suggests that instruction can

divergent thinking skills
Thinking skills that involve solving problems for which there are no single correct answers.

convergent thinking skills
Thinking skills that involve solving problems that have correct answers.

PRACTICE

TABLE 15.4	Bloom's Taxonomy: Levels and Verbs

1. **Knowledge:** arrange, define, duplicate, label, list, memorize, name, order, recognize, relate, recall, repeat, reproduce, state.

2. **Comprehension:** classify, describe, discuss, explain, express, identify, indicate, locate, recognize, report, restate, review, select, translate.

3. **Application:** apply, choose, demonstrate, dramatize, employ, illustrate, interpret, operate, practice, schedule, sketch, solve, use, write.

4. **Analysis:** analyze, appraise, calculate, categorize, compare, contrast, criticize, differentiate, discriminate, distinguish, examine, experiment, question, test.

5. **Synthesis:** arrange, assemble, collect, compose, construct, create, design, develop, formulate, manage, organize, plan, prepare, propose, set up, write.

6. **Evaluation:** appraise, argue, assess, attach, choose, compare, defend, estimate, judge, predict, rate, core, select, support, value, evaluate.

Source: http://www.officeport.com/edu/blooms.htm

focus on the different types of intelligence. For example, in a thematic lesson on Cuba, a teacher might address visual intelligence by having students create political posters pre- and post-Castro and then engage interpersonal intelligence by having students work cooperatively to write a play about the life of a Cuban child. The Classroom Example provides more examples for activities based on the multiple intelligences model. Using this approach as a guide for curriculum development allows the teacher to engage gifted and talented students in a range of ways.

Instructional Procedures

In addition to considering the content of the curriculum, teachers of gifted and talented students must also consider the best way to deliver that content. An array of instructional strategies and approaches have been found to be effective in supporting their learning. In addition to specific instructional strategies, a number of acceleration and enrichment techniques also result in the modification of instructional procedures. These include mentoring, curriculum telescoping and curriculum compacting, use of the enrichment triad, and implementation of several model programs. Many of these acceleration and enrichment options, such as research projects and independent studies, allow the student to work at his or her own pace on topics of particular interest and relevance. Other options are Saturday or summer programs that emphasize fast-paced instruction or problem-based learning. These programs often are housed on university campuses; therefore, coordination with the student's in-school program is necessary (Olszewski-Kubilius, 2003). Finally, when you have gifted and talented students in your class, it is important to keep their parents in mind. Parents should be encouraged to be actively involved in their child's education. When they are involved, they can provide valuable support and experiences to complement your efforts.

Effective Instructional Strategies for the Classroom

When planning instruction for gifted and talented students, it is important to consider the way in which content is presented. In general, teachers should avoid boring, repetitive tasks, and instead present information in such a way that it is challenging and motivating, using a variety of presentation formats, such as lecture, discussion, and visual, rather than just one. This also frequently requires the careful pacing of information so that it is presented rapidly enough to sustain interest. When encouraging learning, teachers also should be aware of the need to engage gifted and talented students in cooperative activities. It has been shown that these students benefit the most when paired cooperatively with another gifted and talented student (Robinson, 2003).

Content Areas

Multiple Intelligences	Language Arts	Social Studies	Math/Science
Verbal-Linguistic	Read and research the works of a contemporary Cuban author. Illustrate or translate the work to share with the class.	Create a 5-minute narrated video production promoting tourism in Cuba.	Create several mathematical word problems using Cuban demographic data.
Logical-Mathematical	Research and report the demographics of the Cuban population including average family income, educational levels, etc.	Create an annotated outline or time line explaining Cuban history.	Compare and contrast the economy of Cuba with a country of your choice.
Visual-Spatial	Create a political poster or a collage of life in Cuba pre- and post-Castro. Write a narrative to explain your work. Research the works of contemporary Cuban artists; use posters and postcards of artists' works and present your findings to the class (written or oral report).	Create and sketch out a political cartoon for a newspaper of your choice.	Design and draw to scale the perfect "raft" to be used by political refugees, and explain why your raft would be superior (weight, dimensions, materials used, etc.).
Musical-Rhythmic	Research the African influence on Cuban music and prepare a written or oral report on your findings.	Research Cuban musical artists; bring samples of their music to class and share your research of their life and musical influence (written or oral report).	
Bodily-Kinesthetic	Role play one of the works of your favorite Cuban authors.	Perform several typical Cuban dances for the class (alone or with a partner).	Investigate the math and science behind the construction of typical Cuban musical instruments.
Naturalistic		Create a diorama depicting Cuba's natural resources.	Design a collage depicting Cuba's climate, wildlife, and natural habitat. Explain your collage.
Interpersonal	In a cooperative group, write a play about the life of a young Cuban child now living in Cuba.	Learn one of the typical Cuban childhood games and teach the class.	
Intrapersonal	Write an essay sharing your personal feelings about Cuba's political situation, OR write a "journal" of your imagined trip to the U.S. aboard a raft.		

Source: Bianco, M. (2004). Unpublished.

Learning activities should be cooperative, not competitive.

Mentoring

Mentoring is matching an individual with a person with more knowledge or skills in a particular area. The mentor could be another student or an adult. For example, a 6th-grade student who is gifted in math might have an 11th-grade gifted student as a mentor. Another example is that of a talented 10th-grade musician who has a university music professor as a mentor. Although this is usually a one-to-one matching, having more than one mentor might be helpful, and "telementoring," in which the student and mentor communicate via the Internet, can be effective as well (Clasen & Clasen, 2003). Research has shown that mentoring programs can and should address nonacademic areas such as motivation and emotional support (Casey & Shore, 2000; Hebert & Neumeister, 2000). One method of addressing nonacademic areas is **double mentoring,** in which an expert mentor works with the student within his or her discipline or area of expertise and a teacher mentor addresses the developmental and affective needs of the student (Clasen & Hanson, 1987).

Curriculum Telescoping and Curriculum Compacting

Two acceleration approaches that are frequently used to help ensure that a gifted student is challenged are curriculum telescoping and curriculum compacting. **Curriculum telescoping** involves providing the typical educational program in less time, for example four years of high school in three years. **Curriculum compacting** is when the teacher allows a student to skip material that has already been mastered (Davis & Rimm, 2004). For example, using pretests, a teacher might determine that Nick has already mastered basic reading skills being taught to the class. Nick would not participate in that unit when those skills are being taught. Rather, he would have an enrichment activity, such as allowing him to read on a subject of his own choosing to reinforce and improve his reading skills.

Enrichment Triad

The **enrichment triad** includes three levels or types of enrichment activities (Renzulli, 1977). In Type I (General Exploratory Activities), the teacher puts the student in contact with areas of study that might be interesting and encourages the student to explore the topic. In Type II (Group Training Activities), the teacher uses training exercises to develop thinking skills in relation to the area of study. According to Renzulli, these first two types can be used with any student, although the student who is gifted will benefit considerably more from them. The Type III activities (Individual and Small

mentoring The pairing of a student with an established expert.

double-mentoring An expert mentor provides support in the student's area of expertise and a teacher addresses the student's affective needs.

curriculum telescoping The provision of an educational program in less time than normally planned for.

curriculum compacting Allowing a student to skip material that he or she has already mastered.

enrichment triad An instructional model that includes three levels of enrichment activities: general exploratory activities, group training activities, and individual and small group investigations of real problems.

Group Investigations of Real Problems) are particularly relevant for gifted students. These involve a real investigation, like a scientific experiment, of the area of study. The students formulate a problem, determine a method to study the problem, collect data or information, and draw their conclusions based on their results. In addition, they develop a tangible product that is presented to a real audience. Gifted students should spend about half of their time in these activities. The Type I and Type II activities are used to prepare the student to be able to do the Type III activities independently.

The teacher's role in the development and initiation of Type III activities is to be a "manager" in the learning process. Specifically the teacher (1) identifies and focuses student interests, (2) finds appropriate outlets for student products, (3) provides students with methodological assistance, and (4) develops a laboratory environment (Maker, 1982). The following is an example of a Type III activity:

> A group of students interested in school rules conducted a survey of all classrooms asking for opinions on (1) the rules most needed and (2) the rules most often broken. The survey resulted in the development of a proposed discipline policy for the school, which was presented to the principal of the school and the executive board of the Parent-Teachers Association. (Maker, 1982, p. 223)

Model Programs

A number of model programs have been developed for students who are gifted and talented. Many of these are designed to provide systemic change to the entire school and affect *all* students, not just gifted students. This is consistent with the principle of universal design discussed throughout this text. Table 15.5 summarizes the goals and components of several popular models.

Three models, in particular, that are frequently implemented in schools are the Schoolwide Enrichment Program (SEM), the Autonomous Learner Model (ALM), and the Integrated Curriculum Model (ICM). The SEM is the most widely publicized and researched program for gifted and talented students. The SEM has been in existence in various forms for a number of years. The goals of the SEM are basically to provide a continuum of services that will challenge students with demonstrated or potential superior performance, to infuse the general education curriculum with a variety of activities that challenge students to perform at advanced levels, and to give teachers the flexibility to provide extended opportunities for students who demonstrate superior interest and performance (Renzulli & Reis, 2003). The SEM has a number of

PRACTICE

TABLE 15.5	Description of Several Curriculum Models Used with Gifted and Talented Students

NAME	DESCRIPTION
Multidimensional Curriculum Model (Morelock & Morrison, 1999)	Based on the Vygotsky principle that optimal learning occurs when learning is neither too difficult nor too easy. The student is taken through five levels of abstractness and complexity with teacher direction.
Parallel Curriculum Model (Tomlinson et al., 2002)	This model is designed for both homogeneous and heterogeneous classrooms. It provides four levels of curriculum content requiring increased intellectual demand.
Purdue Three Stage Enrichment Model (Feldhusen & Kolloff, 1986)	Designed to train divergent and convergent thinking skills, creative problem solving, and independent study skills.
Talents Unlimited Model (Schlicter, 1997)	A teacher training model based on Taylor's Multiple Talent Totem Poles. Teachers are trained to teach several thinking skills.
Structure of Intellect Model (Meeker & Meeker, 1986)	Includes over 100 training modules to teach 90 types of intellectual skills based on Guilford's (1967) SOI model.

integrated components including the enrichment triad, curriculum compacting, enrichment clusters, and acceleration options such as grade skipping and college course enrollment. It also incorporates the Talent Pool Strategy, which encourages the school to identify 15–20% of students who would benefit from the gifted curriculum.

The ALM (Betts & Kercher, 1999) was designed to promote self-directed, independent learning in the cognitive, emotional, and social domains and consists of five major dimensions.

1. Orientation: Self/personal development and group building activities
2. Individual Development: Inter/intrapersonal understanding and the use of technology
3. Enrichment: Cultural activities and community service
4. Seminars: Small group presentations in areas such as futuristic or problematic topics
5. In-Depth Study: Individual and group projects and mentorships

One of the goals of the ALM is to provide the opportunity for in-depth learning in specific areas rather than scratching the surface of a broad range of topics. Figure 15.2 presents a schematic of the ALM.

The ICM (VanTassel-Baska, 2003) involves three dimensions: knowledge of discipline-specific advanced content, higher-order thinking, and learning experiences focusing on real-world issues, ideas, and themes. Specific teaching units in the areas of language arts, social studies, and science have been developed by the College of William and Mary that incorporate the three dimensions of the ICM.

The Parent's Role in Instruction

Parents should be actively involved in their gifted child's education. Clark (2002) identified several roles that parents can play. These included providing the teacher with information on how best to teach their child, acting as advocates for gifted education

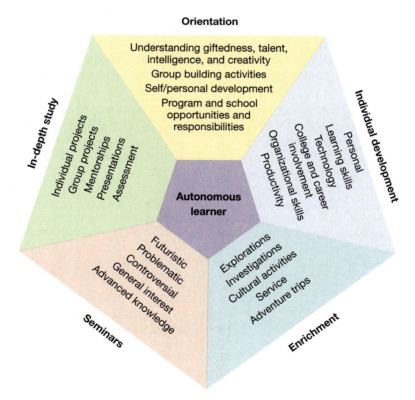

FIGURE 15.2 Schematic of the Autonomous Learning Model

Source: Betts, G., & Kircher, J. (1999). *Schematic of the Autonomous Learning Model.* Greeley, CO: Alps Publishing. Used with permission.

programs, and volunteering to help in the classroom or on field trips. Clark goes on to describe ways for teachers to help involve parents such as including the parents during the planning of their child's educational program and placing the parents on the educational team that makes important decisions. Conversely, there are also potential concerns that parents of gifted and talented children might have that must be addressed. These include coping with their child's heightened sensitivity, intensity, and perfectionism, and facing the possibility of an early "empty nest" because of acceleration programs (Silverman & Kearney, 1989).

Check Your Understanding

1. What are acceleration and enrichment? What are the advantages and disadvantages of each?

2. What are three content areas that should be incorporated in a gifted student's curriculum?

3. How can Bloom's taxonomy and Gardner's theory of multiple intelligences be used in teaching gifted and talented students?

4. What are some specific instructional procedures that can be used with gifted and talented students? What are some model programs that can be considered?

5. What is the parent's role in instruction of gifted and talented students? What are some considerations the teacher should keep in mind regarding these parents?

What Are Other Instructional Considerations for Students Who Are Gifted and Talented?

In addition to instructional content and procedures, two areas of particular importance to teachers of gifted and talented students are the placement of these students and the use of instructional technology. No single placement is used for gifted and talented students. Resources will have an important influence as will the availability of teachers who are certified in the area of gifted education. The reality is that many gifted and talented students are taught by general education teachers in the general education classroom. When there is a trained gifted and talented teacher in a school and the students are taught in the general education classroom, there should be significant collaboration between the two teachers. Technology can provide tremendous opportunities for exploration, analysis, and presentation of information. As Pyryt (2003) stated, "I believe that the possibilities for computer-based instruction with gifted individuals are limited only by our visions. The challenge will be to integrate our technological capabilities with our dreams" (p. 587). On the other hand, teachers must be aware of the potential problem of inappropriate use of computer technology.

The Instructional Environment

There are two considerations related to the instructional environment for students who are gifted and talented. The first has to do with the most appropriate educational placement. Should they be taught in the general education classroom? A separate classroom? A separate school? The placement can be affected based on whether a particular acceleration or enrichment approach is used. For example, a high school student might be enrolled in a university and another student might be placed in a school for the performing arts. Second, if gifted and talented students are taught in a general education classroom, different ways of grouping students must be considered.

Relevant CEC Standard
► Effective management of teaching and learning for students with gifts and talents (GT5K3)

Placement Options

Historically, gifted and talented students have been most frequently taught in separate classrooms or even separate schools. With the emphasis on inclusion that emerged in the 1990s, there has been a movement to teach these students with their nongifted peers in the general education classroom. Some have even argued that separating gifted students and their peers violates the democratic principles associated with public education (McDaniel, 2002), although this is one of a few exceptionalities for which there are many supporters of separate educational environments. This issue of the inclusion of gifted and talented students in the general classroom has led to a debate over the most effective placement of gifted and talented students.

A position paper on inclusion published by the Association for the Gifted (TAG, n.d.), a division of the Council for Exceptional Children, stated that for an inclusion program to be appropriate for gifted and talented students, a one-program-fits-all approach to education should not be used. Further, the inclusion program should address three educationally relevant characteristics of gifted students:

1. A rapid rate of learning and development in some domain
2. An advanced knowledge in areas related to that domain
3. A seriousness about learning

TAG also goes on to say that placing students in situations in which they experience persistent failure and placing students in situations in which they face a chronic lack of challenge are equally inappropriate. This implies that regardless of the educational setting and model employed, the instructional program must meet individual student needs. If this is done in the general education classroom, the teacher will need to provide certain modifications such as differentiated instruction, flexible student groupings, and a mixture of enrichment and acceleration (Hughes, 1999).

There are also those who reject the argument for inclusion and believe that gifted and talented students should be taught separately from their nongifted peers. Page and Keith (1996) strongly supported the homogenous grouping of gifted and talented students, particularly those from minority backgrounds. Kennedy (2002) reported that there were problems teaching a highly gifted student within a general education setting, including lack of attention to emotional needs. Davis and Rimm (2004) made a strong statement about teaching gifted and talented students as a separate group:

> Learning activities can be enriched and accelerated—to fit student capabilities and learning needs, develop creativity and thinking skills, reduce boredom and frustration, and combat underachievement habits by inviting students to work and think for a change. Equally important is the opportunity to interact with others like themselves for social and academic support. (p. 153)

Similarly, the National Association for Gifted Children (2003) reaffirmed the importance of grouping gifted students together. They argued that such grouping allowed the instruction to be more appropriate, rapid, and advanced, matching the skills and capabilities of gifted students. Unfortunately, the existing research on the issue of educational placement is inconclusive, partially as a result of the lack of methodologically appropriate studies (Neber, Finsterwald, & Urban, 2001).

Placement Considerations Related to Acceleration Approaches. Accelerated programs can result in a change of the instructional environment, although the change is somewhat dependent on the age and the characteristics of the students who are gifted and talented. For example, young gifted students might begin school at an early age, although there is some question about whether or not this is appropriate. Sanker-DeLeeuw (2002) found that only 37% of parents and 7% of teachers she surveyed felt that early school entrance was a good idea. At the secondary level, approaches such as correspondence courses and taking college courses in high school might be used.

Older students also might skip grade levels or apply for early college admission. Robinson (1996) described a model program at the University of Washington that admits students ages 14 and under for a radical acceleration program. Although some have argued that these types of programs might have harmful effects, particularly in the social areas, data indicate that the students continue to have high achievement levels and that most adjust well socially to college life (Olszewski-Kubilius, 2002). The graduation in 2003 of 14-year-old Gregory Smith from Randolph Macon College in Virginia with two Nobel Prize nominations brought this option to attention in the national media.

Placement Options Related to Enrichment Approaches. Implementing an enrichment approach to instruction can also affect a gifted or talented student's educational placement. The specific nature of a student's gifts and talents could also affect the physical environment in which she or he receives instruction. For example, a student with extraordinary musical talent might attend a school for the performing arts, and a budding scientist might go to a school such as the Bronx High School of Science. A growing option is the use of state-supported residential high schools available in more than 10 states (Kolloff, 2003).

Enrichment approaches that take the student out of the regular school environment include exchange programs and field-based instruction, such as classes at museums. An example of this is the extensive offerings in the Chicago public school system. A number of museums and institutions including the Historical Society, Art Institute, and the Lincoln Park Zoo offer programs for gifted students in a variety of areas such as art and science. Yet another possibility for enrichment is the use of **magnet schools,** schools that have been earmarked to offer specialized training in given areas. Some magnet schools are developed specifically for gifted and talented students, but many also include students of different ability levels who want to specialize in a certain area. Magnet schools have been found to be a positive alternative for gifted middle school students (Gentry, Rizza, & Owen, 2002).

magnet school A school that offers specialized training in specific areas.

Instructional Grouping

If gifted and talented students are taught in an inclusive classroom, grouping options must be considered. Methods of grouping gifted students that encourage both their learning and that of their nongifted classmates that have been used include XYZ grouping, multiage and multigrade grouping, within-class grouping, and cluster grouping (Kulik, 2003).

Relevant CEC Standard
▶ Grouping practices that support differentiated learning environments (GT5K5)

XYZ Grouping. **XYZ grouping** involves placing students into one of three groups (high, medium, and low) based on their IQs and then using standard teaching methods and materials. The XYZ grouping model has been used by a number of school systems although the positive effects of the approach have been minimal, possibly due to the lack of a differentiated curriculum. The Classroom Suggestions includes several questions that teachers can ask themselves to ensure that the curriculum is being differentiated.

XYZ grouping Grouping students according to their IQ.

Multiage and Multigrade Grouping. In **multiage and multigrade grouping,** students are placed in classes based on their educational performance level, regardless of

multiage and multigrade grouping Grouping students according to their educational level, regardless of their actual age or grade.

Classroom Suggestions Differentiating Curriculum

❑ Do I focus on essentials? Do my lessons highlight the essential concepts, principles, and skills of each area of the curriculum? Do my students find subjects of study meaningful and interesting?

❑ Do I assess and instruct inseparably? Is assessment used as a tool for growth rather than for pointing out mistakes?

❑ Do I modify content (what I teach), process (how I teach), and product (how I measure student learning) according to student readiness? Do I adapt these elements to suit individual student characteristics?

❑ Do I facilitate student learning? Do I collaborate with students in their learning? Is my classroom student-centered?

❑ Do I balance group and individual expectations? Do I allow and encourage each student to be the best he or she can possibly be?

❑ Do I work flexibly in my classroom? Am I flexible in grouping, outcomes, pacing, materials, and resources?

Source: http://www.tki.org.nz/r/gifted/pedagogy/difference.php

In Practice Meet Educator Dian Trompler and Her Student Sara

My 29 years of teaching include experience in elementary and middle schools. I have a graduate degree in gifted education, and my journey with gifted children has spanned 15 years in a variety of programs. Currently, I teach a self-contained multiage class of fourth- and fifth-grade gifted

students in a low-socioeconomic area of an urban district. Students who qualify for gifted services may apply from anywhere in the district to attend this class. The class is part of a multiage kindergarten through fifth-grade gifted program at my school.

I first met Sara when she was nominated for gifted services by her third-grade teacher. Her teacher realized she needed a program that was more consistent with her unique learning characteristics. On the district ability test, Sara scored at the 99th percentile with an IQ of 150. On the Gates-MacGinitie Reading Test, she scored at the 10th grade reading level. When evaluated in math, Sara demonstrated that she already knew 90% of the content at her grade level.

Sara attended my gifted pullout program during third and fourth grades for one day each week. I also made recommendations to her general education teachers about her class work. During fifth grade, she attended my full-time gifted class. Sara's classes in both programs consisted of approximately 15 high-ability students.

In the general education classroom, Sara already knew most of the third-grade content, whereas most of her classmates scored below third grade in reading. She learns new information and skills at a much faster rate and needs much less repetition than her peers to learn new content. Sara became bored waiting for others to catch on to the concepts. She saw no purpose in completing assignments involving information she already knew, and her enthusiasm for learning began to dwindle.

After being identified for gifted services, Sara once again found excitement in learning. The modification to her general education assignments helped her gain knowledge at a pace appropriate for her ability. Sara now attends Advanced Placement classes in middle school.

Instructional Content and Procedures

In planning instruction for gifted students, I look at their unique learning characteristics. For Sara, a typical gifted learner, these include the ability to learn quickly and reason beyond her age. She possesses an extensive vocabulary and a broad knowledge

---

within-class grouping Grouping students according to their ability and teaching using a differentiated curriculum.

cluster grouping The placement of 5–10 gifted and talented students with general education students, who are then taught as a group using a differentiated curriculum.

their age or expected grade level (Kulik, 2003). In other words, you might have students of different ages and grades grouped together because of their similar reading or math ability. Kulik also reported that this model has empirical support and is the basis for a very successful reading program, Success for All (Slavin & Madden, 2000), which has been implemented in almost 2,000 schools nationally. Another benefit of this model is that teachers might be more prone to view their students as diverse rather than similar and subsequently provide more appropriate instruction (Lloyd, 1999).

Within-Class Grouping. In **within-class grouping,** gifted students remain in their classroom but are placed into groups based on their academic ability. The teacher circulates among the groups to differentiate the instruction. Kulik reported that this approach also has been shown to be effective. **Cluster grouping,** considered a type of within-class grouping, usually involves placing 5–10 gifted and talented students with similar learning needs together with a group of general education students with a trained teacher who provides a differentiated curriculum.

JUANITA REVISITED What types of grouping options could Ms. Bertrand use in Juanita's class to support Juanita's learning?

base, prefers complex and challenging learning, and rapidly recognizes relationships between ideas and concepts. She is intense, highly creative, passionate, an avid reader, morally sensitive, and concerned with justice. I modify the content, process, product, and environment of the general education curriculum to ensure enough abstraction and complexity to satisfy such gifted learning characteristics.

Gifted students are global thinkers and readily see the connections between thematic content. Therefore, I plan interdisciplinary units around universal ideas. One unit involves the concept of cultures with a broad generalization concerning global peace. To understand cultures, students explore how native people and immigrants have adapted to living in each geographical region of our country. Students choose literature that depicts multicultural characters. In science, students experiment with the principles related to the regional environment.

Textbooks, the Internet, interviews, primary source documents, simulations, and discussions provide the means to access and assimilate the information. The activities enable students to work like historians, scientists, and geographers. This unit extends the depth and breadth of objectives for social studies, science, and language arts. Products

are developed by the students to demonstrate their learning rather than their performance on tests and worksheets.

Students also explore topics about which they are personally passionate. The goal is to create a real product to present to an authentic audience. Sara chose to study different personality types. She worked with a university professor to compare the personality profiles of her general education class to her gifted class. She presented her findings to university students in a gifted education program.

Instructional Environment and Technology

It is necessary to use flexible grouping to accommodate the wide range of abilities and interests. Students make a choice from a selection of novels with similar themes to create literature circles. For one project, students formed groups based on interest in a topic. Students work in self-selected groups for hands-on inquiry-based science activities. Many gifted students prefer to work independently, and I honor such needs during projects in social studies and language arts.

I pretest all of my students on elementary math standards. Those who demonstrate an understanding of the concepts work in small groups with a mentor to complete algebra projects.

Students rotate in and out of the algebra group depending on the concept being taught. My students have access to a computer lab for research and for technology-based projects. Sara found primary source documents on the Internet to study American history. Her group created a Web site to share their invented technology for the ExploraVision competition. She used library databases to research famous people, to explain the science concepts for ExploraVision, and to find information for independent studies. Most final products are completed with Microsoft Word, PowerPoint, or Publisher. The technology trainer assists students with computer skills. Students have the flexibility to move from the classroom to the computer lab or the library.

Collaboration

I collaborate with general education teachers to help differentiate assignments for gifted students. Working with Sara's fourth-grade teacher, I recommended modifications to the math content. Because she demonstrated proficiency on 90% of the fourth-grade skills, I proposed that she work in a fifth-grade class for math. Another strategy allowed Sara to work on more complex math tasks when she accurately completed five of the hardest problems in a daily assignment.

Instructional Technology

Instructional technology can provide many benefits for gifted and talented students, and can be used to assist in both acceleration and enrichment. Through improved telecommunications, many universities offer advanced courses to the public schools (VanTassel-Baska, 2006). Technology also provides valuable enrichment opportunities for students who are gifted and talented. Computer skills have been identified as one of the 10 most important content areas for gifted and talented students (Davis & Rimm, 2004). Computer technology can be used to enhance learning in many ways, including the use of electronic databases that provide students with access to a variety of data that they can subsequently analyze. There are also "tool skills" such as word processing programs, programs for statistical analysis of data, and presentation modes such as PowerPoint (Pyryt, 2003). Computers can also be used for distance learning and the previously mentioned telementoring. The use of chat rooms for people with similar interests and interactive Web sites are other ways students can gather and share information. An example of the latter is www.nationalgeographic.com/xpeditions, which allows interactive multimedia exploration of various geographic concepts. Graphic design and computer animation software can also assist creative and artistic students.

 Relevant CEC Standard
► Technology for planning and managing the learning environment (GT4K2)

Stettler (1998) identified four types of learning activities that can be conducted using technology:

Acquiring: Student is an information consumer rather than producer

Retrieving: Student is an information searcher or "surfer"

Constructing: Student is an information producer using higher-level thinking skills

Presenting: Student is a conveyor of the produced information to an audience

According to Stettler, typical students should spend about 60% of their technology time acquiring, 15% retrieving, 15% constructing, and 10% presenting. Gifted students, on the other hand, should spend 20%, 25%, 40%, and 15% of their time, respectively, on the four activities.

In addition to being aware of how technology can support the learning of gifted and talented students, teachers should also understand that computer and Internet technology might be a double-edged sword for some gifted students. Pryrt (2003) identified several concerns with what he called "the dark side of technology." To some intellectually gifted students, computer crimes, such as software piracy, hacking, virus infestation, and gaining access to classified information, might be a temptation. In addition, access to inappropriate Web sites needs to be monitored, as well as the time actually spent on the computer because this is time when there is a lack of social interaction.

Check Your Understanding

1. What are the advantages and disadvantages of including gifted and talented students in the general education classroom?

2. What are some acceleration approaches that affect the instructional environment? What are some enrichment approaches?

3. What are XYZ, multiage and multigrade, and within-class grouping structures? What are some advantages of using each of these?

4. What are some ways that computer technology can enhance the educational program for gifted students? What are some possible negative uses of technology teachers should be aware of when using technology with gifted and talented students?

What Are Some Considerations for the General Education Teacher?

Relevant CEC Standard
▶ Teacher attitudes and behaviors that influence behavior of individuals with gifts and talents (GT1K14)

As we have noted throughout this chapter, general education teachers play a significant role in the education of gifted and talented students who are frequently taught in their classrooms. This placement occurs for a variety of reasons, including the lack of formal gifted education programs in some states, inadequate funds, and the movement toward inclusion of *all* students in the general education classroom. It is imperative, therefore, that general education teachers learn about issues related to the identification and subsequent education of students who are gifted and talented. Table 15.6 shares several ways general education teachers can support gifted and talented students in their classrooms.

As discussed earlier, research has shown that teachers have not been particularly successful in identifying students who are gifted and talented, particularly when the student is underachieving, female, has a disability, or is from a culturally and linguistically diverse background. At least a portion of this lack of success has been attributed to uncertainty about the definition and the criteria used to identify students who are gifted and talented. General education teachers must become familiar with the characteristics of these students and look beyond superior intelligence, verbal ability, or academic skills to identify a student. Certainly, the importance of identifying typically underrepresented groups should be acknowledged.

In an inclusive classroom, the general education teacher should be motivated and properly trained, and must be able to address the gifted or talented student's unique educational needs. It is also important that the teacher differentiate the curriculum to

TABLE 15.6	What General Education Teachers Should Do When Working with Gifted and Talented Students

- ❑ Recognize gifted children
- ❑ Provide new challenges
- ❑ Inform child's parents about acceleration
- ❑ Minimize teaching students what they already know
- ❑ Make school a positive experience for all students . . . including your brightest

Source: Colangelo, Assouline, & Gross (2004).

meet all students' needs. By identifying each student's academic level in their classes, teachers can use various approaches of grouping students that might assist *all* students, not just those who are gifted and talented. Of utmost importance is collaboration among general education teachers, gifted education programs, and special education programs. The National Association for Gifted Children (NAGC, 1998) developed a position paper to address this important area. Strategies they suggested to support the collaborative process include the following:

- Redefine the role of educators for gifted education programs
- Allow for cooperative planning time among general and gifted program staffs
- Provide for assurances for continuity of services
- Provide resources to support collaborative efforts

Over 25 years ago, Lindsey (1980) summarized a number of reviews concerned with specific teacher behaviors crucial for effective teaching of students who are gifted or talented (the list is as relevant today as it was then). Those behaviors included the ability to develop a flexible, individualized program; skill in the use of varied teaching strategies; and respect for students' creativity, imagination, and values. Teachers who are successful working with students who are gifted and talented typically are sensitive to others, flexible, enthusiastic, and innovative. Teachers should also not be intimidated by their gifted students who may ask questions the teacher might not be able to answer. In addition, it is important to realize that some students who are gifted may view themselves as different and might possess such characteristics as lowered personal self-esteem or perfectionism. The general education teacher needs to be sensitive to students' emotional needs and to provide increased support to help them reach their potential.

Finally, it is necessary that general education teachers be aware of the various obstacles they might face and to plan for them accordingly. Potential challenges include the possible need for increased preparation and planning time to create activities and lessons that fully engage the gifted student, specialized training to learn strategies to teach gifted students, modification of an engrained instructional style to better meet the needs of a gifted student, and teaching and managing an academically diverse classroom.

JUANITA REVISITED If Juanita was in your general education class, what approaches or procedures might you use to ensure all your students, including Juanita, were receiving quality instruction?

Check Your Understanding

1. What can general education teachers do to help identify gifted and talented students from typically underrepresented areas?

2. What are important characteristics that a general education teacher should display when teaching gifted and talented students?

3. Why is it important for general education teachers to be sensitive to the possible emotional needs of gifted and talented students?

4. What are possible obstacles that a general education teacher might face when teaching gifted and talented students?

Identification Tools: The use of multiple measures using multiple criteria is recommended. *Intelligence Tests:* Wechsler Intelligence Scale for Children–IV, Naglieri Nonverbal Ability Test; *Rating Scales:* Scales for Rating Behavioral Characteristics of Superior Students, Gifted and Talented Evaluation Scales, Gifted Evaluation Scale–Second Edition; *Creativity Tests:* Torrance Tests of Creative Thinking; *Alternative Procedures:* Dynamic Assessment, Portfolio Assessment, and Performance Assessment.

Characteristics	Indicators You Might See
Intellectual	IQ of 130 or higher, advanced logical thinking, early language development, accelerated pace of thought processes, flexibility of thought process.
Academic	Above-average performance in academic subjects, diligent approach to tasks, superior study skills, creative application of course content, engaging in solitary academic activities, asking many questions, learning through observation, desire to learn independently, development of academic skills at an early age.
Creative	Ability to express feelings and emotions, uses humor, original and persistent in problem solving, having many ideas, bored by the routine and obvious, finding unconventional ways to do things.
Social-Emotional	Fear of failure, higher sense of self than peers, high motivation and task persistence, high levels of sensitivity, self-awareness and idealism, perfectionism.

Students with Gifts and Talents

Teaching Implications

Instructional Content
- Consider acceleration or enrichment programs.
- Support thinking, problem-solving, and social-emotional skills.
- Consider Bloom's taxonomy and Gardner's theory of multiple intelligences when selecting content.
- Keep individual student diversity in mind.

Instructional Procedures
- Use higher-level questions, model problem-solving and thinking strategies, reinforce original problems and solutions, develop tasks for generalization.
- Use a variety of presentation formats.
- Consider using cooperative learning.
- Encourage the parent to be active in the student's instruction.

Instructional Environment
- Consider various grouping strategies: XYZ grouping, multiage and multigrade grouping, within-class grouping, and cluster grouping.

Instructional Technology
- Consider types of learning activities that can be done using technology: acquiring, retrieving, constructing, and presenting.
- Keep in mind the negative opportunities technology allows, such as hacking and software piracy.

Methodologies and Strategies to Try
- Mentoring (p. 532)
- Curriculum Telescoping (p. 532)
- Curriculum Compacting (p. 532)
- The Enrichment Triad (p. 532)
- Schoolwide Enrichment Model (p. 533)

Considerations for the General Classroom and Collaboration

Instruction could occur in the general classroom, a special program, or a combination of the general classroom with acceleration and/or enrichment programs.

The general education teacher should:
- Become familiar with the characteristics of students with gifts and talents, and those who are typically underidentified, to improve identification.
- Develop a flexible, individualized plan; be skilled in the use of a variety of strategies; and have respect for the student's creativity, imagination, and values.
- Be prepared for possible increased preparation and planning time, the need to learn strategies to teach gifted students, the modification of a teaching style you are used to, and teaching and managing an academically diverse classroom.
- Time should be allocated for collaboration between general education teachers and gifted education teachers.

Collaboration
General and special educators should consult on:
- Identifying gifted and talented students
- Differentiating curriculum
- Considering acceleration and enrichment options
- Allowing for a continuity of services
- Selecting and using technology

Chapter Summary

Go to the text's Online Learning Center at **www.mhhe.com/taylor1e** to access study resources, Web links, practice quizzes, and extending materials.

What Are the Foundations of Gifts and Talents?

- Gifted and talented individuals have been identified throughout recorded history although gifted education did not begin in the United States until the late 19th century. Today, there are strong proponents for and opponents against gifted education.
- The first federal definition of gifted and talented, called the Marland definition, identified six areas in which a student could be gifted and talented: general intellectual ability, specific academic aptitude, creative or productive thinking, leadership ability, visual and performing arts, and psychomotor ability. Subsequent federal definitions were similar but eliminated psychomotor ability.
- The most recent federal definition, enacted in 1993, identifies gifted and talented students as those who exhibit the capacity for intellectual, creative, or artistic high performance and show unusual leadership ability or excel in an academic field. This current definition uses the term "outstanding talent," rather than "gifts and talents," and emphasizes that they can occur across all cultural and socioeconomic groups.
- Renzulli's three-ring definition states that gifted and talented students possess a combination of above-average ability, task commitment, and creativity.
- Various versions of the current and past federal definitions are used by different states.
- Although it is difficult to determine the actual number of gifted and talented students, the prevalence rate reported for a number of years has been 3–5%. More than 2 million school-aged students receive gifted education.
- Underrepresented groups include underachievers, students with disabilities, females, and culturally and linguistically diverse students.

What Are the Causes and Characteristics of Gifts and Talents?

- There are arguments for both genetic and environmental causes, but it is generally accepted that gifts and talents are caused by an interaction of these factors.
- One of the most widely reported characteristics of gifted and talented students is superior intelligence. When using intelligence as a measure, gifted and talented students typically have an IQ over 130. Gardner's theory of multiple intelligences is also used as a way to view superior intelligence. Gardner identified eight types of intelligence an individual might display: verbal-linguistic, logical-mathematical, musical, spatial, bodily-kinesthetic, interpersonal, intrapersonal, and naturalistic. Existential intelligence is being evaluated.
- Other characteristics of gifted and talented students include superior academic ability and creativity.
- Social-emotional characteristics of gifted and talented students may include high motivation and task persistence; and high levels of sensitivity, self-awareness, and idealism. The characteristics of personal/social adjustment and self-concept have been studied extensively.

How Are Students Who Are Gifted and Talented Identified?

- Multiple procedures should be used to identify students who are gifted and talented as no single method is totally accurate or effective.
- Preschool children are often initially identified as gifted or talented by their parents. Controversy exists as to whether gifts and talents should be identified at such a young age.
- Procedures that can be used to identify school-aged children as gifted or talented include teacher nominations, peer nominations, rating scales, intelligence and achievement testing, and creativity assessment.
- Students who underachieve, students with disabilities, females, and students from culturally and linguistically diverse backgrounds are often underidentified as gifted or talented.
- Alternative approaches to identification include dynamic, portfolio, and performance assessment.

What and How Do I Teach Students Who Are Gifted and Talented?

- Two popular approaches to teaching gifted and talented students are acceleration and enrichment. Acceleration relates to moving a student through the curriculum at a faster pace. Enrichment refers to modifying or adding to the curriculum.
- The actual instructional content of the educational program will largely depend on the nature of an individual's gifts and talents. Content area teachers should consider including the development of thinking, problem-solving, and social-emotional skills.
- Two models that can be used to plan content for gifted and talented students are Bloom's taxonomy and Gardner's theory of multiple intelligences. In Bloom's taxonomy, which includes six levels for cognitive understanding, the focus should be placed on the two or three highest levels of understanding—analysis, synthesis, and evaluation. Gardner's theory of multiple intelligences can be used to plan a lesson around a student's specific area of intelligence.
- It is important to differentiate the curriculum to make it appropriate for all students. Teachers should use strategies that focus on asking higher-level questions, modeling problem-solving and thinking strategies, reinforcing original problems and solutions, and developing tasks for generalization.
- Strategies such as mentoring, curriculum telescoping, curriculum compacting, and the enrichment triad have proved successful for gifted and talented students. Effective model programs include the schoolwide enrichment program, the autonomous learner model, and the integrated curriculum model.

SUMMARY

- Parents of gifted and talented children should be actively involved in their education. Teachers can encourage this through involving parents in planning the child's educational program.

What Are Other Instructional Considerations for Students Who Are Gifted and Talented?

- There is some controversy about whether gifted and talented students should be taught in the general education classroom or grouped and taught separately. Both acceleration and enrichment approaches may affect the instructional environment. XYZ, multiage and multigrade, and within-class grouping can be used when teaching gifted and talented students in general education classrooms.
- Technology can support both acceleration and enrichment approaches to gifted education. Of the four types

of learning activities that can be conducted using technology—acquiring, retrieving, constructing, and presenting—gifted and talented students should spend most of their time on constructing. The inappropriate use of technology, such as hacking and virus infestation, should be monitored.

What Are Some Considerations for the General Education Teacher?

- The general education teacher plays an important role in identifying gifted and talented students, particularly underrepresented groups.
- The general education teacher should provide a flexible, differentiated teaching program.
- There may be a need for more planning time, a need for specialized training, and a need to modify instructional style when teaching students with gifts or talents.

Reflection Questions

1. Do you agree that individuals with superior leadership skills should be considered gifted and talented? Why? How would you define and determine superior leadership skills?
2. What are some of the techniques or approaches that should be used to identify students typically underrepresented in gifted education programs? Use different criteria? Use different assessment procedures? Others? What do you think you would look for?
3. Do you think an individual's gifts and talents are primarily the result of nature or nurture? What implications are there if they are primarily due to nature? To nurture?

4. Think of an individual that you know who you consider to be creative. What specific characteristics does that person have that makes you consider her or him as being creative?
5. If your state adopted Gardner's multiple intelligences model, would it affect the type of student identified as gifted and talented? Why or why not? If so, how?
6. What do you think are the pros and cons of grade skipping? Would you encourage a student or your child to skip a grade? If so, under what circumstances?

Application Activities: For Learning and Your Portfolio

1. (*Portfolio Possibility*) Determine the definition that your state uses for gifted and talented. Compare and contrast it to the current federal definition. If your state does not have a definition for gifted and talented, find out why.
2. Interview a general education teacher about the types of characteristics she or he would look for in a potentially gifted and talented student. What characteristics were mentioned the most?
3. (*Portfolio Possibility*) Write a two-page position paper either in favor of, or against, the use of teacher nomination as the sole procedure to identify gifted and talented students.

4. (*Portfolio Possibility*) Do some research on the schoolwide enrichment model, in general, and the enrichment triad, in particular. Develop an activity that includes the three levels of the enrichment triad.
5. (*Portfolio Possibility*) Included in this chapter was a discussion of the Association for the Gifted's position on inclusion. Write your own position statement on the issue.
6. Check the Internet for interactive Web sites that could be used for instructional purposes for gifted and talented students. Keep track of them realizing that you might be able to use them for all students, not just gifted and talented students.

SUMMARY

Appendixes

Text Appendix

Sample Individualized Education Program

 Online Appendixes www.mhhe.com/taylor1e

Appendix

Part B | INDIVIDUALIZED EDUCATION PROGRAM

The Individualized Education Program (IEP) is a written document that is developed for each eligible child with a disability. The Part B regulations specify, at 34 CFR §§300.320-300.328, the procedures that school districts must follow to develop, review, and revise the IEP for each child. The document below sets out the IEP content that those regulations require.

A statement of the child's present levels of academic achievement and functional performance including:

- How the child's disability affects the child's involvement and progress in the general education curriculum (i.e., the same curriculum as for nondisabled children) **or** for preschool children, as appropriate, how the disability affects the child's participation in appropriate activities. [34 CFR §300.320(a)(1)]

A statement of measurable annual goals, including academic and functional goals designed to:

- Meet the child's needs that result from the child's disability to enable the child to be involved in and make progress in the general education curriculum. [34 CFR §300.320(a)(2)(i)(A)]

- Meet each of the child's other educational needs that result from the child's disability. [34 CFR §300.320(a)(2)(i)(B)]

For children with disabilities who take alternate assessments aligned to alternate achievement standards (in addition to the annual goals), a description of benchmarks or short-term objectives. [34 CFR §300.320(a)(2)(ii)]

U.S. Department of Education
Office of Special Education and Rehabilitative Services,
Office of Special Education Programs

Model Form: Individualized Education Program

A-1

A description of:

- How the child's progress toward meeting the annual goals will be measured.
  [34 CFR §300.320(a)(3)(i)]

- When periodic reports on the progress the child is making toward meeting the
  annual goals will be provided such as through the use of quarterly or other
  periodic reports, concurrent with the issuance of report cards.
  [34 CFR §300.320(a)(3)(ii)]

```



```

A statement of the special education and related services and supplementary aids and
services, based on peer-reviewed research to the extent practicable, to be provided to
the child, or on behalf of the child, and a statement of the program modifications or
supports for school personnel that will be provided to enable the child:

- To advance appropriately toward attaining the annual goals.
  [34 CFR §300.320(a)(4)(i)]

- To be involved in and make progress in the general education curriculum and to
  participate in extracurricular and other nonacademic activities.
  [34 CFR §300.320(a)(4)(ii)]

- To be educated and participate with other children with disabilities and
  nondisabled children in extracurricular and other nonacademic activities.
  [34 CFR §300.320(a)(4)(iii)]

```



```

An explanation of the extent, if any, to which the child will not participate with
nondisabled children in the regular classroom and in extracurricular and other
nonacademic activities. [34 CFR §300.320(a)(5)]

```



```

U.S. Department of Education
Office of Special Education and Rehabilitative Services,
Office of Special Education Programs

Model Form: Individualized Education Program

A-2 Appendix

A statement of any individual appropriate accommodations that are necessary to measure the academic achievement and functional performance of the child on State and districtwide assessments. [34 CFR §300.320(a)(6)(i)]

```



```

If the IEP Team determines that the child must take an alternate assessment instead of a particular regular State or districtwide assessment of student achievement, a statement of why:

- The child cannot participate in the regular assessment.
  [34 CFR §300.320(a)(6)(ii)(A)]

- The particular alternate assessment selected is appropriate for the child.
  [34 CFR §300.320(a)(6)(ii)(B)]

```



```

The projected date for the beginning of the services and modifications and the anticipated frequency, location, and duration of special education and related services and supplementary aids and services and modifications and supports.
[34 CFR §300.320(a)(7)]

Service, Aid or Modification	Frequency	Location	Beginning Date	Duration

U.S. Department of Education
Office of Special Education and Rehabilitative Services,
Office of Special Education Programs

Model Form: Individualized Education Program

Appendix   **A-3**

TRANSITION SERVICES

Beginning not later than the first IEP to be in effect <u>when the child turns 16, or younger if determined appropriate by the IEP Team</u>, and updated annually thereafter, the IEP must include:

- Appropriate measurable postsecondary goals based upon age-appropriate transition assessments related to training, education, employment, and where appropriate, independent living skills. [34 CFR §300.320(b)(1)]

- The transition services (including courses of study) needed to assist the child in reaching those goals. [34 CFR §300.320(b)(2)]

Transition Services (Including Courses of Study)

RIGHTS THAT TRANSFER AT AGE OF MAJORITY

- Beginning not later than one year before the child reaches the age of majority under State law, the IEP must include a statement that the child has been informed of the child's rights under Part B of the IDEA, if any, that will, consistent with 34 CFR §300.520, transfer to the child on reaching the age of majority. [34 CFR §300.320(c)]

U.S. Department of Education
Office of Special Education and Rehabilitative Services,
Office of Special Education Programs

Model Form: Individualized Education Program

A-4   Appendix

Glossary

A

absence seizure An abnormal electrical discharge in the brain in which the individual experiences a momentary loss of consciousness.

acceleration An educational approach that allows a student to cover the usual curriculum content faster.

accommodation A change in the input or output method used by the teacher or the student related to the intended instructional outcome without changing the content or conceptual level.

acronym A word in which each letter represents the first letter in a word or sentence to be remembered.

acrostic A sentence in which the first letter of each word represents the first letter in a word or sentence to be remembered.

adaptation A change made to the curriculum that keeps the academic content the same but slightly changes the conceptual level required of the student.

adaptive equipment Specialized devices designed and used to help a student perform some function.

adventitious hearing loss Deafness acquired after birth.

alternative communication Techniques that substitute for spoken communication for those individuals who appear unable or unlikely to develop spoken language skills.

amblyopia A generally correctable vision defect caused by the suppression of images resulting from strabismus or other eye disorders that causes blurred image in either or both eyes. Also referred to as lazy eye.

anaphylactic reaction A severe allergic reaction that can be potentially life-threatening. It sometimes occurs with asthma.

anoxia Loss of oxygen that can affect a newborn child.

applied behavior analysis The systematic application of behavioral principles to change socially significant behavior.

articulation disorder The atypical production of speech sounds.

assistive technology Any item, equipment, or product system that is used to increase, maintain, or improve functional capabilities.

astigmatism Difficulties in focusing at any visual range.

at-risk infant or toddler Defined by IDEA 2004 as an individual under age 3 who would be likely to experience a substantial developmental delay if early intervention services are not provided.

Attention Trainer A battery-operated device that keeps track of points or point losses.

attribution retraining A procedure to retrain an individual's attributions of success or failure. Possible attributions include ability, effort, task difficulty, and luck.

augmentative communication Methods and devices that supplement existing verbal communication skills to enhance the communication skills that the individual already exhibits.

aura A seizure that only results in a sensory sensation, such as a certain taste or smell. Auras can be used as a warning that a more serious seizure might occur.

B

baseline data Data collected prior to a change in an intervention program.

basic interpersonal communication skills (BICS) Conversational abilities that LEP students may master quite easily.

behavior chain interruption strategy A learning strategy that involves interrupting a task analysis of sequenced or chained steps to encourage communication skill development.

behavior intervention plan An educational program that emphasizes the development of positive behaviors that will serve the same purpose as a negative behavior and the assessment methods that will be used to evaluate progress.

behavioral inhibition The difficulty inhibiting and/or monitoring behaviors.

bibliotherapy The use of literature to help people solve problems and deal with feelings, to teach about a particular disability, or to promote social awareness and acceptance of differences.

buddy system A student is assigned a buddy who will give him or her support by doing such things as going over instructions, explaining rules, or answering questions.

C

chained behaviors A series of discrete behaviors that are sequenced and combined to complete a larger, single behavior.

challenge test A test used to determine the reduction of lung capacity to help diagnose asthma.

classwide peer tutoring (CWPT) A combination of whole class instruction, peer tutoring, and cooperative learning.

cleft palate An organic structural defect caused by the failure of the parts of the mouth or lips (cleft lip) to fuse appropriately during fetal development.

closed head injury A brain injury in which the skull is not penetrated.

cluster grouping The placement of 5–10 gifted and talented students with general education students, who are then taught as a group using a differentiated curriculum.

cognitive academic language proficiency (CALP) The more complex, abstract language use related to problem solving, evaluating, and inferring.

cognitive behavior modification (CBM) An educational approach to help students internalize efficient learning strategies by actively involving them in the learning process using verbalization, modeled strategies, and a planned, reflective goal statement.

cognitive strategies Deliberate, planned activities used to acquire information.

collaboration Process in which two or more equal parties work toward a common goal.

collaborative consultation A model in which general and special education teachers and other professionals are perceived to be equal partners working together to plan programs for students.

communication The process by which one individual relates ideas to another. It includes, among other aspects, language and speech.

community-based instruction Involves teaching students skills in the community environments in which the skills will be used.

complex partial seizure An abnormal electrical discharge in the brain in which the individual displays behaviors such as agitation, eye blinking, facial grimacing, and occasionally aggression.

conditional knowledge The "when and why" of learning; metacognitive strategy knowledge.

conduct disorder A disorder that involves a repetitive and persistent pattern that violates age-appropriate societal norms or the basic rights of others.

conductive hearing loss A hearing loss caused by a problem associated with transmission of sound waves from the outer through the middle ear.

congenital hearing loss Deafness acquired prior to or at birth.

contingency contract An agreement, usually in writing, that specifies consequences for desired performances.

convergent thinking skills Thinking skills that involve solving problems that have correct answers.

cooperative learning A grouping arrangement in which students of various abilities work together and are responsible for both their own learning and the group's reaching specific goals.

cooperative teaching Special and general education teachers sharing in classroom planning and teaching.

cortical visual impairment Loss of vision resulting from brain damage or other conditions.

creative dramatics An improvised drama created by the players.

criterion-referenced curriculum-based assessment A criterion-referenced test using the content of the student's curriculum as the basis for the items.

criterion-referenced tests Tests frequently developed by teachers to determine a student's mastery of content.

cross-age tutoring The tutoring of younger students by older students.

cued speech Uses 36 different manual cues to aid in distinguishing among the 44 sounds of oral English. Cues can represent vowels, consonants, or a combination.

culturally diverse students Those students who come from backgrounds that are not primarily Western European.

curriculum compacting Allowing a student to skip material that he or she has already mastered.

curriculum telescoping The provision of an educational program in less time than normally planned for.

curriculum-based assessment The use of instruments designed to measure the expected curricular outcomes for a student.

curriculum-based measurement A formal type of curriculum-based assessment that uses standard methodology.

D

Deaf with a capital "D" Refers to members of the Deaf culture and community.

deaf with a small "d" Refers to any group of people whose audiological status places them in that range of hearing loss.

declarative knowledge The "what" of learning: knowledge of the facts, concepts, or definitions that must be learned.

developmentally appropriate practice Assumes children develop at different rates and involves engaging each child in activities appropriate to her or his current developmental level to build on skills to learn increasingly higher-level developmental skills.

differential reinforcement Positive reinforcement in which the teacher rewards students for performing behaviors other than, or behaviors that are incompatible with, targeted undesirable ones.

differentiated curriculum An adaptation to the standard curriculum to provide instruction at the students' appropriate level.

dimensional classification system A classification system for emotional disturbance that includes six categories or dimensions.

direct instruction An instructional procedure that maintains several fundamental and sequential components of effective instruction: daily review, presentation, guided practice, independent practice, and weekly and monthly reviews.

disability A limitation that is inherent in an individual as a result of the impairment.

discrete trial training Highly structured adult-directed applied behavior analysis approach to teaching students with autism spectrum disorders using massed trials.

distributed trial teaching An instructional strategy that involves teaching a skill at naturally occurring times and to natural cues in the environment.

divergent thinking skills Thinking skills that involve solving problems for which there are no single correct answers.

double-mentoring An expert mentor provides support in the student's area of expertise and a teacher addresses the student's affective needs.

Duchenne muscular dystrophy The most prevalent type of muscular dystrophy; it primarily affects males. It involves progressive muscle weakness and usually results in death in the early 20s.

due process A safeguard system to ensure that decisions regarding a student's educational program are fair and just.

dynamic assessment A test-train-retest model used to determine how quickly and efficiently an individual learns new material.

E

echolalia The repetition of others' words or phrases.

echopraxia The repetition of others' gestures and movements.

emotional abuse A pattern of behavior that impairs a child's emotional development or sense of self-worth. This may include constant criticism, threats, or rejection, as well as withholding love, support, or guidance. Emotional abuse is almost always present with other forms of abuse.

enrichment An educational approach that involves the modification of, or addition to, the curriculum to make it richer and more varied.

enrichment triad An instructional model that includes three levels of enrichment activities: general exploratory activities, group training activities, and individual and small group investigations of real problems.

exceptional student A student whose educational needs are not being met by traditional education programs. An exceptional student can have a disability or can have gifts and talents.

executive functioning The activation, organization, planning, integration, and management of cognitive functions.

externalizing disorders Disorders that are typically expressed outwardly, including aggression, acting out, and disobedience.

extinction Withholding positive reinforcement for a previously reinforced response.

F

facilitated communication An alternative means of communication in which students are given physical and emotional support to type on an electronic keyboard or point at letters on an alphabet board.

fingerspelling Uses 26 different finger/hand positions to denote each letter of the alphabet.

504 Plan A plan to determine what accommodations will be implemented in the classroom for a student who does not qualify for services under IDEA 04 as per the requirements of Section 504 of the Vocational Rehabilitation Act.

fluency The ability to read quickly and accurately.

fluency disorder The atypical flow of verbal expression, characterized by impaired rate and rhythm.

frequency Refers to the measurement of sound waves and is expressed in cycles per second or hertz.

full inclusion The philosophy that all students with disabilities receive all of their instruction in the general education classroom regardless of their level or type of disability.

full-service schools Schools that include an array of services for students and families such as after- and before-school care, recreation, health service, and counseling in a "one-stop" shopping approach to service identification and delivery.

functional academics Practical, everyday problem-solving skills that will best serve the individual in his or her current and future life.

functional behavior assessment An analysis of what occurs immediately before and after a behavior is exhibited to help determine the purpose of the behavior.

G

generalization When a behavior endures over time, occurs in a variety of settings, or occurs across a set of related behaviors.

generalized tonic-clonic seizure An abnormal electrical discharge in the brain in which the individual becomes extremely rigid, loses consciousness, and displays rhythmic jerking.

H

handicap A problem an individual encounters based on external factors.

hard of hearing Refers to individuals with mild to severe hearing losses.

hearing Refers to individuals with no identified hearing loss.

hearing impairment An impairment in hearing, whether permanent or fluctuating, that adversely affects a child's educational performance.

hidden curriculum The unwritten social conventions of a school or class that typical students intuitively comprehend.

high-stakes assessment Large-scale assessment in which important decisions such as retention and graduation are made.

home base A place in the school where the student can go to escape stress; prevent tantrums, rage, meltdowns or shutdowns; or regain control after a tantrum, rage, or meltdown.

home-based contingency programs Reinforcement is provided at home based on school performance.

hyperopia Farsightedness; near objects appear out of focus but distant objects are in focus.

hypotonia The loss of muscle tone.

I

impairment A loss or abnormality of a psychological, physiological, or anatomical structure or function.

incidence The number of individuals identified as falling into a particular category for the first time during a specific period (such as a year).

incidental teaching Method of instruction that uses applied behavior analysis to teach preacademic skills within typical early childhood activities in preschools or home settings instead of sitting face-to-face with the child at a table in a clinical setting.

inclusive service-learning An approach that allows students with and without disabilities to integrate and apply knowledge and skills learned in school to address needs in their schools and communities through community service activities.

independent group contingencies An instructional grouping method in which group members' individual improvement is evaluated and rewarded.

individualized health (care) plan A plan developed to provide teachers with information about the health care status, prescribed health care procedures, and the physical management procedures for a student.

interagency agreement A formal written agreement that provides commitment of shared responsibility for student learning and a plan on which the school, community, and family collaborate.

interdependent group contingencies An instructional grouping method in which group members' combined performance is evaluated and rewarded.

internalizing disorders Disorders that are typically expressed inwardly, including personality problems, anxiety, and depression.

K

keyword method A method to enhance recall by linking unfamiliar information to more familiar information.

L

language A code in which arbitrary symbols stand for meaning, and the rules that govern that code.

language disorder The impairment or deviant development of comprehension or use of spoken, written, or other symbol system.

learned helplessness Individuals attribute their successes to external factors out of their control and attribute their failures to internal factors.

learning strategies Cognitive tools used to help learn, retrieve, and apply information and skills.

legal blindness Vision of 20/200 or worse in the best eye with the best possible correction.

life skills Life management skills that include community access, daily living, budgeting and finances, independent living, transportation, and social relationships.

linguistically diverse students Those students whose primary language is not English. Sometimes referred to as English language learners or as having limited English proficiency.

loudness Refers to the intensity of a sound and is measured in decibels.

low vision Vision of 20/70 to 20/200 in the best eye with the best possible correction.

low vision specialist An ophthalmologist or optometrist who further specializes in assessment, prescription, and use of low vision devices.

M

magnet school A school that offers specialized training in specific areas.

manifestation determination Procedures used to determine if a behavior requiring disciplinary action is caused by, or related to, the student's disability.

Marland definition A gifted student should demonstrate high performance or potential in either general intellectual ability, specific academic aptitude, creative or productive thinking, leadership ability, visual and performing arts, or psychomotor ability.

massed trial teaching An instructional strategy that involves practicing skills repeatedly in the same teaching session.

meningocele A type of spina bifida in which the membranes surrounding the spinal cord protrude through a hole in the vertebrae forming a sac.

mentoring The pairing of a student with an established expert.

metacognition Regulation of the awareness and use of strategies.

metacognitive strategies Used for planning (deciding what strategy to use), monitoring (checking during use to be sure strategy is working), and checking outcomes of learning (checking after use to be sure strategy worked).

mixed hearing loss A hearing loss that results when an individual experiences a conductive loss in one ear and a sensorineural loss in the other ear.

mnemonics Devices such as acronyms, acrostics, rhymes, or songs used to aid memory.

mobility Moving about an environment safely.

mood disorders A class of disorders that includes manic disorders, depressive disorders, and bipolar disorders.

morpheme The minimally significant unit of meaning.

morphological disorder Omitting or misusing specific morphemes beyond the typical age to do so.

morphology The rules governing the use of minimally significant units of meaning.

motor stereotypies Repetitive motor movements such as hand flapping.

multiage and multigrade grouping Grouping students according to their educational level, regardless of their actual age or grade.

myelomeningocele The most severe type of spina bifida in which the spinal cord protrudes through a hole in the back that can result in paralysis of the lower limbs.

myopia Nearsightedness; distant objects appear out of focus but near objects are in focus.

myringotomy Placing small tubes inside the ears to allow air to vent inside the ear and prevent fluid buildup while relieving the existing pressure.

N

natural environment The setting where the child would be if he or she did not have a disability.

negative reinforcement The presentation of an aversive stimulus and then its removal as a consequence of the student's behavior in order to increase that response.

neglect Failure to provide for a child's basic needs, which may be medical, educational, or emotional.

neologisms Made-up words. Students with autism sometimes use them.

norm-referenced tests Tests that are usually standardized and provide an indication of how much a student knows in comparison to others.

nystagmus Abrupt, jerky movements of the eyes.

O

open head injury A brain injury in which the skull is penetrated and a portion of the brain is exposed.

ophthalmologists Medical doctors who identify and treat eye problems.

opticians Individuals who make or deal in optical devices and instruments.

optometrists Eye doctors who examine eyes for defects and problems in refraction and prescribe corrective lenses.

orientation The process of using sensory input and information to know one's position in an environment.

orthopedic impairment An impairment caused by a congenital anomaly, disease, or other causes such as cerebral palsy.

orthoses Equipment that enhances the use of a body part.

other health impairment An impairment affecting an individual's vitality, strength, or alertness.

otitis media Middle ear infections that can lead to either temporary or permanent hearing loss.

overlapping curriculum A student is involved in the general education curriculum while also working on very different content or curriculum goals.

P

palilalia The repetition of ones own words.

paradoxical effect The mistaken notion that stimulant medications such as Ritalin have an opposite effect on individuals with ADHD than on individuals without ADHD.

parallel curriculum outcome The content is the same as for most students but major changes in the outcome are made within that content.

partial inclusion The philosophy that suggests that students with disabilities should receive most of their instruction in the general classroom but also be taught in other instructional settings when appropriate.

partial participation Individuals are allowed to partially engage in an activity rather than deny or delay their involvement because prerequisite skills have not been learned or mastered.

peer support interventions Procedures used to increase peer interactions between children with and without communication disorders.

peer-assisted learning strategies (PALS) An expansion of the basic structure of the classwide peer tutoring system (CWPT) that engages students in strategic reading activities.

peer-mediated instruction One partner performs while the other monitors and corrects errors, and then roles are switched.

person-centered planning A method by which professionals can better focus on the student and thereby encourage participation.

pharmacological treatment The use of medication to help in controlling some emotional or behavioral disorders.

phoneme The minimally significant unit of sound.

phonological awareness The recognition that words, syllables, or sounds exist in spoken language and the ability to manipulate them by deleting, adding, substituting, and transposing.

phonological disorder Difficulty in learning the rules for using speech sounds in the absence of any obvious physical limitations.

phonological processes Rules that simplify adult speech forms.

phonology The system of speech sounds and the rules governing their use.

physical abuse Physical injury with the intent to hurt as a result of punching, beating, kicking, biting, shaking, throwing, stabbing, choking, hitting, burning, or otherwise harming an individual.

Picture Exchange Communication System A systematic behavioral program that teaches children to use pictures to communicate their needs and desires through approaching a communication partner and exchanging a symbol for the actual object.

pivotal response teaching A modified discrete trial format that relies on interspersed mastery trials using natural reinforcement and child-selected materials.

play therapy The use of a child's play for self-expression and exploring feelings to work through troubling experiences, fears, and anxieties.

portfolio assessment A means of determining students' achievements and abilities using a collection of their work.

positive behavior support A behaviorally based systems change approach to redesigning the environment to minimize problem behaviors.

positive reinforcement The contingent presentation of a consequence following a student response to increase that response.

postlingual hearing loss Deafness occurring after the development of speech and language.

pragmatics A system of rules governing the use and function of language.

pragmatics disorder Difficulty in using language appropriately based on the setting.

prebraille skills Development of tactile perception and hand movements.

precision teaching A system of evaluating and improving instruction characterized by direct, continuous, and precise measurements of student progress using response rate.

prelingual hearing loss Deafness occurring prior to the development of speech and language.

Premack Principle Positive reinforcement procedure that uses student-preferred activities as reinforcers for performing less preferred activities.

prereferral assessment Gathering information, usually informally, before a referral is made.

prereferral intervention A program, designed from the prereferral assessment information, that is implemented before a formal referral is made.

prevalence The total number of individuals who are in a given category at a particular point in time.

prevention An outcome of the process of intervention in an effort to avert learning and/or emotional and social disorders.

procedural knowledge The "how" of learning; cognitive strategy knowledge.

process tests Instruments that purportedly measure how well a person processes information.

prompt An additional stimulus or cue that will increase the chances of a correct response being given.

prostheses Equipment that replaces a body part.

protective factors Factors that may intervene with the harm caused by risk factors, explaining the resiliency of some children.

punishment Contingently applying an aversive consequence following a behavior to reduce the behavior.

R

rapid automatic naming Quickly naming stimuli such as digits, letters, or names of simple objects; related to early reading ability.

recall A level of difficulty that requires the student to remember the response and give it without any choices.

reciprocal tutoring A form of tutoring in which students trade off the roles of tutor and tutee.

recognition A level of difficulty that requires only that the student select the response from multiple choices.

reconstruction A level of difficulty that requires the student to not only recall the information but also produce it.

refraction The focusing of light as it passes through the components of the eye.

Regular Education Initiative A movement that supported the education of all students with special needs without the need for labels through the collaboration of general education and special education teachers.

related services Those activities or services that enable a child with a disability to receive a free, appropriate public education and to benefit from the special education program.

response cards May be laminated cards or signs with preprinted answers on them or blank white boards written on with dry-erase markers that all students will hold up so the teacher can see their responses.

response cost The withdrawal of specific numbers of reinforcers contingent on a behavior's occurrence.

response to intervention Relatively new criterion indicating that a student's lack of response to a scientific, research-based intervention can be considered in identifying a learning disability.

retinopathy of prematurity Vision loss resulting from complications from high oxygen levels given to sustain life in infancy.

reverse-role tutoring A form of tutoring in which the student with the disability is the tutor.

risk factors Those elements of life that can contribute to the probability of developmental delays if no intervention is provided.

S

savant syndrome A condition occurring in approximately 10% of individuals with autism in which extraordinary abilities in areas such as art, music, and mathematics are displayed.

scaffolds Support provided by the teacher until the student is ready to assume control of learning.

schizophrenia A condition characterized by delusions, hallucinations, and disorganized speech and behavior.

self-advocacy Skills that enable individuals with disabilities to speak for themselves and others.

self-determination A combination of skills, knowledge, and beliefs that enable a person to engage in goal-directed, self-regulated, autonomous behavior.

self-monitoring The observation and recording of one's own behavior.

self-regulation Self-control that enables an individual to act in a manner that influences his or her own behavior.

self-reinforcement Evaluating and reinforcing oneself.

semantics A system of rules governing the meaning of words and word combinations.

semantics disorder Difficultly in vocabulary development.

sensorineural loss A hearing loss caused by a problem directly associated with auditory nerve transmission; a problem exists in the inner ear or auditory nerve.

sexual abuse Activities such as fondling a child's genitals, penetration, incest, rape, sodomy, indecent exposure, and exploitation through prostitution or production of pornographic materials.

shunt A surgical procedure for hydrocephaly in which a valve is implanted that directs cerebrospinal fluid from the brain into the bloodstream.

signing exact English Combines existing ASL signs with new signs to create a code to help deaf students learn English. This code represents oral English through hand movements.

simple partial seizure An abnormal electrical discharge in the brain in which the individual might have abnormal muscle movements or sensory sensations such as a certain taste or smell.

social stories Short stories with simple sentences and optional illustrations about specific, commonly encountered social situations.

special education Instruction specifically designed to meet the individual needs of an exceptional student.

specific language impairment (SLI) A child language disorder that exists in the absence of any other developmental disability or obvious structural or neurological problems.

speech The physical production of language.

speech disorder An impairment in the articulation of speech sound, fluency, or voice.

speech or language impairment According to IDEA, this is a communication disorder, such as stuttering, impaired articulation, a language impairment, or a voice impairment, that adversely affects a child's educational performance.

speechreading The process of considering the situational context, facial expressions, gestures, body language, and lip and tongue movements to try to determine what a speaker is saying.

spina bifida occulta A condition in which an opening exists in one or more of the vertebrae in the spinal column.

strabismus Any deviation in the alignment of the eyes as a result of muscle imbalance.

supported employment Can involve the use of job coaches who provide individual help to individuals in learning new job skills and continue to check on the individual across time. Supported employment can also involve more extensive supervision through the employment of small groups of individuals who work in a business, employment of small groups who perform jobs in the community, and employment of individuals within a business that employs both individuals with and without disabilities.

syntactic disorder A disorder in which one uses simple sentences when more complex structures should be used or confuses word order when forming sentences or using more complex structures.

syntax The rules of word function and word order.

T

task analysis The identification of a sequential list of objectives within a skill area.

Terman myth The myth that all gifted individuals are gifted in all possible areas.

theory of mind The ability of an individual to see the world from the perspective of others.

think aloud procedure A diagnostic procedure that allows the student to talk his or her way through the solution of a problem so the teacher can determine the incorrect procedures that are being used.

threshold hypothesis The hypothesis suggesting that heredity is important in setting the intellectual potential of an individual and that the environment determines how much potential is realized.

time-out The contingent removal of the student from a positively reinforcing environment for some predetermined amount of time.

TOAD system An observational system that stands for Talking out, Out of seat, Attention problems, and Distraction.

token economy The contingent presentation of something tangible that can be exchanged later for some preferred reinforcer.

tone-prompt system A tape recorder that intermittently plays soft tones to remind a student to monitor him- or herself.

transfer/generalization The ability of an individual to take new learning and use it in a new environment or situation, or to apply the learning in some manner that was not directly taught.

transition services Coordinated activities for a student within an outcome-oriented process that promote transition from school to adult life.

traumatic brain injury An acquired injury to the brain caused by an external force.

twice exceptional A student who is both gifted and has a disability.

U

universal design The concept that environments, instruction, and assessments should be designed to be accessible to all individuals.

universal intervention An intervention that is used as a general schoolwide or whole classroom strategy for all students with and without disabilities.

universal precautions A set of guidelines designed to prevent exposure to blood-borne pathogens.

V

visual acuity How sharp visual images are perceived.

visual field The scope of what one can see without turning the head or moving the eyes.

voice disorder Atypical production of voice quality, pitch, or loudness.

W

wayfinding Learning a route through an environment and being able to retrace it from memory.

within-class grouping Grouping students according to their ability and teaching using a differentiated curriculum.

working memory Individual's ability to hold information for usage for short periods of time.

X

XYZ grouping Grouping students according to their IQ.

Z

zero tolerance Disciplinary action taken without considering extenuating circumstances.

References

A

About APH: The history of the American Printing House for the Blind: A chronology. (2004). Retrieved October 25, 2004, from www.aph.org/about/hihglite.htm

Achenbach, T. M. (1991). *Achenbach system of empirically based assessment.* Itasca, IL: Riverside.

Achenbach, T. M. (1997). *Achenbach system of empirically based assessment.* Itasca, IL: Riverside.

Achenbach, T. M. (2000). *Achenbach system of empirically based assessment.* Itasca, IL: Riverside.

Achenbach, T. M. (2003). *Achenbach system of empirically based assessment.* Itasca, IL: Riverside.

Achenbach, T. M., & Edelbrock, C. S. (1991), *Child behavior checklist—teacher's report.* Burlington, VT: University Associates in Psychiatry.

Adelman, A., & Taylor, L. (1983). *Learning disabilities in perspective.* Glenview, IL: Scott, Foresman & Company.

Adreon, D., & Stella, J. (2001). Transition to middle and high school: Increasing the success for students with Asperger Syndrome. *Intervention in School and Clinic, 36*(5), 266–271.

Agran, M., Blanchard, C., & Wehmeyer, M. L. (2000). Promoting transition goals and self-determination through student self-directed learning: The self-determined learning model of instruction. *Education and Training in Mental Retardation and Developmental Disabilities, 35*(4), 351–365.

Alberto, P. A., & Troutman, A. C. (2006). *Applied behavior analysis for teachers* (7th ed.). Upper Saddle River, NJ: Merrill/Prentice-Hall.

Alexander, D. (2000, June). *How research advances will affect people with developmental disabilities in the 21st century.* Keynote address presented at the annual meeting of the American Association on Mental Retardation, Washington, DC.

Alexander, H. (2000). Neuroimaging: Applications in disorders of early brain development. *Journal of Developmental and Behavioral Pediatrics, 21,* 291–302.

Alexander Graham Bell Association for the Deaf and Hard of Hearing. (n.d.). *Types of hearing aids.* Retrieved May 25, 2007, from www.agbell.org/DesktopDefault.aspx?p=Types_of_Hearing_Aids

Algozzine B., & Ysseldyke, J. (2006). *Teaching students with sensory disabilities: A practical guide for every teacher.* Thousand Oaks, CA: Corwin Press.

Allen, K. E., & Schwartz, I. S. (2001). *The exceptional child: Inclusion in early childhood education.* Albany, NY: Delmar.

Alper, S. (2003). The relationship between inclusion and other trends in education. In D. L. Ryndak & S. Alper, *Curriculum and instruction for students with significant disabilities* (2nd ed., pp. 13–30). Boston: Allyn & Bacon.

Alter, P. J., & Conroy, M. A. (2006). Preventing challenging behavior in young children: Effective practices. Retrieved June 10, 2006, from www.challengingbehavior.org

Ambrose, G. (2000). Sighted children's knowledge of the environmental concepts and ability to orient in an unfamiliar residential environment. *Journal of Visual Impairment & Blindness, 94*(8), 509–521.

American Academmcy of Otolaryngology. (n.d.). *Perforated eardrum.* Retrieved June 20, 2005, from www.entnet.org/healthinfo/ears/perforation.cfm

American Academy of Pediatrics. (2001). AAP releases new guidelines for treatment of Attention-Deficit/Hyperactivity Disorder. *Pediatrics, 108*(4), 1033–1044.

American Association on Intellectual and Developmental Disabilities. (2007). *Name change.* Retrieved February 8, 2007, from www.aamr.org/About_AAIDD/MR_name_change.htm

American Diabetes Association. (n.d.a). *Diabetes myths.* Retrieved February 10, 2006, from www.diabetes.org/diabetes-myths.jsp

American Diabetes Association. (n.d.b) *The genetics of diabetes.* Retrieved February 10, 2006, from www.diabetes.org/genetics.jsp

American Foundation for the Blind. (2002). *What you need to know about low vision.* Prepared by Jennifer Bell &

Mary Ann Siller. Retrieved February 1, 2007, from www.afb. org/Section.asp?SectionID=44&TopicID=189&DocumentID=1757

American Foundation for the Blind. (2006). *Educating students with visual impairments for inclusion in society: A paper on the inclusion of students with visual impairments.* Retrieved February 1, 2007, from www.afb. org/Section.asp?SectionID=44&TopicID=189&DocumentID=1344

American Printing House for the Blind. (2004). *About APH.* Retrieved July 3, 2007, from www.aph.org/about/hist.html

American Psychiatric Association. (1968). *Diagnostic and statistical manual of mental disorders* (2nd ed.). Washington, DC: Author.

American Psychiatric Association. (1980). *Diagnostic and statistical manual of mental disorders* (3rd ed.). Washington, DC: Author.

American Psychiatric Association. (1987). *Diagnostic and statistical manual of mental disorders* (3rd ed., rev.). Washington, DC: Author.

American Psychiatric Association. (1994). *Diagnostic and statistical manual of mental disorders* (4th ed.). Washington, DC: Author.

American Psychiatric Association. (2000). *Diagnostic and statistical manual of mental disorders* (4th ed., text rev.). Washington, DC: Author.

American Speech-Language-Hearing Association. (n.d.). *Type, degree, and configuration of hearing loss.* Retrieved June 20, 2005, from www.ASHA.org

American Speech-Language-Hearing Association. (1993, March). Guidelines for caseload size and speech language pathology delivery in the schools. *Asha, 35*(Suppl. 10), 33–39.

American Speech-Language-Hearing Association. (1996, Spring). Inclusive practices for children and youth with communication disorders (position statement and technical report). *Asha, 38*(Suppl. 16), 35–44.

American Speech-Language-Hearing Association. (2000). Guidelines on the roles and responsibilities of school-based speech-language clinicians. *ASHA Supplement, 20,* 28–31.

American Speech-Language-Hearing Association. (2005a). Incidence and prevalence of communication disorders and hearing loss in children—2006 edition.

American Speech-Language-Hearing Association. (2005b). *Traumatic brain injury.* Retrieved January 23, 2006, from http://asha.org/public/speech/disorders/Traumatic-Brain-Injury.htm?print=1

American Speech-Language-Hearing Association. (2006a). *Introduction to augmentative and alternative communication.* Retrieved January 23, 2006, from www. asha.org/ public/speech/disorders/Augmentative-and-Alternative.htm.

American Speech-Language-Hearing Association. (2006b). *Stuttering.* Retrieved March 20, 2006, from www.asha.org/ pulic/speech/disorders/stutter.

American Speech-Language-Hearing Association. (2007). *Incidence and prevalence of communication disorders and hearing loss in children, 2008 edition.* Retrieved June 30, 2007, from www.asha.org/members/research/ reports/children.htm

American Speech-Language-Hearing Association, Ad Hoc Committee on Service Delivery in the Schools. (1993). Definitions of communication disorders and variations. *Asha, 35* (Suppl. 10), 40–41.

American Speech-Language-Hearing Association, Ad Hoc Committee on the Roles and Responsibilities of the School-Based Speech-Language Pathologist. (1999). *Guidelines for the roles and responsibilities of the school-based speech-language pathologist.* Rockville, MD: American Speech-Language-Hearing Association.

Anastopoulos, A. D., Rhoads, L. H., & Farley, S. E. (2006). Counseling and training parents. In R. Barkley (Ed.), *Attention-deficit hyperactivity disorder* (3rd ed., pp. 453–479). New York: Guilford Press.

Anderegg, M. L., & Vergason, G. (1988). An analysis of one of the cornerstones of the Regular Education Initiative. *Focus on Exceptional Children, 20,* 1–7.

Andrews, G., & Summers, A. C. (2002). *Voice treatment for children and adolescents* (2nd ed). San Diego, CA: Singular.

Andrews, J. F., Leigh, I. W., & Weiner, M. T. (2004). *Deaf people: Evolving perspectives from psychology, education, and sociology.* Boston: Pearson Education.

Annie E. Casey Foundation. (2005). *KIDS COUNT data book.* Retrieved June 7, 2006, from www.aecf.org/kidscount/

Aratani, L. (2005).*Group seeks to end gifted designation.* Retrieved October 5, 2005, from wwww.washingtonpost. com/ac2/wp-dyn/mailafriend?contentId=AR2005082401173

Archbold, S. M. (2006). Cochlear implantation and deaf education: Conflict or collaboration. In S. B. Waltzman & J. T. Roland Jr. (Eds.), *Cochlear implants* (pp. 183–192). New York: Thieme Medical Publishers.

Arends, R. (2007). *Learning to teach* (7th ed.). Boston: McGraw-Hill.

Armbruster, B. B., & Osborn, J. (2001). *Put reading first: The reading blocks for teaching children to read.* Washington, DC: Partnership for Reading.

Arnos, K. S. (2002). Ethical issues in genetic counseling and testing for deafness (pp. 149–161). In V. Gutman (Ed.), *Ethics in mental health and deafness.* Washington, DC: Gallaudet University Press.

Arnos, K. S., & Pandya, A. (2003). Advances in the genetics of deafness. In M. Marschark & P. E. Spencer (Eds.), *Oxford handbook of deaf studies, language and education* (pp. 392–405). New York: Oxford University Press.

ASLinfo.com (n.d.). Trivia. Deaf time-line. Retrieved June 14, 2005, from www.aslinfo.com/trivia/cfm.

Atkins v. Virginia, 536 U.S. 304 (2002).

Attention Deficit Disorder Association. (2005). *Myths about ADD/AD/HD.* Retrieved June 3, 2005, from www. add.org/articles/myth.html

Autism Society of America. (2003). *Autism facts.* Retrieved August 13, 2005, from www.autism-society.org/site/PageServer/pagename=Autism_Facts

Autism Society of America. (2004). *What is autism?* Retrieved July 12, 2005, from www.autism-society.org/site/PageServer

Avoké, S., & Wood-Garnett, S. (2001). Language minority children and youth in special education. *Teaching Exceptional Children, 33,* 90–91.

Ayres, K. M., & Langone, J. (2005). Intervention and instruction with video for students with autism: A review of the literature. *Education and Training in Developmental Disabilities, 40*(2), 183–196.

B

Babbitt, B. C. (1999). *10 tips for software selection for math instruction.* Retrieved January 13, 2002, from www.ldonline.org/ld_indepth/technology/babbitt_math_tips.html

Bacon, E. H., & Bloom, A. L. (1994). Don't ratl the kiDS. *Journal of Emotional and Behavioral Problems, 3*(1), 8–10.

Baglieri, S., & Knopf, J. (2004). Normalizing difference in inclusive teaching. *Journal of Learning Disabilities, 37,* 525–529.

Bagwell, C., Molina, B., Pelham, W., & Hoza, B. (2001). Attention-deficit hyperactivity disorder and problems in peer relations: Predictions from childhood to adolescence. *Journal of the American Academy of Child and Adolescent Psychiatry, 40,* 1285–1292.

Baldi, P. L. (1998). Encoding, metacognitive, autoattributional processes and memory in mentally retarded adolescents. *Psychological Reports, 82,* 931–945.

Baloglu, M., & Kocak, R. (2006). A multivariate investigation of the differences in mathematics anxiety. *Personality and Individual Differences, 40,* 1325–1335.

Bambara, L. M., & Brantlinger, E. (2002). Toward a healthy sexual life: An introduction to the special series on issues of sexuality for people with developmental disabilities. *Research and Practice for Persons with Severe Disabilities, 27,* 5–7.

Barclay, C. L., Roberts, C. W., & Rutherford, R. B. (2003). The role of the community schools in reintegrating youth with disabilities from juvenile detention. *Beyond Behavior, 12*(3), 25–26.

Barkley, R. A. (1997). *ADHD and the nature of self-control.* New York: Guilford Press.

Barkley, R. A. (1998). *Attention deficit hyperactivity disorder: A handbook for diagnosis and treatment* (2nd ed.). New York: Guilford Press.

Barkley, R. A. (2004). Attention-deficit/hyperactivity disorder and self-regulation: Taking an evolutionary perspective on executive functioning. In R. Baumeister & K. Vohs (Eds.), *Handbook of self-regulation: Research, theory, and applications* (pp. 301–323). New York: Guilford Press.

Barkley, R. A. (2006a). *Attention-deficit hyperactivity disorder: A handbook for diagnosis and treatment* (3rd ed.). New York: Guilford Press.

Barkley, R. A. (2006b). Etiologies. In R. A. Barkley (Ed.), *Attention-deficit hyperactivity disorder* (3rd ed., pp. 219–247). New York: Guilford Press.

Barkley, R. A. (2006c). A theory of ADHD. In R. A. Barkley (Ed.), *Attention-deficit hyperactivity disorder* (3rd ed., pp. 297–334). New York: Guilford Press.

Barkley, R. A., & Biederman, J. (1997). Toward a broader definition of the age-of-onset criterion for attention-deficit/hyperactivity disorder. *Journal of the American Academy of Child and Adolescent Psychiatry, 36,* 1204–1210.

Barkley, R. A., & Edwards, G. (2006). Diagnostic interview, behavior rating scales, and the medical evaluation. In R. A. Barkley (Ed.), *Attention-deficit hyperactivity disorder* (3rd ed., pp. 337–368). New York: Guilford Press.

Barnhill, G. P. (2005). Functional behavioral assessment in schools. *Intervention in School and Clinic, 40*(3), 131–143.

Barnhill, G., Hagiwara, T., Myles, B. S., & Simpson, R. L. (2000). Asperger syndrome: A study of the cognitive profiles of 37 children and adolescents. *Focus on Autism and Other Developmental Disabilities, 15,* 146–153.

Baroff, G. (1999). *Mental retardation: Nature, cause, and management* (3rd ed.). Philadelphia: Brunner, Mazel.

Baron-Cohen, S., Allen, J., & Gillberg, C. (1992). Can autism be detected at 18 months? The needle, the haystack, and the CHAT. *British Journal of Psychiatry, 161,* 839–843.

Barry, L. M., & Messer, J. J. (2003). A practical application of self-management for students diagnosed with attention-deficit/hyperactivity disorder. *Journal of Positive Behavior Interventions, 5*(4), 238–248.

Barry, T., Lyman, R., & Klinger, L. (2002). Academic underachievement and attention-deficit/hyperactivity disorder: The negative impact of symptom severity on school performance. *Journal of School Psychology, 40,* 259–283.

Barton, P. E. (2004). Why does the gap persist? *Educational Leadership, 62*(3), 9–13.

Bat-Chava, Y. (2000). Diversity of deaf identities. *American Annals of the Deaf, 145,* 420–428.

Bateman, B., & Linden, M. (1998). *Better IEPs: How to develop legally correct and educationally useful programs* (3rd ed.). Longmont, CO: Sopris West.

Batshaw, M. L., & Shapiro, B. (2002). Mental retardation. In M. L. Batshaw (Ed.), *Children with disabilities* (5th ed., pp. 287–305). Baltimore, MD: Paul H. Brookes.

Battle, D. E. (1996). Language learning and use by African American children. *Topics in Language Disorders, 16*(4), 22–37.

Bauer, A. M., & Kroeger, S. (2004). *Inclusive classrooms. Video cases on CD-ROM activity and learning guide.* Upper Saddle River, NJ: Pearson.

Bauer, A. M., & Ulrich, M. E. (2002). "I've got a Palm in my pocket": Using handheld computers in an inclusive classroom. *Teaching Exceptional Children, 35*(2), 18–22.

Baum, S., Rizza, M., & Renzulli, S. (2006). Twice-exceptional adolescents: Who are they? What do they need? In F. Dixon & S. Moon (Eds.), *The handbook of secondary gifted education* (pp. 137–164). Waco, TX: Prufrock Press.

Baumgart, D., Brown, L., Pumpian, I., Nisbet, J., Ford, A., Sweet, M., Messina, R., & Schroeder, J. (1982). The principle of partial participation and individualized adaptations in educational programs for students with severe handicaps. *Journal of the the Association for Persons with Severe Handicaps, 7*(2), 17–27.

Becvar, D. S., & Becvar, R. J. (1988). *Family therapy: A systemic integration.* Boston: Allyn & Bacon.

Beech, M. (2003). *Accommodations: Assisting students with disabilities. A guide for educators* (Rev.). Tallahassee, FL: Florida Department of Education, Bureau of Instructional Support and Community Services.

Beegle, D. M. (2003). Overcoming the silence of generational poverty. *Talking Points, 15*(1), 11–20. Retrieved January 22, 2007, from www.combarriers.com/TP0151Overcoming.pdf

Beigel, A. R. (2000). Assistive technology assessment: More than the device. *Intervention in School and Clinic, 35*(4), 237–243.

Bellak, I., & Bellak, S. (1991). *Children's Apperception Test.* San Antonio, TX: The Psychological Corporation.

Bender, W. (2004). *Learning disabilities: Characteristics, identification, and teaching strategies* (5th ed.). Boston: Allyn & Bacon.

Benner, G. J., Nelson, J. R., & Epstein, M. H. (2002). Language skills of children with EBD: A literature review. *Journal of Emotional & Behaviorial Disorders, 10*, 43–59.

Benz, M. R., Lindstrom, L., & Yovanoff, P. (2000). Improving graduation and employment outcomes for students with disabilities: Predictive factors and student perspectives. *Exceptional Children, 66*, 509–529.

Berkson, G. (2004). Intellectual and physical disabilities in prehistory and early civilization. *Mental Retardation, 42*, 195–208.

Berninger, V., & Amtmann, D. (2003). Preventing written expression disabilities through early and continuing assessment and intervention for handwriting and/or spelling problems: Research into practice. In H. L. Swanson, K. Harris, & S. Graham (Eds.), *Handbook of learning disabilities* (pp. 345–363). New York: Guilford Press.

Bernstein, L. E., & Auer Jr., E. T. (2003). Speech perception and spoken word recognition. In M. Marschark & P. E. Spencer (Eds.), *Oxford handbook of deaf studies, language, and education* (pp. 379–391). New York: Oxford University Press.

Best, S. J. (2005). Definitions, supports, issues, and services in schools and communities. In S. J. Best, K. W. Heller, & J. L. Bigge, *Teaching individuals with physical or multiple disabilities* (5th ed., pp. 3–29). Upper Saddle River, NJ: Pearson Education.

Best, S. J., Heller, K. W., & Bigge, J. L. (2005). *Teaching individuals with physical or multiple disabilities* (5th ed.). Upper Saddle River, NJ: Pearson.

Best, S. J., Reed, P., & Bigge, J. L. (2005). Assistive technology. In S. J. Best, K. W. Heller, & J. L. Bigge, *Teaching individuals with physical or multiple disabilities* (5th ed.). Upper Saddle River, NJ: Pearson Education.

Bettleheim, B. (1967). *The empty fortress.* New York: Free Press.

Betts, G., & Kercher, J. (1999). *Autonomous learner model: Optimizing ability.* Greeley, CO: Alps Publishing.

Beyda, S. (2002). Dramatic improvisation for students with EBD. *Beyond Behavior, 11*(3), 34–38.

Bigge, J. L., & Stump, C. S. (1999). *Curriculum, assessment, and instruction for students with disabilities.* Boston: Wadsworth.

Bishop, V. E. (2005). Early childhood. In M. C. Holbrook & A. J. Koenig (Eds.), *Foundation of education: Volume II. Instructional strategies for teaching children and youths with visual impairments* (2nd ed., chap. 7). Retrieved February 12, 2007, from www.afb.org/foe/book.asp?ch=v2ch7

Blackorby, J., & Wagner, M. (1996). Longitudinal postschool outcomes of youth with disabilities: Findings from the National Longitudinal Transition Study. *Exceptional Children, 62*, 399–413.

Blades, M., Lippa, Y., Golledge, R., Jacobson, R., & Kitchin, R. (2002). The effect of spatial tasks on visually impaired people's wayfinding abilities. *Journal of Visual Impairment and Blindness, 96*(6), 407–420.

Blamey, P. J. (2003). Development of spoken language by deaf children. In M. Marschark & P. E. Spencer (Eds.), *Oxford handbook of deaf studies, language, and education* (pp. 232–246). New York: Oxford University Press.

Blanck, P. D. (1998). *The Americans with Disabilities Act and the emerging workforce employment of people with mental retardation.* Washington, DC: AAMR.

Blazer, B. (1999). Developing 504 classroom accommodation plans: A collaborative systematic parent-student-teacher approach. *Teaching Exceptional Children, 32*(2), 28–33. Retrieved January 22, 2006, from www.ldonline.org/ld_indepth/teaching_techniques/504_plans.html

Bloom, B. (1956). *Taxonomy of educational objectives: The classification of education goals.* New York: David McRay.

Bloom, L., & Lahey, M. (1978). *Language development and language disorders.* New York: Wiley.

Board of Education of the Hendrick Hudson Central School District v. Rowley, 102 S. Ct. 3034 (1982).

Boeree, C. G. (2002). The emotional nervous system. Retrieved May 14, 2006, from www.ship.edu/~cgboeree/limbicsystem.html

Bohnert, A. M., Crnic, K. A., & Lim, K. G. (2003). Emotional competence and aggressive behavior in school-age children. *Journal of Abnormal Child Psychology, 31*, 79–91.

Bonds, B. G. (2003). School-to-work experiences: Curriculum as a bridge. *American Annals of the Deaf, 148*(1), 38–48.

Bondy, A., & Frost, L. (1994). The picture exchange communication system. *Focus on Autistic Behavior, 9*, 1–19.

Bonham, G. S., Basehart, S., Schalock, R. L., Marchand, C. B., Kirchner, N., & Rumenap, J. M. (2004). Consumer-based quality of life assessment: The Maryland Ask Me! project. *Mental Retardation, 42*, 338–355.

Bonnaud, C., Jamet, F., Deret, D., & Neyt-Dumesnil, C. (1999). [Translated title] Recognition of human faces with adults with severe mental retardation. *Revue Francophone de la Déficience Intellectuelle, 10*, 5–17.

Booth, J., Burman, D., Meyer, J., Lei, Z., Trommer, B., Davenport, N., Li, W., Parrish, T., Gitelman, D., & Mesulam, M. (2005). Larger deficits in brain networks for response inhibition than for visual selective attention in attention deficit hyperactivity disorder (AD/HD). *Journal of Child Psychology and Psychiatry, 46*, 94–111.

Bos, C. S., Coleman, M., & Vaughn, S. (2002). Reading and students with E/BD: What do we know and recommend? In K. L. Lane, F. M. Gresham, & T. E. O'Shaugnessy (Eds), *Interventions for children with or at risk for emotional and behavioral disorders* (pp. 87–92). Boston: Allyn & Bacon.

Bos, C. S., & Vaughn, S. (2006). *Strategies for teaching students with learning and behavior problems* (6th ed.). Boston: Allyn & Bacon.

Bouchard, D., & Tetreault, S. (2000). The motor development of sighted children and children with moderate low vision aged 8–13. *Journal of Visual Impairment and Blindness, 94*(9), 564–574.

Bouchard, T. J. (1997). IQ similarity in twins reared apart: Findings and responses to critics. In R. J. Sternberg & E. Grigorenka (Eds.), *Intelligence, heredity, and environment* (pp. 126–160). New York: Cambridge University Press.

Bouck, E. C. (2004). State of curriculum for secondary students with mild mental retardation. *Education and Training in Developmental Disabilities, 39*(2), 169–176.

Boulineau, T., Fore, C., Hagan-Burke, S., & Burke, M. D. (2004). Use of story-mapping to increase the story-grammar text comprehension of elementary students with learning disabilities. *Learning Disability Quarterly, 27*(2), 105–121.

Bowe, F. G. (2000). *Physical, sensory, and health disabilities. An introduction.* Upper Saddle River, NJ: Prentice-Hall.

Bowe, F. G. (2002a). Deaf and hard of hearing Americans' instant messaging and e-mail use: A national survey. *American Annals of the Deaf, 147*(4), 6–10.

Bowe, F. G. (2002b). Enhancing reading ability to prevent students from becoming low-functioning deaf as adults. *American Annals of the Deaf, 14*(5), 22–27.

Bower, E. (1960). *Early identification of emotionally handicapped children in the schools.* Springfield, IL: Charles C Thomas.

Bower, E. (1982). Defining emotional disturbance: Public policy and research. *Psychology in the Schools, 19*, 55–60.

Bowers, P., & Ishaik, G. (2003). RAN's contribution to understanding reading disabilities. In H. L. Swanson, K. Harris, & S. Graham (Eds.), *Handbook of learning disabilities* (pp. 140–157). New York: Guilford Press.

Bowman, B., Donovan, M., & Burns, N. (2000). Committee on Early Childhood Pedagogy, National Research Council. *Eager to Learn: Educating our preschoolers.* Washington, DC: National Academy Press.

Boyajian, A. E., DuPaul, G. J., Handler, M. W., Eckert, T. L., & McGoey, K. E. (2001). The use of classroom-based brief functional analyses with preschoolers at-risk for attention deficit hyperactivity disorder. *School Psychology Review, 30*(2), 278–293.

Braddock, D, & Parish, S. (2002). An institutional history of disability. In D. Braddock (Ed.), *Disability at the dawn of the 21st century and the state of the states* (pp. 3–43). Washington, DC: American Association on Mental Retardation.

Bragdon, A., & Gamon, D. (2000). *Brains that work a bit differently.* New York: Bragdon/Barnes & Noble.

Brice, A. E. (2002). *The Hispanic child: Speech, language, culture and education.* Boston: Allyn & Bacon.

Brice, P. J. (2002). Ethical issues in working with deaf children, adolescents, and their families. In V. Gutman (Ed.), *Ethics in mental health and deafness* (pp. 52–67). Washington, DC: Gallaudet University Press.

Bricker, D. B. (1986). *Early education of at-risk and handicapped infants, toddlers, and preschool children.* Glenview, IL: Scott, Foresman.

Brigham, F. J., & Brigham, M. M. (2001). A focus on mnemonic instruction. *Current Practice Alerts, 5.*

Brill, C. (1994). The effects of participation in service-learning on adolescents with disabilities. *Journal of Adolescence, 17*, 369–380.

Brinckerhoff. L. C., McGuire, J. M., & Shaw, S. F. (2002). *Postsecondary education and transition for students with leaning disabilities* (2nd ed.). Austin, TX: Pro-Ed.

Brinton, B., Fujiki, M., Spencer, J. C., & Robinson, L. A. (1997). The ability of children with specific language impairment to access and participate in an ongoing interaction. *Journal of Speech, Language, and Hearing Research, 40*(5), 1011–1025.

Broun, L. T. (2004). Teaching students with autistic spectrum disorders to read: A visual approach. *Teaching Exceptional Children, 36*(4), 36–40.

Browder, D. M., & Snell, M. E. (2000). Teaching functional academics. In M. E. Snell & F. Brown (Eds.), *Instruction of students with severe disabilities* (pp. 493–542). Upper Saddle River, NJ: Prentice-Hall.

Browder, D. M., Spooner, F., Ahlgrim-Delzell, L., Flowers, C., Algozzine, B., & Karvonen, M. (2003). A content analysis of the curricular philosophies reflected in states' alternate assessment performance indicators. *Research and Practice for Persons with Severe Disabilities, 28*, 165–181.

Browder, D. M., Spooner, F., Algozzine, B., Ahlgrim-Delzell, L., Flowers, C., & Karvonen, M. (2003). What we know and need to know about alternate assessment. *Exceptional Children, 70*, 45–61.

Browder, D. M., & Xin, Y. P. (1998). A meta-analysis and review of sight word research and its implications for teaching functional reading to individuals with moderate and severe disabilities. *Journal of Special Education, 32,* 130–153.

Brown, F., Snell, M. E., & Lehr, D. (2006). Meaningful assessment. In M. E. Snell & F. Brown, *Instruction of students with severe disabilities* (pp. 67–110). Upper Saddle River, NJ: Pearson.

Brown, L., Branston, M. B., Hamre-Nietupski, S., Pumpian, I., Certo, N., & Gruenwald, L. (1979). A strategy for developing chronological-age-appropriate and functional curricular content for severely handicapped adolescents and young adults. *The Journal of Special Education, 13,* 81–90.

Brown, L., Nisbet, J., Ford, A., Sweet, M., Shiraga, B., York, J., & Loomis, R. (1983). The critical need for nonschool instruction in educational programs for severely handicapped students. *Journal of the Association of the Severely Handicapped, 8,* 71–77.

Brown, L., Wilcox, B., Sontag, E., Vincent, B., Dodd, N., & Gruenewald, L. (1977). Toward the realization of the least restrictive educational environments for severely handicapped students. *The American Association for the Education of the Severely/Profoundly Handicapped Review, 2*(4). Reprinted in *Research and Practice for Persons with Severe Disabilities* (2004), *29,* 2–8.

Brown, W. H., Musick, K. K., Conroy, M., & Schaeffe, E. H. (2002). A proactive approach to promoting young chldren's compliance. *Beyond Behavior, 11*(2), 3–8.

Brownell, M. T., & Walther-Thomas, C. (2001). An interview with Steven Shore: Understanding the autism spectrum—what teachers need to know. *Intervention in School and Clinic, 36*(5), 293–299, 305.

Bruder, M. (2000). *The Individual Family Service Plan.* Retrieved June 12, 2006, from http://ericec.org/digests/e605.html

Bruininks, R., Woodcock, R., Weatherman, R., & Hill, B. (1996). *Scales of Independent Behavior–Revised.* Chicago: Riverside.

Bryan, T. (1997). Assessing the personal and social status of students with learning disabilities. *Learning Disabilities: Research and Practice, 12*(1), 63–76.

Bryant, D., & Dix, J. (1999). Mathematics interventions for students with learning disabilities. In W. Bender (Ed.), *Professional issues in learning disabilities* (pp. 219–259). Austin, TX: Pro-Ed.

Bryant, D. P. (2003). Promoting effective instruction for struggling secondary students: Introduction to the special issue. *Learning Disability Quarterly, 26*(2), 70–71.

Bryant, D. P., & Bryant, B. R. (1998). Using assistive technology adaptations to include students with learning disabilities in cooperative learning activities. *Journal of Learning Disabilities, 31*(1), 41–54.

Bryant, D. P., & Bryant, B. R. (2003). *Assistive technology for people with disabilities.* Boston: Allyn & Bacon.

Bryant, D. P., Goodwin, M., Bryant, B. R., & Higgins, K. (2003). Vocabulary instruction for students with learning disabilities: A review of the research. *Learning Disability Quarterly, 26,* 117–128.

Buck, G., Polloway, E., Smith-Thomas, A., & Cook, K. (2003). Prereferral intervention processes: A survey of state practices. *Exceptional Children, 69,* 349–360.

Budd, J., & LaGrow, S. (2000). Using a three-dimensional interactive model to teach environmental concepts to visually impaired children. *RE:view, 32*(2), 83–95.

Buege, C. (1993). Effect of mainstreaming on attitude and self-concept using creative drama and social skills training. *Youth Theatre Journal, 7,* 19–22.

Bulgren, J. A., & Lenz, B. K. (1996). Strategic instruction in the content areas. In D. D. Deshler, E. S. Ellis, & B. K. Lenz (Eds.), *Teaching adolescents with learning disabilities: Strategies and methods* (2nd ed., pp. 409–473). Denver: Love.

Bullock, L., Gable, R., & Mohr, D. (2005). Tramatic brain injury: A challenge for educators. *Preventing School Failure, 49,* 6–10.

Bunce, B. H. (1995). *Building a language-focused curriculum for the preschool classroom* (Vol. 2). Baltimore: Paul H. Brookes.

Burch, S. (2002). *Signs of resistance. American deaf cultural history, 1900 to World War II.* New York: New York University Press.

Burlington School Committee v. Department of Education, 471 U.S. 359 (1985).

Burns, E. (2001). *Developing and implementing IDEA IEPs: An individualized education program handbook for meeting Individuals with Disabilities Education Act requirements.* Springfield, IL: Charles C Thomas.

Burns, M., & Senesac, B. (2005). Comparison of dual discrepancy criteria to assess response to intervention. *Journal of School Psychology, 43,* 393–406.

Burns, M., Storey, K., & Certo, N. (1999). Effect of service learning on attitudes towards students with severe disabilities. *Education and Training in Mental Retardation and Developmental Disabilities, 34,* 58–65.

Burrell, B., Wood, S. J., Pikes, T., & Holliday C. (2001). Student mentors and proteges learning together. *Teaching Exceptional Children, 33*(3), 24–28.

Bursuck, W. D., Smith, T., Munk, D., Damer, M., Mehlig, L., & Perry, J. (2004). Evaluating the impact of a prevention-based model of reading on children who are at risk. *Remedial and Special Education, 25*(5), 303–313.

Bush-LaFrance, R. (1988). Unseen expectations of blind youth: Educational and occupational ideas. *Journal of Visual Impairment and Blindness, 82,* 132–136.

Butcher, J., Dahlstrom, W., Graham, A., & Kaemmer, B. (1989). *MMPI–2: Manual for Administration and scoring.* Minneapolis: University of Minnesota Press.

Butler, S., Crudden, A., Sansing, W., & LeJeune, B. J. (2002). Employment barriers: Access to assistive technology and research needs. *Journal of Visual Impairment and Blindness 96*(9), 664–668.

Butterworth, J., Steere, D. E., & Whitney-Thomas, J. (1997). Using person-centered planning to address personal quality of life. In R. L. Schalock (Ed.), *Quality of life. Vol. 2: Application to persons with disabilities* (pp. 5–24). Washington, DC: American Association on Mental Retardation.

Byrne, P. (2000). *Philosophical and ethical problems in mental handicap.* Chippenham, Wiltshire, Great Britain: Antony Rowe.

C

Cade, T., & Gunter, P. L. (2002). Teaching students with severe emotional or behavioral disorders to use musical mnemonic techniques to solve basic division calculations. *Behavioral Disorders, 27*(3), 208–214.

Calderon, R., & Greenberg, M. T. (2003). Social and emotional development of deaf children: Family, school, and program effects. In M. Marschark & P. E. Spencer (Eds.), *Oxford handbook of deaf studies, language and education* (pp. 177–189). New York: Oxford University Press.

Callicott, K. J. (2003). Culturally sensitive collaboration within person-centered planning. *Focus on Autism and Other Developmental Disabilities, 18,* 60–68.

Capone, G. (2001). Down syndrome: Advances in molecular biology and the neurosciences. *Journal of Developmental and Behavioral Pediatrics, 22,* 40–59.

Carbone, E. (2001). Arranging the classroom with an eye (and ear) to students with AD/HD. *Teaching Exceptional Children, 34*(2), 72–81.

Carnine, D. W., Silbert, J., & Kame'enui, E. J. (1997). *Direct instruction reading* (3rd ed.). Upper Saddle River, NJ: Prentice-Hall.

Carnine, D. W., Silbert, J., Kame'enui, E. J., & Tarver, S. G. (2004). *Direct instruction reading* (4th ed.). Upper Saddle River, NJ: Merrill Prentice-Hall.

Carroll, D. (2001). Considering paraeducator training, roles, and responsibilities. *Teaching Exceptional Children, 34,* 60–64.

Carter, E. W., & Wehby, J. H. (2003). Job performance of transition-age youth with emotional and behavioral disorders. *Exceptional Children, 69*(4), 449–465.

Carter, J. A., Lees, J. A., Murira, G. M., Gona, J., Neville, B. G. R., & Newton, C. R. J. C. (2005). Issues in the development of cross-cultural assessments of speech and language for children. In *International Journal of Language & Communication Disorders, 40*(4), 385–401.

Carter, M., & Grunsell, J. (2001). The behavior change interruption strategy: A review of research and discussion of future directions. *Journal of the Association for Persons with Severe Handicaps, 26,* 37–49.

Cartledge, G., Wang, W., Blake, C., & Lambert, M. C. (2002). Middle school students with behavior disorders acting as social skill trainers for peers. *Beyond Behavior, 11*(3), 14–18.

Casey, K. M., & Shore, B. M. (2000). Mentor's contributions to gifted adolescents' affective, social, and vocational development. *Roeper Review, 22*(4), 227–230

CBS Interactive (2007, November 12). Brain maturity may lag in kids with AD/HD. Retrieved November 6, 2007, from http://cbsnews.com/stories/2007/11/12/health/main3492746.shtml.

Center for Applied Special Technology. (2006). *What is Universal Design for Learning?* Retrieved June 10, 2006, from www.cast.org/research/udl/index.html

Centers for Disease Control and Prevention. (2006). *Childhood lead poisoning fact sheet.* Retrieved June 25, 2006, from www.cdc.gov/nceh/publications/factsheets/ChildhoodLeadPoisoning.pdf

Centers for Disease Control and Prevention. (2007). *CDC releases new data on autism spectrum disorders (ASDs) from multiple communities in the United States.* Retrieved April 2, 2007, from www.cdc.gov/od/oc/media/pressrel/2007/r070208.htm

Chalk, J. C., Hagan-Burke, S., & Burke, M. D. (2005). The effects of self-regulated strategy development on the writing process for high school students with learning disabilities. *Learning Disability Quarterly, 28*(1), 75–87.

Chang, S., & Schaller, J. (2002). The views of students with blindness or low vision on the support they received from teachers. *Journal of Visual Impairment and Blindness, 96*(8), 558–575.

Charlop-Christy, M. H., Carpenter, M., Le, L., Leblanc, L. A., & Kellet, K. (2002). Using the picture exchange communication system (PECS) with children with autism: Assessment of PECS acquisition, speech, social-communicative behavior, and problem behavior. *Journal of Applied Behavior Analysis, 35,* 213–231.

Charman, T., & Baird, G. (2002). Practitioner review: Diagnosis of autism spectrum disorder in 2- and 3-year-old children. *Journal of Child Psychology and Psychiatry, 43,* 289–305.

Chaudry, N. M., & Davidson, P. W. (2001). Assessment of children with visual impairment or blindness. In R. J. Simeonsson, & S. L. Rosenthal (Eds.), *Psychological and developmental assessment: Children with disabilities and chronic conditions* (pp. 225–247). New York: Guilford Press.

Chen, D. (2001). *Visual impairment in young children: A review of the literature with implications for working with families of diverse cultural and linguistic backgrounds.* Washington, DC: Special Education Programs (ED/OSERS). (ERIC Document Reproduction Service No. ED 478 932)

Chen, R., & DeStefano, F. (1998). Vaccine adverse events: Causal or coincidental? *Lancet, 351,* 611–612.

Cheramie, G. M., Griffin, K. M., & Morgan, T. (2000). Usefulness of assessment techniques in assessing classification for emotional disturbance and generating classroom recommendation. *Perceptual & Motor Skills, 90*(1), 250–252.

Chesley, G., & Calaluce, P. (1997). The deception of inclusion. *Mental Retardation, 35,* 488–490.

Child Welfare Information Gateway. (2003). *Substance abuse and child maltreatment.* Retrieved July 12, 2006, from www.childwelfare.gov/pubs/factsheets/subabuse_childmal.pdf

Child Welfare Information Gateway. (2004). *Risk and protective factors for child abuse and neglect.* Retrieved July 12, 2006, from www.childwelfare.gov/preventing/programs/whatworks/riskprotectivefactors.pdf

Child Welfare Information Gateway. (2006). *What is child abuse and neglect?* Retrieved July 12, 2006, from www.childwelfare.gov/pubs/factsheets/whatiscan.pdf

Children and Adults with Attention Deficit Disorder. (2001). *The disorder named AD/HD. Fact sheet #1.* Retrieved November 20, 2005, from www.chadd.org/fs/fs1.htm

Children and Adults with Attention Deficit Disorder. (2003). *Evidence-based medication management for children and adolescents with AD/HD. Fact sheet #3.* Retrieved November 20, 2005, from www.chadd.org/fs/fs3.htm

Chopra, R. V., Sandoval-Lucero, E., Aragon, L., Bernal, C., De Balderas, H. B., & Carroll, D. (2004). The paraprofessional role of connector. *Remedial and Special Education, 25,* 219–231.

Ciardiello, A. (1998). "Did you ask a good question today?" Alternative cognitive and metacognitive strategies. *Journal of Adolescent and Adult Literacy, 42,* 210–219.

City of Cleburne, TX v. Cleburne Living Center Inc., 473 U.S. 432 (1985).

Clarfield, J., & Stoner, G. (2005). The effects of computerized reading instruction on the academic performance of students identified with AD/HD. *School Psychology Review, 34*(2), 246–254.

Clark, B. (1992). *Growing up gifted* (4th ed.) Upper Saddle River, NJ: Prentice-Hall.

Clark, B. (2002). *Growing up gifted* (6th ed.) Upper Saddle River, NJ: Prentice-Hall.

Clark, G. M., & Bigge, J. L. (2005). Transition and self-determination. In S. J. Best, K. W. Heller, & J. L. Bigge, *Teaching individuals with physical or multiple disabilities* (5th ed., pp. 367–398). Upper Saddle River, NJ: Pearson.

Clark, S. G. (2000). The IEP process as a tool for collaboration. *Teaching Exceptional Children, 33*(2), 56–66.

Clasen, D., & Clasen, R. E. (2003). Mentoring the gifted and talented. In N. Colangelo & G. Davis (Eds.), *Handbook of gifted education* (pp. 254–267). Needham Heights, MA: Allyn & Bacon.

Clasen, D., & Hanson, M. (1987). Double mentoring: A process for facilitating mentorships for gifted students. *Roeper Review, 10,* 107–110.

Clements, S. (1966). *Minimal brain dysfunction in children: National project on learning disabilities in children.* (NINDS Monograph No. 3, Public Health Service Bulletin No. 1415). Washington, DC: U.S. Department of Health, Education, and Welfare.

Cleveland, H. H., Jacobson, K. C., Lipinski, J. J., & Rowe, D. C. (2000). Genetic and shared environmental contributions to the relationship between the home environment and child and adolescent achievement. *Intelligence, 28,* 69–86.

Cochran, L., Feng, H., Cartledge, G., & Hamilton, S. (1993). The effects of cross-age tutoring on the academic achievement, social behaviors, and self-perceptions of low-achieving African-American males with behavioral disorders. *Behavioral Disorders, 18*(4), 292–302.

Codding, R., & Lewandowski, L. (2003). Academic interventions for children with ADHD: A review of current options. *ADHD Report, 11,* 8–11.

Cohen, S. (2001). Lead poisoning: A summary of treatment and prevention. *Pediatric Nursing, 27,* 125–130.

Colangelo, N. (2003). Counseling gifted students. In N. Colangelo & G. Davis (Eds.), *Handbook of gifted education* (pp. 373–387). Needham Heights, MA: Allyn & Bacon.

Colangelo, N., Assouline, S., & Gross, M. (2004). *A nation deceived: How schools hold back America's brightest students* (Vol. 1). Iowa City: University of Iowa.

Colangelo, N., & Davis, G. A. (Eds). (2003). *Handbook of gifted education.* Boston: Allyn & Bacon.

Colarusso, R., Keel, M., & Dangel, H. (2001). A comparison of eligibility criteria and their impact on minority representation in LD programs. *Learning Disabilities Research and Practice, 16,* 1–7.

Cole, C. M., Waldron, N., & Majd, M. (2004). Academic progress of students across inclusive and traditional settings. *Mental Retardation, 42,* 136–144.

Cole, P. A., & Taylor, O. L. (1990). Performances of working class African American children on three tests of articulation. *Language, Speech, and Hearing Services in Schools, 21*(3), 171–176.

Coleman, M. C., & Vaughn, S. (2000). Reading interventions for students with E/BD. *Behavior Disorders, 25*(2), 93–104.

Coleman, M. C., & Webber, J. (2002). *Emotional and behavioral disorders: Theory and practice* (4th ed.). Boston: Allyn & Bacon.

Collins, B. C. (2007). *Moderate and severe disabilities. A foundational approach.* Upper Saddle River, NJ: Pearson.

Compton, D. (2006). How should unresponsiveness to secondary intervention be operationalized? It is all about the nudge. *Journal of Learning Disabilities, 39,* 170–173.

Conderman, G., & Strobel, D. (2006). Problem solving with guided repeated oral reading instruction. *Intervention in School and Clinic, 42*(1), 34–39.

Cone-Wesson, B. (2003). Screening and assessment of hearing loss in infants. In M. Marschark & P. E. Spencer (Eds.), *Oxford handbook of deaf studies, language, and education* (pp. 420–433). New York: Oxford University Press.

Conley, P. T. (2002). Preparing students for life after high school. *Educational Leadership, 59,* 60–63.

Conlon, C. (1992). New threats to development: Alcohol, cocaine, and AIDS. In M. Batshaw & Y. Perret (Eds.), *Children with disabilities: A medical primer* (3rd ed., pp. 111–136). Baltimore: Paul H. Brookes.

Conners, C. (1997). *Conners Rating Scales-Revised.* N. Tonawanda, New York: Multi-Health Systems.

Connor, D. F. (2006). Stimulants. In R. Barkley (Ed.), *Attention-deficit hyperactivity disorder* (3rd ed., pp. 608–647). New York: Guilford Press.

Conroy, M. A., & Brown, W. H. (2004). Early identification, prevention, and early intervention with young children at risk for emotional or behavioral disorders: Issues, trends, and a call for action. *Behavioral Disorders, 29*(3), 224–236.

Cook, B., Cameron, D., & Tankersley, M. (2007). Inclusive teachers' attitudinal ratings of their students with disabilities. *Journal of Special Education, 40*, 230–238.

Cook, M. (2005). Autism: The mercury trail. *New Statesman, 134*, 4752.

Cook, T., & Swain, J. (2001). Parents' perspectives on the closure of a special school: Towards inclusion in partnership. *Educational Review, 53*, 191–198.

Coolidge, F., Thede, L., & Young, L. (2000). Heritability and the comorbidity of attention deficit hyperactivity disorder with behavior disorders and executive function deficits: A preliminary investigation. *Neuropsychology, 17*, 273–287.

Corn, A. L., DePriest, L. B., & Erin, J. N. (2005) Visual efficiency. In M. C. Holbrook & A. J. Koenig (Eds.), *Foundation of education: Volume II. Instructional strategies for teaching children and youths with visual impairments* (2nd ed., chap. 13). Retrieved February 12, 2007, from www.afb.org/foe/book.asp?ch=v2ch13

Corn, A. L., Hatlen, P., Huebner, K. M., Ryan, F., & Siller, M. A. (1996). Developing the national agenda for the education of children and youths with visual impairments, including those with multiple disabilities [Electronic version]. *Journal of Visual Impairment & Blindness, 28*, 5–17.

Corn, A. L., & Koenig, A. J. (1996). *Foundations of low vision: Clinical and functional perspectives.* New York: American Foundation for the Blind.

Corn, A. L., & Koenig, A. J. (2002). Literacy for students with low vision: A framework for delivering instruction. *Journal of Visual Impairment & Blindness, 96*(5), 305–321.

Corral, N., & Antia, S. D. (1997). Self-talk. *Teaching Exceptional Children, 29*(4), 42–45.

Cosmos, C. (2002). Be a winner in your classroom—attend the CEC annual convention & Expo. *CEC Today, 8*(6), 1, 5, 7.

Costello, E., Messer, S., Bird, H., Cohen, P., & Reinherz, H. (1998). The prevalence of serious emotional disturbance: A reanalysis of community studies. *Journal of Child and Family Studies, 7*, 411–432.

Council for Exceptional Children. (1997). Making assessments of diverse students meaningful. *CEC Today, 4*, 1, 9.

Council for Exceptional Children. (2002). *Addressing over-representation of African American students in special education: The prereferral process.* Arlington, VA: Author.

Council of State Directors of Programs for the Gifted. (2003). *2001–2002 state of the states gifted and talented education report.* Longmont, CA: Author.

Coutinho, M., Oswald, D., Best, A., & Forness, S. (2002). Gender and sociodemographic factors and the disproportionate identification of culturally and linguistically diverse students with emotional disturbance. *Behavioral Disorders, 27*, 109–125.

Cox, P., & Dykes, M. (2001). Effective classroom adaptations for students with visual impairments. *Teaching Exceptional Children, 33*(6), 68–74.

Crago, M. B. (1992). Ethnography and language socialization: A cross-cultural perspective. *Topics in Language Disorders, 12*(3), 28–39.

Craig, A., Hancock, K., Tran, Y., Craig, M., & Peters, K. (2002). Epidemiology of stuttering in the community across the entire life span. *Journal of Speech, Language, and Hearing Research, 45*, 1097–1105.

Craig, C., Hough, D., Churchwell, C., & Schmitt, V. (2002). A statewide study of the literacy of students with blindness or low vision. *Journal of Visual Impairment and Blindness, 96*(6), 452–455.

Crane, K., Gramlich, M., & Peterson, K. (2004, September). Putting interagency agreements into action. *Issue Brief. Examining Current Challenges in Secondary Education and Transition, 3*(2). Retrieved from www.ncset.org

Crenshaw, T. M., Kavale, K. A., Forness, S. R., & Reeve, R. E. (1999). Attention deficit hyperactivity disorder and the efficacy of stimulant medication: A meta-analysis. In T. Scruggs & M. Mastropieri (Eds.), *Advances in learning and behavioral disabilities* (Vol. 13, pp. 117–131). Greenwich, CT: JAI.

CRESPAR (Center for Research on the Education of Students Placed At Risk). (2006). *The mission.* Retrieved June 7, 2006, from http://crespar.law.howard.edu/themission.html

Croen, L., Grether, J., Curry, C., et al. (2001). Congenital abnormalities among children with cerebral palsy: More evidence of prenatal antecedents. *Journal of Pediatrics, 138*, 804–810.

Croen, L., Grether, J., Hoogstrate, J., & Selvin, S. (2002). Changing prevalence of autism in California. *Journal of Autism and Developmental Disorders, 32*, 207–215.

Crook, W. (1983). Let's look at what they eat. *Academic Therapy, 18*, 629–631.

Crozier, S., & Sileo, N. M. (2005). Encouraging positive behavior with social stories: An intervention for children with autism spectrum disorders. *Teaching Exceptional Children, 37*(6), 26–31.

Cruickshank, W. (1967). *The brain-injured child in home, school, and community.* Syracuse, NY: Syracuse University Press.

Cruickshank, W. M., Bentzen, F. A., Ratzeburg, F. H., & Tannhauser, M. T. (1961). *A teaching method for brain-injured and hyperactive children: A demonstration-pilot study.* Syracuse, NY: Syracuse University Press.

Cullinan, D., & Epstein, M. (1995). Behavior disorders. In N. Haring & L. McCormick (Eds.), *Exceptional children and youth* (6th ed.). Upper Saddle River, NJ: Merrill Prentice-Hall.

Cullinan, D., Evans, C. Epstein, M. H., & Ryser, G. (2003). Characteristics of emotional disturbance of elementary school students. *Behavioral Disorders, 28*, 94–110.

Cummins, J. (1984). *Bilingualism and special education: Issues in assessment and pedagogy.* San Diego: College-Hill Press.

Cushing, L. S., Clark, N. M., Carter, E. W., & Kennedy, C. H. (2005). Access to the general education curriculum for students with significant cognitive disabilities. *Teaching Exceptional Children, 38*(2), 6–13.

Cutspec, P. (2004). Influence of dialogic reading on the language development of infants and toddlers. *Bridges, 2*(2), 1–12. Retrieved from www.evidencebasedpractices.org/bridges

Cutting, L., Koth, C., Mahone, E., & Denckla, M. (2003). Evidence for unexpected weaknesses in learning in children with attention-deficit/hyperactivity disorder without reading disabilities. *Journal of Learning Disabilities, 36*, 259–269.

D

D'Allura, T. (2002). Enhancing the social interaction skills of preschoolers with visual impairments. *Journal of Visual Impairment and Blindness, 96*(8), 576–585.

Dahlberg, S., & Gillberg, C. (1989). Symptoms in the first two years of life: A preliminary population study of infantile autism. *European Archives of Psychiatry and Neurological Sciences, 238*, 169–174.

Daley, D. (2006). Attention deficit hyperactivity disorder. A review of the essential facts. *Child Care, Health, and Development, 32*, 193–204.

Davidson Institute on Talent Development. (2007). *Federal policies.* Retrieved April 9, 2007, from www.geniusdenied.com/Policies/StatePolicyDetails.aspx?StateCode=10,000&NavID=6_3

Davies, D., Stock, S., & Wehmeyer, M. L. (2002). Enhancing independent time-management skills for individuals with mental retardation using a palmtop personal computer. *Mental Retardation, 40*(5), 358–365.

Davies, R., & Ferguson, J. (1997). Teachers' views of the role of initial teacher education in developing their professionalism. *Journal of Education for Teaching, 23*(1), 39–56.

Davila, R., Williams, M., & MacDonald, J. (1991). *Clarification of policy to address the needs of children with attention deficit disorders within general and/or special education.* Washington, DC: U.S. Department of Education.

Davis, G. A., & Rimm, S. B. (2004). *Education of the gifted and talented* (5th ed.). Needham Heights, MA: Allyn & Bacon.

Deafculture.com (n.d.). *Comparative chart: Deaf and ethnic cultures.* Retrieved June 16, 2007, from www.deafculture.com./ethnic_culture/

de la Cruz, R. E., Lian, M. G., & Morreau, L. E. (1998). The effects of creative drama on social and oral language skills of children with learning disabilities. *Youth Theatre Journal, 12*, 89–95.

De La Paz, S., & MacArthur, C. (2003) Knowing the how and why of history expectations for secondary students with and without learning disability. *Learning Disability Quarterly, 26*(2), 142–154.

De La Paz, S., Owen, B., Harris, K., & Graham, S. (2000). Riding Elvis' motorcycle: Using self-regulated strategy development to PLAN and WRITE for a state writing exam. *Learning Disabilities Research and Practice, 15*(2), 101–109.

Demchak, M., & Greenfield, R. G. (2003). *Transition portfolios for students with disabilities. How to help students, teachers, and families handle new settings.* Thousand Oaks, CA: Corwin Press.

Denney, M. K., Singer, G. H. S., Singer, J., Brenner, M. E., Okamoto, Y., & Fredeen, R. M. (2001). Mexican immigrant families' beliefs and goals for their infants in the neonatal intensive care unit. *Journal of the Association for Persons with Severe Handicaps, 26*, 148–157.

Denning, C., Chamberlain, J., & Polloway, E. (2000). An evaluation of state guidelines for mental retardation. *Education and Training in Mental Retardation and Developmental Disabilities, 35*, 226–232.

Deno, S. (1985). Curriculum-based measurement: The emerging alternative. *Exceptional Children, 52*, 219–232.

Deno, S., & Fuchs, L. (1987). Developing curriculum-based measurement systems for data-based special education problem solving. *Focus on Exceptional Children, 19*, 1–16.

Denton, C. A., Vaughn, S., & Fletcher, J. M. (2003). Bringing research-based practice in reading intervention to scale. *Learning Disabilities Research & Practice, 18*(3), 201–211.

DePaepe, P., Shores, R., Beck, S., & Denny, R. (1996). Effects of task difficulty on the disruptive and on-task behavior of students with severe behavior disorders. *Behavioral Disorders, 21*, 216–225.

Deshler, D. D., Ellis, E. S., & Lenz, B. K. (1996). *Teaching adolescents with learning disabilities: Strategies and methods* (2nd ed.). Denver: Love.

Deshler, D. D., Warner, M. M., Schumaker, J. B., & Alley, G. R. (1983). Learning strategies intervention model: Key components and current status. In J. D. McKinney & L. Feagans (Eds.), *Current topics in learning disabilities* (Vol. 1, pp. 245–283). Norwood, NJ: Ablex.

DeVault, R., & Joseph, L. M. (2004). Repeated readings combined with word boxes phonics technique increases fluency levels of high school students with severe reading delays. *Preventing School Failure, 49*(1), 22–27.

Devinsky, O. (2004a). *Complex partial seizures.* Retrieved February 10, 2006, from www.epilepsy.com/epilepsy/seizure_complexpartial.html

Devinsky, O. (2004b). *Tonic-clonic seizures.* Retrieved February 10, 2006, from www.epilepsy.com/epilepsy/seizure_tonicclonic.html

Dial, J., Mezger, C., Gray, S., Massey, T., Chan, F., & Hull, J. (1990). *Manual: Comprehensive vocational evaluation system.* Dallas, TX: McCarron-Dial Systems.

Diana v. State Board of Education, No. C-70-37 RFP (N. Cal. 1973).

Diem, R. A., & Katims, D. S. (2002). The introduction of computers in an at-risk learning environment: A seven-year retrospective view. *Computers in the Schools, 19*(1/2), 19–32.

Dillard, J. L. (1972) *Black English: Its history and usage in the United States.* New York: Vintage.

DiPaola, M. F., & Walther-Thomas, C. (2003). *Principals and special education: The critical role of school leaders.* (ERIC Document Reproduction Service No. ED 477 115)

DiPerna, J., & Elliott, S. (2000). *Academic Competence Evaluation Scales.* San Antonio, TX: Psychological Corporation.

Discipline strategies you can use. (2004). *CEC Today, 10*(5), 4–5, 19.

Division on Blindness or Low Vision. (2005). History of the division on visual impairments. Retrieved May 13, 2005, from www.ed.arizona.edu/dvi/history.htm

Dodd, B., Crosbie, S., McIntosh, B. Teitzel, T. & Ozanne, A. (2003) *Pre-Reading Inventory of Phonological Awareness (PIPA).* San Antonio, TX: Psychological Corporation.

Dodge, D. T., & Colker, L. (2002). *The creative curriculum* (5th ed.). Washington, DC: Teaching Strategies.

Dodge, E. P. (2004). Communication skills: The foundation for meaningful group intervention in school-based programs. *Topics in Language Disorders, 24*(2), 141–150.

Dohan, M., & Schulz, H. (1998). The speech-language pathologist's changing role: Collaboration within the classroom. *Journal of Children's Communication Development, 20*(1), 9–18.

Dolch, E. W. (1950). *Teaching primary reading* (2nd ed.). Champaign, IL: Garrard Press.

Doll, B., Sands, D. J., Wehmeyer, M. L., & Palmer, S. (1996). Promoting the development and acquisition of self-determined behavior. In D. J. Sands & M. L. Wehmeyer (Eds.), *Self-determination across the life span: Independence and choice for people with disabilities* (pp. 63–88). Baltimore, MD: Paul H. Brookes.

Donovan, M. S., & Cross, C. T. (Eds.), for the Committee on Minority Representation in Special Education. (2002). *Minority students in special and gifted education.* Washington, DC: National Academy Press.

Dore, R., Dion, E., Wagner, S., & Brunet, J. P. (2002). High school inclusion of adolescents with mental retardation: A multiple case study. *Education and Training in Mental Retardation and Developmental Disabilities, 37*, 253–261.

Douvanis, G., & Hulsey, D. (2002). *The least restrictive environment mandate: How has it been defined by the courts?* Retrieved June 11, 2006, from http://ericec.org/digests/e629.html

Downing, J. A. (2004). Related services for students with disabilities: Introduction to the special issue. *Intervention in School and Clinic, 39*, 195–208.

Downs, A., & Smith, T. (2004). Emotional understanding, cooperation, and social behavior in high-functioning children with autism. *Journal of Autism and Developmental Disorders, 34*, 625–635.

Drasgow, E. (1998). American sign language as a pathway to linguistic competence [Electronic version]. *Exceptional Children, 64*(3), 329–342.

Drew, C. J., Logan, D. R., & Hardman, M. L. (1992). *Mental retardation: A life cycle approach* (5th ed.). New York: Merrill.

Duke, T. S. (2004). Problematizing collaboration: A critical review of the empirical literature on teaching teams. *Teacher Education and Special Education, 27*, 307–317.

Dunlap, G., & Fox, L. (1999). Supporting families of young children with autism. *Infants and Young Children, 12*(2), 48–54.

Dunn, L. M., Smith, J. O., Dunn, L. M., & Horton, K. B. (1981). *Peabody language development kits.* Bloomington, MN: American Guidance Service.

Dunst, C. J., & Kassow, D. Z. (2004). Characteristics of interventions promoting parental sensitivity to child behavior [Electronic version]. *Bridges, 2*(5), 1–17. Retrieved from www.researchtopractice.info/products.php#bridges

DuPaul, G. J., & Eckert, T. L. (1998). Academic interventions for students with attention-deficit/hyperactivity disorder: A review of the literature. *Reading and Writing Quarterly, 14*, 59–82.

DuPaul, G. J., & Ervin, R. A. (1996). Functional assessment of behaviors related to attention-deficit/hyperactivity disorder: Linking assessment to intervention design. *Behavior Therapy, 27*, 601–622.

DuPaul, G. J., Ervin, R. A., Hook, C. L., & McGoey, K. E. (1998). Peer tutoring for children with attention deficit hyperactivity disorder: Effects on classroom behavior and academic performance. *Journal of Applied Behavior Analysis, 31*, 579–592.

DuPaul, G. J., & Henningson, P. N. (1993). Peer tutoring effects on the classroom performance of children with attention deficit hyperactivity disorder. *School Psychology Review, 22*, 134–143.

DuPaul, G. J., & Stoner, G. (2003). *AD/HD in the schools: Assessment and intervention strategies* (2nd ed). New York: Guilford Press.

DuPaul, G. J., & White, G. (2004). An AD/HD primer [Electronic version]. *Principal Leadership Magazine, 5*, 1–7. Retrieved February 18, 2005, from www.naspcenter.org/principals/nassp_AD/HD.html

Durlap, J. A., & Wells, A. M. (1997). Evaluation of indicated preventive intervention (secondary intervention) mental health programs for children and adolescents. *American Journal of Community Psychology, 26*, 775–802.

Durlap, J. A., & Wells, A. M. (1998). Primary prevention mental health programs for children and adolescents: A meta-analytic review. *American Journal of Community Psychology, 25*, 115–152.

Durrer, B., & McLaughlin, T. F. (1995). The use of peer tutoring interventions involving students with behavior disorders. *B.C. Journal of Special Education, 19*(1), 20–27.

Dykeman, B. F. (2003). School-based interventions for treating social adjustment difficulties in children with traumatic brain injury. *Journal of Instructional Psychology, 30*, 225–230.

E

Early Reading Diagnostic Assessment Second Edition (ERDA Second Edition). (2003). San Antonio, TX: Psychological Corporation.

Easterbrooks, S. (1999). Improving practices for students with hearing impairments. *Exceptional Children, 65*, 537–554.

Easterbrooks, S. R., & Baker, S. K. (2001). Enter the matrix! *Teaching Exceptional Children, 33*(3), 70–76.

Eddy, J. M., Reid, J. B., & Curry, V. (2002). The etiology of youth antisocial behavior, delinquency, and violence and a public health approach to prevention. In M. R. Shinn, H. M. Walker, & G. Stoner (Eds.), *Interventions for academic and behavior problems II: Preventive and remedial approaches* (pp. 27–51). Bethesda, MD: National Association of School Psychologists.

Edelson, J. (1999). Children's witnessing of adult domestic violence. *Journal of Interpersonal Violence, 14*(8), 526–534.

Eder, W., & von Mutius, E. (2005).Genetics in asthma: The solution to a lasting conundrum. *Allergy, 60*, 1482–1485.

Edgar, E., & Siegel, S. (1995). Postsecondary scenarios for troubled and troubling youth. In J. M. Kauffman, J. W. Lloyd, D. P. Hallahan, & T. A. Astuto (Eds.), *Issues in educational placement: Students with emotional and behavioral disorders* (pp. 251–283). Hillsdale, NJ: Erlbaum.

Ehren, B. J. (2000). Maintaining a therapeutic focus and sharing responsibility for student success: Keys to in-classroom speech-language services. *Language, Speech and Hearing Services in Schools, 31*, 219–229.

Ehren, B. J. (2002). Speech-language pathologists contributing significantly to the academic success of high school students: A vision for professional growth. *Topics in Language Disorders, 22*(2), 60–80.

Ehren, B. J. (2005). Looking for evidence-based practice in reading comprehension instruction. *Topics in Language Disorders, 25*, 310–321.

Eisen, M. D. (2006). History of the cochlear implant. In S. B. Waltzman & J. T. Roland Jr. (Eds.), *Cochlear implants* (pp. 1–10). New York: Thieme Medical Publishers.

Elbaum, B. E., Schumm, J. S., & Vaughn, S. (1997). Urban middle-elementary students' perceptions of grouping formats for reading instruction. *Elementary School Journal, 97*, 475–500.

Elbaum, B., & Vaughn. S. (2003). Self-concept and students with learning disabilities. In H. L. Swanson, K. Harris, & S. Graham (Eds.), *Handbook of learning disabilities* (pp. 229–241). New York: Guilford Press.

Elbaum, B., Vaughn, S., Hughes, M., & Moody, S. W. (1999). Grouping practices and reading outcomes for students with disabilities. *Exceptional Children, 65*, 399–415.

Eli Lilly and Company. (2005). *Causes of AD/HD.* Retrieved May 23, 2005, from www.strattera.com/1_3_childhood_AD/HD/1_3_1_1_1_causes.jsp

Elks, M. A. (2004). Believing is seeing: Visual conventions in Barr's classification of the "feeble-minded." *Mental Retardation, 42*, 371–382.

Elliot, S. N., & Gresham, G. M. (1991). *Social skills intervention guide: Practical strategies for social skills training.* Circle Pines, NM: American Guidance Service.

Elliot, S., DiPerna, J., & Shapiro, E. (2000). *Academic intervention monitoring system.* San Antonio, TX: Psychological Corporation.

Ellis, A. (2001). *Research on education innovations* (3rd ed.). Larchmont, NY: Eye of Education.

Ellis, E. E., Lenz, B. K., & Sabornie, E. J. (1987). Generalization and adaptation of learning strategies to natural environments: Part 2: Research into practice. *Remedial and Special Education, 8*(2), 6–23.

Emerson, R. W., Corn, A., & Siller, M. A., (2006). Trends in braille and large-print production in the United States: 2000-2004 [Electronic version]. *Journal of Visual Impairment & Blindness, 100*(3), 137–151.

Englert, C. S., & Raphael, T. C. (1988). Constructing well-formed prose: Process, structure, and metacognitive knowledge. *Exceptional Children, 54*, 513–520.

Epilepsy Foundation. (2005a). *Epilepsy and seizure statistics.* Retrieved February 10, 2006, from www.efa.org/answerplace/statistics.cfm

Epilepsy Foundation. (2005b). *First aid for generalized tonic clonic (grand mal) seizures.* Retrieved February 10, 2006, from www. efa.org/answerplace/Medical/firstaid/firstaidkeys.cfm

Estevis, A. H., & Koenig, A. J. (1994). A cognitive approach to reducing stereotypic body rocking. *RE:view, 26*(3), 119–125.

Etscheidt, S. (2002). Extended school year services: A review of eligibility criteria and program appropriateness. *Research and Practice for Persons with Severe Disabilities, 27*, 188–203.

F

Falk, K. B., & Wehby, J. H. (2001). The effects of peer-assisted learning strategies on the beginning reading skills of young children with emotional or behavioral disorders. *Behavioral Disorders, 26*, 344–359.

Falvey, M. (1989). *Community-based curriculum. Instructional strategies for students with severe handicaps* (2nd ed.). Baltimore: Paul H. Brookes.

Falvey, M. (2004). Toward realizing the influence of "Toward realization of the least restrictive educational environments for severely handicapped students." *Research & Practice for Persons with Severe Disabilities, 29*, 9–10.

Falvo, D. (2005). *Medical and psychosocial aspects of chronic illness and disability* (3rd ed.). Sudbury, MA: Jones & Bartlett.

Fantuzzo, J., McWayne, C., & Perry, M. A. (2004). Multiple dimensions of family involvement and their relations to behavioral and learning competencies for urban, low-income children. *School Psychology Review, 33*(4), 467–480.

Farah, M., & Noble, K. (2005). Socioeconomic influences on brain development: A preliminary study. In U. Mayr, E. Awh, & S. Keele (Eds.), *Developing individuality in the human* brain: A tribute to Michael I. Posner. *Decade of behavior* (pp. 189–208). Washington, DC: American Psychological Association.

Faraone, S. (2004). Genetics of adult attention-deficit/hyperactivity disorder. *Psychiatric Clinics of North America, 27*, 303–321.

Faraone, S., Doyle, A., Mick, E., & Biederman, J. (2001). Meta-analysis of the association between the 7-repeat allele of the dopamine D4 receptor gene and AD/HD. *American Journal of Psychiatry, 158*, 1052–1057.

Farlow, L. J., & Snell, M. E. (2006). Teaching self-care skills. In M. E. Snell & F. Brown, *Instruction of students with severe disabilities* (pp. 328–374). Upper Saddle River, NJ: Pearson.

Farmer, T. W. (2000). Misconceptions of peer rejection and problem behaviors: A social interactional perspective of the adjustment of aggressive youth with mild disabilities. *Remedial and Special Education, 4*, 194–208.

Fasold, R., & Wolfram, W. (1978). Some linguistic features of Negro dialect. In P. Stoller (Ed.), *Black American English* (pp. 49–83). New York: Delta.

Federal Register, 34CFR300.506(b)(t)(i). Assistance to States for the Education of Children with Disabilities and Preschool Grants for Children with Disabilities; Final Rule. Meditation. Volume 71, Number 156 (2006).

Federal Register, 34CFR300.320(7)(b). Assistance to States for the Education of Children with Disabilities and Preschool Grants for Children with Disabilities; Final Rule. Definition of the individualized education program. Volume 71, Number 156 (2006).

Federal Register, 34CFR300.154. Assistance to States for the Education of Children with Disabilities and Preschool Grants for Children with Disabilities; Final Rule. Methods of ensuring services. Volume 71, Number 156 (2006).

Federal Register, 34CFR300.8(c)(6). Assistance to States for the Education of Children with Disabilities and Preschool Grants for Children with Disabilities; Final Rule. Child with a disability. Volume 71, Number 156 (2006).

Feingold, B. (1975). *Why your child is hyperactive.* New York: Random House.

Feldhusen, J., & Kollof, P. (1986). The Purdue three-stage enrichment model for gifted education at the elementary level. In J. Renzulli (Ed.), *Systems and models for developing programs for the gifted and talented* (pp. 126–152). Mansfield Center, CT: Creative Learning Press.

Fennick, E. (2001). Coteaching an inclusive curriculum for transition. *Teaching Exceptional Children, 33*(6), 60–66.

Ferguson, R. (1998). Teachers' perceptions and expectations and black-white test score gap. In C. Jencks & M. Phillips (Eds.), *The black-white test score gap* (pp. 273–317). Washington, DC: Brookings Institution.

Ferrell, K. A. (2005). Growth and development of young children. In M. C. Holbrook & A. J. Koenig (Eds.), *Foundations of education: Volume I. History and theory of teaching children and youth with visual impairments* (2nd ed., chap. 4). Retrieved February 2, 2007, from www.afb.org/foe/book.asp?ch=v1ch04

Fiedler, B. C. (2001). Considering placement and educational approaches for students who are deaf and hard of hearing. *Teaching Exceptional Children, 34*(2), 54–59.

Fiedler, C. R., Simpson, R. L., & Clark, D. M. (2007). *Parents and families of children with disabilities. Effective school-based support services.* Upper Saddle River, NJ: Pearson Education.

Field, S. (1997). A historical perspective on student involvement in the transition process: Toward a vision of self-determination for all students. *Career Development for Exceptional Individuals, 19*, 169–176.

Field, S., Martin, J., Miller, R., Ward, M., & Wehmeyer, M. (1998). Self-determination for persons with disabilities: A position statement of the Division on Career Development and Transition. *Career Development for Exceptional Individuals, 21*, 113–128.

Fisher, M., & Meyer, L. H. (2002). Development and social competence after two years for students enrolled in inclusive and self-contained educational programs. *Research and Practice for Persons with Severe Disabilties, 27*, 165–174.

Fitzpatrick, M. (2004). *MMR and autism: What parents need to know.* New York: Routledge.

Flanigan, K., von Niederhausern, A., Dunn, D., Alder, J., Mendell, J., & Weiss, R. (2003). Rapid direct sequence analysis of the dystrophin gene. *American Journal of Human Genetics, 72*, 931–939.

Fleming, J. L., & Monda-Amaya, L. E. (2001). Process variables critical for team effectiveness. *Remedial and Special Education, 22*, 158–171.

Fletcher, J., Francis, D., Morris, R., & Lyon, G. R. (2005). Evidence-based assessment of learning disabilities in children and adolescents. *Journal of Clinical Child and Adolescent Psychology, 34*, 506–522.

Fombonne, E. (2002). Prevalence of childhood disintegrative disorder. *Autism, 6*, 149–157.

Foorman, B. R., & Torgesen, J. (2001). Critical elements of classroom and small-groups instruction promote reading success in all children. *Learning Disabilities: Research & Practice 16*(4), 203–212.

Ford, B. A. (2000). Preview. *Multiple Voices, 4*(1), v–vi.

Forest, M., & Lusthaus, E. (1990). Everyone belongs with the MAPs action planning system. *Teaching Exceptional Children, 22*(2), 32–35.

Forest, M., & Pearpoint, J. (1992). Everyone belongs: Building the vision with MAPS—The McGill Action Planning System. In D. Wetherow (Ed.), *The whole community catalogue: Welcoming people with disabilities into the heart of community life* (pp. 95–99). Manchester, CT: Communitas Inc..

Forgan, J. W. (2002). Using bibliotherapy to teach problem solving. *Intervention in School and Clinic, 38*(2), 75–82.

Forness, S. R., & Kavale, K. A. (2000). Emotional or behavioral disorders: Background and current status of the E/BD terminology and definition. *Behavioral Disorders, 25*(3), 264–269.

Forness, S. R., Kavale, K. A., Crenshaw, T. M., & Sweeny, D. P. (2000). Best practice in treating children with AD/HD: Does not using medication in a comprehensive intervention program verge on malpractice. *Beyond Behavior, 10*(2), 4–7.

Forness, S. R., Kavale, K. A., Sweeny, D. P., & Crenshaw, T. M. (1999). The future of research and practice in behavior disorders: Psychopharmacology and its school treatment implications. *Behavioral Disorders, 24,* 305–318.

Forness, S. R., & Knitzer, J. (1992). A new proposed definition and terminology to replace "serious emotional disturbance" in Individuals with Disabilities Education Act. *School Psychology Review, 21,* 12–20.

Fossett, B., Smith, V., & Mirenda, P. (2003). Facilitating oral language and literacy development during general education activities. In D. L. Ryndak & S. Alper, *Curriculum and instruction for students with significant disabilities* (2nd ed., pp. 173–205). Boston: Allyn & Bacon.

Foster, K. C., Erickson, G. C., Foster, D. F., Brinkman, D., & Torgesen, J. K. (1994). Computer administered instruction in phonological awareness: Evaluation of the Daisy Quest program. *Journal of Research and Development in Education, 27,* 126–137.

Fox, J., Conroy, M., & Heckaman, K. (1998). Research issues in functional assessment of the challenging behaviors of students with emotional and behavioral disorders. *Behavioral Disorders, 24*(1), 26–33.

Fox. L. (2006a). *Program practices for promoting the social development of young children and addressing challenging behavior.* Tampa, FL: Center for Evidence-Based Practice: Young Children with Challenging Behavior. Retrieved June 10, 2006, from http://challengingbehavior.fmhi.usf.edu/

Fox. L. (2006b). *Supporting infants and toddlers with challenging behavior.* Tampa, FL: Center for Evidence-Based Practice: Young Children with Challenging Behavior. Retrieved June 10, 2006, from http://challengingbehavior. fmhi.usf.edu/

Fox, L., Dunlap, G., Hemmeter, M. L., Joseph, G. E., & Strain, P. S. (2003). The teaching pyramid: A model for supporting social competence and preventing challenging behavior in young children. *Young Children, 58*(4), 48–53.

Fox. L., Hemmeter, M. L., Smith, B., & Dunlap, G. (2003). Evidence-based practice for young children with challenging behavior. Paper presented at CEC Annual Convention, Seattle, WA, April 9–12. Retrieved from www. challengingbehavior.org

Frame, M. (2000). The relationship between visual impairment and gestures. *Journal of Visual Impairment and Blindness, 94*(3), 155–172.

Francis, D. J., Shaywitz, S. E., Stuebing, K. K., Shaywitz, B. A., & Fletcher, J. M. (1996). Developmental lag versus deficit models of reading disability: A longitudinal, individual growth curves analysis. *Journal of Educational Psychology, 80*(4), 3–17.

Frank, A. R., & Sitlington, P. L. (1997). Young adults with behavioral disorders—before and after IDEA. *Behavioral Disorders, 23*(1), 40–56.

Frank, J. (2000). Requests by persons with blindness or low vision for large-print accommodation. *Journal of Visual Impairment and Blindness, 94*(11), 716–720.

Frankland, H. C., Turnbull, A. P., Wehmeyer, M. L., & Blackmountain, L. (2004). An exploration of the self-determination construct and disability as it relates to the Diné (Navajo) culture. *Education and Training in Developmental Disabilities, 39*(3), 191–205.

Frasier, M. M., Lee, J., & Winstead, S. (1997). Is the future problem solving program accomplishing its goals? *Journal of Secondary Gifted Education, 8*(4), 157–163.

Frasu, A. (2004). "Which is correct: Deaf, deaf, hard of hearing, or hearing impaired?" *Deaflinx* [Electronic version]. Retrieved June 14, 2005, from www.deaflinx.com/label.html

Freeland, J. T., Skinner, C. H., Jackson, B., McDaniel, E., & Smith, S. (2000). Measuring and increasing silent reading comprehension rates: Empirically validating a repeated readings intervention. *Psychology in the Schools, 37*(5), 415–425.

Freeman, F., & Alkin, M. (2000). Academic and social attainments of children with mental retardation in general education and special education settings. *Remedial and Special Education, 21,* 3–18.

Frey, L. (2003). Abundant beautification: An effective service-learning project for students with emotional or behavioral disorders. *Teaching Exceptional Children, 35*(5), 66–75.

Friend, M. (2002). An interview with Dr. Marilyn Friend. *Intervention in School and Clinic, 37,* 223–228.

Friend, M., & Bursuck, W. D. (2006). *Including students with special needs: A practical guide for classroom teachers* (4th ed.). Boston: Allyn & Bacon.

Friend, M., & Cook, L. (2000). *Interactions. Collaboration skills for school professionals* (3rd ed.). New York: Longman.

Frith, U. (1991). Autistic psychopathy in childhood. In U. Frith (Ed.), *Autism and Asperger syndrome* (pp. 37–92). New York: Cambridge University Press.

Frost, L., & Bondy, A. (1994). *PECS: The Picture Exchange Communication System training manual.* Cherry Hill, NJ: Pyramid Educational Consultants.

Fry, E. (1957). Developing a word list for remedial reading. *Elementary English, 33,* 456–458.

Fry, E. (1972). *Reading instruction for classroom and clinic.* New York: McGraw-Hill.

Fuchs, D., & Fuchs, L. (1989). Effects of examiner familiarity on black, Caucasian, and Hispanic children: A meta-analysis. *Exceptional Children, 55,* 303–308.

Fuchs, D., & Fuchs, L. (2006). Introduction to Response to Intervention: What, why, and how valid is it? *Reading Research Quarterly, 41,* 93–99.

Fuchs, D., Fuchs, L. S., Mathes, P. G., & Simmons, D. C. (1997). Peer-assisted learning strategies: Making classrooms more responsive to diversity. *American Educational Research Journal, 34,* 174–206.

Fuchs, D., Fuchs, L. S., Thompson, A., Svenson, E., Yen, L., Al Otaiba, S., Yang, N., McMaster, K. N., Prentice, K., Kazdan,

S., & Saenz, L. (2001). Peer-assisted learning strategies in reading: Extensions for kindergarten, first grade, and high school. *Remedial and Special Education, 22*(1), 15–21.

Fuchs, D., Mock, D., Morgan, P., & Young, C. (2003). Responsiveness to intervention: Definitions, evidence, and implications for the learning disabilities construct. *Learning Disabilities Research and Practice, 18*, 157–171.

Fuchs, L. S., Fuchs, D., & Kazdan, S. (1999). Effects of peer-assisted learning strategies on high school students with serious reading problems. *Remedial and Special Education, 20*(5), 309–318.

Fuggetta, G., (2006). Impairment of executive functions in boys with attention deficit/hyperactive disorder. *Child Neuropsychology, 12*, 1–12.

Fulk, B. J. M., Mastropieri, M. A., & Scruggs, T. E. (1992). Mnemonic generalization training with learning disabled adolescents. *Learning Disabilities Research, 7*(1), 2–10.

Fulk, B. M., & King, K. (2001). Classwide peer tutoring at work. *Teaching Exceptional Children, 34*(3), 49–53.

G

Gajar, A., Goodman, L., & McAfee, J. (1993). *Secondary and beyond: Transition of individuals with mild disabilities.* New York: MacMillan.

Galili-Weisstub, E., & Segman, R. (2003). Attention deficit and hyperactivity disorder: Review of genetic association studies. *Israel Journal of Psychiatry and Related Sciences, 40*, 57–66.

Gallagher, J. J. (2003). Issues and challenges in the education of gifted students. In N. Colangelo & G. Davis (Eds.), *Handbook of gifted education* (pp. 11–23). Needham Heights, MA: Allyn & Bacon.

Gardner, H. (1983). *Frames of mind.* New York: Basic Books.

Gardner, J., & Bates, P. (1991). Attitudes and attributions on use of microcomputers in school by students who are mentally handicapped. *Education and Training in Mental Retardation, 28*(1), 98–107.

Gardner, L., & Corn, A. (n.d.). *Low vision: Access to print.* Retrieved July 4, 2007, from www.cecdvi.org/ Postion%20Papers/low_vision_print

Gately, S. E., & Gately, F. J. (2001). Understanding coteaching concepts. *Teaching Exceptional Children, 33*(4), 40–47.

Geary, D. (2003). Learning disabilities in arithmetic: Problem-solving differences and cognitive deficits. In H. L. Swanson, K. Harris, & S. Graham (Eds.), *Handbook of learning disabilities* (pp. 199–212). New York: Guilford Press.

Gentry, M., Rizza, M. G., & Owen, S. V. (2002). Examining perceptions of challenge and choice in classrooms: The relationship between teachers and their students and comparisons between gifted students and other students. *Gifted Child Quarterly, 46*(2), 145–55.

Gerber, P. J., & Price, L. A. (2003). Persons with learning disabilities in the workplace: What we know so far in the Americans with Disabilities Act era. *Learning Disabilities Research and Practice, 18*(2), 132–136.

Gersten, R. (1998). Recent advances in instructional research for students with learning disabilities: An overview. *Learning Disabilities Research & Practice, 13*(3), 162–170.

Gersten, R., Baker, S., & Edwards (1999, December). *Teaching expressive writing to students with learning disabilities.* Arlington, VA: The ERIC Clearinghouse on Disabilities and Gifted Education. (ERIC Document Reproduction Service No. E590/EDO-99-16)

Gersten, R., Baker, S., Marks, S. U., & Smith, S. B. (1999). *Effective instruction fo learning disabled or at-risk English-language learners; An integrative synthesis of the empirical and professional knowledge bases.* Report presented at the National Center for Learning Disabilities Summit on Research in Learning Disabilities: Keys to Successful Learning.

Getting ready: Findings from the National School Readiness Indicators Initiative: A 17 state partnership. (2005, February). Rhode Island: KIDS COUNT. Retrieved August 13, 2007, from www.gettingready.org

Giangreco, M. F., & Broer, S. M. (2005). Questionable utilization of paraprofessionals in inclusive schools: Are we addressing symptoms or causes? *Focus on Autism and Other Developmental Disabilities, 20*, 10–26.

Giangreco, M. F., & Doyle, M. B. (2002). Students with disabilities and paraprofessional supports: Benefits, balance, and band-aids. *Focus on Exceptional Children, 34*(7), 1–12.

Gillberg, C., & Coleman, M. (2000). *The biology of the autistic syndromes* (3rd ed.). London: MacKeith Press.

Gillberg, C., & Wing, L. (1999). Autism: Not an extremely rare disorder. *Acta Psychiatrica Scandinavica, 99*, 399–406.

Gilliam, J. (1995). *Attention Deficit/Hyperactivity Test.* Austin, TX: Pro-Ed.

Gilliam, J. (2006). *Gilliam Autism Rating Scale–2.* Austin, TX: Pro-Ed.

Gilliam, W. S. (2005). Prekindergarteners left behind: Expulsion rates in state prekindergarten systems. Retrieved June 24, 2006, from www.fcd-us.org/PDFs/ NationalPreKExpulsionPaper03.02_new.pdf

Gittman, E., & Koster, J. (1999, October). *Analysis of ability and achievement scores for students recommended by classroom teachers to a gifted and talented program.* Paper presented at the Annual Meeting of the Northeastern Educational Research Association, Ellenville, NY. (ERIC Document Reproduction Service No. ED445118)

Glor-Scheib, S., & Telthorster, H. (2006). Activate your student IEP team member using technology: How electronic portfolios can bring the student voice to life! [Electronic version]. *Teaching Exceptional Children Plus, 2*(3). Retrieved May 5, 2006, from http://escholarship.bc. edu/education/tecplus/vol2/iss3/art1

Goddard, H. (1912). *The Kallikak family: A study in the heredity of feeblemindedness.* New York: MacMillian.

Goin, R., & Myers, B. (2004). Characteristics of infantile autism: Moving towards earlier detection. *Focus on Autism and Other Developmental Disabilities, 19*, 5–12.

Goldberg, R. J., Higgins, E. L., Raskind, M. H., & Herman, K. L. (2003). Predictors of success in individuals with learning disabilities: A qualitative analysis of a 20-year longitudinal study. *Learning Disabilities Research & Practice, 18*(4), 222–236.

Goldman, L. S., Genel, M., Bezman, R. J., & Slanetz, P. J. (1998). Diagnosis and treatment of attention-deficit/hyperactivity disorder in children and adolescents. *Journal of the American Medical Association, 279*(14), 1100–1107.

Goldson, E. (2001). Maltreatment among children with disabilities. *Infants and Young Children, 13*(4), 44–54.

Goldstein, A., Glick, B., & Gibbs, J. C. (1998). *Aggression replacement training: A comprehensive intervention for aggressive youth* (Rev. ed.). Champaign, IL: Research Press.

Goldstein, A. P., & McGinnis, E. (1997). *Skillstreaming the adolescent: New strategies and perspectives for teaching prosocial skills.* Champaign, IL: Research Press.

Goldstein, S., & Goldstein, M. (1998). *Managing attention-deficit/hyperactivity disorder in children: A guide for practitioners.* New York: Wiley.

Good, R. H., Kaminski, R. A., Smith, S., Laimon, D., & Dill, S. (2001). *Dynamic Indicators of Basic Early Literacy Skills–5th edition* (DIBELS). University of Oregon: Institute for Development of Educational Achievement. Retrieved from http://dibels.uoregon.edu/

Goshorn, A. (2006). Living in a separate (but gifted) world. In E. Keefe, V. Moore, & F. Duff (Eds.), *Listening to the experts: Students with disabilities speak out* (pp. 165–170. Baltimore: Paul H. Brookes.

Gottesman, I. I., & Reilly, J. (2003). Strengthening the evidence for genetic factors in schizophrenia (without abetting genetic discrimination). *Principles of Experimental Psychopathlogy: Essays in Honor of Brendan A. Maher,* 31–44.

Gottfredson, L. (2004). Realities in desegregating gifted education. In D. Boothe & J. Stanley (Eds.), *In the eyes of the beholder: Critical issues for diversity in gifted education* (pp.139–155). Waco, TX: Prufrock Press.

Gottfried, A. (1984). *Home environment and early cognitive environment: Longitudinal research.* Orlando, FL: Academic Press.

Gottlieb, J. (1974). Attitudes toward retarded children: Effects of labeling and academic performance. *American Journal of Mental Deficiency, 79,* 268–273.

Graham, S. (1999). Handwriting and spelling instruction for students with learning disabilities: A review. *Learning Disability Quarterly, 22,* 78–98.

Graham, S., Harris, K., & Larsen, L. (2001). Prevention and intervention of writing difficulties for students with learning disabilities. *Learning Disabilities Research & Practice, 16*(2), 78–84.

Grandin, T. (n.d.). *An inside view of autism.* Retrieved July 18, 2007, from www.autism.org/temple/inside.html

Grandin, T. (1995). The learning style of people with autism: An autobiography. In K. A. Quill (Ed.), *Teaching children with autism: Strategies to enhance communication and socialization* (pp. 33–52). New York: Delmar.

Graves, D. H. (1983). *Writing: Teachers & children at work.* Exeter, NH: Heinemann.

Graves, D. H. (1985). All children can write. *Learning Disability Focus, 1,* 36–43.

Gray, C. (1993). *The original social stories book.* Austin, TX: Future Horizons.

Gray, C. (1997). Your concerns result in new social story ratio: A closer look at directive sentences. *Access Express, 4,* 4–5.

Gray, C., & Garand, J. (1993). Social stories: Improving responses of students with autism with accurate social information. *Focus on Autistic Behavior, 8,* 1–10.

Green, F., Schleien, S., Mactavish, J., & Benepe, S. (1995). Nondisabled adults' perceptions of relationships in the early stages of arranged partnerships with peers with mental retardation. *Education and Training in Mental Retardation and Developmental Disabilities, 30,* 91–108.

Greene, G. (1999). Mnemonic multiplication fact instruction for students with learning disabilities. *Learning Disabilities Research & Practice, 14*(3), 141–148.

Green, T. D. (2005). Promising prevention and early intervention strategies to reduce the overrepresentation of African American students in special education. *Preventing School Failure, 49*(3), 33–41.

Greenspan, S. (2006). Functional concepts in mental retardation: Finding the natural essence of an artificial category. *Exceptionality, 14*(4), 205–224.

Greenwood, C. R. (1996). Research on the practices and behavior of effective teachers at the Juniper Gardens Children's Project: Implications for the education of diverse learners. In D. Speece & B. Keogh (Eds.), *Research on classroom ecologies: Implications for inclusion of children with learning disabilities* (pp. 36–37). Hillsdale, NJ: Erlbaum.

Greenwood, C. R. (1999). Reflections on a research career: Perspective on 35 years of research at the Juniper Gardens Children's Project. *Exceptional Children, 66*(1), 7–21.

Greenwood, C. R., Arreaga-Mayer, C., Utley, C. A., Gavin, K. M., & Terry, B. J. (2001). Classwide peer tutoring learning management system. *Remedial and Special Education, 22,* 34–47.

Greenwood, C. R., Delquadri, J. C., & Carta, J. J. (1997). *Together we can! Classwide peer tutoring to improve basic academic skills.* Longmont, CO: Sopris West.

Greenwood, C. R., Maheady, L., & Delquadri, J. C. (2002). Class-wide peer tutoring. In G. Stoner, M. R. Shinn, & H. Walker (Eds.), *Interventions for achievement and behavior problems* (2nd ed., pp. 611–649). Washington, DC: National Association of School Psychologists.

Gresham, F. (2005). Response to intervention: An alternative means of identifying students as emotionally disturbed. *Education and Treatment of Children, 28,* 328–324.

Gresham, F., Lane, K., & Beebe-Frankenberger, M. (2005). Predictors of hyperactive-impulsive-inattentive and conduct problems: A comparative follow-back investigation. *Psychology in the Schools, 42,* 721–736.

Gresham, F. M. (1997). Social competence and students with behavior disorders: Where we've been, where we are, and where we should go. *Education and Treatment of Children, 20*, 233–249.

Gresham, F. M. (1998). Social skills training: Should we raze, remodel, or rebuild? *Behavioral Disorders, 24*, 19–25.

Gresham, F. M. (2002). Social skills assessment and instruction for students with emotional or behavioral disorders. In K. Lane, F. M. Gresham, & T. O'Shaughnessy (Eds.), *Interventions for children with or at risk for emotional and behavioral disorders* (pp. 2424–258). Boston: Allyn & Bacon.

Gresham, F. M., & Elliot, S. N. (1990). *Social skills rating system.* Circle Pines, MN: American Guidance Service.

Gresham, F. M., Sugai, G., & Horner, R. (2001). Interpreting outcomes of social skills training for students with high-incidence disabilities. *Exceptional Children, 67*(3), 331–144.

Griffin-Shirley, N., Kelley, P., & Lawrence, B. (2006). *The role of the orientation and mobility specialist in public school.* Division on Visual Impairments, Council for Exceptional Children. Retrieved July 3, 2007, from www.cecdvi.org/Postion%20Papers/060325%20CEC%20O&M%20Position%20Paper.doc

Gronlund, N. (2006). *Assessment of student achievement* (8th ed.). Boston: Allyn & Bacon.

Gross, M. U. (2001). Ability grouping, self-esteem, and the gifted: A study of optical illusions and optimal environments. In N. Colangelo & S. G. Assouline (Eds.), *Talent development IV: Proceedings from the 1998 Henry B. and Jocelyn Wallace National Research Symposium on Talent Development* (pp. 59–88). Scottsdale, AZ: Great Potential Press.

Grossman, H. (Ed.). (1983). *Classification in mental retardation* (Rev. ed.). Washington, DC: American Association on Mental Retardation.

Grushkin, D. A. (2003). The dilemma of the hard of hearing within the U.S. Deaf community. In L. Monaghan, C. Schmaling, K. Nakamura, & G. H. Turner (Eds.), *Many ways to be deaf. International variation in deaf communities* (pp. 1114–1140). Washington, DC: Gallaudet University Press.

Guadalupe v. Tempe Elementary School District. No. 3, 587F. 2d 535 (10th Cir. 1979).

Guetzloe, E. C. (1993). The special education initiative: Responding to changing problems, populations and paradigms (The Forum). *Behavioral Disorders, 18*(4), 303–307.

Guide Dogs for the Blind. (2006). *Frequently asked questions.* Retrieved February 12, 2007, from www.guidedogs.com/ site/PageServer?pagename=about_overview_faq

Guilford, J. (1967). *The nature of human intelligence.* New York: McGraw-Hill.

Gunter, P. L., & Denny, R. K. (1998). Trends and issues in research regarding academic instruction of students with emotional and behavior disorders. *Behavioral Disorders, 24*(1), 45–50.

Gunter, P. L., Miller, K. A., Venn, M. L., Thomas, K., & House, S. (2002). Self-graphing to success: Computerized data management. *Teaching Exceptional Children, 35*(2), 30–34.

Gupta, V. (2003). History, definition, and classification of pervasive developmental disorders. *The Exceptional Parent, 33*, 40–43.

Gupta, V. (2004). History, definition, and classification of autistic spectrum disorders. In V. Gupta (Ed.), *Autistic spectrum disorders in children* (pp. 1–16). New York: Marcel Dekker.

Guralnick, M. J. (1998). Effectiveness of early intervention for vulnerable children: A developmental perspective. *American Journal on Mental Retardation, 102*, 319–345.

H

Haager, D., & Vaughn, S. (1997). Assessment of social competence in students with learning disabilities. In J. W. Lloyd, E. J. Kame'enui, & D. Chard, *LEA's series on special education and disability* (pp. 129–152). Mahwah, NJ: Erlbaum.

Hagberg, B., Aicardi, J., Dias, K., & Ramos, O. (1983). A progressive syndrome of autism, dementia, ataxia, and loss of purposeful hand use in girls: Rett's syndrome: Report of 35 cases. *Annals of Neurology, 14*, 471–479.

Hall, B. J., Oyer, H. J., & Haas, W. H. (2001). *Speech, language, and hearing disorders guide for the teacher* (3rd ed). Boston: Allyn & Bacon.

Hall, J. (2002). Narrowing the breach: Can disability culture and full educational inclusion be reconciled? *Journal of Disability Policy Studies, 13*, 144–152.

Hall, T. (2002, June). *Effective instruction: Effective classroom practices report. National Center on Accessing the General Curriculum.* Retrieved from www.cast.org/publications/ncac/ncac_explicit.html

Hallahan, D. P., & Kauffman, J. M. (2006) *Exceptional learners: An introduction to special education* (10th ed.). Boston: Allyn & Bacon.

Hallahan, D., Lloyd, J., Kauffman, J., Weiss, M., & Martinez, M. (2005). *Learning disabilities: Foundations, characteristics, and effective teaching* (3rd. ed.). Boston: Allyn & Bacon.

Haller, A. K., & Montgomery, J. K. (2004). Noise-induced hearing loss in children. What educators need to know. *Teaching Exceptional Children, 36*(4), 22–27.

Hallowell, E. M., & Ratey, J. J. (1992). *50 tips on the classroom management of attention deficit disorder.* Retrieved March 27, 1999, from www.chadd.org/50class.htm

Halpin, T. (2006, May 17). Mainstram schools can't manage special needs pupils, says teachers. *Timesonline.* Retrieved May 18, 2006, from www.timesonline.co.uk/article/0,,2-2184133,00.html

Hamill, L., & Everington, C. (2002). *Teaching students with moderate to severe disabilities: An applied approach for inclusive environments.* Upper Saddle River, NJ: Merrill.

Handen, B., & Lubetsky, M. (2005). Pharmacotherapy in autism and related disorders. *School Psychology Quarterly, 20*, 155–171.

Hansen, E., Lee, M., & Forer, G. (2002). A "self-voicing" test for individuals with visual impairments. *Journal of Visual Impairment and Blindness, 96*(4), 273–276.

Haring, K. A., & Lovett, D. L. (1997). Early childhood assessment. In R. L. Taylor (Ed.), *Assessment of individuals with mental retardation* (pp. 153–172). San Diego: Singular.

Harkins, J. E., & Bakke, M. (2003). Technologies for communication: Status and trends. In M. Marschark & P. E. Spencer (Eds.), *Oxford handbook of deaf studies, language, and education* (pp. 406–419). New York: Oxford University Press.

Harlaar, N., Spinath, F., Dale, P., & Plomin, R. (2005). Genetic influences on early word recognition abilities and disabilities: A study of 7-year-old twins. *Journal of Child Psychology and Psychiatry, 46*, 373–384.

Harley, R. K., Lawrence, G. A., Sanford, L., & Burnett, R. (2000). *Visual impairment in the schools* (3rd ed.). Springfield, IL: Charles C Thomas.

Harris, K. R., & Schmidt, T. (1997). Learning self-regulation in the classroom. *AD/HD Report, 5*(2), 1–6.

Harris, S., Glasberg, B., & Ricca, D. (1996). Pervasive developmental disorders: Distinguishing among subtypes. *School Psychology Review, 25*, 308–315.

Harris, S., & Handleman, J. (2000). Age and IQ at intake as predictors of placement for young children with autism: A four- to six-year follow-up. *Journal of Autism and Developmental Disorders, 30*, 137–142.

Haslam, N., Williams, B., Prior, M., Haslam, R., Graetz, B., & Sawyer, M. (2006). The latent structure of attention-deficit/hyperactivity disorder: A taxometric analysis. *Australian and New Zealand Journal of Psychiatry, 40*, 639–647.

Hatlen, P. (1996). The core curriculum for blind and visually impaired students, including those with additional disabilities [Electronic version]. *Journal of Visual Impairment & Blindness, 94*(11), 677–694.

Hatlen, P. (2005). Historical perspectives. In M. C. Holbrook & A. J. Koenig (Eds.), *Foundations of education: Volume I. History and theory of teaching children and youth with visual impairments* (2nd ed., chap. 1). Retrieved February 1, 2007, from www.afb.org/foe/book.asp?ch=v1ch01

Hatton, D. (2001). Model registry of early childhood visual impairment: First-year results. *Journal of Visual Impairment and Blindness, 95*(7), 418–433.

Hatton, D. D., McWilliam, R. A., & Winton, P. J. (2002). *Infants and toddlers with visual impairments: Suggestions for early interventionists.* Arlington, VA: ERIC Clearinghouse on Disabilities and Gifted Education. (ERIC Document Reproduction Service No. ED473829)

Hayes, B. K., & Conway, R. N. (2000). Concept acquisition in children with mild intellectual disability: Factors affecting the abstraction of prototypical information. *Journal of Intellectual & Developmental Disability, 25*, 217–235.

Hebert, T. P., & Neumeister, K. L. S. (2000). University mentors in the elementary classroom: Supporting the intellectual, motivational, and emotional needs of high-ability students. *Journal for the Education of the Gifted, 24*(2), 122–148.

Heckaman, K., Conroy, M., Fox, J., & Chait, A. (2000). Functional assessment-based intervention research on students with or at risk for emotional or behavioral disorders in school settings. *Behavioral Disorders, 25*(3), 196–210.

Hegde, M. N., & Maul, C. A. (2006). *Language disorders in children: An evidence-based approach to assessment and treatment.* Boston: Allyn & Bacon.

Heiligenstein, E., Conyers, L. M., Berns, A. R., & Smith, M. A. (1998). Preliminary normative data on *DSM-IV* attention deficit hyperactivity disorder in college students. *Journal of American College Health, 46*, 185–188.

Heiligenstein, E., Guenther, G., Levy, A., Savino, F., & Fulwiler, J. (1999). Psychological and academic functioning in college students with attention deficit hyperactivity disorder. *Journal of American College Health, 47*(4), 181–185.

Heinze, T. (2005). Comprehensive assessment. In M. C. Holbrook & A. J. Koenig (Eds.), *Foundations of education: Volume II. Instructional strategies for teaching children and youth with visual impairments* (2nd ed., chap. 2). Retrieved February 1, 2007, from www.afb.org/foe/book.asp?ch=v1ch02

Heller, K. W., Alberto, P. A., Forney, P. E., & Schartzman, M. N. (1996). *Understanding physical, sensory, and health impairments.* Pacific Grove, CA: Brooks/Cole.

Heller, K. W., Forney, P. E., Alberto, P. A., Schwartzman, M. N., & Goeckel, T. M. (2000). *Meeting physical and health needs of children with disabilities. Teaching student participation and management.* Stamford, CT: Wadsworth/Thomson Learning.

Henry, G. T., Gordon, C. S., Mashburn, A., & Ponder, B. D. (2001). *Pre-K longitudinal study: Findings from the 1999-2000 year.* Atlanta: Georgia State University, Applied Research Center of the Andrew Young School of Policy Studies.

Henry, L. A., & MacLean, M. (2002). Working memory performance in children with and without intellectual disabilities. *American Journal on Mental Retardation, 107*, 421–432.

Herer, G. R., Knightly, C. A., & Steinberg, A. G. (2002). Hearing. Sounds and silences. In M. L. Batshaw (Ed.), *Children with disabilities* (5th ed., pp. 193– 227). Baltimore, MD: Paul H. Brookes.

Hervey-Jumper, H., Douyon, K., & Franco, K. (2006). Deficits in diagnosis, treatment, and continuity of care in African American children and adolescents with ADHD. *Journal of the National Medical Association, 98*, 233–238.

Hesketh, L. J., & Chapman, R. S. (1998). Verb use by individuals with Down syndrome. *American Journal of Mental Retardation, 103*, 288–304.

Hessels-Schlatter, C. (2002). A dynamic test to assess learning capacity in people with severe impairments. *American Journal on Mental Retardation, 107*, 340–351.

Hester, P., & McCarvill, S. (2000). Redefining the structure and culture of schools to create safe and effective learning environments for *all* students. In L. M. Bullock & R. A. Gable (Eds.), *Positive academic and behavioral supports: Creating safe, effective, and nurturing schools for all students*. Highlights from the Forum on Positive Academic and Behavioral Supports. Reston, VA: CCBD.

Hickson, L., Blackman, L., & Reis, E. (1995). *Mental retardation: Foundations of educational programming*. Boston: Allyn & Bacon.

Hill, E., & Ponder, P. (1976). *Orientation and mobility techniques*. New York: American Foundation for the Blind.

Hinshaw, S., & Nigg, J. (1999). Behavior rating scales in the assessment of disruptive behavior problems in children. In D. Shaffer, C. Lucas, & J. Richters (Eds.), *Diagnostic assessment in child and adolescent psychology* (pp. 91–126). New York: Guilford Press.

Hinshaw, S., Owens, E., Sami, N., & Fargeon, S. (2006). Prospective follow-up of girls with attention-deficit/ hyperactivity disorder into adolescence: Evidence for continuing cross-domain impairment. *Journal of Consulting and Clinical Psychology, 74*, 489–499.

Hobbs, N. (1966). Helping the disturbed child: Psychological and ecological strategies. *American Psychologist, 21*, 1105–1115.

Hobson v. Hansen, 269 F. Supp. 401 (D.O.C. 1967).

Hodapp, R. M., & Zigler, E. (1997). New issues in the developmental approach to mental retardation. In W. E. MacLean Jr. (Ed.), *Ellis' handbook of mental deficiency, psychological theory, and research* (3rd ed., pp. 115–136). Mahwah, NJ: Erlbaum.

Holbrook, M. C., & Koenig, A. J. (2005). Basic techniques for modifying instruction. In M. C. Holbrook & A. J. Koenig (Eds.), *Foundation of education: Volume II. Instructional strategies for teaching children and youths with visual impairments* (2nd ed., chap. 5). Retrieved February 12, 2007, from www.afb.org/foe/book.asp?ch=v2c5

Holbrook, M. C., & Koenig, A. J. (2006). Ensuring high-quality instruction for students in braille literacy programs [Electronic version]. *Journal of Visual Impairment & Blindness, 94*(11), 677–694.

Holgate, S., Davies, D., Powell, R., & Holloway, J. (2005). ADAM33: A newly identified gene in the pathogenesis of asthma. *Immunology and Allergy Clinics of North America, 25*, 655–658.

Homes for the Homeless. (1995). *An American family myth: Every child at risk*. New York: Homes for the Homeless & the Institute for Children and Poverty. Retrieved from www.homesforthehomeless.com/

Homes for the Homeless. (1998). *Ten cities 1997-1998: A snapshot of family homelessness across America*. New York: Homes for the Homes & the Institute for Children and Poverty. Retrieved from www.homesforthehomeless.com/

Honaker, M. L. (2005). APA letter to the department of education regarding the implementation of the Individuals with Disabilities Education Improvement Act of 2004. Retrieved from www.apa.org/ppo/issues/idea22805.html

Honda, H., Shimizu, Y., & Rutter, M. (2005). No effect of MMR withdrawal on the incidence of autism: A total population study. *Journal of Child Psychology and Psychiatry, 46*, 572–579.

Honig v. Doe, 108 S. Ct. 592. (1988).

Horn, E., Thompson, B., Palmer, S., Jenson, R., & Turbiville, V. (2004). Preschool. In C. H. Kennedy & E. M. Horn (Eds.), *Including students with severe disabilities* (pp. 207–221). Boston: Pearson Education.

Horvath, K., Stefanatos, G., Sololski, K. N., Wachtel, R., Nabors, L., & Tildon, J. T. (1998). Improved social and language skills after secretin administration in patients with autistic spectrum disorders. *Journal of the Association of Academic Minority Physicians, 9*(1), 10–15.

Hourcade, J. J., Parette, H. P., & Huer, M. B. (1997). Family and cultural alert! Considerations in assistive technology assessment. *Teaching Exceptional Children, 30*(1), 40–44.

Howard, J., Greyrose, E., & Beckwith, L. (1996, Spring). Teacher-facilitated microcomputer activities: Enhancing social play and affect in young children with disabilities. *Journal of Special Education Technology, 13*(1), 36–46.

Huebner, K. M. (2005). Visual impairment. In M. C. Holbrook & A. J. Koenig (Eds.), *Foundations of education: Volume I. History and theory of teaching children and youth with visual impairments* (2nd ed., chap. 2). Retrieved February 1, 2007, from www.afb.org/foe/book. asp?ch=v1ch02

Huebner, K., & Koenig, A. (n.d.) *Student-centered educational placement decisions: The meaning, interpretation, and application of least restrictive environment*. Retrieved July 4, 2007, from www.ed.arizona. edu/dvi/Postion%20Papers/student_centered.htm

Huesmann, L., Moise, J., & Freedman, J. (2005). Issue 15: Does media violence promote violent behavior in young children. In R. Halgin (Ed.), *Taking sides: Clashing views on controversial issues in abnormal psychology* (3rd ed.). New York: McGraw-Hill.

Hughes, C. (2001). Executive dysfunction in autism: Its nature and implications for the everyday problems experienced by individuals with autism. In J. Burack, T. Charmin, N. Yirmiya, & P. Zelazo (Eds.), *The development of autism: Perspectives from theory and research* (pp. 255–275). Mahwah, NJ: Erlbaum.

Hughes, C., Guth, C., Hall, S., Presley, J., Dye, M., & Byers, C. (1999). "They are my best friends." Peer buddies promote inclusion in high school. *Teaching Exceptional Children, 32*, 32–37.

Hughes, L. (1999). Action research and practical inquiry: How can I meet the needs of the high-ability student within my regular education classroom? *Journal for the Education of the Gifted, 22*(3), 282–297.

Hughes, M., Dote-Kwan, J., & Dolendo, J. (1998). A close look at the cognitive play of preschoolers with blindness or low vision in the home. *Exceptional Children, 64*(4), 451–462.

Hulit, L. M., & Howard, M. R. (2002). *Born to talk: An introduction to speech and language development* (3rd ed). Boston: Allyn & Bacon.

Humphries, T. (2004). The modern deaf self: Indigenous practices and educational imperatives. In B. J.

Brueggemann (Ed.), *Literacy and deaf people: Cultural and contextual perspectives* (pp. 29–46). Washington, DC: Gallaudet University Press.

Hune, J. B., & Nelson, C. M. (2002). Effects of teaching a problem-solving strategy on preschool children with problem behavior. *Behavioral Disorders, 27*(3), 185–207.

Hunsaker, S. L., Finley, V. S., & Frank, E. L. (1997). An analysis of teacher nomination and student performance in gifted programs. *Gifted Child Quarterly, 41*, 19–24.

Hunt, J. M. (1961). *Intelligence and experience.* New York: Ronald Press.

Hutinger, P., & Johanson, J. (1998). Software for young children. In S. L. Judge & H. P. Parette (Eds.), *Assistive technology for young children with disabilities* (pp. 76–126). Cambridge, MA: Brookline Books.

Huurre, T., & Aro, H. (2000). The psychosocial well-being of Finnish adolescents with visual impairments versus those with chronic conditions and those with no disabilities. *Journal of Visual Impairment and Blindness, 94*(10), 625–638.

Hwa-Froelich, D. A., & Vigil, D. C. (2004). Three aspects of cultural influence on communication: "A literature review." *Communication Disorders Quarterly, 25*(3), 107–118.

Hyde, M., Zevenbergen, R., & Power, D. (2003). Deaf and hard of hearing students' performance on arithmetic word problems. *American Annals of the Deaf, 148*(1), 56–64.

Hynd, G. (1992). Neurological aspects of dyslexia: Comments on the balance model. *Journal of Learning Disabilities, 25*, 110–113.

Hyter, Y. D., Rogers-Adkinson, D. L., Self, T. L., Simmons, B. F., & Jantz, J. (2001). Pragmatic language intervention for children with language and emotional/behavioral disorders. *Communication Disorders Quarterly, 23*(1), 4–16.

I

Idol, L. (2006). Toward inclusion of special education students in general education. *Remedial and Special Education, 27*, 77–94.

International Dyslexia Association. (2002). *Definition of dyslexia.* Retrieved May 19, 2007, from www.interdys.org/servlet/compose?section_id=5&page_id=79

Iovannone, R., Dunlap, G., Huber, H., & Kinkaid, D. (2003). Effective educational practices for students with autism spectrum disorders. *Focus on Autism and Other Developmental Disabilities, 18*(3), 150–165.

Irgens, K. A. (2001). Assessment of emotional disturbance: A national survey of school psychologists' practices. *Dissertation Abstracts International Section A: Humanities & Social Sciences Univ. Microfilms International, 61*, 4284.

IRIS Center. (2006). *Approaches to RTI.* Retrieved October 30, 2006, from http://iris.peabody.vanderbilt.edu/rti01_overview/rti01_05.html

IRIS Group. (2006). *Legacy training modules: RTI (overview).* Retrieved May 23, 2007, from http://iris.peabody.vanderbilt.edu/rti01_overview/chalcycle.htm

Irlen Institute. (n.d.). *Irlen syndrome/scotopic sensitivity.* Retrieved April 18, 2003, from www.irlen.com/index_sss.html

Irving Independent School District v. Tatro, 104 S. Ct. 3371. 82 Led.2d 664 (1984).

J

Jankowski, K. A. (1997). *Deaf empowerment. Emergence, struggle, and rhetoric.* Washington, DC: Gallaudet University Press.

Janney, R. E., & Snell, M. E. (1997). How teachers include students with moderate and severe disabilities in elementary classes: The means and meaning of inclusion. *The Association for Persons with Severe Handicaps, 22*(3), 159–169.

Janofsky, M. (2005). *Some new help for the extremely gifted.* Retrieved November 8, 2005, from www.nytimes.com/2005/10/26/education/26gifted.html?ex=1131598800&en=fd081f

Jarry, E., Castro, E., & Duff, F. (2006). On the road to co-teaching at the high school level. In E. Keefe, V. Moore, & F. Duff (Eds.), *Listening to the students with disabilities speak out* (pp. 159–164). Baltimore: Paul H. Brookes.

Jennett, H., Harris, S., & Mesibov, G. (2003). Commitment to philosophy, teacher efficacy, and burnout among teachers of children with autism. *Journal of Autism and Developmental Disorders, 33*(6), 583–593.

Jensen, A. (1969). How much can we boost IQ and scholastic achievement? *Harvard Educational Review, 39*, 1–123.

Jick, H., & Kaye, J. (2004). Autism and DPT vaccination in the United Kingdom. *New England Journal of Medicine, 350*, 2722–2723.

Jimerson, S. R., Egeland, B., Sroufe, L. A., & Carlson, B. (2000). A prospective longitudinal study of high school dropouts: Examining multiple predictors across development. *Journal of School Psychology, 38*, 525–549.

Jitendra, A. K., Edwards, L. L., Sacks, G., & Jacobson, L. A. (2004). What research says about vocabulary instruction for students with learning disabilities. *Exceptional Children, 70*(3), 299–322.

Johns, B. (2000). Reaching them through teaching them: Curriculum and instruction for students with E/BD. *Beyond Behavior, 10*(1), 3–6.

Johns, B. H., Crowley, E. P., & Guetzloe, E. (2002). *Effective curriculum for students with emotional and behavioral disorders: Reaching them through teaching them.* Denver: Love.

Johnsen, S. K., & Ryser, G. R. (1996). An overview of effective practices with gifted students in general-education settings. *Journal for the Education of the Gifted, 19*(4), 379–404.

Johnson, C. (2004). Early clinical characteristics of children with autism. In V. Gupta (Ed.), *Autistic spectrum disorders in children* (pp. 85–123). New York: Marcel Dekker.

Johnson, D. W., & Johnson, R. T. (1991). *Learning together and alone* (3rd ed.). Boston: Allyn & Bacon.

Jordan, L., Reyes-Blanes, M. E., Peel, B. B., Peel, H. A., & Lane, H. B. (1998). Developing teacher-parent partnerships across cultures: Effective parent conferences. *Intervention in School and Clinic, 33*(3), 141–147.

Joshi, M. (2005). Vocabulary: A critical component of comprehension. *Reading and Writing Quarterly, 21,* 209–219.

Juel, C. (1988). Learning to read and write: A longitudinal study of fifty-four children from first through fourth grade. *Journal of Educational Psychology, 80,* 437–447.

Justice, L. M. (2004). Creating language-rich preschool classroom environments. *Teaching Exceptional Children, 37*(2), 36–44.

Justice, L. M. (2006). *Communication sciences and disorders: An introduction.* Upper Saddle River, NJ: Prentice Hall.

K

Kabat, S., Masi, W., & Segal, M. (2003). Advances in the diagnosis and treatment of autism spectrum disorders. *Professional Psychology: Research and Practice, 34*(1), 26–33.

Kaduson, H. G., & Schaefer, C. (2000). *Short term play therapy for children.* New York: Guilford Press.

Kahng, S., Iwata, B. A., & Lewin, A. B. (2002). Behavioral treatment of self-injury. *American Journal on Mental Retardation, 107,* 212–221.

Kaiser, A. P., & Grim, J. C. (2006). Teaching functional communication skills. In M. E. Snell & F. Brown, *Instruction of students with severe disabilities* (pp. 447–488). Upper Saddle River, NJ: Pearson.

Kaiser, A. P., Hancock, T. B., & Nietfeld, J. P. (2000). The effects of parent-implemented enhanced milieu teaching on the social communication of children who have autism. *Early Education & Development, 11,* 423–446.

Kaiser, A. P., & Hester, P. P. (1994). Generalized effects of enhanced milieu teaching. *Journal of Speech and Hearing Research, 37.*

Kalb, C. (2005, February 28). When does autism start? *Newsweek,* pp. 45–53.

Kanner, L. (1943). Autistic disturbances of affective contact. *Nervous Child, 2,* 217–250.

Kanner, L. (1964). *History of the care and study of the mentally retarded.* Springfield, IL: Charles C Thomas.

Kanner, L., & Eisenberg, L. (1956). Early infantile autism 1943–1955. *American Journal of Orthopsychiatry, 26,* 55–65.

Kaplan, S. (2004). Where we stand determines the answer to the question: Can the No Child Left Behind legislation be beneficial to gifted students? *Roeper Review, 26,* 124–125.

Kapperman, G., & Sticken, J. (2005). Assistive technology. In M. C. Holbrook & A. J. Koenig (Eds.), *Foundations of education: Volume II. Instructional strategies for teaching children and youth with visual impairments* (2nd ed., chap. 14). Retrieved February 1, 2007, from www.afb.org/foe/book.asp?ch=v1ch02

Karchmer, M. A., & Mitchell. R. E. (2003). Demographic and achievement characteristics of deaf and hard-of-hearing students. In M. Marschark & P. E. Spencer (Eds.), *Oxford handbook of deaf studies, language and education* (pp. 21–37). New York: Oxford University Press.

Karolyi, C., Ramos-Ford, V., & Gardner, H. (2003). Multiple intelligences: A perspective on giftedness. In N. Colangelo & G. Davis (Eds.), *Handbook of gifted education* (3rd ed.; pp. 100–112). Boston: Allyn & Bacon.

Karvonen, M., Test, D. W., Wood, W. M., Browder, D., & Algozzine, B. (2004). Putting self-determination into practice. *Exceptional Children, 71*(1), 23–41.

Katims, D. S. (2000). Literacy instruction for people with mental retardation: Historical highlights and contemporary analysis. *Education and Training in Mental Retardation and Developmental Disabilities, 35,* 3–15.

Katims, D. S. (2001). Literacy assessment of students with mental retardation: An exploratory investigation. *Education and Training in Mental Retardation and Developmental Disabilities, 36*(4), 363–372.

Katsiyannis, A., & Maag, J. (2001). Educational methodologies: Legal and practical considerations. *Preventing School Failure, 46*(1), 31–37.

Kauffman, J. M. (2005). *Characteristics of emotional and behavioral disorders of children and youth* (8th ed.). Upper Saddle River, NJ: Pearson/Merrill Prentice Hall.

Kauffman, J. M., Mostert, M. P., Trent, S. C., & Hallahan, D. P. (2002). *Managing classroom behavior: A reflective case-based approach.* Boston: Allyn & Bacon.

Kaufman, A., & Kaufman, N. (2004a). *Kaufman Brief Intelligence Test–II.* Circle Pines, MN: American Guidance Service.

Kaufman, A., & Kaufman, N. (2004b). *The Kaufman Test of Educational Achievement–II.* Circle Pines, MN: American Guidance Service.

Kavale, K. (2002). Discrepancy models in the identification of learning disability. In R. Bradley, L. Danielson, & D. Hallahan (Eds.), *Identification of learning disabilities: Research to practice* (pp. 369–426). Mahwah, NJ: Erlbaum.

Kaye, H. S. (1997). *Education of children with disabilities.* (Report No. EC305866). San Francisco, CA: University of California, San Francisco. (ERIC Document Reproduction Service No. ED412668)

Kazdin, A. E. (2001). *Behavior modification in applied settings* (6th ed.). Belmont, CA: Wadsworth/Thomson Learning.

Kazdin, A. E., & Bootzin, R. R. (1972). The token economy: An evaluative review. *Journal of Applied Behavior Analysis, 5,* 343–372.

Kef, S. (2002). Psychosocial adjustment and the meaning of social support for visually impaired adolescents. *Journal of Visual Impairment and Blindness, 96*(1), 22–37.

Kehle,T., Bray, M., Theodore, L., Zhou, Z., & McCoach, B. (2004). Emotional disturbance/social maladjustment: Why is the incidence increasing? *Psychology in the Schools, 41,* 861–865.

Kelley, P., & Smith, P. (2005). Independent living skills. In M. C. Holbrook & A. J. Koenig (Eds.), *Foundation of education: Volume II. Instructional strategies for teaching children and youths with visual impairments* (2nd ed., chap. 16). Retrieved February 12, 2007, from www.afb.org/foe/book.asp?ch=v2ch16

Kelly, L. P. (2003). Considerations for designing practice for deaf readers. *Journal of Deaf Studies and Deaf Education, 8*(2), 171–186.

Kemp, C. E., & Parette, H. P. (2000). Barriers to minority family involvement in assistive technology decision-making processes. *Education and Training in Mental Retardation and Developmental Disabilities, 35*(4), 384–392.

Kendziora, K. T. (2004). Early intervention for emotional and behavioral disorders. In R. B. Rutherford, M. M. Quinn, & S. R. Mathur (Eds.), *Handbook of research in emotional and behavioral disorders* (pp. 327–351). New York: Guilford Press.

Kennedy, A. C., & Bennett, L. (2006). Urban adolescent mothers exposed to community, family, and partner violence: Is cumulative violence exposure a barrier to school performance and participation? *Journal of Interpersonal Violence, 21*(6), 750–774.

Kennedy, C. (2004). Students with severe disabilities (pp. 3–16). In C. H. Kennedy & E. M. Horn, *Including students with severe disabilities.* Boston: Pearson.

Kennedy, C. H., & Horn, E. M. (2004). *Including students with severe disabilities.* Boston: Pearson.

Kennedy, D. M. (2002). Glimpses of a highly gifted child in a heterogeneous classroom. *Roeper Review, 24*(3), 120–124.

Kern, L., Hilt, A. M., & Gresham, F.(2004). An evaluation of the functional behavioral assessment process used with students with or at risk for emotional and behavioral disorders. *Education and Treatment of Children, 27*(4), 440–452.

Kerr, B. A., & Nicpon, M. F. (2003). Gender and giftedness. In N. Colangelo & G. Davis (Eds.), *Handbook of gifted education* (pp. 493–505). Needham Heights: Allyn & Bacon.

Kerr, M. M., & Nelson, C. M. (2006). *Strategies for addressing behavior problems in the classroom* (5th ed.). Columbus, OH: Pearson/Merrill-Prentice Hall.

Keyes, G. K. (1994). Motivating reluctant students: The Time on Computer program. *Teaching Exceptional Children, 27*(1), 20–23.

Keyes, M. W., & Owens-Johnson, L. (2003). Developing person-centered IEPs. *Intervention in School and Clinic, 38*, 145–152.

Keyser-Marcus, L., Briel, L., Sherron-Targett, P., Yasuda, S., Johnson, S., & Wehman, P. (2002). Enhancing the schooling of students with traumatic brain injury. *Teaching Exceptional Children, 34*, 62–67.

Kidder-Ashley, P., Deni, J., & Anderton, J. (2000). Learning disability eligibility in the 1990s: An analysis of state practices. *Education, 121*, 65.

King-Sears, M. E. (1997). Best academic practices for inclusive classrooms. *Focus on Exceptional Children, 29*(7), 1–22.

King-Sears, M. E. (2001). Three steps for gaining access to the general education curriculum for learners with disabilities. *Intervention in School and Clinic, 37*(2), 67–76.

Kirk, S. A., Gallagher, J. J., & Anastasiow, N. J. (2006). *Educating exceptional children* (11th ed.). Boston: Houghton Mifflin.

Kirschenbaum, R. J. (1998) Dynamic assessment and its use with underserved gifted and talented populations. *Gifted Child Quarterly, 42*, 40–47.

Kleinert, H., McGregor, V., Durbin, M., Blandford, T., Jones, K., Owens, J., Harrison, B., & Miracle, S. (2004). Service-learning opportunities that include students with moderate and severe disabilities. *Teaching Exceptional Children, 37*(2), 28–34.

Kliewer, C., & Biklen, D. (2001). "School's not really a place for reading": A research synthesis of the literate lives of students with severe disabilities. *Journal of the Association for Persons with Severe Handicaps, 26*, 1–12.

Kluwin, T. N., Stinson, M. S., & Colarossi, G. M. (2002). Social processes and outcomes of in-school contact between deaf and hearing peers. *Journal of Deaf Studies and Deaf Education, 7*(3), 200–213.

Kluth, P. (2000). Community referenced learning and the inclusive classroom. *Remedial and Special Education, 21*, 19–26.

Knoff, H., & Prout, H. (1985). *Kinetic drawing system for family and school: A handbook.* Los Angeles: Western Psychological Services.

Kochhar, C. A., West, L. L., & Taymans, J. M. (2000). *Successful inclusion. Practical strategies for a shared responsibility.* Upper Saddle River, NJ: Prentice-Hall.

Koegel, L. K., Koegel, R. L., Harrower, J. K., & Carter, C. M. (1999). Pivotal response intervention I: Overview of approach. *Journal of the Association for Persons with Severe handicaps, 24*(3), 174–185.

Koenig, A. J. (1990). Exploring decision-making processes for selection of appropriate reading media for individuals with visual impairments [Electronic version]. *Peabody Journal of Education, 67*(2), 74–88.

Koenig A. J., & Holbrook, M. C. (1989). Determining the reading medium for students with visual impairments: A diagnostic teaching approach. *Journal of Visual Impairment and Blindness, 83*(6), 296–302.

Koenig A. J., & Holbrook, M. C. (1995). *Learning media assessment of students with visual impairments: A resource guide for teachers* (3rd ed.). Lubbock, TX: Texas School for the Blind and Visually Impaired.

Koenig, A. J., & Holbrook, M. C. (2000). Ensuring high-quality instruction for students in braille literacy programs. *Journal of Visual Impairment and Blindness, 94*(11), 677–695.

Koenig, A. J., & Holbrook, M. C. (2005). *Literacy skills.* In M. C. Holbrook & A. J. Koenig (Eds.), *Foundation of education: Volume II. Instructional strategies for teaching children and youths with visual impairments* (2nd ed., chap. 8). Retrieved February 12, 2007, from www.afb.org/foe/book.asp?ch=v2ch8

Koenig, A. J., Holbrook, M. C., Corn, A. L., DePriest, L. B., Erin, J. N., & Presley, I. (2005). Specialized assessments for students with visual impairments. In M. C. Holbrook & A. J. Koenig (Eds.), *Foundation of education: Volume II. Instructional strategies for teaching children and youths with visual impairments* (2nd ed., chap. 4). Retrieved February 12, 2007, from www.afb.org/foe/book.asp?ch=v2ch4

Kolloff, P. (2003). State-supported residential high schools. In N. Colangelo & G. Davis (Eds.), *Handbook of gifted education* (pp. 238–246). Needham Heights: Allyn & Bacon.

Konopasek, D. E. (2004). *Medication fact sheets: A medication reference guide for the nonmedical professional.* Longmont, CO: Sopris West.

Konopasek, D. E., & Forness, S. R. (2004). Psychopharmacology in the treatment of emotional and behavioral disorders. In R. B. Rutherford, M. M. Quinn, & S. R. Mathur (Eds.), *Handbook of research in emotional or behavioral disorders* (pp. 352–368). New York: Guilford Press.

Konstantopoulas, S., Modi, M., & Hedges, L. (2001). Who are America's gifted? *American Journal of Education, 109*(3), 344–382.

Kos, J., Richdale, A., & Hay, D. (2006). Children with attention deficit hyperactivity disorder and their teachers: A review of the literature. *International Journal of Disability, Development, and Education, 53,* 147–160.

Kraemer, B. R., McIntyre, L. L., & Blacher, J. (2003). Quality of life for young adults with mental retardation during transition. *Mental Retardation, 41,* 250–262.

Krain, A., & Castellanos, F. X. (2006). Brain development and ADHD. *Clinical Psychology Review, 26,* 433–444.

Kregel, J. (2004). Designing instructional programs. In P. Wehman & J. Kregel (Eds.), *Functional curriculum for elementary, middle, & secondary age students with special needs* (2nd ed., pp. 37–66). Austin, TX: Pro-Ed.

Krupski, A. (1977). Role of attention in the reaction-time performance of mentally retarded adolescents. *American Journal of Mental Deficiency, 82,* 79–83.

Kuder, S. J. (2003). *Teaching students with language and communication difficulties* (2nd ed.). Boston: Allyn & Bacon.

Kuhn, M. R., & Stahl, S. A. (2003). Fluency: A review of developmental and remedial practices. *Journal of Educational Psychology, 95*(1), 3–21.

Kuhne, M., & Wiener, J. (2000). Stability of social status of children with and without learning disabilities. *Learning Disability Quarterly, 23,* 64–75.

Kulik, J. A. (2003). Grouping and tracking. In N. Colangelo & G. Davis (Eds.), *Handbook of gifted education* (pp. 268–281). Needham Heights: Allyn & Bacon.

Kumar, D., Ramasamy, R., & Stefanich, G. (2001). Science for students with blindness or low vision: Teaching suggestions and policy implication for secondary educators. *Electronic Journal of Science Education, 5*(3).

Kuoch, H., & Mirenda, P. (2003). Social story interventions for young children with autism spectrum disorders. *Focus on Autism and Other Developmental Disabilities, 18*(4), 219–227.

Kyle, K. E., DuPaul, G. J., Yugar, J. M., & Lutz, J. G. (1996). *Hyperactivity, number of years in preschool, and aggression: Predictors of future behavior disorders in a school setting.* Atlanta: National Association of School Psychologists.

L

La Malfa, G., Lassi, S., Bertelli, M., Salvini, R., & Placidi, G. (2004). Autism and intellectual disability: A study of prevalence on a sample of the Italian population. *Journal of Intellectual Disability Research, 48,* 262–267.

Lachar, D., & Gruber, C. (2001). *Personality Inventory for Children–Second Edition.* Los Angeles: Western Psychological Services.

Lambert, N., Nihira, K., & Leland, H. (1993). *AAMR Adaptive Behavior Scale–School and Community.* Austin, TX: Pro-Ed.

Landrum, T. J., Tankersley, M., & Kauffman, J. M. (2003). What is special about special education for students with emotional or behavioral disorders? *Journal of Special Education, 37*(3), 148–156.

Lane, K. L. (1999). Young students at risk for antisocial behavior: The utility of academic and social skills interventions. *Journal of Emotional and Behavioral Disorders, 7*(4), 211–223.

Lang, H. G. (2003). Pespectives on the history of deaf education. In M. Marschark & P. E. Spencer (Eds.), *Oxford handbook of deaf studies, language, and education* (pp. 9–20). New York: Oxford University Press.

Larry P. v. Riles, 343 F. Supp. 1306 (N.D. Cal. 1972).

Larsson, H., Lichtenstein, P., & Larsson, J. (2006). Genetic contributions to the development of ADHD from childhood to adolescence. *Journal of the American Academy of Child and Adolescent Psychiatry, 45,* 973–981.

Lawler, C., Croen, L., Grether, J., & Van de Water, J. (2004). Identifying environmental contributions to autism: Provocative clues and false leads. *Mental Retardation and Developmental Disabilities Research Reviews, 10,* 292–302.

Learning Disabilities Association, Educational Services Committee. (1995). Fact sheet: Assistive technology for individuals with learning disabilities. *Newsbriefs,* January/February.

Lee, H., Koehler, D., Pang, C., Levine, R., Ng, P., Palmer, D., Quinton, P., & Hu, J. (2005). Gene delivery to human sweat glands: A model for cystic fibrosis gene therapy. *Gene Therapy, 12,* 1752–1760.

Lee, J. W., & Cartledge, G. (1996). Native Americans. In G. Cartledge & J. F. Milburn, *Cultural diversity and social skills instruction* (pp. 205–243). Champaign, IL: Research Press.

Lee, R. (Ed.). (2004). *A beginner's introduction to deaf history.* Feltham, Middlesex: British Deaf History Society.

Lee, W. W. (1987). Microcomputer courseware production and evaluation guidelines for students with learning disabilities. *Journal of Learning Disabilities, 20,* 436–437.

Lee-Tarver, A. (2006). Are individualized education plans a good thing? A survey of teachers' perceptions of the utility of IEPs in regular education settings. *Journal of Instructional Psychology, 33*, 263–272.

Lentini, R., Vaughn, B. J., & Fox, L. (2004). *Routine based support guide for young children with challenging behavior.* Tampa, FL: University of South Florida, Early Intervention Positive Behavior Support. Retrieved from www.challengingbehavior.org

Lentini, R., Vaughn, B. J., & Fox, L. (2005). *Creating teaching tools for young children with challenging behavior* [CD-ROM]. Early Intervention Positive Behavior Support, The Division of Applied Research and Educational Support, 13301 Bruce B. Downs, Tampa, FL 33612. Retrieved from www.challengingbehavior.org

Leonard, L. B. (1998). *Children with specific language impairment.* Cambridge, MA: MIT Press.

Lerner, J. (2003). *Learning disabilities: Theories, diagnosis, and teaching strategies* (9th ed.). Boston: Houghton Mifflin.

Lerner, J., & Kline, F. (2006). *Learning disabilities and related disorders: Characteristics and teaching strategies* (10th ed.). Boston: Houghton Mifflin.

Leroux, J., & Levitt-Perlman, M. (2000). The gifted child with attention deficit disorder: An identification and intervention challenge. *Roeper Review, 22*, 171–176.

Leslie, M. (2000). The vexing legacy of Lewis Terman [Electronic version]. *Stanford Magazine*, July/August. Retrieved from www.stanfordalumni.org/news/magazine/2000/julaug/articles/terman.html

Lessenberry, B. M., & Rehfeldt, R. A. (2004). Evaluating stress levels of parents of children with disabilities. *Exceptional Children, 70*, 231–244.

Levendosky, A. A., Huth-Boocks, A., & Semel, M. A. (2002). Adolescent peer relationships and metal health functioning in families with domestic violence. *Journal of Clinical and Child and Adolescent Psychology, 31*(3), 206–218.

Levin. J. R. (1993). Mnemonic strategies and classroom learning: A twenty-year report card. *The Elementary School Journal, 94*(2), 235–244.

Levy, S. E., & Hyman, S. L. (2005). Novel treatments for autistic spectrum disorders. *Mental Retardation and Developmental Disabilities Research Reviews, 11*, 131–142.

Levy, S., Coleman, M., & Alsman, B. (2002). Reading instruction for elementary students with emotional/behavioral disorders. *Beyond Behavior, 11*(3), 3–10.

Lewis, B., Frebairn, L., & Terry, H. (2000). Follow-up for children with early expressive phonology disorders. *Journal of Learning Disabilities, 33*, 433–444.

Lewis, J. D. (2001). *Language isn't needed: Nonverbal assessments and gifted learners* (RC 022 965). San Diego, CA: Growing Partnerships for Rural Special Education. (ERIC Document Reproduction Service No. ED453026)

Lewis, R. B., & Doorlag, D. H. (2006). *Teaching special students in general education classrooms* (7th ed.). Upper Saddle River, NJ: Merrill/Prentice Hall.

Lewis, S., & Allman, C. B. (2005). Educational programming. In M. C. Holbrook & A. J. Koenig (Eds.), *Foundations of education: Volume I. History and theory of teaching children and youth with visual impairments* (2nd ed., chap. 9). Retrieved February 1, 2007, from www.afb.org/foe/book.asp?ch=v1ch02

Lewis, T. J., & Sugai, G. (1999). Effective behavior support: A systems approach to proactive school-wide management. *Focus on Exceptional Children, 31*, 1–24.

Leyser, Y., & Heinze, T. (2001). Perspectives of parents of children who are visually impaired: Implications for the field. *RE:view, 33*(1), 37–48.

Liddel, S. K. (2003). *Grammar, gesture, and meaning in American Sign Language.* Cambridge, UK: Cambridge University Press.

Lidz, C. S., & Macrine, S. L. (2001). An alternative approach to the identification of gifted culturally and linguistically diverse learners: The contribution of dynamic assessment. *School Psychology International, 22*(1), 74–84.

Lindegren, M., Steinberg, S., & Byers, R. (2000). Epidemiology of HIV/AIDS in children. *Pediatric Clinics of North America, 47*, 1–20.

Lindsey, M. (1980). *Training teachers of the gifted and talented.* New York: Teachers College Press.

Lindsley, O. R. (1971). Precision teaching in perspective. *Teaching Exceptional Children, 3*, 114–119.

Linn, A., & Myles, B. S. (2004). Asperger syndrome and six strategies for success. *Beyond Behavior, 14*(1), 3–9.

Liptak, G. (2002). Neural tube defects. In M. Batshaw (Ed.), *Children with disabilities* (5th ed., pp. 467–492). Baltimore, MD: Paul H. Brookes.

Lloyd, J. W., Forness, S. R., & Kavale, K. A. (1998). Some methods are more effective than others. *Intervention in School and Clinic, 33*(4), 195–200.

Lloyd, L. (1999). Multi-age classes and high ability students. *Review of Educational Research, 69*(2), 187–212.

Lock, R. H., & Layton, C. A. (2001). Succeeding in postsecondary ed through self-advocacy. *Teaching Exceptional Children, 34*(2), 66–71.

Lonigan, C. J., Anthony, J. L., Bloomfield, B. G., Dyer, S. M., & Samwel, C. S. (1999). Effects of two shared-reading interventions on emergent literacy skills of at-risk preschoolers. *Journal of Early Intervention, 22*, 306–322.

Lorch, E., Eastham, D., Milich, R., Lemberger, C., Sanchez, R., Welsh, R., & van den Broek, P. (2004). Difficulties in comprehending causal relations among children with AD/HD: The role of cognitive engagement. *Journal of Abnormal Psychology, 113*, 56–63.

Lord, C., & Volkmar, F. (2002). Genetics of childhood disorders: XLII. Autism, Part 1: Diagnosis and assessment in autistic spectrum disorders. *Journal of the American Academy of Child and Adolescent Psychiatry, 41*, 1134–1136.

Lovaas, O. I. (1987). Behavioral treatment and normal educational and intellectual functioning in young autistic children. *Journal of Consulting and Clinical Psychology, 55*, 3–9.

Love, J. M., Kisker, E. E., Ross, C. M., Schochet, P. Z., Brooks-Gunn, J., Paulsell, D., Boller, K., Constantine, J., Vogel, C., Fuligni, A., & Brady-Smith, C. (2002). *Making a difference in the lives of infants and toddlers and their families: The impacts of early Head Start. Volume 1: Final technical report.* Washington, DC: U.S. Department of Health and Human Services, Administration for Children and Families.

Lowry, S. S., & Hatton, D. D. (2002). Facilitating walking by young children with visual impairments. *RE:view, 34*(3), 125–133.

Luckasson, R., Borthwick-Duffy, S., Buntinx, Wil H. E., Coulter, D. L., Craig, E. M., Reeve, A., Schalock, R. L., Snell, M. E., Spitalnik, D. M., Spreat, S., & Tassé, M. J. (2002). *Mental retardation: Definition, classification, and systems of supports* (10th ed.). Washington, DC: American Association on Mental Retardation.

Luckasson, R., Coulter, D. L., Polloway, E. A., Reiss, S., Schalock, R. L., Snell, M. E., Spitalnik, D. M., & Stark, J. A. (1992). *Mental retardation: Definition, classification, and system of supports* (9th ed.). Washington, DC: American Association on Mental Retardation.

Luckner, J., Bowen, S., & Carter, K. (2001). Visual teaching strategies. *Teaching Exceptional Children, 33*(3), 38–44.

Luckner, J., & Muir, S. (2002). Suggestions for helping students who are deaf succeed in general education settings. *Communications Disorders Quarterly, 24*, 23–30.

Lue, M. S. (2001). *A survey of communication disorders for the classroom teacher.* Boston: Allyn & Bacon.

Luke S. and Hans S. v. Nix et al., USDC Civ. No. 81-3331 (1984).

Lund, N. J., & Duchan, J. F. (1993). *Assessing children's language in naturalistic contexts* (3rd ed.). Englewood Cliffs, NJ: Prentice-Hall.

M

Maccini, P., & Hughes, C. A. (2000). Effects of a problem-solving strategy on the introductory algebra performance of secondary students with learning disabilities. *Learning Disabilities Research and Practice, 15*, 1–21.

Maccini, P., Gagnon, J. C., & Hughes, C. A. (2002). Technology-based practices for secondary students with learning disabilities. *Learning Disability Quarterly, 25*(4), 247–261.

Maciag, K. G., Schuster, J. W., Collins, B. C., & Cooper, J. T. (2000). Training adults with moderate and severe mental retardation in a vocational skill using a simultaneous prompting procedure. *Education and Training in Mental Retardation and Developmental Disabilities, 35*(3), 306–316.

Mack, C. G., & Koenig, A. J. (n.d.). *Access to technology for students with visual impairments.* Retrieved July 4, 2007, from www.cecdvi.org/Postion%20Papers/technology.htm

Madaus, J. W. (2006). Employment outcomes of university graduates with learning disabilities. *Learning Disability Quarterly, 29*(1), 19–31.

Madsen, C. H., Becker, W. C., & Thomas, D. R. (1968). Rules, praise, and ignoring. Elements of elementary classroom control. *Journal of Applied Behavior Analysis, 1*, 139–150.

Maheady, L. (1997). Preparing teachers for instructing multiple ability groups. *Teacher Education and Special Education, 20*(4), 322–339.

Maheady, L., Harper, G. F., & Mallette, B. (2003). A focus on class-wide peer tutoring. *Current Practice Alerts*, 8.

Mahoney, G., & Perales, F. (2003). Using relationship-focused intervention to enhance the social emotional functioning of children with autism disorders. *Topics in Early Childhood Special Education, 23*(2), 74–86.

Maich, K., & Kean, S. (2004). Read two books and write me in the morning: Bibliotherapy for social emotional intervention in the inclusive classroom [Electronic version]. *Teaching Exceptional Children Plus, 1*(2) Article 4. Retrieved April, 2005, from htpp://escholarship.bc.edu/education/tecplus/vol1/iss2/4

Maker, J. (1982). *Teaching models in education of the gifted.* Rockville, MD: Aspen.

Male, M. (2002). *Technology in inclusion: Meeting the special needs of all students* (4th ed.). Boston: Allyn & Bacon.

Maller, S. J. (2003). Intellectual assessment of deaf people: A critical review of core concepts and issues. In M. Marschark & P. E. Spencer (Eds.), *Oxford handbook of deaf studies, language and education* (pp. 451–463). New York: Oxford University Press.

Malloy, H. L., & McMurray, P. (1996). Conflict strategies and resolutions: Peer conflict in an integrated early childhood classroom. *Early Childhood Research Quarterly, 11*, 185–206.

Malone, D. M., & Gallagher, P. A., & Long, S. R. (2001). General education teachers' attitudes and perceptions of teamwork supporting children with developmental concerns. *Early Education and Development, 12*, 577–592.

Mandlawitz, M. (2006). *What every teacher should know about IDEA 2004.* Boston: Allyn & Bacon.

Mardell-Czudnowski, C., & Goldenberg, D. (1998). *Development Indicators for the Assessment of Learning–3.* Circle Pines, MN: American Guidance Service.

Marks, S. U., Shaw-Hegwer, J., Schrader, C., Longaker, T., Peters, I., Powers, F., & Levine, M. (2003). Instructional management tips for teachers of students with autism spectrum disorder (ASD). *Teaching Exceptional Children, 35*(4), 50–55.

Marland, S. (1972). *Education of the gifted and talented Report to Congress.* Washington, DC: U.S. Office of Education.

Marschark, M., Lang, H. G., & Albertini, J. A. (2002). *Educating deaf students: Research into practice.* New York: Oxford University Press.

Marston, D., Muyskens, P., Lau, M., & Canter, A. (2003). Problem-solving model for decision making with high-incidence disabilities: The Minneapolis experience. *Learning Disabilities Research & Practice, 18*(3), 187–200.

Martin, J., Van Dycke, J., Greene, B., Gardner, J., Christensen W., Woods, L., & Lovett, D. (2006). Direct observation of teacher-directed IEP meetings: Establishing the need for student IEP meeting instruction. *Exceptional Children, 72,* 187–200.

Martin, J. E., Huber Marshall, L., & Maxson, L. L. (1993). Transition policy: Infusing self-determination and self-advocacy into transition programs. *Career Development for Exceptional Individuals, 16,* 53–61.

Martin, J. E., Marshall, L. H., & Sale, P. (2004). A 3-year study of middle, junior high, and high school IEP meetings. *Exceptional Children, 70,* 285–297.

Martin, N. R. M. (2005). *A guide to collaboration for IEP teams.* Baltimore, MD: Paul H. Brookes.

Masi, G., Perugi, G., Toni, C., Millepiedi, S., Mucci, M., Bertini, M., & Pfanner, C. (2006). Attention-deficit hyperactivity disorder comorbidity in children and adolescents. *Bipolar Disorders, 8,* 373–381.

Mastropieri, M. A., & Scruggs, T. E. (1991). *Teaching students ways to remember: Strategies for learning mnemonically.* Cambridge, MA: Brookline Books.

Mastropieri, M. A., & Scruggs, T. E. (1998). Constructing more meaningful relationships in the classroom: Mnemonic research into practice. *Learning Disabilities Research & Practice, 13,* 138–145.

Mastropieri, M. A., & Scruggs, T. E. (2007). *The inclusive classroom: Strategies for effective instruction* (3rd ed.). Upper Saddle River, NJ: Merrill/Prentice-Hall.

Mastropieri, M. A., Scruggs, T. E., & Whedon, C. (1997). Using mnemonic strategies to teach information about U.S. presidents: A classroom-based investigation. *Learning Disability Quarterly, 20,* 13–21.

Mathur, S. R., & Rutherford, R. B. (1996). Is social skills training effective for students with emotional or behavioral disorders? *Behavior Disorders, 22,* 21–28

Matson, J. L., Kiely, S. L., & Bamburg, J. W. (1997). The effect of stereotypies on adaptive skills as assessed with the DASH–II and Vineland Adaptive Behavior Scales. *Research in Developmental Disabilities, 18,* 471–476.

Matthews, D. M., Pracek, E., & Olson, J. (2000). Technology for teaching and learning, In J. L. Olson & J. M. Platt, *Teaching children and adolescents with special needs* (3rd ed., pp. 322–346). Upper Saddle River, NJ: Merrill.

Mattie, H. D. (2001). Generalization effects of cognitive strategies conversation training for adults with moderate to severe disabilities. *Education and Training in Mental Retardation and Developmental Disabilities, 36,* 178–187.

Mayer, G. R., & Leone, P. E. (2002). Developing untapped talents and fostering success with hypermedia. In L. Wilder & S. Black (Eds.), *Integrating technology in program development for children and youth with emotional or behavioral disorders* (pp. 47–60). Arlington, VA: CCBD.

Mayer, G. R., & Sulzer-Azaroff, B. (2002). Intervention for vandalism and aggression. In M. Shinn, H. Walker, & G. Stoner (Eds.), *Interventions for academic and behavior problems II: Preventive and remedial approaches*

(pp. 853–884). Bethesda, MD: National Association of School Psychologists.

Mayes, S. D., Calhoun, S. L., & Lane, S. E. (2005). Diagnosing children's writing disabilities: Different tests give different results. *Perceptual and Motor Skills, 101,* 72–78.

Mayfield, J., & Homack, S. (2005). Behavioral considerations associated with traumatic brain injury. *Preventing School Failure, 49,* 17–22.

McBee, M. (2006). A descriptive analysis of referral sources for gifted identification screening by race and socioeconomic status. *Journal of Secondary Gifted Education, 17,* 103–111.

McBride, B. J., & Schwartz, I. S. (2003). Effects of teaching early interventionists to use discrete trials during ongoing classroom activities. *Topics in Early Childhood Special Education, 23*(1), 5–17.

McBurnett, K. (1995). The new subtype of AD/HD: Predominantly hyperactive-impulsive type. *Attention! 1,* (10–15).

McBurnett, K., Pfiffner, L., Wilcutt, E., Tamm, L., Lerner, M., Ottolini, Y., & Furman, M. (1999). Experimental cross-validation of *DSM-IV* subtypes of attention-deficit/hyperactivity disorder. *Journal of the American Academy of Child and Adolescent Psychiatry, 38,* 17–24.

McCarney, S. (1993). *Prereferral intervention manual and prereferral checklist.* Columbia. MO: Hawthorne Educational Systems.

McCarney, S. (1995). *Attention Deficit Disorders Evaluation Scale–2.* Columbia, MO: Hawthorne.

McCarty, B., & Hazelkorn, M. (2001). Reflection: The key to social-emotional change using service-learning. *Beyond Behavior, 10*(3), 30–35.

McCoach, D. B., & Seigle, D. (2003). The structure and function of academic self-concept in gifted and general education students. *Roeper Review, 25*(2), 61–65.

McCormick, L. (2003a). Language intervention and support. In L. McCormick, D. F. Loeb, & R. Schiefelbusch (Eds.), *Supporting children with communication difficulties in inclusive settings* (2nd ed., pp. 259–297). Boston: Allyn & Bacon.

McCormick, L. (2003b). Language intervention in the inclusive preschool. In L. McCormick, D. F. Loeb, & R. Schiefelbusch (Eds.), *Supporting children with communication difficulties in inclusive settings* (2nd ed., pp. 333–366). Boston: Allyn & Bacon.

McCormick, L., Noonan, M. J., Ogata, V., & Heck, R. (2001) Co-teacher relationship and program quality: Implications for preparing teachers for inclusive preschool settings. *Education and Training in Mental Retardation and Developmental Disabilities, 36*(2), 119–132.

McCormick, L., & Wegner, J. (2003). Supporting augmentative communication. In L. McCormick, D. F. Loeb, & R. Schiefelbusch (Eds.), *Supporting children with communication difficulties in inclusive settings* (2nd ed., pp. 435–459). Boston: Allyn & Bacon.

McDaniel, T. R. (2002). Mainstreaming the gifted: Historical perspectives on excellence and equity. *Roeper Review, 24*(3), 112–114.

McDonnell, J. (1998). Instruction for students with severe disabilities in general education settings. *Education and Training in Mental Retardation and Developmental Disabilities, 33*, 199–215.

McDonnell, J., Thorson, N., Disher, S., Mathot-Buckner, C., Mendel, J., & Ray, L. (2003). The achievement of students with developmental disabilities in inclusive settings: An exploratory study. *Education and Treatment of Children, 26*, 224–236.

McDonnell, J. J., Hardman, M. L., & McDonnell, A. P. (2003). *An introduction to persons with moderate and severe disabilities. Educational and social issues* (2nd ed.). Boston: Allyn & Bacon.

McEachin, J. J., Smith, T., & Lovaas, O. I. (1993). Long-term outcome for children with autism who received early intensive behavioral treatment. *American Journal on Mental Retardation, 97*, 359–372.

McGaha, C., & Farran, D. (2001). Interactions in an inclusive classroom: The effects of visual status and setting. *Journal of Visual Impairment and Blindness, 95*(2), 80–94.

McGee, G. G., Morrier, M. J., & Daly, T. (1999). An incidental teaching approach to early intervention for toddlers with autism. *Journal of the Association for Persons with Severe Handicaps, 24*(3), 133–146.

McGinnis, E., & Goldstein, A. P. (1990). *Skillstreaming early childhood: New strategies and perspectives for teaching prosocial skills.* Champaign, IL: Research Press.

McGinnis, E., & Goldstein, A. P. (1997). *Skillstreaming the elementary school child: New strategies and perspectives for teaching prosocial skills.* Champaign, IL: Research Press.

McGinnis, J. C., Friman, P. C., & Carlyon, W. D. (1999). The effect of token rewards on intrinsic motivation for doing math. *Journal of Applied Behavior Analysis, 32*, 375–379.

McGoey, K. E., Eckert, T. L., & DuPaul, G. J. (2002). Early intervention for preschool-age children with AD/HD: A literature review. *Journal of Emotional and Behavioral Disorders, 10*(1), 14–28.

McGregor, G. (2003).Standards based reform and students with disabilities. In D. L. Ryndak & S. Alper, *Curriculum and instruction for students with severe disabilities in inclusive settings* (2nd ed.). Boston: Allyn & Bacon.

McGregor, D., & Farenkopf, C. (2005). Recreation and leisure skills. In M. C. Holbrook & A. J. Koenig (Eds.), *Foundation of education: Volume II. Instructional strategies for teaching children and youths with visual impairments* (2nd ed., chap. 18). Retrieved February 12, 2007, from www.afb.org/foe/book.asp?ch=v2ch18

McGrew, K. S., & Evans, J. (2003). *Expectations for students with cognitive disabilities: Is the cup half empty or half full? Can the cup flow over?* (Synthesis Report 55). Minneapolis, MN: University of Minnesota, National Center on Educational Outcomes. Retrieved November 17, 2006, from http://education.umn.edu/NCEO/OnlinePubs/Synthesis55.html

McIntosh, R., Vaughn, S., & Bennerson, D. (1995). FAST social skills training for students with learning disabilities. *Teaching Exceptional Children, 28*, 37–41.

McIntyre, D. J., & O'Hair, M. J. (1996). *The reflective roles of the classroom teacher.* Belmont, CA: Wadsworth.

McLean, S. (2001). A survey of middle level teachers' perceptions of inclusion. *Dissertation Abstracts International, 61*(7-A), 2596.

McNally, R., Cole, P., & Waugh, R. (2001). Regular teachers' attitudes to the need for additional classroom support for the inclusion of students with intellectual disability. *Journal of Intellectual and Developmental Disability, 26*, 257–273.

Mechling, L. C., & Ortega-Hurndon, F. (2007). Computer-based video instruction to teach young adults with moderate intellectual disabilities to perform multiple step, job tasks in a generalized setting. *Education and Training in Developmental Disabilities, 42*(1), 24–37.

Meeker, M., & Meeker, R. (1986). The SOI system for gifted education. In J. Renzulli (Ed.), *Systems and models for developing programs for the gifted and talented* (pp. 194–215). Mansfield Center, CT: Creative Learning Press.

Meichenbaum, D. (1977). *Cognitive behavior modification.* New York: Plenum.

Meichenbaum, D. (1980). Cognitive behavior modification with exceptional children: A promise yet unfulfilled. *Exceptional Education Quarterly, 1*(1), 83–88.

Meichenbaum, D., & Biemiller, A. (1998). *Nurturing independent learners: Helping students take charge of their learning.* Cambridge, MA: Brookline Books.

Meichenbaum, D., & Goodman, J. (1971). Training impulsive children to talk to themselves: A means of developing self-control. *Journal of Abnormal Psychology, 77*, 115–126.

Meltzer, L., & Montague, M. (2001). Strategic learning in students with learning disabilities: What have we learned? In B. Keogh & D. Hallahan (Eds.), *Intervention research and learning disabilities.* Hillsdale, NJ: Erlbaum.

Meltzer, L. J., Katzir-Cohen, T., Miller, L., & Roditie, B. (2001). The impact of effort and strategy use on academic performance: Student and teacher perceptions. *Learning Disability Quarterly, 24*, 85–98.

Mercer, C. D., & Mercer, A. R. (2005). *Teaching students with learning problems* (7th ed). Upper Saddle River, NJ: Merrill/Prentice Hall.

Merrell, K., & Walker, H. (2004). Deconstructing a definition: Social maladjustment versus emotional disturbance and moving the EBD field forward. *Psychology in the Schools, 41*, 899–910.

Merrell, K. W., Gill, S. J., McFarland, H., & McFarland, T. (1996). Internalizing symptoms of gifted and non-gifted elementary-age students: A comparative validity study using the Internalizing Symptoms Scale for Children. *Psychology in the Schools, 33*(3), 185–191.

Mesibov, G. B. (2005). An overview of Division TEACCH. Retrieved January 30, 2006, from www.teacch.com/aboutus.htm

Mesibov, G. B., Adams, L., & Klinger, L. (1997). *Autism: Understanding the disorder.* New York: Plenum Press.

Mesibov, G. B., Shea, V., & Schopler, E. (2005). *Structured teaching: The TEACCH approach to working with autism.* New York: Kluwer Academic/Plenum.

Metropolitan Housing Council. (2004). *Moving on: Student mobility and affordable housing.* Lousiville, KY: Author. Retrieved from www.metropolitanhousing.org/studentmobilityreport

Meyer, L. H., Bevan-Brown, J., Harry, B., & Sapon-Shevin, M. (2004). School inclusion and multicultural issues in special education. In J. A. Banks & C. A. McGee Banks (Eds.), *Multicultural education. Issues and perspectives* (5th ed., pp. 350–378). Hoboken, NJ: Wiley.

Michaud, L. J., Semel-Concepcion, J., Duhaime, A-C., & Lazar, M. F. (2002). Traumatic brain injury. In M. Batshaw (Ed.), *Children with disabilities* (5th ed., pp. 525–545). Baltimore, MD: Paul H. Brookes.

Miller, C., Sanchez, J., & Hynd, G. (2003). Neurological correlates of reading disabilities. In H. L. Swanson, K. Harris, & S. Graham (Eds.), *Handbook of learning disabilities* (pp. 242–255). New York: Guilford Press.

Miller, D. (2006). Students with fetal alcohol syndrome: Updating our knowledge, improving their programs. *Teaching Exceptional Children, 38*(4), 12–18.

Miller, J., & Skillman, G. (2003). Assessors' satisfaction with measures of cognitive ability applied to persons with blindness or low vision. *Journal of Visual Impairment and Blindness, 97*(12), 769–774.

Miller, M. M., Menacker, S. J., & Batshaw, M. L. (2002). Vision. Our window to the world. In M. L. Batshaw (Ed.), *Children with disabilities* (5th ed., pp. 165–192). Baltimore, MD: Paul H. Brookes.

Miller, S. P. (2002). *Validated practices for teaching students with diverse needs and abilities.* Boston: Allyn & Bacon.

Miller, S. P., Butler, F. M., & Lee, K. (1998). Validated practices for teaching mathematics to students with learning disabilities. A review of literature. *Focus on Exceptional Children, 30*, 1–16.

Miller, S. P., & Mercer, C. (1997). Educational aspects of mathematics disabilities. *Journal of Learning Disabilities, 30*(1), 47–56.

Mills v. Board of Education of the District of Columbia, 348 F. Suppl 866 (D.D.C. 1972).

Minskoff, E. (1998). Sam Kirk: The man who made special education special. *Learning Disabilities Research and Practice, 13*(1), 15–21.

Minskoff, E., & Allsopp, D. (2003). *Academic success strategies for adolescents with learning disabilities & AD/HD.* Baltimore: Paul H. Brookes.

Mirenda, P. (2003). Toward functional augmentative and alternative communication for students with autism: Manual signs, graphic symbols, and voice output communication aids. *Language, Speech, and Hearing Services in Schools, 34*, 203–216.

Moats, L. C. (1998). Reading, spelling and writing disabilities in the middle grades. In B. Wong (Ed.), *Learning about learning disabilities.* Orlando FL: Academic Press.

Moats, L. C. (2001a). Overcoming the language gap. *American Educator, 5*, 8–9.

Moats, L. C. (2001b). When older students can't read. *Educational Leadership, 58*, 36–40.

Mock, D., & Kauffman, J. (2005). The delusion of inclusion. In J. Jacobson, R. Foxx, & J. Mulick (Eds.), *Controversial therapies for developmental disabilities: Fad, fashion, and science in professional practice* (pp. 113–128). Mahwah, NJ: Erlbaum.

Montague, M. (1997). Cognitive strategy instruction in mathematics for students with learning disabilities. *Journal of Learning Disabilities, 30*(2), 164–177.

Moody, S. W., Vaughn, S., & Schumm, J. S. (1997). Instruction grouping for reading: Teachers' views. *Remedial and Special Education, 18*(6), 347–356.

Moon, S. M. (2003). Counseling families. In N. Colaangelo & G. Davis (Eds.), *Handbook of General Education* (pp. 388–402). Needham Heights: Allyn & Bacon.

Moore, C. L., Harley, D. A., & Gamble, D. (2004). Ex-post-facto analysis of competitive employment outcomes for individuals with mental retardation: National perspective. *Mental Retardation: A Journal of Practices, Policy, and Perspectives, 42*, 253–262.

Moores, D. F. (2001). *Educating the deaf: Psychology, principles, and practices* (3rd ed.). Boston: Houghton Mifflin.

Morelock, M., & Morrison, K. (1999). Differentiating "developmentally appropriate": The multidimensional curriculum model for gifted young children. *Roeper Review, 21*, 195–200.

Moreno, S., & O'Neal, C. (2006). *Online Asperger syndrome information and support (OASIS): Tips for teaching high functioning people with autism.* Retrieved January 30, 2006, from www.udel.edu/bkirby/asperger/moreno_tips_for_teaching.html

Mortweet, S. L., Utley, C. A., Walker, D., Dawson, H. L., Delquadri, J. C., Reddy, S. D., Greenwood, C. R., Hamilton, S., & Ledford, D. (1999). Classwide peer tutoring: Teaching students with mild mental retardation in inclusive classrooms. *Exceptional Children, 65*, 524–536.

Most, T. (2002). The effectiveness of an intervention program on hearing aid maintenance for teenagers and their teachers. *American Annals of the Deaf, 147*(4), 29–37.

Moyes, R. A. (2001). *Incorporating social goals in the classroom: A guide for teachers and parents of children with high-functioning autism and Asperger syndrome.* Philadelphia: Jessica Kingsley.

MTA Cooperative Group. (1999). National Institute of Mental Health multimodal treatment study of AD/HD follow-up: 24-month outcomes of treatment strategies for attention-deficit/hyperactivity disorder. *Pediatrics, 113*, 754–761.

Mukherjee, S., Lightfoot, J., & Sloper, P. (2000). The inclusion of pupils with a chronic health condition in mainstream school: What does it mean for teachers? *Educational Research, 42,* 59–72.

Mull, C., & Sitlington, P. L. (2003). The role of technology in the transition to postsecondary education of students with learning disabilities: A review of the literature. *Journal of Special Education, 37*(1), 26–32.

Muller, E., & Linehan, P. (2001). *Federal disability terms: A review of state use. Quick turn around.* (ERIC Document Reproduction Service No. ED456589)

Murphy, K., & Gordon, M. (2006). Assessment of adults with ADHD. In R. Barkley (Ed.), *Attention-deficit hyperactivity disorder* (3rd ed., pp. 425–450). New York: Guilford Press.

Murray, F. (2002). Increasing reading and language skills with PowerPoint. In L. Wilder & S. Black (Eds.), *Integrating technology in program development for children and youth with emotional or behavioral disorders* (pp. 39–45). Arlington, VA: CCBD.

Murray, H., & Bellak, L. (1973). *Thematic Apperception Test.* San Antonio, TX: Psychological Corporation.

Muscott, H. S. (2000). A review and analysis of service-learning programs involving students with behavioral disorders. *Education and Treatment of Children, 23,* 346–368.

Muscott, H. S. (2001). An introduction to service-learning for students with emotional and behavioral disorders: Answers to frequently asked questions. *Beyond Behavior, 10*(3), 8–15.

Muyskens, P., & Ysseldyke, J. E. (1998). Students' academic responding times as a function of classroom ecology and time of day. *Journal of Special Education, 31*(4), 411–424.

Myles, B. S., & Simpson, R. L. (2001). Understanding the hidden curriculum: An essential social skill for children and youth with Asperger syndrome. *Intervention in School and Clinic, 36,* 279–286.

N

Nagle, K. (2001). Transition to employment and community life for youths with visual impairments: Current status and future directions. *Journal of Visual Impairment and Blindness, 95*(12), 725–738.

Naglieri, J. (2003). *Naglieri Nonverbal Ability Test.* San Antonio: Harcourt Educational Measurement.

Naglieri, J., LeBuffe, P., & Pfeiffer, S. (1993). *Devereux Behavior Rating Scales–School Form.* San Antonio, TX: Psychological Corporation.

Naglieri, J., McNeish, T., & Bardos, A. (1991). *Draw-a-Person: Screening procedure for emotional disturbance.* San Antonio, TX: Psychological Corporation.

National Association for Bilingual Education. (2004). *Why Research Matters.* Retrieved June 28, 2006, from www.nabe.org/research.html

National Association for Gifted Children. (1998). *Collaboration between gifted and general education programs.* Retrieved July 3, 2006, from www.nagc.org/index.aspx?id=462

National Association for Gifted Children. (2003). *Ability grouping.* Washington, DC: Author. Retrieved June 11, 2003, from www.nagc.org/Policy/abilgroup.htm

National Association for Gifted Children. (2005). *Frequently asked questions.* Retrieved April 9, 2007, from www.nagc.org/index.aspx?id=548

National Association of School Psychologists. (2002). *IDEA reauthorization: Challenging behavior and students with disabilities.* Retrieved July 8, 2005, from www.naspcenter.org/factsheets/idea_fs.html

National Autistic Society. (2005). *Some facts and statistics.* Retrieved August 30, 2005, from www.nas.org.uk/nas/jsp/polopoly.jsp?d=235

National Center for Health Statistics. (2005). *Self-inflicted injury/suicide.* Retrieved July 5, 2006, from www.cdc.gov/nchs/fastats/suicide.htm

National Center for Injury Prevention and Control. (2005). *Child maltreatment: Fact sheet.* Retrieved from www.cdc.gov/ncipc/factsheets/cmfacts.htm

National Coalition Against Domestic Violence. (2006). *Domestic violence and housing.* Retrieved June 25, 2006, from www.ncadv.org/files/Housing_.pdf

National Coalition for the Homeless. (2006). *Homeless families with children.* NCH Fact Sheet 12. Retrieved June 25, 2006, from www.nationalhomeless.org

National excellence: A case for developing America's talent. (1993). Retrieved June 4, 2003, from www.ed.gov/pubs/DevTalent/part2.html

National Eye Institute. (2006). *Amblyopia.* Retrieved July 3, 2007, from www.nei.nih.gov/health/amblyopia/index.asp

National Eye Institute. (2007). *Facts about the cornea and corneal disease.* Retrieved July 3, 2007, from www://nei.nih.gov/health/cornealdisease/index.asp

National Heart, Lung, and Blood Institute. (n.d.a). *What causes cystic fibrosis?* Retrieved February 10, 2006, from www.nhlbi.nih.gov/health/dci/Diseases/cf/cf_causes.html

National Heart, Lung, and Blood Institute. (n.d.b). *What is cystic fibrosis?* Retrieved February 10, 2006, from www.nhlbi.nih.gov/health/dci/Diseases/cf/cf_what.html

National Information Center for Children and Youth with Disabilities. (2004). *Spina bifida.* Retrieved February 18, 2006, from www.nichcy.org/pubs/factshe/fs12txt.htm

National Institute of Mental Health. (2001). *Learning disabilities: Decade of the brain.* Retrieved June 1, 2004, from www.ldonline.org/ld_indepth/general_info/gen-nimh-booklet.html

National Institute of Mental Health. (2004). *Autism spectrum disorders (pervasive developmental disorders).* Retrieved August 13, 2005, from www.nimh.gov/publicat/autism.cfm

National Institute of Neurological Disorders and Stroke. (2005). *Autism facts.* Retrieved September 12, 2005, from www.ninds.nih.gov/disorders/autism/detail_autism.htm

National Institute of Neurological Disorders and Stroke. (2006a). *NINDS cerebral palsy information page.* Retrieved February 7, 2006, from www.ninds.nih.gov/disorders/cerebral_ palsy/cerebral_palsy.htm

National Institute of Neurological Disorders and Stroke. (2006b). *NINDS muscular dystrophy information page.* Retrieved February 10, 2006, from www.ninds.nih.gov/disorders/md/md.htm

National Institute of Neurological Disorders and Stroke. (2006c). *NINDS traumatic brain injury information page.* Retrieved March 18, 2006, from www.ninds.nih.gov/disorders/tbi/tbi.htm

National Institute on Deafness and Other Communication Disorders. (2001). *Meniere's disease.* Retrieved June 16, 2007, from www.nidcd.nih.gov/health/hearing/menier.htm

National Institute on Deafness and Other Communication Disorders. (2002). *Otitis media.* Retrieved June 20, 2005, from www.nidcd.nih.gov/health/hearing/otitismedia.asp

National Institute on Deafness and Other Communication Disorders. (2003). *Usher syndrome.* Retrieved June 16, 2007, from www.nidcd.nih.gov/health/hearing/usher.htm

National Institute on Deafness and Other Communication Disorders. (2007a). *Hearing aids.* Retrieved June 16, 2007, from www.nidcd.nih.gov/health/hearing/hearingaid.asp

National Institute on Deafness and Other Communication Disorders. (2007b). *Noise-induced hearing loss.* Retrieved June 16, 2007, from www.nidcd.nih.gov/health/hearing/noise.htm

National Institutes of Health. (1998). *Rehabilitation of persons with traumatic brain injury.* Retrieved April 28, 2006, from http://consensus.nih.gov/1998/1998TraumaticBrainInjury109html.htm

National Joint Committee on Learning Disabilities. (1997, February). *Operationalizing the NJCLD definition of learning disabilities for ongoing assessment in schools: A report from the National Joint Committee on Learning Disabilities.* Austin, TX: Pro-Ed.

National Law Center on Homelessness and Poverty. (2004, January). *Homelessness in the United States and the Human Right to Housing.* Retrieved August 13, 2007, from www.nlchp.org/content/pubs/HomelessnessintheUSandRightstoHousing.pdf

National Reading Panel. (2000). *Teaching children to read: An evidence-based assessment of the scientific research literature on reading and its implications for reading instruction.* Bethesda, MD: National Institutes of Health.

National Research Council. (2001a). *Eager to learn: Educating our preschoolers.* Washington, DC: National Academy Press.

National Research Council. (2001b). *Educating children with autism.* Washington, DC: National Academy Press.

Neal, J., Bibby, L., & Nicholson, R. (2004). Occupational therapy, physical therapy, and orientation and mobility services in public schools. *Intervention in School and Clinic, 39,* 218–222.

Neber, H. (2004). Teacher identification of students for gifted programs: Nominations to a summer school for highly gifted students. *Psychology Science, 46,* 348–362.

Neber, H., Finsterwald, M., & Urban, N. (2001). Cooperative learning with gifted and high-achieving students: A review and meta-analysis of 12 studies. *High Ability Studies, 12*(2), 199–214.

Nelson, J. R. (1996). Designing schools to meet the needs of students who exhibit disruptive behavior. *Journal of Emotional and Behavioral Disorders, 4,* 147–161.

Nelson, J. R., Benner, G., & Cheney, G. (2005). An investigation of the language skills of students with emotional disturbance served in public school settings. *Journal of Special Education, 39,* 97–105.

Nelson, M. (2004). Introduction to Part IV, Intervention and treatment research. In R. B. Rutherford, M. M. Quinn, & S. R. Mathur (Eds.), *Handbook of research in emotional and behavioral disorders* (pp. 321–326). New York: Guilford Press.

Newborg, J. (2004). *Battelle Developmental Inventory, Second Edition (BDI–2).* Itasca, IL: Riverside Publishing.

Newcomer, P. L. (2003). *Understanding and teaching emotionally disturbed children and adolescents.* Austin, TX: Pro-Ed.

Newell, K. M. (1997). Motor skills and mental retardation. In W. E. MacLean Jr. (Ed.), *Ellis' handbook of mental deficiency, psychological theory, and research* (3rd ed., pp. 275–308). Mahwah, NJ: Erlbaum.

Niles, W. J., & Marcellino, P. A. (2004). Needs based negotiation: A promising practice in school collaboration. *Teacher Education and Special Education, 27,* 419–432.

Noonan, M. J., & McCormick, L. (1993). *Early intervention in natural environments: Methods and procedures.* Pacific Grove, CA: Brooks/Cole.

Numminen, H., Service, E., & Ruoppila, I. (2002). Working memory, intelligence, and knowledge base in adult persons with intellectual disability. *Research in Developmental Disabilities, 23,* 105–118.

O

O'Keefe, M. (1998). Factors mediating the link between witnessing interparental violence and dating violence. *Journal of Family Violence, 13*(1), 39–57.

O'Keefe, M., & Lebovics, S. (2005). Adolescents from maritally violent homes. *The Prevention Researcher, 12*(1), 3–7.

O'Shaughnessy, T. E., Lane, K. L., Gresham, F. M., & Beebe-Frankenberger, M. E. (2002). Students with or at risk for leaning and emotional-behavioral difficulties: An integrated system of prevention and intervention. In K. L. Lane, F. M. Gresham, & T. E. O'Shaughnessy, *Interventions for children with or at risk for emotional and behavioral disorders.* Boston: Allyn & Bacon.

O'Shaughnessy, T. E., Lane, K. L., Gresham, F. M., & Beebe-Frankenberger, M. E. (2003). Children placed at risk for learning and behavioral difficulties: Implementing a school-wide system of early identification and prevention. *Remedial and Special Education, 24*(1), 27–35.

Office of Applied Studies. (2003). *Children living with substance-abusing or substance-dependent parents.* Rockville, MD: Substance Abuse and Mental Services Administration.

Office of Special Education and Rehabilitative Services. (2005). *Number of students ages 6 through 21 served under IDEA, Part B, in the U.S. and outlying areas, by disability category, educational environment and year: Fall 1996 through fall 2005.* Retrieved June 16, 2007, from www.ideadata.org/tables29th/ar_2-5.htm

Office of Special Education Programs. (2006). *Individuals with disabilities education act (IDEA) data.* Retreved April 17, 2006, from www.ideadata.org/index.html

Ohtake, Y. (2003). Increasing class membership of students with severe disabilities through contribution to classmates' learning. *Research & Practice for Persons with Severe Disabilities, 28,* 228–231.

Okolo, C. M., Bahr, C. M., & Reith, H. J. (1993). A retrospective view of computer-based instruction. *Journal of Special Education Technology, 12*(1), 1–27.

Olive, M. L., & McEvoy, M. A. (2004). Issues, trends, and challenges in early intervention. In A. M. Sorrels, H. J. Rieth, & P. T. Sindelar (Eds.), *Critical issues in special education: Access, diversity, and accountability* (pp. 92–105). Boston: Pearson/Allyn & Bacon.

Olmedo, R., & Kauffman, J. (2003). Sociocultural considerations in social skills training research with African American students with emotional or behavioral disorders. *Journal of Developmental and Physical Disabilities, 15,* 101–121.

Olson, J., & Platt, J. (2004). *Teaching children and adolescents with special needs* (4th ed.). Upper Saddle River, NJ: Pearson/Merrill/Prentice Hall.

Olszewski-Kubilius, P. (2002). A summary of research regarding early entrance to college. *Roeper Review, 24*(3), 152–157.

Olszewski-Kubilius, P. (2003). Special summer and Saturday programs for gifted students. In N. Colangelo & G. Davis (Eds.), *Handbook of gifted education* (pp. 219–228). Needham Heights, MA: Allyn & Bacon.

Ortiz, A. A. (1997). Learning disabilities occurring concomitantly with linguistic differences. *Journal of Learning Disabilities, 30*(3), 321–332.

Ostrosky, M. M., Jung, E. Y., Hemmeter, M. L., & Thomas, D. (2003). Helping children understand routines and classroom schedules. Retrieved June 10, 2006, from www.csefel.uiuc.edu/whatworks.html

Ostrosky, M. M., & Kaiser, A. P. (1991). Preschool classroom environments that promote communication. *Teaching Exceptional Children, 23,* 6–10.

Oswald, D. P., Coutinho, M. J., Best, A. I. M., & Nguyen, N. (2001). Impact of sociodemographic characteristics on the identification rates of minority students as having mental retardation. *Mental Retardation, 39,* 351–367.

Ota, K. R., & DuPaul, G. J. (2002). Task engagement and mathematics performance in children with attention deficit hyperactivity disorder: Effects of supplemental computer instruction. *School Psychology Quarterly, 17,* 242–257.

Owens, R. E. (2004). *Language disorders: A functional approach to assessment and intervention.* Boston: Allyn & Bacon.

Owens, R. E. (2005). *Language development: An introduction.* Boston: Allyn & Bacon.

Owens, R. E., & Robinson, L. A. (1997). Once upon a time: Use of children's literature in the preschool classroom. *Topics in Language Disorders, 17*(2), 19–48.

Owens-Johnson, L., & Hamill, L. B. (2002). Community-based instruction. In L. B. Hamill & C. Everington, *Teaching students with moderate to severe disabilities: An applied approach for inclusive environments.* Upper Saddle River, NJ: Merrill/Prentice Hall.

Ozonoff, S., & Rogers, S. (2003). From Kanner to the millennium: Scientific advances that have shaped clinical practice. In S. Ozonoff, S. Rogers, & R. Hendren (Eds.), *Autism spectrum disorders: A research review for practitioners* (pp. 3–33). Washington, DC: American Psychiatric Publishing.

P

Padden, C., & Humphries, T. (2005). *Inside Deaf culture.* Cambridge, MA: Harvard University Press.

Page, E., & Keith, T. (1996). The elephant in the classroom: Ability grouping and the gifted. In C. Benbow & D. Lubinski (Eds.), *Intellectual talent: Psychometric and social issues* (pp. 192–210). Baltimore: Johns Hopkins Press.

Palmer, B. C., Miles, J., Schierkolk, S., & Fallik, H. (2002). *Cooperative planning handbook for youth with developmental disabilities.* Denver, CO: Colorado State Department of Human Services. (ERIC Document Reproduction Service No. ED 477 396)

Parette, H. P. (1997). Assistive technology devices and services. *Education and Training in Mental and Developmental Disabilities, 32*(4), 267–280.

Parette, H. P. (1998). Cultural issues and family-centered assistive technology decision-making. In S. L. Judge & H. P. Parette (Eds.), *Assistive technology for young children with disabilities: A guide to providing family-centered services* (pp. 184–210). Cambridge, MA: Brookline.

Parette, H. P., & McMahan, G. A. (2002). What should we expect of assistive technology? Being sensitive to family goals. *Teaching Exceptional Children, 35*(1), 56–61.

Park, H. S., & Lian, M. G. J. (2001). Introduction to special series on culturally and linguistically diverse learners with severe disabilities. *Journal of the Association for Persons with Severe Handicaps, 26,* 135–137.

Park, J., Turnbull, A. P., & Park, H-S. (2001). Quality of partnerships in service provision for Korean American parents of children with disabilities: A qualitative inquiry. *Journal of the Association for Persons with Severe Handicaps, 26,* 158–170.

Parker, W. D. (2000). Healthy perfectionism in the gifted. *Journal of Secondary Gifted Education, 11*(4), 173–182.

Parker, W. D. (2002). Perfectionism and adjustment in gifted children. In G. L. Fleet & P. L. Hewitt, (Eds.), *Perfectionism: Theory, research, and treatment* (pp. 133–148). Washington, DC: American Psychological Association.

Parrish, M. (2004). Urban poverty and homelessness as hidden demographic variables relevant to academic achievement. In D. Booth & J. Stanley (Eds.), *In the eyes of the beholder: Critical issues for diversity in gifted education* (pp. 203–211). Waco, TX: Prufrock Press.

PASE v. Hannon, 506 F. Supp. 831 (N.D. Ill. 1980).

Patton, J. R., Cronin, M. E., Bassett, D. S., & Koppel, A. E. (1997). A life skills approach to mathematics instruction: Preparing students with learning disabilities for the real-life math demands of adulthood. *Journal of Learning Disabilities, 30*(2), 178–187.

Patton, J. R., Cronin, M. E., & Jairrels, V. (1997). Curricular implications of transition: Life skills as an integral part of transition education. *Remedial and Special Education, 18,* 294–306.

Paul, R. (2001). *Language disorders from infancy through adolescence: Assessment and intervention* (2nd ed.). St. Louis, MO: Mosby-Year Book.

Peck, C. A., Staub, D., Galluci, C., & Schwartz, I. (2004). Parent perception of the impacts of inclusion on their nondisabled child. *Research and Practice for Persons with Severe Disabilities, 29,* 135–143.

Pelham, W. E., Wheeler, T., & Chronis, A. (1998). Empirically supported psychosocial treatments for attention deficit hyperactivity disorder. *Journal of Clinical Child Psychology, 27*(2), 190–205.

Pellegrino, L. (2002). Cerebral palsy. In M. Batshaw (Ed.), *Children with disabilities* (5th ed., pp. 443–466). Baltimore, MD: Paul H. Brookes.

Pennsylvania Association for Retarded Citizens (PARC) v. Commonwealth of Pennsylvania, 334 F. Supp. 1257 (E.D. Pa. 1971), 343 F. Supp. 279 (E.D. pa 1972).

Perry, A. (1991). Rett syndrome: A comprehensive review of the literature. *American Journal on Mental Retardation, 96,* 275–290.

Petot, J. (2000). Interest and limitations of projective techniques in the assessment of personality disorders. *European Psychiatry, 15,* 11–14.

Pfeiffer, S., & Stocking, V. B. (2000). Vulnerabilities of academically gifted students. *Special Services in the Schools, 16*(1-2), 83–93.

Pfiffner, L. J., Barkley, R. A., & DuPaul, G. J. (2006). Treatment of AD/HD in school settings. In R. A. Barkley, *Attention-deficit hyperactivity disorder: A handbook for diagnosis and treatment* (3rd ed., pp. 547–569). New York: Guilford Press.

Phillips, B., & Halle, J. (2004). The effects of a teacher-training intervention on student interns' use of naturalistic language teaching strategies. *Teacher Education and Special Education, 27*(2), 81–96.

Phillips, E. (1967). Problems in educating emotionally disturbed children. In N. Haring & E. Phillips (Eds.), *Methods in special education* (pp. 137–158). New York: McGraw-Hill.

Pierangelo, R., & Guiliani, G. A. (2004). *Transition services in special education. A practical approach.* Boston: Pearson/Allyn & Bacon.

Pitman, P., & Huefner, D. S. (2001). Will the courts go bi-bi? IDEA 1997, the courts, and deaf education. *Exceptional Children, 67*(2), 187–198.

Plomin, R., & Price, T. S. (2003). The relationship between genetics and intelligence. In N. Colangelo & G. Davis (Eds.), *Handbook of gifted education* (pp. 113–123). Needham Heights, MA: Allyn & Bacon.

Plotts, C., &Webber, J. (2001-2002). The role of developmental histories in the screening and diagnosis of autism spectrum disorders. *Assessment for Effective Intervention, 27,* 19–26.

Polleux, F., & Lauder, J. (2004). Toward a developmental neurobiology of autism. *Mental Retardation and Developmental Disabilities Research Reviews, 10,* 303–317.

Polloway, E. A., Patton, J. R., & Serna, L. (2005). *Strategies for teaching learners with special needs* (8th ed.). Upper Saddle River, NJ: Merrill/Prentice Hall.

Polloway, E. A., Smith, T. E. C., & Miller, L. (2004). *Language instruction for students with disabilities* (3rd ed.). Denver, CO: Love.

Poon-McBrayer, K. F., & Garcia, S. B. (2000). Profiles of Asian American students with LD at initial referral, assessment, and placement in special education. *Journal of Learning Disabilities, 33*(1), 61–71.

Popkin, J., & Skinner, C. H. (2003). Enhancing academic performance in a classroom serving students with serious emotional disturbance: Interdependent group contingencies with randomly selected components. *School Psychology Review, 31*(2), 282.

Post, M., Storey, K., & Karabin, M. (2002). Supporting students and adults in work and community environments. *Teaching Exceptional Children, 34*(3), 60–65.

Poston, D., Turnbull, A., Park, J., Mannan, H., Marquis, J., & Wang, M. (2003). Family quality of life: A qualitative inquiry. *Mental Retardation, 41,* 313–328.

Powell, T., & Siegle, S. (2000, Spring). Teacher bias in identifying gifted and talented students. *The National Research Center on the Gifted and Talented.* Fifth article.

Power, D., & Leigh, G. R. (2003). Curriculum: Cultural and communicative contexts. In M. Marschark & P. E. Spencer (Eds.), *Oxford handbook of deaf studies, language and education* (pp. 38–51). New York: Oxford University Press.

Powers, K. M., Gil-Kashiwabara, E., Geenen, S. J., Powers, L. E., Balandran, J., & Palmer, C. (2005). Mandates and effective transition planning practices reflected in IEPs. *Career Development for Exceptional Individuals, 28,* 47–59.

Prater, M. A. (2003). She will succeed! Strategies for success in inclusive classrooms. *Teaching Exceptional Children, 35*(5), 58–64.

Premack, D. (1959). Toward empirical behavior laws: 1. Positive reinforcement. *Psychological Review, 66*(4), 219–233.

Pressley, M., Woloshyn, V. E., Burkell, J., Cariglia-Bull, T., Lysynchuk, L., McGoldrick, J. A., Schneider, B., Snyder, B., & Symons, S. (1995). *Cognitive strategy instruction that really improves children's academic performance* (2nd ed.). Cambridge, MA: Brookline Books.

Prickett, J. G., & Welch, T. R. (1998). Educating students who are deafblind. In S. Z. Sacks & R. K. Silberman (Eds.), *Educating students who have visual impairments with other disabilities* (pp. 139–159). Baltimore: Paul H. Brookes.

Prizant, B. M., & Wetherby, A. M. (1998). Understanding the continuum of discrete-trial traditional behavioral to social-pragmatic developmental approaches in communication enhancement for young children with autism/PDD. *Seminars in Speech and Language, 19*(4), 329–352.

The Psychological Corporation. (2001). *Wechsler Individual Achievement Test–II.* San Antonio, TX: Author.

Pugach, M. C., & Johnson, L. J. (1995). *Collaborative practitioners. Collaborative schools.* Denver, CO: Love.

Pyryt, M. C. (2003). Technology and the gifted. In N. Colangelo & G. Davis (Eds.), *Handbook of gifted education* (pp. 582–590). Needham Heights, MA: Allyn & Bacon.

Q

Qin, Z., Johnson, D. W., & Johnson, R. T. (1995). Cooperative versus competitive efforts and problem solving. *Review of Educational Research, 65,* 129–143.

Quay, H., & Peterson, D. (1996). *Revised Behavior Problem Checklist, PAR Edition: Professional manual.* Odessa, FL: Psychological Assessment Resources.

Quinn, M. M., Rutherford, R. B., Leone, P. E., Osher, D. M., & Poirier, J. M. (2005). Youth with disabilities in juvenile corrections: A national survey. *Exceptional Children, 71*(3), 339–345.

R

Raising a reader. Retrieved July 17, 2006, from www.pcf.org/raising_reader.

Ramey, C. T., & Ramey, S. L. (1992). Effective early intervention. *Mental Retardation, 30,* 337–345.

Ramey, E. T., & Campbell, F. A. (1984). Preventative education for high-risk children: Cognitive consequences of Carolina Abecedarian Project. *American Journal of Mental Deficiency, 88,* 515–523.

Ramsey, C. (2004). What does culture have to do with the education of students who are deaf or hard of hearing? In B. J. Brueggemann (Ed.), *Literacy and deaf people: Cultural and contextual perspectives* (pp. 47–58). Washington, DC: Gallaudet University Press.

Raphael, J. (2005). Teens having babies: The unexplored role of domestic violence. *The Prevention Researcher, 12*(1), 15–71.

Raskin, M., & Bryant, B. R. (2002). *Functional evaluation for assistive technology.* Austin, TX. Psycho-Educational Services.

Reichard, A., Sacco, T. M., & Turnbull III, H. R. (2004). Access to health care for individuals with developmental disabilities from minority backgrounds. *Mental Retardation, 42,* 459–470.

Reid, D. K. (1988). *Teaching the learning disabled: A cognitive developmental approach.* Boston: Allyn & Bacon.

Reid, J., & Eddy, J. M. (1997). The prevention of antisocial behavior: Some considerations in the search for effective interventions. *Handbook of Antisocial Behavior,* 343–356.

Reid, R. (1999). Attention deficit hyperactivity disorder: Effective methods for the classroom. *Focus on Exceptional Children, 32*(4), 1–20.

Reid, R., Trout, A. L., & Schartz, M.. (2005). Self-regulation interventions for children with attention deficit/hyperactivity disorder. *Exceptional Children, 71*(4), 361–377.

Reis, S. M. (2002). Gifted females in elementary and secondary school. In M. Neihart, S. Reis, N. Robinson, & S. Moon (Eds.), *The social and emotional development of gifted children* (pp. 125–136). Waco, TX: Prufrock Press.

Reis, S. M., & McCoach, D. B. (2002). Underachievement in gifted and talented students with special needs. *Exceptionality, 10*(2), 113–125.

Reis, S. M., & Renzulli, J. (2004). Current research on the social and emotional development of gifted and talented students: Good news and future possibilities. *Psychology in the Schools, 41,* 119–130.

Renaissance Group. (1999). *Teacher competencies.* Retrieved May 23, 2007, from www.uni.edu/coe/inclusion/standards/competencies.html

Renzulli, J. (1977). *The enrichment triad model: A guide for developing defensible programs for the gifted and talented.* Wethersfield, CT: Creative Learning Press.

Renzulli, J. S. (2003). Conception of giftedness and its relationship to the development of social capital. In N. Colangelo & G. Davis (Eds.), *Handbook of gifted education* (3rd ed., pp. 75–87). Needham Heights, MA: Allyn & Bacon.

Renzulli, J. S., & Reis, S. M. (2002). What is schoolwide enrichment? How gifted programs relate to total school improvement. *Gifted Child Today, 25*(4), 18–29.

Renzulli, J. S., & Reis, S. M. (2003). The schoolwide enrichment model: Developing creative and productive giftedness. In N. Colangelo & G. Davis (Eds.), *Handbook of gifted education* (pp. 184–203). Needham Heights, MA: Allyn & Bacon.

Renzulli, J. S., Smith, L., White, A., Callahan, C., & Hartman, R. (2001). *Scales for Rating the Behavioral Characteristics of Superior Students (Revised Edition).* Mansfield Center, CT: Creative Learning Press.

Reschly, D. (1978). WISC-R factor structure among Anglos, Blacks, Chicanos, and Native American Papagos. *Journal of Consulsting and Clinical Psychlogy, 46,* 417–422.

Reschly, D. (1979). Nonbiased assessment. In G. Phye & D. Reschly (Eds.), *School psychology: Perspective and issues.* New York: Academic Press.

Resnick, R. (2000). *The hidden disorder.* Washington, DC: American Psychological Association.

Reynolds, C., & Kamphaus, R. (2004). *Behavior Assessment System for Children–2.* Circle Pines, MN: American Guidance Service.

Richards, T. (2001). Functional magnetic resonance imaging and spectroscopic imaging of the brain: Appication of fMRI and fMRS to reading disabilities and education. *Learning Disability Quarterly, 24,* 189–203.

Richards, S. B., & Russell, S. C. (2003). Administration of programs and services. In H. R. Weaver, M. F. Landers, T. M. Stephens, & E. A. Joseph (Eds.), *Administering special education programs. A practical guide.* Westport, CT: Praeger.

Richert, E. S. (1997). Excellence with equity in identification and programming. In N. Colangelo & G. Davis (Eds.), *Handbook of gifted education* (2nd ed., pp. 75–88). Needham Heights, MA: Allyn & Bacon.

Rieger, A. (2004). Explorations of the functions of humor and other types of fun among families of children with disabilities. *Research and Practice for Persons with Severe Disabilities, 29,* 194–209.

Rimland, B. (1964). *Infantile autism: The syndrome and its implication for a neural theory of behavior.* Englewood Cliffs, NJ: Prentice-Hall.

Rimm, S. (1990). *Gifted kids have feelings too: And other not-so-fictitious stories for and about teenagers.* Watertown, WI: Apple.

Rimm-Kaufman, S. E., Pianta, R., & Cox, M. J. (2000). Teachers' judgments of problems in the transition to kindergarten. *Early Childhood Research Quarterly, 15,* 147–166.

Risdal, D., & Singer, G. H. S. (2004). Marital adjustment in parents of children with disabilities: A historical review and meta-analysis. *Research and Practice for Persons with Severe Disabilities, 29,* 95–103.

Rivera, D. (1997). Mathematics education and students with learning disabilities: Introduction of special series. *Journal of Learning Disabilities, 30*(1), 2–19, 68.

Robbins, A. M. (2003). Communication intervention for infants and toddlers with cochlear implants. *Topics in Language Disorders, 23*(1), 16–23.

Robbins, R. (2002). The use of traditional American Indian stories and symbols in counseling adolescents with behavioral problems. *Beyond Behavior, 12*(1), 12–19.

Robin, A. L. (2006). Training families with AD/HD adolescents. In R. A. Barkley, *Attention-deficit hyperactivity disorder: A handbook for diagnosis and treatment* (3rd ed., pp. 499–546). New York: Guilford Press.

Robinson, A. (2003). Cooperative learning and high ability students. In N. Colangelo & G. Davis (Eds.), *Handbook of gifted education* (pp. 282–292). Needham Heights, MA: Allyn & Bacon.

Robinson, N. M. (1996). Acceleration as an option for the highly gifted adolescent. In C. P. Benbow & D. J. Lubinski (Eds.), *Intellectual talent: Psychometric and social issues* (pp. 169–178). Baltimore, MD: Johns Hopkins University Press.

Robinson, T. R., Smith, S. W., & Miller, M. D. (2002). Effect of a cognitive-behavioral intervention on responses to anger by middle school students with chronic behavior problems. *Behavioral Disorders, 27*(3), 256–271.

Rogers, E. L., & Rogers, D. C. (2001). Students with E/BD transition to college: Make a plan. *Beyond Behavior, 10*(1), 42–45.

Rogers, K. B. (2002). Effects of acceleration on gifted learners. In M. Neihart & S. Reis (Eds.), *The social and emotional development of gifted children: What do we know?* (pp. 3–12). Waco, TX: Prufrock Press.

Rogers, M. T., & Silverman, L. K. (1998). *Recognizing giftedness in young children.* Denver, CO: Gifted Development Center. (ERIC Document Reproduction Service No. 428471)

Roid, G. (2003). *Stanford-Binet Intelligence Scales–Fifth Edition.* Chicago, IL: Riverside.

Romano, E., Tremblay, R., Vitaro, F., Zoccolillo, M., & Pagani, L. (2001). Prevalence of psychiatric diagnoses and the role of perceived impairment: Findings from an adolescent community sample. *Journal of Child Psychology and Psychiatry, 42,* 451–461.

Rorschach, H. (1932). *Psychodiagnostik: Methodik und ergebrisse etines wahrnehmungsdiagnostischen experiments* (2nd ed.). Bern, Switzerland: Huber.

Roseberry-McKibbin, C. (2007). *Language disorders in children: A multicultural and case perspective.* Boston: Allyn & Bacon.

Rosen, S. (2005). *Academics are not enough: Incorporating life skills in the curriculum for children and youth with blindness or low vision.* Retrieved May 13, 2005, from www.ed.arizona.edu/dvi/Postion%20Papers/academics.htm

Rosenshine, R., & Stevens, R. (1986). Teaching functions. In M. Wittrock (Ed.), *Handbook of research on teaching* (3rd ed., pp. 376–391). New York: Macmillan.

Roskos, K., & Neuman, S. B. (2002). Environment and its influences for early literacy teaching and learning. In S. B. Neuman & D. K. Dickinson (Eds.), *Handbook of early literacy research* (pp. 281–294). New York: Guildford Press.

Ross, D. M., & Ross, S. A. (1979). Cognitive training for the EMR child: Language skills prerequisite to relevant-irrelevant discrimination tasks. *Mental Retardation, 17,* 3–7.

Royal Association for Deaf People. (2005). *Communicating with deaf people.* Retrieved May 25, 2007, from www.royaldeaf.org.uk/page.php?id=100258

Rubin, E., & Lennon, L. (2004). Challenges in social communication in Asperger syndrome and high-functioning autism. *Topics in Language Disorders, 24,* 271–285.

Rubin, R., & Balow, B. (1978). Prevalence of teacher identified behavior problems: A longitudinal study. *Exceptional Children, 45,* 102–111.

Ruble, L., & Gallagher, T. (2004). *Autism spectrum disorders: Primer for parents and educators.* Bethesda, MD: National Association of School Psychologists.

Rueda, R., & Monzo, L. D. (2002). Apprenticeship for teaching: Professional development issues surrounding the collaborative relationship between teachers and paraeducators. *Teaching and Teacher Education, 18,* 503–521.

Runion, H. (1980). Hypoglycemia—Fact or fiction. In W. Cruickshank (Ed.), *Approaches to learning: The best of ACLD* (pp. 111–122). Syracuse, NY: Syracuse University Press.

Rutter, M. (2006). *Genes and behavior: Nature-nurture interplay explained.* Malden, MA: Blackwell.

Rutter, M., & Silberg, J. (2002). Gene-environment interplay in relation to emotional and behavioral disturbance. *Annual Review of Psychology, 53,* 463–490.

Ryan, A. L., Halsey, H. N., & Matthews, W. J. (2003). Using functional assessment to promote desirable student behavior in schools. *Teaching Exceptional Children, 35*(5), 8–15.

Ryndak, D. L., & Alper, S. (2003). *Curriculum and instruction for students with severe disabilities in inclusive settings.* Boston: Allyn & Bacon.

Ryndak, D. L., & Pullen, P. C. (2003). Education teams and collaborative teamwork in inclusive settings. In D. L. Ryndak & S. Alper (Eds.), *Curriculum and instruction for students with significant disabilities in inclusive settings* (2nd ed.). Boston: Allyn & Bacon.

S

Sabornie, E. J., Evans, C., & Cullihan, D. (2006). Comparing characteristics of high-incidence disability groups: A descriptive review. *Remedial and Special Education, 27*(2), 95–104.

Sachs-Ericsson, N., & Ciarlo, J. A. (2000). Gender, social roles, and mental health: An epidemiological perspective. *Sex Roles, 43,* 605–628.

Sacks, S. Z. (1998). Educating students who have blindness or low vision with other disabilities: An overview. In S. Z. Sacks & R. K. Silberman (Eds.), *Educating students with visual impairments and other disabilities.* Baltimore, MD: Paul H. Brookes.

Sacks, S. Z., & Silberman, R. K. (2005). Social skills. In M. C. Holbrook & A. J. Koenig (Eds.), *Foundation of education: Volume II. Instructional strategies for teaching children and youths with visual impairments* (2nd ed., chap. 17). Retrieved February 12, 2007, from www.afb.org/foe/book.asp?ch=v2ch17

Sacramento City Unified School District v. Rachel H., 14 F.3D 1398 (Ninth Court, 1994).

Saddler, B., & Graham, S. (2005). The effects of peer-assisted sentence combining instruction on the writing of more and less skilled young writers. *Journal of Educational Psychology, 97*(1), 43–54.

Sadker, D., Sadker, M., & Zittleman, K. (2008). *Teachers, schools, and society* (8th ed.). Boston: McGraw-Hill Higher Education.

Saenz, T. I., & Huer, M. B. (2003). Testing strategies involving least biased language assessment of bilingual children. *Communication Disorders Quarterly, 24*(4), 184–193.

Safran, J. S. (2002). Supporting students with Asperger's syndrome in general education. *Teaching Exceptional Children, 34*(5), 60–66.

Safran, S. P., Safran, J. S., & Ellis, K. (2003). Intervention ABCs for children with Asperger syndrome. *Topics in Language Disorders, 23*(2), 154–165.

Salend, S. J. (2005). *Creating inclusive classrooms: Effective and reflective practices for all students* (5th ed.). Upper Saddle River, NJ: Merrill/Prentice Hall.

Salend, S. J. (2008). *Creating inclusive classrooms: Effective and reflective practices* (6th ed.). Upper Saddle River, NJ: Merrill/Prentice Hall.

Salend, S. J., & Taylor, L. (2002). Cultural perspectives: Missing pieces in the functional assessment process. *Intervention in School and Clinic, 38*(2), 104–112.

Salvia, J., Ysseldyke, J., & Bolt, S. (2007). *Assessment in special and remedial education* (10th ed.). Boston: Houghton-Mifflin.

Sander, E. K. (1972), When are speech sounds learned? *Journal of Speech and Hearing Disorders, 37,* 55–63.

Sanjuan, J., Tolosa, A., Gonzalez, J., Aguilar, E., Perez-Tur, J., Najera, C., Molto, D., & de Frutos, R. (2006). Association between FOXP2 polymorphisms and schizophrenia with auditory hallucinations. *Psychiatric Genetics, 16,* 67–72.

Sankar-Deleeuw, N. (2002). Gifted preschoolers: Parent and teacher views on identification, early admission, and programming. *Roeper Review, 24*(3), 172–177.

Santos, R. M., & Ostrosky, M. M. (2003) *Understanding the impact of language differences on classroom behavior.* Retrieved June 10, 2006, from www.csefel.uiuc.edu/whatworks.html

Santrock, J. W. (2001). *Educational psychology.* New York: McGraw-Hill.

Santrock, J. W. (2008). *Educational psychology* (3rd ed.). Boston: McGraw-Hill.

Sawa, A., & Kamiya, A. (2003). Elucidating the pathogenesis of schizophrenia: DISC-I gene may predispose to neurodevelopmental changes underlying schizophrenia. *BMJ: British Medical Journal, 327*(7416), 632–633.

Scarborough, A. A., Spiker, D., Mallik, S., Hebbeler, K. M., Bailey, D. B., & Simeonsson, R. J. (2004). A national look at children and families entering early intervention. *Exceptional Children, 70*(4), 469–483.

Schacter, S. (2004). *What causes epilepsy?* Retrieved February 10, 2006, from www.epilepsy.com/101/ep101_cause.html

Scheerenberger, R. (1983). *A history of mental retardation.* Baltimore: Paul H. Brookes.

Scherer, M. J. (2004). *Connecting to learn. Educational and assistive technology for people with disabilities.* Washington, DC: American Psychological Association.

Schick, B. (2004). How might learning through an educational interpreter influence cognitive development? In E. A. Winston (Ed.), *Educational interpreting. How it can succeed* (pp. 73–87). Washington, DC: Gallaudet University Press.

Schlichter, C. (1997). Talents unlimited model in programs for gifted students. In N. Colangelo & G. Davis (Eds.), *Handbook of gifted education* (2nd ed., pp. 318–327). Boston: Allyn & Bacon.

Schloss, P. J., Smith, M. A., & Schloss, C. N. (2001). *Instructional methods for secondary students with learning and behavior problems* (3rd ed.). Boston: Allyn & Bacon.

Schopler, E., Reichler, R., & Renner, B. (1988) *The Childhood Autism Rating Scale.* Los Angeles: Western Psychological Services.

Schroedel, J. G., Watson, D., & Ashmore, D. H. (2003). A national research agenda for the postsecondary education of deaf and hard of hearing students: A road map for the future. *American Annals of the Deaf, 148*(2), 67–73.

Schumaker, J. B., & Deshler, D. D. (2003). Can students with LD become competent writers? *Learning Disability Quarterly, 26*(2), 129–140.

Schumaker, J. B., Deshler, D. D., Nolan, S., Clark, F. L., Alley, G. R., & Warner, M. M. (1981). *Error monitoring: A learning strategy for improving academic performance of LD adolescents.* Lawrence: University of Kansas, Institute for Research on Learning Disabilities.

Schwartz, I. S., Sandall, S. R., McBride, B. J., & Boulware, G. (2004). Project DATA (Developmentally Appropriate Treatment for Autism): An inclusive school-based approach to educating young children with autism. *Topics in Early Childhood Special Education, 24*(3), 156–168.

Schwartz, W. (1997). *Strategies for identifying the talents of diverse students.* (ERIC Document Reproduction Service No. ED410323)

Scott, J., Clark, C., & Brady, M. (2000). *Students with autism: Characteristics and instructional programming.* San Diego: Singular.

Scott, T. M., & Nelson, C. M. (1999). Universal school discipline strategies: Facilitating learning environments. *Effective School Practices, 17,* 54–64.

Scott, T. M., Payne, L. D., & Jolivette, K. (2003). Preventing predictable problem behaviors by using positive behavior support. *Beyond Behavior, 13*(1), 3–7.

Scruggs, T. E., & Mastropieri, M. A. (2000). Mnemonic interventions for students with behavior disorders: Memory of learning and behavior. *Beyond Behavior, 10*(1).

Seattle Committee for Children. (1992). *Second step: A violence prevention curriculum.* Seattle: Author. Retrieved from www.cfchildren.org/program_ss.shtml

Seigneuric, A., & Ehrlich, M. (2005). Contribution of working memory capacity to children's reading comprehension: A longitudinal investigation. *Reading and Writing, 18,* 617–656.

Seligman, M. (2000). *Conducting effective conferences with parents of children with disabilities.* New York: Guilford Press.

Semrud-Clikeman, M. (2001). *Traumatic brain injury in children and adolescents. Assessment and intervention.* New York: Guilford Press.

Sense and sensitivity. (2004). *Bottomlines, 2*(5), 1–2.

Serna, R. W., & Carlin, M. T. (2001). Guiding visual attention in individuals with mental retardation. In L. M. Glidden (Ed.), *International review of research in mental retardation* (Vol. 24, pp. 321–357). San Diego, CA: Academic Press.

Set the scene for social ease. (2004). *Bottomlines, 2*(2), 1–2.

Sexton, C. W. (2001). Effectiveness of the DISTAR Reading I Program in developing first graders' language skills. *Journal of Educational Research, 82,* 291–293.

Shackelford, J. (2006). *State and jurisdictional eligibility definitions for infants and toddlers with disabilities under IDEA (NECTAC Notes No. 21).* Chapel Hill: University of North Carolina, FPG Child Development Institute, National Early Childhood Technical Assistance Center.

Shalev, R., Manor, O., Kerem, B., Ayali, M., Bidici, N., Friedlander, Y., & Gross-Tsur, V. (2001). Developmental dyscalculia is a familial learning disability. *Journal of Learning Disabilities, 34,* 59–65.

Shapiro, J., & Valentine, V. (2006). I. King Jordan: Reflection on a changing culture. *National Public Radio.* Retrieved February 26, 2007, from www.npr.org/templates/story/story.php?storyId=5370327

Shattock, P. (2006). *Back to the future: An assessment of some of the unorthodox forms of biomedical intervention currently being applied to autism.* Paper presented at the Durham conference 1995 [updated December 2006]. Retrieved April 29, 2007, from http://osiris.sunderland.ac.uk/autism/dietinfo.html

Shaughnessy, A., & Sanger, D. (2005). Kindergarten teachers' perceptions of language and literacy development, speech-language pathologists, and language interventions. *Communication Disorders Quarterly, 26*(2), 67–84.

Shaywitz, S. (2003). *Overcoming dyslexia: The new and complete science-based program for reading problems at any level.* New York: Knopf.

Sheets, R. H., & Gay, G. (1996). Students' perceptions of disciplinary conflicts in ethnically diverse classrooms. *NASSAP Bulletin, 80*(580), 84–94.

Sheppard, S. (2001). Tips for teaching: Improving academic success for diverse-language learners. *Preventing School Failure, 45*(3), 132–135.

Shippen, M. E., Simpson, R. G., & Crites, S. A. (2003). A practical guide to functional behavioral assessment. *Teaching Exceptional Children, 35*(5), 36–44.

Shonkoff, J. P., & Phillips, D. A. (Eds.). (2000). *From neurons to neighborhoods: The science of early childhood development.* Washington, DC: National Academy Press.

Shutack, J. (2005). *Spina bifida occulta and open spina bifida: A patient's guide.* Retrieved February 21, 2006, from www.spineuniverse.com/displayarticle234.html?source=overture&key=b

Siegel, L. (2003). Basic cognitive processes and reading disabilities. In H. L. Swanson, K. Harris, & S. Graham (Eds.), *Handbook of learning disabilities*. New York: Guilford Press.

Siegle, D. (2001). Overcoming bias in gifted and talented referrals. *Gifted Education Communicator, 32*, 22–25.

Silliman, E. R., & Scott, C. M. (2006). Language impairment and reading disability: Connections and complexities [Introduction to the special issue]. *Learning Disabilities Research & Practice, 21*(1), 1–7.

Silverman, L., & Kearney, K. (1989). Parents of the extraordinary gifted. *Advanced Development, 1*, 41–56.

Simeonsson, R. J., Wax, T. M., & White, K. (2001). Assessment of children who are deaf or hard of hearing. In R. J. Simeonsson & S. L. Rosenthal (Eds.), *Psychological and developmental assessment: Children with disabilities and chronic conditions* (pp. 248–266). New York: Guilford Press.

Simon, M. (2001). Beyond broken promises: Reflections on eliminating barriers to the success of minority youth with disabilities. *Journal of the Association for Persons with Severe Handicaps, 26*, 200–203.

Simon, M. (2006). School psychologists and emotional and behavior disorders: Definitions, perspectives and assessment practices. *Dissertation Abstracts International, 66*(5-A).

Simons, J. (1998). Response to Chesley and Calaluce on inclusion. *Mental Retardation, 36*, 322–324.

Simonson, M., Smaldino, S., Albright, M., & Zvacek, S. (2006). *Teaching and learning at a distance. Foundations of distance education*. Upper Saddle River, NJ: Pearson.

Simopoulos, A. (1983). Nutrition. In C. Brown (Ed.), *Childhood learning disabilities and prenatal risk*. Skillman, NJ: Johnson & Johnson.

Simpson, A., Langone, J., & Ayres, K. M. (2004). Embedded video and computer based instruction to improve social skills for students with autism. *Education and Training in Developmental Disabilities, 39*(3), 240–252.

Simpson, R. L. (2005). Evidence-based practices and students with autism spectrum disorders. *Focus on Autism and Other Developmental Disabilities, 20*(3), 140–149.

Simpson, R. L., de Boer-Ott, S. R., & Smith-Myles, B. (2003). Inclusion of learners with autism spectrum disorders in general education settings. *Topics in Language Disorders, 23*(2), 116–133.

Simpson, R., Myles, B., Sasso, G., & Kamps, D. (1997). *Social skills for students with autism* (2nd ed.). (ERIC Document Reproduction Service No. ED 414 697)

Singh, D. K. (2001). *Are general educators prepared to teach students with physical disabilities?* Paper presented at the annual convention of the Council for Exceptional Children, Kansas City, MO. (ERIC Document Reproduction Service No. ED 455 635)

Sitlington, P. L., & Clark, G. M. (2004). *Transition education and services for students with disabilities* (4th ed.). Boston: Allyn & Bacon.

Sitlington, P. L., Clark, G. M., & Kolstoe, O. P. (2000). *Transition education and services for adolescents with disabilities* (3rd ed.). Boston: Allyn & Bacon.

Skinner, M. E. (1998). Promoting self-advocacy among college students with learning disabilities. *Intervention in School and Clinic, 33*(5), 278–283.

Slavin, R. (1995). *Cooperative learning* (2nd ed.). Needham Heights, MA: Allyn & Bacon.

Slavin, R., & Madden, N. (2000). Research on achievement outcomes of Success For All: A summary and response to critics. *Phi Delta Kappan, 82*, 38–40, 59–66.

Slenkovich, J. E. (1992). Can the language "social maladjustment" in the SED definition be ignored? *School Psychology Review, 21*, 21–22.

Smiley, L. R., & Goldstein, P. (1998). *Language delays and disorders: From research to practice*. San Diego: Singular.

Smith, A. (2001). A faceless bureaucrat ponders special education, disability, and white privilege. *Journal of the Association for Persons with Severe Handicaps, 26*, 180–188.

Smith, A., Geruschat, D., & Huebner, K. (2004). Policy to practice: Teachers and administrators' views on curricular access by students with low vision. *Journal of Visual Impairment and Blindness, 98*(10), 612–628.

Smith, B. H., Barkley, R. A., & Shapiro, C. J. (2006). Attention-deficit/hyperactivity disorder. In E. J. Mash & R. A. Barkley (Eds.), *Treatment of childhood disorders* (3rd ed). New York: Guilford Press.

Smith, B. J., & Fox, L. (2003). *Systems of service delivery: A synthesis of evidence relevant to young children at risk of or who have challenging behavior*. Tampa, FL: University of South Florida, Center for Evidence-Based Practice, Young Children with Challenging Behavior. Retrieved from www.challengingbehavior.org

Smith, C. R. (2004). *Learning disabilities: The interaction of students and their environments* (5th ed.). Boston: Allyn & Bacon.

Smith, D. D., & Luckasson, R. (1992). *Introduction to special education: Teaching in an age of challenge*. Needham Heights, MA: Allyn & Bacon.

Smith, J. D. (2003). Abandoning the myth of mental retardation. *Education and Training in Developmental Disabilities, 38*, 358–361.

Smith, J. D. (2006). Speaking of mild mental retardation: It's no box of chocolates, or is it? *Exceptionality, 14*(4), 191–204.

Smith, R. H., & Robin, N. H. (2002). Genetic testing for deafness—GJB2 and SLC26A4 as causes of deafness. *Journal of Communication Disorders, 35*, 367–377.

Smith, R. L., Collins, B. C., Schuster, J. W., & Kleinert, H. (1999). Teaching table cleaning skills to secondary students with moderate/severe disabilities: Facilitating observational learning during instructional downtime. *Education and Training in Mental Retardation and Developmental Disabilities, 34*, 342–353.

Smith, S. W., Siegel, E. M., O'Connor, A. M., & Thomas, S. B. (1994). Effects of cognitive-behavior training on angry behavior and aggression of three elementary-aged students. *Behavioral Disorders, 19,* 126–135.

Smith, V. M. (2003). "You have to learn who comes with the disability": Students' reflections on service learning experiences with peers labeled with disabilities. *Research and Practice for Persons with Severe Disabilities, 28,* 79–90.

Snell, M. E., & Brown, F. (2006). Designing and implementing instructional programs. In M. E. Snell & F. Brown (6th ed.), *Instruction of students with severe disabilities* (5th ed., pp. 111–169). Upper Saddle River, NJ: Merrill.

Snow, C. E., Burns, M. S., & Griffin, P. (Eds.). (1998). *Preventing reading difficulties in young children.* Washington, DC: National Academy Press.

Solanto, M., Abikoff, H., Sonuga-Barke, E., Schacar, R., Logan, G., Wigal, T., Hechtman, L., Hinshaw, S., & Turkel, E. (2001). The ecological validity of delay aversion and response inhibition as measures of impulsivity in AD/HD: A supplement to the NIMH multimodal treatment study of AD/HD. *Journal of Abnormal Psychology, 29,* 215–228.

Sonnier-York, C., & Stanford, P. (2002). Leaning to cooperate: A teacher's perspective. *Teaching Exceptional Children, 34*(6), 40–44.

Sousa, D. (1999). *How the brain works* [video]. Thousand Oaks, CA: Corwin Press.

Sparks, B., Friedman, S., Shaw, D., Aylward, E., Echelard, D., Artru, A., Maravilla, K., Giedd, J., Munson, J., Dawson, G., & Dager, S. (2002). Brain structural abnormalities in young children with autism spectrum disorder. *Neurology, 59,* 184–192.

Sparrow, S., Balla, D., & Cicchetti, D. (2005). *The Vineland Adaptive Behavior Scales–II.* Circle Pines, MN: American Guidance Service.

Spearman, C. (1927). *The abilities of man.* New York: Macmillan.

Spencer, T., Biederman, J., Wilens, T., & Faraone, S. (2002). Overview and neurobiology of attention-deficit/hyperactivity disorder. *Journal of Clinical Psychiatry, 63*(Supp. 12), 3–9.

SPeNSE Fact Sheet. (2001). *The role of paraprofessionals in special education.* (ERIC Document Reproduction Service No. ED 469 294)

Spiegel, H., & Bonwit, A. (2002). Acquired Immunodeficiency Syndrome. In M. Batshaw (Ed.), *Children with disabilities* (5th ed., pp. 123–140). Baltimore, MD: Paul H. Brookes.

Spreat, S., & Conroy, J. W. (2001). Community placement for persons with significant cognitive challenges: An outcome analysis. *Journal of the Association for Persons with Severe Handicaps, 26,* 106–113.

Spungin, S. J., & Ferrell, K. A. (2007). *The role and function of the teacher of students with visual impairments.* Retrieved July 4, 2007, from www.cecdvi.org/Postion%20Papers/RevisedRole&FunctionofTVI2006.doc

Sridhar, D., & Vaughn, S. (2000). Bibliotherapy for all: Enhancing reading comprehension, self-concept, and behavior. *Teaching Exceptional Children, 33,* 74–82.

Stainback, S., & Stainback, W. (1992). Schools as inclusive communities. In W. Stainback & S. Stainback (Eds.), *Controversial issues confronting special education.* Boston: Allyn & Bacon.

Stanovich, K. (1986). Matthew effects in reading: Some consequences of individual differences in the development of reading fluency. *Reading Research Quarterly, 21,* 360–407.

Starting points: Meeting the needs of our youngest children. (1994). New York: Carnegie Corporation. Retrieved from www.carnegie.org/starting_points/index.html

Stavinoha, P. (2005). Integration of neuropsychology in educational planning following traumatic brain injury. *Preventing School Failure, 49,* 11–16.

Stein, M., Carnine, D., & Dixon, R. (1998). Direct instruction: Integrating curriculum design and effective teaching practice. *Intervention in School and Clinic, 33,* 227–234.

Stemple, J. C., Glaze, L. E., & Gerderman, B. K. (1995). *Clinical vice pathology: Theory and management* (2nd ed.). San Diego, CA: Singular.

Stephens, K. R., & Karnes, F. A. (2000). State definitions for the gifted and talented revisited. *Exceptional Children, 66,* 219–238.

Stephens, R. D., & Arnette, J. L. (2000, February). From the courthouse to the schoolhouse: Making successful transitions. *Office of Juvenile Justice and Delinquency Prevention, Juvenile Justice Bulletin,* 1–15.

Stephens, T., Blackhurst, A., & Magliocca, L. (1982). *Teaching mainstreamed students.* New York: Wiley.

Sternberg, R., Grigorenko, E., & Kidd, K. (2006). Racing toward the finish line. *American Psychologist, 61,* 178–179.

Stetter, L. (1998). Matching technologies to modes of learning. *Gifted Child Today Magazine, 21*(2), 44–49.

Stevens, R. J., & Slavin, R. E. (1995). The cooperative elementary school: Effects on students' achievement, attitudes, and social relations. *American Educational Research Journal, 32,* 321–351.

Stewart, D. A., & Kluwin, T. N. (2001). *Teaching deaf and hard of hearing students. Content, strategies, and curriculum.* Boston: Allyn & Bacon.

Stinson, M. S. & Kluwin, T. N. (2003). Educational consequences of alternative school placements. In M. Marschark & P. Spencer (Eds.), *Oxford handbook of deaf studies, language, and education,* pp. 52–64. New York: Oxford University Press.

Stodden, R. A., & Whelley, T. (2004). Postsecondary education and persons with intellectual disabilities: An introduction. *Education and Training in Developmental Disabilities, 39*(1), 6–15.

Stokes, S. (2006). *Structured teaching: Strategies for supporting students with autism* (under a contract with CESA 7 and funded by a discretionary grant from the

Wisconsin Department of Public Instruction). Retrieved January 30, 2006, from www.cesa7.k12.wi.us/sped/autism/structure/str10.htm

Stone, W., Lee, E., Ashford, L., Brissie, J., Hepburn, S., Conrad, E., & Weiss, B. (1999). Can autism be diagnosed accurately in children under 3 years? *Journal of Child Psychology and Psychiatry, 40*, 219–226.

Stormont, M., Lewis, T. J., & Beckner, R. (2005). Positive behavior support systems: Applying key features in preschool settings. *Teaching Exceptional Children, 37*(6), 42–9.

Storey, K. (1997). Quality of life issues in social skills assessment of persons with disabilities. *Education and Training in Mental Retardation and Developmental Disabilities, 32*(3), 197–200.

Strain, P. S. (2001). Empirically-based social skill intervention. *Behavioral Disorders, 27*, 30–36.

Strain, P. S., & Hoyson, M. (2000). On the need for longitudinal, intensive social skill intervention: LEAP follow-up outcomes for children with autism as a case-in-point. *Topics in Early Childhood Special Education, 20*(2), 116–122.

Strategies to help students with autism. (2002). *CEC Today, 8*(8), 1, 5–6, 13, 15.

Stromer, R., Kimball, J. W., Kinney, E. M., & Taylor, B. A. (2006). Activity schedules, computer technology, and teaching children with autism spectrum disorders. *Focus on Autism and Other Developmental Disabilities, 21*(1), 14–24.

Stuart, S. (2004). Life is just chance: Voices of girls with EBD. *Beyond Behavior, 13*(2), 3–6.

Stump, C., & Bigge, J. L. (2005). Curricular options for individuals with physical or multiple disabilities. In S. J. Best, K. W. Heller, & J. L. Bigge, *Teaching individuals with physical or multiple disabilities* (5th ed., pp. 113–150). Upper Saddle River, NJ: Pearson Education.

Sturomski, N. (1997). Interventions for students with learning disabilities. *NICHCY News Digest, 25*. Retrieved from www.nichcy.org/pubs/newsdig/nd25txt.htm

Sugai, G., Horner, R., & Gresham, F. (2002). Behaviorally effective school environments. In M. Shinn, H. M. Walker, & G. Stoner (Eds.), *Interventions for academic and behavior problems II: Preventive and remedial approaches* (pp. 315–350). Bethesda, MD: National Association of School Psychologists.

Sullivan, A., & Strang, H. (2002/2003). Bibliotherapy in the classroom. *Childhood Education, 79*(2), 74–80.

Sunderland, L. C. (2004). Speech, language, and audiology services in schools. *Intervention in School and Clinic, 39*, 209–217.

Sundheim, S., & Voeller, K. (2004). Psychiatric implications of language disorders and learning disabilities: Risks and management. *Journal of Child Neurology, 19*, 814–826.

Sutherland, K. S., Copeland, S., & Wehby, J. H. (2001). Catch them while you can: Monitoring and increasing the use of effective praise. *Beyond Behavior, 10*(1), 46–49.

Sutherland, K. S., McMaster, K. L., & Marshall, J. (2003). Maximizing the benefits of cooperative learning for students with learning and/or behavior problems. *Beyond Behavior, 13*(1), 12–16.

Swanson, H. L. (1999a) Instructional components that predict treatment outcomes for students with learning disabilities: Support for a combined strategy and direct instruction model. *Learning Disabilities Research & Practice, 14*(3), 129–140.

Swanson, H. L. (1999b). What develops in working memory? A lifespan perspective. *Developmental Psychology, 35*, 986–1000.

Swanson, H. L., Cooney, J., & McNamara, J. (2004). Learning disabilities and memory. In B. Y. L. Wong (Ed.), *Learning about learning disabilities* (3rd ed.). San Diego: Elsevier Academic Press.

Swanson, H. L., & Hoskyn, M. (1998). Experimental intervention research on students with learning disabilities: A meta-analysis of treatment outcomes. *Review of Educational Research, 68*, 277–321.

Swanson, H. L., & Saez, L. (2003). Memory difficulties in children and adults with learning disabilities. In H. L. Swanson, K. Harris, & S. Graham (Eds.), *Handbook of learning disabilities* (pp. 182–198). New York: Guilford Press.

Swiatek, M. A. (2002). A decade of longitudinal research on academic acceleration through the study of mathematically precocious youth. *Roeper Review, 24*(3), 141–144.

Switlick, D. M. (1997). Curriculum modifications and adaptations. In D. F. Bradley, M. E. King-Sears, & D. M. Switlick (Eds.), *Teaching students in inclusive settings* (pp. 225–251). Needham Heights, MA: Allyn & Bacon.

Switzky, H. (1997). Individual differences in personality and motivational systems in persons with mental retardation. In W. E. MacLean Jr. (Ed.), *Ellis' handbook of mental deficiency, psychological theory, and research* (3rd ed., pp. 343–377). Mahwah, NJ: Erlbaum.

Synhorst, L., Buckley, J., Reid, R., Epstein, M., & Ryser, G. (2005). Cross informant agreement of the Behavioral and Emotional Rating Scale–2nd Edition (BERS–2) parent and youth rating scales. *Child and Family Behavior Therapy, 27*, 1–11.

T

TAG position paper on inclusion. (n.d.). Council for Exceptional Children. Retrieved June 11, 2003, from http://137.99.89.70:8001/siegle/TAG/inclusion.htm

Tager-Flusberg, H. (2001). A reexamination of the theory of mind hypothesis of autism. In J. Burack, T. Charmin, N. Yirmiya, & P. Zelazo (Eds.), *The development of autism: Perspectives from theory and research* (pp. 173–194). Mahwah, NJ: Erlbaum.

Tagler-Flusberg, H., & Sullivan, K. (1998). Early language development in children with mental retardation. In J. A. Burack, R. M. Hodapp, et al. (Eds.), *Handbook of mental retardation and development.* New York: Cambridge University Press.

Tamkin, A. (1960). A survey of educational disability in emotionally disturbed children. *Journal of Educational Research 53*, 313–315.

Tannen, D. (1994). *Gender and discourse.* New York: Oxford University Press.

Tarver, S. G. (1999). Direct instruction. *Current Practice Alerts*, Issue 2.

TASH. (n.d.). Retrieved June 20, 2005, from www.tash.org

Tashjian, M. D., & Schmidt-Davis, H. (2000). *Vocational rehabilitation experiences among individuals who achieved a supported employment outcome: A longitudinal study of the vocational rehabilitation service program.* (ERIC Document Reproduction Service No. ED479979)

Taylor, G. R. (2004). *Parenting skills & collaborative services for students with disabilities.* Lanham, MD: Scarecrow Education.

Taylor, P., Collins, B. C., Schuster, J. W., & Kleinert, H. (2002). Teaching laundry skills to high school students with disabilities: Generalization of targeted skills and nontargeted information. *Education and Training in Mental Retardation and Developmental Disabilities*, *37*(2), 172–183.

Taylor, R. (2009). *Assessment of exceptional students: Educational and psychological procedures* (8th ed.). Boston: Allyn & Bacon.

Taylor, R., Richards, S., & Brady, M. (2005). *Mental retardation: Historical perspectives, current practices, and future directions.* Boston: Pearson.

Taylor, R., Richards, S., Goldstein, P., & Schilit, J. (1997). Teacher perceptions of inclusive settings. *Teaching Exceptional Children*, *29*, 50–54.

Taylor, R., & Ziegler, E. (1987). A comparison of the first principle factor of the WISC–R across ethnic groups. *Educational and Psychological Measurement*, *47*, 691–694.

Taylor, R., Ziegler, E., & Partenio, I. (1985). Factor structure of the WISC–R across ethnic groups: An investigation of construct validity. *Diagnostique*, *11*, 9–13.

Taymans, J. M., & West, L. L. (2001). *Selecting a college for students with learning disabilities or attention deficit hyperactivity disorder (ADHD).* Arlington, VA: The ERIC Clearinghouse on Disabilities and Gifted Education. (ERIC Document Reproduction Service No. E620/ED461957)

Terman, L. (1925). *Genetic studies of genius.* Stanford, CA: Stanford University Press.

Terman, L., & Oden, M. (1947). *Genetic studies of genius: Vol. IV. The gifted child grows up.* Stanford, CA: Stanford University Press.

Terman, L., & Oden, M. (1959). *Genetic studies of genius. Vol. V. The gifted group at midlife.* Stanford, CA: Stanford University Press.

Thapar, A., van den Bree, M., Fowler, T., Langley, K., & Whittenger, N. (2006). Predictors of antisocial behaviour in children with attention deficit hyperactivity disorder. *European Child and Adolescent Psychiatry*, *15*,118–125.

Theodore, L., Akin-Little, A., & Little, S. (2004). Evaluating the differential treatment of emotional disturbance and social maladjustment. *Psychology in the Schools*, *41*, 879–886.

Thoma, C. A., Nathanson, R., Baker, S. R., & Tamura, R. (2002). Self-determination: What do special educators know and where do they learn it? *Remedial and Special Education*, *23*(4), 242–247.

Thomas, C. H., & Patton, J. R. (1986). Characteristics of mentally retarded persons. In J. R. Patton, J. S. Payne, & M. Bierne-Smith (Eds.), *Mental retardation* (2nd ed.). Columbus, OH: Charles E. Merrill.

Thompson, J. R., Bryant, B. R., Campbell, E. M., Craig, E. M., Hughes, C., Rotholz, D. A., Schalock, R. L., Silverman, W. P., Tassé, M. J., & Wehmeyer, M. L. (2007). *Supports Intensity Scale.* Washington, DC: American Association on Intellectual and Developmental Disabilities. Retrieved March 9, 2007, from www.siswebsite.org

Thurlow, M., & Ysseldyke, J. (1997). Large-scale assessment participation and reporting issues: Implications for local decisions. *Diagnostique*, 22, 225–236.

Thurlow, M. L., Ysseldyke, J. E., Wotruba, J. W., & Algozzine, B. (1993). Instruction in special education classrooms under varying student-teacher ratios. *The Elementary School Journal*, *93*(3), 305–320.

Timothy W. v. Rochester School District, 875 F. 2d 954 (1st Cir. 1988).

Tomlinson, C. (1995). *How to differentiate instruction in mixed-ability classrooms.* Alexandria, VA: Association for Supervision and Curriculum Development.

Tomlinson, C., Brighton, C., Hertberg, H., Callahan, C., Moon, T., Brimijoin, K., Conover, L., & Reynolds, T. (2003). Differentiating instruction in response to student readiness, interest, and learning profile in academically diverse classrooms: A review of the literature. *Journal for the Education of the Gifted*, *27*, 119–145.

Tomlinson, C., Kaplan, S., Renzulli, J., Purcell, J., Leppien, J., & Burns, D. (2002). *The parallel curriculum.* Thousand Oaks, CA: Corwin Press.

Tonelson, S., & Butler, C. J. (2000). At promise for success: Improving academic and behavioral outcomes for students with emotional and behavioral disorders. In L. M. Bullock & R. A. Gable (Eds.), *Positive academic and behavioral supports: Creating safe, effective, and nurturing schools for all students.* Highlights from the Forum on Positive Academic and Behavioral Supports. Reston, VA: CCBD.

Topping, K., & Ehly. S. (Eds). (1998). *Peer-assisted learning.* Mahwah, NJ: Erlbaum.

Torgesen, J. K. (1977). Memorization processes in reading-disabled children. *Journal of Educational Psychology*, *69*, 571–578.

Torgesen, J. K. (1999). Assessments and instruction for phonemic awareness and word recognition skills. In H. W. Catts & A. G. Kamhi (Eds.), *Language and reading disabilities* (pp. 128–153). Boston: Allyn & Bacon.

Torgesen, J. K. (2000). Individual differences in response to early interventions in reading: The lingering problem of treatment resisters. *Learning Disabilities Research & Practice 15*(1), 55–64.

Torgesen, J. K. (2004). Avoiding the devastating downward spiral: The evidence that early intervention prevents reading failure. *American Educator, Fall 2004*, 6–9, 12–13, 17–19, 45–47.

Torrance, E. P. (1977). *Creativity in the classroom.* Washington, DC: National Educational Association.

Torrance, E. P. (1981). Non-test ways of identifying the creatively gifted. In J. C. Gowan, J. Khatena, & E. P. Torrance (Eds.), *Creativity: Its educational implications* (2nd ed., pp. 165–170). Dubuque, IA: Kendall/Hunt.

Torrance, E. P. (2000a). *Torrance Tests of Creative Thinking: Manual for scoring and interpreting results. Verbal, Forms A and B.* Bensenville, IL: Scholastic Testing Service.

Torrance, E. P. (2000b). *Torrance Tests of Creative Thinking: Norms-technical manual. Figural, Forms A and B.* Bensenville, IL: Scholastic Testing Service.

Tournaki, N., & Criscitiello, E. (2003). Using peer tutoring as a successful part of behavior management. *Teaching Exceptional Children, 36*(2), 22–25.

Traci, M., & Koester, L. S. (2003). Parent-infant interactions: A transactional approach to understanding the development of deaf infants. In M. Marschark & P. E. Spencer (Eds.), *Oxford handbook of deaf studies, language and education* (pp. 190–202). New York: Oxford University Press.

Trautman, L. S. (2006). *Notes to the teacher: The child who stutters at school.* Stuttering Foundation of America. Retrieved March 2006 from www.stuttersfa.org

Treffert, D. (2005). *Savant syndrome: Frequently asked questions.* Retrieved September 14, 2005, from www.wisconsinmedicalsociety.org/savant/faq.cfm

Trent, J. W., Jr. (1994). *Inventing the feeble mind. A history of mental retardation in the United States.* Berkeley, CA: University of California Press.

Trivette, C. M. (2003). Influence of caregiver responsiveness on the development of young children with or at risk for developmental disabilities. *Bridges, 1*(3), 1–13.

Trivette, C. M. (2004). Influence of the home environment on the social-emotional development of young children. *Bridges, 2*(7), 1–16.

Trout, A., Nordness, P., Pierce, C., & Epstein, M. (2003). Research on the academic status of children with emotional and behavioral disorders: A review of the literature from 1961 to 2000. *Journal of Emotional and Behavioral Disorders, 11*, 198–210.

Tucker, J. (1985). Curriculum-based assessment: An introduction. *Exceptional Children, 52*, 199–204.

Tuttle, D. W., & Tuttle, N. R. (2004). *Self-esteem and adjusting with blindness: The process of responding to life's demands* (3rd ed.). Springfield, IL: Charles C Thomas.

Tuttle, D. W., & Tuttle, N. R. (2005). Psychosocial needs of children and youths. In M. C. Holbrook & A. J. Koenig (Eds.), *Foundations of education: Volume I. History and theory of teaching children and youth with visual impairments* (2nd ed., chap. 6). Retrieved February 1, 2007, from www.afb.org/foe/book.asp?ch=v1ch06

U

U.S. Department of Education. (1998). *To assure the free appropriate public education of all children with disabilities: Twentieth annual report to Congress on the implementation of the Individuals with Disabilities Education Act.* Washington, DC: U.S. Government Printing Office. (ERIC Document Reproduction Service No. ED 424 722)

U.S. Department of Education. (2002). *Twenty-fourth annual report to Congress on implementation of the Individuals with Disabilities Education Act.* Washington, DC: U.S. Government Printing Office.

U.S. Department of Education. (2003a). *Identifying and treating attention deficit hyperactivity disorder: A resource for school and home.* Retrieved July 12, 2004, from www.ed.gov/teachers/needs/speced/AD/HD/AD/HD-resource-pt1.doc

U.S. Department of Education. (2003b). *Twenty-fifth annual report to Congress on the implementation of the Individuals with Disabilities Education Act.* Washington, DC: U.S. Government Printing Office.

U.S. Department of Education. (2005). *Report of children with disabilities receiving special education under Part B of the Individuals with Disabilities Education Act.* Data file, Office of Special Education Programs, Data Analysis System. Retrieved June 8, 2006, from www.ideadata.org/tables

U.S. Department of Education. (2006). *Report of children with disabilities receiving special education under Part B of the IDEA.* Data file, Office of Special Education Programs, Data Analysis System. Retrieved May 17, 2007, from www.ideadata.org

U.S. Department of Health and Human Services. (2005). *Child maltreatment 2003: Reports from the states to the National Child Abuse and Neglect Data System.* Washington, DC: U.S. Government Printing Office, Administration on Children, Youth, and Families. Retrieved from www.acf.dhhs.gov/programs/cb/publications/cm03/

Uberti, H. Z., Scruggs, T. E., & Mastropieri, M. A. (2003). Keywords make the difference! Mnemonic instruction in inclusive classrooms. *Teaching Exceptional Children, 35*(3), 56–61.

Udvari-Solner, A., & Thousand, J. (1996). Creating a responsive curriculum for inclusive schools. *Remedial and Special Education, 17*(3), 182–192.

Ullmann, R., Sleator, E., & Sprague, R. (1991). *ADD-H Comprehensive Teacher's Rating Scale–2.* Los Angeles: Western Psychological Services.

Unnever, J., & Cornell, D. (2003). Bullying, self-control, and AD/HD. *Journal of Interpersonal Violence, 18*, 129–148.

V

Van Riper, C., & Erickson, R. (1996). *Speech correction: An introduction to speech pathology and audiology* (9th ed.). Needham Heights, MA: Allyn & Bacon.

Vandercook, T., York, J., & Forest, M. (1989). The McGill action planning system (MAPS): A strategy for building the vision. *Journal of the Association for Persons with Severe Handicaps, 14*, 205–215.

VanDerHeyden, A., Witt, J., & Barnett, D. (2005). The emergence and possible future of response to intervention. *Journal of Psychoeducational Assessment, 23*, 339–361.

VanTassel-Baska, J. (2003). Content-based curriculum for high-ability learners: An introduction. In J. VanTassel-Baska & C. Little (Eds.), *Content-based curriculum for high-ability learners* (pp. 1–23). Waco, TX: Prufrock Press.

VanTassel-Baska, J. (2006). *Basic educational options for gifted students in schools.* Retrieved September 23, 2006, from www.geniusdenied.com/Articles/Record.aspx?NavID=13_0&rid=12845

VanTassel-Baska, J., Johnson, D., & Avery, L. (2002). Using performance tasks in the identification of economically disadvantaged and minority gifted learners: Findings from Project STAR. *Gifted Child Quarterly, 46*, 110–123.

Vaughn, S., & Fuchs, L. (2003). Redefining learning disabilities as inadequate response to instruction: The promise and potential problems. *Learning Disabilities Research and Practice, 18*, 137–146.

Vaughn, S., Gersten, R., & Chard, D. J. (2000). The underlying message in LD intervention research: Findings from research syntheses. *Exceptional Children, 67*, 99–114.

Vaughn, S., Hughes, M. T., Moody, S. W., & Elbaum, B. (2001). Instructional grouping for reading for students with LD: Implications for practice. *Intervention in School and Clinic, 36*(3), 131–137.

Vaughn, S., Kim, A. H., Sloan, C. V. M., Hughes, M. T., Elbaum, B., & Sridhar, D. (2003). Social skills intervention for young children with disabilities: A synthesis of group design studies. *Remedial and Special Education, 24*(1), 2–15.

Vaughn, S., Linan-Thompson, S., & Hickman, P. (2003). Response to intervention as a means of identifying students with reading/learning disabilities. *Exceptional Children, 69*, 391–409.

Vaughn, S., Moody, S. & Schumm, J. S. (1998). Broken promises: Reading instruction in the resource room. *Exceptional Children, 64*(2), 211–226.

Vaughn, S., Schumm. J. S., Klingner, J. K., & Saumell, L. (1995). Students' views of instructional practices: Implications for inclusion. *Learning Disability Quarterly, 18*(3), 236–248.

Veltman, M., Thompson, R., Craig, E., Dennis, N., Roberts, S., Moore, V., Brown, J., & Bolton, P. (2004). A paternally inherited duplication in the Prader-Willi/Angelman syndrome critical region: A case and family study. *Journal of Neuropsychiatry and Clinical Neurosciences, 16*, 199–213.

Viadero, D. (March 25, 2005). Math emerges as big hurdle for teenagers. *Education Week, 24*(28), 1, 16.

Vialle, W., Ashton, T., Carlon, G., & Rankin, F. (2001). Acceleration: A coat of many colours. *Roeper Review, 24*(1), 14–20.

Vile Junod, R., DuPaul, G., Jitendra, A., Volpe, R., & Cleary, K. (2006). Classroom observations of students with and without ADHD: Differences across types of engagement. *Journal of School Psychology, 44*, 87–104.

Villa, R. A., Thousand, J. S., & Nevin, A. I. (2004). *A guide to co-teaching. Practial tips for facilitating student learning.* Thousand Oaks, CA: Corwin Press.

Visco v. School District of Pittsburgh, 684 F. Supp. 1310 (1988).

Volkmar, F., Lord, C., Bailey, A., Schultz, R., & Klin, A. (2004). Autism and pervasive developmental disorders. *Journal of Child Psychology and Psychiatry, 45*, 135–170.

von Hahn, L. (2003). Traumatic brain injury: Medical considerations and educational implications. *Exceptional Parent, 33*, 40–42.

W

Wadsworth, D. E., & Knight, D. (1999). Preparing the inclusion classroom for students with special physical and health needs. *Intervention in School and Clinic, 34*, 170–175.

Wadsworth, S., Olson, R., Pennington, B., & DeFries, J. (2000). Differential genetic etiology of reading disability as a function of IQ. *Journal of Learning Disabilities, 33*, 192–199.

Wagner, M., Newman, L., Cameto, R., & Levine, P. (2005). *National longitudinal study 2. Changes over time in the early postschool outcomes of youth with disabilities.* Prepared for the Office of Special Education Programs, U.S. Department of Education. Menlo Park, CA: SRI International.

Wakefield, A., Murch, S., Anthony, A., Linnell, D., Casson, D., Malik, M., Berelowitz, M., Dhillon, A., Thomson, M., Harvey, P., Valentine, A., Davies, S., & Walker-Smith, J. (1998). Ileal-lymphoid-nodular hydroplasia, non-specific colitis, and pervasive developmental disorder in children. *The Lancet, 351*, 637–641.

Waldman, I., & Gizer, I. (2006). The genetics of attention deficit hyperactivity disorder. *Clinical Psychology Review, 26*, 396–342.

Walker, H., & Sprague, J. (1999). Longitudinal research and functional behavioral assessment issues. *Behavioral Disorders, 24*, 331–334.

Walker, H. M., Ramsey, E., & Gresham, F. M. (2003-2004a). Heading off disruptive behavior. *American Educator, Winter*, 6–21, 45–46.

Walker, H. M., Ramsey, E., & Gresham, F. M. (2003-2004b). How early intervention can reduce defiant behavior—and win back teaching time. *American Educator, Winter*, 6–15, 18–21, 45–46.

Walker, H. M., Ramsey, E., & Gresham, F. M. (2004). *Antisocial behavior in school: Evidence-based practices* (2nd ed.). Belmont, CA: Wadsworth/Thomson Learning.

Walker, H. M., & Severson, H. H. (1990). *Systematic screening for behavior disorders.* Longmont, CO: Sopris West.

Walker, H. M., & Severson, H. H. (2002). Developmental prevention of at-risk outcomes for vulnerable antisocial children and youth. In K. L. Lane, F. M. Gresham, & T. E. O'Shaughnessy (Eds.), *Interventions for children with or at risk for emotional and behavioral disorders* (pp. 177–194). Boston: Allyn & Bacon.

Walker, H. M., Severson, H. H., & Feil, E. G. (1995). *The Early screening project: A proven child-find process.* Longmont, CO: Sopris West.

Walker, H. M., & Walker, J. E. (1991). *Coping with noncompliance in the classroom: A positive approach for teachers.* Austin, TX: Pro-Ed.

Wall, R., & Corn, A. (2002). Production of textbooks and materials in the United States. *Journal of Visual Impairment and Blindness, 96*(4), 212–223.

Walther-Thomas, C., Korinek, L., & McLaughlin, V. L. (1999). Collaboration to support students' success. *Focus on Exceptional Children, 32*(3), 1–18.

Wang, M., & Birch, J. (1984). Comparison of a full-time mainstreaming program and a resource room approach. *Exceptional Children, 51*, 33–40.

Warger, C. (2002). *Supporting paraeducators: A summary of current practices.* (ERIC Document Reproduction Service No. ED 475 383)

Warren, S. (2002). Presidential address—Genes, brains, and behavior: The road ahead. *Mental Retardation, 40*, 421–426.

Webber, J. (1998). Responsible inclusion: Key components for success. In P. Zionts (Ed.), *Inclusion of students with emotional and behavioral disorders.* Austin, TX: Pro-Ed.

Wechsler, D. (1997). *Wechsler Adult Intelligence Scale–III.* New York: Psychological Corporation.

Wechsler, D. (2002). *Wechsler Preschool and Primary Scale of Intelligence–Revised.* San Antonio, TX: Psychological Corporation.

Wechsler, D. (2003). *Manual for the Wechler Intelligence Scale for Children–Fourth Edition.* San Antonio, TX: Psychological Corporation.

Wehby, J. H., Falk, K. B., Barton-Arwood, S., Lane, K. L., & Cooley, C. (2003). The impact of comprehensive reading instruction on the academic and social behavior of students with emotional and behavior disorders. *Journal of Emotional and Behavioral Disorders, 11*(4), 225–238.

Wehman, P. (1992). *Life beyond the classroom: Transition strategies for young people with disabilities.* Baltimore: Paul H. Brookes.

Wehman, P., & Kregal, J. (Eds.). (2004). *Functional curriculum for elementary, middle, & secondary age students with special needs* (2nd ed.). Austin, TX: Pro-Ed.

Wehman, P., & Targett, P. S. (2004). Principles of curriculum design. In P. Wehman & J. Kregal (Eds.), *Functional curriculum for elementary, middle, & secondary age students with special needs* (2nd ed., pp. 1–36). Austin, TX: Pro-Ed.

Wehmeyer, M. L. (2002). *Teaching students with mental retardation: Providing access to the general curriculum.* Baltimore: Paul H. Brookes.

Wehmeyer, M. L., Agran, M., & Hughes, C. (2000). A national study of teachers' promotion of self-determination and student-directed learning. *Journal of Special Education, 34*, 58–68.

Wehmeyer, M. L., Kelchner, K., & Richards, S. (1996). Essential characteristics of self-determined behaviors of adults with mental retardation and developmental disabilities. *American Journal on Mental Retardation, 100*, 632–642.

Wehmeyer, M. L., & Palmer, S. B. (2003). Adult outcomes for students with cognitive disabilities three years after high school: The impact of self-determination. *Education and Training in Mental Retardation and Developmental Disabilities, 38*(2), 131–144.

Wehmeyer, M. L., Lattin, D., & Agran, M. (2001). Achieving access to the general curriculum for students with mental retardation: A curriculum decision-making model. *Education and Training in Mental Retardation and Developmental Disabilities, 36*(4), 327–342.

Wehmeyer, M. L., Lattin, D., Lapp-Rincker, G., & Agran, M. (2003). Access to the general curriculum of middle school students with mental retardation: An observational study. *Remedial and Special Education, 24*(5), 262–272.

Wehmeyer, M. L., & Schwartz, M. A. (1997). Self-determination and positive adult outcomes: A follow-up study of youth with mental retardation and learning disabilities. *Exceptional Children, 63*, 245–255.

Wehmeyer, M. L., & Schwartz, M. A. (1998). Self-determination and quality of life for students with mental retardation. *Education and Training in Mental Retardation and Developmental Disabilities, 33*, 3–12.

Weikert, D., Bond, J., & McNeil, J. (1978). The Ypsilanti Perry Preschool Project: Preschool years and longitudinal results through fourth grade. *Monographs of the High/Scope Educational Research Foundation, 3.*

Weiler, M., Bernstein, J., Bellinger, D., & Waber, D. (2002). Information processing deficits in children with attention-deficit/hyperactivity disorder, inattentive type, and children with reading disability. *Journal of Learning Disabilities, 35*, 448–461.

Weinstein, S. (2002). Epilepsy. In M. Batshaw (Ed.), *Children with disabilities* (5th ed., pp. 493–524). Baltimore, MD: Paul H. Brookes.

Weiss, H., Caspe, M., & Lopez, M. E. (2006). Family involvement in early childhood education. Harvard Family Research Project Research Brief 1 in a Series: *Family Involvement Makes a Difference.*

Weiss, M. P., & Lloyd, J. (2003). Conditions for co-teaching: lessons from a case study. *Teacher Education and Special Education, 26*(1), 27–41.

Welch, M. (2000). Collaboration as a tool for inclusion. In S. E. Wade (Ed.), *Inclusive education: A casebook and readings for prospective and practicing teachers* (pp. 71–96). Mahwah, NJ: Erlbaum.

Welton, E., Vakil, S., & Carasea, C. (2004). Strategies for increasing positive social interactions in children with autism: A case study. *Teaching Exceptional Children, 37*(1), 4–46.

Wender, P. (2002). *ADHD: Attention deficit hyperactivity in children and adults.* Oxford, England: Oxford University Press.

Westby, C. E. (1995). Culture and literacy: Frameworks for understanding. *Topics in Language Disorders, 16*(1), 50–66.

Westby, C. E. (1998). Assessment of pragmatic competence in children with psychiatric disorders. In D. L. Rogers-Adkinson & P. L. Griffith (Eds.), *Communication and psychiatric disorders in children: Theory and intervention* (pp. 177–258). San Diego: Singular.

Westling, D. L., & Fox, L. (2004). *Teaching students with severe disabilities* (3rd ed.). Upper Saddle River, NJ: Pearson Prentice-Hall.

Weston, S. M. (2001). The effect of peer nomination on the identification of gifted minority students. [Abstract]. *Humanities & Social Sciences Univ. Microfilms International, 61*(10-A), 3895.

Weyandt, L. (2001). *An AD/HD primer.* Boston: Allyn & Bacon.

White, C. R., & Palmer, K. (2003). Technology instruction for students with emotional and behavioral disorders attending a therapeutic day school. *Beyond Behavior, 13*(1), 23–27.

White, M. T., Garrett, B., Kearns, J. F., & Grisham-Brown, J. (2003). Instruction and assessment: How students with deaf-blindness fare in large-scale alternate assessments. *Research and Practice for Persons with Severe Disabilities, 28*, 205–213.

Whitehouse, R., Chamberlain, P., & O'Brien, A. (2001). Increasing social interactions for people with more severe learning disabilities who have difficulty developing personal relationships. *Journal of Learning Disabilities, 5.*

Whitmire, K. (2002). The evolution of school-based speech-language services: A half century of change and a new century of practice. *Communication Disorders Quarterly, 23*(3), 68–76.

Wiederholt, L. (1974). Historical perspectives on the education of the learning disabled. In L. Mann & D. Sabatino (Eds.), *The second review of special education* (pp. 103–152). Austin, TX: Pro-Ed.

Wigle, S., & DeMoulin, D. (1999). Inclusion in a general education setting and self-concept. *Journal of At-Risk Issues, 5*, 27–32.

Wilder, L. K. (2003). Transitioning homeless youth with emotional and behavioral disorders. *Beyond Behavior, 13*(1), 17–19.

Williams, G., & Palmer, A. (2006). Preparing for college: Tips for students with HFA/Asperger's syndrome. Retrieved January 30, 2006, from www.teacch.com/prep4col2.htm

Williams, J. (2003). Teaching text structure to improve reading comprehension. In H. L. Swanson, K. Harris, & S. Graham (Eds.), *Handbook of learning disabilities* (pp. 293–305). New York: Guilford Press.

Williams, K. (2001). Understanding the student with Asperger syndrome: Guidelines for teachers. *Intervention in School and Clinic, 36*(5), 287–292.

Williams, S. C. (2002). How speech-feedback and word-prediction software can help students write. *Teaching Exceptional Children, 34*(3), 72–78.

Willingham, D. (2004-2005). Understanding AD/HD. *American Educator, Winter,* 36–41.

Wing, L. (1981). Asperger's syndrome: A clinical account. *Psychological Medicine, 11,* 115–129.

Wing, L. (1993). The definition and prevalence of autism: A review. *European Child and Adolescent Psychiatry, 2,* 61–74.

Winzer, M. (1993). *The history of special education.* Washington, DC: Gallaudet Free Press.

Wodrich, D., Spencer, M., & Daley, K. (2006). Combining RTI and psychoeducational assessment: What we must assume to do otherwise. *Psychology in the Schools, 43,* 797–806.

Wolery, M. (1995). Experienced teachers' perceptions of resources and supports for inclusion. *Education and Training in Mental Retardation and Developmental Disabilities, 30,* 15–26.

Wolfe, D. A. (1997). Children exposed to marital violence, In O. W. Barnett, C. I. Miller-Perrin, & R D. Perrin (Eds.), *Family violence across the lifespan* (pp. 136–157). Thousand Oaks, CA: Sage.

Wolfe, P. S., & Hall, T. E. (2003). Making inclusion a reality for students with severe disabilities. *Teaching Exceptional Children, 35*(4), 56–61.

Wolfensberger, W. (1972). *The principle of normalization in human services.* Toronto: National Institute on Mental Retardation.

Wolffe, K. E. (2005). Growth and development in middle childhood and adolescence. In M. C. Holbrook & A. J. Koenig (Eds.), *Foundations of education: Volume I. History and theory of teaching children and youth with visual impairments* (2nd ed., chap. 5). Retrieved February 12, 2007, from www.afb.org/foe/book.asp?ch=v2c5

Wolffe, K. E., Sacks, S. Z., Corn, A. L., Erin, J. N., Huebner, K. M., & Lewis, S. (2002). Teachers of students with visual impairments: What are they teaching? [Electronic Version]. *Journal of Visual Impairment & Blindness, 96*(5), 293–304.

Wolfram, W. (1990). *Dialect differences and testing.* Washington, DC: Office of Educational Research and Improvement (ERIC Document Reproduction Service No. ED 323 813)

Wolfram, W., Adger, C. T., & Christian, D. (1999). *Dialects in schools and communities.* Mahwah, NJ: Erlbaum.

Woll, B., & Ladd, P. (2003). Deaf communities. In M. Marschark & P. E. Spencer (Eds.), *Oxford handbook of deaf studies, language, and education* (pp. 151–167). New York: Oxford University Press.

Wong, B. Y. L., & Donahue, M. (2002). *The social dimensions of learning disabilities: Essays in honor of Tanis Bryan.* Mahwah, NJ: Erlbaum.

Wood, J., Nezworski, M., Lilienfeld, S., & Garb, H. (2003). *What's wrong with the Rorschach: Science confronts the controversial inkblot test.* San Francisco: Jossey-Bass.

Wood, W. M., Karvonen, M.., Test, D. W., Browder, D., & Algozzine, B. (2004). Promoting student self-determination skills in IEP planning. *Teaching Exceptional Children, 36*(3), 8–16.

Woodcock, K., & Aguayo, M. (2000). *Deafened people: Adjustment and support.* Toronto: University of Toronto Press.

Woodcock, R., McGrew, K., & Maher, N. (2001). *Woodcock-Johnson–III.* Itasca, IL: Riverside.

Woods, J. J., & Wetherby, A. M. (2003). Early identification of and intervention for infants and toddlers who are at risk for autism spectrum disorder. *Language Speech, and Hearing* Services *in the Schools, 34,* 180–193.

Woolfolk, A. (2001). *Educational psychology* (8th ed.). Needham Heights, MA: Allyn & Bacon.

World Health Organization. (1999). *International classification of diseases* (10th ed.). New York: Author.

X

Xu, C., Reid, R., & Steckelberg, A. (2002). Technology applications for children with AD/HD: Assessing the empirical support. *Education and Treatment of Children, 25*(2), 224–248.

Y

Yehle, A. K., & Wambold, C. (1998). An AD/HD success story: Strategies for teachers and students. *Teaching Exceptional Children, 30*(6), 8–13.

Yell, M. L. (1992). A comparison of three instructional approaches on task attention, interfering behaviors, and achievement of students with emotional and behavioral disorders (Doctoral dissertation). *Dissertation Abstracts International*, No. 9236987.

Yoder, D., Retish, E., & Wade, R. (1996). Service learning: Meeting student and community needs. *Teaching Exceptional Children, 28*(4), 14–18.

Young, M. (2000). *Working memory, language, and reading.* Retrieved December 6, 2006, from www. brainconnection.com/topics/?main=fa/memory-language3

Ysseldyke, J., Algozzine, B., & Epps, S. (1983). A logical and empirical analysis of current practice in classifying students as handicapped. *Exceptional Children, 50,* 160–166.

Ysseldyke, J., & Olsen, K. (1999). Putting alternate assessments into practice: What to measure and possible sources of data. *Exceptional Children, 65,* 175–185.

Ysseldyke, J., Vanderwood, M., & Shriner, J. (1997). Changes over the past decade in special education referral to placement probability: An incredibly reliable practice. *Diagnostique, 23,* 193–202.

Z

Zima, B. T., Forness, S. R., Bussing, R., & Bernadette, B. (1998). Homeless children in emergency shelters: Need for prereferral intervention and potential eligibility for special education. *Behavioral Disorders, 23*(2), 998–110.

Zimmerman I., Steiner, V., & Pond, R. (2002). *Preschool Language Scale–4.* San Antonio, TX: Psychological Corporation.

Zionts, P., Zionts, L., & Simpson, R. L. (2002). *Emotional and behavioral problems: A handbook for understanding and handling students.* Thousand Oaks, CA: Corwin Press.

Zuo, L., & Cramond, B. (2001). An examination of Terman's gifted children from the theory of identity. *Gifted Child Quarterly, 45*(4), 251–259.

Photo Credits

Chapter 12

p. 398: John Birdsall/The Image Works;
p. 399: Syracuse Newspapers/Michelle Gabel/The Image Works; p. 406: Ellen B. Senisi/The Image Works; p. 407: Elena Rooraid/PhotoEdit Inc.; p. 412: Bob Daemmrich/The Image Works; p. 414: Ellen B. Senisi/The Image Works; p. 420: Robin Nelson/PhotoEdit Inc.; p. 421: Will Hart/PhotoEdit Inc.; p. 428: Bob Daemmrich/The Image Works; p. 430: Courtesy of Amanda Norris; p. 431: Jeff Greenberg/PhotoEdit Inc.

Chapter 13

p. 438: Marty Heitner/The Image Works;
p. 439: Ellen B. Senisi/The Image Works;
p. 440T: Ellen B. Senisi/The Image Works;
p. 440B: Geri Engberg/The Image Works;
p. 445: John Birdsall/The Image Works;
p. 450 Creatas/Punchstock; p. 455: Ellen B. Senisi/The Image Works; p. 459: Tony Freeman/PhotoEdit Inc.; p. 461: David Young-Wolff/ PhotoEdit Inc.; p. 466: Courtesy of Christine Honsberger

Chapter 14

p. 474: Bob Daemmrich/The Image Works
p. 475: Ellen B. Senisi/The Image Works;
p. 478: Ellen B. Senisi/The Image Works;
p. 487: Bob Daemmrich/The Image Works;
p. 500: Courtesy of Varie Hudson Hawkins;
p. 502: Bill Aron/PhotoEdit Inc.

Chapter 15

p. 510: Bob Daemmrich/The Image Works;
p. 511: Ellen B. Senisi/The Image Works;
p. 515: Ellen B. Senisi/The Image Works;
p. 517: David Grossman/The Image Works;
p. 523: Ellen B. Senisi/The Image Works;
p. 532: Syracuse Newspapers/Li-Hua Lan/The Image Works; p. 538: Courtesy of Dian Trompler

Name Index

A

Abikoff, H., 483
Achenbach, T. M., 182, 187
Acrey, C., 9
Adams, L., 366
Adelman, A., 31
Adger, C. T., 231
Adreon, D., 386
Agran, M., 151, 153, 163, 166, 379
Aguayo, M., 256
Aguilar, E., 182
Ahlgrim-Delzell, L., 418, 419
Aicardi, J., 361
Akin-Little, A., 177
Albertini, J. A., 255, 262, 263, 264, 265, 268,
    271, 272, 273, 276, 277
Alberto, P. A., 145, 158, 160, 196, 199, 200,
    201, 343, 346, 348, 349, 405, 408, 410, 411,
    413, 414
Albright, M., 347
Alder, J., 337
Alexander, D., 143
Alexander, H., 143
Algozzine, B., 45, 121, 153, 154, 294, 419
Alkin, M., 59
Allen, J., 372
Allen, K. E., 376
Alley, G. R., 111, 116
Allman, C. B., 311
Allsopp, D., 489
Al Otaiba, S., 499
Alper, S., 426, 427
Alsman, B., 189
Alter, P. J., 464, 465
Ambrose, G., 295
Amtmann, D., 102
Anastopoulos, A. D., 490
Anderegg, M. L., 58
Anderton, J., 99
Andrews, G., 236
Andrews, J. F., 262, 263, 265
Anthony, A., 365
Anthony, J. L., 461
Antia, S. D., 118
Aragon, L., 83
Aratani, L., 513

Archbold, S. M., 277
Arends, R., 99
Armbruster, B. B., 109, 111
Arnette, J. L., 193
Arnos, K. S., 265
Aro, H., 296
Arreaga-Mayer, C., 499
Artru, A., 365
Ashford, L., 373
Ashmore, D. H., 270
Ashton, T., 527
Asperger, H., 361
Assouline, S., 522, 524, 526, 527, 528, 541
Auer, E. T., Jr., 258
Avery, L., 526
Avoké, S., 29
Ayali, M., 98
Aylward, E., 365
Ayres, K. M., 389

B

Babbitt, B. S., 126
Bacon, E. H., 208
Baglieri, S., 58
Bagwell, C., 484
Bahr, C. M., 126
Bailey, A., 363, 365
Bailey, D. B., 450
Baird, G., 373
Baker, S., 111, 119
Baker, S. K., 270
Baker, S. R., 153, 154
Bakke, M., 275, 276, 277, 278
Balandran, J., 88
Baldi, P. L., 145
Balla, D., 148
Baloglu, M., 101
Balow, B., 179
Bambara, L. M., 408
Bamburg, J. W., 409
Barclay, C. L., 193
Bardos, A., 187
Barkley, R. A., 478, 481, 482, 483, 486,
    489, 490, 492, 493, 494, 495, 498,
    499, 502

Barnett, D., 106
Barnhill, G. P., 196, 378
Baroff, G., 142
Baron-Cohen, S., 372
Barry, L. M., 490
Barry, T., 483
Barton, P. E., 445, 446, 448, 461, 467
Barton-Arwood, S., 189, 205
Basehart, S., 146
Bassett, D. S., 101
Batshaw, M. L., 136, 143, 147, 288, 293, 294,
    297, 301, 309
Battle, D. E., 230
Bauer, A. M., 126, 339, 501
Baum, S., 525
Baumgart, D., 423
Beck, S., 491
Becker, W. C., 197
Beckner, R., 462, 463
Beckwith, L., 208
Becvar, D. S., 181
Becvar, R. J., 181
Beebe-Frankenberger, M., 189, 441, 453,
    458, 459, 462, 485
Beech, M., 127, 128, 163, 209, 238,
    497, 503
Beegle, D. M., 448
Beigel, A. R., 127
Bell, A. G., 255
Bellak, I., 187
Bellak, S., 187
Bellinger, D., 483
Bender, W., 100, 485
Benepe, S., 146
Benner, G. J., 185
Bennerson, D., 190
Bennett, J., 206–207
Bennett, L., 447
Bentzen, F. A., 496, 497
Benz, M. R., 168
Berelowitz, M., 365
Berkson, G., 136
Bernadette, B., 193

Christian, D., 231
Chronis, A., 490, 502
Churchwell, C., 295
Ciardiello, A., 529
Cicchetti, D., 148
Clarfield, J., 502
Clark, B., 513, 517, 519, 520, 528, 534
Clark, C., 377, 379, 384, 386
Clark, D. M., 75, 76, 341, 346
Clark, F. L., 111
Clark, G. M., 155, 307, 341
Clark, N. M., 167
Clark, S. G., 74
Clasen, D., 532
Clasen, R. E., 532
Cleary, K., 483
Cleveland, H. H., 517
Cochran, L., 205
Codding, R., 490
Cohen, P., 180
Cohen, S., 99
Colangelo, N., 16, 522, 524, 526, 527, 528, 529, 541
Colarossi, G. M., 273
Colarusso, R., 97
Cole, C. M., 145
Cole, P., 60
Cole, P. A., 230
Coleman, M., 189, 205, 366, 367, 368, 369, 370, 372, 373
Coleman, M. C., 176, 196, 489, 503
Colker, L., 464
Collins, B. C., 42, 156, 158, 402, 407, 412, 421
Compton, D., 106
Conderman, G., 110
Cone-Wesson, B., 266
Conley, P. T., 168
Conlon, C., 333
Conners, C., 488
Connor, D. F., 495
Conover, L., 527
Conrad, E., 373
Conroy, J. W., 408
Conroy, M., 195, 196
Conroy, M. A., 194, 205, 453, 464, 465
Constantine, J., 460
Conyers, L. M., 491
Cook, B., 60
Cook, K., 38
Cook, L., 65, 68, 69, 70, 77, 78, 79, 80
Cook, M., 365
Cook, T., 346
Cooley, C., 189, 205
Coolidge, F., 485
Cooney, J., 103
Cooper, J. T., 156
Copeland, S., 197
Corn, A. L., 289, 290, 298, 299, 300, 303, 306, 311, 312
Cornell, D., 484
Corral, N., 118
Cosmos, C., 193
Costello, E., 180
Coulter, D. L., 138, 139, 140, 141, 143, 145, 147, 148, 402, 412
Coutinho, M., 180
Coutinho, M. J., 140

Cox, M. J., 194
Cox, P., 304, 305, 308, 315
Crago, M. B., 231
Craig, A., 228
Craig, C., 295
Craig, E. M., 138, 139, 140, 141, 143, 145, 147, 148, 402, 412
Craig, M., 228
Cramond, B., 518
Crane, K., 89
Crenshaw, T. M., 491, 494
Criscitiello, E., 205
Crites, S. A., 196
Crnic, K. A., 183
Croen, L., 327, 364, 366
Cronin, M. E., 101, 152, 155
Crook, W., 99
Crosbie, S., 454
Cross, C. T., 140
Crowley, E. P., 112, 189, 191, 204, 208, 209
Crozier, S., 383
Crudden, A., 306
Cruickshank, W., 95, 477, 496, 497
Cullihan, D., 194
Cullinan, D., 179, 182
Cummins, J., 232
Curry, C., 327
Curry, V., 195
Cushing, L. S., 167
Cutspec, P., 461
Cutting, L., 483

D

Dager, S., 365
Dahlberg, S., 372
Dahlstrom, W., 187
Dale, P., 98
Daley, D., 480
Daley, K., 105
D'Allura, T., 294
Daly, T., 375, 382
Damer, M., 462
Dangel, H., 97
Darwin, C., 516
Davenport, N., 483
Davidson, P. W., 288
Davies, D., 163, 165, 332
Davies, R., 208
Davies, S., 365
Davila, R., 486
Davis, G. A., 16, 512, 519, 522, 523, 528, 532, 536, 539
Dawson, G., 365
Dawson, H. L., 162
De Balderas, H. B., 83
de Boer-Ott, S. R., 391
DeFries, J., 98
de Frutos, R., 182
de la Cruz, R. E., 201
De La Paz, S., 111, 112
Delquadri, J. C., 122, 162, 499
Demchak, M., 340, 342, 348
DeMoulin, D., 59
Denckla, M., 483
Deni, J., 99
Denney, M. K., 425

Denning, C., 48
Denny, R., 491
Denny, R. K., 189
Deno, E., 57
Deno, S., 43
Deno, S. L., 258
Denton, C. A., 462
DePaepe, P., 491
DePriest, L. B., 298, 299, 303, 312
Deret, D., 407
Deshler, D. D., 111, 116
DeStefano, F., 365
DeVault, R., 110
Devinsky, O., 330, 331
Dhillon, A., 365
Dial, J., 300
Dias, K., 361
Diem, R. A., 207
Dill, S., 454
Dillard, J. L., 231
DiLorenzo, K., 15
Diment, K., 258
Dion, E., 59
DiPaola, M. F., 71, 82
DiPerna, J., 38
Disher, S., 59
Dix, D., 176
Dix, J., 101
Dixon, R., 110
Dodd, B., 454
Dodd, N., 416, 426
Dodge, D. T., 464
Dodge, E. P., 234
Dohan, M., 217, 230, 239, 246
Dolce, K., 383
Dolendo, J., 294
Doll, B., 154
Donahue, M., 103
Donovan, M., 456
Donovan, M. S., 140
Doorlag, D. H., 122
Dore, R., 59
Dote-Kwan, J., 294
Douvanis, G., 56
Douyon, K., 480
Downing, J. A., 14, 15, 84
Downs, A., 370
Doyle, A., 481
Doyle, M. B., 424
Drasgow, E., 265
Duchan, J. F., 229
Duff, F., 60
Dugger, 353
Duhaime, A.-C., 339, 344
Duke, T. S., 65, 69
Dunlap, G., 374, 378, 379, 380, 385, 459, 463
Dunn, D., 234, 337
Dunn, L. M., 234
Dunst, C. J., 460
DuPaul, G. J., 479, 483, 485, 489, 490, 492, 493, 494, 495, 496, 497, 498, 499, 500, 501, 502
Durbin, M., 168
Durlap, J. A., 194
Durrer, B., 205
Dye, M., 387
Dyer, S. M., 461

McWayne, C., 456
McWilliam, R. A., 301
Mechling, L. C., 164
Meeker, M., 533
Meeker, R., 533
Mehlig, L., 462
Meichenbaum, D., 109, 195, 491
Meltzer, L., 118
Menacker, S. J., 288, 293, 294, 297, 301, 309
Mendel, J., 59
Mendell, J., 337
Mercer, A. R., 122
Mercer, C., 111, 122
Merrell, K., 178, 179
Merrell, K. W., 521
Mesibov, G. B., 366, 380, 381
Messer, J. J., 490
Messer, S., 180
Messina, R., 423
Mesulam, M., 483
Meyer, J., 483
Meyer, L. H., 77, 408
Mezger, C., 300
Michaud, L. J., 339, 344
Mick, E., 481
Miles, J., 87, 88
Milich, R., 483
Millepiedi, S., 485
Miller, C., 98
Miller, D., 446
Miller, J., 294, 300
Miller, K. A., 207
Miller, L., 118, 246
Miller, M. D., 190
Miller, M. M., 288, 293, 294, 297, 301, 309
Miller, R., 153, 154, 168
Miller, S. P., 108, 111, 112, 120, 126, 150, 159, 161, 164, 165, 189, 501
Millgan, C., 9
Minskoff, E., 489, 504
Miracle, S., 168
Mirenda, P., 377, 390, 408
Mitchell, R. E., 263
Moats, L. C., 110, 234, 462
Mock, D., 58, 105
Modi, M., 519
Mohr, D., 326, 334, 335
Moise, J., 181
Molina, B., 484
Molto, D., 182
Monda-Amaya, L. E., 72
Montague, M., 111, 116, 118
Monzo, L. D., 83
Moody, S., 121
Moody, S. W., 121, 122, 462
Moon, S. M., 529
Moon, T., 527
Moore, C. L., 147
Moores, D. F., 254, 255, 261, 263, 264, 267, 268
Morelock, M., 533
Moreno, S., 387
Morgan, P., 105
Morgan, T., 188
Morreau, L. E., 201
Morrier, M. J., 375, 382
Morris, R., 106
Morrison, K., 533

Mortweet, S. L., 162
Most, T., 276
Mostert, M. P., 189, 190, 205, 206, 208
Moyes, R. A., 387
Mucci, M., 485
Muir, S., 280
Mukherjee, S., 344, 353
Mull, C., 112
Muller, E., 177
Munk, D., 462
Munson, J., 365
Murch, S., 365
Murira, G. M., 232
Murphy, K., 478
Murray, F., 207
Murray, H., 187
Muscott, H. S., 191, 193
Musick, K. K., 195
Muyskens, P., 120, 462
Myers, B., 373
Myles, B. S., 378, 387

N

Nabors, L., 384
Nagle, K., 306
Naglieri, J., 186, 187, 524
Najera, C., 182
Nathanson, R., 153, 154
Neal, J., 13, 14
Neber, H., 522, 536
Nelson, C. M., 190, 198, 200, 206, 208
Nelson, J. R., 185, 208
Nelson, M., 189
Neuman, S. B., 239
Neumeister, K. L. S., 532
Neville, B. G. R., 232
Nevin, A. I., 82
Newborg, J., 453
Newcomer, P. L., 189, 195, 201, 202
Newell, K. M., 409
Newman, L., 87
Newton, C. R. J. C., 232
Neyt-Dumesnil, C., 407
Nezworski, M., 188
Ng, P., 332
Nguyen, N., 140
Nicholson, R., 13, 14
Nicpon, M. F., 525
Nietfeld, J. P., 422
Nigg, J., 186
Nihira, K., 148
Niles, W. J., 69, 71
Nisbet, J., 406, 423
Noble, K., 517
Nolan, S., 111
Noonan, M. J., 160, 504
Nordness, P., 185
Norris, A., 430–431
Novak, 182
Numminen, H., 145

O

O'Brien, A., 104
O'Connor, A. M., 196
Oden, M., 518
Ogata, V., 504

O'Hair, M. J., 68
Ohtake, Y., 413
Okamoto, Y., 425
O'Keefe, M., 447, 450
Okolo, C. M., 126
Olive, M. L., 159
Olmedo, R., 180
Olsen, K., 418
Olson, J., 120, 122, 126, 155, 492, 499, 501
Olson, R., 98
Olszewski-Kubilius, P., 530, 536
O'Neal, C., 387
Ortega-Hurndon, F., 164
Ortiz, A. A., 231, 232
Orton, S., 17
Osborn, J., 109, 111
O'Shaughnessy, T. E., 189, 441, 453, 458, 459, 462
Osher, D. M., 193
Ostrosky, M. M., 240, 448, 465
Oswald, D., 180
Oswald, D. P., 140
Ota, K. R., 500
Ottolini, Y., 482
Owen, B., 111
Owen, S. V., 537
Owens, E., 482
Owens, J., 168
Owens, R. E., 219, 220, 236, 237, 239
Owens-Johnson, L., 74, 428
Oyer, H. J., 222, 223, 230, 236, 237, 242, 247
Ozanne, A., 454
Ozonoff, S., 366, 373, 379

P

Padden, C., 261
Pagani, L., 180
Page, E., 536
Palmer, A., 379
Palmer, B. C., 87, 88
Palmer, C., 88
Palmer, D., 332
Palmer, K., 207, 208
Palmer, S., 86, 414
Palmer, S. B., 154
Pang, C., 332
Paradis, Maria Theresia von, 288
Parette, H. P., 123, 165
Parish, S., 137
Park, H. S., 425
Park, J., 425
Parker, W. D., 520
Parrish, M., 29
Parrish, T., 483
Partenio, I., 47
Patton, J. R., 101, 120, 121, 146, 147, 152, 154, 155
Paul, R., 446
Paulsell, D., 460
Payne, L. D., 204, 205
Pearpoint, J., 74
Peck, C. A., 433
Peel, B. B., 449
Peel, H. A., 449
Pelegrino, L., 327, 328
Pelham, W., 484
Pelham, W. E., 490, 502

Subject Index

Note: Page references in *italics* refer to figures and tables.

American Association of the Deaf-Blind (AADB), *401*

American Association on Intellectual and Developmental Disabilities (AAIDD), 137–138, 139–140, 141

American Association on Mental Retardation (AAMR), 138–139, *138*, 402. *See also* American Association on Intellectual and Developmental Disabilities

American Council of the Blind, 289

American Indian/Alaska Native children mental retardation identification in, 140 underrepresentation in gifted programs, 525

American Orthopsychiatric Association, 177

American Printing House (APH) for the Blind, 288

American Psychiatric Association (APA), 361, 477

American Sign Language (ASL) in bilingual-bicultural approach, 271 in Deaf culture, 254, 261–263 early exposure to, 265 literacy and, 263 teaching resources, 279

American Speech-Language-Hearing Association (ASHA), 217, 220–221, *241*, 248

Americans with Disabilities Act (ADA; PL 101-335), 22–23, 255, 278

amnesia, following brain injury, 338

amniocentesis, 337

Analogical Reasoning Learning Test (ARLT), 412

anaphylactic reaction, 332

Angelman syndrome, *404*

anoxia, during childbirth, 98, 142

anxiety disorders, 485

APH (American Printing House for the Blind), 288

applied behavior analysis (ABA), 196, 380–382

AP (Advanced Placement) program, 527

ARC, 18, 137, *401*

ARLT (Analogical Reasoning Learning Test), 412

ART (Aggression Replacement Training), 190

articulation, in speech, 217

articulation disorders, 224, 227, 230, 237, 248

ASD. *See* autism spectrum disorders

ASEBA (Achenbach System of Empirically Based Assessment), 187

ASHA (American Speech-Language-Hearing Association), 217, 220–221, *241*, 248

Asian Americans, technology use by, 123

Asian/Pacific Islanders, identification of mental retardation in, 140

ASL. *See* American Sign Language

Asperger syndrome. *See also* autism spectrum disorders characteristics of, 359, *367* definition of, 362 gender differences in, 364 historical recognition of, 361 prevalence of, 363 social skills of students with, 377–378 transition skills for students with, 379

assessments. *See also* evaluation procedures; identification process alternate, 418–419 of at-risk children, 454–455, 470 of at-risk infants and toddlers, 453, 470 for attention deficit/hyperactivity disorder, 487–488 of creativity, 524 curriculum-based, 42–43 discriminatory, 20, 21 dynamic, 412, 525–526 of gifted and talented children, 523–524 high-stakes, 50 of instructional technology use, 348, *349* intelligence tests (*See* intelligence tests) language, 228–232 misuse of testing with deaf students, 266–267 in No Child Left Behind legislation, 23 observational, 41 participation in all, 27 prereferral, 37, 38, 40–41, 43–44 of students with culturally diverse backgrounds, 230–232 of students with severe disabilities, 411–412, 416–419, *417*, *419* vision, 297–301, *299*

assistive technology for at-risk students, 466–468, 471 attention deficit/hyperactivity disorders and, 499–502, 507 for augmentative alternative communication, 243–244, 349–350, 390, 429–430, *431* autism spectrum disorders and, 387–390, 395 blindness or low vision and, 304, 312–314, *313*, 316, 319 communication disorders and, 243–246, 249 deafness or hard of hearing and, 274–279, 283 definition of, 8 diverse families and, 165 in elementary and secondary programs, 124–127, *125* emotional or behavioral disorders and, 206–208, *207*, 211 for gifted and talented students, 539–540, 543 intellectual disabilities and, 163–165, 171 learning activity types using, 540 learning disabilities and, 122–127 physical or health disabilities and, 339, 347–352, *349*, 355 in preschool programs, 123 selection of, 126–127, *126* severe disabilities and, 429–431, *431*, 435 Technology-Related Assistance of Individuals with Disabilities Act requirements, 348

Association for the Gifted, 536

asthma, 326, 331–332, 338, 354

astigmatism, 292

Astro Algebra (software), 125

ataxia, 327, *328*

athetoid cerebral palsy, 327, *328*

at-risk conditions, 439–471 biological/medical risk, 445, 470 collaboration by teachers, 467, 471 definition of, 442–443 early intervention for infants or toddlers, 442–443, 453, 459–460, 464 environmental risk, 445–449, *449*, *450*, 470 established risk, 444–445, 470 general education teachers and students at risk, 468–471 history of, 441–442 identification of children in, 452–455, 470 instructional content, 455–458, 466–467, 471 instructional environment, 464–466, 467, 471 instructional procedures for students in, 458–463, 471 instructional technology, 466–468, 471 intervention example, 460, *461* involvement of families of at-risk children, 456–457, *457*, 460 lack of profile of an at-risk child, 450–451 language and literacy, 460–462 longitudinal study of at-risk children, 450–451, 452 prevalence of students in, 443–444 prevention, 458–460 protective factors, 449–451, *451* routine-based positive support planning form, *468* state laws regarding children in, 453 Universal Design for Learning, 458, 462

at-risk infant or toddler, definition of, 442–443

attention characteristics, in students with severe disabilities, 406

attention deficit disorder (ADD), 477. *See also* attention deficit/hyperactivity disorder

Attention Deficit Disorder Association (ADDA), 476

Attention Deficit Disorders Evaluation Scale–2, 488

attention deficit/hyperactivity disorder (AD/HD), 475–507 causes of, 480–481 characteristics of students with, 481–485, *482*, *484*, 506 coexistence with other exceptionalities, 485, 506 collaboration by teachers of students with, 501, 504–505, 507 diagnostic criteria for, 477–478, *479* 504 plans, 21, 503–504, *505* general education teachers of students with, 503–507, *504*, *505* history of, 477 identification of students with, 485–488, 506 instructional content, 489–491, *490*, 500–501, 507 instructional environment, 496–499, *498* instructional grouping, 498–499 instructional procedures, 491–496, *494*, 507 instructional technology, 499–502, 507

attention deficit/hyperactivity disorder (AD/HD) (*Cont.*)
    medications for, 493–495
    not covered under IDEA 04, 4, 477
    prevalence of, 478–480
    traumatic brain injury and, 325–326
    types of, 480, 506
Attention Deficit/Hyperactivity Disorder Test, 488
attention problems, 103, 144. *See also* attention deficit/hyperactivity disorder
Attention Trainer, 502
attribution retraining, 118
attributions, autism and, 370
audiologists, 266
audiology, as related service, 12
audiometric evaluation, 266
auditory feedback equipment, 245
auditory prompt systems, 165
augmentative and alternative communication (AAC) technology, 243–244, 349–350, 390, 429–430, *431*
aura, 331
autism, 361, *362*, 363, *367. See also* autism spectrum disorders
autism spectrum disorders (ASD), 359–395
    causes of, 365–366
    characteristics of, *362*, 366–372, *367*, *371, 373,* 394
    collaboration by teachers of students with, 389, 391
    criteria for, *362*, 373–374
    definitions of types of, 361–362, *362*
    general education teachers of students with, 391–395, *392–393*
    history of, 360–361
    identification of students with, 372–374, *373*, 394
    inclusion collaboration model, 391
    instructional content, 374–379, *377*, 388–389, 395
    instructional environment, 380, 389, 395
    instructional grouping, 387
    instructional procedures, 379–384, *380*, *383, 392–393,* 395
    instructional technology, 387–390, 395
    prevalence of, 5–7, *6, 7,* 363–364
    secondary language disorders and, 227, 248
    transition of students with, 379
autistic disorder (autism), 361, *362*, 363, *367. See also* autism spectrum disorders
"autistic psychopathy," 361. *See also* Asperger syndrome
Autonomous Learner Model (ALM), 534, *534*

B

Baby DATA, 376
BASC–II (Behavior Assessment System for Children–II), 187, 487
baseline data, 41
basic interpersonal communication skills (BICS), 232
bathroom locations, 204
Battelle Developmental Inventory, Second Edition (BDI–2), 453
Bedlam (St. Mary of Bethlehem asylum), 176

behavior. *See also* emotional or behavioral disorders
    adaptive, 147, 148, 411–412
    applied behavior analysis, 196, 380–382
    assessment systems, 187, 487–488
    chained, 421–422, *422*
    cognitive behavior modification, 195–196, 491–492
    rating scales, 148, 186–187, 300
    repetitive, 369
    self-injurious, 369, 409
    skill development, 344–345, 421
    target, 421
behavioral inhibition, attention deficit/hyperactivity disorder and, 482–483
behavior intervention plan (BIP), 27–28, 196–197
behavioral skill development, 344–345, 421
behavioral techniques intervention, 196, 492–493
Behavior Analysts, 466
Behavior Assessment System for Children–II (BASC–II), 187, 487
behavior chain interruption, 422
behavior contracts, 198–199, *200*
behavior rating scales, 148, 186–187, 300
Bennett, Joanne, profile of, 206–207
Berry, Juliana, profile of, 166–167
Best Buddies International program, 164
bibliotherapy, 202
BICS (basic interpersonal communication skills), 232
Big, Bigger, Borrow strategy, 111
bilingual-bicultural (bi-bi) approach, 271
Binet, Alfred, test development by, 49
BIP (behavioral intervention plan), 27–28, 196–197
bipolar disorder, 184, 485
Black English (BE), 231
The Black Stork (film), 17–18, *18*
blindness or low vision, 287–319
    age of onset, 294
    braille skills, 303–304
    causes of, 292–293, *293*
    characteristics of students with, 294–296, 318
    collaboration by teachers of students with, 317, 319
    definitions of, 290–291, *290*, 318
    general education teachers of students with, 314–319
    history of, 288–289
    identification of students with, 296–301, 318
    inclusion of students with, 310–311, 314–319
    instructional content, 301–306, 316–317, 319
    instructional environment, 304–305, *304*, 309–312, 316, 319
    instructional procedures, 306–309, *309*, 316–317, 319
    instructional technology, 304, 312–314, *313*, 316, 319
    prevalence of, 291
    transition planning for students with, 306, *307*

blood borne pathogens, universal precautions against, 333
blood sugar problems, 333. *See also* diabetes
Bloom's taxonomy, 529, *530*
Boardmaker, 390
Board of Education of the Hendrick Hudson Central School District v. Rowley (1982), *22*, 24
"book cuddling," 456–457
books, 202, 236, 456–457
boys. *See* gender differences
braille, 303–304, 311–312, *313*
Braille2000, *313*
braille translation software, *313*
brain. *See also* traumatic brain injury
    attention deficit/hyperactivity disorder and, 477, 481, 483
    autism causes and, 365–366
    imaging, 337–338, 365
    lobes of, *335*
buddy system, 162, 164
Burlington School Committee v. Department of Education of Massachusetts (1985), *22*
bus rides, students with autism and, 386, *386*

C

CAI (computer-assisted instruction), 500–501
calculators, 164
CALP (cognitive academic language proficiency), 232
career education. *See* employment
Carolina Abecedarian Project, 143–144, 460
cascade of integration options, 168, *168*
cascade of services, 57, *57*
casein intolerance, autism and, 384
catheterization, 343
CBA (curriculum-based assessment), 42–43
CBI (community-based instruction), 154–155, 160, 168–169, 427–428
CBM (cognitive behavior modification), 491–492
CBM (curriculum-based measurement), 43
CDD (childhood disintegrative disorder), 363, 364, *367. See also* autism spectrum disorders
CEC (Council for Exceptional Children), 18, 177
Centers for Disease Control (CDC), 333
cerebral palsy. *See also* physical and health disabilities
    adaptive equipment for students with, 349–350
    causes and characteristics, 327–328, 354
    in history, 324–325
    identification of students with, 337
    individualized health (care) plan for, 343–344, *344*
    profile of student with, 399–400
    voice disorders from, 223
chained behaviors, 421, *422*
challenge test, to identify asthma, 338
changing classes, by students with autism, *386*
Checklist for Autism in Toddlers, 372

dialects, 221, 229, 230–231

Diana v. California State Board of Education (1973), *20*

DIBELS–5 (Dynamic Indicators of Basic Early Literacy Skills), 454

differential reinforcement, 199

differentiated curriculum, 527, *537*

digital clocks, 164

DiLorenzo, Kim, profile of, 15

dimensional classification system, 179

diplegia, 327

Direct Instruction (DI) method
intellectual disabilities and, 156
learning disabilities and, 113–114

direct instruction
attention deficit/hyperactivity disorder and, 491
autism spectrum disorders and, 380
emotional or behavioral disorders and, 195
in reading, 109–110

directive sentences, 383

disabilities. *See also specific disabilities*
definition of, 3
in history, 16–19
prevalence of, 5–7, *6*, *7*
types of students having, 4

discipline, in IDEA 04 legislation, 27–28

discrete trial teaching, 381, 421

discrimination
in assessment, 20, 21, 47, 524–525
court cases on, *20*
in employment, 20–21, 22

distance learning, 339, 347

distractibility, 103

distributed trial teaching, 421

divergent thinking skills, 529

diverse backgrounds. *See* culturally and linguistically diverse backgrounds

Dix, Dorothea, 176

dolphin therapy, 384

domestic violence, 447

double hemiplegia, 327

double mentoring, 532

Down syndrome, *141*, 445

drama, as therapeutic intervention, 201

Draw-a-Person Screening Procedure for Emotional Disturbance, 187

drill-and-practice programs, 502

drug therapy, for attention deficit/hyperactivity disorder, 493–495

drug use during pregnancy, 98, 142

Duchenne muscular dystrophy, 329–330, 337, 343, 354

due process, 21, 25

Duxbury software, *313*

dynamic assessment, 412, 525–526

Dynamic Indicators of Basic Early Literacy Skills (DIBELS–5), 454

dyscalculia, 98

dysfluency, 227–228

dyslexia, 98, 100

E

ear, anatomy of, 256, *256*

early childhood. *See also* infants and toddlers; preschool children

collaboration best practices, 85–87

developmentally appropriate practice in, 414

general curriculum access for students with severe disabilities, 413–415, *415*

intervention for children with emotional or behavioral disorders, 194–195

early identification and assessment. *See also* identification process
of children with severe disabilities, 411
of infants and toddlers, 36–37
as related service, 14

early intervention
with at-risk infants or toddlers, 442–443, 453, 459–460, 464
longitudinal study of at-risk children, 450–451, 452
Operation Head Start, 441–442
for students with emotional or behavioral disabilities, 194–195

Early Reading Diagnostic Assessment Second Edition (ERDA–Second Edition), 454

Early Screen Project, 454

EBD. *See* emotional or behavioral disorders

Ebonics, 231

e-Buddies, 164

echolalia, 227, 368

echopraxia, 368

ecological inventories, 417

ED. *See* emotional disturbance

Edmark Reading Program, 164

Educating Children with Autism, 384

Education for All Handicapped Children Act (PL 94-142), 20–21, 255

Education of the Gifted and Talented (Marland), 513

Education of the Handicapped Act Amendments of 1986 (PL 99-457), 21, 22

Elder, Carol, profile of, 278–279

electroencephalographs (EEG), 337

electromyography (EMG), 337

electronic portfolio presentations, 164

Elementary and Secondary Education Act (ESEA) of 1965 (PL 89-10), *20*, 443, 454

elementary school programs
attention deficit/hyperactivity disorder and, 497–498, *498*
autism spectrum disorders and, 386–387, *386*
blindness or low vision and, 297–298, 302–306
communication disorders and, 240
emotional or behavioral disorders and, 204–205
for gifted and talented students, 522–526
hearing loss and, 266
instructional technology in, 124–127, *125*
learning disabilities and, 120
mental retardation/intellectual disabilities and, 160, 171

eligibility criteria, 45–51
culturally or linguistically diverse backgrounds and, 46–47
evaluation procedures, 48–51
lack of instruction and, 46
state laws on, 47–48, 453, 521

ELLs (English-language learners), 29, 118–119, 448–449

e-mail, 278

embedded skill instruction, 423

EMG (electromyography), 337

emotional abuse of children, 448, *449*

emotional disturbance (ED). *See also* emotional or behavioral disorders
attention deficit/hyperactivity disorder as, 486
IDEA 04 definitions of, 177–178, 210
overrepresentation of African Americans in, 29–30
prevalence of, 5–7, *6*, *7*
variability of characteristics in, 48

emotional or behavioral disorders (EBD), 175–211
age and, 180, *184*
in at-risk children, 454–455
in attention deficit/hyperactivity disorder, *484*, 486
in autism, 368–370
behavioral management intervention in, 196–203, 211
causes of, 181–182
characteristics of students with, 181–185, 210
classification of, 178–179
cognitive behavioral intervention in, 195–196, 211
communication disorders and, 248
definitions of, 177–178, 210
direct/explicit instruction in, 195, 211
early intervention in, 194–195
externalizing characteristics in, 182–183, 210
gender differences in, 180, 183, *183*
general education teachers of students with, 208–209
history of, 176–177
identification of students with, 185–188, 210
instructional content, 189–193, 206–207, 211
instructional environment, 203–206, 207, 211
instructional grouping, 205–206
instructional technology, 206–208, 211
prevalence of, 179–180
secondary language disorders and, 226–227
in students with severe disabilities, 408–409
transition planning for students with, 191–193
in traumatic brain injury, 335

employment. *See also* transition planning
legislation against discrimination in, 20–21, 22
of students with blindness or low vision, 306, *307*
of students with emotional or behavioral disorders, 191–192
of students with intellectual disabilities, 154–155, 160
work environment analysis, *307*

encephalitis, 142, 404

English language learners (ELLs), 29, 118–119, 448–449

enhanced milieu teaching strategies, 422

H

handicap, definition of, 3
handwriting, 101, *102. See also* writing
hard of hearing. *See also* deafness and hard
    of hearing
    definitions of, 254, 256–258
    students as bilingual and bicultural,
        262–263
Hawkins, Varie Hudson, profile of, 500–501
head injuries. *See* traumatic brain injury
Headsprout Early Reading Program, 502
Head Start, 18, 441–442, 453
health impairments. *See* other health
    impairments
hearing, definition of, 254
hearing aids, 275–276, *275*
hearing impairment, 254, 258, 282. *See also*
    deafness and hard of hearing
hearing loss. *See also* deafness and hard of
    hearing
    age of onset, 258
    conductive, 257, 259–260
    degree of, 257
    expressed in decibels, 256, 257, *257*
    sensorineural, 256–257, 260, 276
Helen Keller National Center for Deaf-Blind
    Youths and Adults (HKNC), *401*
hemiplegia, 327
hidden curriculum, 378
high-stakes assessment, 50
Hispanic students
    assessment difficulties, 47
    identification of mental retardation in, 140
    underrepresentation in gifted
        programs, 525
HIV/AIDS, 333–334, *338*, 354
HKNC (Helen Keller National Center for
    Deaf-Blind Youths and Adults), *401*
Hobson v. Hansen (1967), *20*
home base, for students with autism spec-
    trum disorders, 387
home-based contingency programs, 493, *494*
homelessness, 193, 447, 450
homework, for students with attention
    deficit/hyperactivity disorder, 503
Honig v. Doe (1988), *22*
Honsberger, Christine, profile of, 466–467
Honsberger, Toby, profile of, 388–389
hormone therapy, 384
Huisman, Ingrid, profile of, 316–317
human immunodeficiency virus (HIV),
    333–334, *338*, 354
Hurler syndrome, *141, 404*
hydrocephaly, 143, 329
hyperactivity. *See* attention deficit/
    hyperactivity disorder
hyperglycemia, 333
hyperopia, 292
hypoglycemia, 333
hypotonia, 363

I

ICM (Integrated Curriculum Model),
    533–534
IDEA. *See* Individuals with Disabilities
    Education Act of 1990

IDEA 04. *See* Individuals with Disabilities
    Education Act of 2004
identification process, 36–37
    for at-risk children, 452–455, 470
    for gifted and talented children, 521–526
    for infants, toddlers, and preschool
        children, 36–37
    minority students, 19, 29–30, 47
    for school-aged students, 37
    for students with attention deficit/
        hyperactivity disorder, 485–488
    for students with autism spectrum
        disorders, 372–374, *373*, 394
    for students with blindness or low
        vision, 296–301, 318
    for students with communication
        disorders, 228–232, 248
    for students with deafness or hard of
        hearing, 265–267, 282
    for students with emotional or behavior
        disorders, 185–188, 210
    for students with learning disabilities,
        104–108, 130
    for students with mental retardation/
        intellectual abilities, 147–149, 170
    for students with physical or health
        disabilities, 337–338, *338*
    for students with severe disabilities,
        411–413, 434
    for students with traumatic brain
        injury, 338
IEP. *See* individualized education program
IFSP. *See* individual family service plan
IHP (individualized health (care) plans),
    343–344, *344*
impairment, definition of, 3
impulse control, 344–345
incidence, definition of, 5
incidental teaching, 382, 389
inclusion. *See also* program placement
    attitudes towards, *59*, 60
    benefits for peers without disabilities,
        426–427
    cascade of integration options, 168, *168*
    desirable teacher characteristics in, *59*
    for gifted and talented students, 536–537
    partial *vs.* full, 58–59
    philosophy, 10, 11, 15, 58–59
    for students with autism spectrum
        disorders, 391
    for students with blindness or low
        vision, 310–311, 314–319
    for students with deafness or hard of
        hearing, 272–273
    for students with intellectual
        disabilities, 166–169
    for students with physical or health
        disabilities, 344
    for students with severe disabilities,
        414–416, *415, 416*, 426–427, 430–431
inclusive service-learning, 168–169
independent group contingencies, 206
independent living skills, 300–301, 305
Indiana, "at risk" identification in, 453
individualized education program (IEP)
    based on needs not availability of
        services, 311
    content of, 52–54

family involvement in, 74–76
    in IDEA 04 legislation, 24
    IEP multidisciplinary team, 52
    model form for, Appendix
    in PL 94-142 legislation, 21
    program placement, 56–61
    related services in, 12–16
    standards referenced approach in,
        415–416
    student involvement in, 73–74
    transition planning, 87–88
individualized family service plan (IFSP)
    for at-risk children, *457, 458*
    content of, 54–56, *55*
    for infants and toddlers, 24, 30
    services provided as part of, 55
individualized health (care) plans (IHP),
    343–344, *344*
Individuals with Disabilities Education Act
    of 1990 (IDEA; PL 101-476)
    legislation affecting, 21, *22*
    No Child Left Behind Act and, 23
    number of students receiving services
        under, 5–7, *6, 7*
    reauthorizations of, *22*
    related services, 12–16
    terminology in, 3–4
    universal design in, 9, *9*
Individuals with Disabilities Education Act
    of 2004 (IDEA 04; PL 108-446), 23–28
    on assistive technology, 348
    on at-risk infants and toddlers, 443, 446,
        452–453, 470
    attention deficit/hyperactivity disorder
        and, 477, 486, 506
    on autism, 360, 361, *362*, 394
    on communication disorders, 220–221, 248
    on deaf-blindness, 402
    on deafness and hard of hearing, 258, 282
    disciplinary actions, 27–28
    on education and transition of infants
        and toddlers, 30–31
    on emotional and behavioral disorders,
        177–178, 185, 210
    on extended school year services, 429
    on learning disabilities, 96, 130
    on mental retardation, 137, 138, 170
    on multiple disabilities, 402
    on not requiring controlled substances,
        495
    on overrepresentation of students with
        diverse backgrounds, 29–30
    overview of, 20, 23, 24–27
    on physical and health disabilities, 325,
        338, 354
    on teacher qualifications, 28
    on traumatic brain injury, 338
    on visual impairments, 291, 318
infants and toddlers
    at-risk, 442–443, 453, 464
    autism in, 372
    blindness or low vision in, 297, 301
    cochlear implants in, 277
    education and transition of, 30–31
    hearing loss in, 266
    individual family service plans for, 24
    initial identification procedures for, 36–37
    legislated intervention services for, 23

general education teacher considerations, 127–131

history of, 94–96

identification of students with, 104–108

importance of structure in, 112–113

instructional content, 108–112, 131

instructional environment, 120, 131

instructional procedures, 112–119, 131

instructional technology, 122–127, 131

origin of term, 18, 95–96

prevalence of, 5–7, *6*, *7*, 97

secondary language disorders and, 226–227

task analysis for, 113

writing and written expression characteristics, 101–102, *102*

Learning Disabilities Association of America (LDA), 96

learning media assessment (LMA), 298–300

learning sequence, 156, *157*

Learning Strategies Curriculum (LSC), 116–117

least restrictive environment (LRE)

current thinking on, 60–61

in Education for All Handicapped Children Act, 21

general education teachers and, 31–32

in IDEA 04 legislation, 24

interpretation of, 56

statistics on placement, 57–58

for students with blindness or low vision, 310–311

for students with deafness or hard of hearing, 272–273

legal blindness, 290, *290*

legislation. *See also* Individuals with Disabilities Education Act of 1990; Individuals with Disabilities Education Act of 2004

Americans with Disabilities Act, 22–23

Child Abuse Prevention and Treatment Act, 30–31

on discriminatory assessment practices, 20–21, *20*, 22

early, 19–21, *20*

Education for All Handicapped Children Act, 20–21

Education of the Handicapped Act Amendments of 1986, 21, 22

Elementary and Secondary Education Act of 1965, *20*, 443, 454

National Defense Education Act, *20*

No Child Left Behind Act, 23, 526

numbering convention, 20

post-PL 94-142, 21–23, 401

Rehabilitation Act of 1973, 19–21, 340, 476

on special education, 20

Special Education Act, *20*

Technology-Related Assistance of Individual with Disabilities Act, 348

Title I of the Elementary and Secondary Education Act of 1965, 443

Vocational Education Amendments of 1968, *20*

Vocational Rehabilitation Act of 1973, 503–504

LEP (limited English proficiency), 29, 232

Lesch-Nyan syndrome, *404*

level of support classification system, 139–140, *139*, 402–403

life skills. *See also* transition planning

for students with emotional or behavioral disabilities, 191–192

for students with intellectual disabilities, 152–153

for students with physical or health disabilities, 341

limited English proficiency (LEP), 29, 232

linguistically diverse students. *See also* culturally and linguistically diverse backgrounds

definition of, 29

identification difficulties, 46–47

overrepresentation of, 29–30

lipreading, 271

listening skills, 304, 345

literacy. *See also* reading; writing

in at-risk children, 454, 455–456

blindness or low vision and, 295, 303–304

communication disorders and, 234

deafness or hard of hearing and, 263, 268–269

litigation. *See* court decisions

LLD (language learning disabilities), 102

LMA (learning media assessment), 298–300

local educational agency (LEA), 25, 28

loop systems, for students with deafness or hard of hearing, 276

loudness, definition of, 256

low birth weight, 445, 446–447

low vision, definition of, 290, *290. See also* blindness or low vision

LRE. *See* least restrictive environment

LSC (Learning Strategies Curriculum), 116–117

Luke S. and Hans S. v. Nix et al. (1984), *22*

lunchtime, support suggestions for students with autism, *386*

M

macular degeneration, 290, 293

magnet schools, 537

Making Action Plans (MAPs), 74, *74*

mand-model strategy, 422

manic disorders, 184

manifestation determination, 27–28

manual communication, 254

Marland definition, of gifts and talents, 513–514

massed trial teaching, 421

mathematics

in at-risk children, 456

cognitive–metacognitive model in, 116, *116*

instructional technology in, 124–126

instruction in, 111

learning disability characteristics in, 101, 130

metacognitive strategies in, 115–116, *116*

peer-assisted learning strategies for, 499

for students with deafness or hard of hearing, 263–264, *269*

Matthew effect, 100

MBD (minimal brain dysfunction), 95, 477

MBI (minimal brain injury), 95, 98, 477

mediation, 25

medical services for diagnostic purposes, 14

medications, 202–203, 493–495

Megadots, *313*

memory, 103, 145, 295, 407

meningitis, learning disabilities and, 99

meningocele, 328–329, *329*

mental retardation/intellectual disabilities, 135–171

autism and, 370

causes of, 141–143, *141*, *142*

characteristics of students with, 144–147, 170

classification of individuals with, 139–140

communication disorders and, 248

early court cases on, 19, 47

general education teachers of students with, 166–169, 171

history of, 17–18, 136–137

IDEA 04 definition of, 138

identification of students with, 147–149, 170

instructional content, 149–155, 166–167, 171

instructional environment, 159–163, 167, 171

instructional procedures, 156–158, 171

instructional technology, 163–165, 171

overrepresentation of African Americans in, 29–30, 47, 140

prevalence of, 5–7, *6*, *7*, 140

prevention of, 143

secondary language disorders and, 226–227

state law variations in definitions of, 47–48

transition planning, 153–155

use of terms, 4, 4n, 136–138, 140

mentoring, 532

metacognition, 102–103, 115–116

metronomes, 244–245

migrant children, 446, 447

milk (casein) intolerance, autism and, 384

Mills v. Board of Education of the District of Columbia, 19

minimal brain dysfunction (MBD), 95, 477

minimal brain injury (MBI), 95, 98, 477

Minnesota Multiphasic Personality Inventory–2, 187

minorities. *See* culturally and linguistically diverse (CLD) backgrounds

misarticulation, 224, 227, 230, 237, 248

mixed cerebral palsy, 327, *328*

mixed hearing loss, 257, 261

MMR vaccine, autism and, 365

mnemonics, 117–118, *118*, 196

mobility skills, 295–296, 300, 304–305, 343

mobility specialists, 14

modeling, in language disorders, 236

monoplegia, 327

mood disorders, 184. *See also* emotional or behavioral disorders

morphemes, 218, 224

morphological disorders, 225, 248

morphology, 218

motor development, in attention deficit/hyperactivity disorder, *484*

motor stereotypies, 369

Mountbatten Brailler, 304

multiage and multigrade grouping, 537–538

multicultural backgrounds. *See* culturally and linguistically diverse backgrounds

multiple intelligences, Gardner's theory of, 519, *520*, 529–530, *531*

muscular dystrophy, 329–330, 337, 354

myelomeningocele, 328–329, *329*

myopia, 292

myringotomy, 260

N

Naglieri Nonverbal Ability Test, 524

name-memorizing tasks, 145

National Agenda, 289, 302

National Association for Gifted Children, 536, 541

National Association for the Deaf, 255

National Association of Retarded Children (ARC), 18, 137, *401*

National Defense Education Act (PL 85-926), 20

National Early Intervention Longitudinal Study (NEILS), 450–451

National Excellence: A Case for Developing America's Talent, 513, 526

National Federation of the Blind, 289

National Joint Committee on Learning Disabilities (NJCLD), 96–97

National Longitudinal Transition Study–2 (NLTS–2), 87

National Mental Health and Special Education Coalition, 178

National Reading Panel, 454, 462

National Research Council, 366–367, 383–384, 391

natural environment, 159

naturalistic teaching strategies, 421–422

NCLB (No Child Left Behind Act), 23, 28, 526

negative reinforcement, 198

neglect, 446, 447–448, *449*

NEILS (National Early Intervention Longitudinal Study), 450–451

neologisms, 368

neural tube defects, 143

neurological causes of learning disabilities, 98

New England Asylum for the Blind, 288

NFB-Trans software, *313*

NJCLD (National Joint Committee on Learning Disabilities), 96–97

NLTS–2 (National Longitudinal Transition Study–2), 87

No Child Left Behind Act (NCLB; PL 107-110), 23, 28, 526

noncompliance, by students with emotional or behavioral disorders, 194

nondiscriminatory evaluation, 21, 26, 47

Nonverbal Language Kit, 234

normalization, 137

norm-referenced tests, 42, 48, 228

Norris, Amanda, profile of, 430–431

Number Heroes (software), 124

nystagmus, 293

O

observational data
in attention deficit/hyperactivity disorder identification, 488
in emotional or behavioral disorder identification, 185–186
in language disorder identification, 229
in the prereferral process, 41, *41*

observation and error analysis, 41

observation rooms, 204

occupational therapy, 13

ocular motility defects, 292–293

OHI. *See* other health impairments

OI. *See* orthopedic impairment

one teach, one drift model, 79

one teach, one observe model, 78–79

one-to-one instruction, 121, 160–161

open head injury, 334. *See also* traumatic brain injury

Operation Head Start, 441–442, 453

oppositional defiant disorder, 485

optical defects, 292

oralism, 271

oralist movement, 255

Oregon Project for Visually Impaired and Blind Preschool Children, 300

orientation, in students with blindness or low vision, 295–296, 300, 304–305

orientation and mobility (O&M) teachers, 14, 304–305

orthopedic impairment (OI)
causes and characteristics, 327–328, 354
definition of, 325
identification of, 337
muscular dystrophy, 329–330, 337, 354
prevalence of, 326
spina bifida, 328–329, 337, 354

orthosis, 348–349

ostomy management, 343

other health impairments (OHI)
acquired immunodeficiency syndrome, 333–334
asthma, 326, 331–332, 338, 354
attention deficit/hyperactivity disorder as, 476, 486
cystic fibrosis, 332, *338*, 354
definition of, 325
epilepsy, 324, 330–331, *331*, 337–338, 354
identification of, 337–338, *338*, 354
prevalence of, 5–7, *6*, *7*, 325–326

otitis media, 259–260, *260*

OUTLOUD, *313*

overlapping curriculum, 128–129

P

palilalia, 368

PALS (Peer-Assisted Learning Strategy), 205, 499

paradoxical effect, 494

paragraph shrinking, 499

parallel curriculum, 128, 151

parallel talk, 236

parallel teaching, 80

paraplegia, 327

paraprofessionals, 82–83, *82*, *83*, 424

parental participation right, 21

parental stress, 425

parent counseling and training, 15, 460, *461*, 490

parents. *See* families

Parent Training and Information Centers, 73

parity, in collaboration, 69

Part B programs, 23

Part C programs, 23, 26–27, 30–31

partial inclusion, 61

partial participation, 423

partial sight, 291. *See also* blindness or low vision

partner reading, 499

PASE v. Hannon (1980), *20*

PBS (positive behavior support), 204–205, *205*, 387, 462, *468*

PCP (person-centered planning), 74, *74*, 149–150

PDAs (personal digital assistants), 126, 501

PDD–NOS (pervasive developmental disorder–not otherwise specified), 363, *367. See also* autism spectrum disorders

Peabody Language Development Kits-Revised, 234

PECS (Picture Exchange Communication System), 388–389, 390

Peer-Assisted Learning Strategy (PALS), 205, 499

peer buddies, 387

peer-mediated instruction, 499

peer modeling, 242–243

peer nomination, of gifted and talented students, 522–523

peer relationships. *See also* social skills
blindness or low vision and, 296, 314
communication disorders and, 242–243
intellectual disabilities and, 146–147, 164
traumatic brain injury and, 344

peer support interventions, 242–243

peer tutoring
for students with attention deficit/hyperactivity disorder, 99
for students with autism spectrum disorders, 387
for students with emotional or behavioral disorders, 205
for students with intellectual disabilities, 162
for students with learning disabilities, 122
for students with severe disabilities, 427

Pendred syndrome, 260

Pennsylvania Association for Retarded Citizens (PARC) v. Commonwealth of Pennsylvania, 19

perceptual abilities, of students with blindness or low vision, 295–296, 307–308, 318

perceptual shifts, 95, *95*

perfectionism, 520, 529

perforated eardrum, 260

perinatal factors, 98, 142

Perkins Brailler, 303–304

Perry Preschool Project, 459–460

persecution of exceptional individuals, 16

personal digital assistants (PDAs), 126, 501

personality inventories, 185–186, 187

Personality Inventory for Children–2, 187

person-centered planning (PCP), 74, *74*, 149–150

person-first terminology, 3–4

perspective sentences, 383

pervasive developmental disorder–not otherwise specified (PDD–NOS), 363, *367*. *See also* autism spectrum disorders

pharmacological treatment, 202–203, 493–495

phenylketoneuria (PKU), *141*, 445

phonemes, 218, *219*, 224

phonics instruction, 109–110

phonological awareness, 100, 109

phonological processes, 224

phonological processing disorders, 224, 225, 248

phonology, 218, 224

physical abuse of children, 448, *449*

physical and health disabilities, 323–355

   acquired immunodeficiency syndrome, 333–334, *338*, 354

   asthma, 326, 331–332, *338*, 354

   cerebral palsy (*See* cerebral palsy)

   collaboration by teachers of students with, 355

   cystic fibrosis, 332, *338*, 354

   definitions of, 325

   epilepsy, 324, 330–331, *331*, 337–338, 354

   general education teachers of students with, 352–355

   history of, 324–325

   identification of students with, 337–338, *338*, 354

   individualized health (care) plans, 343–344, *344*

   instructional content, 339–342, 350–351, 355

   instructional environment, 346–347, 351, 355

   instructional procedures, 342–345, *344*, 355

   instructional technology, 347–352, *349*, 355

   muscular dystrophy, 329–330, 337, 354

   prevalence of, 325–326

   self-determination skills, 341

   spina bifida, 328–329, 337, 354

   transition planning for students with, 342, *342*

   traumatic brain injury (*See* traumatic brain injury)

physical education, for students with autism, *386*

physical therapy, 13

picture boards, 349–350

Picture Exchange Communication System (PECS), 388–389, 390

PIPA (Pre-Reading Inventory of Phonological Awareness), 454

pivotal response teaching (PRT), 382

PKU (phenylketoneuria), 445

placement. *See* program placement

play-based assessments, 411

play skills, visual impairment and, 294, 318

play therapy, 202

portfolio assessment, 526

positioning of students with physical disabilities, 343, *344*, 348–349

positive behavior support (PBS), 204–205, *205*, 387, 462, *468*

positive reinforcement, 197–198

postlingual hearing loss, 258

postnatal factors, 99, 142

postsecondary education, transition planning for, 54, 112, 193, 379

poverty. *See also* at-risk conditions

   disabilities and, 142–143, 180

   increase in, 443

   IQ and, 517

   risk of failure in school and, 446–447

   role of, 29–30

   specific language impairment and, 223

Pragmatic Activities for Language Intervention, 234

pragmatics, 220

pragmatics disorder, 225, 248

praise, 197–198

prebraille skills, 303

precision teaching, 492

prediction relay, 499

pregnancy

   alcohol use during, 98, 142

   intellectual disability factors in, 142

   learning disorder factors in, 97–98

   prenatal screening and treatment, 143, 337

prelingual hearing loss, 258

Premack Principle, 199, 418

premature birth, 446–447

prenatal factors, 97, 142

prenatal screening, 143, 337

Pre-Reading Inventory of Phonological Awareness (PIPA), 454

prereferral assessment, 37, 38, 40–41, 43–44

prereferral intervention, 37, 38–41, *38*

Prereferral Intervention Manual and Checklist, *38*

prereferral process

   commercial products in, *38*

   criterion-referenced testing, 42

   curriculum-based assessment, 42–43

   observation, 41

   prereferral assessment, 37, 38, 40–41, 43–44

   prereferral intervention, 37, 38–41, *39*

preschool children. *See also* early childhood

   at-risk, 464–466

   with attention deficit/hyperactivity disorder, 482, 497

   with autism spectrum disorders, 375–376, 385

   with communication disorders, 239–240, 242

   with deafness or hard of hearing, 278–279

   with emotional or behavioral disorders, 204

   identifying gifted and talented, 522

   initial identification in, 36–37

   instructional technology use by, 123

   with learning disabilities, 120

   with mental retardation/intellectual disabilities, 159–160, 171

   transition to preschool, 26–27, 30–31

Preschool Language Scale, 278

prevalence, definition of, 5

primary language disorders, 224–226, 248

primary prevention, 458

problem-solving skills, 192, 529

procedural knowledge, 109

procedural safeguards, 25

process tests, 107

program placement, 56–61. *See also* inclusion

   classroom do's and don'ts on, *61*

   for gifted and talented students, 535–538

   least restrictive environment in, 56–58 (*See also* least restrictive environment)

   statistics on, 59–58

   for students with blindness or low vision, 310–311

   for students with physical or health disabilities, 346

Project DATA, 376–377

projective tests, 186, 187–188

Project PRIDE, 462

Project Re-Ed, 177

prompts, 157, *158*, 165

prosthesis, 348–349

protective factors, 449–451, *451*

proxemics, 220

PRT (pivotal response teaching), 382

psychological services, 13

psychosocial factors, in intellectual disabilities, 142–143

psychostimulants, 493–495

pullout programs, for students with communication disorders, *241*, 242

punishment, 201

pure-tone tests, 266

Q

quadriplegia, 327

R

Raising a Reader, 456–457

rapid automatic naming (RAN), 100

reading. *See also* literacy

   braille, 303–304, 311–312, *313*

   by deaf and hard of hearing students, 263

   instructional technology in, 126

   instruction components, 109–111

   learning disability characteristics in, 99–101, 130

   memory problems and, 103

   peer-assisted learning strategies in, 499

   portfolios, 526

   shared storybook reading, 461–462

   by students with communication disorders, 234

   word substitutions, *101*

reading comprehension, 100–101, 109, 110

Reading First, 454

Reading Mastery program, 462

recall, 156

receptive language, 217

reciprocal tutoring, 205

recognition, 156

reconstruction, 156

recreation, 13–14, 305–306

referral process, 44–45

refraction, problems in, 292

"refrigerator mom" theory, 365

Regular Education Initiative (REI), 58

social skills
  in at-risk students, 456, 462–463
  attention deficit/hyperactivity disorder and, 483–484
  autism spectrum disorders and, 377–378
  blindness or low vision and, 300–301, 305
  communication disorders and, 242–243
  curriculum programs, *191*
  emotional or behavioral disorders and, 190, 191
  physical or health disabilities and, 341, 344–345, 353
  pragmatics and, 220
  role-playing activities, 341
  severe disabilities and, 408
  STOP strategy, 195
  universal intervention in, 194–195
Social Skills Intervention Guide (SSIG), *191*
social stories, 382–383, *383*
social withdrawal, 184
social work services, 14–15
socioeconomic status, IQ and, 517. *See also* poverty
SOLO (software toolkit), 126
sound, 256, *256*
Sousa's memory model, 103
spastic cerebral palsy, 327, *328. See also* physical and health disabilities
spatial perception, in students with blindness or low vision, 363–364
special education. *See also* legislation
  collaboration in (*See* collaboration)
  components of, 8
  definition of, 8
  eligibility for, 45–51
  history of, 16–19
  location of, 9–10
  overrepresentation of culturally diverse in, 29–30, 140
  professionals in, 10–12
  referral process, 44–45
  related services, 12–16, 83–85
  role of general education teacher in, 31–32
  universal design in, 8–9, *9*, 339
Special Education Act (PL 87-276), *20*
special education teachers. *See* teachers, special education
specific language impairment (SLI), 223, 224–226
specific learning disabilities (SLD), 486
speech. *See also* speech disorders
  components of language, 218–220, *219*
  definition of, 217
  four systems in production of, 217–218
  talking word processors, *313*
speech disorders. *See also* communication disorders
  in autism, 368
  causes of, 223–224
  characteristics of students with, 227–228
  deafness or hard of hearing and, 264, 282
  definition of, 221
  evaluation of linguistically diverse students, 230–232
  fluency disorders, 227–228, 237–238, 248
  identification of students with, 230, 248

  instructional procedures, 236, 244–245, 249
  misarticulations, 224, 227, 230, 237, 248
  severe disabilities and, 408
  voice disorders, 223, 227, 236–237
speech-language pathologists (SLP), 15, 229–230, 241, 389
speech-language pathology, 12, 15–16
speech or language impairment, definition of, 220–221. *See also* communication disorders; speech disorders
speechreading, 271, 281
speech recognition programs, 123
spelling, 101–102
spina bifida, 328–329, 337, 354
spina bifida occulta, 328
spirometry testing, 338
SRBCSS (Scales for Rating Behavioral Characteristics of Superior Students), 523
SSIG (Social Skills Intervention Guide), *191*
standardized testing, learning disability identification by, 106–108. *See also* assessments; *specific standardized tests*
standards driven approach, 415–416
standards referenced approach, 415–416
Stanford-Binet Intelligence Scale, 49, 148, 373, 518
Starting Points, 442
state laws
  on at-risk infants and toddlers, 453
  on eligibility criteria, 48
  on identification of gifted and talented children, 521
station teaching model, 79
stereotypical behavior, 409
STOP strategy, 195
storytelling, 202, 231
strabismus, 293
stress, parental, 425
study skills, 111–112
stuttering, 223–224, 227–228, 230, 237–238, 244–245
substance abuse, parental, 446
Success for All, 538
supported employment, 420
Supports Intensity Scale, 140, 148
symbol boards, 349–350
Symptoms of Autism Before Age 2 Checklist, 372, 394
syntactic disorders, 225, 248
syntax, 218–219
syphilis, 260
Systematic Screening for Behavior Disorders, 454

T

Talent Pool Strategy, 534
target behaviors, teaching specific, 421
TASH, 401, *401*
task analysis, 42, 113, 156
Tay Sachs disease, *141*, *404*, 411
TBI. *See* traumatic brain injury
TEACCH (Treatment and Education of Autistic and Related Communication Handicapped Children), 380, *380*
teachers, general education
  for at-risk students, 468–471

  attitudes toward inclusion, *59*, 60
  co-teaching models, 78–80, *81*, 209
  for gifted and talented students, 538–539, 540–543, *541*
  role in special education, 31–32
  for students with attention deficit/hyperactivity disorder, 503–507, *504*, *505*
  for students with autism spectrum disorders, 391–395, *392–393*
  for students with blindness and low vision, 314–319
  for students with communication disorders, 246–249
  for students with disabilities not qualifying under IDEA 04, 326
  for students with emotional or behavioral disorders, 208–209
  for students with hearing losses, 280–283
  for students with intellectual disabilities, 166–169, 171
  for students with learning disabilities, 127–131
  for students with physical or health disabilities, 352–355
  for students with severe disabilities, 432–435
teachers, of distance learning courses, 347
teachers, special education
  collaboration with other school personnel, 10–12, 32
  co-teaching models, 78–80, *81*
  highly qualified, 28
Teaching Exceptional Children (journal), 18
teams, in collaboration process, 72, 85–87
team teaching model, 80, *81. See also* co-teaching
technology. *See* assistive technology
Technology-Related Assistance of Individuals with Disabilities Act (1988), 348
teen pregnancy, 443, 447
Telecommunications Relay Service (TRS), 277–278
teleconferencing, 339
telementoring, 532
television violence, 181
tertiary prevention, 459
test-teach-retest paradigm, 412
test-train-test model, 525–526
text telephones (TTY), 277–278
text-to-graphic software, 431
Thematic Apperception Test, 187
theory of mind, autism and, 370
thimerosal, 365
think-aloud procedure, 44
"three-ring" definition of gifted and talented, 514, *514*
threshold hypothesis, 517
time-out, 199–200, 204
Timothy W. v. Rochester School District (1988), *22*
Title I of the Elementary and Secondary Education Act (ESEA) of 1965, 443
TOAD system, 488
toddlers. *See* infants and toddlers
toileting management, 343
token economy, 198
token reinforcement systems, 198, 489–490

tone-prompt system, 502
Torrance Test of Creative Thinking, 519, 524
total communication approach, 271
toxoplasmosis, *142*, 260
transfer/generalization of skills, 145, 407–408, 416
transition phase of learning disability research, 95
transition planning. *See also* employment
   to adult living, 87–90, 342
   to employment, 379, 420
   instructional content, 112
   interagency agreements on, 89–90, *89*
   from juvenile detention, 193
   National Longitudinal Transition Study–2, 87
   planning and programming, 88, 112
   to postsecondary goals, 54, 112, 193, 379
   to preschool programs, 26–27, 30–31
   to school programs, 85–87, 342, *342*
   for students with blindness or low vision, 306, *307*
   for students with deafness or hard of hearing, 270
   for students with emotional or behavioral disabilities, 191–193
   for students with intellectual disabilities, 152–155
   for students with physical or health disabilities, 342, *342*
   for students with severe disabilities, 419–420
transition portfolios, 342, *342*
transportation, as related service, 12
traumatic brain injury (TBI)
   access to the general education curriculum, 339–340
   age when injury acquired, 336
   behavioral and social skill development and, 344–345
   brain anatomy, 334, *335*
   causes and characteristics, 334–336, 354
   definition of, 325
   IDEA 04 qualifications and, 326
   identification of students with, 338
   prevalence of, 5–7, *6*, *7*, 325–326
   seizures and, 330, 334
   severity of, 336
   supporting parents of students with, 345
triad of social impairments, 366–367
triplegia, 327
Trompler, Dian, profile of, 538–539
TRS (Telecommunications Relay Service), 277–278
TTY (text telephones), 277–278
Tuberous sclerosis, *141*
tunnel vision, 290

Turner's syndrome, 445
turn taking, 381–382
twice exceptional, 524–525
twin studies
   in attention deficit/hyperactivity disorder, 481, 485
   in autism, 366
   in gifts and talents, 517
   in learning disabilities, 98
Type 1/Type 2 diabetes, 332–333. *See also* diabetes

U

UCLA Young Autism Project, 375–376
UDL (Universal Design for Learning), 458, 462
ultrasound procedures, 337
underachievers, 524
underdeveloped countries, mental retardation in, 5
undifferentiated attention deficit disorder, 477
United Cerebral Palsy Association, 18
universal design, 8–9, *9*, 339
Universal Design for Learning (UDL), 458, 462
universal intervention, 194–195
universal precautions, 333
University of Kansas Center for Research on Learning, 117–118
Usher syndrome, 260

V

vaccines, autism and, 365
Van Economo's encephalitis, 477
ventilator management, 343
Victor, the Wild Boy of Aveyron, 17, *17*
video games, 164
Vineland Adaptive Behavior Scales–II, 148, 300
vision screening, 298–299
visual acuity, 290, *290*
visual communication technologies, 277–279
visual efficiency skills, for students with blindness or low vision, 303
visual field limitation, 290
visual impairments. *See* blindness or low vision
visual memory, 295
visual schedules, 380, *380*
visual skills, autism and, 371–372, *371*
vocabulary development, 110–111, *152*
vocational assessment services, 89
Vocational Education Amendments of 1968 (PL 90-576), *20*

Vocational Rehabilitation Act of 1973, 503–504
vocational skills. *See* employment
voice disorders, 223, 227, 236–237, 248
voice output communication aids (VOCAs), 244, 390
voice recognition software, 351
voicing, in speech, 217

W

Waardenburg syndrome, 260
wayfinding, 295–296
Wechsler Individual Achievement Test–II (WIAT–II), 50, 148, 488, 524
Wechsler Intelligence Scale for Children–IV (WISC–IV), 49, 148, 524
wedges, *344*, 348
wheelchairs, 339–340, 343
whole group instruction, 122, 162–163
WIAT–II (Wechsler Individual Achievement Test–II), 50, 148, 488, 524
Wilson Reading System, 110
WISC–IV (Wechsler Intelligence Scale for Children–IV), 49, 148, 524
witches, exceptional individuals as, 16
withdrawal, social, 184
within-class grouping, 538
Wolf-Hirschhorn syndrome, *404*
Woodcock-Johnson–III, 148
Woods, Michael, profile of, 124–125
word recognition problems, 98, 100–101
word substitutions, *101*
work carrels, 120
work experiences. *See* employment
working memory, 145, 407
Worrell, Jamie, profile of, 10–11
writing, 101–102, *102*, 116, *118*, 130. *See also* literacy
written expression, 101–102, *102*, 130

X

XYZ grouping, 537

Y

Young Autism Project, 375–376

Z

zero reject, 21
zero tolerance, 27
ZIPPER strategy, 196